# Lecture Notes in Computer Science 3656

*Commenced Publication in 1973*
Founding and Former Series Editors:
Gerhard Goos, Juris Hartmanis, and Jan van Leeuwen

## Editorial Board

David Hutchison
  *Lancaster University, UK*
Takeo Kanade
  *Carnegie Mellon University, Pittsburgh, PA, USA*
Josef Kittler
  *University of Surrey, Guildford, UK*
Jon M. Kleinberg
  *Cornell University, Ithaca, NY, USA*
Friedemann Mattern
  *ETH Zurich, Switzerland*
John C. Mitchell
  *Stanford University, CA, USA*
Moni Naor
  *Weizmann Institute of Science, Rehovot, Israel*
Oscar Nierstrasz
  *University of Bern, Switzerland*
C. Pandu Rangan
  *Indian Institute of Technology, Madras, India*
Bernhard Steffen
  *University of Dortmund, Germany*
Madhu Sudan
  *Massachusetts Institute of Technology, MA, USA*
Demetri Terzopoulos
  *New York University, NY, USA*
Doug Tygar
  *University of California, Berkeley, CA, USA*
Moshe Y. Vardi
  *Rice University, Houston, TX, USA*
Gerhard Weikum
  *Max-Planck Institute of Computer Science, Saarbruecken, Germany*

Mohamed Kamel  Aurélio Campilho (Eds.)

# Image Analysis and Recognition

Second International Conference, ICIAR 2005
Toronto, Canada, September 28-30, 2005
Proceedings

 Springer

Volume Editors

Mohamed Kamel
University of Waterloo
Department of Electrical and Computer Engineering
Waterloo, Ontario N2L 3G1, Canada
E-mail: mkamel@uwaterloo.ca

Aurélio Campilho
University of Porto
Faculty of Engineering
Institute of Biomedical Engineering
Rua Dr. Roberto Friaas, 4200-465 Porto, Portugal
E-mail: campilho@fe.up.pt

Library of Congress Control Number: 2005932546

CR Subject Classification (1998): I.4, I.5, I.3.5, I.2.10, I.2.6, F.2.2

ISSN        0302-9743
ISBN-10     3-540-29069-9 Springer Berlin Heidelberg New York
ISBN-13     978-3-540-29069-8 Springer Berlin Heidelberg New York

This work is subject to copyright. All rights are reserved, whether the whole or part of the material is concerned, specifically the rights of translation, reprinting, re-use of illustrations, recitation, broadcasting, reproduction on microfilms or in any other way, and storage in data banks. Duplication of this publication or parts thereof is permitted only under the provisions of the German Copyright Law of September 9, 1965, in its current version, and permission for use must always be obtained from Springer. Violations are liable to prosecution under the German Copyright Law.

Springer is a part of Springer Science+Business Media

springeronline.com

© Springer-Verlag Berlin Heidelberg 2005
Printed in Germany

Typesetting: Camera-ready by author, data conversion by Scientific Publishing Services, Chennai, India
Printed on acid-free paper    SPIN: 11559573    06/3142    5 4 3 2 1 0

# Preface

ICIAR 2005, the International Conference on Image Analysis and Recognition, was the second ICIAR conference, and was held in Toronto, Canada. ICIAR is organized annually, and alternates between Europe and North America. ICIAR 2004 was held in Porto, Portugal. The idea of offering these conferences came as a result of discussion between researchers in Portugal and Canada to encourage collaboration and exchange, mainly between these two countries, but also with the open participation of other countries, addressing recent advances in theory, methodology and applications.

The response to the call for papers for ICIAR 2005 was encouraging. From 295 full papers submitted, 153 were finally accepted (80 oral presentations, and 73 posters). The review process was carried out by the Program Committee members and other reviewers; all are experts in various image analysis and recognition areas. Each paper was reviewed by at least two reviewers, and also checked by the conference co-chairs. The high quality of the papers in these proceedings is attributed first to the authors, and second to the quality of the reviews provided by the experts. We would like to thank the authors for responding to our call, and we wholeheartedly thank the reviewers for their excellent work, and for their timely response. It is this collective effort that resulted in the strong conference program and high-quality proceedings in your hands.

We were very pleased to be able to include in the conference program keynote talks by two world-renowned experts: Prof. Anastasios (Tas) N. Venetsanopoulos, Dean of the Faculty of Applied Science and Engineering at the University of Toronto, Canada; and Prof. Jelena Kovacevic, Director of the Center for Bioimage Informatics, Departments of Biomedical Engineering & Electrical and Computer Engineering at Carnegie Mellon University, USA. We would like to express our sincere gratitude to each of them for accepting our invitations.

We would like to thank Khaled Hammouda, the webmaster of the conference, for maintaining the Web pages, interacting with the authors and preparing the proceedings; and Cathie Lowell for her administrative assistance. We would also like to thank the members of the Local Organizing Committee for their advice and help. We also appreciate the help of the Springer editorial staff Christine Günther, Anna Kramer, and Alfred Hofmann, for supporting this publication in the LNCS series.

Finally, we were very pleased to welcome all the participants to this conference. For those who did not attend, we hope this publication provides a good view into the research presented at the conference, and we look forward to meeting you at the next ICIAR conference.

September 2005                                          Mohamed Kamel, Aurélio Campilho

# ICIAR 2005 – International Conference on Image Analysis and Recognition

## General Chair

Mohamed Kamel
University of Waterloo, Canada
mkamel@uwaterloo.ca

## General Co-chair

Aurélio Campilho
University of Porto, Portugal
campilho@fe.up.pt

## Local Organizing Committee

Otman Basir
University of Waterloo, Canada
obasir@uwaterloo.ca

Alex Bot
IEEE Toronto Section, Canada
albot@ieee.org

David Clausi
University of Waterloo, Canada
dclausi@engmail.uwaterloo.ca

Mahmoud El-Sakka
University of Western Ontario, Canada
elsakka@csd.uwo.ca

Paul Fieguth
University of Waterloo, Canada
pfieguth@uwaterloo.ca

Rastislav Lukac
University of Toronto, Canada
lukacr@ieee.org

Kostas Plataniotis
University of Toronto, Canada
kostas@dsp.utoronto.ca

Hamid Tizhoosh
University of Waterloo, Canada
tizhoosh@pami.uwaterloo.ca

## Webmaster

Khaled Hammouda
University of Waterloo, Canada
hammouda@pami.uwaterloo.ca

## Supported by

 Pattern Analysis and Machine Intelligence Group, University of Waterloo, Canada

 Department of Electrical and Computer Engineering, Faculty of Engineering, University of Porto, Portugal

 INEB – Instituto de Engenharia Biomédica

 IEEE Toronto Section

 IEEE Kitchener-Waterloo Section

## Advisory and Program Committee

| | |
|---|---|
| M. Abdallah | American University of Beirut, Lebanon |
| P. Abolmaesumi | Queen's University, Canada |
| R. Abugharbieh | University of British Columbia, Canada |
| M. Ahmadi | University of Windsor, Canada |
| M. Ahmed | Wilfrid Laurier University, Canada |
| J. Alirezaie | Ryerson University, Canada |
| A. Amin | University of New South Wales, Australia |
| D. Androutsos | Ryerson University, Canada |
| H. Araujo | University of Coimbra, Portugal |
| J. Barron | University of Western Ontario, Canada |
| O. Basir | University of Waterloo, Canada |
| J. Bioucas | Technical University of Lisbon, Portugal |
| A. Bot | IEEE Toronto Section, Canada |
| B. Boubakeur | University of Windsor, Canada |
| T. Bui | Concordia University, Canada |
| M. Cheriet | University of Quebec, Canada |
| D. Chiu | University of Guelph, Canada |
| D. Clausi | University of Waterloo, Canada |
| L. Corte-Real | University of Porto, Portugal |

| | |
|---|---|
| E. Dubois | University of Ottawa, Canada |
| M. El-Sakka | University of Western Ontario, Canada |
| R. Fazel | University of Manitoba, Canada |
| M. Ferretti | University of Pavia, Italy |
| P. Fieguth | University of Waterloo, Canada |
| M. Figueiredo | Technical University of Lisbon, Portugal |
| A. Fred | Technical University of Lisbon, Portugal |
| G. Freeman | University of Waterloo, Canada |
| L. Guan | Ryerson University, Canada |
| M. Haindl | Institute of Information Theory and Automation, Czech Republic |
| E. Hancock | University of York, UK |
| E. Jernigan | University of Waterloo, Canada |
| J. Jorge | INESC-ID, Portugal |
| G. Khan | Ryerson University, Canada |
| S. Krishnan | Ryerson University, Canada |
| A. Krzyzak | Concordia University, Canada |
| R. Laganière | University of Ottawa, Canada |
| R. Lins | Universidade Federal de Pernambuco, Brazil |
| S. Lu | Memorial University of Newfoundland, Canada |
| R. Lukac | University of Toronto, Canada |
| J. Marques | Technical University of Lisbon, Portugal |
| A. Mendonça | University of Porto, Portugal |
| J. Orchard | University of Waterloo, Canada |
| A. Ouda | University of Western Ontario, Canada |
| A. Padilha | University of Porto, Portugal |
| P. Payeur | University of Ottawa, Canada |
| F. Perales | University of the Balearic Islands, Spain |
| F. Pereira | Technical University of Lisbon, Portugal |
| N. Peres de la Blanca | University of Granada, Spain |
| E. Petrakis | Technical University of Crete, Greece |
| P. Pina | Technical University of Lisbon, Portugal |
| A. Pinho | University of Aveiro, Portugal |
| J. Pinto | Technical University of Lisbon, Portugal |
| F. Pla | University of Jaume I, Spain |
| K. Plataniotis | University of Toronto, Canada |
| T. Rabie | University of Toronto, Canada |
| P. Radeva | Universitat Autònoma de Barcelona, Spain |
| L. Rueda | University of Windsor, Canada |
| F. Samavati | University of Calgary, Canada |
| B. Santos | University of Aveiro, Portugal |
| G. Schaefer | Nottingham Trent University, UK |
| P. Scheunders | University of Antwerp, Belgium |
| J. Sequeira | Ecole Supérieure d'Ingénieurs de Luminy, France |
| M. Sid-Ahmed | University of Windsor, Canada |

| | |
|---|---|
| J. Silva | University of Porto, Portugal |
| W. Skarbek | Warsaw University of Technology, Poland |
| B. Smolka | Silesian University of Technology, Poland |
| J. Sousa | University of Coimbra, Portugal |
| C. Suen | Concordia University, Canada |
| S. Sural | Indian Institute of Technology, Kharagpur, India |
| G. Thomas | University of Waterloo, Canada |
| H. Tizhoosh | University of Waterloo, Canada |
| D. Vandermeulen | Catholic University of Leuven, Belgium |
| A. Venetsanopoulos | University of Toronto, Canada |
| M. Vento | University of Salerno, Italy |
| E. Vrscay | University of Waterloo, Canada |
| R. Ward | University of British Columbia, Canada |
| M. Wirth | University of Guelph, Canada |
| J. Wu | University of Windsor, Canada |
| J. Yeow | University of Waterloo, Canada |
| J. Zelek | University of Waterloo, Canada |
| X. Zhang | Ryerson University, Canada |

## Reviewers

| | |
|---|---|
| W. Abd-Almageed | University of Maryland, USA |
| A. Adegorite | University of Waterloo, Canada |
| N. Alajlan | University of Waterloo, Canada |
| B. Ávila | Universidade Federal de Pernambuco, Brazil |
| T. Barata | Instituto Superior Técnico, Portugal |
| E. Cernadas | University of Vigo, Spain |
| L. Chen | University of Waterloo, Canada |
| S. Chowdhury | University of Waterloo, Canada |
| M. Correia | University of Porto, Portugal |
| R. Dara | University of Waterloo, Canada |
| A. Dawoud | University of South Alabama, USA |
| O. El Badawy | University of Waterloo, Canada |
| I. El Rube' | University of Waterloo, Canada |
| J. Glasa | Slovak Academy of Sciences, Slovakia |
| V. Grau | University of Oxford, UK |
| C. Hong | Hong Kong Polytechnic, Hong Kong, China |
| A. Kong | University of Waterloo, Canada |
| J. Martínez | University of Jaume I, Spain |
| B. Miners | University of Waterloo, Canada |
| A. Monteiro | University of Porto, Portugal |
| F. Monteiro | IPB, Portugal |
| D. Oliveira | Universidade Federal de Pernambuco, Brazil |
| A. Picariello | University of Naples, Italy |
| A. Puga | University of Porto, Portugal |

S. Rahnamayan        University of Waterloo, Canada
R. Rocha             INEB — Instituto de Engenharia Biomédica, Portugal
M. Sabri             University of Waterloo, Canada
F. Sahba             University of Waterloo, Canada
A. Silva             Universidade Federal de Pernambuco, Brazil
B. van Ginneken      Image Sciences Institute, Netherlands
C. Vinhais           ISEP, Portugal
D. Xi                University of Waterloo, Canada
C. Yang              National Dong Hwa University, Taiwan
Q. Yu                University of Waterloo, Canada

# Table of Contents

## Image Segmentation

Localization Scale Selection for Scale-Space Segmentation
  *Sokratis Makrogiannis, Nikolaos Bourbakis* .................... 1

Image Segmentation for the Application of the Neugebauer Colour Prediction Model on Inkjet Printed Ceramic Tiles
  *P. Latorre, G. Peris-Fajarnes, M.A.T. Figueiredo* ................ 9

FCM with Spatial and Multiresolution Constraints for Image Segmentation
  *Adel Hafiane, Bertrand Zavidovique* .......................... 17

Combined Color and Texture Segmentation Based on Fibonacci Lattice Sampling and Mean Shift
  *Yuchou Chang, Yue Zhou, Yonggang Wang* ..................... 24

Unsupervised Image Segmentation Using Contourlet Domain Hidden Markov Trees Model
  *Yuheng Sha, Lin Cong, Qiang Sun, Licheng Jiao* ................ 32

A Novel Color C-V Method and Its Application
  *Li Chen, Yue Zhou, Yonggang Wang* .......................... 40

SAR Image Segmentation Using Kernel Based Spatial FCM
  *Xiangrong Zhang, Tan Shan, Shuang Wang, Licheng Jiao* ......... 48

Segmentation of Nanocolumnar Crystals from Microscopic Images
  *David Cuesta Frau, María Ángeles Hernández-Fenollosa, Pau Micó Tormos, Jordi Linares-Pellicer* ...................... 55

## Image and Video Processing and Analysis

Mutual Information-Based Methods to Improve Local Region-of-Interest Image Registration
  *K.P. Wilkie, E.R. Vrscay* ..................................... 63

Image Denoising Using Complex Wavelets and Markov Prior Models
  *Fu Jin, Paul Fieguth, Lowell Winger* ........................... 73

A New Vector Median Filter Based on Fuzzy Metrics
  *Samuel Morillas, Valentín Gregori, Guillermo Peris-Fajarnés,
  Pedro Latorre* .................................................. 81

Image Denoising Using Neighbor and Level Dependency
  *Dongwook Cho, Tien D. Bui, Guangyi Chen*...................... 91

Time Oriented Video Summarization
  *Chaoqiang Liu, Tao Xia, Hui Li* ................................. 99

Shadow Removal in Gradient Domain
  *Zhenlong Du, Xueying qin, Hai Lin, Hujun Bao* ................. 107

Efficient Global Weighted Least-Squares Translation Registration in
the Frequency Domain
  *Jeff Orchard* .................................................. 116

Isotropic Blur Identification for Fully Digital Auto-focusing
  *Jeongho Shin, Sunghyun Hwang, Seong-Won Lee, Joonki Paik* ...... 125

Edge Detection Models
  *Q.H. Zhang, S. Gao, Tien D. Bui*............................... 133

Video Stabilization Using Kalman Filter and Phase Correlation
Matching
  *Ohyun Kwon, Jeongho Shin, Joonki Paik* ........................ 141

Wavelet Image Denoising Using Localized Thresholding Operators
  *M. Ghazel, G.H. Freeman, E.R. Vrscay, R.K. Ward*............... 149

Type-2 Fuzzy Image Enhancement
  *P. Ensafi, H.R. Tizhoosh* ..................................... 159

A Multi-level Framework for Video Shot Structuring
  *Yun Zhai, Mubarak Shah*........................................ 167

All-in-Focus Imaging Using a Series of Images on Different Focal Planes
  *Mark Antunes, Michael Trachtenberg, Gabriel Thomas, Tina Shoa* .. 174

Skew Estimation and Correction for Form Documents Using Wavelet
Decomposition
  *Dihua Xi, Mohamed Kamel, Seong-Whan Lee* ...................... 182

Scalable e-Learning Multimedia Adaptation Architecture
  *Mazen Almaoui, Konstantinos N. Plataniotis* ................... 191

Highlight Detection and Removal Based on Chromaticity
  *Shu-Chang Xu, Xiuzi Ye, Yin Wu, Sanyuan Zhang* ............... 199

Digital Video Scrambling Using Motion Vector and Slice Relocation
  *Sang Gu Kwon, Woong Il Choi, Byeungwoo Jeon* ................ 207

Weighted Information Entropy: A Method for Estimating the Complex Degree of Infrared Images' Backgrounds
  *Lei Yang, Jie Yang, Ningsong Peng, Jianguo Ling* ............... 215

Neural Network Adaptive Switching Median Filter for the Restoration of Impulse Noise Corrupted Images
  *Pavel S. Zvonarev, Ilia V. Apalkov, Vladimir V. Khryashchev, Irina V. Reznikova* ............................................ 223

A Shot Boundary Detection Method for News Video Based on Rough Sets and Fuzzy Clustering
  *Xin-bo Gao, Bing Han, Hong-bing Ji* ........................... 231

Image Enhancement via Fusion Based on Laplacian Pyramid Directional Filter Banks
  *Hai-yan Jin, Xiao-hui Yang, Li-cheng Jiao, Fang Liu* ............. 239

Wavelet-Based Methods for Improving Signal-to-Noise Ratio in Phase Images
  *Héctor Cruz-Enriquez, Juan V. Lorenzo-Ginori* .................. 247

Image Evaluation Factors
  *Hongxun Yao, Min-Yu Huseh, Guilin Yao, Yazhou Liu* ............ 255

Monoscale Dual Ridgelet Frame
  *Tan Shan, Licheng Jiao* ....................................... 263

Description Selection Scheme for Intermediate Frame Based Multiple Description Video Streaming
  *S. Pavan, G. Sridhar, V. Sridhar* ............................... 270

Background Removal of Document Images Acquired Using Portable Digital Cameras
  *André R. Gomes e Silva, Rafael Dueire Lins* .................... 278

Comparison of the Image Distortion Correction Methods for an X-Ray Digital Tomosynthesis System
  *J.Y. Kim* .................................................... 286

## Image and Video Coding

An Efficient Video Watermarking Scheme Using Adaptive Threshold and Minimum Modification on Motion Vectors
*Kyung-Won Kang, Kwang-Seok Moon, Gwang-Seok Jung, Jong-Nam Kim* .............................................. 294

Lossless Compression of Correlated Images/Data with Low Complexity Encoder Using Distributed Source Coding Techniques
*Mortuza Ali, Manzur Murshed* ................................... 302

Automatically Detecting Symmetries in Decorative Tiles
*Rafael Dueire Lins, Daniel Marques Oliveira* ..................... 310

A Fast Video Mixing Method for Multiparty Video Conference
*Xin-Gang Liu, Kook-Yeol Yoo, Kwang-Deok Seo* .................. 320

Grayscale Two-Dimensional Lempel-Ziv Encoding
*Nathanael J. Brittain, Mahmoud R. El-Sakka* .................... 328

Unequal Error Protection Using Convolutional Codes for PCA-Coded Images
*Sabina Hosic, Aykut Hocanin, Hasan Demirel* .................... 335

Design of Tree Filter Algorithm for Random Number Generator in Crypto Module
*Jinkeun Hong, Kihong Kim* ...................................... 343

Layer Based Multiple Description Packetized Coding
*Canhui Cai, Jing Chen* ......................................... 351

Extended Application of Scalable Video Coding Methods
*Zhi-gang Li, Zhao-yang Zhang, Biao Wu, Ying Zhang* ............. 359

Accelerated Motion Estimation of H.264 on Imagine Stream Processor
*Haiyan Li, Mei Wen, Chunyuan Zhang, Nan Wu, Li Li, Changqing Xun* ................................................. 367

MPEG-2 Test Stream with Static Test Patterns in DTV System
*Soo-Wook Jang, Gwang-Soon Lee, Eun-Su Kim, Sung-Hak Lee, Kyu-Ik Sohng* .................................................. 375

Speed Optimization of a MPEG-4 Software Decoder Based on ARM Family Cores
*Linjian Mo, Haixiang Zhang, Jiajun Bu, Chun Chen* .............. 383

## Shape and Matching

Marrying Level Lines for Stereo or Motion
  *Nikom Suvonvorn, Samia Bouchafa, Bertrand Zavidovique* ......... 391

Envelope Detection of Multi-object Shapes
  *N. Alajlan, O. El Badawy, M.S. Kamel, G. Freeman* .............. 399

Affine Invariant, Model-Based Object Recognition Using Robust Metrics and Bayesian Statistics
  *Vasileios Zografos, Bernard F. Buxton* .......................... 407

Efficient Multiscale Shape-Based Representation and Retrieval
  *I. El Rube, N. Alajlan, M. Kamel, M. Ahmed, G. Freeman* ......... 415

Robust Matching Area Selection for Terrain Matching Using Level Set Method
  *Guo Cao, Xin Yang, Shoushui Chen* ............................... 423

Shape Similarity Measurement for Boundary Based Features
  *Nafiz Arica, Fatos T. Yarman Vural* ............................. 431

## Image Description and Recognition

Image Deformation Using Velocity Fields: An Exact Solution
  *Jeff Orchard* ................................................... 439

Estimating the Natural Number of Classes on Hierarchically Clustered Multi-spectral Images
  *André R.S. Marçal, Janete S. Borges* ............................ 447

Image Space $I^3$ and Eigen Curvature for Illumination Insensitive Face Detection
  *Christian Bauckhage, John K. Tsotsos* ........................... 456

Object Shape Extraction Based on the Piecewise Linear Skeletal Representation
  *Roman M. Palenichka, Marek B. Zaremba* .......................... 464

A Generic Shape Matching with Anchoring of Knowledge Primitives of Object Ontology
  *Dongil Han, Bum-Jae You, Yong Se Kim, Il Hong Suh* .............. 473

Statistical Object Recognition Including Color Modeling
  *Marcin Grzegorzek, Heinrich Niemann* ............................ 481

Determining Multiscale Image Feature Angles from Complex Wavelet Phases
*Ryan Anderson, Nick Kingsbury, Julien Fauqueur* .................. 490

Cylinder Rotational Orientation Based on Circle Detection
*Gabriel Thomas, John E. Kaye, Rajat Jayas, Cam Kaye* ........... 499

Lip Reading Based on Sampled Active Contour Model
*Takeshi Saitoh, Ryosuke Konishi* ................................. 507

Fast Viseme Recognition for Talking Head Application
*Mariusz Leszczynski, Władysław Skarbek, Stanisław Badura* ........ 516

Image Analysis by Discrete Orthogonal Hahn Moments
*Jian Zhou, Huazhong Shu, Hongqing Zhu, Christine Toumoulin, Limin Luo* .................................................... 524

On Object Classification: Artificial vs. Natural
*Minhwan Kim, Changmin Park, Kyongmo Koo* .................... 532

Recognition of Passports Using a Hybrid Intelligent System
*Kwang-Baek Kim, Sungshin Kim, Sang-An Ha* .................... 540

Description of Digital Images by Region-Based Contour Trees
*Shinobu Mizuta, Tetsuya Matsuda* ................................ 549

Compressing 2-D Shapes Using Concavity Trees
*O. El Badawy, M.S. Kamel* ...................................... 559

# Image Retrieval and Indexing

Content-Based Image Retrieval Using Perceptual Shape Features
*Mei Wu, Qigang Gao* ........................................... 567

Compressed Telesurveillance Video Database Retrieval Using Fuzzy Classification System
*Samia F. Khelifi, M. Elarbi Boudihir, Rachid Nourine* ............. 575

Machine-Learning-Based Image Categorization
*Yutao Han, Xiaojun Qi* ......................................... 585

Improving Shape-Based CBIR for Natural Image Content Using a Modified GFD
*Yupeng Li, Matthew J. Kyan, Ling Guan* ........................ 593

Probabilistic Similarity Measures in Image Databases with SVM Based
Categorization and Relevance Feedback
   *Md. Mahmudur Rahman, Prabir Bhattacharya, Bipin C. Desai* ..... 601

## 3D Imaging

3D Geometry Reconstruction from a Stereoscopic Video Sequence
   *A. Salgado, J. Sánchez* ......................................... 609

Three-Dimensional Planar Profile Registration in 3D Scanning
   *João Filipe Ferreira, Jorge Dias* ................................. 617

Text-Pose Estimation in 3D Using Edge-Direction Distributions
   *Marius Bulacu, Lambert Schomaker* ............................. 625

A Neural Network-Based Algorithm for 3D Multispectral Scanning
Applied to Multimedia
   *Alamin Mansouri, Alexandra Lathuiliere, Franck S. Marzani,*
   *Yvon Voisin, Pierre Gouton* ..................................... 635

A Novel Stereo Matching Method for Wide Disparity Range Detection
   *Dongil Han, Dae-Hwan Hwang* .................................. 643

Three-Dimensional Structure Detection from Anisotropic Alpha-Shapes
   *Sébastien Bougleux, Mahmoud Melkemi, Abderrahim Elmoataz* ...... 651

## Morphology

A Morphological Edge Detector for Gray-Level Image Thresholding
   *Bin Chen, Lei He, Ping Liu* ..................................... 659

Vector Morphological Operators for Colour Images
   *Valérie De Witte, Stefan Schulte, Mike Nachtegael,*
   *Dietrich Van der Weken, Etienne E. Kerre* ....................... 667

Decomposition of 3D Convex Structuring Element in Morphological
Operation for Parallel Processing Architectures
   *Syng-Yup Ohn* .................................................. 676

## Colour Analysis

Soft-Switching Adaptive Technique of Impulsive Noise Removal in
Color Images
   *Bogdan Smolka, Konstantinos N. Plataniotis* .................... 686

Color Indexing by Nonparametric Statistics
    *Ian Fraser, Michael Greenspan* .................................. 694

High Order Extrapolation Using Taylor Series for Color Filter Array
Demosaicing
    *J.S. Jimmy Li, Sharmil Randhawa* ............................. 703

Adaptive Colorimetric Characterization of Digital Camera with White
Balance
    *Soo-Wook Jang, Eun-Su Kim, Sung-Hak Lee, Kyu-Ik Sohng* ........ 712

A New Color Constancy Algorithm Based on the Histogram of Feasible
Mappings
    *Jaume Vergés–Llahí, Alberto Sanfeliu* .......................... 720

A Comparative Study of Skin-Color Models
    *Juwei Lu, Qian Gu, K.N. Plataniotis, Jie Wang* .................. 729

## Texture Analysis

Hermite Filter-Based Texture Analysis with Application to Handwriting
Document Indexing
    *Carlos Joel Rivero-Moreno, Stéphane Bres, Véronique Eglin* ........ 737

Rotation-Invariant Texture Classification Using Steerable Gabor Filter
Bank
    *Wumo Pan, T.D. Bui, C.Y. Suen* ............................... 746

Multiresolution Histograms for SVM-Based Texture Classification
    *Srinivas Andra, Yongjun Wu* ................................... 754

Texture Classification Based on the Fractal Performance of the Moment
Feature Images
    *Guitao Cao, Pengfei Shi, Bing Hu* .............................. 762

## Motion Analysis

Mapping Local Image Deformations into Depth
    *Stephen Benoit, Frank P. Ferrie* ................................ 770

Motion Segmentation Using a K-Nearest-Neighbor-Based Fusion
Procedure of Spatial and Temporal Label Cues
    *Pierre-Marc Jodoin, Max Mignotte* .............................. 778

2D Shape Measurement of Multiple Moving Objects by GMM
Background Modeling and Optical Flow
　　*Dongxiang Zhou, Hong Zhang* .................................... 789

Dynamic Water Motion Analysis and Rendering
　　*Yunjun Zhang* .................................................. 796

A Fast Real-Time Skin Detector for Video Sequences
　　*Farhad Dadgostar, Abdolhossein Sarrafzadeh* ..................... 804

Efficient Moving Object Segmentation Algorithm for Illumination
Change in Surveillance System
　　*Tae-Yeon Jung, Ju-Young Kim, Duk-Gyoo Kim* ..................... 812

## Tracking

Maintaining Trajectories of Salient Objects for Robust Visual Tracking
　　*Filiz Bunyak, S.R. Subramanya* ................................. 820

Real Time Head Tracking via Camera Saccade and Shape-Fitting
　　*Jason Z. Zhang, Ye Lu, Q.M. Jonathan Wu* ....................... 828

A Novel Tracking Framework Using Kalman Filtering and Elastic
Matching
　　*Xingzhi Luo, Suchendra M. Bhandarkar* .......................... 836

Singularity Detection and Consistent 3D Arm Tracking Using
Monocular Videos
　　*Feng Guo, Gang Qian* ........................................... 844

Predictive Estimation Method to Track Occluded Multiple Objects
Using Joint Probabilistic Data Association Filter
　　*Heungkyu Lee, Hanseok Ko* ...................................... 852

## Biomedical Applications

A Model-Based Hematopoietic Stem Cell Tracker
　　*Nezamoddin N. Kachouie, Paul Fieguth, John Ramunas,
　　Eric Jervis* .................................................... 861

Carotid Artery Ultrasound Image Segmentation Using Fuzzy Region
Growing
　　*Amr R. Abdel-Dayem, Mahmoud R. El-Sakka* ....................... 869

Vector Median Root Signals Determination for cDNA Microarray Image Segmentation
*Rastislav Lukac, Konstantinos N. Plataniotis* .................... 879

A New Method for DNA Microarray Image Segmentation
*Luis Rueda, Li Qin* ........................................ 886

Comparative Pixel-Level Exudate Recognition in Colour Retinal Images
*Alireza Osareh, Bita Shadgar, Richard Markham* ................. 894

Artificial Life Feature Selection Techniques for Prostrate Cancer Diagnosis Using TRUS Images
*S.S. Mohamed, A.M. Youssef, E.F. El-Saadany, M.M.A. Salama* .... 903

A Border Irregularity Measure Using a Modified Conditional Entropy Method as a Malignant Melanoma Predictor
*Benjamin S. Aribisala, Ela Claridge* ........................... 914

Automatic Hepatic Tumor Segmentation Using Composite Hypotheses
*Kyung-Sik Seo* ............................................. 922

Automated Snake Initialization for the Segmentation of the Prostate in Ultrasound Images
*S. Rahnamayan, H.R. Tizhoosh, M.M.A. Salama* ................. 930

Bayesian Differentiation of Multi-scale Line-Structures for Model-Free Instrument Segmentation in Thoracoscopic Images
*Luke Windisch, Farida Cheriet, Guy Grimard* .................... 938

Segmentation of Ultrasonic Images of the Carotid
*Rui Rocha, Aurélio Campilho, Jorge Silva* ...................... 949

Genetic Model-Based Segmentation of Chest X-Ray Images Using Free Form Deformations
*Carlos Vinhais, Aurélio Campilho* ............................. 958

Suppression of Stripe Artifacts in Mammograms Using Weighted Median Filtering
*Michael Wirth, Dennis Nikitenko* .............................. 966

Feature Extraction for Classification of Thin-Layer Chromatography Images
*António V. Sousa, Ana Maria Mendonça, Aurélio Campilho, Rui Aguiar, C. Sá Miranda* ..................................... 974

A New Approach to Automatically Detecting Grids in DNA Microarray
Images
  *Luis Rueda, Vidya Vidyadharan* .................................. 982

Ultrafast Technique of Impulsive Noise Removal with Application to
Microarray Image Denoising
  *Bogdan Smolka, Konstantinos N. Plataniotis* ..................... 990

Detection of Microcalcification Clusters in Mammograms Using a
Difference of Optimized Gaussian Filters
  *Samuel Oporto-Díaz, Rolando Hernández-Cisneros,
  Hugo Terashima-Marín* ........................................... 998

A Narrow-Band Level-Set Method with Dynamic Velocity for Neural
Stem Cell Cluster Segmentation
  *Nezamoddin N. Kachouie, Paul Fieguth* .......................... 1006

Multi Dimensional Color Histograms for Segmentation of Wounds in
Images
  *Marina Kolesnik, Ales Fexa* .................................... 1014

## Face Recognition and Biometrics

Robust Face Recognition from Images with Varying Pose
  *Jae-Young Choi, Murlikrishna Viswanathan, Taeg-Keun Whangbo,
  Young-Gyu Yang, Nak-Bin Kim* .................................... 1023

Feature Extraction Used for Face Localization Based on Skin Color
  *Juan José de Dios, Narciso García* ............................. 1032

Rotation-Invariant Facial Feature Detection Using Gabor Wavelet and
Entropy
  *Ehsan Fazl Ersi, John S. Zelek* ................................ 1040

Face Recognition Using Optimized 3D Information from Stereo Images
  *Changhan Park, Seanae Park, Jeongho Shin, Joonki Paik,
  Jaechan Namkung* ................................................ 1048

Face Recognition – Combine Generic and Specific Solutions
  *Jie Wang, Juwei Lu, K.N. Plataniotis, A.N. Venetsanopoulos* .... 1057

Facial Asymmetry: A New Robust Biometric in the Frequency Domain
  *Sinjini Mitra, Marios Savvides, B.V.K. Vijaya Kumar* ........... 1065

Occluded Face Recognition by Means of the IFS
  *Andrea F. Abate, Michele Nappi, Daniel Riccio, Maurizio Tucci* .... 1073

Verification of Biometric Palmprint Patterns Using Optimal Trade-Off
Filter Classifiers
  *Pablo Hennings, Marios Savvides, B.V.K. Vijaya Kumar* .......... 1081

Advanced Correlation Filters for Face Recognition Using
Low-Resolution Visual and Thermal Imagery
  *Jingu Heo, Marios Savvides, B.V.K. Vijaya Kumar* ............... 1089

Robust Iris Recognition Using Advanced Correlation Techniques
  *Jason Thornton, Marios Savvides, B.V.K. Vijaya Kumar* .......... 1098

Secure and Efficient Transmissions of Fingerprint Images for Embedded
Processors
  *Daesung Moon, Yongwha Chung, Kiyoung Moon, SungBum Pan* .... 1106

On the Individuality of the Iris Biometric
  *Sungsoo Yoon, Seung-Seok Choi, Sung-Hyuk Cha, Yillbyung Lee,
  Charles C. Tappert* ............................................. 1118

Facial Component Detection for Efficient Facial Characteristic Point
Extraction
  *Jeong-Su Oh, Dong-Wook Kim, Jin-Tae Kim, Yong-In Yoon,
  Jong-Soo Choi* ................................................. 1125

The Effect of Facial Expression Recognition Based on the Dimensions
of Emotion Using PCA Representation and Neural Networks
  *Young-Suk Shin* ............................................... 1133

Enhanced Facial Feature Extraction Using Region-Based
Super-Resolution Aided Video Sequences
  *T. Celik, C. Direkoglu, H. Ozkaramanli, H. Demirel, M. Uyguroglu* .. 1141

Efficient Face and Facial Feature Tracking Using Search Region
Estimation
  *C. Direkoğlu, H. Demirel, H. Özkaramanlı, M. Uyguroğlu* .......... 1149

# Image Secret Sharing

A Step Towards Practical Steganography Systems
  *Abdelkader H. Ouda, Mahmoud R. El-Sakka* ...................... 1158

New Aspect Ratio Invariant Visual Secret Sharing Schemes Using Square Block-Wise Operation
*Ching-Nung Yang, Tse-Shih Chen* ................................. 1167

Minimizing the Statistical Impact of LSB Steganography
*Zoran Duric, Dana Richards, Younhee Kim* ...................... 1175

Extended Visual Secret Sharing Schemes with High-Quality Shadow Images Using Gray Sub Pixels
*Ching-Nung Yang, Tse-Shih Chen* ................................ 1184

A Steganographic Method for Digital Images Robust to RS Steganalysis
*André R.S. Marçal, Patricia R. Pereira* ......................... 1192

## Single-Sensor Imaging

Estimation of Target Density Functions by a New Algorithm
*Askin Demirkol, Zafer Demir, Erol Emre* ........................ 1200

A Neural Network for Nonuniformity and Ghosting Correction of Infrared Image Sequences
*Sergio N. Torres, Cesar San Martin, Daniel G. Sbarbaro, Jorge E. Pezoa* ................................................ 1208

## Real-Time Imaging

Real-Time Image Processing Using Graphics Hardware: A Performance Study
*Minglun Gong, Aaron Langille, Mingwei Gong* ................... 1217

Real-Time and Robust Background Updating for Video Surveillance and Monitoring
*Xingzhi Luo, Suchendra M. Bhandarkar* ......................... 1226

Evaluation and Improvements of a Real-Time Background Subtraction Method
*Donatello Conte, Pasquale Foggia, Michele Petretta, Francesco Tufano, Mario Vento* ................................ 1234

Fixed Pixel Threshold PDC Algorithm and Its Implementation for Full Search Block Matching Motion Estimation
*Lynn Yang, Majid Ahmadi* ...................................... 1242

Robust Global Mosaic Topology Estimation for Real-Time Applications
  *Nuno Pinho da Silva, João Paulo Costeira* .......................  1250

Real-Time Digital Image Warping for Display Distortion Correction
  *Dongil Han* ...................................................  1258

Complexity-Controllable Motion Estimation for Real-Time Video
Encoder
  *Zhi Yang, Haixiang Zhang, Jiajun Bu, Chun Chen* ................  1266

**Author Index** ................................................  1275

# Localization Scale Selection for Scale-Space Segmentation

Sokratis Makrogiannis and Nikolaos Bourbakis

ITRI/CSE Department, Wright State University,
3640 Colonel Glenn Hwy, Dayton, OH, 45435-0001, USA
smakrogi@cs.wright.edu

**Abstract.** In this work the relation between scale-space image segmentation and selection of the localization scale is examined first, and a scale selection approach is consequently proposed in the segmentation context. Considering the segmentation part, gradient watersheds are applied to the non-linear scale-space domain followed by a grouping operation. A report on localization scale selection techniques is carried out next. Furthermore a scale selection method that originates from the evolution of the probability distribution of a region uniformity measure through the generated scales is proposed. The introduced algorithm is finally compared to a previously published approach that is also introduced into the segmentation context to indicate its efficacy.

## 1 Introduction

The topic of color image segmentation represents a popular and interesting research area. Several methods have been proposed in the past depending on the nature of the problem involved [8], [11], [12]. Previous works have shown that region based approaches outperform other methods in terms of segmentation accuracy and satisfactory results have been presented by many researchers. Recent segmentation methods tend to incorporate the multiscale nature of images. This allows the integration of both the deep and superficial image structure [11]. A popular subcategory of these approaches employs the scale-space theory to generate the domain of multiple scales.

The interaction of localization scale selection techniques and scale-space segmentation is studied in this paper. More specifically the localization scale in this work represents the starting point of the segmentation method. In the employed segmentation scheme, gradient watersheds are applied to the generated non-linear scale-space stack and a multiscale region grouping/merging process follows to form the final segmentation results. In the segmentation context, the selected localization scale should not contain excessive or lacking information, since this would produce an over- or under- segmented final result respectively. Previous considerations for automated scale selection [1], [4] are reported and a scale selection criterion is finally proposed and compared to the approach proposed by Lin and Shi in [1].

## 2 Outline of the Segmentation Scheme

The employed segmentation scheme may be divided into three stages; application of watersheds in scale-space, multiscale dissimilarity estimation and finally region grouping.

*Generation of Scale-Space and Watershed Segmentation.* The domain of multiple scales is generated by the iterative application of an inhomogeneous filter that reduces the amount of diffusion at those locations, which have a larger likelihood to be edges [9]. This likelihood is measured by the squared gradient. The PDE equation of the filtering process is expressed by:

$$\delta_t \cdot u = div(g(|\nabla u|^2) \cdot \nabla u) \quad (1)$$

where $g(.)$ is a function that determines the amount of diffusion and is referred to as diffusion tensor.

The watershed is subsequently applied to the modulus of the color gradient of the generated scales, where the appropriate color distance is estimated by local non-parametric density kernel estimation [3]. The linking of the watershed regions for successive scales is applied using a spatial proximity criterion [10].

*Region Dissimilarity at Multiple Scales.* In this work the inter-region (dis) similarity relation is represented by a Region Adjacency Graph (RAG) built on the localization i.e. the starting scale. The RAG edge weights are determined by a multiscale region dissimilarity measure. The employed region features are the dynamics of contours and the relative entropy of the region distributions. These are used as fuzzy variables in a fuzzy rule based scheme to measure the dissimilarity of two adjacent regions in each scale. Given the linking information from the previous stage, the outcome of the fuzzy logic system is subsequently summed up over the successive scales to obtain a more robust dissimilarity measure. The multiresolution dissimilarity measure is expressed by the following equation:

$$RD(p,q) = \sum_{i=So}^{Sa} F(DC_i^{L(p,q)}, RE_i^{L(p,q)}) \quad (2)$$

where $p$ and $q$ are two adjacent regions at the localization scale $S_o$, $L_{p,q}$ is the linking list derived from the scale space generation stage, $DC_i$ denotes the dynamics of contours in each scale $i$, $RE_i$ symbolizes the relative entropy of the sample distributions of the two examined regions in scale $i$ and $F(.,.)$ denotes the fuzzy inference scheme that estimates the pairwise dissimilarity.

The *Dynamics of Contours* is a contrast measure based on the notion of dynamics of the minima that were tracked during the watershed process and the flooding scenario of the watershed transform. The latter is used to locate the most significant minimum of the flooding chain [7].

The *Relative Entropy* is a stochastic dissimilarity measure between two distributions, estimated here by a variation of the Kullback-Leibler distance:

$$REp,q = \sum_{g=0}^{255} \left[ P_p(g) \cdot \log_{10}(\frac{P_p(g)}{P_q(g)}) + P_q(g) \cdot \log_{10}(\frac{P_q(g)}{P_p(g)}) \right] \quad (3)$$

Parzen kernels are also utilized to estimate the multivariate probability density.

*Fuzzy Inference Scheme.* The employed fuzzy inference scheme uses as input variables the dynamics of contours and the relative entropy and as output variable the degree of dissimilarity. Both input variables are divided into two sets, namely SMALL and LARGE. The output variable comprises two fuzzy sets called SIMILAR and NOTSIMILAR.

The fuzzy inference includes the following rules:

1. If dynamics_of_contours (SMALL) AND relative_entropy (SMALL) THEN output (SIMILAR)
2. If dynamics_of_contours (LARGE) OR relative_entropy (LARGE) THEN output (NOT_SIMILAR).

*Region Grouping.* A subtractive nearest neighbor finding approach may be applied to the RAG graph edges using the estimated dissimilarity measure $RD(p,q)$ as the graph edge weight. An additional algorithm was also employed, based on a minimax operation on the RAG structure to produce the different groups of regions (denoted by RAG-Minimax) [5]. RAG-Minimax derived better segmentation results and was finally adopted in this work.

The nodes linked by the remaining edges are subsequently merged and updated until the termination criterion is met. The termination criterion is determined by means of thresholding on the global distribution (histogram) of the graph edge weights.

## 3 Selection of the Localization Scale

The overall performance of the proposed multiscale scheme is strongly dependent on the number and significance of the regions present in the localization scale $S_0$. This is mainly due to the application of the watershed algorithm on the original image to produce the initial region set. The number of regions may be reduced by some type (Gaussian or Anisotropic Diffusion) of smoothing on the original image; the smoothed image corresponds to the localization scale. Our task here is to determine the amount of diffusion that needs to be applied, so that the problems of over- and under- segmentation, and the dislocation of contours are reasonably reduced.

The field of scale selection has been previously studied in the literature. Some of the related approaches take into consideration the evolution of the top points of the gradient image across scales [2], or the correlation of signal and noise [6], when the image is corrupted by noise. Besides that, an interesting approach was also presented in [1], where the appropriate scale is selected by calculating a smoothness variable across scales and estimating the minimum of its second order derivative (see Figure 1). The main idea is that if a noisy area is supposed to be flat (i.e. small gradient magnitude) and it becomes smooth enough (i.e. the weighted sum of the second order derivatives of the image is small) after some iterations, the algorithm stops. As a result, the employed smoothness variable is defined as the ratio of the flat pixels over the number of smooth pixels. If $t_0$

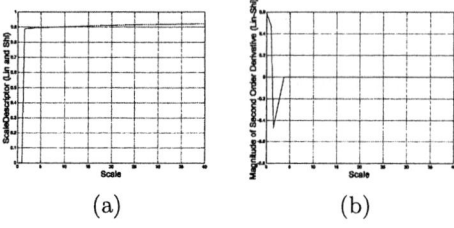

**Fig. 1.** Lin and Shi (a) scale descriptor and (b) second order derivative of (a) for image Lena

denotes the scale that corresponds to the second order derivative global minimum of the smoothness variable, then the selected scale $t_1$ is given by:

$$t1 = 2 \cdot t0. \tag{4}$$

In the following sections a brief study is conducted on selecting the localization scale for watershed-based segmentation. Our objective is to determine an initial scale that is characterized by the smallest possible over-segmentation, while preserving all significant watershed lines. In order to quantify this requirement, a scale descriptor has to be defined.

### 3.1 Scale Description Function

If we consider the scale selection as an interpretation problem, a global feature should be defined to express the degradation of details in the context of segmentation. In this work it is expressed by the portion of dissimilar regions in the over-segmented image that is produced by the watershed transform in each scale. Similarly, this corresponds to the probability of occurrence of dissimilar regions i.e. visually significant contours.

The region dissimilarity measure adopted in this work is the relative entropy between the distributions of two adjacent regions (see section 2). This dissimilarity value is attributed to each watershed line. It is worth noting that the feature of dynamics of contours is excluded from the scale descriptor calculation. This is due to the fact that the dynamics of contours involves also information from the flooding history in the watershed process, therefore it is not a pure statistical homogeneity measure.

The scale description function can be considered as a stochastic process, the distribution of which changes with scale. The proposed Scale Descriptor ($SD$) is thus expressed by the following relation:

$$SD(t) = P(RE(t) > T) = 1 - P(RE(t) \leq T). \tag{5}$$

The quantity $SD$ is thus defined as the probability of relative entropy $RE$ to be larger than $T$ ($T$ is regularly set to 1). This probability is given by the density estimation of $RE$ *for a given scale $t$*. It is calculated as the ratio of the contours with $RE > T$ over the total number of contours for scale $t$ or equally, from the

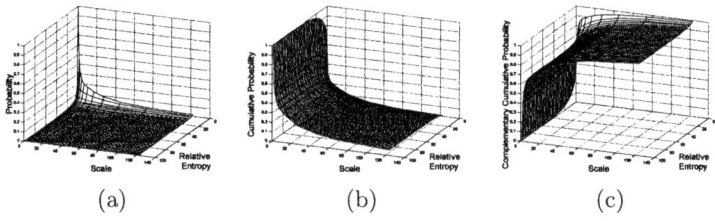

**Fig. 2.** Three-dimensional plot of (a) the probability density of Relative Entropy as a function of scale (image Lena), (b) the corresponding probability distribution (cumulative) function and (c) the complementary of (b)

complement of the probability distribution function. This may be also defined as the perpendicular intersection of the complementary distribution function (Figure 2c) for a specific value $T$ of the Relative Entropy quantity across different time scales. Figure 2 displays the evolution of the probability density of relative entropy in successive scales (Figure 2a), the corresponding cumulative distribution (Figure 2b) and the complementary quantity of (b) with respect to the value 1 (in Figure 2c). The evolution of $SD$ is depicted in Figure 3a for the image Lena.

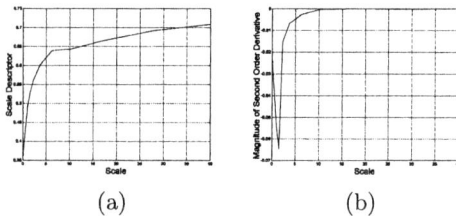

**Fig. 3.** Graph of (a) evolution of the scale descriptor SD and (b) its second order derivative for image Lena

### 3.2 Scale Selection Approaches

According to $SD$, the localization scale is defined as the scale that follows an abrupt loss of information. This is interpreted as a rapid decrement of the slope of this function and is given by the global minimum of the second order derivative (Figure 3b). This selected localization scale is therefore estimated by:

$$t_{req} = k \cdot \arg\min(\frac{\partial^2 SD}{\partial t^2}). \tag{6}$$

The $k$ parameter was experimentally set to 2.

Some other variations of the above scale selection approach have also been considered before concluding with the proposed method [4]. One consideration was based on a normalized scale descriptor that was given by the probability of $RE > T$ over the total amount of contours that were estimated *on all the* generated time scales. It was observed that this scale description function has an approximately exponential shape and several scale selection approaches were accordingly developed. The first localization scale selection criterion was readily estimated by the slope of the normalized scale descriptor itself. Another idea was to approximate the normalized scale description function using exponential approximation by solving the equivalent problem of an $RC$ electronic circuit. Two cases were examined here; the first one is to estimate the scale that is equivalent to the $RC$ parameter of an $RC$ filter, when the capacitor is practically charged. According to the other case the localization scale is estimated as the scale that is located closer to the corner of the exponential approximation. However it was experimentally found that these three scale selection approaches often produce under-segmented results, i.e. some important visual information is lost [4]. Therefore the scale selection approach defined by (5) and (6) was found to be more suitable for the proposed scheme and is also compared to [1] in the following section.

## 4 Experimental Results and Conclusion

The proposed scale selection approach is compared to the Lin and Shi Selection approach (denoted by LSS) using both qualitative and quantitative measures. The qualitative evaluation is carried out by visually examining the delineation accuracy and region uniformity of the final results. The quantitative evaluation is obtained using the Yang and Liu criterion [12]:

$$YLGC = \sqrt{\frac{R}{h \cdot w \cdot c}} \cdot \sum_{i=1}^{R} \sigma i^2 \cdot \sqrt{Ai} \qquad (7)$$

where $h$, $w$ and $c$ is the number of rows, columns and channels of the image respectively, $R$ the total number of regions, $\sigma_i^2$ the color error over region $i$, $A_i$ the number of pixels of region $i$. This criterion expresses the trade-off between the suppression of heterogeneity and preservation of details. Smaller values of $YLGC$, denote more accurate and concise segmentation results.

Table 1 summarizes the evaluation and comparison study of our proposed approach for the localization scale selection (denoted by SODM: Second Order Derivative Minimum), versus the Lin and Shi approach [1] adapted to the image segmentation context. Furthermore, Figure 4 illustrates the localization scale segmentation results of the compared methods for our test images. Figure 5 depicts the corresponding final results based on the different localization scales to evaluate the overall system performance. *Qualitatively*, the SODM criterion outperforms the LSS approach for every test image, i.e. the detected regions represent more accurately the visual content. From the *quantitative YLGC* segmentation measure it becomes obvious that both of the examined methods produce almost equal results, with the SODM approach being marginally better in three cases.

In conclusion, the applicability of a localization scale selection to multiscale image segmentation is examined in this paper. A study of scale selection methods

**Table 1.** Scale selection results in terms of number of regions and segmentation accuracy

| Test Image | Parrots | | Peppers | | Tree | | Woman | |
|---|---|---|---|---|---|---|---|---|
| Scale selection method | LSS | SODM | LSS | SODM | LSS | SODM | LSS | SODM |
| No. of Wat. Regions (orig. image) | 1621 | 1621 | 2239 | 2239 | 2582 | 2582 | 1345 | 1345 |
| Selected Scale (t) | 3.75 | 2.25 | 6.25 | 2.25 | 1.5 | 6.25 | 6.25 | 10.25 |
| No. of Wat. Regions (local. scale) | 896 | 1020 | 937 | 1152 | 2056 | 1800 | 220 | 150 |
| Segmentation Measure (local. scale) | 187.74 | 212.19 | 138.49 | 170.53 | 527.88 | 315.02 | 22.24 | 16.28 |
| No. of Regions (final) | 120 | 120 | 100 | 100 | 200 | 200 | 25 | 25 |
| Segmentation Measure (final) | 69.40 | 67.98 | 52.46 | 47.57 | 98.66 | 94.26 | 6.82 | 7.05 |

**Fig. 4.** Contour maps of the localization scale (initial segmentation). First row: test images Parrots, Tree and Woman. Second Row: Selected scale using LSS. Third Row: SODM results.

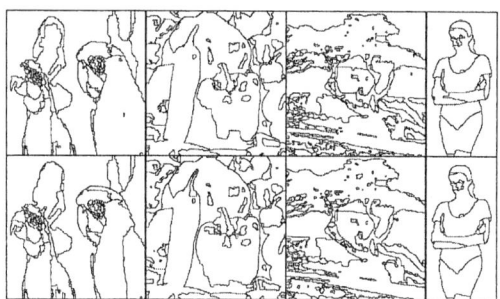

**Fig. 5.** Final segmentation results. First Row: LSS results. Second Row: SODM results.

has been conducted in order to automatically determine the localization scale of the presented segmentation method. A novel scale descriptor has been proposed that uses the relative entropy feature and several selection criteria have been tested and compared to a previously reported scale selection approach.

# References

1. Z. Lin and Q. Shi: An Anisotropic Diffusion PDE for Noise Reduction and Thin Edge Preservation. Proc. Int. Conf. on Image Analysis and Processing, (1999) 102–107.
2. T. Lindeberg: Feature Detection with Automatic Scale Selection. Int. Journal of Computer Vision Vol. 30, No. 2 (1998) 79–116.
3. G. Economou, A. Fotinos, S. Makrogiannis and S. Fotopoulos: Color Image Edge Detection Based on Nonparametric Estimation. Proc. IEEE Int. Conf. on Image Processing (ICIP 2001), Vol. 1 (2001) 922–925.
4. S. Makrogiannis I. Vanhamel and H. Sahli: Scale Space Segmentation of Color Images. IRIS-Technical Report No. 0076, ETRO Dept., Vrije Universiteit Brussel (2001) 1–44.
5. S. Makrogiannis, G. Economou, S. Fotopoulos and N.G. Bourbakis: Segmentation of Color Images Using Multiscale Clustering And Graph Theoretic Region Synthesis. IEEE Trans. on Systems, Man and Cybernetics: Part A, Vol. 35, No. 2 (2005) 224–238.
6. P. Mrazek and M. Navara: Selection of Optimal Stopping Time for Nonlinear Diffusion Filtering. Int. Journal of Computer Vision, Vol. 52, No. 2/3 (2003) 189–203.
7. L. Najman and M. Schmitt: Geodesic Saliency of Watershed Contours and Hierarchical Segmentation. IEEE Trans. on PAMI, Vol. 18, No. 12 (1996) 1163–1173.
8. N.R. Pal and S.K. Pal: A Review on Image Segmentation Techniques. Pattern Recognition, Vol. 26, No. 9 (1993) 1277–1294.
9. P. Perona and J. Malik: Scale-Space and Edge Detection Using Anisotropic Diffusion. IEEE Trans. on PAMI, Vol. 12, No. 7 (1990) 629–639.
10. I. Pratikakis, H. Sahli and J. Cornelis: Hierarchical Segmentation using Dynamics of Multiscale Gradient Watershed. Proc. $11^{th}$ Scandinavian Conference on Image Analysis 99, 1999 577–584.
11. P. de Smet, R. Pires, D. De Vleeschauwer and I. Bruyland: Activity Driven Nonlinear Diffusion for Color Image Watershed Segmentation. SPIE Journal of Electronic Imaging, Vol. 8, No. 3 (1999) 270–278.
12. Y.-H. Yang and J. Liu: Multiresolution Image Segmentation. IEEE Trans. on PAMI, Vol. 16 (1994) 689–700.

# Image Segmentation for the Application of the Neugebauer Colour Prediction Model on Inkjet Printed Ceramic Tiles

P. Latorre[1], G. Peris-Fajarnes[1], and M.A.T. Figueiredo[2]

[1] Depto Exp Grafica en la Ingenieria, Universidad Politecnica Valencia
Ctra. Nazaret-Oliva s.n., 46730, Grao de Gandia, Valencia, Spain
{platorre, gperis}@degi.upv.es
[2] Instituto de Telecomunicaçoes, Instituto Superior Tecnico
Torre Norte, Piso 10, Av. Rovisco Pais, 1049-001, Lisboa, Portugal
mtf@lx.it.pt

**Abstract.** Colour prediction models (CPM) can be used to analyze the printing quality of halftone-based color printing systems. In this paper, we consider the Neugebauer CPM which requires as input the fraction of occupation of each primary. To obtain these numbers, we apply several image segmentation algorithms, with and without contextual information. These segmentation algorithms are evaluated with respect to another technique based on mixtures of factor analyzers. More importantly, the segmentation results are evaluated with respect to the performance of the Neugebauer CPM when used with the obtained fractions of occupation. This evaluation is carried out by comparing the predicted color against that measured with a spectrophotometer, and testifies for the adequacy of the approach.

## 1 Introduction

The macroscopic color of a halftone design depends on several factors, including the morphology, ink distribution, and occupation area of the printed dots. Several approaches allow relating the microscopic distribution of dots with the resulting average macroscopic color [12]. These approaches, which are important in practice since they allow controlling the printing process, can be divided into two classes:

**Regression-based:** Some regression curve is adjusted to experimental data (usually in a minimum mean squared error sense), without considering the physics of the printing process. There are several regression-based models, such as Neugebauer, Murray-Davies, Yule-Nielsen, modified Neugebauer, and others [12].
**From "first principles":** These approaches are based on physical models of the processes occurring during and after printing; they are harder to implement and, as far as we know, haven't achieved the performance of regression-based methods [12].

In this paper we apply the *Neugebauer color prediction model* (N-CPM) to printed ceramic tiles. The N-CPM requires as input the relative area coverage of each printing primary. To obtain estimates of these numbers, we apply several non-contextual and contextual segmentation algorithms to the microscopic images of the printed surfaces. All algorithms are tested on two color spaces: RGB and the so-called *opponent color space* (OCS) [13], which were previously shown to give good results with one kind of printed dot [6]. As far as we know, CPMs have only recently been applied to ceramic tiles, but not using image analysis methods [4].

Section 2 describes the N-CPM and the experimental methods used to obtain the printed ceramic tiles and the corresponding images. In Section 3, we briefly discuss color image smoothing and the segmentation algorithms. Section 4 describes the generation of "ground-truth" images based on mixtures of factors analyzers [3]. Experimental results are reported in Section 5. The paper is concluded in Section 6.

## 2 The Neugebauer Color Prediction Model and the Experimental Procedure

We consider halftone designs of two inks, printed with an industrial binary CMYK inkjet printer for ceramic tiles [5]. For this type of printer, there are $2^4$ basic colors, called Neugebauer primaries [12]: the single colors cyan (C), magenta (M), yellow (Y), and black (K); all binary overlaps (CM, CY, MY, CK, MK, YK); all ternary overlaps (CMY, CMK, CYK, MYK), the single full overlap (CMYK), and the background.

According to the spectral Neugebauer CPM (N-CPM) [12], the overall reflectance of a halftone pattern is predicted as

$$R(\lambda) = \sum_i a_i R_i(\lambda), \qquad (1)$$

where $\lambda$ denotes wavelength, $R_i(\lambda)$ is the spectral reflectance curve (as a function of wavelength) of the $i^{th}$ Neugebauer primary at full colorant coverage, and $a_i$ is the fractional relative area coverage of that printing primary (with $\sum_i a_i = 1$).

To assess the N-CPM for two kinds of dots, we digitally created and printed two rows of $3 \times 3$ $cm^2$ halftones with the two inks, one of them with a theoretical dot area percentage fixed at 20%, and the other increasing from 20% to 80% in 10% steps (see Fig. 1, Left) on $20cm \times 30cm$ tiles with engobe and matt glaze layers on a fired biscuit base (for better consistency). Each square is named with the corresponding colors and dot area percentages; *e.g.*, C20M30 refers to 20% cyan and 30% of magenta (theoretical). We also created $3 \times 3$ $cm^2$ color squares with 100% occupation of the corresponding Neugebauer primaries for these halftones; *e.g.*, for cyan and magenta, these would be cyan, magenta, and overlapping, at 100% occupation, as well as background.

We acquired images using a CCD color camera with a zoom lens, under a bank of two 36-Watt daylight fluorescent lamps. The imaged area was $7mm \times 8.5mm$, at $50cm$ distance from the base of the camera to the tile surface (see Fig. 1).

For the application of the N-CPM, we measured reflectance curves of a $8mm$ radius circle of each halftone square patch, as well as of each Neugebauer primary with an *integrating sphere MINOLTA CM-508i spectrophotometer*, with illumination-geometry $D65/10°$. The spectral range covered is $[400 - 700]$ $nm$, in $10nm$ steps.

The segmentation algorithms will provide estimates of the $a_i$ parameters for use in (1). This allows comparing the N-CPM predicted reflectance curve with the corresponding spectrophotometer curve to assess its validity.

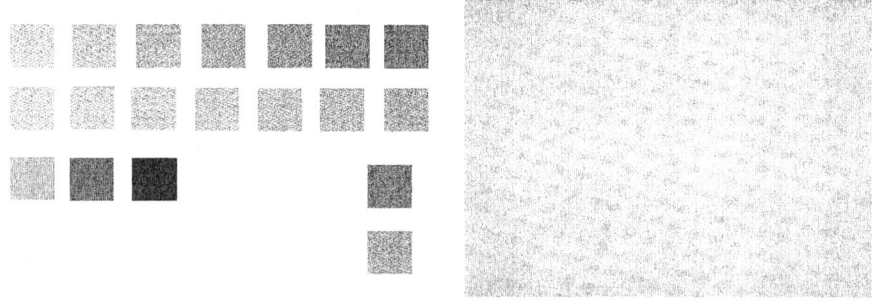

**Fig. 1.** Left: Digitally created file for $C$ and $M$. First row, Cyan fixed at 20%. Second row, Magenta fixed at 20%. Right: Image of $C$ at 30% and $M$ at 20% acquired with the Zoom lens.

## 3  Segmentation Algorithms to Estimate Dot Area

Due to the noise in the acquired images, they are pre-processed by a non-linear, edge-preserving, multichannel smoothing filter called *adaptive nearest neighbor filter*, the details of which are found in [6] and [2]. To segment the images, we used the following techniques, both in $RGB$ and OCS: fuzzy C-means (FCM); FCM with contextual information based on a Markov random field (FCM-MRF) [11]; mixture of Gaussians (MoG); contextual MoG, via the iterated conditional modes (ICM) algorithm [7], [8]; a new MoG method which also smoothes the posterior class probability estimates. For a detailed description of the FCM and FCM-MRF approaches, we refer the reader to [11].

The MoG model for images with two types of dots (say, cyan and magenta) considers each pixel as a sample of a random variable in $I\!R^3$ (RGB or OCS) with a 4-component MoG probability density function,

$$p(y) = \sum_{j=1}^{4} a_j \, \mathcal{N}(y|\mu_j, C_j);$$

the four Gaussian components correspond to the four Neugebauer primaries: pure cyan, pure magenta, overlap, and background. Parameters $\mu_j$ and $C_j$ are the mean vector and covariance matrix of each component, while $a_j$ is the weight of component $j$, to be used in the N-CPM equation (1). The standard expectation-maximization (EM) algorithm [7] obtains estimates of these parameters from a set of samples (pixels) $\{y_i, i = 1, ..., N\}$ by iterating two steps:

**E-step:** Compute the *a posteriori* probability that pixel $i$, for $i = 1, ..., N$, was produced by component $j$ (given the current estimates $\widehat{a}_j$, $\widehat{\mu}_j$, and $\widehat{C}_j$)

$$\tau_{ij} = \frac{\widehat{a}_j \, \mathcal{N}(y_i|\widehat{\mu}_j, \widehat{C}_j)}{\sum_{k=1}^{4} \widehat{a}_k \, \mathcal{N}(y_i|\widehat{\mu}_k, \widehat{C}_k)}, \qquad \text{for } j = 1, 2, 3, 4; \qquad (2)$$

**M-step:** Update the parameter estimates according to (for $j = 1, 2, 3, 4$)

$$\widehat{a}_j = \frac{\sum_i \tau_{ij}}{N}, \qquad \widehat{\mu}_j = \frac{\sum_i y_i \tau_{ij}}{\sum_i \tau_{ij}}, \qquad \widehat{C}_j = \frac{\sum_i (y_i - \widehat{\mu}_j)(y_i - \widehat{\mu}_j)^T \tau_{ij}}{\sum_i \tau_{ij}}.$$

The ICM approach is based on the same MoG model. The first phase of this approach is to run the EM algorithm until convergence. In the second phase, a modified EM algorithm is applied, based on a modified E-step in which the *a posteriori* probabilities are spatially smoothed using a window centered on that pixel:

$$\tau'_{ij} = \frac{\eta_{ij} \mathcal{N}(y_i|\widehat{\mu}_j, \widehat{C}_j)}{\sum_{k=1}^{4} \eta_{ik} \mathcal{N}(y_i|\widehat{\mu}_k, \widehat{C}_k)}, \quad \text{with} \quad \eta_{ij} = \frac{\exp(\beta \sum_{n \in W_i} \tau_{nj})}{\sum_{k=1}^{4} \exp(\beta \sum_{n \in W_i} \tau_{nj})}, \quad (3)$$

where $W_i$ is a window centered around pixel $i$ and the $\tau_{ij}$ are computed according to the standard E-step (2). The smoothed $\tau'_{ij}$ posterior probabilities are then used in the standard M-step.

We also propose a new method to smooth the *a posteriori* probabilities. The key idea is that each set of *a posteriori* probabilities $\{\tau_{i1}, ..., \tau_{i4}\}$, which have to be nonnegative ($\tau_{ij} \geq 0$) and normalized ($\tau_{i1} + ... + \tau_{i4} = 1$), can be expressed by 3 unconstrained real variables $\{\alpha_{i1}, \alpha_{i2}, \alpha_{i3}\}$ using a so-called multinomial logistic transformation:

$$\tau_{i1} = \frac{e^{\alpha_{i1}}}{1 + \sum_{j=1}^{3} e^{\alpha_{ij}}}, \quad \tau_{i2} = \frac{e^{\alpha_{i2}}}{1 + \sum_{j=1}^{3} e^{\alpha_{ij}}}, \quad \tau_{i3} = \frac{e^{\alpha_{i3}}}{1 + \sum_{j=1}^{3} e^{\alpha_{ij}}}, \quad \tau_{i4} = \frac{1}{1 + \sum_{j=1}^{3} e^{\alpha_{ij}}}.$$
(4)

This transformation is of course invertible according to

$$\alpha_{i1} = \log\left(\frac{\tau_{i1}}{\tau_{i4}}\right), \quad \alpha_{i2} = \log\left(\frac{\tau_{i2}}{\tau_{i4}}\right), \quad \alpha_{i3} = \log\left(\frac{\tau_{i3}}{\tau_{i4}}\right). \quad (5)$$

The proposed approach consists of computing the $\alpha_{ij}$ variables according to (5) after the last E-step, spatially smoothing these variables using any filter (since these variables are under no constraints) and then recomputing the $\tau_{ij}$ variables using (4).

## 4  Obtaining the "Groundtruth" Segmentations

In [6] it was shown, for one type of printed dot, that singular value decomposition (SVD) could be used to create images that can be seen as *groundtruth*. In fact, the SVD was just the first of a series of steps which included morphological operations and the *connected components labelling* method; see [6] for full details. For images of two printed dots, we propose the use of mixtures of factors analyzers (MFA) [3], which can be seen as a local generalization of factor analysis (FA, [1]). For lack of space, we can not give details of the MFA approach, and the reader is referred to [3] for more information. Fig. 2 shows examples of these segmentations obtained by MFA, after some post-processing steps [6], as well as segmentations obtained by the ICM algorithm described in Section 3.

## 5  Results and Discussion

### 5.1  Segmentation Results

To compare the segmentation results produced by the algorithms described in Section 3 with the MFA-based segmentations, we computed sensitivity *per class* (SC)

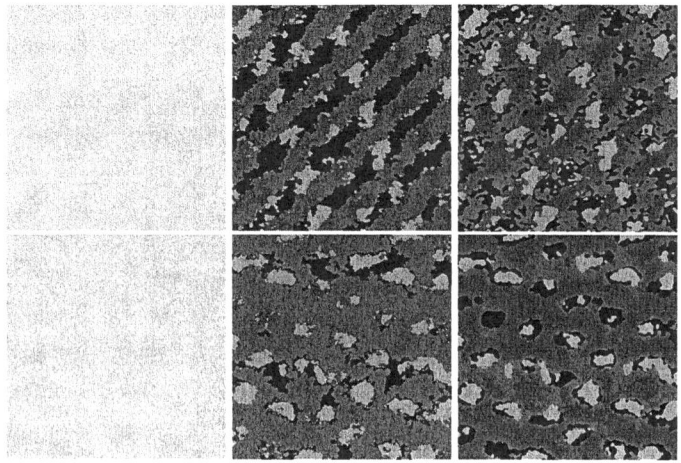

**Fig. 2.** Left column: original images of $C50Y20$ and $M20Y80$. Center column: corresponding MFA-generated *groundtruth*. Right column: ICM based segmentation results.

**Table 1.** Sensitivities (per class) and overall accuracies. $GS1$ means Gaussian smoothing with standard deviation $\sigma = 0.3$ with a $3 \cdot 3$ window size. $GS2$, standard deviation $\sigma = 1.0$ with a $3 \cdot 3$ window size. $GS3$, standard deviation $\sigma = 1.0$ with a $5 \cdot 5$ window size. $GS4$, standard deviation $\sigma = 3.0$ with a $5 \cdot 5$ window size. ANN is the adaptation of the Adaptive Nearest Neighbour Filter, as in [2], applied on a $3 \cdot 3$ window.

|  | SC-C | SC-M | SC-Y | SC-CM | SC-CY | SC-MY | SC-Back | Overall accuracy |
|---|---|---|---|---|---|---|---|---|
| FCM | 67,23 | 67,41 | 69,37 | 61,66 | 54,75 | 66,64 | 75,81 | 64,46 |
| FCM-MRF | 67,53 | 65,61 | 69,77 | 62,24 | 56,43 | 66,87 | 75,72 | 64,75 |
| EM | 67,54 | 74,70 | 71,62 | 70,26 | 57,42 | 82,60 | 81,20 | 73,64 |
| EM-ICM | 68,17 | **75,72** | **72,32** | 70,90 | **58,34** | 82,18 | **82,31** | **74,08** |
| EM GS1 | 67,86 | 74,58 | 72,28 | 70,75 | 57,83 | 83,04 | 81,23 | 74,02 |
| EM GS2 | 67,99 | 74,29 | 72,07 | 70,67 | 57,84 | 82,95 | 81,15 | 73,94 |
| EM GS3 | 68,15 | 74,07 | 71,93 | 70,87 | 58,07 | 83,07 | 81,03 | 73,90 |
| EM GS4 | 68,23 | 73,69 | 71,55 | 71,02 | 58,24 | 83,05 | 80,74 | 73,73 |
| EM ANN | 67,53 | 74,52 | 71,95 | 70,22 | 57,90 | 82,39 | 81,07 | 73,79 |

values as well as overall accuracies (OA). These quantities are given by: $SC = TP/(TP + FN)$, where $TP$ stands for "true positives" and $FN$ for "false negatives"; $OA = NCC/(NCC + NIC)$, where $NCC$ denotes the "number of correct classifications" and $NIC$ means "number of incorrect classifications". Table 1 reports results for all segmentation methods in $RGB$ (all methods did worse in OCS, so we omit those results). We see that the ICM algorithm gives the best results in terms of $OA$. The alternative method that we have proposed performs only slightly worse, with the advantage that the contextual part is applied only once.

### 5.2 Assessing the Neugebauer Model

We assess the N-CPM by comparing the experimentally measured spectral reflectance for each printed patch (see Section 2) against the spectral curves predicted by the N-

**Table 2.** Comparing spectrophotometer and model predicted reflectance curves: first row in each case is the MFA-based result, the second row is the result by the ICM algorithm

|  | RMS value (%) | DeltaE76 | DeltaE00 | MI00 |
|---|---|---|---|---|
| C20M20 | 6,74 | 4,86 | 3,66 | 1,99 |
|  | 5,31 | 3,27 | 2,30 | 1,36 |
| C20M30 | 8,15 | 5,50 | 3,98 | 1,74 |
|  | 4,69 | 2,93 | 2,39 | 1,48 |
| C20M40 | 8,75 | 6,90 | 5,09 | 1,70 |
|  | 6,81 | 4,84 | 4,02 | 2,07 |
| C20M50 | 7,73 | 4,98 | 3,80 | 1,63 |
|  | 5,82 | 5,25 | 4,53 | 1,89 |
| C20M60 | 5,12 | 3,97 | 3,07 | 1,24 |
|  | 5,98 | 4,22 | 3,27 | 1,38 |
| C20M70 | 3,69 | 6,25 | 4,37 | 0,44 |
|  | 4,79 | 6,86 | 4,99 | 1,28 |
| C20Y20 | 2,25 | 1,34 | 1,00 | 0,53 |
|  | 5,56 | 3,58 | 2,58 | 1,16 |
| C20Y30 | 7,77 | 7,66 | 5,71 | 2,33 |
|  | 4,37 | 3,54 | 2,54 | 1,31 |
| C20Y40 | 6,20 | 3,98 | 2,68 | 1,72 |
|  | 5,52 | 5,63 | 3,87 | 1,62 |
| C20Y50 | 4,96 | 6,05 | 4,03 | 0,94 |
|  | 3,97 | 3,14 | 2,02 | 1,15 |
| C20Y60 | 1,55 | 1,24 | 1,04 | 0,22 |
|  | 1,87 | 1,13 | 1,11 | 0,15 |
| C20Y70 | 6,57 | 10,25 | 6,00 | 1,05 |
|  | 6,27 | 9,26 | 5,39 | 0,76 |
| M20Y20 | 4,30 | 2,89 | 2,14 | 0,72 |
|  | 4,83 | 3,76 | 2,68 | 0,67 |
| M20Y30 | 6,40 | 5,03 | 3,43 | 0,78 |
|  | 5,05 | 3,75 | 2,64 | 0,76 |
| M20Y40 | 8,40 | 7,30 | 6,91 | 1,02 |
|  | 8,76 | 7,50 | 6,99 | 1,03 |
| M20Y50 | 5,48 | 5,01 | 3,07 | 0,77 |
|  | 8,89 | 7,69 | 7,06 | 1,06 |
| M20Y60 | 4,95 | 3,88 | 2,66 | 0,79 |
|  | 4,76 | 5,86 | 5,13 | 0,91 |
| M20Y70 | 5,47 | 5,99 | 4,95 | 0,89 |
|  | 3,95 | 4,39 | 3,39 | 0,80 |

CPM based on the *groundtruth* segmentation and the one obtained by the ICM algorithm described in Section 3. The predicted spectral curves are obtained by plugging the estimated dot area coverage (parameters $a_i$ from the segmentations) and the reflectance curves of the Neugebauer primaries into (1). To compare predicted and mea-

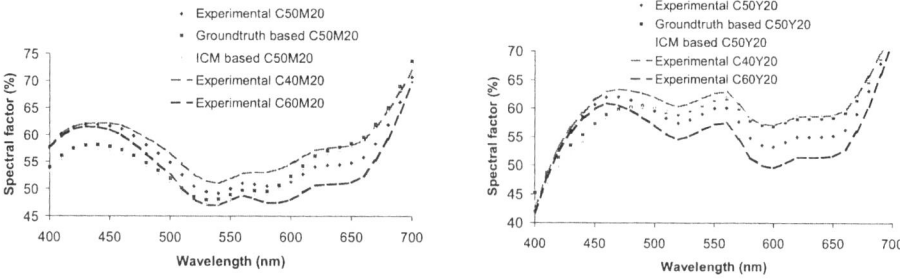

**Fig. 3.** Model predicted spectral reflectance curves of $C50M20$ and $C50Y20$

sured spectral reflectance curves, we use the following quantities [10]: the root mean squared (RMS) error between the two curves; the $\Delta E_{L^*a^*b^*}$ color difference; the $\Delta E_{00}$ color difference; and the metameric index $MI_{00}$. The $\Delta E_{L^*a^*b^*}$ and $\Delta E_{00}$ colour differences are particularly relevant since they try to match the human color perception. The procedure to obtain an $L^*a^*b^*$ color from a spectral reflectance curve is described in [6].

Table 2 shows values for a set of test images. It is known that humans can only discern color differences when $\Delta E_{L^*a^*b^*} > 3.5$ [9]. Thus, we can state that the MFA-based results and the results produced by the ICM algorithm yield good colour predictions with the Neugebauer model.

In Fig. 3 we can see the experimental and predicted reflectance curves for two cases: $C50Y20$ and $C50M20$. For $C50Y20$, we also show $C40Y20$ and $C60Y20$ reflectance curves, and for $C50M20$, we show the $C40M20$ and $C60M20$ curves. These curces can be seen as a kind of bounds for the predicted reflectances. These two plots show a slight limitation in the lower part of the spectrum, for these two cases, of the prediction capability.

## 6 Conclusion

We have investigated the use of some non-contextual and contextual segmentation algorithms for images of halftone patterns with two types of printed dots, taken from ink-jet printed ceramic surfaces. *Groundtruth* and ICM segmentation results are used to feed a Neugebauer colour prediction model which outputs predictions of spectral reflectance curves. These predicted curves were compared with experimental ones (obtained with a spectrophotometer) under several error measures (some of them of perceptual nature). We have concluded that the predicted colors are close to the measured ones.

This paper has established a color prediction framework for ink-jet printing technology on ceramic tiles for four-color patterns. The next step will be to analyze images with three types of printed dots ($C$, $M$ and $Y$), which implies the existence of 8 ($2^3$) different clusters, four of which correspond to overlapping of inks.

## Acknowledgements

This work has been partially funded by the European Project MONOTONE (G1RD-CT-2002-00783).

# References

1. A. Basilevsky, *Statistical Factor Analysis and Related Methods.* John Wiley & Sons New York (1994).
2. M. J. Cree, "Observations on Adaptive Vector Filters for Noise Reduction in Color Images," *IEEE Signal Processing Letters,* vol. 11, no. 2 (2004) 140-143.
3. Z. Ghahramani, G. Hinton, *The EM algorithm for Mixtures of Factor Analyzers.* Technical Report CRG-TR-96-1 University of Toronto (1996).
4. L. Iovine, S. Westland, T. L. V. Cheung, "Application of Neugebauer-based Models to Ceramic Printing," *IS&T / SID Twelfth Color Imaging* (2004) 176-180.
5. Kerajet Ink-Jet printing system. http://www.kerajet.com
6. P. Latorre, G. Peris-Fajarnes, M. Mirmehdi, B. Thomas, "Assessing the Neuegbauer Colour Prediction Model for Ink-jet Printed Ceramic Tiles," *Proceedings of the 4th IASTED International Conference on Visualization, Imaging, and Image Processing,* (2004) 636-641.
7. G. McLachlan, D. Peel, *Finite Mixture Models,* John Wiley & Sons New York (2000).
8. G. McLachlan, S. K. Ng, G. Galloway, D. Wang, "Clustering of Magnetic Resonance Images," *Proceedings of the American Statistical Association (Statistical Computing Section).* (1996) 12-17.
9. M. Stokes, M. D. Fairchild, R. S. Berns, "Colorimetrically Quantified Visual Tolerances for Pictorial Images," *Proceedings of TAGA,* (1992) 757-778.
10. L. A. Taplin, R. S. Berns, "Spectral Color Reproduction Based on Six-color Inkjet Output System," *Proceedings of the Ninth Color Imaging Conference: Colour Science and Engineering, Systems, Technologies, and Applications,* Springfield (2000) 209-213.
11. R. Wiemker, "Unsupervised Fuzzy Classification of Multispectral Imagery Using Spatial-Spectral Features," *Proceedings of the 21st Annual Meeting of the Gessellschaft für Klassifikation – GfKI'97,* pp. 12-14, Postdam, 1997.
12. D. Wyble, "A Critical Review of Spectral Models applied to Binary Color Printing," *Color Research and Applications,* vol. 25, (2000) 4-19.
13. X. Zhang, B. A. Wandell, "A Spatial Extension of Cielab for Digital Color Image Reproduction," *Society for Information Display* (1996).

# FCM with Spatial and Multiresolution Constraints for Image Segmentation

Adel Hafiane and Bertrand Zavidovique

Institut d'Electronique Fondamentale,
Université de Paris-Sud, Bâtiment 220,
F-91405 Orsay Cedex, France

**Abstract.** A modified FCM algorithm based on spatial and multiresolution constraints is described in this paper. First the pyramid is built from the original image then in each level FCM parameters are computed under a neighborhood spatial constraint. The coarse membership functions propagate down to fine layers to improve segmentation accuracy. The algorithm is tested on both synthetic and multispectral images. Experimental results are presented, showing the effectiveness of the method.

## 1 Introduction

Image segmentation is a key step in image processing and computer vision. It appears fundamental towards semantic Data Base retrieval, in partitioning an image into homogeneous regions with similar visual aspect from color, texture or spectral features. Such segmentation can be formalized as a classification problem where each pixel is assigned to a specific class. Clustering techniques – unsupervised classification – have thus gained considerable attention lately for these applications [1,2]. Widely used in this purpose Fuzzy C-Means (FCM) algorithm [3] shows good clustering performance[4]. The segmentation is obtained by minimizing a criterion based on a fuzzy distance between the prototypes and the image pixels. Although the original FCM algorithm yields good results in segmenting noise-free images, it generally fails to segment images corrupted by noise, outliers and other imaging artifacts. Therefore segmenting real world images such as remote sensing images by FCM can lead to unreasonably inconsistent segmentation. One way to deal with this problem is filtering images before to apply FCM. However filtering may loose some important information. To deal with this problem earlier works [5,6] show the improvement in segmentation results by incorporating the spatial information into the FCM algorithm. Other approaches incorporate a second constraint term for the membership function to be influenced by neighborhood membership functions [7]. Likewise, the second term added to the FCM objective function can deal straight with distances of neighbors to prototypes [8]. Those methods favour a direct contribution of neighbors' intensity values while other properties of that neighborhood could be taken into account.

In this paper we present an approach based on spatial and multiresolution constraints for FCM. We do not consider only the spatial information in the image plan, but also at different levels of resolution. The clustering process operates at each level of resolution, so that each point be influenced by its spatial neighborhood and its immediate ancestor in the pyramid. Two terms have been added to the original FCM objective function. The first one constrains the membership function of a given pixel to follow the neighbors' membership function. The second propagates in a similar way the father membership function to influence the child.

The paper is organized as follows. Section 2 describes the pyramidal representation. The new algorithm with the modified FCM is described in section 3. Our segmentation method being tested on both synthetic and real images, results are illustrated in section 4. The paper concludes in section 5.

## 2 Pyramidal Representation

Multiresolution methods are meant to provide a global view of an image by examining it at various frequency ranges. Different types of details are put forward at different levels in the associated pyramid structure. Also, it installs a set of relationship between image elements in different layers. Therefor such representation allows building some consistency property. Indeed, for instance if one pixel belongs to a specific class with a high membership value at a level $n$ and its ancestor at level $(n-1)$ belongs to the same class with also a high membership value, therefore the pixel assignment to this class gains higher confidence. In most pyramidal decomposition schemes the image is successively decomposed into (low-pass) versions by combination of convolution and sub-sampling. Given an $NxN$ image $g$ and using an appropriate filter $h$ with size $LxK$, the image at lower resolution $(n-1)$ is given by

$$g^{n-1}(x,y) = \sum_{i=1}^{L}\sum_{j=1}^{K} h(i,j) g^{n}(2x-i, 2y-j) \quad (1)$$

A popular filter is the Gaussian (low-pass), other filters may turn appropriate depending on applications and types of features to enhance. The pyramid is obtained thereby applying the procedure described in (1) at successive levels, making the size of images decrease continuously. For instance, a quad tree image representation handles a pyramid structure where each element at level $(n-1)$ has four children at level $(n)$ see figure 1. Note that usually the higher level in the pyramidal representation has 0 index and the lowest gets $n$.

## 3 Spatial Multiresolution Constraint

The traditional FCM algorithm minimizes the objective function $J(U,V)$ defined as a sum of similarity measures. It is given by

$$J(U,V) = \sum_{i=1}^{C}\sum_{j=1}^{N} u_{ij}^{m} \| x_j - v_i \|^2 \quad (2)$$

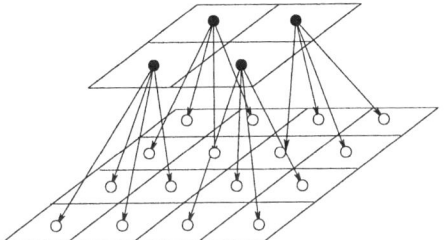

**Fig. 1.** Pyramidal representation

where $X = \{x_1, x_2, ..., x_N\}$ denotes the set of data $x_k$ corresponds to feature vector. $V = \{v_1, v_2, ..., v_C\}$ represents the prototypes, known as the cluster centers. $U = [u_{ij}]$ is the partition matrix which satisfies the following conditions:

$$U \left\{ u_{ij} \in [0,1] \;\; \forall i,j \quad 0 < \sum_{j}^{N} u_{ij} < N \;\; \forall i \quad \sum_{i}^{C} u_{ij} = 1 \;\; \forall j \right\} \quad (3)$$

$m$ is a fuzzifier that indicates the membership fuzziness for each point. FCM algorithm is an iterative process by minimizing the distance from each point to the prototypes. The FCM objective function in Eq. 2 does not incorporate any spatial context. This can lead to undesirable region formation. More over the classification process is extremely noise sensitive, as any smoothing effect would require neighbors. In order to overcome the problem, a regularization term will be added to constrain Eq. 2 so that classification of each point be influenced by its neighborhood and its immediate ancestor in the pyramidal representation. The modified objective function becomes:

$$J_{SCM}(U,V) = \sum_{i=1}^{C}\sum_{j=1}^{N} u_{ij}^m \| x_j - v_i \|^2 + \frac{n}{2}\alpha \sum_{i=1}^{C}\sum_{j=1}^{N} u_{ij}^m e^{-\sum_{k \in \Omega} u_{ik}^m}$$
$$+ \quad \beta \sum_{i=1}^{C}\sum_{j=1}^{N} u_{ij}^m f_i^{(n-1)}(x_j) \quad (4)$$

where $\Omega$ is a set of neighbors ($k \neq j$). $f_i^{(n-1)}(x_j)$ is the point $x_j$ 's ancestor membership function to the $i^{th}$ cluster in lower layer $(n-1)$. Parameters $\alpha$ and $\beta$ are weights to control the influence of the related term. $\alpha$ is multiplied by a scale factor $(\frac{n}{2})$ to diminish the importance of the spatial constraint at lower levels. The objective function (4) is now comprised of three terms. The first is the same as in regular FCM. The second is a penalty term that incorporates spatial relationships in the neighborhood. It tends to forcing a pixel belong to the same class as its neighbors thereby using the membership functions to correlate the class of a point with classes of its spatial neighbors. This second term reaches a minimum when the membership value of neighbors for a particular cluster is large. Remains to incorporate the relationship between classes of elements at different resolution levels for more feature consistency thus more confidence in the pixel classification. The third term conveys an influence of the father on the labeling of a pixel. The membership function at a coarser level precisely provides the fine level with information about the father membership value to a peculiar cluster. Optimizing (4) with respect to $U$ will be completed in a classical way by a Lagrange multiplier technique.

$$J_{SCM}(U,V) = \sum_{i=1}^{C}\sum_{j=1}^{N} u_{ij}^m \left( \| x_j - v_i \|^2 + \frac{n}{2}\alpha e^{-\sum_{k\in\Omega} u_{ik}^m} + \beta f_i^{(n-1)}(x_j) \right)$$
$$+ \sum_{j=1}^{N} \lambda_j (1 - \sum_{i=1}^{C} u_{ij}) \qquad (5)$$

The derivative of (5) versus $u_{ij}$ is

$$\frac{\partial J_{SCM}}{\partial u_{ij}} = m u_{ij}^{m-1} \left( \| x_j - v_i \|^2 + \frac{n}{2}\alpha e^{-\sum_{k\in\Omega} u_{ik}^m} + \beta f_i^{(n-1)}(x_j) \right) - \lambda_j \qquad (6)$$

Solving for $u_{ij}$ gives

$$u_{ij} = \left( \frac{\lambda_j}{m(\| x_j - v_i \|^2 + \frac{n}{2}\alpha e^{-\sum_{k\in\Omega} u_{ik}^m} + \beta f_i^{(n-1)}(x_j))} \right)^{\frac{1}{m-1}} \qquad (7)$$

Solving for $\lambda_j$ with respect to the constraint (3), it comes

$$\sum_{i=1}^{C} \left( \frac{\lambda_j}{m(\| x_j - v_i \|^2 + \frac{n}{2}\alpha e^{-\sum_{k\in\Omega} u_{ik}^m} + \beta f_i^{(n-1)}(x_j))} \right)^{\frac{1}{m-1}} = 1 \qquad (8)$$

As $\lambda_j$ does not depend in any term of the sum this yields

$$\lambda_j^{\frac{-1}{m-1}} = \sum_{i=1}^{C} \left( m \| x_j - v_i \|^2 + \frac{n}{2}\alpha e^{-\sum_{k\in\Omega} u_{ik}^m} + \beta f_i^{(n-1)}(x_j) \right)^{\frac{-1}{m-1}} \qquad (9)$$

Eventually substituting in (7) the following update membership is obtained

$$u_{ij} = \frac{1}{\sum_{p=1}^{C} \left( \frac{\| x_j - v_i \|^2 + \frac{n}{2}\alpha e^{-\sum_{k\in\Omega} u_{ik}^m} + \beta f_i^{(n-1)}(x_j)}{\| x_j - v_p \|^2 + \frac{n}{2}\alpha e^{-\sum_{k\in\Omega} u_{pk}^m} + \beta f_p^{(n-1)}(x_j)} \right)^{\frac{1}{m-1}}} \qquad (10)$$

As seen from (10) the membership value of a point $j$ to cluster $i$, defined by $u_{ij}$, depends on membership values of its neighbors and ancestor in the pyramidal representation. At a given level of resolution, for a point to have a high membership value to a particular cluster depends on how its neighbors and father belong to this cluster. The amount of regularization is controlled by the weights $\alpha$ and $\beta$. In the particular case when $\alpha = \beta = 0$ the membership value, $u_{ij}$, is the standard FCM membership function. Increasing the values of $\alpha$ or $\beta$ increases the smoothness. The effect of spatial regularization is more important in higher levels of the pyramid than in low levels possibly causing over smoothness. Actually, the influence of the spatial constraint should be weaker at higher levels. Therefore we chose to multiply $\alpha$ by a half of the level index —i.e. the scale factor— . As a result, the importance of the spatial contribution effect increases from top to bottom. Further achieving better performance is a matter of trade-off between terms.

The prototype update equation is the same as in standard FCM, since the second component of (4) does not depend on $v_i$. Centroids update obeys the following equation:

$$v_i = \frac{\sum_{j=1}^{N} u_{ij}^m x_j}{\sum_{j=1}^{N} u_{ij}^m} \tag{11}$$

The Fuzzy Spatially-Constrained C Means in Multiresolution, FSC$^2$M$^2$ , algorithm consists in computing the parameters at each level of resolution with a constant number of clusters for all levels. The FSC$^2$M$^2$ can be summarized by the following steps:

**Step 1** Fix the number of clusters
*At each level:*
**Step 2** Initialize the centers and $u_{ij}$
**Step 3** Compute the distance $\| x_j - v_i \|^2$
**Step 4** Update the partition matrix using (10)
**Step 5** Update centroids using (11)
**Step 6** Repeat step 3 to step 5 till convergence
**Step 7** Defuzzification at the bottom layer

Note that at level 0 $f_i^{(n-1)}(x_j)$ is set to 0
The convergence is achieved when the change in membership values at layer $n$ is less than a threshold.

## 4 Experiments

Experiments have been carried out to check effectiveness of the proposed algorithmic improvement. We adopt two kinds of test images: Synthetic and remote sensing (RS) images. FSC$^2$M$^2$ is applied to images and results are compared with those of standard FCM and sole spatial constraint – FSC$^2$M –. The multiresolution scheme is the Gaussian pyramid and three levels are used for the experiments. The weights $\alpha$ and $\beta$ were set respectively to 180 and 100. In all experiments the fuzzifier $m$ is set to 2.

Fig. 2 shows results for an RGB color image (in (a)) corrupted by 30% of shotnoise. The image contains four class patterns. Fig. 2 (b) shows the results of the FCM algorithm, and (c) the results of FSC$^2$M ($\beta$ =0). FSC$^2$M$^2$ results on these synthetic images are illustrated in Fig. 2 (d). In all such cases FSC$^2$M$^2$

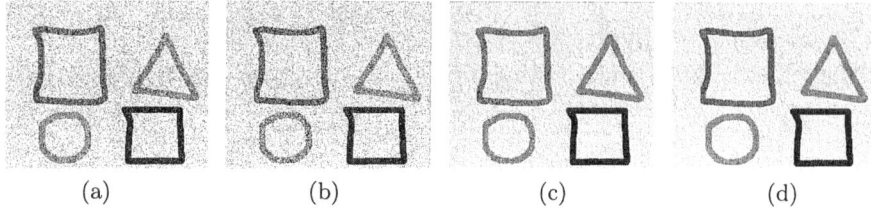

**Fig. 2.** Segmentation results for synthetic images

outperforms FCM and $FSC^2M$. Unlike FCM, $FSC^2M$ detects correctly the different classes, although some over segmentation due to noise remains that vanish with $FSC^2M^2$. Also $FSC^2M^2$ proves more robustness of segmentation.

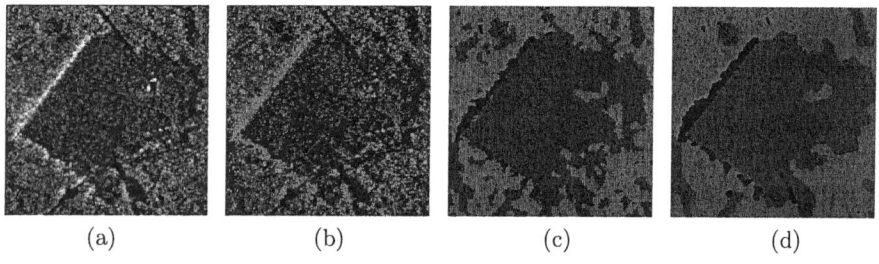

**Fig. 3.** Segmentation results for one band RS images

**Fig. 4.** Segmentation results for 3 bands RS images

In a second experiment real multispectral test images were obtained from CCRS (http://www.ccrs.nrcan.gc.ca). The image was created by a C/X band SAR system: in each pixel 3 bands represent the spectral characteristics. These images contain many kinds of noise and artifacts due to the sensor, atmospheric distortions.... Such conditions make it difficult to segment those images by classical FCM. However to evaluate our algorithm for RS images and study the effect of bands information upon the segmentation we test one band and three bands images.

Fig. 3 (a) shows forests as confirmed by the ground truth and in this case we consider only one band. (b) shows FCM segmentation results in which many regions are not well segmented. From the same Fig the image (c) displays FSC$^2$M results. It can be seen that the case (d) (FSC$^2$M$^2$) provide a better matching with perceptual regions and boundaries.

Fig. 4 (a) represents agricultural fields in 3 bands. The segmentation results yielded by FCM, FSC$^2$M and FSC$^2$M$^2$ are shown respectively in Figs. 4 (b)(c) and (d). One can notice that FCM segmentation produces a lot of insignificant regions, that make it less accurate than FSC$^2$M$^2$. The proposed method outperforms FCM and brings out satisfactory segmentation: the difference with FCM remains qualitatively consistent on samples from a dozen of similar images(eg. agricultural, forest, urban,...).

## 5 Conclusion

In this paper we proposed a new method for image segmentation. The FSC$^2$M$^2$ algorithm uses a modified version of the FCM objective function to increase performance and robustness. We incorporate spatial and multiresolution informations, aiming at more effective segmentation. The results show that FSC$^2$M$^2$ proves a better accuracy than FCM on both synthetic and RS images.

However automatic determination of the number of classes is known as the drawback of FCM algorithm. That is true as well for FSC$^2$M$^2$. Several algorithms have been proposed to outcome this problem, they possibly combine with FSC$^2$M$^2$ the same way as with FCM. In the present work weights are set heuristically but we will now introduce stochastic methods benefiting from the pyramid structure to compute them.

## References

1. Jain, A. K., Musty, M. N., Flynn, P. j.: Data Clustering: A Review. ACM Comput Surv. **31** (1999) 264–323
2. Kaufman, L., Rousseeuw, P.: Finding Groups in Data, An Introduction to Cluster Analysis. John Wiley&Sons. (1990)
3. Bezdek, J. C.: Pattern Recognition With Fuzzy Objective Function Algorithm. Plenum Press. New York. (1981)
4. Krishnapuram, R., Keller, J: Fuzzy and Possibilistic Clustering Methods for Computer Vision. Neural and Fuzzy Systems. **31** (1994) 133–159
5. Tolias, Y. A., Panas, S. M.: Image Segmentation by A Fuzzy Clustering Algorithm Using Adaptive Spatially Constrained Membership Functions. IEEE Trans. on Systems, Man and Cybernetics. **28** (1998) 359–369
6. Tolias, Y. A., Panas, S. M.: On applying Spatial Constraints in Fuzzy Image Clustering Using a Fuzzy Rule–Based System. IEEE Signal Processing Letters. **5** (1998) 245–247
7. Pham, D. L.: Spatial Models for Fuzzy Clustering. Computer Vision and Image Understanding. **84** (2001) 285–297
8. Ahmed, M. N., Yamany, S. M., Mohamed, N., Frag. A. A., Moriatry, T.: A Modified Fuzzy C-means Algorithm for Bias Field Estimation and Segmentation of MRI Data. IEEE Trans. on Medical Imaging. **21** (2002) 193–199

# Combined Color and Texture Segmentation Based on Fibonacci Lattice Sampling and Mean Shift

Chang Yuchou, Zhou Yue, and Wang Yonggang

Institute of Image Processing and Pattern Recognition,
Shanhai Jiaotong University, 200030 Shanghai, China
{ycchang, zhouyue, yonggangwang}@sjtu.edu.cn

**Abstract.** A novel segmentation algorithm for natural color image is proposed. Fibonacci Lattice-based Sampling is used to get the color labels of image so as to take advantage of the traditional approaches developed for gray-scale images. Using local fuzzy homogeneity derived from color labels, texture component is calculated to characterize spatial information. Color component is obtained by peer group filtering. To avoid over-segmentation of texture areas in a color image, these color and texture components are jointly employed to group the pixels into homogenous regions by the mean shift based clustering. Finally, experiments show very promising results.

## 1 Introduction

Image Segmentation is an important precondition in image analysis and visual pattern recognition. Although there have been hundreds of segmentation algorithms, they were developed only for gray scale images and could not be simply extended to color counterparts [1][2]. The difficulty mainly lies in the inherent correlation of multiple bands of color images. To circumvent this problem, two straightforward ways have been adopted in the previous works. One is to choose a color space with independent intensity and chromaticity channels, such as CIE LUV [3], HSV [4], etc. Another way is to reduce the dimensionality of the original color image. In [5], the original RGB space was transformed into the XYZ space which, subsequently, was used to form the xyY space. Using xyY, a measure of the chromatic information is derived, combining the (x, y) pair of chromaticity values into a single quantity. Deng and Manjunath [3] proposed an unsupervised image segmentation method called JSEG in which a 3-band color image was converted into a scalar map, i.e. color class map, after the color quantization step. In principle, every color quantization method can result in a class map after the pixels' color values are labeled by indices. However, these indices themselves do not typify the true color information and are only used to search quantized colors in the color palette. As an exception, Mojsilovic and Soljanin [6] presented an image-independent quantizer based on Fibonacci lattice sampling to form a structured palette by which the quantized images are more amenable to the type of processing used for grayscale ones. In our study, we apply this technique to the color image and in turn some features are extracted for image segmentation.

In addition, texture also exists in images, which usually represents inhomogeneous areas. If only using color information, textural areas may be over-segmented where the colors are different to some extent and hence the segmented images will be inconsistent with semantic understanding of humans. JSEG [3] is a popular color texture segmentation method proposed recently. The basic idea of JSEG is to separate the segmentation process into two stages: color quantization and spatial segmentation. The decoupling of color similarity from spatial distribution in JSEG allows for the development of more tractable algorithms for each of the two processing stages. On the other hand, color quantization plays a crucial role to the segmentation result because it provides a precondition for spatial segmentation. In fact, it is important to design an elegant color quantization algorithm and inappropriate ones may lead to under-segmentation or over-segmentation results.

We argue that joint color-texture features should be used to represent the spatial interactions within and between spectral bands more effectively. In this paper, we propose a novel color image segmentation method based on the Fibonacci lattice sampling and the mean shift algorithm. Color and textural features are extracted from the quantized images based on Fibonacci lattice sampling, where color components are obtained by peer group filtering and texture components are constructed by fuzzy homogeneity. Then, a clustering technique based on mean shift is applied to the feature vectors to form the final homogenous regions. The paper is organized as follows. Section 2 depicts the construction of color and texture components based on Fibonacci lattice sampling. A joint color-texture segmentation method based on mean shift is developed in Section 3 and some experimental results are given in Section 4. We conclude this paper in Section 5.

## 2 Construction of Color Component and Texture Component

Representing the color and texture information in a color image appropriately is a challenging work due to the spatial interactions between its color bands. In virtue of color space sampling based on Fibonacci lattice proposed in [6], we can construct these two components conveniently.

### 2.1 Color Space Sampling Based on Fibonacci Lattice

The Fibonacci lattice sampling scheme proposed in [6] provides a uniform quantization of the CIE Lab color space and a way to establish a partial order relation on the set of points. At each different level of L values in the CIE Lab color space, a complex plane in polar coordinates is used to define a spiral lattice as a convenient means for sampling. The following set of points on (a, b) plane constitutes a spiral lattice:

$$z_n = n^{\delta} e^{j2\pi n\tau}, \tau, \delta \in R, n \in Z \quad (1)$$

Fig. 1 shows a spiral lattice for $\tau = (\sqrt{5}-1)/2$ and $\delta = 1/2$, which is called Fibonacci lattice. Each point $z_n$ is identified by its index n. Parameter $\tau$ and $\delta$ determines the axial distribution and the radial distribution of the points respectively. If there exist $N_L$ L values and $N_P$ colors in the corresponding (a, b) plane, for each point in the palette, the corresponding symbol is composed by adding its chrominance index $n$ to a multiple of its luminance index $i$

$$q = n + N_p \bullet i,  \qquad (2)$$

Consequently, the L, a and b values for any color from the palette can be reconstructed from its symbol $q$. For a pixel $p$, with color components $L_p$, $a_p$ and $b_p$, the process of determining the closest palette point starts with finding the closest luminance level $L_s$ from the $N_L$ levels available in the palette. The luminance level $L_s$ determines an (a, b) plane and one of the points $z_n$, $0 \le n < N_p$, in that plane is the minimum mean square error (MSE) solution. It means that the solution $q$ is the point whose squared distance to the origin is closest to $r_p^2 = a_p^2 + b_p^2$.

**Fig. 1.** Points of the Fibonacci lattice in a complex plane

**Fig. 2.** (a) Original image, (b) color quantized version using a Fibonacci palette with 540 colors and (c) Fuzzy Homogeneity of image displayed by gray levels

In order to achieve as accurate color representation as possible, in our experiment, we use VQ quantization to extract L values. These L values can approximately denote the luminance levels of the image. Since the plane of (a, b) is not circular, there will be points in the Fibonacci lattice whose colors are not valid in the RGB space. Thus we label all these points as range invalid. The points are given by $z_n = s\sqrt{n} e^{j(2\pi n \tau + \alpha_0)}$, where $\tau = (\sqrt{5}-1)/2$, $\alpha_0 = 0.5$ and $s = 1$. In Fig. 2(a), L component is quantized into {53, 60, 64, 66, 68, 71, 75, 79, 97} and using these L values and $N_p = 60$ points in each plane to constitute the palette. Therefore the size of palette is $9 \times 60 = 540$, on the other hand, the number of colors in valid RGB space is 523. Fig. 2(b) shows the quantized image in which it uses 71 valid colors in the palette. Thus, each pixel is labeled by the symbol $q$, which not only is the index of the palette, but also typifies the color information to some extent.

## 2.2 Construction of Texture Component by Fuzzy Homogeneity

Benefiting from the structure of the above color palette, it is possible to extend the processing methods for gray-scale images to color ones. Images usually contain both the textural and smooth areas. While smooth areas contain similar colors locally, textural areas may have different colors. Therefore it is important to consider both color and texture variation simultaneously to avoid over-segmentation of textural areas. In order to estimate smooth or textural areas, fuzzy homogeneity is used to describe local coarseness. In [7], intensities of three color components in RGB color space were extracted to calculate fuzzy homogeneity values. However, RGB representation does not coincide with psychology of human eyes and there is high correlation among its three components. Considering the fine characters of Fibonacci symbols, we apply them to constitute fuzzy homogeneity. For an $M \times N$ image, each pixel value $g_{ij} \in [1, N_Q]$ is the corresponding symbol of palette, $N_Q$ is palette size. Apart from invalid symbols in RGB space, all $M \times N$ pixels only occupy a subset of palette symbol values, $N_{vsub}$. In this subset, symbol values are used to compute fuzzy homogeneity which is defined as

$$\mu_h^\lambda(i,j) = \left\{ \overline{\ell_{X \times Y}^\lambda(g_{ij}) \vee \eta_{X \times Y}^\lambda(g_{ij})} \middle| g_{ij} \in N_{vsub}, 1 \leq i \leq M, 1 \leq j \leq N \right\} \qquad (3)$$

where $\mu_h^\lambda(i,j)$ is the fuzzy homogeneity value at position $(i,j)$ and $X \times Y$ is the local window size which is $5 \times 5$ in the experiment. $\ell^\lambda(\cdot)$ is Laplacian operator, representing the discontinuity such as abrupt changes of the corresponding color symbols, and $\eta^\lambda(\cdot)$ represents the standard deviation which describes the contrast of the color symbols within a local region. See [7] for the detailed presentation. The composition rule is used to find fuzzy homogeneity of the pixel. Fig. 2(c) shows the fuzzy homogeneity of the image which is displayed by gray levels.

Coarser the local region surrounding a pixel is, the less the homogeneity value the pixel has. Different normalized fuzzy homogeneity ranges denote corresponding levels of homogeneous areas. We use fuzzy homogeneity $\mu_h^\lambda(i,j)$ which is computed in the $3 \times 3$ or $5 \times 5$ local windows as texture component $T_c(i,j)$.

## 2.3 Construction of Color Component by Peer Group Filtering

In the global window, how to specify the center pixel's color is related with that of adjacent pixels. In the smooth areas, because of similar colors around the center pixel, the center pixel can be replaced by averaging most colors of adjacent pixels so as to keep uniform visual perception. On the other hand, in the texture areas, we use the average colors which is similar to the center pixel to represent its color and discard other distinct colors. Hence, remaining pixels keep the principal colors relevant with the center pixel and make for extracting main color parts in texture. Peer group filtering (PGF) whose purpose is to smooth image and remove impulse noises [8] is a nonlinear algorithm classifying pixels into sets by means of similar colors. Assuming that there exist several clusters of colors in the global window, one set is similar colors with the center pixel and others are distinct ones, we use the mean of former set to replace the center pixel color.

After specifying the size of global window $L_{side}$ according to image itself, we calculate the distances of the color values of neighbor pixels $p_k(n)$ in the global window to the center pixel $p_0(n)$. Then all neighbor pixels in this window are sorted according to these distances. The peer group, which contains the center pixel and the neighbors of similar colors, is formed by choosing the $m$ pixels with the minimum distances. The size of peer group $m(n)$ is decided by

$$m(n) = \arg\max \frac{|a_1(i) - a_2(i)|^2}{s_1^2(i) + s_2^2(i)}, i = 0, \cdots, L_{side}^2 - 1 \tag{4}$$

where

$$a_1(i) = \frac{1}{i}\sum_{j=0}^{i-1} d_j(n) \text{ and } a_2(i) = \frac{1}{k+1-i}\sum_{j=i}^{k} d_j(n), \tag{5}$$

$$s_1^2(i) = \sum_{j=0}^{i-1}|d_j(n) - a_1(i)|^2 \text{ and } s_2^2(i) = \sum_{j=i}^{k}|d_j(n) - a_2(i)|^2 \tag{6}$$

After the classification, we can compute the average color of the peer group based on their corresponding pixels' symbols. If the average value is invalid in the palette, we specify its nearest valid symbol as its color component:

$$C_c(i,j) \cong (\text{int}) \frac{\sum_{k=0}^{m(n)-1} q(p_k(n))}{m(n)} \tag{7}$$

## 3  Joint Color-Texture Segmentation Based on Mean Shift

The color and texture components can be combined together to be a real number to represent homogeneous regions, however, it may lose some information since both components interfere with each other. In order to avoid this limitation, after the normalization of color and texture component, homogeneity vector is formed:

$$v_{i,j}(c,t) = \langle C_c(i,j), T_c(i,j) \rangle \tag{8}$$

According to these feature vectors, we use a clustering technique namely mean shift to group pixels into homogeneous regions to gain final results.

## 3.1 Mean Shift Based Clustering

Mean shift is a simple, nonparametric technique for estimation of the density gradient. Recently the idea is widely applied to several computer vision problems. As to the detail algorithm, please refer to [9].

Let $f(x)$ be the probability density function underlying a $p$-dimensional feature space, and $\mathbf{x}_i$ the available data points in this space. Under its simplest formulation, the mean shift property can be written as

$$\hat{\nabla} f(x) \sim \left( \underset{\mathbf{x}_i \in S_{h,\mathbf{x}}}{ave} [\mathbf{x}_i] - \mathbf{x} \right) \qquad (9)$$

where $S_{h,\mathbf{x}}$ is the $p$-dimensional search window with radius $h$ centered on $\mathbf{x}$. The mean shift algorithm is described briefly as follows:

1) Choose the radius $h$ of the search window;
2) Choose the initial location of the window;
3) Compute the mean shift vector and translate the window by that amount;
4) Repeat till convergence.

## 3.2 Joint Color-Texture Segmentation

In [10], the mean shift algorithm was applied to color image segmentation. However, the method restricts analysis to the color space and do not take into account the spatial texture information, which affects the segmentation results. The approach in this work takes both color and texture into account. To conclude, the complete color image segmentation procedure is as follows.

1) At first, Fibonacci lattice sampling is used to get the symbols of the pixels;
2) In the symbol map, texture and color components are derived;
3) The mean shift based clustering technique is used to group the pixels into several homogeneous regions according to the feature vectors;
4) An agglomerative clustering algorithm [11] is performed on the cluster centroids to further merge close clusters such that the minimum distance between two centroids satisfies a preset threshold.

# 4 Experimental Results

To test the proposed algorithm, we have applied it on a number of real natural images from WWW. Fig. 3 and 4 show the two experimental results of the proposed method and the method of JSEG [3]. Fig. 3 (b) demonstrates that the proposed method posses great capabilities to distinguish different regions. Although JSEG segment main homogeneous areas, it neglects the stone in swamp and a part of hills which have different colors in comparison with around pixels. Comparing to JSEG which does not consider the spatial information in process of color quantization, we quantize image using combination of color and texture components which describe the space relations. Moreover, JSEG uses color distribution to form pixels' J values firstly and uses them to indicate whether the local area is in the texture region interiors or near boundaries, hence J value itself does not contain color values directly. Our algorithm not only considers texture distribution, but also calculates color component as descriptor. In general, the segmentation results match well with perceived boundaries.

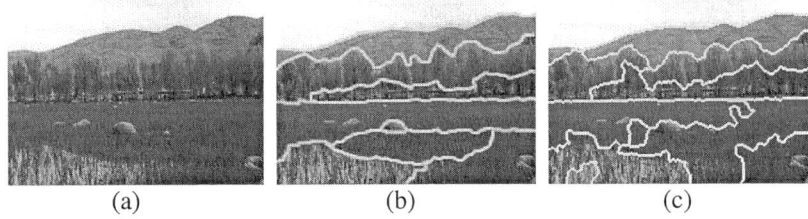

**Fig. 3.** (a) Original image; (b) Segmentation by proposed method; (c) Segmentation by JSEG

**Fig. 4.** (a) Original image; (b) Segmentation by proposed method; (c) Segmentation by JSEG

## 5 Conclusions

Color and texture are two most important ingredients in human visual perception. Many segmentation approaches used both of them to get homogeneous regions. In this work, a novel segmentation algorithm is proposed, which considers interaction of texture distribution and local color information. Using Fibonacci lattice-based quantization helps us calculate fuzzy homogeneity and obtain the texture representation. Peer Group Filtering is used to get the local major colors. We cluster these feature vectors jointly by means of mean shift method to get the final segmentation results. The proposed algorithm can detect small homogeneous regions surrounded by other ones and give effective results.

## References

1. Pal, N.R., Pal, S.K.: A review on Image Segmentation Techniques. Pattern Recognition, Vol.26. (1993) 1277–1294
2. Cheng, H.D., Jiang, X.H., Sun, Y., Wang, J.: Color Image Segmentation: Advances and Prospects, Pattern Recognition, Vol.34 (2001) 2259–2281
3. Deng, Y., Manjunath, B.S.: Unsupervised Segmentation of Color-Texture Regions in Image and Video, IEEE Transactions on Pattern Analysis and Machine Intelligence, Vol.23 (2001) 800–810

4. Xu, J., Shi, P.F.: Natural Color Image Segmentation, IEEE International Conference on Image Processing, Vol.1 (2003) 973–976
5. Paschos, G., Valavanis, K.P: Chromatic Measures for Color Texture Description and Analysis, Proc.10th IEEE International Symposium on Intelligent Control, (1995) 319–325
6. Mojsilovic, A., Soljanin, E.: Color Quantization and processing by Fibonacci Lattices, IEEE Transactions on Image Processing, Vol.10 (2001) 1712–1725
7. Cheng, H.D, Li, L.: Fuzzy Homogeneity and Scale Space Approach to Color Image Segmentation, Pattern Recognition, Vol.36 (2003) 1545–1562
8. Deng, Y., Kenney, C., Moore, M.S., Manjunath, B.S.: Peer Group Filtering and Perceptual Color Image Quantization, Proc. IEEE International Symposium on Circuits and Systems, Vol.4 (1999) 21–24
9. Comaniciu, D.: An Algorithm for Data-driven Bandwidth Selection, IEEE Transactions on Pattern Analysis and Machine Intelligence, Vol.25 (2003) 281–288
10. Comaniciu, D.: and Meer, P.: Robust Analysis of Feature Spaces: Color Image Segmentation, Proc. IEEE Computer Society Conference on Computer Vision and Pattern Recognition, (1997) 750–755
11. Duda, R.O., Hart, P.E.: Pattern Classification and Scene Analysis, John Wiley & Sons, New York (1970)

# Unsupervised Image Segmentation Using Contourlet Domain Hidden Markov Trees Model

Yuheng Sha, Lin Cong, Qiang Sun, and Licheng Jiao

Institute of Intelligent Information Processing and National Key Lab for Radar
Signal Processing , Xidian University, Xi'an, 710071 China
yuhengsha@yahoo.com.cn

**Abstract.** A novel method of unsupervised image segmentation using contourlet domain hidden markov trees model is presented. Fuzzy C-mean clustering algorithm is used to capture the likelihood disparity of different texture features. A new context based fusion model is given for preserve more interscale information in contourlet domain. The simulation results of synthetic mosaics and real images show that the proposed unsupervised segmentation algorithm represents a better performance in edge detection and protection and its error probability of the synthetic mosaics is lower than wavelet domain HMT based method.

## 1 Introduction

Wavelet analyses have good non-linear approximation performance for piecewise smooth functions in one dimension. In essence, wavelets are good at catching point or zero-dimensional singularities, but bi-dimensional piecewise smooth functions resembling images have one-dimensional discontinuities. This indicates that more powerful representations of image are needed in higher dimensions. The Multiscale Geometric Analysis takes up with the optimal presentation of multidimensional function. Ridgelet[1] represent good approximation performance while the target function has linear singularity. However, the approximation performance of rigelet for non-linear singularity functions will be equal to wavelets. Monoscale ridgelet[2] resolve the problem of sparse approximation of multi-variable functions, but the decompose scale is fixed. Curvelet[3] can decompose images at any scale and has better approximation performance than wavelets and rigelet. However, the existence of Randon transform in curvelet determines a higher complexity and redundancy which limited its applications. Inspired by curvelet, M.N.Do and Martin Vetterli present a "true" representation of bi-dimensional image: Contourlet[4]. It inherits the multiscale feature of curvelet transform, and it can be view as another realization of curvelet in certain meaning.

In[5], hidden Markov tree (HMT) was proposed in the wavelet domain to achieve the statistical information of images by capturing interscale dependencies of wavelet coefficients across scales. Many unsupervised image segmentation algorithms[6,7] using wavelet domain HMT model are proposed and achieved satisfied results. Contourlet transform also provide a natural multiscale structure of image analysis, and contourlet domain HMT models[8] can characterize more anisotropic information than wavelet domain HMT model. Inspired by above methods, an unsupervised image segmentation method is developed based on contourlet domain HMT models. If an image contains different textures, hard clustering algorithm could be misclassified during the clustering process. Soft clustering algorithm FCM is used to capture the likelihood disparity of different texture features. A new context based interscale model named multiscale neighborhood context model is presented in this paper. This model considers the coefficients relationship in different scale. Simulation results of synthetic mosaics and real images show that this method is feasible and effective.

## 2 Contourlet Domain Hidden Markov Trees Model

### 2.1 Contourlet Approximation

The contourlet transform not only has the multiscale and time-frequency-localization properties of wavelets, but also offers a high degree of directionality and anisotropy. Specifically, contourlet transform involves basis functions that are oriented at any power of two numbers of directions with flexible aspect ratios. With such a rich set of basis functions, contourlets can represent a smooth contour with fewer coefficients compared with wavelets. Due to this cascade structure, multiscale and directional decomposition stages in the contourlet transform are independent of each other. This feature makes contourlets a unique transform that can achieve a high level of flexibility in decomposition while being close to critically sampled (up to 33% overcomplete, which comes from the Laplacian pyramid) 1[4].

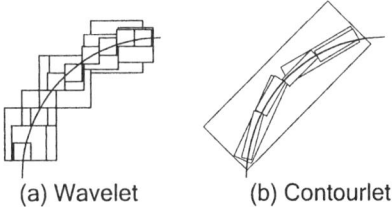

(a) Wavelet      (b) Contourlet

**Fig. 1.** Wavelets have square supports that can only capture point discontinuities. Whereas contourlets have elongated supports that can capture linear segments of contours, and thus can effectively represent a smooth contour with fewer coefficients.

Fig.2 shows example contourlet transforms of the "Barbara" image. For the visual clarity, only two-scale decompositions are shown. Each image is decomposed into a lowpass subband and several bandpass directional subbands.

It is worth notice that only contourlets that match with both location and direction of image contours produce significant coefficients. Thus, the contourlet transform effectively explores the fact image edges are localized in both location and direction. Contourlet transform based on an efficient bi-dimensional multiscale and directional filter bank that can deal effectively with images having anisotropic information, and has many good properties such as multiresolution, localization, and anisotropy.

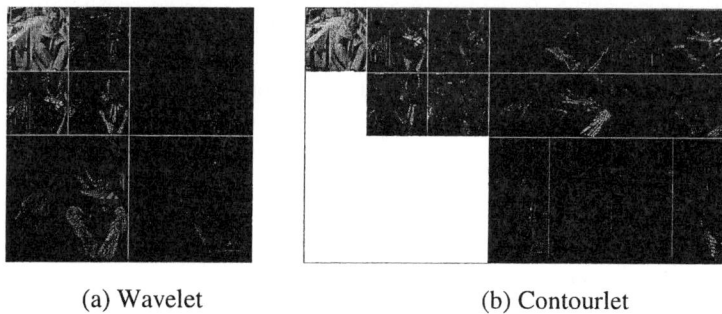

(a) Wavelet          (b) Contourlet

**Fig. 2.** The image is decomposed into two pyramidal levels, which are then decomposed into four and eight directional subbands

### 2.2 Contourlet Domain Hidden Markov Trees Model

We first study the marginal statistics of the wavelet and contourlet coefficients of natural images. The followed figure plots the histograms of two finest subbands of image "Barbara".

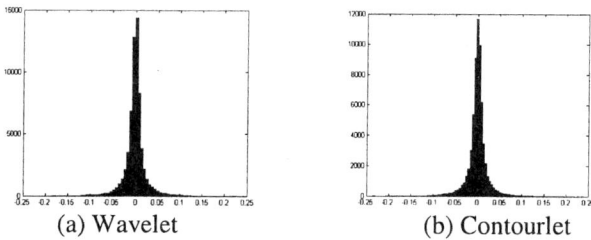

(a) Wavelet          (b) Contourlet

**Fig. 3.** One subband of wavelet and contourlet coefficients histogram of Barbara image

These distributions exhibit a sharp peak at zero amplitude and heavy tails to both sides of the peak. This implies that the wavelet and contourlet transforms are sparse, at the majority of coefficients are close to zero. The kurtosis of the two shown distribution are 21.03 and 20.59, which are much higher than the kurtosis of 3 for Gaussian distributions. Similar distributions are also observed at all subbands of other test images. Thus, the subband marginal distributions of natural images in wavelet and contourlet domain are highly non-Gaussian.

Compare with wavelet HMT model, the contourlet HMT model has a major advantage is that it accounts for inter-direction dependencies, while the wavelet HMT model does not. There are two direction relationships in contourlet HMT model. The first one is like wavelet HMT model, the parent-children relationship are transfer in mono-direction. The other one is that a parent coefficient can have its children spread over two directional subbands.

For preserve the scale characterizes with original image, the first parent-children relationship is adopted in our algorithm. The second one could be used in image denoising, texture retrieval [8].

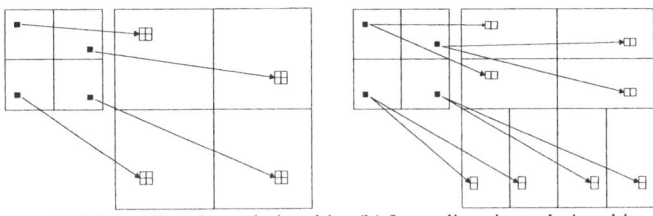

(a) Mono-direction relationship  (b) Inter-direction relationship

**Fig. 4.** Parent-children relationships for a possible contourlet decomposition

## 3 Unsupervised Image Segmentation Using Contourlet Domain Hidden Markov Trees Model

### 3.1 Supervised Bayesian Segmentation

Image segmentation aims at addressing the problem of identifying different regions of homogeneous "textural" characteristics within the image. Supervised Bayesian image segmentation approach classifies an image using both image features and prior knowledge. Usually maximum a posteriori (MAP) estimation is involved[7],i.e.,

$$\hat{x} = \arg\max_{x} E[C_{MAP}(X,x) | Y = y] \qquad (1)$$

where $C_{MAP}(X,x)$ is the cost function that assigns equal cost to any single erroneous estimation. To overcome the expensive computation intrinsic by MAP estimator, a sequential MAP (SMAP) estimator was developed with an alternative weighted cost function $C_{SMAP}(X,x)$ in [9]. Assume $Y^{(n)}$ is an image block at scale $n$, and $X^{(n)}$ is its class label. $y^{(n)}$ and $x^{(n)}$ are the particular values of them. The SMAP estimator can be reformulated as[4]:

$$\hat{x}^{(n)} = \arg\max_{x^{(n)}}\{\log p_{y^{(n)}|x^{(n)}}(y|x^{(n)}) + \log p_{x^{(n)}|x^{(n+1)}}(x^{(n)}|\hat{x}^{(n+1)})\} \qquad (2)$$

The two terms in (2) are the likelihood function of an image block and the contextual information from the next coarser scale, respectively. As for the second part of (2), a context-based Bayesian segmentation algorithm, HMTseg, was presented by H.Choi et al in [5] where the contextual information is modeled as a context vector $v^{(n)}$. The contextual prior $p_{x^{(n)}|v^{(n)}}(c|u)$ is involved in the SMAP as the second part of (2). Assume there are $N$ different textures and SMAP estimate can be obtained by

$$\hat{x}^{(n)} = \arg\max_{x^{(n)}} p_{x^{(n)}|v^{(n)}, y^{(n)}}(x^{(n)}|\hat{v}^{(n)}, y^{(n)}) \qquad (3)$$

Where

$$p_{x^{(n)}|v^{(n)}, y^{(n)}}(x^{(n)}|\hat{v}^{(n)}, y^{(n)}) = \frac{p_{x^{(n)}}(x^{(n)}) p_{v^{(n)}|x^{(n)}}(\hat{v}^{(n)}|x^{(n)}) f(x^{(n)}|v^{(n)})}{\sum_{c=1}^{N} p_{x^{(n)}}(c) p_{v^{(n)}|x^{(n)}}(\hat{v}^{(n)}|x^{(n)} = c) f(y^{(n)}|x^{(n)} = c)}$$

where $p_{x^{(n)}}(c)$ is the probability mass function of class $c$ at scale $n$ and $f(y^{(n)} \mid x^{(n)} = c)$ is the likelihood function of image block $y^{(n)}$ with respect to class $c$ that can be calculated with one upward sweep process in the EM algorithm[10].

In HMTseg, the HMT model was applied to characterize texture images, aiming at capturing interscale dependencies of wavelet coefficients with the assumption of subband independence. Alternatively, an improved hidden Markov model, HMT-3S [11], was presented to characterize not only the dependencies of wavelet coefficients between different scales but those across wavelet subbands to enhance the accuracy of characterizing image statistics. Meanwhile, JMCMS was combined with HMT-3S to propose in [12] to capture more robust contextual information with multiple context models to improve the segmentation performance around boundaries. But above segmentation methods belongs to supervised image segmentation, i.e., all image features are given in terms of HMT or HMT-3S models. Consequently, we propose an unsupervised image segmentation based on Fuzzy C-means clustering, an efficient approach to soft clustering.

## 3.2 Unsupervised Image Segmentation Using Likelihood Disparity

The unsupervised Bayesian image segmentation can be represented as: without any feature prototypes or training data, find the region of interest or all the non-overlapping distinct regions in an image. Multiscale analysis gives us a natural mul-

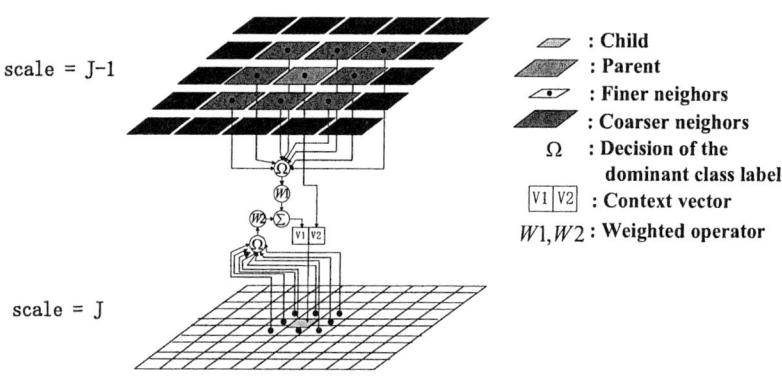

**Fig. 5.** Multiscale neighborhood context model

tiresolution framework and contourlet domain HMT model are capable of capturing statistical properties of texture images. The unsupervised method is based on only the coarsest scale, corresponding to a large window size of localization operation in parameter estimation. At the coarsest scale in contourlet HMT model each node contains the statistical information from all other descendants at finer scales and can give us an robust computation of the model likelihood. Because of the tying within the subband during the model training, the whole image will be considered as one texture by using the Expectation Maximization (EM) training algorithm and only one global model can be obtained. Due to the different goodness of fit between this global model and local texture regions, we can use the likelihood disparity to obtain a raw segmentation map by using the FCM clustering at the coarsest scale, where each node covers the largest area with the robust likelihood computation. Then the unsupervised segmentation process is converted to the self-supervised process.

A new context based interscale model named multiscale neighborhood context model is presented in this paper. This model represents a good performance in multiscale fusion process. The weight operator can preserve the outline information in coarser scale and the detail information in finer scale simultaneity.

## 4 Simulation Results and Analysis

Here we test our methods on synthetic mosaics, aerial photo and synthetic aperture radar (SAR) images. Comparison results of our method and the wavelet based one are given. Wavelet transform we use DB4 three level decompose, and contourlet transform we use classical '9-7' LP and DFB three level decompose.

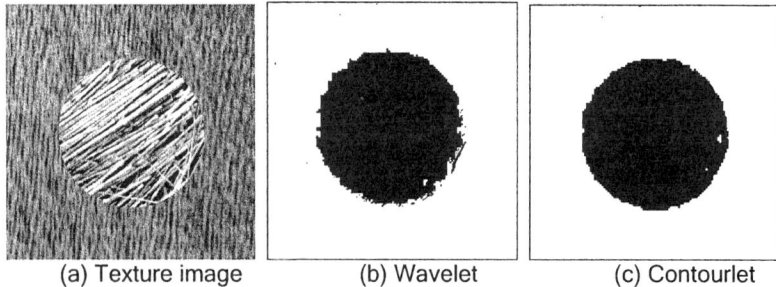

(a) Texture image    (b) Wavelet    (c) Contourlet

**Fig. 6.** Synthetic mosaic image segmentation results

Here we give the error segment probability to evaluate the segmentation result.

$$p_{error} = e_i / e_{total} \tag{4}$$

Where $e_i$ is the number of error pixel points and $e_{total}$ is the total pixel number in the No.i class. The smaller error probability, the better result we achieved.

**Table 1.** The error segmentation probability

| $P_{error}(\%)$ | Mosaic1 | Mosaic2 | Average |
|---|---|---|---|
| Wavelet HMT | 9.30 | 3.98 | 6.64 |
| Contourlet HMT | 8.96 | 3.84 | 6.40 |

For illustrate the effectiveness of our algorithm, we present segmentation results of other three images.

From the above results we can see that the results based on our method has better performance in detecting and protecting directional edges. The more important is that it can detect more detail and mingle directional information.

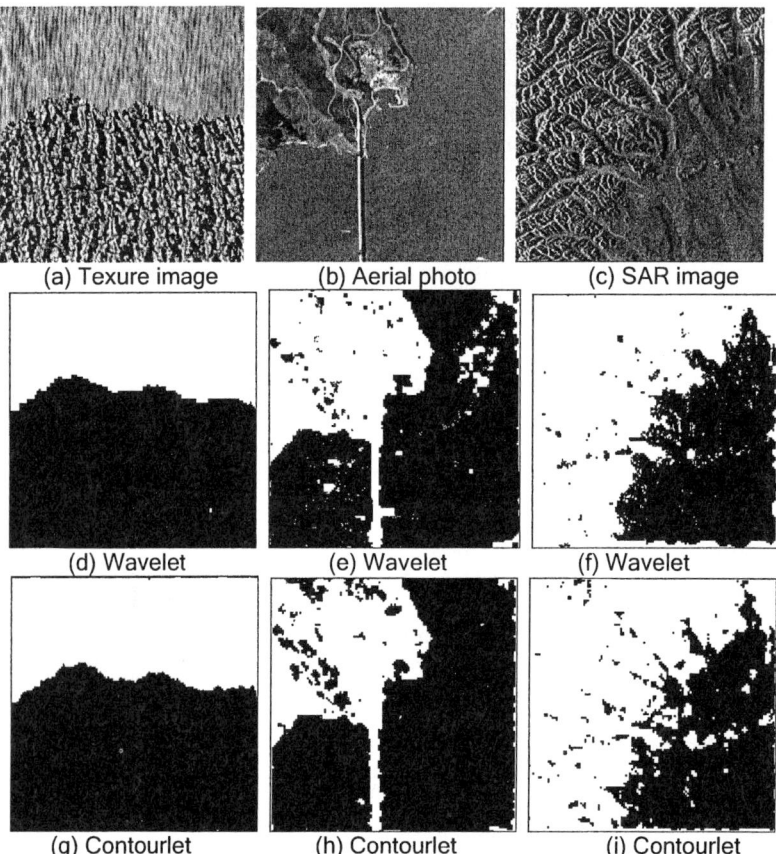

**Fig. 7.** Experimental results of other images

## 5 Conclusion and Discussion

The unsupervised image segmentation algorithm presented in this paper achieves better results than wavelet HMT based one. The effective representation of multidimensional singularity information in image is known well by researchers in image processing field increasingly. The appearance and the development of the image multi-scale geometric analysis must bring vital forces in information processing. How to achieve an effective evaluation of real images is still a problem.

## References

1. E. J. Candès. Ridgelet: theory and applications. Ph.D. Thesis, Department of statistics Stanford Univ. 1998.
2. E. J. Candès. Monoscale Ridgelets for the representation of Images with Edges. Tech. Report, Stanford Univ. 1999.
3. E. J. Candès, D. L. Donoho. Curvelets. Tech. report, Stanford Univ. 1999.

4. M.N.Do, M. Vetterli. "Contourlet," Beyond Wavelets, G.V.Welland ed., Academic Press, New York, 2003
5. Hyeokho Choi, Richard G. Baraniuk, Multiscale Image Segmentation Using Wavelet-Domain Hidden Markov Models, IEEE Transactions on Image Processing. Vol.10, No 9,1309-1321, Sep. 2001.
6. Qiang SUN, Shuiping GOU ,Licheng JIAO, A New Approach to Unsupervised Image Segmentation based on Wavelet-domain Hidden Markov Tree Models. ICIAR2004, Porto, Portugal, Sep 29-Oct 1, 41-48, 2004.
7. X. M. Song, G. L. Fan. Unsupervised Bayesian image segmentation using wavelet domain hidden Markov models. IEEE International Conference on Image Processing (ICIP2003), Barcelona, Spain, Sept. 2003
8. Duncan D.-Y.Po, M.N.Do, Directional Multiscale Modeling of Images using the Contourlet Transform, Statistical Signal Processing, 2003 IEEE Workshop on: 262-265, 28 Sept.-1 Oct, 2003.
9. C.A. Bouman, M Shapiro, A multisclae random field model for Bayesian image segmentation. IEEE Trans. on Image Processing, vol.3, no.2, pp.162-177, March 1994
10. M. S. Crouse, R. D. Nowak, and R. G. Baraniuk, Wavelet-based signal processing using hidden Markov models. IEEE Trans. on Signal Processing, vol. 46, no. 4, pp. 886-902, April 1998
11. G. L. Fan and X. G. Xia, Wavelet-based texture analysis and synthesis using hidden Markov models. IEEE Trans. on Circuits and Systems, Part I, vol. 50, no. 1, pp. 106-120, Jan. 2003
12. G. L. Fan and X. G. Xia, A joint multi-context and multiscale approach to Bayesian image segmentation, IEEE Trans.on Geoscience and Remote Sensing, vol. 39, no. 12, Dec. 2001.

# A Novel Color C-V Method and Its Application

Li Chen, Yue Zhou, and Yonggang Wang

Institute of Image Processing and Pattern Recognition, Shanghai Jiaotong University,
Shanghai, 200030, China
{ahli1981, zhouyue, yonggangwang}@sjtu.edu.cn

**Abstract.** C-V method, an active contour model developed by Chan and Vese, has been successfully applied to solve the problem of object detection in grayscale images. In this paper, a novel color C-V method which takes into account of color information and global property is presented. Choosing the appropriate color space for this model is also introduced. Finally, the applications of the proposed method to natural color images and microscopic halftone printing images are given and the experimental results show robust performance especially in case of weak edges and noisy inputs.

## 1 Introduction

Active contours or snakes [1] are used to detect the objects in a given image using techniques of curve evolution. This model can obtain accurate boundary of objects by deforming the initial curve which is defined in advance. The deformation process is guided by minimizing with respect to the initial curve a functional, whose local minimum is given by boundary of objects.

The classical active contours are based on gradient to detect boundary. In this way, only local information of boundary is used, thus it is fairly difficult to get ideal results dealing with fuzzy edge and discrete edge. To circumvent this problem, Chan and Vese [2] developed an active contour model, namely C-V method, which is based on Mumford-Shah model [3] and the level set approach [4]. C-V method [2] relies on the global information of homogeneous regions instead of local gradient; therefore it can obtain relatively better results in fuzzy or discrete cases. Besides, C-V method need not make restriction to the position of initial curve, and it is still effective to those images with abundant noise so that a process of denoising is not in need.

Most existing active contours are confined to scalar segmentation. For a color image, the usual approaches are either converting it into a scalar image beforehand or carrying out segmentation in each color channel respectively and then simply synthesizing the result. However, neither of them can utilize color information effectively. The former approach neglects a fact that objects in color images usually have different shapes in different color channels, so converting color images into scalar counterparts one may lose some useful features of the objects. In particular, C-V method will be invalid in the cases that the object and the background have the same intensity. As to the latter approach, the correlation between different color channels is not considered so that the segmentation accuracy cannot be ensured.

Obviously, the segmentation of color images can not achieve satisfactory results if purely relying on scalar methods of segmentation. Only by integrating information in the three color channels, can we segment color images effectively. Chan and Vese have proposed a method [5] similar to this idea, but the way of integration is still weighted sums of the channels, which does not differ from the method of transforming color images into scalar images in nature (for the transformation is also weighted sums). As a result, this method still cannot collect sufficient information. Besides, there are too many parameters in the model, which lower the robustness.

The aim of this paper lies in the extension of the original gray-scale C-V method to color images, making full use of color information to overcome the weakness of scalar segmentation. In Section 2, we review the classical C-V method briefly. Section 3 presents a novel color C-V method. We also modify the original C-V formulation to achieve better global property. The applications of our method to natural color images and microscopic halftone printing images are discussed in Section 4 and we conclude this paper in Section 5.

## 2 Classical C-V Method

Chan and Vese [2] proposed a method which employs active contours to segment images based on Mumford-Shah model [3]. This method is adapted to detect edges either with or without gradient. The particular details of it are following.

Let $\Omega$ be a bounded open subset of $IR^2$. Let $I(x,y)$ be a given image so that $I(x,y): \bar{\Omega} \to IR$. Let $C$ be the current active contour which divides the image into several parts and $C_0$ be the boundary of objects in the image. Let $I_0(x,y)$ be the segmented image. Then the aim of Mumford-Shah model is to find the true boundary $C_0$ which divides the image into some approximately homogenous parts, when difference between $I_0(x,y)$ and $I(x,y)$ becomes least in this partition. The problem turns to minimizing the following energy functional:

$$F^{MS}(I_0, C) = \mu Length(C) + \lambda \int_\Omega |I - I_0|^2 \, dxdy + \int_{\Omega/C} |\nabla I_0|^2 \, dxdy \qquad (1)$$

A simplified segmentation model is proposed by Chan and Vese based on this functional. That is, assuming the gray-scale of each homogenous region be constant: in region $R_i \subset \Omega/C$, $I(R_i) = C_i$, $C_i$ is constant. In this case, to minimize the energy functional is to find the best $C_0$, which minimize the difference between the segmented image and the original image.

Let the image be divided by $C$ into two parts: object $\omega_o$ and background $\omega_b$, and the means of them are $c_o$ and $c_b$ respectively. Then the simplified energy functional proposed by Chan and Vese is:

$$F(C, c_o, c_b) = \mu L(C) + \nu S_o(C) + \lambda_o \int_{inside(C)} |I - c_o|^2 \, dxdy \\ + \lambda_b \int_{outside(C)} |I - c_b|^2 \, dxdy \qquad (2)$$

where $C$ is a random close active contour. $L(C)$ is the length of $C$; $S_o(C)$ is the area of the closed region; $\mu, \nu \geq 0$, $\lambda_o, \lambda_b > 0$. The sum of the two latter terms is minimized when $C$ fits the boundary of homogenous regions. We can obtain the best result of global segmentation from minimizing the energy function (2).

The method of level set [4, 6] is applied to solve the model: let $\phi$ be the value of SDF based on initial curve $C_0$, $\{C_0 \mid \phi_0(x,y) = 0\}$. Each pixel has their own value of $\phi$. Let $\phi[inside(C)] > 0$, $\phi[outside(C)] < 0$. We define Heaviside Function:

$$H(z) = \begin{cases} 1, z > 0, \\ 0, z < 0. \end{cases} \quad (3)$$

Then the final style of energy functional is:

$$F(C, c_o, c_b) = \mu \int_\Omega \delta(\phi) |\nabla \phi| dxdy + v \int_\Omega H(\phi) |\nabla \phi| dxdy \\ + \lambda_o \int_{inside(C)} |I - c_o|^2 dxdy + \lambda_b \int_{outside(C)} |I - c_b|^2 dxdy. \quad (4)$$

Employing Euler-Lagrangian method to solve (4), we obtain:

$$\begin{cases} c_o(\phi) = \dfrac{\int_\Omega I(x,y) H_\varepsilon(\phi) dxdy}{\int_\Omega H_\varepsilon(\phi) dxdy}, \; c_b(\phi) = \dfrac{\int_\Omega I(x,y)[1 - H_\varepsilon(\phi)] dxdy}{\int_\Omega [1 - H_\varepsilon(\phi)] dxdy} \\ \dfrac{\partial \phi}{\partial t} = \delta(\phi)[\mu \nabla \cdot \dfrac{\nabla \phi}{|\nabla \phi|} - v - \lambda_o [I(x,y) - c_o]^2 + \lambda_b [I(x,y) - c_b]^2] \end{cases} \quad (5)$$

By solving (5) in numerical way, we obtain the value of $\phi$ on the whole image. Then we can update the level set to lead the curve evolving to the boundary of objects.

## 3 Color C-V Method

Few efforts have been put on the extension of scalar C-V method to color counterpart. In [5], a color C-V method was proposed in which the result of segmentation in each color channel is synthesized by weighted sums. However, in vector valued image, the relation between vectors cannot be fully delivered by weighed sums, so there still exist some deficiencies in segmentation. We present a new color C-V method thinking much of using color information efficiently, which shows advantageous ability in segmentation to color images with weak edges, holes, and noise.

### 3.1 A Novel Color C-V Method

For vector valued images (e.g. sonar images and color images), because of the values of pixels are vectors, to apply directly C-V method to these images usually cannot get pleasant results: if we transform vector valued images to scalar images, the information cannot be sufficiently used; if we segment the images from channel to channel, the relation between channels would be neglect thus the information would not be well utilized either. Therefore, we propose a new C-V method for vector valued images. Our method is based on vector space, gray-scale C-V method and human vision to overcome the shortages of original methods.

Let $u_{0,i}$ be the $i$-th channel of value of the pixels in vector valued images, $i = 1,...N$, $C$ is active contour. In N-dimension space, let $\overline{c^+} = (c_1^+,...,c_N^+)$, $\overline{c^-} = (c_1^-,...,c_N^-)$ be N-dimension vectors. Substituting gray-scale in (2) by Euclidean distance between these vectors, we can obtain the color C-V method for N-dimension segmentation:

$$F(\overline{c^+},\overline{c^-},\phi) = \mu \cdot L(C) + v S_o(C) + \int_{inside(C)} \frac{1}{N}\sqrt{\sum_{i=1}^{N}(\lambda_i^+)^2 (u_{0,i}(x,y) - c_i^+)^2}$$
$$+ \int_{outside(C)} \frac{1}{N}\sqrt{\sum_{i=1}^{N}(\lambda_i^-)^2 (u_{0,i}(x,y) - c_i^-)^2}\,dxdy \quad (6)$$

where $\lambda_i^+ > 0$, $\lambda_i^- > 0$, they are weights of each channel.

From the functional above, we conclude that the model is to find the best approximation of $\overline{c^+}$ and $\overline{c^-}$ which minimizes $F(\overline{c^+},\overline{c^-},\phi)$. Active contour $C$ is the boundary between two homogenous regions. The former two terms are smooth terms, and the latter two terms are energy terms. In this case, we employ Euclidean distance to combine information in the N channels according to the theory of vector spaces. In this way, boundary information in each channel is effectively used, avoiding the problem bought by the weighting method, and the obtained distances between vectors are more accordant to the physical understanding of multi-dimension spaces.

In the formulation of level set, we can rewrite (6) as:

$$F(\overline{c^+},\overline{c^-},\phi) = \mu \int_\Omega \delta(\phi(x,y)) |\nabla \phi(x,y)|\,dxdy + v \int_\Omega H(\phi(x,y))\,dxdy$$
$$+ \int_\Omega \frac{1}{N}\sqrt{\sum_{i=1}^{N}(\lambda_i^+)^2 (u_{0,i}(x,y) - c_i^+)^2}\,H(\phi(x,y))$$
$$+ \int_\Omega \frac{1}{N}\sqrt{\sum_{i=1}^{N}(\lambda_i^-)^2 (u_{0,i}(x,y) - c_i^-)^2}\,(1 - H(\phi(x,y)))\,dxdy \quad (7)$$

where $\mu$ and $\lambda_i$ represent the sensitivity of boundary detection. The more $\mu$ and $\lambda_i$ are, the easier it is to remove high-frequency noise; instead, the less $\mu$ and $\lambda_i$ are, the better effect of the segmentation of minutiae boundary in the model.

Employing Euler-Lagrangian equation to solve (7), we obtain:

$$\frac{\partial \phi}{\partial t} = \delta_\varepsilon[\mu \cdot div(\frac{\nabla \phi}{|\nabla \phi|}) - \frac{1}{N}\sqrt{\sum_{i=1}^{N}\lambda_i^+(u_{0,i}-c_i^+)^2} + \frac{1}{N}\sqrt{\sum_{i=1}^{N}\lambda_i^-(u_{0,i}-c_i^-)^2}\,]. \quad (8)$$

From (8), we find that the available range of $\delta$ would affect the global property of the model. Therefore, we employ the method as following: substituting $|\nabla \phi|$ for $\delta$ in (8) to strengthen the global property of this equation. In this way, the available range of the equation extends to the whole area of images. After substituting, (8) will become:

$$\frac{\partial \phi}{\partial t} = |\nabla \phi|[\mu \cdot div(\frac{\nabla \phi}{|\nabla \phi|}) - \frac{1}{N}\sqrt{\sum_{i=1}^{N}\lambda_i^+(u_{0,i}-c_i^+)^2} + \frac{1}{N}\sqrt{\sum_{i=1}^{N}\lambda_i^-(u_{0,i}-c_i^-)^2}] \qquad (9)$$

For color images, N=3, we employ entropy average [6] method to solve (9):

$$\phi_{i,j}^{n+1} = \phi_{i,j}^n + \Delta t[\max(F_{m-s},0)\nabla^+ +$$
$$\min(F_{m-s},0)\nabla^+ + \mu k_{i,j}[(D_{i,j}^{0y})^2 + (D_{i,j}^{0x})^2]^{1/2}]$$

where

$$F_{m-s} = -v - \frac{1}{3}\sqrt{\sum_{i=1}^{3}\lambda_i^+(u_{0,i}-c_i^+)^2} + \frac{1}{3}\sqrt{\sum_{i=1}^{3}\lambda_i^-(u_{0,i}-c_i^-)^2} .$$

Based on M-S model, our color C-V method is not only able to obtain pleasant results when segmenting color images heavily polluted by noise or involving fuzzy edges, but also able to achieve good global property, which helps resolve the problem in segmentation to those images within holes. Fig. 1(a) is an image having holes far from their exterior boundary; Fig. 1(b) is the result of segmentation based on original C-V method; Fig. 1(c) is the result of segmentation based on our novel color C-V method.

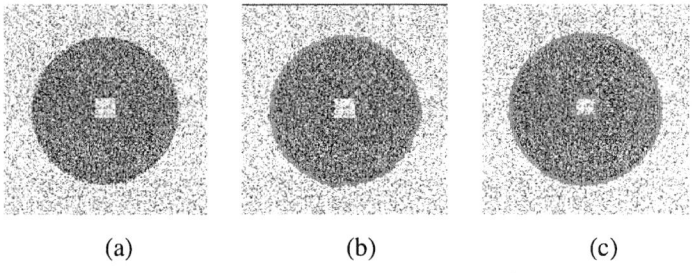

(a)  (b)  (c)

**Fig. 1.** (a) An image containing holes far from boundary and much noise. (b) Result of segmentation using the C-V method proposed in [5]. (c) Result of the segmentation using our proposed method.

We can find from Fig. 1: our color C-V method can detect those holes deep in the center of objects, raising the effect of segmentation. Besides, this method is robust to the position and shape of initial curve. By experiments, we demonstrate that no matter how position and shape of the initial curve is like, by color C-V method, we can obtain the same correct result from each of them. This fact infers that the result of segmentation is unrelated to initial curve.

### 3.2 Choice of Color Space

In most cases, RGB color space cannot really reflect the difference between various colors in human vision. Normally the distance between two distinct colors in our vision may be very tiny in RGB color space, thus the difference between these two colors would be neglected. For example, in Fig. 2(a), the lower square cannot be detected using RGB color space, and the result is Fig.2 (b). For the purpose of obtaining better results, we adopt LUV color space which is more even in distribution and more accordant with human vision. We find that, by transforming from RGB color space to LUV color space, the method can detect some objects and edges which cannot be detected using RGB color space. For example, in Fig. 2(c), the lower square is detected after the transformation.

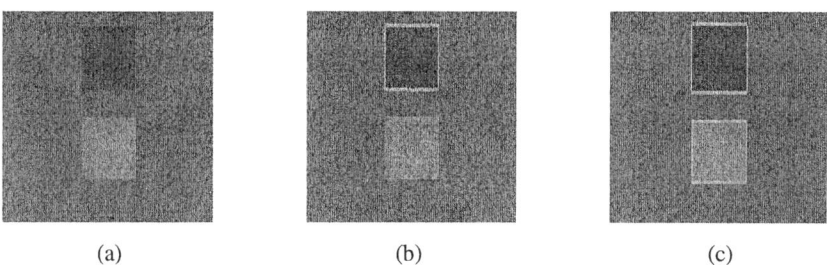

(a) (b) (c)

**Fig. 2.** (a) A color image. (b) Result of segmentation using RGB space. (c) Result of segmentation using LUV space.

Experiments demonstrate that by this transformation, color C-V method becomes more sensitive to boundary in images, avoiding the distortion of segmentation caused by tiny distance in RGB color space, and more accordant with human vision.

## 4 Applications and Experimental Results

The novel color C-V method can be applied to various domains. In this section, we will use natural color images and microscopic halftone printing image to show its performance.

Fig. 3(a) is a natural color image. The image consists of flowers and leaves. Because of illumination, the values of pixels in the image vary from place to place. Besides, there are some holes among the flowers and the buds are different from petals. Fig. 3(b) is the result of segmentation using original C-V method while Fig. 3(c) is the result of segmentation using our color C-V method. It is obvious that in Fig. 3(c), all of the pedals of the flowers are definitely separated from leaves and the background, while the holes and buds are detected too.

In color printing images, halftone dot, visible only under a microscope, is the basic unit used to transfer color inks and organize tones of images. To get color prints with high quality, detecting and controlling the variation of dots with different ink colors (such as cyan, magenta and yellow) in printing process is very important. Microscopic halftone image segmentation is one of the significant steps in the computerized system of printing quality control.

Halftone image segmentation is affected by various factors: fuzzy edge and uneven density of halftone dot, complex background and abundant noise, all of which lead to high difficulty of segmentation. Classical methods applied to halftone image include the entropy method [7] and the Otsu method [8] which both require a conversion from the original color images to gray-scale ones. In this work, we employ the color C-V method to segment the microscopic halftone images. Fig. 4 illustrates the segmentation results to a microscopic halftone image using classical methods in contrast to our method.

From Fig. 4(b) and Fig. 4(c), we find that these traditional methods fail to correctly segment the halftone image for too much noise and the complex background. Instead, the color C-V method can obtain the satisfactory edges of halftones, unaffected by the severe noise and complex background. Two more examples are given in Fig. 5 where the color C-V method can deal with the weak edges in the halftone images elegantly.

**Fig. 3.** (a) A natural color image. (b) Result of segmentation using Color C-V method without global property. (c) Result of segmentation using our color C-V method.

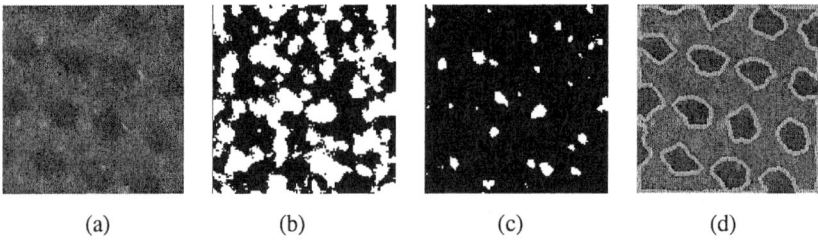

**Fig. 4.** (a) A halftone image. (b) Result of segmentation using Otsu method. (c) Result of segmentation using entropy method. (d) Result of segmentation using our color C-V method.

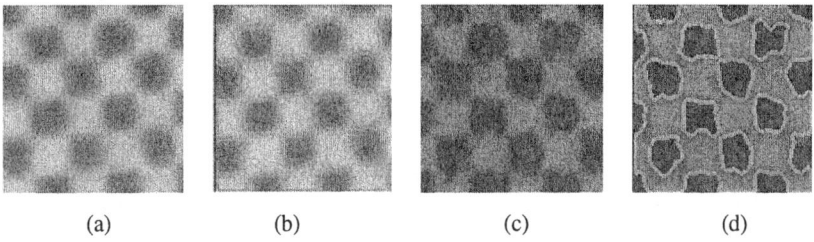

**Fig. 5.** (a) A halftone image. (b) Result of segmentation using our color C-V method. (c) A halftone image. (d) Result of segmentation using our color C-V method.

## 5 Conclusion

In this paper, we propose a novel color C-V method. Considering the correlation between different color channels, we treat the color components of pixels in a color image as vectors and thus extend the original C-V method to the color case. The global property is incorporated into this model to deal with the cases of small holes occurring in color images. Besides, the suitable color space is also chosen for segmentation according to human visual perception. Finally, we apply the proposed method to natural color images and microscopic halftone printing images and the results demonstrate that the proposed method is promising in detecting poor-contrast boundaries even with noisy inputs in color images.

## References

1. Kass, M., Witkin, A. and Terzopoulos, D.: Snakes: Active contour models. Int. J. Computer. Vision. 4 (1987) 321–331
2. Chan, F.T., Vese, L.: Active contours without edges. IEEE Trans Image Processing. 2 (2001) 266–277
3. Mumford, D. and Shah, J.: Optimal approximation by piecewise smooth functions and associated variational problems. Comm. Pure Appl. Math. 42 (1989) 557–685
4. Zhao, H.K., Chan, T., Merriman, B. and Osher, S.: A variational level set approach to multiphase motion. J. Commput. Phys. 127 (1996) 179–195
5. Chan, F.T., Vese, L.: Active contours without edges for vector-valued Images. Journal of Visual Communication and Image Representation. 11 (2000) 130–141
6. Osher, S., Sethian, J, A.: Fronts propagating with curvature-dependent speed: algorithms based on Hamilton-Jacobi formulations. Journal of Computational Physics. 1 (1998) 12–49
7. Wang, Y., Yang, J.: A new printing measurement method and structure feature extraction of microscopic dot. Proceedings of the World Congress on Intelligent Control and Automation. 4 (2004) 3658–3661
8. Otsu, N.: A threshold selection method from gray-level histograms. IEEE Trans. Syst. Man, Cybern. 1 (1979) 62–66

# SAR Image Segmentation Using Kernel Based Spatial FCM

Xiangrong Zhang, Tan Shan, Shuang Wang, and Licheng Jiao

National Key Lab for Radar Signal Processing and Institute of Intelligent
Information Processing, Xidian University, Xi'an, Shaanxi 710071, China
xrzhang@mail.xidian.edu.cn

**Abstract.** The presence of speckle in synthetic aperture radar (SAR) images makes the segmentation of such images difficult. In this paper, a set of energy measures of channels of the undecimated wavelet decomposition is used to represent the texture information of SAR image efficiently. Furthermore, the kernel FCM incorporating spatial constraints, which is characteristic of robustness to noise, is applied to the SAR image segmentation. A synthesized texture image and a Ku-band SAR image are used in experiments and the successful segmentation results show the validation of the method.

## 1 Introduction

Recently, SAR image segmentation was attempted to use the spatial association of elements based on pixel intensities. Texture is just this kind of important characteristic that represents not only the gray level statistic information of image but also the structural arrangement of surfaces and their relationship to the surrounding environment. In SAR image, it can be considered that texture is an innate property of all surfaces and different surface coarseness of land covers presents different texture [1]. Therefore, the segmentation of SAR images usually uses texture measures as features for the segmentation algorithm in order to improve its performance.

Despite the lack of a complete and formal definition of texture, there are various methods available for texture extraction. More recently, the methods of multi-channel or multiresolution have received much attention in texture analysis [2] [3]. In all cases, a multiscale feature extraction with two or three levels led to better results than a single resolution analysis. The multiresolution properties of the wavelet transform are beneficial for texture discrimination. Due to the translation-invariant property, the undecimated wavelet decomposition [4] is used to represent the texture of the SAR image in this paper. Then stable texture features can be achieved.

On the basis of feature extraction, the next step of SAR image segmentation involves clustering. Fuzzy c-means algorithm (FCM) has been efficiently applied in the segmentation of SAR images [5] [6]. But it is also showed that the algorithm is sensitive to the noise. Unfortunately, it is well know that there exist speckles in SAR image, which needs robust clustering methods for segmentation. The kernel-based FCM incorporating spatial constraints (Kernel SFCM) is introduced in paper [7], where the potential ability of this algorithm to restrain noise is demonstrated for MRI image segmentation. In this paper, Kernel SFCM is applied to the segmentation of the land covers in SAR image, and the high performance achieved suggests that this approach performs better than traditional clustering algorithms in SAR image segmentation.

## 2   Wavelet Energy Measures for Texture Feature

The use of a pyramid-structured wavelet transform for texture analysis was first suggested in the pioneering work of Mallat [8]. Subsequently, various texture measures based on the wavelet decomposition energies are presented. In paper [9], [10] and [3], wavelet transform, tree-structured wavelet transform and wavelet packet are respectively used for texture analysis and are applied to texture segmentation and classification. For downsampling wavelet decomposition, there is neither loss nor redundancy of information between the levels. However, the downsampling has a drawback that the decomposition is not translation-invariant. On the contrary, the undecimated wavelet decomposition can provide robust texture features due to the translation-invariant property. The energy of each subimage can be a favorable feature of texture because it indicates dominant spatial-frequency channels of the original image. We use the energy measures ($l_1$-norm) as texture features in this paper. And the texture features are made up of the energies of subimages by the undecimated wavelet decomposition over a window centered on the current spatial location, which makes the difference between classes more distinguish.

It is also clear that a multiresolution feature extraction with 2 or 3 levels is preferable to a local analysis with one level only. Then we implement 3-level wavelet decomposition. The feature vector of each pixel can be represented as the 10-dimension vector $(e_{LL-1}, e_{LH-1}, e_{HL-1}, e_{HH-1}, e_{LH-2}, e_{HL-2}, e_{HH-2}, e_{LH-3}, e_{HL-3}, e_{HH-3})$, in which, for example $e_{LL-1}$ denotes the energy of the LL subimage in the first level. And LL subimage is obtained by lowpass filtering in both row and column directions, The detail images, LH, HL, and HH, contain high frequency components.

## 3   Kernel SFCM for SAR Image Segmentation

Speckles are another source of fluctuation existed in SAR image. Traditional clustering approaches are sensitive to noise and the performances are affected by the distribution of the dataset greatly. Intuitively, because Euclidean distance is used for the comparability measure in these methods, the samples that are close to each other will be clustered together in the sample space. If the sample space can be clustered linearly, high performance will be achieved using the classical clustering algorithms. But when the sample space can be clustered non-linearly, the performance using the classical clustering algorithm is limited. Therefore, modified methods of the comparability measure have been put forward. Du and Lee [6] applied FCM clustering to segment SAR images using a distance measure based on the Wishart distribution, namely, the Euclidean squared distance in the objective function of FCM is replaced by the Wishart measure. In paper [11], an additional constraint is placed on the membership functions within the objective function of FCM that forces them to be spatially smooth. Paper [12] proposed a spatial FCM in which the neighborhood information is added to the objective function of FCM to improve the robustness to the noise.

In addition, some kernel clustering algorithms have been proposed [7] [13] because of the particular processing ability of kernel. In these methods, the scalar product in the objective function is replaced by the kernel function. In paper [7], the spatial FCM (SFCM) is extended to Kernel SFCM with kernel technique. The applications of kernel and spatial constraints enhance the robustness of the algorithm so that it is much more appropriate for the segmentation of SAR image.

In SFCM, the median of the region around the central pixel is introduced to the objective function of FCM. The objective function is given by

$$J_m = \sum_{i=1}^{c}\sum_{k=1}^{N} u_{ik}^m \|x_k - v_i\|^2 + \alpha \sum_{i=1}^{c}\sum_{k=1}^{N} u_{ik}^m \|\bar{x}_k - v_i\|^2 \tag{1}$$

where $c$ is the number of classes, $N$ is the number of samples, $u_{ik}$ is the membership of the sample $x_k$ to the prototype $v_i$, $\bar{x}_k$ denotes the median of the region around the central pixel. The real constant $m$ is a weighting exponent on each fuzzy membership. The parameter $\alpha$ controls the effect of the penalty term. Lower image signal-to-noise ratios (SNR) would require a higher value of the parameter $\alpha$.

Under the constraint of $\sum_{k=1}^{c} u_k(x_i) = 1$, $i = 1, 2, \cdots, c$, the iterative functions of the cluster prototype $v_i$ and the membership $u_{ik}$ can be obtained from equation (1).

$$u_{ik} = \frac{\left(\|x_k - v_i\|^2 + \alpha \|\bar{x}_k - v_i\|^2\right)^{-1/(m-1)}}{\sum_{j=1}^{c}\left(\|x_x - v_j\|^2 + \alpha \|\bar{x}_k - v_j\|^2\right)^{-1/(m-1)}}. \tag{2}$$

$$v_i = \frac{\sum_{k=1}^{n} u_{ik}^m (x_k + \alpha \bar{x}_k)}{(1+\alpha)\sum_{j=1}^{c} u_{ik}^m}. \tag{3}$$

Replacing the scalar product in (1) with a kernel function, the objective function of the Kernel SFCM is defined as

$$J_m = \sum_{i=1}^{c}\sum_{k=1}^{N} u_{ik}^m (1 - K(x_k, v_i)) + \alpha \sum_{i=1}^{c}\sum_{k=1}^{N} u_{ik}^m (1 - K(\bar{x}_k, v_i)) \tag{4}$$

where $K(x, y)$ is the kernel function. Then the iterative functions of the cluster prototype $v_i$ and the membership $u_{ik}$ can be obtained from equation (4).

$$u_{ik} = \frac{((1-K(x_k,v_i)) + \alpha(1-K(\bar{x}_k,v_i)))^{-1/(m-1)}}{\sum_{j=1}^{c}((1-K(x_x,v_j)) + \alpha(1-K(\bar{x}_k,v_j)))^{-1/(m-1)}} \quad (5)$$

$$v_i = \frac{\sum_{k=1}^{n} u_{ik}^m (K(x_k,v_i)x_k + \alpha K(\bar{x}_k,v_i)\bar{x}_k)}{\sum_{j=1}^{c} u_{ik}^m (K(x_x,v_j) + \alpha K(\bar{x}_k,v_j))} \quad (6)$$

The iterative procedure of (5) and (6) is the Kernel SFCM algorithm. In this way, Kernel SFCM for SAR image segmentation can be summarized as follow.

*Step1*: The original SAR image is extended near the edge in a mirror manner first. For each center pixel in a region of a sliding window, the 3-level undecimated wavelet decomposition is applied and the energy measures of channels are made up of the feature vector $x$ for each pixel. And then standardize the feature vectors in order to balance the role of each feature for segmentation.

*Step2*: Evaluate the median filter image of the original image, which puts the relation between gray levels of neighboring pixels into consideration. Perform the procedure same as the Step1, and get the feature vector $\bar{x}$ of each pixel in the median filter image.

*Step3*: Set cluster number $c$ and constant $m = 2$. Initialize the prototypes and set the threshold $\varepsilon > 0$ for a small value. Set the iteration counter $g = 1$.

*Step4*: Repeat the following iteration

1) Update the partition matrix $U$ with (5).
2) Update the prototypes $V$ with (6).
3) $g = g + 1$.

Until $\|V_{g+1} - V_g\| < \varepsilon$

*Step5*: Defuzzy and assign all pixels to the corresponding class label.

## 4 Experiments and Analysis

Segmentations of synthesized texture image and SAR image have been carried out to test the efficiency of the proposed method in this paper. In comparison, FCM, SFCM and Kernel SFCM are respectively used for segmentation.

In the first experiment, the synthesized texture image consists of three textures. The sliding window size is of 16×16 (pixels) for undecimated wavelet-decomposed. The RBF kernel function is used in Kernel SFCM, in which the width of RBF kernel $\sigma = 1$ and the parameter $\alpha = 0.5$. The results of the experiment are shown in Fig.1.

From Fig. 1, it is obvious that the segmentation results with SFCM (Fig.1.(c)) and with Kernel SFCM(Fig.1.(d)) are better than that with FCM (Fig.1.(b)) for the reason

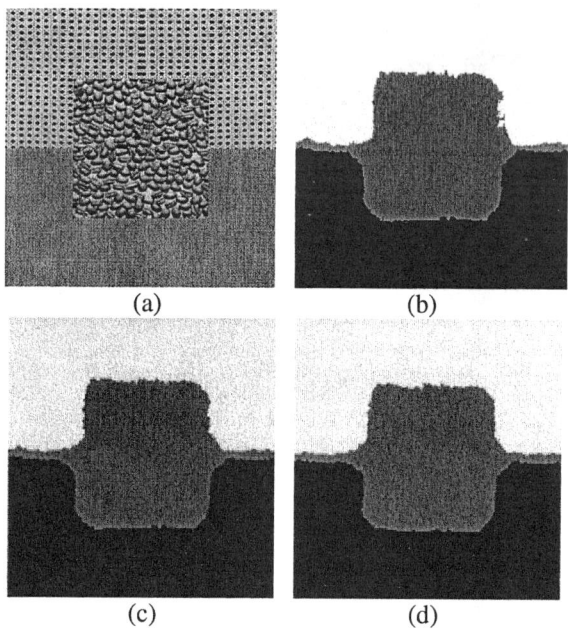

**Fig. 1.** Comparison of segmentation results on a natural texture image (a) test image; (b) with FCM; (c) with SFCM; (d) with Kernel SFCM

that the spatial constraints are taken into consideration. In addition, the boundary is more correct in Fig.1.(d).

Further experiment is carried out on the sub-image of the SAR image with 1-m resolution, Ku-band coming from the Rio Grande River near Albuquerque, New Mexico. The image is of $256 \times 256$ pixels in size. It is segmented into three different landcover regions. The sliding window size is of $32 \times 32$ (pixels) for texture feature extraction by undecimated wavelet-decomposed. Parameter $\alpha = 3$. Experimental results are shown in Fig. 2.

From Fig. 2, the observation is that we can get the satisfied results based on FCM, SFCM and the Kernel SFCM respectively with the undecimated wavelet decomposition energy measures as the texture features. However, there is much background noise in Fig.2. (b). In Fig.2. (c), the spatial information is considered, so there is less noise than the result in Fig.2 (a). While there is little noise in Fig.2.(d) and the land covers are clustered correctly.

## 5 Conclusion

In this paper, the SAR image segmentation is investigated. A set of energy measures of channels of the undecimated wavelet decomposition is introduced to represent the texture information of SAR image efficiently. Considering the characteristic that there

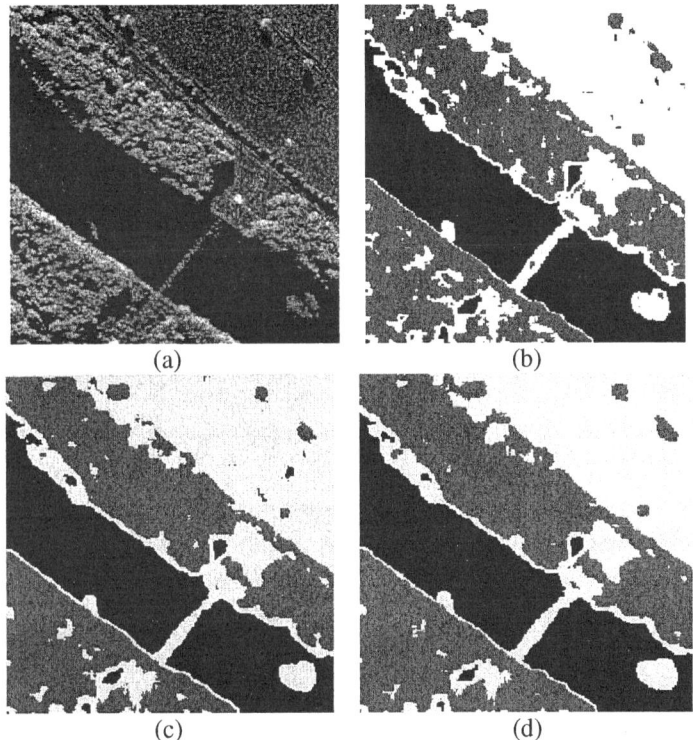

**Fig. 2.** Comparison of segmentation results on a Ku-band SAR subimage (a) original image; (b) with FCM; (c) with SFCM; (d) with Kernel SFCM

exist speckles in SAR image, the Kernel SFCM characterized by robustness to noise is applied to the SAR image segmentation. A synthesized texture image and a Ku-band SAR subimage are used in experiments. As have been demonstrated by experiments, the successful segmentation results show the feasibility and validity of the method.

# References

1. Ulaby, F.T., Kouyate, F., Brisco, B., Williams,L.: Textural Information in SAR Images. IEEE Trans. Geosci. Remote Sensing. GE-24 (1986) 235–245
2. Unser, M.: Texture Classification and Segmentation Using Wavelet Frames. IEEE Trans. Image Processing. 4 (1995) 1549–1560
3. Laine, A., Fan, F.: Texture Classification by Wavelet Packet Signatures. IEEE Trans. Pattern Analysis and Machine Intelligence. 15 (1993) 1186–1191
4. Fukuda, S., Hirosawa, H.: A Wavelet-Based Texture Feature Set Applied to Classification of Multifrequency Polarimetric SAR Images. IEEE Trans. on Geoscience and Remote Sensing. 37 (1999) 2282–2286

5. Lee, J.S., Grunes, M.R., Ainsworth, T.L., Du, L., Schuler, D.L., Cloude, S.R.: Unsupervised Classification Using Polarimetric Decomposition and Comples Wishart Classifier. In: Proceedings of IGARSS 98. Seattle, WA, (1998) 2178–2180
6. Du, L., Lee, J.S.: Fuzzy Classification of Earth Terrain Covers Using Complex Polarimetric SAR Data. Int. J. Remote Sensing. 17 (1996) 809–926
7. Zhang, D.Q., Chen, S.C.: Kernel-Based Fuzzy Clustering Incorporating Spatial Constraints for Image Segmentation. In: Proceedings of 2th International Conference on Machine Learning and Cybernetics. (2003) 2189–2192
8. Mallat, S.G.: A Theory of Multiresolution Signal Decomposition: The Wavelet Representation. IEEE. Trans. Pattern Analysis and Machine Intelligence. 11 (1989) 674–693
9. Lu, C.S., Chung, P.C., Chen, C.F.: Unsupervised Texture Segmentation via Wavelet Transform. Pattern Recognition. 30 (1997) 729–742
10. Chang, T., Kuo, C.C.J.: Texture Analysis and Classification with Tree-Structured Wavelet Transform. IEEE Trans. Image Processing. 2 (1993) 429–441
11. Pham, D.L.: Robust Fuzzy Segmentation of Magnetic Resonance Images Computer-Based Medical Systems. In: Proceedings of 14th IEEE Symposium on CBMS. (2001) 127–131
12. Ahmed, M.N., Yamany, S.M., Mohamed, N., Farag, A.A., Moriarty, T.: A Modified Fuzzy C-means Algorithm for Bias Field Estimation and Segmentation of MRI data. IEEE Trans. on Medical Imaging. 21 (2002) 193–199
13. Zhang, L., Zhou, W.D., Jiao, L.C.: Kernel Clustering Algorithm. Chinese J. Computer. 25 (2002) 587–590

# Segmentation of Nanocolumnar Crystals from Microscopic Images

David Cuesta Frau[1], María Ángeles Hernández-Fenollosa[2], Pau Micó Tormos[1], and Jordi Linares-Pellicer[3]

[1] DISCA Department, Polytechnic University of Valencia, Alcoi Campus,
Plaza Ferràndiz i Carbonell, 2,
03801 Alcoi, Spain
{dcuesta, pabmitor}@disca.upv.es
http://gedaii.epsa.upv.es

[2] Department of Applied Physics, Polytechnic University of Valencia,
Camíde Vera s/n, 46071 Valencia, Spain
mhernan@fis.upv.es

[3] DSIC Department, Polytechnic University of Valencia, Alcoi Campus,
Plaza Ferràndiz i Carbonell, 2, 03801 Alcoi, Spain
jlinares@dsic.upv.es

**Abstract.** This paper addresses the segmentation of crystalline Zinc oxide nanocolumns from microscopic images. ZnO is a direct band semiconductor suitable for many applications whose interest has been growing recently. One of these applications are light-collecting devices such as solar cells, using nanostructured substrates. Electrodeposition is a low cost technique very suitable for the preparation of nanostructured ZnO, producing nanocolumnar ZnO crystals with a morphology that depends on the deposition parameters and the substrate characteristics. The parameters of the sample can be determined processing images of the nanostructures, which is the objective of this study.

## 1 Introduction

Zinc oxide (ZnO) has some unique physical properties that make it very interesting from the point of view of many technological applications. To realize any type of device technology it is important to have control over the concentration of intentionally introduced impurities, called dopants, which are responsible for the electrical properties of ZnO. The dopants determine whether the current (and, ultimately, the information processed by the device) is carried by electrons or holes. In semiconducting oxides, it is generally possible to achieve one or other of these types, but not both. The dopants are also called shallow level impurities because they introduce energy levels close to one of the allowed energy bands in the material and are easily ionized as a result. There may also be unintentional impurities introduced during the growth of ZnO that have a deleterious effect on the properties of the material. These are called deep level defects or impurities and may be either elemental impurities arising from contamination of the

**Fig. 1.** Example of nanocolumns of ZnO. Image obtained using scanning electron microscopy.

growth environment or structural defects in the ZnO crystal lattice. These structural defects can be vacancies in the crystal structure or interstitials, i.e. atoms sitting in the open regions around lattice sites. In both cases, they may introduce energy levels deep within the forbidden band gap of ZnO and act as traps for carriers in the material. These uncontrolled defects make it very difficult to obtain reproducible device performance and reliability.

One of the applications of ZnO, in the form of nanocolumns (Fig. 1), is light-collecting devices such as solar cells. Electrodeposition is a low cost technique very suitable for the preparation of nanostructured ZnO, producing nanocolumnar ZnO crystals with a morphology that depends on the deposition parameters and the substrate characteristics [1]. The parameters of the sample can be determined processing images of the nanostructures. This paper deals with the segmentation of crystalline Zinc oxide nanocolumns from microscopic images for parameter estimation and, thus, physical properties monitorization.

Electrodeposition procedure consists of a three electrode electrochemical cell and a solution. The conducting substrate is set up as a working electrode. Three growth variables are controlled during the deposition process: current intensity, time and temperature. Images of the samples are obtained using scanning electron microscopy (SEM), using a Jeol JSM6300 [2].

As has already been stated, the morphology of ZnO layers depends on deposition conditions and parameters. We will focus our attention to nanocolumns of ZnO obtained by electrodeposition over GaN substrates after 30 minutes, a current intensity of $2.5 mA/cm^2$, and a temperature of $65^oC$ (see Fig.2). ZnO columns grown on GaN are at least twice higher than those grown on other substrates. They are perfectly vertical aligned and oriented, and have approximately the same size. The density is lower than using other substrates.

We propose in this work to utilize image processing techniques for an automatic analysis of images of nanocolumns of ZnO grown on GaN substrates.

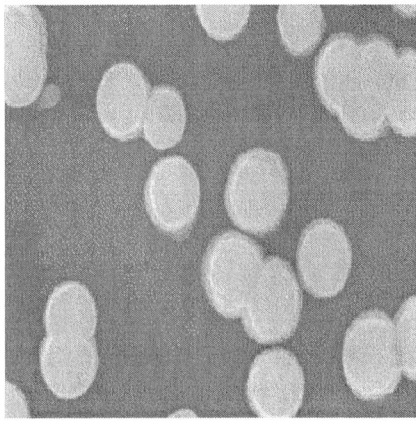

**Fig. 2.** Example of nanocolumnar ZnO grown on GaN substrate (top view)

Based on other similar applications of these techniques [3,4,5,6], the objective is to measure the dimension, overlapping, and density of such nanocolumns in SEM images to determine and monitorize the physical properties of the sample.

Thus, the method starts with a typical image preprocessing stage aimed at obtaining a better version of the input image. Then, the output of the preprocessing stage is binarized using a thresholding algorithm in order to clearly separate the background from the foreground (nanocolumns). Next, a contour extraction stage takes place. This stage comprises other substages such as: negative of the image, erosion, edge detection and thinning. The goal of this stage is to obtain a chain of pixels for each 8-connected region. Finally, the resulting columns (including overlappings and occlusions) are segmented and measured using a raster-to-vector conversion algorithm and an arc segmentation method. The stages of this method are shown in Fig.3.

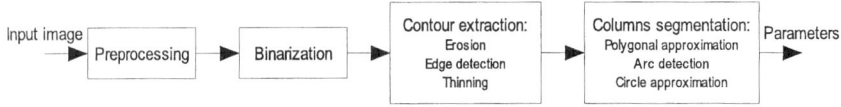

**Fig. 3.** Diagram of the stages

For the practical application of the method proposed, we developed a software tool for daily use in our physics laboratory. Programming has been done using C++ language under Windows and Linux, using Borland C++ Builder and Kylix compilers, respectively[1]. Next sections describe the stages of the process.

---

[1] Windows is a trademark of Microsoft Corporation, and C++Builder and Kylix are trademarks of Borland Software Corporation.

## 2 Image Preprocessing

Top view images of ZnO nanocolumns usually have a reasonable good quality because they are tall enough to enhance the contrast between the base and the top of the columns. Therefore, columns correspond to bright pixels (foreground), and background, dark pixels, corresponds to the base of the columns. Anyway, in order to make the borders of the columns look sharper and more homogeneous, we apply a noise reduction filter based on the median filtering, known as Tri-State median filter [7]. We have succesfully applied this filter to similar cases because it provides a good tradeoff between noise supression and edge preservation.

Being $X(i,j)$ the input image, the output image $Y(i,j)_{TSM}$ is given by:

$$Y(i,j)_{TSM} = \begin{cases} X(i,j), T \geq d_1 \\ Y(i,j)_{CWM}, d_2 \leq T < d_1 \\ Y(i,j)_{SM}, T < d_2 \end{cases} \quad (1)$$

namely, the output is one out of three possible values, depending on the relationship between a threshold $T$ and two distances, $d_1 = |X(i,j) - Y(i,j)_{SM}|$ and $d_2 = |X(i,j) - Y(i,j)_{CWM}|$. The respective outputs of filters CWM and SM are a centered weighted median, and a standard median.

Other defects that may appear on the image are holes and spots. We apply a method based on contour following [8] to remove them, according to a predefined threshold.

## 3 Image Binarization

In order to separate background from foreground, that is, columns, an image thresholding algorithm has been applied. There are many image thresholding techniques available nowadays. However, due to the good separability of dark and bright regions in these images, we chose a well known method of global thresholding, Otsu's method [9]. This algorithm has become a classical tool for image binarization for its simplicity and good results.

## 4 Contour Extraction

The binarization stage outputs a monochrome image where the columns and the background are clearly separated. Negative of the image is then computed in order to make columns correspond to black pixels and background to white pixels. Then image is eroded by means of mathematical morphology, using as the structuring element the typical 4-connected cross, to remove small isthmuses between neighbouring columns.

Next, a classical edge detector is applied [10], and the resulting image is thinned [11] so as to obtain a one-pixel wide contour of each column or overlapping columns. Thinning is the classical approach to skeletonization. As in other stages of the process described in this work, there are many thinning algorithms reported in the technical literature. We chose the method described in [11] due to its simplicity, high speed, and accuracy. In addition, the method is rotation invariant. This algorithm is iterative, deleting those object pixels that lie on its outer boundaries at each iteration. The core of the method is the use of 20 empirical rules to decide whether a foreground pixel belongs to the object skeleton or not. Considering the 8 neighbours of any pixel in the image as LU (Left Up), L (Left), LD (Left Down), CU (Center Up), CD (Center Down), RU (Right Up), R (Right), and RD (Right Down), the expression that combines these 20 rules is:

$$\begin{aligned}
&\left(LU * L * LD * CD * \overline{RU} * \overline{R}\right) + \left(LU * L * LD * CU * \overline{RD} * \overline{R}\right) + \\
&\left(LU * \overline{LD} * CU * \overline{CD} * RU * R\right) + \left(LU * L * CU * \overline{CD} * \overline{RD} * RU\right) + \\
&\left(LU * L * \overline{CD} * \overline{RD} * \overline{R} * \overline{RU}\right) + \left(LU * \overline{LD} * CU * \overline{CD} * \overline{RD} * \overline{R}\right) + \\
&\left(LU * L * LD * CU * CD * RD * \overline{R} * RU\right) + \\
&\left(LU * L * LD * CU * \overline{CD} * RD * R * RU\right) + \\
&\left(L * LD * \overline{CU} * \overline{RD} * \overline{R} * \overline{RU}\right) + \left(\overline{LU} * LD * \overline{CU} * CD * \overline{R} * \overline{RU}\right) + \\
&\left(\overline{L} * \overline{LD} * CU * \overline{CD} * \overline{RD} * RU\right) + \left(\overline{L} * \overline{LD} * \overline{LU} * \overline{CD} * RU * R\right) + \\
&\left(\overline{L} * \overline{LU} * CD * \overline{CU} * \overline{RU} * RD\right) + \left(\overline{L} * \overline{LU} * \overline{LD} * \overline{CU} * R * RD\right) + \\
&\left(\overline{L} * LU * LD * CU * CD * R * RD * RU\right) + \\
&\left(L * LU * LD * \overline{CU} * CD * R * RD * RU\right) + \\
&\left(\overline{L} * \overline{LU} * CD * R * RD * RU\right) + \left(L * \overline{LD} * CU * R * RD * RU\right) + \\
&\left(\overline{LU} * LD * \overline{CU} * CD * R * RD\right) + \left(L * LD * \overline{CU} * CD * \overline{RU} * RD\right)
\end{aligned}$$

where overlined pixel values correspond to background pixels. If this expression is true, the pixel could be considered as background since it does not belong to the skeleton. However, these 20 rules are not enough to obtain a connected representation of some horizontal or vertical lines of width 2 pixels in the input image. Extremities of zigzag diagonal lines can also be incorrectly deleted. To solve these problems, the procedure is slightly modified by adding some new decision rules to the initial 20. These details can be found in [11]. These rules are iteratively applied to every pixel in the image until no change takes place. The state of the image at this point is shown in Fig.4.

## 5 Columns Segmentation

Before segmentation itself can take place, thinned contours are vectorized using line following and a polygonal approximation algorithm, with a error threshold of one pixel. The output of this vectorization process is a list of polygonal lines (basic primitives are lines) that fit each contour. This list is the input to an arc segmentation algorithm aimed at obtaining a higher order approximation, using circular arcs. This algorithm is a simplification of that described in [12], based on the following general principles to consider a polyline as an arc:

- Curvature. All segments should turn in the same direction, in other words, the polyline is either concave or convex, but not both.
- Length. Segments are of approximately equal length.
- Shape. Points lie approximately on the same circle.

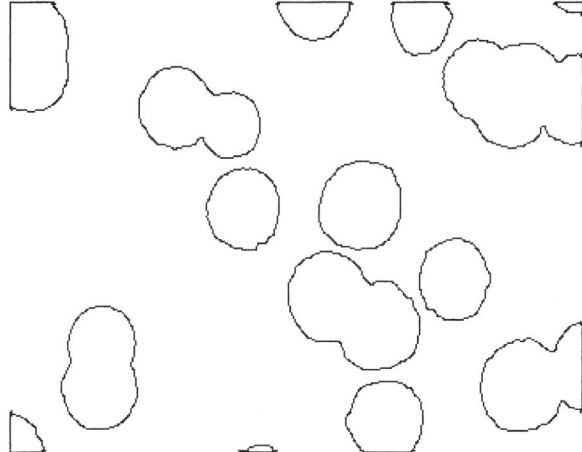

**Fig. 4.** Columns contours extracted after edge detection and thinning of the thresholded image

These principles can be completed with additional information of these specific images: only circular arcs are present, and line width is always 1 pixel. The algorithm proceeds iteratively until all the polylines of each contour have been merged or split to form suitable circular arcs. Starting with the first three vertices of each polyline, the initial parameters of a circle (center and radius) are computed. Then, following points are added provided a criterion, based on curvature, length, and shape, is met, and parameters are recomputed. Else, a new arc starts and the previous steps are repeated until there are no points left.

Once the contour of each column or groups of columns is extracted, it must be analized in order to segment each one and therefore be able to measure the parameters of the columns. There are some possible situations for each contour, depending on the case:

- Isolated and complete columns. This is the optimal case, clean, complete, and single column border is represented by a 8-connected chain of pixels.
- Two columns overlapping. Sometimes to columns grow too close that some parts of the borders may merge. As a result, a figure with a shape similar to the 8 number appears.
- Columns at edges of the image. The image usually does not comprise the whole ZnO sample and therefore some incomplete columns may appear at the edges of the image, represed by circular arcs.
- Multiple overlapping. In some cases, more than two columns grow very close and consequently the resulting border is an irregular combination of circular arcs from where true circles should be extracted.

The resulting approximation is therefore classified as one of the previous cases: if the two enpoints coincide, it represents a full circle, else, it is an arc featuring an incomplete border of a column. In this last case, according to the position of the arcs, namely, if they intersect with the edges of the images, they correspond to columns at edges of the images, otherwise they are overlapping columns. In both cases, arcs are approximated with full circles. More than an arc can correspond to the same circle. An example of the result of this process is shown in Fig.5.

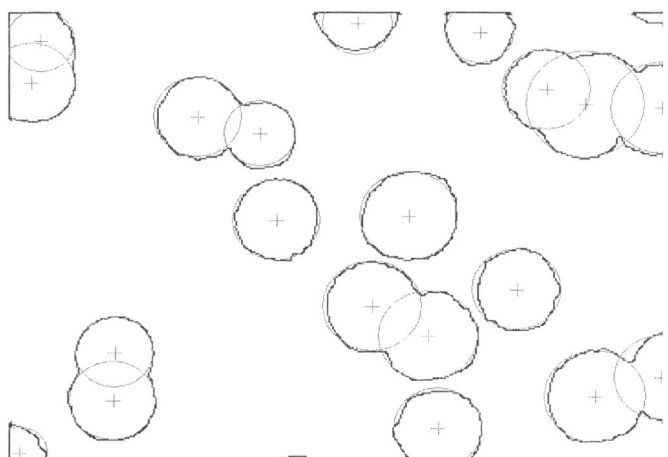

**Fig. 5.** Segmentation and circle approximation of nanocolumns after vectorization and arc detection

Finally, the software application computes the average area and dimension of the circles, percentage of image area, and percentage of overlapping circle areas. This last calculation is easily obtained using a circle intersection method and computing the common area of the meeting circles.

## 6 Discussion and Conclusion

We have described a method to automatically measure some parameters of SEM images of ZnO nanocolumns grown on GaN subtrates. This is of great interest since ZnO is becoming one of the most popular semiconductors nowadays, with many technological uses. This method has been implemented in a real software application.

Our method outputs a circle approximation of the nanocolumns detected in the image, and thus, a quantitative measure of their parameters can be obtained. Circle approximation of nanocolumns accuracy is sufficient for our measures. However, sometimes the error is too big because there are many stages involved in this circle approximation: thinning, polygonal aproximation and arc segmentation. We plan to apply a more direct method based on circle detection, and therefore omit some stages. Circle detection can be performed using the popular Hough transform, but other methods with lower computational cost and less memory requirements have appeared recently [13]. Some of these methods will be studied as future work.

This method could also be utilized in other similar applications such as cell detection, particle picking, and, in general, in any case where images of circular features is of interest. Replacing circle detection procedure by an ellipse detection [14], this scheme can be applied even in more situations.

# References

1. Cembrero,J., Elmanouni,A., Hartiti,B., Mollar, M., Mar, B.: Nanocolumnar ZnO Films for Photovoltaic Applications. Thin Solid Films. Elsevier (2004) 198–202
2. Damonte,L.C.,Mendoza,L.A.,Mar,B.,Hernández,M.A.: Nanoparticles of ZnO Obtained by Mechanical Milling. Powder Technology, Vol.148. Elsevier (2004) 15–19
3. Yu, Z., Bajaj, C.: Detecting Circular and Rectangular Particles Based on Geometric Feature Detection in Electron Micrographs. Journal of Structural Biology, Vol. 145. Elsevier (2004) 168–180
4. Zhu, Y. et al: Automatic Particle Selection: Results of a Comparative Study. Journal of Structural Biology, Vol. 145. Elsevier (2004) 3–14
5. Prasad, D., Ray, N., Acton, S.T.: Level Set Analysis for Leukocyte Detection and Tracking. IEEE Transactions On Image Processing, Vol.13, No.4. (2004) 562–572
6. Yue, Z.Q., Chen, S.., Tham, L.G.: Finite Element Modeling of Geomaterials Using Digital Image Processing. Computers and Geotechnics, Vol.30. Elsevier (2003) 375–397
7. Chen,T., Ma, K.K., Chen, L.H.: Tri-State Median Filter for Image Denoising. IEEE Transactions on Image Processing, Vol. 8, No. 12. (1999) 1834–1838
8. Ablameyko, S., Pridmore, T.: Machine Interpretation of Line Drawing Images, Technical Drawings, Maps and Diagrams. Springer-Verlag, Berlin Heidelberg (2000)
9. Otsu, N.: A Threshold Selection Method from Gray Level Histograms. IEEE Transactions on Systems, Man and Cybernetics, Vol.9, No.1. (1979) 62–66
10. Canny, J.: A Computational Approach to Edge Detection. IEEE Transactions on Pattern Analysis and Machine Intelligence, Vol.1, No.11. (1986) 679–698
11. Maher, A., Rabab, W.: A Rotation Invariant Rule-Based Thinning Algorithm for Character Recognition. IEEE Transactions on Pattern Analysis and Machine Intelligence, Vol. 24, **12** (2002) 1672–1678
12. Wenyin, L., Dori, D.: Incremental Arc Segmentation Algorithm and Its Evaluation. IEEE Transactions on Pattern Analysis and Machine Intelligence, Vol.20, No.4. (1998) 424–430
13. Qiao, Y., Ong, S.H.: Connectivity-based Multiple-circle Fitting. Pattern Recognition, Vol.37. Elsevier (2004) 755–765
14. Zhang, S.C., Liu,Z.Q.: A Robust, Real-time Ellipse Detector. Pattern Recognition, Vol.38. Elsevier (2005) 273–287

# Mutual Information-Based Methods to Improve Local Region-of-Interest Image Registration

K.P. Wilkie and E.R. Vrscay

Department of Applied Mathematics,
University of Waterloo, Waterloo, Ontario, Canada N2L 3G1
{kpwilkie, ervrscay}@uwaterloo.ca

**Abstract.** Current methods of multimodal image registration usually seek to maximize the similarity measure of mutual information (MI) between two images over their region of overlap. In applications such as planned radiation therapy, a diagnostician is more concerned with registration over specific regions of interest (ROI) than registration of the global image space. Registration of the ROI can be unreliable because the typically small regions have limited statistics and thus poor estimates of entropies. We examine methods to improve ROI-based registration by using information from the global image space.

## 1 Introduction

We are concerned with multimodal image registration – the geometric alignment of images obtained from different modalities [2]. A typical example occurs in the planning of cancer treatment by radiation therapy, where it is common to use data from both computer tomography (CT) and positron emission tomography (PET), to obtain anatomical and functional information, respectively.

Most image registration procedures compare images directly, with specific attention to landmarks, surfaces, or pixel/voxel intensity values. Limitations of these procedures have led to the use of information theoretic methods to characterize image alignment in terms of pixel correlations. Mutual information (MI), introduced in [5], has become a standard measure of image registration – see [3] for further developments.

Registration involves finding a spatial transformation to align a study image $Y$ to a target image $X$. In simple cases, affine transformations suffice, but, non-linear transformations, based on elasticity for example, are required to account for deformations caused by patient positioning and internal organ movement.

In cancer treatment, it is common for diagnosticians to be most concerned with a particular region of the image, e.g., a cancerous lesion. Alignment is more important over the regions of interest (ROIs) than over the global images, and diagnosticians commonly improve ROI alignment by perturbing the global registration result. Directly registering ROIs by estimating MI is prone to error: The limited statistics provided by small regions are highly sensitive to noise and to the region of overlap.

The region of overlap is the common area contained within both the target and transformed study images. It is a function of the transformation, and changes during registration. Pixels contained in the region of overlap determine the overlap statistics used to estimate MI. Overlap statistics can cause artificial increases in MI as images move out of alignment. To counteract this, Studholme et al. [4] proposed normalized mutual information (NMI) which is invariant of overlap statistics. Unfortunately, as we will show in Section 2.1, the limited statistics of small regions inhibit the effectiveness of NMI.

To improve ROI registration, we examine similarity measures that combine global image information with ROI information. Our methods employ convex combinations of either the MI of the images and ROIs, or the distributions of the images and ROIs. The extreme limits of such convex combinations correspond to registering the ROIs or registering the images. Our methods seem to improve the registration of ROIs when compared to global image registration.

## 2 Mathematical Preliminaries

We consider an image $X$ as an array of pixels with greyscale values $x_k$, where $x_k$ are random variables that assume the discrete greyscale values $g_1, g_2, \cdots, g_N$. Our images are rescaled to 8 bits/pixel, so that $N = 2^8 = 256$ and $g_k = k - 1$. Associated with $X$ is the greyscale probability distribution $\mathbf{p} = (p_1, p_2, \cdots, p_N)$. Here $p_k$ is the frequency of occurence of greyscale value $g_k$, normalized so that $\sum p_k = 1$. The *entropy* of $X$ is defined as

$$H(X) = H(\mathbf{p}) = -\sum_{k=0}^{N-1} p_k \log p_k, \tag{1}$$

where log denotes $\log_2$, and $H$ is measured in "bits." Entropy is a convex down function: For two probability distributions $\mathbf{p}$ and $\mathbf{q}$, and for $c \in [0,1]$, entropy satisfies.

$$H(c\mathbf{p} + (1-c)\mathbf{q}) \geq cH(\mathbf{p}) + (1-c)H(\mathbf{q}). \tag{2}$$

Consider two images, $X$ and $Y$, with respective distributions $\mathbf{p}$ and $\mathbf{q}$. The *relative entropy* between $\mathbf{p}$ and $\mathbf{q}$ is defined as [1]

$$D(\mathbf{p}\|\mathbf{q}) = \sum_{k=1}^{N} p_k \log \frac{p_k}{q_k}, \tag{3}$$

where by convention $0 \log \frac{0}{q} = 0$ and $p \log \frac{p}{0} = \infty$. Relative entropy is non-negative, and zero if and only if $\mathbf{p} = \mathbf{q}$, but it is not a metric since it is not symmetric and it does not satisfy the triangle inequality.

Now let $\mathbf{r}$ denote the joint distribution associated with images $X$ and $Y$: for $1 \leq i, j \leq N$, $r_{ij}$ is the probability of finding the greyscale values $(g_i, g_j)$ in corresponding pixel pairs. It follows that $\mathbf{p}$ and $\mathbf{q}$ are marginals of $\mathbf{r}$, i.e.

$$\sum_{i=1}^{N} r_{ij} = q_j, \quad \sum_{j=1}^{N} r_{ij} = p_i. \tag{4}$$

If the pixels of $X$ and $Y$ are independent, then $r_{ij} = p_i q_j$ and the joint distribution is the product distribution **d**, where $d_{ij} = p_i q_j$.

*Mutual information*, $I(X,Y)$, is defined as the relative entropy between the joint distribution **r** and the product distribution **d**, i.e.

$$I(X,Y) = \sum_{i,j} r_{ij} \log \frac{r_{ij}}{p_i q_j}. \qquad (5)$$

It is a measure of the distance from the joint distribution to the product distribution. The higher $I(X,Y)$ is, the more correlated are corresponding pixel pairs. Hence, mutual information is maximized when the two images are most correlated and the joint distribution is "furthest" from the product distribution. As pointed out in [1], $I(X,Y)$ is a measure of the amount of information that one random variable contains about another random variable. If the random variables $x_i$ and $y_i$ are independent for all $i$, then $I(X,Y) = 0$.

The *joint entropy* associated with the pair of images $X$ and $Y$ is

$$H(X,Y) = H(\mathbf{r}) = -\sum_{i,j} r_{ij} \log r_{ij}, \qquad (6)$$

i.e. the entropy of the joint distribution. ¿From Equation (4), $H(X,X) = H(X)$. Mutual information can thus be expressed in terms of entropy,

$$I(X,Y) = H(X) + H(Y) - H(X,Y). \qquad (7)$$

Note that $I(X,X) = H(X)$. The relationship between $H(X)$, $H(Y)$, $H(X,Y)$ and $I(X,Y)$ is expressed in a Venn diagram, as shown in Figure 2.2 of [1]. We will compare this to NMI, defined in [4] by

$$\hat{I}(X,Y) = \frac{H(X) + H(Y)}{H(X,Y)}. \qquad (8)$$

## 2.1 Some Simple Examples Tailored to the Registration Problem

In Figure 1 we plot $I(X,Y)$ vs. $n$, where the target $X$ is the $512 \times 512$ pixel *Lena* image, and $Y$ is the same image shifted horizontally by $n$ pixels. In the left plot, $Y$ is periodic; the image wraps around the computation window which is fixed to the size of the target image. This case, though not realistic, is used to demostrate the effects of overlap statistics. In the right plot, $X$ and $Y$ are cropped to the region of overlap. This region decreases as $|n|$ increases, which adversely affects the statistics: As $|n|$ approaches the target image boundary, $I(X,Y)$ falsely indicates registration. In each case, $I(X,Y)$ shows a strong peak at registration, i.e. at $n = 0$. Note, noise greatly reduces the amplitude of these peaks.

To examine effects of limited statistics, we use two transaxial magnetic resonance (MR) brain images, the target is proton density (PD) weighted and the study is T2 relaxation time (T2) weighted; see Figure 2. Figure 3 shows registration curves for horiziontal shifts calculated for three ROIs of various size. The

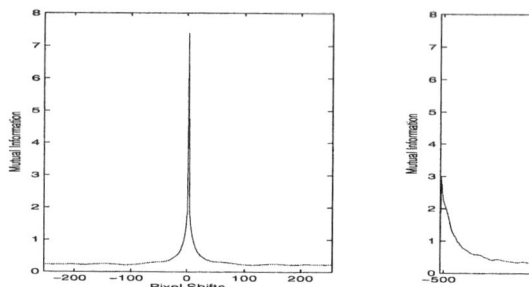

**Fig. 1.** MI for *Lena* and a horizontally shifted *Lena* using a fixed computation window with periodic boundary conditions (*left*) and the region of overlap (*right*)

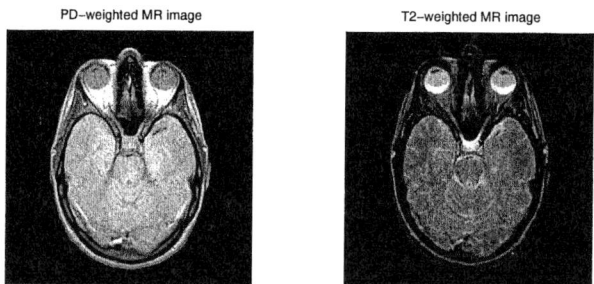

**Fig. 2.** PD-weighted (*left*) and T2-weighted (*right*) MR brain images

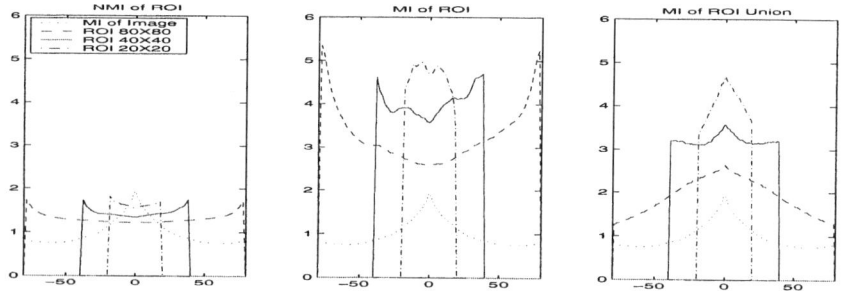

**Fig. 3.** Registration curves PD- and T2-weighted MR images and three ROI using NMI (*left*), MI (*middle*), and MI computed with ROI union statistics (*right*)

left and middle plots display NMI and MI respectively, both are computed with ROI overlap statistics (contributing pixels lie in the intersection of the ROIs). The right plot displays MI computed with ROI union statistics (contributing pixels lie in the union of the ROIs). Note the left and middle registration curves are distorted by the limited statistics of the ROI overlap: In both cases, no peaks occur at registration. The use of ROI union statistics, however, produce registration curves with clearly defined peaks.

These results suggest important consequences for medical image registration. For example, in prostate-focused registration, a typical 256 × 256 pixel image displays the prostate as a circle of radius 23 pixel-widths, an area of 1661 pixels. If the 40 × 40 pixel ROI from Figure 3 approximates the prostate, then even by quadrupling the number of pixels used to estimate MI, using the 80 × 80 pixel ROI, a meaningless registration curve will still be obtained.

## 3 Proposed Methods to Improve ROI Registration

As mentioned in Section 1, diagnosticians may be more concerned that images are most accurately aligned over a region of interest, as opposed to the global image. Small ROIs possess insufficient statistics to accurately estimate MI, but still contain useful information. We present two methods to perform ROI registration by "blending" the information of the ROI with that of the global image.

### 3.1 Method 1: Weighted Mutual Information

A crude way of performing such blending is to construct a convex combination of the MI for two separate problems, namely, $(i)$ the registration of the ROIs and $(ii)$ the registration of the global images. Thus we define

$$\begin{aligned} J(X, Y; c) &= (1 - c)I(X_{ROI}, Y_{ROI}) + cI(X, Y), \\ &= (1 - c)I(\mathbf{p}_{ROI}, \mathbf{q}_{ROI}) + cI(\mathbf{p}, \mathbf{q}), \quad 0 \leq c \leq 1. \end{aligned} \quad (9)$$

Here, $X_{ROI}$ and $Y_{ROI}$ denote the ROIs of images $X$ and $Y$, with distributions $\mathbf{p}_{ROI}$ and $\mathbf{q}_{ROI}$, respectively. The case $c = 0$ corresponds to registration of the ROIs and $c = 1$ corresponds to registration of the global images. $J(X, Y; c)$, which we call *weighted mutual information* (WMI), performs a linear interpolation between these two cases. Note that WMI is *not* a mutual information function in the strict sense.

To facilitate optimization, a desirable feature of such blending would be to enhance the peak of the similarity measure at registration. This, however, may not be achievable: Since the distributions in Equation (9) do not depend on $c$, it follows that

$$\frac{\partial J(X, Y; 0)}{\partial c} = I(\mathbf{p}, \mathbf{q}) - I(\mathbf{p}_{ROI}, \mathbf{q}_{ROI}). \quad (10)$$

Hence, it is not guaranteed *a priori* that this derivative is positive. Depending upon the nature of the ROIs, it is possible that the RHS of Equation (10) is negative, implying an initial *decrease* in WMI by the inclusion of global image statistics. However, it is not only the *amplitude* of the peaks which is of concern but also the *location* of the peaks, i.e., the point of registration.

This method can be altered to use the normalized mutual information from each of the ROI and image, instead of the mutual information. We call this function WNMI, and it is computed in an analagous way to WMI, see Equation (9).

## 3.2 Method 2: Mutual Information of Weighted Distributions

We now propose a method that employs weighted probability distributions – a kind of statistical blending of an image with its ROI. For images $X$ and $Y$, we define the following weighted distributions ($N$-vectors), for $0 \leq c \leq 1$:

$$\mathbf{p}_c = (1-c)\mathbf{p}_{ROI} + c\mathbf{p}$$
$$\mathbf{q}_c = (1-c)\mathbf{q}_{ROI} + c\mathbf{q}, \qquad (11)$$

and the following weighted joint distribution ($N \times N$ matrix),

$$\mathbf{r}_c = (1-c)\mathbf{r}_{ROI} + c\mathbf{r}. \qquad (12)$$

By construction, the above weighted distributions are probability distributions that linearly interpolate between the ROI and global image statistics.

To construct a similarity measure, we use these weighted distributions in the definition of mutual information. From Equation (7), we define

$$K(X,Y;c) = H(\mathbf{p}_c) + H(\mathbf{q}_c) - H(\mathbf{r}_c). \qquad (13)$$

$K(X,Y,c)$ is the *mutual information of weighted distributions* (MIWD) derived from the global images and their regions of interest. Note the two limiting cases,

1. $K(X,Y;0) = I(X_{ROI}, Y_{ROI})$, the MI of the ROIs of images $X$ and $Y$.
2. $K(X,Y;1) = I(X,Y)$, the MI of images $X$ and $Y$.

Using the convexity of entropy, Equation (2), and the fact that $\log(x)$ is an increasing function of $x$, one can derive the following inequality from Equation (13) to relate WMI and MIWD (see Appendix for details):

$$K(X,Y;c) \geq J(X,Y;c) - E(c), \qquad (14)$$

where

$$E(c) = -(1-c)\log(1-c) - c\log c. \qquad (15)$$

Note that $E(c)$ is the entropy of a binary random variable with distribution $(c, 1-c)$, so $E(0) = E(1) = 0$ and $E(1/2) = 1$.

In Figure 4 we see the relationship between WMI and MIWD for our PD- and T2-weighted MR images at registration, using two different ROIs for weighting: a brain matter ROI and an eye socket ROI. Notice that as the weighting parameter $c$ changes, moving from the ROI to the global image, WMI is a linear interpolation of the two values, whereas the behaviour of MIWD is dependent on the statistics of the ROIs and images. (From the plot, we see that the MIWD function is not convex.) The value of $c$ which provides the right amount of mixed statistics to most accurately register regions of interest is difficult to determine, and the subject of future investigations. In the discussions to follow, we have used $c = \frac{1}{2}$, corresponding to an equal weighting of both the image and the ROI statistics.

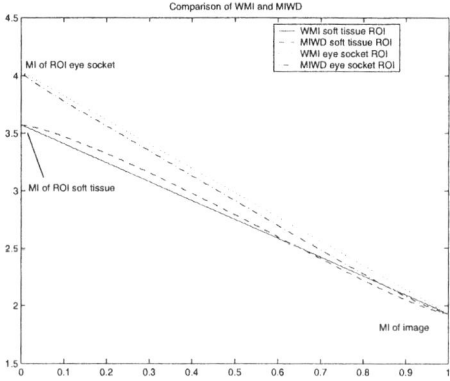

**Fig. 4.** WMI and MIWD *vs.* the weighting parameter $c$, for PD- and T2-weighted MR brain images at registration using a flat ROI (*dashed*) and an active ROI (*dotted*)

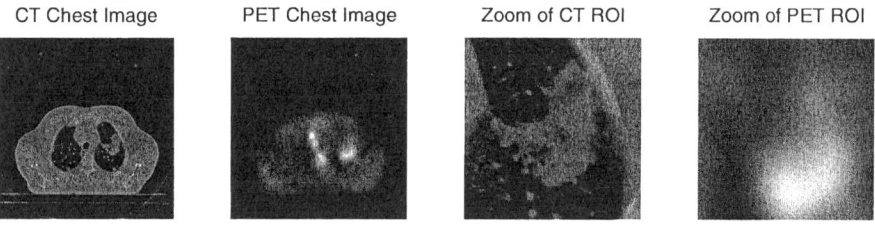

MI of Zoom = 1.5471

**Fig. 5.** Original CT and PET transaxial chest images (*left*). Zooms of the regions of interest in CT image space (*right*).

## 4 Results of an ROI-Based Registration Experiment

We have constructed a simple experiment using PET and CT transaxial chest images that were manually aligned by a rigid-body transformation based on fiducial point matching. Our goal is to improve the alignment of the unusually bright area in the PET image with the visible tumor in the CT image. The ROIs were independently defined for each image as approximately 3700 pixel polygons. The images and a zoom of the ROIs (as defined by the target CT image) are shown in Figure 5. Notice the poor alignment of the tumor regions.

For simplicity, the registration transformation was limited to vertical translations. The resulting curves are shown in Figure 6. Negative shifts correspond to upward translations, and positive to downward translations, of the study PET image with respect to the target CT image. The curves for WNMI, WMI, and MIWD were computed using two rules:

1. If the ROIs do not overlap, use the value of the global MI or NMI (set $c = 1$).
2. If the ROIs overlap, weight using ROI union statistics.

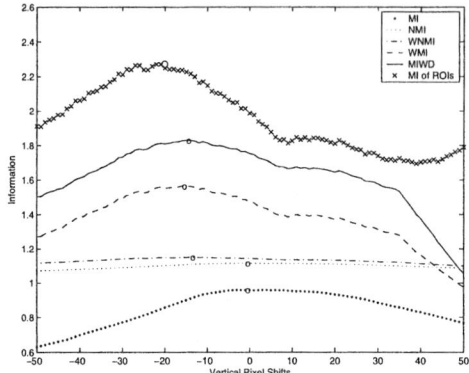

**Fig. 6.** Registration curves for vertical translations of the PET image with respect to the CT image, using ROI union statistics when needed. The curves represent MI (*dots*), NMI (*dotted*), WNMI (*dash-dot*), WMI (*dashed*), MIWD (*solid*), and MI of the ROIs (*xxx*). The maximum of each curve is indicated by a circle.

In order to maintain continuity of the similarity measure, for optimization purposes, the value of $c$ is made to decrease continuously from $c = 1$, at no ROI overlap, to the desired weighting factor, here $c = \frac{1}{2}$, at and above some percentage of ROI overlap. One can think of this as slowly zooming in the statistics from the global images to the local ROIs.

In Figure 6, each curve's maximum determines the vertical shift required to register the images (and ROIs) according to the similarity measure defining the curve. The registration transformations determined by MI and NMI are small translations, about 1 pixel, vertically up from the original position. The transformation determined by registering only the ROIs, using ROI union statistics, is a much larger upward translation, about 20 pixels. However, the registration transformations determined by WNMI, WMI, and MIWD, lie in between these two extremes with vertical translations around 13 pixels. Shifts of 13 pixels – roughly 11 mm – are acceptable and may be compensating for internal organ deformations caused by different positioning of the patient in PET and CT.

The registration curve for MI of ROIs, in Figure 6, demonstrates that it is a poor similarity measure. The curve is rough with multiple local maxima which inhibit optimization. Furthermore, it may not be desirable to discard the global image information even when performing ROI-based image registration.

Figure 7 shows the results of registration by each similarity measure over the zoomed region. Below each image is the mutual information calculated over the zoomed region. While MI is affected by the limited statistics of the zoom region ($90 \times 90$ pixels), we use it as a quantitative measure of alignment for lack of something more robust. MI is highest for registration by MI of the ROIs, and second highest for registration using mixed statistics. Visually, the ROIs in the bottom row (registration by WNMI, WMI, and MIWD) are more accurately registered than those in the top row (registration by MI, NMI, and MI of ROIs).

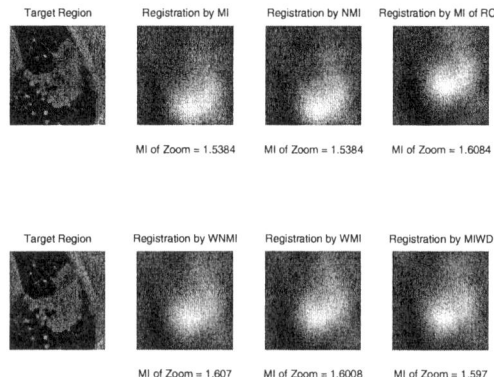

**Fig. 7.** Zoom of ROI as defined in the CT image (*top row left*). Results of registration using MI, NMI, and MI of ROIs (*top row left to right*), and using WNMI, WMI, and MIWD (*bottom row left to right*).

## 5 Summary and Concluding Remarks

In this paper, we have proposed two methods of blending image statistics with ROI statistics to improve the registration of small regions. The first method, WMI, is a simple convex combination of the mutual information of the global images with that of the ROIs. The second method, MIWD, takes the mutual information of the convex combinations of the marginal and joint probability distributions from both the global images and ROIs.

We also explored the use of ROI union statistics as opposed to ROI overlap statistics when dealing with small regions. Using the ROI union region is a reasonable way to avoid the problems associated with using the overlap region, especially for regions that are small to begin with. Taking the union region of global images will reduce the effect of overlap statistics, but may have the possibly negative effect of causing a registration of the background instead of the foreground objects. This is not a problem for ROI-based registration, especially in medical images, where the ROIs typically lie inside the foreground object.

The experiments presented above suggest the best registration result for small ROIs may be obtained by maximizing WNMI, WMI, or MIWD using ROI union statistics. We are still investigating the robustness of these similarity measures with respect to the weighting parameter $c$ as well as the content of the images and regions of interest.

In applications, the ROI can be any interesting area (or areas) of the image, for example significant edges. Our methods are easily modified for these cases. One of the original motivations of this study was the idea of an "activity-based" registration procedure, where the ROIs of an image are decided by some criteria, e.g., variance or local entropy.

Finally, there may well be other mathematical ways of combining region statistics, a subject that we are currently exploring.

## Acknowledgements

We thank Dr. R. Barnett, Medical Physics Division, Grand River Regional Cancer Center, Kitchener, Ontario, for suggesting this problem, for helpful conversations and for supplying the CT and PET data. We also thank Prof. J. Orchard, School of Computer Science, University of Waterloo, for the two MR brain images. This research has been supported in part by the Natural Sciences and Engineering Research Council of Canada in the form of a Postgraduate Scholarship (KPW) and Individual Research Grant (ERV).

## References

1. T.M. Cover and J.A. Thomas, *Elements of Information Theory* (Wiley, New York, 1991).
2. J.V. Hajnal, D.L.G. Hill and D.J. Hawkes, Editors, *Medical Image Registration* (CRC Press, Boca Raton, 2001).
3. F. Maes, A. Collignon, D. Vandermeulen, G. Marchal and P. Suetens, Multimodality image registration by maximization of mutual information, IEEE Trans. Image Proc. **16**, 187-198 (1997).
4. C. Studholme, D.L.G. Hill, D.J. Hawkes, An overlap invariant entropy measure of 3D medical image alignment, Pattern Recognition. **32**, 71-86 (1999).
5. P. Viola and W.M. Wells, III, Alignment by maximization of mutual information, Proc. 5th Int. Conf. Computer Vision, 16-23 (1995).

## Appendix

In this Appendix, we derive the inequality in Eq. (14). From the convexity property of entropy,

$$H(\mathbf{p}_c) \geq (1-c)H(\mathbf{p}_{ROI}) + cH(\mathbf{p})$$
$$H(\mathbf{q}_c) \geq (1-c)H(\mathbf{q}_{ROI}) + cH(\mathbf{q}). \qquad (16)$$

As for the final term in (14) (we use superscripts for $c$ and $ROI$ to minimize notational complexity)

$$\begin{aligned}
-H(\mathbf{r}_c) &= \sum r_{ij}^c \log r_{ij}^c \\
&= \sum \left[(1-c)r_{ij}^{ROI} + cr_{ij}\right] \log \left[(1-c)r_{ij}^{ROI} + cr_{ij}\right] \\
&= (1-c) \sum r_{ij}^{ROI} \log \left[(1-c)r_{ij}^{ROI} + cr_{ij}\right] + \\
&\quad + c \sum r_{ij} \log \left[(1-c)r_{ij}^{ROI} + cr_{ij}\right] \\
&\geq (1-c) \sum r_{ij}^{ROI} \log \left[(1-c)r_{ij}^{ROI}\right] + c \sum r_{ij} \log \left[cr_{ij}\right] \\
&= (1-c) \sum r_{ij}^{ROI} \log r_{ij}^{ROI} + c \sum r_{ij} \log r_{ij} + (1-c)\log(1-c) + c\log c \\
&= -(1-c)H(\mathbf{r}_{ROI}) - cH(\mathbf{r}) + (1-c)\log(1-c) + c\log c.
\end{aligned}$$

We have used the fact that the elements of $\mathbf{r}$ and $\mathbf{r}_{ROI}$ sum to unity. Combining these results yields the desired inequality.

# Image Denoising Using Complex Wavelets and Markov Prior Models

Fu Jin, Paul Fieguth, and Lowell Winger

Dept. of Systems Design Engineering, Univ. of Waterloo,
Waterloo, Ontario, Canada N2L 3G1
{fjin, pfieguth, lwinger}@uwaterloo.ca

**Abstract.** We combine the techniques of the complex wavelet transform and Markov random fields (MRF) model to restore natural images in white Gaussian noise. The complex wavelet transform outperforms the standard real wavelet transform in the sense of shift-invariance, directionality and complexity. The prior MRF model is used to exploit the clustering property of the wavelet transform, which can effectively remove annoying pointlike artifacts associated with standard wavelet denoising methods. Our experimental results significantly outperform those using standard wavelet transforms and are comparable to those from overcomplete wavelet transforms and MRFs, but with much less complexity.

**Keywords:** image denoising, complex wavelet transform, Markov random field.

## 1 Introduction

Images and image sequences are frequently corrupted by noise in the acquisition and transmission phases. The goal of denoising is to remove the noise, both for aesthetic and compression reasons, while retaining as much as possible the important signal features. Traditionally, this is achieved by approaches such as Wiener filtering, which is the optimal estimator in the sense of mean squared error (MSE) for Gaussian processes. However, the Wiener filter requires stationarity and an accurate statistical model of the underlying process, these performing poorly for natural images failing these assumptions. In practice, adaptive methods [1,2] were mostly used. These methods are good in that they are fast and can effectively suppress noise for most *natural* images. More importantly their adaptivity allows them to work for non-stationary processes (it is well-known the natural images are non-stationary). The main problem with such methods is their assumption that the natural images are independent random processes, which usually is not true. For example, image textures are correlated and are successfully modelled as Gaussian MRF (GMRF).

The last decade has seen a good deal of effort in exploiting the wavelet transform to suppress noise in natural images [3,4,5,7], because of its effectiveness and simplicity. It is now well-known that wavelet transforms with some regularity have strong decorrelation ability, thus well-representing many natural images with relatively few large coefficients. So it is thus far more reasonable to assume that the wavelet coefficients are independent, than the original spatial domain pixels. This explains why good denoising results have been achieved by simply thresholding or shrinking each wavelet coefficient *independently* [3,4]. Indeed, this kind of approach has much better results than traditional methods [1,2], both subjectively and objectively. However, for natural images the wavelet transform is not quite equivalent to the ideal eigen value/Karhunen-Loeve decomposition, so some correlation (dependence) still exists among the wavelet coefficients. For example, large (in magnitude) wavelet coefficients tend to be clustered within a scale and across scales. If these characteristics could be exploited in some way for denoising, better performance might be expected. Indeed, MRF models have been used for this very reason [5,7] and significantly better results obtained, both subjectively and objectively. Specifically, pointlike artifacts associated with the independence model have been effectively suppressed.

Considering the shift-variability of standard wavelets, or the complexity of shift-invariant (undecimated) transforms, in this paper we propose to use complex wavelet transform together with a MRF model for image denoising. A different formulation of the problem is also proposed. Sec. 2 describes the problem formulation. Sec.3 introduces the basic ideas of the complex wavelets and its useful properties. Sec.4 is about the probability models we use in the paper. In Sec.5 we show some experimental results with discussions.

## 2 The Denoising Method

Standard wavelet-based denoising methods consist of three steps:

1. The wavelet decomposition of the image is computed:
   Given noise-free image $\underline{x}_o$ and wavelet transform $H$, then

$$\underline{x} = H\underline{x}_o$$
$$\underline{y} = H\underline{y}_o = H(\underline{x}_o + \underline{w}_o) \quad (1)$$

   where $\underline{y}$ are the noisy observations.

2. The obtained wavelet coefficients are modified:

$$\hat{\underline{x}} = f(\underline{y}) \quad (2)$$

   where $f()$ denotes our proposed estimator.

3. The cleaned image is obtained from the modified wavelet coefficients by inverse wavelet transform:

$$\hat{\underline{x}}_o = H^{-1}\hat{\underline{x}}(\underline{y}) \quad (3)$$

For the first step we need to choose the "best" wavelet transform for an application. Commonly used wavelets include Daubechies orthogonal wavelets with the lengths from 2 to 10, bi-orthogonal wavelets with symmetry and several regular (smooth) overcomplete wavelets implemented by the *a trous* algorithm . Generally speaking, overcomplete wavelets outperform the fully decimated wavelets for signal and image denoising because they are shift-invariant. For images, wavelets with good orientation-selectivity (e.g. curvelet, ridgelet) are preferred. In this paper we use the dual-tree complex wavelet proposed by Kingsbury [8] because of its shift-invariance and orientation-selectivity properties. These properties will be shown in Section 3.

For Step two we propose to use a Bayesian decision and estimation method to modify the wavelet coefficients [5,7]. We classify the wavelet coefficients into two groups: $H_0$ and $H_1$, representing noise and signal, respectively. Then the $ith$ coefficient is changed to minimize the mean square error:

$$\hat{x}_i = E(x_i|y)$$
$$= E(x_i|y, L_i = H_0)P(L_i = H_0|y)$$
$$+ E(x_i|y, L_i = H_1)P(L_i = H_1|y) \qquad (4)$$

where $E()$ denotes expectation. $L_i \in \{H_0, H_1\}$ is the label of the $ith$ coefficient.

In practice, we can assume $E(x_i|y, H_0) = 0$. There are several methods to evaluate $E(x_i|y, H_1)$. In this paper we simply set $E(x_i|y, H_1) = y_i$. Thus we have

$$\hat{x}_i = P(L_i = H_1|y) \cdot y_i \qquad (5)$$

So to find $\hat{x}_i$ the only unknown quantity is $P(L_i = H_1|y)$. To get $P(L_i = H_1|y)$ one method is to find $P(\underline{L}|y)$ first [5,7], using the Bayesian rule

$$P(\underline{L}|y) = \frac{P(y|\underline{L})P(\underline{L})}{P(y)} \qquad (6)$$

where $\underline{L}$ is the label field. Then based on models $P(y|\underline{L})$ and $P(\underline{L})$ we can use stochastic sampling to find the joint probability $P(\underline{L}|y)$ and then the marginal probability $P(L_i = H_1|y)$. However, it is usually difficult to model $P(y|\underline{L})$; in [5,7], $y$ was heuristically assumed to be an independent process given $\underline{L}$.

In this paper we find $\hat{x}_i$ in a different way, separating detection and estimation. First we find the label field $\underline{L}$ by maximizing a *posteriori* probability (MAP)

$$\max_{\underline{L}} P(\underline{L}|\underline{m}) \propto \max_{\underline{L}} P(\underline{m}|\underline{L}) \cdot P(\underline{L}) \qquad (7)$$

where $\underline{m}$ is the feature vector for the classification. In Sec. 4 we also empirically model $P(\underline{m}|\underline{L})$ as an independent process. However, it should be noted this model is just used for *detecting* labels, not directly for *estimating* $x_i$. This means we only require the model of $P(\underline{m}|\underline{L})$ be good enough to classify labels correctly. With $\underline{L}$ known we can then estimate $x_i$ by

$$\hat{x}_i = E(x_i|y_i, \underline{L}_{(-i)})$$
$$\approx P(L_i = H_1|y_i, \underline{L}_{(-i)}) \cdot y_i \qquad (8)$$
$$= \frac{P(y_i|L_i = H_1, \underline{L}_{(-i)}) \cdot P(L_i = H_1|\underline{L}_{(-i)})}{\sum_{k=0}^{1} P(y_i|L_i = H_k, \underline{L}_{(-i)}) P(L_i = H_k|\underline{L}_{(-i)})} \cdot y_i$$

where $\underline{L}_{(-i)}$ is the whole label field $\underline{L}$ excluding $L_i$.

The required probability models ($P(\underline{m}|\underline{L})$, $P(y_i|L_i = H_1, \underline{L}_{(-i)})$ and $P(L_i = H_1|\underline{L}_{(-i)})$) are discussed in Sec. 4.

## 3 The Complex Wavelet Transform

The present standard wavelet transforms are almost all *real-value* transforms, such as Daubechies and biorthogonal wavelets [6]. They have some interesting properties and are successfully used in many image processing applications (e.g., compression, denoising, feature extraction). However, under the constraint of being real-valued they suffer from a few disadvantages [8]:

1. The real-valued orthogonal wavelet can not be symmetric, which is expected for some applications;
2. Lack of shift invariance, which means small shifts in the input signal can cause major variations in the distribution of energy between coefficients at different scales;
3. Poor directional selectivity for diagonal features, when the wavelet filters are real and separable.

A well-known way of providing shift-invariance is to use the undecimated form of the dyadic filter tree, which is implemented most efficiently by the algorithm *a trous*. However, this suffers from substantially increased computation requirements compared to the fully decimated DWT. In addition, separable $2D$ overcomplete wavelet transforms still have poor directional selectivity. Designing non-separable direction-selective $2D$ wavelet bases is usually a complicated task.

If the wavelet filters are allowed to be complex-valued (this results in single-tree complex wavelet (ST-CWT)) all the above three problems can be overcome [8]. However, though (ST-CWT) can solve these problems it suffers from poor frequency selectivity. Thus, Kingsbury [8] proposed the dual-tree complex wavelet transform (DT-CWT) (Fig. 1). DT-CWT uses two real DWT trees to implement its real part and imaginary part, separately. In addition to the other attractive properties of the ST-CWT, DT-CWT has good frequency selectivity and easy to achieve perfect reconstruction. Indeed, Selesnick [9] found that the real and imaginary parts of the DT-CWT can be linked by the Hilbert transform. This observation further explains why DT-CWT has those useful characteristics.

The $2D$ DT-CWT can be easily implemented by the tensor products of $1D$ DT-CWT. Because the $1D$ filters are complex the $2D$ DT-CWT consists of six wavelets (Fig. 2). Note the good directionality of the wavelet bases.

## 4 The a Prior Models

1. $P(\underline{m}|\underline{L})$

As mentioned in Sec.2 $P(\underline{m}|\underline{L})$ is modelled as an independent process, i.e.

$$P(\underline{m}|\underline{L}) = \prod_{i=1}^{N} P(m_i|L_i) \qquad (9)$$

where $\underline{m}$ is the feature vector and $\underline{L}$ is the label field. We use the magnitude of complex wavelet coefficient as the feature:

$$m(u,v) = \sqrt{r_e^2(u,v) + i_m^2(u,v)}, \quad u,v = 1,2,...,N \qquad (10)$$

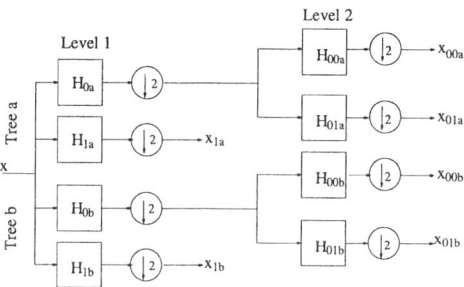

**Fig. 1.** *two*-level dual-tree complex wavelet transform

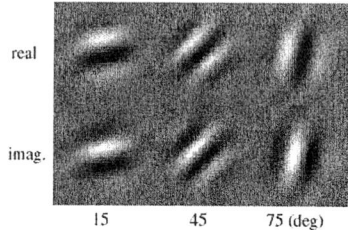

**Fig. 2.** 2D dual-tree complex wavelet bases (only three orientations are shown)

where $u, v = 1, 2, ..., N$ are coordinates of the image field. $r_e(u,v)$ and $i_m(u,v)$ are the real and imaginary parts, respectively

$$y(u,v) = r_e(u,v) + \sqrt{-1} \cdot i_m(u,v) \qquad (11)$$

In this paper we assume $r_e(u,v)$ and $i_m(u,v)$ are Gaussian, as did in several other papers (e.g. [3]). Thus, a good approximate model for $m(u,v)$ is Rayleigh distribution. Fig. 3 shows the histogram (from a group of natural images) of $m(u,v)$ and estimated Rayleigh function.

2. $P(y_i|L_i = H_k, \underline{L}_{(-i)}), \quad k = 0, 1$
We assume a conditional independence

$$P(y_i|L_i = H_k, \underline{L}_{(-i)}) = P(y_i|L_i = H_k) \qquad (12)$$

and then model $P(y_i|L_i = H_k)$ as complex Gaussian.

3. $P(L_i = H_1|\underline{L}_{(-i)})$
The label process $\underline{L}$ is modelled as a MRF. Specifically we use the auto-logistic model [5]. This kind of models have also been successfully applied for texture segmentation. It is described as

$$P(\underline{L}) = 1/Z \cdot exp(-V(\underline{L})) \qquad (13)$$

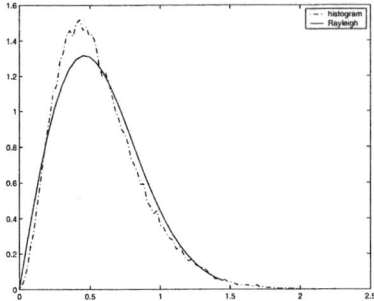

**Fig. 3.** Histogram of the magnitude and estimated Rayleigh function $P(m_i|L_i = H_1)$

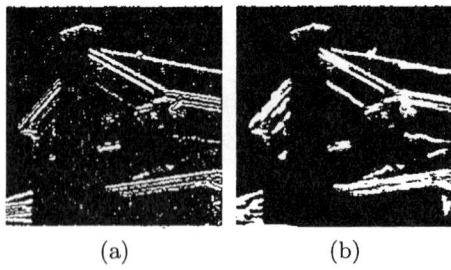

**Fig. 4.** Labels without (a) and with (b) a priori model for one wavelet orientation ($15°$)

where the energy function $V(\underline{L}) = \sum_i V_{Ni}(\underline{L})$ and the clique potentials are defined as

$$V_{Ni}(\underline{L}) = \sum_{j \in Ni} V_{i,j}(L_i, L_j) \quad \text{with}$$

$$V_{i,j}(L_i, L_j) = \begin{cases} -\gamma \text{ if } L_j = L_i \\ \gamma \text{ if } L_j \neq L_i \end{cases} \quad (14)$$

where $\gamma$ is a positive scalar. $N_i$ is the first-order neighborhood system.

This *a priori* model for the label field tries to exploit the clustering property of the wavelet coefficients. It has been shown to be useful for suppressing separate noise artifact [5]. In Fig. 4 the influence of the *a priori* model is illustrated. We used iterated conditional mode (ICM) in the maximization process.

## 5  Experimental Results and Discussions

We applied the proposed technique to several natural images with artificial additive Gaussian noise. One result is shown in Fig. 5. For comparison we also show the denoising result from [3]. This method is widely used in references for comparison. It did not employ any *a priori* label model. Visually, Fig. 5(d) looks

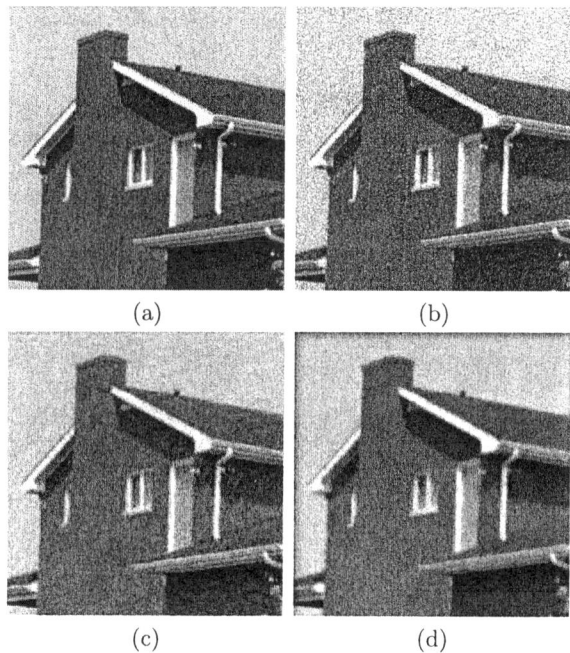

**Fig. 5.** (a) original (b) noisy (c) denoised image by adaptive thresholding [3] (d) proposed method

much cleaner and thus more pleasing than Fig. 5(c), though the latter looks a little bit sharper. Objectively the proposed approach is also about $1dB$ better in the sense of SNR.

We also compared with the methods in [5,7] because they also used MRF *a priori* model. We found the results looks similar and the differences in SNR are less than $0.5dB$. However, in [5,7] *undecimated* overcomplete wavelets were used. Thus their complexity is much higher than the *decimated* complex wavelet (For example for $2D$ decomposition the complex wavelet transform has a redundancy of 4, independent of number of levels. But for the overcomplete wavelet transform the redundancy is $4+3(NL-1)$, where $NL$ denotes the number of levels). This is especially true in the MRF iteration process. Furthermore, $2D$ complex wavelets have better direction-selectivity which means potential for better denoising performance. It should also be noted our problem formulation is different. We first find edge masks according to *MAP* and then combine this knowledge with the measurement to evaluate the conditional probability $P(L_i = H_1|y_i, \underline{L}_{(-i)})$.

# References

1. Kuan D., Sawchuk A., Strand T., Chavel P.: Adaptive noise smoothing filter for images with signal-dependent noise. IEEE Trans. PAMI **2**(7) (1985) 165–177
2. Lee J.: Digital image enhancement and noise filtering by use of local statistics. IEEE Trans. PAMI. **2**(2) (1980) 165–168

3. Chang S. and Bin Y. and Vetterli M.: Spatially adaptive wavelet thresholding with context modeling for image denoising. IEEE Trans. on Image Processing., **9**(9) (2000) 1522 - 1531
4. Mihcak M. and Kozintsev I. and Ramchandran K. and Moulin P.: Low-complexity image denoising based on statistical modeling of wavelet coefficients. IEEE Sig Proc.Lett., **12**(6) (1999) 300 - 303
5. Malfait M. and Roose D.: Wavelet-based image denoising using a Markov random field a prior model. IEEE Trans. Imag Proc.,**4**(6) (1997) 545 - 557
6. Daubechies I.: Orthonormal Bases of Compactly Supported Wavelets. Comm. Pure Appl. Math. **5** 41 (1988) 909-996
7. Pizurica A., Philips W., Lemahieu I. and Acheroy M.: A joint inter- and intrascale statistical model for Bayesian wavelet based image denoising. IEEE Trans. Imag Proc.,**5**(11) (2002) 545 - 557
8. kingsbury N.: Image processing with complex wavelets. Phil. Trans. Royal Society London A, **9**(29), (1999) 2543 – 2560
9. Selesnick I.: The design of approximate Hilbert transform pairs of wavelet bases. IEEE Trans. Signal Processing, **5**(50), (2002) 1144 - 1152.

# A New Vector Median Filter Based on Fuzzy Metrics

Samuel Morillas[1,*], Valentín Gregori[2,**], Guillermo Peris-Fajarnés[1],
and Pedro Latorre[1]

[1] Universidad Politécnica de Valencia, E.P.S. de Gandia, Departamento de Expresión Gráfica en la Ingeniería, Carretera Nazaret-Oliva s/n, 46730 Grao de Gandia (Valencia), Spain
[2] Universidad Politécnica de Valencia, E.P.S. Gandia, Departamento Matemática Aplicada, Carretera Nazaret-Oliva s/n 46730 Grao de Gandia (Valencia), Spain

**Abstract.** Vector median filtering is a well known technique for reducing noise in color images. These filters are defined on the basis of a suitable distance or similarity measure, being the most common used the Euclidean and City-Block distances. In this paper, a Fuzzy Metric, in the sense of George and Veeramani (1994), is defined and applied to color image filtering by means of a new Vector Median Filter. It is shown that the standard Vector Median Filter is outperformed when using this Fuzzy Metric instead of the Euclidean and City-Block distances.

## 1 Introduction

Images are acquired by photoelectronic or photochemical methods. The sensing devices and the transmission process tend to degrade the quality of the digital images by introducing noise, geometric deformation and/or blur due to motion or camera misfocus [8,27]. The presence of noise in an image may be a drawback in any subsequent processing to be done over the noisy image such as edge detection, image segmentation or pattern recognition. As a consequence, filtering the image to reduce the noise without degrading its quality, preserving edges, corners and other image details, is a major step in any computer vision application [28].

One of the most important families of nonlinear filters is based on the ordering of vectors in a predefined sliding window [27,28]. The output of these filters is defined as the lowest ranked vector according to a specific ordering criterion using a particular *distance measure*. Probably, the most well-known vector filter is the *vector median filter* (VMF) [3] which uses the $L_1$ (City-Block) or $L_2$ (Euclidean) norm to order vectors according to their relative magnitude differences. The direction of the image vectors can also be used as an ordering criterion to remove vectors with atypical direction, which means atypical chromaticity. The *basic vector directional filter* (BVDF) [33] parallelizes the VMF operation employing the angle between color vectors as a distance criterion. The BVDF uses only information about directions, so, it is not able to remove achromatic noisy pixels from the image. The *Directional Distance Filter* (DDF) [16] overcomes the difficulties of the BVDF by using both magnitude and direction in the distance criterion.

---

* The author acknowledges the support of Spanish Ministry of Education and Science under program "Becas de Formación de Profesorado Universitario FPU".
** The author acknowledge the support of Spanish Ministry of Science and Technology "Plan Nacional I+D+I", and FEDER, under Grant BFM2003-02302.

However, those vector filters are designed to perform a fixed amount of smoothing and they are not able to adapt to local image statistics. Within this aim, many different filters have been recently introduced in the literature [1,2,17,19,20,21,22,23,24,25,31,32].

In the color image processing field both magnitude and chromatic relations play a major role [6]. These relationships are usually represented using a distance or similarity measure. Many different distance and similarity measures have been introduced in the literature [28,6,7,35,36,29]. Some of them are based on fuzzy theory [6,7,35,36,29] and have been recently applied with many different purposes in image processing, such as, image retrieval [9], image comparison [34], object recognition [11], or region extraction [10].

In this paper, a fuzzy metric in the terms of George and Veeramani [12] is defined and applied to color image filtering by adapting the well-known VMF. The paper is organized as follows. The fuzzy metric is defined in section 2. In Section 3, the proposed filtering is explained. In section 4, some experimental results are shown. Finally, conclusions are presented in section 5.

## 2 An Appropriate Fuzzy Metric

One of the most important problems in Fuzzy Topology is to obtain an appropriate concept of fuzzy metric. This problem has been investigated by many authors from different points of view. In particular, George and Veeramani [12] have introduced and studied the following notion of fuzzy metric which constitutes a slight modification of the one due to Kramosil and Michalek [18].

According to [12] a fuzzy metric space is an ordered triple $(X, M, *)$ such that $X$ is a (nonempty) set, $*$ is a continuous t-norm and $M$ is a fuzzy set of $X \times X \times ]0, +\infty[$ satisfying the following conditions for all $x, y, z \in X$, $s, t > 0$:

(FM1) $M(x, y, t) > 0$
(FM2) $M(x, y, t) = 1$ if and only if $x = y$
(FM3) $M(x, y, t) = M(y, x, t)$
(FM4) $M(x, z, t + s) \geq M(x, y, t) * M(y, z, s)$
(FM5) $M(x, y, \cdot) : ]0, +\infty[ \longrightarrow [0, 1]$ is continuous.

$M(x, y, t)$ represents the degree of nearness of $x$ and $y$ with respect to $t$. If $M(x, y, *)$ is a fuzzy metric space we will say that $(M, *)$ is a fuzzy metric on $X$. In the following, by a fuzzy metric we mean a fuzzy metric in the George and Veeramani's sense.

The authors proved in [12] that every fuzzy metric $(M, *)$ on $X$ generates a Hausdorff topology on $X$. Actually, this topology is metrizable as it was proved in [13,14], and so the above definition can be considered an appropriate concept of fuzzy metric space.

A fuzzy metric $(M, *)$ on $X$ is said to be stationary if $M$ does not depend on $t$, i.e. for each $x, y \in X$ the function $M_{x,y}(t) = M(x, y, t)$ is constant [15].

A subset $A$ of $X$ is said to be F-bounded [12] if there exist $t > 0$ and $s \in ]0, 1[$ such that $M(x, y, t) > s$ for all $x, y \in A$.

Example 4.4 of [30] suggests the next proposition.

**Proposition 1.** *Let $X$ be the closed real interval $[a, b]$ and let $K > |a| > 0$. Consider for each $n = 1, 2, \cdots$ the function $M_n : X^n \times X^n \times ]0, +\infty[ \longrightarrow ]0, 1]$ given by*

$$M_n(x, y, t) = \prod_{i=1}^{n} \frac{min\{x_i, y_i\} + K}{max\{x_i, y_i\} + K} \quad (1)$$

*where $x = (x_1, \cdots, x_n), y = (y_1, \cdots, y_n)$, and $t > 0$. Then, $(M_n, \cdot)$ is a stationary F-bounded fuzzy metric on $X^n$, where the t-norm $\cdot$ is the usual product in $[0, 1]$.*

*Proof.* Axioms (FM1)-(FM3) and (FM5) are obviously fulfilled. We show, by induction, the triangular inequality (FM4).

An easy computation shows that $M_1$ verifies (FM4). Now, suppose it is true for $M_{n-1}$. Then, for each $x = (x_1, \ldots, x_n), y = (y_1, \ldots, y_n), z = (z_1, \ldots, z_n)$ and for each $t, s > 0$ we have

$$M_n(x, z, t+s) = \prod_{i=1}^{n} \frac{min\{x_i, z_i\}+K}{max\{x_i, z_i\}+K} = \prod_{i=1}^{n-1} \frac{min\{x_i, z_i\}+K}{max\{x_i, z_i\}+K} \cdot \frac{min\{x_n, z_n\}+K}{max\{x_n, z_n\}+K} \geq$$
$$\geq \prod_{i=1}^{n-1} \frac{min\{x_i, y_i\}+K}{max\{x_i, y_i\}+K} \cdot \prod_{i=1}^{n-1} \frac{min\{y_i, z_i\}+K}{max\{y_i, z_i\}+K} \cdot \frac{min\{x_n, y_n\}+K}{max\{x_n, y_n\}+K} \cdot \frac{min\{y_n, z_n\}+K}{max\{y_n, z_n\}+K} = \quad (2)$$
$$= \prod_{i=1}^{n} \frac{min\{x_i, y_i\}+K}{max\{x_i, y_i\}+K} \cdot \prod_{i=1}^{n} \frac{min\{y_i, z_i\}+K}{max\{y_i, z_i\}+K} = M_n(x, y, t) \cdot M_n(y, z, s),$$

so $M_n$ is a fuzzy metric on $X^n$, for $n = 1, 2, \ldots$ and clearly it is stationary.

Finally, $X^n$ is F-bounded, for $n = 1, 2, \ldots$ Indeed, if we write $\mathbf{a} = (\overbrace{a, \ldots, a}^{n})$ and $\mathbf{b} = (\overbrace{b, \ldots, b}^{n})$, then for each $x, y \in X^n$ and $t > 0$ we have

$$M_n(x, y, t) \geq M_n(\mathbf{a}, \mathbf{b}, t) = \left(\frac{a+K}{b+K}\right)^n > 0, \text{ for } n = 1, 2, \ldots \quad (3)$$

□

In next sections we will use the above fuzzy metric and it will be denoted $M_n(x, y)$, since it does not depend on $t$.

### 2.1 Computational Analysis

Computationally efficient distances are of interest in the field of order statistic filters [4,5]. For this reason, the use of the $L_1$ Norm is preferred to the $L_2$ Norm in many cases [28].

The particular case of the proposed fuzzy metric $M_n$ suitable for 3-channel image processing tasks will be $M_3$, where $M_3(\mathbf{I}_i, \mathbf{I}_j)$ will denote the fuzzy distance between the pixels $\mathbf{I}_i$ and $\mathbf{I}_j$ in the $\mathbf{I}$ image. For each calculation of $M_3$: 3 comparisons, 6 additions, 3 divisions and 2 products have to be computed. In the case of $L_1$ Norm are necessary 3 comparisons (absolute value), 3 subtractions and 2 additions whereas for the $L_2$ Norm 3 subtractions, 3 powers, 2 additions and 1 square-root have to be done. As can be seen in Table 1, the computational complexity of $M_3$ is even higher than the $L_2$ Norm. However, an optimization in the computation of $M_3$ (Fast $M_3$) may be applied.

Given a fixed parameter $K$ in (1), numerator and denominator of each division in (1) are in a bounded set $[K, 255 + K]$ when processing RGB images. All the possible divisions can be precalculated in a square matrix $C$ where

$$C(i,j) = \frac{min\{i,j\} + K}{max\{i,j\} + K} \quad i,j \in [0, 255] \qquad (4)$$

Using the pre-computation matrix, the calculation of Fast $M_3$ for two pixels $\mathbf{I}_i = (\mathbf{I}_i(1), \mathbf{I}_i(2), \mathbf{I}_i(3))$, $\mathbf{I}_j = (\mathbf{I}_j(1), \mathbf{I}_j(2), \mathbf{I}_j(3))$ is reduced to

$$M_3(\mathbf{I}_i, \mathbf{I}_j) = \prod_{l=1}^{3} C(\mathbf{I}_i(l), \mathbf{I}_j(l)) \qquad (5)$$

By means of this optimization, 3 accesses to matrix and 2 products are enough to make the computation.

The time measured for the construction of the matrix $C$ is about 0.8 seconds in a Pentium IV 2.4GHz. Although it supposes an initial cost, the gain is approx. $8\mu s$ (see Table 1) in each computation, so, the initial cost is compensated when $10^5$ computations have to be done (which is roughly the computation involved in the filtering of a $50 \cdot 50$ pixels image[1]).

**Table 1.** Computational comparison between the classical metrics $L_1$ and $L_2$ and the proposed fuzzy metric $M_3$ measured in a Pentium IV 2.4GHz

| Metric | 1 Computation ($\mu s$) | Computations per second |
|---|---|---|
| $L_1$ Norm | 28.37 | 3.524 $10^4$ |
| $L_2$ Norm | 30.10 | 3.322 $10^4$ |
| $M_3$ | 34.68 | 2.883 $10^4$ |
| Fast $M_3$ | 26.98 | 3.706 $10^4$ |

The results presented in Table 1 show that the $M_3$ Fuzzy Metric is computationally cheaper than the classical $L_1$ and $L_2$ Norms when the optimization of the precomputation matrix is applied.

## 3 Image Filtering

### 3.1 Classical Vector Median Filter [3,28]

Let $\mathbf{I}$ represents a multichannel image and let $W$ be a window of finite size $n$ (filter length). The noisy image vectors in the filtering window $W$ are denoted as $\mathbf{I}_j, j = 0, 1, ..., n-1$. The *distance* between two vectors $\mathbf{I}_i, \mathbf{I}_j$ is denoted as $\rho(\mathbf{I}_i, \mathbf{I}_j)$. For each vector in the filtering window, a global, accumulated distance to all other vectors in the window has to be calculated. The scalar quantity $R_i = \sum_{j=0}^{n-1} \rho(\mathbf{I}_i, \mathbf{I}_j)$, is the distance associated to the vector $\mathbf{I}_i$. The ordering of the $R_i$'s: $R_{(0)} \leq R_{(1)} \leq ... \leq R_{(n-1)}$, implies the same ordering of the vectors $\mathbf{I}_i$'s: $\mathbf{I}_{(0)} \leq \mathbf{I}_{(1)} \leq ... \leq \mathbf{I}_{(n-1)}$. Given this order, the output of the filter is $\mathbf{I}_{(0)}$.

---
[1] For all the filters studied in this article has been used a 8-neighborhood $3 \times 3$ size window $W$.

## 3.2 Proposed Vector Median Filter

The proposed filter will parallelize the operation of the classical VMF with just one modification. The ordering criterion usually used as defined above has to be inverted due to the axiom (FM2) of the Fuzzy Metric (1), and then the vector median must now be defined as the vector in the sliding window that maximizes the *accumulated* fuzzy distance, as follows.

Being the fuzzy distance between two pixels $\mathbf{I}_i, \mathbf{I}_j$ of the image $\mathbf{I}$ in the $n$ length sliding window $W$ denoted as $M_3(\mathbf{I}_i, \mathbf{I}_j)$, the scalar quantity $M^i = \sum_{j=0, j \neq i}^{n-1} M_3(\mathbf{I}_i, \mathbf{I}_j)$, is the accumulated fuzzy distance associated to the vector $\mathbf{I}_i$. According to VMF, the ordering of the $M^i$'s is now defined as: $M^{(0)} \geq M^{(1)} \geq ... \geq M^{(n-1)}$, therefore, the ordering of the vectors $\mathbf{I}_i$ is: $\mathbf{I}_{(0)} \geq \mathbf{I}_{(1)} \geq ... \geq \mathbf{I}_{(n-1)}$. Given this order, the output of the filter $\mathbf{I}_{out}$ is defined as $\mathbf{I}_{(0)}$.

This is, in general, the straightforward adaptation of the VMF when using a similarity measure instead of a distance measure [28].

## 4 Experimental Results

In this section, the classical gaussian model for the thermal noise and the impulsive noise model for the transmission noise, as defined in [28,32], has been used to add noise to the well-known images Lenna ($256 \cdot 256$), Peppers ($512 \cdot 512$) and Baboon ($512 \cdot 512$). The performance of the filter has been evaluated by using the common measures MSE, SNR and NCD as defined in [32].

Three different types of noise, according to the models in [28,32], have been considered in this section:

- Type A = low contaminated impulsive noise $p = 7\%, p_1 = p_2 = p_3 = 0.3$
- Type B = high contaminated impulsive noise $p = 30\%, p_1 = p_2 = p_3 = 0.3$
- Type C = mixed gaussian impulsive noise $\sigma = 10, p = 15\%, p_1 = p_2 = p_3 = 0.3$

### 4.1 Adjusting the K Parameter

The $K$ parameter included in the definition of the Fuzzy Metric $M_3$ (1) has an important influence on the filter performance. The metric is non-uniform in the sense that the measure given by $M_3$ for two different pairs of consecutive numbers (or vectors) may not be the same. However, this feature may be very interesting since it is known that the human perception of color is also non-uniform [26]. Clearly, increasing the value of $K$ reduces this non-uniformity. This effect is shown in Fig. 1 where the content of the matrix $C$ (4) for different values of $K$ is presented.

After performing several tests, the results seem to show that a suitable value for the $K$ parameter for a variety of noise types is $K = 2^{10}$. The dependence of the performance on the value of $K$ is shown in Fig. 2. The use of a proper value for $K$ may lead to an improvement of the filter performance up to $60\%$. In Fig. 2 the performance (MSE) of the filter dependent on $K$ is shown for the filtering of the Lenna image contaminated with type B noise. For other performance measures as SNR and NCD the behavior is similar to MSE. The performance is low for lower values of $K$. Increasing $K$ leads to

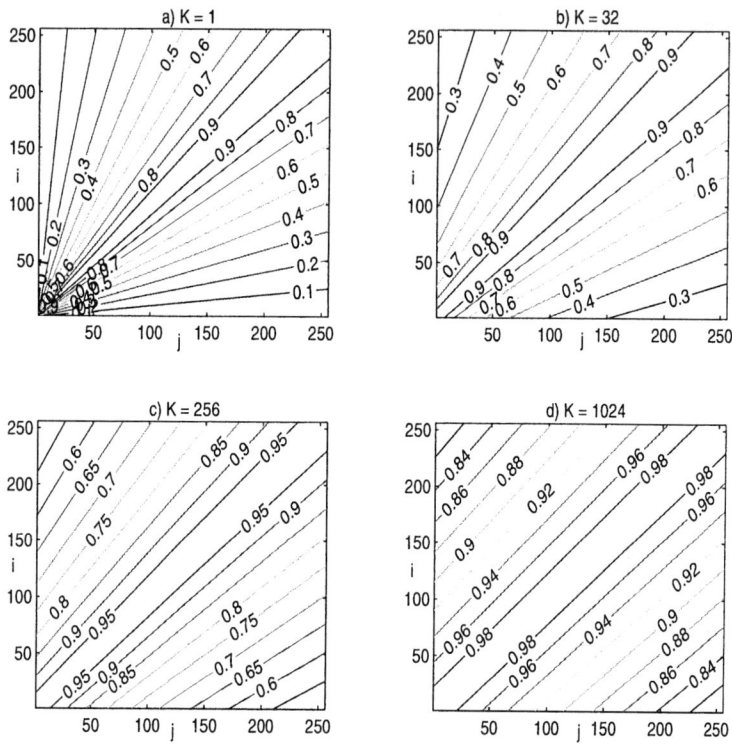

**Fig. 1.** Content of the pre-computation matrix $C(i,j)$ for several values of $K$

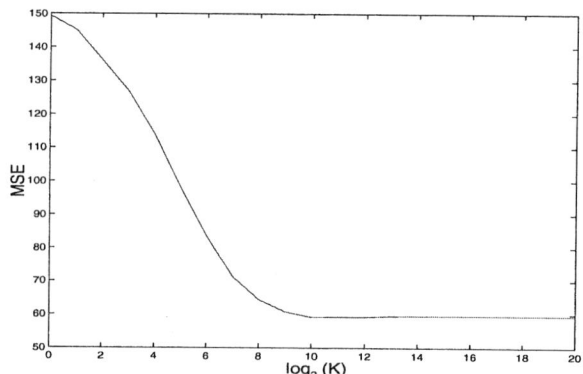

**Fig. 2.** Performance of the VMF using $M_3$ in terms of MSE depending on $K$ using the Lenna image contaminated with type B noise

a maximum performance and then it decreases slightly for higher values of $K$. Finding the optimum $K$ is a problem we are trying to solve since it depends on the particular image and noise. In spite of it, it has been found that in the most of the tested cases the optimum is in the range $[2^9, 2^{15}]$, as the case shown in Fig. 2.

## 4.2 Comparing Performances

In order to compare the performance of the VMF using the metrics $L_1$, $L_2$ and $M_3$, different images contaminated with different types of noise have been used as commented in section 4.

The results of the performance measured in tems of MSE, SNR and NCD are shown in Tables 2,3 and 4. Fig. 3 presents the peppers image contaminated with type B noise (30% impulsive) and the output of the compared filters, standing out a detail of each image.

**Table 2.** Comparison of the performance measured in terms of MSE, SNR and NCD using the Lenna image contaminated with different types of noise

| Filter | A Noise ||| B Noise ||| C Noise |||
|---|---|---|---|---|---|---|---|---|---|
|  | MSE | SNR | $NCD_{Lab}$ | MSE | SNR | $NCD_{Lab}$ | MSE | SNR | $NCD_{Lab}$ |
| None | 552.9 | 15.17 | $4.92\ 10^{-2}$ | 2318.51 | 9.35 | $20.80\ 10^{-2}$ | 1246.86 | 12.04 | $17.90\ 10^{-2}$ |
| VMF $L_1$ | 42.18 | 26.75 | $1.81\ 10^{-2}$ | 59.63 | 25.25 | $2.19\ 10^{-2}$ | 91.59 | 23.38 | $6.40\ 10^{-2}$ |
| VMF $L_2$ | 45.56 | 26.41 | $1.79\ 10^{-2}$ | 76.05 | 24.19 | $2.46\ 10^{-2}$ | 97.01 | 23.13 | $6.35\ 10^{-2}$ |
| VMF $M_3$ | 41.81 | 26.78 | $1.80\ 10^{-2}$ | 59.18 | 25.28 | $2.17\ 10^{-2}$ | 90.49 | 23.43 | $6.36\ 10^{-2}$ |

**Table 3.** Comparison of the performance measured in terms of MSE, SNR and NCD using the Peppers image contaminated with different types of noise

| Filter | A Noise ||| B Noise ||| C Noise |||
|---|---|---|---|---|---|---|---|---|---|
|  | MSE | SNR | $NCD_{Lab}$ | MSE | SNR | $NCD_{Lab}$ | MSE | SNR | $NCD_{Lab}$ |
| None | 566.94 | 14.42 | $4.84\ 10^{-2}$ | 2493.27 | 7.99 | $21.09\ 10^{-2}$ | 1324.56 | 10.73 | $19.66\ 10^{-2}$ |
| VMF $L_1$ | 18.87 | 29.19 | $4.84\ 10^{-2}$ | 35.49 | 26.45 | $2.34\ 10^{-2}$ | 63.10 | 23.95 | $7.53\ 10^{-2}$ |
| VMF $L_2$ | 19.30 | 29.10 | $1.88\ 10^{-2}$ | 40.37 | 25.89 | $2.46\ 10^{-2}$ | 64.98 | 23.82 | $7.51\ 10^{-2}$ |
| VMF $M_3$ | 18.71 | 29.23 | $1.86\ 10^{-2}$ | 33.35 | 26.72 | $2.29\ 10^{-2}$ | 62.10 | 24.02 | $7.48\ 10^{-2}$ |

**Table 4.** Comparison of the performance measured in terms of MSE, SNR and NCD using the Baboon image contaminated with different types of noise

| Filter | A Noise ||| B Noise ||| C Noise |||
|---|---|---|---|---|---|---|---|---|---|
|  | MSE | SNR | $NCD_{Lab}$ | MSE | SNR | $NCD_{Lab}$ | MSE | SNR | $NCD_{Lab}$ |
| None | 535.33 | 15.52 | $4.83\ 10^{-2}$ | 2301.44 | 9.18 | $20.76\ 10^{-2}$ | 1238.64 | 11.88 | $17.37\ 10^{-2}$ |
| VMF $L_1$ | 287.66 | 18.22 | $4.07\ 10^{-2}$ | 326.93 | 17.66 | $4.48\ 10^{-2}$ | 350.65 | 17.36 | $7.93\ 10^{-2}$ |
| VMF $L_2$ | 295.07 | 18.11 | $4.02\ 10^{-2}$ | 351.71 | 17.34 | $4.61\ 10^{-2}$ | 359.89 | 17.24 | $7.72\ 10^{-2}$ |
| VMF $M_3$ | 287.98 | 18.21 | $4.05\ 10^{-2}$ | 326.73 | 17.67 | $4.46\ 10^{-2}$ | 350.27 | 17.36 | $7.88\ 10^{-2}$ |

The results show that the VMF using the proposed fuzzy metric may give better performance than using the classical metrics.

## 5 Conclusions

The metric (1) proposed in section 2, which has been proved to be a Fuzzy Metric in the sense of George and Veeramani [12], is a suitable fuzzy metric to be used in multichan-

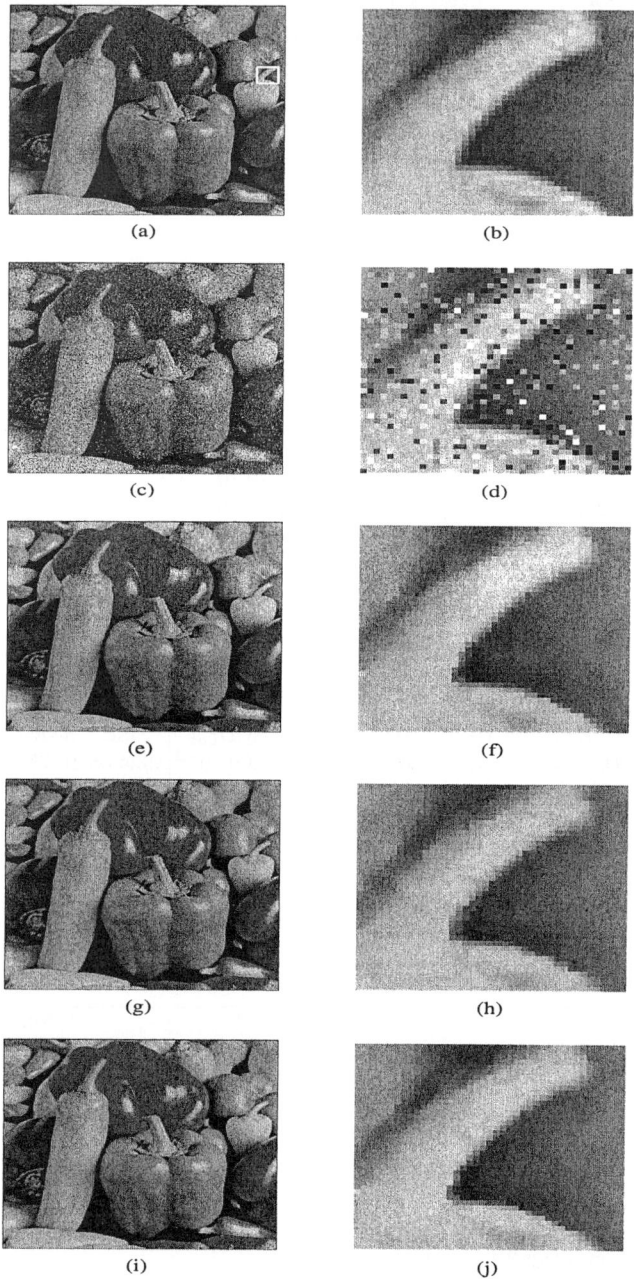

**Fig. 3.** (a) Original image peppers pointing out the detailed area, (b) detailed area, (c) peppers corrupted with noise type B and (d) detail, (e) result of the VMF using $L_1$ and (f) detail, (g) result of the VMF using $L_2$ and (h) detail, (i) result of the proposed filter using $M_3$ and (j) detail

nel image filtering. The adaptation of the Vector Median Filter (section 3) for the use of the proposed fuzzy metric outperforms the usual VMF's using the classical metrics $L_1$ and $L_2$, specially when the impulsive noise present in the image is high, as has been shown in section 4. Moreover, the proposed metric presents a nice computational cost (see section 2.1).

Fuzzy Metrics are a powerful tool which may be successfully applied in image processing tasks since they are able to represent more complex relations than the classical metrics.

# References

1. H. Allende, J. Galbiati, *A non-parametric filter for image restoration using cluster analysis*, Pattern Recognition Letters 25 8 (2004) 841-847.
2. K. Arakawa, *Median filter based on fuzzy rules and its application to image restoration*, Fuzzy Sets and Systems 77 1 (1996) 3-13.
3. J. Astola, P. Haavisto, Y. Neuvo,*Vector Median Filters*, Proc. IEEE. 78 4 (1990) 678-689.
4. M. Barni, F. Buti, F. Bartolini, V. Capellini, *A Quasi-Euclidean Norm to Speed Up Vector Median Filtering*, IEEE Transactions on Image Processing 9 10 (2000) 1704-1709.
5. M. Barni, *A Fast Algorithm for 1-Norm Vector Median Filtering*, IEEE Transactions on Image Processing, 6 10 (1997) 1452-1455.
6. I. Bloch, *Fuzzy spatial relationships for image processing and interpretation: a review*, Image and Vision Computing 23 2 (2005) 89-110.
7. I. Bloch, *On fuzzy spatial distances*, Advances in imaging and electron physics 128 (2003).
8. C. Boncelet,*Image noise models*, in: A. Bovik (Ed.), Handbook of Image and Video Processing. Academic Press, 2000.
9. T. Chaira, A.K. Ray, *Fuzzy Measures for color image retrieval*, Fuzzy Sets and Systems 150 3 (2005) 545-560.
10. T. Chaira, A.K. Ray, *Fuzzy approach for color region extraction*, Pattern Recognition Letters 24 12 (2003) 1943-1950.
11. O. Coillot, A.V. Tuzikov, R.M. Cesar, I.Bloch, *Approximate reflectional simmetries of fuzzy objects with an application in model based object recognition*, Fuzzy Sets and Systems 147 1 (2004) 141-163.
12. A. George, P. Veeramani,*On Some results in fuzzy metric spaces*, Fuzzy Sets and Systems 64 3 (1994) 395-399.
13. A. George, P. Veeramani, *Some theorems in fuzzy metric spaces* , J. Fuzzy Math. 3 (1995) 933-940.
14. V. Gregori, S. Romaguera, *Some properties of fuzzy metric spaces*, Fuzzy Sets and Systems 115 3 (2000) 477-483.
15. V. Gregori, S. Romaguera, *Characterizing completable fuzzy metric spaces*, Fuzzy Sets and Systems 144 3 (2004) 411-420.
16. D.G. Karakos, P.E. Trahanias, *Generalized multichannel image-filtering structures* , IEEE Transactions on Image Processing 6 7 (1997) 1038-1045.
17. L. Khriji, M. Gabbouj, *Adaptive fuzzy order statistics-rational hybrid filters for color image processing*, Fuzzy Sets and Systems 128 1 (2002) 35-46.
18. I. Kramosil, J. Michalek, *Fuzzy metric and statistical metric spaces*, Kybernetica 11 (1975) 326-334
19. R. Lukac, B. Smolka, K.N. Plataniotis, A.N. Venetsanopoulos, *Selection weighted vector directional filters*, Computer Vision and Image Understanding 94 (2004) 140-167.

20. R. Lukac, *Adaptive vector median filtering*, Pattern Recognition Letters, 24 12 (2003) 1889-1899.
21. R. Lukac, B. Smolka, K. Martin, K.N. Plataniotis, A.N. Venetsanopoulos, *Vector Filtering for Color Imaging*, IEEE Signal Processing Magazine, Special Issue on Color Image Processing, 22 1 (2005) 74-86.
22. R. Lukac, K.N. Plataniotis, B. Smolka, A.N. Venetsanopoulos, *Generalized Selection Weighted Vector Filters*, EURASIP Journal on applied signal processing, Special Issue on Nonlinear signal and image processing 12 (2004) 1870-1885.
23. R. Lukac, K.N. Plataniotis, B. Smolka, A.N. Venetsanopoulos, *A Multichannel Order-Statistic Technique for cDNA Microarray Image Processing* IEEE Transactions on Nanobioscience 3 4 (2004) 272-285.
24. R. Lukac, K.N. Plataniotis, B. Smolka, A.N. Venetsanopoulos, *cDNA Microarray Image Processing Using Fuzzy Vector Filtering Framework* Fuzzy Sets and Systems, Special Issue on Fuzzy Sets and Systems on Bioinformatics 152 1 (2005) 17-35.
25. R. Lukac, *Adaptive Color Image Filtering Based on Center Weighted Vector Directional Filters* Multidimensional Systems and Signal Processing 15 (2004) 169-196.
26. D.L. MacAdam, *Visual sensitivities to color differences in daylight*, J. Opt. Soc. Am., 33 (1942) 247-274
27. I. Pitas, *Digital image processing algorithms and applications*, John Wiley & Sons, 2000.
28. K.N. Plataniotis, A.N. Venetsanopoulos, *Color Image processing and applications*, Springer-Verlag, Berlin, 2000.
29. S. Santini, R. Jain, *Similarity Measures*, IEEE Transactions on pattern recognition and machine intelligence 21 9 (1999) 871-883.
30. A. Sapena, *A contribution to the study of fuzzy metric spaces* Appl. Gen. Topology 2 1(2001) 63-76.
31. B. Smolka, R. Lukac, A. Chydzinski, K.N. Plataniotis, W. Wojciechowski *Fast adaptive similarity based impulsive noise reduction filter* Real-Time Imaging 9 4 (2003) 261-276.
32. M. Szczepanski, B. Smolka, K.N. Plataniotis, A.N. Venetsanopoulos, *On the distance function approach to color image enhancement*, Discrete Applied Mathematics 139 (2004) 283-305.
33. P.E. Trahanias, D. Karakos, A.N. Venetsanopoulos, *Vector Directional Filters: a new class of multichannel image processing filters*, IEEE Trans. Image Process. 2 4 (1993) 528-534.
34. D. Van der Weken, M. Nachtegael, E.E. Kerre, *Using similarity measures and homogeneity for the comparison of images*, Image and Vision Computing 22 9 (2004) 695-702.
35. W.J. Wang, *New similarity measures on fuzzy sets and on elements*, Fuzzy sets and systems 85 3 (1997) 305-309.
36. D. Yong, S. Wenkang, D. Feng, L. Qi, *A new similarity measure of generalized fuzzy numbers and its application to pattern recognition*, Pattern Recognition Letters 25 8 (2004) 875-883.

# Image Denoising Using Neighbor and Level Dependency*

Dongwook Cho[1], Tien D. Bui[1], and Guangyi Chen[2]

[1] Department of Computer Science and Software Engineering, Concordia University,
Montréal, Québec, Canada, H3G 1M8
{d_cho, bui}@cse.concordia.ca
[2] Department of Computer Science, McGill University,
Montréal, Québec, Canada, H3A 2A7

**Abstract.** In this paper, we present new wavelet shrinkage methods for image denoising. The methods take advantage of the higher order statistical coupling between neighboring wavelet coefficients and their corresponding coefficients in the parent level. We also investigate a multiplying factor for the universal threshold in order to obtain better denoising results. An empirical study of this factor shows that its optimum value is approximately the same for different kinds and sizes of images. Experimental results show that our methods give comparatively higher peak signal to noise ratio (PSNR), require less computation time and produce less visual artifacts compared to other methods.

## 1 Introduction

For the last decade, various denoising approaches using wavelet transform have been proposed and proved to be efficient for images as well as signals. It has been shown that denoising using wavelet transforms produces superb results. This is because wavelet transform has the compaction property of having only a small number of significant coefficients and a large number of very detailed coefficients. Therefore, it is possible to suppress the noise in the wavelet domain by killing some detailed coefficients which represent the detailed information as well as the noise.

Recently, several important approaches have been proposed by considering the influence of other wavelet coefficients on the current wavelet coefficient to be thresholded. Cai and Silverman [1] proposed a thresholding scheme by taking the immediate neighbor coefficients into account. Their experimental results showed apparent advantages over the traditional term-by-term wavelet denoising. Chen and Bui [2] extended this neighboring wavelet thresholding idea to the multi-wavelet case. Sendur and Selesnick [3] proposed bivariate shrinkage functions for denoising. It is indicated that the estimated wavelet coefficients also depend on the parent coefficients. The smaller the parent coefficients, the greater the

---

* This work was supported by research grants from the Natural Sciences and Engineering Research Council of Canada.

shrinkage. In [4] Azimifar et al. observed statistical correlations between wavelet coefficients. Mihcak et al. [5] performed an approximate maximum *a posteriori* (MAP) estimation of the variance for each coefficient, using the observed noisy data in a local neighborhood. Crouse et al. [6] developed a framework for statistical signal processing based on wavelet-domain hidden markov models (HMM). The framework enables us to concisely model the non-Gaussian statistics of individual wavelet coefficients and capture statistical dependencies between coefficients. Portilla et al.[7] presented an image denoising algorithm which is based on a Gaussian scale mixture (GSM) model using an overcomplete multiscale oriented basis. They define a vector using neighboring coefficients and obtain an accurate estimate by the vector operations. Also Cho and Bui developed a generalized denoising algorithm using a multivariate statistical model and Bayesian estimator in [8]. All these works show that incorporating different information like neighbors and parents is helpful to remove noise and preserve details for natural image denoising.

In this paper, we develop new shrinkage approaches by a hybrid combination of different schemes. Experimental results show that these methods obtain comparatively higher peak signal to noise ratio (PSNR) for all the tested noisy images.

## 2 Shrinkage Approaches for Denoising

In the wavelet domain, despite the decorrelating properties of the wavelet transform, there still exist significant residual statistical dependencies between neighboring wavelet coefficients. Our goal is to exploit this dependency to improve the estimation of a coefficient given its noisy observation and a *context* (spatial and scale neighbors).

Recently, there have been several works which try to use the context in the wavelet domain [1][3][4][5][9]. Among them, Cai and Silverman in [1] proposed a simple and effective approach for a 1D signal by incorporating the neighboring coefficients. Their *block thresholding* method has excellent asymptotic properties and attains the optimal rate of convergence in the Besov sequence space. This means that the least upper bound of the expected denoised error is close to zero when the length of the signal tends to infinity.

We define some common notations first. Let $A$ be a clean natural image with size $N \times N$, $B$ the noisy image which can be expressed as $B = A + \sigma C$, and $C$ the zero-mean Gaussian white noise, which is $C \sim N(0,1)$. $\sigma^2$ is noise variance. After performing multiresolution wavelet decomposition on $B$, we get the wavelet coefficient $y_{j,k}$, which is the $k$-th wavelet coefficient in $j$-th level for $B$. Due to the linearity of the wavelet transform, we have:

$$y_{j,k} = x_{j,k} + \sigma z_{j,k}, \tag{1}$$

where $x_{j,k}$ and $z_{j,k}$ are the wavelet coefficients of $A$ and $C$ respectively in the same location as $y_{j,k}$.

## 2.1 Method 1

One of the simplest wavelet shrinkage rules for a noisy image is the universal threshold $\lambda = \sqrt{2\sigma^2 \log N^2}$ suggested by Donoho in [10]. The universal threshold grows asymptotically and removes more noise coefficients as $N$ tends to infinity. The univeresal threshold is designed for smoothness rather than for minimizing the errors. So $\lambda$ is more meaningful when the signal is sufficiently smooth or the length of the signal is close to infinity. Natural image, however, is usually neither sufficiently smooth nor composed of infinite number of pixels. In fact, if we suppose that an optimal threshold $\lambda^*$ which minimizes mean squared error (MSE), $\lambda^* = \alpha\lambda$, $\alpha$ is always much less than 1.0 for natural images. We obtained $\alpha$ in the range [0.2, 0.3] with Daubechies 8 filter, which is similar for different kinds and sizes of images when we applied soft thresholding rule. We extend *NeighCoeff* in [1] to 2D image based on this observation as follows:

$$\hat{x}_{j,k} = y_{j,k}\left(1 - M^2\lambda^{*2} \Big/ \sum_{s_l \in N_{j,k}} s_l^2 \right)_+, \qquad (2)$$

where $N_{j,k}$ is an $M \times M$ window which consists of the thresholded coefficient and its neighbors. In the experiments, we investigate the optimal threshold by varying $\alpha$ and $M$.

## 2.2 Method 2

Although Method 1 yields very good performance, a constant $\alpha$ must be chosen empirically. If we substitute $\lambda^*$ in Eq. 2 by a nonparametric threshold with minimum risk, we may not need to use the universal threshold with a constant $\alpha$ to build a robust shrinkage method. One of the existing optimal thresholding methods is *SureShrink*, which uses an adaptive threshold by minimizing Stein's unbiased risk estimation(*SURE*) for each wavelet decomposition level [11]. When $\mathbf{w}_j$ is an $n \times n$ wavelet subband in level $j$, *SURE* threshold $\lambda^*$ is

$$\lambda^* = \arg\min_\lambda SURE(\mathbf{w}_j, \lambda)$$
$$= \arg\min_\lambda \left[ n^2 - 2 \cdot \#\{k : |y_{j,k}| \leq \lambda\} + \sum_k^{n^2} \min(|y_{j,k}|, \lambda)^2 \right]. \qquad (3)$$

Then a new shrinkage rule can be obtained from Eq. 2 by substituting the nonparametric threshold $\lambda^*$ in Eq. 3 instead of the universal threshold.

## 2.3 Method 3

Here we suggest one more method so as to distinguish it from the other two methods.

For the previous two methods, we have considered neighbor dependency. There is another possible correlation between the wavelet coefficients lying in different decomposition levels. The statistical correlation between parent and child coefficients has been widely recognized in image coding and denoising [9][6][7][3][12] since *zerotrees* were introduced by Shapiro [12]. Parent and child have interdependency similar to neighbors. Therefore, if we can utilize neighbors spreaded both vertically and horizontally as shown in Fig. 1, a better performance can be expected.

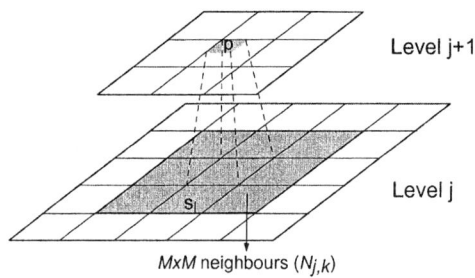

**Fig. 1.** Choosing context for Method 3

According to this idea, we propose the following criterion by applying the coefficients in the coarser level to Eq. 2:

$$\hat{x}_{j,k} = y_{j,k} \left[ 1 - (M^2 + 1){\lambda^*}^2 \bigg/ \left( \sum_{s_l \in N_{j,k}} s_l^2 + p^2 \right) \right]_+, \qquad (4)$$

where $\lambda^* = \alpha\lambda$ like Method 1, $s_l$ denotes the coefficient to be thresholded and its neighbors in an $M \times M$ window, and $p$ is a parent of the coefficient to be thresholded, which is a coefficient matched in the coarser level (see Fig. 1). In Eq. 4, it should be noted that a normalized factor, $M^2 + 1$, is used which is the number of correlated elements in the context. By this rule, the effect of the local variance from the parent level is considered as well as from the current level.

The three proposed shrinkage rules have a common feature: Local sample coefficients are taken from an $M \times M$ window $N_{j,k}$ for Method 1 and Method 2, and $N_{j,k}$ and a parent coefficient $p$ for Method 3 as shown in Fig. 1. If we assume that the mean of the sample coefficients is zero, the local variance of $y_{j,k}$ can be defined as $\sigma_{y_{j,k}}^2 = \sum a_i^2/m$, where $a_i$ denote the sample coefficients ($s_l$ and $p$) and $m$ is the number of local samples. In this case, we can notice that both Eqs. 2 and 4 become $\hat{x}_{j,k} = y_{j,k}\left(1 - {\lambda^*}^2/\sigma_{y_{j,k}}^2\right)_+$.

In [5], linear minimum mean squared error-like (MMSE-like) estimator of $x_{j,k}$ is given by $\hat{x}_{j,k} = y_{j,k} \frac{\hat{\sigma}_{x_{j,k}}^2}{\hat{\sigma}_{x_{j,k}}^2 + \sigma^2}$, where $\hat{\sigma}_{x_{j,k}}^2$ is an estimated variance of $x_{j,k}$. They have computed an approximate maximum likelihood (ML) estimator for $\hat{\sigma}_{x_{j,k}}^2$ as $\left( \frac{1}{M^2} \sum_{s_l \in N_{j,k}} s_l^2 - \sigma^2 \right)_+$. In other words, $\hat{\sigma}_{x_{j,k}}^2 = \left( \sigma_{y_{j,k}}^2 - \sigma^2 \right)_+$. Therefore, linear

MMSE estimator can be rewritten as $\hat{x}_{j,k} = y_{j,k}\left(1 - \sigma^2/\sigma^2_{y_{j,k}}\right)_+$. Since $\lambda^* \propto \sigma$ for the universal threshold used in Method 1 and Method 3, the shrinkage rule of linear MMSE estimator is the same as that of these two methods if we assume that $\alpha\sqrt{2\log N^2} = 1$. In this sense, it could be said that Method 3 uses the local variance considering both neighbor and level dependency. And our thresholds have strong connection with the estimator based on the probability density of the wavelet coefficients and *prior* like linear MMSE estimator.

## 3 Experimental Analysis and Evaluation

In our experiments, we have carried out various experiments using different parameters and several kinds of gray-level images with $256 \times 256$ and $512 \times 512$ sizes. Among them three $512 \times 512$ images, which are *Lena*, *Boat* and *Barbara*, are used in this paper for comparison purposes. We assume that the noise model is Gaussian additive white noise $N(0, \sigma^2)$. We have chosen Daubechies wavelet D8 which is one of the most popular mother wavelets for denoising and the dual tree complex wavelet transforms (CWT) [13]. In addition, Tranlation-invariant (TI) CWT has been used by combining both TI and CWT. Since CWT has the near shift-invariant property, TI CWT gives only slightly better results than CWT.

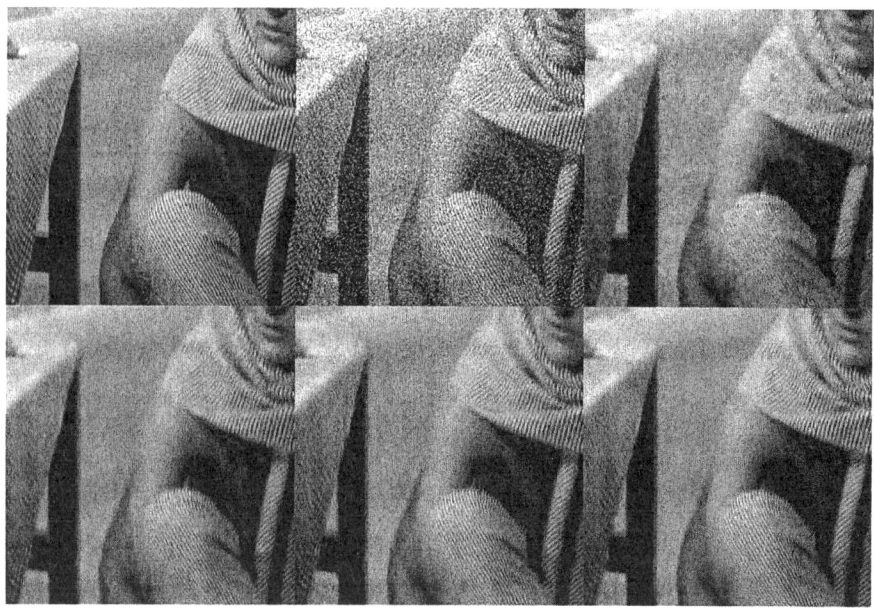

**Fig. 2.** Cropped images (256×256) using proposed algorithms for 512×512 *Barbara* image with $\sigma$=30 : Original (top-left), Noisy (top-center; 18.58dB), *Wiener* filter (top-right; 24.73dB), Method 2 (bottom-left; 27.35dB), Method 1 (bottom-center; 27.92dB), Method 3 (bottom-right; 27.96dB)

**Fig. 3.** Cropped images (128×128) using proposed algorithms for 512×512 *Boat* image with $\sigma=20$ : Original (top-left), Noisy (top-center; 22.10dB), *Wiener* filter (top-right; 28.09dB), Method 2 (bottom-left; 29.81dB), Method 1 (bottom-center; 29.97dB), Method 3 (bottom-right; 30.17dB)

For our proposed shrinkage algorithms, determining an optimal constant $\alpha$ in Eqs. 2 and 4 for Method 1 and Method 3 is required. $\alpha$ can be chosen experimentally. We found that the value is empirically similar to the optimal value for universal soft-thresholding in [10] and located in a particularly narrow range even for diverse types of images with different sizes and noise levels.

We set $\alpha$ to 0.16 ~ 0.19 for both Method 1 and Method 3 depending on the sizes of the neighboring and parent windows when we use CWT. In CWT, a threshold should be doubled since it is compared with the sum of the squares of the magnitudes calculated from both real and imaginary parts.

To evaluate and analyze our proposed algorithms, we compared them with the existing effective approaches. Denoised images can be compared both visually and numerically. We use PSNR for numerical measurement, which is the most representative numerical measures for image quality.

A comparison of selected methods is given in Figs. 2 and 3 for a 512×512 size *Boat* and *Barbara* images. For the varied noise variances, the measured PSNR values are plotted in Fig. 4 for our proposed methods and other available existing methods. We compared our method with the existing algorithms proposed in [3], [7], [9], [14], and [15].

In [7], an image denoising algorithm using Gaussian scale mixtures is proposed. In their experiments, the results are only 0.1dB ~ 0.2dB better than ours as shown in Fig. 4. However, it may not be proper to compare our results because

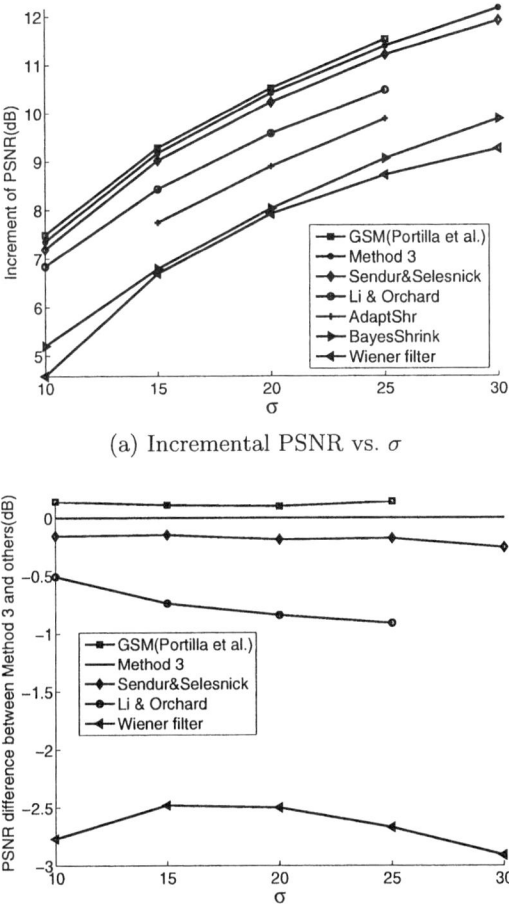

(a) Incremental PSNR vs. $\sigma$

(b) PSNR differences between Method 3 (zero horizontal line) and other approaches

**Fig. 4.** Comparison graphs for some principal approaches from 512×512 *Lena* image

Portilla et al. use a customized wavelet called *steerable pyramid* while we use the usual orthogonal wavelets and CWT. The emphasis of our paper is in the study of the effects of neighboring and level dependencies on thresholding the wavelet coefficients. Moreover, our Matlab program takes 3 seconds for a 512×512 image with CWT on 2.4GHz Pentium IV, whereas their Matlab implementation takes roughly 40 seconds for a 256×256 image on 1.7 GHz Pentium III according to [7]. One of the advantages of our methods is the low computational requirement which makes our methods very competitive in real applications.

## 4 Conclusion

We have presented algorithms which take advantage of the higher order statistical coupling between neighbor wavelet coefficients and their corresponding coefficients in the parent level with effective translation-invariant wavelet transforms. Also the multiplying constant of a threshold which produces lower MSE for image denoising has been introduced and chosen empirically. Our methods give fairly satisfying results in both visual and numerical aspects. In addition, they are considerably fast and effective for thresholding and easy to implement.

# References

1. Cai, T.T., Silverman, B.W.: Incorporating information on neighbouring coefficients into wavelet estimation. Sankhya: The Indian Journal of Statistics, Series A **63** (2001) 127–148
2. Chen, G.Y., Bui, T.D.: Multiwavelet denoising using neighbouring coefficients. IEEE Signal Processing Lett. **10** (2003) 211–214
3. Sendur, L., Selesnick, I.W.: Bivariate shrinkage with local variance estimation. IEEE Signal Processing Lett. **9** (2002) 438–441
4. Azimifar, Z., Fieguth, P., Jernigan, E.: Wavelet shrinkage with correlated wavelet coefficients. In: IEEE Int. Conf. on Image Processing. Volume 3. (2001) 162–165
5. Mihcak, M.K., I. Kozintsev, K.R., Moulin, P.: Low-complexity image denoising based on statistical modeling of wavelet coefficients. IEEE Signal Processing Lett. **6** (1999) 300–303
6. Crouse, M.S., Nowak, R.D., Baraniuk, R.G.: Wavelet-based signal processing using hidden markov models. IEEE Trans. Signal Processing **46** (1998) 886–902
7. Portilla, J., V. Strela, M.W., Simoncelli, E.P.: Image denoising using scale mixtures of gaussians in the wavelet domain. IEEE Trans. Image Processing **12** (2003) 1338–1351
8. Cho, D., Bui, T.D.: Multivariate statistical modeling for image denoising using wavelet transforms. Signal Processing: Image Communications **20** (2005) 77 – 89
9. Chang, S.G., Yu, B., Vetterli, M.: Spatially adaptive wavelet thresholding with context modeling for image denoising. IEEE Trans. Image Processing **9** (2000) 1522–1531
10. Donoho, D.L.: Denoising by soft-thresholding. IEEE Trans. Inform. Theory **41** (1995) 613–627
11. Donoho, D.L., Johnstone, I.M.: Adapting to unknown smoothness via wavelet shrinkage. Journal. Amer. Stat. Assoc. **90** (1995) 1200–1224
12. Shapiro, J.M.: Embedded image coding using zerotrees of wavelet coefficients. IEEE Trans. Signal Processing **41** (1993) 3445–3462
13. Kingsbury, N.G.: Image processing with complex wavelets. Phil. Trans. Royal Society London A **357** (1999) 2543–2560
14. Chang, S.G., Yu, B., Vetterli, M.: Adaptive wavelet thresholding for image denoising and compression. IEEE Trans. Image Processing **9** (2000) 1532–1546
15. Li, X., Orchard, M.T.: Spatially adaptive image denosing under overcomplete expansion. In: IEEE Int. Conf. on Image Processing. Volume 3. (2000) 300–303

# Time Oriented Video Summarization

Chaoqiang Liu[1], Tao Xia[2], and Hui Li[1]

[1] Temasek Laboratories and Centre for Wavelets,
Approximation and Information Processing, National University of Singapore
[2] Centre for Wavelets, Approximation and Information Processing,
National University of Singapore

**Abstract.** This paper addresses a novel video summarization procedure that produces a dynamic (video) abstract of the original video sequence. To remain temporal characteristic in the video abstract, a newly time-oriented feature is introduced. The approach relies on time instances, frame rate of the original video sequence and display speed of the video summary to select frames for a video abstract. This method preserves the time-evolving dynamic nature of the video content. Based on a input video sequence, real-time video summarization can be achieved at different display speed.

## 1 Introduction

The emergence of digital videos has triggered an interest in various video-processing fields especially video abstracting. There have been research efforts that strive to output motion video summaries to accommodate better content overviews. To date, the most common approach is to use a set of keyframes extracted from the input video for its content summary. Many systems extract a constant number of keyframes from each video shot [1]-[3], while sophisticated systems assign more keyframes to scene shots with more changes [4]-[6]. To remove redundancies and duplicates from keyframes, there are also methods clustering keyframes based on their visual similarities [7]-[9]. However, while keyframes are effective in helping the user to spot the desired shots from a video, they are insufficient for the user to get a general idea of the video content. Furthermore, another common drawback is that it simply presents a sequence of key frames at a certain fixed rate without considering any time relationship between successive key frames.

There also have been research efforts on dynamic video abstract based on adaptive and dynamic sampling of sub-shots units of the video sequence,to preserve the video content and time relationship [10]. Whereas, based on such a method, once the video is given, the video abstract is fixed. User cannot have video abstracts at different display speed and real-time video abstract cannot be realized.

In this paper, a time oriented video summarization (TOVS) method is proposed to generate a real time video summary at different display speed. This method keeps the temporal characteristics of the video content and performs direct fast playback based on the compressed video stream. Algorithms of related works and the TOVS procedure are described in Section II. Based on TOVS, several algorithms are developed due to different purposes. Simulation results are presented and analysed in Section III. Finally, some conclusions and discussions are given in Section IV.

## 2 Time Oriented Video Summarization

As well known, the video stream is stored frame by frame. For video summarization, If the original video stream is compressed, we define the corresponding reconstructed frames as $\widetilde{F}_0, \widetilde{F}_1, ..., \widetilde{F}_{N-1}$. If it is not compressed, let $F_0, F_1, F_2, F_3, ..., F_{N-1}$ representing the frames in the original video stream, where $N$ is the total number of the frames, and the frames displayed in the video summarization are denoted as $G_0, G_1, ..., G_{M-1}$. With $C$ denoting the frame rate, the video duration of the original video stream is $\frac{N}{C}$. The key frames are defined as $F_i, i \in I_K := \{J_k\}_{k=0,...,L-1}$. As video summarization is based on the original video sequence, a variable $R$ is introduced to denote how many times the video summarization is faster than original video sequence from vision effect. This $R$ is used to extract frames from original video sequence for video abstract and can be specified by the laymen. Hence the corresponding video length of the video summarization is $\frac{N}{CR}$.

Most video compression methods exploit motion estimation and compensation [11]-[12]. Therefore the videos consist of two types of frames, key frames (including scene transition frames and the compulsory frames compressed by intraframe compression) and motion frames (frames in between two adjacent key frames). As the data of a motion frame is dependent on some relevant motion frames and the relevant key frame, so in order to reconstruct a motion frame from a compressed video stream, those relevant frames also need to be reconstructed. Meanwhile, video codec transmits two parts of data for a motion frame $F_i$, one is motion vector field $F_{i,m}$, and the other is displaced frame difference (DFD) $F_{i,d}$. The reconstructed motion frame is given by

$$\widetilde{F}_i = M(F_{i,m}, \widetilde{F}_{i-1}) + D(F_{i,d}), \tag{1}$$

where the function $M$ is a motion prediction unit based on motion vector field $F_{i,m}$ and the reconstructed previous frame $\widetilde{F}_{i-1}$, and $D$ is an operator to generate a DFD image from the compressed DFD data $F_{i,d}$.

Most researchers focus on retrieving the key frames to represent the content of a segment of video sequences. With notions defined above, their common idea can be described as

$$G_k = \widetilde{F}_{J_k}, \text{ or } G_k = F_{J_k}, \tag{2}$$

depending on whether the input video stream is compressed or not. Basically, the extracted keyframes are presented in the video summary uniformly.

Unlike the reported work in the literature, we propose a video summarization method with time-oriented features. Without loss of generality we assume the initial time instance when we start the procedure is $t_0$, and current time instance is $t$. Thus, the index of the current frame in the input compressed video is $j = [(t-t_0)*C*R]$. Such a index $j$ will be used to select frames to be presented in the video summary. After that, the index $j$ is updated as the current time instance $t$ varies. The process is repeated until the whole input video sequence is read through. In other words, the frames in the video summary are selected based on current time instance, frame rate of the input video stream, and display speed of the video summary. Due to different purposes, several different video summary algorithms are implemented based on TOVS.

## 2.1 TOVS Based on Key Frames

If we only display the key frames, TOVS is developed as TOVS Algorithm Based on Key Frames only (TOVS-K). As mentioned, the index of the current frame in the input compressed video clip is $j = [(t-t_0)*C*R]$. Then we use this index to find the relevant key frame $k_{near} = \max_{k \in I_k, k \leq j}\{k\}$ as shown in Figure 1. If $k_{near}$ is already displayed in the video summary, then $G_i = G_{i-1}$, which means $k_{near}$ will be displayed again. If $k_{near}$ is not displayed yet, then $k_{near}$ will be selected into the video summary and displayed. The process is repeated until the entire input video sequence has been read through.

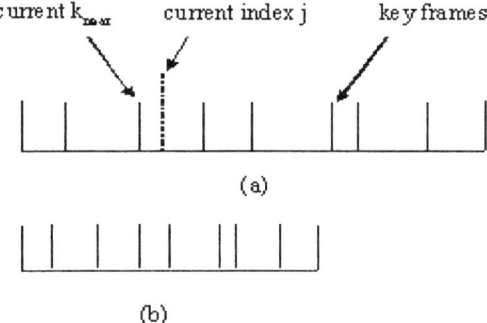

**Fig. 1.** TOVS-K: (a) key frames in original video stream (b) displayed frames in video summarization

TOVS-K is obtained by adding time-oriented features to those related video summarization methods based on key frames, as mentioned in last section. The difference between TOVS-K and traditional video summarization methods based on key frames lies in that, the distributions of the keyframes in TOIVS-K is proportional to their distributions in the original video clip, while in other methods, keyframes are displayed uniformly. As shown in Figure1, it is clear that the displayed key frames in the video summary still keep the temporal characteristics of the original video stream.

## 2.2 TOVS Based on Idea Motion Compensation

Key frames are insufficient for the non-expert end-users to get a general idea of the video content. Our research aims to develop a summarizing approach in the compressed domain, to display not only keyframes but also some relevant frames to make the video summary more natural. From such a point of view, TOVS is developed as TOVS Based on Ideal Motion Compensation (TOVS-IMC) as shown in Figure 2.

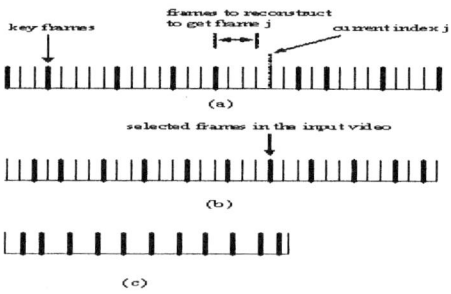

**Fig. 2.** TOVS-IMC: (a) frames in original video (b) selected frames in original video (c) frames in video summarization

As noted, at time instance $t$, $j = [(t - t_0) * C * R]$ stands for the index of the current frame in the input compressed video stream. Instead of displaying relevent key frames as in TOVS-K, this frame $j$ will be displayed in the video summary. In order to reconstruct this frame, all the relevant frames need to be reconstructed up to the previous key frame. After that, we repeat the process by updating the index j as current time instance changes, until the value of j exceeds N.

So compared with other traditional video abstract generation methods, TOVS-IMC is different in several aspects. Since our simulations are complemented by computers, the following are observed under pc environment. First, with a time-oriented feature, TOVS-IMC may generate different number of frames if it is repeated. Second, at each instance of TOVS-IMC, the time interval between two successive frames may vary due to the variation of CPU and memory usage of the system. Third, TOVS-IMC is an application in the sense that no extra information is generated. At last, if the system performance is very good (CPU of the computer is quite fast), TOVS-IMC will increase the frame rate accordingly, which will result in a smoother video.

## 2.3 TOVS Based on Maximum Decoding Length

For real-time video summarization, the computation complexity has to be considered while it is not considered in TOVS-IMC. When $R = 1$, which means the video summarization is the same as the original video sequence, it is possible to reach real-time video abstract. However, for a given $R$, the video abstract is $R$ times faster and the decoder $D(F_{i,d})$ will generate $R$ times frames comparing when $R = 1$. The computational complexity is highly increased. Therefore it is impossible to realize TOVS-IMC real time for a large $R$. Since most of the computation cost is spent on evaluating $D(F_{i,d})$, it is necessary to reduce the computation complexity on it to achieve the real-time process. In view of the fact that the motion prediction image $M(F_{i,m}, \widetilde{F}_{i-1})$ is a good approximation of $\widetilde{F}_i = M(F_{i,m}, \widetilde{F}_{i-1}) + D(F_{i,d})$, so $\widetilde{F}_i$ is substituted by $M(F_{i,m}, \widetilde{F}_{i-1})$ to enable video summarization to be implemented in real time. This gives rise to TOVS with a Maximum Decoding Length K (TOVS-MCK).

The process of TOVS-MCK is similar as the TOVS-IMC, the only difference lies in the computation complexity. In TOVS-MCK, for a current selected frame j in the original video stream, which will be displayed in the video summarization, while reconstructing all the relevant frames to reconstruct frame j, we use $\widetilde{F}_j = M(F_{j,m}, \widetilde{F}_{j-1}) + D(F_{j,d})$ when $i = j$ and $\widetilde{F}_i = M(F_{i,m}, \widetilde{F}_{i-1})$ when $i \neq j$. That means the displayed frame difference is only used to refine the approaximation for frame $j$, while motion prediction image is taken to be the approaximation for rest frames. So the computation complexity is highly reduced. Meanwhile, another important idea for real-time process in TOVS-MCK is to introduce a maximum decoding length K. Instead of reconstructing all the relevant frames up to the relevant key frames, we reconstruct a number of K frames only. For a current selected frame $j$ in a compressed video sequence, when the index of the relevant key frame is $i$, if $i + K < j$, then we reconstruct frame $i$ to frame $i + K$, and the frame $i + K$ is displayed in the video summarization instead of frame $j$. Obviously, through such a process, the quality of the video summarization is affected and the time accurancy of the frames displayed in the video summarization may be lost. However, the video quality still can be controlled through selecting and testing different value of K, and through TOVS-MCK, the video abstract is becoming smoother comparing with the video summarization generated by TOVS-IMC. Based on the observation that smoothness is more important than time stamp accuracy of every displayed frame, such a trade-off is worthwhile for real time applications. The selection of maximum decoding length K depends on the performance of the system. If the CPU speed is quite fast, $K$ could be very large. The upper limit of $K$ is the key frame rate of original compressed video clip. To properly choose this maximum decoding length $K$, the video summarization generated by TOVS-MCK can approach the quality of video abstract produced by TOVS-IMC, meanwhile, it can be realized real-time. In a word, TOVS-MCK is a trade-off between speed and the video quality in video summary applications.

## 3 Simulation Results

Although video summarization by TOVS-IMC cannot be realized real-time, it still can be regarded as a ideal case for video summarization applications from view point of quality, so it could be thought of a target to reach. Based on two sets of test data, test data I and test data II, which are real video streams extracted from two movies, we have tested TOVS-K and TOVS-MCK to generate real time video summarization. The parameters of test data I, test data II and the video abstracts generated are presented in Table 1.

**Table 1.** Test Data I and Test Data II

|  | Test Data I | Test Data II |
|---|---|---|
| Video Frame Size | 320*240 | 320*174 |
| Video Length | 61.60(s) | 68.42(s) |
| Key Frame Rate | 16(f/s) | 16(f/s) |
| Frame Rate C | 15(f/s) | 12(f/s) |
| R | 5 | 5 |
| Data Rate(kbps) | 314 | 396 |
| Summary Length | 12.32(s) | 13.68(s) |

As test results of the two methods look similar from view point of whole summary length, so it is necessary to zoom in the figures of the simulation results, and eventually we get the curves as shown in Figure 3 and Figure 4.

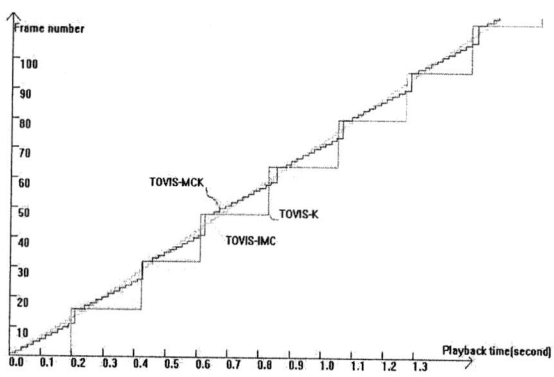

**Fig. 3.** Video summaries generated based on test data I

It is clear from Figure 3 and Figure 4 that, only key frames are displayed in the video summarization generated by TOVS-K, while the video summarization generated by TOVS-MCK is approaching the one generated by TOVS-IMC and the video content is more natural with more frames presented. Through the simulation, we also found out that, the better the system performance (the faster the CPU speed), the better the video quality and the smoother the video summarization.

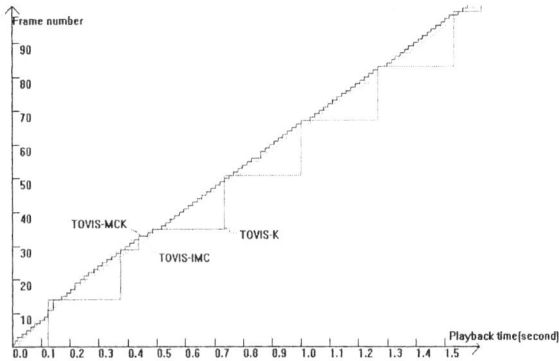

**Fig. 4.** Video summaries generated based on test data II

## 4 Conclusion

In this paper, we have presented a novel time-oriented video summary method. Three algorithms are proposed. The first (TOVS-K) is based on only key frames, the second (TOVS-IMC) uses ideal motion compensation in addition to key frames, while the third (TOVS-MCK) is a computationally efficient trade-off of the second algorithm. These video summary algorithms can be used for any compressed video clip if the compression codec exploits motion compensation. Among the three methods, the video summarization generated by TOVS-IMC has the best quality but it cannot be realized real-time. TOVS-K and TOVS-MCK can both produce real-time video summarization, and the video abstract made by TOVS-MCK can almost reach the quality as by TOVS-IMC. Our procedures keep the temporal characteristics of the original video sequence and make the video content in the video summarization more natural.

## Acknowledgment

The authors would like to thank DSTA funding for support of the programme "Wavelets and Information Processing".

## References

1. A. Ferman and A. Tekalp, "Multiscale content extraction and representatoin for video indexing", in *Multimedia Storage and Archiving System II*, Proc. SPIE 3229, Dollas, TX, pp. 23-31, 1997.
2. Y. Tonomura, A. Akustu, K. Otsuji, and T. Sadakata, "Videomap and videospace-icon: tools for anatomizing video content," In *Proc. ACM INTERCHI'93*, pp. 131-141, 1993.
3. H. Ueda, T. Miyatake, and S. Yoshizawa, "Impact:an interactive natural-motion-picture dedicated multimedia authoring system," in *Proc. ACM SIGCHI'91*, New Orleans, Apr. 1991.

4. D. Dementhon, V. Kkbla and D. Doermann, "Video summarization by curve simplification", Tech. Rep. LAMP-TR-018, Language and Media Processing Laboratory, Univeristy of Maryland, 1998.
5. B. Gunsel, Y. Fu, and A. M. Tekalp, "Hierarchical temporal video segmentation and content characterization", in *Multimedia Storage and Archiving System II, Proc. SPIE 3229*, Dollas, TX, pp. 46-56, 1997.
6. H. J. Zhang, C. Y. Low, S. W. Smoliar, and J. H. Wu, "Video parsing, retrieval and browsing:an integrated and content-based solution," *ACM Multimedia 95*, San Francisco, CA, pp. 15-24, 1995.
7. A. Girgensohn and J. Boreczky, "Time-constrained keyframes selection techniques", in *Proc. IEEE Multimedia Computing and Systems (ICMCS'99)*, 1999.
8. M. Yeung, B. Yeo,W. Wolf, and B. Liu, "Video browsing using clustering and scene transitions on compressed sequences," in *Proc, SPIE on Multimedia Computing and Networking*, vol. 2417, 1995.
9. Y. Gong and X. Liu,"Video summarization with minimal visual content redundancies," in *Image Processing, 2001. Proceedings. 2001 International Conference*, vol. 3, pp. 362-365, 2001.
10. J. Nam and A. H. Tewfik, "Video abstract of video", in *IEEE 3rd workshop*, Dept. of Electrical and Computer Eng., University of Minnesota at Twin Cities, 1999.
11. F. Dufaux, F. Moscheni,"Motion estimation techniques for digital TV: a review and a new contribution", *Proceedings of the IEEE*, vol. 83, pp. 858-876, June. 1995.
12. J. K. Su, R. M. Mersereau, "Motion estimation methods for overlapped block motion compensation", *IEEE Trans. Image Processing*, vol. 9, pp. 1509-1521, Sept. 2000.

# Shadow Removal in Gradient Domain

Zhenlong Du, Xueying qin, Hai Lin, and Hujun Bao

State Key Lab of CAD&CG, Zhejiang University, P.R. China
{duzhl, xyqin, lin, bao}@cad.zju.edu.cn

**Abstract.** Shadow removal is of significance in computer vision. Shadow usually adheres to texture, and it is difficult to decouple shadow from texture without any assumptions. In this paper, we suppose that the texture beneath shadow should bear the similar patterns, which makes the problem of simultaneously recovering the reflectance and light attenuation factor solvable with sole image. A novel shadow removal method is proposed, which is fulfilled by complementing the lost radiance in shadow region. Experiments show that our proposed approach could maintain the texture structure and the coherent lighting with the intact region.

## 1 Introduction

Removing shadow in image is of significance to scene cognition, object tracking, and image composition. Shadow often adheres to texture, the dependent relation of shadow and texture causes shadow processing along with texture processing.

Shadow removal relates to the type of texture. Textures could be categorized as two kinds: strong and weak according to the denseness/sparseness degree of the constituent structure. Although humans' eyes can distinguish shadow from whichever texture, this procedure becomes rather difficult in machine vision, the key point is how to fully comprehend those explicit and implicit informations. It should be noted that the texture type is not invariant at all times, it varies with the alteration of perspective depth and view position.

There exists the potential irradiance relationship between illumination and shadow regions to be exploited for shadow removal. Illumination and shadow (including umbrae and penumbrae) regions simultaneously appear in the same image, illumination region receives total irradiance, while the shadow region receives part irradiance. If knowing the irradiance difference between illumination and shadow regions, we can remove shadow by completing the lost irradiance in shadow region. Our inspiration is partly influenced by Sato and Ikeuchi's [1] method, which estimated the irradiance with the priorly known object shape and the requirement to input many images. Our approach could recover the approximate irradiance from only one image without knowing the object shape in advance.

After we know the relative irradiance of sun and environment light (for convenient description, the sun has a alias of direct light, the sky light is also named to environment light), the reflectance of pixel should be known, and could be used for shadow removal. Removing shadow and acquiring the reflectance are ill-posed problem with one image input, and these two problems are interweaved. We reasonably limit the problem scope, which requires the specified regions must appear with similar textural patterns, hence these two problems could be solved. The presented limitation in the paper is not sole, we believe there should exist others. Based on the limitation, the ratio of pixel's intensity to mean intensity of the same region serves as the relative reflectance of pixel.

The input image involving ambiguous shadow is solved in our succeeding technical report. The approach of this paper mainly concentrates on the image, from which observer could discern different kinds of regions effortlessly.

When the light irradiance changes, the captured radiance of camera alters too. To simulate this kind of physical phenomena, we use a virtual light source to relight the pixel. The pixel radiance rises with the increase irradiance of light source, and vice versa. During the irradiance tuning process, when light irradiance reaches a certain threshold, pixel's radiance would go beyond displayable bound. Oppositely decreasing the irradiance of light source, pixel's radiance would fall into the radiance distribution of shadow region. Since the shadow and illumination regions are given priorly, the tunable irradiance range can be determined. We exploit the tuned irradiance amount and initial setting value of light source to extract the coarse shadow matte, and employ the complement space of color to remove shadow. The conception of the complement space is somewhat similar to the inverse-chromaticity space proposed by Tan [16], whose method is based on the statistical technique, while ours stresses the property of individual pixel, and could keep the structure of complex texture. Finlayson [13,14,15] proposed the intrinsic image, and used it serve the reflectance scalar for shadow removal, but the accurate acquisition of intrinsic image need input more than one image.

The paper contains three contributions: acquiring the irradiance of image, extracting shadow matte and smoothing coarse shadow matte. The acquired irradiance is used for relighting the shadow region, and the shadow matte describes the occlusion degree to irradiance of each pixel. Meanwhile, smoothing the shadow matte is for more realistic result, these steps consolidate to remove the shadow in single outdoor image.

This remainder of the paper is organized as follows: in section two we review the related work, and present the derivation of the associated formulations which serve as the theoretical basis for implementation in section three. We discuss two key steps, the extraction of the coarse shadow matte and smoothing to the pulled shadow matte, and summarize our work in last section.

## 2 Related Work

Shadow generation is from the object occlusion to light propagation. For the existed shadow, moving object or moving light source can bring about moving shadow. The shadow moving shadow [6,9,12] could be removed by using the sufficient information in image sequence. These methods are difficult to be applied to single outdoor image, for in one image less information could be exploited.

Cham [4] and Jaynes [5] presented the approach of shadow removal by employing the feedback information from the camera, this kind of shadow removal manner is appropriate for indoor cinema or exhibition hall. Intrinsic image [9] is a image of lighting elimination, and it essentially serves as the reflectance, but the acquisition of accurate intrinsic image needs input more than one image.

If the shadow region is viewed as *hole*, some filling-in approaches of image processing could be employed for removing shadow. Bertalmio [20] proposed the *inpainting* method, which performs well when inpainting the small-patch region, and could preserve the structure of texture and image simultaneously, however the extension of *inpainting* to the large-patch hole brings about heavy computation. Perez and Blake [18] introduced PDE method to image editing, which would be applied to fill the *hole*. The *hole* contour, which lies between illumination and shadow regions, would preserve because Poisson approach operates in gradient domain. Drori [19] presented an image completion approach based on fragment, which also could fill-in the large hole, while the process of searching and matching leads to non-interactive response. For matting and compositing shadow, Chuang [10] obtained the geometrical information of shadow caster via passive way, Chuang's method only fits for the small-scale scene.

## 3 Estimation of Irradiance and Reflectance

As Fig. 1 illustrates, $R_{illu}$, $R_{shadow}$ and $R_{pro}$ require user to specify in advance, $R_{illu}$, $R_{shadow}$ and $R_{pro}$ are denoted by contours with color of black, white and yellow separately. The *illumination region* $R_{illu}$ is entirely illuminated by solar light $E_{sun}$ and environmental light $E_{env}$, and the *umbrae region* $R_{shadow}$ is merely by $E_{env}$, while the *penumbrae region* $R_{penu}$ is by the blending of $E_{sun}$ and $E_{env}$. The solar light attenuation factor $\alpha$ is introduced to describe the occlusion degree to $E_{sun}$, and $\alpha$ also represents the region type, **one** corresponds to $R_{illu}$, **zero** to $R_{shadow}$, and values within interval [0, 1] to $R_{pro}$.

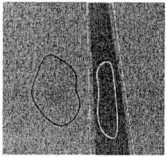

**Fig. 1.** Regions of Required to specify

For each pixel $X(x, y)$ and color component $K = R, G, B$, the spectral power distribution of incident light is $E(\lambda)$, $S(\lambda)$ is the surface spectral reflectance function. The pixel received irradiance of each color component, regardless of the material type as well as the shape of object, can be described as [15,16]:

$$I_K(X) = \int_\Omega S(\lambda, X) E(\lambda, X) q_K(\lambda) d\lambda \tag{1}$$

where $q_K(\lambda)$ is the sensor spectral sensitivity, $I_K(X)$ is the color response of sensor, $\Omega$ is the scope of visible spectrum.

An image of opaque dielectric-inhomogeneous objects taken by a digital color camera can be described as:

$$I_K(X) = K_d(X) \int_\Omega S_d(\lambda, X) E(\lambda, X) q_K(\lambda) d\lambda + K_s(X) \int_\Omega E(\lambda, X) q_K(\lambda) d\lambda \quad (2)$$

where $K_d(X)$ and $K_s(X)$ are the diffuse and specular reflection factor respectively. If the specular objects in image is absent, the last term of right hand side in Eq. 2 can be omitted. And then, the total receiving irradiance of pixel in color component $K$ is that:

$$I_K(X) = K_d(X) \int_\Omega S_d(\lambda, X) E(\lambda, X) q_K(\lambda) d\lambda \quad (3)$$

It is the common assumption that the camera sensitivity has the narrow-band characteristic that follows the Dirac Delta function [15], hence the $E(\lambda, X)$ could be approximated to the sum of $\alpha E_{sun}$ and $E_{env}$, and we introduce the notation $\rho$ as:

$$\rho = \int_\Omega S_d(\lambda, X) q_K(\lambda) d\lambda \quad (4)$$

Thus the Eq. 3 can be rewritten as:

$$I_K(X) = K_d(X)(\alpha E_{sun} + E_{env})\rho \quad (5)$$

where $\alpha$ is the solar light attenuation factor.

In region $R$, the mean radiance $\overline{I}_K$ can be discretely described as:

$$\overline{I}_K = \sum_{X \in R} K_d(X)(\alpha E_{sun} + E_{env})\rho / N_R \quad (6)$$

where $N_R$ is the total number of pixels within $R$. In addition, the denotations of $\overline{K_d}$ and $K_d$ are the mean and relative reflectance respectively.

Because $\alpha$ is zero in $R_{shadow}$ and $\alpha$ is one in $R_{illu}$, this means that in Eq. 5 the term of $\alpha E_{sun} + E_{env}$ keeps constant in the same type of region, so we could derive $K_d(X)$ by division of Eq. 6 to Eq. 5:

$$\overline{K_d}(X) = K_d(X) N_R / (\sum_{X \in R} K_d(X)) = I_K(X) / \overline{I}_K \quad (7)$$

Under the assumption of similar patterns appearing in $R_{illu}$ and $R_{shadow}$, we approximately regard $\overline{K_d}$ to be equal between $R_{illu}$ and $R_{shadow}$, so we could derive the Eq. 8 and Eq. 9:

$$E_{env} = \sum_K \sum_{X \in R_{shadow}} I_K(X) / N_R \quad (8)$$

$$E_{sun} = \sum_K \sum_{X \in R_{illu}} I_K(X) / N_{R_{illu}} - \sum_K \sum_{X \in R_{shadow}} I_K(X) / N_{R_{shadow}} \quad (9)$$

Eq. 8 and Eq. 9 are the approximate estimation to solar light and environmental light separately.

After gaining $E_{sun}$ and $E_{env}$, we relight each pixel to remove the shadow. Accurate irradiance acquisition [2,3] need input many sample images, and depends on some prior constraints. In the paper, our goal is to remove the shadow in one image, and produce the visually plausible effect.

## 4 Implementation of Shadow Removal

There are four unknowns in one equation of Eq. 5, we estimate these unknowns step by step. Computation of $K_d$ is given in subsection 4.1, followed by the extraction of coarse shadow matte, next presented the smoothing to the extracted matte.

### 4.1 Computation of $K_d$

Diffuse reflectance scalar might be accurately represented either by BRDF [3] or by BTF [17], the limitation of these methods is difficult to be applied to outdoors. As we know, the observer is more sensitive to the relative radiance variation than the absolute radiance, hence we remove the shadow by modifying the relative variation of pixel color.

Eq. 5 involves two unknowns: $\alpha$ and $K_d$, after having known $E_{sun}$ and $E_{env}$. In this step $K_d$ of $R_{pro}$ is evaluated by Eq. 7. We store each pixel's $K_d$ into an image, which is referred to as $K_d$ map.

### 4.2 The Coarse Shadow Matte Extraction

From Eq. 5, we know that when the amount of total irradiance of $E_{sun}$ increases, the pixel becomes more brighter, this means less irradiance is occluded, therefore $\alpha$ should decrease correspondingly, and vice versa. This process follows the physical phenomena. To simulate this kind of phenomena, we imagine the image is lighted by the virtual light whose irradiance is tunable. We impose a virtual light at every pixel in order to mat shadow. We continuously increase irradiance of the virtual light till pixel intensity reaches the maximal displayable bound. There is no doubt that $\alpha$ equals to 0 at this time. Oppositely decreasing the irradiance of virtual light, the pixel intensity falls into the radiance distribution of umbrae region, the $\alpha$ at this time is 1. It should be noted that, due to the existence of texture, whether in illumination or shadow regions, there exists some pixels exhibiting the opposite attribute to the region that they belong to, that is, though one pixel lies in the illumination region, its intensity satisfies with the intensity distribution of shadow region, so does this case for some pixels of shadow region. The phenomena are more apparent in strong texture than weak texture. We eliminate the texture influence by Gabor filters bank [8,11].

The initial irradiance of virtual light depends on the given illumination and shadow regions. In most cases, the initial irradiance is set to the mean value of $R_{shadow}$.

We store each pixel's $\alpha$ of into an image, which is referred to as $\alpha$ map. The introductions of $\alpha$ and $K_d$ map borrow from the conception of image processing.

## 4.3 Smoothing the Coarse Shadow Matte in Gradient Domain

The shadow generated in outdoors is a whole body of continuity and smoothness. The transition area between umbrae and penumbrae exhibits smooth, no abrupt change. In addition, the umbrae does not display entirely black. The pulled coarse $\alpha$ map only manifests the light attenuation degree of individual pixel, this is evident from Figure 2(c). We impose the constraint of continuity and smoothness to make the shadow map more realistic.

Every $\alpha(X)$ should satisfy dual smoothness constraints: global and local. The global smoothness constraint requires that within the whole region $\alpha(X)$ should approach to the actual value $\widehat{\alpha}(X)$, and the local smoothness constraint requires that $\widehat{\alpha}(X)$ should be close to the neighborhood for maintaining the smoothness, which is equivalent to the requirement that the second-order derivative of $\widehat{\alpha}(X)$ keep minimal variation. The smoothing constraint is given in least squares sense:

$$E = \sum_X [\alpha(X) - \widehat{\alpha}(X)]^2 + \lambda \sum_X [(\partial_{xx}\alpha(X))^2 + (\partial_{yy}\alpha(X))^2 + (\partial_{dd}\alpha(X))^2 + (\partial_{DD}\alpha(X))^2] \quad (10)$$

where $\lambda$ is the adjustor to smoothness degree, $\partial_{dd}$ and $\partial_{DD}$ are the second-order partial derivative along primary and secondary diagonal.

Take partial derivative on both sides of Eq. 10, substitute the forward difference of first-order and second-order into the associated items, then derive Eq. 11 as that:

$$(1 + 24\lambda)\widehat{\alpha}(x,y) + \lambda \begin{cases} -4\widehat{\alpha}(x+1,y) - 4\widehat{\alpha}(x+1,y-1) - 4\widehat{\alpha}(x,y-1) - 4\widehat{\alpha}(x-1,y-1) \\ -4\widehat{\alpha}(x-1,y) - 4\widehat{\alpha}(x-1,y+1) - 4\widehat{\alpha}(x,y+1) - 4\widehat{\alpha}(x+1,y+1) \\ + \widehat{\alpha}(x+2,y) + \widehat{\alpha}(x+2,y-2) + \widehat{\alpha}(x,y-2) + \widehat{\alpha}(x-2,y-2) \\ + \widehat{\alpha}(x-2,y) + \widehat{\alpha}(x-2,y+2) + \widehat{\alpha}(x,y+2) + \widehat{\alpha}(x+2,y+2) \end{cases} = \alpha(x,y) \quad (11)$$

where $(x,y)$ denotes the pixel location. Applying Eq. (11) at every $(x,y)$ within $R_{pro}$, produces the linear equations. The number of equations increases with the size of process region. In ideal case, the variation range of $\widehat{\alpha}(x,y)$ lies between 0 and 1. Due to the existence of noise, the scope of $\alpha$ becomes broader than ideal case, and the actual range is between -0.2 and 1.2. The limited variation of $\widehat{\alpha}(x,y)$ somewhat reduces the computation time. Furthermore, the convergency accuracy might be set to be 0.1. If $\alpha$ is beneath 0.1, the observer hardly discerns the visual variation. The recommended accuracy is 0.05. Therefore the limited solution interval and small accuracy setting guarantee the smoothing procedure with interactive response.

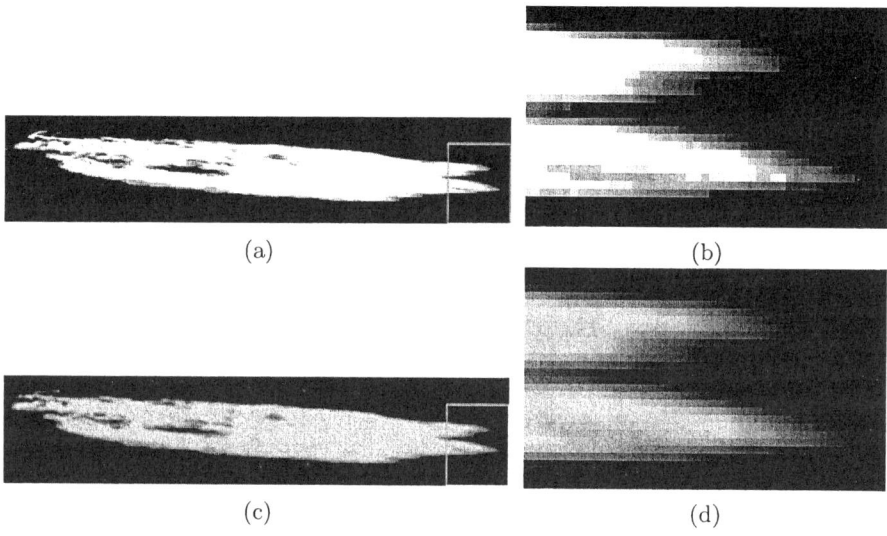

**Fig. 2.** Matter Optimization

In Fig. 2, the smoothed $\alpha$ matte (c) is more approaching to outdoors than coarse $\alpha$ matte (a), from the comparison of (b) and (d), the smoothness degree is dramatically improved by smoothing. Setting adjustor $\lambda$ to different values leads to different smoothness degree.

It should be noted that the introduction of second order derivatives along principle and secondary diagonal direction promotes the smoothness degree of $\alpha$ map.

## 5 Conclusion

Shadow is like a sword with dual blades. Sometimes shadow needs to be removed from the image or video because its existence is an obstacle to cognition, segmentation, or tracking, however sometimes shadow plays an important role in enhancing the realism of scene and understanding the spatial relationship of objects. In a word, shadow is not always adverse.

Reducing the number of images for the task of shadow removal is our effort. Whether as few as possible, even only one image suffices to accomplish the shadow removal has a trial answer. Under the assumption that the similar pattern appears in specified regions, we solved the ill-posed problem of simultaneously acquiring the pixel reflectance and light attenuation factor from one illuminating equation. It should be noted that the visual satisfaction is our pursuit.

Computing the irradiance of image is also addressed in the paper. We exploited the irradiance relationship among different kinds of regions, and devised an approach to recover the irradiance from image. It should be noted that our method performs well in point light source or approximatable point light than non-point light source, which does not mean the extension to the environment of non-light source could not fulfill.

Extracting shadow matte is also given in the paper. Taking advantage of the pulled matte, it is smooth to realistically composite the shadow into synthetic scene. This dramatically reduces the load of modelling and rendering of geometry object, especially the complex object.

# References

1. I. Sato, Y. Sato, K. Ikeuchi. Illumination from shadows. IEEE Trans. on PAMI, 25(3):290–300. March 2003.
2. M. Goesele, X. Granier, W. Heidrich and H.-P. Seidel. Accurate light source acquisition and rendering. In Proc. of SIGGRAPH 2003, 2003.
3. X. Granier, W. Heidrich. A simple layered RGB BRDF model. In Proc. of Pacific Graphics '02. 2002.
4. T.J. Cham, J. Rehg, R. Sukthankar, G. Sukthankar. Shadow elimination and occluder light supression for multi-projector sisplays. In Proc. of Computer Vision and Pattern Recognition, 2003.
5. C.Jaynes, S. Webb, R.M. Steele. Camera-based detection and removal of shadows from interactive multiprojector displays. IEEE Trans. on Visualization and Computer Graphics. 10(3):290–301, May/June, 2004.
6. J.W. Hsieh, W.F. Hu, C.J. Chang, Y.S. Chen. Shadow elimination for effective moving object detection by Gaussian shadow modeling. Image and Vision Computing. 21(6):505–516, 2003.
7. P.E. Debevec, J. Malik. Recovering high dynamic range radiance maps from photographs. In Proc. of SIGGRAPH 1997, 1997.
8. D.R. Martin, C.C. Fowlkes, J. Malik. Learning to detect natural image boundaries using local brightness, bolor and texture cues. IEEE Trans. PAMI, 26(5):530–549, May, 2004..
9. Y. Weiss. Deriving intrinsic images from image sequences. ICCV 2001, 2001.
10. Y.Y. Chuang, D.B. Goldman, B. Curless, D.H. Salesin, et.al. Shadow matting and compositing. In Proc. of SIGRAPH 2003, Aug. 2003.
11. Y. Rubner, C. Tomasi. Coalescing texture descriptors. In Proc. ARPA Image Understanding Workshop, 1996.
12. S. Nadimi, B. Bhanu. Moving shadow detection using a physics-based approach. In Proc. of Sixteen Intl. Conf. on Pattern Recognition, Canada, pp. 701–704, 2 (2002).
13. G.D. Finlayson, S.D. Hordley, M.S. Drew. Removing shadows from images. In Proc. of Intl. Conf. Computer Vision 2001, 2001.
14. G.D. Finlayson, M.S. Drew, C. Lu. Intrinsic images by entropy minimization. In Proc. of European Conference of Computer Vision 2004(ECCV 2004), 2004.
15. G.D. Finlayson. Coefficient color constancy. Ph.D. Dissertation of Simon Fraser Univ. Apr. 1995.
16. R.T. Tan. Illumination color and intrinsic surface properties - Physics-Based color analysis from a single image. Ph.D. Dissertation of Univ. of Tokyo, Dec. 2003.
17. X. Liu, Y. Hu, J. Zhang, X.. Tong, et al. Synthesis and rendering of bidirectional texture functions on arbitrary surfaces. IEEE Trans. PAMI, vol. 10, no. 3, pp. 278-289, May/June, 2004.

18. P. Perez, M. Gangnet, A. Blake. Poisson image editing. In Proc. of SIGGRAPH'2003, 2003.
19. I. Drori, D. Choen-Or, H. Yeshurum. Fragment-Based image completion. In Proc. of SIGGRAPH'2003, 2003.
20. M. Bertalmio, L. Vese, G. Sapiro, S. Osher. Simultaneous structure and texture image inpainting. IEEE Trans. on Image Processing, 2003, 12(8): 882–889.

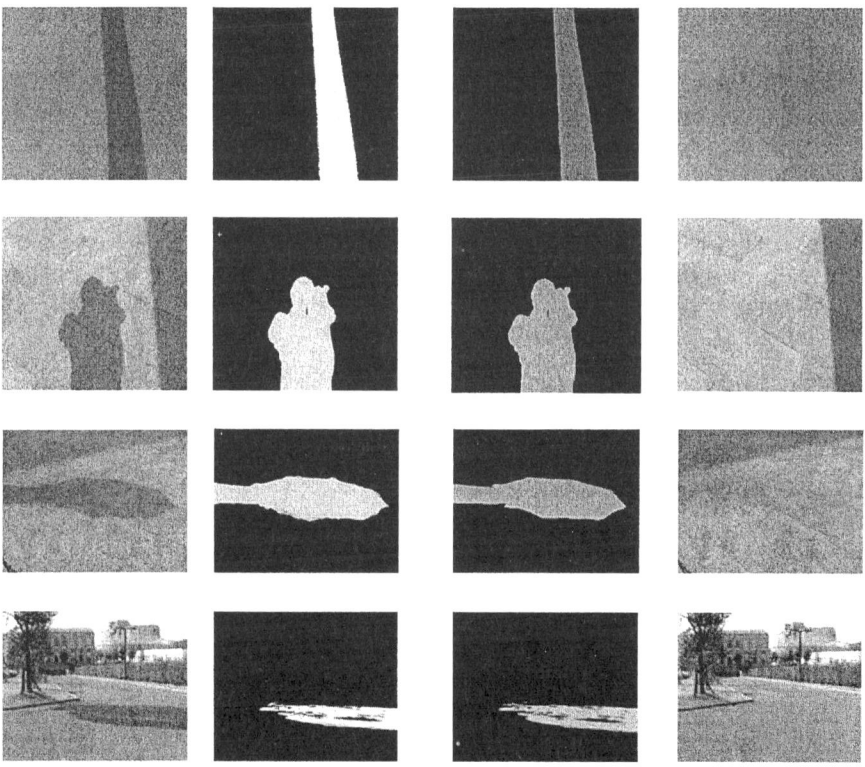

(a)Original image  (b)Coarse shadow matte  (c)Smoothed shadow matte  (d)Shadow removal

**Fig. 3.** Some results

In Figure 3, four groups of result are presented. The second and third columns of each row are coarse and smoothed shadow matte, respectively. The forth column of the corresponding row is the result of shadow removal. From the compare of second and third columns, it is obvious that the smoothed shadow matte is more approach to the outdoors. Meanwhile, the shadow removal results are rather perfect, though only one image is provided.

# Efficient Global Weighted Least-Squares Translation Registration in the Frequency Domain

Jeff Orchard

University of Waterloo, Waterloo Ontario N2L 3G1, Canada
jorchard@cs.uwaterloo.ca

**Abstract.** The weighted sum of squared differences cost function is often minimized to align two images with overlapping fields of view. If one image is shifted with respect to the other, the cost function can be written as a sum involving convolutions. This paper demonstrates that performing these convolutions in the frequency domain saves a significant amount of processing time when searching for a global optimum. In addition, the method is invariant under linear intensity mappings. Applications include medical imaging, remote sensing, fractal coding, and image photomosaics.

## 1 Introduction

One of the most common error metrics used in scientific applications is the sum of squared differences (SSD). In image processing, the SSD cost function is frequently used to asses the degree of similarity between two images. Image registration, in particular, often uses this metric when judging what spatial transformation brings two images of the same scene into alignment. It has been shown that for images differing only by additive Gaussian noise, the SSD cost function is the optimal choice [1]. Any problem that seeks to minimize the SSD is called a "least-squares" problem.

Another common error metric is cross-correlation [2]. One of the reasons for its popularity is the fact that its computation is equivalent to a convolution and can therefore be evaluated efficiently in the frequency domain (see section 2.1 below). Without this speedup, performing image registration would be too slow, particularly for 3D datasets or for large images (bigger than $1024 \times 1024$) such as those common in X-ray imaging and remote sensing. This method is common practice in medical image registration [3, 4].

In many image registration applications, only a small portion of each image is used to register the images. For example, one might have two overlapping aerial photographs, as in Fig. 1. If you can outline a window of the overlap in one of the photos, then finding the correct alignment of the two photos can be achieved by shifting one image over the other and evaluating the error norm in that window. The offset that gives the optimum norm value is called the optimal registration, and should correspond to the correct position. This windowed registration is

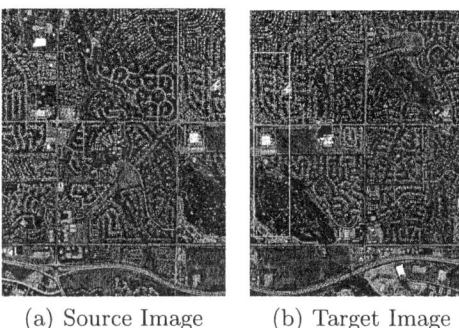

(a) Source Image    (b) Target Image

**Fig. 1.** Overlapping aerial photographs. A region of the overlap is outlined in the target image.

equivalent to a weighted registration problem, where all the pixels outside the windowed region have a weight of zero.

It is sometimes necessary to cast the intensities of an image down to a scale that has a limited range. For example, suppose the intensity values of two overlapping images have to be mapped to the range $[0, 255]$. The way the cast is typically done is to create a linear map such that the lowest intensity in the image maps to 0, and highest to 255. If the intensity ranges of two overlapping images is different, the intensity remappings will be different. This intensity casting causes corresponding pixels in the two images to have different intensities. The mismatch confuses the cross-correlation and SSD cost functions, and can lead to an incorrect registration result.

This paper proposes a method to efficiently compute the weighted SSD cost function by representing it as a combination of convolutions. Also, the optimal linear intensity remapping is determined with little additional effort.

## 2 Theory

### 2.1 Correlation Coefficient

When it comes to comparing images or functions, a common metric to measure the degree to which functions are similar is the Pearson's cross-correlation, defined as [2]

$$C(a) = \frac{\int f(x)g(x-a)dx}{\sqrt{\int f^2(x)dx \int g^2(x)dx}} . \tag{1}$$

In this context, $C(a)$ measures the correlation between the function $f(x)$ and the shifted function $g(x - a)$. For example, if $g$ is equal to $f$, then $C(a)$ achieves its maximum value when $a$ is zero (corresponding to no shift). This measure has been used in automatic alignment algorithms in medical imaging [5,3,6].

It is well known that the operation of convolution can be carried out by a multiplication in the frequency domain. The convolution of two functions, $f(x)$ and $g(x)$, is defined as

$$(f \star g)(a) = \int_{-\infty}^{\infty} f(x)g(a-x)dx \ . \quad (2)$$

That is, the function $g$ is flipped about $x = 0$ and shifted along the negative $x$-axis by a distance $a$. To turn the numerator of (1) into a convolution, we define a new function $\bar{g}(x)$ that is equal to $g(-x)$. Then, we replace $g(x-a)$ in (1) with $\bar{g}(a-x)$. Now the numerator of (1) is a convolution between $f(x)$ and $\bar{g}(x)$.

Consider the Fourier transform of the convolution, $\mathcal{F}\{(f \star \bar{g})(a)\}$. It is not difficult to show that the Fourier transform of a convolution is equivalent to the component-wise product of the two Fourier transforms (see Appendix B of [7]). That is, $\mathcal{F}\{(f \star \bar{g})(a)\} = \mathcal{F}\{f(x)\}(s) \cdot \mathcal{F}\{\bar{g}(a-x)\}(s)$. Thus, the numerator of the cross-correlation function can be evaluated for all values of $a$ by taking the Fourier transform of each of $f$ and $\bar{g}$, multiplying the two sets of coefficients, and then applying the inverse Fourier transform to the result. Finding the maximum of this function with respect to $a$ is simply a matter of scanning the evaluated function $C(a)$ for its maximum value. Note that if $f$ and $g$ are real-valued, then $C(a)$ will also be real-valued.

One of the problems with the correlation coefficient cost function is that it cannot be used as a measure for weighted registration problems. For weighted registration problems, we turn to the sum of squared differences (SSD) cost function.

## 2.2 Weighted Sum of Squared Differences

Given the functions $f(x)$ and $g(x-a)$ as before, the weighted sum of squared differences (SSD) registration of $g$ to $f$, with weighting function $w$, corresponds to the value of $a$ that minimizes

$$L_W(a) = \int \left[f(x) - g(x-a)\right]^2 w(x-a)dx \ . \quad (3)$$

The weighting function, $w$, is greater than or equal to zero over its entire domain. For example, $w$ could be a piecewise constant function that is zero everywhere except in a region where the registration is to operate – there its value is 1. Then, minimizing (3) is the same as moving $w$ in concert with $g$, and limiting the domain of the SSD calculation to only the region where $w$ is non-zero. By expanding the square brackets in (3), we get

$$L_W(a) = \int f^2(x)\bar{w}(a-x)dx + \int \bar{g}^2(a-x)\bar{w}(a-x)dx$$
$$- 2\int f(x)\bar{g}(a-x)\bar{w}(a-x)dx \ , \quad (4)$$

where $\bar{g}$ is defined as before, and $\bar{w}$ is defined similarly. As with the evaluation of the cross-correlation function, the weighted SSD cost function includes convolution-like terms. The first integral is a convolution between $f^2$ and $\bar{w}$, and changes with different values of $a$. We will denote it $e_1(a)$. The second integral is a constant with respect to $a$ since the weighting function moves with $\bar{g}$. We will denote this value as $e_2$. Combining $\bar{g}$ and $\bar{w}$ so that their product $\bar{g}(x)\bar{w}(x)$ equals $\bar{h}(x)$, the last integral of (4) becomes the convolution $\int f(x)\bar{h}(a-x)dx$. We will denote this last integral as $e_3(a)$. Thus, the weighted SSD cost function for a given displacement $a$ is

$$L_W(a) = e_1(a) + e_2 - 2e_3(a) \ . \tag{5}$$

## 2.3 Intensity Remapping

In addition to finding the best match over all shifts, we can also find the best match over all linear intensity remappings. That is, we wish to find the optimal shift in conjunction with the optimal contrast and brightness adjustment to make the corresponding parts of the two images as similar as possible. This is analogous to replacing the intensity $g(x)$ with $sg(x) + t$ for some constants $s$ and $t$. Naturally, the optimal $s$ and $t$ will depend on the shift, $a$. With an intensity-remapped $g$, the weighted SSD error measure can be written

$$L_R(a,s,t) = \int \left[ f(x) - s\ g(x-a) - t \right]^2 w(x-a)dx \ . \tag{6}$$

Now the problem becomes a minimization over $a$, $s$ and $t$. In particular, for every value of $a$, we wish to find the corresponding optimal values for $s$ and $t$. The optimal values can still be found efficiently since the convolution integrals that arise can still be evaluated in the frequency domain. Writing $F$, $G$ and $W$ instead of $f(x)$, $g(x-a)$ and $w(x-a)$, respectively, we expand the brackets in (6) to get,

$$L_R(a,s,t) = \int F^2 W + s^2 G^2 W - 2sFGW + t^2 W - 2tFW - 2tsGW\, dx \tag{7}$$
$$= e_1(a) + s^2 e_2 - 2se_3(a) + t^2 e_4 - 2te_5(a) + 2tse_6 \ . \tag{8}$$

Notice that (8) implies that $e_1$, $e_3$ and $e_5$ are functions of $a$, while $e_2$, $e_4$ and $e_6$ are constants (since $g$ and $w$ shift with each other). Only the integrals that involve $f$ with $g$ or $w$ change with respect to $a$. For any given value of $a$, (8) is a paraboloid in $s$ and $t$ that opens upward. The minimum value of the paraboloid can be determined analytically by solving a simple $2 \times 2$ linear system of equations. Hence, for a fixed $a$-value, the optimal $s$- and $t$-values are given by

$$\begin{bmatrix} s \\ t \end{bmatrix} = \frac{1}{e_2 e_4 - e_6^2} \begin{bmatrix} e_4 & -e_6 \\ -e_6 & e_2 \end{bmatrix} \begin{bmatrix} e_3 \\ e_5 \end{bmatrix} . \tag{9}$$

Although the theory derived here is for 1D functions, it can easily be generalized to higher dimensions. For the remainder of this paper, we will focus on 2D images.

## 2.4 Algorithmic Complexity

All the above analysis involving the Fourier transform also carries over to the discrete Fourier transform (DFT). The discrete 2D analog for (3) is

$$L_W(a) = \sum_{i=1}^{N} \sum_{j=1}^{N} [f_{i,j} - g_{i-a,j-b}]^2 \, w_{i-a,j-b} \, . \tag{10}$$

In this section, we compare the cost (measured in floating point operations, or flops) of computing the optimal solution for (10) by the direct computation method, to the cost of evaluating (10) by performing convolution in the frequency domain.

Suppose $f$ and $g$ are $N \times N$ images. The direct method to evaluate (10) involves simply evaluating the double-sum for every valid shift $(a, b)$. For a single value of $(a, b)$, evaluating the double-sum requires adding together $N^2$ terms, and each term requires one subtraction and two multiplications (since squaring is a multiplication). Thus, at 3 flops per term, the double-sum takes $(3N^2 + N^2 - 1)$ flops to evaluate. Since there are $N^2$ values of $(a, b)$, evaluating (10) for all values of $(a, b)$ takes $(4N^4 - N^2)$ flops.

However, evaluating (10) by calculating the convolutions in the frequency domain (via the form in (4)) takes $\mathcal{O}(N^2 \log N)$ flops. This is because the Fast Fourier Transform (FFT) of an $N \times N$ image takes at most $4N^2 \log_2 N$ complex operations (a complex multiplication followed by a complex addition) [8]. Each complex operation requires 8 flops, so the FFT takes at most $32N \log_2 N$ flops. To find the minimum of (4), a total of 5 FFTs need to be performed: FFTs of $f$, $f^2$, $\bar{w}$, $\bar{h}$, and an inverse FFT to transform the measure back to the spatial domain. This brings the total number of flops to perform the FFTs to $160N^2 \log_2 N$. Other than the FFTs, the remaining tasks are all $\mathcal{O}(N^2)$. These tasks include evaluating the middle term in (4), and performing the element-by-element multiplication of the Fourier transforms.

In many applications, the weighting function $w$ is zero for a large portion of the domain. To analyze this situation, assume that $w$ is non-zero over a domain of size $M \times M$, where $M < N$. Then, the sum in (10) has only $M^2$ terms, and hence the cost of evaluating it directly for a single value of $a$ is $(3M^2 + M^2 - 1)$ flops, and the cost of evaluating it directly for all values of $a$ is $(4N^2M^2 - N^2)$ flops, or $\mathcal{O}(N^2M^2)$.

Unfortunately, the Fourier method is not any cheaper to evaluate when $M < N$; the cost is the same as if $w$ were nonzero everywhere. However, the Fourier method is still cheaper than the direct method if $M^2 > \log N$.

The above complexity analysis is for the simple weighted SSD cost function that does not include any intensity remapping. However, similar results are obtained for the more complicated intensity remapping method. In (8), the terms $e_1(a)$, $e_3(a)$ and $e_5(a)$ all involve convolutions.

## 3 Methods

We implemented both the direct method and the Fourier method in the C++ programming language. All the Fourier transforms were done using the FFTW library [9]. Image data was stored in contiguous memory to improve the cache coherency (i.e. to cut down on the number of cache misses). The direct method evaluates the error norm for only those shifts that have the entire window (non-zero part of $w$) completely inside $f$.

On a set of satellite images from Intermap Technologies Inc. (Englewood, Colorado), we timed how long each method took to find the optimal shift and intensity remapping parameters. The timings were run on a 2.4 GHz Intel Pentium 4 machine with 2 gigabytes of RAM.

The images were shrunken to various sizes to get a more complete picture of their performance on different scales. Figure 1 shows the two images that were used, and the window for comparison. For the largest set of images, $f$ had dimensions $3008 \times 3780$, $g$ and $w$ had dimensions $3078 \times 3845$, and the window had dimensions $490 \times 2460$. The four scaled-down sets of images had roughly $\frac{1}{2}$, $\frac{1}{4}$, $\frac{1}{9}$ and $\frac{1}{25}$ the number of pixels in each image.

## 4 Results and Discussion

In all tests, both methods successfully determined the optimal translation and intensity remapping parameters. Figure 2 shows the absolute difference image of the two images merged using the optimal shift. The region of overlap is nearly zero, indicating that the match is excellent.

The timing results are summarized in Fig. 3(a). The figure is a log-log plot graphing the number of pixels in $f$ (the source image) against the running time in seconds. Note that $f$, $g$ and $w$ were all scaled equally for each execution. The straight line of the direct method indicates that there is a power-law relationship between the scale of the problem (in terms of number of pixels in $f$) and the running time. The fact that the slope of the line is approximately 2 (with respect to the logarithm of the axis labels) fits with the algorithmic complexity derived earlier. In particular, it says that the computation time is proportional to the square of the number of pixels in $f$ (where $f$ is $N \times N$).

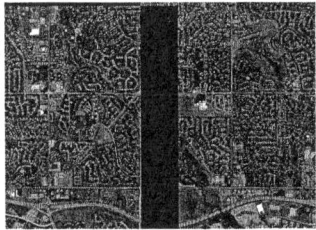

**Fig. 2.** Difference image of registered images

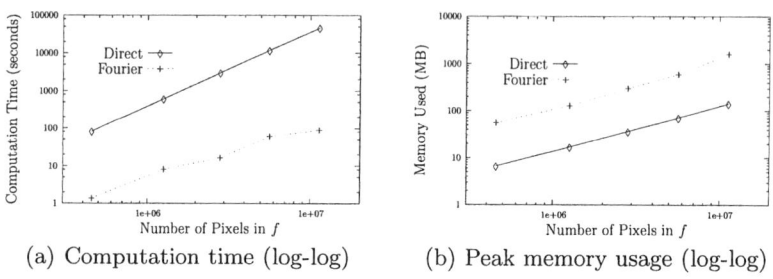

(a) Computation time (log-log)   (b) Peak memory usage (log-log)

**Fig. 3.** Computation time and peak memory usage for the direct method and the Fourier method. For each run, each of the images $f$, $g$ and $w$ were resized using the same scale factor. Note that all axes are plotted in log scale.

The graph for the Fourier method is not as easy to interpret. However, the graph is consistent with the complexity class derived above: $\mathcal{O}(N^2 \log N)$.

To get a better feel for the meaning of Fig. 3(a), let us consider some example timings. For the smallest dataset, in which $f$ and $g$ are roughly 615 × 760 and the window is 96 × 480, the Fourier method took 1.36 seconds and the direct method took 83.7 seconds. For the largest images, in which $f$ and $g$ are roughly 3008 × 3780 and the window is 490 × 2460, the Fourier method took 88 seconds and the direct method took 46,873 seconds (just over 7 hours).

It should be noted that the prime factorization of the dimensions of $f$ play a role in the speed of the Fourier method. The FFT is a divide-and-conquer algorithm and is most efficient when the length of the data can be factored into a product of small prime numbers. The above experiments represent a rather optimistic scenario, in which the dimensions of $f$ have lots of small prime factors: $3008 = (2)^6(47)$, and $3780 = (2)^2(3)^3(5)(7)$. However, the slow-down is not terribly significant for less fortunate image dimensions. If $f$ has dimensions 3019 × 3796 (3019 is a prime number, and $3296 = (2)^2(13)(73)$), the Fourier method takes 168 seconds, slower by a factor of approximately 2.

The memory use by the two methods is also quite different. Figure 3(b) is a log-log plot showing the peak memory usage (in megabytes), again with the number of pixels in $f$ on the horizontal axis. Both methods show a straight line with a slope of roughly 1 (with respect to the log of the axis labels). Hence, as we might expect, the memory requirements go up linearly with the number of pixels. However, the Fourier method used about eight times as much memory as the direct method (using over 1.5 gigabytes to process the largest image set). The reason for this is that the images have to be stored as complex numbers (single-precision). Another reason is that the Fourier method has to compute and store $e1$, $e3$ and $e5$ in their entirety before evaluating $L_R(a,s,t)$. The direct method can calculate these values one trial shift at a time. Furthermore, the direct method does not need to store all of $g$ and $w$, only the parts corresponding to where $w$ is non-zero. Our implementation takes advantage of this shortcut.

## 5 Conclusions and Future Work

When registering two images that are translated with respect to each other, the SSD cost function involves a convolution term. Variants of the problem, including the addition of a weighting factor and linear intensity remapping, still yield convolution terms. The computational advantage of evaluating these terms in the frequency domain is very substantial. In our experiments, the Fourier method was at least 60 times faster (in some cases over 500 times faster) than the direct method. The trade-off is the mount of memory required by the methods; the Fourier method used about eight time as much memory as the direct method.

In most imaging applications, the original data to be aligned is real-valued (i.e. the imaginary part is zero). For real-valued data, the FFT can be done faster by taking advantage of the symmetry in the Fourier coefficients. Indeed, the FFTW library has methods to compute the FFT of a real-valued dataset, outputting a half-size set of Fourier coefficients (avoiding the redundancy caused by the symmetry). Adapting the Fourier method described in this paper to take advantage of this efficiency is trivial.

It should be noted that the direct method has some advantages. For example, the cost function can be evaluated for a subset of trial shifts, while the Fourier method is an inherently global operation. Thus, if the approximate registration is known, it might be more effective to directly evaluate the cost function for sample shifts around that initial guess rather than performing a global search using the Fourier method. However, for the direct method to be faster on the largest image set, fewer than 0.2% of the possible shifts could be sampled. More than that and the Fourier method would be faster.

The SSD error measure is not necessarily the best cost function for registering images. Which error norm is best will depend on a number of factors, such as the type of noise present in the images. Some examples of other norms are the $\mathcal{L}^1$ norm, total variation [10], and robust estimators [11,12]. It may be feasible to expand these error norms using a Taylor series. The convolution terms in the Taylor series could then be evaluated in the frequency domain. The problem is that more terms makes the Fourier method more expensive, and it is not clear which error norms will still be faster using this approach. More work to investigate other norms is needed.

## Acknowledgment

We would like to thank Intermap Technologies Inc. for supplying the satellite image dataset. We also thank the Natural Science and Engineering Research Council (NSERC) of Canada for their financial support.

## References

1. Hill, D.L.G., Hawkes, D.J.: Across-modality registration using intensity-based cost functions. In Bankman, I., ed.: Handbook of Medical Imaging: Processing and Analysis. Academic Press (2000) 537–553

2. Woods, R.P.: Within-modality registration using intensity-based cost functions. In Bankman, I.N., ed.: Handbook of Medical Imaging: Processing and Analysis. Academic Press (2000) 529–536
3. Maas, L.C., Frederick, B.D., Renshaw, P.F.: Decoupled automated rotational and traslational registration for fMRI time series data: the DART registration algorithm. Magnetic Resonance in Medicine **37** (1997) 131–139
4. Pipe, J.G.: Motion correction with PROPELLER MRI: Application to head motion and free-breathing cardiac imaging. Magnetic Resonance in Medicine **42** (1999) 963–969
5. Ehman, R.L., Felmlee, J.P.: Adaptive technique for high-definition MR imaging of moving structures. Radiology **173** (1989) 255–263
6. Wang, Y., Grimm, R., Felmlee, J., Riederer, S., Ehman, R.: Algorithms for extracting motion information from navigator echoes. Magnetic Resonance in Medicine **36** (1996) 117–123
7. Orchard, J.: Simultaneous Registration and Activation Detection: Overcoming Activation-Induced Registration Errors in Functional MRI. PhD thesis, Simon Fraser University (2003)
8. Cooley, J.W., Tukey, J.W.: An algorithm for the machine calculation of complex fourier series. Mathematics of Computation **19** (1965) 297–301
9. Frigo, M., Johnson, S.G.: The design and implementation of FFTW3. Proceedings of the IEEE, Special Issue on Program Generation, Optimization, and Platform Adaptation **93** (2005) 216–231
10. Li, Y., Santosa, F.: A computational algorithm for minimizing total variation in image restoration. IEEE Transactions on Image Processing **5** (1994) 987–995
11. Nestares, O., Heeger, D.J.: Robust multiresolution alignment of MRI brain volumes. Magnetic Resonance in Medicine **43** (2000) 705–715
12. Nikou, C., Heitz, F., Armspach, J.P., Namer, I.J., Grucker, D.: Registration of MR/MR and MR/SPECT brain images by fast stochastic optimization of robust voxel similarity measures. NeuroImage **8** (1998) 30–43

# Isotropic Blur Identification for Fully Digital Auto-focusing*

Jeongho Shin, Sunghyun Hwang, Seong-Won Lee, and Joonki Paik

Image Processing and Intelligent Systems Laboratory,
Department of Image Engineering,
Graduate School of Advanced Imaging Science, Multimedia, and Film,
Chung-Ang University, 221 Huksuk-Dong, Tongjak-Ku, Seoul 156-756, Korea
paikj@cau.ac.kr
http://ipis.cau.ac.kr

**Abstract.** In this paper, we propose a blur identification for fully digital auto-focusing (FDAF) techniques under the assumption of isotropic point spread function (PSF). The proposed blur identification starts with the estimation of one-dimensional (1D) step response, and estimate the two-dimensional (2D) PSF using the fundamental relationship between the step and the impulse responses. For more accurate blur identification, we present the PSF interpolation method that fills out the PSF element off the concentric circle. We also propose least squares 2D PSF solutions that robustly estimates the strength of the concentric circles under noisy, incomplete observation environment. Experimental results prove that the proposed blur identification method outperforms the existing ones in the sense of both accuracy and efficiency.

## 1 Introduction

As digital image processing techniques widely spread to various application areas, low-cost, high-quality imaging technology gains attraction in consumer, communication, and computer industry. However, degradation of image quality is unavoidable due to unskillful user's operation or the insufficient depth-of-field of camera lens. Among various image degradation factors, focusing is the most important one that determines the quality of processed image. In order to prevent out-of-focus in an image acquisition process, most commercial products adopt an auto-focusing (AF) system. A fully digital auto-focusing (FDAF) consists of analysis and control modules, both of which are completely realized by digital signal processing only [1]. The FDAF's analysis module estimates a point spread function (PSF) to measure a degree-of-focus on hand. In the control module, an out-of-focus image is restored with the PSF estimated in the analysis module.

---

* This work was supported by Korean Ministry of Science and Technology under the National Research Laboratory Project, by Korean Ministry of Information and Communication under the Chung-Ang University HNRC-ITRC program, and by the Korea Research Foundation Grant funded by Korean Government (MOEHRD)(R08-2004-000-10626-0).

Because the PSF should be obtained from the blurred image itself, the FDAF falls into the category of blind image restoration.

In this paper, we extensively unfold and improve the algorithm proposed in [1,3] to estimate the PSF for the analysis module based on boundary information from the image itself, which are the degraded edges. Moreover, we propose an interpolated isotropic PSF model and an associated algorithm to find useful edges and estimate more accurate PSF coefficients. By modeling the isotropic PSF as a function of linear combination of the PSF coefficients, we can reduce the number of PSF coefficients. An out-of-focused input image is modeled as the output of a two-dimensional (2D) linear system with finite impulse response, and it is assumed that the original image involves ideal step edges. The edges blurred by 2D convolution of the ideal step edges with 2D PSF then provide information of the transfer function in the degradation system. After gathering the information of the PSF from blurred edges, we can estimate the PSF by solving linear simultaneous equations which will be derived from relation between 2D PSF and blurred edge later. This relationship and the corresponding method for solving the linear simultaneous equations will be intensively covered in this paper.

In Section 2, a novel blur identification algorithm is proposed. We also present a new representation model of isotropic PSF and a robust 2D PSF estimation in the same section. In section 3, we demonstrate the better performance of the proposed blur identification algorithm, and the results identifying the synthetic blurs with various types are compared to the existing blur identification techniques. Finally, we conclude this paper in Section 4.

## 2 Isotropic Blur Identification

In this section, we present a blur identification algorithm for the FDAF under the assumption of isotropic PSF.

### 2.1 2D Isotropic PSF Model

The discrete approximation of an isotropic PSF is shown in Fig. 1. As shown in Fig. 1, many pixels are locate off concentric circles within the region defined as

$$S_R = \left\{ (m,n) \big| \sqrt{m^2 + n^2} \leq R \right\}, \quad (1)$$

where $R$ is the radius of the PSF and $(m,n)$ represents the position of pixels in the 2D coordinate. Elements of the PSF within $S_R$ are geometrically represented in Fig. 1. Each pixel within the support $S_R$ is located either on the concentric circles or not. Pixels on a concentric circle follow the model described in [1]. On the other hand, pixels off a concentric circle should be interpolated by using adjacent pixel on the concentric circle as

$$h(m,n) = \begin{cases} \alpha a_r + \beta a_{r+1}, & \text{if}(m,n) \in S_R, \\ 0, & \text{elsewhere,} \end{cases} \quad (2)$$

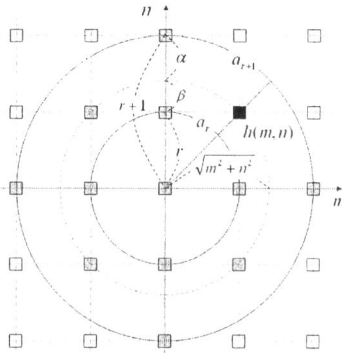

**Fig. 1.** Geometrical representation of a 2D isotropic discrete PSF: The gray rectangles represent pixels within the radius of PSF and the empty ones are pixels out of the radius of PSF

where $a_r$ and $a_{r+1}$ respectively represent the $r$th and the $r+1$st entries of the vector, $\mathbf{a} = [a_0 a_1 \cdots a_R]^T$. In (2), the index $r$ is determined as

$$r = \lfloor \sqrt{m^2 + n^2} \rfloor, \qquad (3)$$

where $\lfloor \cdot \rfloor$ is the truncation operator to integer. Based on Fig. 1, $\alpha$ and $\beta$ are determined as

$$\alpha = r - 1 + \sqrt{m^2 + n^2}, \text{ and } \beta = 1 - \alpha. \qquad (4)$$

This approximation of 2D discrete PSF is available to the popular isotropic blurs, such as Gaussian out-of-focus blur, uniform out-of-focus blur, and x-ray scattering.

### 2.2 Detection of Feasible Edges

In order to get extract PSF information from a blurred edge, there should not be any influence on the corresponding edge from any other adjacent edges. We call it a feasible edge that satisfies two conditions: (i) linearity and (ii) uniqueness in the region-of-interest. In order to detect the feasible edge, we first find vertical and horizontal edge maps. By applying each *Sobel operator* to the blurred image, we can separately get vertical and horizontal edge maps. By merging these edge maps using the logical sum of Boolean operation, we get a new edge map containing both vertical and horizontal edges. Then, for finding edges that satisfy the uniqueness condition, we apply a spatial shape constraints to the edge map.

### 2.3 Least Squares PSF Estimation

In this subsection, we propose an advanced PSF estimation algorithm without any recursive procedure or iterative optimization. In order to estimate all PSF coefficients, we use the fundamental relationship between 2D PSF and 1D step response. The in-focused pattern image $f_P(k,l)$ can be represented as

$$f_P(k,l) = \begin{cases} i_L, & \text{if } 0 \leq k < N, \text{ and } 0 \leq l < t, \\ i_H, & \text{if } 0 \leq k < N, \text{ and } t \leq l < N, \end{cases} \quad (5)$$

where the constant $t$ represents the boundary of left and right in the pattern image, i.e. the pattern image has two regions whose flat intensity values are $i_L$ and $i_H$, respectively. The blurred pattern image $g_P(k,l)$ is obtained by convolving (2) and (5) as

$$g_P(k,l) = \begin{cases} i_L, & \text{if } 0 \leq k < N, \text{ and } 0 \leq l < t - R, \\ s(l), & \text{if } 0 \leq k < N, \text{ and } t - R \leq l \leq t + R, \\ i_H, & \text{if } 0 \leq k < N, \text{ and } t + R < l < N, \end{cases} \quad (6)$$

where $R$ is the radius of the PSF, and the sequence $s(l)$ represents the 1D step response and $\{s(l)\}_{l=t-R}^{t+R} = \{s(t-R), \cdots, s(t), \cdots, s(t+R)\} = \{s_0, s_1, \cdots, s_{2R}\}$. The radius of the PSF is straightforwardly determined by the starting and ending positions of the 1D step response as,

$$R = \frac{\text{Ending position-Starting position-1}}{2}. \quad (7)$$

At each feasible edge point obtained in the previous subsection, the 1D step response is extracted along the direction orthogonal to the edge. For suppressing noise effect, if the number of useful edge points is $K$, all 1D step responses are averaged as

$$\bar{\mathbf{s}} = \frac{1}{K} \sum_{j=1}^{K} \mathbf{s}^j, \quad (8)$$

where $\mathbf{s}^j$ represents the vector of step response corresponding to the $j$th edge. The normalized 1D step response is obtained as

$$\hat{\mathbf{s}} = \frac{1}{s_{2M}} \left( \bar{\mathbf{s}} - [i_L]_{(2M+1) \times 1} \right), \quad (9)$$

where $[i_L]_{(2M+1) \times 1}$ denotes a $(2M+1) \times 1$ dimensional vector whose elements are equal to $i_L$.

Each observed 1D step response corresponds to partial summation of the PSF as

$$s_i = (i_H - i_L) \left[ \sum_{m=-R}^{R} \sum_{n=-R}^{-R+i} h(m,n) \right] + i_L, \quad 0 \leq i \leq 2R. \quad (10)$$

After unpacking the summation in (10), simplifying the equation yields the following 2R+1 linear simultaneous equations:

$$\begin{aligned} s_0 &= (i_H - i_L)\{h(0,-R) + 2[h(1,-R) + \cdots + h(R,-R)]\} + i_L, \\ s_1 &= (i_H - i_L)\{h(0,-R+1) + 2[h(1,-R+1) + \cdots + h(R,-R+1)]\} + s_0, \\ &\vdots \\ s_{2R} &= (i_H - i_L)\{h(0,R) + 2[h(1,R) + \cdots + h(R,R)]\} + s_{2R-1}. \end{aligned} \quad (11)$$

Furthermore, using the discrete approximation, we can substitute all PSF elements into linear combination of free coefficients of the PSF as derived in (2). For examples, the first and the last equations in (11) always become

$$s_0 = (i_H - i_L)a_R + i_L, \quad \text{and} \quad s_{2R} = (i_H - i_L)a_R + s_{2R-1}. \tag{12}$$

Equations (11) can be rewritten in a compact matrix-vector form as

$$\mathbf{s} = \mathbf{D}\mathbf{a}, \tag{13}$$

where $s$ is a $2R+1$-dimensional vector defined as

$$\mathbf{s} \equiv \frac{1}{(i_H - i_L)}\begin{bmatrix} s_0 - i_L & s_1 - i_L & \cdots & s_{2R} - i_L \end{bmatrix}^T, \tag{14}$$

and $\mathbf{a}$ is a $R+1$ dimensional coefficients vector. The $(2R+1) \times (R+1)$ matrix $\mathbf{D}$ is not specified in a closed form, but has a form of

$$\mathbf{D}^T = \begin{pmatrix} 0 & \cdots & 0 & \times & \cdots & \times \\ \vdots & & & \times & \cdots & \times \\ 0 & \times & \cdots & \times & \cdots & \times \\ \times & \times & \cdots & \times & \cdots & \times \end{pmatrix}, \tag{15}$$

where ×'s denote arbitrary nonzero entries. In equation (14) uncorrupted data $\mathbf{s}$ should be contaminated by the noise which was added to the degradation process. If $\mathbf{s}$ contains measurement error, then the corrupted version $\hat{\mathbf{s}}$ can be represented as

$$\hat{\mathbf{s}} = \mathbf{D}\mathbf{a} + \mathbf{e}. \tag{16}$$

Because the measurement error $\mathbf{e}$ is unknown, the best we can then do is to choose an estimator $\hat{\mathbf{a}}$ that minimizes the effect of the errors in some sense. For mathematical convenience, a natural choice is to consider the least-squares criterion,

$$\varepsilon_{LS} = \frac{1}{2}\|\mathbf{e}\|^2 = \frac{1}{2}(\hat{\mathbf{s}} - \mathbf{D}\mathbf{a})^T(\hat{\mathbf{s}} - \mathbf{D}\mathbf{a}) \tag{17}$$

Minimization of the least-squares error in (17) with respect to the unknown coefficients a leads to so-called *normal equations* [4]

$$(\mathbf{D}^T\mathbf{D})\hat{\mathbf{a}}_{LS} = \mathbf{D}^T\hat{\mathbf{s}}, \tag{18}$$

which determines the least-squares estimate $\hat{\mathbf{a}}_{LS}$ of $\mathbf{a}$. Note that the shape of the observation matrix $\mathbf{D}$ guarantees its columns to be independent. Thus, the $(R+1) \times (R+1)$ *Grammian matrix* is *positive-definite* [4] and we can explicitly solve the normal equations by rewriting (18) as

$$\hat{\mathbf{a}}_{LS} = (\mathbf{D}^T\mathbf{D})^{-1}\mathbf{D}^T\hat{\mathbf{s}} = \mathbf{D}^+\hat{\mathbf{s}}, \tag{19}$$

where $(\mathbf{D}^T\mathbf{D})^{-1}\mathbf{D}^T$ is the pseudoinverse of $\mathbf{D}$. The optimal coefficients $\hat{\mathbf{a}}_{LS}$ are used in constructing PSF which was modeled in (2).

Once the PSF has been constructed, our blind image restoration now becomes a general image restoration problem [6]. Although we use a constraint least squares (CLS) filter to resolve the image restoration problem with *a posterior* PSF, any image restoration technique can be applied.

## 3 Experimental Results

In this section, we present various experimental results not only for comparison with the conventional PSF estimation algorithms but also for evaluating the proposed algorithm with real out-of-focus images. Test images were captured with the Nikon-D100 digital camera on a gas-stabilized optical table to avoid another blurring artifact such as motion blur.

The algorithms to be compared include the nonparametric expectation maximization (EM) algorithm [2] and the isotropic blur estimation-based algorithm proposed [1,3]. In order to show the performance of the proposed blur identification algorithm, we deal with the synthetically blurred images by two different types of PSFs. For the simulation, we used a 256×256 resolution chart image. We synthetically made an out-of-focused version of the original image by convolving with truncated 3 × 3 Gaussian as

$$\begin{bmatrix} 0.0751 & 0.1238 & 0.0751 \\ 0.1238 & 0.2042 & 0.1235 \\ 0.0751 & 0.1235 & 0.0751 \end{bmatrix} \qquad (20)$$

where the variance of Gaussian function, $\sigma_G = 1$, was used. BSNR 30dB Gaussian noise was added after the simulated out-of-focus blur. As the first step of the proposed AF algorithm, the feasible edges should be extracted from the blurred image according to the algorithm described in Section 2.2. The 1D step responses used for estimating the 2D PSF was obtained from the final edge map by using the scheme proposed in Section 2.3. As the result of the averaging and normalizing, each step response could be estimated. In this case, the resulting, normalized 1D step response is overestimated because the entire energy of unknown PSF is included. Threrefore, we overestimate the radius of the 2D PSF to extract more samples in the 1D step responses. This process can cover the modeling error mentioned in Section 2.1. Both PSFs obtained by the proposed method and by other existing algorithms are given in Table 1. The PSF identified

**Table 1.** 2D PSF estimated with various algorithms for 3×3 truncated Gaussian out-of-focus blur

| The algorithm proposed in [1] | Nonparametric EM algorithm [2] | Proposed algorithm |
|---|---|---|
| $\begin{bmatrix} 0.0000 & 0.1699 & 0.0000 \\ 0.1699 & 0.3202 & 0.1699 \\ 0.0000 & 0.1699 & 0.0000 \end{bmatrix}$ | $\begin{bmatrix} 0.0842 & 0.1106 & 0.0787 \\ 0.1095 & 0.2338 & 0.1095 \\ 0.0787 & 0.1106 & 0.0842 \end{bmatrix}$ | $\begin{bmatrix} 0.0731 & 0.1699 & 0.0731 \\ 0.1242 & 0.2074 & 0.1242 \\ 0.0731 & 0.1242 & 0.0731 \end{bmatrix}$ |

by the nonparametric EM algorithm was obtained using 56 iterations including the other parameters as: two noise variances are $\sigma_v = 282.94$ and $\sigma_w = 4.1035$, and image model coefficients, $a_{01} = 0.8814$, $a_{10} = 0.8969$, and $a_{10} = -0.7812$. In this experiment, the EM algorithm started with $\sigma_v = 1.0$ and $\sigma_w = 1.0$, and the initial PSF being unit impulse. As shown in Table 1, the PSF estimated by the proposed algorithm is the most close to the Gaussian used for the simulated blur.

**Table 2.** 2D PSF estimated with various algorithms for 3×3 unform out-of-focus blur

| The algorithm proposed in [1] | Nonparametric EM algorithm [2] | Proposed algorithm |
|---|---|---|
| $\begin{bmatrix} 0.0000 & 0.1704 & 0.0000 \\ 0.1704 & 0.3202 & 0.1704 \\ 0.0000 & 0.1704 & 0.0000 \end{bmatrix}$ | $\begin{bmatrix} 0.0366 & 0.1623 & 0.0295 \\ 0.1634 & 0.2480 & 0.1634 \\ 0.0295 & 0.1623 & 0.0366 \end{bmatrix}$ | $\begin{bmatrix} 0.0000 & 0.1978 & 0.0000 \\ 0.1978 & 0.2087 & 0.1978 \\ 0.0000 & 0.1978 & 0.0000 \end{bmatrix}$ |

Uniform out-of-focus blur synthetically produced was also used for another experiment. The 2D PSF is as

$$\begin{bmatrix} 0.0 & 0.2 & 0.0 \\ 0.2 & 0.2 & 0.2 \\ 0.0 & 0.2 & 0.0 \end{bmatrix} \tag{21}$$

and BSNR 30dB additive Gaussian noise was further added to the blurred image. The correspondingly identified PSFs using three algorithms are tabulated in Table 2. The result of the EM algorithm is obtained using 66 iterations including

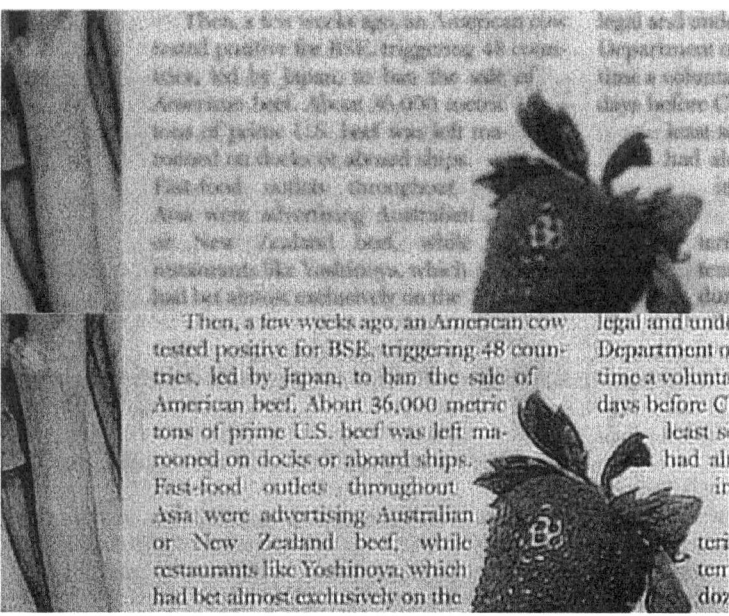

**Fig. 2.** The result of the proposed digital auto-focusing

$\sigma_v = 329.45$ and $\sigma_w = 4.5836$, $a_{01} = 0.8919$, $a_{10} = 0.9024$, and $a_{10} = -0.7977$ with the same initial condition of the previous experiment. While the algorithms proposed in [1] and [2] are not adequate for unknown type of PSF with support over $5 \times 5$ respectively because of inaccurate PSF model and the excessive number of parameters. In case of $5 \times 5$ blur, 17 parameters are needed. The proposed blur identification algorithm can estimate the PSF of relatively big size without any prior knowledge.

Finally, in order to show the performance of the proposed FDAF algorithm, out-of-focus images were restored. In Figs. 2, the upper and lower images respectively show an out-of-focused image and the corresponding restored image.

## 4 Conclusions

We have introduced a signal identification for FDAF technique under the assumption of isotropic PSF. The proposed identification method is compared with the similar, introductory version proposed by Kim [1] and a nonparametric EM-based algorithm by Lagendijk [2]. The two existing methods gives acceptable PSF identification results with synthetic, relatively small support ($3 \times 3$ in the experiment) out-of-focus blur. Kim's method, however, fails in estimation of the PSF when the support increases because of its PSF model is limited to a very small support. Similarly, the EM-based method also fails with larger, realistic out-of-focus blur because it requires estimation of 17 parameters for a $5 \times 5$ PSF and the estimation errors dramatically increases with larger supports. Application areas of the AF technique using the proposed blur identification include: light-weight, low-cost mobile imaging system, and automatic tracking and high-resolution recognition in video surveillance system.

## References

1. Kim, S.K., Park, S.R., Paik, J.K.: Simultaneous out-of-focus blur estimation and restoration for digital auto-focusing system. IEEE Trans. Consumer Electronics **34** (1998) 1071–1075
2. Lagendijk, R.L., Biemond, J., Boekee, D.E.: Identification and restoration of noisy blurred image using the expectation-maximization algorithm. IEEE Trans. Acoustic, Speech and Signal Processing **38** (1990) 1180–1191
3. Kim, S.K., Paik, J.K.: Out-of-focus blur estimation and restoration for digital auto-focusing system. Electronics Letters **34** (1998) 1217-1219
4. Noble, B., Daniel, J.: Applied Linear Algebra. Prentice Hall (1988)
5. Lun, D.P.K., Chan, T.C.L., Hsung, T.C., Feng, D.D., Chan, Y.H.: Efficient blind restoration using discrete periodic radon transform. IEEE Trans. Image Processing **13** (2004) 188–200
6. Katsaggelos, A.K.: Iterative image restoration algorithms. Optical Engineering **287** (1989) 735–748
7. Kundur, D., Hatzinakos, D.: Blind Image Deconvolution. IEEE Signal Processing Mag. **4** (1996) 43–64

# Edge Detection Models*

Q.H. Zhang, S. Gao, and Tien D. Bui

Department of Computer Science and Software Engineering,
Concordia University, Montreal, QC, Canada, H3G 1M8

**Abstract.** In this paper, the Mumford-Shah (MS) model and its variations are studied for image segmentation. It is found that using the piecewise constant approximation, we cannot detect edges with low contrast. Therefore other terms, such as gradient and Laplacian, are included in the models. To simplify the problem, the gradient of the original image is used in the Rudin-Osher-Fatemi (ROF) like model. It is found that this approximation is better than the piecewise constant approximation for some images since it can detect the low contrast edges of objects. Linear approximation is also used for both MS and ROF like models. It is found that the linear approximation results are comparable with the results of the models using gradient and Laplacian terms.

## 1 Introduction

One of the most difficult problems in image processing is image segmentation. In principle, we cannot formally define what is image segmentation. However, in practice, we have the following observations: For an observed image $u_0$ (possibly with noise), we try to find an optimal piecewise smooth approximation $u$ of $u_0$ for each specific region. The regions are denoted by $\Omega_i, i = 1, 2, ..., n$. The function $u$ varies smoothly within each $\Omega_i$, and rapidly or discontinuously across the boundaries of $\Omega_i$. The process of finding the boundaries of $\Omega_i$ is called segmentation. The boundaries of all $\Omega_i$ are denoted as $C$ and $\Omega_i$ is an open set. Therefore the whole image can be expressed as $\Omega = \bigcup \Omega_i \bigcup C$.

To find the boundary, many methods have been suggested. For example, Sobel and Laplace edge detectors have been used successfully to detect sharp edges of images. However Sobel and Laplace methods calculate the gradient and the second order derivative for each pixel of the observed image. Therefore, only the property of the neighboring pixels is used. These are local approaches. The global property of the input image is neglected in the these methods.

On the other hand, Mumford and Shah have proposed the following minimization problem [8,1,16,17]:

$$inf_{u,C}\{E_{MS}(u,C) = \alpha \int_{\Omega \setminus C} (u - u_0)^2 dxdy + \mu \int_{\Omega \setminus C} |\nabla u|^2 dxdy + \nu |C|\}, \quad (1)$$

---

* This work was supported by research grants from the Natural Sciences and Engineering Research Council of Canada.

where $\mu, \nu, \alpha > 0$ are parameters which can be considered as weight factors. The problem is to find $u$ and $C$ such that the above energy is minimal. $C$ is the set of segmentation curves and $u$ is the approximation of $u_0$. Since this approach takes the whole image into consideration, and tries to minimize the energy of the observed image, it is a global approach.

There are many variations of the Mumford-Shah model such as Rudin-Osher-Fatemi (ROF)[18] like model which can be expressed as the following minimization problem:

$$inf_{u,C}\{E_{ROF}(u,C) = \alpha \int_{\Omega \backslash C} (u-u_0)^2 dxdy + \mu \int_{\Omega \backslash C} |\nabla u| dxdy + \nu |C|\}, \quad (2)$$

The difference between MS and ROF like models comes from the second term. In the MS model, the $L^p$ norm with $p = 2$ of the gradient allows us to remove the noise but unfortunately penalizes too much the gradients corresponding to edges. One could then decrease $p$ in order to preserve the edges as much as possible. One of the first work in this direction is the ROF model[18].

## 2 Piecewise Constant Approximation

If we assume that $u$ is a constant in each region ($u = c$), Eq.(1) and Eq.(2) are of the same form, that is

$$inf_{u,C}\{E(u,C) = \alpha \int_{\Omega \backslash C} (c-u_0)^2 dxdy + \nu |C|\}. \quad (3)$$

Using the level set function $\phi(x,y)$[10]

$$\phi(x,y,t) = \begin{cases} > 0 & \text{if } (x,y) \text{ in } \Omega \\ = 0 & \text{if } (x,y) \text{ in } \delta\Omega \\ < 0 & \text{if } (x,y) \text{ in } \bar{\Omega} \end{cases}$$

and the Heaviside function $H(x)$, the two-phase version of Eq.(3) can be written as[2,13,14,4,5]

$$E(c_1, c_2, \phi) = \alpha \int_{inside\ C} (c_1 - u_0)^2 dxdy + \alpha \int_{outside\ C} (c_2 - u_0)^2 dxdy + \nu |C|$$
$$= \alpha \int_{\Omega} (c_1 - u_0)^2 H(\phi) dxdy + \alpha \int_{\Omega} (c_2 - u_0^2)(1 - H(\phi)) dxdy$$
$$+ \nu \int_{\Omega} |\nabla H(\phi)| dxdy \quad (4)$$

where $c_1$ and $c_2$ are constants.

We have the following level set equation:

$$\frac{\partial \phi}{\partial t} = -\delta(\phi)[(c_1 - u_0)^2 - (c_2 - u_0)^2 - \nu \nabla \cdot (\frac{\nabla \phi}{|\nabla \phi|})] \quad (5)$$

with the boundary condition $\frac{\delta(\phi)}{|\nabla\phi|}\nabla\phi\cdot\hat{n} = \frac{\delta(\phi)}{|\nabla\phi|}\frac{\partial\phi}{\partial n} = 0$. The final solution of Eq.(5) will minimize the function $E(c_1, c_2, \phi)$. Because $c_1$ and $c_2$ are constants, we have $\frac{\partial E}{\partial c_1} = \frac{\partial E}{\partial c_2} = 0$. Therefore, $c_1(\phi) = \frac{\int_\Omega u_0 H(\phi)dxdy}{\int_\Omega H(\phi)dxdy}$ and $c_2(\phi) = \frac{\int_\Omega u_0(1-H(\phi))dxdy}{\int_\Omega (1-H(\phi))dxdy}$.

## 3  ROF Model with Gradient Term

For the piecewise constant approximation, the second term of equations (1) and (2) does not appear and the MS and ROF models are the same. In this case, the whole image is segmented into different regions such that the variance inside each region is small. Therefore the low contrast edges in a region will not be detected since it will not cause much changes to the variance inside that region. In order to detect these small differences, we need to include the gradient term in Eq.(2) in our calculation. To include the gradient in the calculation means that we need to solve two PDEs[1,3,9,12]: one for $u$ inside and one for $u$ outside curve $C$. To simplify the problem we use the fact that the final solution of $u$ should be approximately $u_0$, we replace the second term of Eq.(2) by $\int |\nabla u_0|dxdy$. Thus, the ROF model becomes:

$$inf_{u,C}\{E(u,C) = \alpha \int_{inside\ C}(c_1-u_0)^2 dxdy + \alpha \int_{outside\ C}(c_2-u_0)^2 dxdy$$
$$+ \mu \int_{inside\ C}|\nabla u_0|dxdy + \nu|C|\}, \qquad (6)$$

Notice that for the gradient term, we only calculate the gradient inside $C$. The advantage of this approximation compared to the original ROF model is that the calculation is fast since we do not need to solve two coupled PDEs for $u$ inside and outside respectively. Therefore, it would be more useful for practical applications. The advantage of this approximation over the piecewise constant case is that more edges can be detected.

The level set equation becomes:

$$\frac{\partial\phi}{\partial t} = -\delta(\phi)[(c_1-u_0)^2 - (c_2-u_0)^2 + \mu|\nabla u_0| - \nu\nabla\cdot(\frac{\nabla\phi}{|\nabla\phi|})], \qquad (7)$$

with the boundary condition $\frac{\delta(\phi)}{|\nabla\phi|}\nabla\phi\cdot\hat{n} = 0$. It is clear that when $\mu \to 0$, Eq.(6) becomes Eq.(4).

## 4  ROF Model with High Order Derivative

In both the MS and the ROF original models, high order derivatives of $u$ are not included. We of course can include high order derivative term of $u$ in the models. For example, if we include second derivative of $u$ in ROF, then the ROF model becomes:

$$\inf_{u,C}\{E(u,C) = \alpha \int_{\Omega\setminus C}(u-u_0)^2 dxdy + \mu \int_{\Omega\setminus C}|\nabla u|dxdy +$$
$$+ \lambda \int_{\Omega\setminus C}|\Delta u|dxdy + \int \nu|C|\}, \tag{8}$$

In order to study only the Laplacian term effects on the segmentation, we will take $\mu = 0$ in Eq.(8). Using $u = u_0$ approximation in the third term of Eq.(8), the above equation for two phases becomes:

$$\inf_{u,C}\{E(u,C) = \alpha \int_{inside\ C}(c_1-u_0)^2 dxdy + \alpha \int_{inside\ C}(c_2-u_0)^2 dxdy$$
$$+ \lambda \int_{inside\ C}|\Delta u_0|dxdy + \int \nu|C|\}, \tag{9}$$

In the above, we have only included the Laplace term for the inside region. Thus, the level set equation changes to

$$\frac{\partial \phi}{\partial t} = -\delta(\phi)[(c_1-u_0)^2 - (c_2-u_0)^2 + \lambda|\Delta u_0| - \nu\nabla\cdot(\frac{\nabla\phi}{|\nabla\phi|})] \tag{10}$$

with the boundary condition $\frac{\delta(\phi)}{|\nabla\phi|}\nabla\phi\cdot\hat{n} = 0$

In ref[6], Lee, BenHamza and Krim have also included the Laplace term in their analysis. Where they have constructed an energy function as

$$\inf_{u,C}\{E(u,C) = \alpha \int_{inside\ C}(c_1-u_0)^2 dxdy + \alpha \int_{inside\ C}(c_2-u_0)^2 dxdy$$
$$+ \int \nu|C| + \beta A -$$
$$\gamma[\int_{inside\ C}|\Delta u_0|dxdy - \int_{outside\ C}|\Delta u_0|dxdy]\}, \tag{11}$$

Here $A$ is the area inside the curve. Due to the fact that $\int|\Delta u_0|dxdy$ is a constant for a given image. Therefore, the largest value of $\int_{outside\ C}|\Delta u_0|dxdy - \int_{inside\ C}|\Delta u_0|dxdy$ is the same as the minimum value of $\int_{inside\ C}|\Delta u_0|dxdy$. Therefore the model in Ref.[6] is similar to the above model. If $\lambda = 0$, Eq.(9) becomes Eq.(4).

## 5  Linear Approximations of MS and ROF Models

In the MS model, the second term in Eq.(1) leads $u$ to be smooth in each region. However $|\nabla u|$ becomes very large across the boundary line. Therefore the MS model can be used to detect discontinuities in the image surface. They can also be detected by the Chan-Vese (CV) model due to the fact that the variation of the image intensity across the regions becomes very large if the boundaries are step edges. But if the step edge is small, then this kind of boundary will be hard to detect.

In the following, we will use linear approximation instead of constant approximation. We will use a linear planar surface, $u(x,y) = a + b \cdot x + c \cdot y$, to approximate the inside of each region in this section. Here $a, b, c$ are constants. From here onward $\int$ means $\int_\Omega$ but for simplicity the $\Omega$ is omitted.

For the two-phase case, Eq.(1) and Eq.(2) become:

$$E_{MS}(u_1, u_2, \phi) = \alpha_1 \int (a_1 + b_1 x + c_1 y - u_0)^2 H(\phi) dx dy$$
$$+ \alpha_2 \int (a_2 + b_2 x + c_2 y - u_0)^2 (1 - H(\phi)) dx dy$$
$$+ \mu(b_1^2 + c_1^2) \int H(\phi) dx dy + \mu(b_2^2 + c_2^2) \int (1 - H(\phi)) dx dy +$$
$$\nu \int |\nabla H(\phi)| dx dy. \qquad (12)$$

and

$$E_{ROF}(u_1, u_2, \phi) = \alpha_1 \int (a_1 + b_1 x + c_1 y - u_0)^2 H(\phi) dx dy$$
$$+ \alpha_2 \int (a_2 + b_2 x + c_2 y - u_0)^2 (1 - H(\phi)) dx dy$$
$$+ \mu\sqrt{(b_1^2 + c_1^2)} \int H(\phi) dx dy + \mu\sqrt{(b_2^2 + c_2^2)} \int (1 - H(\phi)) dx dy +$$
$$\nu \int |\nabla H(\phi)| dx dy. \qquad (13)$$

We obtain the following level-set equations for Eq.(12) and Eq.(13):

$$\frac{\partial \phi}{\partial t} = -\delta(\phi)[-\nu \nabla \cdot \frac{\nabla \phi}{|\nabla \phi|} + \alpha_1 (a_1 + b_1 x + c_1 y - u_0)^2 + \mu(b_1^2 + c_1^2)$$
$$-\alpha_2 (a_2 + b_2 x + c_2 y - u_0)^2 - \mu(b_2^2 + c_2^2)] \qquad (14)$$

and

$$\frac{\partial \phi}{\partial t} = -\delta(\phi)[-\nu \nabla \cdot \frac{\nabla \phi}{|\nabla \phi|} + \alpha_1 (a_1 + b_1 x + c_1 y - u_0)^2 + \mu\sqrt{(b_1^2 + c_1^2)}$$
$$-\alpha_2 (a_2 + b_2 x + c_2 y - u_0)^2 - \mu\sqrt{(b_2^2 + c_2^2)}] \qquad (15)$$

with the same boundary condition as Eq.(5).

We can calculate $a_1, b_1, c_1$ via the following equations ($\alpha_1 = \alpha_2 = 1$)

$$a_1 \int H(\phi) dx dy + b_1 \int H(\phi) x dx dy + c_1 \int y H(\phi) dx dy = \int u_0 H(\phi) dx dy$$

$$a_1 \int x H(\phi) dx dy + b_1 \int (x^2 + \mu) H(\phi) dx dy$$
$$+ c_1 \int xy H(\phi) dx dy = \int x u_0 H(\phi) dx dy \qquad (16)$$

$$a_1 \int yH(\phi)dxdy + +b_1 \int xyH(\phi)dxdy + c_1 \int (y^2 + \mu)H(\phi)dxdy$$
$$= \int yu_0 H(\phi)dxdy$$

We have similar equation for $a_2, b_2, c_2$ but with $1 - H(\phi)$ replacing $H(\phi)$.

For the ROF model, we can calculate the $a_1, b_1, c_1$ using the following equations:

$$a_1 \int H(\phi)dxdy + b_1 \int H(\phi)xdxdy + c_1 \int yH(\phi)dxdy = \int u_0 H(\phi)dxdy$$

$$a_1 \int xH(\phi)dxdy + b_1 \int (x^2)H(\phi)dxdy + \frac{\mu b_1}{2\sqrt{b_1^2 + c_1^2}} \int H(\phi)dxdy$$

$$+c_1 \int xyH(\phi)dxdy = \int xu_0 H(\phi)dxdy \tag{17}$$

$$a_1 \int yH(\phi)dxdy + +b_1 \int xyH(\phi)dxdy + c_1 \int (y^2)H(\phi)dxdy$$

$$+\frac{\mu c_1}{2\sqrt{b_1^2 + c_1^2}} \int H(\phi)dxdy = \int yu_0 H(\phi)dxdy$$

We have similar equation for $a_2, b_2, c_2$ but with $1 - H(\phi)$ replacing $H(\phi)$.

## 6 Experimental Results

We have implemented the above models using one level set function. In Fig.1, the segmentation results of all the above models are shown. It is clear that the CV constant model cannot detect all the boundaries in the image. On the other hand, all other models give better segmentation results. This is not surprising at all. Since it is well known that gradient and Laplacian terms can detect the boundary very well for sharp edges. Therefore including the gradient and Laplacian terms in the CV model can give us better results. For linear approximation model of the MS and ROF models, we can expect some detail information inside each region $\Omega_i$.

In Fig.2, we have also used Chan-Vese piecewise constant approximation model, ROF like model with the gradient and Laplacian terms, the MS and ROF models with linear approximation for the car plate image. It is found that Chan-Vese piecewise constant approximation cannot detect the number 8 in the image while it is detected by other models.

## 7 Conclusions

We have applied different variations of the MS model and the ROF model for images segmentation. It is found that the piecewise constant approximation CV model cannot detect the edges with low contrast in the image. For this kind

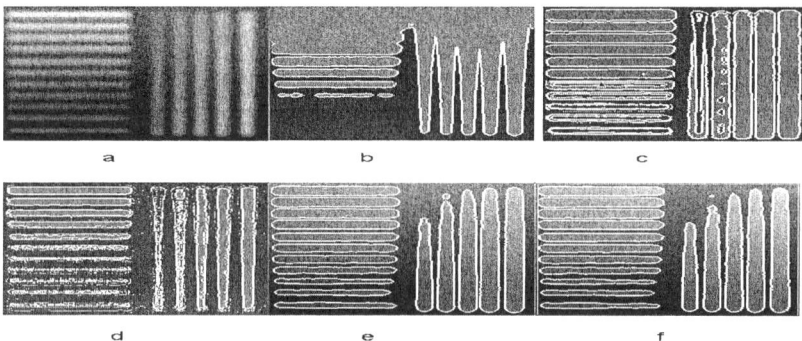

**Fig. 1.** First row: (a) original image, (b) Chan-Vese piecewise constant approximation. (c) ROF model with the gradient term. Second row: (d) ROF model with Laplacian term, (e) MS model with linear approximation, (f) ROF like model with linear approximation.

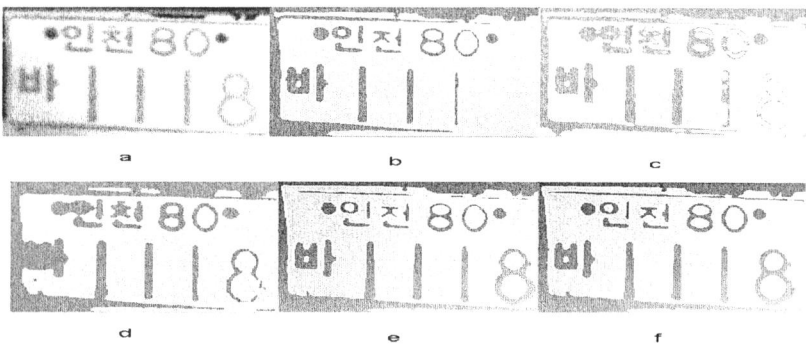

**Fig. 2.** First row: (a) original image, (b) Chan-Vese piecewise constant approximation. (c) ROF model with the gradient term. Second row: (d) ROF model with Laplacian term, (e) MS model with linear approximation, (f) ROF like model with linear approximation.

of edges, we need to include the gradient term in the original models. To do this, we can either use the original image to calculate the gradient or use linear approximation of the image function $u$. Linear approximation ROF-like model is also applied here and we find it produces similar results as the linear approximation of MS model. We also include the Laplacian term in the ROF model and we have found that ROF model with Laplacian term can produce better results than the piecewise constant approximation CV model.

# References

1. G. Aubert and P. Kornprobst, Mathematical Problems in Image Processing: Partial differential equations and the Calculus of Variations, Vol. 147 of Applied Mathematical Sciences, Springer-Verlag, 2002.

2. T. F. Chan and L. A. Vese, Active Contours without edges, IEEE transactions on Image Processing, 2001, 10(2): 266-277.
3. P. Charbonnier, L. Blanc-Feraud, G. Aubert, and M. Barlaud, Deterministic edge-preserving regularization in computer imaging, IEEE Trans. Image Process. 6, 1997, 298-311.
4. S. Gao and Tien D. Bui, Image Segmentation and Selective Smoothing by Using Mumford-Shah Model, to be published in IEEE Transaction on Image Processing.
5. S. Gao and Tien D. Bui, A new image segmentation and smoothing model, Proc. of IEEE int. Symposium on Biomedical Imaging: From Nano to Macro, pp. 137-140, Arlington, V.A., April 15-18, 2004.
6. B. R. Lee, A. Ben Hamza and H. Krim, An active contour model for image segmentation: a variational perspective. Proc. IEEE international conference on acoustics speech and Signal processing, Orlando, May 2002.
7. S. Z. Li, Roof-Edge Preserving Image Smoothing Based on MRFs, IEEE Transactions on Image Processing, Vol. 9, No. 6, June 2000, pp.1134-1138.
8. D. Mumford, and J. Shah, Optimal approximation by piecewise smooth functions and associated variational problems. Comm. Pure Appl. Math. 42 (1989) 577 -685.
9. F.A. Pellegrino, W. Vanzella, and V. Torre, Edge Detection Revisited, IEEE Transactions on Systems, Man, and Cybernetics Part B: Cybernetics, Vol. 34, No. 3, June 2004, pp.1500-1517.
10. J. A. Sethian, Level Set Methods and Fast Marching Methods, Cambridge University Press, 1999.
11. S. Teboul, L. Blanc-Feraud, G. Aubert, and M. Barlaud, Variational Approach for Edge-Preserving Regularization Using Coupled PDEs, IEEE Transactions on Image Processing, Vol. 7, No. 3, March 1998 387-397.
12. A. Tsai, A. Yezzi, and Alan S. Willsky, Curve Evolution Implementation of the Mumford-Shah Functional for Image Segmentation, Denoising, Interpolation, and Magnification, IEEE Tran. on Image Processing, Vol. 10 (8), 2001, 1169-1186.
13. L. Vese and T. F. Chan, A Multiphase Level Set Framework for Image Segmentation Using the Mumford and Shah Model, International Journal of Computer Vision 50(3), 271-293, 2002.
14. L. A. Vese, Multiphase Object Detection and Image Segmentation, in "Geometric Level Set Methods in Imaging, Vision and Graphics", S. Osher and N. Paragios (eds), Springer Verlag, 2003, pp. 175-194.
15. R.A. Weisenseel, W.C. Karl, D.A. Castanon, A region-based alternative for edge-preserving smoothing, Proceedings of the International Conference on Image Processing, 2000. pp. 778-781. Vancouver, BC, Canada.
16. A. Blake and A. Zisserman, Visual Reconstruction, The MIT Press Cambridge, Massachusetts, 1987.
17. W. Vanzella, F.A. Pellegrino, and V. Torre, Self-Adaptive Regularization, IEEE Transactions on PAMI, Vol. 26, No. 6, June 2004, pp.804-809.
18. L. Rudin, S. Osher and E. Fatemi, Nonlinear Total Variation Based Noise Removal, Physica D, Vol. 60 , 1992, 259-268.

# Video Stabilization Using Kalman Filter and Phase Correlation Matching*

Ohyun Kwon, Jeongho Shin, and Joonki Paik

Image Processing and Intelligent Systems Laboratory, Department of Image Engineering,
Graduate School of Advanced Imaging Science, Multimedia, and Film, Chung-Ang University,
221 Huksuk-Dong, Tongjak-Ku, Seoul 156-756, Korea
paikj@cau.ac.kr
http://ipis.cau.ac.kr

**Abstract.** A robust digital image stabilization algorithm is proposed using a Kalman filter-based global motion prediction and phase correlation-based motion correction. Global motion is basically estimated by adaptively averaging multiple local motions obtained by phase correlation. The distribution of phase correlation determines a local motion vector, and the global motion is obtained by suitably averaging multiple local motions. By accumulating the global motion at each frame, we can obtain the optimal motion vector that can stabilize the corresponding frame. The proposed algorithm is robust to camera vibration or unwanted movement regardless of object's movement. Experimental results show that the proposed digital image stabilization algorithm can efficiently remove camera jitter and provide continuously stabilized video.

## 1 Introduction

The unwanted movements and vibration caused by unstable camera support may critically degrade the quality of video in both objective and subjective senses. Such movement in a camera shot often causes an incorrect superposition of the current and the reference images as well as malfunction of typical change-detection algorithms. Since compact consumer video cameras with powerful zooms are often subject to amplified fluctuation of images caused by hand motion, various digital image stabilizing systems have been developed to improve the visual quality [1]. The digital image stabilization system can be divided into motion estimation and motion compensation systems. The motion estimation system computes inter-frame global motion vectors, which are forwarded to the motion compensation system. The motion compensation system stabilizes the image sequence according to the motion vector. Various digital image stabilizing systems have been developed to minimize motion degradation. A digital image stabilizer generally consists of motion estimation and motion compensation systems. Most motion estimation systems adapt either block matching [2,3,4] or phase correlation algorithms [5,6,7]. In block matching, various matching criteria

---

* This research was supported by Korean Ministry of Science and Technology under the National Research lab. Project and by Korean Ministry of Information and Communication under HNRC-ITRC program at Chung-Ang university supervised by IITA.

such as: point matching [3], edge pattern matching [2], gray-coded bit-plane matching [1], and block motion vectors filtering have been developed. However, block matching does not properly work without any clear pattern in the estimation region. Therefore, we use phase correlation for motion estimation.

In this paper, we propose digital image stabilization with Kalman filtering-based motion prediction and novel sub-pixel phase correlation-based motion correction. A frame motion vector (FMV) is estimated from local motion vectors (LMVs) of four rectangular sub-images, where phase correlation (PC)-based motion estimation is performed. Multiple LMVs are compared with the predicted FMV obtained by Kalman filter, and only qualified LMVs are averaged to produce the current frame's FMV. The finally obtained FMV performs the correction in the Kalman filter for the next frame prediction. Fig.1. shows the block diagram of proposed system. The FMV is accumulated to the previous match accumulated motion vector (AMV) to the current frame's position to that of the reference frame.

This paper is organized as follows: In Sec. 2, we summarize the sub-pixel phase correlation-based LMV estimation algorithm. Kalman filter-based FMV computation algorithm is described in Sec. 3. Experimental results and conclusions are respectively given in Secs. 4 and 5.

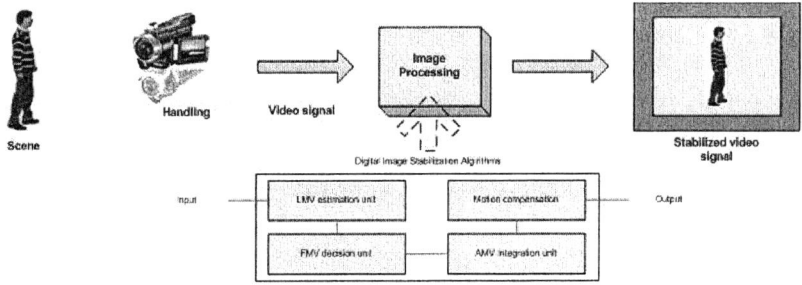

**Fig. 1.** Block diagram of the proposed digital image stabilization system

## 2   LMV Estimation by Phase Correlation

### 2.1   Phase Correlation

The phase correlation algorithm is based on the Fourier transform's shift property, which states that a shift in the coordinate frames of two functions is transformed to linear phase difference in the Fourier domain. This can be described as follows.

Let $f_k(x,y)$ and $f_{k+1}(x,y)$ be two functions that are absolutely integrable over $R^2$, and have the relationship as

$$f_{k+1}(x,y) = f_k(x-d_1, y-d_2). \tag{1}$$

According to the Fourier shift property we have that

$$\hat{f}_{k+1}(u,v) = \hat{f}_k(u,v)\exp\{-j2\pi(ud_1 + vd_2)\}, \tag{2}$$

where $\hat{f}$ represents the Fourier transform of $f$. Hence the normalized cross power spectrum is given as

$$\frac{\hat{f}_{k+1}(u,v)\hat{f}_k^*(u,v)}{\left|\hat{f}_k(u,v)\hat{f}_k^*(u,v)\right|} = \exp\{-j2\pi(ud_1 + vd_2)\}, \qquad (3)$$

where * represents the complex conjugate of the complex number. The normalized cross power spectrum may also be viewed as the cross power spectrum of whitened signals. There are two possible ways to solve (3) for $(d_1, d_2)$. One is to use, in the Fourier domain, a three-dimensional (3-D) Euclidean space whose canonical reference frame is given by the two frequency axes and the phase difference between the two images. A more practical, robust approach is to perform inverse Fourier transform of the normalized cross power spectrum. It becomes then straightforward to determine $(d_1, d_2)$, since, from (3), $\delta(x - d_1, y - d_2)$ is the Dirac delta function centered at $(d_1, d_2)$, which represents the displacement between the two images.

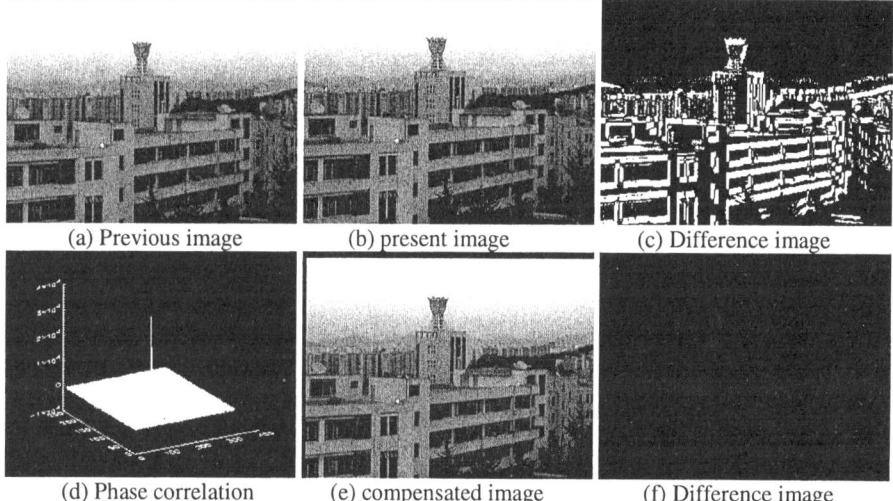

**Fig. 2.** (a) and (b) experimental images with a certain amount of displacements, (c) difference image between (a) and (b), (d) phase correlation, (e) compensated image, and (f) difference between (a) and (e)

### 2.2 LMV Estimation

In each image frame of a video, four sub-images are defined as shown in Fig. 3(a). These sub-images are used to determine LMVs using phase correlation. For efficient FFT computation, sub-images have square shape with horizontal and vertical pixel dimensions being a power of two. Typically a sub-image size of $64 \times 64$ is preferred to reduce the computational and at the same time keep sufficiently large area for correct estimation.

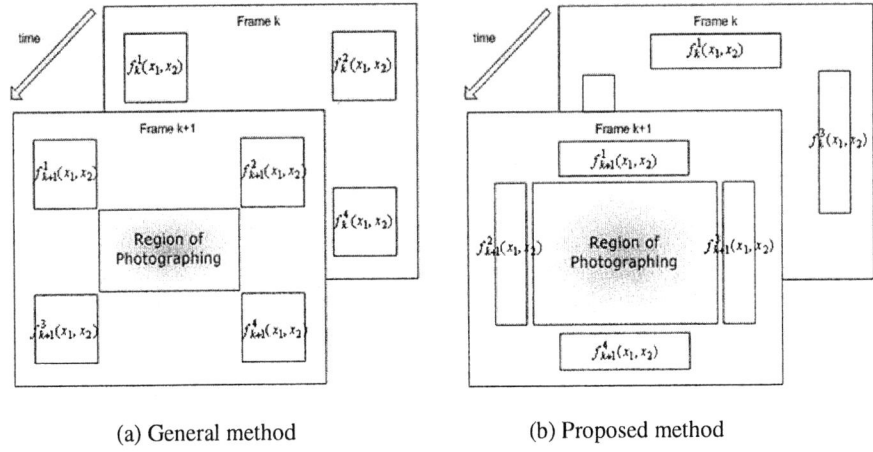

(a) General method      (b) Proposed method

**Fig. 3.** Two different arrangements of four sub-images

For all four sub-images in an image frame, LMVs are estimated from the corresponding sub-images of the previous frame based on phase correlation. For each sub-image the largest peak amplitude location of the corresponding phase correlation surface is assigned as the LMV with the corresponding peak amplitude. The FMV the image frame can then be decided by suitably combining information from four LMVs.

Fig. 3(a) shows a general method that uses square-shaped sub-images. In order to get more robust estimation, we proposed rectangular blocks as shown in Fig. 3(b). For efficient FFT computation, two blocks are combined into one square block as shown in Fig. 4. Fig. 4(a) could get more correct vertical motion vector and (b) could get more correct horizontal motion vector.

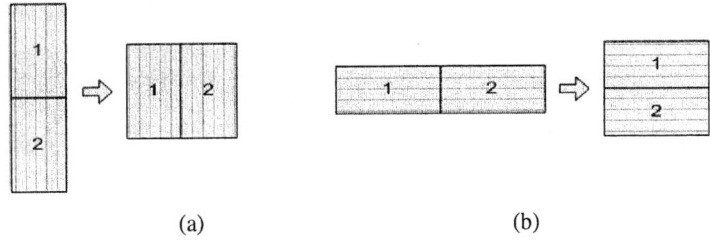

(a)      (b)

**Fig. 4.** Square block made by combining two rectangular blocks for phase correlation

The conceptual block diagram of the proposed stabilization system is shown in Fig. 1. The LMV estimation unit produces LMVs from sub-image in different positions of the frame. The FMV decision unit determines the FMV by processing four LMVs and the FMVs in the previous frames. The AMV integration unit accumulates FMVs in the consecutive image frames to produce the optimal motion vector that compensates the current frame to the reference frame. Finally, the stabilized image is generated by reading out the proper region of fluctuated image in the frame memory. The proposed motion estimation algorithm is shown in Fig. 5.

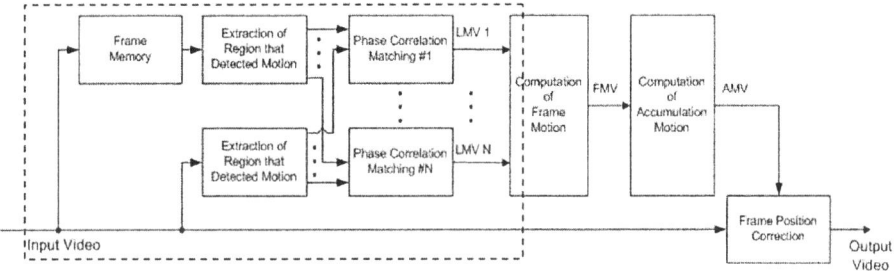

**Fig. 5.** Proposed motion estimation algorithm of stabilization system

## 3 FMV Prediction Using Adaptive Kalman Filter

In general, an LMV from a subimage with moving objects tends to be erroneous. So it should be excluded from the FMV decision process. Since the hand movement is relatively slower than the frame rate of the video camera, FMVs of two successive

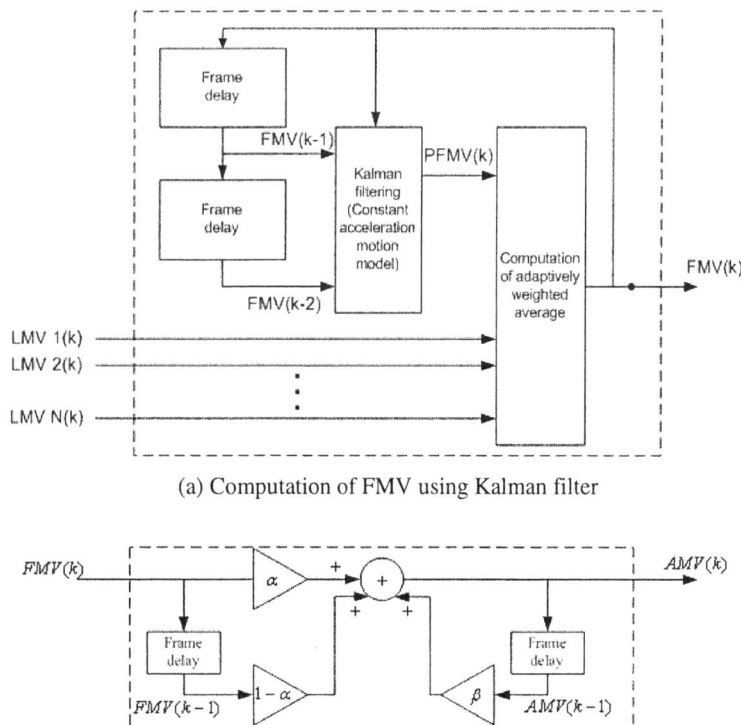

(a) Computation of FMV using Kalman filter

(a) Computation of AMV

**Fig. 6.** Block diagram of the proposed motion compensation system

frames fluctuated by camera's jitter should be similar. Based on these properties of camera's motion, we use a simple and robust motion prediction and correction scheme in which the FMV is determined by separately selecting the most maximum peak of each motion vector elements from subimage and using Kalman filter for selecting LMVs that are close to the predicted FMV. After determining the FMV, the motion correction system shown in Fig. 6 decides whether camera's motion or unintentional panning affects the motion of a frame.

An important point in motion compensation is the distinction between jiggling and panning. Jiggling is the oscillatory movement that has to be stabilized. It has no constant direction on consecutive frames and its amplitude is generally small. Panning is the wanted motion that user does to capture a wide area of the scene. It is directed in the same direction and displacements are bigger than jiggling. Vella presented distinction between jiggling and panning by a threshold, T, in [4]. If the absolute value of an FMV is larger than T, panning occurs non-preferably. In the similar way, even if the absolute value of the FMV is smaller than T, jiggling starts and it makes the image to become unstable. In this paper, we use AMV to deal with panning and jiggling [2]. The AMV computation procedure is given as

$$AMV[t] = kAMV[t-1] + \{\alpha FMV[t] + (1-\alpha)FMV[t-1]\}, \qquad (4)$$

where $t$ represents time index, the constant $k$, $0 \le k \le 1$ is used for smooth panning and virtually enlarging the effective AMV range, and $\alpha$, $0 \le \alpha \le 1$, is used for filtering out the unexpected noise effect on the AMV. The proposed motion compensation system is shown in Fig. 6.

## 4 Experimental Results

In order to demonstrate the performance of the proposed algorithm, we used a single image frame from SONY DCR-TRV900 camcorder. We tested $640 \times 480$ images in both outdoor and indoor. Block diagram of the experimental set up is shown in Fig. 7. We connected the camcorder to a computer by using a frame grabber. From RGB color image, we extracted only luminance component for motion estimation. After motion estimation and compensation we can display both the original and stabilized images at the same time.

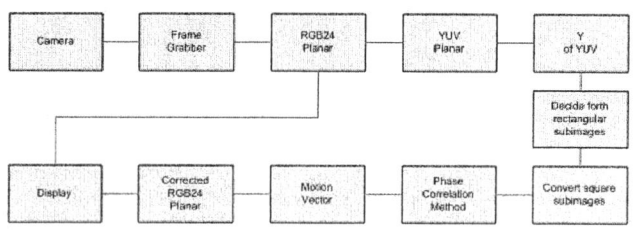

**Fig. 7.** Block diagram of the experimental set up

To show the performance of the proposed algorithm, Figure 8 shows the original image, stable image, and difference image in indoor and outdoor.

**Fig. 8.** Experimental results in indoor and outdoor

Table 1 shows that the decision FMV using square block like a Fig. 3(a), and average for correction (A1), change position of block as a cross (A2) and rectangular block + Kalman filter for correction (P). From the experiments the proposed method gives the best results. The performance is evaluated in the sense of root mean square (RMS) error. The proposed method provides better results than most of other existing methods with a block matching and phase correlation.

**Table 1.** Motion vectiors comparison between the proposed method and others

| | Frame | LMV1 | LMV2 | LMV3 | LMV4 | FMV | LMV1 | LMV2 | LMV3 | LMV4 | FMV |
|---|---|---|---|---|---|---|---|---|---|---|---|
| A1 | 1~2 | 2 | 0 | 3 | 4 | 2 | 1 | 1 | 2 | 2 | 1 |
| | 2~3 | 5 | 0 | 5 | 0 | 2 | 1 | 1 | 1 | 0 | 0 |
| | 3~4 | 5 | 0 | 4 | 4 | 3 | 0 | 1 | 0 | 0 | 0 |
| | 4~5 | 0 | 0 | 4 | 7 | 2 | 27 | 2 | -1 | 0 | 7 |
| | 5~6 | 0 | 0 | 11 | 0 | 2 | -6 | -27 | 11 | -15 | -9 |
| A2 | 1~2 | 3 | 2 | 0 | 0 | 1 | 2 | 1 | 1 | 1 | 1 |
| | 2~3 | 4 | 3 | 3 | 0 | 2 | 1 | 0 | 1 | 0 | 0 |
| | 3~4 | 5 | 5 | 4 | 0 | 3 | 0 | 0 | 0 | 0 | 0 |
| | 4~5 | 8 | 5 | 0 | 0 | 3 | 0 | -1 | 7 | 1 | 1 |
| | 5~6 | 0 | 13 | 20 | 10 | 10 | -23 | 8 | 21 | 3 | 2 |
| P | 1~2 | 3 | 4 | 3 | 4 | 4 | 2 | 0 | 2 | 2 | 2 |
| | 2~3 | 7 | 0 | 8 | 7 | 7 | 2 | 0 | 2 | 2 | 2 |
| | 3~4 | 9 | 9 | 0 | 10 | 9 | 2 | 2 | -25 | 2 | 2 |
| | 4~5 | 14 | -32 | 11 | 11 | 11 | 2 | 1 | 1 | 2 | 1 |
| | 5~6 | 18 | 0 | -32 | 18 | 18 | 3 | 6 | 0 | 1 | 3 |

## 5 Conclusions

In this paper, we proposed a digital image stabilization algorithm to remove unwanted motion by hand shaking. The proposed stabilization algorithm is based on rectangular sub-image phase correlation for motion estimation and Kalman filtering for motion prediction and correction. For efficient calculation, the luminance image is used. Robust digital image stabilization is realized by systematically estimating LMVs, FMV, and AMV and removing panning and jiggling. In experimental results, we showed that the proposed stabilization algorithm could efficiently remove the unwanted displacement from the image even with moving objects. In addition, the proposed digital image stabilization algorithms can be applied to the video surveillance system to enhance face recognition rate and human tracking performance [8].

## References

1. S. Ko, S. Lee, S. Jeon, and E. Kang, "Fast digital image stabilizer based on gray-coded bit-plane matching," *IEEE Trans. Consumer Electronics*, vol. 45, pp. 598-603, 1999.
2. J. Paik, Y. Park, and D. Kim, "An adaptive motion decision system for digital image stabilizer based on edge pattern matching," *IEEE Trans. Consumer Electronics*, vol. 38, pp. 607-615, 1992.
3. K. Uomori, A. Morimura, H. Ishii, and Y. Kitamura, "Automatic image stabilization system by full-digital signal processing," *IEEE Trans. Consumer Electronics*, vol. 36, pp. 510-519, 1990.
4. F. Vella, A. Castorina, Massimo, and G. Messina, "Digital image stabilization by adaptive block motion vectors filtering," *IEEE Trans. Consumer Electronics*, vol. 48, pp. 796-801, 2002.
5. S. Erturk, "Digital Image Stabilization with Sub-Image Phase Correlation Based Global Motion Estimation," *IEEE Trans. Consumer Electronics*, vol. 49, pp. 1320-1325, 2003.
6. S. Erturk and T. J. Dennis, "Image sequence stabilization based on DFT filtering," *Proc. Image Vision and Signal Processing*, vol. 127, pp. 95-102, 2000.
7. H. Foroosh, J. Zerubia, and M. Berthod, "Extension of phase correlation to subpixel registration," *IEEE Trans. Image Processing*, vol. 11, pp. 188-200, 2002.
8. L. Marcenaro, G. vernazza, and C. S. Regazzoni, "Image stabilization algorithms for video-surveillance applications," *Proc. Int. Conf. on Image Processing*, vol. 1, pp. 349-352, 2001.

# Wavelet Image Denoising Using Localized Thresholding Operators

M. Ghazel[1], G.H. Freeman[2], E.R. Vrscay[3], and R.K. Ward[1]

[1] Department of Electrical and Computer Engineering,
University of British Columbia, Vancouver, BC V6T 1Z4
[2] Department of Electrical and Computer Engineering
[3] Department of Applied Mathemarics,
University of Waterloo, Waterloo, ON N2L 3G1

**Abstract.** In this paper, a localized wavelet thresholding strategy which adopts context-based thresholding operators is proposed. Traditional wavelet thresholding methods, such as VisuShrink, LevelShrink and BayesShrink, apply the conventional hard and soft thresholding operators and only differ in the selection of the threshold. The conventional soft and hard thresholding operators are point operators in the sense that only the value of the processed wavelet coefficient is taken into consideration before thresholding it. In this work, it will be shown that the performance of some of the standard wavelet thresholding methods can be improved by applying a localized, context-based, thresholding strategy instead of the conventional thresholding operators.

## 1 Introduction

Over the past decade, various wavelet-based methods have been proposed for the purpose of image enhancement and restoration. Basic wavelet image restoration techniques are based on thresholding in the sense that each wavelet coefficient of the image is compared to a given threshold; if the coefficient is smaller than the threshold, then it is set to zero, otherwise it is kept or slightly reduced in magnitude. The intuition behind such an approach stems from the fact that the wavelet transform is efficient at energy compaction, thus small wavelet coefficients are more likely due to noise, and large coefficients are generally due to important image features, such as edges. Most of the efforts in the literature have concentrated on developing threshold selection criteria. Originally, Donoho and Johnstone proposed the use of a *universal* threshold applied uniformly throughout the entire wavelet decomposition tree [3,4]. Then the use of different thresholds for different subbands and levels of the wavelet tree was found to be more efficient [5]. Some methods of selecting thresholds that adapt to different spatial characteristics have recently been proposed and investigated [1]. It was found that such adaptivity in the threshold selection tends to improve the wavelet thresholding performance because it accounts for additional local statistics of the image, such as smooth or edge regions.

Although adaptive wavelet thresholding methods attempt to employ thresholds that are adaptive to the local characteristics of the wavelet coefficients of the signal, they still apply the conventional hard and soft thresholding operators. These thresholding operators are point operators which are applied on each wavelet coefficients independently of its location or context. While it is generally assumed that the wavelet transform performs a significant degree of decorrelation between neighboring pixels, it is evident that some degree of dependence between neighboring wavelet coefficients remains. Intuitively, it seems more reasonable that when thresholding a wavelet coefficient, other neighboring coefficients should also be taken into consideration.

In this paper, localized, context-based hard and soft thresholding operators, which take into consideration the content of an immediate neighborhood when thresholding a wavelet coefficient, are proposed. It will be experimentally shown that the performance of three traditional wavelet thresholding methods, namely *VisuShrink, LevelShrink* and *BayesShrink*, may be significantly improved by using these new context-based thresholding operators instead of the conventional point operators.

This paper is organized as follows: Standard wavelet thresholding for image denoising is briefly discussed in section 2. The localized thresholding operators are then introduced in section 3. Section 4 includes the use of the cycle spinning algorithm for enhancing the denoised estimates. Experimental results and concluding remarks are given in sections 5 and 6, respectively.

## 2 Wavelet Thresholding for Image Denoising

Standard wavelet thresholding can be performed in the following steps:

1. Compute a linear forward discrete wavelet transform of the noisy signal.
2. Perform a nonlinear thresholding operation on the wavelet coefficients of the noisy signal.
3. Compute the linear inverse wavelet transform of the thresholded wavelet coefficients.

The second step in the above wavelet thresholding algorithm involves the selection of the threshold, $\lambda$, and the application of a thresholding operator. While the selection of the threshold differs from one method to another, most traditional wavelet thresholding methods apply the conventional hard and soft thresholding operators, described next.

### 2.1 Conventional Thresholding Operators

Traditional wavelet thresholding methods have adopted the following conventional operators corresponding to a threshold $\lambda$,

- The *hard thresholding* operator is defined as:

$$\hat{\mathbf{X}} = T_h(\mathbf{Y}, \lambda) \text{ such that } \hat{x}_{ij} = T_h(y_{ij}, \lambda) = \begin{cases} y_{ij} & \text{if } |y_{ij}| \geq \lambda, \\ 0 & \text{otherwise.} \end{cases} \quad (1)$$

- The *soft thresholding* operator is defined as:

$$\hat{\mathbf{X}} = T_s(\mathbf{Y}, \lambda) \text{ such that } \hat{x}_{ij} = T_s(y_{ij}, \lambda) = \begin{cases} y_{ij} - \lambda & \text{if } y_{ij} \geq \lambda, \\ y_{ij} + \lambda & \text{if } y_{ij} \leq -\lambda, \\ 0 & \text{otherwise,} \end{cases} \quad (2)$$

where $\mathbf{X} = [x_{ij}]$, $\mathbf{Y} = [y_{ij}]$ and $\hat{\mathbf{X}} = [\hat{x}_{ij}]$ denote the wavelet coefficients of the original noiseless image, the noisy image and the denoised estimate, respectively.

The main difference among standard wavelet thresholding methods lies in the selection of the threshold $\lambda$. Next, three commonly known traditional wavelet thresholding methods are briefly described.

## 2.2 Standard Wavelet Thresholding Methods

In this section, three increasingly adaptive standard wavelet thresholding methods are reviewed.

- *VisuShrink:* Consists of applying the above thresholding operators using the universal threshold $\lambda_{univ} = \sqrt{2\ln(M)}\sigma_\mathbf{w}$, for a noisy signal of size $M$ and noise intensity $\sigma_w$ [3,4].
- *LevelShrink:* Account for some of the variability within the wavelet tree structure by using different thresholds for different decomposition levels. More specifically, a level-dependent threshold is given by $\lambda_j = \sqrt{2\ln(M)} \times \sigma_\mathbf{w} \times 2^{-(J-j)/2}$, for $j = 1, 2, \ldots J$, where $J$ is the total number of decomposition levels and $j$ is the scale level where the wavelet coefficient to be thresholded is located [5].
- *BayesShrink:* Assumes that the probability distribution of the noiseless wavelet coefficients follows a generalized Gaussian distribution [1]. An estimate of the optimal threshold, $\lambda$, is then selected by minimizing the mean-squared error between the noiseless wavelet coefficients, $\mathbf{X}$, and their denoised estimates, $\hat{\mathbf{X}}$. Based on this model for wavelet coefficients, it was experimentally shown that the following threshold:

$$\hat{\lambda}_j^{sub*} = \begin{cases} \frac{\sigma_\mathbf{w}^2}{\sqrt{\sigma_{\mathbf{Y}_j^{sub}}^2 - \sigma_\mathbf{w}^2}} & \text{if } \hat{\sigma}_{\mathbf{Y}_j^{sub}}^2 >> \hat{\sigma}_\mathbf{w}^2, \\ \max_{m=1,2,\ldots,M_j}\{|Y_{j,m}^{sub}|\} & \text{otherwise,} \end{cases} \quad (3)$$

is near optimal [1].

## 2.3 Remarks

The three standard wavelet thresholding methods described above apply the conventional hard and soft thresholding operators, defined in Eqs. (1) and (2). For a given threshold $\lambda$, these operators are point operators which are applied on each wavelet coefficient independently of their location or context. Consequently, the value of each thresholded wavelet coefficient depends only on the value of its noisy counterpart. While it is generally assumed that the wavelet transform performs a significant degree of decorrelation between neighboring pixels, it is well appreciated that some degree of dependence between neighboring wavelet coefficients remains. In fact, natural images' structures generally demonstrate similarities across a number of resolution scales of their wavelet coefficients. For instance, wavelet coefficients corresponding to a high activity subregion (i.e., edges) are generally clustered together and copied across the various resolutions and subbands of the wavelet tree. One should therefore expect some degree of dependence between neighboring wavelet coefficients corresponding to high activity subregions of the image. Thus, a more efficient thresholding operator should take advantage of this type of redundancy among neighboring wavelet coefficients.

## 3 Localized Wavelet Thresholding Operators

We now describe a context-based thresholding strategy that thresholds a noisy wavelet coefficient based not only on its value but also on the values of some of its neighbors. This method can be outlined as follows:

1. For each wavelet coefficient to be thresholded, $y_{ij}$, its neighborhood consists of an $m \times m$ mask centered at (but excluding) $y_{ij}$ and is denoted by $\mathcal{C}_{m \times m}(y_{ij})$.
2. The maximum value (in magnitude) of the neighboring wavelet coefficients within the mask, $M_{ij} = \max_{\{(k,l) \neq (i,j)\} \in \mathcal{C}_{m \times m}(y_{ij})} |y_{kl}|$, is then computed.
3. Now for a given threshold $\lambda$, consider the following localized hard and soft thresholding operators:
   - The localized hard thresholding operator is defined by $\hat{\mathbf{X}} = T_h^{loc}(\mathbf{Y}, \lambda)$, such that:
   
   $$\hat{x}_{ij} = T_h^{loc}(y_{ij}, \lambda) = \begin{cases} y_{ij} & \text{if } |y_{ij}| \geq \lambda \text{ OR } M_{ij} \geq \lambda, \\ 0 & \text{otherwise.} \end{cases} \quad (4)$$
   
   - The localized soft thresholding operator is defined by $\hat{\mathbf{X}} = T_s^{loc}(\mathbf{Y}, \lambda)$, such that:
   
   $$\hat{x}_{ij} = T_s^{loc}(y_{ij}, \lambda) = \begin{cases} y_{ij} - \lambda & \text{if } y_{ij} \geq \lambda, \\ y_{ij} + \lambda & \text{if } y_{ij} \leq -\lambda, \\ y_{ij} & \text{if } |y_{ij}| < \lambda \text{ AND } M_{ij} \geq \lambda, \\ 0 & \text{otherwise.} \end{cases} \quad (5)$$

These simple, localized and context-based thresholding operators are presented as alternatives to the conventional hard and soft thresholding operators defined in Eqs. (1) and (2). The selection of these localized thresholding operators is explained and motivated in the following observations:

- These localized thresholding operators clearly take the values of the neighboring coefficients, located within the defined mask, into consideration before thresholding each wavelet coefficients. Thus, taking advantage of the dependence among neighboring wavelet coefficients.
- Note that only those wavelet coefficients that are insignificant and also surrounded by insignificant coefficients are set to zero. However, an insignificant coefficient is kept unchanged if it is located near a significant one.
- The issue of selecting the neighborhood and its size was investigated. It was observed that larger masks result in sharper, but noisier estimates, exhibiting more artifacts. On the other hand, smaller masks yield results that are closer to the standard wavelet thresholding methods. It was experimentally observed that a 3×3 window yields the best results for the three thresholding methods, studied in the previous section.

## 4 Enhancement Using Cycle Spinning

The denoised estimates obtained by wavelet thresholding methods often exhibit disturbing visual artifacts. In particular, pseudo-Gibbs phenomena tend to be noticeable in the vicinity of edges and other sharp discontinuities. The idea of using the cycle spinning algorithm has been previously proposed for the purpose of reducing the pseudo-Gibbs disturbing artifacts that are often present in wavelet-based image reconstruction and denoised estimates [2]. This procedure may be summarized as follows:

$$\hat{\mathbf{x}}_K = \frac{1}{K} \sum_{h=0}^{K-1} D_{-h}(IDWT(T_\lambda(DWT(D_h(\mathbf{y}))))), \qquad (6)$$

where the noisy image, $\mathbf{y}$, is first shifted, using a diagonal shifting operator, $D_h$, the DWT is then computed, and the thresholding method of choice, $T_\lambda$, is then applied. Then the IDWT is computed and the denoised image is unshifted. This process is repeated for each shift, $k = 1, 2, \ldots, K$, and the respective results are then averaged to obtain one denoised and enhanced estimate of the image.

## 5 Experimental Results

First, we present some results before and after the incorporation of the cycle spinning idea, for the commonly used test image of *Lena* (512 × 512 pixel, 8 bits per pixel) and its noisy observation as corrupted by an AWGN noise with intensity $\sigma_w = 25$, as illustrated in Fig. 1. We then present additional experimental results using various noisy images.

### 5.1 Before Cycle Spinning

Table 1 illustrates a quantitative comparison of the quality of the denoised estimates obtained by the three wavelet thresholding methods using the conventional

Original image　　　　　　　　Noisy test image: $\sigma_w = 25$
512 × 512 pixels　　　　　　　RMSE=25.00, PSNR=20.17

**Fig. 1.** The original and the noisy version of the test image of *Lena*

**Table 1.** Conventional vs. context-based thresholding comparison

|  | Conventional thresholding | | | | Context-based thresholding | | | |
| --- | --- | --- | --- | --- | --- | --- | --- | --- |
|  | Hard | | Soft | | Hard | | Soft | |
|  | RMSE | PSNR | RMSE | PSNR | RMSE | PSNR | RMSE | PSNR |
| **VisuShrink** | 12.37 | 26.28 | 15.76 | 24.18 | 10.21 | 27.95 | 14.16 | 25.11 |
| **LevelShrink** | 10.01 | 28.11 | 11.30 | 27.07 | *9.37* | *28.69* | 10.07 | 28.07 |
| **BayesShrink** | 10.07 | 28.07 | 9.93 | 28.19 | 10.02 | 28.11 | 9.02 | 29.02 |

as well as the context-dependent hard and soft thresholding operators. In view of these results, we make the following observations:

- For the studied wavelet thresholding methods, there is an improvement in the quality of the denoised estimates obtained using the localized thresholding operators compared to the denoised images obtained by traditional thresholding schemes.
- The improvement achieved by the proposed localized thresholding operators is more evident for the case of the *VisuShrink* and *LevelShrink* than it is for the *BayesShrink* method. This can be explained by the fact that the optimal threshold corresponding to BayesShrink was originally derived specifically for the purpose of conventional soft thresholding as defined in Eq. (2). Thus this threshold may no longer be optimal when using the localized thresholding operators.

### 5.2 After Cycle Spinning

The cycle spinning algorithm was incorporated in order to enhance the denoised estimates obtained by the studied wavelet thresholding methods using the con-

**Table 2.** Conventional vs. context-based thresholding comparison after incorporating the cycle spinning idea with $K = 16$ shifts

|  | Conventional thresholding | | | | Context-based thresholding | | | |
| --- | --- | --- | --- | --- | --- | --- | --- | --- |
|  | Hard | | Soft | | Hard | | Soft | |
|  | RMSE | PSNR | RMSE | PSNR | RMSE | PSNR | RMSE | PSNR |
| VisuShrink | 10.27 | 27.90 | 14.94 | 24.64 | 8.87 | 29.18 | 12.76 | 26.01 |
| LevelShrink | 8.34 | 29.70 | 10.61 | 27.61 | *8.06* | *30.00* | 8.71 | 29.33 |
| BayesShrink | 8.64 | 29.40 | 8.66 | 29.38 | 8.71 | 29.33 | 8.36 | 29.69 |

ventional as well as the context-based hard and soft thresholding operators and the results are illustrated in Table 2. In view of these results we make the following observations:

- When comparing the results illustrated in Tables 1 and 2, it is evident that the quality of the denoised images is significantly improved by using the cycle spinning method.
- Generally, the use of the proposed localized thresholding operators yields better results than using the conventional thresholding operators before and after incorporating the cycle spinning idea.
- Experimentally, it was observed that the quality of the denoised estimate improves significantly after only a few shifts and then becomes stable and little or no further gains are achieved through additional shifts. In our case, a total of $K = 16$ diagonal shifts were used.
- Fig. 2 illustrates the results obtained by the *LevelShrink* method using the conventional as well as the context-based hard thresholding operators, before and after incorporating the cycle spinning algorithm. The context-based *LevelShrink* hard thresholding method yields the best results before and after the cycle spinning algorithm.
- Clearly the cycle spinning algorithm may be rather computationally expensive. Indeed, when incorporating this algorithm with $K$ shifts for any denoising method, the computational complexity is multiplied by a factor of $K$.

### 5.3 Additional Experimental Results

Fig. 3 illustrates the results of denoising four different test images, *Lena, Boat, Peppers* and *San Francisco*, which were corrupted by an AWGN noise with varying intensity; $\sigma_w = 10, 20, 30$ and $40$, using the *BayesShrink* method before and after the incorporation of the cycle spinning (C.S.) algorithm. Again, two versions of the *BayesShrink* scheme were implemented: the conventional *BayesShrink* technique which adopts the conventional soft thresholding operator and a Context-Based (C-B) *BayesShrink* scheme which applies the proposed context-based soft thresholding operator.

(a) Standard hard *LevelShrink*  (b) Context-based hard *LevelShrink*
RMSE=10.01, PSNR=28.11        RMSE=9.37, PSNR=28.69

Before cycle spinning

(c) Standard hard *LevelShrink*  (d) Context-based hard *LevelShrink*
RMSE=8.34, PSNR=29.70         RMSE=8.06, PSNR=30.00

After cycle spinning

**Fig. 2.** A sample of the results

In view of these experimental results, we make the following observations:

- The results obtained by the C-B *BayesShrink* wavelet thresholding method are consistently better than those obtained by the conventional *BayesShrink* scheme. Indeed, this is the case for all test images and noise intensities.
- This improvement is even more evident before using the cycle spinning idea than after applying this enhancement method. This is probably because the use of the cycle spinning idea has benefited both methods by reducing most

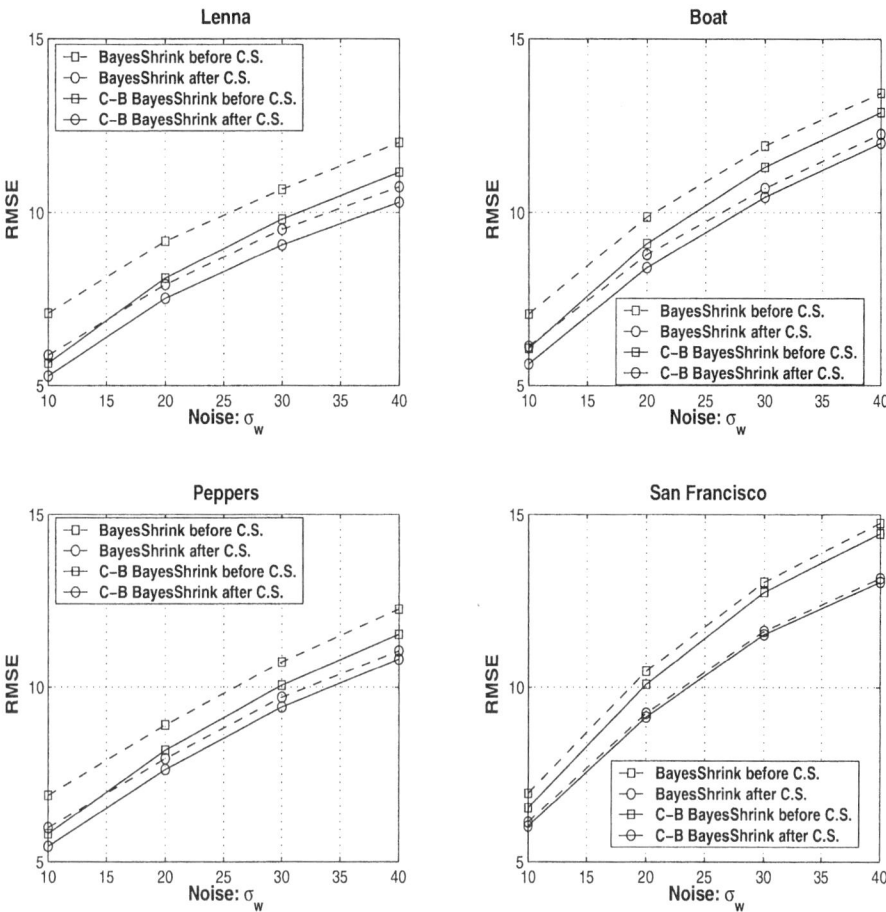

**Fig. 3.** Conventional vs. context-based (C-B) thresholding comparison for *BayesShrink* before and after applying the cycle spinning (C.S.) idea with $K = 16$ shifts

of the artifacts, hence yielding closer enhanced denoised estimates for both thresholding schemes.
- The cycle spinning idea is computationally expensive. In practice, some applications may not allow for this time complexity. Thus, the fact that the proposed context-based thresholding strategy yields significantly better results than the conventional thresholding operator without applying the cycle spinning idea is of great practical significance.

Based on the experimental results presented so far, it may be reasonable to conclude that, in general, the proposed context-based thresholding operators yield better results than the conventional thresholding operators.

## 6 Concluding Remarks

In this paper, we have proposed a generalized class of localized, context-based soft and hard wavelet thresholding operators that also depend upon the neighboring coefficient values. Our experiments have shown that these operators yield significant improvements over the conventional hard and soft thresholding point operators, especially for the *VisuShrink* and *LevelShrink* methods. The incorporation of cycle spinning further improves the results, but at significant computational expense.

## References

1. S.G. Chang, B. Yu, and Martin Vetterli, "Spatially adaptive wavelet thresholding with context modeling for image denoising," *IEEE Trans. on Image Proc.*, vol. 9, no. 9, pp. 1522-1531, 2000.
2. R.R. Coifman, and D.L. Donoho, "Translation-invariant denoising," in A. Antoniadis, and G. Oppenheim, editors, Wavelets and Statistics, vol. 103 of Springer Lecture Notes in Statistics, pp. 125-150, New York, Springer-Verlag 1995.
3. D.L. Donoho, "Denoising and soft-thresholding," *IEEE Trans. Infor. Theory*, vol. 41, pp. 613-627, 1995.
4. D.L. Donoho, and I.M. Johnstone, "Ideal spatial adaptation via wavelet shrinkage," *Biometrika*, vol. 81, pp. 425-455, 1994.
5. S. Zhong, and V. Cherkassky, "Image denoising using wavelet thresholding and model selection," *Proc. IEEE Int. Conf. on Image Proc. (ICIP)*, Vancouver, B.C., Sept. 2000.

# Type-2 Fuzzy Image Enhancement

P. Ensafi and H.R. Tizhoosh

Systems Design Engineering, University of Waterloo,
200 University Avenue West, Waterloo, Ontario
pensafi@engmail.uwaterloo.ca
tizhoosh@uwaterloo.ca

**Abstract.** In the classical image processing paradigm, the fundamental idea of image enhancement is to produce a new image such that it exposes information for analysis more than the original image. Fuzzy Logic methods are one of valuable and frequently used techniques among many other image enhancement approaches. In this work we demonstrate that a type-2 fuzzy logic system is able to perform image contrast enhancement better than its type-1 counterpart. Examples are provided. Results are discussed.

**Keywords:** Locally adaptive techniques; Fuzzy image enhancement; Type-2 Fuzzy Sets.

## 1 Introduction

Fuzzy logic is a type of logic, in which fundamental issues of reasoning are approximate instead of exact. Research has shown that type-1 fuzzy logic systems have difficulties in modeling and minimizing the effect of uncertainties [10,11,12]. One reason that limits the ability of type-1 fuzzy sets to handle uncertainty is that the membership function for a particular input is a crisp value [10,11]. Recently, type-2 fuzzy sets, characterized by membership functions that are fuzzy themselves, have been attracting interest. Moreover, it is becoming increasingly important for image processing systems to have adequate solutions for representing and manipulating the uncertainties involved at every processing stage. Tizhoosh [14] has already established a measure of ultrafuzziness and used fuzzy sets type-2 for image thresholding. This motivated the authors to create a type-2 fuzzy image enhancement algorithm based on extension of existing techniques. Among various methods, local contrast enhancement approaches have generally better results compared to global techniques [3,6,9]. Hence, we consider one of these techniques, namely the locally adaptive fuzzy histogram hyperbolization method, represented in [3], as a framework for our study. This method is based on type-1 fuzzy sets. In this paper, we have improved its performance by extending it to a type-2 algorithm.

The paper is organized as follows: Sections 2 and 3 are devoted to fuzzy image definition and fuzzy hyperbolization. The locally adaptive image enhancement method presented in [3] is described in section 4.

Section 5 discusses the concept of type-2 fuzzy sets. In section 6 our proposed approach for type-2 fuzzy image enhancement is explained. Section 7 contains the experimental results and provides some further discussion.

## 2 Fuzzy Image Definition

According to the concept of fuzzy set theory, introduced by Zadeh [1,2], a mathematical framework for image processing problems can be established [4,5,8]. For the image $I$, when $g_{mn}$ represents the intensity of the $mn$-th pixel and $\mu_{mn}$ its membership value, then $I$ can be represented as an array of membership values [6]:

$$I = \bigcup_{m}^{M} \bigcup_{n}^{N} \frac{\mu_{mn}}{g_{mn}}, \qquad (1)$$

where $m = 1, 2, 3 \ldots M$ and $n = 1, 2, 3 \ldots N$. Using the linear index of fuzziness we can calculate the image fuzziness [5]:

$$\gamma(I) = \frac{2}{MN} \sum_{i=1}^{N} \sum_{j=1}^{M} \min[\mu_I(g_{ij}), \overline{\mu}_I(g_{ij})], \qquad (2)$$

where $\mu_I(g_{ij})$ is the membership function of grey level $g_{ij}$ and $\overline{\mu}_I(g_{ij}) = 1 - \mu_I(g_{ij})$.

## 3 Fuzzy Hyperbolization

The concept of histogram and fuzzy histogram hyperbolization is described in [7], [9], and [13]. In the method presented in [3], the membership value for each grey level is calculated as

$$\mu(g_{mn}) = \frac{g_{mn} - g_{\min}}{g_{\max} - g_{\min}}, \qquad (3)$$

where the image minimum and maximum grey level is represented by $g_{\min}$ and $g_{\max}$, respectively. Then using parameter $\beta$ as a fuzzifier and the desired number of grey levels $L$, the new grey levels can be calculated using the following transformation [3]:

$$g'_{mn} = (\frac{L-1}{e^{-1}-1}) \times [e^{-\mu(g_{mn})^{\beta}} - 1]. \qquad (4)$$

## 4 Locally Adaptive Image Enhancement

Among different methods of image enhancement, local enhancement techniques are frequently used. In the method proposed in [3] a locally adaptive approach is employed to divide an image into several sub-images. Based on the value of homogeneity, expressed by equation:

$$\mu_{Homo} = (1 - \frac{g_{\max\_Local} - g_{\min\_local}}{g_{\max\_global} - g_{\min\_global}})^2, \qquad (5)$$

and given minimum and maximum size of the local window, using a fuzzy if-then-else rule, the local window size surrounding each supporting point is calculated. The center of each neighborhood moves among center points of local windows. In order to avoid loss of information during the interpolation, the size of the larger window is chosen so that local windows have enough overlap with each other.

Two matrixes of size $M \times N$ contain minimum and maximum grey levels of each sub-image. Using a 2-D interpolation function the membership value of every pixel can be calculated. Using these interpolated membership values and equation (4) will lead us to an enhanced image with the higher level of contrast [3].

## 5 Type-2 Fuzzy Sets

The idea of type-2 fuzzy sets was introduced by Zadeh [12] as an extension to the ordinary or type-1 fuzzy sets [10,11]. Type-2 fuzzy sets are useful in situations where it is difficult to agree on the accurate membership function for a fuzzy set because there is an uncertainty in its shape, its location or in its other parameters [11]. Hence, the additional third dimension in type-2 fuzzy logic systems gives more degrees of freedom for better representation of uncertainty compared to type-1 fuzzy sets.

Four sources of uncertainties have been identified for type-1 fuzzy logic systems: (i) uncertain meaning of the words, (ii) consequences associated with a histogram of values, (iii) uncertain measurements, and (iv) noisy data [10].

These uncertainties in fuzzy sets result in an uncertain membership function. The fact that type-1 fuzzy sets have crisp membership functions makes them unable to model such uncertainties.

A type-2 fuzzy set can be obtained by blurring the membership function of a type-1 fuzzy set [10] (Fig. 1, 2).

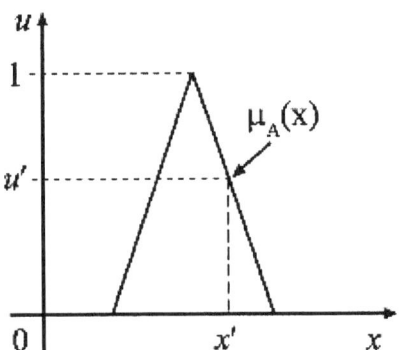
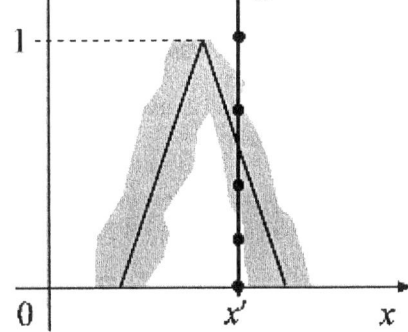

**Fig. 1.** Membership function of a Type-1 Fuzzy Set [10]

**Fig. 2.** Membership function of a Type-2 Fuzzy Set [10]

Now for the value of $x'$, instead of a single value membership function $u'$, the membership function takes on values wherever the vertical line intersects the blur (Fig. 2). Because there is no need to weight those values the same, we can assign an amplitude distribution to all of them. Doing this for all, we create a three-dimensional membership function, which is a type-2 membership function that characterizes a type-2 fuzzy set.

We can characterize a type-2 fuzzy set $\tilde{A}$ as [10]:

$$\tilde{A} = \{((x,u), \mu_{\tilde{A}}(x,u)) \mid \forall x \in X, \forall u \in J_x \subseteq [0,1]\}, \tag{6}$$

where $J_x$ is the primary membership of $x$ and $\mu_{\tilde{A}}(x,u)$ is a type-2 membership function and $0 \leq \mu_{\tilde{A}}(x,u) \leq 1$. The footprint of uncertainty (FOU), which represents the uncertainty in the primary memberships of the type-2 fuzzy set $\tilde{A}$, is expressed as [10]:

$$FOU(\tilde{A}) = \bigcup_{x \in X} J_x. \tag{7}$$

The shaded region in Fig. 2 indicates FOU. In [11] the authors indicate that "...in order to develop a type-2 fuzzy logic system, we need to be able to: (i) perform set theoretic operations on type-2 sets; (ii) know properties of membership grades of type-2 sets; (iii) deal with type-2 fuzzy relations and their compositions; and, (iv) perform type reduction and defuzzification to obtain a crisp output from the fuzzy logic system".

## 6 Proposed Technique

In this section, we introduced our type-2 fuzzy set image enhancement method. This study is conducted by utilizing a type-2 fuzzy image processor, which is designed using a partially dependent approach. First, one of the best possible type-1 fuzzy logic systems [3,5,9] is chosen, and is subsequently used to initialize the parameters of the type-2 algorithm. Such an approach has the following advantages: (i) smart initialization of the factors of the type-2 fuzzy set, and ii) having a fundamental system whose performance can be compared with that of the new one.

As mentioned before, a type-2 fuzzy set may be obtained by blurring a type-1 membership function. For this purpose we use interval-based sets to construct the type-2 fuzzy set by defining the upper and lower membership values using

$$\mu_{UPPER}(x) = (\mu(x))^{0.5}, \tag{8}$$

and

$$\mu_{LOWER}(x) = (\mu(x))^2, \tag{9}$$

where $0 \leq \mu(x) \leq 1$ is the membership function for value $x$ (Fig. 3).

Applying a few changes in the method presented in [3], in addition to matrixes containing minimum and maximum grey level of sub-images, a third matrix with the mean value of sub-images is generated. Interpolated values are calculated by a linear 2-D interpolation function. After calculation of $\mu(x)$ using equation (3), $\mu_{UPPER}$ and $\mu_{LOWER}$ are calculated from equations (8) and (9), respectively. Now, the blurred area, referred to as the Footprint of Uncertainty, is bounded by upper and lower membership functions (Fig. 3). Points within the blurred area' have membership grades given by type-1 membership function $\mu$. Thus, FOU provides an additional dimension, thereby enabling the uncertainties in the shape and position of the type-1 fuzzy set to be represented. Here, $\mu_{T2}$ the proposed membership function is expressed as:

$$\mu_{T2}(g_{mn}) = (\mu_{LOWER} \times \alpha) + (\mu_{UPPER} \times (1-\alpha)), \tag{10}$$

where $0 \leq \alpha \leq 1$ and

$$\alpha = \frac{g_{Mean}}{L}. \tag{11}$$

$g_{Mean}$ symbolizes the corresponding mean value of each sub-image and $L$ is the number of grey levels.

Using $\mu_{T2}$ values results in new grey levels and our proposed enhanced image. The idea behind equation (10) is that pixels in a very dark neighborhood will get a greater proportion of $\mu_{UPPER}$ thus higher grey values. Therefore, the image would be brighter in dark areas and thereby obtains a higher level of contrast.

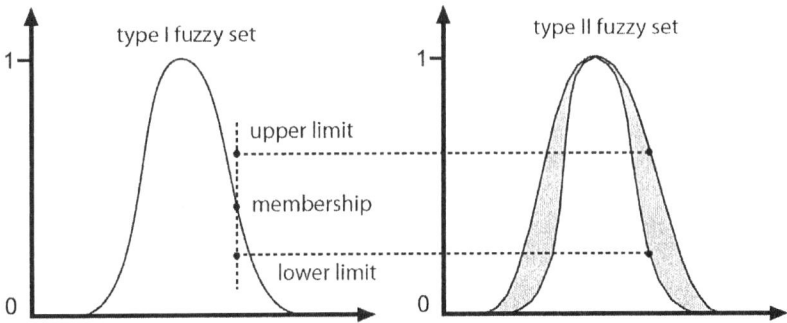

**Fig. 3.** Upper and Lower limits of a membership function and type-2 construction [14]

## 7 Experimental Results

In this section, the result of the proposed method is presented. Figure 4 shows the test images. The first four rows are X-ray images, and the last row is the Lena images. The first column of each row is the original version, the second column shows the result of locally adaptive type-1 fuzzy approach presented in [3], the third is the result of the same approach using $\mu_{LOWER}(x) = (\mu(x))^2$, and the last column is the result of the proposed approach. In all 3 methods fuzzifier $\beta = 1.1$ and the minimum and maximum size of local windows are set to 10 and 20, respectively.

To achieve a reliable subjective assessment on the proposed method, the results were presented to 15 observers (mostly medical experts). The test persons evaluated the quality of the images based on the ranking scale 1 (excellent) up to 5 (very bad).

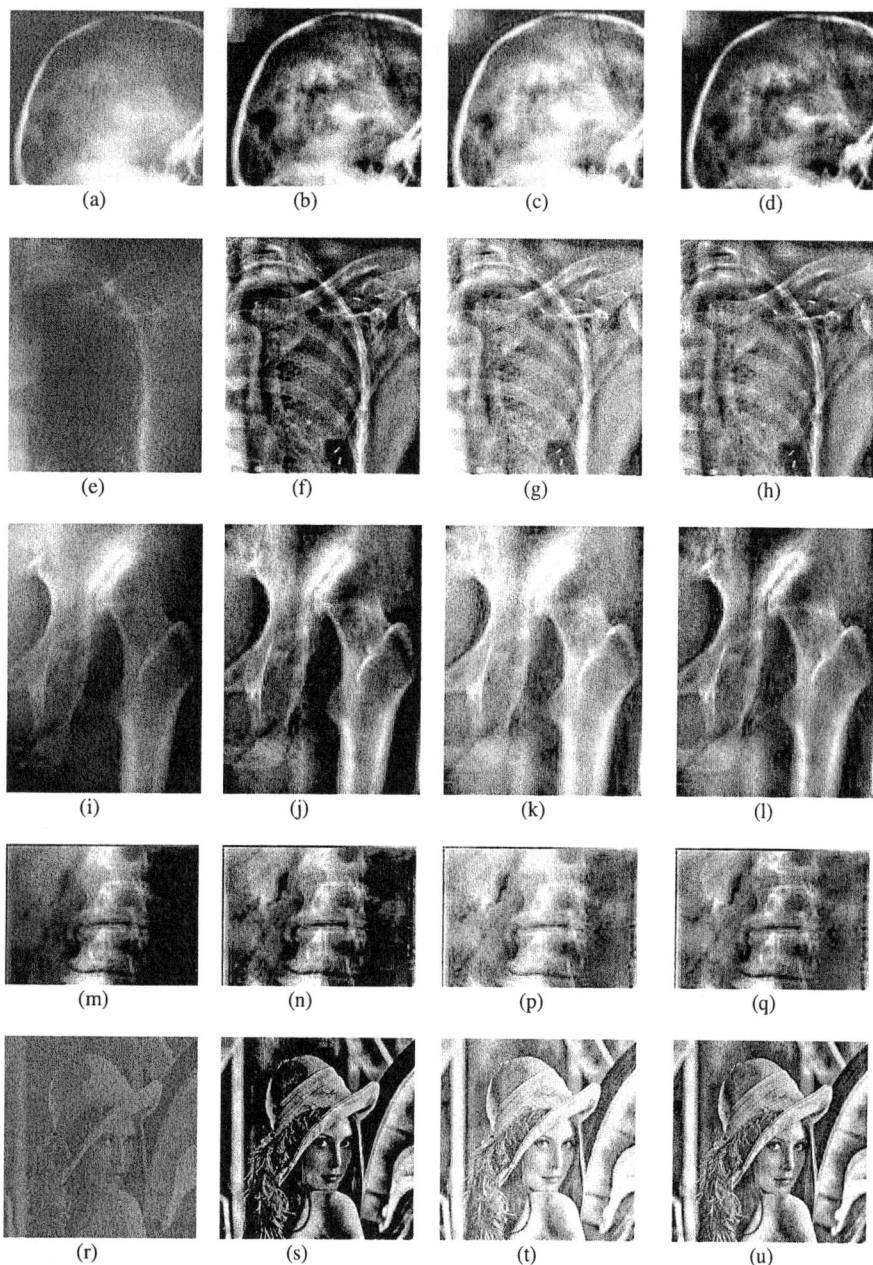

**Fig. 4.** (a), (e), (i), (m) and (r) original low contrast versions; (b), (f), (j), (n) and (s) results of type-1 fuzzy method in [3]; (c), (g), (k), (p) and (t) results of type-1 fuzzy method in [3] with membership function $\mu_{UPPER}$; (d), (h), (l), (q) and (u) results of the proposed method

Mean Opinion Score (MOS) has been calculated to find an overall evaluation (Table 1). The results show that the proposed method has the highest scores (highlighted rows) hence better quality of contrast.

Table 1. MOS Evaluation

| Figure | MOS | Figure | MOS |
|--------|------|--------|------|
| 4(b)   | 3    | 4(n)   | 3    |
| 4(c)   | 3.47 | 4(p)   | 3.27 |
| 4(d)   | 2    | 4(q)   | 1.73 |
| 4(f)   | 3.2  | 4(s)   | 2.73 |
| 4(g)   | 3.4  | 4(t)   | 3    |
| 4(h)   | 2.73 | 4(u)   | 1.74 |
| 4(j)   | 2.2  |        |      |
| 4(k)   | 3.47 |        |      |
| 4(l)   | 1.93 |        |      |

## 8 Conclusion

In this paper, we have proposed an elementary type-2 fuzzy image contrast enhancement algorithm that is based on a locally adaptive type-1 fuzzy histogram hyperbolization method. The results shown here demonstrate the effectiveness of type-2 fuzzy logic in image enhancement approaches. However, more experimental results are required in order to establish a reliable comparison. Type-2 fuzzy sets and their design and implementation is, compared to ordinary fuzzy sets, quite challenging. This paper should be understood as an initial attempt to apply the type-2 idea on image enhancement. Further investigations are necessary to exploit the potentials of type-2 fuzzy sets for image quality improvement.

## References

[1] Zadeh, L. A., "A Fuzzy- set- theoretic Interpretation of Linguistic Hedges", Journal of Cybernetic, vol. 2, pp. 4-34, 1972.
[2] Zadeh, L. A., "Fuzzy Sets", Information and Control, vol. 8, pp 338-353, 1965.
[3] Tizhoosh, H.R. Krel, G. and Muchaelis, B., "Locally Adaptive Fuzzy Image Enhancement", In: Computational Intelligence, Theory and Applications; proceeding of 5th fuzzy days'97, Dortmund, Germany, Springer, pp.272-276, 1997.
[4] Tizhoosh, H.R.,"Fuzzy Image Enhancement: An Overview", In: Kerre, E., Nachtegael, M. (Eds.): Fuzzy Techniques in Image Processing, Springer, Studies in Fuzziness and Soft Computing, pp. 137-171, 2000, ISBN: 3-7908-1304-4.
[5] Tizhoosh, H.R., "Fuzzy Image Processing: Potentials and State of the Art", IIZUKA'98, 5th International Conference on Soft Computing, Iizuka, Japan, October 16-20, 1998, vol. 1, pp. 321-324.

[6] Krell, G., Tizhoosh, H.R., Lilienblum, T., Moore, C.J., Michaelis, B., "Fuzzy Image Enhancement and Associative Feature Matching in Radiotherapy", proceedings of 1997 IEEE International Conference on Neural Networks, vol. 3, p 1490, pt. 3, 1997.
[7] Banks, S., "Signal Processing, Image Processing and Pattern Recognition", Prentice Hall International, Great Britain, 1990.
[8] Pal, S.K., Dutta, Majumder D., "Fuzzy Mathematical Approach to Pattern Recognition", John Wiley & Sons., New York, 1986.
[9] Tizhoosh, H.R., Fochem, M., "Image Enhancement with Fuzzy Histogram Hyperbolization", proceedings of EUFIT'95, vol. 3, pp. 1695-1698, Achen, Germany, 1995.
[10] Mendel, J.M., John, R.I.B., "Type-2 Fuzzy Sets Made Simple", IEEE Transactions on Fuzzy Systems, vol. 10, no. 2, pp. 117-27, April 2002.
[11] Karnik, N.N., Mendel, J.M., "Introduction to Type-2 Fuzzy Logic Systems", 1998 IEEE International Conference on Fuzzy Systems Proceedings. IEEE World Congress on Computational Intelligence, vol.2, p 915-935, pt. 2, 1998
[12] Zadeh, L. A., "The Concept of A Linguistic Variable and Its Application to Approximate Reasoning - 1" , Information Sciences 8, pp. 199 - 249, 1975.
[13] Schneider, M., Craig, M., "On the Use of Fuzzy Sets in Histogram Equalization", Fuzzy Sets and Systems, vol. 45, n. 3, pp. 271-279, 1992.
[14] Tizhoosh, H.R., "Image Thresholding Using Type II Fuzzy Sets", to be published in Pattern Recognition, 2005.

# A Multi-level Framework for Video Shot Structuring

Yun Zhai and Mubarak Shah

School of Computer Science,
University of Central Florida, Orlando, Florida 32816

**Abstract.** Video shots provide the most basic meaningful segments for video analysis and understanding. In this paper, we present a detection and classification framework for the video shot segmentation in a coarse-to-fine fashion. The initial transitions are detected from a sub-sampled video space. These coarse segments are later refined in the original video space with the technique of illumination artifacts removal and transition finalization. The transition type (abrupt or gradual) are finally determined by exploiting the histogram intersection plot. The proposed method has been tested on a large amount of videos, which contain a variety of types of shot transitions. Accurate and competitive results have been obtained.

## 1 Introduction

The increasing amount of video data available to us poses challenges to develop tools for video indexing and searching, so that users can efficiently navigate through it. As the most based semantic meaningful segments of the video, detecting shots becomes an important and interesting problem in video processing and analysis. A video shot is defined as a sequence of frames taken by a single camera with no major changes in the visual content. The transitions between shots can be categorized into two types: abrupt and gradual. The abrupt transitions is generated by directly appending one shot after another. On the other hand, the gradual transitions are generated to present production effects, e.g., wipes, fade-in, fade-out, dissolve, etc. The goal in the shot detection usually contains two parts: transition localization and transition type determination.

Many efforts have been devoted into this area for the past years, and they can be differentiated by their underlying mechanisms. Boreczky *et al.* [2] has proposed a shot detection method based on the direct comparison of the pixels in the consecutive frames. One modification of this approach [8] is to count the number of pixels that are significantly changed. They work well for sequences taken by still camera, but is highly sensitive to the camera and scene object motion. Another group of approaches use the similarity measures between global feature vectors. One popular feature used is the color histogram. Yeo *et al.* [9] proposed an difference measure by computing the sum of absolute differences between corresponding bins in the histogram. Furht *et al.* [3] has used the color histograms in HSV space to make the system less sensitive to the lighting conditions. An alternative to the global comparison is the block-wise histogram comparison proposed by Nagasaka *et al.* [7]. There methods are robust against the motion. However, they do not perform well on slow gradual transitions. Another important feature have been used is the edge information. Zabih *et al.* [10] has proposed an edge-based similarity measure between frames. After motion compensation, the percentage of edge pixels exiting from one frame to its following frames is computed. Even though it is robust against global motion, the computational complexity is high.

In this paper, we present a coarse-to-fine approach for not only detecting the transitions between video shots, but also classifying the transitions into one of the two types: abrupt transition and gradual transition. The video is first segmented into coarse segments by analyzing in the sub-sampled video space. The shots transitions then are refined by illumination artifacts removal technique and are finalized in the original video space. The types of the transitions are determined by looking at the neighborhoods of the initial transition boundaries. The rest of this paper is organized as follows: Section 2 discusses the overall algorithm, including boundary initialization, illumination artifact removal, transition type determination and transition boundary finalization; Section 3 presents the system evaluation results; finally, Section 4 concludes our work.

## 2 Proposed Framework

### 2.1 Transition Boundary Initialization

During a shot transition, the visual similarity of the consecutive frames changes. This can be detected by observing the color histograms of the frames. We use a 3-D color histogram in RGB space, allocating 8 bins for each dimension. Let $D(i)$ represents the histogram intersection between frames $f^{i-1}$ and $f^i$, which is computed as,

$$D(i) = \sum_{allbin\ b} min(H_{i-1}(b), H_i(b)), \quad (1)$$

where $H_{i-1}$ and $H_i$ are histograms of frames $f^{i-1}$ and $f^i$ respectively, and $b$ is the individual bins. A transition boundary at $f^i$ is found if:

$$D(i-1) - D(i) > T_{color},$$
$$D(i+1) - D(i) > T_{color}, \quad (2)$$

where $T_{color}$ is the threshold that captures the significant difference between the color statistics of two frames.

For abrupt transitions (Fig.1(a)), where the difference in color distribution is large enough, the above frame-to-frame histogram intersection performs well. However, for the gradual transitions (Fig.1(b)), the color differences between consecutive frames are not sufficiently significant to be captured, miss detection occur. To solve this problem, we first temporally sub-sample the original video sequences (every fifth frame in the experiments). The histogram intersection is then applied to the sub-sampled sequences, thus amplifying the frame-to-frame visual differences (Fig.1(c)). This initial estimate of shot boundary, which may not be accurate, is refined in the next step.

Once the approximate location of a transition boundary is obtained, we localize it at the highest sampling rate. This is achieved by finding the frame corresponding to the

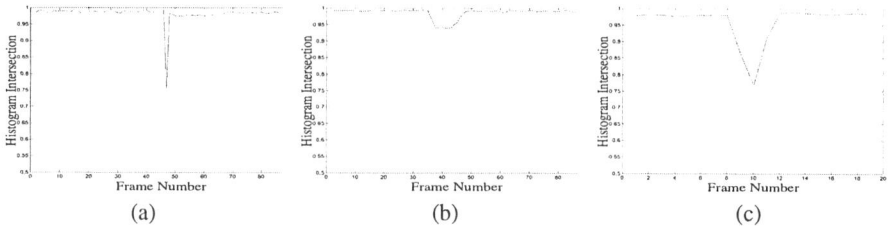

**Fig. 1.** (a). Histogram intersection plot for a short video containing an abrupt transition; (b). Histogram intersection plot for a sequence containing a gradual transition; (c). Histogram intersection plot for the sub-sampled video in (b) with sampling at every fifth frame

local minimum of the color histogram intersection plot. Let $P$ be the initial estimate of the transition boundary and $a$ be the search range, the localized transition boundary at frame $M$ is determined as,

$$M = arg\ min(\{D(P-a), ..., D(P+a)\}). \tag{3}$$

### 2.2 Illumination Artifact Removal

The detection of the shot transitions is followed by the removal of outliers. We have observed that in many videos that relate to meetings, briefings, celebrities, politicians, the most common outliers are caused by the camera flashes. In such cases, the illumination of consecutive frames abruptly changes and results in over detection of the transition boundaries. To remove such outliers, we compute the average color statistics, $K_L$ and $K_R$, of the immediate left and right neighborhoods of a candidate transition boundary. The visual similarity of these two neighbors is computed in terms of the Bhattacharya distance $d_B$ between $K_L$ and $K_R$,

$$Sim(K_L, K_R) = exp\Big(-d_B^2(K_L, K_R)\Big), \tag{4}$$

where $d_B = -ln(\sum_{b=1}^{k} \sqrt{K_L^b, K_R^b})$. The candidate boundary is removed if both of the neighborhoods present high similarity.

### 2.3 Determining Transition Type

Once the transition boundaries are localized, they are then classified into one of two categories: abrupt and gradual. Examples of gradual transitions are dissolves, fade-ins, fade-outs, wipes, and etc, and they often last for longer temporal periods. The length of transition, however, may differ for different types of transitions. Since the estimated initial boundaries from previous steps are represented by single frames, the gradual transition could take place before the initial boundary, after the initial boundary, or across the initial boundary (Fig.2(b)).

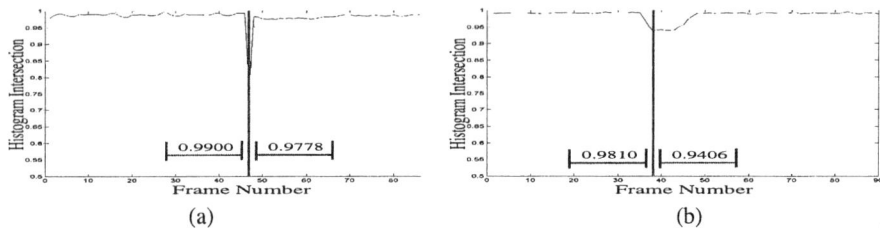

**Fig. 2.** (a). Histogram intersection plot for a sequence with an abrupt transition; (b). Histogram intersection plot for a sequence with a gradual transition. The average histogram intersection of the neighbors around the initial transitions are shown in the figure. The windows size is 30 frames in the experiment.

To determine the transition type, we consider frames in a neighborhood of size $b$, on each side of the detected transition boundary $P$. If the transition is a gradual transition, either one of the neighborhoods or both of them higher visual activity. The visual activity of each neighborhood is computed as the average histogram intersections $D_L$ and $D_R$ in each neighbor,

$$D_L = \frac{1}{b} \sum_{i=1}^{b} D(P - i),$$

$$D_R = \frac{1}{b} \sum_{i=1}^{b} D(P + i). \qquad (5)$$

If both $D_L$ and $D_R$ are high (visually smooth), the transition is categorized as abrupt (Fig.2(a)). Otherwise, the transition is classified as gradual. Examples for both of the types are shown in Fig.2(b) with visual activities in their neighborhoods.

### 2.4 Gradual Transition Boundary Determination

Once the transition type is determined, the exact starting and ending locations of the boundaries need to be determined. The determination for the abrupt transitions is straightforward, since the transition only takes place in two frames. It is more important to locate the beginning and ending frames of the gradual transitions, such the accurate shot representation can be found and used in future video analysis and understanding.

We assume that the transition length is not infinite long. If we pick a point that is far away from the initial boundary, and that point is inside the shot instead of on the transition, then, the neighborhood around that point should be visually smooth. As we move this point towards the initial boundary, the visual activity level in its neighborhood starts raising up at the places where the transition starts or ends. If the point comes from the left side of the initial boundary, the raising up point is the starting frame of the transition. If it comes from the right side of the boundary, it is the ending frame of that transition. This process is demonstrated in Fig.3 .

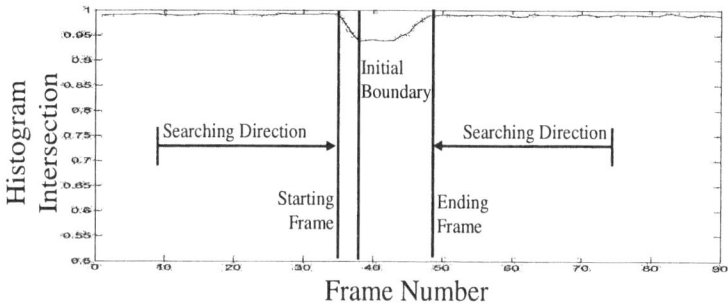

**Fig. 3.** Locating the starting and ending frames in a gradual transition

## 3 System Evaluation Results

The data set we have experimented our framework on is provided by the US National Institute of Technologies and Standards (NIST). The data set is an open benchmark which contains 13 MPEG-1 news videos from CNN, ABC and C-SPAN news networks. It has been used for the TRECVID forum in 2003 [1]. Each video is around thirty minutes long. The news videos from CNN and ABC contain both news program and commercials, while the videos from C-SPAN only contain news programs. The reason of testing on news videos is that there are a rich amount of shots transitions covering both abrupt and gradual types. Furthermore, since it is a Television program, many variation of the gradual transitions are present. Therefore, it is a good testing bed for shot transition detection and type determination.

We have applied our framework on all 13 news videos. There are three types of accuracy measurements:

- Precision/Recall for Abrupt Transitions:

$$Precision = \frac{A_{abrupt}}{X_{abrupt}}, \quad Recall = \frac{A_{abrupt}}{Y_{abrupt}}, \tag{6}$$

where $A_{abrupt}$ is the number of matched abrupt transitions, $X_{abrupt}$ is the number of detected abrupt transitions, and $Y_{abrupt}$ is the number of reference abrupt transitions.

- Precision/Recall for Gradual Transitions:

$$Precision = \frac{A_{gradual}}{X_{gradual}}, \quad Recall = \frac{A_{gradual}}{Y_{gradual}}, \tag{7}$$

where $A_{gradual}$ is the number of matched gradual transitions, $X_{gradual}$ is the number of detected gradual transitions, and $Y_{gradual}$ is the number of reference gradual transitions.

- Frame Based Precision/Recall for Gradual Transitions:

$$Precision = \frac{A'_{gradual}}{X'_{gradual}}, \quad Recall = \frac{A'_{gradual}}{Y'_{gradual}}, \tag{8}$$

where $A'_{gradual}$ is the total number of frames in the overlapping regions in matched gradual transitions, $X'_{gradual}$ is the total number of frames in the detected gradual transitions, and $Y'_{gradual}$ is the total number of frames in the reference gradual transitions.

| Filename | Type | Cut Recall | Cut Precision | Grad Recall | Grad Precision | Frame Recall | Frame Precision |
|---|---|---|---|---|---|---|---|
| 19990303.121216 | CSPAN | 1.000 | 1.000 | 0.000 | 0.000 | 0/0 | 0/0 |
| 19980619_ABC | ABC | 0.890 | 0.934 | 0.811 | 0.673 | 1150/1711 | 1150/1314 |
| 19980224_ABC | ABC | 0.820 | 0.874 | 0.717 | 0.648 | 970/1733 | 970/1074 |
| 19980425_ABC | ABC | 0.732 | 0.896 | 0.872 | 0.570 | 1522/2287 | 1522/1815 |
| 19980222_CNN | CNN | 0.737 | 0.904 | 0.712 | 0.365 | 735/1439 | 735/1043 |
| 19980515_CNN | CNN | 0.770 | 0.923 | 0.824 | 0.545 | 1252/2063 | 1252/1747 |
| 19980531_CNN | CNN | 0.757 | 0.897 | 0.824 | 0.494 | 749/1255 | 749/937 |
| 19980412_ABC | ABC | 0.800 | 0.907 | 0.861 | 0.598 | 1105/2118 | 1105/1301 |
| 2001614.1647460 | CSPAN | 1.000 | 1.000 | 0.000 | 0.000 | 0/0 | 0/0 |
| 19980308.1216980 | CSPAN | 1.000 | 1.000 | 0.000 | 0.000 | 0/0 | 0/0 |
| 20010628.1649460 | CSPAN | 0.962 | 0.916 | 0.000 | 0.000 | 0/0 | 0/0 |
| 20010702.1650112 | CSPAN | 1.000 | 1.000 | 0.000 | 0.000 | 0/0 | 0/0 |
| 19980203_CNN | CNN | 0.732 | 0.843 | 0.853 | 0.626 | 1478/2221 | 1478/1697 |
| Mean | | 2097/2644 | 2097/2285 | 887/1090 | 887/1616 | 8961/14827 | 8961/10928 |
| | | 0.793 | 0.918 | 0.814 | 0.550 | 0.604 | 0.820 |

**Fig. 4.** System evaluation results for the first run of the proposed method. Since there is no gradual transition in the C-SPAN videos, the corresponding precision and recall measures are set to zeros.

| Filename | Type | Cut Recall | Cut Precision | Grad Recall | Grad Precision | Frame Recall | Frame Precision |
|---|---|---|---|---|---|---|---|
| 19990303.121216 | CSPAN | 1.000 | 1.000 | 0.000 | 0.000 | 0/0 | 0/0 |
| 19980619_ABC | ABC | 0.890 | 0.940 | 0.826 | 0.677 | 1163/1734 | 1163/1326 |
| 19980224_ABC | ABC | 0.820 | 0.886 | 0.725 | 0.641 | 980/1745 | 980/1084 |
| 19980425_ABC | ABC | 0.718 | 0.898 | 0.866 | 0.561 | 1514/2279 | 1514/1818 |
| 19980222_CNN | CNN | 0.728 | 0.914 | 0.722 | 0.361 | 738/1475 | 738/1039 |
| 19980515_CNN | CNN | 0.766 | 0.923 | 0.824 | 0.545 | 1252/2063 | 1252/1747 |
| 19980531_CNN | CNN | 0.740 | 0.898 | 0.833 | 0.491 | 753/1266 | 753/964 |
| 19980412_ABC | ABC | 0.794 | 0.907 | 0.861 | 0.595 | 1101/2114 | 1101/1292 |
| 2001614.1647460 | CSPAN | 1.000 | 1.000 | 0.000 | 0.000 | 0/0 | 0/0 |
| 19980308.1216980 | CSPAN | 1.000 | 1.000 | 0.000 | 0.000 | 0/0 | 0/0 |
| 20010628.1649460 | CSPAN | 0.962 | 0.916 | 0.000 | 0.000 | 0/0 | 0/0 |
| 20010702.1650112 | CSPAN | 1.000 | 1.000 | 0.000 | 0.000 | 0/0 | 0/0 |
| 19980203_CNN | CNN | 0.675 | 0.887 | 0.894 | 0.607 | 1544/2320 | 1544/1774 |
| Mean | | 2065/2644 | 2065/2193 | 898/1090 | 898/1687 | 9045/14996 | 9045/11044 |
| | | 0.781 | 0.942 | 0.824 | 0.532 | 0.603 | 0.819 |

**Fig. 5.** System evaluation results of the second run

After the completion of the processing pipeline, transitions that are less than 5 frames long are declared as abrupt, and shots shorter than 20 frames are merged with its previous one.

We have experimented for two runs with different processing parameters and the evaluation results generated from the matching program provided by NIST are shown in Fig.4 and Fig.5. Since there is no gradual transition in the C-SPAN videos, the corresponding precision and recall measures are set to zero.

## 4 Conclusions

In this paper, we have presented a framework for the detection transitions between video shots and the determination of their corresponding types. The method utilizes the visual features in the video frames and performs in a coarse-to-fine fashion. The framework contains four steps: Transition Boundary Initialization, Illumination Artifact Removal, Transition Type Determination and Gradual Transition Boundary Localization. The process is straightforward and easy for implementation. It has been tested on an open benchmark data set provided by NIST, and competitive results have been obtained.

## References

1. http://www-nlpir.nist.gov/projects/tv2003/ tv2003.html
2. J.S. Boreczky and L.A. Rowe, "A Comparison of Video Shot Boundary Detection Techniques", *Journal of Electronic Imaging*, 5(2), April 1996.
3. B. Furht, S. W. Smoliar and H. Zhang, "Video and Image Processing in Multimedia Systems". Norwell, MA: Kluwer, 1995.
4. A. Hanjalic, "Shot Boundary Detection: Unraveled and Resolved?", *IEEE Transactions on Circuits and Systems for Video Technology*, 2002.
5. R. Lienhart, "Reliable Transition Detection In Videos: A Survey and Practitioner's Guide", *International Journal of Image and Graphics*, 2001.
6. X. Liu and T. Chen, "Shot Boundary Detection Using Temporal Statistics Modeling", ICASSP, 2002.
7. A. Nagasaka and Y. Tanaka, "Automatic Video Indexing and Full-Video Search For Object Appearances", *Visual Database Systems II*, 1992.
8. K. Otsuji, Y. Tonomura and Y. Ohba, "Video Browsing Using Brightness Data", SPIE/IST VCIP, 1991.
9. B.-L. Yeo and B. Liu, "Rapid Scene Analysis On Compressed Video," *IEEE Trans. Circuits and Systems for Video Technology*, 1995.
10. R. Zabih, J. Miller, and K. Mai, "A Feature-Based Algorithm For Detecting Cuts and Classifying Scene Breaks", *ACM Multimedia*, 1995.
11. D. Zhang, W. Qi and H.J. Zhang, "A New Shot Detection Algorithm", *IEEE Pacific-Rim Conf on Multimedia*, 2001.

# All-in-Focus Imaging Using a Series of Images on Different Focal Planes

Mark Antunes, Michael Trachtenberg, Gabriel Thomas, and Tina Shoa

Department of Electrical and Computer Engineering at the University of Manitoba
Winnipeg, Manitoba, R3T 5V6
{umantune, umtracht}@cc.umanitoba.ca
{thomas, tshoa}@ee.umanitoba.ca

**Abstract.** In all-in-focus imaging, a series of photographs taken of the same objects, on different focal planes, are analyzed to create an entirely in-focus final image. Edge detection techniques determined by variable thresholds are applied to the 512x512 input images and they are then progressively subdivided into smaller, $2^N$ sized blocks, varying in size from 256x256 pixels down to 1x1 pixel. The 1x1 blocks are used to determine actual edges and the areas around them are then filled with progressively larger block sizes. The particular image that is most in-focus over a given region is determined by comparing the sums of edge pixels for the corresponding blocks of the different input images. Beyond aesthetic value, all-in-focus imaging may be used in applications ranging from pattern recognition and object detection to biometrics. We have successfully detected in-focus regions in an image and have generated final, all-in-focus images with only minor errors.

## 1 Introduction

When photographing a person who is several hundred meters in front of the Eiffel Tower, a decision must be made as to whether to focus on the subject in the foreground or the Tower in the background. Either choice results in the other object being out of focus. This is because like the human eye, current digital photography is only able to focus on a single focal plane at a time and as a result, objects which do not lie on that plane appear blurred.

The *focal plane* is a flat plane orthogonal to the optical axis on which a lens is focused. Objects are typically located at distinct focal plane distances, with the last focal plane representing the "infinite plane". All-in-focus imaging provides a method for capturing images on multiple focal planes and transferring them on a single image in which all objects are in-focus.

In the past, several methods have been proposed to obtain all-in-focus images. The *select and merge method* generates a focused image from two differently focused ones [1] by blurring an image using a *Point Spread Function* (PSF) which is approximated by a *Gaussian function*. This technique yields unsatisfactory results when applied to more than two images [2]. Attempts to extend the select and merge method to handle multiple images by comparing each image to its neighbours and selecting the focused regions have been unsatisfactory. Other auto-focusing systems

[3] use a PSF to determine whether or not the input image is focused, but these systems are generally unsuccessful due to the difficulty of accurately determining the blur parameters. Another proposed method for generating a focus image is based on image fusion [4]. This method must be optimized for the fusion algorithm parameters which are expected to affect the contrast and stability of the image. Hui, et al. [5] generate an all-in-focus image from two images using a combination of image fusion, the wavelet transform, and an area-based maximum selection scheme. This technique generally does not perform well around boundary regions [1].

Shoa et al. [6] created all-in-focus images of micromechanical systems based on gradient operators and the premise that in-focus objects exhibit sharp edges. A light microscope equipped with a CCD camera with different focus settings was used. Our goal in this paper is to extend this approach into the realm of general photography of images taken with a commercial digital camera.

## 2 Image Acquisition

Sample images were acquired with a 6.3 Megapixel EOS Digital Canon Rebel Camera set atop of a tripod. All camera settings were manually adjusted, with the focal planes uniquely determined based on the objects' locations. The images were then resized to 512x512 pixels and converted from colour to grayscale. In order to get the best results, the nearest objects are placed approximately 10cm away from the camera, while the farthest objects were placed approximately 8-10m away. Below are example input images that will be referred to later in the paper.

**Fig. 1.** Two sets of input images taken from the same position in which objects become in-focus on different focal planes

Additionally, contrast enhancement is applied so that objects become more distinct and isolated. Our algorithm uses a simple power law transformation with a $\gamma$ value of 0.2 for this purpose. This technique enhances the desired edges of the objects to be identified as belonging to a region with the correct focal settings.

## 3 Edge Detection as a Focusing Metric

Light refracts when it passes through a lens. The degree to which light waves in a lens bend upon exiting depends on their relative location to the lens, but to a first order approximation, all of the exiting beams converge at a specific point S from the lens. This location is called the focal point, and it defines the image plane that is most in focus. Any other location S' will be blurred, and the degree of blurriness is correlated with the relative distance between S and S'. The blurring appears as a circle of radius $b$, whose relationship to the distance $v''$ and lens diameter $a$ is given by [6]

$$v'' = \frac{a+b}{a} v. \qquad (1)$$

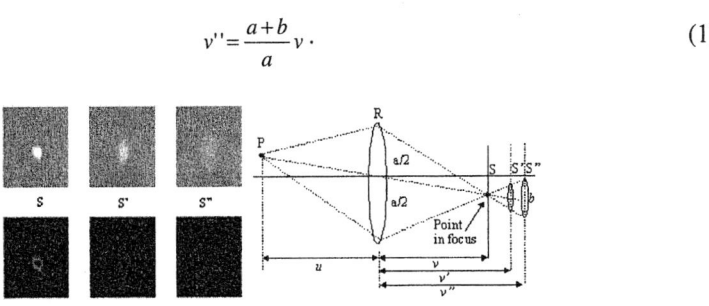

**Fig. 2.** A *point P* appears out of focus and it is imaged as a blurred disc at image planes different than $S$ that violate the lens equation. Original grayscale images *(top row)* and their corresponding gradients *(bottom row)*.

The above image pairs show the original and gradient images at three different image focal planes. The blurring follows the smooth transition from the background and the gradient can therefore be used as a metric to measure the focal areas of more complex images. The blurring effect can be explained using the following two systems:

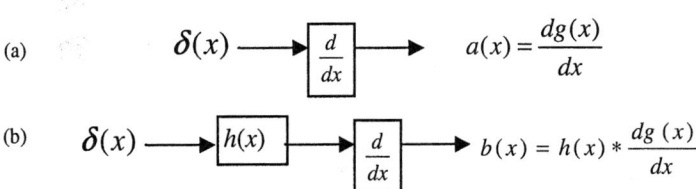

**Fig. 3.** (a) Modeling the image gradient using correct focus settings. (b) Image gradient when a different focal plane is chosen. The convolution increases the images radius and blurs the image.

Although images are generally two-dimensional, a one-dimensional analysis is used here to simplify the explanation. The output of Fig. 3(a) represents the derivative of the impulse-like image. Because the partial derivatives of the image with respect to $x$ and $y$ can be calculated using convolution and the derivative of a Gaussian, the output is solely the derivative of a Gaussian function, which has one positive and one negative peak. The gradient of the focused point in Fig. 2 is a ring whose magnitude has been plotted.

The system in Fig. 3(b) describes what occurs when the impulse-like image has been degraded by selecting a focal plane in which the point is not in-focus. This is modeled as the convolution of the input impulse and a PSF, which is modeled in two dimensions as:

$$h(x,y) = \begin{cases} 0 & \sqrt{x^2+y^2} > b \\ (1/\pi b^2) & \sqrt{x^2+y^2} \leq b \end{cases} \quad (2)$$

where $b$ depends on the extent of the focus defect. The value of $b(x)$ decays as a function of the focal settings:

$$b(x) = \int_{x-c/2}^{x+c/2} \frac{-2c\tau}{\pi b^2} e^{-c\tau^2} d\tau \quad (3)$$

and its maximum value is found by:

$$\max\{b(x)\} = \int_{-b}^{0} \frac{-2c\tau}{\pi b^2} e^{-c\tau^2} d\tau = \frac{\left(1 - e^{-cb^2}\right)}{\pi b^2} \quad (4)$$

The rapid decay in amplitude is evident in the two images of Fig. 2 which were taken at erroneous focal settings S' and S'' [7].

## 4 The Proposed Method Algorithm

At this point in the algorithm the images have been pre-processed with the power law transformation for contrast enhancement and the gradient images have been computed using Roberts masks using a variable threshold.

### 4.1 Variable Thresholding

The use of a single threshold value as in [6] is insufficient when working with general commercial photographic images. This is because detailed images contain many variations in shape and texture and there is no universal edge detection indicator. A large threshold value results in only very distinct edges being selected. The selected image components are virtually guaranteed to be in-focus, but sections of an image which are in-focus may be neglected if they don't have sharp edges. Low threshold values in contrast, identify slower transitions in pixel values as edges. Although more image components are identified, the edges of blurry objects are included in the edge detected image.

In our algorithm, a default maximum value is defined for the threshold and then applied to the images to determine the sections which are in-focus. Once the resulting data is collected and processed, the threshold is then reduced by a variable amount and reapplied to the images so that areas which have not previously been detected at a higher threshold can now be identified. This process continues over a range of threshold values until a predetermined number of iterations have been reached.

The varying amount by which the threshold is decremented is calculated by finding the midway point between the current threshold and a default minimum threshold. This approach has been chosen because small variations at high thresholds do not significantly affect a gradient image, whereas, small variations at low thresholds can affect the gradient image tremendously. Optimal results with reasonable execution times have occurred by using a maximum threshold of 0.500 and a minimum value of 0.100 with 5 iterations. Thus, threshold values of 0.500, 0.300, 0.200, 0.150, and 0.125 are used.

### 4.2 Image Subdivision and Edge Summation

Each of the gradient images is progressively subdivided into $2^N$ block sizes ranging from 256x256 to 1x1 pixel(s). For each threshold value, the sum of identified edge pixels in the gradient image is stored for each of the different sized blocks. This process is performed on each input image. The algorithm then uses these values to determine which of the input regions is the most in-focus for the given region.

### 4.3 Detecting In-focus Regions

The block that contains the most edge pixels is then mapped to a corresponding label image. A label image tracks which gradient image has the most edges for a given region at a given block size. The various block sizes and the data they contain are stored in separate labelled images until the final decisions are made in the weighted voting section. This process also occurs for each threshold value, and a block ceases to be processed if a label image has already been established.

In Fig. 4, the contents of the nine labelled images can be seen at the algorithm progresses. From this figure, it is clear that the smaller sized blocks yield the high precision that is needed to reconstruct an all-in-focus image; however, these images show that there are still many regions that don't have a label assigned to them. Thus, the larger block sizes are used to fill-in the surrounding pixels. Also, as the threshold lowers, the labelled images also become more complete because there a many more edges in the gradient images from which these labelled images were created. Each of the various shades of gray represents one of the four input images as being selected to be the most in-focus for the corresponding block size. The input images on the closer focal planes result in a dark colour and the input images on the farther focal planes result in a light colour.

### 4.4 Weighted Voting and Final Pixel Selection

Once the input images have been processed and the labelled images created for each block size, the various input image sections that will be mapped to the final, all-in-focus image must be selected on a pixel-by-pixel basis. In order to create the final image, different weighting is assigned based on a) the size of the blocks which were used to create labelled image; and b) the iteration level in which the label was assigned. In the first scheme, the 1x1 pixel blocks are assigned the highest weighting and the lowest weighting to the 256x256 pixel blocks. The reason behind this approach is that the 1x1 pixel blocks contain the most specific information pertaining to an edge being detected. Essentially, the 2x2 pixel blocks are used to fill in around

All-in-Focus Imaging Using a Series of Images on Different Focal Planes    179

the 1x1 blocks and the 4x4 blocks are used to fill in around the 2x2 blocks. This approach assumes that pixels near distinct edges are also in-focus or in other words, pixels which are in the same general region lie on the same focal plane.

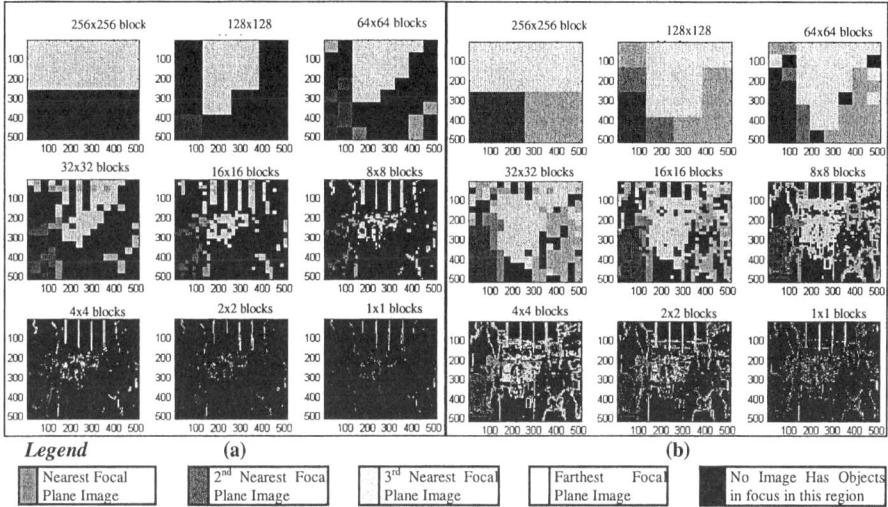

**Fig. 4.** (a) Initial label images for each block subdivision at the highest threshold for the bottom row of images in *Fig. 1* (b) Final label images for each block subdivision at the lowest threshold for the bottom row of images in *Fig. 1*

However, as objects become increasingly out-of-focus they begin to dilate as can be seen in Fig. 2 which results in boundary problems. As the edge detection threshold continues to decrease, pixels in the vicinity of an object's actual edge may become falsely selected into the labelled images because they appear in the gradient image. As a result, simply assigning the highest weight to the 1x1 pixel blocks will not yield optimal results. Therefore, the algorithm also keeps track of which iteration it was on when the labelled pixel was selected and assigns a higher weighting to pixels which were selected at higher thresholds. Using this approach, it is possible for the information in the labelled images created with larger sized blocks to be used over the information in labelled images with smaller block sizes so long as that the pixel label was determined at an earlier iteration for the larger block size.

Specifically, the final value of any input pixel $r_{xy}$ is determined by referencing its pixel value in the 1x1 pixel labelled image. If the label image has a label assigned at that location and that label was assigned on the first iteration, then that {x,y} coordinate in the final labelled image gets the value indicated by the label. Now, if no label is associated with the $r_{xy}^{th}$ pixel at the 1x1 level, the algorithm then looks at that pixel location in the 2x2 labelled image to the label at that coordinate. If however, there is a label assigned to that location in the 1x1 labelled image but it was selected on the second iteration with a lower threshold, the algorithm then looks to see if there are labels assigned at the 2x2 level for that pixel. If the labels at the 2x2 level were selected in the first iteration, then the corresponding location in the final labelled image will come from the 2x2 labelled image and not the 1x1 labelled image. This continues until the 256x256 block sizes are reached. Explicitly, 1x1 blocks can be outweighed by 2x2 blocks if, at the coordinate {x,y}, the labels were assigned to the 2x2 blocks at least one iteration before the 1x1 blocks; but in this case they would not be outweighed by 4x4 blocks. Furthermore, the 2x2 blocks, can be outweighed by 8x8 blocks, if the labels were assigned to the 8x8 blocks at least two iterations before the 2x2 blocks.

For both sets of input images in Fig. 1, the final labelled images can be seen below with the darkest shade of gray representing the nearest focal plane input image.

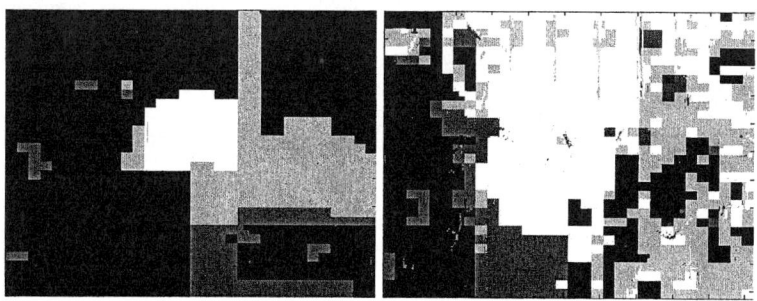

**Fig. 5.** Final labelled image used to produce the final, all-in-focus image of the top row of input images from Fig. 1 *(left)* and the bottom row of input images *(right)*

### 4.5 Creating an All-in-Focus Image

Creating the final, all-in-focus image is simply a matter of traversing the final labelled image pixel by pixel in order to determine which input image has been selected as being in-focus. Next, the algorithm simply extracts the pixel intensity value from the corresponding image, and stores the value at the same location in the final image. The result of applying our algorithm to the images in Fig. 1 can be seen below.

**Fig. 6.** The final, all-in-focus image all-in-focus image of the top row of input images from Fig. 1 *(left)* and the bottom row of input images *(right)*

## 5 Conclusions

As seen in Fig. 6, an all-in-focus image can be extracted from a series of images taken at different focal lengths with minor errors. Currently, the algorithm takes approximately 20 minutes to run on a Pentium 4, 2.5 GHz PC. By optimizing the algorithm and with the ever increasing speed of integrated circuits, our approach may soon be an attractive technique for generating all-in-focus images in real time.

## References

[1] K. Kodama, K. Aizawa and M. Hatori, "Iterative Reconstruction of an All-Focused Image by Using Multiple Differently Focused Images, " *IEEE Proceedings of 1996 International Conference on Image Processing*, Vol. III, pp.551-554, 1996.

[2] Y. Tsubaki, A. Kubota, K. Kazuya, K. Aizawa "All-focused image generation and 3D modeling of microscopic images of insects", *IEEE Proceedings 2001 International Conference on Image Processing*, Volume: 2, Page(s): 197 -200, 2001

[3] S. Ku Kim, S. Rae Park; J. Ki Paik, "Simultaneous out-of-focus blur estimation and restoration for digital auto-focusing system," *IEEE Transactions on Consumer Electronics,* Volume: 44 Issue: 3, Page(s): 1071 –1075, Aug 1998

[4] P.J. Burt, R.J. Kolczynski, "Enhanced image capture through fusion ," *IEEE Proceedings Fourth International Conference on Computer Vision*, 11-14, Page(s): 173 –182, May 1993

[5] L. Hui, B.S. Manjunath, S.K. Mitra, "Multi-sensor image fusion using the wavelet transform," *IEEE Proceedings 1994 International Conference on Image Processing*, Volume: 1, Page(s): 51 -55, Nov. 1994

[6] Tina Shoa, Gabriel Thomas, Cyrus Shafai, Alireza Shoa "Extacting a Focused Image From several out-of-focus Micromechanical Structure Images, " *ICASSP,* 2004

[7] Blind deconvolution of spatially invariant image blurs with phase *Cannon,M.;* Acoustics, Speech, and Signal Processing, IEEE Transactions on ,Volume: 24 , Issue: 1 , Feb 1976 Pages: 58 – 63

# Skew Estimation and Correction for Form Documents Using Wavelet Decomposition*

Dihua Xi[1], Mohamed Kamel[1], and Seong-Whan Lee[2]

[1] Pattern Analysis and Machine Intelligence Research Group,
Department of Electrical and Computer Engineering,
University of Waterloo, Waterloo, Canada
{dhxi, mkamel}@pami.uwaterloo.ca
[2] Center for Artificial Vision Research,
Korea University, Seoul, Korea
swlee@image.korea.ac.kr

**Abstract.** Form document image processing has become an increasingly essential technology in office automation tasks. One of the problems is that the document image may appear skewed for many reasons. Therefore, the skew estimation plays an important role in any automatic document analysis system. In the past few years, many algorithms have been developed to detect the skew angle of text document images. However, these algorithms suffer from two major deficiencies. Firstly, most of them suppose that the original image is monochrome and therefore they are not suitable to apply to documents with a complicated background. Secondly, most of the current methods were developed for general document images that are not as complicated as form documents. In this paper, we present a new approach to skew detection for grey-level form document images. In our system, image decomposition by 2D wavelet transformations is used to estimate the skew angle.

## 1 Introduction

Form documents play an important role in people's daily lives. Various categories of form documents, such as bank checks, invoices, flight tickets, etc., are widely used and are generally processed manually. However, the manual processing method is very tedious and expensive. Therefore, the development of an automatic system for the processing of these forms is very much needed. In general, there are three interrelated steps involved in dealing with the automatic processing of form documents, namely, *preprocessing, form layout analysis* and *form data interpretation and recognition*. The final step can be solved by adopting conventional optical character recognition (OCR) techniques. The second step is to locate and extract the key items which need to be interpreted and recognized. The accuracy of such system is primarily affected by the preprocessing step, which may include skew estimation and correction, line extraction, binarization, etc.

---

* This research was supported by Natural Sciences and Engineering Research Council of Canada (NSERC).

The estimation of the skew angle and skew correction affects almost all of the subsequent processing steps and, therefore, this step is very important. However, in the previous methods, input images are always assumed with no or very slightly skewed ($\leq 2°$). Image skewness affects almost all of the subsequent pressing steps and therefore, skew correction is very important for the development of an accurate and efficient form processing system. The most difficult problem is the estimation of the skew angle, since the skew correction can be implemented using many traditional methods. Many skew estimating algorithms have been developed for general document processing. O'Gorman [1] classified these algorithms into three categories those based on the projection profile [2], Hough transform [3] and nearest neighbor clustering techniques [4]. However, few papers have considered the skew problem of form documents.

Although many algorithms in the above three categories of techniques are satisfactorily accurate and fast for some general documents, none of these approaches is suitable for complicated form documents. The skew estimation of form documents is very difficult, due to their specific characteristics, namely:

- The type and size of the fonts may vary in a form document.
- Form document consists of table lines. In some cases, several categories of table lines may appear simultaneously in one form.
- Handwriting strokes may be included. The size, stroke thickness, baseline and color, etc. may vary significantly between forms filled in by different fillers.
- The problem of overlap may occur between the strokes, table lines and printed fonts.
- A form document may include photos or a complicated background.
- Moreover, the color or intensity of the background, lines and strokes may also vary in a form document.

Furthermore, most of those algorithms are only appropriate for machine-printed pages without overlap. In practice, however, filled-in handwriting strokes and overlap always appear in form documents. Moreover, almost all of the proposed methods are limited to binarized document images. There is an increasing number of forms that are used in daily life. Unfortunately, one can never expect perfect results, especially for an image with a complicated background. Therefore, it is difficult to process complex images using such approaches.

In this paper, we proposed a novel methodology based on 2D wavelet decomposition technique, which has been used efficiently for the extraction of reference lines and filled in strokes from form document images [5]. In our approach, wavelet decomposition is an essential step, which is used to restrain the complicated background and then estimate the local directions of the important components. Our system can still work well, even if the grey values on the line and background change continuously.

## 2 Form Image Decomposition

In this section, we explain the basic notation of wavelet decomposition and then describe the construction of 2D wavelets with adjustable rectangular supports for skew image processing.

## 2.1 Construction of Non-orthogonal Wavelet with Adjustable Rectangle Support

According to the wavelet theory [6, 7], an orthogonal wavelet can be defined by its own scaling function $\varphi(x)$ and wavelet function $\psi(x)$. The 2D wavelet is usually constructed from 1-D wavelet, by define $\varphi(x)\varphi(y)$ as wavelet function, $\psi(x)\varphi(y)$, $\varphi(x)\psi(y)$ and $\psi(x)\psi(y)$ as scaling functions. These functions can be used to decompose any function $f(x,y) \in L^2(R^2)$ into four sub functions, as follows:

$$f(x,y) = f_{V \otimes V}(x,y) \oplus f_{V \otimes W}(x,y) \oplus f_{W \otimes V}(x,y) \oplus f_{W \otimes W}(x,y), \quad (1)$$

Where the symbol $A \otimes B$ stands for the tensor product of the two spaces, $A$ and $B$.

The support of a 2-D wavelet is usually a square area, because the same support exists for both the scale and wavelet function of 1-D orthogonal wavelet. Therefore, we introduce a method of constructing a 2D wavelet with rectangle support using two 1D wavelets. Let $\varphi(x), \psi(x)$ and $\varphi'(x), \psi'(x)$ be wavelet and scaling functions corresponding to two wavelets may with different supports. Then, $\varphi(x)\varphi'(y)$, $\varphi(x)\psi'(y)$, $\psi(x)\varphi'(y)$, and $\psi(x)\psi'(y)$ are a 2-D wavelet. As in the case of equation (1), any $f(x,y) \in L^2(R^2)$ can be decomposed as

$$f(x,y) = f_{V \otimes V'}(x,y) \oplus f_{V \otimes W'}(x,y) \oplus f_{W \otimes V'}(x,y) \oplus f_{W \otimes W'}(x,y). \quad (2)$$

The constructed 2D wavelet might have adjustable rectangle support according to the practice conditions. Similar to orthogonal wavelet, the decomposition of a 2D function by the proposed adjustable wavelet can also be accomplished by a two times integral, due to the fact that the wavelet and scaling functions are still separable.

## 2.2 Wavelet Decomposition of Skew Form Document Image

Two of these four sub-images in equation 2, LH and HL, incorporate various responses to lines with different skew angles, as will be shown in Fig. 5. We use of this property in order to estimate the skew angle of a form.

### 2.2.1 Mathematical Description

Suppose that the parameter equation of a straight line on a plane can be written in the form

$$l_c : \begin{cases} x = x_0 + k_1 t \\ y = y_0 + k_2 t \end{cases}, \quad t \in [a, b], \quad (3)$$

which passes through the fixed point $(x_0, y_0)$ and the slope of the line can be evaluated by $\tan \alpha = \frac{k_2}{k_1}$, where $k_1$ and $k_2$ satisfy the constraint $k_1^2 + k_2^2 \neq 0$.

Although, from the mathematical point of view, a line does not possess any width in practice as shown in Fig. 1, a real line in an image should have a width, $w$, and a slope angle, $\alpha$. Suppose that the center line is $l_c$, and $l_p$ is a line parallel to $l_c$. The widths in the horizontal and vertical directions are $w_x = \frac{w}{\sin \alpha}$ and $w_y = \frac{w}{\cos \alpha}$, respectively.

A grey image containing this line can be represented by

$$f(x,y) = \begin{cases} f_{line}(x,y), & |k_2(x - x_0) + k_1(y - y_0)| < k_2 w_x \text{ or } k_1 w_y \\ f_{background}(x,y), & otherwise \end{cases} \quad (4)$$

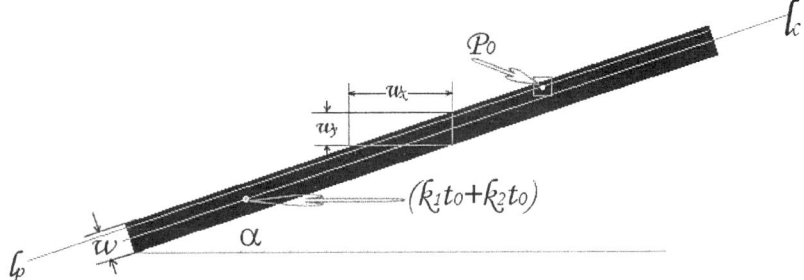

**Fig. 1.** Description of a line with width $w$ and slope angle $\alpha$

For a compact supported wavelet, suppose that its support window is a rectangle $[a,b] \times [c,d]$, then

$$f_{V \otimes W'}(x,y) = \int_a^b \varphi(\frac{u}{2})du \int_c^d f(u+2x, v+2y)\psi'(\frac{v}{2})dv. \qquad (5)$$

As in the case of equation (5), the projection onto $W \otimes V'$ can be calculated by $\Psi^2(x,y) = \varphi'(x)\psi(y)$ as

$$f_{W \otimes V'}(x,y) = \int_a^b \varphi'(\frac{v}{2})dv \int_c^d f(u+2x, v+2y)\psi(\frac{u}{2})du \qquad (6)$$

In fact, the width and height of the sub-image are only half that of the original image, which allows the computational speed to be increased.

### 2.2.2 Choose Proper Wavelet Support

In this section, we discuss how to choose a proper rectangle support. We consider two factors: the slope and width of the line to be extracted.

- The choice of support: with various types of rectangles.
- The response to different lines (angles, width) and at different positions.

If the skew angle is not close to $\frac{\pi}{4}$, it is better to use a rectangle support by choosing different support Coiflet wavelets. There are two advantages to using a rectangle support. Firstly, it can save computing time. Secondly, a better result can be obtained when we decide the threshold to use and estimate the skew angle later on. In our experiments, the 2-D Coiflet-Coiflet (C-C) wavelet filter [8] with rectangular supports which are used for estimating the LH and HL sub images, is illustrated in Fig. 3. These wavelets are constructed by the 1-D Coiflets at order 1 and 2, whose support width are 5 and 11, respectively. We give an example in Fig. 4 to show the LH and HL sub-images under the C1-C2 wavelets shown in Fig. 3.

### 2.2.3 Characteristics of Form Document Decomposition

An artificial image is presented in Fig. 5 to illustrate the properties described above. The input image $(a)$ shown in the upper middle of Fig. 5 consists of various lines with

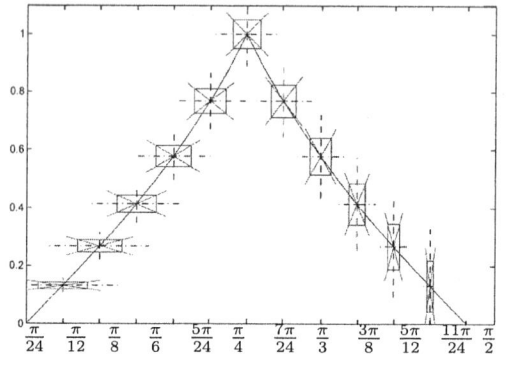
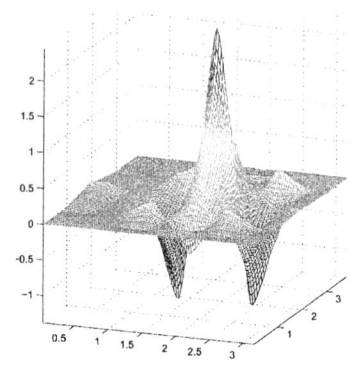

**Fig. 2.** The various types of ideal wavelet rectangular supports corresponding to the angle of a line and horizontal direction

**Fig. 3.** The 2-D Coiflet wavelet functions: $\varphi(x)\psi'(y)$

different slopes. On the left side, the LH sub-image corresponding to the projection onto $V \otimes W'$ is shown. The HL sub-image is located on the right side. One can see from Fig. 5 that the response in the LH sub-image becomes weaker, whereas the response in the HL sub-image becomes stronger, as the direction of the lines changes from horizontal to vertical.

Fig. 6 illustrates an example of line whose point intensity changes frequently. One can see that a strong response is still obtained near the edge using the constructed wavelet decomposition.

## 3  Determination of the Skew Angle

According to section 2.2, a form document image can be decomposed into two sub-images, named LH and HL. The complexity of the background is well restrained in both sub-images. Therefore, the lines can be distinguished from the background, regardless of the response intensity.

A form is primarily composed of two perpendicular sets of lines. Some forms include only one set of lines. To decide the skew angle, we only need to find the direction of the main set of lines. Our algorithm to estimate the skew angle and furthermore the skew correction can be divided into the following steps.

**Step 1: Binarization of Sub-images**
Using the intensity distribution of LH and HL sub images, the binarization thresholds can be estimated.

**Step 2: Orientation of each Point in the Foreground**
The orientation of a point $(x, y)$ in the foreground is estimated by

$$\varphi(x,y) = \frac{1}{2}\arctan(\frac{2*\mu_{1,1}}{\mu_{2,0}-\mu_{0,2}}), \tag{7}$$

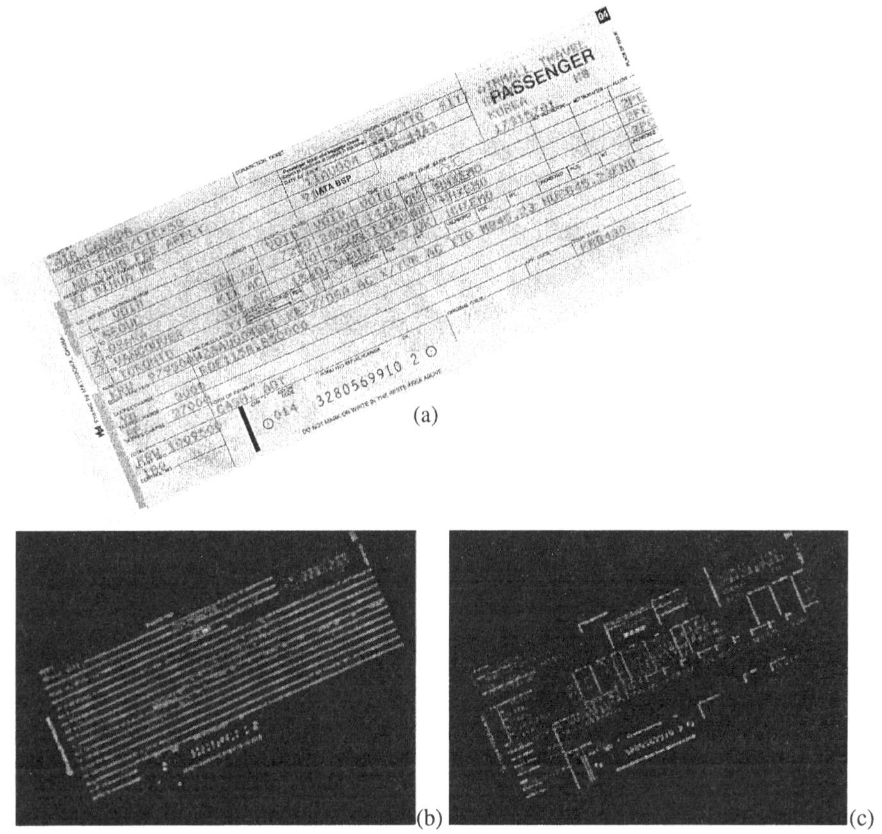

Skew Estimation and Correction for Form Documents Using Wavelet Decomposition 187

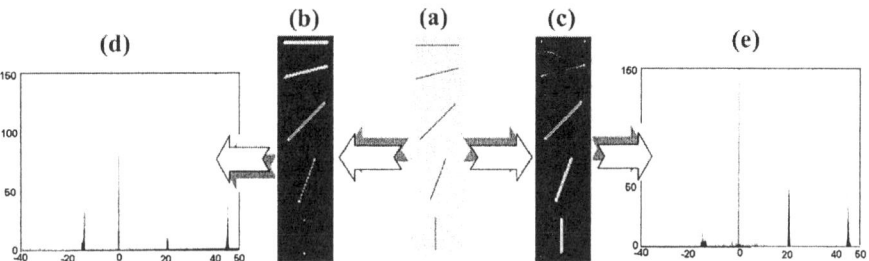

**Fig. 4.** Wavelet decomposition of a Canadian Flight ticket using C-C wavelets. (a) Original skew image; (b) & (c) LH and HL sub-images of (a), respectively.

**Fig. 5.** Responses of different slope lines. (a) Original image; (b) & (c) The LH and HL sub-images of (a); (d) & (e) The distribution histograms for different orientations of the LH and HL sub-images, respectively.

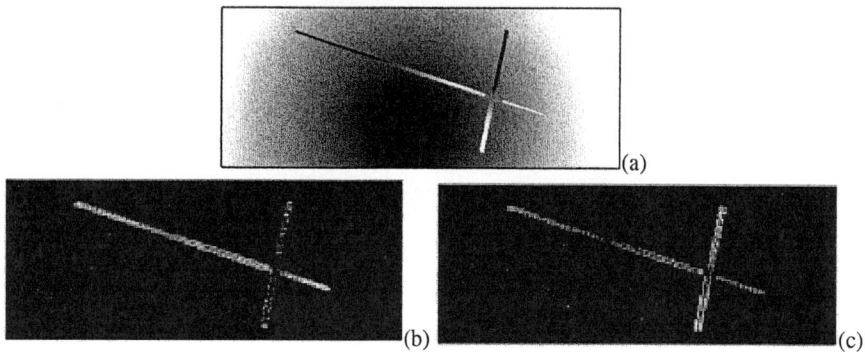

**Fig. 6.** The wavelet decomposition of an image with complex line and background. (a) Original image; (b) & (c) The LH and HL sub-images of (a), respectively.

where

$$\mu_{p,q} = \sum_{i=-N_x}^{N_x} \sum_{j=-N_y}^{N_y} (x+i-\bar{x})^p (y+j-\bar{y})^q, \; if \; f(x+i, y+j) \; is \; a \; point \; in \; the \; foreground.$$

The center of mass $(\bar{x}, \bar{y})$ and the $(p, q)$ order central moments $\mu_{p,q}$ are calculated as:

$$\begin{cases} \bar{x} = \frac{1}{M} \sum_{i=-N_x}^{N_x} \sum_{j=-N_y}^{N_y} (x+i), & if \; f(x+i, y+j) \; is \; a \; point \; in \; the \; foreground \\ \bar{y} = \frac{1}{M} \sum_{i=-N_y}^{N_y} \sum_{j=-N_y}^{N_y} (y+j), & if \; f(x+i, y+j) \; is \; a \; point \; in \; the \; foreground. \end{cases} \quad (8)$$

**Step 3: Estimation of the Skew Angle**
The skew angle can be estimated from the distribution of the number of points for different orientations, because the directions for all of the points near a line are approximately parallel to the line. For an image containing a table, the majority of the points have orientations which are parallel to the direction of the group of lines.

Suppose the table in a form document image mainly consists of two groups of perpendicular lines. Representing the two perpendicular directions as one unique direction provides a convenient and reasonable method of finding the skew angle, because we can rectify the result by means of the two angles obtained from the LH and HL sub-images. Simultaneously, the range of $\varphi(x, y)$ can be reduced by half. Here, we obtain the skew angle in the interval $(-\frac{\pi}{4}, \frac{\pi}{4}]$, by

$$\phi(x,y) = \begin{cases} \varphi(x,y), & if \; |\varphi| \leq \frac{\pi}{4} \\ -sign(\varphi)(\frac{\pi}{2} - |\varphi|), & if \; |\varphi| > \frac{\pi}{4} \end{cases} \; where \; sign(x) = \begin{cases} 1, & if \; x > 0 \\ 0, & if \; x = 0 \\ -1, & if \; x < 0 \end{cases}$$

is the sign function.

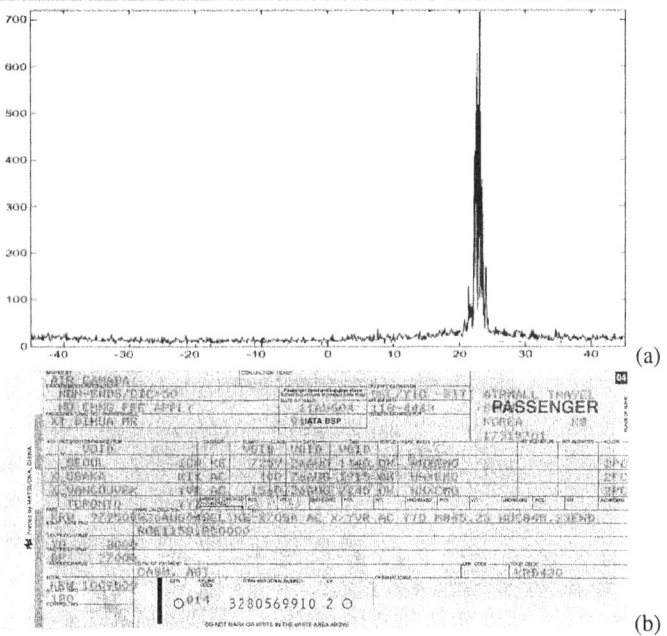

**Fig. 7.** Skew correction of a Canadian bank cheque shown in Fig. 4. (a) Histograms of different gradient orientations of LHsub-image; (b) The skew corrected image.

In fact, $\phi(x, y)$ can be interpreted as a periodic function with a period $\frac{\pi}{2}$. The most straight-forward way of estimating the skew angle is to use the histogram of the number of points for different orientations in the foreground of the image. The orientation histogram plots the number of pixels against the orientation. Fig. 5 is used to illustrate the responses of different directional lines. For an image with two sets of lines, a common approximate peak is reached in both histograms of the LH and HL sub-images. For an image mainly containing one set of lines, the peak will appear at least in one histogram. The peak value corresponds to the skew angle of the original form document image. Therefore, only one of the LH and HL sub-images is needed to estimate the skew angle.

Fig. 7a shows the distribution of the numbers of points for different orientations of the LH sub-image. The skew angle obtained from the histogram is about 23 degrees.

**Step 4: Skew Correction Using Estimated Skew Angle**

Using the skew angle $\theta$ obtained in the preceding section, the skew form document image can be aligned by the rotation transformation

$$\begin{cases} x' = x\cos\theta + y\sin\theta \\ y' = -x\sin\theta + y\cos\theta \end{cases}, \qquad (9)$$

where $(x, y)$ is the coordinate before being deskewed, and $(x', y')$ is the coordinate after being deskewed.

Fig. 7b shows the skew correction result for the original skewed document image shown in Fig. 4a.

## 4 Experiments and Conclusions

In this section, we first introduce the experimental results and then provide a discussion of them.

The performance of the proposed algorithm was tested using a form documents image database containing more than 300 skewed form document images, comprising several categories of forms, such as sales slips, airplane tickets, bank checks, telephone bills, and forms used in post offices, supermarket, schools, etc. The original images were imported using optical scanners and were subsequently converted into gray scale images. The scanning resolution range was from 200 to 600 DPI. The width or height of the images in the database varies from 300 to 7000 pixels. Most of the form images have a complicated background. The correction rate (considering the difference of the angles from their theoretical values to be less than $\pm 0.2°$) is more than 95 percent. The few examples of failure are due to the number of form lines being too small and the presence of too much "noise", such as that resulting from characters, filled-in information and the background.

The main contribution of this paper is the construction of a family of wavelet transforms with adjustable rectangular supports. Compared to the classical approaches, such as those based on the Hough transform, our system can be used for grey-level form document images with complicated backgrounds, which those traditional methods may not succeed on. At the same time, the computing complexity of our approach is low, mainly due to the use of wavelet decomposition. The experimental results confirm the excellent performance of this techniques.

## References

[1] O'Gorman, L.: The document spectrum for page layout analysis. IEEE Trans. on Pattern Analysis and Machine Intelligence **15** (1993) 1162–1173
[2] Pavlidis, T., Zhou, J.: Page segmentation and classification. Compute Vision, Graphics and Image Processing **54** (1992) 184–496
[3] Jiang, H.F., Han, C.C., Fan, K.C.: A fast approach to the detection and correction of skew documents. Pattern Recognition Letters **18** (1997) 675–686
[4] Gatos, B., Papamarkos, N., Chamzas, C.: Skew detection and text line position determination in digitized documents. Pattern Recognition **30** (1997) 1505–1519
[5] Xi, D., Lee, S.W.: Extraction of reference lines and items from form document images. Pattern Recognition **38** (2005) 289–305
[6] Mallat, S.: A Wavelet Tour of Signal Processing. Academic Press, San Diego (1998)
[7] Donoho, D., Mallat, S., von Sachs, R., Samuelides, Y.: Signal and covariance estimation with macrotiles. IEEE Trans. on Signal Processing **53** (2003) 614–627
[8] Daubechies, I.: Orthonormal bases of compactly supported wavelets. Communications on Pure and Applied Mathematics **41** (1988) 909–996

# Scalable e-Learning Multimedia Adaptation Architecture

Mazen Almaoui and Konstantinos N. Plataniotis

Dept. of Electrical and Computer Engineering, University of Toronto
{mazen, kostas}@dsp.utoronto.ca

**Abstract.** A neglected challenge in existing e-Learning (eL) systems is providing access to multimedia to all users regardless of environmental conditions such as diverse device capabilities, the heterogeneity of the underlying IP network, and user modality preference. This paper proposes a novel two-tier transcoding framework capable of adapting eL multimedia to meet the end-user environmental challenges. This two-tier architecture consists of 1)an application layer transcoder that adapts the presentation format of the eL content as viewed in a browser to meet device capabilities and user modality preference, 2) a bitstream transcoder that transforms multimedia streams to conform to the device's processing capabilities and to adapt the encoding rate to meet the network's fluctuating bandwidth. Results demonstrate the eL multimedia transcoding for mobile devices and its low overhead delays.

## 1 Introduction

The maturity of the Internet has given rise to effective collaborative e-Learning (eL) webcasting. Such applications allow various people from different physical locations to communicate and interact together over the Internet. Fig. 1 shows a screen shot of the web interface for the ePresence eL webcasting system that has the capability of streaming video, audio, text, and slides to the end-user [1].

The increasing multimedia processing capability of mobile devices such as Personal Digital Assistants (PDA), Pocket PCs, and Smart Phones as well as advances in wired and wireless networks in terms of multimedia delivery have added a new dimension to how people collaborate. Conventional eL applications such as ePresence cannot support multimedia delivery that adapts to unique device and network conditions. In light of this fact, there is a growing aspiration for a Universal Multimedia Access (UMA) Framework [2] that provides seamless access of multimedia to anyone, at anytime, by adapting eL content to unique device capabilities, unreliable IP networks, and user personal preferences.

End-user devices differ in a multitude of processing capabilities such as framerate, resolution, and number of audio channels supported. This diversity in device capabilities requires media content to be adapted, and media streams that cannot be processed by the device to be dropped. This must be performed in real-time to avoid delays in delivering eL content and to provide the user with the experiences that an individual attending the actual live event would have [3].

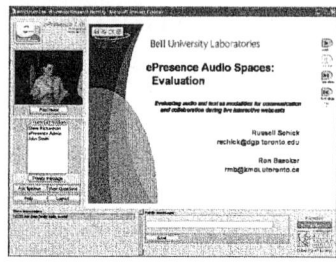

**Fig. 1.** ePresence: interactive e-Learning application

The second challenge to consider relates to the underlying network's bandwidth capacity and fluctuations determined by factors such as packet loss, delay, and jitter [4]. This diversity in bandwidth characteristics gives rise to a need for multimedia adaptation to provide variable bit-rate multimedia encoding.

Lastly, we address the challenge of delivering a given quality of experience [2] to the end user. This involves negotiation of a Quality of Service (QoS) based on personal preferences and preferred modality. This must be negotiated, not granted because not all devices are capable of processing all types of media.

In order to resolve the three key challenges, multimedia transcoding [5] is utilized to adapt eL content. Here, two types of transcoding are required; application layer transcoding and multimedia bitstream transcoding. Application layer transcoding adapts the presentation format of the eL content [6] to meet device processing capabilities and user preferences (Fig. 1). Bitstream transcoding [5] is performed on the the actual media to parse, transform, and truncate the underlying multimedia streams to adapt the encoding rate to the network's fluctuating bandwidth capacity. Both transcoding approaches require descriptions of varying device capabilities, network conditions, and user preferences. This can be done using metadata, a tool used for describing, indexing, and searching the properties of the user's environmental conditions, and properties of the actual media. Thus, metadata-driven transcoding [6] is needed to achieve application layer transcoding and to provide adaptation parameters to achieve bitstream transcoding. This paper proposes a novel scalable two-tier architecture for implementing metadata-driven transcoding. Section 2 gives a brief overview of existing eL systems architectures. Section 3 explains the proposed two-tier transcoding architecture. Section 4 visually demonstrates the importance of transcoding for an eL system by applying our approach to the ePresence architecture and provides the delay implications of real-time bitstream transcoding.

## 2 Related Work

Web-based eL systems such as the ones discussed in [7,3] include a combination of video, audio, slides, chat session, and whiteboard functionality. A four-tier electronic educational system (EES) model was proposed in [8] that provides a degree of data personalization to the end-user. The top layer (instructional layer) allows educators to specify which media to include in the system (video, slides, etc.). However, the end-user, does not have the flexibility to specify which eL material they desire and no consideration is put forth concerning what modalities individual user devices can process. The lower layers take the instructions from this layer to create the final presentation format as seen through a browser. Similarly, a metadata-based approach to delivering personalized course material for a specific user learning needs was proposed in [9]. In particular, IEEE LTSC Learning Object Metadata (LOM) is used to allow professors to deliver personalized material. For example, the user can choose the language or difficulty level of the eL material. Programmable models such as Netscript [1], ANTS[2], and SmartPackets[3] provide solutions for handling network traffic, however do not address adaption to meet device and user preference needs.

These eL solutions do not adapting multimedia to meet each user's unique device capabilities, modality preference, and adapting the media encoding rate to take into account fluctuating network conditions. Transcoding must be incorporated into existing eL applications all of the above mentioned user needs.

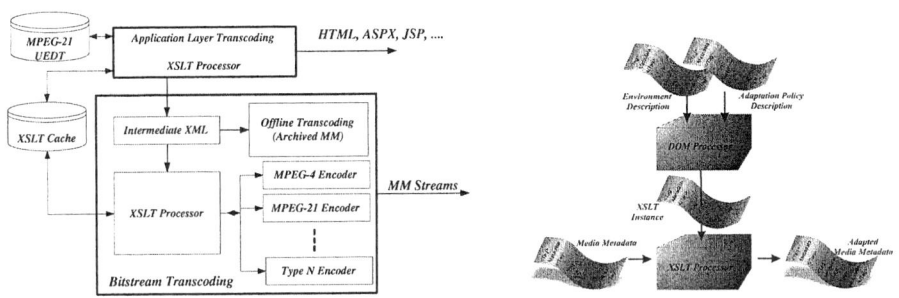

(a) Proposed two-tier metadata-driven transcoding architecture

(b) Metadata Transformation Engine

**Fig. 2.** System overview

## 3 Proposed System

The objective of the proposed transcoding system is to adapt eL multimedia to match a user's environment characteristics (device capability, network conditions, modality preference). The proposed architecture is shown in Fig 2(a).

Section 1 presented a motivation for metadata-driven transcoding. Metadata syntax is represented using Extensible Markup Language (XML). Metadata description can be done through the MPEG-21 standard [10]. The tools offered by the standard include the Usage Environment Description Tool (UEDT) [2] to describe device capabilities, network conditions, and user characteristics as

---

[1] http://www1.cs.columbia.edu/dcc/netscript/
[2] http://www.cs.washington.edu/homes/djw/papers/00755004.pdf
[3] http://www.net-tech.bbn.com/smtpkts/smtpkts-index.html

well as the natural environment characteristics. The processing and transformations of this metadata can be accomplished using Extensible Stylesheet Language Transformation (XSLT) [5]. Application layer transcoding requires transformation rules to process user metadata in order to determine the presentation preferences. Bitstream transcoding requires these rules to process intermediate XML and physically adapt multimedia to match the device's processing capabilities and network available bandwidth. Due to the short length of this paper, details of XSLT sheets will not be explained, refer to [10] for more detail.

A generic metadata transformation system is proposed in [11] as shown in Fig. 2. This solution consist of a Document Object Model (DOM) processor that creates XSLT sheets and an XSLT processor that transforms XML with the created XSLT sheet. The problem with DOM processing is its computational cost making it an unviable solution for a real-time eL application. Our method performs DOM processing a priori and caches XSLT sheets for transcoding. Here, an XSLT rule for providing multimedia adaptation is chosen from a set of previously cached sheets to provide best-effort service by replacing the DOM processor with a selection phase that is more efficient for real-time transcoding.

The XSLT sheet selection processes is comprised of three steps. First, the cached sheets are pre-filtered to determine a small set of possible sheets matching the user request. The pre-filtering is done based on parameters that remain *unchanged* throughout a session assuming the same device is used from the beginning of the eL webcast until the session is terminated. Then, one of the sheets from this set is chosen to be used during transcoding. Finally, the XSLT sheets chosen are passed to transcoding modules to transform XML metadata to produce the appropriate presentation template and to transcode the multimedia streams. This will be explained in more detail in subsequent sections. The process of determining which sheet to select is up to the system designer.

Application layer transcoding begins by obtaining the user's UEDT metadata. The main idea behind the application layer transcoding module is to choose the best matching XSLT rule from the XSLT cache that will adapt the eL content layout (which is represented by an XML file) to meet user environment characteristics. The sheet selected depends on the user's device capabilities and the desired modalities. This module produces and outputs the proper template that will display the desired modalities in a browser (Fig. 1). The template produced depends on the underlying eL system interface (e.g. HTML, JSP, etc.). The application layer transcoding module then passes control to the bitstream transcoding module to adapt multimedia streams as shown in Fig. 2(a).

The next step in the adaptation process is bitstream transcoding. The bitstream transcoding module utilizes adaptation parameters from the application layer module to transform the underlying streams. Depending on the implementation of the eL system, some of the components shown in Fig. 2(a) can be excluded. This will depend on whether transcoding will be conducted offline (i.e. on-demand) or in real-time (i.e. live and on-demand). As shown in Fig.2(a), the bitstream transcoding engine consists of the intermediate XML, offline and real-time (MPEG-4) encoders, and the XSLT processor.

As a residual of application layer transcoding, intermediate XML metadata is passed to the bitstream transcoding module. This intermediate XML contains the metadata describing the modality and resolutions reserved for each as supported by the browser template produced by the application layer transcoder. Additional information included are name and address of the multimedia that the browser embedded protocols will attempt to access eL multimedia and other optional parameters as required by the system.

Offline bitstream transcoding is in essence scalable coding [2]. Multiple scaled copies of the same media are encoded and stored on the content server. The multimedia copy that best matches the end-user's environment parameters is delivered. Scalable coding can only be used for on-demand eL systems and is not a viable solution for live webcasting. In contrast, real-time bitstream transcoding requires only one version of the multimedia to be stored on the content server. Multimedia is adapted in real-time to meet the end users environmental needs. There are various bitstream encoding solutions [5] capable of providing real-time transcoding. The XSLT processor in Fig. 2(a) can be used to transform the intermediate XML metadata to any format required by the underlying eL system's encoder in order to perform metadata-driven transcoding. For example, if the MPEG-21 Framework is used, the intermediate XML could be the environment description and the the bitstream description (BSD) [5] of the multimedia streams. The XSLT processor would process the user's environment description to determine which XSLT sheet to retrieve from the cache in order to adapt the requested multimedia streams. The output of the XSLT processor can be the bitstream adaptation rules required by the MPEG-21 encoder to transcode the multimedia streams to meet the end-user environmental needs.

The MPEG-4 Standard scalable tools are used to provide temporal, spatial, and SNR scalability, hence can serve as the bitstream transcoder. The set of rules obtained from the XSLT cache together with the intermediate XML serve as input into the XSLT processor. The intermediate XML contains parameters for temporal (e.g 15 f/s for PDA, 25 f/s for PC) and spatial (qcif for PDA, 4cif for PC) scaling of video and slides and audio scaling parameters. The XSLT processor outputs a script file that take into account the user's environment characteristics. This script is utilized by the MPEG-4 encoder to transcode the multimedia streams. Real-time transcoding solutions are not limited to the proposed MPEG-21 and MPEG-4 encoding solutions. The important point of the XSLT processor (in combination with the intermediate XML) is to provide an extensible architecture to incorporate any bitstream encoding solution that is a viable or desired solution to virtually any eL system.

## 4 Results

Experimental results of our system for achieving application layer and bitstream transcoding will be presented in this section. This will demonstrate why application layer transcoding is crucial to delivering personalized eL material to meet the user's device, network, and personal preference to in order to affectively utilize ePresence interface functionality. Results of the proposed bitstream transcoding approach will also be evaluated in terms of how delay will affect real-time multimedia adaptation and delivery of ePresence material. Testing is conducted using an FFMPEG encoder [4], Darwin Streaming Server [5], and a QuickTime Player to provide an end-to-end MPEG-4 delivery framework. Note that multicasting is not used because (a) the ePresence server resides over a restricted unicast network gateway and (b) eL material needs to be delivered to each user separately to match their unique environmental needs. However, a multicast solution would be an important research topic to investigate for ePresence.

**Application Layer Transcoding:** Fig. 1 shows the current browser template used to represent eL content. This template is intended for PCs with suitable multimedia capabilities with a large enough real-estate to display and process all available modalities shown. Our application layer transcoding decision process produces the same template if it is determined that the end-users device is capable of processing all available modalities. Hence this guarantees our solution meets the interface requirements of the current ePresence system.

Application layer transcoding becomes crucial for mobile devices accessing ePresence that have minimal multimedia processing capabilities as it determines which XSLT rule is needed to match the device's capabilities in processing the requested modality. Fig. 3(a) clearly displays this problem. Fig 3a(i) and 3a(ii) show how the display size affects the clarity of the delivered media for a PDA and Smart Phone (SP) on the current ePresence system. Hence, it would not be logical to stream all the available media to a PDA or Smart Phone. Fig 3a(iii) and 3a(iv) show how the application layer transcodor takes all these factors into account and logically adapts the available media and presentation format using XSLT rules. Note that other possible adaptations (i.e. choice of modalities) can be chosen for a PDA and SP. This ensures the proper delivery of material to meet the device needs while trying to meet the end users modality request.

**Bitstream Transcoding:** Real-time video delivery applications must stream content with negligible delay in order to produce a live lecture experience. The Real Time Streaming Protocol (RTSP) [4] can deliver a continues flow of video (e.g. 28Kb/s for dial-up to a PDA, 100-300Kb/s for high speed to a PC) with negligible streaming delays . This invovles pre-buffering a portion of video at the user device to ensure that the buffer can maintain a steady flow of media to playback while the rest is streamed over the webcast session. Although RTSP can ensure a steady flow of media in the user device buffer, the effect of transcoding delay must also be addressed and how it effect this steady flow. Transcoding inevitably will cause delay due to the fact that video must be converting between formats (e.g raw video to MPEG-4 format) or scaled (e.g. change frame-rate).

One of the key challenges that designers of transcoding servers face is making sure that the streaming server always has a continues flow of buffered media to deliver. Fig. 3b shows an approximation of start-up delays at the beginning of an eL webcasting session as a result of transcoding. These results are from real

---

[4] sourceforge.net/projects/ffmpeg/
[5] http://developer.apple.com/darwin/projects/streaming/

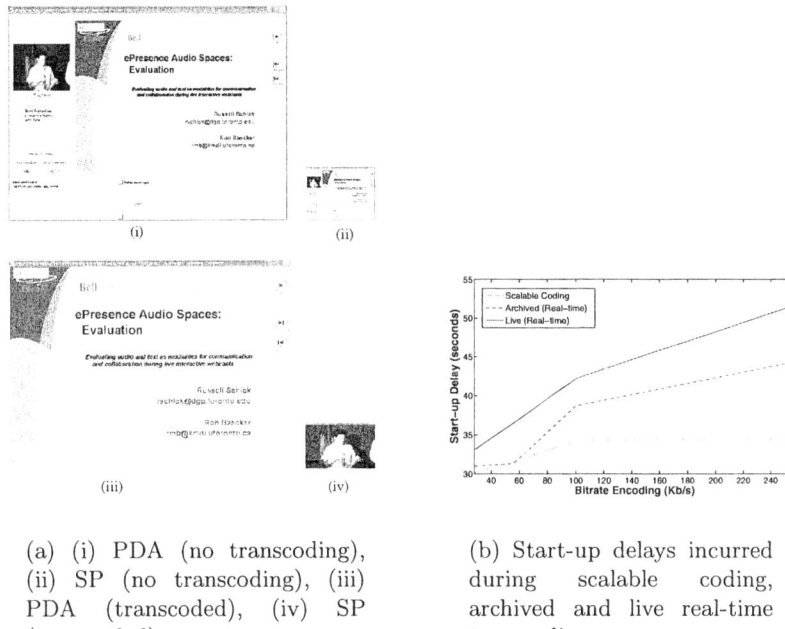

(a) (i) PDA (no transcoding), (ii) SP (no transcoding), (iii) PDA (transcoded), (iv) SP (transcoded)

(b) Start-up delays incurred during scalable coding, archived and live real-time transcoding

**Fig. 3.** Results: (a) Application layer transcoding, (b) Bitstream transcoding

experiments using the above mentioned streaming framework to a user that is 50Km away from the eL system server. It is expected that scalable coding will producing the lowest overhead due to the fact that no transcoding is needed. The start-up overhead observed is due to pre-buffering at the user device. As mentioned in Section 3, scalable coding can only be used for on-demand eL systems and cannot be used for live sessions. eL sessions are archived using MPEG-4 encoding. This archived multimedia is transcoded by scaling the video and audio to match the end users environmental characteristics. As Fig. 3b shows, there is a noticeable delay increase in comparison to scalable coding (which skips the transcoding step). The amount of delay increases proportional to the encoding bit-rate. This is due to the computational intensity and memory usage that the transcoder experiences as the target encoding bit-rate (e.g. 100Kb/s) increases. For live eL sessions, the encoder requires the aid of a capturing device to transfer and synchronize live video and audio from devices (e.g. video camera). As shown in Fig. 3b, transcoding live session incurs the highest amount of delays. This additional overhead is due to two factors: 1) delay from the capturing device, 2) high computational intensity of transcoding raw video and audio to MPEG-4.

The encouraging conclusion that can be drawn from Fig. 3b is that start-up delay overhead is going to be roughly under one minute. Assuming that an eL session will be on average one hour in duration (e.g. course lecture), this is an acceptable delay for the end-user to cope with. The benefits of adding transcoding to the current ePresence architecture will be worthy of the tradeoff of a one minute start-up delay that the system will incur. Note that this delay will probably increase as the user's distance from the server increases (e.g overseas).

## 5 Conclusions

This paper has addressed the problem of Universal Multimedia Access in the context of an e-Learning applications. More specifically, seamless delivery of multimedia content to diverse end-users in unreliable network conditions has been considered. The proposed solution is a real-time application level and bitstream transcoding solution that can be be accomplished with low delay overhead to deliver eL content to any user, despite there environmental restrictions.

## References

1. Baecker, R., Moore, G., Zijdemans, A.: Reinventing the lecture: Webcasting made interactive. In: Proc. of HCI Int'l. Volume 1. (2003) 896–900
2. Bormans, J., Gelissen, J., Perkis, A.: MPEG-21: The 21st century multimedia framework. IEEE Signal Processing Magazine **20** (2003) 53–62
3. Deshpande, S., Hwang, J.: A real-time interactive virtual classroom multimedia distance learning system. IEEE Trans. on Multimedia **3** (2001) 432–444
4. Schulzrinne, H., Rao, A., Lanphier, R.: Rfc 2326: Real time streaming protocol (rtsp). Technical report (2004)
5. Timmerer, C.: Resource Adaptation using XML with the MPEG-21 Multimedia Framework. PhD thesis, Institut fur Informaionstechnologie, Universitat Klagenfurt, Germany (2003)
6. van Beek, P.: Metadata-driven multimedia access. IEEE Signal Processing Magazine **20** (2003) 40–52
7. Brotherton, J., Bhalodia, J., Abowd, G.: Automated capture, integration, and visualization of multiple media streams. In: Proc. of the IEEE Int'l Conf. on Multimedia Computing and Systems. (1998) 54–63
8. Cloete, E.: Electronic education system model. Computers and Education **36** (2001) 171–182
9. Paris, A., Simos, R., et al.: Developing an architecture for the software subsystem of a learning technology system-an engineering approach. In: Proc. of the IEEE Int'l Conf. Advanced Learning Technologies. (2001) 17–20
10. Vetro, A., Trimmerer, C.: Information technology-multimedia framework MPEG-21-part7: Digital item adaptation. Technical Report 21000-1:2007, ISO/IEC (2003)
11. Kinno, A., Yonemoto, Y., et. al.: Environment adaptive XML transformation and its application to content delivery. In: Symposium of Applications and the Internet. (2003) 31–36

# Highlight Detection and Removal Based on Chromaticity

Shu-Chang Xu, Xiuzi Ye, Yin Wu, and Sanyuan Zhang

College of Computer Science, Zhejiang University,
310027 Hangzhou, China

**Abstract.** The presence of highlight can lead to erroneous results in Computer Vision applications such as edge detection, and motion tracking. Many algorithms have been developed to detect and remove highlight. In this paper, we propose a simple and effective method for detecting and removal of highlight. We first use a window to help to remove the noise and reduce the data amount for analysis. We then apply K-means algorithm in a 5-D vector space to computer diffuse chromaticity. In the case of non-white illuminant, illuminant chromaticity is estimated in the inverse-intensity space, and we use Fuzzy C-mean clustering and linear fitting to get illuminant chromaticity. Finally, we use Specular-to-Diffuse mechanism to separate specular reflection component from image. Experiments show that it is robust and can give good results.

## 1 Introduction

How to detect and remove highlight reflected from inhomogeneous object is a hot research topic in Computer Vision. The existence of highlight can induce incorrect results in, e.g. edge detection, image segmentation and object tracking algorithms.

Many algorithms have been developed to detect and remove highlight. in recent years. Light polarization analysis was used in early methods. Wolff[1] et al. introduce polarizing filter to remove highlight. Nayar [2] et al. extended this work by taking object color into account and produce impressive results. In general, methods with polarization analysis are limited by hardware. Sato [3] et al. introduce a 4-D temporal-color space by considering a series of images irradiated by the same illuminant in different directions. In the case of single color object, the requirement of the image series limits the applications of the algorithm. This method though can handle multi-colored objects, requiring the users manually selecting different colors. Shafer[4] proposed the well-known Dichromatic Reflection Model, which deem illuminated by a single light source. A cluster of uniformly colored object in RGB space forms a parallelogram distribution defined by two vectors, namely surface (specular) and body (diffuse) reflection components. Body reflection component represents the object color, and the surface reflection component approximately has the same property as the illuminant. Based on Shafer's work, Klinker[5] et al. found the cluster actually forms a slope T-shape and developed methods to determine the two component vectors. Though using only a single image as input, without requiring hardware and image series, the T-shape is difficult to extract because of the presence of the noise and that operating in 3-D space is not an easy task. To reduce computational complexity, Karsten[6] proposed a global method based on the 2-D UV space. Tan[7] et. al. developed the STD (Specular-to-Diffuse) mechanism which is based on *max intensity-chromaticity space*. Tan's algorithm is robust and easier than existing algorithms. Unfortunately, it is based on the assumption that the camera noise shows in linear. Furthermore, the process of finding diffuse pixel candidate is non-trivial.

Based on the work in Tan[7] et. al., in this paper, we first propose to use the Best Fit Window. Then, a method based on *max intensity-chromaticity space* is proposed to detect highlight regions. In the case of non-white illuminant, we use a simple approach to estimate illuminant chromaticity. Finally, we use the STD mechanism to separate the specular component from images.

## 2 Reflection Model

Dichromatic Reflection Model describes the color of the reflected light as a combination of surface reflection and body reflection (Figure 1) as follows:

$$L(\lambda, \theta) = L_b(\lambda, \theta) + L_s(\lambda, \theta) \tag{1}$$

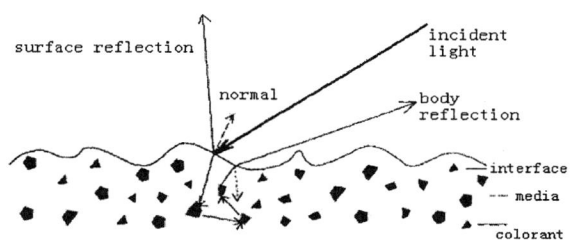

**Fig. 1.** Dichromatic Reflection Model (from [4])

Here, L, $L_b$ and $L_s$ denote the reflected light, body reflection component and surface reflection component respectively. $\lambda$ denotes the wavelength and parameters $\theta$ include the direction angles needed for describing the reflection geometry. Separating the spectral reflection property of $L_b$, $L_s$ and considering them as products of spectral power distributions $C_b$, $C_s$ and geometric concerning factors $m_b$, $m_s$, we have

$$L(\lambda) = m_b C_b(\lambda) + m_s C_s(\lambda) \tag{2}$$

After spectral integration, we have the following image formation of digital camera:

$$I(x, y) = m_s \int_\Omega C_s(\lambda) h(\lambda) d\lambda + m_b \int_\Omega C_b(\lambda) h(\lambda) d\lambda \tag{3}$$

where h(.) represents the camera sensor response function of incident light and $\Omega$ represents the visible spectrum region. I(*x*, *y*) is the pixel intensity at location (x, y). We can rewrite the above equation as the following:

$$I(x, y) = m_s I_s + m_b I_b \tag{4}$$

where $I_s = \int_\Omega C_s(\lambda)h(\lambda)d\lambda$ and $I_b = \int_\Omega C_b(\lambda)h(\lambda)d\lambda$. The two parts of right side of equation (4) denote specular reflection component and diffuse reflection component respectively. As Tan[7] described, we can get a new formula from equation (4) expressed by chromaticity:

$$I(x,y) = \overline{m_s}\Gamma_s + \overline{m_b}\Gamma_b \tag{5}$$

Where $\Gamma_s = I_s / \sum_{RGB} I_s$ and $\Gamma_b = I_b / \sum_{RGB} I_b$ represent specular chromaticity and diffuse chromaticity respecitively. Obviously, $\sum_{RGB} \Gamma_s = \sum_{RGB} \Gamma_b = 1$.

## 3 Highlight Detection

To separate the specular component using STD mechanism, diffuse chromaticity is required. For the objects with ideal Lambert surface, diffuse chromaticity is a constant but specular chromaticity is a variant. In this section, we obtain the diffuse chromaticity based on a local window BFW for detecting highlight regions.

### 3.1 The Best Fit Window

Global specular information is considered in many previous methods [1, 2, 5], which is noise-sensitive and time-consuming in computation. Statistically, highlight regions are local with high intensity pixels. Assuming uniformly colored surfaces, any local diffuse chromaticity should be the same as the global one. We hence introduce a local window called the Best Fit Window (BFW, see Figure 2), and all the analysis followed in the paper will be based on this window.

We locate the BFW by intensity: given a window, moving from the upper-left corner of the image and counting the number of pixels (denoted by $s$) in the window with intensity value larger than the global average intensity $L1_{ave}$. We choose the corresponding window of max($s$) as the BFW. Our experiments show the result of one time computation is not satisfactory, especially for images with many low-intensity background pixels. We then calculate the new average intensity $L2_{ave}$ from the pixels whose intensity value larger than $L1_{ave}$. Replace $L1_{ave}$ with $L2_{ave}$ and repeat the above procedure to find a better BFW. Generally, one more iteration can already produce an acceptable BFW. In our experiments, the size of BFW is set to 1/9 of the image size. It is worthy pointing out that: (1) Both diffuse and specular pixels should be included in the BFW. Therefore, existing methods such as the one described in [16] to determine the edges of highlight regions cannot be applied here; (2) The size of BFW, in theory, should be dependent on the scene contents (object size and orientation). It's a

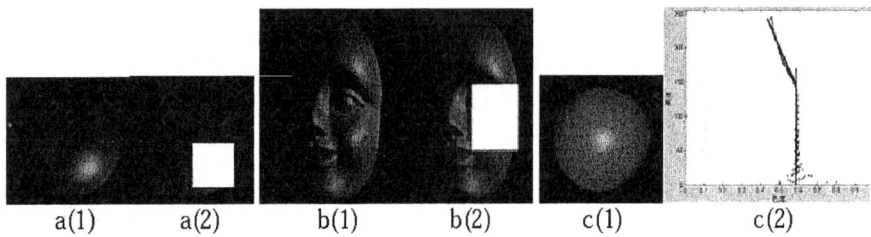

| a(1) | a(2) | b(1) | b(2) | c(1) | c(2) |

**Fig. 2.** The BFW and *max intensity-chromaticity space*. White window in a(2) and b(2) denotes BFW; c (2) depicts the *max intensity-chromaticity space* of c(1).

hard task to determine it based on the scene contents. In stead, in this paper, we simply set it to be 1/3 of the image size; (3) BFW can be used to remove noise and improve performances by reducing analysis data. Only if the objects in the scene are almost white we may then get a wrong BFW: in this case, other information other than intensity should be considered in determining the BFW. Actually, this is a difficultcase for all highlight detection and removal algorithms.

### 3.2 Diffuse Chromaticity Estimation

Tan [7] et al. introduced the *max intensity-chromaticity* space in which, a specular pixel A is closer to the left of the X axis than a diffuse pixel B with the same surface color. In Figure 2-c(2), the chromaticity of diffuse pixels is constant and the corresponding points are located at the right side. However, the chromaticity of specular pixels is variable (the curve in the left). Actually, the beeline and the curve can be completely confused because of noise and un-uniform surface properties in real cases. Figure c(2) is actually composed of three parts: the left, middle and right parts. In the left part, chromaticity value closes to 1/3 which means it contains specular pixels with high brightness and pixels in shadow only illuminated by environment lights. The middle part mainly includes specular pixels with low brightness; and the right part mainly includes diffuse pixels. Background pixels and noise can make the separation very difficult. That's the main reason why we use BFW: it can help to remove noise.

Considering the *max intensity- chromaticity space* in BFW will be easier than in the entire BFW space. We build a 5-dimensional vector space composed of CIE La*b* color space (with weight of 4/5) and pixel location $(x, y)$ (with weight of 1/5). We then apply K-means algorithm to cluster the data in the 5-D space into 2 regions based on Euclidian distances. We select a region with lower intensity, and then remap the data back to *max intensity-chromaticity* space (see Fig. 3), with the reasonable assumption that the pixels are candidates of diffuse pixels. We can then get the diffuse chromaticity using statistical histogram with 1% accuracy tolerance (see Fig. 3).

Tan [7] et al. introduced a color ratio space to avoid noise. The process is not very convenient. Their algorithm assumes that the camera has linear noise. Our method doesn't have this constraint: using BFW, the diffuse chromaticity can be simply obtained. Moreover, our experiments show that the results are satisfactory (see Figure 5).

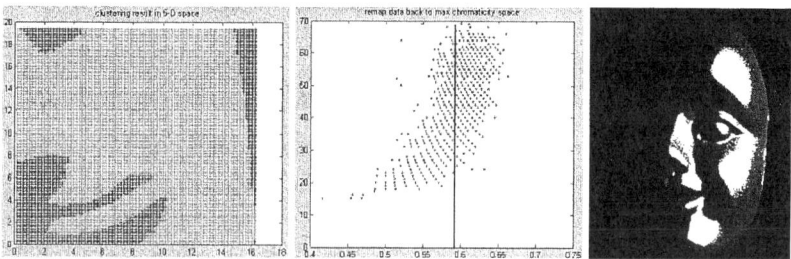

**Fig. 3.** Estimating the diffuse chromaticity using K-mean algorithm in 5-D space. Original image is b(1) in Fig 2. (**Left**) cluster 5-D vector into 2 regions. (**Middle**) remap data from region with lower intensity back to the max intensity-chromaticity space. (**Right**) Result for the highlight region detection.

## 4 Non-white Illuminant

The STD mechanism assumed pure white illuminant. Unfortunately, this is almost impossible in the real world. To apply STD mechanism to separate the specular component, we need the illuminant chromaticity. The estimation of illuminant chromaticity involves the color constancy problem [8~10] and many correlative methods have been developed [11~12]. We present a simple method based on inverse-intensity space [13] to estimate illuminant chromaticity. In the RGB color space, every color can be expressed by chromaticity as follows: $\kappa(rr, gg, bb) = (R, G, B)/(R+G+B)$. Based on Equation (5) in Section 2, we can rewrite the chromaticity as:

$$\kappa = \frac{\overline{m}_s \Gamma_s + \overline{m}_b \Gamma_b}{\overline{m}_s \sum_{RGB} \Gamma_s + \overline{m}_b \sum_{RGB} \Gamma_b} \tag{6}$$

Since the $\Sigma$ parts are equal to 1, by substituting Equation (5) into (6), we have:

$$I(x, y) = \overline{m}_b (\Gamma_b - \Gamma_s) \frac{\kappa}{\kappa - \Gamma_s} \tag{7}$$

Define $a = \overline{m}_b (\Gamma_b - \Gamma_s)$, Equation (7) can be described as:

$$\kappa = a / \sum_{RGB} I(x,y) + \Gamma_s \tag{8}$$

Equation (8) shows that we can estimate the illuminant chromaticity $\Gamma_s$ if the image chromaticity $\kappa$ and pixel intensity $\Sigma I(x, y)$ can be obtained.

We project all pixels in the BFW into the inverse-intensity space. Obviously, diffuse pixels locate towards the right of the x-axis. Pixels with low brightness illuminated only by environment lights may also close to the right. For the distribution of

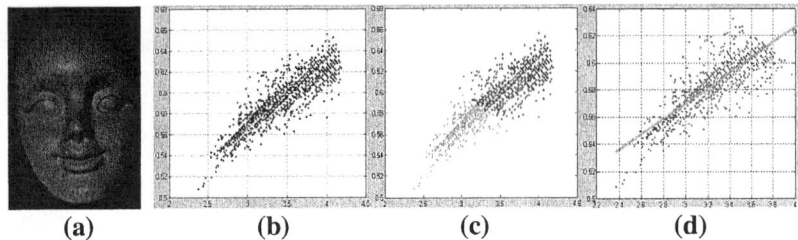

**Fig. 4.** Estimation of tlluminant chromaticity: **(a):** the original image **(b):** BFW pixels projecting into inverse-intensity space. **(c):** fuzzy C-mean clustering (3 clusters). **(d):** linear fitting of the first 2 clusters.

the specular pixels, we simply choose the pixels with brightness values larger than the average of the BFW for analysis. Those pixels are then normalized with zero-mean and one-deviation, and a Fuzzy C-mean clustering is applied. In our experiments, all pixels are grouped into 3 clusters (see Figure 4 c). We then find the cluster whose center has the biggest x-coordinate (it includes some specular pixels), and perform linear fitting to the other two clusters. The intercept value is taken as the estimated value of the illuminant chromaticity (see Figure 4).

## 5 Experiments

Figure 5-6 show some results of our algorithm applied to a variety of images. In Figure 5, our algorithm outperforms the algorithm in Tan [7] et al. for multi-object cases (see images (a) and (b)); and their algorithm fails in (b) since when they remap pixels with the same color ratio value in color ratio space back to the *max intensity-*

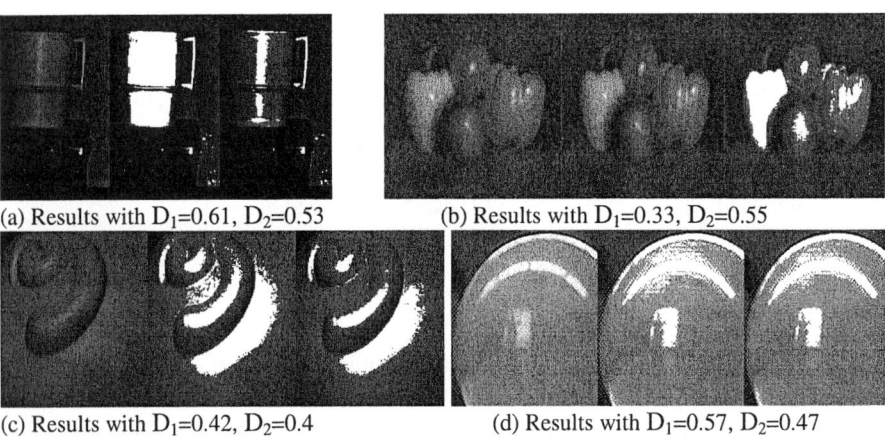

(a) Results with $D_1=0.61$, $D_2=0.53$   (b) Results with $D_1=0.33$, $D_2=0.55$

(c) Results with $D_1=0.42$, $D_2=0.4$   (d) Results with $D_1=0.57$, $D_2=0.47$

**Fig. 5.** Some highlight detection results. The left, middle and right images in each group are original images, resultant images of the algorithm in Tan [7] et al. (with diffuse chromaticity denoted by D1) and our algorithm (with diffuse chromaticity denoted by D2), respectively.

*chromaticity space*, the candidate diffuse pixels are very likely belonging to different objects which have different diffuse chromaticity. It can also be noticed that there is no clear difference between their algorithm and ours in (d), though the chromaticity values are largely different, this is because of the big gap between the max chromaticity value of specular and diffuse pixels. In this case, different values of diffuse chromaticity in some allowable ranges can slightly change the detection results.

Once we have detected the highlight regions, the STD mechanism is applied to separate the diffuse and specular reflection components. The method described in Section 4 is used to estimate illuminant chromaticity in the non-white illuminants cases. Images then can be normalized by dividing each pixel's RGB with illuminant chromaticity. Figure 6 shows some such examples after highlights are removed.

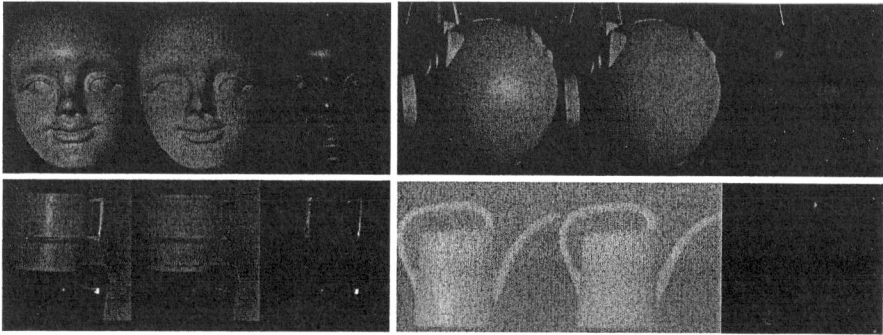

**Fig. 6.** Highlight removal results. The left, middle and right images in each group are original images, diffuse reflection specular reflection component, respectively.

## 6 Conclusions

In this paper, we propose to use the BFW to help to remove image noise and reduce the amount of the analysis data. Based on BFW, a weighted K-means algorithm is applied in a 5-D space to estimate diffuse chromaticity. In order to get non-white illuminant chromaticity, we perform fuzzy clustering and linear fitting in the inverse-intensity space. Experiments show that our method is robust and can produce good results. Our method eliminates the assumption of linear noise of camera. Furthermore, our method of highlight region detection is separable and can be used independently. For example, we can first detect highlight regions using our algorithm and then use the inpainting algorithm to correct the color [14~15].

## Acknowledgements

The authors would like to thank the support from the China NSF under Grant #60273060, China Ministry of Education under Grant #20030335064, and Education Office of Zhejiang Province under Grant #G20030433.

# References

1. Wolff L.B, Boult T.: Constraining object features using polarization reflectance model. IEEE Trans. on Pattern Analysis and Machine Intelligence, (1991), 13(7):635–657.
2. Nayar S.K., Fang X.S and Boult T.: Separation of reflection components using color and polarization. International Journal of Computer Vision, (1996) 21(3).
3. Sato Y. and Ikeuchi K.: Temporal-color space analysis of reflection. Journal of Optics Society of America A., 11, (1994).
4. Shafer S.A.: Using color to separate reflection components. Color Research and Applications, 10, (1985).
5. Klinker G.J., Shafer S.A., and Kanade T.: The measurement of highlights in color images. International Journal of Computer Vision, (1990) 2:7–32,
6. Karsten.S., Andreas K. Global and Local Highlight Analysis in Color Images, Proc. 1st Int. Conf. on Color in Graphics and Image Processing (CGIP), Saint-Etienne, France, Oct. 1-4, (2000) 300–304.
7. Tan R.T., Nishino K., Ikeuchi K.: "Separating Reflection Components Based on Chromaticity and Noise Analysis", IEEE Transaction on Pattern Analysis and Machine Intelligence (PAMI) 26(10), October (2004) 1373–1379.
8. Geusebroek J.M., Boomgaard R., Smeulders S.: and T. Gevers.: A physical basis for color constancy. In The First European Conference on Color in Graphics, Image and Vision, (2002) 3–6.
9. Brainard D. H. and Freeman W. T.: Bayesian color constancy. Opt. Soc. Am. A 14, (1997) 1393–1411.
10. Funt B. V. and Finlayson G. D.: Color constant color indexing, IEEE Trans. Pattern Anal. Mach. Intell. (1995).17, 522–533.
11. Lee H.C.: Method for computing the scene-illuminant from specular highlights. Journal of Optics Society of America A., (1986) 3(10):1694–1699.
12. Lehmann T.M. and Palm C.: Color line search for illuminant estimation in real-world scene. Journal of Optics Society of America A., (2001) 18(11):2679–2691.
13. Tan R.T., Nishino K., Ikeuchi K.: Illumination Chromaticity Estimation using Inverse-Intensity Chromaticity Space, in proceeding of IEEE Computer Society Conference on Computer Vision and Pattern Recognition (CVPR 2003) June 18-20, (2003) 673–680.
14. Marcelo B., Sapiro G., Ballester C., Caselles V.: Image inpainting. In: Computer Graphics, SIGGRAPH 2000. (2000) 417–424.
15. Tan P., Yang J., Lin S., Shum H.: Illumination-Constrained inpainting for single image highlight removal. Journal of Software, China. (2004), 15(1):33–40

# Digital Video Scrambling Using Motion Vector and Slice Relocation

Sang Gu Kwon, Woong Il Choi, and Byeungwoo Jeon

School of Information and Communication Engineering,
Sungkyunkwan University,
300 Chunchun-Dong Jangan-Gu Suwon, Korea
iamant1039@skku.edu, creata@ece.skku.ac.kr, bjeon@yurim.skku.ac.kr

**Abstract.** As digitalized content rapidly proliferates in networked systems, content security necessarily arises as one of the most important issues. Many developers have studied techniques for allowing only authorized persons to access content. Recently, video scrambling techniques, one type of the authorizing tools, have been introduced. However, they change the original video data, which often increases the bit rate of the source data. To overcome this problem, we propose a scrambling technique which deliberately distorts the original video sequences in a reversible way by arbitrarily relocating the differential motion vectors and MB (macroblock) starting positions in a slice. This method can be applied to most common video coding techniques such as MPEG-1/2/4, and H.264.

## 1 Introduction

As digital contents have been increasingly abundant everywhere, adequate protection of multimedia contents is highly required. Digital video sequences are routinely distributed through non-private channels such as satellite links, cable television networks, wireless networks, and the Internet. Accordingly, video content providers demand more secure yet simple techniques such as video scrambling. Digital video scrambling method deliberately distorts video signals in order to discourage unauthorized viewing. For authorized clients, the descrambler can properly restore the original video by referring to a legitimate key while unauthorized clients can decode the scrambled video but resulting in an unpleasant distorted video. In recent years, many researchers have proposed various scrambling techniques [1]- [6]. The transform-based scrambling method utilizes residual coefficient in frequency domains such as wavelet or DCT [4], [5]. Wavelet-based schemes use such techniques as selective bit scrambling, block shuffling, and block rotation [4], [5]. For the DCT-based schemes, there are DCT coefficient scrambling, motion vector scrambling, and sign encryption [4], [5]. Other existing methods are motion vector scrambling [3] and the intra prediction mode scrambling [6]. Motion vector scrambling changes the codeword of motion vector in accordance to the value of CBP [3].

However, those methods except intra prediction mode scrambling [6] cause increase of bit rate after scrambling. To overcome this problem, this paper proposes two novel scrambling methods which are based on relocation of motion vector and slice position in inter frame. Motion vectors are the key information conveyed in most video coding techniques. If motion vectors are not properly recovered by the decoder, the reconstructed video sequences will be distorted severely. This proposed method can be applied to most video coding techniques. We note that video sequences can be easily distorted by arbitrarily relocating them using a slice scrambling method within a frame.

## 2 Proposed Scrambling Methods

We propose to relocate motion vector and slice positions in a deliberate but reversible way for scrambling. The former exchanges a differential motion vector DMV with one another, and the latter changes the location of slice within a frame to give wrong information about MB positions to the video decoder.

### 2.1 Motion Vector Relocation

Temporal redundancy is removed by motion compensation in inter frame. In motion estimation, a vector describing relative position between a given block and the block in the reference frame which has minimum block matching error is called the motion vector. For encoding the motion vector, differential value of the motion vector and the predicted motion vector which is obtained from neighboring blocks is encoded by a variable length code. The proposed method utilizes this DMV for scrambling video data. The proposed method arbitrarily relocates one DMV component in one block with a DMV component in another block within the same slice or frame.

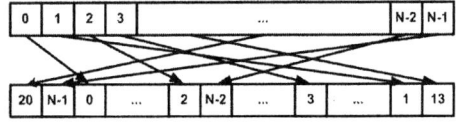

**Fig. 1.** Relocating x and y components of DMVs

The main idea of relocating DMVs is shown in Fig. 1. Where top line is the original bitstream and bottom one is the bitstream after scrambling. 'x' and 'y' in the figure indicate the compressed information of the x and y component of a DMV. Since the codeword of each DMV component is simply relocated in the bitstream, total size of the bitstream is not changed as long as Huffman coding scheme is used. When arithmetic coding scheme is used, total size of bitstream may not be identical to original bitstream because symbols are jointly coded in arithmetic coding, but it is expected almost the same with the size of the original one.

In the proposed method, we can see that the distortion of the scrambled video is increased as the difference between the original DMV and the relocated one is increased. A rule for the relocation of the DMV components uses a pseudo random sequence generated by a key. For example, the first 4 bits of the sequence decide how many places the DMV components are rotated to the right, and the remaining bits decide whether one DMV component is swapped with next one. If the sequence is '1101110...', for instance, the first 4 bits are '1101', so the order of the DMV components is right-rotated by 13 places. If the DMV components '0 1 2 3 4 5 6 7 8 9 A B C D E F' were right-rotated by 13, for example, the result would be '3 4 5 6 7 8 9 A B C D E F 0 1 2.' The remaining bits of the sequence can then further modify order of the components. In this example the fifth bit is '1', so the first DMV component in the rotated list is swapped with the second one, the sixth bit is '1', so the second component is swapped with the third one, and the seventh bit is '0', so the third is not changed, etc. This would result in '4 5 3 6 7 8 9 A B C D E F 0 1 2' until process of the first 7 bits. This relocation rule is only an example. The content owner can change the relocation rule as the one wishes.

If there are sufficient number of DMVs within one frame, security is also guaranteed. If there are N DMVs and those vectors are relocated randomly, the combination of DMV arrays is up to $(2N)!$. Therefore it is too difficult to guess right location of the DMV components without the authorized key. This method is easy to implement and does not cause much computational complexity. The detailed scrambling procedure for the encoder and decoder is as follows.

In the encoder, a pseudo random sequence of a certain length is generated according to a specific key. After encoding one inter frame, the encoder reads the pseudo random sequence to determine how to arbitrarily relocate the DMVs. Then the encoder relocates the codewords of all DMV components of the bitstream in that frame. This procedure is executed for every frame. The descrambling procedure is similar to the scrambling in the decoder. After the decoder reads the bitstream for one frame, a pseudo random sequence is generated by the same specific key to determine the relocation rule.

Since the codewords of the DMV components are changed in the bitstream, before decoding one frame procedure, the decoder first has to read whole bitstream for one frame, then relocate all DMV components using a pseudo random sequence in the bitstream in advance; therefore bitstream parsing is required twice. After this process is finished, the decoder starts decoding MBs process with corrected bitstream, but it does not cause any more delay in decoding.

Only an authorized person who knows the key can properly reconstruct the original video sequence. A non-authorized decoder uses wrong DMV components for motion compensation of certain blocks, so the reconstructed pictures are severely distorted.

## 2.2 Slice Relocation

The motion vector relocation scheme does not affect skipped blocks or intra blocks which contain no motion vector. Background regions are likely to be encoded as skip mode due to their low spatial detail or little motion. For those areas such as the background, a slice relocation method is proposed. A frame consists of slices, and a slice consists of MBs. Since the proposed method relocates the position of each slice within a frame, the spatial position of total MB data in a slice can be changed. Through slice relocation, skipped MBs in a background region can be replaced by inter MBs having motion vectors in the foreground region. The proposed method modifies the MB starting position in each slice header to relocate slices.

Fig. 2 shows the slices in one frame; the left side indicates the slice ordering before scrambling and the right side after scrambling. The relocation scheme used here is the same as the one used in the example in Section 2.1. In Fig. 2, for example, the slice # 4 is changed to the slice # 0, so the MB starting position of the slice # 4 is changed to the one of the slice # 0. In the same way, the MB starting position of the slice # 5 is changed to the one of the slice # 1, and so on.

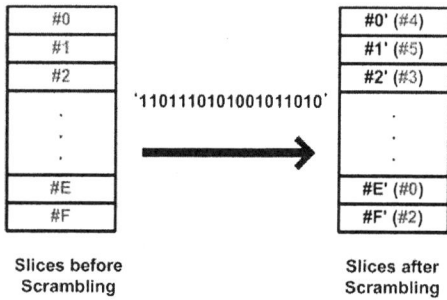

**Fig. 2.** An example of a slice relocation rule

The proposed slice relocation method for scrambling does not require any overhead in the bitstream. In order to relocate the slices, the number of MBs and the structure of slice should be the same with each other. Besides a frame should consist of at least two slices for using this scheme. Since it is likely to be visible how slices are relocated in I (intra) slices, we don't apply our scheme to I slice. I slice can be scrambled by the method using intra prediction modes proposed in [6]. The proposed method can be performed under the flexible MB ordering (FMO) scheme adopted in the H.264 standard. The FMO technique can flexibly change slice structure in various ways, so we can achieve more efficient scrambling.

In the encoder and decoder, the scrambling and descrambling procedures are similar to that of the motion vector relocation method. Before encoding one frame, the encoder and the decoder check whether the frame is an I picture before processing one frame. If the frame is an I picture, the encoder and decoder do not read the pseudo random sequence by a specific key, otherwise they read it to decide relocation rule and reversible relocation rule. In encoding one slice, the encoder changes MB starting position in a slice using relocation rule. In decoding one slice, the decoder find the right position of slice using given starting MB position from the encoder and reversible relocation rule which is derived from the pseudo random sequence. A non-authorized decoder uses wrong starting MB positions of slices, so the decoder places decoded slices at wrong positions within a frame.

The proposed slice relocation method changes slice positions in a frame, so all information in the original one is changed. This includes motion vectors, intra blocks, and residual blocks. Therefore the video sequence is severely distorted.

## 3 Experimental Results

For the test sequence of our experiment, we used 'Mother and daughter' and 'Foreman' sequences of CIF size. We implemented our scheme on the H.264 reference software, JM 9.0. We tested it under H.264 baseline profile. Only the first frame of each sequence is encoded as an I picture, and each frame contains 36 slices each of which consists of 11 MBs.

To see the effect of the proposed method, the scrambled sequences by motion vector and slice relocation methods are shown in Fig. 3 and Fig. 4. In Fig. 3 and Fig. 4, (a), (c), (e), and (g) show the scrambled sequences by motion vector relocation method only, and (b), (d), (f), and (h) show the scrambled sequences by both motion vector and slice relocation methods.

Note that the frames in (a) and (b) in Fig. 3 and Fig. 4 are not distorted because the proposed scheme does not affect intra blocks. Thus the $1^{st}$ frame is decoded correctly. As shown in (c), (e) and (g) in Fig. 3 and Fig. 4, the video sequences are gradually distorted as frame number is increased due to relocation of the DMV.

In comparison to the 'Mother and daughter' sequence, we can see that the 'Foreman' is more severely distorted. It has many motion vectors not only in foreground but also in background region due to the camera panning. Therefore, background region is also distorted by the proposed motion vector relocation method.

However, we can see that some regions are not properly distorted by motion vector relocation method in Fig. 4(g) and Fig. 3, because the 'Mother and daughter' sequence has many background region and the Foreman sequence has many intra blocks in certain frames. The background region is likely to be coded by skip mode that just copies the collocated block in reference frame. Since the skipped MB does not have the motion vector, the proposed motion vector relocation method is not applied in that area. In Fig. 4(g), we can see the hand clearly in right-bottom region because MBs of this region are coded as intra blocks.

In order to distort the static region, the slice relocation scheme is additionally applied. In Fig. 3 and Fig. 4, (d), (f), and (h), we can see that the background region is getting worse by addition of slice relocation scheme due to dislocation of slices. In Fig. 4(h), the $155^{th}$ frame shows that right-bottom area are severely distorted as compared to Fig. 4(g). However, if many MBs in a slice are coded as intra blocks in Fig. 4(h), the slice can not be distorted efficiently. Intra prediction mode scrambling resolves this problem [6].

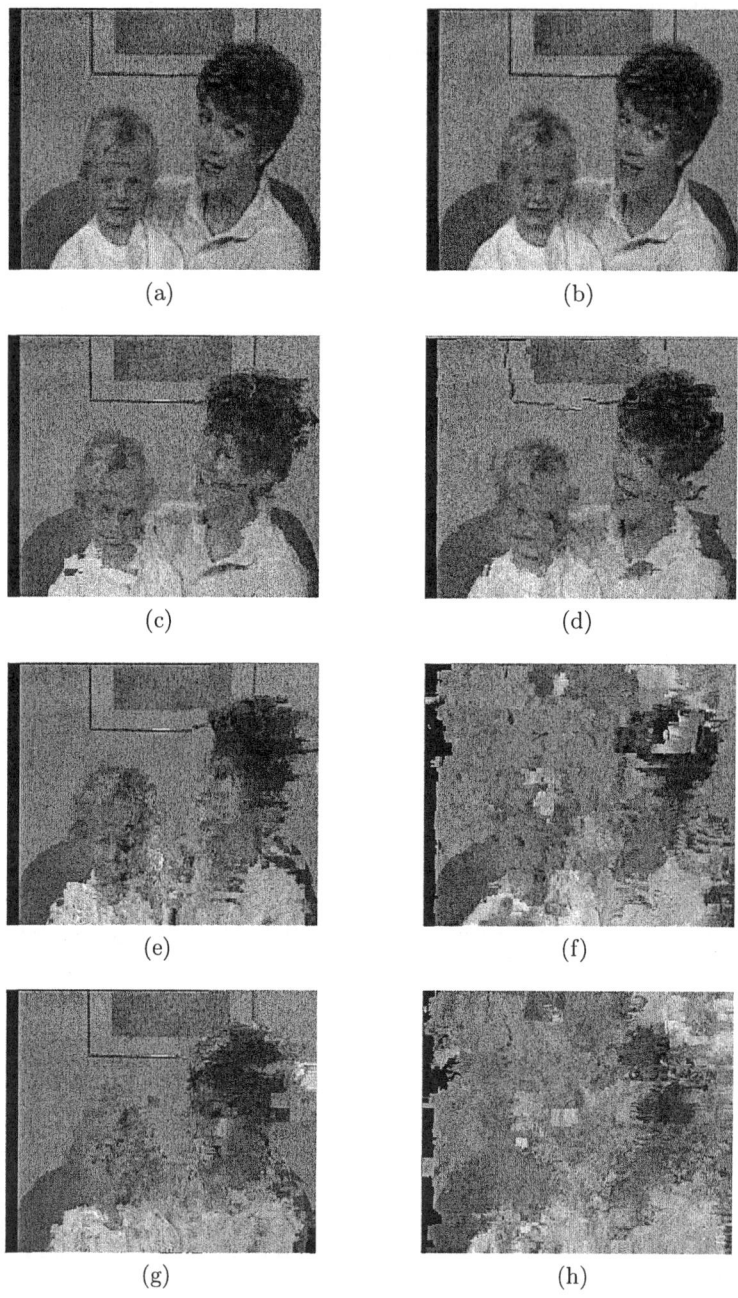

**Fig. 3.** Scrambled 'Mother and daughter' sequence; (a), (c), (e), and (g) are distorted by motion vector relocation method, and (b), (d), (f), and (h) are distorted by motion vector and slice relocation methods: (a) $1^{st}$ frame, (b) $1^{st}$ frame, (c) $51^{st}$ frame, (d) $51^{st}$ frame, (e) $101^{st}$ frame, (f) $101^{st}$ frame, (g) $201^{st}$ frame, (h) $201^{st}$ frame

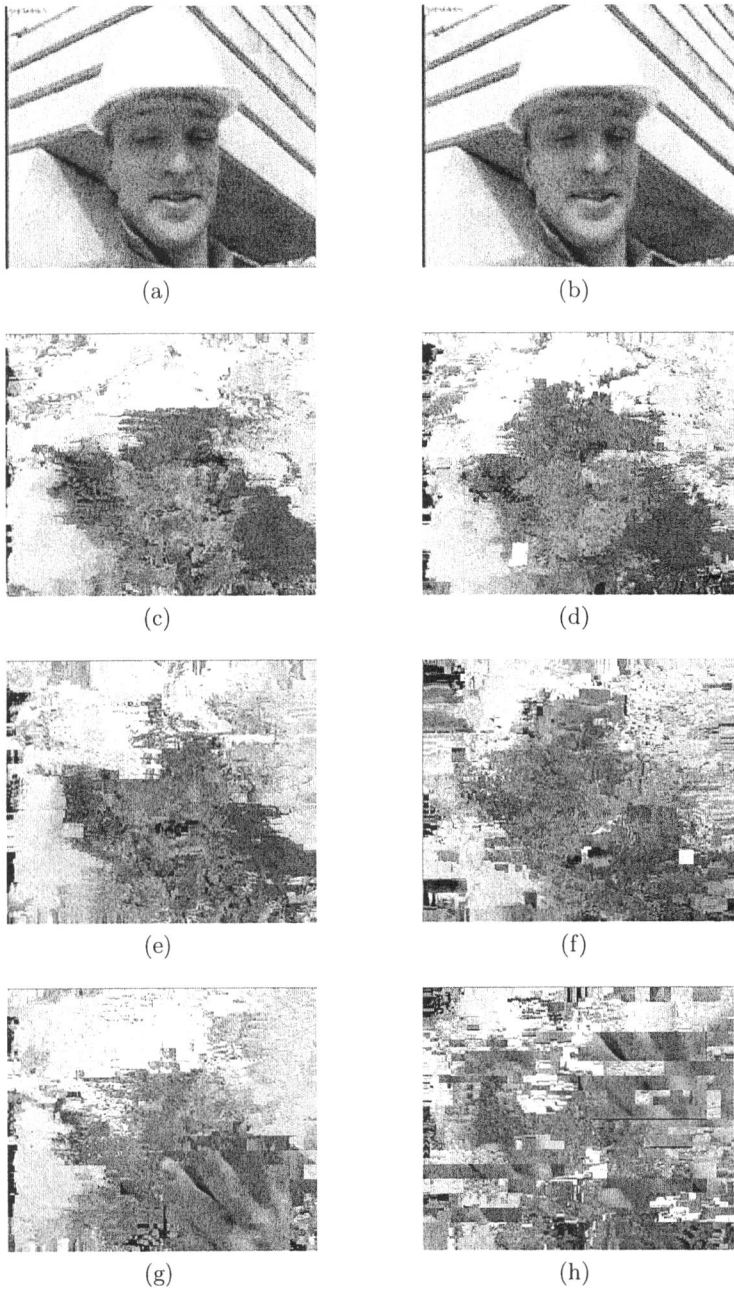

**Fig. 4.** Scrambled 'Foreman' sequence; (a), (c), (e), and (g) are distorted by motion vector relocation method, and (b), (d), (f), and (h) are distorted by motion vector and slice relocation methods: (a) $1^{st}$ frame, (b) $1^{st}$ frame, (c) $51^{st}$ frame, (d) $51^{st}$ frame, (e) $101^{st}$ frame, (f) $101^{st}$ frame, (g) $155^{th}$ frame, (h) $155^{th}$ frame

This experiment shows that the motion vector relocation method does not sufficiently scramble the sequence when the background of the original video sequence does not have any motion or foreground has little motion. The slice relocation method resolves this problem. Additionally, only the I picture can be correctly reconstructed; the other frames are unpleasantly distorted. In the same manner, successive frames refer to distorted blocks in their previous frames and dislocate the position of each slice in the current frame. The proposed methods can be applied with intra prediction mode scrambling [6] in H.264 for I picture and intra blocks. Thus scrambling error can be drifted as motion compensation is processed. As a result, we can obtain scrambling effects through the proposed methods.

## 4 Conclusion

In this paper, two scrambling methods were proposed. One is the motion vector relocation method and the other is the slice relocation method. Both methods are designed to scramble only the inter frames. Since the proposed method only relocates the codeword of motion vector and first MB position in slice within video bitstream, there is no difference in total size of bitstream when it is coded as Huffman coding. Besides, the motion vector relocation method can be applied to most video coding techniques. The encoder and decoder can know relocation information by referring to a specific key exchanged in a different channel, so security is increased. The proposed methods just require parsing bitstream twice, but there is no other encoding and decoding process delay. The experimental result showed that video sequences can substantially be distorted by the proposed method. They will be attractive for providing content protection in digital video.

When arithmetic coding scheme is used with the motion vector relocation method, the bitstream may not be identical to original one, so it needs further study to implement the method under the arithmetic coding scheme.

**Acknowledgment.** This work has supported by the Korea Research Foundation Grant (KRF-2003-041-D20405).

## References

1. B. Macq and J. Quisquate, "Digital images multiresolution encryption," *Interactive Multimedia Assoc. Intell. Property Proj.*, Jan 1994, pp. 179-186.
2. N. Katta et al, "Scrambling apparatus and descramble apparatus," U.S. patent 5377266, Dec 27. 1994.
3. J. Jang, "Digital video scrambling method," Korean patent 0151199, Jun 18. 1998.
4. W. Zeng and S. Lei, "Efficient frequency domain video scrambling for content access control," *ACM Multimedia '99*, Nov 1999.
5. W. Zeng and S. Lei, "Efficient frequency domain selective scrambling of digital video," *IEEE Transactions on Multimedia*, pp. 118- 129, March 2003.
6. J. Ahn, H. Shim, B. Jeon and I. Choi "Digital Video Scrambling Method Using Intra Prediction Mode" *LNCS* vol.3333, pp.386-393, Springer Verlag, Nov. 2004.

# Weighted Information Entropy: A Method for Estimating the Complex Degree of Infrared Images' Backgrounds

Lei Yang, Jie Yang, Ningsong Peng, and Jianguo Ling

Institute of Image Processing and Pattern Recognition, Shanghai Jiaotong University,
P.O. Box 69, 1954 Huashan Road, Shanghai, 200030, P. R. China
{tristoney, jieyang, pengningsong, lingjianguo76}@sjtu.edu.cn

**Abstract.** The validity of using the weighted information entropy to estimate the complex degree of the infrared images' backgrounds is discussed in this paper. A Butterworth high pass filter whose cut-off frequency can be adaptively regulated to meet the different backgrounds is proposed to restrain the different clutters. Since the backgrounds usually have some random change in the video sequences, an adaptive binarisation criterion for small target detection is also presented. Experimental results show the robustness of our method.

## 1 Introduction

In the actual sea-sky conflicts, the background of target is usually complex. The robustness of target detection is a crucial factor for tracking target. By the reason of the sunshine's refraction, the ocean wave may generate many regions where the grey-values in infrared images change dramatically, which is so-called "sea clutter". It has been regarded as a difficult task to detect or trace small target under this condition. If we do not care more about the models of the backgrounds, the spatial high pass filtering is normally used to detect the small target. Victor et al. put forward the morphologic operators for small target detection according to the prior knowledge of targets [1]. Peng et al. designed a $5 \times 5$ high pass template filter for real-time target detection [2]. Both two methods have good practicability for detecting the small target under the mild backgrounds, but they do not have the same performances in the sea clutter. Denney et al. presented a small target detective method based on the predication under the adaptive auto-regressive background [3]. Many researchers have analyzed and confirmed the chaotic nature of the radar sea clutter signal [4, 5]. Leung and Lo presented a method for signal detection in the sea clutter based on prediction of chaotic characteristics [6]. In general, the different backgrounds ask different suitable methods for target detection. Based on the analysis of various target detective methods, Hilliard pointed out that low pass IIR filter has a better comprehensive performance for clutter prediction [7]. In this paper, the validity of using the weighted information entropy to estimate the complex degree of the infrared images' backgrounds is discussed, and then an adaptive Butterworth high pass filter (BHPF) is designed to restrain the different clutters. To handle the random change of the complex backgrounds in the video sequences, an adaptive binarisation criterion for small target detection is also presented. Experimental results show the robustness of our method.

## 2 Theory Foundation: Butterworth High Pass Filter

In order to separate small target from the complex backgrounds, we analyzed the characteristics of the images with infrared small target through their frequencies' distribution. For the mild sky background, the images are mainly consisted of low frequency components. For the complex sea clutter background, the images mostly consist of middle frequency components. For the small target under the backgrounds mentioned above, it consists of high frequency components of the images. So the key problem is how to effectively separate the middle frequency from the high frequency. BHPF is a simple filter in frequency domain, which possesses some distinguished features not only maximum flat amplitude in the pass band, but also smooth transition between low frequency and high frequency. The transfer function of BHPF usually can be expressed as follows:

$$H(u,v) = \frac{1}{1+(\sqrt{2}-1)(D_0/D(u,v))^{2r}} \quad (1)$$

where $r$ is the order of the filter, which decides the slope of the curve diagram for the property of filtering. In our research case, since the order is not the key factor which influents frequency separation, we set $r=2$ to simplify our discussion. $D_0$ is the cut-off frequency which decides the position of frequency separation in BHPF. $D(u,v) = \sqrt{u^2+v^2}$ is the Euclidean distance between the point $(u,v)$ and the origin in Fourier spectrum. By regulating $D_0$, the filtering characteristics can be changed to meet different filtering requirements.

## 3 Using Weighted Information Entropy to Estimate the Complex Degree of Infrared Images' Backgrounds

Due to the fact that the variance of a grey-level image only describes the deviation degree between pixels' grey and their mean in the meaning of statistics, it can't provide any spatial information regarding the grey-value distribution of the images. Therefore, we propose an adaptive regulation scheme in terms of cut-off frequency based on the information entropy of different infrared images.

### 3.1 A New Idea

The information entropy is an efficient approach to illustrate the complex degree of grey-value distribution upon an infrared image. Let $S$ denote the set of grey-values in an infrared image with 256 grey-levels, and $p_s$ be the probability of grey-value $s$ occurred in the set $S$, the information entropy of the image can be defined as follows

$$H(S) = -\sum_{s=0}^{255} p_s \log p_s, \text{ when } p_s = 0, \text{ define } p_s \log p_s = 0 \quad (2)$$

The information entropy of an image denotes the average information about the image, but it neglects the importance of grey information. It can not represent our subjective judgments about the background of the image. Thus, we give some modification to Eq. (2).

Roughly speaking, in the infrared images with complex backgrounds, the small target and the clutter are normally appeared in the form of high grey-level. This largely impacts the direction of our subjective judgment for the image's information. In order to emphasis the contribution of high grey-value components to the information entropy of an image, we specify the grey-value $s$ which corresponds to the probability $p_s$ to the weight coefficient, and then modify Eq. (2) as follows

$$H'(S) = -\sum_{s=0}^{255} s \cdot p_s \log p_s, \text{ when } p_s = 0, \text{ define } p_s \log p_s = 0 \quad (3)$$

$H'(S)$ is named weighted information entropy (WIE) of the image. It provides an effective way to describe the information incorporated in different backgrounds because it combines the grey distribution information of the infrared images with our subjective judgments.

### 3.2 Discussion of the Validity

To explain the validity of using the WIE to describe the complex degree of the infrared images' backgrounds, we will discuss three representative cases as follows.

I. In the case of a grey-level image which only includes $m$ ($m \in N, 1 \leq m \leq 256$) kinds of grey-value $s_1, s_2, \cdots, s_m$, if the probability of each kind value to appear is equal, the weighted information entropy of the image is expressed as

$$H'(S) = -\left\{ s_1 \frac{1}{m} \log \frac{1}{m} + s_2 \frac{1}{m} \log \frac{1}{m} + \cdots + s_m \frac{1}{m} \log \frac{1}{m} \right\}$$
$$= \left( \frac{s_1 + s_2 + \cdots + s_m}{m} \right) \cdot \log m \quad (4)$$

The formula (4) denotes that the mean of grey-values is an effective way to describe the complex degree of an image when it has the same probability distribution. For example, it can be comprehended into that the background of small target can be estimated roughly by the mean brightness of the images when we observe some infrared images which have even grey change.

Ⅱ. As for two infrared images which both include $r(1 \leq r \leq 256)$ kinds of grey-values, if their grey-values respectively are $s_1, s_2, \cdots s_r$ and $as_1, as_2, \cdots as_r$ (where $a$ is an intensity factor, and $0 < a \leq 255/\max\{s_1, s_2, \cdots s_r\}$), and the probability of each grey-value in these two images is equal respectively, i.e. $p_{s_1} = p_{as_1}, p_{s_2} = p_{as_2} \cdots, p_{s_r} = p_{as_r}$, the two WIE values $H_1'(S)$ and $H_2'(S)$ of these two images will satisfy the following equation

$$H_2'(S) = -\sum_{m=1}^{r} as_m \cdot p_{s_m} \log p_{s_m} = aH_1'(S) \qquad (5)$$

It can be considered that general grey intensity is an important property to evaluate the backgrounds' complex degree of the infrared images which have the same grey-value distribution. For example, influenced by some uncertain factors such as sunshine's refraction in the sea clutter or gain drift of the detective devices, the general grey intensity of the infrared image will be shifted randomly. Sometimes this shift or these shifts will badly weaken the Signal-to-Clutter Ratio (SCR) of the infrared images. The WIE of the images can accurately represent the shift of the general grey intensity, and it is advantageous for us to choose an appropriate detective method.

Ⅲ. For an image which includes $r(1 \leq r \leq 256)$ kinds of known grey-values $s_1, s_2, \cdots s_r$, the relationship between the WIE and the probabilities of the different grey-values of the image can be expressed as follows.

Let $\alpha > 0$ is an undetermined constant. An auxiliary function is defined as

$$F(p_{s_1}, p_{s_2} \cdots p_{s_r}) = H'(S) + \alpha \left[1 - \sum_{m=1}^{r} p_{s_m}\right] = -\sum_{m=1}^{r} s_m \cdot p_{s_m} \log p_{s_m} + \alpha \left[1 - \sum_{m=1}^{r} p_{s_m}\right] \qquad (6)$$

If we calculate the first-order partial derivative for the $r$ variables $p_{s_m}$ $(1 \leq m \leq r)$ in the function $F(p_{s_1}, p_{s_2} \cdots p_{s_m})$, and set them to zero, the probabilities of the different grey-values which make the WIE reach the maximum can be written as [8]

$$p_{s_m} = \exp\left(-\frac{\alpha}{s_m} - 1\right), (m = 1, 2, \cdots r), \text{ when } s_m = 0, \text{ define } p_{s_m} = 0 \qquad (7)$$

Then we get the maximum value of the WIE

$$H'(S)_{\max} = \alpha + \sum_{m=1}^{r} s_m \exp\left(-\frac{\alpha}{s_m} - 1\right) \qquad (8)$$

By calculating the first order derivation for the variable $s_m$ in Eq. (7), we obtain

$$\frac{dp_{s_m}}{ds_m} = \frac{\alpha}{s_m^2} \exp\left(-\frac{\alpha}{s_m} - 1\right) > 0 \qquad (9)$$

The probabilities $p_{s_m}$ which make the WIE reach the maximum is a monotonic increasing function in the domain of variables $s_m$, as shown in Eq. (9). In other words, if the grey-values of the image are known and the WIE of an image reaches the maximum, the probability distribution of the different grey is proportional to different grey-values, which is corresponding to the basic motivation for using the WIE to indicate our subjective judgment about the image. At the same time, we notice that the high grey-values should be controlled in some ranges. Eq. (7) indicates that $p_{s_m} < e^{-1} \approx 0.368$ is an important condition that should be met to get the maximum value of the WIE, which obviously shows that the joint distribution of the different grey-values corresponding to the infrared images which have complex backgrounds, such as the sea clutter.

We have analyzed the validity of using the WIE to estimate the complex degree of the infrared image's background. An adaptive small target detective method is presented in the following sections.

## 4 Adaptively Detect the Small Target in the Video Sequences

Based on the analysis above, we can establish a connection between the weighted information entropy and the BHPF's cut-off frequency. Our regulation scheme can be described by the following two steps: first, storing the WIE and the appropriate cut-off frequency from some typical images with different backgrounds according to the *prior* knowledge; second, calculating the cut-off frequency of the BHPF by using piecewise linear interpolation method in real-time system.

In the infrared video sequences, the backgrounds of the consecutive frames usually have some random change, so the WIE and the corresponding cut-off frequency of the BHPF of these two frames will also be changed. Obviously, it leads to the general grey intensity of the filtered images increase or decrease in different degree, so we can not detect the small target by a fixed binarisation threshold. Observe the two filtered images of the consecutive frames, suppose that the maximum of the target region's grey-values in the previous frame is $s_{pm}$ and the mean grey-values of these two frames are $s_{pe}$ and $s_{ne}$ respectively, since the property of the small target in the consecutive frames does not change a lot, we can obtain an adaptive binarisation threshold of the next frame $\Theta_n$ by

$$\Theta_n = (1-\varepsilon) \cdot s_{pm} + s_{ne} - s_{pe} \qquad (10)$$

where $\varepsilon (0 \leq \varepsilon \leq 1)$ is a factor for keeping some grey margin (in our system, we set $\varepsilon = 0.1$). Experiments show that this criterion can not only utilize the new information of the target, but also avoid losing targets in the multiple targets cases.

The outline of the whole small target detective process is shown in Fig 1.

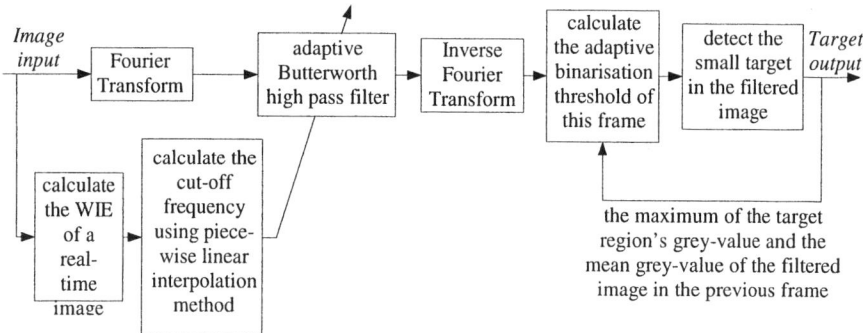

**Fig. 1.** Outline of the whole small target detective process in the infrared video sequences

## 5 Experiments and Results

In Fig. 2, several images selected from an infrared video sequence are shown to confirm the validity of our method. Two common metrics can be used to evaluate the performance of the filters [7], they are defined as follows

$$\text{Signal-to-Clutter Ratio Gain: } SCR\ Gain = \frac{(S/C)_{out}}{(S/C)_{in}} \tag{11}$$

$$\text{Background Suppression Factor: } BSF = \frac{C_{in}}{C_{out}} \tag{12}$$

where $S$ is the signal amplitude, $C$ is the clutter standard deviation within a single frame. The experimental data are listed in table 1, which shows that the filtering performances of several common filters are very close with each other when they are used for the mild background of infrared images [see row A1 in table 1]. However, once the images are influenced by clutter, the filtered effect of median and wavelet modulus are better than 5×5 high pass template. Because Wavelet modulus filter essentially is an edge detection method, its filtering performance will be worse when the grey of background changes dramatically [see row E1, F1 in table 1]. It is obvious that our adaptive BHPF keeps better performance for small target detection under the different backgrounds. The column 3 in Fig. 2 is the binarisation results of the filtered images. Experiments show that the whole detective process of us is robust.

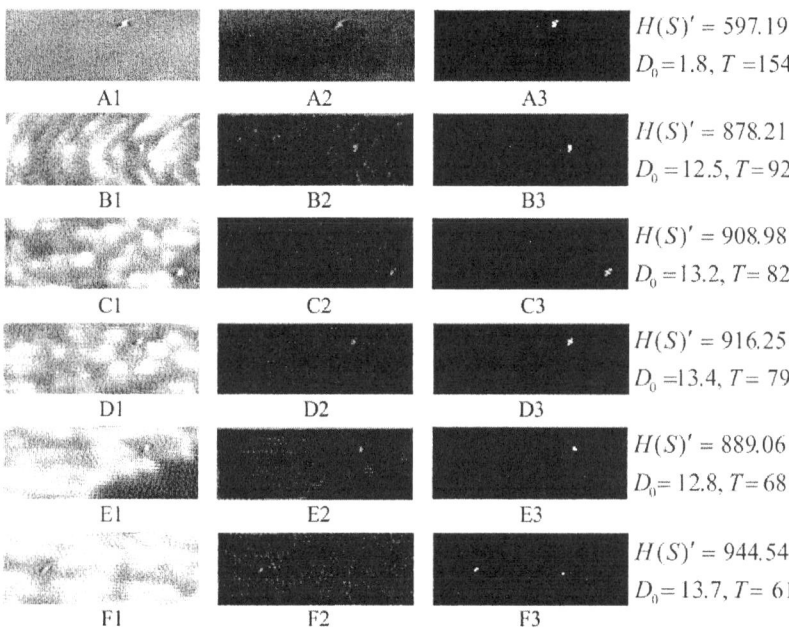

**Fig. 2.** Small target detective samples based on adaptive BHPF (Column 1: original infrared images in a video sequence; Column 2: filtered results of adaptive BHPF; Column 3: binarization results; $H'(S)$: the weighted information entropy of original image; $D_0$: cut-off frequency of adaptive BHPF; $T$: binarisation threshold in the video sequences)

**Table 1.** Comparison of several small target detective method (A1, B1, C1, D1, E1, F1: original infrared images which are showed in Fig. 2)

| filtering method | median | | 5×5 high pass template | | wavelet modulus | | adaptive BHPF | |
|---|---|---|---|---|---|---|---|---|
| Metrics | SCR Gain | BSF | SCR Gain | BSF | SCR Gain | BSF | SCR Gain | BSF |
| A1 | 1.089 | 1.399 | 0.555 | 0.533 | 1.718 | 1.299 | 1.420 | 1.420 |
| B1 | 2.545 | 2.334 | 1.697 | 1.247 | 3.254 | 1.629 | 3.929 | 3.979 |
| C1 | 3.741 | 2.638 | 2.072 | 1.362 | 4.398 | 2.218 | 5.529 | 5.115 |
| D1 | 2.396 | 2.569 | 1.735 | 1.406 | 2.836 | 1.375 | 4.476 | 4.640 |
| E1 | 12.339 | 4.428 | 8.179 | 2.391 | N/A | N/A | 17.619 | 6.433 |
| F1 | 27.076 | 2.121 | 14.393 | 1.053 | 7.978 | 1.001 | 21.677 | 3.869 |

## 6 Conclusions

In this paper, we use the weighted information entropy to describe the complex degree of the infrared images' backgrounds, and then an adaptive BHPF whose cut-off frequency can be regulated to meet the different backgrounds is proposed to restrain the different clutters. Since the backgrounds usually have some random change in the infrared video sequences, we also present an adaptive binarisation criterion for detection. The experimental results confirm that the WIE is an effective method for evaluating the complex degree of the infrared images' backgrounds, and the robustness of our method is embodied. In real-time system, a small tracing window will be established in terms of the correlative relationship for positions in the consecutive frames, which will dramatically decrease the complexity of algorithm.

# References

1. Victor T. T., Tamar P., Leung M. and Joseph E. B.: Morphology-based Algorithm for Point Target Detection in Infrared Backgrounds. Signal and Data Processing of Small Targets 1993, (1993) 2-11
2. Peng J. X. , Zhou W. L.: Infrared Background Suppression for Segmenting and Detecting Small Target. Acta Electronica Sinica,27, (1999), 47-51
3. Denney B. S. and de Figuriredo R. J. P.: Optimal Point Target Detection Using Adaptive Auto Regressive Background Predictive. Signal and Data Processing of Small Targets 2000, (2000) 46-57
4. Leung, H. and Haykin, S.: Is there a radar attractor. Appl. Phys. Lett. 56, (1990) 593-595
5. He, N. and Haykin, S.: Chaotic modeling of sea clutter. Electron. Lett. 28, (1992) 2076-2077
6. Leung, H. and Lo, T.: Chaotic radar signal processing over the sea. IEEE J. Oceanic Eng. 18,(1993) 287-295
7. Hilliard, C.: Selection of a Clutter Rejection Algorithm for Real-time Target Detection from an Airborne Platform. Signal and Data Processing of Small Targets 2000. (2000) 74-84
8. Jiang, D.: Information Theory and Coding. University of Science and Technology Of China Press. 2001

# Neural Network Adaptive Switching Median Filter for the Restoration of Impulse Noise Corrupted Images

Pavel S. Zvonarev, Ilia V. Apalkov, Vladimir V. Khryashchev,
and Irina V. Reznikova

Digital Circuits and Signals Laboratory,
Department of Physics,
Yaroslavl State University,
150000, Russia Yaroslavl, Sovetskaya st., 14
dcslab@uniyar.ac.ru

**Abstract.** A new neural network adaptive switching median (NASM) filter is proposed to remove salt-and-pepper impulse noise from corrupted image. The algorithm is developed by combining advantages of the known median-type filters with impulse detection scheme and the neural network was included into impulse detection step to improve its characteristics. Comparison of the given method with traditional filters is provided. A visual example is given to demonstrate the performance of the proposed filter.

## 1 Introduction

Images are often corrupted by impulse noise due to errors generated in noisy sensors or communications channels. It's important to eliminate noise in images before edge detection, image segmentation or object recognition procedures. The well known median filter and its derivatives have been recognized as effective means of impulse noise removal [1-3]. The success of median filters is based on two main properties: edge preservation and efficient noise attenuation with robustness against impulsive-type noise. Edge preservation is essential in image processing due to the nature of visual perception [4].

However, median filtering also removes very fine details and sometimes changes signal structure. The main reason is that the median filter uses only rank-order information of the input data within the filter window, and discards its original temporal-order information. To avoid the damage of "good" image pixels the switching scheme is introduced [5]. The idea of this median filter modification is based on impulse noise detection. If the impulses can be detected and their positions are correctly located in the image, it is feasible to replace the impulses by the best estimates using only uncorrupted pixels. Self-organizing neural networks [6], fuzzy techniques [7] or other methods can be used on the detection step.

In the work [8] authors present a median-based switching filter, which is called progressive switching median (PSM), where both the impulse detector and the noise filter are applied progressively in iterative form. The main advantage of such method is that some impulse pixels located in the middle of large noise blotches can also be properly detected and filtered. Another interesting approach for impulse noise removal is adaptive median (AM) filter [9]. It has variable window size for removal of impulses while preserving sharpness. Simulations on test images with PSM and AM filters confirm that these algorithms are superior to standard median filters in removing impulse noise.

The new based-median neural network adaptive switching (NASM) filter is introduced in this paper. It uses advantages of filters considered above. The neural network was included into impulse detection step to improve algorithm characteristics.

The main tasks of this work are the development and testing of complex NASM algorithm and its comparison with different median type filters modifications with impulse detection scheme. The paper is organized as follows: in Section 2 we describe the proposed NASM algorithm. Section 3 shows the simulation results. Conclusions and directions for future work are given in Section 4.

## 2 Impulse Noise Detection and Removing

The noise considered in this work is bipolar salt-and-pepper impulsive noise which means fixed values 0 (pepper) and 255 (salt) for all the impulses. This model is mathematically expressed as

$$x_i = \begin{cases} 0 & \text{with probability } p_n \\ 255 & \text{with probability } p_p \\ \varphi_i & \text{with probability } 1-(p_n+p_p) \end{cases} \quad (1)$$

where $p_n = p_p = 0.5R$, $\varphi_i$ denotes the uncorrupted (good) pixel values, 0 – fixed value of the negative impulses, 255 – fixed value of positive impulses, $R$ – noise ratio ($0 \le R \le 1$) and $x_i$ denotes the pixel values of the degraded image.

### 2.1 Impulse Detection

Impulse detection procedure includes two steps: the first step is the preliminary impulse detection and the second step is the neural network impulse detection which is used to correct the preliminary result. The preliminary impulse detector can find almost all impulses for salt-and-pepper noise model, but some "good" pixels with values equal to salt or pepper values could be detected as impulses too. Network allows distinguishing such pixels from impulses and it is used to obtain final result of impulse detection.

**Preliminary Impulse Detection.** Preliminary impulse detection algorithm uses two images. The first represents corrupted image $\{x_i\}$, which displays values of pixel at position $i = (i_1, i_2)$. The second is a binary flag image $\{f_i\}$, where the binary value $f_i$ is used to indicate whether the pixel $i$ has been detected as an impulse, i.e., $f_i = 0$ means the pixel $i$ is good and $f_i = 1$ means it is an impulse. In the beginning, we assume that all the image pixels are good, i.e., $f_i \equiv 0$.

Then for each pixel $x_i$ we find the minimum and maximum values of the samples in a $W_D \times W_D$ window ($W_D$ is an odd integer not smaller than 3). If we use $\Omega_i^W$ to represent the set of the pixels within a $W \times W$ window centered about $i$

$$\Omega_i^W = \{ j = (j_1, j_2) | i_1 - (W-1)/2 \le j_1 \le i_1 + (W-1)/2, \\ i_2 - (W-1)/2 \le j_2 \le i_2 + (W-1)/2 \} \qquad (2)$$

then we have

$$\min{}_i = \min\{ x_i | j \in \Omega_i^{W_D} \}, \\ \max{}_i = \max\{ x_i | j \in \Omega_i^{W_D} \}. \qquad (3)$$

After this we use simple measurement to detect impulses

$$f_i = \begin{cases} 0, & \text{if } \min{}_i < x_i < \max{}_i \\ 1, & \text{else.} \end{cases} \qquad (4)$$

The received binary flag image $\{f_i\}$ is the result of preliminary detection step.

**Neural Network Impulse Detection.** Neural network impulse detection algorithm uses three images. The first represents corrupted image $\{y_i\}$. The second is a binary flag image $\{f_i\}$ obtained by preliminary impulse detection. And the third is also a binary flag image $\{g_i\}$ which is used to write the final impulse detection result. At start we assume $\{g_i\}$ equal preliminary impulse detection result, i.e., $g_i \equiv f_i$.

For each pixel detected as an impulse by preliminary detection we apply a network. There are two premises for network topology selection. The first is the size of input vector and the second is the size of output vector. During examination of training data we found that the most information consists in seven local characteristics of pixel. They are pixel value, medians and dispersions for different neighborhoods of estimated pixel. Here we use only pixels with $f_i = 0$ for calculating of such values. Let $M^W$ denote the number of the pixels with $f_i = 0$ in the $W \times W$ window. If $M^W$ is even, the median calculates as arithmetic mean of two middle elements of sorted data. Then, if $M^3$ more then 0, we preset elements of input network vector $v$

$$v_0 = y_i$$
$$v_1 = \text{Med}\{ y_j | f_j = 0, j \in \Omega_i^3 \} - y_i \qquad v_2 = \text{Disp}\{ y_j | f_j = 0, j \in \Omega_i^3 \}$$
$$v_3 = \text{Med}\{ y_j | f_j = 0, j \in \Omega_i^5 \} - y_i \qquad v_4 = \text{Disp}\{ y_j | f_j = 0, j \in \Omega_i^5 \} \qquad (5)$$
$$v_5 = \text{Med}\{ y_j | f_j = 0, j \in \Omega_i^7 \} - y_i \qquad v_6 = \text{Disp}\{ y_j | f_j = 0, j \in \Omega_i^7 \}.$$

The dimension of output vector in compliance with current task was selected to be equal to one in the case of two different output states ("good" and "bad"). In our algorithm three-layer network with $S_D$ neurons in hidden layer is used. During experimental work we found out that $S_D$ can't be less than five.

Let $D_i$ denote the output value of network with range $[0;1]$ for pixel at position $i$, where $D_i$ approaches to 1 confirms that the pixel was detected as an impulse correctly and if $D_i$ approaches to 0 means that the pixel with high probability is "good". Then we use simple measurement to pass corrected solution about pixel

$$g_i = \begin{cases} 0, & \text{if } f_i = 1; \ D_i < 0.1; \ M^3 > 0 \\ g_i, & \text{else.} \end{cases} \quad (6)$$

The received binary flag image $\{g_i\}$ is the result of impulse detection procedure.

## 2.2 Noise Filtering

Two image sequences are generated during the filtration procedure. The first is a sequence of gray scale images, $\{\{z_i^{(0)}\},\{z_i^{(1)}\},\cdots,\{z_i^{(n)}\},\cdots\}$, where $z_i^{(0)}$ denotes the pixel value at position $i$ in the initial noisy image, and $z_i^{(n)}$ represents pixel value at position $i$ in the image after the $n$th iteration. The second is a binary flag image sequence, $\{\{h_i^{(0)}\},\{h_i^{(1)}\},\cdots,\{h_i^{(n)}\},\cdots\}$, where the binary value $h_i^{(n)} = 0$ means the pixel $i$ is good and $h_i^{(n)} = 1$ means it is an impulse. The initial flag image $\{h_i^{(0)}\}$ is the impulse detection result $\{g_i\}$, i.e., $h_i^{(0)} \equiv g_i$.

In the $n$th iteration $(n=1,2,\cdots)$, for each pixel $z_i^{(n-1)}$, we first find its median value $m_i^{(n-1)}$ of a $W_F \times W_F$ ($W_F$ is an odd integer and not smaller than 3) window centered about it. The median value here selected from only good pixels with $h_i^{(n-1)} = 0$ in the window. Let $M$ denote the number of all the pixels with $h_i^{(n-1)} = 0$ in the $W_F \times W_F$ window. If $M$ is even, then median calculates as arithmetic mean of two middle elements of sorted data. If $M > 0$, then

$$m_i^{(n-1)} = \text{Med}\{z_j^{(n-1)} | h_j^{(n-1)} = 0, j \in \Omega_i^{W_F}\}. \quad (7)$$

The value of $z_i^{(n)}$ is modified only when the pixel $i$ is an impulse and $M$ is greater than 0:

$$z_i^{(n)} = \begin{cases} m_i^{(n-1)}, & \text{if } h_i^{(n)} = 1; M > 0 \\ z_i^{(n-1)}, & \text{else.} \end{cases} \quad (8)$$

Once an impulse pixel is modified, it is considered as a good pixel in the subsequent iterations

$$h_i^{(n)} = \begin{cases} h_i^{(n-1)}, & \text{if } z_i^{(n)} = z_i^{(n-1)} \\ 0, & \text{if } z_i^{(n)} = m_i^{(n-1)}. \end{cases} \quad (9)$$

The procedure stops after the $N_F$th iteration when all of the impulse pixels have been modified, i.e.,

$$\sum_i h_i^{(N_F)} = 0. \quad (10)$$

Then we obtain the image $\{z_i^{(N_F)}\}$ which is restored output image.

## 3 Simulation Results

In our experiments, the original test images are corrupted with fixed valued salt-and-pepper where negative and positive values are 0 and 255 respectively with equal probability. Mean square error (MSE) is used to evaluate the restoration performance in our experiments. MSE is defined as

$$MSE = \frac{1}{N}\sum_i (u_i - \varphi_i)^2 \quad (11)$$

where $N$ is the total number of pixels in the image, $u_i$ and $\varphi_i$ are the pixel values at position $i$ in the test and the original images respectively.

To implement NASM filter we need to define three parameters: $W_D$, $S_D$ and $W_F$. They are not sensitive to noise ratio and the best results for the most of the test images were obtained with $W_D = 7$, $S_D = 5$ and $W_F = 3$.

Average representation of neural network influence on the algorithm performance for the set of test images is shown on Fig. 1, where ASM and NASM algorithms with switched off and switched on neural network detection step respectively.

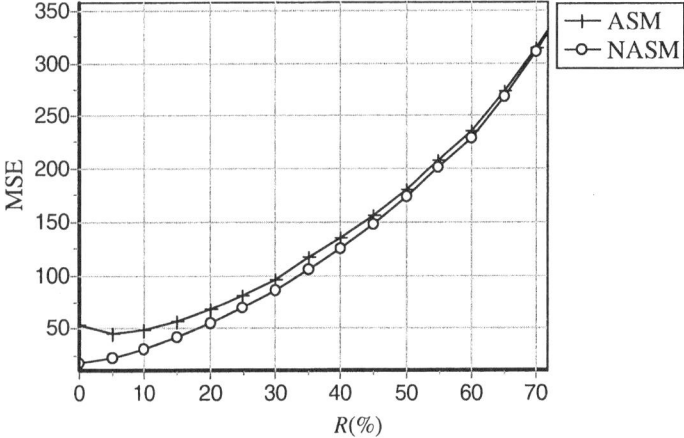

**Fig. 1.** Influence of neural network on the algorithm performance

From Fig. 1, we can observe that neural network including gives sizeable positive effect on the algorithm performance, especially when the noise ratio is not too high.

A comprehensive evaluation is reported in Fig. 2 and Fig. 3 that compare MSE for two images with different detail degree corresponding to six different algorithms: 1) simple median filter with window size $3 \times 3$, 2) AM filter for window size from 3 to 15, 3) PSM filter, 4) iterative median (IM) filter (iterative apply the simple median filter) with $3 \times 3$ window and 10 iterations, 5) center weighted median filter (CWM) with window size $5 \times 5$ and a center weight of 3 [10], 6) proposed NASM filter.

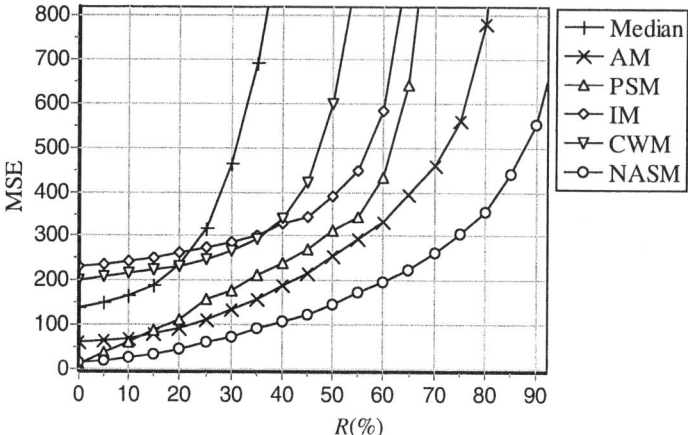

**Fig. 2.** A comparison of different median-based noise removal algorithms for the test image "Stream and Bridge"

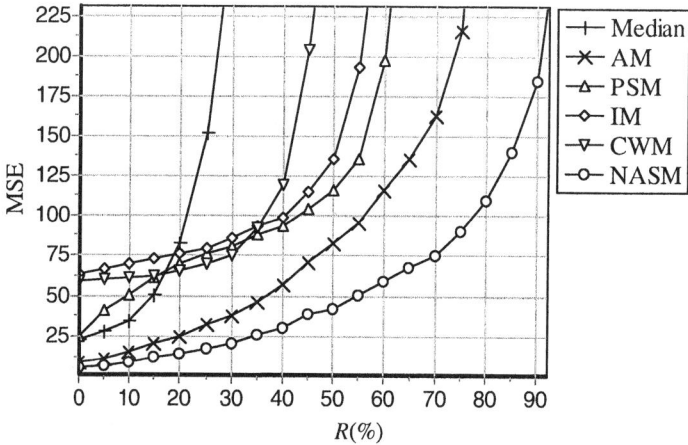

**Fig. 3.** A comparison of different median-based noise removal algorithms for the test image "Peppers"

The MSE curves demonstrate that in the presence of salt-and-pepper type of noise NASM algorithm is better than the other median-based methods on both images on all range of noise ratio. The algorithm was tested on many others images and the similar results were obtained.

In Fig. 4, are shown the restoration results of different filtering methods for the test image "Lena" highly corrupted with 60% salt-and-pepper noise. Simple median filter can preserve image details but many noise pixels are remained in the image. CWM filter performs better than simple median filter, but also misses many impulse noises. IM filter can remove more impulses then CWM, but many good pixels are also modified, as the result we have the blurred image. PSM filter has problem in case of

**Fig. 4.** Restoration results of different median-based filters. (a) Corrupted image "Lena" with 60% salt-and-pepper noise. (b) Median filter with 3×3 window size. (c) CWM filter with 5×5 window size and a center weight of 3. (d) IM filter with 3×3 window and 10 iterations. (e) PSM Filter. (f) AM filter. (g) Proposed NASM filter. (h) Original test image of "Lena".

noise blotches (a place in image where a large number of impulse pixels may connect). AM filter shows height result. It can remove most of the impulses, preserving details but edges in image are defected. The best result is obtained using NASM algorithm. It removes all of the noise pixels while preserving image details and edges very well.

## 4 Conclusion

The idea of new impulse noise removal algorithm has arisen on the basis of analysis of two known effective algorithms PSM and AM. The basic problem of PSM algorithm is the filtration of highly corrupted images by the salt-and-pepper noise. In this case noisy pixels are grouped in blocks. PSM algorithm is unable to remove them. AM filter cannot distinguish "good" pixels of image with values equal to salt or pepper values from impulses, that is why AM filter defects borders of objects in image. The algorithm submitted in this work includes advantages of the filters considered above, eliminating their basic lacks. Also algorithm was improved with a help of neural network. Neural network positive effect appears especially when original image corrupted with salt-and-pepper noise has "good" pixels with values equal to salt or pepper values. Network provides the possibility to distinguish such pixels from impulses. Proposed algorithm demonstrates high results on overwhelming majority of test images. It removes the most of noise pixels while preserving details and edges of the objects even in highly corrupted images. This property is important for further processing (edges detection or objects recognition).

## References

1. I. Pitas and A. Venetsanopoulos, Nonlinear Digital Filters: Principles and Applications. Boston, MA: Kluwer, 1990.
2. S. Mitra and G. Sicuranza, Nonlinear Image Processing. Academic Press, 2000.
3. T. Nodes and N. Gallagher, "Median Filters: Some Modifications and Their Properties," IEEE Trans. ASSP, vol. ASSP-30, no. 5, 1982.
4. L. Yin, R. Yang, M. Gabbouj, Y. Neuvo, "Weighted Median Filters: A Tutorial," IEEE Trans. Circuits Systems, vol. 43. no. 3, pp. 157-192, 1996.
5. T. Sun and Y. Neuvo, "Detail-Preserving Median Based Filters in Image Processing," Pattern Recognit. Lett., vol. 15, pp. 341-347, 1994.
6. H. Kong and L. Guan, "A Neural Network Adaptive Filter for the Removal of Impulse Noise in Digital Images," Neural Networks, vol. 9, no. 3, pp.373-378, 1996.
7. D. Zhang and Z. Wang, "Impulse Noise Detection and Removal Using Fuzzy Techniques," Electron. Lett., vol. 33, pp. 378-379, 1997.
8. Z. Wang and D. Zhang, "Progressive Switching Median Filter for the Removal of Impulse Noise from Highly Corrupted Images," IEEE Trans. Circuits Systems – II, vol. 46, no. 1, pp. 78-80, 1999.
9. H. Hwang and R. Haddad, "Adaptive Median Filters: New Algorithms and Results," IEEE Trans. on Image Processing, vol. 4, no. 4, pp. 499-502, 1995.
10. S. Ko and Y. Lee, "Center Weighted Median Filters and Their Applications to Image Enhancement," IEEE Trans. Circuits Systems, vol. 38, no. 9, pp. 984-993, 1991.

# A Shot Boundary Detection Method for News Video Based on Rough Sets and Fuzzy Clustering[1]

Xin-bo Gao, Bing Han, and Hong-bing Ji

School of Electronic Engineering, Xidian Univ., Xi'an 710071, China

**Abstract.** With the rapid growing amount of multimedia, content-based infomation retrieval has become more and more important. As a crucial step in content-based news video indexing and retrieval system, shot boundary detection attracts much more research interests in recent years. To partition news video into shots, many metrics were constructed to measure the similarity among video frames based on all the available video features. However, too many features will reduce the efficiency of the shot boundary detection. Therefore, it is necessary to perform feature reduction for every decision of shot boundary. For this purpose, the classification method based on rough sets and fuzzy c-means clustering for feature reduction and rule generation is proposed. According to the particularity of news scenes, shot transition can be divided into three types: cut transition, gradual transition and no transition. The efficacy of the proposed method is extensively tested on more than 2 h of news programs and 98.0% recall with 96.6% precision have been achieved.

## 1 Introduction

With the increasing proliferation of digital video contents, efficient techniques for analysis, indexing, and retrieval of videos according to their contents have become evermore important. A common first step for most content-based video analysis techniques available is to segment a video into elementary shots, each comprising a continuous in time and space. These elementary shots are composed to form a video sequence during video sorting or editing with either *cut* transitions or *gradual* transitions of visual effects such as fades, dissolves, and wipes.

In recent years, a large number of metrics have been proposed to segment a video into shots by measuring the dissimilarity, or distance, between two or a short sequence of adjacent frames [1-3]. These metrics make use of such frames or video features as pixel values, statistic features, intensity and color histogram and *etc*. If the measured dissimilarity is greater than some predetermined threshold, the shot boundary is assumed. How to adequately use features available is becoming the hot topic on shot boundary detection to improve the detection efficiency with keeping the detection accuracy, it is necessary to perform feature reduction for every decision of shot boundary. To this end, the rough set (RS) and fuzzy *c*-means (FCM) algorithm based

---

[1] This work was supported by National Natural Science Foundation of China (No.60202004) and the Key Project of Chinese Ministry of Education (No.104173).

feature reduction and rule generation method is presented. First, features of video sequences used as conditional attributes are extracted and the decision attributes are also given. By calculating the correlation between conditional attributes, the importance of conditional attributes can be obtained. The final features can be achieved by clustering feature attributes with FCM. For each class, the fuzzy *if-then* rule is generated for decision with fuzzy inference. The experimental results with real news videos demonstrate the effectiveness of the proposed scheme.

## 2 Basic Concepts of Rough Sets

The rough sets theory introduced by Pawlak in early 1980s[4-6] is an effective mathematical analysis tool to deal with vagueness and uncertainty in the areas of machine learning, decision analysis, knowledge discovery from database, inductive reasoning, pattern recognition and *etc.*.

**Definition 1:** Let $R$ be an equivalence relation on a universal set $X$. Moreover, let $X/R$ denote the family of all equivalence classes introduced on $X$ by $R$. One such equivalence class in $X/R$, which contains $x \in X$, is designated by $[x]_R$. For any output class $A \subseteq X$, we can define the lower and upper approximations, denoted as $\underline{R}(A)$ and $\overline{R}(A)$, which approach $A$ as closely as possibly from inside and outside respectively. Here, the union of all equivalence classes in $X/R$ that are contained in $A$ and the union of all equivalence classes in $X/R$ that overlap with each other in $A$ are defined respectively as

$$\underline{R}(A) = \bigcup \{[x]_R | [x]_R \subseteq A, x \in X\} \qquad (1)$$

$$\overline{R}(A) = \bigcup \{[x]_R | [x]_R \cap A \neq \emptyset, x \in X\} \qquad (2)$$

**Definition 2[7]:** Let $U$ be a finite set of *objects* called the universe. $A$ is a finite set of *attributes*, and $V$ is a set of attribute values, where

$$V = \bigcup_{a \in A} V_a ,$$

$V_a$ is called the domain of $a$. $f$ is an *information function*, $f: U \times A \to V$, for every $x \in U$ and $a \in A, f(x,a) \in V_a$. By the *information system* we will understand a quadruple $S = <U, V, f, A>$. Then, a decision table is defined as an information system, $A = (U,V,f,C \cup D)$. The positive region of $C$ to $D$ is defined as

$$\text{POS}_C(D) = \bigcup_{X \in U/IND(D)} \underline{C}(X) \qquad (3)$$

In condition attributes, some attributes play an important role for classification results, while the others may not be more effects on classification results. So the importance or dependence of attributes can be used to measure the importance of classification results and the attributes can be deducted.

**Definition 3:** Let $P$ and $Q$ be the attribute sets (such as condition attributes and decision attributes). $P \subseteq R, Q \subseteq R : U/P = \{X_1, X_2, \cdots, X_i\}$, $U/Q = \{Y_1, Y_2, \cdots, Y_j\}$. We say that $Q$ depends on $P$ in the degree of $k$ on $P$ if

$$k = \gamma_P(Q) = \frac{|POS_P(Q)|}{|U|} \quad (4)$$

Where $|\cdot|$ denotes the cardinality of a given set. Thus the coefficient $k$ expresses the ratio of all elements of the universe which can be properly classified into blocks of the partition $U/I(Q)$ with employing attributes $P$. It can be used to deal with consistency of information.

## 3 Shot Boundary Detection Scheme Based on RS and FCM

As mentioned in literatures, the selected low-level features are essential to achieve high accuracy for shot boundary detection. But there are too many features available in the video. By choosing the most appropriate features to represent a shot or video, the computational burden will be reduced which induces high efficiency. So, the feature optimal choice method based on RS and FCM algorithm is introduced.

### 3.1 Fuzzy c-Mean Algorithm

As an effective unsupervised analysis tool, the FCM algorithm has been widely used in many fields, including communication [8], medical treatment [9], training of neutral network [10] *etc*. Recently, it has been introduced into content based video indexing and browsing by more and more researchers [11, 12]. In addition, the researchers used the RS and $K$-means clustering to segment images [13]. Shi [14] developed the hyper spectral band reduction based on RS and fuzzy $c$-means clustering. Here, we introduce the RS and fuzzy clustering into the field of shot boundary segmentation. The basic FCM algorithm can be referred to [15] for more detailed discussion.

### 3.2 Feature Selection Based on RS and FCM

To detect the video shot boundaries, 12 candidate features are usually extracted for common use as follows.

  (1) The red (R), green (G) or blue (B) component in RGB model;
  (2) The hue (H), saturation(S) or value (V) component in HSV model;
  (3) Gray-histogram (G-H);
  (4) Color-histogram: the color histogram of RGB model (Rgb-H) and the color histogram of HSV model (Hsv-H) respectively ;
  (5) Statistic features: mean (M), variance (St) and skewness (P).

Here, the extracted features from news videos are served as condition attribute set $P = \{c_1, c_2, \cdots, c_n\}$ and the corresponding transition types of shots is defined as decision attribute set, $Q = d$. To select the primary features for decision, the FCM algorithm is employed to analyze the classifying capability of various features

$$x_k = \gamma_{c_k}(d), \quad k = 1, 2, \cdots, n \quad (8)$$

Through clustering, the closest feature to the center is selected as the primary feature. While, $\gamma_{c_i}(d)$ reflects the whole classification capability of features. The classification capability of different features is different for various video transitions. So it is not enough accurately for measuring similarity to directly use $\gamma_{c_i}(d)$ as clustering feature vectors. The definition above can be modified as

$$x_k = \{x_{k1}, x_{k2}, \cdots, x_{km}\} \quad (9)$$

where, $x_{k,j} = |c_k(Y_j)|/Y_j$, $j = 1, 2, \cdots, m$, which represents the recognition rate of each shot transition to the $k$-th feature. For the same transition shots, the features that have the same classification results are thought to be similar. Through classifying, the $x_k$ ($k = 1, 2, \cdots, n$) can be divided into feature groups with the similar classification capability. Then according to maximum membership rules and the characteristics of strong correlation between closed features, one feature is selected in each feature groups. Then, an equivalence deduction of original high dimension features is obtained.

### 3.3 Rules Generation

There is a shot transition or no transition in each demonstration, including *cut* transition, *dissolve* transition, *wipe* transition, zoom, pan, object motions, flash, the affects of caption appearance and disappearance in a shot. Then decision set includes *cut*, *gradual* and *no transition*. Table 1 gives the information of 30 test video clips with their features and fuzzy membership of variables. The fuzzy membership functions of features are shown in Fig.1.

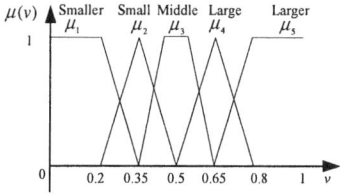

**Fig. 1.** Definition of the fuzzy variable in Table 1

From the decision table, the feature vector for FCM clustering, the classifiable ability of every feature to different shot transition can be calculated by (9). $x_{1,1}=8/12$, $x_{2,1}=8/12$, $x_{3,1}=7/12$, $x_{4,1}=11/12$, $x_{5,1}=0$, $x_{6,1}=7/12$, $x_{7,1}=7/12$, $x_{8,1}=10/12$, $x_{9,1}=11/12$, $x_{10,1}=8/12$, $x_{11,1}=9/12$, $x_{12,1}=10/12$; $x_{1,2}=11/12$, $x_{2,2}=11/12$, $x_{3,2}=0$, $x_{4,2}=10/12$, $x_{5,2}=11/12$, $x_{6,2}=11/12$, $x_{7,2}=11/12$, $x_{8,2}=12/12$, $x_{9,2}=12/12$, $x_{10,2}=8/12$, $x_{11,2}=9/12$, $x_{12,2}=10/12$; $x_{1,3}=0$, $x_{2,3}=0$, $x_{3,3}=10/12$, $x_{4,3}=0$, $x_{5,3}=0$, $x_{6,3}=1/6$, $x_{7,3}=0$, $x_{8,3}=0$, $x_{9,3}=0$, $x_{10,3}=0$, $x_{11,3}=0$, $x_{12,3}=6/6$. And the clustering results are shown in Fig.2 and Fig.3.

According to the clustering results and maximum membership rules, the rules of shot transition can be obtained as follows.

(1) If $H = \mu_5$ or $H = \mu_4$ and $Hsv - H = \mu_5$ or $Hsv - H = \mu_4$ and $m = \mu_5$ or $m = \mu_4$, Then there is *no transition*;

(2) If $V = \mu_1$ or $V = \mu_2$ and $G - H = \mu_1$ or $G - H = \mu_2$ and $m = \mu_1$ or $m = \mu_2$, Then there is a *cut transition*;

(3) If $V = \mu_3$ and $P = \mu_3$, Then there is a *gradual transition*.

**Table 1.** The decision table for shot transition

| No. | Condition Attributes Set | | | | | | | | | | | Decision Set | |
|---|---|---|---|---|---|---|---|---|---|---|---|---|---|
| | R | G | B | H | S | V | G-H | Rgb-H | Hsv-H | M | St | P | Type | D |
| 1 | L | L | L | Sr | L | L | M | M | M | L | Sr | Sr | Zoom | N |
| 2 | Lr | Lr | Lr | Lr | Lr | Lr | Lr | Lr | Lr | L | L | L | Cut | C |
| 3 | Sr | Sr | Sr | Sr | L | Sr | Sr | Sr | Sr | S | Sr | Sr | Pan | N |
| 4 | Sr | Sr | Sr | Sr | Sr | Sr | Sr | Sr | Sr | Sr | Sr | Sr | No | N |
| 5 | Lr | Lr | Lr | Lr | Lr | Lr | Lr | Lr | Lr | Lr | Lr | Lr | Cut | C |
| 6 | M | M | L | M | L | M | M | M | M | M | M | M | Wipe | G |
| 7 | Sr | Sr | Sr | Sr | Sr | L | Sr | Sr | L | Sr | Sr | Sr | No | N |
| 8 | Lr | Lr | Lr | Lr | Lr | Lr | Lr | Lr | Lr | Lr | Lr | Lr | Cut | C |
| 9 | Lr | Lr | Lr | Lr | Lr | Lr | Lr | Lr | Lr | Lr | Lr | Lr | Cut | C |
| 10 | Lr | Lr | Lr | Lr | Lr | Lr | Lr | Lr | Lr | Lr | Lr | Lr | Cut | C |
| 11 | M | M | M | M | Sr | M | M | S | S | M | M | Sr | No | N |
| 12 | M | M | M | M | M | M | M | M | M | M | M | M | Wipe | G |
| 13 | Lr | Lr | Lr | S | Lr | Lr | Lr | Lr | Lr | Lr | Lr | Lr | Cut | C |
| 14 | M | M | M | L | L | M | M | M | M | M | M | M | Wipe | G |
| 15 | Lr | Lr | Lr | Lr | S | Lr | Lr | Lr | Lr | Lr | S | Lr | Cut | C |
| 16 | Lr | Lr | Lr | Lr | Lr | Lr | Lr | Lr | Lr | Lr | Lr | Lr | Cut | C |
| 17 | Sr | Sr | Sr | Sr | Sr | Sr | Sr | Sr | Sr | Sr | Sr | Sr | Zoom | N |
| 18 | M | M | S | Sr | Sr | Sr | SRr | Sr | Sr | M | Sr | Sr | Zoom | N |
| 19 | Sr | S | S | Sr | Sr | Sr | Sr | Sr | Sr | Sr | Sr | Sr | No | N |
| 20 | Lr | Lr | Lr | M | Lr | Lr | Lr | Lr | Lr | L | Lr | Lr | Cut | C |
| 21 | S | S | Sr | Sr | Sr | M | Sr | Sr | Sr | S | L | L | Zoom | N |
| 22 | Sr | Sr | Sr | Sr | Sr | Sr | L | M | M | S | Sr | Sr | Pan | N |
| 23 | Lr | Lr | Lr | Lr | Lr | Lr | Lr | Lr | Lr | Lr | Lr | Lr | Cut | C |
| 24 | M | M | M | M | M | S | M | M | M | M | M | M | Dissolve | G |
| 25 | M | M | L | M | M | M | M | S | SR | S | S | S | Zoom | N |
| 26 | Sr | Sr | Sr | Sr | Sr | Sr | L | Sr | L | Sr | Sr | Sr | No | N |
| 27 | M | M | S | M | M | M | M | M | M | S | M | M | Dissolve | G |
| 28 | M | M | M | M | M | M | M | M | M | M | M | M | Dissolve | G |
| 29 | L | L | L | L | L | L | L | Lr | LR | L | L | L | Cut | C |
| 30 | Lr | Lr | Lr | Lr | Lr | Lr | Lr | Lr | Lr | Lr | Lr | Lr | Cut | C |

*Notice: Lr: Larger; L: Large; M: Middle; S: Small; Sr: Smaller; C: Cut transition; G: Gradual transition; N: No transition; D: Decision.*

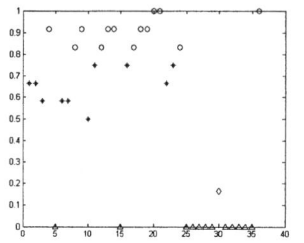 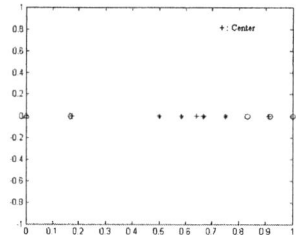

**Fig. 2.** Clustering result in the data space   **Fig. 3.** The position of clustering centers

## 4 Experimental Results

The method described above is applied to 5 news programs from CCTV-1, whose frame size is 352×240 and frame rate is 30 frames per second, which include cut, fade and dissolve, as well as zoom, pan and other camera motions and object motions. The detail information is shown in Table 2.

**Table 2.** The detailed information on the news programs

| News program | 1 | 2 | 3 | 4 | 5 | Total |
|---|---|---|---|---|---|---|
| Duration | 34'55" | 30'2" | 36'26" | 24'47" | 15'44" | 141'54" |
| Video shots | 374 | 323 | 396 | 247 | 187 | 1527 |
| Cut shots | 339 | 315 | 390 | 237 | 178 | 1459 |
| Gradual shots | 35 | 8 | 6 | 10 | 9 | 68 |

**Table 3.** The comparison of our method with the histogram method (DOH)

| Program video | | News 1 | News 2 | News 3 | News 4 | News 5 | Average |
|---|---|---|---|---|---|---|---|
| Proposed method | Hits | 370 | 320 | 388 | 245 | 182 | 1605 |
| | Misses | 12 | 10 | 16 | 7 | 8 | 53 |
| | False | 8 | 7 | 8 | 5 | 3 | 31 |
| | Recall | 97.8% | 97.6% | 98.2% | 98.0% | 98.3% | 98.0% |
| | Precision | 96.6% | 97.8% | 96.1% | 97.2% | 95.8% | 96.7% |
| DOH method | Hits | 380 | 350 | 400 | 250 | 190 | 1570 |
| | Misses | 30 | 15 | 46 | 22 | 17 | 130 |
| | False | 36 | 42 | 50 | 25 | 20 | 173 |
| | Recall | 91.8% | 95.1% | 88.2% | 91.0% | 90.8% | 91.4% |
| | Precision | 90.3% | 88.1% | 87.2% | 90.2% | 89.3% | 89.0% |

Here, we conduct an experiment with our method and the histogram-based method [15] on the same video clips respectively. The experimental results are summarized in Table 3. To evaluate the performance of the proposed scheme of gradual transition segmentation, we use the standard *recall* and *precision* criteria [12].

Based on the 1,527 shot boundary detected, we achieves 98.0% recall with 96.7% precision. And there are two types of false detections in videos. One results from the existence of irregular camera operations during the gradual transitions. The other is due to a lot of flash effects in a shot. The misses are mainly due to the small content change between the frame pairs at some shot boundaries.

In addition, the total classification capability of each feature, $\gamma_{c_k}(d)$, is used as the feature vector for clustering, $x_1$=19/30, $x_2$=19/30, $x_3$=7/30, $x_4$=20/30, $x_5$=11/30, $x_6$=19/30, $x_7$=18/30, $x_8$=19/30, $x_9$=23/30, $x_{10}$=14/30, $x_{11}$=18/30, $x_{12}$=27/30. Then the clustering results are shown in Fig.4 and Fig.5.

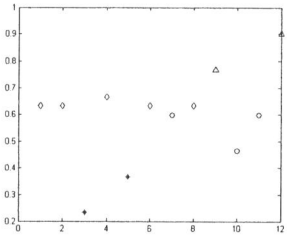 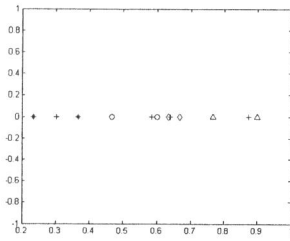

**Fig. 4.** Clustering result in the data space    **Fig. 5.** The position of clustering centers

So the selected features for detecting shot boundary are B, H, S, G-H, S, P and decision rules can be obtained as follows

(1) If $B = \mu_5$ or $B = \mu_4$ and $H = \mu_5$ or $H = \mu_4$ and $S = \mu_5$ or $S = \mu_4$ and $G - H = \mu_5$ or $G - H = \mu_4$ and $S = \mu_5$ or $S = \mu_4$, $P = \mu_5$ or $P = \mu_4$, Then there is *no* transition;

(2) If $B = \mu_1$ or $B = \mu_2$ and $H = \mu_1$ or $H = \mu_2$ and $S = \mu_1$ or $S = \mu_2$ and $G - H = \mu_1$ or $G - H = \mu_2$ and $S = \mu_1$ or $S = \mu_2$, and $P = \mu_1$ or $P = \mu_2$, Then there is a *cut* transition;

(3) If $B = \mu_3$ and $H = \mu_3$ and $S = \mu_3$ and $G - H = \mu_3$ and $S = \mu_3$ and $P = \mu_3$, Then there is a *gradual* transition.

The results from the above decision rules achieve 95% recall with 94% precision on the same video programs. Though it achieves good performance, the CPU time of the method based on the total classification capability is much higher than our method, obviously because there are more features used in the former method than in our method. And our method has a high accuracy because it is more accordant to the actual situation than the former one.

## 5 Conclusions

This paper presents a feature reduction method based on RS and FCM, by which the rules for shot boundary detection are obtained. Due to differences of the correlation between features, their classification capability is different for various shot boundary.

In addition, based on the characteristics of differences from the classification capability of various features to different shot transition, the correlation between features can be defined using the classification ability of attributes (or dependence between attributes) in RS theory. Then, by FCM algorithm, the optimal feature reduction can be obtained. According to the reduction results, we achieve the decision rules for shot boundary detection. Experimental results on five real news videos illustrate the effectiveness and the efficiency of the proposed method.

## References

1. John S. Boreczky, Lawrence A. Rowe. Comparison of video shot boundary detection techniques. In SPIE Conf. Storage & Retrieval for Image & Video Databases, Vol.2670, (1996) 170-179
2. Gargi, U., Kasturi, R., Strayer, S.H. Performance characterization of video-shot-change detection methods. IEEE Trans. on CSVT, Vol.10(1) (2000) 1-13
3. Ford, R.M., et al. Metrics for shot boundary detection in digital video sequences. Multimedia Syst., (2000) 37-46
4. Pawlak Z. Rough Set. Int. J. of Comput. Inf. Sci.. Vol. 11(5) (1982) 341-356
5. Pawlak Z. Vagueness and Uncertainty: A Rough Set Perspective. ICS Research Reports 19, Warsaw Univ. of Technology, (1994)
6. Pawlak Z., Grzymala-Busse J., Slowinski R., and Ziarko W. Rough sets. Comm. ACM. Vol.38(11) (1995) 89-95
7. Guo-Yin Wang, Jun Zhao, Jiu-Jiang An, Yu Wu. Theoretical study on attribute reduction of rough set theory: comparison of algebra and information views. ICCI, (2004) 148-155
8. Sheng C., Bernard M., Peter M. G. A clustering technique for digital communications channel equalization using radial basis function networks. IEEE Trans. on NN, Vol.4(4) (1993) 570-579
9. Bezdek J.C., Fordon W.A. The application of fuzzy set theory to the medical diagnosis. In Advances of Fuzzy Sets and Theories, North-Holland, Amsterdam, (1979) 445-461
10. Karayiannis N.B., Mi G.W. Growing radial basis neural networks: merging supervised and unsupervised learning with network growth techniques: IEEE Trans. on NN, Vol.8(6) (1997) 1492-1506
11. Xinbo Gao, Xiaoou Tang. Unsupervised model-free news video segmentation. IEEE Trans. on CSVT, Vol.12(9) (2002) 765-776
12. Han Bing, Gao Xin-bo, Ji Hong-bin. An efficient algorithm of gradual transition for shot boundary segmentation. SPIE on MIPPR, Vol. 5286(2) (2003) 956-961
13. Liu Yan, Yue Y., et al. Application of rough set and $K$-means clustering in image segmentation (in Chinese). Infrared and Laser Engineering, Vol.33(3) (2004) 300-302
14. Shi Hong, Shen Yi, Liu Zhi-yan. Hyperspectral band reduction based on RS and fuzzy $c$-means clustering (in Chinese). Journal of Electronics & Information Technology, Vol.4 (2004) 619-624
15. Bezdek J C. Pattern Recognition with Fuzzy Objective Function Algorithm. Plenum Press, New York, (1981)
16. Zhang H.J. and Smoliar S.W. Developing power tools for video indexing and retrieval. Proceedings of the SPIE: Storage and Retrieval for Image and Video databases II, San Jose, CA, Vol.2185 (1994) 140-149

# Image Enhancement via Fusion Based on Laplacian Pyramid Directional Filter Banks

Hai-yan Jin[1], Xiao-hui Yang[1], Li-cheng Jiao[1], and Fang Liu[2]

[1] Institute of Intelligent Information Processing and National Key Lab for Radar Signal Processing, Xidian University, Xi'an, 710071 China
hy_jin823@yeah.net
[2] School of Computer Science, Xidian University, Xi'an, 710071 China

**Abstract.** Based on the directionality of images and combining the direction information with multiple resolution analysis, an image enhancement idea via fusion based on directional filter banks is presented in this paper. Combining with LP analysis further, an image fusion method based on LPDFB is given in the paper. Using the experiments to compare the results, they prove its feasibility and validity.

## 1 Introduction

Image fusion processing has become a key point in image processing field as an important part of information fusion. It is a new technique to deal with different source images synthetically. To a two-dimensional image, the intention of fusion is to obtain a more exact, comprehensive and reliable image representation for a scene or a target by information exaction and integration. The reliability and automatic level of recognition can be improved by image fusion. Recently, image enhancement via fusion has been widely used in multi-spectrum image comprehension, medical image processing, remote image processing and weather forecast field and so on.

Generally, image fusion processing is carried out in the following three levels: pixel fusion, feature fusion, and decision fusion. Pixel fusion is the lowest-level fusion, which analyzes and integrates the information before the original information is estimated and recognized. This process retains information as much as possible and provides the detail information with high precision. Feature fusion is done in the middle level, which analyzes and deals with the feature information such as edge, contour, direction obtained by pretreatment and feature extraction. Decision fusion is the highest-level fusion, which points to the actual target. Before fusion, the data should be pre-cured to gain the independent decision result, so the cost is high and at the same time the information lose can not be avoided. At present, most study is concentrated in the pixel fusion and representative methods are based on the pyramid transform [1], wavelet transform (WT) [2-4] and so on. The conventional WT idea considers the maximal absolute value of wavelet coefficients or local feature of two images. Wavelets are very effective in representing objects with isolated point singularities, while wavelet bases are not the most significant in representing objects with singularities along lines. As a consequence, the method based on the WT can not excavate the edge quality and detail information, especially for SAR images with abundant texture information and much high frequency information included in the edges. The smoothness and lightness of fusion image are the key point of image fusion. Aimed at the disadvantages of wavelets, the direction information is combined with multi-resolution analysis in this paper and we construct an effective directional filter banks (DFB) [5-6], further combining with LP decomposition. A method of image Enhancement via fusion based on Laplacian Pyramid directional filter banks (LPDFB) is presented in this paper.

## 2 Image Enhancement via Fusion Based on the DFB and LP

### 2.1 Laplacian Pyramid (LP) Decomposition

LP [7-8] is a multi-scale data representation. It captures data in a hierarchical manner where each level corresponds to a reduced resolution approximation. The basic idea of the LP is as Fig.1. The process can be iterated on the coarse version.

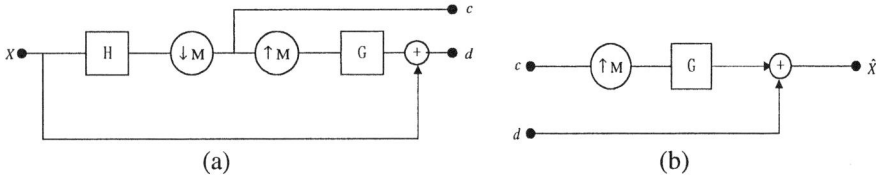

**Fig. 1.** LP analysis and synthesis sketch map. (a) Analysis. The outputs are a coarse approximation $c$ and a difference $d$ between the original signal and the prediction. (b) Usual synthesis.

We use a $d \times d$ nonsingular integer matrix **M** to represent the sampling operation. For an M-fold down-sampling, the input $x[n]$ and the output $x_d[n]$ are related by [9]

$$x_d[n] = x[\mathbf{M}n] \tag{1}$$

For an M-fold up-sampling, the input $x[n]$ and the output $x_u[n]$ are related by

$$x_u[n] = \begin{cases} x[k] & \text{if } n=\mathbf{M}k, k \in Z^d \\ 0 & \text{otherwise} \end{cases} \tag{2}$$

The coarse approximation signal

$$c[n] = \sum_{k \in Z^d} x[k] h[\mathbf{M}n-k] = \langle x, \tilde{h}[\cdot - \mathbf{M}n] \rangle \tag{3}$$

where we denote $\tilde{h}[n] = h[-n]$. The up-sampling and filtering operation results in

$$p[n] = \sum_{k \in Z^d} c[k] g[n - \mathbf{M}k] = \sum_{k \in Z^d} \langle x, \tilde{h}[\cdot - \mathbf{M}k] \rangle g[n - \mathbf{M}k] \tag{4}$$

Writing signals as column vectors, for example, $x = (x[n] : n \in \mathbb{Z}^d)^T$, we can express these operations as left matrix multiplications

$$c = \mathbf{H}x \quad \text{and} \quad p = \mathbf{G}c \qquad (5)$$

where $\mathbf{H}$ and $\mathbf{G}$ correspond to $(\downarrow \mathbf{M})\mathbf{H}$ and $\mathbf{G}(\uparrow \mathbf{M})$, respectively. We denote $\mathbf{I}$ as the identity matrices with appropriate sizes depending on the context. Using this matrix notation and according to (5), the difference signal of the LP can be written as

$$d = x - p = x - \mathbf{GH}x = (\mathbf{I} - \mathbf{GH})x \qquad (6)$$

Writing (6) as matrix notation and combining with (5), we can write the analysis operator of the LP as follows

$$\underbrace{\begin{pmatrix} c \\ d \end{pmatrix}}_{y} = \underbrace{\begin{pmatrix} \mathbf{H} \\ \mathbf{I} - \mathbf{GH} \end{pmatrix}}_{\mathbf{A}} x \qquad (7)$$

In the LP structure, each level generates only one band-pass signal, so the resulting band-pass signals of the LP do not suffer from the "scrambled" frequencies.

## 2.2 A Construction Method for DFB

In 1992, Bamberger and Smith [10] explored non-separable filter banks in constructing a 2-D DFB. Minh N Do and Martin Vetterli et al. studied the structured linear extension [6]. But by far, the application of DFB is limited in image processing.

We define sampling operation on lattices in multi-dimensional $z^d$ system in this paper. Using a $d \times d$ nonsingular integer matrix $\mathbf{M}$ to represent the lattice as

$$LAT(\mathbf{M}) = \{\mathbf{M}n, n \in Z^d\}, \qquad (8)$$

The two-dimensional two-channel tree-structured filter banks decomposition is adopted in this paper. Using quincunx sampling lattice, the following matrices are possible representations of the two-dimensional quincunx sub-lattice [11]

$$\mathbf{Q}_0 = \begin{pmatrix} 1 & -1 \\ 1 & 1 \end{pmatrix}, \quad \mathbf{Q}_1 = \begin{pmatrix} 1 & 1 \\ -1 & 1 \end{pmatrix} \qquad (9)$$

The following four basic unimodular matrices are used in the DFB in order to provide the equivalence of the rotation operation

$$\mathbf{R}_0 = \begin{pmatrix} 1 & 1 \\ 0 & 1 \end{pmatrix}, \quad \mathbf{R}_1 = \begin{pmatrix} 1 & -1 \\ 0 & 1 \end{pmatrix}, \quad \mathbf{R}_2 = \begin{pmatrix} 1 & 0 \\ 1 & 1 \end{pmatrix}, \quad \mathbf{R}_3 = \begin{pmatrix} 1 & 0 \\ -1 & 1 \end{pmatrix} \qquad (10)$$

Here, we use a useful tool — the Smith form, which can diagonalize any integer matrix $\mathbf{M}$ into a product $\mathbf{UDV}$, where $\mathbf{U}$ and $\mathbf{V}$ are unimodular integer matrices and $\mathbf{D}$ is an integer diagonal matrix [12]. The quincunx matrix in (9) can be expressed in the Smith form as

$$Q_0 = R_1 D_0 R_2 = R_2 D_1 R_1 \text{ and } Q_1 = R_0 D_0 R_3 = R_3 D_1 R_0 \tag{11}$$

Where

$$D_0 = \begin{pmatrix} 2 & 0 \\ 0 & 1 \end{pmatrix}, \quad D_1 = \begin{pmatrix} 1 & 0 \\ 0 & 2 \end{pmatrix} \tag{12}$$

are two 2-D diagonal matrices that correspond to dyadic sampling in each dimension.

At the first two decomposition levels of the DFB, quincunx filter banks (QFB) are used at each level. We choose the sampling matrices in the first and second level to be $Q_0$ and $Q_1$. From the third level, expand the rest of the tree. To achieve finer frequency partition, we use QFB together with re-sampling operations. Re-sampled QFB's of $R_0$ and $R_1$ are used in the first half of DFB channels, which lead to sub-bands corresponding to basically horizontal directions or directions between +45° and -45°. $R_2$ and $R_3$ are used in the second half of the DFB channels and lead to sub-bands corresponding to the remaining directions.

DFB can capture the high frequency information of the image, but on the contrary for the low frequency information. So before applying DFB, we combine it with multi-resolution analysis. We choose LP to pre-treat here. In the LP structure, each pyramid level generates only one band-pass signal, so the result signals do not suffer from the frequency scrambling effect. The following is the image enhancement method via fusion based on the Laplacian Pyramid Directional Filter Banks (LPDFB).

### 2.3 The Image Fusion Algorithm Based on LPDFB

Step1: Initialize parameters. We choose "9-7" filter as the LP decomposition filter and tree- structured DFB in this paper. The maximal decomposition level is 5.
Step2: Decompose two local blurry input images respectively using LP and then we can obtain coarse approximation images "low1" and "low2" at half size respectively and detail images "high1" and "high2" at full size.
Step3: Using DFB constructed by above method to decompose the detail images "high1" and "high2" in step2 independently, and we can get directional sub-band images "high-dir1" and "high-dir2" at this level.
Step4: Take the coarse approximation images "low1" and "low2" in step2 apart as input and do the step2 iteratively until complete the initialized decomposition level.
Step5: Add band-pass directional sub-bands information "high-dir1" and "high-dir2" as the row vectors to the final output "y1" and "y2".
Step6: Low-pass filter the decomposition results "y1" and "y2" and obtain two groups of coefficients "c1" and "c2".
Step7: Construct a set of new coefficients "c" by finding maximal absolute value of corresponding position of "c1" and "c2".
Step8: Take "c" as the input parameter of LPDFB and reconstruct the image to obtain the fusion results.

## 3 Numerical Experiments and Analysis

### 3.1 The Evaluation Standard of the Effect of Image Fusion

At present, there is not a general and uniform standard to evaluate the fusion image. So we use information entropy, average grads and standard deviation to analyze the fusion images.

(1) Information Entropy(IE)[13]: According to information theory, the information entropy of an 8 bit image is

$$E = -\sum_{t=0}^{255} p_t \log_2 p_t \qquad (13)$$

where $p_t$ is the probability that pixel value is t. Information entropy indicates the change of information capability after fusion. The greater the entropy is, the more information in images. So the better fusion images are.

(2) Average Grads(AG)[13]: We use $\overline{g}$ to represent average grads. It can reflect the detail contrast of images sensitively. Therefore we can use it to evaluate the clearness of images. The formula is

$$\overline{g} = \frac{1}{(M-1)(N-1)} \times \sum_{i=1}^{(M-1)} \sum_{j=1}^{(N-1)} \sqrt{\left(\left(\frac{\partial f(x_i, y_j)}{\partial x_i}\right)^2 + \left(\frac{\partial f(x_i, y_j)}{\partial x_j}\right)^2\right) / 2} \qquad (14)$$

where $f(x, y)$ is image function, $M$ and $N$ are the number of row and column respectively. In general, the greater it is, the clearer the image.

(3) Standard deviation(STD) [13]: We use std to indicate sample standard deviation. It is an important index to weigh the information capability of images, also can evaluate the contrast. The formula is

$$std = \left(\frac{1}{n-1} \sum_{i=1}^{n} (x_i - \overline{x})^2\right)^{\frac{1}{2}} \qquad (15)$$

where $\overline{x}$ is the mean of pixels, $x_i$ the pixels value. In general, the greater it is, the more information it increased. That is to say, we can find more information in it.

### 3.2 Numerical Experiments

To show the performance of the method in this paper, we choose a common natural image and a SAR image to experiment. Both the images are 512×512. In the experiments, we use "sym4" wavelets, which is a family of near symmetry wavelets. To obtain external results, we do 2-level and 5-level WT decomposition respectively.

### 3.2.1 Clock Image Fusion Experiments

(a) clock No.1 blurred image   (b) clock No.2 blurred image   (c) 2-level WT fusion result

(d) 5-level WT fusion image   (e) LP directional filter banks fusion result

**Fig. 2.** clock image fusion results

**Table 1.** Comparison of "clock" image fusion results using different methods

| Images | IE | AG | STD |
|---|---|---|---|
| clock No.1 blurred image | 4.8370 | 3.1994 | 51.0468 |
| clock No.2 blurred image | 4.7995 | 2.3342 | 51.3058 |
| 2-level WT fusion result | 5.0952 | 3.2933 | 51.6693 |
| 5-level WT fusion result | 5.1094 | 3.8666 | 52.1719 |
| LP directional filter banks result | 5.1158 | 4.0440 | 52.3658 |

### 3.2.2 SAR Image Fusion Experiments

(a) SAR image No.1   (b) SAR image No.2   (c) 2-level WT fusion result

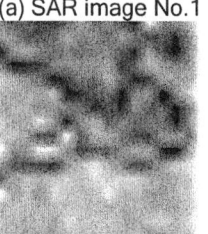 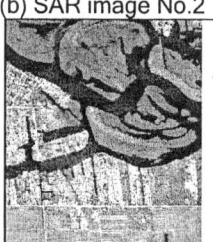

(d) 5-level WT fusion image   (e) LP directional filter banks fusion result

**Fig. 3.** SAR image fusion results

**Table 2.** Comparison of SAR image fusion results using different methods

| Images | IE | AG | STD |
|---|---|---|---|
| SAR image No.1 | 3.7441 | 8.9689 | 65.2375 |
| SAR image No.2 | 3.7806 | 8.2740 | 66.4160 |
| 2-level WT fusion result | 5.0756 | 5.3747 | 61.1428 |
| 5-level WT fusion result | 5.0706 | 1.3382 | 55.1222 |
| LP directional filter banks result | 5.0793 | 11.8071 | 69.4398 |

### 3.3 Experiments Analysis

From the above experiments, we obtain two groups of numerical data (see Table 1 and Table 2). According to the index in section 3.1 and combining visual effect, firstly we can find that the information entropy of the images after fusion by several methods is higher than original images. It shows that the information capacity is increased. Further more the information entropy obtained by LPDFB method is higher than by 2-level and 5-level WT methods. Also the average grads and standard deviation of fusion images are increased. It shows that fusion images reflect the detail feature of images better and each index obtained by LPDFB method is higher than by 2-level and 5-level WT methods. It is benefit for target estimation and autoclassification. In SAR image experiment section 3.2.2, the fusion results by WT idea not good and the average grads of fusion images are even lower than original images. It indicates that wavelets are not good at capture the detail and texture feature while LPDFB technique can.

From the visual effect, in section 3.2.1, the blurred parts are enhanced by several methods after fusion. 2-level WT method makes the detail part of the image not clear, for example, the plate of the clock is still vague, while 5-level wavelet transform makes the images more clear but the serrate edges in quadrate clock is appeared. The method presented in this paper not only makes the detail image inosculate together but reconstructed fusion result is clear and overcome the serrate edge. In SAR image experiment section 3.2.2, 2-level WT enhances the information of original images, but makes texture of the light area vague, while 5-level WT result is dissatisfied. The reason is that for SAR images with inherent speckle noise, WT strips the low frequency information directly. Consequently the detail information is lost in a certain extent. The loss is related to the decomposition level. The less level is, the more loss of detail information with more spectral information retained, and the more level is, the better spatial detail information representation with worse spectral performance. The method presented in this paper enhances the information of original images, also retains the texture and detail effectively and leads to the clear enhancement images, especially for SAR images. In conclusion, combining the indexes and the visual effect of fusion results, the method in this paper is preponderant.

## 4 Conclusion

Based on the wavelets, a Laplacian Pyramid Directional Filter Banks (LPDFB) is constructed in this paper. Furthermore a method of image enhancement via fusion based on the Laplacian Pyramid Directional Filter Banks (LPDFB) is given. It considers that the directional information can be reconstructed and the edge contour can be retained effectively, especially for the texture feature of SAR images. The main idea of this method is as follows. Firstly, LP decomposition is carried to each original image. Each pyramid level generates only one band-pass signal, even for multi-dimensional cases. The resulting band-pass signals of the LP do not suffer from the "scrambled" frequencies by down-sampling the low-pass channel only. Furthermore, each detail part is decomposed by directional filter banks (DFB) respectively, and leads to two groups of coefficients. Then, according to the rule of finding maximal absolute value of corresponding position, we construct a new group of coefficients. Finally, reconstruct the fusion images in term of new coefficients. The validity has been proved by the emulation experiments.

## References

1. Gui-xi Liu, Wan-hai Yang. A Multiscale Contrast-Pyramid-Based Image Fusion Scheme and Its Performance Evaluation. Optics Journal. 2001.21(11): 1336-1342.
2. Gui-xi Liu, Wan-Hai Yang. A WAVELET-DECOMPOSITION-BASED IMAGE FUSION SCHEME AND ITS PERFORMANCE EVALUATION. ACTA AUTOMATICA SINICA. 2002.11(28): 927-934.
3. Xiao-yu Jiang, Zhi-yun Gao, Li-wei Zhou. Multispectral Image Fusion Using wavelet Transform. ACTA ELECTRONICA SINICA. 1997.8(25): 105-108.
4. PU Tian, FANG Qing-zhe, NI Guo-qiang. Contrast-Based Multiresolution Image Fusion. ACTA ELECTRONICA SINICA. 2000.12.(28): 116-118.
5. M. N. Do and M. Vetterli. Curvelets and filter banks. IEEE Trans. Image Proc., 2001.
6. M. N. Do and M. Vetterli. Pyramidal directional filter banks and curvelets. In Proc. IEEE Int. conf. On Image Proc., Thessaloniki, Greece, Oct. 2001.
7. M. N. Do. Directional Multiresolution Image Representations. PhD thesis, Swiss Federal Institute of Technology, Lausanne, Switzerland, December 2001.
8. M. N. Do, M. Vetterli. Framing pyramids. IEEE Trans. Signal Proc., 2002.
9. E. Viscito and J.P. Allebach. The analysis and design of multidimensional FIR perfect reconstruction filter banks for arbitrary sampling lattices. IEEE Trans.Circ. and Syst., 38(1):29-42, January 1991.
10. R. H. Bamberger, M. J. T. Smith. A filter bank for the directional decomposition of images: Theory and design. IEEE Trans. Signal Proc., April 1992. 40(4):882–893.
11. M. Vetterli. Multidimensional subband coding: Some theory and algorithms. Signal Proc., 6(2): 97-112, February 1984.
12. P. P.Vaidyanathan. Multirate Systems and Filter Banks. Prentice-Hall, Englewood Cliffs, NJ, 1993.
13. Hai-hui Wang, Jia-xiong Peng, Wei Wu. Remote Sensing Image Fusion Using Wavelet Packet Transform. Journal of Image and Graphics. 2002.9(7): 922-937.

# Wavelet-Based Methods for Improving Signal-to-Noise Ratio in Phase Images

Héctor Cruz-Enriquez and Juan V. Lorenzo-Ginori

Center for Studies on Electronics and Information Technologies, Universidad Central de Las Villas, Carretera a Camajuaní, km 5 ½, Santa Clara, VC, CP 54830, Cuba
{hcruz, juanl}@uclv.edu.cu
http://www.fie.uclv.edu.cu

**Abstract.** Complex images with low signal to noise ratio (SNR) appear in various applications. To recover the associated phase images, noise effects, as loss of contrast and phase residues that can deteriorate the phase unwrapping process, should be reduced. There are various methods for noise filtering in complex images, however most of them deal only with the magnitude image. Only few works have been devoted to phase image de-noising, despite the existence of important applications like Interferometric Synthetic Aperture Radar (IFSAR), Current Density Imaging (CDI) and Magnetic Resonance Imaging (MRI). In this work, a group of de-noising algorithms in the wavelet domain were applied to the complex image, in order to recover the phase information. The algorithms were applied to simulated and phantom images contaminated by three different noise models, including mixtures of Gaussian and Impulsive noise. Significant improvements in SNR for low initial values (SNR<5 dB) were achieved by using the proposed filters, in comparison to other methods reported in the literature.

## 1 Introduction

Images produced by systems such as Synthetic Aperture Radars (IFSAR), Current Density Imaging (CDI) and Magnetic Resonance Imaging (MRI) appear as arrays of complex numbers with a poor signal to noise ratio (SNR) in many cases.

Examples of noise sources in the complex images can be the acquisition hardware, physiological noise from patients, noisy artifacts provoked by movements during image acquisition (MRI, CDI) and phase jitter appearing in IFSAR. In all these cases noise produces a deterioration in SNR and a loss of contrast in the image, as well as phase residues that deteriorate the phase unwrapping process, used in most applications.

In this paper we pursue to show some issues related to wavelet de-noising for phase images that differ from its application to magnitude images.

Three noise models were considered in this work, which consisted in combinations of additive white Gaussian (AWGN) and impulsive noise. Results obtained in [1] as well as the algorithms shown in [2, 3] for magnitude images, have been considered as a reference for comparison. The noise models associated to complex images have been discussed in [2, 3]. Most de-noising algorithms developed for complex images have assumed zero-mean AWGN, contaminating independently the real and imaginary parts. Noise distribution in the magnitude image is usually assumed to have a zero-mean Rician distribution, which behaves as a Gaussian distribution for high SNR and as a Rayleigh one for low SNR. This paper deals with phase images in low SNR environments.

## 2 Materials and Methods

### 2.1 Simulated Image

The complex simulated image consisted [1, 2] in a magnitude image formed as a 64 x 64 pixels square with intensity 210 (bright region) centered inside another square of size 128 x 128 with 90 units intensity (dark region). The original unwrapped phase image was defined as the bi-dimensional Gaussian function

$$\varphi_{uv} = A \exp\left(\frac{(u-64)^2}{\sigma_u^2} + \frac{(v-64)^2}{\sigma_v^2}\right), \quad (1)$$

with $A = 7\pi$, $\sigma_u^2 = 3500$ and $\sigma_v^2 = 1000$.

The complex image was formed from the magnitude and phase images. Its real and imaginary parts were contaminated with the combinations of AWGN and impulsive noise shown in Table 1, where σ is the standard deviation for a Gaussian process with zero mean and $P_I$ represents the percentages of impulsive noise

The impulsive noise was modeled in the same way as in [1], where the probability of occurrence of an impulse for any part, real or imaginary, is given by

$$p = 1 - \sqrt{1 - P_I} \quad . \quad (2)$$

In Table 1 are shown the global percentage $P_I$ of the impulses to be generated. Both the image and the noise were modeled considering and 8-bit resolution for the representation of their numerical values.

**Table 1.** Noise models

| NOISE MODEL | σ | $P_I$, % |
|---|---|---|
| 1 | 60 | 0 |
| 2 | 70 | 3 |
| 3 | 90 | 5 |

### 2.2 Measurement Parameters

A set of measurements similar to those performed in [1] were performed, where we determined the values of SNR, the number of phase residues (RES), the standard deviation (STDEV) and the normalized mean square error (NMSE), defined as

$$NMSE = \frac{\sum_i \sum_j \|\varphi(i,j) - \hat{\varphi}(i,j)\|^2}{\sum_i \sum_j \|\varphi(i,j)\|^2}, \tag{3}$$

where $\varphi$ is the original unwrapped phase, $\hat{\varphi}$ is the recovered unwrapped phase after filtering and $(i, j)$ are the píxel values in the direction $(u, v)$. SNR was calculated as

$$SNR = 10\log_{10}\left(\frac{1}{NMSE}\right). \tag{4}$$

The amount of phase residues that appear both in the noisy and in the denoised signals were calculated by applying systematically the expression

$$\varphi(r) = \oint_C \nabla\varphi(r) \cdot dr = 2K\pi. \tag{5}$$

Here $\varphi(r)$ is the signal phase, $\nabla\varphi(r)$ is the phase gradient and $K$ is an integer number that accounts for the phase residues enclosed in the region $C$.

## 2.3 Analysis of Noisy Complex Images

A noisy complex image $z_n$ perturbated by the presence of AWGN, is given by

$$z_n = (\rho\cos\varphi + \eta_r) + j(\rho\sin\varphi + \eta_i) \tag{6}$$

Here $\rho$ is the module or magnitude, $\varphi$ is the argument or phase and $\eta = \eta_r + j\eta_i$ is the complex AWGN, with zero mean and variance $\sigma$.

By expressing the squared noisy magnitude, and grouping terms, we obtain

$$\rho_n^2 = \rho^2 + 2\rho(\eta_r \cos\varphi + \eta_i \sin\varphi) + (\eta_r^2 + \eta_i^2) \tag{7}$$

It is desired that $\rho_n^2 \cong \rho^2$. The rest of the expression is the noisy influence, having AWGN from the real and imaginary parts and a mixture of the noiseless phase and magnitude with the noise components. The effect of noise in the magnitude image might influence the de-noising process applied to the real and imaginary parts independently. To alleviate this problem, the use of unit magnitude phasors (e.g., substituting the noisy magnitude by a unit value) was introduced and tested. In this case, if $z_n = \rho_n \angle \varphi_n$, then $z_u = 1\angle\varphi_n$.

The unit magnitude noisy phasor in a Cartesian coordinate system is

$$z_u = \cos\varphi_n + jsen\varphi_n. \tag{8}$$

When de-noising is applied to the real and imaginary parts of the complex image, a more direct relationship to the phase components will exist without the noisy influence from the magnitude. This improved phase recovery from the image.

## 2.4 De-noising Algorithms

A set of filtering algorithms in the wavelet domain was introduced here to improve SNR in phase images. The filtering processes begin with the application of the bi-dimensional Discrete Wavelet Transform (DWT-2D) to both the real and imaginary parts of the noisy complex image $z_n$. From this transformation, the noisy DWT-2D complex coefficients $c_{j,o}^{ch}$ are obtained, where the index $ch$ indicates whether the coefficient belongs to the real ($re$) or imaginary ($im$) part of the complex image, while the terms $j$ and $o$ indicate the decomposition level and the orientation (horizontal, vertical or diagonal), respectively.

The expression of the transformation $T$ for the DWT-2D is given by

$$c_{j,o}^{ch} = T_{DWT-2D}[z_n] \,. \tag{9}$$

The synthesis equation associated to equation (9) was applied to filter the thresholded wavelet coefficients $\hat{c}_{j,o}^{ch}$, as

$$\hat{z} = T_{DWT-2D}^{-1}[\hat{c}_{j,o}^{ch}] \,. \tag{10}$$

The first filtering method described is based in the classical soft thresholding of the wavelet coefficients (called SOFT here). Thresholding was applied independently to the real and imaginary parts, as

$$\hat{c}_{j,o}^{ch}\Big|_{SOFT} = T_{THR\_SOFT}[c_{j,o}^{ch}] = \begin{cases} \operatorname{sgn}(c_{j,o}^{ch}) \times (|c_{j,o}^{ch}| - thr) & |c_{j,o}^{ch}| \geq thr \\ 0 & |c_{j,o}^{ch}| < thr \end{cases}, \tag{11}$$

where $thr$ is the threshold value, which will be discussed in paragraph 2.6.

The second filtering method (called SOFT_UN) is performed by applying the threshold to the wavelet coefficients obtained from the unit-magnitude phasors, as

$$z_u = T_U[z_n] = z_n / \rho_n \,, \tag{12}$$

where $\rho$ is the magnitude image that corresponds to $z$, and

$$c_{u\,j,o}^{ch} = T_{DWT-2D}[z_u] \,. \tag{13}$$

Now equation (11) is applied to these coefficients and we obtain

$$\hat{c}_{j,o}^{ch}\Big|_{SOFT\_UN} = T_{THR\_SOFT}\left[c_{u\,j,o}^{ch}\right] \,. \tag{14}$$

In the third filtering algorithm (HARD), the wavelet coefficients of the real and imaginary parts of the noisy complex image were hard-thresholded independently.

$$\hat{c}_{j,o}^{ch}\Big|_{HARD} = T_{THR\_HARD}\Big[c_{j,o}^{ch}\Big] = \begin{cases} c_{j,o}^{ch} & \left|c_{j,o}^{ch}\right| \geq thr \\ 0 & \left|c_{j,o}^{ch}\right| < thr \end{cases}. \quad (15)$$

The fourth filtering algorithm (COMP_UN) used hard thresholding followed by soft thresholding, where the latter was applied to the unit magntude phasors

$$\hat{c}_{j,o}^{ch}\Big|_{COMP\_UN} = T_{THR\_SOFT}\left[T_{DWT-2D}\left[T_U\left[T_{DWT-2D}^{-1}\left[\hat{c}_{j,o}^{ch}\Big|_{HARD}\right]\right]\right]\right]. \quad (16)$$

In the fifth filter (called AB_HARD), thresohlding was applied to the magnitude coefficients, instead of doing this for the real and imaginary parts independently.

$$\left|c_{j,o}\right| = \sqrt{\left(c_{j,o}^{RE}\right)^2 + \left(c_{j,o}^{IM}\right)^2}. \quad (17)$$

The filtering transformation was in this case

$$\left|\hat{c}_{j,o}\right|_{AB\_HARD} = T_{THR\_AB\_HARD}\left[\left|c_{j,o}\right|\right] = \begin{cases} \left|\hat{c}_{j,o}\right| & \left|\hat{c}_{j,o}\right| \geq thr_G \\ 0 & \left|\hat{c}_{j,o}\right| < thr_G \end{cases}. \quad (18)$$

The threshold is obtained from the thresholds for the real and imaginary parts as

$$thr_G = \left[(thr_{RE})^2 + (thr_{IM})^2\right]^{\frac{1}{2}}.$$

The sixth filter (A_H_S_U.) used hard thresholding of the magnitude coefficients, followed by soft thresholding of the coefficients of the real and imaginary parts of the unit magnitude phasors. Here

$$\left|\hat{c}_{j,o}\right|_{AB\_HARD\_SOFT\_UN} = T_{SOFT}\left[T_{DWT-2D}\left[T_U\left[T_{DWT-2D}^{-1}\left[\left|\hat{c}_{j,o}\right|_{AB\_HARD}\right]\right]\right]\right]. \quad (19)$$

Other filtering alternatives were also studied, including the Wiener filtering [2, 3]. We have illustrated here only the cases with which we obtained the best results.

## 2.5 Threshold Calculation

Threshold calculation was made through the median absolute deviation (MAD) estimate used in [4], with which the resulting threshold is

$$thr = \frac{\sqrt{2 \cdot \log(n)} \cdot median(\left|c_{1,o}^{ch}\right|)}{0.6745}, \quad (20)$$

where $n$ is the number of pixels in the image and $median(\left|c_{1,o}^{ch}\right|)$ is the value of the statistical median of the array formed by the absolute value of the wavelet coefficients from the first decomposition level.

## 3 Results

Performance evaluation for the filters was realized using the simulated complex image described in 2.2, as well as an RMI phantom. Tables 2 and 3 show the results obtained for three out of the six filters described above, corresponding to SNR and NMSE for noise models 2 and 3. In all filters the wavelet *Bior2.6* was employed, with

**Table 2.** Results of filtering in terms of NMSE and SNR, noise models 2 and 3

Image: Image 1  Wavelet: Bior2.6  Noiseless residues: 0  Trials: 20

| Filter | Noise model 2 | | | Noise model 3 | | |
|---|---|---|---|---|---|---|
| | NMSE | STDV | SNR | NMSE | STDV | SNR |
| NONE | 0.9144 | 5.39e-001 | 0.97 | 1.2821 | 7.85e-001 | -0.61 |
| COMP_UN | 0.0181 | 5.70e-002 | 23.32 | 0.0137 | 7.95e-003 | 19.47 |
| AB_HARD | 0.0021 | 2.86e-003 | 29.11 | 0.0085 | 7.66e-003 | 22.39 |
| A_H_S_U | 0.0018 | 2.81e-003 | 30.41 | 0.0079 | 7.77e-003 | 22.78 |

**Table 3.** Results of filtering in terms of phase residues, noise models 2 and 3

Image: Image 1  Wavelet: Bior2.6  Noiseless residues: 0  Trials: 20

| Filter | Noise model 2 | | Noise model 3 | |
|---|---|---|---|---|
| | Nres | stdv | Nres | stdv |
| NONE | 1396.80 | 47.75 | 2149.70 | 44.17 |
| COMP_UN | 6.50 | 3.30 | 12.35 | 4.85 |
| AB_HARD | 2.50 | 2.67 | 5.10 | 3.08 |
| A_H_S_U | 2.00 | 2.43 | 4.40 | 2.56 |

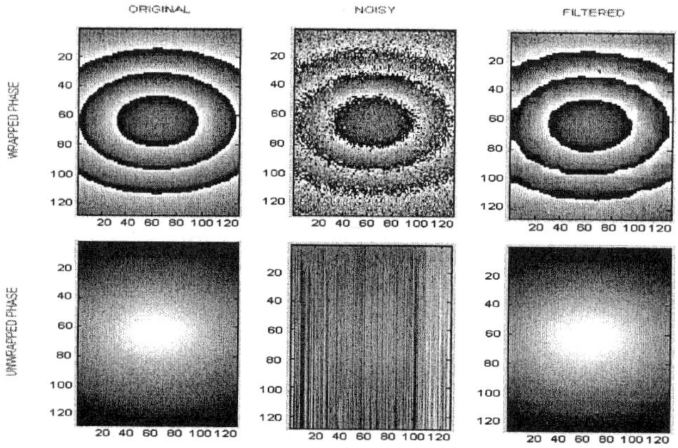

**Fig. 1.** De-noising of simulated image, wavelet Bior2.6, $J=4$, filter COMP_UN

$J = 4$. In all cases the SNR of phase images was less than 5 dB, to consider only low SNR environments. Figure 1 shows in the first column the original (wrapped and unwrapped) simulated images, in the second column the contaminated images (wrapped and unwrapped with an algorithm that does not tolerate phase residues) and in the third one the results obtained by using the filter COMP_UN. The simulated complex image was contaminated with noise model 2.

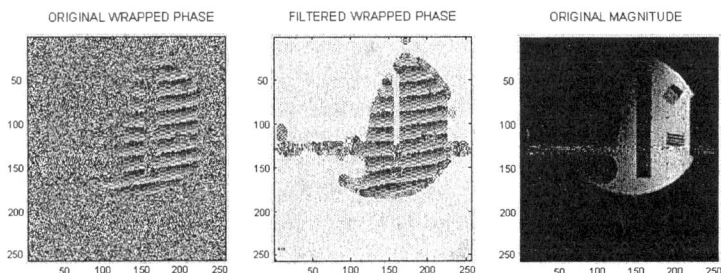

**Fig. 2.** De-noising of phantom image. Wavelet Bior2.6, $J=4$, filter AB_HARD

Figure 2 shows a phantom image in its original version, where a total of 28097 phase residues were detected. After filtering with AB_HARD, the number of remaining phase residues was 4990 for an 82% decrement. In this case, once the de-noising process has finished, further processing was applied in order to make more uniform the intensity of the background pixels, making the filtered image values in purely noisy regions to have low intensity.

## 4 Discussion and Conclusions

The proposed methods constitute a new alternative for phase image de-noising that differ from the traditional wavelet domain methods [2, 3, 4, 5] that are based in Wiener filtering or in soft thresholding and phase preservation of the wavelet coefficients. The filters introduced here showed very good SNR gain, as well as good preservation of edges and details in the phase image. This can be attributed to the use of hard thresholding in the first filtering stage.

Soft thresholding showed a high SNR gain for all the noise models used in this work, however low edge preservation in some regions of interest was observed. At the same time a high suppression of background noise and phase residues was obtained, that justified its usage in the second filtering stage.

The use of unit magnitude phasors showed to be effective to improve SNR. It was observed also that it was the magnitude image, and not the phase one, the most sensitive to phase changes in the wavelet coefficients. The magnitude image was degraded when the real and imaginary parts of the wavelet coefficients were filtered independently, while this process led to an improvement of the phase image.

The noise reduction levels obtained surpass previous results reported in the literature [1] without the need of a high computational burden. The usage of concatenated filtering and unitary magnitude phasors together with combined thresholding, while not useful for magnitude images, showed a high effectiveness as a novel procedure for phase image de-noising in the wavelet domain.

## References

1. Lorenzo-Ginori, J. V., Plataniotis, K. N. and Venetsanopoulos, A. N.: Non linear filtering for phase image de-noising.. IEE Proc.-Vis. Image Signal Process, Vol 49(5) 290-296, October 2002.
2. Alexander, M. E. , Baumgartner, R., Summers, A. R., Windischberger, C. , Klarhoefer, M., Moser, E. and Somorjai, R. L,: A Wavelet-based Method for Improving Signal-to-noise Ratio and Contrast in MR Images. Magnetic Resonance Imaging 18 (2000) 169-180.
3. R. D.Nowak: Wavelet-Based Rician Noise Removal for Magnetic Resonance Imaging. IEEE Transactions on Image Processing Vol. 8 (10) 1408-1419, 1999.
4. H.Braunisch, W. Bae-ian, and J. A.Kong,: Phase unwrapping of SAR interferograms after wavelet de-noising. In: IEEE Geoscience and Remote Sensing Symposium, IGARSS 2000. 2 (2000) 752 -754.
5. S. Zaroubi, and G. Goelman: Complex De-noising of MR Data Via Wavelet Analysis: Application to Functional MRI. Magnetic Resonance Imaging 18 (2000) 59-68.

# Image Evaluation Factors

Hongxun Yao[1], Min-Yu Huseh[2], Guilin Yao[1], and Yazhou Liu[1]

[1] Dept. Computer Science, Harbin Institute of Technology, China 150001
{yhx, glyao, yzliu}@vilab.hit.edu.cn
[2] NEC Laboratories, China 100084
minyu @research.nec.com.cn

**Abstract.** We describe a method for objective and quantitative evaluation of image quality. The method represents a novel use of image enhancement concepts. It employs three new measures that evaluate the definition of contours, uniform intensity distribution, and noise rate in determining the image quality. Because the three measures have clear physical meanings, they can be selectively applied according to the viewer's evaluation criteria. The three measures are relatively inexpensive to compute, making them suitable for automated ranking of image quality in personal digital imaging devices, such as digital cameras. However, the method is equally adept at evaluating other digital images such as those on the Internet. Experiments with the method show good correlation with visual quality assessment for various image subject types.

## 1 Introduction

With the advent of digital photography, especially the availability of affordable digital cameras and camera-equipped mobile phones, there is a flood of digital images taken with such equipment and kept in our PCs or on the Web. We need technologies that can evaluate the quality of such images to help users select the best ones for viewing and storing. In particular, such technologies should be computationally inexpensive so they could be implemented in the digital imaging devices. Also, it is desirable that the technologies provide meaningful and objective evaluation criteria so as to satisfy users' individual selection needs.

Certain progress has been made in image quality evaluation in various other image processing fields, such as photographic print [1], metallographic microstructure pictures [2], medical images [3], satellite photos and video after compression [4-6]. For objective evaluation of photographic images, a quality measure based on DCT [7] can compare differently processed versions of the same image. The IQM measure proposed by Nill [8] can compare different images but is computationally intensive and lack physical meaning.

For effective and high-speed evaluation of image quality, we developed a new image quality evaluation method that employs three computationally inexpensive and physically meaningful measures to help identify high-quality images. The three measures evaluate the definition of contours, uniform intensity distribution, and the noise rate of an image. In fact, the three measures are conceptually complementary to similar criteria used in image enhancement, which has seen good progress and real-world applications in recent years [9,10]. Our work is an important innovation that links image quality to enhancement needs, which can help automate the selection of applicable enhancement techniques.

In this paper, we give the derivation of our evaluation measures and demonstrate their use and results in trial applications. We also compare our method with the image quality measure proposed by Nill [8] analytically and with experimental results.

## 2 Related Work

### 2.1 Image Quality Measure (IQM)

Norman B. Nill [8] proposed an image quality measure (IQM) in 1992, which is derived from digital image power spectra. The main idea is that all scenes have the same power spectrum because of a double stochastic Poisson process. IQM is given by

$$IQM = \frac{1}{n_1 \times n_2} \sum_{\theta=-180°}^{180°} \sum_{\rho=0.01}^{0.5} W(\rho) A^2(T\rho) P(\rho,\theta) \qquad (1)$$

where $P(\rho,\theta)$ is polar coordinate form of the normalized power spectrum of a given 2-D image consisting of $n_1 \times n_1$ pixels, and $A(T\rho) = (0.2 + 0.45T\rho)\exp(-0.18T\rho)$ denotes the modulation transfer function (MTF) for computing the human visual system (HVS) characteristics. The constant $T$ fixes the spatial frequency of the peak of the HVS MTF with respect to the image's Nyquist frequency; here $T = 51.1$. $W(\rho)$ is a modified Wiener noise filter.

### 2.2 Analysis of IQM

The IQM measure is a perspective computing for normally acquired arbitrary scenes, by filtering noises and considering the human visual system influence. It is shown to be an effective measure for assessing quality of aerial images. However, it is sensitive to power spectra changes rather than scene definition or intensity distribution changes. Because of IQM's emphasis on the effect of power spectra, it is sensitive to image energy. As a result, it often happens that an image with a high IQM score (which suggests a high quality image) is not necessarily better looking from a subjective point of view than an image with a lower IQM score. Table 1 demonstrates a case where a picture with the best contour definition and clarity (the left side picture) receives the lowest IQM score.

The examples shown in Table 1 and other similar examples suggest that we cannot rely on IQM in evaluating the quality of general images. In the following we describe a novel evaluation method that represents a significant innovation in image quality assessment. We base our method on image enhancement concepts and define our image evaluation factors based on image enhancement technology.

**Table 1.** Examples show visually clearer pictures may receive lower IQM scores

| Sample images | | | |
|---|---|---|---|
| IQM | 98.5 | 148.6 | 154.3 |

## 3 Image Evaluation Factors

There are two types of methods in image enhancement technology. One is to enhance contour information of images; the second is to filter noises from images. In section 3.1, we define a contour-volume factor $Ft_{CV}$, which computes a mean contour volume per pixel in an image as a measure of the details in the image. In section 3.2, we define a noise-rate factor $Ft_N$ to consider the noise influence on the image. From the information entropy viewpoint, we define a uniform intensity-distribution factor $Ft_{UD}$ in section 3.3 to measure the color and intensity distribution of an image. All of them have clear physical meanings.

### 3.1 The Contour-Volume Factor

The contour-volume factor $Ft_{CV}$ measures the definition or details of an image. If the value $Ft_{CV}$ does not reach a given threshold, it means the image is not clear enough. We define the Contour-Volume Factor $Ft_{CV}$ by the following formula:

$$Ft_{CV} = \frac{1}{N} \sum_{over\ all\ m_1} \sum_{over\ all\ m_2} |G(m_1, m_2)| \qquad (2)$$

where $G(m_1, m_2)$ is a convoluted result array, obtained by the discrete convolution of the input image array $F(n_1, n_2)$ with the array $H$ in equation (4). $N$ is the number of image pixels. The relation between $G$, $F$, and $H$ is:

$$G(m_1, m_2) = \sum_{over\ all\ n_1} \sum_{over\ all\ n_2} F(n_1, n_2) H(m_1 - n_1 + 1, m_2 - n_2 + 1). \qquad (3)$$

The convolution array of the high-pass (the Laplacian operator) form is:

$$H = \begin{pmatrix} -1 & -1 & -1 \\ -1 & 8 & -1 \\ -1 & -1 & -1 \end{pmatrix}. \qquad (4)$$

Table 2 shows the $Ft_{CV}$ values of three pictures and demonstrates that the clearest image receives the highest $Ft_{CV}$ value while the most blurred picture receives the lowest $Ft_{CV}$ value.

**Table 2.** Representing image quality (detail and clarity) by $Ft_{CV}$ values

| Sample images | | | |
|---|---|---|---|
| $Ft_{CV}$ | 53.9 | 24.0 | 16.9 |
| IQM | 189.2 | 114.2 | 82.6 |

Note that for this set of images, IQM also gives the correct score trend. Experiment results show the contour-volume factor $Ft_{CV}$ and IQM values correlate positively in general as shown in Figure 1 below.

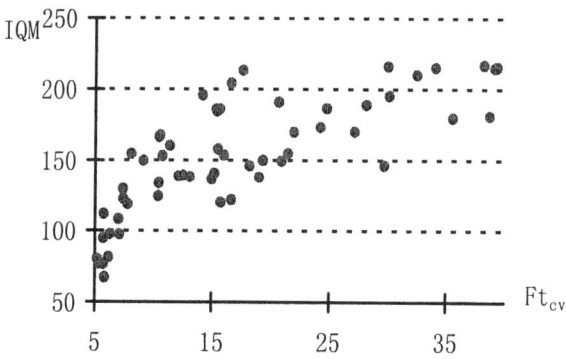

**Fig. 1.** Positive correlation between experimental values of IQM and $Ft_{CV}$

We have applied the contour-volume factor $Ft_{CV}$ to many real-world images and proved that it works well in measuring image clarity. It even works well for misty or foggy scenes as shown in Table 3. Note, however, in this case of foggy scenes, IQM's scoring trend is different from that of $Ft_{CV}$. We consider the $Ft_{CV}$ scoring trend shown in Table 3 to be closer to what pleases the human visual experiences.

The contour-volume factor $Ft_{CV}$ can be affected by noises, because noise points may be mistaken for contour points since they are both high frequency components, thereby raising the $Ft_{CV}$ value. The noise-filtering factor described in the next section can help overcome this potential problem as well as distinguish noisy (e.g., dark) images from the less noisy ones in general.

**Table 3.** Measuring foggy images by $Ft_{CV}$ values

| Sample images | | | |
|---|---|---|---|
| $Ft_{CV}$ | 55.9 | 28.1 | 13.3 |
| IQM | 250.2 | 179.4 | 228.6 |

### 3.2 The Noise-Rate Factor

According to image enhancement technology, a noise image $F(n_1, n_2)$ could convolute with the Median Filter $\mathbf{H}_{MF}$ to produce a filtered image $G(n_1, n_2)$. We define the noise-rate factor as

$$Ft_N = 1 - \sqrt[3]{\frac{\delta^2}{\varepsilon^2}}. \qquad (5)$$

Where $\delta^2 = \sum_{n_1}\sum_{n_2}[\mathbf{G}(n_1, n_2) - \mathbf{F}(n_1, n_2)]^2$. $\delta^2$ is the noise volume index; the higher the $\delta^2$ value, the larger volume of noise of the image. The noise volume index is normalized by the energy of original image, $\varepsilon^2 = \sum_{n_1}\sum_{n_2} F^2(n_1, n_2)$, to make the $Ft_N$ value between 0 and 1.

Pictures captured under dark illumination condition generally have lower (noisier) noise-rate factor $Ft_N$ values, as illustrated in Table 4 below. Also, pictures with coarse grains (due to improper enlargement, for example) have lower noise-rate factor values.

As discussed at the end of section 3.1, the noise-rate factor $Ft_N$ can be used to compensate for errors in contour-volume $Ft_{CV}$-based ranking of image quality. For example, the $Ft_{CV}$ values for the sample pictures in Table 1 are (from the left to the right) 37.1, 32.2, and 34.0, respectively. While this trend is better than that of IQM's, it still gives the rightmost, blurriest picture a higher score than the middle, clearer version of the same picture. However, the product $Ft_N$ with $Ft_{CV}$ gives the correct ranking; the resulting product values are 34.1, 28.0, and 26.5 respectively.

**Table 4.** $Ft_N$ values is lower for a darker (noisier) picture

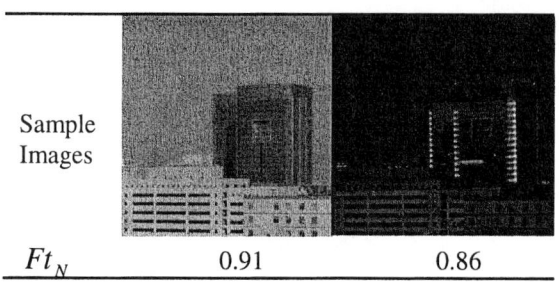

| Sample Images | | |
|---|---|---|
| $Ft_N$ | 0.91 | 0.86 |

### 3.3 The Uniform Intensity-Distribution Factor

From information theory, the more uniform the intensity distribution of an image, the higher information entropy it contains. So, we define the uniform intensity-distribution factor $Ft_{UD}$ as follow:

$$Ft_{UD} = \frac{\log\left[\prod_{k=0}^{L-1}(n_k+1)\right]}{\log\left(\frac{\sum_{k=0}^{L-1}n_k}{L}+1\right)^L} = \frac{\sum_{k=0}^{L-1}\log(n_k+1)}{L\log\left(\frac{\sum_{k=0}^{L-1}n_k}{L}+1\right)} \quad (6)$$

where $L$ is the color depth, and $n_k$ denotes the number of all pixels whose values equal to the $k^{th}$ color of the color depth.

$Ft_{UD}$ is defined as a ratio of a pair of logarithm operators to score the extent of the distribution uniformity. $Ft_{UD}$ ranges between 0 and 1, because

$$0 < \prod_{k=0}^{L-1} n_k \leq \left(\frac{\sum_{k=0}^{L-1}n_k}{L}\right)^L < \infty \; .$$

Note the argument of the numerator in Equation 6 denotes the product of all color or intensity distribution for an image, and the argument of the denominator is the product of the number of each color in the ideal case – the most equalization in color distribution. In order to avoid calculating logarithm of 0, add 1 to each factor, and then we see the form $\dfrac{\log\left[\prod_{k=0}^{L-1}(n_k+1)\right]}{\log\left(\frac{\sum_{k=0}^{L-1}n_k}{L}+1\right)^L}$ instead of $\dfrac{\log\left[\prod_{k=0}^{L-1}n_k\right]}{\log\left(\frac{\sum_{k=0}^{L-1}n_k}{L}\right)^L}$.

The $Ft_{UD}$ factor is used to pick out pictures with uniform intensity or color distribution. Table 5 shows an example of such an application. From Table 5, it is clear that the uniform intensity-distribution factor $Ft_{UD}$ reflects the rich hierarchy of images. The images from the left to the right with decreasing values of $Ft_{UD}$, shown in Table 5, are downtrend in color distribution.

**Table 5.** Flower images ranked by descending $Ft_{UD}$ values

| Flower images | | | | |
|---|---|---|---|---|
| $Ft_{UD}$ | 0.86 | 0.84 | 0.83 | 0.77 |

## 4 Computational Efficiency

The IQM computation is more complex than our method. Its three components, $W(\rho)$, square of $A(T\rho)$, and $P(\rho,\theta)$ each contains one or more exponentiation as shown in equations 7 through 9 below. Furthermore, the exponentiations are done (M x M) times where $M = n_1 = n_2$ as required by IQM.

$$W(\rho) = \left[ \frac{2\pi a \sigma_s^2 \exp(-\rho^2/\sigma_g^2)}{2\pi a \sigma_s^2 \exp(-\rho^2/\sigma_g^2) + \kappa_1 (a^2 + \rho^2)^{1.5} |N(\rho)|^2} \right]^{\kappa_2} \quad (7)$$

$$A(T\rho) = (0.2 + 0.45T\rho)\exp(-0.18T\rho) \quad (8)$$

$$P(\rho,\theta) = \frac{|H(\rho,\theta)|^2}{\mu^2 M^2} \quad (9)$$

where $H(u,v)$ is the discrete Fourier transform of the original image, $u,v = -\frac{M}{2},\cdots,\frac{M}{2}$, $\rho = \sqrt{u^2+v^2}/M$, $\theta = \tan^{-1}\frac{v}{u}$.

In contrast, the most time-consuming part in our method is the $Ft_N$ computation's processing with the Median Filter. Experiment results show clear computational efficiencies of our method compared with the IQM. On a Pentium4 3.0GHz PC with 1GB of main memory, an IQM computation requires 0.511 second whereas applying our method to the same images of 256×256 resolution requires only 0.012 second for $Ft_{CV}$, 0.038 second for $Ft_N$, and 0.003 second for $Ft_{UD}$, respectively.

## 5 Conclusion

In this paper, we describe a novel method that represents a breakthrough in image quality assessment. Our work provides a computationally inexpensive technical means to assess image quality. The three measures used in our evaluation method, namely, the contour-volume factor $Ft_{CV}$, the noise-rate factor $Ft_N$, and the uniform intensity-distribution factor $Ft_{UD}$ all have clear physical meanings. They may be applied individually or jointly to help select images that satisfy specific user criteria.

The derivation of our evaluation measures follows certain key concepts of classical image enhancement technology, which has seen decades of use in processing images. The usefulness of such measures can be seen clearly from the results of our experiments with a large number and varieties of real-world images. As a potential future extension of our work, our measures' consistency with image enhancement techniques could make it possible to employ the measures to automate the determination of what enhancement to apply to an image.

## Acknowledgments

This work was supported by NEC Laboratories, China, and was performed in it.

## References

[1] N. Otaki. Colour Image Evaluation Systems. OKI Technical Review. April 2003/Issue 194 Vol.70 No.2, 68-73
[2] P. Velecký, J. Pospísil. Digital Image Evaluation of Metallographic Microstructure of Sintered Carbides. ACTA UNIV. PALACKI. OLOMUC., FAC. RER. NAT. (1999), PHYSICA 38, 105-113
[3] J.E. Wilhjelm, M.S. Jensen, S.K. Jespersen, B. Sahl, E. Falk. Visual and quantitative evaluation of selected image combination schemes in ultrasound spatial compound scanning, IEEE Transactions on Medical Imaging, ISSN: 0278-0062, Feb. 2004, Volume: 23, Issue: 2, 181- 190
[4] Application Boards - Image Evaluation Kits C6000. For customers requiring a high-end, high-performance solution Kane Computing can offer the following Image Evaluation Kits.
[5] I.M. Walter, P.C. Lockemann, H.H. Nagel. Database Support for Knowledge-Based Image Evaluation. ACM Proceedings of the 13th International Conference on Very Large Data Bases, September 1-4, 1987: 3 – 11
[6] M. P. Eckstein, J. L. Bartroff, C. K. Abbey, J. S. Whiting, and F. O. Bochud, University of California Santa Barbara. Automated computer evaluation and optimization of image compression of x-ray coronary angiograms for signal known exactly detection tasks. Optics Express, March 10, 2003, Vol. 11, No. 5: 460 – 475
[7] J. A. Saghri, P. S. Cheatham, and A. Habibi. Image Quality Measure Based on a Human Visual System Model, Optical Engineering, 1989, 28 (7): 813-818
[8] N. B. Nill, B. H. Bouzas. Objective Image Quality Measure Derived from Digital Image Power Spectra, Optical Engineering, 1992, 31(4):813 – 825
[9] J. Canny. *A Computational Approach to Edge Detection*, IEEE Transactions on Pattern Analysis and Machine Intelligence, 1986, 8(6): 679 – 698.
[10] D. Comaniciu and P. Meer. *Mean Shift: A Robust Approach toward Feature Space Analysis.* IEEE Trans. Pattern Anal. Mach. Intell., 2002,24(5):603–619.

# Monoscale Dual Ridgelet Frame

Tan Shan and Licheng Jiao

National Key Lab for Radar Signal Processing and Institute of Intelligent,
Information Processing, Xidian University,
Xi'an, 710071, China
tanshan5989@yahoo.com.cn

**Abstract.** A new system—Monoscale Dual Ridgelet Frame (MDRF) is constructed in this paper, which can be viewed as a generalized version of Monoscale Ridgelet introduced by Candes. The MDRT takes the Dual Ridgelet Frame as its basic component. We show that localizing the Dual Ridgelet Frame into small squares, dyadic partition of $[0, 1]^2$, constitutes a dual frame in $L^2[0,1]^2$ again. As an example, the high performance of the MDRF for image denoising is demonstrated experimentally.

## 1 Introduction

It is well known that separable wavelet system in 2 dimensions can efficiently deal with point singularity but fails at dealing with straight singularity. Ridgelet system, introduced by Candes in [1], provides a new tool that can optimally represent functions with straight singularity [2]. Donoho introduced an orthonormal basis for $L^2(R^2)$—Orthonormal Ridgele that can be thought of as a $L^2$ substitute of Candes' Ridgelet system and also performs many of the same tasks as the later, for example, Orthonormal Ridgelet can also optimally represent functions with straight singularity [2]. Orthonormal Ridgelet is constructed as the isometric image of a special wavelet basis for Radon space. To obtain orthogonality, Donoho made use of two special properties of Meyer wavelet, i.e., closure property under reflection about the origin in the ridge direction: $\psi_{j,k}(-t) = \psi_{j,1-k}(t)$, and closure property under translation by half a cycle in the angular direction: $w_{i,l}(\theta + \pi) = w_{i,l+2^{i-1}}(\theta)$. Note that the latter closure property would not hold for other prominent wavelet families such as Daubechies' compactly supported wavelet families. It is the closure properties that make it possible to construct orthonormal basis by removing the duplications. By substituting other orthonormal wavelet systems for Meyer wavelet, one can obtain a tight frame instead of orthonormal basis since the two special closure properties don't hold anymore [4]. In paper [5], we constructed a system of this kind with frame bound 1 and called it Ridgelet Frame. Furthermore, in paper [6], we developed a new dual system for $L^2(R^2)$ called Dual Ridgelet Frame constructed using biorthonormal wavelet basis, which can be viewed as the generalized version of Orthonormal Ridgelet and Ridgelet Frame.

These Ridgelet-type methods (in this paper by Ridgelet-type methods we mean Ridgelet system, Orthonormal Ridgelet, Ridgelet Frame and Dual Ridgelet Frame) deal with straight singularity by transforming them into point singularity first, then the resulting point singularity is dealt with by 1-D wavelet in the case of Candes' Ridgelet system, 2-D Meyer wavelet in the case of Donoho' Orthonormal Ridgelet, common 2-D orthonormal wavelet in the case of Ridgelet Frame and biorthogonal wavelet in the case of Dual Ridgelet Frame.

Based on a partition principle, Monoscale Ridgelet was constructed in paper [7], which took Candes' Ridgelet system as basic component and can also efficiently deal with curvilinear singularity with very low curvature in 2-D. In this paper, we show that by localizing the Dual Ridgelet Frame into dyadic partition of $[0, 1]^2$, one can obtain a dual frame again, and we call the resulting frame Dual Monoscale Ridglet Frame (DMRF). The DMRF can be viewed as a generalized version of Monoscale Ridgelet and can also deal with curvilinear singularity with very low curvature in 2-D.

## 2  Dual Ridgelet Frame and Dual Monoscale Ridgelet Frame

It is well known that there exists an isometric map from Radon domain $\Re$ to spatial domain $L^2(R^2)$ [8]. To construct a dual frame, we first constructed a dual frame in Radon domain using biorthogonal wavelet basis. Then, under the isometric map, the image of the resulting dual frame in Radon domain is also a dual frame in $L^2(R^2)$ [6].

Let $\{\psi_{j,k}, \tilde{\psi}_{j,k} : j,k \in Z\}$ and $\{\omega_{i,l}, \tilde{\omega}_{i,l} : i,l \in Z\}$ be two biorthogonal wavelet systems in $L^2(R)$. For convenience below, we denote the former one by $\psi$ and $\tilde{\psi}$. Analogously, we denote the periodization version of the latter one on $[0, 2\pi)$ by $\omega := \omega_{i,l}^{per}(\theta)$ and $\tilde{\omega} := \tilde{\omega}_{i,l}^{per}(\theta)$. Obviously, the tensor product $\{w_\lambda'' = \psi \otimes \omega : \lambda \in \Lambda\}$ and $\{\tilde{w}_\lambda'' = \tilde{\psi} \otimes \tilde{\omega} : \lambda \in \Lambda\}$ is a biorthogonal system for $L^2(R \otimes [0, 2\pi))$, here $\Lambda$ is the correlative index set.

Define orthoprojector $P_\Re$ from $L^2(R \otimes [0, 2\pi))$ to Radon domain by

$$(P_\Re F)(t,\theta) = (F(t,\theta) + F(-t, \theta + \pi))/2 . \tag{1}$$

where $F \in L^2(R \otimes [0, 2\pi))$.

Let $w_\lambda' := 2\sqrt{\pi} w_\lambda''$ and $\tilde{w}_\lambda' := 2\sqrt{\pi} \tilde{w}_\lambda''$. Then, applying $P_\Re$ on $w_\lambda'$ and $\tilde{w}_\lambda'$, we obtain

$$w_\lambda := P_\Re(w_\lambda') = (\frac{I + T \otimes S}{2}) w_\lambda' = 2\sqrt{\pi} P_\Re(w_\lambda'') \tag{2}$$

$$\tilde{w}_\lambda := P_\Re(\tilde{w}_\lambda') = (\frac{I + T \otimes S}{2}) \tilde{w}_\lambda' = 2\sqrt{\pi} P_\Re(\tilde{w}_\lambda'') \tag{3}$$

where operator $T$ is defined by $(Tf)(t) = f(-t)$ and operator $S$ is defined by $(Sg)(\theta) = g(\theta + \pi)$.

We had shown that $(w_\lambda)_{\lambda\in\Lambda}$ and $(\tilde{w}_\lambda)_{\lambda\in\Lambda}$ are dual frame in $\Re$ 6. Now let $(\rho_\lambda)_{\lambda\in\Lambda}$ and $(\tilde{\rho}_\lambda)_{\lambda\in\Lambda}$ denote respectively the images of $(w_\lambda)_{\lambda\in\Lambda}$ and $(\tilde{w}_\lambda)_{\lambda\in\Lambda}$ under the isometric map from Radon domain $\Re$ to spatial domain $L^2(R^2)$. Then it follows that $(\rho_\lambda)_{\lambda\in\Lambda}$ and $(\tilde{\rho}_\lambda)_{\lambda\in\Lambda}$ are dual frame also which we called Dual Ridgelet Frame (DRF). It follows that for $\forall f \in L^2(R^2)$, we have

$$A\|f\|^2_{L^2(R^2)} \leq \sum_{\lambda\in\Lambda} |<f,\rho_\lambda>|^2 \leq B\|f\|^2_{L^2(R^2)}. \tag{4}$$

$$B^{-1}\|f\|^2_{L^2(R^2)} \leq \sum_{\lambda\in\Lambda} |<f,\tilde{\rho}_\lambda>|^2 \leq A^{-1}\|f\|^2_{L^2(R^2)} \tag{5}$$

And

$$f = \sum_{\lambda\in\Lambda} <f,\rho_\lambda> \tilde{\rho}_\lambda = \sum_{\lambda\in\Lambda} <f,\tilde{\rho}_\lambda> \rho_\lambda \tag{6}$$

Below, we will show that based on a localization principle used in [7], a localized dual frame can be constructed using DRF.

Suppose to deal with a bivariate function $f$ that is smooth away from smooth edges and supported on unit square $[0,1]^2$. We partition the unit square using uniformly dyadic squares, and each dyadic square can be expressed as [7]

$$Q = [2^{-s}k_1, 2^{-s}(k_1+1)) \times [2^{-s}k_2, 2^{-s}(k_2+1)) \tag{7}$$

where $s$ is the scale parameters, both $s \geq 0$ and $k_1, k_2$ are integers. Consider the resulting small squares intersected with the smooth edge of $f$. Hypothesize the edge has very low curvature relative to the partition scale. Consequently, it is fairly straight in the associated small square, as shown in Fig.1.

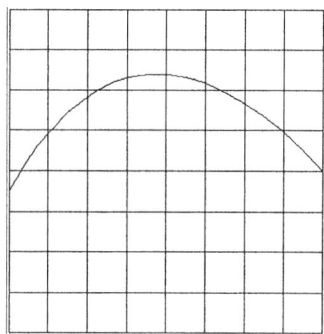

**Fig. 1.** Partitioning of the support of $f$

Let $Q_s$ denote the collection of all dyadic squares at scale s. Then, the function $f$ is localized smoothly near each of the dyadic squares of $Q_s$ by windows $w_Q$, an orthonormal partition of unity selected such that $\sum_{Q \in Q_s} w_Q^2 = 1$. We localize DRF $(\rho_\lambda)_{\lambda \in \Lambda}$ and $(\tilde{\rho}_\lambda)_{\lambda \in \Lambda}$ to each dyadic square $Q$. By $(\rho_{Q,\lambda})_{Q \in Q_s, \lambda \in \Lambda}$ and $(\tilde{\rho}_{Q,\lambda})_{Q \in Q_s, \lambda \in \Lambda}$ we denote the resulting localized dual frame satisfying

$$A\|fw_Q\|^2_{L^2[0,1]^2} \leq \sum_{\lambda \in \Lambda} |< fw_Q, \rho_{Q,\lambda} >|^2 \leq B\|fw_Q\|^2_{L^2[0,1]^2} \tag{8}$$

$$B^{-1}\|fw_Q\|^2_{L^2[0,1]^2} \leq \sum_{\lambda \in \Lambda} |< fw_Q, \tilde{\rho}_{Q,\lambda} >|^2 \leq A^{-1}\|fw_Q\|^2_{L^2[0,1]^2} . \tag{9}$$

And

$$fw_Q = \sum_{\lambda \in \Lambda} |< fw_Q, \rho_{Q,\lambda} >|\tilde{\rho}_{Q,\lambda} = \sum_{\lambda \in \Lambda} |< fw_Q, \tilde{\rho}_{Q,\lambda} >|\rho_{Q,\lambda} \tag{10}$$

Summing (8) and (9) on all squares $Q_s$, we obtain

$$\sum_{Q \in Q_s} A\|fw_Q\|^2_{L^2([0,1]^2)} \leq \sum_{Q \in Q_s} \sum_{\lambda \in \Lambda} |< fw_Q, \rho_{Q,\lambda} >|^2 \leq \sum_{Q \in Q_s} B\|fw_Q\|^2_{L^2([0,1]^2)} \tag{11}$$

$$\sum_{Q \in Q_s} B^{-1}\|fw_Q\|^2_{L^2([0,1]^2)} \leq \sum_{Q \in Q_s} \sum_{\lambda \in \Lambda} |< fw_Q, \tilde{\rho}_{Q,\lambda} >|^2 \leq \sum_{Q \in Q_s} A^{-1}\|fw_Q\|^2_{L^2([0,1]^2)} \tag{12}$$

Using $\sum_{Q \in Q_s} w_Q^2 = 1$, we have

$$A\|f\|^2_{L^2([0,1]^2)} \leq \sum_{Q \in Q_s} \sum_{\lambda \in \Lambda} |< f, w_Q \rho_{Q,\lambda} >|^2 \leq B\|f\|^2_{L^2([0,1]^2)} \tag{13}$$

$$B^{-1}\|f\|^2_{L^2([0,1]^2)} \leq \sum_{Q \in Q_s} \sum_{\lambda \in \Lambda} |< f, w_Q \tilde{\rho}_{Q,\lambda} >|^2 \leq A^{-1}\|f\|^2_{L^2([0,1]^2)} \tag{14}$$

Multiplying each side in (10) by $w_Q$, it follows that

$$fw_Q^2 = \sum_{\lambda \in \Lambda} |< fw_Q, \rho_{Q,\lambda} >|w_Q \tilde{\rho}_{Q,\lambda} = \sum_{\lambda \in \Lambda} |< fw_Q, \tilde{\rho}_{Q,\lambda} >|w_Q \rho_{Q,\lambda} \tag{15}$$

Again, summing this equality on all squares $Q_s$ and using $\sum_{Q \in Q_s} w_Q^2 = 1$, we obtain

$$f = \sum_{Q \in Q_s} \sum_{\lambda \in \Lambda} |< f, w_Q \rho_{Q,\lambda} >|w_Q \tilde{\rho}_{Q,\lambda} = \sum_{Q \in Q_s} \sum_{\lambda \in \Lambda} |< f, w_Q \tilde{\rho}_{Q,\lambda} >|w_Q \rho_{Q,\lambda} \tag{16}$$

Now, from (13), (14) and (15), we obtain our conclusion that $(w_Q \rho_{Q,\lambda})_{Q \in Q_r, \lambda \in \Lambda}$ and $(w_Q \tilde{\rho}_{Q,\lambda})_{Q \in Q_r, \lambda \in \Lambda}$ is a dual frame in $L^2[0,1]^2$, which we call Dual Monoscale Ridgelet Frame (DMRF).

## 3 Image Denosing Application

Below, we will show the performance of DMRF for image denoising application through experiments. In these experiments, we employ decimated biorthogonal wavlet transform (DWT, 7/9 filter) and undecimated biorthogonal wavlet transform (UDWT, 7/9 filter) in DMRF respectively, and denote below the former as D_DMRF, the latter, U_DMRF. We compare the performance of D_DMRF and U_DMRF with those of DWT (7/9 filter) and UDWT (7/9 filter).

**Table 1.** Comparison of performance using different transforms for image denoising on a synthesis image in terms of PSNR

| $\sigma$/PSNR | DWT | UDWT | D_DMRF | U_DMRF |
|---|---|---|---|---|
| 10/28.1492 | 34.5271 | 36.1701 | 34.8398 | **36.6972** |
| 15/24.6368 | 31.6652 | 33.5429 | 32.652 | **34.7966** |
| 20/22.0855 | 29.3786 | 31.5276 | 31.0169 | **33.5218** |
| 5/20.1862 | 28.075 | 30.2295 | 29.8569 | **32.3877** |
| 30/18.5734 | 26.9885 | 29.1608 | 28.5179 | **31.425** |

A synthesis image of size 256*256 with 255 gray levels is tested in our experiments. For DMRF, the partition scale is fixed 3. In all settings, we use the simply thresholding procedures ($3\sigma$). To study the dependency of the denoising methods on different noise levels, the original image is contaminated by additive Gaussian white noise with different standard variances, 10, 15, 20, 25 and 30. The PSNR of the denoised images, which are obtained by different transforms, versus the full range of input noise levels are listed in Table 1.

Obviously, the denoising method based on U_DMRF substantially outperforms those based on others over all noise levels. In addition, for the original image over all noise levels, D_DMRF are 1-2 dB higher than DWT but slightly lower than UDWT, say, 0.3dB and or so.

To compare the visual effect of different methods, partial experimental results are shown in Fig. 2. Here the noise level is of standard variance 20. When DWT is used, artifacts blemish the resulting image seriously (see Fig. 2 (c)). In the case of using UDWT, there are few artifacts, however the line-type structures contained in the original images blur obviously (see Fig. 2 (d) ). On the contrary, the line-type structure is well recovered by using DMRF (see Fig. 2 (e), (f)).

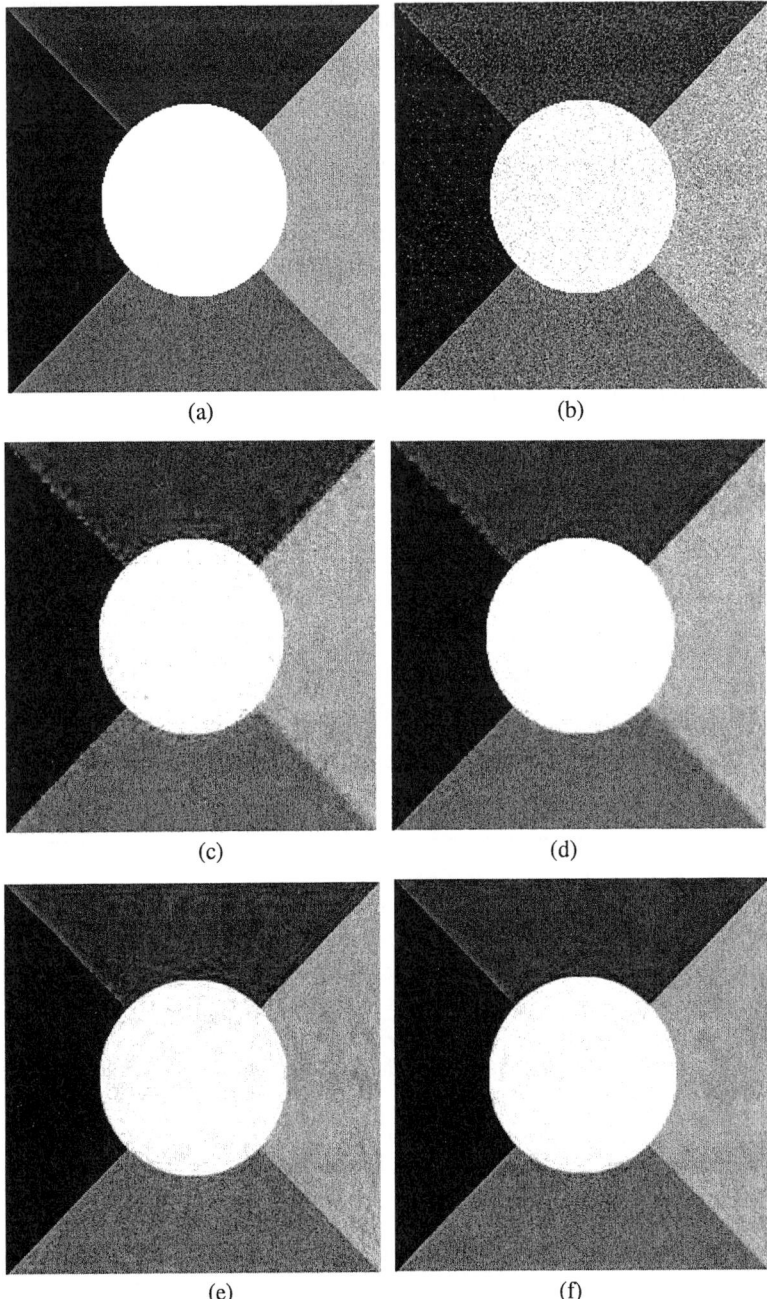

**Fig. 2.** Denoised images for visual comparison using different methods on a synthesis image (with additive Gaussian white noise of standard variance 20) (a) Original image, (b) Noisy image, PSNR=22.0855dB, (c) DWT (7/9 filter), PSNR=29.3786dB, (d) UDWT (7/9 filter), PSNR=31.5276dB, (e) D_DMRF, PSNR=31.0169dB, (f) U_DMRF, PSNR=33.5218dB

## 4 Conclusion

We have developed DMRF, which is a dual frame in $L^2[0,1]^2$. DMRF is based on a localization principle and hence, it also can efficiently deal with edges of very low curvature as Monoscale Ridgelet. DMRF provides a new tool with potential power for various applications, especially for image processing application. Experimentally, the high performance of DMRF for image denoising has been obtained on the test image. These initial experimental results are very promising. Furthermore, DMRF consists of biorthogonal wavelet basis. An outstanding property of biorthogonal wavelet is its symmetry that corresponds to linear phase in signal processing application. The advantages arisen from the introduction of biorthogonal wavelet into DMRF, we believe, will be demonstrated in signal processing especially in image processing applications.

## References

1. Candès, E.J.: Harmonic Analysis of Neural Netwoks. Appl. Comput. Harmon. Anal.. 6 (1999) 197–218
2. Candès, E.J.: On the Representation of Mutilated Sobolev Functions. SIAM J. Math. Anal.. 1 (1999) 2495-2509 1999.
3. Donoho, L.: Orthonormal Ridgelet and Straight Singularities. SIAM J. Math Anal.. 31 (2000) 1062–1099
4. Flesia, G., Hel-Or, H., Averbuch, A., Candès, E.J., Coifman, R.R., Donoho, D.L.: Digital Implementation of Ridgelet Packets. In: Stoeckler, J., Welland, G.V. (Eds.): Beyond Wavelets. Academic Press, (2003) 31–60
5. Tan Shan, Jiao, L.C. and Feng, X.C.: Ridgelet Frame. In: Proceedings of. Int. Conf. Image Analysis and Recognition. Campilho, Aurélio, Kamel, Mohamed (Eds.): Springer Lecture Notes in Computer Science (2004) 479–486
6. Tan Shan, Zhang, X.R., Jiao, L.C.: Dual Ridgelet Frame Constructed Using Biorthonormal Wavelet Basis. In: Proceedings of IEEE International Conference on Acoustics, Speech, and Signal. Philadelphia, PA, USA. March 2005. To appear.
7. Candès, E.J.: Monoscale Ridgelet for the Representation of Images with Edges. Dept. Statist., Stanford Univ., Stanford, CA, Tech. Rep.. (1999)
8. Deans, S.R.: The Radon Transform and Some of Its Applications. New York: Wiley. (1983)

# Description Selection Scheme for Intermediate Frame Based Multiple Description Video Streaming

S. Pavan, G. Sridhar, and V. Sridhar

Applied Research Group, Satyam Computer Services Limited,
SID Block, IISC Campus, Bangalore, India 560 012
{Pavan_S, Sridhar_Gangadharpalli, Sridhar}@satyam.com

**Abstract.** Real time video streaming applications over the internet pose several challenging problems due to the time-varying loss/delay network characteristics. Multiple description video coding is one method to alleviate the detrimental effects caused by these channel variations. However the selection of the source that is right for the channel having a desired cost is fundamental to the success of the multiple description technique. The proposed approach selects the set of descriptions which minimize an objective function for the streaming distortion.

## 1 Introduction

Path diversity is generally employed to improve the robustness of communication systems to propagation errors. The transmission of information over multiple paths with different channel characteristics improves the probability of receiving the information from atleast one of the channels. The Internet being a best effort service is characterized by variable channel bandwidths, delays and packet losses. Thus for real-time streaming applications over the internet the use of buffers or the retransmission of the data (ARQ) is not desired. One approach to improve the quality of service is by the use of multiple description (MD) video coding technique [1]. The MD video coding method provides good error resiliency without adding any excessive delays.

In an MD video coding system the video sequence is encoded into two or more independently decodable descriptions and sent over separate paths through the network. The descriptions can be decoded independently. If all the descriptions are correctly received and decoded then the highest level of signal fidelity is achieved. However, if atleast one of the descriptions is correctly received, then the receiver can still reconstruct the signal with acceptable quality.

One of the methods to generate multiple descriptions is by the use of a scalar quantizer. Vaishampayan in [2] has suggested the use of complementary quantizers, wherein each quantizer coarsely describes a single source but when combined together provides a more refined description. An alternative method to create multiple descriptions is segmentation of the video sequence in the transform domain using decorrelating transforms like the DCT. However, the removal of the correlation between the coefficients will lead to a less accurate estimate of the source when some of the descriptions are lost. This inefficiency can be mitigated to some extent by the use of correlating transforms as in [3], which restores the correlation by introducing statistical redundancies. An improvement over the DCT based transform domain approach is suggested by Ashwin et al in [4], wherein a partial decorrelation of the source is obtained using the wavelet transform. The major drawback of the above-mentioned approaches is that they are stand-alone codecs which are not compatible with the commonly employed video standards such as H.26x or MPEG standards.

The segmentation of the video sequence in temporal space will provide the desired compatibility with the commonly used standard codec. Apostolopoulos in [5] has suggested a temporal segmentation method by splitting the video sequence into even and odd sub-sequences. The major drawback of this method is reduction in the compression efficiency. This decrease in the compression efficiency is due to the decrease in temporal correlation between successive frames present in the sub-sequences. Also, the prediction error at the decoder end to reconstruct the original source in case one of the descriptions is lost, would be more since the odd frames need to be predicted from odd frames and even from even. This problem can be solved to some extent by introducing extra redundancies between the frames present in the odd and even subsequences as described in [6]. However the extra redundancies added would not be useful when both the descriptions are received.

In one of our recent work [7] we proposed an improved temporal segmentation method by creating multiple intermediate sequences to retain the correlation between the adjacent frames present in the original source sequence. However the success of the proposed MD approach depends on dynamically matching the source characteristics with that of the channel. Ali et al in [8] proposed a heuristic based solution to find the set of channel paths which minimized the streaming distortion for a given set of MD sources. This would be intractable in the case of large internet topologies. A more practical way of solving this problem is by the selection of the set of sources which will suit the channel characteristics.

In this paper, we consider a scenario where multiple descriptions are to be optimally matched with multiple channels so as to deliver the video stream with minimum distortions at receiver end; and propose an approach to achieve the same.

## 2 Intermediate Frame Based Multiple Descriptions

The MD coding scheme divides the source video data stream to 'n' (n>1) different descriptions. These 'n' different descriptions are coded independently and sent over 'n' different channels. The reception of any single description will guarantee a minimum quality of service and more descriptions together improves the quality. The correlation between the frames within a particular description is dependent on the temporal difference between the same two frames when they were a part of the original data stream. In order to obtain the best compression efficiency along with good error resiliency this correlation should be the same as that of consecutive frames in the original data stream. The segmentation of the source data stream into even and odd sub-streams [5] will reduce the correlation between the frames in the individual descriptions resulting in a decrease in compression efficiency and error resiliency. The insertion of redundant frames as suggested in [6] improves the correlation to some extent, but will decrease the MD system performance in the case of reception of more than one description. The Intermediate frame based temporal segmentation approach proposed in one of our recent work [7] retains the correlation between the frames in the original data stream leading to an improved performance in both the compression efficiency and error resiliency. In the Intermediate frame based MD approach the temporal spacing between two adjacent frames is divided into 'n' intermediate descriptions as shown in Fig. 1.

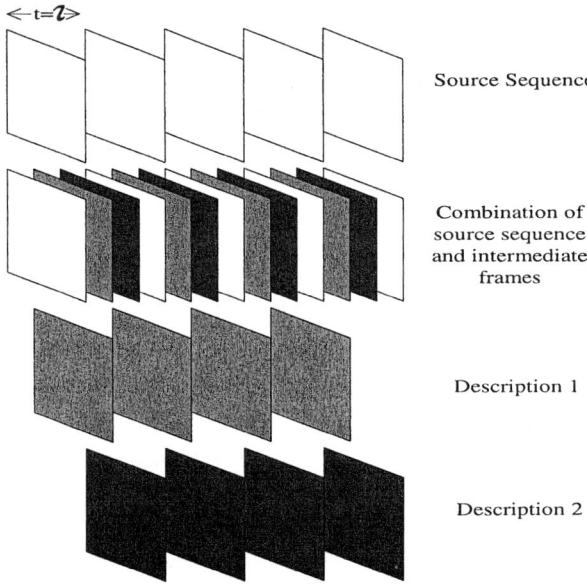

**Fig. 1.** Generation of Intermediate frames for n=2 descriptions

The problem of estimating an intermediate frame given the previous and next frame is represented using a conditional probability model. The states in the model represent the positions of the macroblock within a pre-defined search region. The time 't' represents the instant between two adjacent frames at which the intermediate frame is to be estimated. The model estimates the probability of finding a macroblock present in the intermediate frame to be in a particular state $s_j$ at a given time 't', given the states of the macroblock in the previous and next frame respectively. The state which yields the maximum probability 'p' for a particular 't' is selected as the position of the macroblock in the intermediate frame being estimated. Let $g_1(x, y)$ and $g_2(x, y)$ represent the forward and backward estimate of a pixel in the intermediate frame obtained from the previous and next frames respectively. The two estimates are weighted in the ratio of p and (1-p) to obtain the bidirectional estimate of the pixel $g(x, y)$ in the intermediate frame.

$$g(x,y) = p * g_1(x,y) + (1-p) * g_2(x,y) \qquad (1)$$

A methodology to select the set of intermediate frame descriptions which minimize the streaming distortion to suit the individual channel constraints is described in the next section.

## 3 Problem of Selection of Description That Best Suits Given Channel

The selection of the source description that is right for the channel is fundamental to the success of the multiple description technique. The utilization of the error resiliency performance of the MD approach depends on the compatibility of the description characteristics with the channel constraints like bandwidth, delays/losses. The error resiliency of the MD approach can be evaluated by the streaming distortion parameter. Thus the objective is to select the set of source descriptions that minimize the streaming distortion. The streaming distortion parameter depends mainly on the following two factors:

(1) The number of packets of data which are lost during transmission through the channel. Each individual frame in the video description is transmitted in the form of packets. The number of packets required for a frame depends on the significance of the frame in the sequence. For example, the 'I' frame is coded with more number of bits and the 'B' frame with the least number of bits. Thus the streaming distortion is significant in case of loss of a frame with high amount of information such as an 'I' frame.

(2) The bit-rate of the description that is to be transmitted through the channel. A decrease in the bit-rate represents a more compressed data. Any loss of data in the compressed bit-stream will result in more distortion when the data is decoded.

The objective is to minimize the effective distortion at the receiver by selecting N source descriptions from a finite set of available descriptions, for transmitting on N channels with specific characteristics. Objective function in terms of Streaming distortion is formulated as:

$$\text{Minimize Streaming distortion, D} = \sum_{i=1}^{N} \left[ \frac{\sum_{j=1}^{M} \left\{ \frac{Pk_{ij}}{t_{ij}} - \left( \frac{Pk_{ij}}{t_{ij}} \times (1 - pe_{ij}) \right) \right\}}{MN \times B_i} \right] \quad (2)$$

where $Pk_{ij}$ is the number of packets transmitted for the $j^{th}$ frame in the $i^{th}$ description in a unit time $t_{ij}$ which is the time taken to transmit the corresponding frame, $pe_{ij}$ is the packet error probability for the $j^{th}$ frame in the $i^{th}$ description, M is the number of frames in a description, N is the number of available channels and $B_i$ is the bit-rate associated with the $i^{th}$ description.

Channel characteristics are time varying and we consider the transmission errors are mainly due to burst characteristics which result in packet drops. This implies the error probability $pe_{ij}$ takes a value of either 1 or zero indicating the successful transmission of a packet or dropping of the packet as the case may be. In equation (2) term $Pk_{ij} / t_{ij}$, represents normally transmitted packet and $Pk_{ij} / t_{ij} \times pe_{ij}$ represents transmitting error.

The equation (2) simplifies to:

$$D = \sum_{i=1}^{N} \left[ \frac{\sum_{j=1}^{M} \left\{ \frac{Pk_{ij}}{t_{ij}} \times pe_{ij} \right\}}{MN \times B_i} \right] \quad (3)$$

As an illustration consider a simple case of transmission through two channels. The Streaming distortion for the first frame in description-1 and description-2 is given by:

$$D = \left[ \frac{\left\{ \frac{Pk_{11}}{t_{11}} \times pe_{11} \right\}}{2B_1} + \frac{\left\{ \frac{Pk_{21}}{t_{21}} \times pe_{21} \right\}}{2B_2} \right] \quad (4)$$

The optimum minimum value of streaming distortion can be obtained using a discrete search over the solution space. The solution space is the set of intermediate frame descriptions each represented by a unique value of bit-rate (B) and the error –resiliency (L) performance for a known channel loss distribution. The distortion parameter for each description is different even if the descriptions are passed through the same channel having a particular packet loss distribution. A modified heuristic tabu-search algorithm to find the optimum description is described in Fig. 2. The proposed algorithm is computationally efficient in the sense that the objective function is evaluated only for the recent solution set, $S=\{S_1, S_2, S_3\}$.

## 4 Results and Discussion

In order to quantitatively validate the error-resiliency performance of the proposed approach, experiments have been conducted on the first 100 frames of the Foreman sequence in the QCIF-YUV 4:2:0 format.
The frame rate and the GOP size has been set to 30 frames/second and 20 respectively. The standard ITU-T H.264 video codec is used to encode and decode the

Modified tabu-search description selection algorithm

*Steps*:
1) Choose an initial solution $(B_i, L_i)$ in solution space $S\{B, L\}$.
2) The solution space can be split into four sub-sets:
   $S_1$ = {set of solutions which have Bit-rate>$B_i$ and losses<$L_i$}
   $S_2$ = {set of solutions which have Bit-rate>$B_i$ and losses>$L_i$}
   $S_3$ = {set of solutions which have Bit-rate<$B_i$ and losses<$L_i$}
   $S_4$ = {set of solutions which have Bit-rate<$B_i$ and losses>$L_i$}
3) If $S_4$ exists for a particular $(B_i, L_i)$ then form a new set $S = \{S_1, S_2, S_3\}$ and repeat from step-1.
4) If $S_4$ does not exist then evaluate the objective function for each parameter in the recent solution set and find the minimum.

**Fig. 2.** Algorithm to select the optimum description

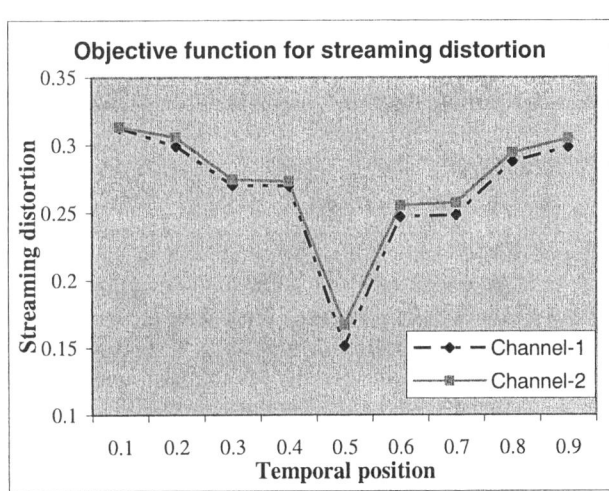

**Fig. 3.** Streaming distortion in channel-1 and channel-2 for a set of 9 descriptions

descriptions. For the verification of the proposed description selection algorithm the number of available channels has been set to 2. The descriptions are subjected to different loss characteristics corresponding to the two different channels. The proposed description selection algorithm is applied over the entire description solution set. An Intermediate frame description (say (x,1-x)) is referred based on the temporal position(x) of each frame in the description with respect to the adjacent previous frame and temporal position(1-x) with respect to next frame when it was a part of the source sequence. The descriptions with temporal positions (0.5, 0.5) and (0.6, 0.4) were selected as the optimal descriptions for channel-1 and channel-2 respectively based on the proposed description selection algorithm. In Fig. 3 the results for the streaming distortion value are reported for a set of 9 descriptions (represented by their temporal position(x) in the source sequence) for channel-1 and channel-2. It can be observed that the optimum for channel-2 is the same description (0.5, 0.5). But, since transmitting the same description over both the channels will not yield any improvement in

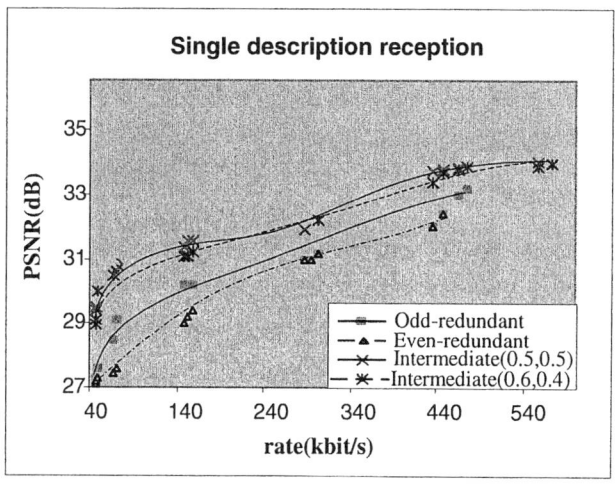

**Fig. 4.** PSNR in dB vs. Bit-rate in kbit/s for the single description reception

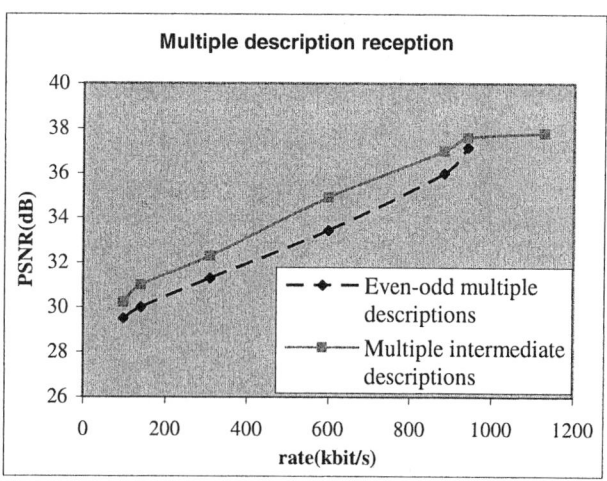

**Fig. 5.** PSNR in dB vs. Bit-rate in kbit/s for the multiple description reception

performance in the case of multiple description reception, the description (0.6, 0.4) is selected as the one to be transmitted through channel-2. The performance of the selected descriptions is compared with the even-odd redundant sequence approach proposed in [6]. In Fig.4 the PSNR values are reported versus the bit-rate used for the single-description case. The performance of the intermediate sequence descriptions for the cases ((0.5, 0.5) and (0.6, 0.4)) are reported. This performance is compared with an odd and even sequence of frames having an additional redundancy of 12 frames. It is clear from Fig.4 that the intermediate-frame MD approach results in an improved performance over the odd and even redundant sequence approach. In Fig.5 the performance comparison of the intermediate frame MD approach with the odd-even redundant sequence approach in the case of multiple description reception is reported. It can be inferred from Fig.5 that the Intermediate frame MD approach yields an improved performance.

## 5 Conclusion

In this paper we presented a formulation for description selection as an optimization problem to select the set of descriptions which suit the channel characteristics. This optimization contributes to the error-resilient performance of the Intermediate frame MD approach proposed in our previous work. The proposed approach can be applied to a varying number of channels each having different channel bandwidth and loss characteristics.

## References

1. Goyal, V.: Multiple Description Coding: Compression meets the network. In: IEEE Signal Processing Magazine (2001)
2. Vaishampayan, V.: Design of Multiple Description Scalar Quantizers. In: Transactions on Information theory. Vol. 39. (1993)
3. Wang, Y., Orchard, M., Reibman A.: Multiple Description Coding Using Pairwise Correlating Transforms. In: IEEE Transactions on Image Processing. Vol. 10. No. 3. (2001)
4. Ashwin, A.C., Ramakrishnan, K.R., Srinivasan, S.H. : A Multiple Description Method for Wavelet based Image Coding. In: IEEE International Conference on Image Processing. (2002)
5. Apostolopoulos, J. : Error-resilient Video Compression through the use of Multiple States. In: IEEE International Conference on Image Processing. Vol. 3. (2000)
6. Tammam Tillo, Gabriella Olmo : Low Complexity Pre-Post-Processing Multiple Description Coding for Video Streaming. In: IEEE International Conference on Information and Communication Technologies: from Theory to Applications (ICTTA). (2004)
7. Pavan, S., Sridhar, G., Sridhar, V. : A Novel Multiple Description Scheme based on Intermediate Frame Estimation. Submitted to: IEEE International Symposium on Signal Processing and its Applications (ISSPA). (2005)
8. Ali, C.B., Yucel Altunbasak, Ozlen Ergun : Fast Heuristics for Multi-path Selection for Multiple Description Encoded Video Streaming. In: IEEE International Conference on Multimedia and Expo. (2003)

# Background Removal of Document Images Acquired Using Portable Digital Cameras

André R. Gomes e Silva and Rafael Dueire Lins

Universidade Federal de Pernambuco, Recife - PE, Brazil
rdl@ufpe.br

**Abstract.** Portable digital cameras have widespread recently. Their image quality, low cost and portability have drastically changed the culture of photography, today. Many professionals start to take photos of documents, instead of photocopying them. This paper presents an algorithm designed to remove the background of document images acquired through portable digital cameras.

**Keywords:** Digital Cameras, Document Image Analysis, Background removal.

## 1 Introduction

The last five years have witnessed a fast growth on image quality of portable digital cameras. Their image grew in resolution to close to an order of magnitude while their price dropped by a factor of at least three. This price-performance improvement widened enormously the number of users of digital cameras burgeoning several new applications. One of them, completely unforeseen is using portable digital cameras for digitalising documents. Professionals of many different areas now use those devices as a fast way to acquire document images, taking advantage of their low weight, portability, low cost, small dimensions, etc. That attitude gave birth to a new research area [5] that is evolving fast in many different directions.

This paper focus on the automatic background border removal of images of documents obtained with portable digital cameras. An algorithm for that purpose should impose as few restrictions as possible, because users tend to acquire those document images in non-ideal conditions of colour, texture, illumination of the surface the document is placed on for digitalisation, perspective camera-document, etc.

The problem presented bears some resemblance with removing borders of monochromatic documents digitalized with automatically fed scanners [1][2][3][4][9]. Depending on a number of factors such as the size of the documents, its state of conservation and physical integrity, the presence or absence of dust in the document and scanner parts, etc. very frequently the image generated is framed either by a solid or stripped black border. This undesirable artifact, also known as *marginal noise*, not only drops the quality of the resulting image for CRT screen visualization, but also consumes space for storage and large amounts of toner for printing. Removing such frame manually is not practical due to the need of a specialized user and time consumed in the operation.

Although the disadvantages and problems introduced by background borders in images acquired with portable digital cameras were the same as in monochromatic scanned documents, the solutions to the two problems are completely unrelated. The main aspect is that the "nature" of the background noise introduced by digital cameras may be completely unpredictable. To the best of the authors' knowledge, the algorithm presented herein is the first of its kind.

## 2 Document Features

The test images for the algorithm proposed here were bureaucratic document images, pages extracted from magazines and phone directories. The bureaucratic documents range from typeset letters, hand filled-in forms, to handwritten documents. Most documents make use of translucent paper in such a way that back-to-front interference was not observed [5][8]. No glossy paper was tested. Documents range in size from A5 to Legal, with predominance of size around A4. Some of them may include black-and-white or colour photograph. The state of conservation of documents also varies widely. Documents may have damages that make noisy borders irregular in shape, thus increase the computational difficulty for their automatic removal. The only restriction imposed to documents is that there is an at least 2-pixel separation frame between the document background (paper) and document information. Figures 01 to 04 exemplify some of the document images tested for border removal.

The background to be removed served as support for taking the photography of the document and may be of any kind of colour or texture, provided that there is a colour

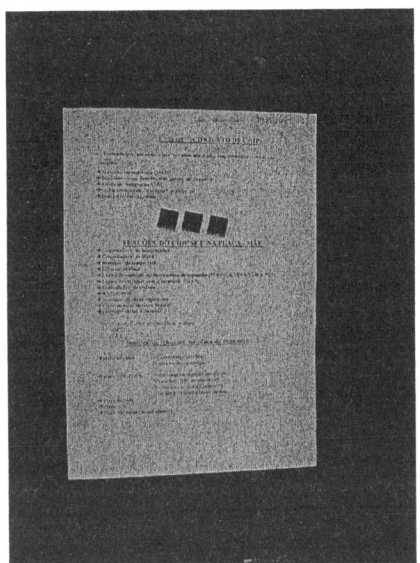
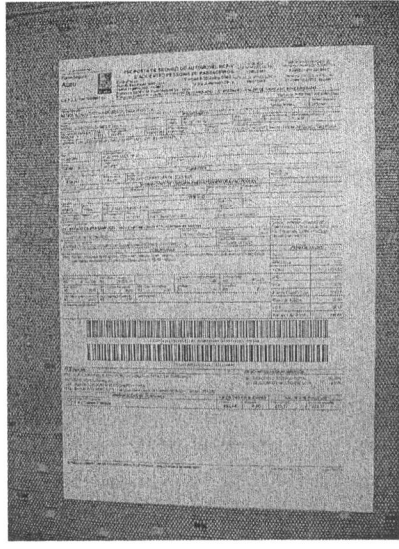

Fig. 1. B&W document on dark background (Size 140.5 KB JPEG)

Fig. 2. B&W document on light non-uniform background with texture (Size 367 KB JPEG)

 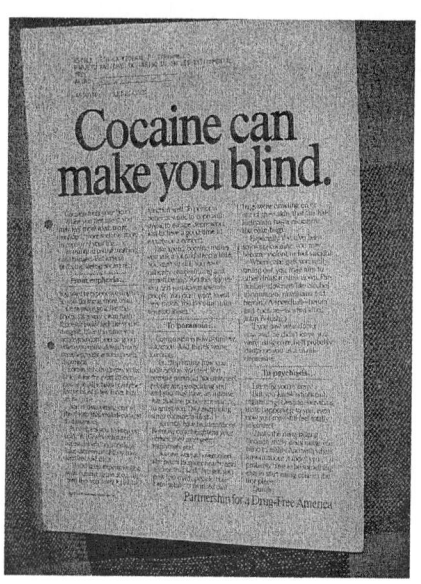

**Fig. 3.** Colour document on non-uniform colour background with texture (375.6 KB)

**Fig. 4.** B&W document with text highlighted on colour background with texture (338.9 KB)

difference of at least 32 levels between the image background and at least one of the RGB components of the most frequent colour of the document background (paper). The way the most frequent colour is found is explained below.

## 3 The New Algorithm

The proposed algorithm starts by splitting the image into nine regions. Statistical analysis is made in the central region to identify the colour of the pixel that corresponds to the background information of the document. Two axes are "drawn" on the photo frame. From the origin of the axes the algorithm moves outwards looking for the document border in the image. Once identified the intersection of the document border and the axes, the algorithm defines four border regions. Pixels in each of these regions are classified and the border contour is found. The document image is cropped as the internal area of the contour. In what follows, the algorithm is detailed.

### 3.1 File Format Conversion

The first step of the algorithm is to open the original JPEG-compressed image acquired from the camera and generate an uncompressed BMP equivalent. Any standard tool for image processing may be used for this file format conversion. The BMP file is used to generate a matrix of pixels with the corresponding RGB components of the image.

## 3.2 Region Splitting

The image is divided into nine regions of similar areas. The most frequent colour of pixels of the central region is found and stored in a variable *fcc*.

## 3.3 Axes Drawing and Scanning

The central point in the image is used to set the origin of two orthogonal axes that split the image in four regions. Scanning the axes from the origin outwards one analyses the colour of each pixel. If the colour of a pixel is within the sphere *S*, centred on *fcc*, with radius *t* *(tolerance)* one considers the pixel as document background. A pixel may also be considered as document background if two of its colour components lie within S, but the third one lies within the concentric outer sphere *S'* of radius 2t. For the documents analysed *t=16*.

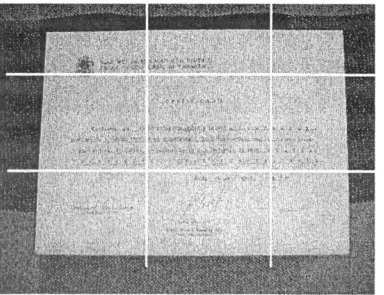

**Fig. 5.** Document with regions

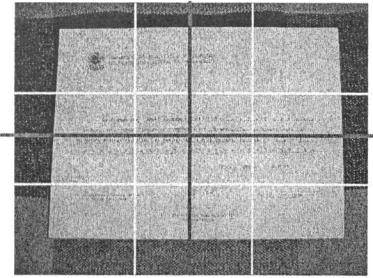

**Fig. 6.** Document with axes

There is no restriction either on document information or on colour/texture of the border, thus the analysis of the continuity of background information will provide the only clue for image segmentation.

Whenever scanning the horizontal axis outwards if a pixel $p_{i0}$ is not considered as document background that information is annotated. If the colour of the next pixel outwards $p_{(i-1)0}$ is within a sphere of radius 8 centred on the colour of pixel $p_{(i+2)0}$ then pixel $p_{i0}$ is considered as document background and the scan process moves further outwards. In this case, most possibly $p_{(i+1)0}$ and $p_{i0}$ are pixels of the

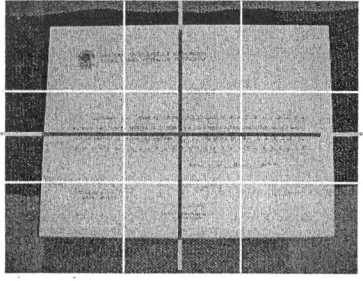

**Fig. 7.** Pixels from axes classified

document information (notice that this distance is related to image resolution, for the camera used 72 dpi).

Otherwise ($p_{(i+2)0}$ is not considered document background), one checks if for at most two of the RGB-component the colour difference between $p_{(i-1)0}$ and $p_{i0}$ is of less than 16 levels, then there is a smooth colour transition between non-background pixels. Otherwise, there was an abrupt colour transition thus there are chances of having reached the framing border or some sort of picture within the document. In this case, one tests if the colour of $p_{(i-1)0}$ is within S and $p_{(i-1)0}$ is considered document background. Otherwise, the document background may have varied (due to the position of the flash, environment illumination, etc.) and one tests if the colour of pixel $p_{(i-1)0}$ is within a sphere of radius 16 centred on the colour of pixel $p_{(i+2)0}$. If this requirement is not met then $p_{(i-1)0}$ is labelled as non-background. The algorithm now moves on analysing the next pixel outwards.

The same procedure is performed on the other three axes to classify their pixels.

### 3.4 Marginal Region Definition

Once the pixels on the axes have been classified and the document limits on them have been identified, four marginal regions of 25-pixel width are drawn (20 pixels inwards, 5 pixels outwards). These marginal regions are analysed finding parameters that compensate differences in illumination. For each of the four marginal regions the most frequent colour $fc_i$ is found.

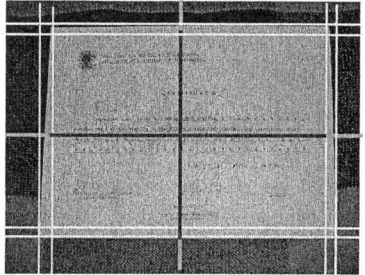

**Fig. 8.** Marginal regions drawn

If any of the RGB-colour components of the $fc_i$ obtained has 32 or more levels distant from $fcc$, $fc_i$ is not considered and $fcc$ is used as the most frequent colour for that region.

### 3.5 Border Detection

The limits of the document are found scanning the image having as starting point the bottommost projection of the limit pixel on the horizontal axis.

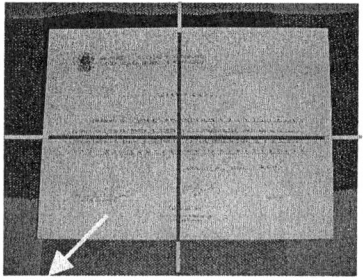

**Fig. 9.** Border detection starting point

The scan moves vertically until meeting two consecutive pixels of colour within a sphere centred on the $fc_i$ of the leftmost marginal region with radius 32 (*border finding step*). This pixel is marked as document border.

Now, the algorithm moves left one and bottom five pixels. Then the border finding step is repeated until reaching the topmost pixel. The abscissa of the leftmost point marked as border serves as the left-cropping limit.

The procedure described in this paragraph is used for cropping the other margins.

## 4  Results Obtained

The algorithm presented above was programmed in C and its code is available under e-mail request to one of the authors. It was executed on an Intel Pentium IV, 2.4 GHz clock, 512MB RAM and HD IDE and elapsed on average 1.2 seconds per image. One must remark that there was no concern about total run-time for the algorithm and that there are plenty of possibilities for optimisations. Over 380 images with different features were tested yielding satisfactory results. Figures 10 to 13 below present some of the results obtained.

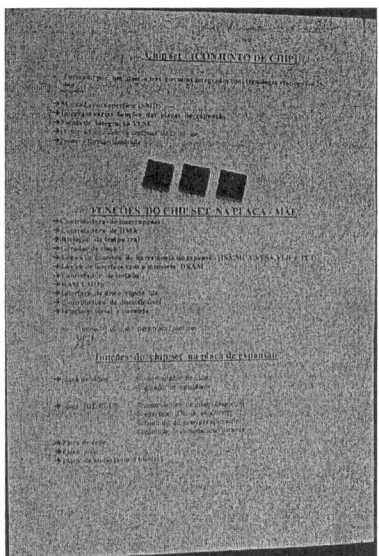

**Fig. 10.** Cropped document of Figure 1 (Size 78,9 KB JPEG)

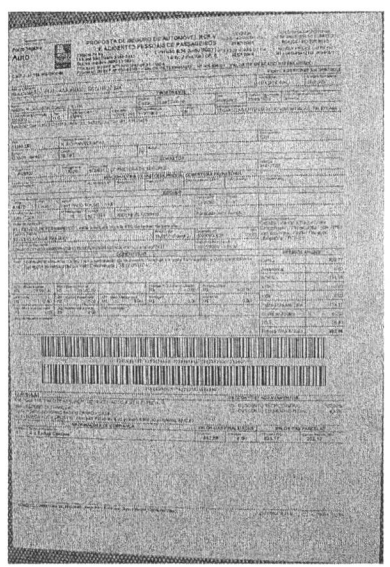

**Fig. 11.** Cropped document of Figure 2 (Size 222 KB JPEG)

**Fig. 12.** Cropped document of Figure 3 (Size 282.9 KB JPEG)

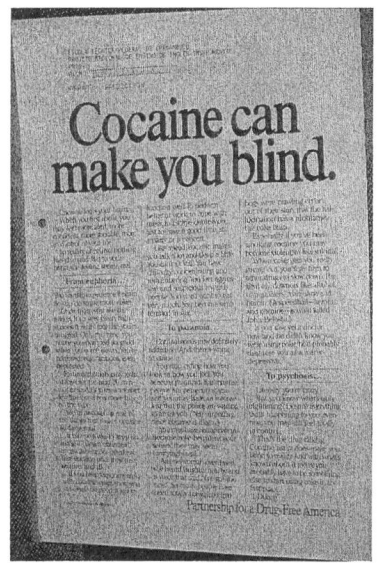

**Fig. 13.** Cropped document of Figure 4 (Size 263.3 KB JPEG)

In only two cases there were problems in the direct application of the algorithm. The first of them is in the case of glossy backgrounds of colour documents and photos taken with flash (see Figure 14). In this case, the image presents a large colour variation from the mode in a non-uniform way. This sort of image did not allow the minimal cropping of the border and thus some of the background border remained in the resulting image, as may be observed on Figure 15.

**Fig. 14.** Colour document in glossy background      **Fig. 15.** Cropped image of Figure 14

From the 380 images tested, only the one presented on Figure 16 presented problems of loss of information, due to cropping only a part of the document image.

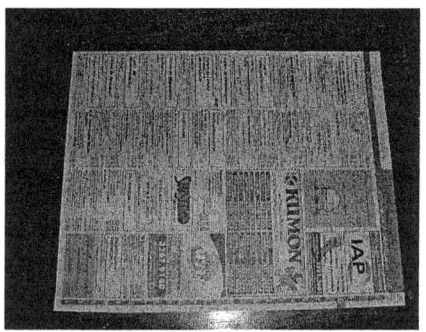 

**Fig. 16.** Colour document in glossy background      **Fig. 17.** Cropped image of Figure 16

One must observe that the documents exhibited in Figures 14 and 16 are highly complex exhibiting a large gamut (almost 200,000 colours), several illustrations and drawings, very high entropy, printed in low quality paper, etc.

## 5   Conclusions and Lines for Further Work

Portable digital cameras are a technological reality today that opens a wide number of challenges in image processing, including document image processing. This paper presents a simple, yet efficient algorithm for removing the background of the surface that served as support for document during digitalization.

The new algorithm was tested on 380 images of documents. In all but two of the images the background was suitably removed. The two unsatisfactory results were found in the case of photos of documents taken with flash on a glossy surface. The application of the algorithm introduced provided and average saving on space for image storage of over 40%, thus also saving bandwidth for image transmission through networks, and automatically zooming document image for browsers.

The average processing time was 1.2 s per image, but there is room for introducing a large number of code optimizations to make the process much faster.

The presented algorithm is the first step towards an environment for processing photos of document images. The next steps include filling in the remaining background border with document background, skew detection and correction, compensating lens and perspective deformations, automatic image-to-text transcription, amongst other things.

## Acknowledgements

Research reported herein was partly sponsored by CNPq-Conselho Nacional de Pesquisas e Desenvolvimento Tecnológico of the Brazilian Government, to whom the authors express their gratitude.

## References

[1] B.T.Ávila and R.D.Lins, A New Algorithm for Removing Noisy Borders from Monochromatic Documents, Proc. of ACM-SAC'2004, pp 1219-1225, Cyprus, ACM Press, March, 2004.
[2] H.S.Baird, Document image defect models and their uses, Proc. $S^{nd}$ Int. Conf. on Document Analysis and Recognition, Japan, IEEE Comp. Soc., pp. 62-67, 1993.
[3] K.C.Fan, Y.K.Wang, T.R.Lay, Marginal noise removal of document images, Patt.Recog. 35, 2593-2611, 2002.
[4] T.Kanungo, R.M.Haralick, I.Phillips, Global and local document degradation models, Proc. Snd Int. Conf. Doc. Analysis and Recognition, pp. 730-734, 1993.
[5] J. Liang, D. Doermann and H. Li. Camera-Based Analysis of Text and Documents: A Survey. *International Journal on Document Analysis and Recognition*, 2005. (TO APPEAR).
[6] R.D.Lins, M.S.Guimarães Neto, L.R. França Neto, and L.G. Rosa. An Environment for Processing Images of Historical Documents. Microprocessing & Microprogramming, pp. 111-121, North-Holland, January 1995.
[7] R.D.Lins and D.S.A.Machado, A Comparative Study of File Formats for Image Storage and Transmission, vol 13(1), pp 175-183, 2004, Journal of Electronic Imaging, Jan/2004.
[8] C.A.B.Mello and R.D.Lins. Image Segmentation of Historical Documents, Visual 2000, Aug. 2000, Mexico.
[9] L.G.Shapiro and G.C.Stockman, Computer Vision, March 2000. http://www.cse.msu.edu/~stockman/Book/book.html.

# Comparison of the Image Distortion Correction Methods for an X-Ray Digital Tomosynthesis System

J.Y. Kim

Dept. of Mechatronics Engineering, Tongmyong University of Information Technology,
535 Yongdang-dong, Nam-gu, Busan 608-711, Korea
kjy97@tit.ac.kr

**Abstract.** X-ray digital tomosynthesis (DT) is very useful to PCB inspection because it can obtain a cross-sectional image of a local inspection area quickly. The image intensifier, which is usually used in DT, distorts X-ray images in shape and intensity. Therefore, image distortion correction is one of the most important issues in realizing DT system. In this paper, two image distortion correction methods for an X-ray DT system are presented and their performances are compared. The first method is to use a simplified distortion model by a distance ratio function in intensity correction, and by 2D point mapping polynomials in shape correction. The second method is to use a general polynomial distortion model. The experimental results show a great improvement of the second method in compensation speed and accuracy.

## 1 Introduction

X-ray technology has been widely used in many industrial applications for inspecting inner defects which can hardly be found by normal vision systems. PCB solder joint inspection such as ball grid array (BGA) or flip chip array (FCA) is one of the applications that require such an X-ray inspection system[1]. An X-ray cross-sectional image can be obtained from two or more images projected from different directions by the methods such as tomography[2], laminography[3], or digital tomosynthesis.

The principle of laminography comes from the geometric focusing effect by a synchronized motion between an X-ray source and a detector, which is shown in Fig. 1. Digital tomosynthesis is a digital version of laminography, where a set of images of different views are stored and synthesized through computational operations in a computer[4]. It is one of the most useful X-ray cross-sectional imaging methods for PCB inspection because it can obtain a cross-section of a local inspection area quickly. Thus it has been often applied to PCB solder joint inspection[1,4-7]. However, the shape and the intensity of the X-ray images obtained by DT are distorted because of the image intensifier used in DT systems. This distortion breaks the correspondences between those images and prevents us from acquiring accurate cross-sectional images. Therefore, image distortion correction is one of the most important issues in realizing DT system.

In this paper, two image distortion correction methods for an X-ray DT system are presented and their performances are compared. The first method is to use a simplified distortion model that is built by uniformly spaced grids and their distorted images. The intensity distortion model is based on the distance ratio function between two grids, and the shape distortion model is based on two-dimensional point mapping polynomials. The second method is to use a general polynomial distortion model, which can cope with arbitrary, more complex and various forms of distortion. Experimental results show a great improvement of the second method in correction speed and accuracy. Also a series of experiments for PCB solder joint image acquisition is performed, and the correction performances by the proposed methods are compared.

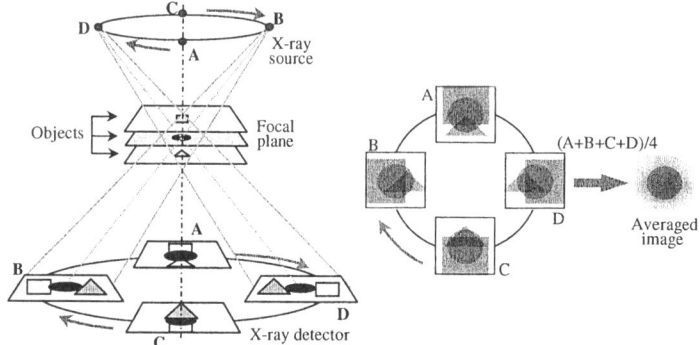

**Fig. 1.** The principle of Laminography and Digital Tomosynthesis

## 2 System Configuration and Image Distortion

Fig. 2(a) shows a configuration of the developed X-ray DT system, which is composed of a scanning X-ray tube, an image intensifier, a view selector and a zoom camera[7]. An image intensifier with a large input screen is used as an X-ray detector so as to get all images projected at various directions. The region of interest of a PCB

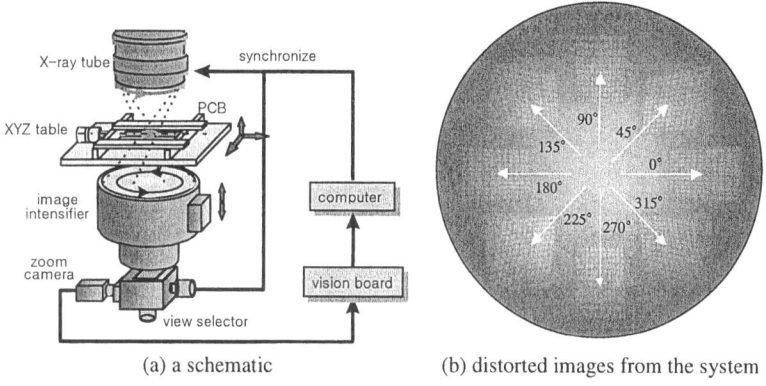

(a) a schematic  (b) distorted images from the system

**Fig. 2.** The configuration of an X-ray Digital Tomosynthesis system

is projected on a circular trajectory on the image intensifier as the X-ray is steered on the trajectory, and eight or more images are sequentially acquired by the zoom camera through a view selector. A galvanometer or a rotating prism can be used as a view selector. The captured images are saved in the digital memory of a computer, and then synthesized to generate a cross-sectional image.

The curved image input surface of the intensifier, however, distorts both of the shape and the intensity of the X-ray images. Fig. 2(b) shows eight distorted images of an uniformly spaced grid pattern projected onto the image intensifier according to the steered X-ray source location. It is not possible to get an accurate cross-sectional image from these distorted images, since the correspondences between the images are not maintained anymore.

## 3 Distortion Correction by Using a Distance Ratio Function

### 3.1 Intensity Distortion Correction

The central area of the image intensifier is brighter than the peripheral area, since the incident angle of the X-ray to the curved input surface of the intensifier varies with the incident locations. To compensate for the distorted intensity and make it uniform over the image, the distorted intensity should be scaled up to the maximum level of the image. In order to do it, intensities are sampled over the image area and the distribution is modeled numerically.

The distorted intensity $\Phi_d(i, j)$ at a point $(i, j)$ of an image can be corrected to the compensated intensity $\Phi_c(i, j)$ by dividing by the distance ratio function $f(L_d)$ for the point, as given in Eq. (1).

$$\Phi_c(i, j) = \Phi_d(i, j) / f(L_d). \tag{1}$$

$$f(L_d) = c_0 + c_1 L_d + c_2 L_d^2 + c_3 L_d^3. \tag{2}$$

$$L_d(i, j) = \sqrt{(i - i_H)^2 + (j - j_H)^2} \tag{3}$$

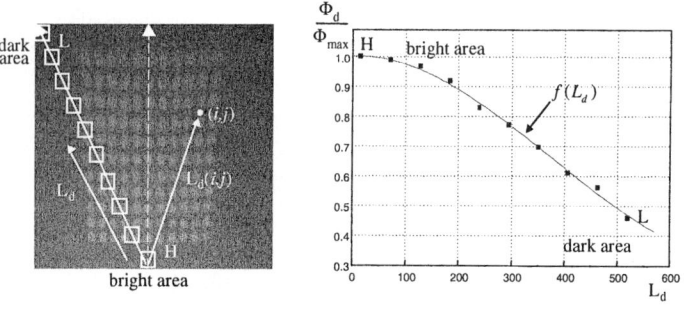

**Fig. 3.** Distorted intensity profile for a distance ration function

where $L_d(i,j)$ is defined as the distance from the highlight point $H = (i_H, j_H)$ to the point $(i,j)$. The distance ratio function $f(L_d)$ has a value decreasing with $L_d$ between 0 and 1, thus plays a role of correcting an intensity $\Phi_d$ to $\Phi_c$. To build the ratio function $f(L_d)$, 10 intensity values are sampled from the 10 small areas on the path from the point H to the point L, as shown in the Fig. 3. The coefficients of the polynomial $f(L_d)$ can be determined by least square method.

### 3.2 Shape Distortion Correction

The shape distortion can be corrected by finding a mapping relationship between the uniformly spacing grid image and its distorted image. Thus, a point $(i,j)$ in the original undistorted image is mapped to a point $(x,y)$ in the distorted image by the mapping relation, as shown in Fig. 4. As the sample data for distortion modeling, this paper used the data sets which consist of the uniformly spaced grid points of 11*11. There are two features in the shape distortion. One is that the distorted images are always symmetric with the projection center line of the x-ray. The other is that the peripheral area of the image intensifier is more elongated than the central area. Based on the two features, the mapping relationship can be represented by the following equations.

$$y_k(i,j) = \alpha_k(j)\{x(i,j) - x_c\}^2 + P_k(j). \tag{4}$$

$$x_k(i,j) = \beta_k(j) \cdot i + i_c. \tag{5}$$

$$\begin{aligned} P_k(j) &= p_0^k + p_1^k \cdot j + p_2^k \cdot j^2 + p_3^k \cdot j^3 \\ \alpha_k(j) &= a_0^k + a_1^k \cdot j + a_2^k \cdot j^2 + a_3^k \cdot j^3 \\ \beta_k(j) &= b_0^k + b_1^k \cdot j + b_2^k \cdot j^2 + b_3^k \cdot j^3 \end{aligned} \tag{6}$$

A distorted line, which is a distortion of an original horizontal line, is modeled by using a 2nd order polynomial as shown in Eq. (4). On the other hand, the x coordinate

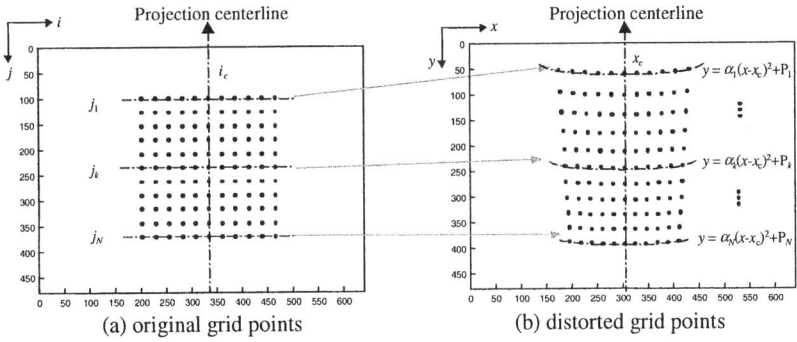

**Fig. 4.** Two-dimensional point mapping for shape distortion correction

values $x_k(i,j)$ of the distorted line are modeled as shown in Eq. (5). The parameters $P_k(j)$, $\alpha_k(j)$, $\beta_k(j)$ are functions of $j$, and they can be modeled by using 3rd order polynomials as shown in Eq. (6). The coefficients $p_0^k \sim p_3^k$, $a_0^k \sim a_3^k$, $b_0^k \sim b_3^k$ are determined by using least square fitting.

## 4 Distortion Correction by Using a General Polynomial Model

### 4.1 Intensity Distortion Correction

In this section, the ratio of the intensity of an arbitrary position to the highest intensity is modeled by using a general polynomial. Let us assume that the ratio $\Phi$ of the intensity in an arbitrary position $(x, y)$ to the highest intensity of an image is modeled in the format of a general polynomial, which can represent an arbitrary form of distortion on two dimensional plane. For example, if the ratio is modeled by a 3rd order polynomial, a ratio $\Phi_k$ in a position $(x_k, y_k)$ can be expressed as

$$\Phi_k = Q_k^T \cdot C \tag{7}$$

Where $\Phi_k = [1, x_k, y_k, x_k^2, x_k y_k, y_k^2, x_k^3, x_k^2 y_k, x_k y_k^2, y_k^3]^T$,
$C = [c_0, c_1, c_2, c_3, c_4, c_5, c_6, c_7, c_8, c_9]^T$.

Assuming that $\Phi_{mk}$ denotes an actual measurement value of the ratio $\Phi_k$ in a position $(x_k, y_k)$, the error $E_{\Phi k}$ between $\Phi_k$ and $\Phi_{mk}$ is given by $E_{\Phi k} = Q_k^T \cdot C - \Phi_{mk}$. The coefficient vector $C$ of a distortion model can be obtained by least square method. The squared error $E_\Phi^2$ can be obtained as follows:

$$E_\Phi^2 = \sum_k E_{\Phi k}^2 = \sum_k E_{\Phi k}^T E_{\Phi k} = C^T \sum_k Q_k Q_k^T C - 2\sum_k \Phi_{mk} Q_k^T C - \sum_k \Phi_{mk}^2 \tag{8}$$

From $\dfrac{\partial E_\Phi^2}{\partial C} = 0$, the coefficient vector C minimizing $E_\Phi^2$ is obtained by

$$C = (\sum_k Q_k Q_k^T)^{-1} \sum_k \Phi_{mk} Q^k \tag{9}$$

Therefore, an intensity model $\Phi_k$ can be obtained by Eq. (7), and it is used as a normalizing function to make the intensities uniformly distributed over the whole image area. An original intensity value $I_0(x, y)$ at a point $(x, y)$ can be scaled into $I(x, y)$ by

$$I(x, y) = I_{max} \cdot \frac{I_0(x, y)}{Q^T \cdot C} \tag{10}$$

where $I_{max}$ is the desired maximum intensity value after intensity distortion compensation.

## 4.2 Shape Distortion Correction

This section uses a general polynomial model on two dimensional plane to represent an arbitrary form of shape distortion. Let us denote the coordinates of an original reference pattern as $(x, y)$ and those of its distorted one as $(X, Y)$. For example, if the distortion is modeled by a 2nd order polynomial, the distorted coordinates $(X_k, Y_k)$ in a position $(x_k, y_k)$ can be expressed as $(X_k, Y_k) = (S_k^T \cdot F, S_k^T \cdot G)$ where $S_k = [1, x_k, y_k, x_k^2, x_k y_k, y_k^2]^T$, $F = [f_0, f_1, f_2, f_3, f_4, f_5]^T$, $G = [g_0, g_1, g_2, g_3, g_4, g_5]^T$, $F$ and $G$ are the coefficient vectors of a distortion model.

Assuming that $(X_{mk}, Y_{mk})$ denotes the actual measurement coordinates of a distorted pattern in a position $(x_k, y_k)$, the error $E_k$ between $(X_k, Y_k)$ and $(X_{mk}, Y_{mk})$ is given by

$$E_k = \begin{bmatrix} E_{Xk} \\ E_{Yk} \end{bmatrix} = \begin{bmatrix} X_k - X_{mk} \\ Y_k - Y_{mk} \end{bmatrix} = \begin{bmatrix} S_k^T \cdot F - X_{mk} \\ S_k^T \cdot G - Y_{mk} \end{bmatrix}. \tag{11}$$

The coefficient vectors $F$ and $G$ can be obtained by least square method. The squared error $E_X^2$ and $E_Y^2$ can be obtained as follows:

$$\begin{bmatrix} E_X^2 \\ E_Y^2 \end{bmatrix} = \begin{bmatrix} \sum_k E_{Xk}^2 \\ \sum_k E_{Yk}^2 \end{bmatrix} = \begin{bmatrix} \sum_k E_{Xk}^T E_{Xk} \\ \sum_k E_{Yk}^T E_{Yk} \end{bmatrix} = \begin{bmatrix} F \sum_k S_k S_k^T F - 2 \sum_k X_{mk} S_k^T F - \sum_k X_{mk}^2 \\ G \sum_k S_k S_k^T G - 2 \sum_k Y_{mk} S_k^T G - \sum_k Y_{mk}^2 \end{bmatrix}. \tag{12}$$

From $\frac{\partial E_X^2}{\partial F} = 0$ and $\frac{\partial E_Y^2}{\partial G} = 0$, the coefficient vectors $F$ and $G$ minimizing $E_X^2$ and $E_Y^2$ each are obtained by

$$\begin{bmatrix} F \\ G \end{bmatrix} = \begin{bmatrix} (\sum_k S_k S_k^T)^{-1} \sum_k X_{mk} S_k \\ (\sum_k S_k S_k^T)^{-1} \sum_k Y_{mk} S_k \end{bmatrix}. \tag{13}$$

Therefore, by using $F$ and $G$ of Eq. (13), an arbitrary point $(X, Y)$ in the distorted image can be mapped into a point $(x, y)$ in the reference pattern. Increasing the polynomial order will definitely result in a more accurate mapping model. Fig. 5 shows the result of intensity and shape distortion correction by using a general polynomial model.

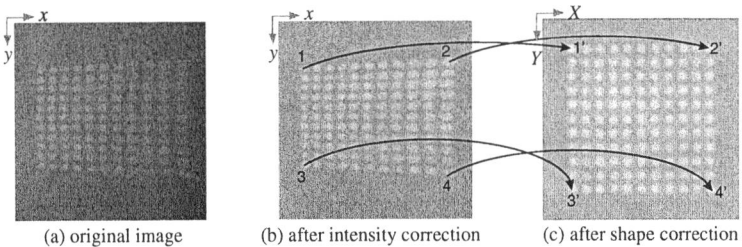

(a) original image     (b) after intensity correction     (c) after shape correction

**Fig. 5.** Image distortion correction by using a general polynomial model

## 5 Comparison of Distortion Correction Performances

A series of experiments to get the DT images of BGA was performed by using the X-ray DT system shown in Fig. 2(a). In the acquired images shown in Fig. 6, the dark regions represent the cross-section of the focal plane. The cross-section at the middle of the lead ball has the maximum diameter. These DT images were acquired by integrating the 8 images taken from 8 different off-axis images which are corrected by using the distortion correction methods presented in above sections.

In case of the first method using a distance ratio function, it took 1.81sec in correcting intensity distortion and 1.53sec in correcting shape distortion. In case of the second method using a general polynomial model, it took 0.32sec in correcting intensity distortion and 0.26sec in correcting shape distortion. So to speak, the second correction method improved the correction speed by 82.6%. On the other hand, the accuracy performance results after intensity and shape correction are as follows: the error between the corrected images and the original images is about 2.2 pixels in the image of 640*480 pixels in case of the first method using a distance ratio function, and the error is about 1.5 pixels in case of the second method using a general polynomial model. So to speak, the second correction method improved the correction accuracy by 31.8%.

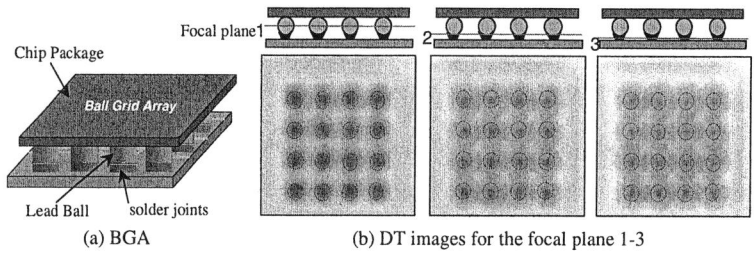

(a) BGA    (b) DT images for the focal plane 1-3

**Fig. 6.** X-ray DT images of BGA

## 6 Conclusions

In order for image distortion correction in an X-ray DT system, this paper presented two methods and compared their performances. The first method is to use a simplified distortion model by a distance ratio function in intensity correction, and by 2D point mapping polynomials in shape correction. The second method is to use a general polynomial distortion model. It can model arbitrary, more complex and various forms of image distortion on two-dimensional plane. And a series of experiments to get DT images of BGA was performed by using the presented correction methods. The experimental results showed that the second method improved the correction speed by 82.6% and the correction accuracy by 31.8% in an image of 640*480 pixels.

## Acknowledgements

This work was supported by Tongmyong University of Information Technology Research Fund of 2004.

## References

1. Adams, J.: X-ray laminography analysis of ultra fine pitch solder connections on ultra-thin boards. SPIE Integrated Circuit Metrology, Inspection, and Process Control V, Vol. 1464. (1991) 484-497
2. Bossi, R. H. and Georgeson, G. E.: Casting development savings with X-ray computed tomography. Casting (1993) 181-188
3. Bocage, E. M.: French Patent 536464 (1922)
4. Rooks, M. and Sack, T.: X-ray inspection of flip chip attach using digital tomosynthesis. Surface Mount Int. Conf., San Jose (1994) 51-55
5. Bord, S., Clement, A., Lecomte, J. C., Marmeggi, J. C.: An X-ray tomography facility for IC industry at STMicroelectronics Grenoble. Microelectronic engineering, Vol. 62. (2002) 1069-1075
6. Sumimoto, T., Maruyamay, T., Azuma, Y., Goto, S., Mondo, M., Furukawa, N., Okada, S.: Detection of defects at BGA solder joints by using X-ray imaging. 2002 IEEE Int. Conf. on Industrial Technology, Vol. 1. (2002) 238-241
7. Roh, Y. J., Ko, K. W., Cho, H. S., Kim, J. Y., Byun, J. E.: The calibration of X-ray digital tomosynthesis system including the compensation of the image distortion. SPIE Symp. on Intelligent Systems and Advanced Manufacturing VII, Vol. 3528. (1998) 248-259

# An Efficient Video Watermarking Scheme Using Adaptive Threshold and Minimum Modification on Motion Vectors

Kyung-Won Kang[1], Kwang-Seok Moon[1], Gwang-Seok Jung[2], and Jong-Nam Kim[1,*]

[1] Division of Electronic Computer and Telecommunication Engineering,
Pukyong National University, Busan, 608-737, Korea
kangkw@mail1.pknu.ac.kr
{moonks, jongnam}@pknu.ac.kr
[2] Departments of Math and Computer Science,
Lehman Colleague of The City University of New York, Bronx, NY 10468-1589
GWANG.JUNG@lehman.cuny.edu

**Abstract.** This paper proposes an efficient video watermarking scheme using adaptive threshold and minimum modification of motion vectors. Our proposed algorithm guarantees the amount of embedded watermark data and minimizes modification of original motion vectors to avoid degradation of video quality without reducing payloads. Besides, our algorithm can embed and retrieve watermark data without any increment of bit rate and original video contents. Experimental result shows that the proposed scheme obtains better video quality than other previous algorithms by about 0.5~1.1dB. Our scheme can be useful to real-time video watermarking which must be compatible to MPEG video coding.

## 1 Introduction

The rapid growth of digital media such as DVD, VOD and HDTV has caused an overflowing of illegal copies because digital media can be easily replicated without any loss. Thus, digital watermarking technology becomes more attractive in researching for their copyright protection and product authentication. A good digital watermarking system should satisfy the two fundamental requirements [1-3]. Firstly, the watermark must be robust against watermark attacks applied to the media content for the purposes of editing, compression or even deliberate attacks. Secondly, the watermark must be embedded in a transparent way to avoid degrading the perceptual quality of the original media. Apparently, these requirements may conflict with each other, so a good digital watermarking technique is a trade-off between invisibility and robustness. Video watermarking techniques have some other features compared with general watermarking techniques. The first one is that video watermarking must use blind detection in which the detection of the watermarking is performed without any original data. The second one is that the watermarking operation should be carried out on real time for actual application. The third one is that it must be compatible with the

---

* Corresponding author.

present video coding standards. A wide range of modifications in any domain can be used for video watermarking techniques. One technique is digital video watermarking which is focused on information hiding in the original video [4,5]. This method inserts a watermark by changing the least significant bit or modifying a statistical property quickly. However, this is not robust enough to attacks such as filtering. Another technique challenges the compress domain such as DCT domain [6-8]. This method is robust enough to attacks but must modify the encoder because the watermark is inserted after DCT or quantization process. Another technique modifies video bitstream [9-11]. This method does not increase bit rate and does not degrade picture quality but the amount of watermark data are limited because of the specification of standards. Several video watermarking schemes based on motion estimation and motion vector have been published [12-14]. In most of the video coding standards, the motion compensation prediction is commonly used. This is a powerful tool to reduce temporal redundancies in frames except intra video frames. The concept of the scheme is that watermark data are embedded quickly into motion vectors without change of the decoding speed and without any incremental change of bit rate in video stream. Besides, this method can embed watermark data on both the compressed and the uncompressed video bitstream. Furthermore, it can retrieve the embedded information without original video contents.

Thus, in this paper, we propose an efficient video watermarking scheme using adaptive threshold and minimum modification on motion vectors. There are two main ideas of our proposed algorithm. One is to guarantee the amount of the embedded watermark using adaptive threshold according to the accumulation number of the desired watermark data and the other is to minimize degradation of video quality when the watermark information is embedded to in original data. Therefore, our scheme will be useful for software-based real-time video watermarking system which must be compatible to MPEG video coding.

## 2 State of the Art in Video Watermark on Motion Vectors

In order to embed watermark information in original data, watermarking techniques apply slight modifications to the original data in a perceptually invisible method. To hide watermark information in motion vectors one can exploit more efficiently the information without any incremental change of bit rate in video bitstream and detect the watermark quickly. Zhao et al. [12] proposed a video watermarking scheme. However, this method relies on the procedure of motion estimation for detecting watermark. Zhongjie et al. [13] embedded watermark information into motion vectors on MPEG-2 compressions process. In this method, the watermark information is embedded into the horizontal or vertical component of motion vectors according to watermark bits. In this scheme, all motion vectors should be updated by the even number values beforehand and the watermark was embedded into motion vectors and could be extracted blindly. However, this method required too much change of the motion vectors. Thus, the change of the motion vectors resulted in the degradation of video quality. Zhang et al.[14] proposed a video watermarking method that embedded information into larger value motion vectors. The larger motion vector magnitude indicated the faster physical moving of the macroblocks. In this case, human eyes cannot perceive well the change of the original motion vector compared with the small magnitude of motion vectors. This scheme was that watermark information was embedded into the modified motion vectors only in the condition of large motion vectors. However, this method does not guarantee the amount of the embedded watermark data because of the fixed threshold value. The probability of a motion vector to be modified by the embedded procedure is greater than 1/2. Therefore, we proposed a method that can avoid degradation of video quality without reducing the payloads and retrieve the embedded watermark exactly and blindly.

## 3 Proposed Video Watermark Scheme

### 3.1 The Principle for Watermark Embedding

We embedded the watermark in the macroblocks that were in the larger motion vector magnitudes. The two main ideas for the algorithm, called the adaptive threshold and the other is minimum modification on motion vectors. They are as follows: At first, the threshold $\varepsilon$ value is set adaptively according to the number of the desired watermark data using the histogram of the amplitude of the motion vectors. This process guarantees the amount of the embedded watermark data. After calculating the threshold value, we define the feature vectors with two symbols (-1 or 1) which map each value to 0 and 1 value respectively. This is used to minimize the modification of the motion vectors when the pseudo-random sequence is used as the watermark. It means that the average probability of each watermark symbol is 1/2.

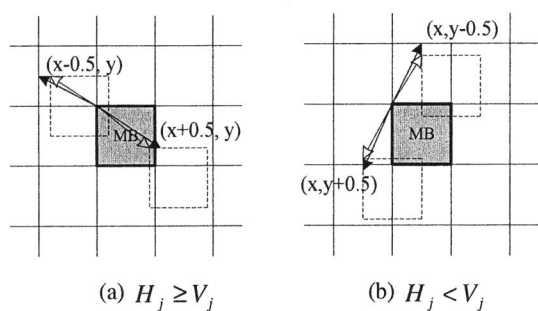

(a) $H_j \geq V_j$  (b) $H_j < V_j$

**Fig. 1.** Modification process for watermarking

The principle for watermark embedding is to modify motion vectors when the feature vectors and watermark sequences are different. Thus our proposed algorithm replaces an original motion vector by the larger motion vector which doesn't change the feature vectors. The larger motion vector indicates the faster physical moving of the macroblocks. In this case, to change the motion vector will be less perceivable by comparing with changing the same value in motion vector when the macroblocks are in lower motion vector. This modification process of motion vector is illustrated in Figure 1. Our watermarking scheme proceeds as follows:

(1) Set the threshold $\varepsilon$ according to the accumulation number of the desired watermark data using histogram technique.
(2) Calculate the magnitude of the motion vector $PMV_i$.

$$|PMV_i| = \sqrt{H_i^2 + V_i^2}, \quad (0 < i < MB), \quad H_i = 2 \times h_i, \quad V_i = 2 \times v_i \quad (1)$$

Where, $MB$ is the number of the total macroblocks. The $h_i / v_i$ is the $i$ th horizontal/vertical component of motion vector. The precision of motion vector is half-pixel accuracy.

(3) Select the set $E$ that is the set of the macroblocks for watermarking.

$$E_i = M_i \cdot F_i, \quad M_i = \begin{cases} 1, & |PMV_i| \geq \varepsilon \\ 0, & |PMV_i| < \varepsilon \end{cases}, \quad (0 < i < MB) \quad (2)$$

Where, $F$ is a frame, $M$ is the selected macroblocks by the threshold $\varepsilon$.

(4) Define the feature vector $\rho[j]$ of $H[j], V[j]$.

$$\rho[j] = H[j] \oplus V[j], \quad (j \in E_i, 0 \leq j < n) \quad (3)$$

Where, the symbol $\oplus$ means XOR(exclusive OR) operation and $H[j]$ and $V[j]$ mean modulo 2 operator of X with respect to 2 such as $H[j] = \mod(H_j, 2) \quad V[j] = \mod(V_j, 2)$.

(5) Updating the feature vector is equal to watermark sequences. It means that we always have the probability of which motion vectors are modified less than 1/2 by the selective inversion of all feature vectors. This process is required for the preparatory operation in watermarking, but result of this calculation is so negligible that it may be ignored.

$$q = \sum_{j=1}^{n} \rho[j] \oplus W[j], \quad \begin{cases} q \leq n/2 \rightarrow \text{don't change all feature vectors} \\ q > n/2 \rightarrow \text{invert all feature vectors} \end{cases} \quad (4)$$

(6) The principle for watermark embedding is to modify motion vectors when the feature vectors and watermark sequences are different. The watermarking procedure is shown below.

```
program watermarking()
  foreach( j in E ) q+= ρ[j]⊕W[j];
  if (q>n/2 ) invert all ρ[];
  foreach( j in E) {
    if ( ρ[j]≠W[j]) {
      if (H_j≥V_j)       h_j = h_j +0.5;
      else               v_j = v_j +0.5;
    }
  }
```

## 3.2 Watermark Detection Approach

The retrieval process is very simple. This is an inverse process of embedding watermarking. The algorithm of extracting watermark is described as follows:

(1) Find the macroblock $E$ that has the watermark using magnitude of the motion vector $PMV_i$ and threshold $\varepsilon$ such as embedding process.
(2) Detect the watermark data using the feature vectors.

$$W_1[j] = \rho[j] \text{ or } W_2[j] = \sim \rho[j], \; \rho[j] = H[j] \oplus V[j], \; (j \in E_i, 0 \leq j < n) \tag{5}$$

(3) Finally decide $W[j]$ between $W_1[j]$ and $W_2[j]$ by correlation of original watermark data. This means that the correct watermark has a greater correlation value than the other value.

## 4 Experimental Results

To verify the effectiveness of the proposed video watermarking procedure, we conducted an experiment that compared with Zhang's method and Zhongjie's method. The proposed algorithm has been tested on standard monochrome video sequence "football", "flower garden" and "mobile". The first sequence has very fast movement of the object and background, the second sequence has medium movement of the object and background and the last sequence has very slow movement of the object and background. All the frames of the video sequences are 352×240 pixels. The rate is 30 frames per second. We can use Hadamard matrix for watermark data which map each value to 0 and 1 respectively.

Figure 2 presents original video frame and the watermarked video frame before the motion compensation. It is clear that the loss of watermarked image is very small and does not affect the image visual quality.

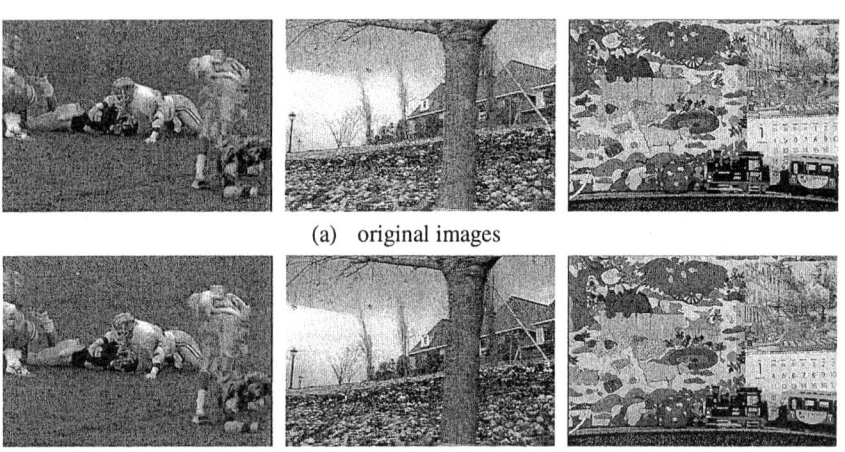

(a) original images

(b) watermarked images

**Fig. 2.** Experimental results with the proposed algorithm

Table 1 shows the performance of the proposed method in terms of the video quality of the embedded macroblocks. The measure of invisibility is defined by average PSNR considering statistical characteristics because watermark data are embedded in the different motion vectors in the proposed method as well as other methods. Zhongjie's method is ignored in our results because the modification of motion vector appeared greater than our method and Zhang's method. The proposed algorithm is superior to Zhang's algorithm in average PSNR by about 0.5~1.1dB because this reduces more the modification of the motion vectors than conventional ones. It is clear that the loss of PSNR of watermarked frames is very small. Thus, this method has more invisibility.

**Table 1.** The average PSNR of the propsed method and other methods

| Sequences | Proposed Method | Zhang's Method | Zhongjie's Method |
|---|---|---|---|
| Football | 42.72 dB | 41.64 dB | 32.81 dB |
| Flower Garden | 41.10 dB | 40.62 dB | 30.94 dB |
| Mobile | 31.80 dB | 31.12 dB | 27.26 dB |

Figure 3 shows the modified motion vectors that watermark information are embedded by the proposed method and Zhang's method on the sixth football image. We have confirmed that two vectors are unequal to each other as difference of the feature vectors.

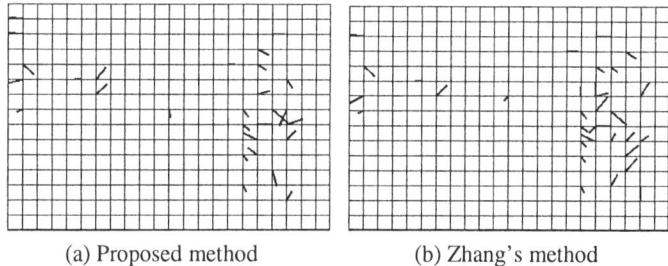

(a) Proposed method       (b) Zhang's method

**Fig. 3.** The motion vectors of the modified macroblocks

Table 2 shows the number of the modified motion vectors when embedded 64 watermark data. The proposed method 1 means with feature vectors to minimizing the modification of the motion vectors and the proposed method 2 means without feature vectors. The proposed method 1 can guarantee the probability less than 1/2 for the minimum modification of motion vectors.

**Table 2.** The number of the modified MVs of the proposed method and other methods

| Sequences | Proposed Method 1 | Proposed Method 2 | Zhang's Method | Zhang's Method |
|---|---|---|---|---|
| Football | 28.55 / 64 | 30.55 / 64 | 31.86 / 64 | 130.34 / 64 |
| Flower Garden | 26.97 / 64 | 31.38 / 64 | 32.28 / 64 | 114.52 / 64 |
| Mobile | 31.10 / 64 | 31.58 / 64 | 31.00 / 64 | 83.93 / 64 |

Figure 4 shows the PSNR result of a few frames. The proposed method has higher average than the other method except the little frames. This exception case is due to difference of the conditions on methods.

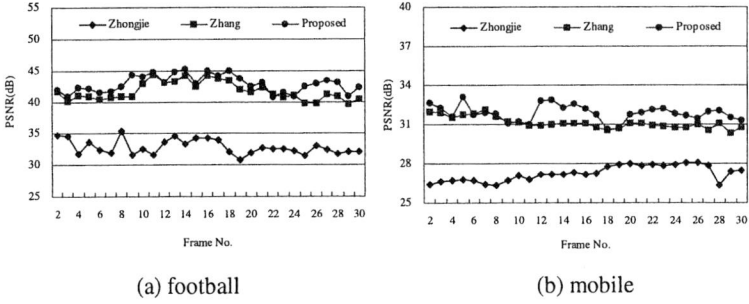

(a) football   (b) mobile

**Fig. 4.** The PSNR comparison of a few frames

In the experiment, we corrupted the watermarked video by adding the uniform distributed noise with different intensity. The comparison results are shown in Figure 5, in which the $x$-axis represents error rate slots, and the $y$-axis shows the detected key value in each error rate slot. This means that the robustness is very strong because the watermark key is detected when the probability of 0.35 errors is given.

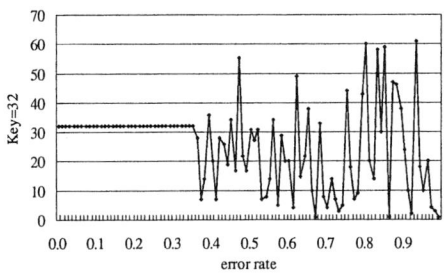

**Fig. 5.** The watermark detection results with error rate (key = 32)

## 5 Conclusions

Digital watermarking is recognized by the very important technology for copyright or ownership of digital multimedia data. Video watermarking systems require real-time applications and blind watermark detection. Thus, we proposed the efficient video watermarking method that was embedded without change of the encoding speed as well as bit rate and retrieved the embedded information quickly without original video contents. In particular, our proposed algorithm guaranteed the amount of embedded watermark data and minimized modification of original motion vectors to avoid degradation of video quality without reducing payloads. Besides, our scheme was used to watermark directly on both the compressed and the uncompressed video bitstream.

Experimental results showed obviously that our algorithms got better video quality compared to conventional algorithms by about 0.5~1.1dB and got robustness against bit errors. Our scheme can be useful to real-time video watermarking which must be compatible to MPEG video coding.

## Acknowledgements

This work was supported by the Regional Research Centers Program(Research Center for Logistics Information Technology), granted by the Korean Ministry of Education & Human Resources Development.

## References

1. I. J. Cox, J. P. M. G. Linnartz, "Public watermarks and resistance to tampering," Proceeding of the IEEE international conference on image processing, vol. 3. pp. 3-6, 1997.
2. C. I. Podilchuk, W. Zeng, "Digital image watermarking using visual models," Proceeding of the SPIE conference on human vision and electronic imaging, vol. 3016, pp. 100-111, 1997.
3. R. G. van Schyndel, A. Z. Tirkel and C. F. Osborne, "A digital watermark," Proceeding of the IEEE international conference on image processing, vol. 2. pp. 86-90, 1994.
4. M. Barni, F. Bartolini, R. Caldelli, A. De Rosa and A. Piva, "A robust watermarking approach for raw video," PV2000 10th international packet video workshop, May 2000.
5. J. Chae, B. Manjunath, "Data hiding in video," Proceedings of the 1999 international conference on image processing, vol. 1, pp. 311-315, October 1999.
6. A. Kusanagi, H. Imai, "A method of watermarking for compressed video," Symposium on cryptography and information security, SCIS'99-W4-2.3, Kobe, 1999.
7. D. Ghosh, K. Ramakrishna, "Watermarking compressed video stream over Internet," Proceedings of IEEE APCC 2003, vol. 2. pp. 711-715, September 2003.
8. M. Kutter, F. Jordan, T. Ebrahimi, "Proposal of a watermarking technique for hiding/retrieving data in compressed and decompressed video," Technical report M2281, ISO/IEC document, JTC1/SC29/WG11, 1997.
9. F. Hartung, B. Girod, "Digital watermarking of MPEG2 coded video in the bitstream domain," Proceedings of IEEE ICASSP '97, vol. 4, pp. 2621-2624, April 1997.
10. Y. Dai, L. Zhang, Y. Yang, "A new method of MPEG video watermarking technology," Proceedings of the ICCT international conference on communication technology, vol. 2. pp. 1845-1847, April 2003.
11. J. Zhang, H. Maitre, J. Li, L. Zhang, "Embedding watermark in MPEG video sequence," Multimedia signal processing, 2001 IEEE Fourth workshop, pp. 535-540, 2001.
12. Z. Zhao, N. Yu, X. Li, " A novel video watermarking scheme in compressed domain based on fast motion estimation," Proceedings of the ICCT 2003, vol. 2, pp. 1878-1882, April 2003.
13. Z. Zhongjie, J. Gangyi, Y. Mei, W. Xunwei, "New Alogorithm for video watermark," ICSP, vol. 1, pp. 760-763, August, 2002.
14. J. Zhang, J. Li, L. Zhang, "Video watermark technique in motion vector," XIV Brazilian symposium on computer graphics and image processing, pp. 179-182, October 2001.

# Lossless Compression of Correlated Images/Data with Low Complexity Encoder Using Distributed Source Coding Techniques

Mortuza Ali and Manzur Murshed

Gippsland School of Comp. and IT, Monash University, Churchill VIC 3842, Australia
{Mortuza.Ali, Manzur.Murshed}@infotech.monash.edu.au

**Abstract.** This paper presents a novel lossless compression technique to transmit correlated images or data within sensor networks of inexpensive devices by exploiting the temporal correlation under the distributed source coding paradigm where the complexity of the encoder is much lower than that of the decoder. The technique operates in pixel-domain to avoid any lossy transform and relies on syndrome decoding of trellis codes by innovatively encoding the final state of the trellis. Experimental results on standard test video sequences proved superiority of this technique against the entropy based LZW lossless coding as well as a recently developed asymptotically lossless distributed source coding technique.

## 1 Introduction

Consider a wireless encoding device, which transmits highly correlated data or images to a decoder. Conventional coding architectures, with computationally complex encoder and relatively simple decoder, are not suitable as power and memory are scarce at the encoder. Although distributed source coding refers to the compression of correlated sources which are not co-located, the similar techniques can be used to compress correlated as well as co-located data or images with a shift of computational complexity from the encoder to the decoder [1]–[3].

A mathematical model addressing this problem was first proposed in [1] based on the three decade old distributed source coding theories developed by Slepian and Wolf [4] for lossless compression, which was later extended for lossy compression by Wyner and Ziv [5]. This radical idea divides the source data space into a finite number of cosets [6], using channel coding techniques, where the distance among the elements of each coset is maintained greater than twice of the correlation noise in the data set. Compression of this technique stems from transmitting only the coset index instead of the actual value. The decoder is then able to extract the actual value from the given coset as long as some from of *side information* is already available at the decoder such that distance between the actual value and the side information is less than half of the distance among the elements in the coset. Considering the fact that consecutive video frames have very high temporal correlation, this mathematical model was then applied for video coding in [2] using *trellis codes* [7]. However, the proposed codec lacks sufficient details for any practical implementation. Since then a number of lossy video codecs have been proposed within the distributed source coding paradigm. Pixel-domain and transform-domain codecs using *turbo codes* were proposed in [8]–[10] and [11], [12] respectively. But these codecs assume feedback from the decoder to the encoder and ideal detection of error at the decoder, neither of which is practical. The former precludes broadcast model of video transmission; while the latter leaves very little room for decoding. Moreover, none of the existing distributed video coding system is lossless. If the side information is not close enough to the original data the decoder fails to give exact output. Besides, use of any transforms at the encoding side inherently renders the system to be lossy.

Lossless compression of correlated images can find its application in the transmission of medical images where a sensor is used to monitor a patient's condition. Although there is high temporal correlation among the successive images transmitted by any monitoring device, existing lossless compression techniques exploits only spatial correlation. For the compression of correlated images, distributed source coding technique was first used in [13]. The system assumes that gray levels of the co-located pixels in correlated images differ by at most some fixed value and thus coset construction is done by modulo encoding rather than using any channel coding technique. This practice however cannot perform well when the correlation is non-uniform. The idea was later extended in [14] by applying turbo coding on modulo encoded gray level values. This work assumed an upper bound of $10^{-6}$ symbol error rate and thus can be considered lossless only asymptotically.

In this paper we present for the first time a truly lossless codec for correlated image or data sequence within the distributed source coding paradigm. The proposed scheme operates in pixel domain to avoid any lossy transform and uses trellis code to generate coset index to exploit inter-frame temporal correlation. In order to keep the complexity of the encoder low, this scheme does not take any advantage from intra-frame spatial correlation. Experimental results showed that the compression ratio of the proposed scheme increases exponentially with the inter-frame correlation. The proposed scheme also consistently outperformed the scheme in [14].

The rest of the paper is organized as follows. Section 2 presents the preliminary informatic results and the concept of syndrome (coset index) coding that form the basis of distributed source coding. The proposed lossless codec is detailed in Section 3. Simulation results and comparison with other compression schemes are presented in Section 4. Section 5 concludes the paper.

## 2 Preliminaries

Consider the communication system in Fig. 1 where $X$ and $Y$ are correlated discrete-alphabet memoryless sources. If $Y$ were known both at the encoder and the decoder, one can compress $X$ at the theoretical rate of its conditional entropy given $Y$, $H(X|Y)$ (see Fig. 1(a)). But surprisingly enough Slepian and Wolf [4] theoretically showed that by just knowing the joint distribution of $X$ and $Y$ one can compress $X$ at the same rate in certain cases, even if $Y$ is not known at the encoder (see Fig. 1(b)) [3]. Any practical realization of this theory would lead to a new paradigm of low-complexity video encoders that can be used on devices with limited power and memory. However, the joint distribution of $X$ and $Y$ for any practical problem e.g., image sequence coding, is impossible to model. As a compromise, Puri and Ramchandran [2] and Girod et al. [8] independently developed lossy distributed video coding techniques using channel coding concepts. Although $Y$ is assumed available at the encoder, these techniques do not allow full exploitation of the correlation between $X$ and $Y$ using computationally expensive operations, such as motion search (see Fig. 1(c)).

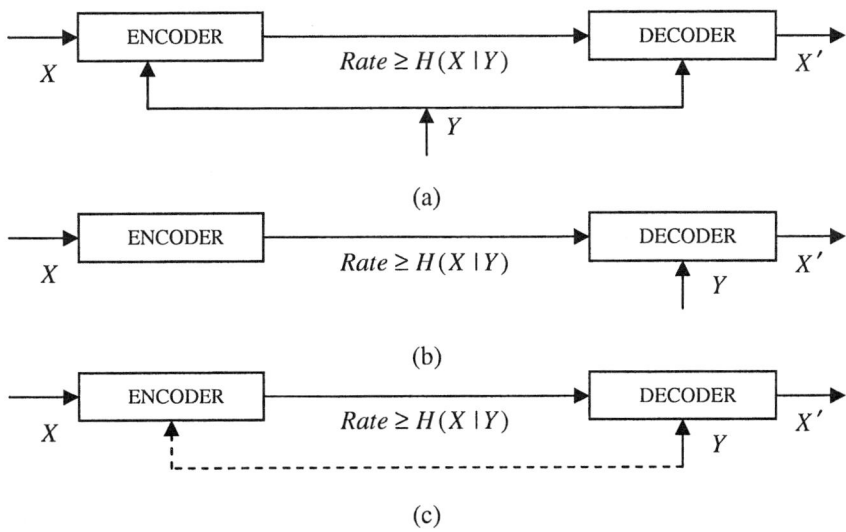

**Fig. 1.** Communication system: the decoder has full access to the side information while the encoder has (a) full access; (b) no access; and (c) minimal access to the side information

The main idea of distributed source coding in [3] is as follows. Let $\mathbf{H}$ be the parity check matrix of a systematic binary linear block code $C(n,k,d)$, where $n$ is the code length, $k$ is the massage length, and $d$ is the minimum Hamming distance of the code. It may be noted that $C$ is a $k$ dimensional subspace of the $n$ dimensional vector space $\{0,1\}^n$ and hence, it induces a partition of the $n$ dimensional space into $2^{n-k}$ cosets each containing $2^k$ codewords of length $n$. In each coset the Hamming distance property of $C$ is preserved. The $i$-th coset of $C$ is associated with a unique index of length $(n-k)$, known as the syndrome $\mathbf{s}_i = \mathbf{c}_{i,j}\mathbf{H}^T$, where $\mathbf{c}_{i,j}$ is the $j$-th codeword of this coset for all $j$ and $i$. Obviously the coset with syndrome $\mathbf{0}$ is the code itself. In compressing an $n$ bit sequence $X$ with correlated side information $Y$ available at the decoder, $X$ is mapped into the $(n-k)$ syndrome bits associated with the coset containing $X$. Upon receiving this syndrome, the decoder decodes $X$ in the corresponding coset by choosing the codeword $X'$ closest to $Y$ in Hamming distance. Thus the compression ratio achieved with this scheme is $n:n-k$. If $Y$ is at a

Hamming distance less than or equal to $\lfloor (d-1)/2 \rfloor$ from $X$, clearly $X' = X$, which is the basis of the lossless compression scheme developed in the next section.

## 3 An Asymmetric Lossless Compression Scheme

The compression scheme presented in this paper is based on the concept of syndrome coding and syndrome decoding using trellis code similar to the technique in [3].

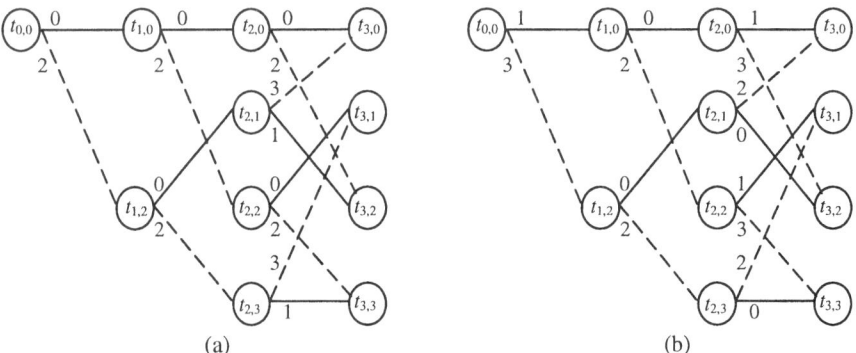

**Fig. 2.** (a) The principal trellis $T_0$ and (b) the trellis $T_i$ with the syndrome $\mathbf{s}_i = [101]$ of a rate ½ memory 2 trellis code having 3 stages where solid and dashed lines distinguish inputs 0 and 1 respectively. The coset associated with trellis $T_i$ has four codeword pairs [101] & [302], [121] & [322], [103] & [300], and [123] & [320] having final state $t_{3,0}$, $t_{3,1}$, $t_{3,2}$, and $t_{3,3}$ respectively.

*Syndrome Coding*: Consider rate $(r-1)/r$, memory $v$, one dimensional, systematic, and distance invariant trellis codes having $L$ stages. Let $\nabla = \{0,1,...,2^r - 1\}$ be the set of all unsigned integers of bit length $r$, which is partitioned into $\nabla_1 = \{0,2,...,2^r - 2\}$ and $\nabla_2 = \{1,3,...,2^r - 1\}$ keeping the minimum Euclidian distance between any two elements in each partition as large as possible. Stage $j = 0,1,...,L$ of the principal trellis has $u_j = \min(2^{(r-1)j}, 2^v)$ nodes, $t_j = \{t_{j,0},...,t_{j,u_j-1}\}$. Each node of all but stage $L$ has $2^{(r-1)}$ labeled branches to the nodes in the next stage with all the labels taken from either $\nabla_1$ or $\nabla_2$. Each of the abovementioned trellis code is a subspace of $\nabla^L$. Altogether there are $2^L$ distinct trellises (cosets) each containing $2^{(r-1)L}$ codewords. A codeword is an ordered sequence of branch labels corresponding to a path from node $t_{o,o}$ to a node in $t_L$ (see Fig. 2). Note that $rL$ and $(r-1)L$ correspond to $n$ and $k$ respectively of the previous section.

Let the trellis associated with $i$-th coset be $T_i$ and the label of the branch (if exists) between nodes $t_{j,a}$ and $t_{j+1,b}$ be $l_i(t_{j,a}, t_{j+1,b})$. Each trellis $T_i$ is associated with a unique syndrome $\mathbf{s}_i \in \{0,1\}^L$ and without any loss of generality, $T_0$ denotes the trellis with syndrome **0**. For a given $rL$-bit codeword $\mathbf{x} = (x_0, x_1, ..., x_{L-1})$ in $T_i$ (say), the $L$-bit syndrome $\mathbf{s}_i$ is obtained by algorithm ENCODE in Fig. 3. It may be noted that for lossless compression it is also necessary to send the final state $f \in t_L$ along with the syndrome, which will be explained later in this section, leading to a compression ratio of $r : (1 + v/L) \approx r : 1$ for $L \gg v$.

Algorithm $(\mathbf{s}_i, f) = \text{ENCODE}(T_0, \mathbf{x})$
$f \leftarrow 0$;
FOR $j = 0, 1, ..., L-1$
  IF $\exists b : l_0(t_{j,f}, t_{j+1,b}) = x_j$ THEN
    $s_{i,j} \leftarrow 0$;
  ELSE
    $\exists b : l_0(t_{j,f}, t_{j+1,b}) \oplus 1 = x_j$;
    $s_{i,j} \leftarrow 1$;
    $f \leftarrow b$;

Algorithm $\mathbf{x}' = \text{DECODE}(T_0, \mathbf{s}_i, \mathbf{y}, f)$
$T_i \leftarrow \text{TRELLIS}(T_0, \mathbf{s}_i)$;
$\mathbf{x}' \leftarrow \text{VITERBI}(T_i, \mathbf{y}, f)$;

Algorithm $T_i = \text{TRELLIS}(T_0, \mathbf{s}_i)$
FOR $j = 0, 1, ..., L-1$
  $\forall a \forall b : l_i(t_{j,a}, t_{j+1,b}) \leftarrow$
    $l_0(t_{j,a}, t_{j+1,b}) \oplus s_{i,j}$;

**Fig. 3.** The encoding and decoding algorithms

*Syndrome Decoding*: It is assumed that the decoder has a side information codeword $\mathbf{y} = (y_0, y_1, ..., y_{L-1})$, which is correlated to $\mathbf{x}$. Once the syndrome $\mathbf{s}_i$ and the final state $f$ are received, the encoded codeword is retrieved using algorithm DECODE in Fig. 3 as follows: first the corresponding trellis $T_i$ is generated using algorithm TRELLIS. This trellis is then used in the Viterbi algorithm to find the codeword $\mathbf{x}'$, which is closest to $\mathbf{y}$ in Euclidian distance and corresponds to a path terminating at state $f$. The minimum squared distance $d_{free}^2$ of a trellis is defined to be $\min_{\forall \alpha \forall \beta \neq \alpha} \|\alpha - \beta\|^2$ where $\alpha$ and $\beta$ are distinct paths in the trellis having the same initial and final states [6]. If $\mathbf{y}$ is at a Euclidian distance less than or equal to $\lfloor (d_{free}^2 - 1)/2 \rfloor$ from $\mathbf{x}$, clearly $\mathbf{x}' = \mathbf{x}$.

*Lossless CODEC*: The proposed lossless compression scheme for correlated frames of image or data, each treated as a collection of non-overlapping $m \times m$-pixel blocks, employs the abovementioned syndrome encoding and decoding techniques using trellis codes of $m^2$ stages. The first frame is transmitted using any conventional lossless coding technique. Each of the remaining frames is transmitted in order as follows. The encoder computes the Euclidian distance between the block to be encoded and the co-located block in the previous frame, used as the side information at the decoder. If the distance is zero, the encoder transmits only the SKIP signal indicating that the block is same as the side information. If the distance is less than or equal to $\lfloor (d_{free}^2 - 1)/2 \rfloor$, the side information is guaranteed to reconstruct the block at the decoder without any loss from the syndrome of the block and the final state of the trellis that are only transmitted. Otherwise, the syndrome coding is discarded in favor of any conventional lossless coding technique due to the poor correlation of the side information.

The decoder always has the lossless previous frame. Whenever it receives the SKIP signal it outputs the co-located block from the previous frame. For the syndrome coded blocks, it takes the co-located block in the previous frame as the side information to reconstruct the block from the received syndrome bits and the final state of the trellis. The conventionally coded blocks are reconstructed accordingly.

## 4 Experimental Results

The proposed scheme was implemented in MATLAB where the syndrome coding used a memory 7 rate 3/4 trellis code with natural mapping into one dimension. The connector coefficients of the trellis code were set as $h^{(0)} = 277$, $h^{(1)} = 54$, $h^{(2)} = 54$, and $h^{(3)} = 0$ [7]. After considerable experimentation we were convinced that its minimum squared distance, $d_{free}^2 = 16$. Since consecutive video frames have very high temporal correlation, frames from six standard QCIF test video sequences were used in our experiment to represent correlated images. The inter-frame correlation among the frames of standard test sequences *Football, Foreman, Carphone, Mother & Daughter, Miss America*, and *Grandmother* are in order from the lowest to the highest. A rate $(r-1)/r$ trellis code can only be used to compress correlated images having at most $r$-bit gray levels per pixel. As we used a rate 3/4 trellis code, 8-bit gray level frames of the standard test sequences were down sampled to 4-bit gray levels by shifting the 8-bit value of each pixel to the right by 4 bits.

Fig. 4 compares the performance of the proposed lossless distributed source codec against the widely used LZW entropy codec. First twenty frames from each of the six test video sequences were compressed using both the codecs and then compression ratios of the twenty frames were averaged for each of the six sequences. Correlations between successive frames for the video sequences were calculated and the averages were taken as its representative measure of temporal correlation of respective videos. The compression ratio of the proposed codec improved exponentially as the degree of temporal correlation increased in the test video sequences. Despite considering only the intra-frame spatial correlation, the LZW codec also improved compression efficiency with the increase in temporal correlation. This anomaly was primarily due to the down sampling of gray scale frames, which increased spatial correlation as fewer levels were used. As expected, the proposed codec outperformed the entropy codec in terms of compression ratio for the last three standard sequences where the temporal correlation among the frames was significantly high. The gap between the compression ratios widened with the increase in correlation. For the remaining three test sequences with relatively low inter-frame temporal correlation, the entropy codec proved better in compression as the proposed codec could not exploit any spatial correlation.

Fig. 5 depicts the performance of the proposed codec against the lossless LZW codec as well as the asymptotically lossless codec developed in [14] by compressing artificially generated images as used in [14]. Six noisy versions of the first frame of each of the test sequences *Mother & Daughter*, *Miss America*, and *Grandmother* were generated by adding AWGN. These noisy frames were then compressed using the

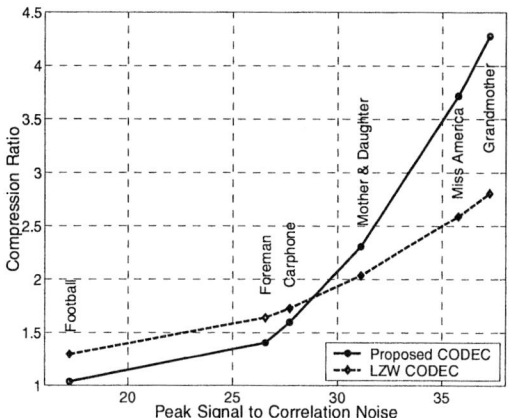

**Fig. 4.** Compression efficiency against the degree of temporal correlation in six standard test video sequences using the proposed and an entropy based codec

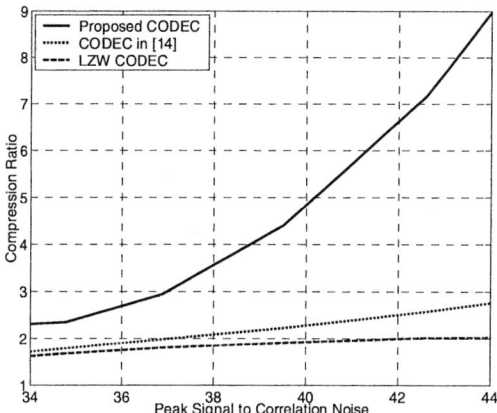

**Fig. 5.** Compression efficiency against the temporal correlation by adding AWGN to standard image frames using the proposed codec, the codec in [14], and an entropy based codec

three codecs with the first frame as the side information. The compression ratios were then averaged for the three sequences. The superiority of the proposed codec was revealed as the compression ratio obtained increased exponentially with the degree of temporal correlation; while the same obtained by the other two codecs increased linearly.

## 5 Conclusions

A lossless coding technique to compress correlated images or data under the distributed source coding paradigm has been presented in this paper. Simulation results showed that compression ratio as high as 4.25:1 was achieved for certain video sequences. The encoder is computationally very simple using only integer operations. On the other hand the decoder is comparatively complex than the encoder due to its reliance on the Viterbi decoding. However, the proposed technique exploits only temporal correlation, and our future work aims to exploit both temporal and spatial correlation under the distributed source coding paradigm.

## References

1. Pradhan, S. S., Ramchandran, K.: Distributed source coding using syndromes (DISCUS): Design and construction. In Proc. IEEE DCC (1999) 158–167.
2. Puri, R., Ramchandran, K.: PRISM: A new robust video coding architecture based on distributed compression principles. In Proc. ACCCC (2002).
3. Pradhan, S. S., Ramchandran, K.: Distributed source coding using syndromes (DISCUS): Design and construction. IEEE Trans. on Info. Theory, Vol. 49, No. 3 (2003) 626–643.
4. Slepian, J. D., Wolf, J. K.: Noiseless coding of correlated information sources. IEEE Transactions on Information Theory, Vol. IT-19 (1973) 471–480.
5. Wyner, A. D., Ziv, J.: The rate-distortion function for source coding with side information at the decoder. IEEE Trans. on Information Theory, Vol. IT-22, No. 1 (1976) 1–10.
6. Forney, G. D.: Coset Codes-Part I: Introduction and Geometrical Classifcation. IEEE Transactions on Information Theory, Vol. 34 (1988) 1123–1151.
7. Schlegel, C. B., Perez, L. C.: Trellis and Turbo Coding. Wiley-IEEE Press, 2004.
8. Girod, B., Aaron, A., Rane, S., Monedero, D. R.: Distributed Video Coding. In Proc. IEEE Vol. 93, Issue 1 (2005) 71–83.
9. Aaron, A., Setton, E., Girod, B.: Towards practical Wyner-Ziv coding of video. In Proc. ICIP (2003).
10. Aaron, A., Zhang, R., Girod, B.: Wyner-Ziv coding of motion video. In Proc. Asilomar Conference on Signals and Systems (2002).
11. Aaron, A., Rane, S., Setton, E., Girod, B.: Transform-domain Wyner-Ziv codec for video. In Proc. VCIP (2004).
12. Aaron, A., Rane, S., Girod, B.: Wyner-Ziv coding with hash-based motion compensation at the receiver. In Proc. ICIP (2004).
13. Ozonat, K.: Lossless distributed source coding for highly correlated still images. Tech. Rep. Electrical Eng. Dept. Stanford University (2000).
14. Liveris, A., Xiong, Z., Georgihades, C.: A Distributed Source Coding Technique for Highly Correlated Images Using Turbo Codes. In Proc. ICASSP (2002).

# Automatically Detecting Symmetries in Decorative Tiles

Rafael Dueire Lins and Daniel Marques Oliveira

Universidade Federal de Pernambuco, Recife - PE, Brazil
rdl@ufpe.br, dmo@cin.ufpe.br

**Abstract.** Symmetry information is used as the basis of a compression algorithm for images of decorative tiles yielding a compact representation. This allows faster network transmission and less space for storage of tile images. This paper presents an algorithm capable of automatically detecting the patterns of symmetry of images of tiles. The methodology developed may apply to any sort of repetitive symmetrical colour images and drawings.

**Keywords:** Image compression, web pages, ceramic tiles.

## 1 Introduction

Searching the Internet, one finds several hundred sites related to ceramic tiles all over the world. Those sites range from virtual museums to manufacturer catalogues. "The decorative tile - azulejo in Portuguese (the word comes from the Arabic *az Zulayj*, "burnished stone") – was considered a fine element of decoration by all ancient civilizations. Persia was the centre for development of almost all the tile-producing techniques used in Europe and was probably also the birthplace of the azulejo. The Arabs took it from their lands in the East to Italy and Spain." [4]. From Europe tiles spread worldwide, being one of the most important finishing and decorative points in architectural design today, overall in warm weather countries.

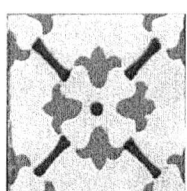  

**Fig. 1.** Portuguese, 14x14 cm  **Fig. 2.** One-eight of Tile 1  **Fig. 3.** Transf. image
Size: 97kB (JPEG)                Size: 15kB (JPEG)              Size: 15kB (JPEG)

Tiles are seldom used in isolation. In general, they form panels applied to floors and walls. Since their very beginning, until today, the motifs are geometric figures with well-defined contours, painted in solid colours. Very rarely a ceramic tile exhibits more than four or five colours.

In a recent paper [16], Lins proposes a taxonomy and file format for tiles, based on the symmetry of their geometrical patterns. This minimises their drawing information and store them in a very efficient way. The pattern images are compressed and stored using formats such as JPEG [18][19] [26] or TIFF [18]. Figure 1 presents an example of a beautiful Portuguese tile whose pattern can be rebuilt from the "seed" exhibited on Figure 2 or more regularly presented on the rectangle of Figure 3. The original image was obtained by scanning a colour photograph from [4] with a flatbed scanner manufactured by Hewlett Packard, model ScanJet 5300, in true-colour 300 dpi. The total number of colours in the image of Figure 1 is around 60,000. Notice that all relevant information such as texture, predominant colours, etc. is still in the reduced image. The original size of tile 01 under JPEG compression is 97kB, while its seed is only 15kB under JPEG. Whenever the visualisation of files is needed, applets are loaded to assemble the original tile image from its components. Today, these applets work with compression algorithms only. However, there is work on progress to make them with progressive file formats, saving time in the transmission of these images through networks. In general, the progressive algorithms split up the original image into different "resolution layers". Additional control information is used to reassemble the layers forming the original image. The increase in size observed in the progressive versions of GIF [18][19] and PNG [18] file formats was of less than 5% of the size without such facility, largely justifying their use. Surprisingly enough was the behaviour presented by JPEG, whose size of progressive compression schemes reached 10% less than the size of plain JPEG compression [15]. The only drawback of such algorithms is the larger computational effort involved in processing the image for its decomposition, which may involve several scans of the original image. As processing time is by far smaller than network transmission the use of progressive algorithms is largely recommended for images visualised through a network.

This paper shows how to automatically detect symmetry patterns in images of ceramic tiles. The algorithm presented may be easily adapted to any other sort of repetitive symmetrical colour images and drawings.

## 2 Detecting Symmetries

Completely asymmetrical patterns are seldom found in decorative tiles, being more common in large wall tile panels with religious motifs. In that case, little can be done in a systematic way to compress images based on geometry. This section analyses the patterns of the tiles presented which show some sort of geometrical symmetry. Symmetry detection has been reported as part of several pattern recognition schemes and even image segmentation strategies. However, it is important to stress that reference [16] reports for the first time in the literature symmetry detection as the basis for an image compression scheme.

Early studies in geometry and theoretical mathematics addressed the evaluation of symmetry of convex sets [9]. These studies approach symmetry evaluation from the theoretical point of view and no method has been suggested to efficiently evaluate those measures. The transformation of the symmetry detection problem to a pattern matching problem introduces efficient algorithms for detection of mirror and rotational symmetries and location of symmetry axis [13][7][11][1][27]. These algorithms assume noise free input and detect symmetry, if it exists, in collections of features such as points and line segments. Any minor perturbation of the input yields a wrong result in symmetry detection. However, upper bounds on the complexity of symmetry detection with limited error tolerance are reported in reference [1].

Symmetry in 2D can be discussed either as a *global* or *local* feature [31]. In the case of global symmetry all points in the image contribute to determining the symmetry. On the other hand, in the case of local symmetry every symmetry element is supported locally by some subset of the object, i.e. by smaller parts of the image. Globally symmetric methods are much more efficient at run time. They usually have a linear time complexity. However, they are generally sensitive to noise and occlusion. Local symmetry methods are more robust to noise and occlusion, are easily parallelizable, but also exhibit a high time complexity.

Detection of 2D symmetry in digital images follows four different approaches. The first approach, also known as the *direct* approach, has as general principle to apply the symmetry transformation (i.e. reflection or rotation) to the image and then compare it to the original image [25][13][6][12]. These methods assume that an object is either perfectly symmetric or it is completely non-symmetrical. Thus, they are highly sensitive to noise and occlusion. Kuehnle [13] follows this strategy to make comparisons of an image and its reflection for detection of vehicles, however.

The second approach uses a voting scheme. It is based on the fact that the symmetry axis or point of rotation is determined by two points in the object. Pairs of points are tested and vote for their preferred symmetry axis. The oriented line with highest vote is selected [22][21][14][23][24][20][31] as the symmetry axis. These voting schemes are complex, thus several methods have been suggested to reduce complexity by grouping points into regions or into curve segments. This strategy reduces the possible number of voting pairs. Voting schemes are robust under noise and occlusion in the input image and generally approach symmetry as a binary feature, where thresholding is performed to overcome noise in the input.

The third approach [29][30][31] introduces the notion of a continuous measure, the symmetry distance. This approach is an evolution of the idea of *Measure of Chirality*, a measure of deviation from mirror-symmetry, described in references [3][8][10]. This approach produces the "degree" of symmetry of the image in relation to a given axis, instead of a "yes" or "no" response to symmetry.

Finally, the most recent approach to symmetry detection is presented by Manmatha and Sawhney in reference [17]. They approach symmetry detection as an aid to identify the significant structure of images. Gaussians and their derivatives at multiple scales are used to find symmetry axis.

## 3 A New Algorithm

The new algorithm presented herein merges some of the elements of the first and third approaches presented in the previous section in a completely novel way. From the direct method it borrows the idea of trying to compare pixel to pixel parts from the overlapped image. The third method contributes with the notion that symmetry is not a binary feature, but that it is a continuous measure. However, instead of seeing the absence of symmetry as a *shape distortion function*, symmetry is detected by analysing pixel to pixel *distance in the colour space*. Thus, the algorithm produces a measure of how *different* colours of pixels are. Although the scheme presented herein is tuned to work with images of ceramic tiles, there is no intrinsic reason why it could not work to detect symmetries in other kinds of images, such as textiles, papers, etc. Images to be studied and classified have well defined symmetric patterns. Their direct size compression for the raster image is shown on column to the right. The tile presented in Figure 01 exhibits a symmetry pattern of type horizontal-vertical-left-right-diagonal, thus its seed has only one-eighth of the image original size. Some 19th century French tiles presented in reference [4] exhibit a higher degree of symmetry and a seed of only 1/32 of its original size would be enough for the generation of the original pattern. Its symmetry pattern is obtained by recursively applying the detection algorithm. It is worth observing that the higher the degree of symmetry the higher the gains in the compressed image [16]. Ceramic tiles may make symmetry detection easier than some other applications:

- ❖ Images have simple geometrical motifs.
- ❖ Tiles tend to use few colours.
- ❖ Tiles have standard sizes, in general.
- ❖ The axis of symmetry of tiles tends to correspond to the symmetry axis of the tile image or is deviated of a few pixels.

**Removing Borders**

A careful look at the image of the tile presented in Figure 01 shows that on the left side the image presents some "stains". This sort of problem is common whenever dealing with images of historical tiles, such as the ones in [4]. Those stains were introduced by time, inappropriate conservation, excess of plaster when the tile was set, etc. They are not part of the tile "information" as such and can be seen as "noise" added to the image. Thus it must be filtered out before the symmetry detection process starts. Cropping an area of about 80% of the original image not only avoids the border noise but also increase the efficiency of the algorithm, as a smaller number of points is analysed. Figure 4 shows the selected area for analysis from the tile presented in Figure 1. One may observe no border noise present in the selected area. For a matter of simplicity one assumes that the pattern of interest is at the centre of original image (small deviations from the centre cause no problem to symmetry detection).

**Fig. 4.** Work area

**Image Segmentation**

The analysis of symmetry proposed herein checks the number of pixels that coincide under transformation and makes some statistics on them. However, not all pixels carry the same "degree of information". Pixels from the background "cluster" need to be recognised and dealt with in a proper manner. Figure 5 presents the image of a non-symmetric tile where the number of background pixels by far exceeds the number of "information pixels" (in blue). Any symmetry detection scheme that simply counts the number of "coincident" pixels would wrongly conclude that there is a vertical symmetry in the image. Thus, a segmentation strategy is introduced: the first step of the algorithm is to find the colour pixel distribution. In general, colour pixel distribution form a multi-modal gaussian distribution centred on the background and each of the "important" colour in the image. The image of the non-symmetric tile exhibited in Figure 5 has 22K colours and its histogram is presented in Figure 6, where one can observe a bi-modal (two-cluster) distribution with predominance to the right of the gaussians that form the image background. In reality the number of background pixels "distorts" the histogram and does not allow one to see that the colour pixel distribution is tri-modal with centre in "white", orange and dark blue.

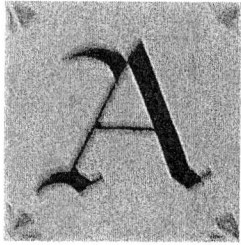 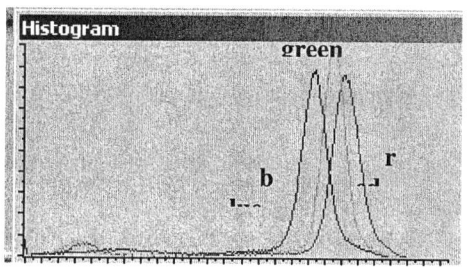

**Fig. 5.** Tile 02, Portuguese tile        **Fig. 6.** Colour histogram of tile 02

The segmentation using the most frequent colour as threshold may lead to errors. There may be a large number of hues in the background and a colour of an information pixel may surpass in absolute value the frequency of background colours. The background colour is calculated by taking the colour frequency distribution and applying a cluster variation to each of them and re-calculating the number of members of the colour "cluster". The cluster with the largest number of members is taken as the most frequent background colour. This part of the segmentation algorithm may be implemented in two steps. In the first one a table is formed while scanning the image. For each pixel read all entries on the table that correspond to the colour and variation of the pixel are incremented. The background cluster corresponds to the entry on the table with the largest value. The cluster variation of ±2 for each RGB component was found adequate for our purposes. All pixels whose colours belong to the sphere centred on the background cluster with radius (tolerance) $t$ are mapped onto white. Otherwise, the pixel has its colour changed into black. The experiments performed pointed at a value of tolerance $t=40$. Figure 07 shows the image of tile 01 with the left-hand side of the analysis area shown with background pixels in white and information pixels in black. In reality, the whole image is segmented.

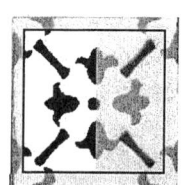

**Fig. 7.** Segmented

## Symmetry Statistics

The segmented image and the original image are both used in the statistics performed to detect the existing pattern of symmetry in images. Four patterns of symmetry depicted on Figure 08 are analyzed to start with. Each pattern splits the image in two regions: *origin* and *target*.

**Fig. 8.** Patterns of Symmetry

Each region is split into four sub-regions of equal sizes, corresponding to a different colour in each pattern of Figure 8. Seven parameters are measured: **i** – the number of information pixels in the segmented image (si); **b** – the number of background pixels in the segmented image (si); **ii** – the number of matching information pixels at origin and target sub-regions in si; **bb** – the number of matching background pixels at origin and target sub-regions in si; **bi** – the number of background pixels mapped onto information pixels in the sub-region of si; **ib** – the number of information pixels mapped onto background pixels in the sub-region of si; **dif_ii** – the sum of the squares of the RGB-component distance of the pixels in **ii** of the non-segmented (original) image.

The parameter *ldii* calculated as presented on Table 02 is a variant of the calculus of Peak-Signal-to-Noise-Ratio (PSNR). The PSNR provides a measure of the quality of the generated image. The higher the PSNR the "better-quality" the generated image is. The following formula is the most common way of calculating it:

$$PSNR = 20\log_{10} \frac{255}{\sqrt{\frac{\sum [f(i,j) - F(i,j)]^2}{N \times M}}}$$

$f(i, j)$ - value of pixel $(i,j)$ in original image.
$F(i,j)$ - value of pixel $(i,j)$ in "noisy" image
$N$ and $M$ are the number of columns and lines in original image.

**Table 2.** Statistical Parameters of Tile Symmetry

| Description | Formula | Description | Formula |
|---|---|---|---|
| % Matching Background for each sub-region in the origin. | $pbb = \frac{bb}{bb+bi}$ | Information Deviation of the whole image. | $Id = \frac{\|2*(ii+ib) - i\|}{2*(ii+ib)}$ |
| % Mismatching Background Pixels for each sub-region. | $pmn = \frac{ib+bi}{(ib+bi+bb)}$ | Background Deviation of the whole image. | $Bd = \frac{\|2*(bb+bi) - b\|}{2*(bb+bi)}$ |
| Mean distance in the color space between the pixels of information | $ldii = 10\log\left(\frac{dif\_ii}{ii^2}\right)$ | % Matching Info for each sub-region in the origin. | $pii = \frac{ii}{ii+ib}$ |

The parameters presented on Table 01 feed the algorithm presented for testing the existence of the pattern of symmetry in the image. The adjustment parameters, empirically found for each pattern are presented on Table 2.

**Algorithm for Symmetry Detection**

```
COUNT = 0;
FOR EACH sub-region DO
    IF (tol_Pbb < pbb) COUNT += kbb;
    IF (tol_Pii < pii) COUNT += kii;
    IF (tol_Pmn > pmn) COUNT += kmn;
    IF (tol_Pldii > ldii) COUNT += kldii;
    IF (tol_Id > Id) COUNT += kId;
    IF (tol_Bd > Bd) COUNT += kBd;
    IF (COUNT > Correct) then SYMMETRIC;
```

**Table 3.** Statistical Parameters

| Parameter | HVSymm. | D Symm. |
|---|---|---|
| Correct | 28 | 32 |
| tol_pii | 80 | 64 |
| tol_Id | 2 | 0 |
| tol_pbb | 88 | 70 |
| tol_Bd | 2 | 2 |
| tol_pnm | 0 | 0 |
| ldii | 8 | 4 |
| kpii | 2 | 4 |
| kpip | 3 | 4 |
| kpbb | 2 | 3 |
| kBd | 2 | 1 |
| kpnm | 1 | 2 |
| kldii | 4 | 3 |

The algorithm as presented above is able to detect the highest level of symmetry in tile images. If any symmetry pattern is found the algorithm should be applied recursively until no further symmetry is detected.

## 4 Results Obtained

The algorithm presented without recursion was tested on a group of images of 187 tiles. The number of images that had their highest-level symmetry correctly detected was of 133, 71.13% of the images tested. There were only 6 false-positive results, meaning that in 3.2% of the tested images there was symmetry detected where there was none. On the other hand, 48 images produced false-negative results, i.e. in 25.6% of the tested images there was undetected symmetrical patterns. The results presented are very conservative as the images tested presented a fair degree of complexity to verify the robustness of the algorithm. In general terms, whenever there was symmetry it was detected by the algorithm. However, as explained below, some images present an almost symmetric pattern that is difficult to detect as non-symmetric, even by humans.

## 5 Algorithm Limitations

The parameters presented on Table 3 were set to provide conservative results and making the number of false-positive results minimal. The beautiful Turkish tiles presented in Figure 9 are responsible for three of the six false positive results obtained for the batch of 187 tiles tested. One must admit that the degree of complexity of the first and second tiles is so high that even humans have difficulty is realizing that they are not symmetrical.

Fig. 9. Non-symmetric Turkish tiles

## 6 Conclusions

Symmetry information may be used to make network transmission and storage of images more efficient. Automatic symmetry detection is far from being a simple problem. Several researchers have attempted different ways with relative success. This paper presents a new algorithm to find symmetries in images of ceramic tiles based on statistical analysis of images. The same approach may also be used in other materials such as textiles and carpets due to the similarity of their print. Modern tiles are produced by machines and pattern variation is minimal, thus making easier automatic recognition of the symmetry pattern. On the other hand, historical tiles were hand made and patterns vary not only between pieces, but also within each piece. Criteria are being developed for better automatic pattern classification.

As already mentioned, the images presented herein were obtained by scanning the most beautiful tile images presented in reference [4] and from the Internet. This process, however presents the drawback of providing non-uniform final image resolution as the images presented in [4] vary in size. Thus, it is under consideration to obtain new images by direct digitally photographing those historical tiles, having the pioneer work of the late researcher António Menezes e Cruz extended by Silvia Tigre Cavalcanti, reported in reference [4] as a guidebook. One fundamental issue is also being addressed: what is the appropriate (minimal) resolution images should have in order to provide enough details to observe the beauty of the tiles at the lowest storage and network transmission costs.

## Acknowledgements

The research reported herein was partly sponsored by CNPq-Conselho Nacional de Desenvolvimento Científico e Tecnológico of the Brazilian Government, to whom the authors express their gratitude.

## References

[1] H.Alt, et al.Congruence, similarity and symmetries of geometric objects. ACM J.Comp., 4:308-315, 1987.
[2] M.Atallah. On symmetry detection. IEEE Transactions on Computers, 34(7):663-666, 1985.
[3] D.Avnir and A.Y.Meyer. Quantifying the degree of molecular shape deformation: a chirality measure. J. Molecular Structure (Theochem), 94:211-222, 1991.

[4] S.Cavalcanti and A.Menezes e Cruz. Tiles in the Secular Architecture of Pernambuco, 19th Century, Metalivros, 2002.
[5] M.Berger, Computer Graphics with Pascal. Addison-Wesley, 1986.
[6] F.W.Burton, J.G.Kollins, and N.A.Alexandridis. An implementation of the exponential pyramid data structure with applications etc. Computer Vision, Graphics, and I.Processing, 25:218-225, 1984.
[7] P.Eades. Symmetry finding algorithms, Computational Morphology, pp 41-51, Elsevier, 1988.
[8] G.Gilat. Chiral coefficient – a measure of the amount of structural chirality. J.Ph. A: 22:545-545, 1989.
[9] B.Grunbaum. Measures of symmetry for convex sets. Symp. P.Math: A.Math.Soc, 7:233-270, 1963.
[10] Y.Hel_Or, S.Peleg, and D.Avnir. Chararcterization of right handed and left handed shapes. Computer Vision, Graphics, and Image Processing, 53(2), 1991.
[11] P.T.Highnam. Optimal algorithms for finding the symmetries etc. Inf.Proc.Lett, 22:219-222, 1986.
[12] J.L.Krahe. Detection of symmetric and radial structures in images. In International Conference on Pattern Recognition, pp. 947-950, 1986.
[13] J.L.Kuehnle. Symmetry-based recognition of vehicle rears. Patt. Recognition Letters, 12: 249—258, 1991.
[14] T.S.Levitt. Domain independent object description and decomposition, in Proceedings American Association of Artificial Intelligence, pp. 207-211, 1984.
[15] R.D.Lins and D.S.A.Machado, A Comparative Study of File Formats for Image Storage and Transmission, vol. 13(1), pp 175-183, 2004, Journal of Electronic Imaging, Jan/2004.
[16] R.D.Lins, A New File Format for Decorative Tiles, LNCS 3211:175-182, Springer Verlag, Sep 2004.
[17] R.Manmatha and H.S.Sawhney. Finding Symmetry in Intensity Images, IBM Tech. Rep., Almaden, 1995.
[18] J.Miano. Compressed Image File Formats: JPEG, PNG, GIF, XBM, BMP. Addison Wesley, 1999.
[19] J.D.Murray, D.James and W. vanRyper. Encyclopedia of Graphics File Formats. O'Reilly, 1996.
[20] R.Nevatia and T.O.Binford. Description and recognition complex curved obj. Art.Intell, 8:77-98, 1977.
[21] H.Ogawa. Symmetry analysis of line drawings etc.. Patt. Recog. Letters, 12: 9-12, 1991.
[22] S.K.Parui and D.D.Majumder. Symmetry analysis by computer. Patt. Recog., 16:63-67, 1983.
[23] J.Ponce. On characterising ribbons and finding skewed symmet. C.Vision, G. I.Proc, 52:328-340, 1990.
[24] S.Posch. Detecting skewed symmetries. Inter. Conf. Patt. Recog., pp. 602-606, August 2002.
[25] A.A.Vasilier. Recognition of symmetrical patterns in images. Int.Conf.Patt.Recog., pp 1138-1140, 1984.
[26] G.K.Wallace. The JPEG Still Picture Compression Standard. CACM(34):31-44, April 1991.
[27] J.Wolter, T.Woo, and R.Volz. Optimal algorithms for symmetry detection in two and three dimensions. The Visual Computer, 1:37-48, 1985.

[28] E. Hamilton. JPEG File Interchance Format. V 1.02, C-Cube Microsystems, September 1992.
[29] H. Zabrodsky, S. Peleg and D. Avnir. A measure of symmetry based on shape similarity. In IEEE Conference on Computer Vision and Pattern Recognition, pp. 703-706, June 1992.
[30] H. Zabrodsky, S. Peleg and D. Avnir. Completion of occluded shapes using symmetry. IEEE Comp. Vision Patt. Recog., pp 678-679, 1993.
[31] H. Zabrodsky, Computational Aspects of Pattern Characterization – Continous Symmetry, PhD Thesis, Hebrew University of Jerusalem, June 1993.
[32] T. Zielke, M. Brauckmann, and W. von Seelen. Intensity and edge-based symmetry detection applied to car-following. In European Conference on Computer Vision, pages 865-873, May 1992.

# A Fast Video Mixing Method for Multiparty Video Conference*

Xin-Gang Liu[1], Kook-Yeol Yoo[1], and Kwang-Deok Seo[2]

[1] Department of Information and Communication Engineering,
University of Yeungnam, South Korea
liuxingang78@yahoo.com.cn, kyoo@yu.ac.kr
[2] Computer and Telecomm. Eng. Division, Yonsei University, South Korea
kdseo@dragon.yonsei.ac.kr

**Abstract.** In this paper, we propose a fast video mixing method for reducing the computational complexity in the MCU (Multipoint Control Unit) used in the video conferencing. The conventional mixing method is based on the pixel-domain transcoder, of which computational complexity is linearly increased as the number of participants is increased. Basically the method requires many decoders and one huge encoder to mix the multiple bitstreams. To reduce the computational complexity, we propose a hybrid mixing method based on the syntax-based bitstream modification and pixel-domain transcoder. The proposed method reduces the computational complexity about 45% at the improved quality, compared with the conventional mixing method based on the pixel-domain transcoder.

## 1 Introduction

With the broad deployment of the Internet, videoconference is now becoming more and more popular nowadays. For the better management of the multiple bitstreams from the participants in the videoconference, the MCU (Multipoint Control Unit) is often used. One of the important functions in the MCU is the mixing of the video bitstreams to distribute the mixed video bitstream to the participants. The computational complexity of the video mixing, however, is drastically increased as the number of participants is increased. For instance, if there are N participants in the video conference, the MCU requires the N video decoders and one video encoder to produce the video bitstream of the mixed video signals. It means that the computational complexity is impractical for the practical application though the MCU in the video conference provides better organization of video conference.

To use the MCU for the practical videoconference system, the reduction of computation-al complexity in the video mixing is critically necessary. In this paper, we propose a hybrid video mixing method based on the syntax-based bitstream modification and pixel-domain transcoding methods. From the analysis in our previous work [4], we showed that the compressed video signals are mixed with the additional header

---

* This work was supported by Yeungnam University Research Grant (000A106113).

description for the reference of the spatial DPCM. The additional header description is used at the boundary of the mixed video signals. For instance, the additional header description of H.263 [1] can be defined with the Annex K. In general, most video decoders in the market used the baseline codec of H.263 for the patents issues and computational complexity. For the reduction of computational complexity in the mixing system, we use the syntax-based modification method for the bitstream corresponding to the left side of the mixed video signals and apply the pixel-domain transcoder for the right-side of the mixed video signals. The simulation results show that the proposed method reduces the computational complexity about 45% at the improved quality, compared with the conventional mixing method based on the pixel-domain transcoders.

This paper is organized as follows: in Section 2, several conventional video mixing techniques are discussed. A proposed hybrid method applied in video mixing will be presented in Section 3. And in Section 4 the experimental results of the proposed method compared with the conventional methods are shown. The conclusions are drawn in Section 5.

## 2 Conventional Video Mixing Methods

There reported several mixing methods for multipoint videoconference. One of the direct techniques is pixel-domain mixing, which uses a transcoder [2, 3]. For instance, let's consider four-party videoconference as shown in Fig. 1. The pixel-domain mixing method is depicted in Fig. 2. Each of the four participants generates a H.263 QCIF bitstream by encoding its own frame sequence. The mixer consists of four cascaded decoders, one pixel mixer and one encoder as shown in Fig.2. Each bitstream is decoded and reconstructed by the transcoder in the mixer. In detail, all of the four reconstructed QCIF video signals are mixed into a CIF video signal in pixel-domain. Following, the encoder in the transcoder re-encodes the new mixed video sequence into a CIF bitstream. The terminal of each participant, decodes the mixed bitstream and displays a CIF video including all of the four QCIF participants in real time.

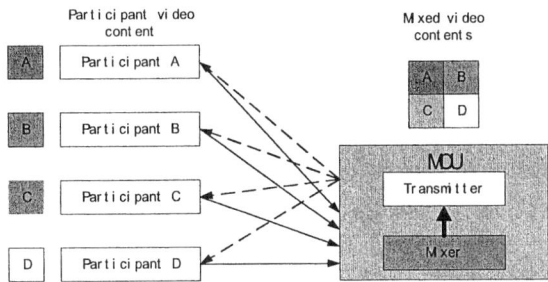

**Fig. 1.** Four-party videoconference

The mixer based on pixel-domain transcoder is more flexible in terms of picture manipulation. However, this method has two major problems. The first is computational complexity. The mixer system should independently decode the bitstreams and the raw video signals are mixed together. And the encoder re-encodes the mixed video signals into a single bitstream. So, four decoders, one encoder and pixel mixer are needed here. It requires large amount of memory and codec capacity. The other drawback in the transcoder is the quality degradation because the mixed video bitstream is a result of double encoding. Further, the re-encoding operation will cause more delay because of the steps of decoding and encoding as shown in Fig.2.

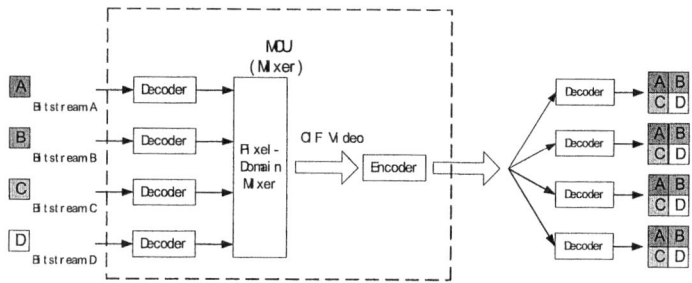

**Fig. 2.** Pixel-domain Transcoder mixing technique

To reduce the computational complexity, we proposed the syntax-based mixing method in [4]. Its basic concept is shown in Fig. 3. This method only need to analyze the bitstream based on syntax of video coding standard and modifies the control information without changing the video signal information in the video bitstream under certain constraints. Because this method uses simple bitstream copy-and-paste operation, it greatly reduces the computational complexity and reduces processing time. Further, it removes the re-encoder step, so the quality of the output signals will be increased compared with the mixer based on pixel-domain transcoder.

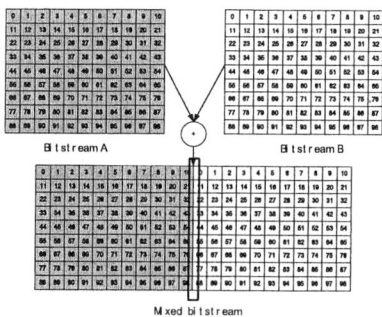

**Fig. 3.** Bitstream-domain mixing system of two bitstream (Horizontal mixing)

In our previous work [4], we assume that the quantization step sizes of all the bitstreams are same. If the change of the quantizer exceeds the bound (-2 to 2) at the boundary of A and B, H.263 baseline codec cannot support the exact description of quantization step size and the incorrect dequantization causes quantization noise drift.

To solve this problem, H.263 Annex K method is used for the description of the quantization step size [4]. In general, most video decoders in the market use the baseline codec of H.263 for the patents issues and computational complexity. For this reason, the constraints on the quantization step sizes should be solved in [4].

In [6, 7], the video mixing method for moving video signals are proposed which investigate the general framework to transcode the video signal. However, the method also requires DCT-domain motion estimation and compensation process. So the reduction of computational complexity is negligible.

## 3 Proposed Hybrid Mixing Technique

From the survey on the conventional methods, the mixing method based on pixel-domain transcoder reduces the quality of videos and also has high complexity of computation. Although the bitstream-domain mixer requires low computation and also has good output quality, the demerit is that the Annex K of H.263 is necessary. It is not realistic for the mixing system because of the popularity of market and additional cost. To solve these problems, we propose a new hybrid video mixing method shown in Fig. 4. Through investigating, we know that bitstream-domain video mixing method is efficient in both complexity and visual quality. But for the bitstream from B and D, we cannot apply the bitstream-domain video mixing method because of the quantization step sizes. Since the sub-pictures from A and C start from the left side of pictures, there is no constraint on the quantization step size. So we use the syntax-based modifications for the bitstreams A and C. and we use the pixel-domain transcoders for the bitstream B and D to solve the constraint on the quantization step size.

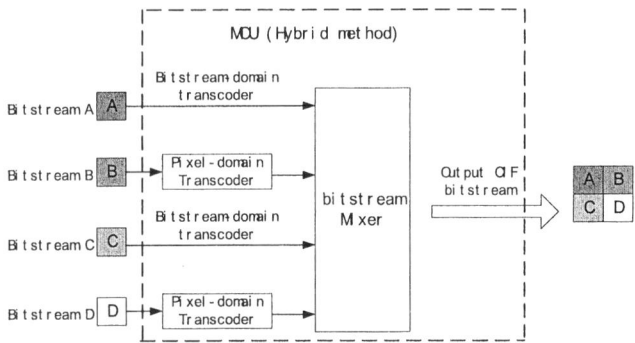

**Fig. 4.** Structure of the proposed hybrid video mixing method

## 4 Simulation Results

For the evaluation of the proposed video mixing method, we perform some simulations, and the simulation environments are given in Table 1.

**Table 1.** Simulation Environments

| Recommendation | Picture Name | Source format | Encoding bit-rate | Frame umber |
|---|---|---|---|---|
| H.263 | A: Forman | QCIF, 176*144 4:2:0, 10kHz | 64kbps | 300 |
| H.263 | B: Akiyo | QCIF, 176*144 4:2:0, 10kHz | 64kbps | 300 |
| H.263 | C: News | QCIF, 176*144 4:2:0, 10kHz | 64kbps | 300 |
| H.263 | D: Silent | QCIF, 176*144 4:2:0, 10kHz | 64kbps | 300 |

### 4.1 Comparison Between Pixel-Domain and Bitstream-Domain Transcoder Method

First we compare the performance between pixel-domain transcoder and syntax-based methods. Four QCIF bitstreams listed in Table 1 are coded by these two methods. The comparisons of PSNR and CPU time for each video comparison are drawn in Fig. 5. The configurations of the simulation computer are: Pentium IV CPU 2.89 GHz, 1.00 GB memory. PSNR comparison shows that the quality of video using pixel-domain transcoder method is reduced due to the re-encoding. Further more, the computational complexity of transcoder is much higher than bitstream-domain method because of its decoding-encoding steps. In Fig.5, CPU time comparison proves that the computation of transcoder method is more complex. This is the reason why we select bitstream-domain mixing method as the main basic idea of the proposed hybrid mixing method.

### 4.2 Performance Comparison of Various Mixing Methods

Then, we do the simulation with two mixing methods: pixel-domain transcoder mixing method and proposed hybrid mixing method. Fig. 6 gives the PSNR comparison of the two video mixing methods. In the proposed method, up-left and down-left parts used syntax-based mixing method and upright and downright parts use pixel-domain transcoder mixing method.

From Fig.6 we can know that the quality of subimages A and C output sub-pictures utilizing proposed hybrid mixing method is better than that those using pixel-domain transcoder method, respectively. On the other hand, the qualities of B and D output sub-pictures are very similar with utilizing pixel-domain transcoder mixing method, respectively. With the same simulation computer, Table 2 shows the CPU times for mixing by the two methods. It means, that the proposed method is more efficient in computational complexity than the pixel-domain transcoder video mixing method, and it reduces the computational complexity about 45%. Further more, although the proposed method is less efficient than the method of syntax-based video mixing proposed in [5], it does not use H.263 Standard Annex K to deal with the problem of DQUANT. For this reason, the proposed method in this paper is more suitable for practical application.

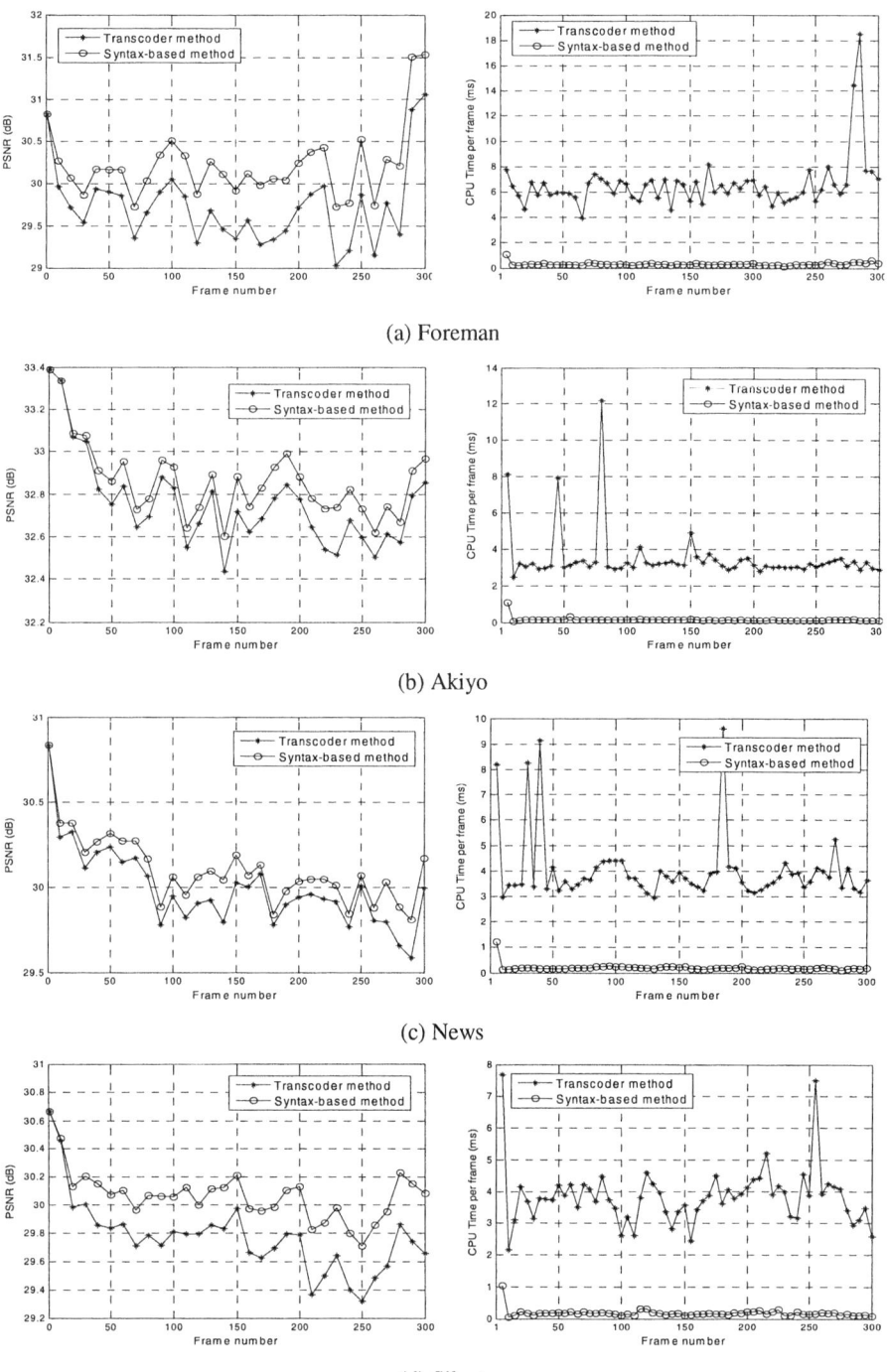

(a) Foreman

(b) Akiyo

(c) News

(d) Silent

**Fig. 5.** Performance comparison in PSNR and CPU time

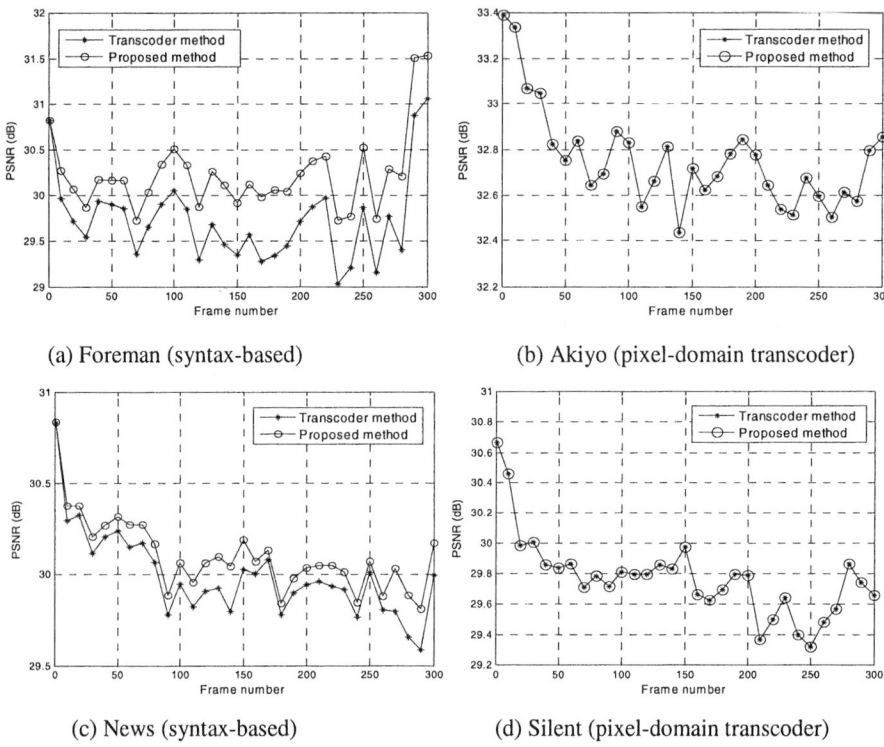

(a) Foreman (syntax-based)　　　(b) Akiyo (pixel-domain transcoder)

(c) News (syntax-based)　　　(d) Silent (pixel-domain transcoder)

**Fig. 6.** PSNR Comparison between proposed and pixel-domain transcoder mixing method

**Table 2.** Simulation time compare

| Method / Compare option | Pixel-domain Transcoder method | Proposed method |
|---|---|---|
| CPU time (Microsecond) | 17.57 | 9.65 |

## 5 Conclusion

In this paper, we propose a new hybrid video mixing method for the videoconference system. From the study of video mixing techniques we know that the conventional video mixing method based on pixel-domain transcoder requires the higher computational complexity: four decoders and on encoder with four times encoding speed and memories. There exists additive delay due to the steps of four-decoder→pixel-domain mixer→one-encoder. And this method also reduces quality of video as a result of double encoding. Although the bitstream-domain mixing method is smart, it requires Annex K of Recommendation H.263 to prevent DQUANT drift error. To reduce the computational complexity, we propose a hybrid mixing method based on the syntax-based bitstream modification and pixel-domain transcoder. The proposed method reduces the computational complexity about 45% at the improved quality, compared with the conventional mixing method based on the pixel-domain transcoders. This new hybrid video mixing method for videoconference improves the efficiency of video mixing. We believe that this video mixing system is valuable for practical implementation such as videoconference system, video chatting and so on.

# References

[1] ITU-T Recommendation H.263, "Video coding for low bit rate communication", Nov. 1995
[2] A. Vetro, C. Christopoulos, and H.Sun, "Video transcoding architecture and techniques: an overview", *IEEE Signal Processing Magazine*, vol. 20, no. 2 pp. 18-29, March 2003
[3] M.Lukacs, "An Advanced digital network video bridge for multipoint with individual customer control," *Bell Commun, Res.*, NJ. May 1992
[4] T.Shanableh and M.Ghanbari, "Transcoding architectures for DCT-domain heterogeneous video transcoding" Proc. Of *IEEE Int'l Conf. of Image Processing*, vol. 1, pp. 433-436, Oct.2001
[5] Kook-yeol, Yoo and Kwang-deok Seo, "Syntax-based mixing method of H.263 coded video bitstreams," Proc. Of *IEEE Int'l Conf. of Consumer Electronics*, p. 9.18, Jan. 2005
[6] Niklas Bjork, Charilaos Christopoulos, "Transcoder architectures for video coding," *IEEE Trans. on Consumer Electronics*, vol. 44, no. 1, pp. 88-98, Feb. 1998
[7] T. Shanableh and M. Ghanbari, "Transcoding architectures for DCT-domain heterogeneous video transcoding" Proc. of *IEEE Int'l Conf. Of Image Processing*, vol, 1, pp. 433-436, Oct. 2001
[8] S. -F. Chang and D.G. Messerschmitt, "Manipulation and compositing of MC-DCT compressed video," *IEEE Journal of Selected Areas in Communications (JSAC)*, vol. 13, no. 1, pp. 1 – 11, Jan. 1995
[9] K.R. Rao and J.J. Hwang, Techniques & Standards for Image, Video, and Audio Coding, Prentice Hall, 1995
[10] Khanlid Sayood, *Introduction to data compression*, $2^{nd}$ ed., Academic Press, 2000
[11] W. H. Chen. C. H. Smith, and S. Fralick, "A fast computational algorithm for the discrete cosine transform," *IEEE Trans. on Commun.*, vol. COM-25. pp. 1004-1009, Sept. 1977.
[12] R. M. Haralick, "A storage efficient way to implement the discrete cosine transform."*IEEE Trans. Computer,* vol. C-25, pp. 764-765, July 1976.
[13] R. C. Reininger and J. D. Gibson. "Distributions of the two dimensional DCT coefficients for images." *IEEE Trans. on Commun.*, vol. COM-31, pp. 835-839, June 1983.

# Grayscale Two-Dimensional Lempel-Ziv Encoding

Nathanael J. Brittain and Mahmoud R. El-Sakka, Senior Member, IEEE

Computer Science Department, University of Western Ontario, London, Ontario, Canada
{njbritta, elsakka}@csd.uwo.ca

**Abstract.** Dictionary-based compression methods are a popular form of data file compression. LZ77, LZ78 and their variants are likely the most famous of these methods. These methods are implemented to reduce the one-dimensional correlation in data, since they are designed to compress text. Therefore, they do not take advantage of the fact that, in images, adjacent pixels are correlated in two dimensions. Previous attempts have been made to linearize images in order to make them suitable for dictionary-based compression, but results show that no single linearization is best for all images. In this paper, a *true* two-dimensional dictionary-based lossless image compression scheme for grayscale images is introduced. Testing results show that the compression performance of the proposed scheme outperforms and surpasses any other existing dictionary-based compression scheme. The results also show that it slightly outperforms JPEG-2000's compression performance, when it operates in its lossless mode, and it is comparable to JPEG-LS's compression performance, where JPEG-2000 and JPEG-LS are the current image compression standards.

## 1 Introduction

In the field of image compression there are two major approaches, lossless and lossy compression. In lossless compression, when an image is compressed and then decompressed, the reconstructed image is an exact copy of the original. In lossy compression, some information about the image is discarded to achieve better compression. This means only a close replica of the original image can be retrieved from the compressed data. The compression scheme presented in this paper is a lossless scheme.

Among the most popular methods of lossless compression are dictionary-based schemes. Dictionary compressors encode a string of data by partitioning the string into many sub-strings, and then replacing each sub-string by a codeword. Communication between the compressor and decompressor is done using messages. Each message consists of a codeword and possibly other information. The dictionary in these schemes is the set of every possible codeword. LZ77 [1] and LZ78 [2] are two of the most famous dictionary-based compression schemes.

In LZ77, the dictionary is a portion of the most recently encoded data. This is also called the search buffer. Codewords for sub-strings are pointers to the longest match for the sub-string found in the search buffer. Each message consists of the codeword for the sub-string, the length of the match and the code of the next symbol.

There are many modifications to the original LZ77 scheme. Rodeh *et al.* introduced LZR [3], a scheme that uses LZ77 but with variable-size pointers. This means the pointer can index a sub-string anywhere in the previously encoded data, rather than just a previous portion. Storer *et al.* introduced LZSS [4], in which a flag bit is used to distinguish two types of messages, a pointer or a character. Bell introduced LZB [5], which also uses LZSS but with variable sized pointers as in LZR. In software, the PNG file format is based on LZ77.

In LZ78, the dictionary codewords correspond to previously encountered substrings. Each codeword consists of two parts, a pointer to the dictionary and the code of the next symbol.

As in LZ77, there are many modifications to the original LZ78 scheme. Welch introduced LZW [6], which is similar to LZ78, but its dictionary initially contains an entry for every possible symbol. At each step, a new dictionary entry is formed, by composing the last codeword sent with the next symbol to be encoded. Thus, LZW eliminated the need to include the code of the next symbol in messages. Miller *et al.* introduced LZMW [7]. LZMW is similar to LZW but is slightly modified when adding dictionary entries. Where LZW composes the last codeword sent with the next symbol to be encoded, LZMW composes the last codeword sent with the entire next codeword. Jakobsson introduced LZJ [8], which is similar to LZW but when the dictionary becomes full, codewords that have only been used once are replaced. Tischer introduced LZT [9]. In this scheme, the dictionary entries are arranged according to recent use. When the dictionary becomes full, each new entry replaces the least recently used entry. In software, Unix Compress and the GIF file format are based on LZW.

Fiala *et al.* introduced LZFG [10], which is similar to LZ77 because it uses a sliding window but also similar to LZ78 because only particular codewords are stored in the dictionary.

LZ77, LZ78, and their variants, take advantage of the fact that adjacent data values are highly correlated. These dictionary-based schemes are designed to compress text and so only reduce one-dimensional correlations in data. Therefore, they do not take advantage of the fact that, in images, adjacent data values (pixels) are highly correlated in two dimensions.

To adapt LZ compressors to suit the two-dimensional nature of images, Amir *et al.* [11] attempt to find ways to linearize images to facilitate the use of one-dimensional LZ compressors. However, tests show that no one linearization is best for all images.

Dia *et al.* [12] present a two-pass two-dimensional LZ77-based scheme for *binary* images. In this scheme, pixels are encoded by searching for exact matching between these pixels and the already encoded pixels. Once such a match is found, the pixels are encoded by encoding the match location information instead. However, it is expected that this scheme will not perform well in the case of grayscale or color images, since the chances of finding large *exact* matches would be very small.

Storer *et al.* and Rizzo *et al.* present a generalization of LZ77 to lossless compression of *binary* images [13,14]. The algorithm, known as *two-dimensional sliding window block matching*, uses a wave heuristic to scan the image and a multishape *two-dimensional suffix trie* data structure to represent the dictionary, which is a window in previously encoded pixels. As in Dia *et al.* [12], it is likely that, if this scheme is applied on grayscale or color images, it would not achieve very good results, due to the small chances of finding large exact matches.

The dictionary-based scheme presented in this paper is designed to take advantage of the two-dimensional correlation between pixels in grayscale images. It is similar to Dia *et al.* [12], Storer *et al.* and Rizzo *et al.* [13,14] two-dimensional dictionary encoding schemes, but it allows for *approximate* matches since it is designed to compress grayscale images.

The rest of this paper is organized as follows. Section 2 describes the proposed scheme in details. Section 3 presents the results. Finally, Section 4 offers the conclusions of this paper.

## 2 The GS-2D-LZ Scheme

*Grayscale Two-Dimensional Lempel-Ziv* (denoted as GS-2D-LZ) is an image compression scheme that is based on the popular family of LZ text compression schemes. However, its dictionary is built on the image history in two-dimensions, rather than in a linear fashion. Hence, it can take advantage of the two-dimensional correlations in image data.

In GS-2D-LZ, an image is encoded in raster scan order, one block of pixels at each step. For each block of pixels an *approximate* match is searched for in previously encoded data. The block is encoded as a pointer to the location of this approximate match, along with the dimensions of the match and residual information to ensure that the compression is lossless. If no suitable match can be found, a block of pixels is encoded using a simple DPCM prediction scheme. After the entire image has been encoded in this fashion, the match location, match position, residual and predicted values are separately encoded using a statistical compression scheme.

### 2.1 Search and Encoding Strategies

The search area, in which matches are considered for a block, is rectangular in shape and located above and to the left of the encoder position. The search region is a function of *search-width* and *search-height* variables, which are adjustable parameters that identify the horizontal and vertical search distances, respectively.

When searching for a match of the block rooted at the encoder position, each pixel in the search region represents a block of pixels rooted at the same position. There are *search-width* × *search-height* − 1 unique blocks to be considered (since the block rooted at the encoder position is not a possibility).

In some cases, it is possible to extend matches into the region of un-encoded pixels. However, this must be carefully done so as not to allow matches that cannot be reconstructed by the decoder. The shape and positioning of the search region in GS-2D-LZ has been designed to account for these facts.

For a particular root pixel in the search region, the algorithm calculates the difference between that pixel and the pixel at the encoder position. To be considered as a possible match, the difference of these two pixels can not exceed the value of a variable called *threshold*, which is an adjustable parameter that identifies the maximum allowable error between pixels. If a pixel is qualified as a root of a potential match, the match is then extended to the right as wide as possible using the same criteria, i.e., in order for the match to be extended one pixel to the right, the difference between corresponding pixels in the potential match and the block being encoded must be less than the *threshold*.

Once a mismatch occurs, the match is then extended down as far as possible. This step is similar to the case when a match is extended right. When a mismatch occurs in a row extension, the width of the match is simply reduced in order to allow the match to continue extended downwards. Extending the match further downward by this manner will eventually force a reduction of the potential width to be less than 1. When this occurs, the algorithm deems that all possible matches at this root are exhausted and all found matches are evaluated in two different ways:

1. The match must be large enough that more new pixels than the value of a variable called *minimum-match-size* are being encoded. The variable *minimum-match-size* is an adjustable parameter. Due to the nature of the variable block size scheme that we use, encoded blocks will sometimes overlap with previously encoded pixels. In this situation, it does not matter that these pixels match or not, nor do these pixels count as new pixels.
2. The potential matching block *mean-square-error* (MSE) is less than the value of a variable called *maximum-MSE*, which is an adjustable parameter.

After considering every match rooted at each pixel in the search region, the largest match is selected and encoded. In the case where no match satisfies the above two conditions, the algorithm encodes a small block of pixels rooted at the position of the encoder, in order to ensure that progress is made. The dimensions of this block are fixed to *no-match-block-width* × *no-match-block-height*, where *no-match-block-width* and *no-match-block-height* are two adjustable parameters. To keep the algorithm fast and efficient, a simple DPCM [15] scheme is used to encode these pixels.

The adjustable parameters in the GS-2D-LZ scheme have been empirically chosen, where *search-width*, *search-height*, *threshold*, *minimum-match-size*, *maximum-MSE*, *no-match-block-width*, and *no-match-block-height* are set to 4, 4, 27, 17, 2.5, 5, and 5, respectively.

### 2.2 Data Structures Defined

There are five tables that are used to record the matching information. These tables are called: *Match Flag*, *Match Location*, *Match Dimensions*, *Residual*, and *Prediction Errors*.

The *Match Flag* table contains a Boolean value for each block of pixels, where a value of *true* is recorded in the table when a suitable match for the block is found and *false* otherwise. When a suitable match is found for a block, the position of the match, relative to the block being encoded, is recorded in the *Match Location*. At the same time, the width and height of the block being encoded are recorded in the *Match Dimensions* tables. Moreover, the difference between each pixel of the actual block and the corresponding pixel in the match found for the block is recorded in the *Residual* table. On the other hand, when no suitable match can be found, the *Prediction Errors* table is used to hold the errors between the DPCM predicted pixel values and the actual pixel values for each pixel of the block.

After the entire image has been scanned, each table is encoded using PAQ6 [16]. Note that, a benchmark was made using a variety of statistical encoders (including

Huffman, Dynamic Huffman and Arithmetic) to find the best scheme to compress these tables. It turns out that the best scheme for this job was PAQ6.

## 3 Experimental Results

The GS-2D-LZ scheme described above was tested on a set of 16 different grayscale natural scene images, shown in Fig. 1.

**Fig. 1.** Test images

For each of these images, the compression performance (in bits per pixel) of the GS-2D-LZ scheme was compared to the compression performance of GIF, Unix-Compress, PNG, BZIP2, JPEG2000 and JPEG-LS schemes, as shown in Table 1. Note that, GIF and Unix-Compress are based on LZW scheme, PNG is based on

LZ77 scheme, BZIP2 [17] is based on the Burrows Wheeler transformation, JPEG2000 [18] is the current JPEG lossy compression standard but operated in its lossless mode, and JPEG-LS [19] is the current JPEG lossless compression standard.

**Table 1.** Compression performance measured in bits per pixel

| Image name | GS-2D-LZ | GIF | Unix-Compress | PNG | BZIP2 | JPEG2000 | JPEG-LS |
|---|---|---|---|---|---|---|---|
| baboon–512x512 | 5.84 | 8.98 | 7.84 | 6.01 | 6.38 | 5.88 | 5.82 |
| barbara–720x580 | 4.75 | 8.74 | 7.73 | 5.23 | 5.92 | 4.69 | 4.74 |
| boats–720x576 | 4.01 | 3.93 | 6.34 | 4.33 | 5.00 | 4.07 | 3.93 |
| bridge–512x512 | 5.35 | 5.44 | 5.00 | 4.94 | 4.30 | 5.74 | 5.50 |
| camera–256x256 | 4.38 | 6.77 | 6.68 | 4.67 | 5.12 | 4.54 | 4.31 |
| columbia–480x480 | 3.47 | 6.61 | 6.21 | 3.92 | 4.45 | 3.52 | 3.43 |
| couple–512x512 | 4.69 | 7.59 | 6.82 | 4.88 | 5.37 | 4.84 | 4.68 |
| crowd–512x512 | 4.05 | 6.89 | 6.01 | 4.53 | 4.71 | 4.20 | 3.91 |
| Lake–512x512 | 5.08 | 8.18 | 7.42 | 5.37 | 5.68 | 5.15 | 4.98 |
| lax–512x512 | 5.81 | 8.64 | 7.73 | 5.98 | 6.38 | 5.96 | 5.76 |
| Lena–512x512 | 4.06 | 7.66 | 6.68 | 4.39 | 5.07 | 4.06 | 3.99 |
| Man–512x512 | 4.58 | 7.90 | 6.95 | 4.93 | 5.49 | 4.69 | 4.50 |
| milkdrop–512x512 | 3.74 | 6.43 | 5.97 | 3.97 | 4.37 | 3.77 | 3.63 |
| peppers–512x512 | 4.65 | 4.54 | 7.22 | 4.91 | 5.37 | 4.63 | 4.51 |
| woman1–512x512 | 4.75 | 6.94 | 6.14 | 4.98 | 5.00 | 4.81 | 4.67 |
| woman2–512x512 | 3.37 | 6.60 | 5.73 | 3.77 | 4.19 | 3.32 | 3.30 |
| Average | 4.54 | 6.99 | 6.65 | 4.80 | 5.18 | 4.62 | 4.48 |

From Table 1, we can see that the compression performance of the GS-2D-LZ scheme surpasses the compression performance of the other dictionary encoding schemes, i.e., GIF, Unix-Compress, and PNG. Note that, in some cases, e.g., baboon–512x512, barbara–720x580, lake–512x512, and lax–512x512, GIF scheme produces compressed files that are bigger than the original files. This is because the GIF scheme does not evaluate the compression performance before producing the compressed file. In Unix-compress, this issue has been considered and that is why the sizes of compressed files are smaller than or equal to the sizes of original images.

Meanwhile, GS-2D-LZ scheme slightly outperforms JPEG2000, when operated in its lossless mode. At the same time, its compression performance is comparable to JPEG-LS's performance.

It is worth mentioning that while all other compression schemes (including JPEG2000 and JPEG-LS), are heavily optimized, the proposed scheme is not, since it was implemented just as a proof of concept. Moreover, there is a great deal of room for improvement in the proposed scheme, including the use of a better compression scheme that just DPCM to compress the mismatched blocks.

## 4 Conclusions

In this paper, a novel two-dimensional dictionary-based scheme is introduced. Experimental results showed that the compression performance of GS-2D-LZ scheme outperforms and surpasses any other dictionary-based compression scheme. At the same time, it performs slightly better than JPEG2000 and is comparable to JPEG-LS. This implies that dictionary-based compression schemes can be as efficient as the current state of the art compression scheme.

## References

1. J. Ziv and A. Lempel, "A Universal Algorithm for Data Compression", IEEE Transactions on Information Theory, Volume 23, No. 3, pp. 337-343, May 1977.
2. J. Ziv and A. Lempel, "Compression of Individual Sequences via Variable-Rate Coding", IEEE Transactions on Information Theory, Volume 24, No. 5, pp. 530-536, September 1978.
3. M. Rodeh, V. Pratt, and S. Even, "Linear Algorithm for Data Compression via String Matching", Journal of the ACM, Volume 28, No. 1, pp. 16-24, January 1981.
4. J. Storer and T. Syzmanski, "Data Compression via Textual Substitution", Journal of the ACM, Volume 29, pp. 928-951, 1982.
5. T. Bell, "Better opm/l Text Compression", IEEE Transactions on Communications, Volume COM-34, pp. 1176-1182, 1986.
6. T. Welch, "A Technique for High-Performance Data Compression", IEEE Computer, pp. 8-19, June 1984.
7. V. Miller and M. Wegman, "Variations on a Theme by Lempel and Ziv", Combinatorial Algorithms on Words, pp. 131-140, 1985.
8. M. Jakobsson, "Compression of the Character Strings by an Adaptive Dictionary", BIT, Volume 25, No. 4, pp. 593-603, 1985.
9. P. Tischer, "A Modified Lempel-Ziv-Welch Data Compression Scheme", Australian Computer Science Communications, Volume 9, No. 1, pp. 262-272, 1987.
10. E. Fiala and D. Greene, "Data Compression with Finite Windows", Communications of the ACM, Volume 32, pp. 490-505, 1989.
11. A. Amir, G. Landau and D. Sokol, "Inplace 2D matching in compressed images", Journal of Algorithms, Volume 49, No. 2, pp. 240-261, November 2003.
12. V. Dai and A. Zakhor. "Lossless layout compression for maskless lithography", Proceedings of the SPIE, Volume 3997, pp. 467-477, 2000.
13. J. Storer and H. Helfgott, "Losless Image Compression by Block Matching", The Computer Journal, Volume 40, No. 2-3, pp. 137-145, 1997.
14. F. Rizzo, J. Storer and B. Carpentieri, "LZ-based image compression", Information Sciences, Volume 135, No. 1-2, pp. 107-122, June 2001.
15. C. Cutler, Differential quantization for television signals, U.S. Patent 2,605,361, July 29, 1952.
16. M. Mahoney, The PAQ6 data compression programs, http://www.cs.fit.edu/~mmahoney/compression/, 2004.
17. M. Burrows and D. J. Wheeler, "A Block-Sorting Lossless Data Compression Algorithm", Digital SRC Research Report 124, 10th May 1994.
18. D. Taubman and M. Weinberger, "JPEG2000: Image Compression Fundamentals, Standards and Practice", Kluwer Academic Publishers, 2002.
19. M. Weinberger, G. Seroussi, and G. Sapiro, "The LOCO-I Lossless Image Compression Algorithm: Principles and Standardization into JPEG-LS", IEEE Transactions on Image Processing, Volume 9, No. 8, pp.1309-1324, August 2000.

# Unequal Error Protection Using Convolutional Codes for PCA-Coded Images

Sabina Hosic, Aykut Hocanin, and Hasan Demirel

Eastern Mediterranean University, Electrical and Electronic Engineering Department,
Gazimagusa, North Cyprus
{sabina.hosic, aykut.hocanin, hasan.demirel}@emu.edu.tr

**Abstract.** Image communication is a significant research area which involves improvement in image coding and communication techniques. In this paper, Principal Component Analysis (PCA) is used for face image coding and the coded images are protected with convolutional codes for transmission over Additive White Gaussian Noise (AWGN) channel. Binary Phase Shift Keying (BPSK) is used for the modulation of digital (binarized) coded images. Received binarized coded images are first decoded by the convolutional decoder using the Viterbi algorithm and then PCA decoded for recognition of the face. Unequal error protection (UEP) with two convolutional encoders with different rates is used to increase the overall performance of the system. The recognition rate of the transmitted coded face images without any protection is 35%, while equal protection with convolutional codes gives rates up to 85% accuracy. On the other hand, the proposed UEP scheme provides recognition rates up to 95% with reduced redundancy.

## 1 Introduction

Image communication is becoming increasingly important for diverse applications such as mobile communications, biomedical imaging, remote security systems etc. Hence, image communication problems are the focus of most recent scientific research, aiming efficient and error-resilient image communication systems with improvement in image coding as well as in communication techniques.

In this paper, eigenfaces technique is used for image coding. It is one of the most frequently used methods based on PCA which maps high dimensional data into a low dimensional space, saving memory and time [1]. PCA-coded images are used for image compression, recognition and transmission. BPSK is used for the modulation of image representation vectors transmitted over an AWGN channel. Transmitting coded images is predisposed for high errors at the receiver side since every entry of representation vector carries much more image information than a single pixel. Therefore, it is very important to minimize errors due to channel noise. Employing UEP on particular bits of the transmitted coefficient increases the overall system performance.

Convolutional codes are frequently used to protect source-coded data by adding redundant bits to it. Complicated convolutional codes perform better than the simple ones but require much more processing power and expensive circuitry. In order to satisfy performance and implementation requirements, in this paper, UEP is implemented such that a few most significant bits (i.e. first 7 bits) are encoded with low-rate convolutional codes while the remaining bits are encoded with a relatively simpler encoder (i.e. rate ½ encoder). Fig. 1 shows a general block diagram of the system.

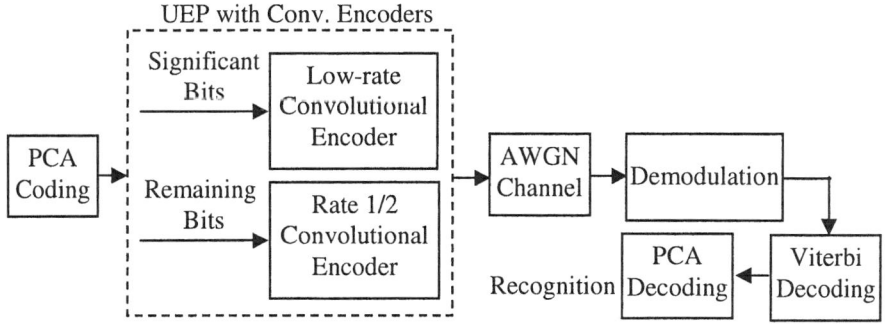

**Fig. 1.** Block Diagram of the System

The main idea in PCA is to decompose a "face space" into a small set of characteristic feature images called "eigenfaces", which, when linearly combined represent one single face. Every eigenvector (eigenface), has a different eigenvalue which determines its contribution in representation of a face image [1]. Eigenvectors with larger eigenvalues have the highest contribution in representation while the effect of others is not so significant, especially if the number of eigenfaces is large [2]. In order to implement identification process for the large data set, data compression is necessary.

In this paper, section 2 describes the eigenfaces approach in detail. Section 3 discusses the transmission of the projection vectors and unequal error protection of representation coefficients. Most significant bits of each coefficient are encoded by convolutional codes with lower rate (with more redundancy) while the rest of the bits are encoded at a higher rate. Projection vectors are then sent over the AWGN channel. Using this UEP scheme, important information that affects face recognition the most is highly protected. Received coded images are decoded first by the Viterbi algorithm. Then PCA decoding is used which includes the recognition of the face. Section 4 includes the results of simulations and the conclusions are stated in section 5.

## 2 Principal Component Analysis

Eigenface method is based on the linear PCA where a face image is encoded to a low dimensional vector. All face images are decomposed into a small set of characteristic feature images called eigenfaces. Each face image is projected on the subspace of meaningful eigenfaces (ones with the nonzero eigen-values). In this way, the collection of weights describes each face. Recognition of a new face is performed by projecting it on the subspace of eigenfaces and then comparing its weights with corresponding weights of each face from a known database.

### 2.1 Calculating Eigenfaces

Suppose that all face images in database are of the same size $w \times h$. Eigenfaces are obtained as eigen-vectors of the covariance matrix of the data points.

Let $\Gamma_i$ be an image from the collection of $M$ images in database. Face image is a 2-dimensional array of size $w \times h$, where $w$ and $h$ are width and height of the image, respectively. Each image can be represented as a vector of dimension $wh$ and the average image, $\Psi$, is defined as:

$$\Psi = \frac{1}{M} \sum_{i=1}^{M} (\Gamma_i) . \qquad (1)$$

Each image, $\Gamma_i$, differ from the average image $\Psi$ by the vector $\Phi_i = \Gamma_i - \Psi$.

The difference vectors are used to set up the covariance matrix $C$, as shown below [4].

$$C = \frac{1}{M} \sum_{i=1}^{M} (\Phi_i \Phi_i^T) = \Lambda \Lambda^T . \qquad (2)$$

$$\Lambda = [\Phi_1 \Phi_2 \Phi_3 ... \Phi_M] . \qquad (3)$$

Since there are $M$ images in database, the covariance matrix $C$ has only $M-1$ meaningful eigenvectors. Those eigenvectors, $u_l$, can be obtained by multiplying eigenvectors, $v_l$, of matrix $L = \Lambda^T \Lambda$ (of size $M \times M$) with difference vectors in matrix $\Lambda$ [4].

$$u_l = \sum_{k=1}^{M} v_{lk} \Phi_k . \qquad (4)$$

The eigenvectors, $u_l$, are called the eigenfaces [4]. Eigenfaces with higher eigenvalues contribute more in representation of the image. Therefore such eigefaces are used for construction of the "face subspace" for image projections which are employed in face identification, classification or recognition. Projection (representation) vectors for every image are defined as

$$\Omega = [\omega_1, \omega_2, ..., \omega_M]. \qquad (5)$$

$\omega_k$ is the $k^{th}$ coordinate of the image $\Phi$ in the face subspace and is calculated as [4]:

$$\omega_k = u_k^T (\Gamma_k - \Psi), \quad k=1, ..., M. \qquad (6)$$

The projection (representation) vectors are indispensable in face recognition tasks, due to their uniqueness.

### 2.2 Recognition

As mentioned above, the projection vector, $\Omega$, is necessary for reconstruction and recognition of the image. Euclidian distance between representations of two different images ($\Omega_1$ and $\Omega_2$) is used for the determination of the recognition rate.

$$E = \sqrt{\sum_{i=1}^{M}(\omega_{1i} - \omega_{2i})^2}. \tag{7}$$

While for perfect reconstruction of the face image all the coefficients may be needed, for recognition only the most significant ones play an important role. Figure 2 shows recognition rates for 80 test images (2 per person) and 320 training images (8 per person) evaluated for different number of coefficients used. In the system described above (8 poses for each person) recognition rate saturates at 95% after 10 coefficients have been used in recognition. The same rate is obtained even if all 320 representation coefficients were used. This implies that it is enough to use only a certain number of most significant coefficients with larger corresponding eigen-values in order to have the maximum recognition rate. Minimum number of coefficients, required for successful recognition rates depends on the data used in training as well as the test images.

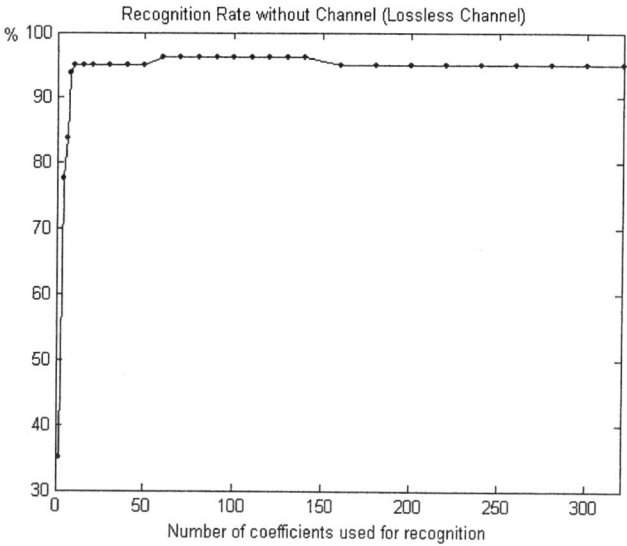

**Fig. 2.** Recognition Rate versus the number of coefficients used for recognition

## 3 UEP Using Convolutional Codes for PCA Coded Images

Transmitting all the pixels of an image at a time requires a huge bandwidth and a large bit rate, which in practice is not available. Therefore, concentrated and compressed form of data should be sent over the channel in order to meet consumer requirements. This compressed form of data may be a coded image where amount of information per bit is substantially increased. Hence a single bit error may result in considerable decrease in performance [3].

In this paper, PCA is used for image coding, where coded information for each image is carried in its projection (representation) vector. Most significant coefficients in the vector are shown to have higher contribution in representation of the face. Unfortunately, this property of projection coefficients and eigenfaces cannot be used in noisy channels due to randomness of the noise and unequal ratio of the error on each coefficient. For instance, small coefficients originally with almost no contribution, after transmission may become large and can even have a different sign. Therefore it is important to protect least significant coefficients just like the most significant ones in transmission of projection vectors. One way to protect bits is to increase redundancy of the source signal and make it less susceptible to the effects of AWGN channel. This is successfully done by convolutional codes where the code rate determines the amount of redundancy.

### 3.1 UEP of Projection Coefficients Using Convolutional Codes

Protecting all coefficients would require larger bandwidth and delay which would not allow much improvement as compared to pixel transmission. Fortunately, errors in the fractional part of each coefficient will not result in considerable representation change compared to errors on integer or sign part. Since every coefficient is transformed into a sequence of binary digits, it is enough to protect a first few bits representing the sign and the integer parts of each coefficient. The most significant bits are hence encoded using a low rate convolutional code with more redundant bits and noise resilience and the remaining bits are encoded with a simple rate 1/2 convolutional code [4]. After encoding, all bits are modulated and transmitted over AWGN channel. At the receiver side, coded bit streams are decoded by the corresponding convolutional decoders. The UEP method is applied on bit level and protects all the coefficients in the projection vector, providing sufficiently small bandwidth and transmission $Eb/N_0$.

Simulations are performed to assess the performance of the UEP scheme. Projection vectors are binarized using a 64 bit quantizer, where the most significant 5 bits represent the integer part and the sign of the coefficient and the remaining 59 are used for the fractional part. This particular arrangement of the bits depends on the nature of the data used in simulations and it can be varied to meet specific requirements. The maximum value of the coefficients is 16 and hence 4 bits are assigned for integer part and an additional bit is assigned for the sign. After projection vectors are digitized, UEP method is applied on a bit level. As previously mentioned, bits which correspond to the sign and the integer part are encoded using a lower rate convolutional encoder while a simpler, rate 1/2 encoder is used for the remaining bits. In the simulations, 7 bits are protected with a lower rate covolutional code in order to increase performance even more. Those received coefficients are used for recognition of the face (Fig. 1).

## 4 Results and Discussion

400 face images from ORL face database are used in this work (10 various poses for 40 different persons) where 320 images (8 per person) are used for training and 80 (2 per person) for testing [5]. Eigen-subspace is constructed from 320 training images and the remaining 80 test images are only used in recognition analysis.

Convolutional codes used for the simulation have rates 1/2, 1/3 and 1/4. The most important criterion for optimal codes is maximizing *minimum free distance* $d_{free}$, which determines the error correction capability of the code and determines performance at high $Eb/N_0$ values. The second criterion is minimizing the number of *nearest-neighbors*, $Ad_{free}$ whose influence increases as the $Eb/N_0$ decreases [6]. The codes used in the simulations are chosen to satisfy the both criteria. The results for performance analysis are based on comparison of recognition rates for transmitted coded images with:

- UEP using rate 1/4 + rate 1/2 convolutional code
- UEP using rate 1/3 + rate 1/2 convolutional code
- All bits equally treated using: rate 1/2, rate 1/3 and rate 1/4.

Performance of above mentioned models are also examined for 8-state and 32-state convolutional codes.

### 4.1 Face Recognition of 80 Received Coded Images (Projection Vectors)

Projection vectors of 80 test images are transmitted over the channel with AWGN. These vectors are received with errors, decreasing recognition rate significantly. Performance is better for higher values of average $Eb/N_0$ but the aim is to keep $Eb/N_0$ as low as possible. Applying previously described UEP, encoding the first 7 bits of each coefficient with a low rate convolutional code, provides significant increase in performance. By this way number of redundant bits is not very high and performance is satisfactory. Furthermore, recognition rates approach the ideal case even for the relatively small values of $Eb/N_0$.

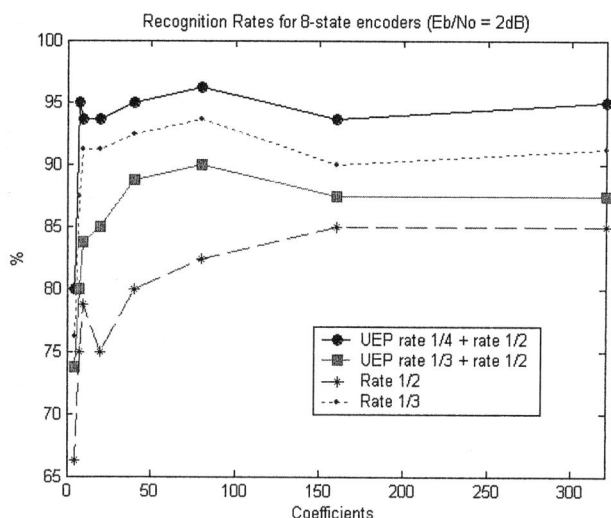

**Fig. 3.** Recognition Rate with and without UEP for 8-state encoders at 2dB

Fig. 3 and 4 compare the performance of the systems with 8-state and 32-state convolutional encoders in AWGN, with and without UEP for $Eb/N_0=2dB$, respectively. Without UEP and for low rate encoders, the number of encoded bits becomes large, increasing the data rate requirements. UEP reduces the number of bits for transmission, providing satisfactory results at a low $Eb/N_0$.

In Fig. 3, it is seen that at a low value of $Eb/N_0 = 2dB$, *UEP rate 1/4 + rate 1/2* scheme increases recognition rate by approximately 5% compared with the *equal rate 1/3* encoding for all bits. This is true even though the UEP scheme has a lower redundancy. For each coefficient, the UEP system results in $7 \cdot 4 + 57 \cdot 2 = 158$ bits while the *Rate 1/3* code requires $64 \cdot 3 = 192$ bits. In order to improve recognition performance, more complicated convolutional codes may be used. Fig. 4 shows that the increasing number of states of the encoders does not provide further performance gains.

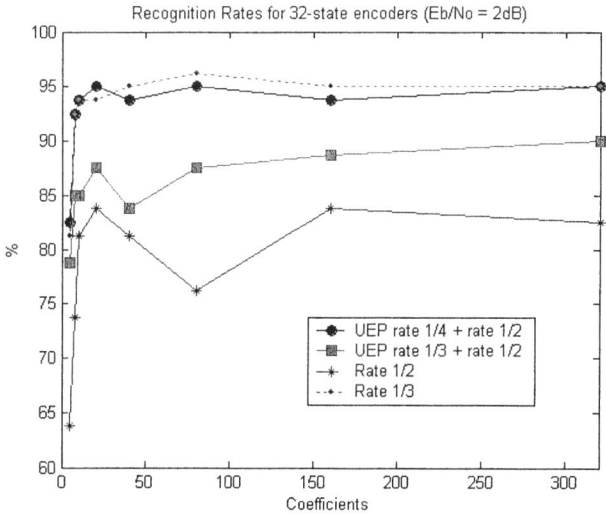

**Fig. 4.** Recognition Rate with and without UEP for 32-state encoders at 2dB

## 5 Conclusion

Coefficients of PCA-coded images, when transmitted over a noisy channel, are all equally important for image representation. Therefore protecting the first few bits of each coefficient is more useful than only protecting coefficients with higher corresponding eigenvalues. Error correcting codes used to protect these coefficients must be carefully chosen to minimize the effects of the channel without increasing the added redundancy. It is shown that the proposed UEP scheme increases overall system performance for face recognition at low $Eb/N_0$ values. Face recognition rates for the UEP with rate 1/4 + rate1/2 Convolutional Codes reaches recognition rates up to 95% and is higher than that of the equal protection with a rate 1/3 convolutional code. This is especially important considering that the UEP scheme requires much less redundancy. Increasing the complexity of the convolutional codes with larger number of encoding states does not result in considerable increase in recognition performance. The proposed scheme may be efficiently employed for face recognition in adverse channel conditions where $E_b/N_0$ is low with minimal added redundancy for error protection.

## References

1. Turk, M., & Pentland, A.,"Eigenfaces for Recognition", *Journal of Cognitive Neuroscience*, vol. 3, no.1, pp 72-86, 1991.
2. Carl G. Looney, *Pattern Recognition Using Neural Networks: Theory and Algorithms for engineers and Scientists*, 1st ed., Oxford: University Press, 1997.
3. Sheila, S., H., "Robust Image Communication over Wireless Channels", *IEEE Communications Magazine*, November 2001.
4. Desai,V., Classon, B., Blankenship, Y.,W., & Jhonson, J., "Unequal Error Protection Design Using Convolutional Codes", , *IEEE International Conference on Communications*, vol. 2, pp 836-840, 2002.
5. O.R.L. Face Database, Retrieved May 12, 2003 from: http://mambo.ucsc.edu/psl/olivetti.html
6. Lin, S., & Costello, D.J., *Error Control Coding*, 2nd ed., New Jersey: Pearson Prentice Hall, 2004

# Design of Tree Filter Algorithm for Random Number Generator in Crypto Module

Jinkeun Hong[1] and Kihong Kim[2]

[1] Division of Information & Communication, Cheonan University,
115 Anseo-dong, Cheonan-si, Chungnam, 330-704, Korea
jkhong@cheonan.ac.kr
[2] Graduate School of Information Security, Korea University,
1, 5-Ka, Anam-dong, Sungbuk-ku, Seoul, 136-701, Korea
hong0612@hanmir.com

**Abstract.** For a hardware random number generator (RNG) in a crypto module, it is important that the RNG hardware offers an output bit stream that is always unbiased. J. H., et al. proposed a combination of the hardware component and a software filter algorithm. However, even though the hardware generating processor generates an output bit stream quickly, if the software filter algorithm is inefficient, the RNG becomes time consuming, thereby restricting the conditions when an RNG can be applied. Accordingly, this paper proposes an effective method of software filtering for an RNG processor in a crypto module. To consistently guarantee the randomness of the output sequence from a RNG, the origin must be stabilized, regardless of any change in circumstances. Therefore, a tree model is proposed to apply the filter algorithm, making it less time consuming than J. H.'s conventional filter algorithm scheme.

## 1 Introduction

Ubiquitous computing is continuing to grow, resulting in the construction of massively distributed computing environments, such as the global positioning system (GPS) [1][2]. However, the particular constraints imposed by ubiquitous computing, including computational power and energy consumption, raise significantly different security issues, such as authentication, confidentiality, and integrity, along with more general issues, such as convenience, speed, and so on. A hardware random number generator uses a non-deterministic source to produce randomness, and more demanding random number applications, such as cryptography, a crypto module engine, and statistical simulation, then benefit from the sequences produced by an RNG, a cryptographic system based on a hardware component [1]. As such, a number generator is a source of unpredictable, irreproducible, and statistically random stream sequences, and a popular method for generating random numbers using a natural phenomenon is the electronic amplification and sampling of a thermal or Gaussian noise signal. However, since all electronic systems are influenced by a finite bandwidth, $1/f$ noise, and other non-random influences, perfect randomness cannot be preserved by any practical system. Thus, when generating random numbers using an electronic circuit, a low power white noise signal is amplified and then sampled at a constant sampling frequency. Yet, when using an RNG with only a hardware component, as required for statistical randomness, it is quite difficult to create an unbiased and stable random bit stream. The studies reported in [3][4][5] show that the randomness of a random stream can be enhanced when combining a real RNG, LFSR number generator, and hash function. Hence, in previous studies about RNG schemes in the security area, F. Cortigiani, et al. (2000) examined a very high speed true random noise generator, S. Rocchi and V. Vignoli (1999) proposed a high speed chaotic CMOS true random analog/digital white noise generator, Adel, et al. (2001) investigated the design and performance analysis of a high speed AWGN communication channel emulator, and a noise-based random bit generator IC for applications in cryptography was considered (Craig S, et al. 1998 [4]).

However, the randomness of such combined methods is still dependent on the security level of the hash function and LFSR number generator. Thus, a previous paper proposed a real RNG that combines an RNG and filtering technique that is not dependent on the security level of the period. Therefore, controlling a stable input voltage for an RNG is an important aspect of the design of an RNG. In particular, it is important that the RNG hardware offers an output bit stream that is always unbiased. Thus, J. H., et al. [5] proposed a method that combines the hardware component with a software filter algorithm. Nonetheless, even though the hardware generating processor generates an output bit stream quickly, if the software filter algorithm is inefficient, the RNG becomes time consuming, thereby restricting the conditions when an RNG can be applied. Accordingly, this paper proposes an effective method of software filtering for an RNG processor in a crypto module. To consistently guarantee the randomness of the output sequence from an RNG, the origin must be stabilized, regardless of any change of circumstances.

Hereinafter, section 2 reviews the framework of an H/W RNG of crypto module, then section 3 examines the filter algorithm in J. H., et. al.'s model and introduces the proposed filter algorithm. Experimental results and some final conclusions are given in sections 4 and 5.

## 2 Framework of RNG in Crypto Module

An H/W random number generator includes common components for producing random bit streams, classified as follows: characteristics of the noise source, amplification of the noise source, and sampling for gathering the comparator output [4][6]. The applied noise source uses Gaussian noise, which typically results from the flow of electrons through a highly charged field [7][8][9]. Ultimately, the electron flow is the movement of discrete charges, and the mean flow rate is surrounded by a distribution related to the launch time and momentum of the individual charge carriers entering the charged field. The Gaussian noise generated in a PN junction has the same mathematical form as that of a temperature-limited vacuum diode. The probability density $f(x)$ of the Gaussian noise voltage distribution function is defined by Eq. (1).

$$f(x) = \frac{1}{\sqrt{2\pi\sigma^2}} e^{-\frac{x^2}{2\sigma^2}} \qquad (1)$$

where, $\sigma$ is the root mean square value of the Gaussian noise voltage. However, for the proposed Gaussian noise random number generator, the noise diode was a diode with white Gaussian distribution. The power density for the noise was constant with a frequency from 0.1Hz to 10MHz and the amplitude had a Gaussian distribution. The noise comes from the agitation of the electrons within a resistance, which sets a lower limit on the noise present in a circuit. Thus, when the frequency range is given, the voltage of the noise is decided by a factor of the frequency. The crest factor of a waveform is defined as the ratio of the peak to the *rms* value, and here a crest value of approximately 4 was used for the noise. However, with the proposed real random number generator, since the noise diode is a noise diode with a white Gaussian distribution, the noise must be amplified to a level where it can be accurately thresholded with no bias using a clocked comparator.

A hardware random number generator includes common components for producing random bit streams, classified as follows: characteristics of the noise source, amplification of the noise source, and sampling for gathering the comparator output. The applied noise source uses Gaussian noise, which typically results from the flow of electrons through a highly charged field, such as a semiconductor junction.

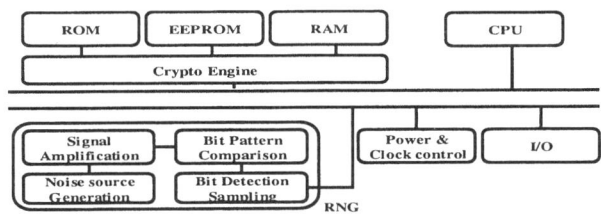

**Fig. 1.** The architecture of random number generator in crypto module

The microcomputer chips in most crypto modules consist of a CPU, ROM, RAM, I/O, EEPROM, etc. A crypto module also includes some form of power and clock control circuitry, BUS, and I/O interface.

## 3 The Filter Model of H/W Random Number Generator

### 3.1 Filter Algorithm in Conventional Model

The conventional filter algorithm is applied in the next process of the output stream of the sampler to reduce the biased statistical randomness [5]. If the optimum buffer size [32bits] and significance level [$\gamma$] are established, this supports unbiased and stable randomness. In the conventional model, a static buffer [S] memory of 32bits is used to buffer the "pass data" in the decision boundary, and the significance level for the *P* value is between 0.9995 and 1.0005.

$$P = \frac{\tau}{T} \quad (2)$$

where, the total sum $\tau$ is the sum of the number of "1" bit patterns and the total length *T* is half the value of the static length.

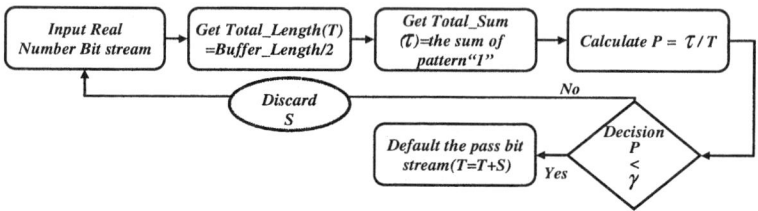

**Fig. 2.** Process of conventional filter algorithm model

where, $D$ is the sum of the passed/failed bit streams, $W$ is the window step size (32bits), and $n$ is the iteration of evaluation (1024$^{th}$ round). When the static buffer is fixed at 64bits, the half value of the static length is 32bits. If the value of {Σ{the number of a pattern "1"bit} / the half value of the static length within the total length} is included within the significance level, the decision will be the state of "pass". In step 1, if the condition of "pass" is decided, this is added as pass data to the buffer memory. In steps 3-4, if "fail" is decided, through the conventional filtering process, this is included in the decision process. The process is then completed when the size of the desired bit stream is gathered. The failed bits (32bits, S) are then made uniform by conventional filter (i.e., the duty distribution of the bit stream "0" and "1" is normalized). In conventional model, the output bit stream is expanded in steps of 32bits, while simultaneously evaluating the significance level. If the value of the duty cycle of the collected output bit stream, $P$, satisfies the condition of significance level, the 32bit stream is added, otherwise it is discarded. As such, this filter process guarantees that the output bit stream has unbiased characteristics.

### 3.2 Proposed Filter Algorithm for Tree Model

A tree filter model is applied in the next process of the output stream of the sampler to reduce the characteristics of a biased bit stream and as an efficient method that can reduce the time consumption.

In Fig. 3, the domain of the output bit stream, $D$ is denoted as $\{D_0, D_1\} = \{D_{00}, D_{01}, D_{10}, D_{11}\} = \{D_0, ..., {}_0, ..., D_1, ..., {}_1\}$. In level $2^i$, $i$ is 1, ..., 10. The evaluation of the significance level is performed on the basis of the level $2^i$ unit. For example, if $w$ is 32bits and $n$ is 1024, then the collected bit stream $D$ is 32768 bits. The levels are processed from level $2^0$ to level $2^i$ according to the increase in degree $i$ for each level, thereby reducing the bit stream size. In level $2^0$, if P is included within the significance level, all evaluations are completed in the 1$^{st}$ round. Alternatively, if $P$ does not satisfy the condition of significance level, it is divided by the tree from $I = 0$, then the divided sets $D_0$ and $D_1$ out of set $D$ are evaluated in level $2^1$, and all evaluations for sets $D_0$ and $D_1$ proceed in the 2$^{nd}$ round.

If $P$ for set $D_0$ is included within the significance level and does not satisfy the condition of significance level for the set $D_1$ node, the bit stream for set $D_0$ is collected, while the set $D_1$ node is divided by the tree architecture into set $D_{10}$ and $D_{11}$ nodes and the evaluation of the significance level proceeds for the set $D_{10}$ and $D_{11}$ nodes. Therefore, for the level $2^2$ tree, the evaluation only proceeds after the tree division of sets $D_{10}$ and $D_{11}$. Given the condition that set $D_1$ does not satisfy the condition of significance level, if $D_{10}$ is within the significance level, it is difficult for the $P$ of $D_{11}$ to be within the significance level. Thus, in the level $2^3$ trees, the $D_{11}$ node is divided, then the divided set $D_{110}$ and $D_{110}$ nodes are evaluated individually. If the evaluation of set $D_{110}$ passes, then the collected bit stream is {$D_0$, $D_{10}$, $D_{110}$} and the evaluation of set $D_{111}$ can proceed. For the tree condition with the proposed filter model, the integer $i$ is expanded from 0 to 10. In the case of conventional model the process is performed through 1024 rounds, however, with the proposed model, the computational iteration of 1024 rounds correspond to the worst case under the same conditions. Most of the evaluations are decided in the medium level, which is not last level ($i=10$). Moreover, various representations of trees and mapping methods are possible. Yet, to simplify the tree filter algorithm, the filter trees are kept in a normalized form: the nodes are always labeled in a $2^i$ order. Where $i$ is 1, 2, ...., $n$. $n$ is the order of the lowest and smallest bit stream set that is not within the accepted level of significance in the worst case.

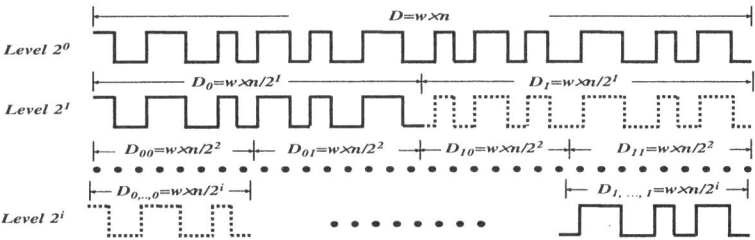

**Fig. 3.** Process of proposed filtering algorithm

```
Algorithm: TreeBasedFilter for filter tree
TreeBasedFilter()::
  1. Let Significance level γ : 0.9995≤ γ ≤1.0005, width: w=[32];
  2. Given RNGSequence size:d=2n*w/2i, i={0, ...,n}, n={10};
  3. for i={0,...,n} times do
  4. if(i==0) j==0 Goto EvaluationTest
  5. else for j={1,...,2i} times do
  6.   Let D be RNGSequence[i*d++][j]; Compute EvaluationTest();
  7. End for
  8. End for
EvaluationTest( )::
  1. If $|D| \leq \gamma$, then D is PassedBitStream, SaveBitstream=D;
  2. Else, D is divided into set D₀ and D₁
  3. If $|D_0| \leq \gamma$ or $|D_1| \leq \gamma$, set D₀ or D₁ is PassedBitStream, SaveBitstream = D₀ or D₁
  4. Else, $|D_0| \succ \gamma$ or $|D_1| \succ \gamma$ then D₀ or D₁ is divided into D₀₀/D₀₁ or D₁₀/D₁₁
```

## 4 Experimental Results

A multiple bit stream of consecutive bits as the output from the RNG was subjected to a mono bit test (such as Eq. (2)), et al. [10][11]. If any of the tests fail, the module then enters an error state. The statistical RNG test method of FIPS140-1 is used, as derived using Eq. (2) on the basis of the statistical RNG randomness.

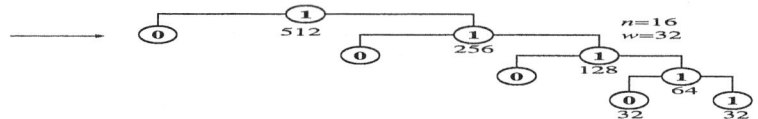

**Fig. 4.** Evaluation example 1 according to proposed tree scheme (failed prob. is 10%)

According to Eq. (2), when the RNG has an output bit stream of 512bits, the window size is 32bits, As such, in the case of conventional model, 16 rounds need to be processed for the filter evaluation, as if the output bit stream (512bits) is divided into a window size of 32bits, this makes 16 fields. If $P$ is not satisfactory for 1 field out of the 16 fields, i.e., the level of passed probability is 90%, the evaluation test start in the level of 256bits, this creates the tree division shown in Fig.4. When the failed probability presents a probability that does not satisfy the significance level in 20 levels consisting of 512bits, the mother tree is divided into the left child node and the right child node consisting of 256bits, respectively. In the case of one failed field, zero out of the one failed field occur in the left child node, while one out of the one failed field occur in the right child node. If it is assumed that one of the failed field in level $2^2$ (128bit units) diverge into a passed field unit in the left child node and a failed field unit the right child node, in $2^3$ level (64bit units), one node occur that are not failed field, while one node occurs as failed field. Therefore, the nodes about the nodes that do not occur as failed fields are not processed. Accordingly, in the case of the combined method consisting of a hardware method and software filtering to create the output bit stream of the RNG, whereas conventional model needed 16 rounds to evaluate the 16 fields, the proposed model only took 8 rounds.

In Fig. 5, when $P$ for the output bit stream of the RNG during the evaluation interval satisfied the significance level, i.e., the passed probability was about 90%, the computational burden for evaluating the significance level with conventional model was set at 100%, meaning the computational burden for the proposed tree model was only about

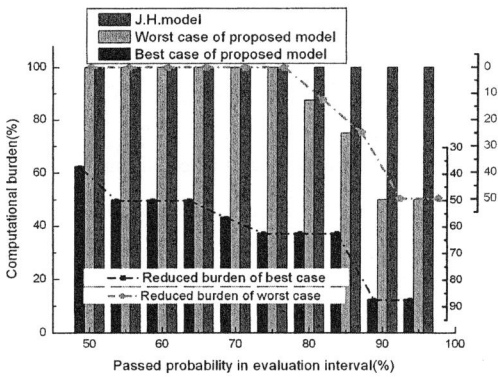

**Fig. 5.** Computation efficiency between conventional and proposed model

50%. As the computational burden was considered in relation to the passed probability of the significance level, the tree node level of the passed probability, which had an upper bound of 85%, was reduced to 12.5% with respect to the computational burden. But at a 75% passed probability for the output stream, the computational burden was not reduced to 0%. In the interval of lower bound of 75%, the proposed algorithm did not have effected. But in the interval of other condition, as $P$ for the passed probability during the evaluation interval decreased, the computational burden increased. Therefore, with regard to the passed probability and computational burden, the performance of the proposed tree model was superior to that of the conventional model.

Meanwhile, Table 1 presents a comparison of the time consumption between conventional and the proposed model in worst case. When the output bit stream of the RNG had gathered about 1.024Mbits, at an 80% passed probability, the time consumed using the conventional model was about 5sec. However, the time consumed by the proposed model was about 4.375sec. Therefore, the time performance of the proposed model was better than that of the conventional model.

**Table 1.** Time consumption between conventional and proposed tree model according to passed probability in worst case (to obtain 1.024Mbits)

| Time consumed with each model (sec) | Passed probability in evaluation interval (%) | | | | |
|---|---|---|---|---|---|
| | 50 | 60 | 70 | 80 | 90 |
| With conventional model | ≈ 6.2 | ≈ 5.6 | ≈ 5.4 | ≈ 5 | ≈ 4.5 |
| With proposed model | ≈ 6.2 | ≈ 5.6 | ≈ 5.4 | ≈ 4.375 | ≈ 2.25 |
| Reduced time | ≈ 0 | ≈ 0 | ≈ 0 | ≈ 0.25 | ≈ 2.25 |

Table 2 presents a comparison of the number of rounds processed between conventional and the proposed model.

**Table 2.** Filtering processing efficiency between conventional and proposed tree model according to passed probability in worst case (to obtain 1.024Mbits)

| Number of iterations for each model (rounds) | Passed probability in evaluation interval (%) | | | | |
|---|---|---|---|---|---|
| | 50 | 60 | 70 | 80 | 90 |
| With conventional model | ≈ 52800 | ≈ 48000 | ≈ 45920 | ≈ 42667 | ≈ 36000 |
| With proposed model | ≈ 52800 | ≈ 48000 | ≈ 45920 | ≈ 37334 | ≈ 18000 |
| Reduced iterations | ≈ 0 | ≈ 0 | ≈ 0 | ≈ 5333 | ≈ 18000 |

After gathering 1.024Mbits, the passed probability was 80% and the number of rounds with the conventional model was 42667, while the number with the proposed tree model was 37334. Therefore, with regard to the time consumption, computational burden, and number of iterations, the performance of the proposed model was superior to that of conventional model when applied to guarantee the stability of the hardware output bit stream of the random number generator.

## 5 Conclusions

A previous paper proposed a real RNG that combines an RNG and filtering technique that is not dependent on the security level of the period. Therefore, it is important that the RNG hardware offers an output bit stream that is always unbiased. Therefore, J. H., et al. proposed the combination of the hardware component with a software filter algorithm. However, even though the hardware generating processor generates an output bit stream quickly, if the software filter algorithm is inefficient, the RNG becomes time consuming, thereby restricting the conditions when an RNG can be applied.

Accordingly, this paper proposes an effective method of software filtering for an RNG processor in a crypto module. To consistently guarantee the randomness of the output sequence from a RNG, the origin must be stabilized, regardless of any change in circumstances. Therefore, a RNG is proposed that applies a filter algorithm that is less time consuming than conventional filter algorithm scheme. In addition, the computational burden is also analyzed when applying the filter algorithm.

## References

1. Alireza h., Ingrid V.: High-Throughput Programmable Crypto-coprocessor, IEEE Computer Society, 2004.
2. Jalal A. M, Anand R., Roy C., M. D. M: Cerberus: A Context-Aware Security Scheme for Smart Spaces, IEEE PerCom'03, 2003.
3. Robert Davies: True Random Number, http://webnz.com/robert/true_rng.html
4. C. S. Petrie and J. A. Connelly: A Noise-Based Random Bit Generator IC for Applications in Cryptography, ISCAS'98, 1998.
5. J. H., et. al.: Design of Real Random Number Generator, CSN'03, 2003.
6. M. D. Restituto, F. Medeiro, and A. R. Vasquez: Nonlinear Switched-Current CMOS IC for Random Signal Generation, IEE Electronic Letters, vol. 29, 1993.
7. http://www.io.com/~ritter/RES/NOISE.HTM
8. http://www.clark.net/pub/cme/P1363/ranno.html
9. Boris Ya, Ryabko and Elena Matchikina: Fast and Efficient Construction of an Unbiased Random Sequence, IEEE Trans. on Information Theory, vol. 46, 2000.
10. FIPS 140-1: Security Requirements for Cryptographic Modules, U.S. Department of Commerce/NIST, 1994.
11. Diehard: http://stat.fsu.edu/~geo/diehard.html, 1998.

# Layer Based Multiple Description Packetized Coding

Canhui Cai and Jing Chen

Institute of Information Science and Technology, Huaqiao University,
Quanzhou, Fujian, 362011, China
chcai@hqu.edu.cn
blackmil@vip.sina.com

**Abstract.** A novel multiple description coding framework, called Layered Multiple Description Packetized Coding (LMDPC) is proposed in this paper. We first develop a two description coding scheme from SNR scalable layer coding, where the base layer is duplicated into both descriptions and enhancement layer was split into two parts and sent to separate descriptions, respectively. Two descriptions are then partitioned horizontally and vertically, forming row packets and column packets for transportation. Because each row packet and column packet has only limited intersection, even packets lost happen on both descriptions, the proposed algorithm still has very good error resilient ability. Experimental results have verified the performance of the proposed MDC framework.

## 1 Introduction

Most of communication networks used nowadays are packet switching networks. Since packet loss in transmission occurs every now and then due to the network congestion and channel failure, robust transmission frameworks are requisite in such packet erasure networks. Multiple Description Coding (MDC) emerges as a predominant method for overcoming transmission errors in unreliable packet switching network and wireless channels and has received considerably attention [1].

The basic idea of the MDC is coding a single source into several self-decodable bit streams called descriptions and delivered them over different channels to the receiver. If all the descriptions are received correctly, the decoder can have a high fidelity source reconstruction. If only some description is available, the decoder is still able to retrieve some information of the lost parts of signals resulting in a reconstructed image with an acceptable quality.

The first MDC scheme, Multiple Description Scalar Quantizer (MDSQ) is proposed by Vaishampayan[2]. An alternate scheme, Multiple Description Transform Coding (MDTC) is introduced in [3, 4]. Both MDSQ and MDTC provide effective schemes to alleviate the effects of the transmission errors. However, the requirement for index assignments in MDSQ calls for complicated system design, while MDTC requires another correlating transform besides the conventional decorrelation transform. To simplify the system implementation, Jiang and Ortega proposed a wavelet based MDC framework, Polyphase Transform and Selective Quantization (PTSQ), where zerotrees are separated into multiple phases and data from one phase and the protection information for another are composed to form a description [5]. Miguel et al. developed a multiple protection MDC scheme, called SPIHT for generalized multiple description coding (MD-SPIHT) in a similar way, yielding better error resilience results with 16 descriptions [6]. In [7], Servetto et al. provided a coding scheme by combining multiple description scalar quantizers with subband coders. Cai et al. suggested another novel subband MDC coder by splitting the significant coefficients in [8]. To exploit the advantages of both MDC and layer coding, Chou et al. [9] split multiple descriptions of FEC-MDC into layers, forming layered multiple description coding (LMDC).

In this paper, we propose a new MDC framework, Layer Based Multiple Description Packetized Coding (LBMDPC), based on layered coding. Instead of forming LMDC, we employ the idea of SNR scalability to form MDC in this work. In the case of two descriptions, the base layer, which contains all critical information of the source, is duplicated and coded into both descriptions, and the enhancement layer, in which information is not so important as the former ones, is partitioned into two parts and coded in separate description. Both descriptions are then split to packets and separately dispatched by diverse channels.

The rest of this paper is organized as follows: Section 2 describes the proposed MDC scheme, including the decomposition, reconstruction procedures, and simulation results to illustrate the improved performances of the proposed framework. Section 3 discusses the measure of packetization and related experimental results. The concluding remarks are given in Section 4.

## 2 The Layer Based Multiple Description Coding

### 2.1 The Framework of the Layer Based Multiple Description Coding

Fig. 1 shows the framework of the proposed Layer Based Multiple Description Subband Coding (LBMDC), where DWT and IDWT denote the forward wavelet transformer and the invert wavelet transformer; CQ and FQ represent the coarser quantizer and the finer quantizer, and $CQ^{-1}$ and $FQ^{-1}$ stand for their counterparts. C indicates a zerotree [10,11] or X-tree coder [12]. From the Fig. 1, one can find that the encoder of the proposed multiple description framework is no more than a SNR scalability codec. Only difference between the Fig. 1 and ordinary layered coding is that the enhancement layer is now divided into two parts and separately coded.

### 2.2 The Layer Based Multiple Description Subband Coding

Wavelet coefficients from the forward transformer is firstly coarsely quantized and coded by a SPIHT encoder to form the primary information. This primary information is then coded and copied to both descriptions to protect the key information of the source. The coefficients is then subtracted by the dequantized coarse coefficients and quantized one more time by a finer quantizer. Finally, the outputs of the finer quantizer are down-sampled, coded, and transmitted from different channels. Similar to PTSQ and MD-SPIHT, we use SPIHT as the codec to make our conclusion more eloquent. Besides, it facilitates the down sampling process on the enhancement layer. In this context, the down sampling on the enhancement layer can be easily realized by decimating both significant coefficient list and insignificant coefficient list in SPIHT codec.

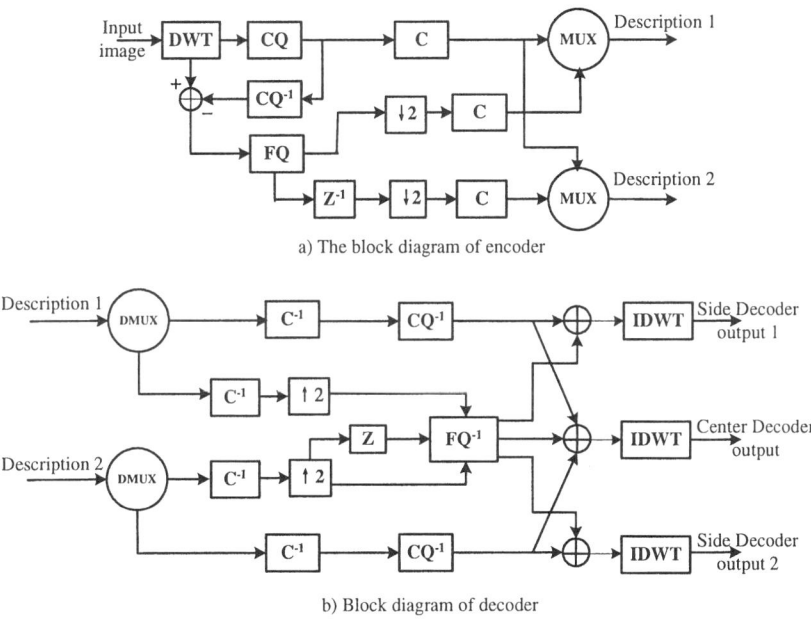

**Fig. 1.** The diagram block of the proposed MDC

If both channels are available, we can reconstruct the wavelet coefficients from the central decoder with base layer information and total enhancement layer information from both channels. If one channel is erased, we can still reconstruct the wavelet coefficients from one of the side decoder with total information in the base layer and half of information in the enhancement layer from the available channel.

### 2.3 The Simulation Results by Layer Based Multiple Description Subband Coding and Discussion

The 7/9 biorthogonal wavelet filters introduced in [13], a five level dyadic wavelet transform, and a SPIHT codec [11] along with an arithmetic coder [14] are used in all our experiments in this work. Fig. 2 shows the reconstructed "Lena" images obtained using LBMDC for a bit rate of 0.5 bpp in about 25% redundancy rate. The redundancy $\rho$ is defined as follows:

$$\rho = (R_1 + R_2 - R_0) / R_0 \qquad (1)$$

Where, $R_1$, and $R_2$ stand for the bit rate used in both side decoders and $R_0$ is the desired bit rate by a normal (single description) codec with the same distortion as the outcome of the center decoder.

Fig. 3 – Fig. 5 show the simulation results obtained using the PTSQ [4], the MDSQ subband coding [6], and the proposed LBMDC, respectively. As can be seen from the plots, the proposed LBMDC algorithm consistently outperformed the PTSQ and the MDSQ subband coding algorithms for the target rate of 0.25 bpp, 0.50bpp, and 1.0 bpp.

**Fig. 2.** The simulation results of the proposed LBMCD algorithm on "Lena" (Bit rate = 0.5 bpp)

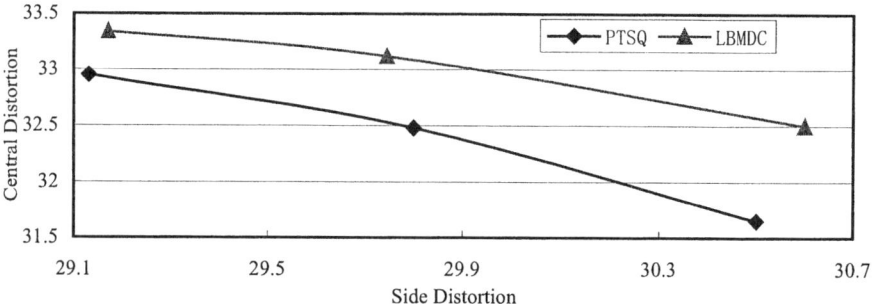

**Fig. 3.** The simulation results by the proposed LBMCD, PTSQ and MDC Subband Coding on "Lena" (Bit rate = 0.25 bpp)

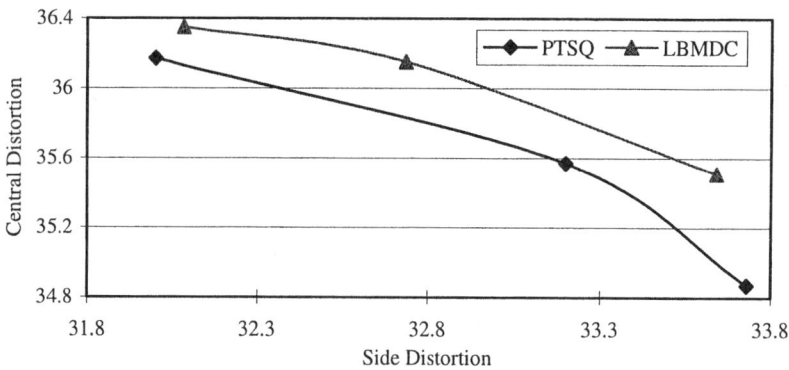

**Fig. 4.** The simulation results by the proposed LBMCD, PTSQ and MDSQ Subband Coding on "Lena" (Bit rate = 0.50 bpp)

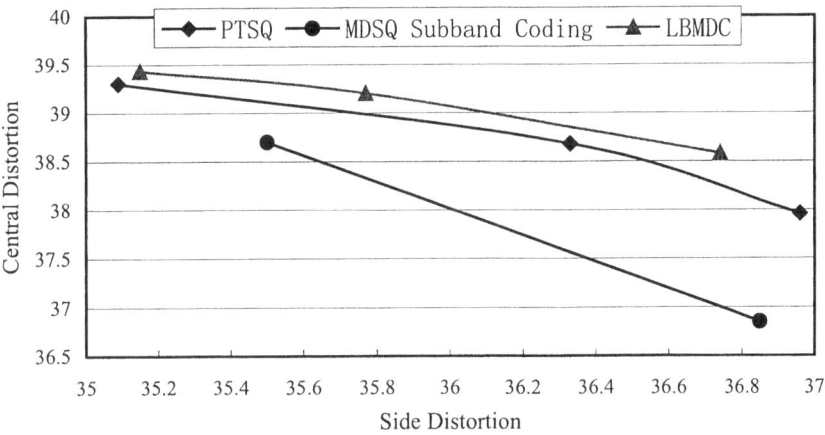

**Fig. 5.** The simulation results by the proposed LBMCD, PTSQ and MDC Subband Coding on "Lena" (Bit rate = 1.00 bpp)

## 3 The Layer Based Multiple Description Packetized Coding

The problem with LBMDC is that most of communication channels used nowadays are mainly packet switching networks, to fit in with such networks, the descriptions must be packetized before dispatched. Since transmitting networks are packet erasure channels, all available packets should be taken into account to improve the quality of the reconstructed image.

### 3.1 The Realization of the Layer Based Multiple Description Packetized Coding Framework

A spontaneous idea is to divide the transformed image into N sub-images and apply LBMDC on the sub-images to produce packets. However, if two sub-descriptions in a sub-image are totally lost, the reconstructed image will be degraded severely. coeffi

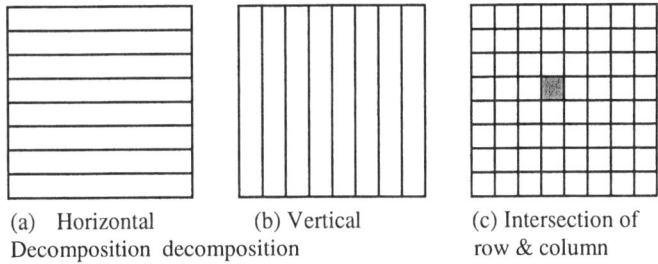

(a) Horizontal Decomposition  (b) Vertical decomposition  (c) Intersection of row & column

**Fig. 6.** Horizontal and vertical decomposed sub-descriptions and their intersections

cients into two descriptions by LBMDC, and then split these two descriptions horizontally and vertically (Fig. 6) separately, forming row sub-descriptions and column sub-descriptions, which are packed and dispatched through variety channels.

Since each row sub-description and each column sub-description have only limited intersection, the lost of row sub-descriptions as well as few column sub-descriptions will not introduce serious distortions, and vice versa. Besides, we can reconstruct the lowest frequency band of the lost sub-image from its neighbor row and column sub-descriptions.

The decoder of the LBMDPC firstly groups all available sub-descriptions to reconstruct the wavelet coefficients, and then estimate missed coefficients in the lowest band by their neighbors and set all other miss coefficients to zero. The received image is finally reconstructed from the coefficients.

### 3.2 Experimental Results by the Layer Based Multiple Description Packetized Coding

As mentioned before, we used the 7/9 biorthogonal wavelet filters, a five-level-pyramid-decomposition, and a SPIHT codec with an arithmetic coder in our experiments. The computer simulation results on image "Lena" is shown in Fig. 7. Where, LBMDPC1denotes the outcomes of the proposed algorithm in the case of only row packets or column packets lost, and LBMDPC2, in the case of packets lost happened on both row and column descriptions. From this figure, one can see in the first case, the outcome of LBMDPC, LBMDPC1 has the best results. Even packets lost happen on both row and column descriptions, LBMDPC2, the outcome by the LBMDPC, are still better than that of PTSQ and comparable with MD-SPIHT's.

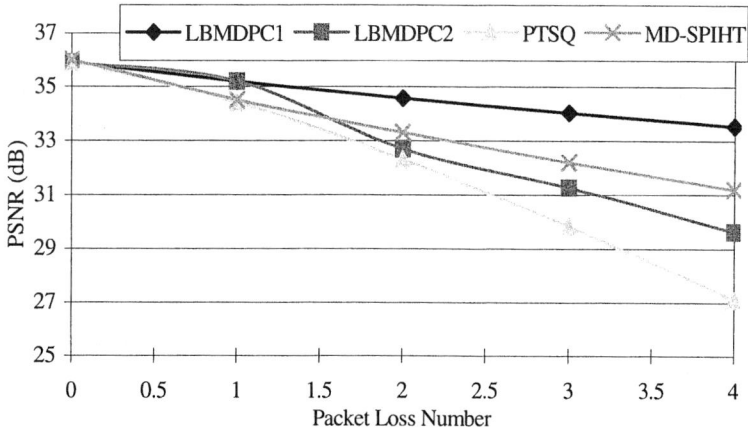

**Fig. 7.** The relationship of PSNR and lost packet number in image "Lena" by PTSQ, MD-SPIHT, and the proposed algorithm

## 4 Concluding Remarks

This paper has developed a new MDC framework, Layer Based Multiple Description Packetized Coding (LBMDPC) for image transmission in the packet erasure channels. Based on the layered coding, we first introduced a new scheme to split each wavelet coefficient of the image to form two bit streams, and then exploited an efficient way to packetize the streams to form row packets and column packets for transmission in packet erasure channels. Combined with the SPIHT codec, the proposed MDC scheme was developed into a new MDC system.

Computer simulating results have shown that the proposed MDC framework has very good error resilient ability if only row packets or column packets are lost. Because each row packet and column packet has only limited intersection, even packets lost happen on both row and column descriptions, the outcome of the proposed algorithm still better than that of PTSQ and are comparable with MD-SPIHT.

## Acknowledgements

This work is partially supported by the National Natural Science Foundation of China under grant 60472106 and the Fujian Province Natural Science Foundation under Grant A0410018.

## References

1. Goyal, V.K.: Multiple Description Coding: Compression Meets the Network. IEEE Signal Processing Magazine 18 (2001) 74–93
2. Vaishampayan, V.A.: Design of Multiple Description Scalar Quantizers. IEEE Trans. on Information Theory 39 (1993) 821-834.
3. Battlo, J.C., Vaishampayan, V.: Asymptotic Performance of Multiple Description Transform Codes. IEEE Trans. on Information Theory 43(1997): 703-707.
4. Wang, Y., Orchard, M.T., Reibman, A.R.: Multiple Description Image Coding for Noisy Channels by Pairing Transform Coefficients. In: Proc. of the First IEEE Workshop on Multimedia Signal Processing (1997) 419-424.
5. Jiang, W., Ortega, A.: Multiple Description Coding via Polyphase Transform and Selective Quantization. In: Proc. of Visual Communications and Image Processing (1999) 998-1008.
6. Miguel, A.C., Mohr, A.E., Riskin, E.A.: SPIHT for Generalized Multiple Description Coding. In: Proc. of ICIP (1999) 842-846.
7. Servetto, S.D.: Multiple Description Wavelet Based Image Coding. IEEE Trans. on Image Processing 9 (2000) 813-26.
8. Cai, C., Chen, J.: Structure Unanimity Based Multiple Description Subband Coding. In: Proc. of ICASSP2004, vol. 3 (2004) 261-264.
9. Chou, P.A., Wang, H.J. Padmanabhan, V.N.: Layered Multiple Description Coding. In: Proc. of Packet Video Workshop (2003)
10. Shapiro, J.M.: Embedded Image Coding Using Zerotrees of Wavelet Coefficients. IEEE Trans. on Signal Processing 41 (1993) 3445-3463.

11. Said A., Pearlman W. A.: A New, Fast, and Efficient Image Codec Based on Set Partitioning in Hierarchical Trees. IEEE Trans. on Circuits Syst., Video Technol. 6 (1996) 243-250.
12. Cai, C., Mitra, S.K., Ding, R.: Smart Wavelet Image Coding: X-Tree Approach. Signal Processing 82 (2002) 239-249
13. Antonini, M., Barlaud, M., Mathieu. P, Daubechies, I.: Image Coding Using Wavelet Transform. IEEE Trans. on Image Processing 4 (1992) 205-221.
14. Witten, I.H., Neal, R.M., Cleary, J. G.: Arithmetic Coding for Data Compression. Commun. ACM 30 (1987) 520-540.

# Extended Application of
# Scalable Video Coding Methods

Zhi-gang Li[1], Zhao-yang Zhang[2], Biao Wu[1], and Ying Zhang[1]

[1] School of Communication and Information Engineering,
Shanghai University, Shanghai 200072, China
jakelee@graduate.shu.edu.cn, ww5bb@sina.com,
zhgyg@mail.shu.edu.cn
[2] Key Laboratory of Advanced Displays and System Application,
Ministry of Education
zhyzhang@yc.shu.edu.cn

**Abstract.** SP(Synchronization-Predictive) frame coding, which enables high efficiency of switching between two video bitstreams with different qualities, is supported by H.264/AVC. And FGS(Fine-Granular-Scalability) coding is supported by MPEG-4 video standard. This paper proposes a solution for combination these two tools with each other so as to adapt to high bandwidth variations of Internet or wireless networks and to low bandwidth variations flexibly for transmitted video streams. Experimental results show that our proposed system outperforms FGS coding by 0.47dB and the H.264/AVC-based video stream switching approach by 0.23dB on average.

## 1 Introduction

It is a hot focus of current researches in video standards that how to transmit video streams over Internet and wireless networks. Two methods, stream switching(SS) and FGS(Fine-Granular-Scalability) video encoding, are settled on to the problem of random variations of bandwidth in these transmission environments.

FGS video encoding has already been adopted by MPEG-4 video standard, which can provides better balance between coding efficiency and scalability than other scalable video codings, while maintaining a very flexible video coding structure. But its defect is the low encoding efficiency compare to other video encoding tools. A comparison with the traditional method under same bandwidth is conducted in [1] and the result shows FGS has 2-3dB disadvantages in its performance. Thus come so many improvements on promotion of the FGS performances such as [2,3], some of which attempt to use in H.264/AVC, however getting a limited effect.

SP(Synchronization-Predictive) frame has been adopted in H.264/AVC for allowing high efficiency of stream switching methods among several bitstreams so as to elevate encoding efficiency[4,5]. Identical reconstructions of the SP frames are permitted even when different reference frames are being used during the period of bitstream switching. One of its advantages is its adaptation to the large scale of bandwidth changes, but having no flexibility of FGS.

Lately X. Sun et al propose a seamless switching scheme[6] to switch down at any frame or switch up at one expected SP frame to other scalable stream. Extra bitstream is needed in the case of switching up process, in which the current scalable bitstream is switched to one operated at higher rates. The most important deficit is that the complexity of its decoder in decoding the high-bit-rate scalable bitstream is about three times of that of a standard MPEG-4 decoder.

In order to overcome the shortcomings of these schemes above, we propose a method to combine the feature of FGS, i.e. the flexible adaption of varying bandwidth in a short span of range, together with the feature of SP frame's bitstream switching, i.e. the high coding efficiency of two or more pre-encoded bitstream with different rates to adapt to higher fluctuated bandwidth change, to use in H.264/AVC. The rest of this paper is organized as follows: section 2 and section 3 are the brief overviews of FGS coding and video bitstream switching, respectively. Section 4 presents the proposed combination solution. The experimental results and concluding remarks are in Section 5 and section 6, respectively.

## 2  H.264/AVC-Based FGS Coding

Our FGS structure consists of an H.264/AVC non-scalable base layer encoded at $R_{base}$ and an MPEG-4 enhancement layer encoded using bitplane coding at a maximum bit-rate $R_{max}$. During transmission, the enhancement layer can be truncated at the rate $R_{available}$ in order to fully utilize the available bandwidth. Fig. 1 illustrates the bitplane coding structure for the enhancement layer of FGS. The residue between the original image and the reconstructed image of base layer is compressed with bit plane coding technique for the DCT coefficients to form the enhancement bitstream. Since the bit plane coding produces an embedded bitstream with fine granularity scalability, it is possible for the server to truncate the enhancement layer in order to match the outgoing bit-rate with the channel capacity variations.

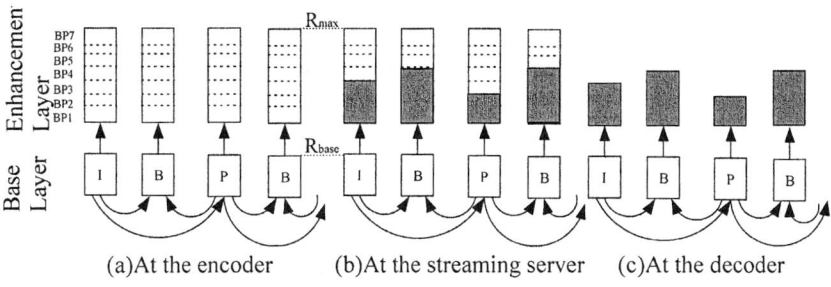

**Fig. 1.** FGS scalability structure. BP1, BP2, ..., BP7 are the bitplanes for the enhancement layer.

If a channel capacity is 80kbps and output frame rate is 10 frames/second, we have to code each frame with an average of 8000 bits. If a rate control is imposed on the base layer such that it is coded with 6000 bits on average, we have to cut the FGS-EL(Enhancement Layer) after 2000 bits on average, depending on the exact value of the actual number of bits we use.

## 3 Video Bitstream Switching

SP frame is one of the features in Extended Profile of H.264/AVC video standard to provide one with a high efficiency of switching among different video streams with similar contents but with different rates. One can insert SP frames in the bitstream to create drift-free switching positions to vary the transmitted bitrate/quality. Fig. 2 shows that one can set up pictures $SP_1$ in a low quality stream, and set up pictures $SP_2$ in a high quality stream, and finish the process switching from the low quality stream to high quality stream within the same sequence by using the secondary SP frame, i.e. pictures $SP_{12}$. Note that the number of bits for $SP_{12}$ is usually far more than that for $SP_1$ or for $SP_2$. The process switching from the high quality stream to low quality stream is alike. So the method of SP frame is a scalability tool with coarse granularity, which is with a feature of large scale of scalability but with less fine-granularity or less flexibility than FGS.

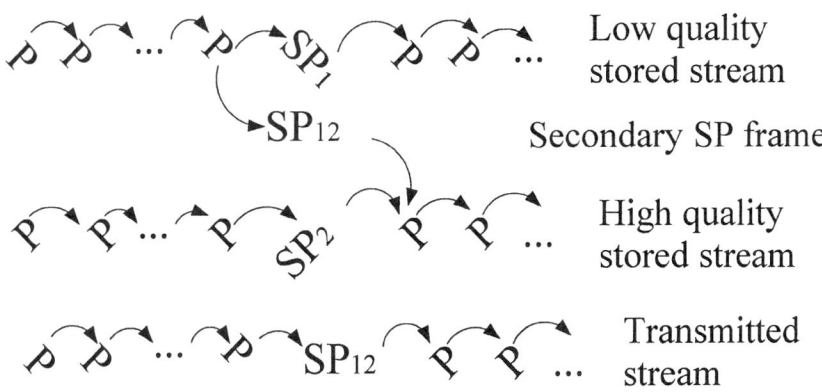

**Fig. 2.** Switching from low quality video stream to high quality one

## 4 Combination of FGS Coding and Video Bitstream Switching

Table 1 gives a brief comparison of video stream switching and FGS coding approach and tells one that the advantages and disadvantages of them are mutually complementary. The combination with each other can enhance the scalable effects for the video bitstreams.

Before our video bitstream switching, there is an adaptive bit-rate selection. Assumed that the available bandwidth fluctuates in the range [$R_{min}$, $R_{max}$], and that two streams are used to cover this bandwidth range, one with low quality and the other

**Table 1.** Comparison of video stream switching and FGS coding

| Comparison | Stream switching | FGS |
|---|---|---|
| Coding Efficiency | High | Become lower when increasing enhancement layer bit-rates |
| Bandwidth Utilization | Low | High, close to 100% |
| Adaptation to bandwidth variation | Only take effects at key frames | Depending on streaming server, it can be done instantly |
| Scalability step | Coarse Granularity | Fine Granular |

with higher quality with bit-rates $R_1$ and $R_2$, respectively, such that $R_{min} \leq R_1 \leq R_2 \leq R_{max}$. In order to be able to send a stream at any given bandwidth, the bit-rate of the lowest quality stream should not be higher than the minimum available bandwidth. For this reason, $R_1$ is selected to be equal to $R_{min}$. The bit-rate $R_2$ for the higher quality stream is chosen to minimize the total distortion D of the fluctuating bandwidth range as follows:

$$D = \sum_{R_{aval}=R_{min}}^{R_{aval}=R_2} D_1 + \sum_{R_{aval}=R_2}^{R_{aval}=R_{max}} D_2, \quad R_{min} < R_2 < R_{max} . \quad (1)$$

Where $D_1$ and $D_2$ are the calculated distortions of the low and high quality decoded streams respectively, and are measured in terms of mean square error. Although in theoretical the bit rate of each enhancement layer bitstream can be truncated up to $R_{max}$, it is not necessary in our proposed combination scheme. The maximum bit rate covered by low quality stream is selected to be slightly higher than $R_2$. With these two scalable bitstreams, any desired bit rate within the band-width range can be achieved by selecting the proper scalable video bitstream and truncating the enhancement layer bitstream. For example, if the available channel bandwidth is less than $R_2$, then low quality video stream is sent to the client; otherwise the high quality one is sent.

Our H.264/AVC-based FGS coding use two adaptive quantization techniques, i.e. selective enhancement and frequency weighting simultaneously. Selective enhancement can be used to enhance a particular region of the video pictures, while frequency weighting can be employed effectively to reduce some of the block artifacts throughout an FGS coded video frame. The new value $c'(i; j; k)$ of a coefficient i of block j(within macroblock k) can be expressed as follows:

$$c'(i,j,k) = 2^{n_{se}(k)} \cdot 2^{n_{fw}(i)} \cdot c(i,j,k) . \quad (2)$$

Where $c(i,j,k)$ is the original value of the coefficient, $n_{se}(k)$ and $n_{fw}(i)$ are the shifted number of bitplanes for selected macroblocks' selective enhancement and selected DCT coefficients' frequency weighting, respectively.

Our proposed combination scheme with two scalable video bitstreams is depicted in Fig. 3. Small bandwidth change is accommodated by the truncation of FGS enhancement layer, and large bandwidth variation is then allowed by starting up switching from the low quality stream 1 to high quality stream 2 within the same sequence with the extra secondary SP frame $SP_{12}$ to take place of primary SP frame $SP_1$ or $SP_2$ or vice versa.

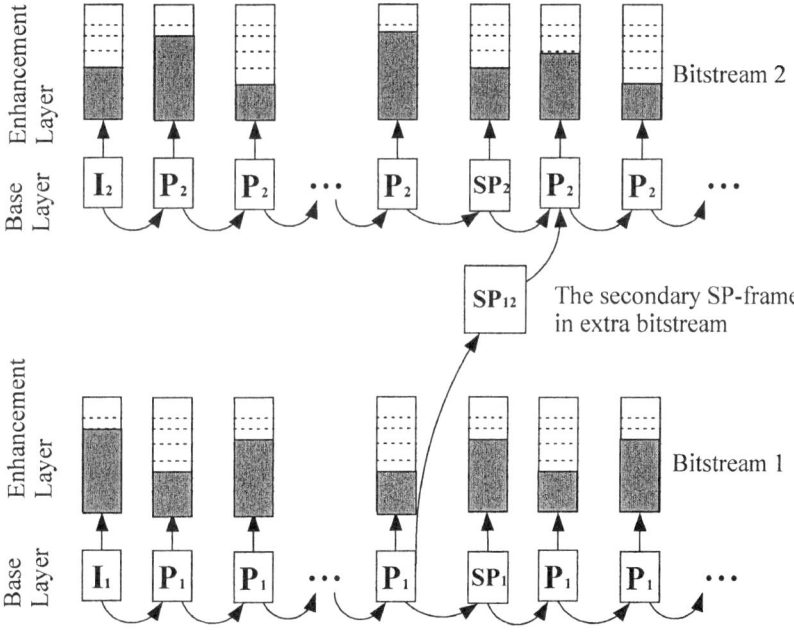

**Fig. 3.** Combining FGS coding with video stream switching

## 5 Experimental Results

The number of frames to be encoded is 30 in the simulations. The first frame is encoded as an I-frame and at fixed intervals, 1s, the frames are encoded as I- or SP-frames whereas the remaining frames are encoded as P-frames under Extended Profile of H.264/AVC. The H.264/AVC encoder parameters are shown in Table 2.

**Table 2.** Encoding parameters for the H.264/AVC base layers

| Test sequence | Foreman |
|---|---|
| Spatial resolution | QCIF(176*144) |
| Encoded frame rate | 10fps |
| SP Picture Periodicity | 10Hz |
| Quantization Parameter of SP-Pictures for Prediction Error (QPSP) | QP-2, where QP represents the quantized parameter used for P frames. |
| Quantization Parameter of SP-Pictures for Predicted Blocks (QPSP2) | QP-1 |
| Number of reference frames | SP frame and P frame both use 1 reference frame. |
| Frame Structure | I P P…P SP P P … |
| Rate-distortion optimization option | Enabled |
| Entropy coding | CAVLC |

The choice of the QPSP2 value in Table 2 can be application dependent: when SP pictures are used to facilitate random access, due to that SP frames placed within a single bitstream will have the major influence on compression efficiency, QPSP2 value should be small; on the other hand, when SP pictures are used for video streaming rate control, QPSP2 value should be kept close to QPSP since SP-pictures sent during switching from one bitstream to another will have large share of the overall bandwidth. We first set the quality of the non switching SP frames by using QPSP, then fine tuning the tradeoff between the size of the switching SP frames and non switching SP frames by using QPSP2.

In our experiment, the bit rate periodically switches from 64 to 128 kbps. Each cycle starts at 64kbps for 1s and then changes to 128kbps for 1s and then changes to 64kbps for 1s. The overhead bits for switching are also included in this simulation. Apparently, the proposed scheme can achieve the best performance among these 3 evaluated schemes from Fig. 4a and Fig. 4b. The performance of 2 different schemes compare to each other in terms of bandwidth adaptation in Fig. 4a: FGS coding and our proposed algorithm(FGS coding+video stream switching). The PSNR of Y components of luma for proposed method have a gain of 0.47dB on average than FGS scheme. We know that our proposed method better than FGS coding by about 2dB after switching up, whereas the second switching(switching down) leads to a little degradation. The main reason of this degradation is that the same set of motion vectors obtained from the high bit-rate bitstream is used to encode the low bit-rate video in the proposed scheme, and the coding efficiency of the low bit-rate bitstream is going to drop.

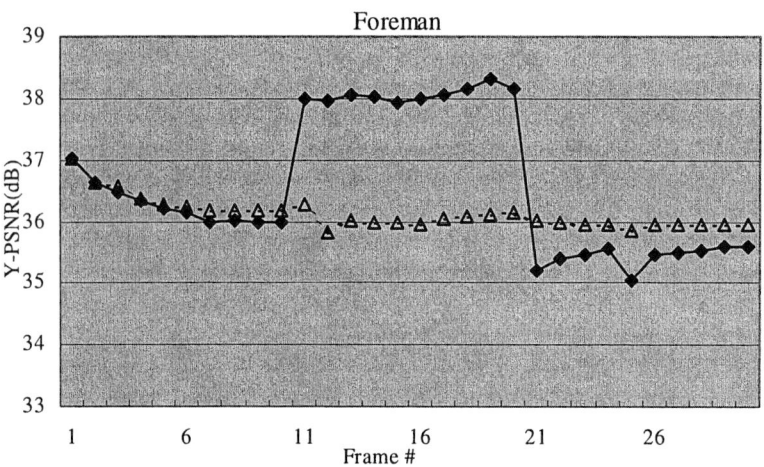

**Fig. 4a.** Dynamic performance of proposed method(*solid line with diamond tags*) vs. FGS coding(*dashed line with triangle tags*)

Fig. 4b compares our proposed method with the individual video stream switching under the same conditions. The PSNR of Y components for the former scheme have a gain of 0.23dB on average than the latter one.

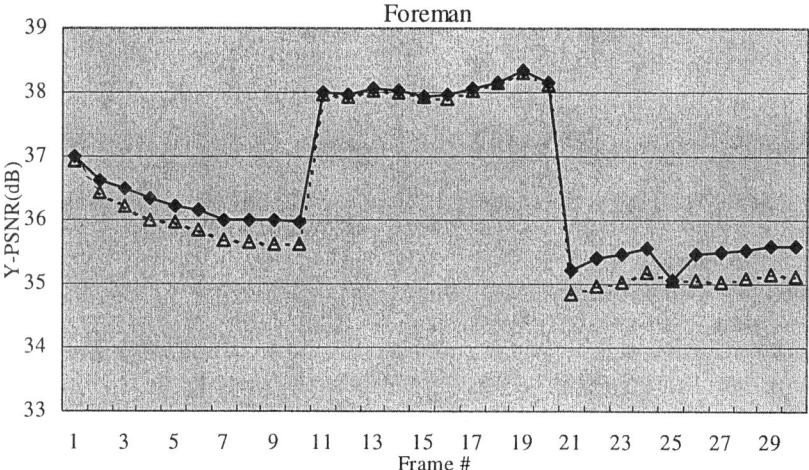

**Fig. 4b.** Dynamic comparison of proposed method(*solid line with diamond tags*) vs. video stream switching(*dashed line with triangle tags*)

## 6 Conclusions

A solution provided herein combining the FGS characteristics, with video stream switching based on H.264/AVC's SP frame coding concept, is implemented into H.264/AVC reference software JM8.6. The base layer is encoded with H.264/AVC, and the enhancement layer is encoded with FGS coding. Our proposed switching scheme among scalable video bitstreams improves the efficiency of video streaming over a broad range of bit rates. And the switching among scalable video bitstreams is drifting-free.

## Acknowledgement

This work was supported by the National Natural Science Foundation of P.R. China under Grants 60332030 and 60372091.

## References

1. H. Radha, M. van der Schaar, and Y. Chen, "The MPEG-4 Fine-Grained Scalable Video Coding Method for Multimedia Streaming Over IP", IEEE Transactions on Multimedia, vol. 3, no. 1, pp. 53~68, Mar. 2001
2. Feng Wu, Shipeng Li, Ya-Qin Zhang, "A Framework for Efficient Progressive Fine Granular Scalable Video Coding", IEEE Trans. On Circuit and Systems for Video Technology, pp. 332-344, Vol. 11, No. 3, March 2001

3. K. Ugur and P. Nasiopoulos, "Design Issues and a Proposal for H.264-based FGS", MPEG03/M9505, ISO/IEC JTC1/SC29/WG11, Pattaya, Thailand, March 2003.
4. Karczewicz, M.; Kurceren, R., The SP- and SI-frames design for H.264/AVC, Circuits and Systems for Video Technology, IEEE Transactions on, Volume: 13 , Issue: 7 , July 2003, Pages:637 - 644
5. Xiaoyan Sun; Shipeng Li; Feng Wu; Jacky Shen; Wen Gao, The improved SP frame coding technique for the JVT standard, Image Processing, 2003. Proceedings. 2003 International Conference on , Volume: 3 , 14-17 Sept. 2003, Pages:III - 297-300
6. X. Sun, F. Wu, S. Li, W. Gao, and Y. Q. Zhang, "Seamless Switching of Scalable Video Bitstreams for Efficient Streaming", Multimedia, IEEE Transactions on , Volume: 6 , Issue: 2 , April 2004, Pages:291 - 303

# Accelerated Motion Estimation of H.264 on Imagine Stream Processor

Haiyan Li, Mei Wen, Chunyuan Zhang, Nan Wu, Li Li, and Changqing Xun

School of Computer Science, National University of Defense Technology,
Chang Sha, Hu Nan, P. R. of China, 410073
xing_can@163.com

**Abstract.** Imagine is a stream-based prototype processor designed for media processing. It uses a three-level bandwidth hierarchy to exploit parallelism and data locality. It has good performance in media processing. H.264 is the newest digital video coding standard. It can achieve high coding efficiency at the cost of complex computation. In addition, video pictures have natural stream features, such as good special locality and limited temporal dependency. This paper presents an accelerated implementation of motion estimation, which is the most time-consuming part in H.264 coding framework, on Imagine stream processor. Experimental results show that the coding efficiency for QCIF format can be up to 372fps and surpass real-time requirement. The acceleration of stream processing is significant. It proves that H.264 coding is suited for implementation on Imagine.

## 1 Introduction

Imagine is a prototype processor of stream architecture developed by Stanford University in 2002. We have done much research on Imagine stream architecture [1,2]. The stream model decomposes applications into a series of computation kernels that operate on data streams. A kernel is a small program executed in arithmetic clusters that is repeated for each successive element of its input streams to produce output stream for the next kernel in the application. Streams are ordered finite-length sequences of data records. Each record in a stream is a collection of related data words of the same type [3]. Imagine can provide high performance in many domains such as media processing and signal processing. For example, Imagine is able to sustain performance of 15.35 giga operations per second (GOPS) in MPEG-2 encoding application, corresponding to 287 frames per second (fps) on a 320*288-pixel, 24-bit color image [4].

H.264 [5], proposed by Joint Video Team (JVT), is a new digital video coding standard. It aims to high compression, high quality, and flexible network adaptability. Especially, it surpasses MPEG-4 in low-rate video coding, and is suited for the requirement of network video application with low bandwidth but high quality. H.264 is widely-used in video telephony, videoconferencing, television broadcasting, video surveillance, stream media applications and so on.

H.264 has high coding efficiency at the cost of complex computation. In addition, video pictures have natural stream features, such as good spatial locality and limited temporal dependency. Considering the high performance of MPEG-2 on stream architecture, it is inferred that H.264 can increase its coding efficiency by stream processing. If so, not only one video coding standard can be implemented efficiently on Imagine. Even for different algorithms in the same standard, stream architecture may satisfy them in virtue of its programmability.

Analyzing each module in H.264 encoder, it can be seen that motion estimation may consume 60% (1 reference frame) to 80% (5 reference frames) of the total encoding time of the H.264 codec and much higher proportion can be obtained if RD optimization or some other tool is invalid and larger search range (such as 48 or 64) is used [6]. Thus, the key of H.264 encoding optimization is how to improve motion estimation algorithms and how to implement existing algorithms efficiently.

This paper introduces H.264 motion estimation algorithm and maps it onto Imagine stream processor. The experimental results show that the coding efficiency for QCIF image format can be up to 372 fps, which exceeds real-time requirement greatly. Compared with V1304 H.264 encoder [7], the speed up is 14.88 times and the acceleration of stream processing is significant. It proves that H.264 is suited for implementation on Imagine.

## 2 UMHexagonS Motion Estimation Algorithm [6]

UMHexagonS algorithm proposed by Tsinghua University can solve "local-minimum" problem well, and therefore it is adopted by H.264 formally. This algorithm uses the hybrid and hierarchical motion search strategies. It includes four steps with different kinds of search pattern: 1) Predictor selection and prediction mode reordering; 2) Unsymmetrical-cross search; 3) Uneven multi-hexagon-grid search; 4) Extended hexagon-based search. With the second and third step, the motion estimation accuracy can be nearly as high as that of full search. But the computation load and operations can be reduced even more.

Unsymmetrical-cross search uses prediction vector as the search center and extends in the horizontal and vertical directions respectively. Uneven multi-hexagon-grid search includes two sub-steps: First a full search is carried out around the search center. And then a 16-HP multi-hexagon-grid search strategy is taken. Extended hexagon-based search is used as a center biased search algorithm, including hexagon search and diamond search in a small range.

## 3 Imagine Stream Processor [8]

Imagine is a programmable coprocessor that directly executes applications mapped to streams and kernels. Fig.1 diagrams the Imagine stream architecture. Kernels typically loop through all input-stream elements, performing a compound stream operation on each element. A compound stream operation reads an element from its input stream(s) in the stream register file (SRF). During computation, all temporary data are stored in the local register file (LRF) of each cluster. And the computed results in a kernel are sent back to the output stream in the SRF. Only the initial and final data streams need to be transferred to the off-chip SDRAM. This storage bandwidth hierarchy is able to meet the large instruction and data bandwidth demands of media processing well.

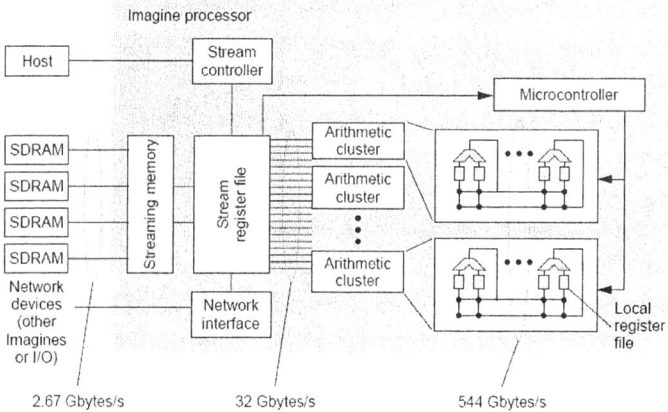

**Fig. 1.** Imagine stream architecture

Programming on Imagine is divided into two levels: stream level (using StreamC) and kernel level (using KernelC). These levels are corresponding to stream scheduling and stream processing in logic view respectively. Programmers can be absorbed in the stream framework definition and kernel partition at the stream level. While at the kernel level, programmers should pay attention to the implementation and optimization of the whole program. Imagine provides three kinds of parallelisms: instruction-level parallelism (ILP), data-level parallelism (DLP) and task-level parallelism (TLP). The choice of these three parallelism modes during the implementation depends on the characteristics of a practical application and the power of hardware resources.

## 4 Implementation of H.264 Motion Estimation

H.264 supports a range of block sizes (from 16*16 down to 4*4). Here we take 8*8 block size as an example to describe our motion search kernel (called *blocksearch*).

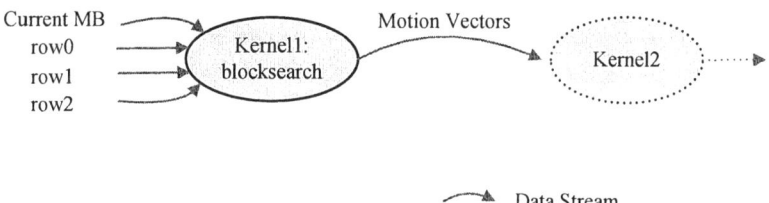

**Fig. 2.** Diagram of *blocksearch* kernel

The input and output streams of *blocksearch* are shown in Fig.2. The motion search window as reference frame is 24*24 and is loaded by way of three input streams. And the sequence of current blocks to be encoded is organized into one input stream. Motion vectors for each block produced by *blocksearch* will be the input for the next kernel.

All these four input streams are of *ubyte4* type (a basic data type in KernelC language [9]), which is composed of 4 packed 8-bit unsigned bytes. Thus, an *ubyte4* stream element can contain four luminance components of horizontally-adjacent pixels in the same block. Fig.3 illustrates the distribution of input stream in eight clusters. It can be seen that each cluster processes a row of pixels in an 8*8 block.

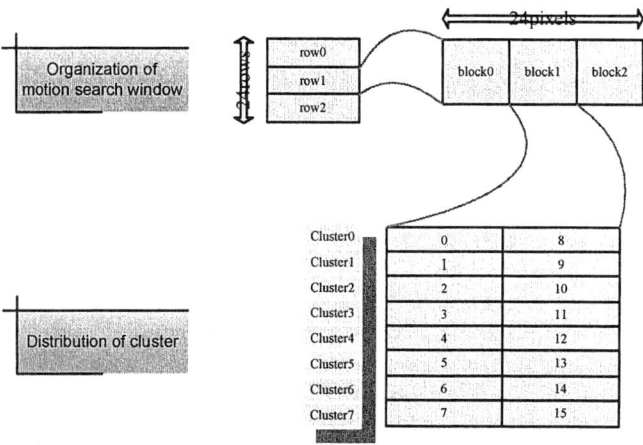

**Fig. 3.** Organization of motion search window and distribution of cluster

Unsymmetrical-cross search operates the blocks in *row1* first, that means the search process begins in the horizontal direction. The sum of absolute difference (SAD) is chosen as our matching criterion. The black and dark gray points in Fig.4 form an 8*8 block. After computing SAD between this block and current block in *Current MB*, the black points in the left column are freed. And load the next column of pixels (gray points) to generate a new 8*8 block for the following search.

When the left four columns of pixels are freed totally, eight corresponding stream elements are consumed, which are not reused in the following search. The search process in the horizontal direction of motion search window needs 17 times SAD computation. The vertical direction performs similar search process. The motion vector with the minimum SAD will be chosen as search center of next search step.

A simple multi-hexagon-grid search is shown in Fig.5 (a full search in a small range is not described here.). The white points are processed in the previous unsymmetrical-cross search; the gray point presents the result position of unsymmetrical-cross search; and the black points are indicators of reference block used in multi-hexagon-grid search. It can be seen that the reference block stream is irregular, not in the horizontal direction or in the vertical direction. Thus, the data rearrangement is needed to organize reference blocks in the order as Fig.5 shows. Index stream or communication kernel is feasible for complex stream rearrangement.

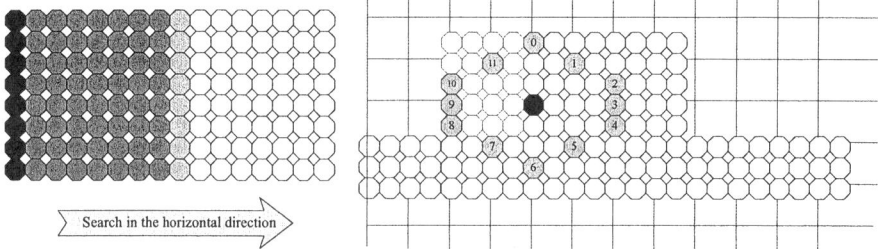

**Fig. 4.** Load and free pixels in unsymmetrical-cross search

**Fig. 5.** Search process of a simple multi-hexagon-grid search

There is large potential data-level parallelism in the block search process. We exploit the parallelism in two approaches, shown in Fig.6. One approach described above, uses four pixels as a stream element that we called pixel stream. SAD computation for different rows of a block can be processed simultaneously in eight clusters of Imagine. Data transfer is implemented through inter-cluster communication. While the second approach uses coarse-grain parallelism called macorblock stream, processing eight different blocks in its own motion search window to produce eight motion vectors simultaneously. The inter-cluster communication will be decreased. However, the number of stored reference block becomes larger. In addition, the motion search windows for each coding block may overlap and bring large redundancy. As a result, the requirement of SRF and LRF bandwidth will increase. Table 1 gives the comparison between pixel stream approach and macroblock stream approach.

**Table 1.** Comparison between two approaches - pixel stream and macroblock stream

|  | Pixel stream | Macroblock stream |
| --- | --- | --- |
| Stream organization | Natural | Complex |
| Record Size | 1 word | 16 words |
| Loading overhead | Little | Large |
| Bandwidth requirement | Low | High |
| Communication | Large | Little |

## 5 Result Analysis

For QCIF image format accepted by H.264 encoder, its definition is PAL: 176*144. At 500MHz on the simulator of Imagine (ISIM), Imagine stream processor can provide 897 cycles to execute unsymmetrical-cross search, and 1581 cycles for uneven multi-hexagon-grid search in pixel-stream approach. Processing 8*8 block needs 2478 cycles, namely 4.956ns. Thus, the total time for processing a frame of QCIF image, which has 396 invocations of kernel, is 1.96ms. Some techniques like loop unrolling or software pipelining may optimize kernel's implementation and improve system performance. For example after unrolling loop twice, 569 cycles is needed for unsymmetrical-cross search and 1165 cycles for uneven multi-hexagon-grid search. In this instance, 1.37ms is enough for encoding one frame and the total performance improves nearly 30%.

While in macroblock-stream approach, it needs 5646 cycles for eight different macroblocks. The run time of kernel is 2.5 times faster than that of pixel-stream approach. However, it is only an ideal result. In practice, it will be limited by large overhead of stream loading. So we implemented our H.264 encoder by using pixel-stream approach.

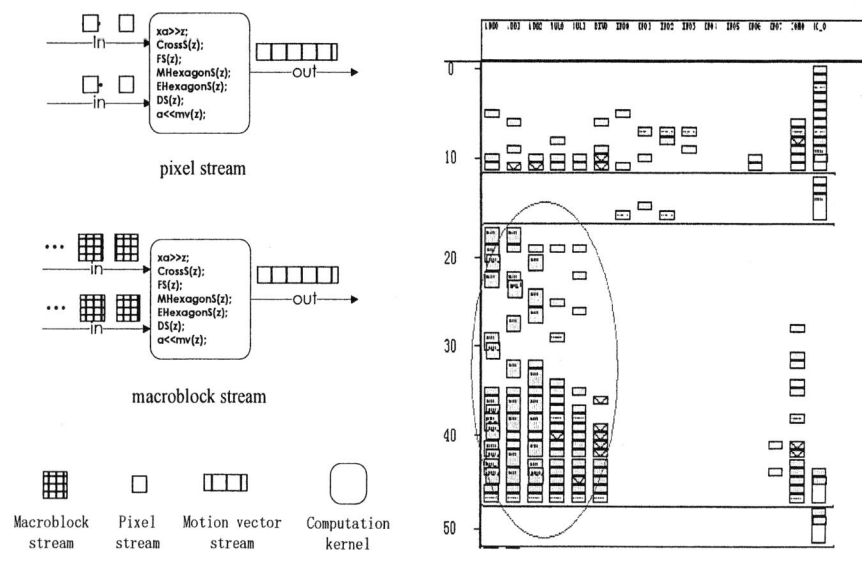

**Fig. 6.** Kernel diagram of pixel stream and macroblock stream

**Fig. 7.** Schedule diagram of *blocksearch*

Using our H.264 encoder including basic parameter-I slices, P slices and CAVLC, the coding efficiency for QCIF image on Imagine stream processor can be up to 372fps. Table 2 illustrates the comparison of an average encoding time for each QCIF frame among JM50 reference program (written by JVT), ShowVideo encoder (with an improved algorithm) [10], V1304 (developed by DSP Research, Inc.) [7] and our implementation on Imagine. Though our experiment excludes extended hexagon based search, the motion estimation accuracy can satisfy the requirement of application. It can be seen that the speed of H.264 motion estimation on Imagine surpasses that of JM reference program greatly, and achieves more obvious performance improvement than that of improved algorithm on general PC. Compared with 25fps of V1304 H.264 encoder, the speed up is 14.88 times. It profits from that stream architecture can support a great deal of ALUs for computation-intensive application, and provide enough instructions and data to fill ALUs in order to keep ALU utilization high (see the circle in Fig.7, where horizontal axis displays hardware resources and vertical axis displays time. A rectangle within the axes indicates using a resource over a period of time. ). The actual coding efficiency may be lower than theoretic value that is because the data stream has extra loading overhead and the functional units keep idle until all required data stream elements are loaded in each cluster. How to organize input/output stream efficiently and exploit parallelism to the utmost extent, is the key of improving the performance of application.

**Table 2.** Comparison of different implementation for H.264 motion estimation

|  | System Environment | Chosen Algorithm | Motion Estimation Range | Average Encoding Time |
|---|---|---|---|---|
| Imagine Implementation | Imagine | UMHexagonS | 24 | 1.37ms/frame |
| JM50 Reference Program | AMD 1.2G + DDR256M | UMHexagonS | 32 | 447.5ms/frame |
| ShowVideo | AMD 1.2G + DDR256M | new algorithm in [10] | 32 | 22.5ms/frame |
| V1304 H.264 Encoder | V1304 | - | - | 40ms/frame |

(Data for JM50 and ShowVideo refer to [10])

## 6 Conclusion

UMHexagonS motion estimation algorithm of H.264 encoder is mapped onto Imagine stream processor in this paper. We have achieved good performance that the coding efficiency for QCIF image format is up to 372fps. We can infer that H.264 coding standard is suited for Imagine based on the implementation of H.264 core algorithm. Thus, Imagine can implement many video-coding standards (MPEG-2, H.264 etc.). The flexibility is comparable with DSP, but the performance can be increased significantly. Imagine has such a great advantage in video coding domain. Our future work is optimizing the H.264 encoder on Imagine. It can provide experience and reference for mapping other video standard on Imagine, and make a contribution to application extension of Imagine.

**Acknowledgements.** We thank High Performance Group of School of Computer Science in National University of Defense Technology for helpful discussions and comments on this work. We thank Imagine project group of Stanford University for providing the Imagine simulator. We thank Xiang Zhong for providing necessary application support. We also thank the reviewers for their insightful comments. This work was sponsored by National Natural Science Foundation of China under Grant 60473080.

## References

1. Mei Wen, Nan Wu, Haiyan Li, and Chunyuan Zhang, Research and Evaluation of Imagine Stream Architecture, *Advances on Computer Architecture, ACA'04*, August 2004
2. Mei Wen, Chunyuan Zhang, Nan Wu, Haiyan Li, and Li Li, A Parallel Reed-solomon Decoder on the Imagine Stream Processor, *Second International Symposium on Parallel and Distributed Processing and Applications, ISPA'04*, December 2004

3. Scott Rixner, William J. Dally, Ujval J. Kapasi, Brucek Khailany, Abelarbo Lopez-Lagunas, Peter R. Mattson, and John D. Owens, A Bandwidth-Efficient Architecuture for Media Processing, Appears in *Micro-31*, 1998
4. John D.Owens, Scott Rixner, Ujval J.Kapasi, Peter Mattson, Brian Towles, Ben Serebrin, and William J. Dally, Media Processing Application on the Imagine Stream Processor, Appears in *the Proceedings of the 2002 International Conference on Computer Design*, 2002
5. Thomas Wiegand, Draft Text of Final Draft International Standard (FDIS) of Joint Video Specification (ITU-T Rec. H.264 | ISO/IEC 14496-10 AVC), *7th Meeting: Pattaya*. March 2003
6. Zhibo Chen, Peng Zhou, and Yun He, Fast Integer Pel and Fractional Pel Motion Estimation for JVT, *6th Meeting: Awaji*, December 2002
7. DSP Research, Inc. V1304:H.264/MPEG4-AVC Encoder, http://www.dspr.com
8. Brucek Khailany, William J. Dally, Ujval J. Kapasi, Peter Mattson, Jinyung NamKoong, John D. Owens, Brian Towles, Andrew Chang, and Scott Rixner, Imagine: Media Processing with Streams, *IEEE Micro*, March-April 2001
9. Abhishek Das, Peter Mattson, Ujval Kapasi, John Owens, Scott Rixner, and Nuwan Jayasena, Imagine Programming System User's Guide 2.0, http://cva.stanford.edu, June 2004
10. Cao Wenfeng, Zhang Ying, Zhang Zhaoyang, and Zhang Yijun, "An Integer Pixel Motion Estimation Algorithm Applicable to H.264", *Journal of Shanghai University (Natural Science)*, August 2004

# MPEG-2 Test Stream with Static Test Patterns in DTV System

Soo-Wook Jang[1], Gwang-Soon Lee[2], Eun-Su Kim[1], Sung-Hak Lee[1], and Kyu-Ik Sohng[1]

[1] School of Electronic Engineering and Computer Science,
Kyungpook National University 1370, Sankyug-Dong, Buk-Gu, Daegu,
702-701, Korea
{jjang, saeloum, shark2, kisohng}@ee.knu.ac.kr
[2] Electronics and Telecommunications Research Institute,
161 Gajeong-Dong, Yuseong-Gu, Daejeon, 305-350, Korea
gslee@etri.re.kr

**Abstract.** MPEG-2 test stream for evaluation the static picture quality of digital television (DTV) should meet both good picture quality and stable bit rate. In this paper, we present a method for generating a high quality test stream to evaluate the static picture quality in DTV receiver. The proposed method is suitable for encoding the static test pattern, such as multiburst and crosshatch, and is based on user-defined quantization and adaptive zero stuffing algorithm. The user-defined quantization is suitable for minimizing the quantization error, which is the reason of degradation of picture quality, and the adaptive zero stuffing algorithm is used to solve the overflow of video buffer verifier (VBV) buffer while encoding process by MPEG-2 encoder. Experimental results show that the average PSNR and the bit rate of the proposed method have more efficient and stable than those of the conventional.

## 1 Introduction

The basic structure of current TV system is newly created by digital technology, delivering high quality video, audio, and data. As the DTV service becomes more widely used than traditional analog TV system, how to measure a picture quality in DTV becomes the main problem. So, the need for a reference test stream to evaluate the picture quality of DTV has substantially increased [1]. The test streams are needed to perform the role traditionally taken by static analogue test patterns and are must satisfied MPEG-2 regulation [2]. From equipment manufacture to system monitoring, the test stream are must guarantee the good picture quality and stable bit rate during the decoding process to evaluate the picture quality [3], [4].

At the heart of coding in MPEG-2 is the discrete cosine transform (DCT). When the DCT is computed for a block of pels, it is desirable to represent the coefficients for high spatial frequencies with less precision, which is considered the spatial frequency response of the human visual system (HVS). This is done by a process called quantization. However, if the spatial frequencies become higher and higher, quantization errors are increased. There is the reason of degradation of picture quality at high spatial frequencies.

For the bit rate control in MPEG-2, if more coding bit than the allocated target number are exhausted, the remaining bit resource in the GOP is getting smaller, In such a case, insufficient coding bits can be allocated to the pictures at the end of the GOP, which may result in severe degradation of picture quality if buffer overflow. C.-T. Ahn et al. [5] proposed zero bit stuffing to prevent the VBV buffer overflow which can cause annoying picture quality degradation. But this method is used simply to prevent buffer overflow without improving picture quality, so that it is difficult to expect good picture quality. if the target number of bits and the number of actual coding bits for each picture do not match well, than the degradation of picture quality and buffer overflow may occur at the end of the GOP. J. W. Lee et al. [6] proposed target bit matching for MPEG-2 video rate control to solve this problem. This algorithm is based on accurate bit estimation, but there is only better than the MPEG-2 Test Model 5 (TM5)[7] algorithm for the complex and fast-moving sequence, while both algorithms yield similar performances for the simple and slowly-moving sequence [6].

This paper proposed a new method for generating the reference test stream to evaluate the picture quality of DTV. The test stream is encoded the static test pattern, such as multiburst and crosshatch, by using MPEG-2 encoder. In order to obtain the test stream with good picture quality, we propose a new user-defined quantization and an adaptive zero stuffing algorithm. The user-defined quantization table is suitable for minimizing the quantization error which is the reason of degradation of picture quality, and the adaptive zero stuffing algorithm that determines the number of zero stuffing bits for preventing buffer overflow and maintaining good picture quality at the same time.

To evaluate the proposed method, we generate the test pattern stream using MPEG-2 encoder with and without the proposed algorithm respectively. Experimental results show that the test pattern stream has a stable bit rate during the decoding process, and the PSNR of the proposed method is about 4 dB higher than that of the conventional cases. The proposed method has a stable bit rate and good picture quality and it is suitable for evaluation a DTV receiver.

## 2 The Proposed Algorithm

To obtain a test stream with good picture quality and stable bit rate, this paper proposed a new algorithm, which is suitable for encoding the static test pattern. The proposed method is shown in Fig. 1.

### 2.1 Proposed User-Defined Quantization

DCT and visually-weighted quantization of the DCT are key parts of the MPEG-2 coding system. Quantization is basically a process for reduction the precision of the DCT coefficients. It is desirable to represent the coefficients for high spatial frequencies with less precision, which is considered the spatial frequency response of the HVS. However, in case of quantizing with default weighting table, if the spatial frequencies become higher and higher then quantization errors increased, which is the reason of degradation of picture quality and undesirable result. The new user-defined quantization is proposed to solve this problem. The proposed weighting table values are set by the minimum value so that there is no degradation of picture quality during quantization process, as shown in Fig. 2. Moreover, proposed weighting table is transmitted to one part of sequence header and is available without change of decoder.

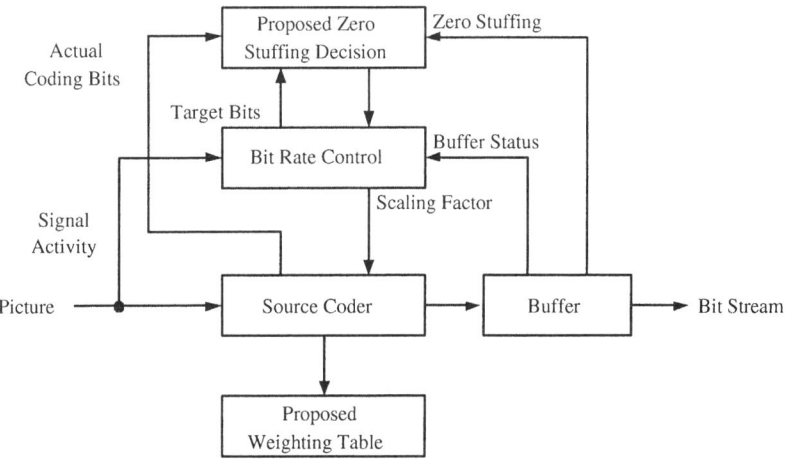

**Fig. 1.** Block diagram for video compression by proposed algorithm

| 8  | 16 | 19 | 22 | 26 | 27 | 29 | 34 |
|----|----|----|----|----|----|----|----|
| 16 | 16 | 22 | 24 | 27 | 29 | 34 | 37 |
| 19 | 22 | 26 | 27 | 29 | 34 | 34 | 38 |
| 22 | 22 | 26 | 27 | 29 | 34 | 37 | 40 |
| 22 | 26 | 27 | 29 | 32 | 35 | 40 | 48 |
| 26 | 27 | 29 | 32 | 35 | 40 | 48 | 58 |
| 26 | 27 | 29 | 34 | 38 | 46 | 56 | 69 |
| 27 | 29 | 36 | 38 | 46 | 56 | 69 | 83 |

(a)

| 8 | 8 | 8 | 8 | 8 | 8 | 8 | 8 |
|---|---|---|---|---|---|---|---|
| 8 | 8 | 8 | 8 | 8 | 8 | 8 | 8 |
| 8 | 8 | 8 | 8 | 8 | 8 | 8 | 8 |
| 8 | 8 | 8 | 8 | 8 | 8 | 8 | 8 |
| 8 | 8 | 8 | 8 | 8 | 8 | 8 | 8 |
| 8 | 8 | 8 | 8 | 8 | 8 | 8 | 8 |
| 8 | 8 | 8 | 8 | 8 | 8 | 8 | 8 |
| 8 | 8 | 8 | 8 | 8 | 8 | 8 | 8 |

(b)

**Fig. 2.** (a) Default and (b) proposed quantization weighting table

## 2.2 Proposed Zero Stuffing Algorithm

We propose a new algorithm that determines the number of zero stuffing bits for preventing VBV buffer overflow and maintaining the high picture quality at the same time. The proposed method is shown in Fig. 3.

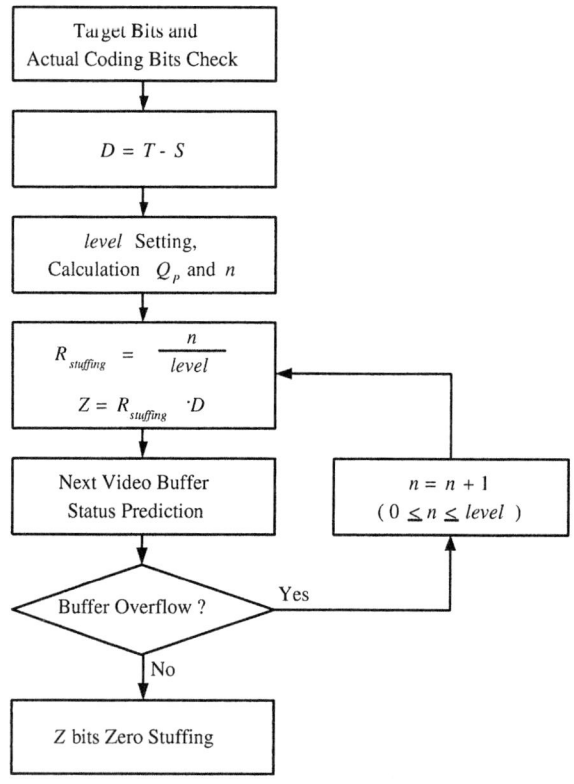

**Fig. 3.** Flowchart of the proposed zero stuffing algorithm

For this operation, we can exploit the relationship between the number of actual coding bits and the number of target bits. The difference $D_{i,p,b}$ can be determined by the following relation.

$$D_{i,p,b} = T_{i,p,b} - S_{i,p,b} \tag{1}$$

where $T$ and $S$ are target number of bits and actual coding bits respectively. And subscription $i$, $p$, and $b$ correspond to a picture type I, P, and B respectively. If the target number of bits and the number of actual coding bits for each picture do not match well, then the degradation of picture quality and buffer overflow may occur at the end of the GOP. However, if the number of zero stuffing bits is allocated as much as $D_{i,p,b}$ to prevent buffer overflow, then the remaining bit resource in the next GOP is getting smaller. As a result, insufficient coding bits are allocated to the pictures of the next GOP, and the severe degradation of picture quality may occur. Therefore we propose a formulation that determines the number of zero stuffing bits $Z_{i,p,b}$ and the initial buffer fullness $d_0^{i,p,b}$

$$Z_{i,p,b} = R_{stuffing} \cdot D_{i,p,b} \qquad (2)$$

and

$$d_0^{i,p,b} = d_0^{i,p,b} + (S_{i,p,b} + Z_{i,p,b} - T_{i,p,b}) \qquad (3)$$

respectively. The initial buffer fullness is updated per each picture. The ratio of zero stuffing $R_{stuffing}$ is

$$R_{stuffing} = \frac{1}{level} \cdot n \qquad (4)$$

where *level* is set by the complexity of encoder, and $n$ is calculated as follows:

$$\alpha - 1 < n < \alpha, \quad n : interger \qquad (5)$$

$$\alpha = \frac{Q_P - Q_{Pmin}}{Q_{Pmax} - Q_{Pmin}} \cdot level \qquad (6)$$

where the $Q_P$ is the PSNR of current picture, the $Q_{Pmin}$ and the $Q_{Pmax}$, the minimum and the maximum PSNR, are updated or maintained by PSNR of current picture, $Q_P$. We set the initial $Q_{Pmin}$ and $Q_{Pmax}$ to 20dB and 90dB respectively. The setting up algorithm of $Q_{Pmin}$ and $Q_{Pmax}$ is shown in Fig. 4. If buffer overflow is predicted at the next picture, then we increase the number of zero stuffing bits through updating the $R_{stuffing}$ and we can prevent buffer overflow. Fig. 5 illustrates relationship between $n$ and $Q_P$.

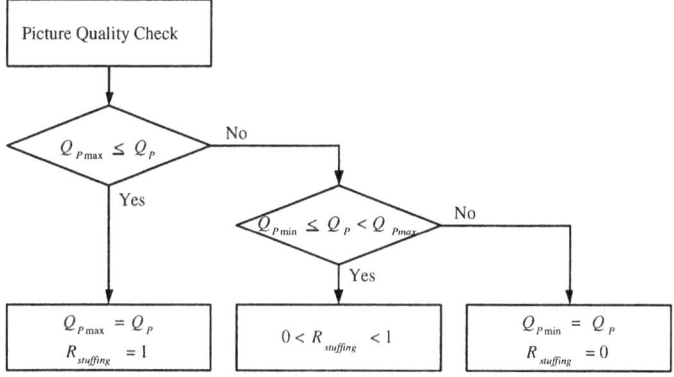

**Fig. 4.** The setting up algorithm of $Q_{Pmin}$ and $Q_{Pmax}$

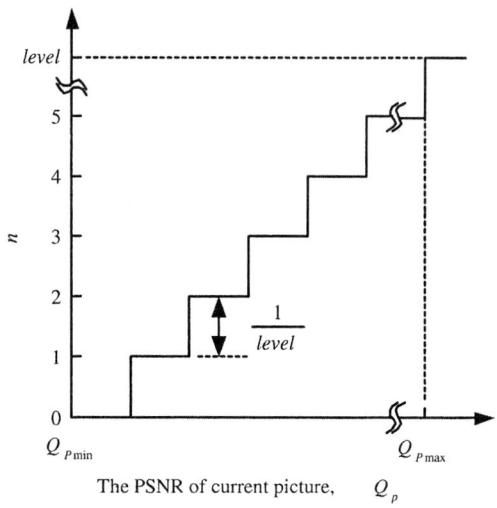

**Fig. 5.** Relationship between $n$ and $Q_P$

## 3 Experiments and Results

We have tested the performance of proposed algorithm with two static test patterns, multiburst and crosshatch as shown in Fig. 6. They are encoded by MPEG-2 encoder with and without the proposed algorithm. Bit rate, VBV buffer size, and *level* are 12 Mbps, 9.78 Mbits, and 9, respectively. And TM5 is used for rate control.

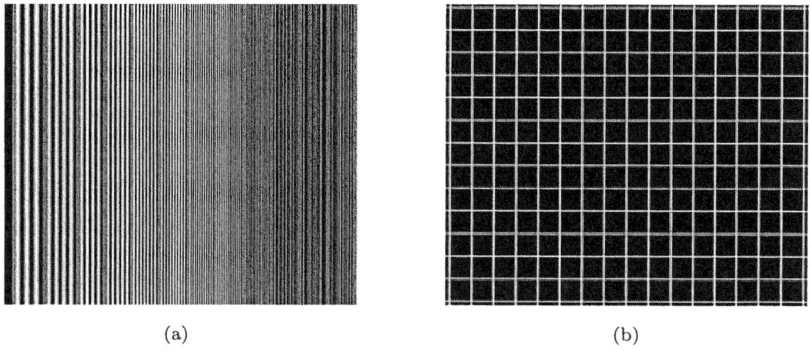

**Fig. 6.** (a) Multiburst (1280 ×720) and (b) crosshatch (1920 ×1080)

Fig. 7(a) and Fig. 8(a) show the PSNR of the test streams. From those figures, we can see that the proposed method is about 4.5 dB more efficient than the conventional cases. Fig. 7(b) and Fig. 8(b) plot the VBV buffer state

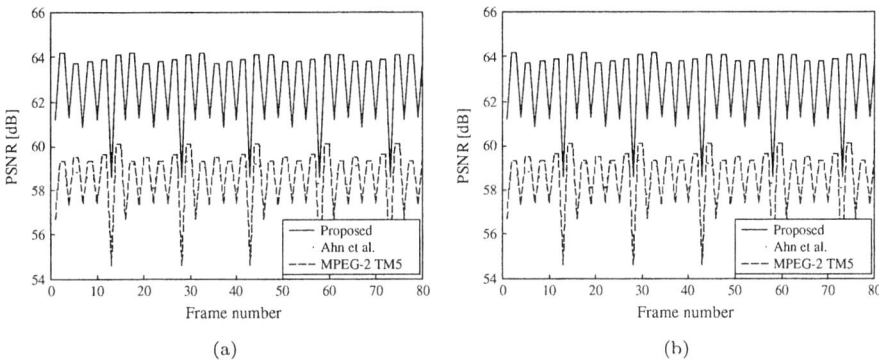

**Fig. 7.** (a) PSNR and (b) VBV buffer state of multiburst pattern encoded

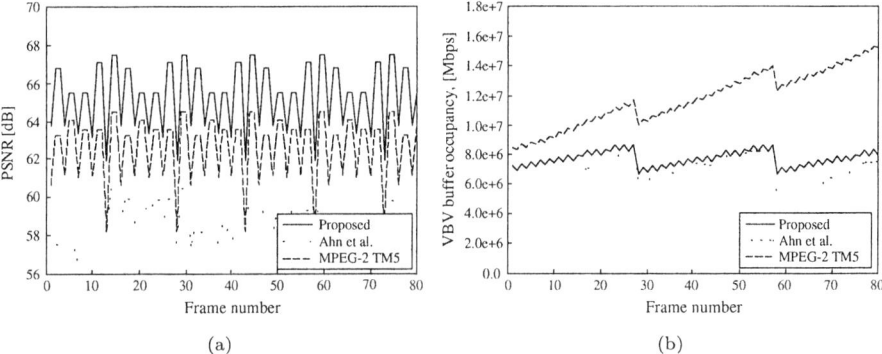

**Fig. 8.** (a) PSNR and (b) VBV buffer state of crosshatch pattern encoded

of the test streams. In both figures, the proposed test stream has a very stable bit rate, while large fluctuation or overflow is occurred in the others'. Therefore, we have not experienced any buffer overflow with the proposed algorithm while high picture quality is to be maintained. The average PSNR of proposed and conventional methods are shown in Table 1.

## 4 Conclusions

High quality test and measurement in the MPEG domain is required to evaluate the static picture quality of DTV receiver. Therefore, high quality test stream is essential if stable bit rate is to be maintained. This paper proposes a new method for generating a high quality test stream to evaluate the static picture quality of DTV receiver. Moreover the proposed method is suitable to compression of the static test pattern. In order to obtain the test stream with good picture quality, we propose a new user-defined quantization for minimizing the quantization

**Table 1.** The average PSNR of the proposed method and the conventional methods

| Test Images | Video Rate [Mbps] | PSNR[dB] | | |
| :---: | :---: | :---: | :---: | :---: |
| | | Proposed | Ahn et al. [5] | MPEG-2 TM5 |
| Multiburst | 12 | 62.8 | 58.7 | 58.6 |
| Crosshatch | 12 | 65.4 | 58.6 | 62.7 |

error and an adaptive zero stuffing algorithm that determines the number of zero stuffing bits for preventing buffer overflow and maintaining good picture quality at the same time. To evaluate the proposed method, we generate the test pattern streams by using MPEG-2 encoder with and without the proposed algorithm. Experimental results show that the proposed test pattern stream has a stable bit rate during the decoding process, and the PSNR of the proposed method is about 4 dB higher than that of the conventional cases. The proposed method has a stable bit rate and good picture quality and it is suitable for evaluation a DTV receiver.

# References

[1] W. Sohn and J. H. Kim: System Test of Digital DBS System for Video and Audio Signals. IEEE Transactions on Broadcasting, Vol. 45, No. 2, (1999) 187-191
[2] K. D. McCann: Testing and Conformance Checking in the Digital Television Environment. IEE International Broadcasting Convention, No. 428, (1996) 331-336
[3] A. N. Rau: Automated Test System for Digital TV Receivers. IEEE International Conference on Consumer Electronics, (2000) 228-229
[4] C. M. Kim, B. U. Lee, and R. H. Park: Design of MPEG-2 Video Test Bitstreams. IEEE Transactions on Consumer Electronics, Vol. 45, No. 4, (1999) 1213-1220
[5] C. T. Ahn and H. S. Chang: A Parallel Processing Architecture for HDTV Encoding System. International Workshop on HDTV96, (1996) 162-168
[6] J. W. Lee and Y. S. Ho: Target Bit Matching for MPEG-2 Video Rate Control. IEEE Region 10 International Conference on Global Connectivity in Energy, Computer, Communication, and Control, Vol. 1, (1998) 66-69
[7] ISO/IEC JTC1/SC29/WG11. Test Model 5, Draft, (1993)

# Speed Optimization of a MPEG-4 Software Decoder Based on ARM Family Cores

Linjian Mo, Haixiang Zhang, Jiajun Bu, and Chun Chen*

College of Computer Science, Zhejiang University, 310027 Hangzhou, P.R. China
zhhx@vip.sina.com
{molin, bjj, chenc}@zju.edu.cn

**Abstract.** MPEG-4 visual simple profile is a widely used video compression standard for mobile solutions. In general, MPEG-4 video decoder requires high computation power for its complex algorithms. It's difficult to implement MPEG-4 video decoder on hand-held devices directly. In this paper, we proposed a novel color space transform algorithm and optimized the memory access operations. Moreover, the multiperless integer IDCT is adopted to further speed up the decoder. Our optimization is based on ARM7TDMI and ARM920T, which are very desirable cores to mobile solutions for low power consumption. Experimental results show that the optimized decoder acts about 5 times faster than existing XVID MPEG-4 video decoder with small video quality degradation and supports real-time video applications.

## 1 Introduction

MPEG-4 is an ISO/IEC standard developed by the Moving Pictures Expert Group (MPEG) [1]. With the rapid development of Internet, MPEG-4 video is adopted in real-time video communications, such as video telephone, video conferencing and video-on-demand (VOD). In order to improve the compression ratio, many effective but complex algorithms are applied in MPEG-4 standard. However, due to limited computation power, the complex algorithms become a bottleneck of real-time video applications, especially in mobile environment. Optimization of those complex algorithms is inevitable.

There are three time-consuming modules of an actual implementation of MPEG-4 visual simple profile decoder; namely, Frame Display (including the color space transformation, through Frame Display is not part of the MPEG-4 standard, it's an important module for actual application), Memory Access (including VOP reconstruction) and IDCT. Above 50% of the decoding time is taken by these three parts [3].

Many researchers are working on the MPEG-4 video decoder optimization. Roughly, current speed optimization for MPEG-4 software video decoder can be classified into two approaches which are platform-independent and platform-dependent. The former optimizes algorithms and data structures, which can be

---

* The work was supported by National Natural Science Foundation of China (60203013), 863 Program (2004AA1Z2390) and Key Technologies R&D Program of Zhejiang Province (2005C23047 & 2004C11052).

applied in all kinds of platform, such as [3,4,11]; the latter mostly works on special hardware platform, for example, [2] works for ARM7TDMI and [7] proposes the optimization based on multiprocessors.

Although significant performance improvements are achieved with approaches stated above, most of them only take consideration on CPU computing ability rather than memory cache. According to [6], the decoding performance with different memory cache is very different. ARM7TDMI, one of the most widely used cores on mobile phone, does not encompass memory caches and the CPU is usually lower than 100MHZ. The bottleneck is not only low CPU computing ability but also small memory. The work done by [2] is much similar to ours which is also based on MPEG-4 visual simple profile and hand-held devices, but they haven't considered the modules, File Input and Frame Display. Referring to [3], these two parts take up the 37.6% of total decoding time. So optimization of the whole decoding process is valuable for practical application.

ARM family cores are widely used in hand-held devices due to low power consumption. In this paper, we present several speed optimization techniques for MPEG-4 visual simply profile based on the architecture features of ARM cores, especially the memory caches. Our focus is on real-time decoding and the foundation of our approach is time profile result of the XVID software decoder [8]. We classified the decoder modules into CPU intensive and memory intensive modules. Referring to the time profile result, the most time-consuming modules are selected for optimization. A fast color space transformation technique and multiplierless integer IDCT are employed with about 10 times speed up and 0.5 PSNR drop. Furthermore, several optimized memory operating and other algorithms are suggested to reduce the number of memory access.

The rest of this paper is organized as follows. Section 2 describes the details of our approach. We present the experiment results in Section 3 and draw the conclusions in Section 4.

## 2 Speed Optimization Techniques

The MEPG-4 visual simply profile decoding process can decompose into following modules:

- Access Memory: VOP Reconstruction and other memory access operation.
- Color Space Transformation (CST): e.g. Converting from YUV to RGB565.
- IDCT: Fast Inverse Discrete Cosine Transform.
- Inverse Quantization (IQ): Dequantization.
- Motion Compensation (MC): Motion compensation.
- Padding: Rectangular padding for unrestricted motion estimation.
- Pixel Interpolation (Interp): Interpolation of pixels motion compensation.
- Saturation: Limiting the decoded pixel values to special range.
- Others: Routines that do not belong to any other modules.

Profiling the XVID decoder, we found that the decoding process is mainly classified into two parts which are CPU intensive modules and memory access intensive modules.

Table 1 is the profile information of decoding process before optimization.
According to the time profile results, we focus on the color space transform, IDCT and memory access process which include Access Memory and Padding. Optimizing the memory access is much more important on ARM7TDMI because these are no memory cache, and all data is from external memory.

**Table 1.** Time profile information of decoding process before optimization. (Obtained by the *Akiyo* (SQCIF) sequence).

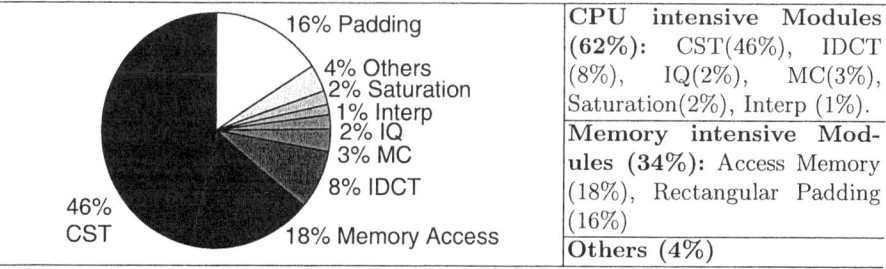

| | |
|---|---|
| CPU intensive Modules (**62%**): CST(46%), IDCT (8%), IQ(2%), MC(3%), Saturation(2%), Interp (1%). | |
| Memory intensive Modules (**34%**): Access Memory (18%), Rectangular Padding (16%) | |
| Others (4%) | |

## 2.1 Converting YUV to RGB565

RGB565 is more widely used color format on hand-held display device rather than YUV, which is the color space MPEG-4 standard based on. To display the video on RGB565 based device, nearly half of the CPU cycles are consumed by the color space transform due to pixel by pixel processing. A lookup table from YUV to RGB565 is suggested to avoid the complex computing.

However, it's too large to setup the full lookup table from YUV to RGB565 directly on common embedded devices, because $255 \times 255 \times 255 \times 2 = 32MB$ space is needed if each entry takes 2 bytes. Some simplification should be done.

It's well known that the human eye is more sensitive to luminance than chroma. Hence the U and V components may be under-sampled to lower the byte size of an image, for improving transmission speeds and saving disk space. Meanwhile, only the high bytes of RGB format are employed in the RGB565. The transfer formula is linear, so the YUV values' low bytes do not have significant impact. As a result, only the high 6, 5, 5 bits of the YUV values are used for forming the lookup table. New table has only $2^6 \times 2^5 \times 2^5 = 2^{16}$ entries, and each entry is still 2 Bytes. The size of the reconstructed table is reduced to 128KB, only 1/256 of the previous one.

The table is constructed by the following equations from (U' V' Y') to (R' G' B'):

$$(Y\ U\ V)^T = (Y'\ U'\ V')^T .* (3\ 7\ 7)^T + (1.5\ 3.5\ 3.5)^T \quad (1)$$

$$\begin{pmatrix} R \\ G \\ B \end{pmatrix} = \begin{pmatrix} 1.164 & 0 & 1.596 \\ 1.164 & -0.391 & -0.813 \\ 1.164 & 2.018 & 0 \end{pmatrix} \left( \begin{pmatrix} Y \\ U \\ V \end{pmatrix} - \begin{pmatrix} 16 \\ 128 \\ 128 \end{pmatrix} \right) \quad (2)$$

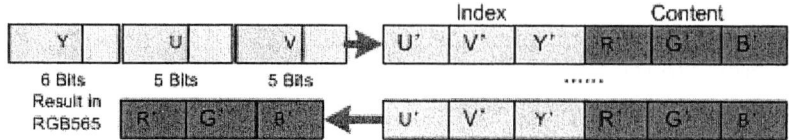

**Fig. 1.** Converting from YUV to RGB565 with simplified table. All components like X' should be complemented which are less than 8 bits. High-bits of the YUV components are selected to form the index.

$$(R'\ G'\ B')^T = (R\ G\ B)^T ./ (7\ 3\ 7)^T \qquad (3)$$

Where $(1.5\ 3.5\ 3.5)^T$ is added to reach the average value and minimize the deviation. ".*", "./" mean applying multiplication or division operations on the corresponding elements of the two matrixes.

The PSNR result in section 3 shows the quality drop is acceptable, especially on low-resolution mobile devices with small LCD display.

On the other hands, the transform is a process performed pixel by pixel which means a very large loop. For example, with the SQCIF (128 × 96) sequences, the loop count reaches $128 \times 96 = 12288$. The decoder will be significantly speeded up even with small optimization on the loop body.

To avoid unnecessary data loading from memory, we limit the variables which are used in the loop body to 14. Although ARM has 16 general proposal registers, two of them should be reserved during the executing. They are *pc* which point to the next instruction and *sp* which is the address of the stack.

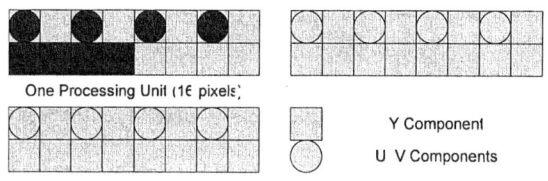

**Fig. 2.** Four YUV components are loaded at the same time during the color space transformation. Here the pixels with the same color are in one load-unit. Each loop processes 16 pixels. (YCbCr 4:2:0 sampled).

Furthermore, in order to minimize the memory access, we process 16 pixels at once. Y, U and V components are represented by 8 bits but the bandwidth of ARM family is 32-bit. Four 8 bits U and V component can be loaded at once to maximize the utility of the system's bandwidth. Following the YCbCr 4:2:0 format, another 16 Y component should be loaded (Fig.2). Finally, only 6 loads should be done compared to the original $16 + 4 + 4 = 24$.

Also the index structure of lookup table will affect the memory access count. In each 2 × 2 pixel region YCbCr 4:2:0 uses four bytes for the Y component and one byte for each of the two chroma components. On the architecture with memory cache such as ARM920T, a memory block named memory page will be

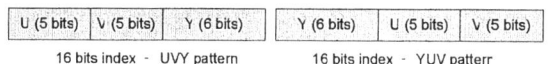

**Fig. 3.** 16 bits index for color space transformation lookup table. (UVY pattern V.S. YUV pattern) The former encounters more cache hits.

fetched at once. The UVY index pattern has much more chance to encounter the *cache hit* than YUV pattern (Fig.3), because it keeps the high bits of the index (UV) unchanged during the 2 × 2 region converting process.

### 2.2 Using Multiplierless Integer Transform

Inverse discrete cosine transform (IDCT) is a computationally intensive module in video decoder. In some complexity mobile sequences, it may even consume about 25% of decoding time. The standard DCT&IDCT is based on floating-point computation. Although, many approximate integer-computation methods are adopted to replace floating-point computation, the integer-computation-based DCT&IDCT is still very complex due to many multiplicative operations. In order to further reduce the complexity, we make use of multiplierless integer transform algorithm to realize the conventional DCT&IDCT.

According to Y.J Chen's algorithm [10], through Walsh-Hadamard transform and lifting scheme, the DCT&IDCT can be processed without multiplication which are replaced by adds and shifts, e.g. $x*5$ can be converted to $x << 2 + x$. So the multiplierless integer DCT&IDCT only utilize shift and add operations and no multiplication is needed. Eight coefficients transform only requires 45 adds and 18 shifts operations, which significantly reduces the complexity compared to the conventional one. Moreover, the multiplierless integer DCT&IDCT inherits all desirable features of conventional DCT and adopting the new transform algorithm will result in negligible video quality degradation.

### 2.3 Memory Access Optimizing

The memory access optimizing techniques are widely applied in our decoder, especially, the VOP reconstruction module. ARM7TDMI, which does not have memory cache, gets more benefit from these techniques.

*Remove the padding process*

Padding is a process adapt to the unrestricted motion estimation. If motion estimation range can be limited into the VOP's bounds during encoding, the padding process can be discarded in decoder. After this, the compression rate raises about 1%-3%, but 16% decoding time is saved.

*Memory allocation pattern*

Better organized data structure is a powerful tool to reduce the number of memory access. Fixed Allocation pattern [9] can protect system from crash which is caused by unprepared memory over use. It's adopted mainly for rapidly memory allocation. It can be found in almost all of the optimized decoder, for example, the process pre-fetching the encoded data from the files.

*Rewrite memset and memcpy function for small size memory operation*

The C library functions memset and memcpy are designed for all type data size, including several checks for different cases. When the transformation data is small, these checks will cause processing time increasing. So we can customize these functions for special requirements.

*32-bit aligned load/store*

The bandwidth of ARM is 32-bit, and the time used to access (load / store) 8-bit data from memory equals that of 32-bit. So we can integrate four 8-bit into one 32-bit when the content is continuous. This technique speed up decoder about 4 times. And it is widely used for all matrix operation in VOP Reconstruction and MC processes.

*Better use the register*

To eliminate unnecessary memory accesses, we limit the parameters of a function no more than four. Moreover, as the analysis of the section 2.1, the performance will be effectively enhanced, if the parameters and temporary variables of a performance critical function, such as the color space transfer process, are limited to be no more than 14.

*Block data transfer instructions*

LDMIA and STMIA are instructions which load and store multiple words from continue addresses into different registers. These instructions are helpful to reduce the CPU cycles compared to the single data transfer instructions.

*Merging the IQ and IDCT modules*

Merging IQ and IDCT processes can reduce the number of the memory access. IDCT process the dequantization result directly rather than storing then reload it from memory. It can also be applied for Saturation control.

## 3 Experimental Results

To verify our optimization results, four SQCIF (128*96) and four CIF (352*288) sequences, "Akiyo", "Container", "Foreman", and "Mobile" are selected to show the results. They are encoded by XVID encoder under MPEG-4 visual simply profile. The devices used for the simulations are 30MHZ ARM7TDMI without memory cache and 200 MHZ ARM920T with 16K memory cache. The other settings are as follows: all the sequences are defined in a static coding structure, i.e., one I-frame is followed by nineteen P-frames (1I19P), QP = 28, 32, 36 and 40 with a frame rate of 30 frames per second and no skip frame throughout the 200 frames.

Our decoder is written by C and compiled by ARM c-compiler. The performance-critical parts are written by assembly language. The profile tool is *GProf*.

The comparison of each module's decoding time for *Akiyo* between XVID [8] and optimized decoder is shown in Fig.4.

Table 2 gives the frame rate (fps), speed up rate and PSNR of the eight test sequences. As the module analysis result of Fig.4, the gain of saved time is mainly from CST which is a stationary process and only decided by the picture size rather than the texture and motion complexity. The sequence *Mobile*

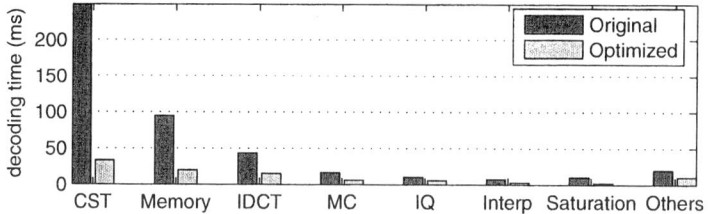

**Fig. 4.** Decoding time comparison of each module for *Akiyo* sequence (SQCIF) between XVID [9] and the optimized Decoder on ARM7TDMI. (Padding process is omitted).

has strenuous motion and complex texture, so the time consumed on IDCT and Memory Access sharply increased. As a result, the speed up gain on stationary sequences, such as *Akiyo*, are more than that on the sequences like *Mobile*. Average PSNR drop is about 0.5, and it's more on *mobile* sequence. Fig.5 (a) shows the PSNR of optimized decoder compared to the original for Foreman sequence with 100k bitrate, 30kps and QP = 28; and Fig.5(b) gives the PSNR under different bitrates. On ARM7TDMI (30MHZ, no memory cache), the decoding time is

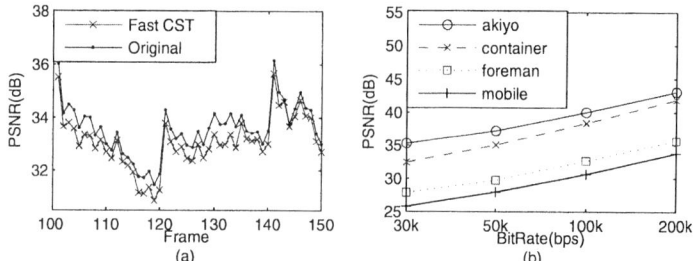

**Fig. 5.** *Foreman* with 100k bit rate, 30kfps and QP = 28. (a) R-D curve of original pictures compared to the decoding result with fast CST. (b) PSNR values for different bitrates.

about 10 frames per second for SQCIF sequences. Also we implemented the optimized decoder on the devices based on ARM920T (200MHZ, with 16k memory cache), the decoding speed is about 40 frames per second for CIF sequences.

Furthermore, we find that the performance on ARM920T is about 4 times better than that on ARM7TDMI though the testing sequences are about 8 times bigger than that for ARM7TDMI. Except the special instructions for multimedia application on ARM920T, the memory cache may be the key factor.

## 4 Conclusions

This paper presents various methods to optimize the MPEG-4 visual simple profile software-based decoder. A fast color space transform algorithm is proposed

**Table 2.** Decoding results on ARM7TDMI and ARM920T

| Sequence | ARM7TDMI (30MHZ, no cache) (SQCIF sequences) | | | ARM920T (200MHZ, 16K Cache) (CIF sequences) | | |
|---|---|---|---|---|---|---|
| | fps | Speedup gain | PSNR drop | fps | Speedup gain | PSNR drop |
| Akiyo | 13.6 | 6.8 | −0.1 (db) | 46.2 | 5.2 | −0.1 (db) |
| Foreman | 12.1 | 5.2 | −0.7 (db) | 44.0 | 4.2 | −0.7 (db) |
| Container | 13.0 | 6.3 | −0.4 (db) | 45.9 | 4.9 | −0.3 (db) |
| Mobile | 8.6 | 4.3 | −0.9 (db) | 35.0 | 3.3 | −0.9 (db) |

to tackle the most time consuming part of the MPEG-4 video decoder. Multiplierless integer IDCT is introduced to further speed up the decoder. We also removed the padding process and optimized various memory access operations, without significant bitrate growing. The optimized decoder is about 5 times faster than the XVID decoder and supports the real-time video applications.

However, the aforementioned techniques, fast color space transformation and multipierless integer IDCT, may cause display quality loss. Though PSNR drop is small and the actual display quality is satisfactory on low resolution mobile devices, we will overcome this problem in the future works.

# References

1. ISO/IEC 14496-2:2001, Coding of Audio-Visual Objects - Part 2: Visual, 2nd Edition (2001)
2. Ramkishor, K.: Real Time Implementation of MPEG-4 Video Decoder on ARM7TDMI, Proc. IEEE International Symposium on Intelligent Multimedia, Video, and Speech Processing, May (2001)
3. Hovden, G., Ling, N.: On Speed Optimization of MPEG-4 Decoder for Real-Time Multimedia Applications, Third International Conference on Computational Intelligence and Multimedia Applications, September (1999)
4. Jung, J., Antonini M., Barlaud M.: Optimal Decoder for Block-Transform Based Video Coders, IEEE Trans. on Multimedia, Vol.5, No.2, June (2003)
5. Panda, P. R. , Catthoor, F.: Data and Memory Optimization Techniques for Embedded Systems, ACM Trans. on Design Automation of Electronic Systems, Vol. 6, No. 2, April (2001) 149–206.
6. Patel, K., Smith, B. C., Rowe, L. A.: Performance of a Software MPEG Video Decoder, ACM Multimedia Conference, Anaheim, CA (1992)
7. Bilas, A., Fritts, J., Singh, J. P.: Real-Time Parallel MPEG-2 Decoding in Software, Proc. of the 11th International Symposium on Parallel Processing (1997)
8. XVID v1.0.2, http://www.xvid.org/
9. Noble, J., Weir, C.: Small Memory Software Patterns for system with limited memory, Addison-Wesley Professional; 1st edition, November (2000)
10. Chen, Y. J., Amaratunga, K.: Multiplierless Approximation of Transforms with Adder Constraint, IEEE Trans. Signal Processing, Vol. 49, No. 12, December (2001)
11. Chau, L. P., Ling, N., Hovden, G., Lan, H., NG, H. C., Lim, K. P.: A Real-Time Realization of MPEG-4 Video Decoder, IEEE International Conference on Image Processing, Kobe, Japan, Vol. 1, October (1999) 249–253

# Marrying Level Lines for Stereo or Motion

Nikom Suvonvorn, Samia Bouchafa, and Bertrand Zavidovique

Institut d'Electronique Fondamentale, Université Paris 11,
Bâtiment 220 - 91405 Orsay Cedex

**Abstract.** Efficient matching methods are crucial in Image Processing. In the present paper we outline a novel algorithm of "stable marriages" that is also fair and globally satisfactory for both populations to be paired. Our applicative examples here being stereo or motion we match primitives based on level lines segments, known for their robustness to contrast changes. They are separately extracted from images, and we draft the corresponding process too. Then for marriages to be organised each primitive needs to be given a preference list sorting potential mates in the antagonist image: parameters of the resemblance founding preferences are explained. Eventually all operators above are embedded within a recursive least squares method and results are shown and compared with a successful Hough based matching that we had used so far.

## 1 Introduction

Efficient matching methods are needed in all areas of Image Processing, ranging from Segmentation - e.g. motion detection or 3D reconstruction from stereo - to actual Pattern Recognition - e.g. model fitting or classification. Efficiency then gets multiple meanings and can address properties as different as easy data extraction and coding format, model simplicity, limited prior assumptions, robustness against ambiguities, conflict freeness etc. not to forget computability. Within that frame, general enough methods are still to be produced. We tested several, from Dynamic Warping on edge or region chain codes [1] for instance to more recently Hough Transform on level lines [2]. In the latter we showed how using n-tuples of carefully coded level line segments, sorted into several sub populations according to the confidence in them, leads to an efficient multipass voting process. Efficiency here is in the sense of "fighting ambiguities (e.g. repetitive patterns) thanks to a reinforcement of stronger by weaker features at a limited enough computing expense". In a wider approach to segmentation that aimed at exhibiting nD image features in gathering (n-1)D ones [3] – edges from points of interest, regions from edges etc – an interesting paradigm of optimisation on bi-partite graphs was tested against Bayesian techniques and shown to sustain comparison well with them. It is called the "stable marriage problem", of which the main interest is to guarantee no logical contradiction in the pairing process provided two different sets of items are genuinely distinguished to be cross-matched one-to-one and each item sorts every member of the antagonist set in a so-called "preference list". Efficiency in that case stresses disambiguation again and we thought to try the method to limit or skip multipass voting in the preceding scheme. The present paper is devoted to preliminary experimentations in that direction for 3D Reconstruction and Motion finding.

It is organized as follows: first, we describe the level-lines' junction extraction resulting into primitives. Second, the preference list construction is explained. Then, the stable marriages algorithm we designed for such matching is outlined. After explaining how outliers are eliminated, we describe shortly the image transformation estimation. Eventually, some results are displayed for comments.

## 2 Image Features

The feature type plays a significant role in the choice of a matching strategy. Less reliable features may lead to very complex matching processes. The level-line is chosen here for being a robust/reliable feature, its invariance property towards contrast changes is known [4][5]. $I_\mathbf{p}$ being the image intensity at pixel $\mathbf{p}$, the *level set* $N_\lambda$ of image $I$ is made of the pixels which intensities are equal or larger than $\lambda$, $N_\lambda = \{\mathbf{p}/I(\mathbf{p}) \geq \lambda\}$. Borders of such level sets are called *level lines* $L_\lambda$. One important property of level lines is that they can overlay but cannot cross. Let $F_\lambda$ be a set of overlaying level lines, called *level line flow*, defined by $F_\lambda = \{L_\lambda^I/\lambda \in [u,v]\}$. $(v-u)$ is called the *flow extension* $\mathcal{E}$. The method proposed in [6][7] extracts the level lines by tracking such flows. In an image, the point where two level line flows merge or split is called a *flow junction*.

The extraction process, under the form of a recursive automaton, performs in 3 steps. First step consists of finding the level line flows at the left-top of each pixel. The following flows are calculated for four directions: top down, right left, bottom up, and left right. Then, flow extension is checked. If there are at least two flows with extensions greater than a threshold, go for the second step, if not pass to the next pixel. The second step consists in validating the flow according to its length despite variations in the flow extension that may make it a subset of the original flow found at first step. So the integral subset flow is looked for continuation in every direction as respecting the following conditions: (1) the predecessor flow must be subset of the successor flow (2) the integral flow does not turn back towards its starting point (3) the integral flow must remain a straight line. Then, we validate flows longer than a threshold. Each validated flow is approximated by a line segment $S$ characterized by the following 4-vector: starting point $\mathbf{p}$, length $l$, orientation $\theta$ and contrast $(c_l, c_r)$ (average grey level on the left/on the right), $\vec{S} = [\mathbf{p}\ \theta\ l\ (c_l, c_r)]$. Its *reliability* is defined as the product $\mathcal{E} \times l$ of the extension by the length. The last step consists in validating the junction. A junction combines separate flows at a given point −at least two validated flows ( line segments)− . As a *primary variable* $P$, the junction is characterized by five or seven parameters: $\Delta\theta$ being the angle between any two line segments, $\vec{P} = [\mathbf{p}\ \vec{S}_1\ \vec{S}_2\ \vec{S}_3\ \Delta\theta_1\ \Delta\theta_2\ \Delta\theta_3]$.

## 3 Matching Candidate

When the primitives have been extracted separately from each image, following the method introduced above, candidates have to be prepared for matching.

Each primitive will create a preference list containing its potential mates (the primitives of the other image to be possibly paired). Matching candidates are searched for inside a bounded window the size of which results from a trade off between computation cost and application constraints. The compatibility between primitives is first tested following three constraints on the junction properties : (1) there is at least one common level line between two junctions (2) they must have the same order of area's intensities (3) angles between any two level line flows cannot change by more than 180 degrees. Note that preference lists are thus incomplete (not all primitives in the other image belong to the list) and likely have different number of matching candidates for different primitives. The preferences are set then based on the junction similarity. Two categories are distinguished according to the transformation range in the targetted application.

(1) if the images to match show an important displacement between them, we rather use the junction properties for its similarity $\mathcal{S}$: it is a weighted sum of three separate terms: (1) junction reliability $\mathcal{F}$, (2) region characteristics around the junction $\mathcal{R}$, and (3) geometric invariance $\mathcal{G}$.

$$\mathcal{S} = \alpha\mathcal{F} + \gamma\mathcal{R} + \delta\mathcal{G}$$
$$\mathcal{F} = \frac{\sum_i^N \mathcal{F}_i}{N}$$
with $\mathcal{F}_i$ the segment reliability, $N$ the segment number

$$\mathcal{R} = \frac{\sum_{i=0}^N \left\| I(\mathcal{R}_i) - I(\mathcal{R}'_i) \right\|^2}{N}$$
with $I(\mathcal{R}_i)$ the contrast $(c_l, c_r)$

$$\mathcal{G} = \sum_{i=0}^N \left| \frac{l_i}{l_{i+1}} - \frac{l'_i}{l'_{i+1}} \right| + \sum_{i=0}^N |\Delta\theta_i - \Delta\theta'_{i+1}| \quad (1)$$

(2) if the displacement is small (like in limited motion analysis) a classic similarity can be used, as the correlation or the sum of differences.

## 4 Stables Marriages Matching

After preselecting matching candidates by creating the preference list for each primitive, an algorithm of stables marriages suitably designed for such problems (see algo.1) will be used for actual matching. Let us first explain the stable marriages paradigm ([8], [9]). In this problem, two finite sub-sets $M$ and $W$ of two respective populations, say men and women, have to match. Assume $n$ is the number of elements, $M = \{m_1, m_2, ..., m_n\}$ and $W = \{w_1, w_2, ..., w_n\}$. Each element $x$ creates its preference list $l(x)$ i.e. it sorts all members of the opposite sex from most to less preferred. A matching $\mathcal{M}$ is a one to one correspondence between men and women. If $(m, w)$ is a matched pair in $\mathcal{M}$, we note $\mathcal{M}(m) = w$ and $\mathcal{M}(w) = m$ and $\rho_m$ is the rank of $m$ in the list of $w$ (resp. $\rho_w$ the rank of $w$ in the list of $m$). Man $m$ and woman $w$ form a blocking pair if $(m, w)$ is not in $\mathcal{M}$ but $m$ prefers $w$ to $\mathcal{M}(m)$ and $w$ prefers $m$ to $\mathcal{M}(w)$. If there is no blocking pair, then the matching $\mathcal{M}$ is stable.

A reliable algorithm of stable marriages in stereo or motion that is global fitting from local attraction, should fulfill three criteria: stability (i.e. no local questionning of more global associations), sex equality (i.e. local/global balance of the resemblance to matching) and global satisfaction (i.e. limited amount of local counter run).

Classic stable marriage algorithms (see [8]) of complexity $O(n^2)$ guarantee the stability only. The solution can be such that every primitive has a weak fit. The proposed algorithm *Blocked Zigzag* (*BZ*) (algo.1) meets the three criteria thanks to a novel representation, called *marriage table*, that translates and supplements the preference lists. The *marriage table* is a table with $(n+1)$ lines and $(n+1)$ columns. Lines (resp. columns) frame the preference orders of men, $\{1 \cdots p \cdots N \infty\}$ (resp. women, $\{1 \cdots q \cdots N \infty\}$). The cell $(p,q)$ contains pairs $(m,w)$ such that $w$ is the $p^{th}$ choice of $m$, and $m$ is the $q^{th}$ choice of $w$. Cells can thus contain more than one pair or none. The cell $(p, \infty)$ (resp. $(\infty, q)$) contains the pairs where the woman is the $p^{th}$ choice of the man (resp the $q^{th}$ choice of the woman) but the man does not exist in her preference list (resp. the woman is not in his preference list). A key feature of this table in the "complete list" case is that each line contains all men once and each column contains all women once (see figure 1(a)).

Stable matchings are looked for by scanning this latter array and suitable properties of the solution are associated to the type of scan. Indeed, one advantage of the marriage table is that satisfaction, equality of sex and stability show concurrently in the same representation. A solution with maximum global satisfaction would display matched pairs as close around the origin (table bottom-left) as mutual exclusion allows. More generally the table representation is indicative of a result global satisfaction through the lay out of the selected couples. Intuitively the closer to the diagonal the more balanced treatment. Elements of a pair in a cell close to the diagonal are equally satisfied or unsatisfied, depending on the distance to the origin. Stability gets a graphic translation too in the marriage table.

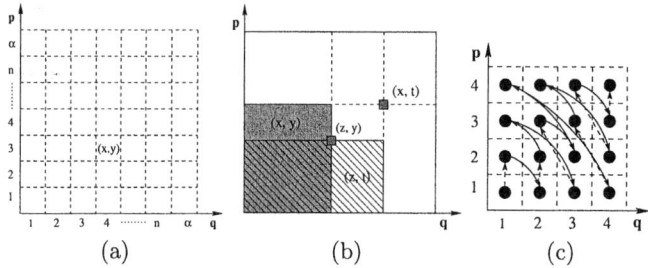

**Fig. 1.** (a) Marriage table : the pair (x,y), y is the $3^{th}$ choice of x and x is the $4^{th}$ choice of y. (b) Blocking situation in marriage table. (c) *BZ* algorithm.

The *BZ* algorithm scans anti-diagonals of the table forward from maximum to minimum global satisfaction but each one is read in swinging from center to sides meaning maximum to minimum sex equality (see figure 1(c)). In each cell, all pairs are accepted for marriage if their components are free. After all cells have been considered, the table is then revisited up to complete removal of blocking situations as follows: potential blocking pairs are matched upon detection (test according to figure 1(b)) while both blocked couples are broken and complementary elements are freed. To overcome cycles in the assignment the number of rescanning is limited to the population size. Scan directions together with questioning all previous marriages on demand guarantees the better at end. However, $BZ$ shows an increase in complexity to $O(n^3)$ due to systematic test added.

**Algorithm 1.** Blocked zigzag algorithm

```
begin
    while there is a bloking pair and rescan number < population size do
        foreach anti-diagonal, maximum to miminum global satisfaction do
            foreach diagonal, maximum to miminum sex equality back and forth
            do
                foreach pair (m, w) do
                    if m and w are free then
                        Marry m with w

        foreach anti-diagonal, maximum to miminum global satisfaction do
            foreach diagonal, maximum to miminum sex equality back and forth
            do
                foreach pair (m, w) do
                    if (m, w) is blocking pair then
                        Free m and w and their spouse
                        Marry m with w
end
```

## 5  Eliminating Outliers

$BZ$ organizes the best correspondence possible for each primitive. Still, when corresponding primitives do not exist in either image, the matching couple cannot be else than a mismatch or a missing match, called *outlier*. We draft here the simple method for eliminating outliers. Considering each couple as an "optical flow" and assuming there are only small displacements locally in images, such optical flow gets same length and direction in average. Whence the algo.2:

## 6  Global Image Transformation

After matching and outliers elimination, couples can be assumed reliable enough to estimating the global transformation between images. We outline here the estimation process in the case of perspective transformation model that requires

**Algorithm 2.** Outliers elimination algorithm

```
begin
    foreach optical flow in small window do
        foreach x ∈ {angle, length} do
            Find neighbors-optical flows-
            Order neighbors by x
            Compute x between any two close flows
            Order x from min to max
            Find optimal threshold (x histogram)
            Compute x in order (current flow, neighbors)
            if x > optimal threshold then
                Delete the current optical flow
end
```

to estimate 8 parameters. Model is of the form $\mathbf{y} = \mathbf{Xh}$, where $h$ is the parameters column: it follows 2.

$$\begin{bmatrix} x'_0 \\ y'_0 \\ \vdots \\ y'_N \end{bmatrix} = \begin{bmatrix} x_0 & y_0 & 1 & 0 & 0 & 0 & -x'_0 x_0 & -x'_0 y_0 \\ 0 & 0 & 0 & x_0 & y_0 & 1 & -y'_0 x_0 & -y'_0 y_0 \\ \vdots & \vdots & \vdots & \vdots & \vdots & \vdots & \vdots & \vdots \\ 0 & 0 & 0 & x_N & y_N & 1 & -y'_N x_N & -y'_N y_N \end{bmatrix} \begin{bmatrix} h_0 \\ h_1 \\ \vdots \\ h_7 \end{bmatrix} \quad (2)$$

And using the least square recursive method in [10], the transformation parameters are given by $\mathbf{h} = (\mathbf{X}^H \mathbf{X})^{-1} \mathbf{X}^H \mathbf{y}$, $\mathbf{h} = \mathbf{X}^\# \mathbf{y}$, hence $\mathbf{h}_n = \mathbf{Q}_n \mathbf{X}^H \mathbf{y}_n$, $\mathbf{Q}_n = (\mathbf{X}_n^H \mathbf{X}_n)^{-1}$

## 7 Experimental Results

In the sequel two series of test results are shown. First one compares the multi pass Hough transform on extracted level-line-segment based primitives, with the stable marriage algorithm run on the same. The difference between original and transformed back images are displayed to that purpose. It is obvious to the naked eye that results are quite comparable, although the BZ Marriages seem to spread errors more all over the picture an in a lesser amount. Each method gets areas where it performs comparatively better − strong primitives orthogonal to the average displacement for Hough and aligned with it for Marriages− . The same phenomenon occurs on all similar images of the type that algorihms were tried on, as long as the transformation to be exhibited is not too complex (limited number of parameters). The present example is extracted from the vision of a car getting out of a parking and involves translations and planar rotations merely. Therefore in a second series of experiments, results of primitive marriages are shown on stereo images extracted from the data base "http://www.gravitram.com/stereoscopic_photography.htm" of monuments. The algorithm again performs qualitatively well despite projections involved. Good news is that large structures are well distinguished, relatively

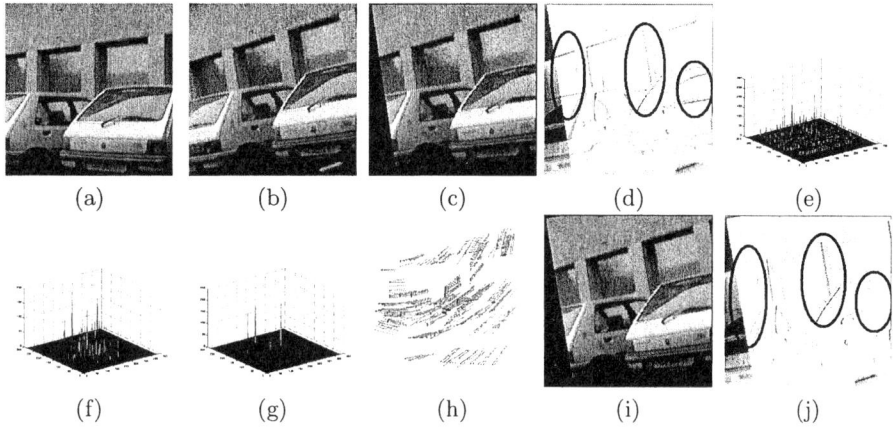

**Fig. 2.** (a)(b) Original images to match, (c) Affine transformation by Hough: $\alpha = -9.0$, $\psi = 1.0096$, $T_x = 5$ and $T_y = 3$, (d) The difference between (b) and (c), (e) The vote space after Hough $1^{st}$ round, (f) $2^{sd}$ round, (g) $3^{rd}$ round, (h) Matching result by $BZ$, (i) Affine transformation by $BZ$: $\alpha = -9.95$, $\psi = 0.9977$, $T_x = 4.10$ and $T_y = 6.73$, (j) The difference between (b) and (i)

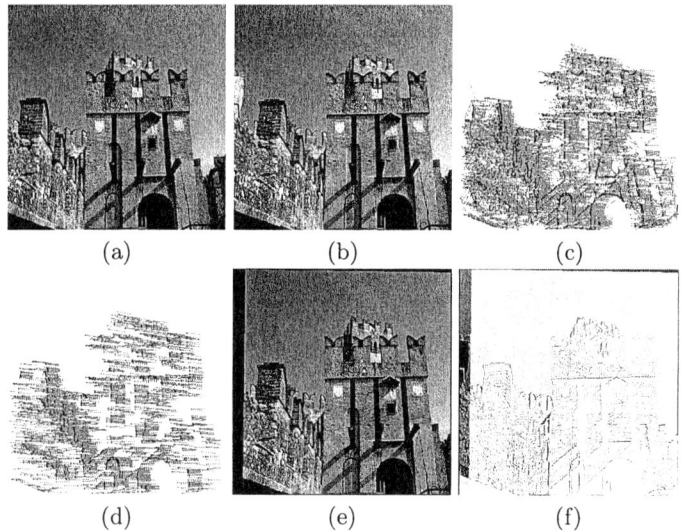

**Fig. 3.** (a)(b) The stereo images, (c) Matching results by $BZ$, (d) Result after elimination of outliers, (e) Perspective transformation: $h_0 = 1.018769$, $h_1 = -0.010705$, $h_2 = 20.975390$, $h_3 = 0.013266$, $h_4 = 0.986765$, $h_5 = 2.239246$, $h_6 = 0.000062$, $h_7 = -0.000035$ and $h_8 = 1.000000$, (f) The difference between (b) and (e)

bad news is that it seems to be to the detriment of more tiny details. That would ask further study of the minimization precision vs. the size of considered primitives, and more generally the impact of the features of selected segments (length, contrast, orientation etc.).

## 8 Conclusion

Stable marriages run comparatively well on image couples or sequences segmented into level line based primitives. Our main applications being car driving and experimental physics (electron microscopy, MRI etc.), they involve images with potential high rate of ambiguities. We thus need to compare results with our Hough technique satisfactorily used so far in a more quantitative way and find explanations why one performs better that the other in which cases. That is our next step in the study, as the whole matching process currently under investigation and drafted in the present paper stands, better than many, the growth of the transform parameter number.

## References

1. B. Burg and B. Zavidovique. Pattern recognitions and image compression by means of a time warping algorithm. *ICPR Paris*, Octobre 1986.
2. S. Bouchafa and B. Zavidovique. Stratégie de vote pour la mise en correspondance de lignes de niveaux. *RFIA'04*, January 2004.
3. K. Zemirli, G. Seetharamann, and B. Zavidovique. Stable matching for selective junction points grouping. *IEEE JCIS*, February 2000.
4. V. Caselles, B. Coll, and J. Morel. Topographic maps and local contrast changes in natural images. *International Journal of Computer Vision*, 33(1):5–27, September 1999.
5. P. Monasse and F. Guichard. Fast computation of a contrast-invariant image representation. *IEEE Trans. on Image Proc.*, 9(5):860–872, 1998.
6. N. Suvonvorn, S. Bouchafa, and L. Lacassagne. Fast reliable level-lines segments extraction. *ICTTA*, 2004.
7. S. Bouchafa and B. Zavidovique. Cumulative level-line matching for image registration. *IEEE 12th International Conference on Image Analysis and Processing*, pages 176–180, September 2003.
8. D. Gal and L.S. Shapley. College admissions and the stability of marriage. *American Mathematical Monthly*, 69:9–15, 1962.
9. D. G. McVitie and L. B. Wilson. Three procedures for the stable marriage problem. *Communications of the ACM*, 14,7:491–492, July 1971.
10. Grard Blanchet and Maurice Charbit. *Signaux et images sous Matlab*. HERMES Science Europe Ltd, 2001.

# Envelope Detection of Multi-object Shapes

N. Alajlan[1,2,3], O. El Badawy[1,2,4], M.S. Kamel[1,2,3], and G. Freeman[1,3]

[1] University of Waterloo, Waterloo, Ontario, N2L 3G1, Canada
[2] Pattern Analysis and Machine Intelligence Research Group
[3] Dept. of Electrical and Computer Engineering
[4] Dept. of Systems Design Engineering

**Abstract.** The purpose of this paper is to allow for high level shape representation and matching in multi-object images by detecting and extracting the envelope of object groupings in the image. The proposed algorithm uses hierarchical clustering to find object groupings based on spatial proximity as well as low-level shape features of objects in the image. Each grouping is then merged using a morphological algorithm. The envelope is extracted by reconstructing the object from its dynamically pruned concavity tree. We test our approach on a set of 45 multi-object trademark images and we report results on object groupings and envelope extraction.

## 1 Introduction

In the last decade, content-based image retrieval (CBIR) has received great attention from researchers in various fields; for instance, image processing, computer vision, pattern recognition, and database systems. This trend is mainly motivated by the ever increasing number of images generated every day, and the rapid developments in digital imaging technologies. Image comparisons in CBIR are traditionally either intensity based (color and texture), or geometry based (shape). Many systems have been proposed for content-based image retrieval. Among the most popular ones are QBIC from IBM [1], Virage [2], and Photobook from MIT labs [3]. Shape-based image retrieval is generally harder and less developed than color- and texture-based retrieval; for example, QBIC is relatively more successful in intensity-based than in shape-based search [4]. A common limitation of existing shape-based retrieval systems is that they do not take into consideration the spatial arrangement of the objects (components) in an image, which may reveal important properties of the scene being analyzed. For instance, they may form a high-level boundary (called an envelope).

Semantic image retrieval has recently emerged as a result of the fact that most users do not require to retrieve images based on only their low-level features [5]. Existing techniques fall behind that target. The ability of a CBIR system to extract all or most relevant information from an image is a necessary first step for the understanding of its content. As an example, multi-object images contain more shape information than the mere sum of the shape information of the individual components. For instance, a group of objects can be spatially arranged such that their envelope has a semantically high-level shape. Detection of such boundaries, or envelopes, is useful as a mean for higher interpretation of the shape information in the scene. (It may as well be an end by itself, as in image restoration applications for example.)

Segmentation of the objects in an image is an important process for successful automatic image retrieval. For natural images, this process is very challenging and beyond the scope of this paper. Therefore, we assume that objects are already segmented and their boundaries are well identified. Many powerful techniques have been proposed for the representation and matching of single closed-boundary shapes [6, 7, 8], but their application to multi-object shapes is not straightforward.

An important visual property of a group of objects is how they are perceived as a whole. In this paper, an approach for envelope detection and extraction in multi-object shapes is proposed. It consists of two main stages. In the first, a hierarchical clustering algorithm is used to group objects based on both their "physical" proximity, as well as their shape similarity. This idea has been suggested in [9] in the context of concavity graphs. In the second stage, morphological operations are used to merge the components in each of the groupings identified in stage one without changing their size. The envelope is then extracted by reconstructing the merged component from its pruned concavity tree. The remainder of this paper is organized as follows. Section 2 reviews some psychological findings about human perceptual grouping of objects and Section 3 introduces the proposed approach. Experimental results are provided in Section 4. Finally, we conclude our work in Section 5.

## 2 Perceptual Grouping

Gestalt theory provides an interpretation of the human perception of visually similar objects into groups [10]. The most significant principles of perceptual grouping are proximity and similarity. The spatial distances between objects are critical in grouping them. Also, objects of similar shape, size or orientation are more likely to form envelopes than objects differing along these features. Other findings by Biederman [11] suggest that the human visual system quickly assumes and uses collinearity, curvature, parallelism, and adjacency of a group of objects in order to perceive them as a whole.

Although the grouping task is made by humans effortlessly, it is not the case for machines. Mathematical models tend to describe low-level features effectively but fail in high-level interpretation. Our approach for objects grouping is based on the perceptual grouping principles, where low-level image features and a set of rules are employed to make decisions about the proximity, shape similarity, and orientation of a group of objects.

## 3 The Proposed Approach

Given a multi-object binary image, our aim is to detect and extract any envelope formed by a group of objects. This is achieved in two stages. First, hierarchical clustering is used to group the objects based on their proximity and their shape similarity. Second, morphological operations are used to merge the objects in each grouping and the envelope is then extracted by reconstructing the merged object from its pruned concavity tree; thus removing any artifacts along the boundary.

## 3.1 Object Grouping

Brain research showed experimentally that the processing of proximity and other features are performed separately [10]. Therefore, in our approach, objects are grouped separately based on their proximity, shape similarity, and orientation using hierarchical clustering. Then, two alternative groupings are considered. In the first, objects that belong to the same proximal and shape similarity groups are judged as one group. The second alternative regards objects of the same proximal and orientation groups as one group. The alternative that results in a lower number of groups is considered as the final grouping.

Srivastava et al. applied hierarchical clustering to group similar silhouettes to search shape databases efficiently [12]. Here, a hierarchical clustering algorithm [13] is applied to the distance matrices of proximity, shape similarity, and orientation. The result is a hierarchical tree, called dendrogram, which is not a single set of clusters, but rather a multi-level hierarchy, where clusters at one level are joined as clusters at the next higher level. In our application, clusters are defined when there is a clear cut in the dendrogram. In this case, the compactness of a cluster is defined by how similar its members are. For proximity and shape similarity groupings, the standard deviation values of the distances under each node in the dendrogram are used to decide where to cut. In order to achieve scale invariance, these values are normalized to have zero mean and unity variance, then the cut is made at the node with the largest normalized standard deviation and higher than a certain threshold (which is evaluated experimentally to be equal to one). For orientation-based grouping, the dendrogram cut is made directly at the desired angle, which is considered to be ten degrees.

An illustrative example is shown in Fig. 1. Panel (a) shows the input multi-object shape. The results of hierarchical clustering based on proximity, shape similarity, and orientation are shown in panels (b), (d), and (e), respectively. The dashed horizontal line shows the location of deciding the groups. Grouping based on proximity and shape similarity results in six groups (note that the members of each group fall in the same clusters of both proximity and shape similarity), whereas grouping based on proximity and orientation gives only two groups. Thus, the latter grouping is considered. The outcome of the object grouping stage is shown in panel (c). In the following, the proximal, shape similarity, and orientation distances between two objects are defined.

**Proximity.** The definition of a spatial distance between two objects that reflects the human judgment of such distance is not yet clear. Clearly, the shortest distance is totally independent of their shape. However, a desirable property of the distance is for it to be sensitive to all points in both objects. Therefore, the

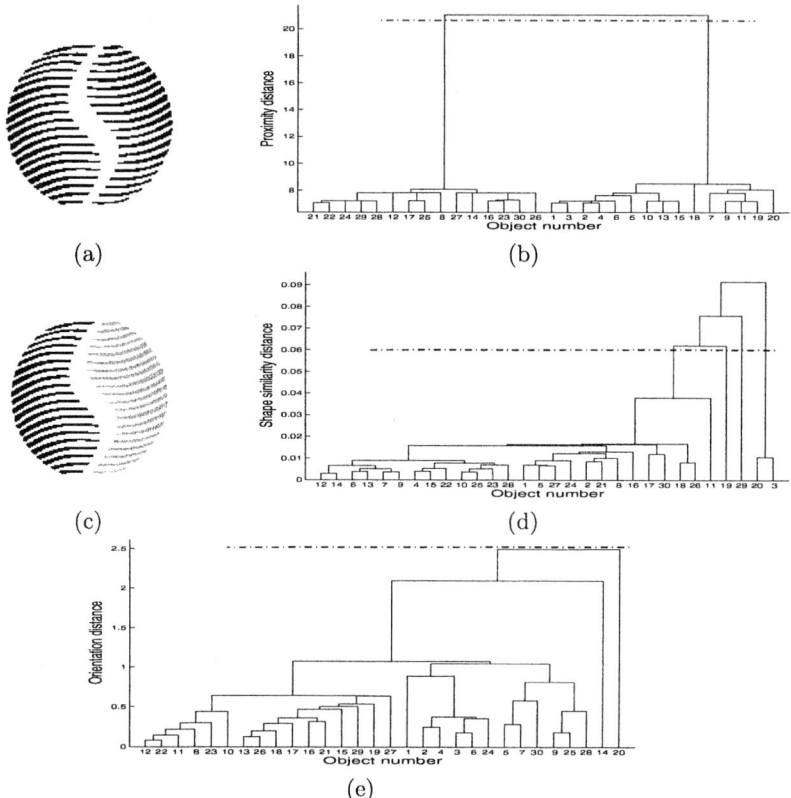

**Fig. 1.** An example of object grouping and envelope extraction. See text for details.

Hausdorff distance is adopted [14]. The Hausdorff distance between two sets of points is the maximum distance of a set to the nearest point in the other set. More formally, the Hausdorff distance $h(X,Y)$ between two objects $X$ and $Y$ is defined as:

$$h(X,Y) = \max_{x \in X} \left\{ \min_{y \in Y} \{d(x,y)\} \right\} \tag{1}$$

where $x$ and $y$ are points of objects $X$ and $Y$, respectively, and $d$ is the Euclidean distance. In order to make the distance function symmetric, a more general definition of Hausdorff distance would be:

$$H(X,Y) = \min \{h(X,Y), h(Y,X)\} \tag{2}$$

It is sufficient to consider only the boundary points of the two objects. However, we consider only the vertices of their convex hulls. This reduces the computations dramatically with minor effect on the performance.

**Shape Similarity.** Based on the observation that objects forming an envelope do not have complex boundaries, global shape descriptors are expected to describe the objects effectively. Another reason for choosing global descriptors is their compactness, which allows efficient computation of the distances between them. Here, the shape of an object is described by its eccentricity and solidity [15].

**Orientation.** The orientation of an object is taken as the orientation of its major axis, which is the straight line segment joining the two points farthest from each other. The major axis orientation is defined as the angle between the horizontal axis and the axis around which the object can be rotated with minimum inertia [15]. This feature is particularly important because objects may form an envelope, although they are not similar in shape, when they are aligned in parallel or in series.

### 3.2 Envelope Detection

This is the second stage towards the extraction of the semantic envelope. The input to this stage is the output of the object grouping stage; specifically, a label matrix of the object groupings in the image. There are two sub-steps in this stage: the first is to morphologically merge the objects in each grouping; whereas the second is to extract the envelope of the merged objects using a contour-based concavity tree extraction algorithm. A requirement of the second stage is that it is passed an image with a *single component*.

**Merging the Groups.** For each grouping identified in stage one, the constituent objects are repeatedly dilated using a 3×3 structuring element until the resulting grouping has only one component. If the dilation operation was performed $n$ times, and the envelope is extracted at this stage, it would be $n$ pixels larger than it should (because of the dilation). We need then to shrink the merged component $n$ pixels, but without splitting it. The shrinking can be done using an erosion operation with a $(2n+1) \times (2n+1)$ structuring element. However, the erosion might (or might not) split the merged component. A splitting will occur if the (square) structuring element cannot slip through the neck joining pairs of (original) components. To get around this problem, we morphologically close the merged component with a diamond shaped structuring element with a main-diagonal of $2n+1$ pixels. This will always guarantee that the subsequent erosion will not split the merged component, as the square structuring element will now be always guaranteed to pass through the necks. If we proceed with the envelope extraction at this stage, the resulting envelope will then be tightly snug around the components, as we need it to be.

**Extracting the Envelope.** The merged component identified in stage one can now be used to extract the envelope. The contour of the merged component could be used as the envelope at this stage, however, it needs to be smoothed. This task is delegated to a contour-based concavity tree extraction algorithm [16] that will ignore concavities that are smaller than a given threshold. This threshold

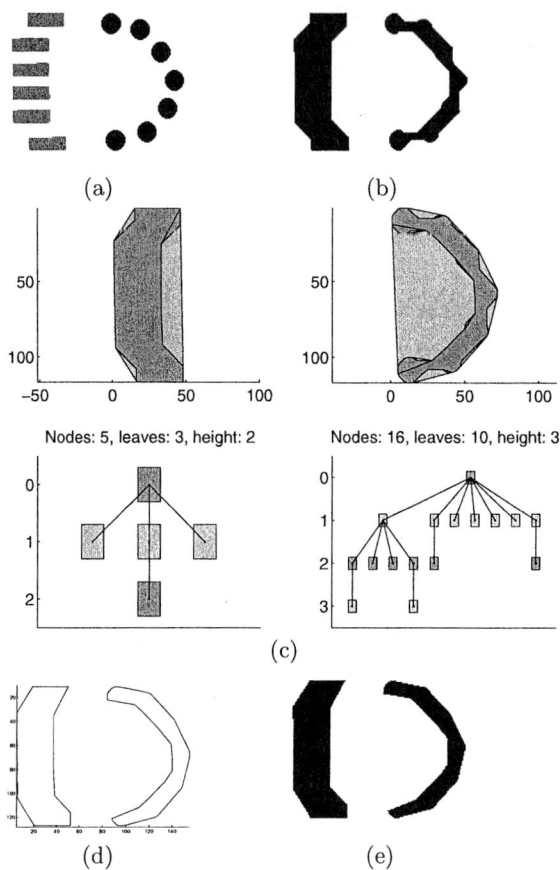

**Fig. 2.** Illustration of the merging and envelope extraction process. Input image (two groupings) (a), result of merging (b), concavity trees used to extract the envelope (c), resulting envelope (d), and output image (e).

varies with the gaps in between the original components. It is currently set to four times the area of the structuring element used in the erosion step. Fig. 2 illustrates the merging and envelope extraction process. We note that effectively only two tree nodes (including the root) were used in the reconstruction of the two envelopes from their corresponding concavity trees.

## 4 Experimental Results

A trademark image is a good example where multiple objects and their spatial arrangement play the major role in the identity of the trademark. The proposed approach was implemented and its performance evaluated on 45 trademark images containing a varying number of objects with various orientations and shapes.

**Fig. 3.** Envelope extraction: examples

The outcome of the object grouping stage was subjectively correct for 39 images (out of 45). Moreover, when the envelope extraction algorithm was applied to each of the 39 correctly grouped images, a subjectively correct envelope was extracted. Fig. 3 shows samples of correct grouping and envelope extraction.

## 5 Conclusions

Envelope extraction is a very important stage towards high-level shape representation and similarity matching. In this paper, an approach for object grouping and envelope detection is introduced. The proposed approach utilizes the proximity and shape similarity between objects, as well as their orientations, for grouping them. Hierarchical clustering allows such utilization. Then, the envelope of each group of objects is approximated by means of morphological operations. A contour-based approach for concavity tree reconstruction is employed to smooth the extracted envelope.

The proposed technique was tested using a diverse set of 45 (multi-object) trademark images. The object grouping was subjectively accurate for 39 images. In each of these 39 images, the (subjectively) correct envelope was extracted. Our future work includes the evaluation of our algorithm with more multi-object images and the extension to shape-based image retrieval.

## References

1. Flickner, M., Sawhney, H., Niblack, W., Ashley, J., Huang, Q., Dom, B., Gorkani, M., Hafner, J., Lee, D., Petkovic, D., Steele, D., Yanker, P.: Query by image and video content: The QBIC system. IEEE Computer **28** (1995) 23–32
2. Bach, J., Fuller, C., Gupta, A., Hampapur, A., Horowitz, B., Humphrey, R., Jain, R., Shu, C.: Virage image search engine: An open framework for image management. In: Storage and Retrieval for Image and Video Databases (SPIE). (1996) 76–87
3. Pentland, A., Picard, R., Sclaroff, S.: Photobook: content-based manipulation of image databases. Int. J. Comput. Vision **18** (1996) 233–254

4. Vetkamp, R.C., Hagedoorn, M.: State of the art in shape matching. In Lew, M.S., ed.: Principles of Visual Information Retrieval. Springer (2001)
5. Eakins, J.P.: Towards intelligent image retrieval. Pattern Recognition **35** (2002) 3–14
6. Adamek, T., O'Connor, N.: A multiscale representation method for nonrigid shapes with a single closed contour. IEEE Trans. on Circuits and Systems for Video Tech. **14** (2004) 742–753
7. Mokhtarian, F.: Silhouette-based isolated object recognition through curvature scale space. IEEE Trans. on PAMI **17** (1995) 539–544
8. Zhang, D., Lu, G.: Review of shape representation and description techniques. Pattern Recognition **37** (2004) 1–19
9. El Badawy, O., Kamel, M.: Shape representation using concavity graphs. In: Proceedings of the 16th International Conference on Pattern Recognition. Volume 3. (2002) 461–464
10. Thorisson, K.: Simulated perceptual grouping: An application to human computer interaction. In: Proceedings of the 16th Annual Conference of Cognitive Science Society, Atlanta, GA (1994) 876–881
11. Biederman, I.: Recognition by components: A theory of human image understanding. Psychological Review **94** (1987) 115–147
12. Srivastava, A., Joshi, S., Mio, W., Liu, X.: Statistical shape analysis: Clustering, learning, and testing. IEEE Trans. on PAMI **27** (2005) 590–602
13. Jain, A.K., Murty, M.N., Flynn, P.J.: Data clustering: a review. ACM Computing Surveys (CSUR) **31** (1999) 264–323
14. Rote, G.: Computing the minimum hausdorff distance between two point sets on a line under translation. Information Processing Letters **38** (1991) 123–127
15. Costa, L.F., Cesar, R.M.: Shape Analysis and Classification: Theory and Practice. CRC Press, Inc. (2000)
16. El Badawy, O., Kamel, M.: Hierarchical representation of 2-D shapes using convex polygons: a contour-based approach. Pattern Recognition Letters **26** (2005) 865–877

# Affine Invariant, Model-Based Object Recognition Using Robust Metrics and Bayesian Statistics

Vasileios Zografos and Bernard F. Buxton

Department of Computer Science, University College London,
Gower Street, London WC1E 6BT, UK
{v.zografos, b.buxton}@cs.ucl.ac.uk

**Abstract.** We revisit the problem of model-based object recognition for intensity images and attempt to address some of the shortcomings of existing Bayesian methods, such as unsuitable priors and the treatment of residuals with a non-robust error norm. We do so by using a reformulation of the Huber metric and carefully chosen prior distributions. Our proposed method is invariant to 2-dimensional affine transformations and, because it is relatively easy to train and use, it is suited for general object matching problems.

## 1 Introduction

In this paper we will examine the view-oriented case for model-based object recognition, in which 2-dimensional representations of 3-dimensional objects are used, called aspects or characteristic views [1]. Such methods have recently become quite popular because of their applicability in many areas and their ease of implementation, since they avoid storing and reconstructing a full 3d model. In addition, there is evidence to suggest that view-oriented representations are used by the human visual system for object recognition [2]. The view-oriented object recognition problem for a single view can be formulated as follows:

**Definition 1.** *Suppose that we have a prototype template function $F_0$, an image function $I$ and a transformation $T$ that transforms the template as $F = TF_0$. The goal of object recognition is to minimise the expression:*

$$\min_{\xi} S = \int_{R(\xi)} g(I(x), F(x)) d^2 x , \qquad (1)$$

*with respect to the transformation parameters $\xi$, where $g(.,.)$ is an error metric and $R$ the parameter space. If the minimum is less than or equal to some threshold $\tau$, then we have a match.*

The main problem that arises from this formulation is the determination of the parameters $\xi$ that minimise the above expression. Solving for $\xi$ depends on the transformation $T$. For complicated transformations $T$, the optimisation is a nonlinear process and the minimum is found using an iterative algorithm.

## 1.1 Our Approach and Related Work

We have based our approach on previous popular work by [5] and [6]. First Grenander et al. proposed a general deformable template model, by representing deformations of the template as probabilistic transformations, for Bayesian inference on contour shape. Jain et al. used this approach together with a snake-like potential function to influence the template toward edge positions in the image. A similar scheme has been used by Cootes et al. [10], where the template is represented by the mean shape of a training set and a linear combination of the most important eigenmodes of the variation from the mean. The Bayesian object localisation method introduced by Sullivan et al. [8] is another interesting approach. Distributions of the template over the foreground and background are learned from training images, and used as the likelihood in a Bayesian inference scheme.

In our approach we use intensity information, without the need to extract features from the image. Also, we use novel distributions for the prior and do not assume that all transformations are equally possible. This disallows trivial solutions of the transformation parameters. Finally, our likelihood function is based on a more robust error metric that currently tends to one distribution when the template overlaps with an object (foreground) and to another when the template is on the background. A Bayesian formulation, that combines this prior knowledge together with information from the input image, the likelihood, is used in order to find a match between the image and the template. This combination is realised in the posterior probability, a maximum of which may indicate a possible match.

## 2 Deformation Model

The deformation model we propose consists of a prototype model template of the representative shape of an object, a selection of parametric transformations that act on the template, and a set of constraints that bias the choices of possible deformation parameters.

### 2.1 Prototype Template Representation

The prototype template consists of the pixels (grey levels) within a (for convenience) rectangular boundary, chosen as a representative example of an object or object class. The prototype is based on our prior knowledge about the objects of interest, and is usually obtained from training samples. Such training could be based on Principal Components Analysis (PCA), shape alignment, or the prototype could simply be the mean shape of the class. Unlike other methods, our model is not parameterised, but instead the transformation is. The model we are using contains grey level and boundary information in the form of a bitmap, and thus is appropriate for general object recognition tasks, since in order to apply the same method to a different class of objects we only need to generate a new prototype image of this class.

## 2.2 Parametric Transformations

Although the prototype template represents the most likely a-priori instance of the object, we still need to deform it to match the image. The parametric transformations consist of a global affine transformation $A$, and a local deformation $D$. It is necessary to compose $A$ as a product of individual meaningful transformations (primitive matrices). Such a composition is not unique, but by adopting a canonical order for the transformations, we could say, for example: $A = SRU_x + d$ where $S$ is an anisotropic scale matrix, $R$ is a rotation matrix, $U_x$ an angular shear matrix on the x-axis, and $d = (d_x, d_y)$ a translation vector.

The local deformation $D$ is a 2d continuous mapping $(x,y) \rightarrow (x,y) + [D_x(x,y), D_y(x,y)]$, defined as a simple sinusoidal function:

$$D_\psi(x,y) = [D_x(x,y), D_y(x,y)] = [\alpha \cos(2\pi k_x \Delta), \beta \cos(2\pi k_y \Delta)] \;, \qquad (2)$$

where $\psi = (\alpha, \beta, k_x, k_y, x_0, y_0)$ are the deformation parameters, with $\alpha, \beta$ being the wave amplitudes, $k_x, k_y$ the wavenumbers, and $\Delta = \sqrt{(x-x_0)^2 + (y-y_0)^2}$ is the Euclidean distance from the centre point $(x_0, y_0)$. We thus suppose that we have a prototype template function $F_0(x,y)$ and a transformation $T$ that transforms the template as follows:

$$TF_0(x,y) = F_0(SRU_x(x,y) + D_\psi(x,y) + (d_x, d_y)) \;. \qquad (3)$$

This is the parametric transformation that will deform the template to match the image. This transformation is realised by shearing the template by angle $\varphi$, then rotating by an angle $\vartheta$, scaling the result by $s_x$, $s_y$ along directions $x$ and $y$ respectively, locally deforming the resulting template by $\psi$ and finally a translation by $d$.

## 2.3 Probabilistic Constraints

Since not all choices of transformation parameters will produce a template that resembles the object(s) in the image, it is necessary to restrict their variability. We do so by imposing a probability density function (p.d.f) on the transformation $T$.

Consider the local deformation $D_\psi(x,y)$ first. We have chosen uniform distributions for the wave centre parameters $x_0, y_0$, since any centre point has an equal probability of producing a valid sinusoid. We further assume that the two sinusoids in (2) have amplitudes $\alpha$ and $\beta$ that are independently and identically normally distributed with zero mean and variance $\sigma_{\alpha\beta}^2$. For the wavenumbers $k_x$ and $k_y$, we also assume zero mean, independent and identical normal distributions with variance $w^2$. This results in a prior distribution for the shape parameters $\psi$:

$$Pr(\psi) = \frac{1}{4\pi\sigma_{\alpha\beta}^2 w^2} \exp\left\{-\frac{\alpha^2 + \beta^2}{2\sigma_{\alpha\beta}^2} - \frac{k_x^2 + k_y^2}{2w^2}\right\} \;, \qquad (4)$$

that favours small deformations of the object in preference to large ones.

For the rotation and translation, we can assume that all rotations and translations are equally possible and thus we can consider their parameters $\vartheta, d$ as being uniformly distributed. However, the scale and shear transformations require a different approach, and special care is required for choosing their p.d.f.s. The reason for this comes from the behaviour of the error function (1), for certain values or ranges of values of the parameters $s = (s_x, s_y)$ and $\varphi$. More specifically, if one or both of the scale parameters are very small, $F(x, y)$ will collapse into a single point or a line respectively. This of course is not going to be a valid representation for the template but the error function will undoubtedly have a minimum for these values of the scale parameters. Such trivial solutions should not be allowed. Similar behaviour occurs with the shear angle $\varphi$, which for $\varphi = \pm\frac{\pi}{2}$, will collapse the object into a line.

To avoid these problems, we need to forbid such values for the scale and shear parameters. To do so, we define a prior for these parameters that will bias them away from such values. A good choice for the scale parameters $s_x$ and $s_y$ is the inverse Gaussian (Wald) distribution [11], which, if we assume that $s_x$ and $s_y$ are independent, that their mean scale $\bar{s}$ is 1, and that their scale parameter is $\sigma_s$, leads to:

$$Pr(s) = \frac{\sigma_s \exp\left[-\frac{\sigma_s}{2}\left(-4 + \frac{1}{s_x} + s_x + \frac{1}{s_y} + s_y\right)\right]}{2\pi\sqrt{s_x^3 s_y^3}}. \tag{5}$$

The Wald distribution is ideal because it assigns very low probability to quantiles close to zero, while it allows us to determine the probability of large values of the scale parameter $s$ by adjusting the tail of the p.d.f.. For the shear angle, we would like to introduce a bias in favour of small deformations, and to rule out the values $\varphi = \pm\frac{\pi}{2}$. Furthermore, when the mean shear angle is zero, the distribution must be symmetric. On the other hand, if the mean angle is close to $-\frac{\pi}{2}$ then the distribution for negative values must fall sharply, whilst the distribution for high values must exhibit similar behaviour when the mean angle is close to (but not quite) $\frac{\pi}{2}$. We have therefore chosen a mixture model of two Gumbel distributions [11], with:

$$Pr(\varphi) = \frac{(1-A)e^{-\frac{\varphi-\bar{\varphi}}{b} - e^{-\frac{\varphi-\bar{\varphi}}{b}}} + Ae^{\frac{\varphi-\bar{\varphi}}{b} - e^{\frac{\varphi-\bar{\varphi}}{b}}}}{b}, \tag{6}$$

where $b$ is the shape parameter and $A = \frac{\bar{\varphi}+\frac{\pi}{2}}{\pi}$. Since the individual transformation parameters were assumed independent, the total prior p.d.f. $Pr(\xi)$, is the product of the individual p.d.f.s (4),(5) and (6).

## 3 Objective Function

Two commonly used metrics in template matching applications are the $L_2$ metric and the $L_1$ metric which are valid from a maximum likelihood perspective, if the error residuals are normally distributed or exponentially distributed respectively. However, [7] have shown that additive noise in real images is generally not normally distributed, and the majority of the variation comes from illumination changes and in-class object variation. In addition, [8] have shown that when using an error metric (such as the $L_2$) and considering only the portion of the image under the template, then the observations $I$ are a function of the hypothesis $\xi$. That is not valid in a Bayesian framework, since $I$ should be considered as fixed. In [8] a learning process is therefore used to model the different foreground and background distributions. Here, we use a simple parametric distribution to interpolate between the foreground and background behaviour. Since, in general we know little about the latter it should be based on a robust statistic. The $L_1$ metric, although robust, is singular when the residual goes to zero, and makes the optimisation process difficult. For this reason, we have chosen as a metric, a reformulation of the Huber norm [9]. This *smooth Huber norm*, is $C^2$ continuous and defined as:

$$g_\tau(x) = \sqrt{1 + \frac{x^2}{\tau^2}} - 1 , \qquad (7)$$

where $\tau$ is the threshold between the $L_1$ and $L_2$ norms. The smooth Huber norm treats residuals close to zero (template over the foreground) with the $L_2$ norm and large residuals (template over the background) with the $L_1$ norm. By using equations (1), (3) and (7) we obtain the combined objective function $S$ which needs to be minimized:

$$\min_\xi S(u,v) = \int_{R(\xi)} \left\{ \sqrt{1 + \frac{[I(u+x, v+y) - TF_0(x,y)]^2}{\tau^2}} - 1 \right\} dx dy . \qquad (8)$$

If we reformulate (8) as a p.d.f we see that the likelihood of observing the input image given the deformations on the prototype template is:

$$Pr(I|\xi) = C_1 \exp\left\{-S(u,v)\right\} , \qquad (9)$$

where $C_1$ is a normalising constant, equal to $1/2(eK_1(1)\tau)$ where $e$ is the exponential and $K_1$ is a modified Bessel function.

Finally, we may use the fact that $Pr(\xi|I) \propto Pr(I|\xi)Pr(\xi)$ and combine equations (4), (5), (6) and (9) to obtain the posterior p.d.f. of the parameters given an image $I$. The parameters may therefore be obtained by minimising the corresponding negative log-likelihood which for example, if the mean shear angle $\overline{\varphi}$ in (6) is zero, is given by:

$$\min_\xi \{-\log Pr(\xi|I)\} = \log(\sqrt{s_x^3 s_y^3}) - \log\left(e^{-\frac{\varphi}{b}} - e^{-\frac{\varphi}{b}} + e^{\frac{\varphi}{b}} - e^{\frac{\varphi}{b}}\right) + \frac{k_x^2 + k_y^2}{w^2}$$

$$+ \sigma_s \left(\frac{1}{s_x} + s_x + \frac{1}{s_y} + s_y - 4\right) + \frac{\alpha^2 + \beta^2}{\sigma_{\alpha\beta}^2} + S(u,v) , \qquad (10)$$

where $\xi = (s_x, s_y, \varphi, k_x, k_y, \alpha, \beta, x_0, y_0, d_x, d_y, \vartheta)$ are the transformation parameters. Note that the distribution shape parameters $b$, $w$, $\sigma_s$, $\sigma_{\alpha\beta}$ and the threshold $\tau$ are treated as constant.

## 4 Experimental Results

We have experimented with greyscale images of faces, such as those shown in Fig. 1 and 2 . First, we present the effects of an appropriately chosen prior on the error function. In this example, we have isolated the scale space by choosing a rectangular template (the female face on the bottom right of the picture) and varying the scale parameters $s_x, s_y$ while keeping all other parameters constant. The resulting sum of square differences error (normalised to a value of 1) can be seen on the top-right of Fig. 1. Note, that the desired solution is at $s_x = s_y = 1$ and trivial solutions are located at values of either of the parameters $s$ close to zero. If we now choose a Wald prior, with a peak at $(1,1)$ (bottom-left), and calculate the inverse log-probability, we get the surface on the bottom-right. The trivial solutions have now become maxima, and the global minimum is at the desired solution $(1,1)$. Compared to the original function, the log-posterior surface is convex with a very large basin of attraction. We also show some optimisation results, where a template is taken from the image (Fig. 2), and is randomly affine transformed and locally deformed. We then use numerical optimisation to match the deformed template to the original image and see if we can find the correct

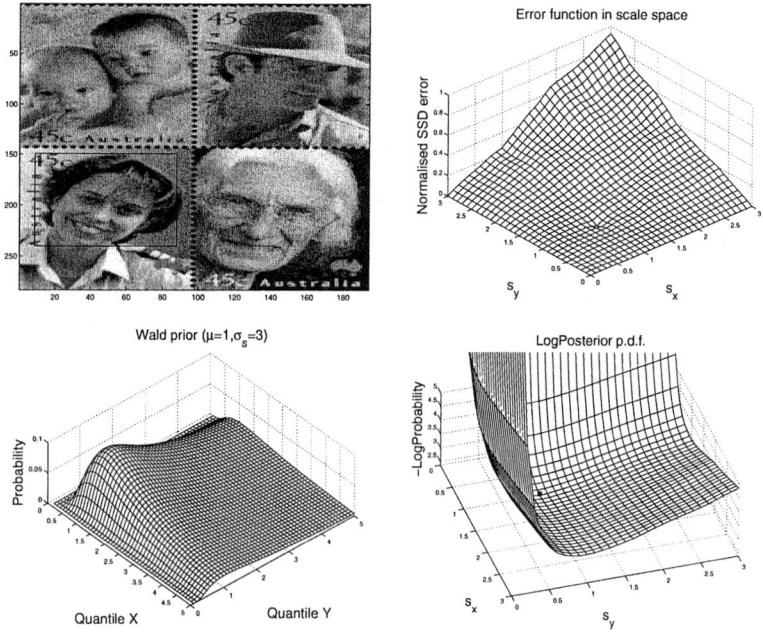

**Fig. 1.** The test image and template (*top left*) and the error function for the scale parameters (*top right*). The desired solution is at $s_x = s_y = 1$. The chosen Wald prior is illustrated (*bottom left*) and the resulting negative log-posterior probability (*bottom right*). The desired solution remains at the same position but without the trivial solutions.

**Fig. 2.** A randomly transformed template is placed on the image (*left*), and by means of numerical optimisation we find the parameters for which the log-posterior has a minimum value. The results can be seen on the (*right*).

**Table 1.** Comparison between actual and estimated values of the transformation parameters from Fig. 2

| Transformation | Actual | Estimated | Absolute deviation |
|---|---|---|---|
| Rotation ($\vartheta$) | $30.47°$ | $29.7046°$ | $0.7654°$ |
| Translation ($d_x, d_y$) | $211, 37$ | $213, 38$ | $2, 1$ |
| Scale ($s_x, s_y$) | $1.3077, 1.1923$ | $1.3125, 1.2719$ | $0.0048, 0.0796$ |
| Shear ($\varphi$) | $27°$ | $24.6776°$ | $2.3224°$ |
| Sinusoid ($\alpha, k$) | $1.96, 0.0327$ | $0.0032, 0.0069$ | $1.9568, 0.0258$ |

parameters of the transformation. The template is placed on the image (Fig. 2, left) and an exhaustive search is used on the translation parameters $d_x, d_y$, in order to find a good starting location for the optimisation algorithm. Using, for simplicity, a variation of the Simplex algorithm [12], we minimise the parameters $\xi$ and obtain the resulting template which is superimposed on the right image of Fig. 2. Visually, the results are quite pleasing, with the affine parameters being correctly identified within an appropriate error deviation (see Table 1).

## 5 Conclusions and Future Work

We have presented a robust treatment of the view-oriented object recognition problem for intensity images under a Bayesian formulation. We have introduced prior distributions to bias appropriately a template which is deforming under affine transformation and a sinusoidal geometric deformation. Also, we have addressed the problem of different distributions of the foreground and background by using the robust smooth Huber metric. Some preliminary results obtained with our methods were presented.

There are many issues that we would like to examine in future work. In particular, we have only discussed grey-level imagery. Extension to colour imagery is needed. In addition, we would like to experiment with other metrics, more closely related to what is known about the statistics of images of natural and man-made scenes [13]. We would also like to experiment with explicit modeling of the foreground and background distributions from training samples, using a statistical mixture model. Finally, in this early stage of our work, we have not discriminated between *intrinsic* variations of the template, that is variations of the shape of the object that depend only on the properties of the object and *extrinsic* variation which may depend on the viewpoint [14]. We hope to introduce models for the *extrinsic*, viewpoint variations in the future.

**Acknowledgement.** The primary author has been supported by a grant from the EPSRC.

# References

1. Koenderink, J., van Doorn, A.: The internal representation of solid shape with respect to vision. Biological Cybernetics **32** (1979) 211–216
2. Tarr, M. J., Williams, P., Hayward, W.G., Gauthier, I.: Three dimensional object recognition is viewpoint dependent. Nature Neuroscience **1** (1998) 275–277
3. Grimson, W. E. L.: Disambiguating Sensory Interpretations Using Minimal Sets of Sensory Data. IEEE Computer Society Int. Conf. on Robotics and Automation (1986) 286–292
4. Faugeras, O. D., Hebert, M.: A 3-D Recognition and Positioning Algorithm Using Geometrical Matching Between Primitive Surfaces. Proc. 8th Int. Joint Conf. Artificial Intell.(1983) 996–1002
5. Grenander, U., Chow, Y., Keenan, D. M.: Hands: A Pattern Theoretic Study of Biological Shapes. Springer (1991)
6. Jain, A. K., Zhong, Y., Lakshmanan, S.: Object Matching Using Deformable Templates. IEEE PAMI **18** (1996) 267–278
7. Tian, Q., Yu, J., Xue, Q., Sebe, N., Huang, T. S.: Robust Error Metric Analysis for Noise Estimation in Image Indexing. Conference on Computer Vision and Pattern Recognition Workshop **9** (2004) 140–146
8. Sullivan, J., Blake, A., Isard, M., MacCormick, J.: Bayesian Object Localisation in Images. Int. J. Computer Vision **44** (2001) 111–136
9. Huber, P. J.: Robust regression: Asymptotics, Conjectures and Monte Carlo. The Annals of Statistics **1** (1973) 799–821
10. Cootes, T. F., Edwards, G. J., Taylor, C. J.: Active Appearance Models. IEEE Pattern Analysis and Machine Intelligence **23** (2001) 681–685
11. Evans, M., Hastings, N., Peacock, B.: Statistical Distributions. Third Edition. Wiley Series in Probability and Statistics (2000)
12. Nelder, J. A., Mead, R.: A simplex method for function minimization. Computer Journal **7** (1965) 308–313
13. Huang, J., Mumford, D.: Statistics of Natural Images and Models. Computer Vision and Pattern Recognition **1** (1999) 1541–1547
14. Dias, M. B., Buxton, B. F.: Separating Shape and Pose Variations. Image and Vision Computing **22** (2004) 851–861

# Efficient Multiscale Shape-Based Representation and Retrieval

I. El Rube[1], N. Alajlan[2], M. Kamel[2], M. Ahmed[3], and G. Freeman[2]

[1] Systems Design Eng., University of Waterloo, Canada
[2] Electrical and Computer Eng., University of Waterloo, Canada
[3] Physics and Computer Science Dep., WLU, Canada

**Abstract.** In this paper, a multiscale representation and retrieval method for 2D shapes is introduced. First, the shapes are represented using the area of the triangles formed by the shape boundary points. Then, the Wavelet Transform (WT) is used for smoothing and decomposing the shape boundaries into multiscale levels. At each scale level, a triangle-area representation (TAR) image and the corresponding Maxima-Minima lines are obtained. The resulting multiscale TAR (MTAR) is more robust to noise, less complex, and more selective than similar methods such as the curvature scale-space (CSS). The proposed method is tested and compared to the CSS method using the MPEG-7 CE-shape-1 dataset. The results show that the proposed MTAR outperforms the CSS method for the retrieval test.

## 1 Introduction

Shape analysis and matching depend mainly on the underlying shape representation method. The criteria that govern the performance of a shape representation method include its invariance, robustness, stability, and uniqueness. Researchers from various fields such as pattern recognition and computer vision have proposed several techniques for 2D shape representation and matching. Examples of these techniques include curvature scale space (CSS) [1],[2] and [3], fuzzy-based matching [4], Fourier descriptors [5], and wavelet descriptors [6]. A recent review paper can be found in [7].

The formulation of shape representation as a multiscale process has at least two advantages. Firstly, the human perception of shapes can be viewed as a multiscale by nature since many interesting shape properties are revealed at different scale levels. Secondly, multiple scales achieve invariance to moderate amounts of deformation and noise. A well established multiscale method is the wavelet transform WT. It has been used in many disciplines including shape analysis and recognition [8], and [9]. Many researchers have adopted the WT in shape representation and matching [10], [6], [11], [12], and [13].

In this paper, a shape representation for closed boundaries that is called multi-scale triangle-area representation (MTAR) is introduced. This representation possesses many advantages over the similar technique, the curvature scale space (CSS) representation [1]. Utilizing the WT makes the MTAR more robust to noise and provides selectivity in the matching process, that is, coarse-to-fine matching.

Mokhtarian and Mackworth [14], [1] proposed the curvature scale space (CSS) method, which is considered one of the most well-researched closed-boundary shape representations and it has been selected for MPEG-7 standardization [15]. In their method, a Gaussian kernel with increasing standard deviation $\sigma$ is used to gradually smooth the contour at different scale levels. At each scale, the curvature of each contour point is measured by:

$$c(u,\sigma) = \frac{\dot{x}(u,\sigma)\ddot{y}(u,\sigma) - \ddot{x}(u,\sigma)\dot{y}(u,\sigma)}{(\dot{x}(u,\sigma)^2 + \dot{y}(u,\sigma)^2)^{3/2}} \quad (1)$$

Where $c$ is the curvature at location $u$ and scale $\sigma$, $\dot{x}$ and $\ddot{x}$ are the first and second derivatives of $x$, respectively. By setting (1) to zero, the inflection points (or curvature zero crossings) are located at each scale. This results in a binary image, called CSS image, which shows the end-points of the concave segments along the contour at each scale level. As the scale level increases, the smoothing effect increases and the number of inflection points decreases until the contour becomes totally convex.

When matching two shapes, only the maxima of contours in their CSS images are used [16]. A near optimal correspondence between two maxima sets is computed efficiently using many heuristics. However, CSS is concavity-based representation and, therefore, can not describe totally convex shapes such as circles and squares. Another disadvantage of CSS is that it requires a large number of iterations to obtain the CSS image (may exceed 200).

An efficient computation of the curvature scale space representation using B-spline wavelets was proposed by Wang et al. [17], [18]. Their method provides an alternative to the classical Gaussian-based scale space representation while being much more efficient and relying on the well-established wavelet theory.

The remainder of this paper is organized as follows. In Section II, the proposed representation is introduced. Section III presents the matching approach. The experimental results are shown in Section IV. Lastly, Section V concludes our work and suggests future work.

## 2 Multi-scale Triangle-Area Representation (MTAR)

In the following, we give a brief explanation of how to obtain the TAR for an arbitrary closed contour. Then, the MTAR images using the WT are shown. Also the effect of general affine transformations on MTAR images is introduced.

### 2.1 TAR Signatures

The TAR signature is computed from the area of the triangles formed by the points on the shape boundary. Each contour point is represented by its $x$ and $y$ coordinates. Then, separated parameterized contour sequences $x(n)$ and $y(n)$ are obtained in order to facilitate applying 1D techniques on each sequence alone. The contour is re-sampled to $N$ points and the curvature of each point is measured using the triangle area representation (TAR), as follows. For each three equai-distant points $P^1, P^2$ and $P^3$, the signed area $A$ of the triangle formed by these points is computed. For the complete boundary points, the TAR signature equation equals,

$$A(i) = \frac{1}{2}(-P_x^i P_y^{i-1} + P_x^{i+1} P_y^{i-1} + P_x^{i-1} P_y^i - P_x^{i+1} P_y^i - P_x^{i-1} P_y^{i+1} + P_x^i P_y^{i+1}), \quad i = 1 : N \quad (2)$$

where N is the total number of points on the shape boundary. The triangles at the edge points are formed by considering the periodicity of the closed boundary. When the contour is traversed in CCW direction, positive, negative and zero values of $A$ mean convex, concave and straight-line points, respectively. Fig. 1 demonstrates these three types of the triangle areas and shows the complete TAR signature for the bird shape.

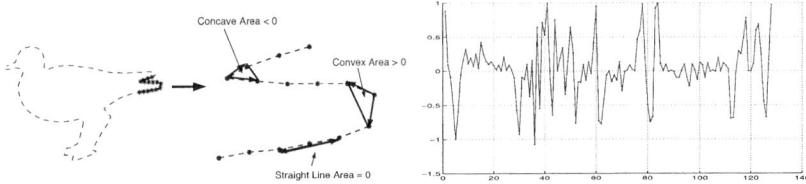

**Fig. 1.** Three different types of the triangle-area values and the TAR signature for the bird shape

When the length of the triangle sides is increased, i.e., by considering farther points, the function of $A$ will represent longer variations along the contour.

A TAR image is a binary image that is obtained by thresholding $A(i)$ at zero and taking the locations of the negative values at different values of triangle sides, as shown in Fig. 2. Thus, the horizontal axis in a TAR image shows the locations of the contour points and the vertical axis represents the triangle side length.

## 2.2 MTAR Images

The dyadic WT is applied to each contour sequence obtaining various decomposed levels. This reduces the effect of noise especially at low values of triangle side lengths, as shown in the first column of Fig. 3. Only the approximation coefficients are adopted in order to reduce the noise effect. At each scale level, the same process of obtaining the TAR image in section 2.1 is also adopted here. The result is the MTAR, which contains $L+1$ TAR images, where $L = log_2(N)$. Fig. 3 also shows that only small number of iterations (vertical axis) are required to obtain each TAR image. This is an advantage for the MTAR over the CSS method which required large number of iterations for its images.

## 2.3 Maxima and Minima Points

Other important features that can be derived from the TAR signatures are the maxima and minima points of these functions. For simplicity, only the locations

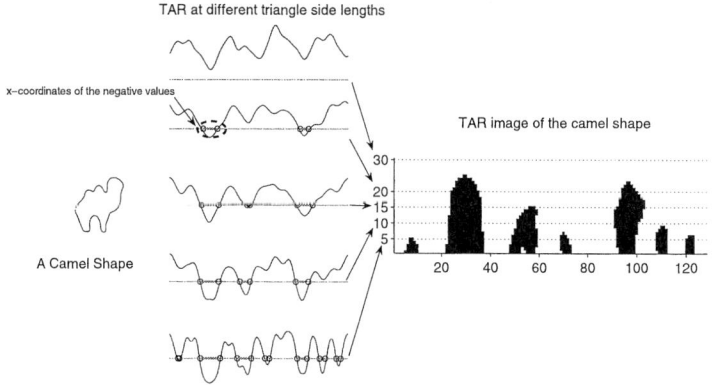

**Fig. 2.** Illustration of the computation of the TAR image. The second column shows the TAR signatures computed at specific triangle-side lengths. The TAR image (third column) is obtained using all the triangle-side lengths from 1 to 30.

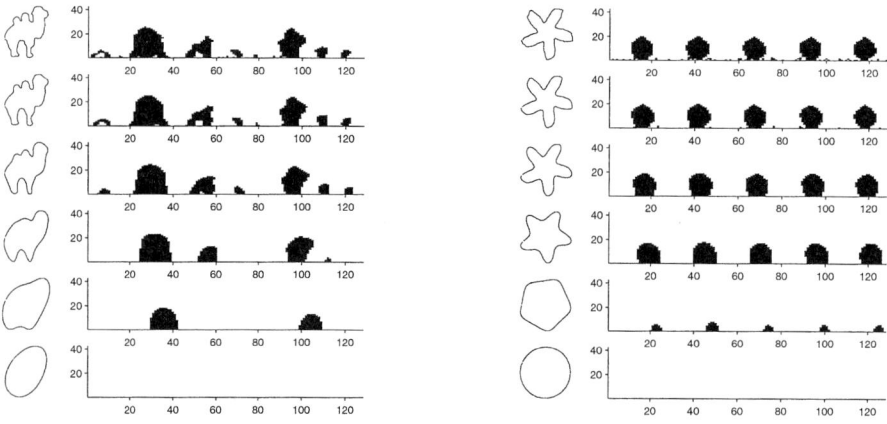

**Fig. 3.** Examples of MTAR images for two different shapes at different wavelet scale level (starting from l=0)

of these features are used in this paper at each triangle-side length. Fig. 4 illustrates a star shape represented by its concavity regions, maxima lines, and minima lines. The maxima points indicate the local convex points that correspond to a convex region. This region can occur in a totally convex area or within a concave region. For example, the small convexity region that is in the same direction as the East is located within a larger concavity. This is shown in the TAR image as a white (background color) region surrounded by the dotted ∩-shape concavity region. The minima points also could occur in both regions, as shown in the same figure. It should be noted that even when the shape become convex

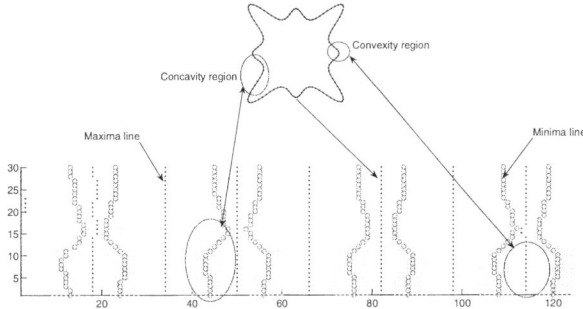

**Fig. 4.** A star shape and its TAR image showing the corresponding concavity region (dotted area), convexity region (background), maxima lines (dotted lines), and minima lines (circles lines)

(no concavity regions), the local maxima and minima are still tracked. This is because that although the TAR becomes totally positive for large triangle-side lengths, it still has the minima and maxima segments.

## 3 Matching

MTAR and CSS images, produced for the same shape, have many properties in common. Both representations are concavity-based methods. However, CSS method measures the curvature as the contour is smoothed by the Gaussian functions at different scales. On the other hand, each MTAR image represents the locations of the concavities using different triangle sides at a specific wavelet-smoothed scale level. Therefore, we followed a similar approach to that of CSS [19] for matching two MTAR image sets of two shapes. Matching is performed in two stages as follows.

In the first stage, a set of global features are used to eliminate very dissimilar shapes and exclude them from further processing. In our work, these features include aspect ration $AR$, circularity $C$, eccentricity $E$ and solidity $S$. In the second stage, a similarity measure $D_s$ between each two MTAR images of the two shapes at certain scale is computed as described in [16].

As indicated before, the MTAR and the CSS images are concavity-based representation methods which mean that they can't differentiate between totally convex shapes (e.g., circles and squares) easily. In order to increase the discrimination of the MTAR method, the average sum of the maxima and minima points $M_t$ for each TAR image is added.

The dissimilarity measure between each two MTAR images at a specific scale is a weighted sum of the global parameters, $M_t$, and $D_s$. Consequently, the final dissimilarity distance between two shapes is a weighted sum of the dissimilarity measures between their MTAR images.

## 4 Experimental Results

The MPEG-7 CE-shape-1 dataset is chosen to evaluate MTAR and compare its performance with that of CSS method. This dataset consists of 1400 shapes grouped in 70 classes. Recently, this dataset has been widely used for shape matching and retrieval.

The retrieval performances of the MTAR and the CSS methods are evaluated in this test. The performances of the methods are assessed using the precision-recall curves. Since the MTAR includes multiscale TAR images, the scale levels from $l = 1$ to $l = 4$ of the MTAR are evaluated and compared to each other. The corresponding average sum of the maxima and minima points are added to each level. Fig. 5 shows that the first three scale levels of the MTAR have close precision-recall values. However, scale levels $l = 2$ and $l = 3$ are less sensitive to noise than the level $l = 1$ and hence needs less time for computation. Also the discrimination of these two scales is higher than the scale level $l = 4$.

Fig. 6 shows that the combined MTAR achieves higher accuracy than the CSS at all recall values. It also shows that the second scale is slightly better than the CSS, whereas the third scale of the MTAR has comparable performance vs the CSS method.

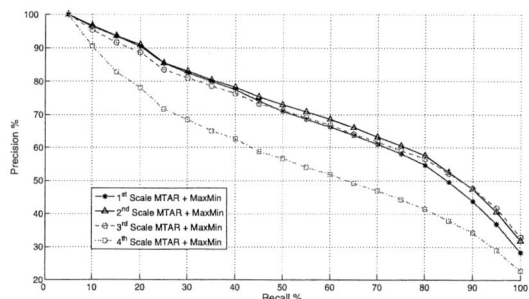

**Fig. 5.** Precision-recall curves for the scale levels $l = 1$ to $l = 4$ of the MTAR with the corresponding MaxMin

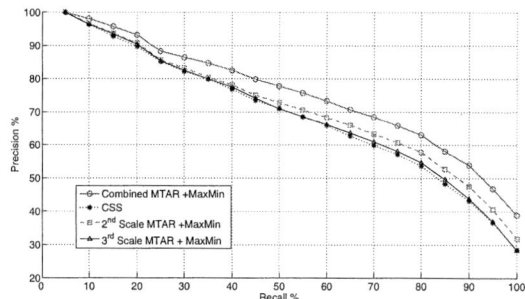

**Fig. 6.** Retrieval precision-recall curves for the combined MTAR+MaxMin, CSS, the 2nd scale of MTAR+MaxMin, and the 3rd scale of MTAR+MaxMin

**Table 1.** Processing times per single query for the MTAR and the CSS

| Method | Representation | Feature Extraction | Matching |
|---|---|---|---|
| $2^{nd}Scale$ MTAR | 15.6ms | 35ms | 1.5ms |
| Combined MTAR | 76.7ms | 100ms | 5.2ms |
| CSS | 3382.7ms | 174ms | 1.8ms |

In order to assess the MTAR, it is compared with the similar method, the CSS. The CSS has been selected for the MPEG-7 system after thorough and comprehensive tests for different shape descriptors. The results of Fig. 6 show that while the combined and the second scale have higher performance than the CSS, the third scale level has almost the same accuracy of the CSS with advantage of being less complex. This indicates that only one scale level can be used for shape retrieval with the advantages of less sensitivity to noise, and less complexity than the CSS.

The complexity of the MTAR and the CSS methods is tested using the Matlab©(ver. 6.5) program on Pentium IV 3.0 GHz PC. It is noticeable from this table that the MTAR is less complex than the CSS method, especially in the representation stage.

## 5 Conclusions

In this paper, a multiscale shape representation and retrieval method is introduced. The application of the WT in this method reduces the noise and the small boundary distortions, which accordingly improves the performance of the representation. The computed average sum of the maxima and minima points at each scale level increases the discrimination power of the proposed MTAR method. The conducted experiment investigates the retrieval performance of the MTAR at various scale levels. When compared to the related representation method, the results show that MTAR outperforms the CSS method. Furthermore, using only one scale level (especially, when $l = 2$ or $l = 3$) attains comparable results and less complexity than the CSS method. The importance of comparing with the CSS is that it is already chosen as an MPEG-7 shape descriptor. Furthermore, several methods are compared to the CSS in the literature including the MPEG-7 experiment tests. In this paper, the MTAR outperforms the CSS even though using a matching algorithm similar to that in [19], which was originally designed for the CSS method.

## References

1. Mokhtarian, F., Mackworth, A.: A theory of multi-scale, curvature-based shape representation for planar curves. IEEE Trans. on PAMI **14** (1992) 789–805
2. Abbasi, S., Mokhtarian, F.: Affine-similar shape retrieval: application to multiview 3-d object recognition. IEEE Trans. on Image Processing **10** (2001)

3. Mokhtarian, F., Bober, M.: Curvature Scale Space Representation: Theory, Applications, and MPEG-7 Standardization. Kluwer Academic Publishers (2003)
4. Chen, Y., Wang, J.: A region-based fuzzy feature matching approach to content-based image retrieval. IEEE Transactions on Pattern Analysis and Machine Intelligence **24** (2002) 1252–
5. Bui, T., Chen, G.: Multiresolution moment-wavelet-fourier descriptor for 2-D pattern recognition. Proceedings of SPIE-The International Society for Optical Engineering **3078** (1997) 552–557
6. Chauang, G., Kuo, C.: Wavelet descriptor of planar curves: Theory and applications. IEEE Transaction on Image Processing **5** (1996) 56–70
7. Zhang, D., Lu, G.: Review of shape representation and description techniques. Pattern Recognition **37** (2004) 1–19
8. Mallat, S.: A Wavelet Tour of Signal Processing. second edn. Academic Press (1999)
9. Costa, L., Jr., R.C.: Shape Analysis and Classification, Theory and Practice. CRC Press LLC (2001)
10. Tsang, K.: Recognition of 2-D stanalone and occluded objects using wavelet transform. International Journal of Pattern Recognition and Artificial Intelligence **15** (2001) 691–705
11. Alferez, R., Wang, Y.: Geometric and illumination invariants for object recognition. IEEE Trans. on PAMI **21** (1999) 505–536
12. Khalil, M., Bayoumi, M.: A dyadic wavelet affine invariant function for 2-D shape recognition. IEEE Trans. on PAMI **23** (2001) 1152–1164
13. ElRube, I., Kamel, M., Ahmed, M.: 2-d shape matching using asymmetric wavelet-based dissimilarity measure. In: ICIAR (1). (2004) 368–375
14. Mokhtarian, F., Mackworth, A.: Scale-based description and recognition of planar curves and two-dimensional shapes. IEEE Trans. on PAMI **8** (1986) 34–43
15. Page, T.M.H.: (http://www.chiariglione.org/mpeg/index.htm)
16. Abbasi, S., Mokhtarian, F., Kittle, J.: Curvature scale space image in shape similarity retrieval. MultiMedia Systems **7** (1999) 467–476
17. Wang, Y.P., Lee, S.L., Toraichi, K.: Multiscale curvature-based shape representation using b-spline wavelets. IEEE Trans. on Image Processing **8** (1999)
18. Wang, Y.P., Lee, S.L.: Scale-space derived from b-splines. IEEE Trans. on PAMI **20** (1998) 1040–1055
19. Pratt, W.K.: Digital Image Processing. Second edn. John Wiley and sons Inc (1991)

# Robust Matching Area Selection for Terrain Matching Using Level Set Method

Guo Cao, Xin Yang, and Shoushui Chen

Institute of Image Processing and Pattern Recognition, Shanghai Jiao Tong University,
Shanghai, 200030, P.R.China
{gcao_jn, yanxin, sschen}@sjtu.edu.cn

**Abstract.** To enhance the reliability of path planning in scenery guidance system, it's very important to select reliable or high matching probability areas from the navigation reference images for performing unmanned aerial vehicles localization. This paper applies three measures and proposes a new selection scheme base on a simplified Mumford-Shah model. The proposed method artfully avoids selecting thresholds to separate the feature images and optimally selects robust-matching areas by evolving the level set function. Experiments of the selection show that the proposed method is efficient.

**Keywords:** Navigation reference image, correlation matching, DCT, level set method.

## 1 Introduction

Unmanned aerial vehicle (UAV) must know where it is in the environment in order to perform useful tasks. Scene matching is one of the widely adopted techniques in navigation system for UAV. The real-time images acquired by the navigation system on-board during flight are compared with a prior-stored reference image to find the correct position of UAV at that time. Although the scene matching method is theoretically simple, it is essential to select robust-matching areas (RMA) in reference images for scene matching to optimize the reliable localization.

Hall[1] presented a method for selecting the best subset of a scene where best is defined in terms of the minimum correlation length which is measured as the 50 percent width of the correlation peak between the original and selected regions, but he didn't take into account the disturbance of sub-peaks. Goldgof[2] et al. present an algorithm which uses Gaussian curvature for extracting special points on the terrain and use these points for recognition of particular regions of the terrain. Xiao[3] made use of the variance of image, continuity of the edges, the length of correlation etc. as measures to select RMA. Sim and Dudek [4] consider image locations with high edge density as possible landmarks, which are represented using an appearance-based method. Olson[5] describe a method based upon a maximum-likelihood robot localization to select landmarks by matching terrain maps. In another paper he[6] use image entropy for performing registration between images and the best registration is determined using normalized correlation. Toshimitsu Kaneko[7] present a feature selection method based on the upper bound of the average template matching error for reliable tracking. Most methods described above have a high computation complexity. So, in this paper we try to use some effective features to give a fast and reasonable selection.

The RMA Selection from navigation reference images is in fact a partition of RMA and non-RMA. This paper presents a novel method based on Mumford-Shah model and integrates different feature information: track-ability, entropy and DCT edge density. The proposed method avoids selecting thresholds to separate the feature images since improper thresholds may result large segmentation errors and uses a level set algorithm for minimizing the Mumford-Shah model energy by evolving a zero level set function. The selection border may change topology, break, merge and form sharp corners easily as the level set function evolves. The paper is organized as follows: section 2 presents details of the extraction of features. Section 3 describes the full selection algorithm. Then, section 4 presents several tests and results. Finally, conclusions are given in section 5.

## 2 Features Extraction

It is possible to significantly improve matching performance by choosing the best feature space. In this section, we describe the features used here.

### 2.1 Track-Ability

Shi and Tomasi[8] propose a method to select features with good texture properties and show how to monitor the quality of image feature dissimilarity that quantifies the change of appearance of a feature between two frames. Given the image $I(\mathbf{x})$ and a window $Win(\mathbf{x})$ in image $I(\mathbf{x})$, the center of $Win(\mathbf{x})$ is $\mathbf{x}$. $w(\mathbf{x})$ is a weighting function. Features of the point $\mathbf{x}$ can be measured use the matrix:

$$Z(\mathbf{x}) = \iint_{Win(\mathbf{x})} G(\mathbf{x}+\mathbf{y})w(\mathbf{x}+\mathbf{y})d\mathbf{y} \qquad (1)$$

$$Tr(\mathbf{x}) = \min(\mu_1, \mu_2) \qquad (2)$$

Where $\mu_1, \mu_2$ are the eigenvalues of the matrix $Z$.

Small $Tr(\mathbf{x})$ values mean a roughly constant intensity profile within a window. Large $Tr(\mathbf{x})$ values can represent corners, salt-and-pepper textures, or any other pattern that can be tracked or matched reliably.

### 2.2 Entropy

Considering an image $I(\mathbf{x})$, with a probability function $P_I(k), k \in \{0,...,255\}$, Fisher's information quantity $q$ is defined as:

$$q_I(k) = -\log P_I(k), \quad \forall k \in \{0,...,255\}$$

$q(k)$ is the amount of information brought by a pixel **x** whose gray level is $k$. The information brought by an image window $Win(\mathbf{x})$ is the average of $q$ in it. Called the entropy $H_{Win}(\mathbf{x})$:

$$H_{Win}(\mathbf{x}) = \frac{1}{N_l \times N_c} \sum_{i=0}^{N_l-1} \sum_{j=0}^{N_c-1} q_I(\mathbf{x}) \tag{3}$$

The size of the window is $N_l \times N_c$. The entropy transformation captures the amount of local variation at each location in the image. They are insensitive to many issues in multi-sensor registration while retaining much image information.

### 2.3 DCT Edge Density

Randen [9] reviews most texture feature extraction approaches and performs a comparative study. Relatively the DCT approach is excellent due to its good overall performance and low complexity. We use DCT approach to extract the texture edge features since using traditional edge detection operators such as Laplace, Canny etc can produce clutters within the textures that we are not interested in.

Two-dimensional $N \times N$ DCT coefficients $v(k,l)$ of an image block $W_{N \times N}(\mathbf{x})$ ( **x** is the center of the block) are given as

$$v(k,l) = \sum_{m=0}^{N-1} \sum_{n=0}^{N-1} \alpha(k,l,m,n) I(m,n) \quad 0 \leq k, l \leq N-1 \tag{4}$$

Define the DCT edge as:

$$DCT_E(\mathbf{x}) = \sqrt{\sum_{l=1}^{N-1} v(0,l)^2 + \sum_{k=1}^{N-1} v(k,0)^2 + \sum_{k=1}^{N-1} \sum_{l=1}^{N-1} v(k,l)^2} \tag{5}$$

The size of the block can be 8×8, 16×16… according to the variety of textures. The feature density of a block $Win(x)$ is the mean value of $DCT(x)$ in it.

## 3 Segmentation Method

Measures discussed above can be represented as a vector $\mathbf{MV}(\mathbf{x}) = (Tr(\mathbf{x}), H(\mathbf{x}), ED(\mathbf{x}))$. They represent the information of an area for robust matching. We need to integrate these three measures to get an effective selection. We can select a threshold for each feature image and use mathematical morphology to get RMA, but improper thresholds may result large selection errors. In fact the selection is a separation of robust matching areas from non-robust matching areas. Chan and Vese[10] proposed an algorithm based on Mumford-Shah model, which could give an optimal partition of robust matching areas. This model has been widely used for image smoothing, segmentation, and surface reconstruction. We modify the algorithm for evolving interfaces to extract the goal areas.

Let $\Omega$ be the image domain for intensity gray image $I(x, y)$. Let $C$ be a smooth, closed initial curve in $R^2$ which separates the image into two areas $I_o(x, y)$, $I_b(x, y)$. $\omega_o$ is the object area and $\omega_b$ is the background. $c_o$ is the mean value inside of the curve $C$, $c_b$ is the mean value outside of the curve $C$. The goal of the model is to find true edges $C_o$ between RMA and non-RMA. The energy function is as follows:

$$F(C) = F_o(C) + F_b(C) = \int_{inside(C)} |I - c_o|^2 dxdy + \int_{outside(C)} |I - c_b|^2 dxdy \quad (6)$$

The minimum of the above energy will be an optimal piecewise-smooth approximation of the edge. We use level set formulation and algorithm for minimizing the Mumford-Shah energy introduced by S.Osher and J.Sethian.[11] In level set equation

$$\phi_t + F|\nabla \phi| = 0, \text{ given } \phi(x,t) = 0. \quad (7)$$

$F$ is the speed function, the position of the closed curve is given by the zero level set of $\phi$, $\phi$ is the level set function. A partial differentiate equation on the implicit function $\phi$ is as follows:

$$\begin{cases} c_o(\varphi) = \dfrac{\int_\Omega I(x, y) H(\varphi) dxdy}{\int_\Omega H(\varphi) dxdy}, \quad c_b(\varphi) = \dfrac{\int_\Omega I(x, y)(1 - H(\varphi)) dxdy}{\int_\Omega (1 - H(\varphi)) dxdy} \\ \dfrac{\partial \varphi}{\partial t} = \delta(\varphi) \left[ \mu \nabla \cdot \dfrac{\nabla \varphi}{|\nabla \varphi|} - v - \mu_o (I(x, y) - c_o)^2 + \mu_b (I(x, y) - c_b)^2 \right] \\ \varphi(0, x, y) = \varphi_0(x, y) \end{cases} \quad (8)$$

Where $H$ is the Heaviside function, $H(z) = \begin{cases} 1 & \text{if } z > 0 \\ 0 & \text{if } z < 0 \end{cases}$.

When we use the numerical algorithm for solving the above Euler-Lagrange equations, we use $|\nabla \phi(x, y)|$ to replace Dirac function $\delta(\phi(x, y))$ in order to expand the evolving space to the whole image.

From equation (8), we obtain the evolving equation to segment navigation reference images.

$$\frac{\partial \varphi}{\partial t} = |\nabla \varphi| \left[ \mu \nabla \cdot \frac{\nabla \varphi}{|\nabla \varphi|} - \frac{1}{3} \left( \sum_{k=1}^{3} \mu_k^i \left( MV_k(\mathbf{x}) - \overline{MV}_k^i \right)^2 + \sum_{k=1}^{3} \mu_k^o \left( MV_k(\mathbf{x}) - \overline{MV}_k^o \right)^2 \right) \right]$$

(9)

Where $MV_k(\mathbf{x})$ is the $k$ th value of vector $MV(\mathbf{x})$, $\overline{MV}_k^i$ is the $k$ th mean value of the inside closed curve and $\overline{MV}_k^o$ is the outside one. $\mu_k^i, \mu_k^o$ denote the weighting parameters. Given an initial closed curve in the reference image. The speed of the curve depends on the curvature of the curve and three measures. Update and evolve the level set function $\phi$ according to (9) until the stop criterion is met. The areas inside the closed curves are the robust matching areas we aim to achieve.

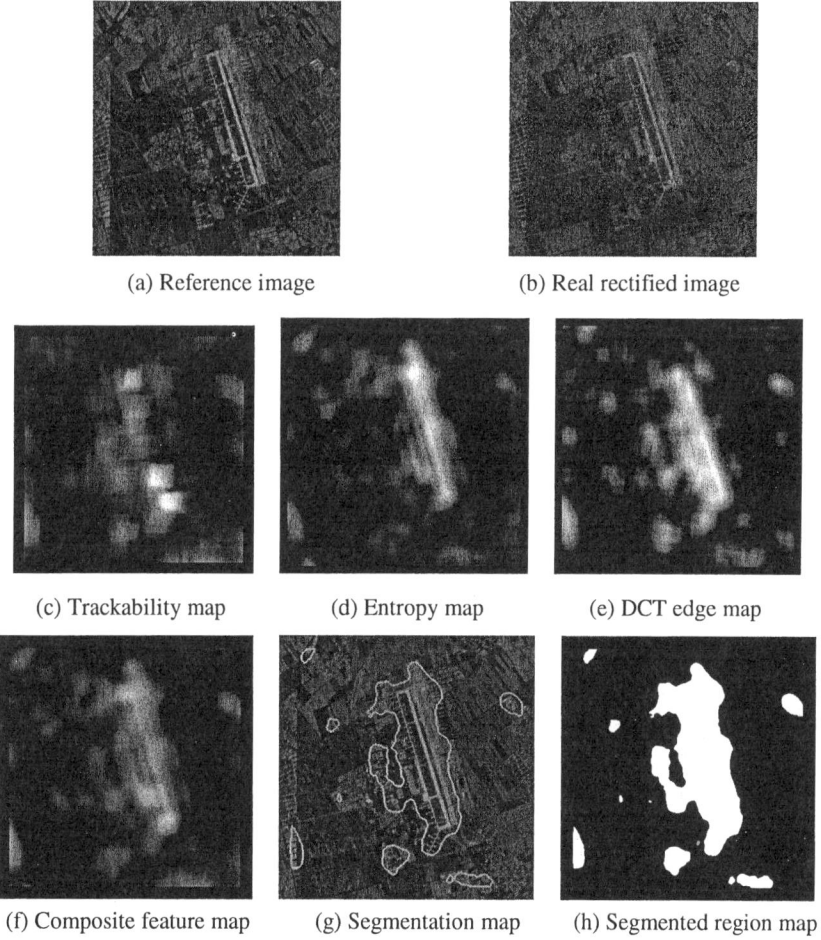

(a) Reference image  (b) Real rectified image

(c) Trackability map  (d) Entropy map  (e) DCT edge map

(f) Composite feature map  (g) Segmentation map  (h) Segmented region map

**Fig. 1.** Results of selection

## 4 Experimental Results

In this section, performance of our proposed algorithm is evaluated using two real images. The experimental platform used is a Pentium 4 1.7G processor-based PC, 256M memory. In these experiments, we set the size of the image block $36\times 36$ when computing the track-ability and entropy information, and set it $8\times 8$ for $DCT$ edge density.

### 4.1 Example 1

In this experiment, the real images Fig.1 (a) and (b) are used as test images with 256 gray levels. The size of the images is $401\times 401$ pixels. Fig.1 (c), (d) and (e) are the feature map which has been discussed above. The total calculating time of the three features is 8.8 seconds. The brighter areas are corresponding to the salient feature areas such as the airport region. Fig.1 (f) is color vector-valued map. There are almost no salient features in the dark regions, which are corresponding to the farmlands. Fig.1 (g) shows the robust matching areas selection results in the reference image. It cost 6.8 seconds to segment the reference image. The areas inside the green closed curve are the regions we aim to achieve. From these images and table 1 we can see that the selected regions have salient features and these regions are robust to match.

### 4.2 Example 2 and 3

Another two examples will now be given to further demonstrate the technique we described. Fig.2 (a) is an airport region gray images which size is pixels. We can see that the airport areas have salient features, which was approved by Fig.2 (b). The total selection time is only 19s while the correlation matching method needs about one and a half hours. Fig.2 (d) was digitized at 240 by 240 pixel resolution with 256 gray levels. From these figures we can see that almost all salient feature areas are selected and the matching probability of these areas is much more high than other areas.

### 4.3 Verification of RMA

In order to evaluate the matching performance of RMA, We use a pair of images: rectified real-time image $R(x',y')$ and reference image $I(x,y)$. Every point in $R(x',y')$ has a matching point in $I(x,y)$ within an error. We select every point in reference image as observational point $p(x,y)$. There is a point $p'(x',y')$ in $R(x',y')$ matching with the observational point $p(x,y)$. Now we choose a square $S(p')$ as a matching template. The template side is $d$ and center is point $p'$. Then, we use image correlation algorithm to search the matching area in $I(x,y)$. It's a successful matching and we define $C(p)=1$ if the distance between point $p$ and result matching point $m$ is smaller than a given threshold $\varepsilon$ ( $D(m,p) = \sqrt{(m_x - p_x)^2 + (m_y - p_y)^2} < \varepsilon$ ), otherwise we define $C(p)=0$ if it's a failure. Take into account all the points in the RMA we can calculate the probability of RMA:

$$P_{RMA} = (\sum_{p \in RMA} C(p))/N_{RMA} \tag{10}$$

The matching is more reliable if the probability of RMA is high. Here we set $\varepsilon = 3$ and the size of square matching template is $36 \times 36$. The probability of RMA and non-RMA can be calculated by using correlation-matching method. Table 1 shows the matching probabilities calculated by using three reference sample images.

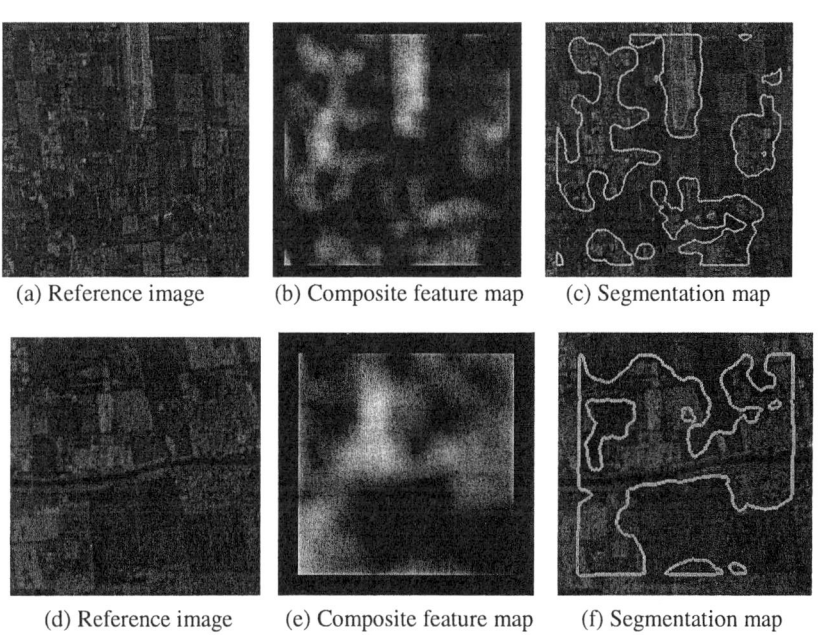

Fig. 2. Results of selection

**Table 1.** Comparison of correct-matching probability and computing time for 3 sample images

| Example No. | Probability of RMA | Probability of non-RMA | Computing time of our proposed method | | Computing time of correlation method |
|---|---|---|---|---|---|
| | | | Feature extraction and Segmentation time | | |
| 1 | 0.9388 | 0.7852 | 8.8s | 6.8s | 5473.8s |
| 2 | 0.9418 | 0.4467 | 7.4s | 11.6s | 5334.5s |
| 3 | 0.8523 | 0.4251 | 2.9s | 3.1s | 1893.4s |

## 5 Conclusions

The selection of RMA in reference image is very significant for path planning in navigation system. In this paper we appliedd three features to characterize the stability of matching performance. These features are fast to calculate and insensitive to illumination changes etc. Our proposed method is based on Mumford-Shah model, which can give an optimal segmentation. We use a level set formulation and algorithm for minimizing the Mumford-Shah energy function with the three features. Experiments have shown that our proposed method is fast and effective. The selected regions are reliable to match.

## References

1. Hall E L, Davies D L, The selection of critical subsets for signal, image, and scene matching, IEEE Transactions on Pattern Analysis and Machine Intelligence, 1980,2(4), pp.313-322.
2. Goldgof, D.B. Huang, T.S. Lee, H, Feature extraction and terrain matching. Computer Vision and Pattern Recognition, Proceedings CVPR '88, Computer Society Conference on 5-9 June 1988. pp 899 – 904
3. Xiao, Yijun, Ding, Mingyue, Zhou, Chengping. Matching suitability analysis of reference map for scene-matching-based navigation. Proc. SPIE 1998,Vol. 3545, International Symposium on Multi-spectral Image Processing, pp. 100-103.
4. Sim.R. and Dudek.G. Mobile robot localization from learned landmarks, In Proceedings of the IEEE/RSJ International Conference on Intelligent Robots and Systems, 1998, pp. 1060-1065.
5. Clark F.Olson, Image registration by aligning entropies, In proceedings on Computer Vision and Pattern Recognition, 2001, 2, pp.331-336.
6. Clark F.Olson, Selecting Landmarks for Localization in Natural Terrain, Autonomous Robots, 2002,12, pp.201-210.
7. Toshimitsu Kaneko,Osamu Hori, Feature Selection for Reliable Tracking using Template Matching, Proceedings CVPR '03, Computer Society Conference on 18-20 June 2003. pp 796-802.
8. Shi Jianbo, Tomasi C, Good Features to Track, In the IEEE Conference on Computer Vision and Pattern Recognition, Seattle, 1994, pp.593-600.
9. Trygve Randen, John Hakon husoy, Filtering for Texture Classification: A Comparative Study, IEEE Transactions on PAMI, 1999, 21(4), pp.291-309.
10. Chan F T, Vese L, Active contours without edges, IEEE Transactions on Image Processing, 2001,10(2), pp.266-277.
11. Sethian J A, Level Set Methods and Fast Marching Methods: Evolving Interfaces in Computational Geometry, Fluid Mechanics, Computer vision, and Materials Science, $2^{nd}$ Edition, Cambridge University Press, 1999.

# Shape Similarity Measurement for Boundary Based Features

Nafiz Arica[1] and Fatos T. Yarman Vural[2]

[1] Department of Computer Engineering, Turkish Naval Academy,
34942, Tuzla, Istanbul, Turkey
narica@dho.edu.tr
[2] Department of Computer Engineering, Middle East Technical University,
06531 Ankara, Turkey
vural@ceng.metu.edu.tr

**Abstract.** In this study, we propose two algorithms for measuring the distance between shape boundaries. In the algorithms, shape boundary is represented by the Beam Angle Statistics (BAS), which maps 2-D shape information into a set of 1-D functions. Firstly, we adopt Dynamic Time Warping method to develop an efficient distance calculation scheme, which is consistent with the human visual system in perceiving shape similarity. Since the starting point of the representations may differ in shapes, the best correspondence of items is found by shifting one of the feature vectors. Secondly, we propose an approximate solution, which utilizes the cyclic nature of the shape boundary and eliminates the shifting operation. The proposed method measures the distance between the features approximately and decreases the time complexity substantially. The experiments performed on MPEG-7 Shape database show that both algorithms using BAS features outperform all the available methods in the literature.

## 1 Introduction

In Content Based Image Retrieval Systems (CBIR), the major goal is to search all the images in the database that are "similar" to a query image according to some predefined criterion. Usually, the images within a given distance from the query or the first few images that have the smallest distance to the query are retrieved as a result of the query operation. The similarity is measured by a distance function defined over the feature space of the images. The objective in most of the similarity measurement methods is to minimize the distance between two vectors by allowing deformations.

Although a sound mathematical basis exists, similarity measurement between the shape features is a serious problem in the shape retrieval and indexing applications. The shapes, which are visually similar, may not be "close" to each other in the vector space, defined over a particular distance measure. Another problem in similarity measurement is the complexity of the algorithms. Since the distance is calculated between the query and each database shapes, the time complexity of the process is crucial for large databases. Current studies on boundary based shape similarity use exhaustive search in matching the starting point of the shape descriptors so that the minimum distance can be found [1], [4], [5]. The problem gets even more complicated, when the dimension of the vector space is large.

The first motivation in this paper is to develop an efficient distance calculation method, which is consistent with the human visual system in perceiving similarity and possesses a remarkable robustness to distortions. For this purpose, we adopt Dynamic Time Warping algorithm, to the boundary based shape features. The shape boundary is represented using the Beam Angle Statistics (BAS) method, which represents 2-D shape information with a set of 1-D functions.

It is well-known that the starting point of the representations may differ in shapes. The proposed algorithm finds the best correspondence of items by shifting one of the feature vectors. However, this process increases the time complexity of the algorithm so that it may not be practical to search for the optimal solution especially for the database applications, which require large number of comparisons. For this reason, instead of finding the exact distance, the suboptimal solutions which measures the distance between the features approximately, may be more appropriate. Secondly, we develop an efficient method which utilizes the cyclic nature of the shape boundary and eliminates the shifting operation.

The performances of algorithms are tested using the data set of MPEG 7 Core Experiments Shape-1 Part B, which is the main part of the Core Experiments. The experiments show that the proposed similarity measurement algorithm outperforms the available methods in the literature.

The paper is organized as follows. Section 2 provides a summary of the shape representation based on BAS, proposed in [1]. Section 3 describes an improved version of Dynamic Time Warping algorithm used for the similarity measurement of BAS features. Section 4 explains a fast cyclic measurement between shape boundaries. The experiments performed on MPEG-7 Shape Database are presented in section 5. Finally, the last section concludes the paper and proposes future studies.

## 2 Shape Representation Based on Beam Angle Statistics (BAS)

BAS is based on the beams, which are the lines connecting the reference point with the rest of the points on the boundary [1]. The characteristics of each boundary point are extracted by using the beam angles in a set of neighborhood systems. The angle between each pair of beams is taken as the random variable at each point on the boundary. Then, the moments provide the statistical information about the shape. In the first moment, each valley and hill corresponds to a concave and convex visual part of the object shape. The other moments increase the discriminative power of the representation. An example of the proposed representation is shown in figure 1.

The BAS representation eliminates the use of any heuristic rule or empirical threshold value of shape boundaries in a predefined scale. BAS, also, gives globally discriminative features to each boundary point by using all other boundary points. Another advantage of BAS representation is its simplicity, yet consistency with the human perception through preserving visual parts of the shapes. The representation is scale, rotation and translation invariant. It is also insensitive to noise and occlusion. The details of the BAS representation can be found in [1].

Next step in shape description is to describe the 1-D BAS functions in a compact way. For this purpose, we adopt piecewise constant approximation method. The BAS function is segmented into equal size frames and each frame is represented by the segment average. Intuitively, in order to reduce the dimension of BAS function from N to T, the data is divided into T equal-size frames. The average value of the data falling within a frame is calculated and the value obtained at each segment becomes the entries of the feature vector with dimension T.

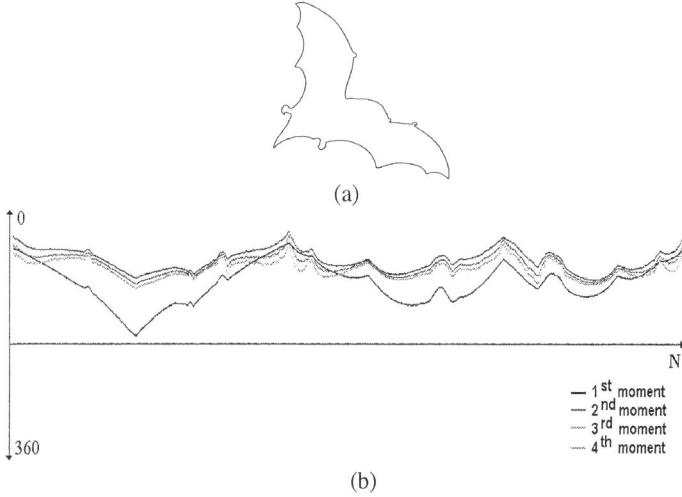

**Fig. 1.** (a) A sample shape boundary and (b) its fourth order statistics of Beam Angle

## 3 Dynamic Warping with Penalty

The matching process needs to compensate the slight variations on the BAS functions appropriately by compressing the function at some places and expanding it at others. The classical DW algorithm achieves this goal by finding an optimal match between two sequences, which allows stretching and compression of the sequences.

In order to align two sequences, $A=A_1,...,A_N$ and $B=B_1,...,B_M$ using DW, we construct an *N-by-M* matrix, where each element *(i,j)* contains the distance between the points $A_i$ and $B_j$. The goal is to find a path through the matrix, which minimizes the sum of the local distances of the points, starting from *(1,1)* and ending at *(N,M)*. This path is called warping path. If *D(i,j)* is the global distance up to *(i,j)* and the local distance at *(i,j)* is given by *d(i,j)*, then DW algorithm uses the following recurrence relation:

$$D(i,j) = d(A_i, B_j) + \min \begin{cases} D(i-1, j-1), \\ D(i-1, j), \\ D(i, j-1). \end{cases} \qquad (1)$$

Given $D(1,1)=d(A_1,B_1)$ as the initial condition, we have the basis for an efficient recursive algorithm for computing $D(i,j)$. The algorithms starts from $D(1,1)$ and iterates through the matrix by summing the partial distances until $D(N,M)$, which is the overall matching score of the sequences $A$ and $B$. DW is accomplished with a time and space complexity of $O(NM)$.

DW algorithm as described above, while not permitting changes in the ordering of the sequence items, allows unconstrained compression and expansion of the items of the two sequences. This may be suitable for some applications, such as speech recognition, where the sequences of the same class may be traced out more slowly during one portion of the speech and more quickly during another portion. In order to allow such variations, it is necessary to distort the time axis appropriately. For this reason, the DW algorithms used for speech recognition does not need to penalize the expansion and compression of the sequences in the matching process. However, in shape boundary, the free expansion and compression of some part of the sequence change the visual appearance of the shape. These variations may carry meaningful information used to distinguish visually different parts of the shape boundary.

The above discussion leads us to the consideration of constraining the warping path to limit the amount of compression and expansion to a certain extent in the matching process. In this study, we propose to assign penalties for expansion and compression of the BAS function. For this purpose, the horizontal and vertical moves in the DW matrix are penalized by a constant. This modification improves the performance of the similarity measurements in BAS descriptors. The proposed Dynamic Warping with Penalty (DWP) algorithm for calculation of distance between two BAS vectors $\Gamma_q$ and $\Gamma_t$ is given below:

---

**1. Initialization :**
  $D(1,1)= d(\Gamma_q(1), \Gamma_t(1))$;
  for $2 \leq i \leq N$
    $D(i,1)=D(i-1,1) + d(\Gamma_q(i), \Gamma_t(1))$;
  for $2 \leq j \leq M$
    $D(1,j)=D(1,j-1) + d(\Gamma_q(1), \Gamma_t(j))$;

**2. Iteration:**
  for $2 \leq i \leq N$
    for $2 \leq j \leq M$
      $D(i,j)=d(\Gamma_q(i), \Gamma_t(j)) + min \{D(i-1,j-1),$
                                                  $D(i-1,j) +penalty,$
                                                  $D(i-1,j) +penalty \}$;

**3. Termination:**
  return $(D(N,M))$

---

## 4 Cyclic Sequence Comparison

The BAS function, which is based on the shape boundary, is considered as a cyclic sequence. In order to align two BAS feature vectors, the starting boundary point is to be matched. This requires to define a unique starting point for each shape, which is not practically possible. For this reason, the alignment computation must determine the amount of cyclic shift that has taken place in order to find the optimal match.

The easiest method of solving cyclic sequence comparison problem is to shift any of the sequences one item at a time and recompute the alignment. The optimal alignment is, then, found by the cyclic shift which results with a minimum distance [1], [2]. However, shifting the elements of any sequence at each time, makes the complexity of the algorithm $O(MN^2)$ for the sequences with lengths $M$ and $N$.

Searching for strict optimality is not practical and efficient in image databases, which contain large number of shapes. Therefore, in practical problems, it is worth to find a suboptimal solution by approximate distance measures, rather than exact solution. The approximate approaches [6], [7], [8], double one of the sequences and then find the subsequence therein that best resembles the other sequence, which computes in time $O(MN)$.

In this study, we, also, approximate the optimal solution for the sack of efficiency and improve the method proposed in [8]. The original algorithm is developed for the partial matching of shape boundaries. However, our aim in BAS comparison is to find a matching between all the items of feature vectors. Thus, we improve the performance of the algorithm by assigning penalties in order to control the length of the warping path in the algorithm.

Given two cyclic sequences $A$ and $B$ with lengths N and M respectively, a minimum distance table with M columns and 2N rows constructed by concatenating the sequence A with itself ($A^2$). Paths start from the first N entries of the first column and end at various points in the last column. $D(i,j)$ is defined as the total distance on the minimum distance path from the $(i,j)$ entry of the distance table to the end of the path at some point in the last column. The value of $D(i,j)$ is evaluated as;

$$D(i,j) = \min \begin{cases} d(A_{i+1}, B_{j+1}) + D(i+1, j+1), \\ d(A_{i+1}, B_j) + D(i+1, j) + penalty, \\ d(A_i, B_{j+1}) + D(i, j+1) + penalty, \end{cases} \quad (2)$$

for $i=1,...,2N-1$ and $j=1,...M-1$. The boundary conditions are

$$D(i, M) = 0, \quad i = 1,...,2N \quad \text{and} \quad (3)$$

$$D(2N, j) = d(A_{2N}, B_{j+1}) - D(2N, j-1), \quad j = 1,..., M - 1. \quad (4)$$

Finally let

$$D(i,0) = d(i,1) - D(i,1). \quad (5)$$

The values of $D(i,0)$, $i=1,...N$ are the total distances of the paths through the minimum distance table from each starting point $i$ in A running from the first point to the last point of B. The path with the lowest $D(i,0)$ is the minimum distance path in the table.

Now, we are ready to give CSC algorithm for the BAS features. Given two BAS feature vectors $\Gamma_q$ and $\Gamma_t$, the cyclic sequence comparison method can be summarized by the following algorithm:

> **1. Initialization :**
>    for $1 \leq i \leq 2N\text{-}1$
>       $D(i,M)=0;$
>    for $1 \leq j \leq M\text{-}1$
>       $D(2N,j)=D(2N,j+1) + d(\Gamma_q(2N), \Gamma_t(j+1));$
> **2. Iteration:**
>    for $2N\text{-}1 \geq i > 1$
>      for $M \geq j \geq 1$
>        $D(i,j)= min \{ \ D(i+1,j+1) + d(\Gamma_q(i+1), \Gamma_t(j+1))$,
>                    $D(i+1,j) + d(\Gamma_q(i+1), \Gamma_t(j)) + penalty,$
>                    $D(i\text{-}1,j) + d(\Gamma_q(i), \Gamma_t(j+1)) + penalty \};$
>    for $1 \leq i \leq N$
>       $D(i,0) = d(\Gamma_q(i), \Gamma_t(1)) + D(i,1);$
> **3. Termination:**
>    return $min_{1 \leq i \leq N} \{ D(i,0) \}$

Note that, we change the recurrence relation by giving a constant penalty to the horizontal and vertical moves through the matrix. Although there is no theoretical reason for giving penalties, the discussion about this revision on the algorithm can be given by the following arguments:

Given two sequences A and B, the algorithm given in [8], finds a subsequence Z of $A^2$, which is most similar to B. In the computation, there is no control over the length of minimum distance path. Therefore, the length of the subsequence Z, |Z| may tend to go far from |A|. This leads to the following consequences in the matching process. The algorithm in [8] calculates a partial matching of A against B. However, our aim is to measure the overall distance between the sequences. This requires to find a complete correspondence between items of the sequences. The algorithm approximates the optimal solution and estimates a lower bound of the exact cyclic distance [7].

The proposed algorithm gives penalties for horizontal and vertical moves and controls the length of the path. This heuristic enforces the path to go through the diagonal and approximate |Z| to |A|. By this way, the complete correspondence between the items of two sequences is computed and the optimal solution is approximated by stimulating the matching score. Another reason for using penalties lies within the same proposition as in the DW case.

## 5 Experiments

The performance of the BAS descriptor is tested in the data set of MPEG 7 Core Experiments Shape-1 Part B, which is the main part of the Core Experiments.

In the first set of experiments, the effect of modification in DW algorithm is tested. The exact cyclic distance between the BAS features is calculated by keeping one of the sequences fix and shifting the other one item at a time. The classical DW is recomputed over and over again. The minimum distance is taken as the exact distance between the sequences. The penalty value in DW recurrence relation is taken as 50 for this particular test data. The constant value used as a penalty in the algorithm improves the similarity rates almost 2% at all sampling rates. This is depicted in Table 1.

Table 1. Comparison of DWP and DW Algorithms (%)

| Algorithm | Length of Sequence | | | | |
|---|---|---|---|---|---|
| | 10 | 20 | 30 | 40 | 50 |
| DW | 62.96 | 76.03 | 79.75 | 81.02 | 81.13 |
| **DWP** | **65.85** | **77.57** | **81.26** | **82.23** | **82.26** |

Another set of experiments are performed in order to compare the proposed cyclic sequence comparison algorithm with the original one in [8]. The penalty value remains as 50 in this set of experiments. The proposed method outperforms the original algorithm almost 5 % at all sampling rates.

Table 2. Comparison of Cyclic Sequence Comparison Algorithm and the algorithm proposed in [8] (%)

| Algorithm | Length of Sequence | | | | |
|---|---|---|---|---|---|
| | 10 | 20 | 30 | 40 | 50 |
| **Cyclic DTW** | **63.35** | **76.02** | **80.82** | **81.60** | **81.82** |
| Partial Shape Matching | 59.15 | 71.19 | 76.70 | 77.59 | 77.98 |

In Table 3, the comparison of the BAS function with the recently reported results of [3] (Shape Context), [4] (Tangent Space), [5] (Curvature Scale Space), [9] (Zernika Moments), [10] (Wavelet) and [11] (Directed Acyclic Graph) is provided. As it is seen from the table, the proposed descriptor performs better then the best-performance descriptors available in the literature, for the data set of MPEG CE Shape-1 part B.

Table 3. Comparison of Proposed Algorithms with BAS vector size 50 and recent studies

| Shape Context | Tangent Space | CSS | Zernika Moment | Wavelet | DAG | BAS with DWP | BAS with CSS |
|---|---|---|---|---|---|---|---|
| 76.51 | 76.45 | 75.44 | 70.22 | 67.76 | 60 | **82.26** | **81.82** |

# 6 Conclusion

In this study, we propose some improvements in two different similarity distance methods defined on the BAS feature space. The first method used for similarity measurement is Dynamic Warping (DW), which is widely used in speech recognition. The DW algorithm finds an optimal match between two sequences, which allows stretching and compression of sections in the subsequences. However, in shape boundary representation, the expansion and compression of some part of the sequence change the visual appearance of the shape. Therefore, the expansion and compression of BAS functions should be handled with a specific care, unlikely in speech case. For this reason, we propose to give penalties for subsequence expansion and compression of the BAS function. This simple modification of the cost function provides substantial improvement on the overall performance of the DW algorithm.

The second method is cyclic sequence matching algorithm, which approximates the optimal solution. To ensure a consistent description of a shape, which is cyclic in nature, a unique starting point must be defined for each shape. Since this is impractical to achieve, the alignment computation must determine the amount of cyclic shift that has taken place in order to find the optimal solution. However, this process increases the computational cost during the similarity measurement, resulting impractical computational cost for large databases. In order to avoid this complexity, we propose an efficient cyclic sequence comparison algorithm. In the performance evaluation of proposed methods, we use the dataset of MPEG 7 Core Experiments Shape-1. It is observed that the proposed shape descriptor outperforms all the methods in the literature in this particular data set.

# References

1. Arica N., Yarman-Vural F. T, BAS: A Perceptual Shape Descriptor Based On The Beam Angle Statistics, Pattern Recognition Letters, vol: 24/9-10, (2003) 1627-1639.
2. Sankoff D., Kruskal J., Time Warps, String Edits and Macromolecules, CLSI Publications, 1999.
3. Belongie, S., Malik, J., Puzicha, J., Shape Matching and Object Recognition Using Shape Contexts. IEEE Trans. PAMI, 24, 4, (2002) 509-522
4. Latecki, L. J., Lakamper, R., Shape Similarity Measure Based on Correspondence of Visual Parts. IEEE Trans. PAMI, 22, 10, (2000) 1185-1190.
5. Mokhtarian, F., Abbasi, S., Kittler, J., Efficient and Robust Retrieval By Shape Content Through Curvature Scale Space. Image Databases and Multimedia Search, A. W. M. smeulders and R. Jain ed., 51-58 World Scientific Publication (1997)
6. Bunke H., Buhler U., Applications Of Approximate String Matching To 2-D Shape Recognition, Pattern Recognition, 26 (12), 1797-1812, 1993.
7. Mollineda, R. A., Vidal E., Casacuberta F., Cyclic Sequence Alignments: Approximate Versus Optimal Techniques, International Journal Of Pattern Recognition and Artificial Intelligence, 16 (3), 291-299, 2002.
8. Gorman J. W., Mitchell O. R., Kuhl F, P., Partial Shape Recognition Using Dynamic Programming, IEEE Trans. PAMI, 10 (2), 257-266, 1988.
9. Khotanzad, A., Hong, Y. H., Invariant Image Recognition By Zernike Moments. IEEE Trans. PAMI, 12, (1990) 489-497.
10. Chuang, G., Kuo, C. –C., Wavelet Descriptor of Planar Curves: Theory and Applications. IEEE Trans. Image Processing, 5, (1996) 56-70.
11. Lin, L. –J., Kung, S. Y.,. Coding and Comparison of Dags as a Novel Neural Structure With Application To Online Handwritten Recognition. IEEE Trans. Signal Processing, (1996).

# Image Deformation Using Velocity Fields: An Exact Solution

Jeff Orchard

University of Waterloo, Waterloo Ontario N2L 3G1, Canada
jorchard@cs.uwaterloo.ca

**Abstract.** In image deformation, one of the challenges is to produce a deformation that preserves image topology. Such deformations are called "homeomorphic". One method of producing homeomorphic deformations is to move the pixels according to a continuous velocity field defined over the image. The pixels flow along solution curves. Finding the pixel trajectories requires solving a system of differential equations (DEs). Until now, the only known way to accomplish this is to solve the system approximately using numerical time-stepping schemes. However, inaccuracies in the numerical solution can still result in non-homeomorphic deformations. This paper introduces a method of solving the system of DEs exactly over a triangular partition of the image. The results show that the exact method produces homeomorphic deformations in scenarios where the numerical methods fail.

## 1 Introduction

Digital images can be "warped" or deformed using a non-rigid deformation. Each pixel can have its own displacement vector indicating where it moves to. There are different methods of determining these displacement vectors. One family of methods, which includes elastic deformation [1] and thin plate splines [2], uses a set of image control points that are moved, and the pixels in the image move with them as if attached to a rubber sheet. These methods work well for small control-point displacements, but large displacements can lead to non-homeomorphic deformations [3]. That is, the spatial transformation may not conserve local topology and therefore not be invertible. In applications such as medical imaging and remote sensing, a non-homeomorphic deformation is not desirable.

Deforming an image usually proceeds by traversing the pixels of the **deformed** image, determining a colour (or intensity) for each pixel. If one knows where the pixel was moved from in the original image, the new pixel's colour can be found by interpolating the original image at that location. This process requires the inverse of the deformation. For this reason, one usually stores the inverse of the desired deformation. The deformation map consists of a displacement vector for each pixel. In this context, the vector indicates where the pixel was displaced from.

There is no efficient way to find the inverse of a deformation defined using control-point displacement maps. Simply negating the displacement vectors does not suffice.

Instead of defining the deformation using control points, the pixels can be moved by flowing along a velocity field [4]. A continuous velocity field is defined over the image, typically by interpolating between a finite set of velocity vectors assigned in the image. These methods are often called "flow methods". The velocity fields can be derived in conjunction with other constraints such as smoothness and incompressibility [5, 6, 7].

However, given a velocity field, the operation of deriving the pixel trajectories can be challenging, and amounts to solving a system of differential equations (DEs) for each pixel. How easy the system is to solve depends on the type of DEs. Some systems are solvable, while others have no known closed-form solution (i.e. we cannot write down the solution in terms of combinations of transcendental functions). For such situations, we can approximate the solution using numerical time-stepping schemes [4]. This, too, has problems. The solution is only an approximation and can contain inaccuracies.

In this paper, we show that by performing linear interpolation on triangular cells in the image, the resulting system of DEs is linear and can be solved analytically. Thus, we derive homeomorphic deformations while avoiding the inaccuracies of numerical approximate solutions.

## 2 Methods

### 2.1 Velocity Fields

Let $f : \mathbb{R}^2 \to \mathbb{R}^2$ be a continuous function that represents the velocity field over a 2D image. Hence, $f(x, y)$ is the velocity vector at location $(x, y)$. We can model deformations as the movement of pixels as they follow this velocity field. Determining the path of a pixel is then a matter of solving the system of DEs

$$\begin{bmatrix} \frac{dx(t)}{dt} \\ \frac{dy(t)}{dt} \end{bmatrix} = f(x(t), y(t)) , \qquad (1)$$

where $f(x(t), y(t))$ is a vector-valued velocity function. Note the introduction of the parameter $t$. For a particular deformation, the system is integrated (backward or forward in time) to a predetermined stop time. The final resting point of each pixel is where that pixel is displaced to in the deformation.

A velocity field is better than a control-point displacement map because a velocity field is easily inverted by simply reversing the velocity vectors. A velocity field also offers continuous deformations so that intermediate deformations can be attained.

If velocity vectors are defined in our image (for example, at a subset of pixel locations), we can define a continuous velocity field over the domain of the image by interpolating between these velocity vectors. Bilinear interpolation can

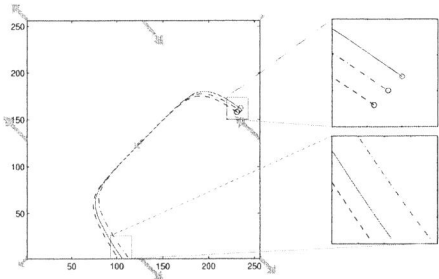

**Fig. 1.** Crossing pixel trajectories resulting from using a numerical solver. The gray arrows represent the velocity vectors at the pixel locations where they are specified. The velocity field is continuously interpolated between these vectors.

be used to interpolate between velocity vectors defined on a rectangular grid. In this case, the system of DEs that governs the motion of pixels in the image is

$$\begin{cases} x'(t) = Ax(t) + By(t) + Cx(t)y(t) + D \\ y'(t) = Ex(t) + Fy(t) + Gx(t)y(t) + H \end{cases} \quad (2)$$

where $x'(t)$ and $y'(t)$ are time derivatives, and $A, \ldots, H$ are constants based on nearby velocity vectors, $\boldsymbol{f}$. This system is the same as the interacting species model, and is non-linear because of the "$x(t)y(t)$" corss-terms. There is no known closed-form general solution to (2).

An alternative is to find an approximate solution to the system of DEs using a numerical method. That is, the movement of each pixel through the velocity field is estimated in discrete time steps using a numerical scheme. However, depending on the characteristics of the velocity field, this can be problematic. Figure 1 shows three numerical solution trajectories that cross each other. The underlying velocity field is continuous, so the solution curves should not cross. Hence, the error introduced by the time-stepping method changed the topology of the solutions.

Consider performing linear interpolation on triangular cells instead of rectangular cells. Since each of the $x$- and $y$-components of the velocity field can be uniquely represented as a linear function in a triangular cell, the resulting system of DEs is linear,

$$\begin{cases} x'(t) = Ax(t) + By(t) + D \\ y'(t) = Ex(t) + Fy(t) + H \end{cases} \quad (3)$$

Linear systems of DEs are easy to solve [8], so the movement of the pixels through the velocity field can be known exactly, and written as a combination of transcendental functions.

### 2.2 Implementation

For a given image and velocity field, the deformation proceeds by first propagating each pixel through the velocity field. The propagation of the trajectories runs from an initial time $t_0$ until a final time $t_f$. During that time, each pixel flows with the velocity field to another location (unless it happens to rest on an equilibrium point). The displacement map for the deformation is simply a record of where each pixel rests at time $t_f$.

A system has been built in MATLAB (MathWorks Inc., Natick, Massachusetts) to derive image deformations by finding the exact solution of pixel trajectories. The image is broken into triangles, the vertices of which are nine pixels from the image[1]. The following is an outline of the methodology for finding the exact trajectory of a pixel through a triangular cell.

Suppose we are starting from the point $(x_i, y_i)$ at time $t_i$ in triangle $T$.

1. The three velocity vectors assigned to the vertices of $T$ are used to define two linear functions over $T$: one for the velocity's $x$-component, and one for its $y$-component.
2. Compute the coefficients for the triangle's system of DEs using the linear functions from step 1.
3. Find and store the general solution for the system of DEs. This involves finding the (generalized) eigenvalues and eigenvectors of the system matrix [8]. This general solution still has two unknown constants of integration.
4. Use the initial data (initial point $(x_i, y_i)$ and initial time $t_i$) to determine values for the unknown constants.
5. Two cases remain: either the trajectory stays inside triangle $T$ for the remainder of the propagation, or the trajectory intersects one of the triangle's edges at some time $t_{\text{exit}} < t_f$.
   (a) If the trajectory remains inside $T$, simply evaluate the solution at $t = t_f$.
   (b) If the trajectory leaves $T$, find the exit time $t_{\text{exit}}$ and evaluate the exit location $(x_{\text{exit}}, y_{\text{exit}})$. Use this exit point as a new initial point. Find out which triangle the trajectory is entering, and go back to step 1 until the final time has been reached.

For the sake of brevity, many of the details are omitted here. It is worth noting that finding the time at which the solution curve intersects one of the triangle's edges results in a nonlinear algebraic equation in $t$ that is not generally solvable. However, fast and accurate solvers exist for such algebraic equations. We use MATLAB's `fzero` function, in conjuction with multiple samples of the trajectory, to find the exit time if it exists.

We also implemented a numerical method for propagating the solution through the triangular cells. The method is written as a MATLAB script. Its velocity function is derived from the same triangulation as the exact method above, but instead of seeking an exact solution, it uses MATLAB's `ode45` function, an implementation of a 4th/5th-order Runge-Kutta time-stepping method [9].

## 2.3 Experiments

The exact method and the numerical method are compared through a series of experiments. For testing purposes, a $256 \times 256$ image is partitioned into a triangle

---

[1] Our implementation is not limited to pixel locations for triangle vertices. The vertices can occur at any location.

mesh of eight triangles. Each triangle is an isosceles right-triangle, measuring 128 pixels on the short sides (see Fig. 2). Velocity vectors are defined at the nine vertices of the triangle mesh.

In each experiment, three different sets of results are produced for the numerical method, each using a different maximum time step. In MATLAB's numerical DE solvers, the user can specify the maximum time step. In our experiments, we derived three test values based on the Courant-Friedrichs-Levy (CFL) condition [10]. We took the CFL condition to mean that the time step should be short enough so that a single step, taken at the maximum velocity in the velocity field, cannot be larger than 128 pixels (the width of a triangle). We will refer to this maximum time step as the CFL step. In our experiments, the tested maximum time-step sizes are 60%, 70% and 80% of the CFL step size.

In the first experiment, we compare the trajectories of three pixels through a challenging velocity field that makes the trajectories converge toward each other, and then diverge again. The purpose is to see if changing the step-size constraint changes the solution significantly, and to see if the solution trajectories cross over each other.

In the second experiment, the numerical and exact methods are each used to produce a displacement map. Each displacement map has two components: an $x$-component and a $y$-component. For each pixel, the corresponding value in the $x$-component gives the $x$-coordinate of the location where that pixel came from. The $y$-component is defined similarly.

## 3 Results

Figures 2(a)-(c) contrast several pixel trajectories for the numerical method under different maximum time-step sizes. Notice that, despite the same underlying velocity field, the numerical methods give qualitatively different solutions for different step-size constraints. In particular, the order of the trajectory curves is not preserved in (a) and (c). Solution curves cannot cross over each other when the velocity field is continuous. Even the strictest step-size solution (Fig. 2(a)) gives solutions that are qualitatively different from those of the exact method.

The displacement maps for the exact and numerical methods are shown in Fig. 3. The figure shows the $x$-component for the displacement maps corresponding to the numerical method with max time-step set to 60% of the CFL step, and the exact method. The $y$-components are not shown here, but exhibit similar results. Since the underlying velocity field is continuous, we expect the displacement map to be smooth. However, notice the banding in the displacement map for the numerical method. The artifact is not present in the displacement map for the exact method.

## 4 Discussion and Conclusions

The velocity fields chosen for these experiments are somewhat pathological, specifically designed to exhibit, in an obvious way, the sort of errors that the

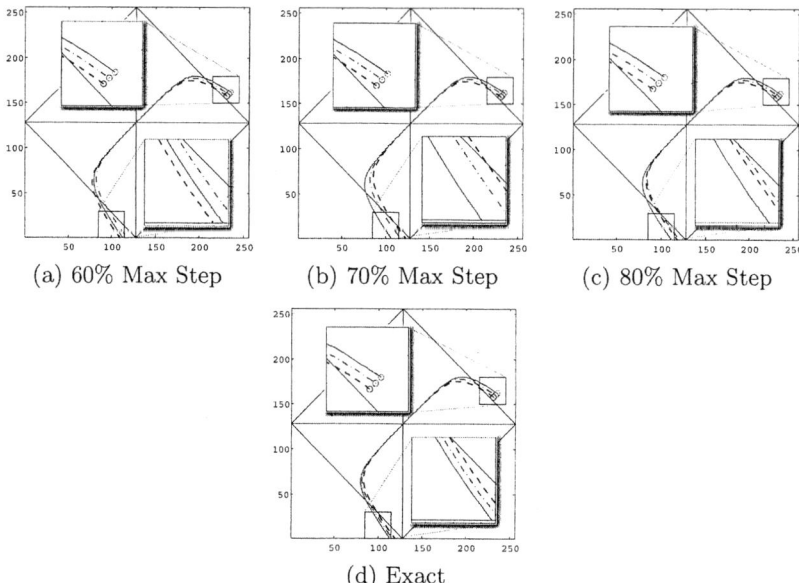

**Fig. 2.** Pixel trajectories for numerical and exact solution methods. Each trajectory starts at the circle marker. The insets magnify the starting and ending of each trajectory.

numerical methods can produce. However, such errors can occur in more subtle scenarios. The examples in this paper illustrate that simply taking a shorter time step does not necessarily lead to a qualitatively correct solution.

The banding observed in Fig. 3 seems to be related to the maximum step size because the other numerical results showed similar bands of different widths.

The "exact" method is not truly exact since the point where the trajectories exit one triangle (and enter the next) have to be located numerically. However, finding the solution of a single algebraic equation is much easier than numerically solving a system of DEs. The algebraic equation gives concrete feedback about the error in the solution. The feedback available to numerical DE solvers is far more nebulous.

Methods exist to remove redundant triangles from a triangulation [11]. If a region of the velocity field is highly linear, it can be modeled by a single triangle. Removing redundant triangles can help speed up the processing time of these methods.

The deformation methods outlined in this paper are for 2D images. However, they can easily be extended to higher dimensions. Higher-order linear systems of DEs are still quite easy to solve exactly.

A 3D application for this type of exact solution method is in the field of magnetic resonance (MR) diffusion tensor tractography. In this field, information about the preferential direction of diffusion of water in the brain is collected using an MR scanner. Since water in a nerve fiber bundle preferentially diffuses

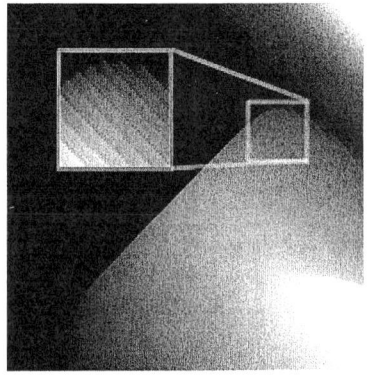 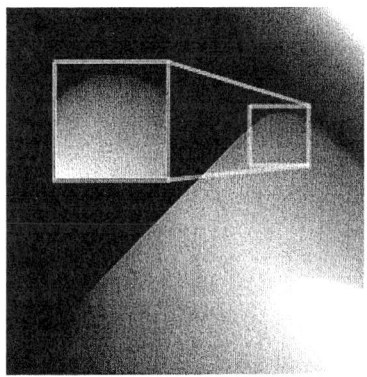

(a) Numerical $x$-component  (b) Exact $x$-component

**Fig. 3.** Displacement maps for the numerical method (with maximum time step set to 60% of the CFL step size), and for the exact method. The inset shows a contrast-enhanced magnification of part of the map.

along the fiber's axis, following these diffusion vectors can give doctors information about long-range nerve connections in the brain. This technique, known as "diffusion tensor tractography", is similar in nature to following the velocity vectors in image deformation. Current methods use discrete time-stepping techniques to trace the nerve fiber bundles through a 3D dataset [12,13,14]. Often, bundles converge with other bundles, and then separate again. Numerical methods to approximate the fiber tracts are subject to the same inaccuracy issues as the numerical methods studied in this paper [12]. Although the spatial resolution of a diffusion tensor image is somewhat coarse compared to the size of the nerve fiber bundles, an exact solution might yield more consistent and possibly more accurate results than the numerical methods.

Finally, more research needs to be done to investigate other methods of interpolation to see if the resulting system of DEs can be solved exactly. So far we have briefly considered Fourier basis functions and radial basis functions, but believe that neither option leads to a solvable system.

## Acknowledgment

We would like to thank the Natural Science and Engineering Research Council (NSERC) of Canada for their financial support.

## References

1. Bajcsy, R., Kocacic, S.: Multiresolution elastic matching. Computer Vision, Graphics and Image Processing **46** (1989) 1–12
2. Bookstein, F.L.: Principal warps: thin-plate splines and the decomposition of deformations. IEEE Transactions on Pattern Analysis and Machine Intelligence **11** (1989) 567–585

3. Christensen, G.E.: Deformable shape models for anatomy. PhD thesis, Washington University, St. Louis, Missuori (1994)
4. Christensen, G.E., Rabbit, R.D., Mill, M.I.: Deformable templates using large deformation kinematics. IEEE Transactions on Image Processing **5** (1996) 1435–1447
5. Beg, M.F., Miller, M., Trouv'e, A., Younes, L.: Computing large deformation metric mappings via geodesic flows of diffeomorphisms. Journal of Computer Vision **61** (2005) 139–157
6. Christensen, G.E., Joshi, S.C., Miller, M.I.: Volumetric transformation of brain anatomy. IEEE Transactions on Medical Imaging **16** (1997) 864–877
7. Joshi, S.C., Miller, M.I.: Landmark matching via large deformation diffeomorphisms. IEEE Transactions on Image Processing **95** (2000) 1357–1370
8. Nagle, R.K., Saff, E.B.: Fundamentals of Differential Equations. Second edn. Benjamin Cummings (1989)
9. Burden, R.L., Faires, J.D.: Numerical Analysis. Fourth edn. PWS-Kent (1989)
10. Haberman, R.: Elementary Applied Partial Differential Equations. Prentice Hall (1987)
11. Schroeder, W.J., Zarge, J.A., Lorensen, W.E.: Decimation of triangle meshes. Computer Graphics **26** (1992) 65–70
12. Basser, P.J., Pajevic, S., Pierpaoli, C., Duda, J., Aldroubi, A.: In vivo fiber tractography using DT-MRI data. Magnetic Resonance in Medicine **44** (2000) 625–632
13. Pajevic, S., Aldroubi, A., Basser, P.J.: A continuous tensor field approximation of discrete DT-MRI data for extracting microstructural and architectural features of tissue. Journal of Magnetic Resonance **154** (2002) 85–100
14. Poupon, C., Clark, C.A., Frouin, V., Regis, J., Bloch, I., Bihan, D.L., Mangin, J.F.: Regularization of diffusion-based direction maps for the tracking of brain white matter fascicles. NeuroImage **12** (2000) 184–195

# Estimating the Natural Number of Classes on Hierarchically Clustered Multi-spectral Images

André R.S. Marçal and Janete S. Borges

Faculdade de Ciências, Universidade do Porto,
DMA, Rua do Campo Alegre, 687, 4169-007 Porto, Portugal

**Abstract.** Image classification is often used to extract information from multi-spectral satellite images. Unsupervised methods can produce results well adjusted to the data, but that are usually difficult to assess. The purpose of this work was to evaluate the Xu internal similarity index ability to estimate the natural number of classes in multi-spectral satellite images. The performance of the index was initially tested with data produced synthetically. Four Landsat TM image sections were then used to evaluate the index. The test images were classified into a large number of classes, using the unsupervised algorithm ISODATA, which were subsequently structured hierarchically. The Xu index was used to identify the optimum partition for each test image. The results were analysed in the context of the land cover types expected for each location.

## 1 Introduction

Image classification techniques are frequently used to produce land cover maps from multi-spectral satellite images. Usually a supervised classification approach is preferred, making use of training areas to characterise the spectral signature of each class looked for in the image. The results are often disappointing, mainly due to the presence of mixed pixels and an inadequacy between the classes anticipated and the classes actually present in the data. A class identified in training might not be spectrally distinguishable from the other classes. In contrast, there might be some classes in the data, clearly distinguishable from the signal point of view, which were not predicted a-priori. These issues are partly solved when an unsupervised algorithm is applied to the data, but other problems do arise. Unsupervised classification algorithms explore the multi-spectral feature space, looking for densely occupied areas, or clusters, to which classes are assigned. The classes obtained by this process are in principle better suited to the data, but the results can be dependent on the algorithm and the choice of parameters used. This is certainly an important aspect, as the cluster configuration is only considered to be valid if clusters cannot reasonably occur by chance or as a beneficial artefact of a clustering algorithm [1]. Even when this issue is sorted out, there is still a difficulty: labelling the classes produced by the unsupervised classifier. This post-classification labelling is sometimes difficult due to the large number of classes usually created (K). An effective method to assist on this process is to structure the classes hierarchically. A set of K-1 solutions is thus made available (classified images with 2, 3, ..., K classes), which brings a new question: which one is the best partition? Or, in an alternative form, what is the "natural" number of classes in the dataset? This is a well-known problem in statistics, but not much explored in image processing, due to the large number of patterns to cluster. This is even more significant in remote sensing, as multi-spectral satellite images are huge data volumes, which are not well manageable for computationally demanding methods.

The validation of a clustering result can be accomplished by carefully applying statistical methods and testing hypotheses [1]. The use of an external index of agreement, such as the Rand index, is appropriate for ascertaining whether the data justify the number of a-priori clusters [2]. Internal examination of validity tries to determine if the structure is intrinsically appropriate for the data [1]. Milligan and Cooper [3] performed a comparative study of 30 similarity indices. However, the large majority of these indices are very demanding computationally, and thus inappropriate for digital images. One criterion that can be applied to large datasets is based on the Minimum of Between Cluster Distance (MBCD) [4]. An improved version of this criterion is proposed by Xu et al. [4]. The purpose of this work was to estimate the usefulness of the Xu similarity index to identify the natural number of clusters in a multi-spectral satellite image.

## 2 Method

### 2.1 Similarity Index

Let $\mathbf{x}_1, \mathbf{x}_2, ..., \mathbf{x}_N$ be the patterns to classify, and $\mathbf{x}_i$ a vector of the $d$-dimension feature space. For digital images, the patterns are the image pixels. The classification of the image corresponds to the establishment of a partition $C_1, C_2, ..., C_k$ for the $N$ patterns, so that $i \in C_k$ if $\mathbf{x}_i$ belongs to the class $k$. The centre of class $k$ is a vector $\mathbf{m}_k$, of dimension $d$, given by Equation (1), where $n_k$ is the number of patterns assigned to class $k$.

$$\mathbf{m}_k = \frac{1}{n_k} \sum_{i \in C_k} \mathbf{x}_i \quad (1)$$

The Sum-of-Squared Error (SSE) for class $k$ ($J_k$) is the sum of the quadratic distances between all its elements and the class centre. The distance $\delta(\mathbf{x}, \mathbf{y})$ between two vectors $\mathbf{x}$ and $\mathbf{y}$ is computed using a metric, such as the Minkowski distance or the Euclidian distance [2]. The Ward distance (Equation 3) is used to evaluate the distance between two clusters $i$ and $j$ [4].

$$J_k = \sum_{i \in C_k} \delta^2(\mathbf{x}_i, \mathbf{m}_k) \quad (2)$$

$$\delta_{ij}^w = \sqrt{\frac{n_i \times n_j}{n_i + n_j}} \times |\mathbf{m}_i - \mathbf{m}_j| \quad (3)$$

A dissimilarity measure ($M$), in terms of the Minimum of Between-Cluster Distances (MBCD), can be defined for a partition with $k$ classes (Equation 4). Both SSE and MBCD alone are insufficient to establish a criterion for the best partition. However, the two can be used together to form an index, as proposed by Xu et al [4].

$$M = min_{i<j}\ \delta_{ij}^w \qquad i,j = 1,2,\ldots,k \tag{4}$$

The initial classification procedure establishes a partition of the data in $k$ classes, which is then hierarchically clustered, producing $k-1$ partitions (with a number of classes $h = k, k-1, \ldots, 2$ classes). The index proposed by Xu, $E(h)$, evaluates the level $h$ of the hierarchical structure by comparing the SSE and MBCD of this level with the proceeding level. The index $E(h)$ is computed using Equation 5, where $J(h)$ is the sum of the $J_k$ for all clusters of partition $h$.

$$E(h) = \frac{M(h) - M(h+1)}{\sqrt{J(h)} - \sqrt{J(h+1)}} \tag{5}$$

When plotting the index $E$ as a function of $h$, a significant maximum of $E(h)$ should be expected to appear at level $h^*$, where lie $h^*$ natural groupings or clusters [4]. An example of a plot $E(h)$ is presented in Figure 1. The figure shows two partitions, 5 and 8 classes, and the Xu similarity index plot. In this case there is a clear maximum for $h = 5$, indicating that the clustering in 5 classes is the most natural choice for this particular dataset.

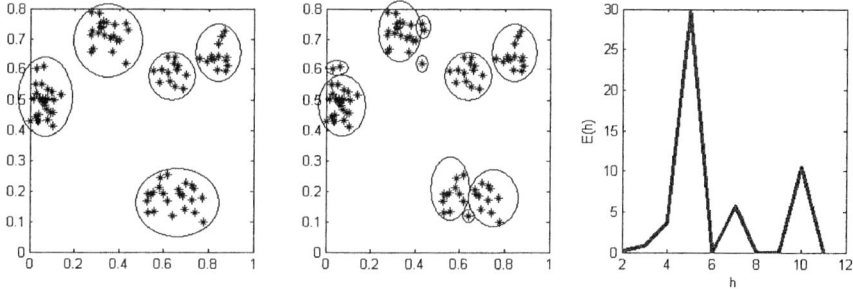

**Fig. 1.** Example of the Xu index applied to synthetic data. Data classified into 5 classes (left), 8 classes (centre) and Xu index plot (right).

## 2.2 Hierarchical Classification of Digital Images

Hierarchical clustering methods require the user to specify a measure of dissimilarity between groups of observations. Agglomerative strategies for hierarchical clustering start at the bottom of the hierarchical structure (the level where each cluster contains a single observation) and at each level recursively merge a selected pair of clusters into a single cluster. This produces a hierarchical structure where each level of the hierarchy represents a particular grouping of the data into disjoint clusters of observations. The indices presented in the previous section can be used to decide which level actually represents a "natural" clustering in the sense that observations within each of its groups are sufficiently more similar to each other than to observations assigned to different groups at that level [5]. Hierarchical clustering algorithms are widely used in some applications as botany and medical diagnosis because they are extremely easy to comprehend [6]. However, the direct application of hierarchical agglomerative methods to digital images is not viable due to the large number of patterns, and, as a result, the enormous computational effort required. An alternative approach is to use an efficient data-clustering algorithm (for example ISODATA) to establish an initial partition of the image data. The tens (or few hundreds) of clusters of this initial partition can then be easily managed to form a hierarchical clustered structure.

The ISODATA (Iterative Self-Organizing Data Analysis Technique) unsupervised classification method is a modification of the k-means algorithm [7]. Both are iterative processes, but the k-means method requires knowledge of the number of classes present in the data. Initially, k centres are seeded along the diagonal (or in other locations) of the feature space. Each pattern (or pixel, for a digital image) is assigned to the class whose centre is closest, according to a given metric (Euclidian distance, for example). Once all patterns are distributed amongst the classes, an updated centre is computed for each class. The process is repeated until all class centres are stable (up to a threshold value), or the iteration limit is reached. The number of classes produced by the ISODATA classifier can vary, within a pre-established range. In each iteration, two or more classes can be merged, a class can be removed or split in two. These decisions are controlled by a set of parameters, which will naturally influence the final results. In the combined methodology, the clusters produced by the ISODATA classifier are used as the initial observations to form the hierarchical clustered structure for the digital images.

## 3 Index Performance with Synthetic Data

The performance of the Xu index was initially evaluated with synthetic data. Each test was performed on a set of 100 elements, randomly generated with Gaussian distribution curves. The following parameters were considered: data dimensionality ($d$), number of Gaussians ($n$), standard deviation of the Gaussians ($\sigma$). The number of classes that should be expected is $n$, although this will be strongly dependent on the random generation process. Each pattern is a $d$-dimension vector with components between 0 and 1.

The synthetic data generation followed a similar process to the method used by Dubes [2]. It assures that a minimum number of elements are assigned to each cluster, but allows some variability in the number of elements per cluster. The process starts by randomly establishing the $n$ Gaussian centres, assuring that they are at least $2\sigma$ apart from each other, and at least at a distance $\sigma$ from the feature space edges. The number of patterns (100) is divided in $n+1$ groups.

Each Gaussian curve is assigned a group, and the elements of the remaining group are randomly assigned to any of the Gaussians.

Each dataset generated was classified in $k$ classes (with $k = 2, 3, \ldots, 12$), using MATLAB algorithm ClusterData [8]. The Xu index was computed for each partition, and a plot of the index versus the number of classes created for each dataset. As an illustration, Figure 1 shows the data and the $E(h)$ plot for a test with $d = 2$, $n = 8$, $\sigma = 0.04$. In this case, the number of classes suggested by the index was 5, instead of the 8 expected. However, a visual inspection of the data plot seems to suggest that the choice of 5 classes is actually a reasonable one.

### 3.1 Evaluation of the Index Performance

A total of 140 sets of parameters were tested: $d = 2, 3, 4, 5$; $n = 4, 5, 6, 7, 8$; $\sigma = 0.01, 0.02, 0.03, 0.04, 0.05, 0.07, 0.10$. For each set of parameters, a total of 200 data sets were produced and evaluated, each with 100 patterns. The number of times that the Xu index plot indicated the expected number of clusters was registered, and the success rate computed. Table 1 shows the success rate (in %) for 24 sets of parameters ($n = 6$). For example, for $d = 3$, $n = 6$, $\sigma = 0.02$, the Xu index selected 6 as the natural number of classes 140 out of 200 times, or 70.0 %. The results presented in Table 1 show that the effectiveness of the index decreases with increasing $\sigma$ and decreasing $d$. Although not shown in Table 1, the effectiveness of the index also decreases with an increase of the number of Gaussian curves ($n$), as expected. It is worth mentioning that for high values of $\sigma$, the number of classes selected by the index is very often different than the number of Gaussians used to generate the data, but still a reasonable choice. This is illustrated in the example of Figure 1. This helps explaining the low success rate of the index for high values of $\sigma$.

**Table 1.** Success rate of the Xu index with synthetic data (6 Gaussians), for various values of data dimensionality ($d$) and standard deviation of the Gaussians ($\sigma$)

|       | $\sigma = 0.01$ | $\sigma = 0.02$ | $\sigma = 0.03$ | $\sigma = 0.04$ | $\sigma = 0.05$ | $\sigma = 0.07$ | $\sigma = 0.10$ |
|-------|-----------------|-----------------|-----------------|-----------------|-----------------|-----------------|-----------------|
| $d=2$ | 86.5%           | 57.5%           | 33.5%           | 18.5%           | 11.5%           | 7.5%            | 6.5%            |
| $d=3$ | 94.0%           | 70.0%           | 56.5%           | 31.5%           | 27.5%           | 10.0%           | 4.0%            |
| $d=4$ | 87.0%           | 78.0%           | 60.5%           | 52.0%           | 36.0%           | 22.0%           | 12.5%           |
| $d=5$ | 83.5%           | 69.0%           | 61.5%           | 54.0%           | 45.5%           | 22.5%           | 8.0%            |

## 4 Results with Image Data

Four test images were selected to evaluate the performance of the Xu similarity index. The images selected are small sections (of 512 by 512 pixels) extracted from Landsat TM images of Portugal and Spain, acquired in October 1997.

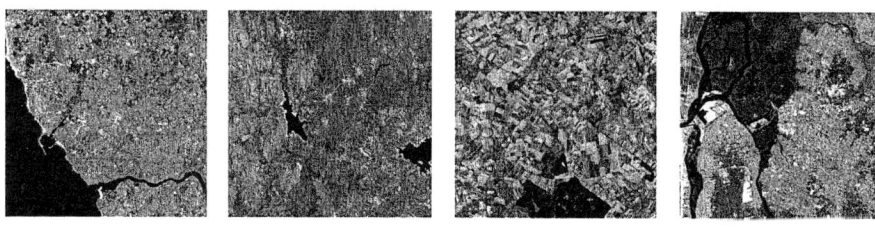

**Fig. 2.** First principal component of the test images I-Porto, II-Geres, III-Castela, IV-Aveiro (from left to right)

The multi-spectral images have 6 bands, with a 30-meter pixel resolution. The thermal band of Landsat TM was not used due to the lower spatial resolution [9]. The first principal component of each test image is shown in Figure 2, from left to right: I-Porto, II-Geres, III-Castela, IV-Aveiro. The first principal components featured in Figure 2 were only used for displaying purposes. They retained 82.4%, 64.9%, 88.5% and 83.3% of the total variance of the multi-spectral test images I, II, III and IV, respectively.

### 4.1 Image Classification and Clustering

Each test image was classified using the algorithm ISODATA implemented on the software PCI Geomatics [10]. The same set of parameters was used throughout, including the range of classes allowed (20-40). The classifier converged for a solution with 27 classes for test image III, and with 40 classes for the remaining test images. The classification results were hierarchically structured, using the Euclidian distance metric between the class centres ($\mathbf{m}_k$) as the agglomerative criterion. This produced 39 classified images for test images I, II and IV (with 40, 39, ..., 2 classes), and 26 classified images for test image III.

### 4.2 Analysis

The Xu similarity index was computed for each classified image, and a plot $E(h)$ produced for each test image. The plots are presented in Figure 3, as a function of the level on the hierarchical structure — the number of classes $h$. An initial inspection of these plots seems to suggest that the optimum solution, or the natural number of classes, is not always a unique choice.

For test image I, an urban area (the city of Porto), the index has 4 strong maximums for $h = 5, 9, 11$ and 18. In urban areas such as this one, with a pixel size of 30 meters, a great number of mixed pixels should be expected. This can help explaining why there are several possible choices for the "natural" number of classes. The best choice according to the index is for $h = 9$, which was the classified image selected for Figure 4 (left).

Test image II covers a mountainous region (Geres, Portugal), with some bodies of water. In this case the Xu index clearly points to a partition with $h = 4$.

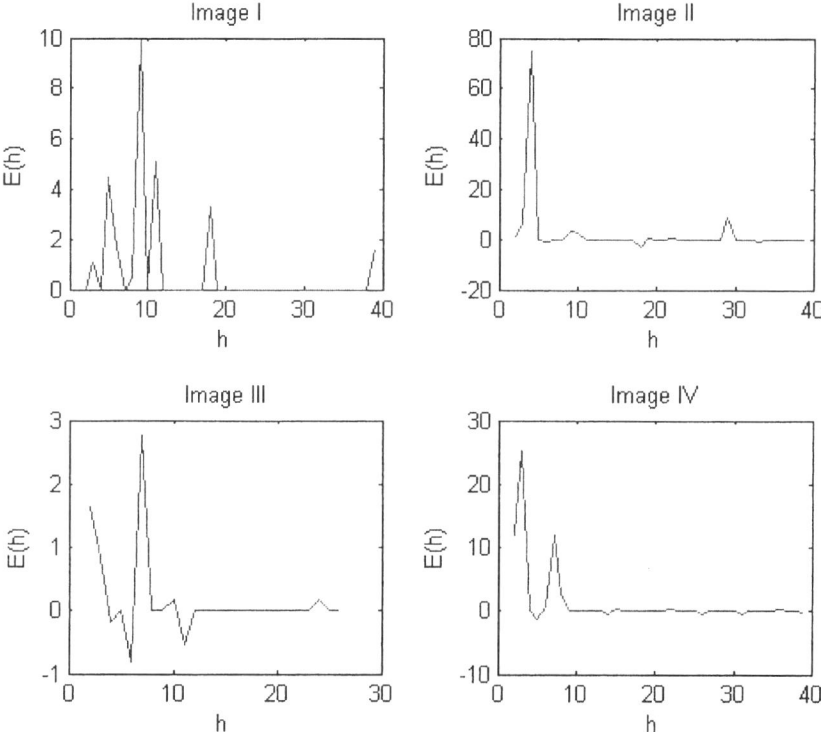

**Fig. 3.** Xu index plots for test images I(top left), II (top right), III (bottom left), IV (bottom right)

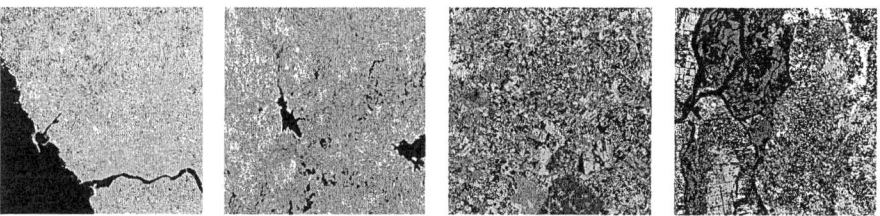

**Fig. 4.** Classification levels selected for test images I ($h = 9$), II ($h = 4$), III ($h = 7$), IV ($h = 7$) (from left to right)

This is a consistent result, corresponding to four classes with well-distinguished spectral signatures: water, bare soil, sparse and dense vegetation. The magnitude of the index for $h = 4$, compared to the other values of $h$, suggests that this is the only natural choice for this image, although very subtle local maximum do appear for $h = 9$ and $h = 29$. The result for $h = 4$ is presented in Figure 4.

Test image III covers an agricultural area (in Castela, Spain), with a small urban sector. The index plot seems to indicate a selection of $h = 7$, although the magnitude is in this case rather low. A choice of $h = 3$ could also be done, but the level of discrimination (only 3 classes) is perhaps inappropriate, from a user perspective. The classified image at this level is presented in Figure 4 (3rd from left). There are two well-distinguished classes in a large field in the bottom part of the image. The remaining classes are assigned to smaller fields spread throughout the image.

Test image IV includes a variety of land covers in the Estuary nearby Aveiro, Portugal. There are deep and shallow water, sand, vegetation and urban areas. The plot of $E(h)$ points towards two possible choices: $h = 3$ or $h = 7$. The magnitude of the index is higher for $h = 3$, but from a user perspective, perhaps the partition of the data into 7 classes is a more meaningful one. This later choice is presented in Figure 4 (right).

An additional evaluation of the Xu index adequacy for estimating the number of classes on a multi-spectral satellite image could be done using ground truth data. However, this is a difficult task, as the existing land cover maps (COS90) were produced by air photo interpretation [11]. The land cover maps have much greater spatial detail and diversity of classes than what can be realistically expected from a Landsat TM image. A considerable effort in data generalisation in the existing land cover maps is therefore required in order to make a meaningful comparison between the two datasets.

## 5 Conclusions

Unsupervised classification methods have great potential for the classification of multi-spectral satellite images, as they permit the identification of the classes that are naturally distinguishable in the data. One of the reasons that justify the fact that these methods are often neglected for satellite image classification is the difficulty in assessing the results produced. A number of statistical indices have been developed and used to assess the classification results [3], but few are applicable to large data volumes, such as multi-spectral satellite images.

The method tested here starts by clustering the multi-spectral image, using an unsupervised classification algorithm, into a manageable number of classes. These are then structured hierarchically, and the Xu internal similarity index is used to select the "natural" number of classes from this set of classified images. The final result is a single classified image, although multiple results at multiple levels of the hierarchic structure can also be provided. One aspect that should be taken into account is the fact that the accuracy of the final classified image selected is limited by the initial clustering. Another aspect is that hierarchical methods impose hierarchical structuring whether or not such structure actually exists in the data. The results suggest nevertheless that the method proposed is effective in achieving a coherent result from the data perspective. The results also seemed to be reasonable from an end user point of view, as the number of classes selected were consistent with the diversity of land cover types expected for each test image.

# References

1. Jain, A. K., Murty, M. N., Flynn, P. J.: Data clustering: A review. ACM Computing Surveys **31** (1999) 264–323
2. Dubes, R. C.: How many clusters are best - an experiment. Pattern Recognition **20** (1987) 645–663
3. Milligan, G. W., Cooper, M. C.: An examination of procedures for determining the number of clusters in a data set. Psychometrika **50** (1985) 159–179
4. Xu, S., Kamath, M. V., Capson, D. W.: Selection of partitions from a hierarchy. Pattern Recognition Letters **14** (1993) 7–15
5. Hastie, T., Tibshirani, R., Friedman, J.: The Elements of Statistical Learning: data mining, inference, and prediction. Springer, New York (2001)
6. Ripley, B. D.: Pattern Recognition and Neural Networks. Cambridge University, Cambridge (1996)
7. Tou, J. T., Gonzalez, R. C.: Pattern Recognition Principles. Addison-Wesley (1974)
8. The Math Works: MATLAB The Language of Technical Computing - Using MATLAB : version 6. The Math Works, Inc. (2000)
9. Lillesand, T. M., Kiefer, R. W.: Remote Sensing and Image Interpretation, 4th edition. John Wiley and Sons, New York (2000)
10. PCI Geomatics: X-Pace Reference Manual, Version 8.2. PCI Geomatics, Ontario, Canada (2001)
11. CNIG: Carta de Ocupao do Solo (COS' 90). Centro Nacional de Informao Geogrfica, Lisboa, Portugal (1990)

# Image Space $\mathbb{I}^3$ and Eigen Curvature for Illumination Insensitive Face Detection

Christian Bauckhage and John K. Tsotsos

Centre for Vision Research, York University, Toronto, ON, M3J 1P3
http://cs.yorku.ca/LAAV

**Abstract.** Generally, the performance of present day computer vision systems is still very much affected by varying brightness and light source conditions. Recently, Koenderink suggested that this weakness is due to methodical flaws in low level image processing. As a remedy, he develops a new theory of image modeling. This paper reports on applying his ideas to the problem of illumination insensitive face detection. Experimental results will underline that even a simple and conventional method like principal component analysis can accomplish robust and reliable face detection in the presence of illumination variation if applied to curvature features computed in Koenderink's image space.

## 1 Motivation and Related Work

In a recent paper on image processing methodology [1], Koenderink fiercely criticized the common practice to understand digital greyscale images as entities embedded in $\mathbb{R}^3$. He observes that if an image was indeed a set of points $(x_i, y_i, z_i)_{i=1...M} \in \mathbb{R}^3$ where the intensity values $z_i = f(x_i, y_i)$ define a surface above the $X, Y$ plane, the geometry of $\mathbb{R}^3$ would allow to rotate this surface about an arbitrary axis. However, such a rotation might cause intensity values to lie in the image coordinate plane and image coordinates to be parallel to the intensity direction. Koenderink argues that a structure that allows for operations leading to physically senseless configurations is not the most reasonable choice for image modeling. As a more appropriate approach to mathematical image modeling he proposes a structure which he calls *image space* $\mathbb{I}^3$. The basic idea is to define $\mathbb{I}^3$ as a fiber bundle that locally looks like $\mathbb{P}^2 \times \mathbb{L}$ where the base manifold $\mathbb{P}^2$ corresponds to the picture plane and the fibers $\mathbb{L}$ are logarithmic scales of the intensity. An analysis of the (differential) geometry of this image space reveals that images in $\mathbb{I}^3$ are (by construction) invariant under different brightness transformations.

In this contribution, we explore the merits this model offers for computer vision. The application domain for our investigation will be illumination insensitive face detection.

Face detection and recognition are arguably among the most popular topics in computer vision and respective publications are almost innumerable. In fact, the field is so active, it already produced its meta literature (cf. e.g. [2,3,4]). A complete survey of face detection techniques therfore is far beyond the prospects of this report but we shall single out a few contributions which are relevant for our discussion.

Since they were first considered by Sirovich and Kirby [5] and popularized by Turk and Pentland [6], Principal Component Analysis (PCA) based approaches have become a widespread tool in face detection. Although there are other subspace techniques like Linear Discriminant Analysis, Independent Component Analysis, or kernelized PCA, simple PCA is still among the most reliable methods [7,8]. However, its performance is known to depend on light source conditions. Recent contributions aiming at illumination invariance hence measure the *gradient similarity* statistics [9] or combine *edge phase congruency* information with local intensity normalization [10]. Others render *eigen-harmonics* to recover a standard illumination [11] or use *eigen light-fields* [12].

Three general trends become apparent from this rough survey: i) Gradient information (i.e. information from the realm of differential geometry) is considered to provide an avenue to illumination invariance. ii) PCA based methods prove to be persistent and are now being applied to more sophisticated data than the mere pixel values of old. iii) There are attempts to embed the abstract concept of *face space* into richer mathematical structures than the usual vector spaces over the field of real numbers.

In the following, we will bring together all these trends. First, we will survey differential geometry in $\mathbb{I}^3$ and investigate the features it provides for illumination invariant face detection. Then, we will discuss how these feature might be put forth into a PCA based framework. We will address the use of real and complex valued feature vectors and then shall present experimental results. A conclusion will close this contribution.

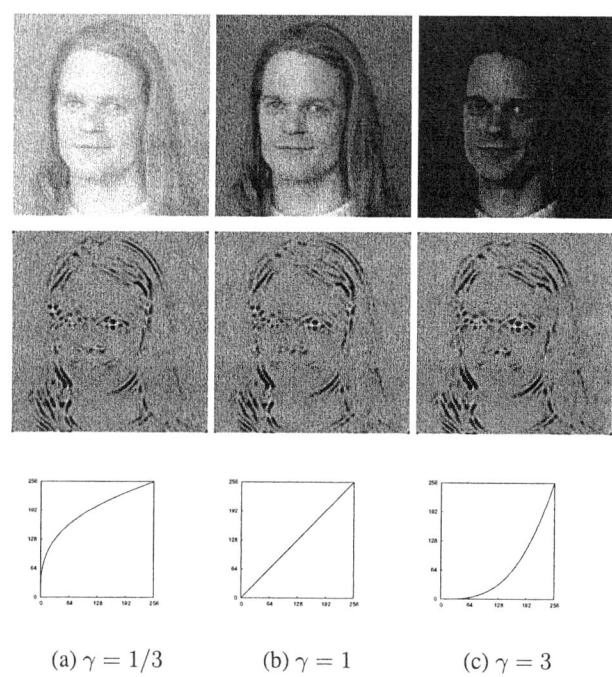

(a) $\gamma = 1/3$  (b) $\gamma = 1$  (c) $\gamma = 3$

**Fig. 1.** Gamma transformations of an image and level sets of the corresponding Gaussian curvature $K$ in $\mathbb{I}^3$

## 2  Curvature Features for Face Detection

As a first step towards a more proper mathematical model for image processing, Koenderink examines the most suitable scale for the intensity dimension. Given that the photon count on a CCD chip is Poisson distributed and assuming observations based on different time scales, he shows that a time independent estimation of the Poisson parameter $\lambda$ leads to a uniform distribution on the log-intensity scale. As a consequence, he proposes to use $Z(x,y) = \log(z(x,y)/z_0)$ for the intensity dimension where $z_0$ is an arbitrary unit of intensity. Points in $\mathbb{I}^3$ are thus specified by coordinates $\{x, y, Z\}$.

Since his primary concern is a space where the intensity domain and the image plane cannot interfere, Koenderink lists geometric constraints for $\mathbb{I}^3$. The resulting group of possible transformations is the group of direct isotropic similarities. Since these do not affect relations among a set of parallel 3D lines, they do not affect the curvature of surfaces in $\mathbb{I}^3$. Moreover, as the geometry of $\mathbb{I}^3$ comes along with a degenerate metric, Gaussian curvature and Mean curvature of surfaces are given by notably simple expressions. In contrast to the lengthy formulas known from Euclidean geometry they simply correspond to

$$K(x,y) = Z_{xx}Z_{yy} - Z_{xy}^2 \quad \text{and} \quad H(x,y) = \frac{Z_{xx} + Z_{yy}}{2}. \tag{1}$$

where $Z_{xx} = \partial^2 Z/\partial x^2$, $Z_{yy} = \partial^2 Z/\partial y^2$, and $Z_{xy} = \partial^2 Z/\partial x \partial y$.

Using the example of Gaussian curvature $K$, Fig. 1 underlines that image intensity transformations barely affect surfaces in $\mathbb{I}^3$. In the figure's top row, we see an image whose intensity was subjected to the gamma-transformations that are indicated in the bottom row of the figure. The middle row shows a level set representation of the corresponding Gaussian curvature where bright spots indicate points of high curvature. Obviously, $K$ remains nearly constant across the different transformations.

Using curvature features derived in the fiber bundle $\mathbb{I}^3$ to tackle illumination invariant face detection is thus a tempting idea. In fact, curvature has been used in face recognition before. In [13], a system is presented that combines curvature maps with results from PCA based eye detection in order to improve facial part detection. And [14] reports on using local principal curvature to register 2D face images with 3D models. However, given the ease and success of PCA in face detection and recognition, it is surprising that there are yet no contributions that apply curvature features instead of intensity information to compute eigenfaces.

Extending PCA to curvature features is of course straightforward. Given an input image $I(x,y)$, we can compute the curvature maps $K(x,y)$ and $H(x,y)$. Like in the intensity approach, patches of $m$ pixels can be represented as objects in $\mathbb{R}^m$, i.e. as vectors $\boldsymbol{k}$ and $\boldsymbol{h}$, respectively. Therefore, given a set of $n$ patches representing faces stored in a $m \times n$ data matrix $\boldsymbol{A}$, *eigen curvature faces* can be computed.

In contrast to the intensity based approach, however, curvature based face detection offers a choice of two feature vectors for every pixel. The question is thus if and how to combine Mean and Gaussian curvature? The intuitive approach is to consider the direct sum $\boldsymbol{k} \oplus \boldsymbol{h} \in \mathbb{R}^{2m}$. However, dealing with PCA and a set of $n$ examples where $n \ll m$, we note that even if the data matrix $\boldsymbol{A}$ is a $2m \times n$ matrix, the matrix $\boldsymbol{A}^T\boldsymbol{A}$ used to compute eigenvectors will remain $n \times n$. Hence, doubling the dimension of the data vectors will still result in a maximum of $n$ eigenvectors. Moreover, with $\boldsymbol{A}_K = [\boldsymbol{k}_1, \boldsymbol{k}_2, \ldots, \boldsymbol{k}_n]$ and $\boldsymbol{A}_H = [\boldsymbol{h}_1, \boldsymbol{h}_2, \ldots, \boldsymbol{h}_n]$ denoting the original data matrices and $\boldsymbol{A} = \boldsymbol{A}_{K \oplus H}$ denoting the one resulting from the embedding in $\mathbb{R}^{2m}$, we will have

$$\boldsymbol{A}^T\boldsymbol{A} = \begin{bmatrix} \boldsymbol{A}_K^T \boldsymbol{A}_H^T \end{bmatrix} \begin{bmatrix} \boldsymbol{A}_K \\ \boldsymbol{A}_H \end{bmatrix} = \boldsymbol{A}_K^T \boldsymbol{A}_K + \boldsymbol{A}_H^T \boldsymbol{A}_H \tag{2}$$

I.e. up to this point the embedding in $\mathbb{R}^{2m}$ yields a mere additive connection of the information contained in the vectors $k_i$ and $h_i$ where $i \in \{1,\ldots,n\}$. Of course, the characteristic polynomial in the next step of the computation of eigenvectors introduces products and nonlinearity. But nevertheless, it seems worthwhile to consider a more complex entanglement of the two feature spaces.

A more *complex* entanglement is indeed possible if we consider the embedding $c = k + ih \in \mathbb{C}^m$. Since the new data matrix $C$ is composed of complex vectors, the standard approach to computing its eigenvectors requires multiplication with the conjugate transpose $C^\dagger$. And as

$$\left(C^\dagger C\right)_{ij} = c_i^* c_j = \sum_l k_{i_l} k_{j_l} + h_{i_l} h_{j_l} + i(k_{i_l} h_{j_l} - h_{i_l} k_{j_l}) \qquad (3)$$

we see that for an embedding in $\mathbb{C}^m$ mixed terms already appear before characteristic polynomials are computed. Note that since $C^\dagger C$ is a Hermitian matrix, its eigenvalues will be real but its eigenvectors will be complex.

## 3 Experiments

The utility of the above features and feature combinations for illumination insensitive face detection was evaluated by means of different experiments. This section summarizes our findings concerning the following six feature spaces

- $I^m$, the common $m$ dimensional intensity space
- $Q^m$, the corresponding intensity space after histogram equalization (often done in the literature to compensate for illumination variation)
- $K^m$, the Gaussian curvature space resulting from computations in $\mathbb{I}^3$
- $H^m$, the corresponding Mean curvature space
- $K^m \oplus H^m$, the $2m$ dimensional space combining Gaussian- and Mean curvature
- $K^m + iH^m$, the $m$ dimensional complex space combining the curvature features

All experiments reported below were based on the same *small* training set of $n = 34$ images (note that recent approaches based on intensity cues require several thousand training images to cope with lighting variations [3]). The gallery was retrieved from the Internet [15] and shows 27 male and 7 female faces, eleven people are wearing glasses, one person is bearded, 33 subjects are of Caucasian ancestry and one is Asian. All images show frontal views of faces recorded under ambient daylight.

In order to obtain accurate curvature images $K(x,y)$ and $H(x,y)$ all necessary derivations were computed using precise recursive Gaussian filtering [16]. Training data resulted from cropping $80 \times 80$ windows (i.e. $m = 6400$) centered at the nose. After vectorization, the data were normalized to unit length and zero mean. Eigenfaces were obtained from a singular value decomposition of the (complex) data matrices. For each of the considered features, the projection of image patches into the corresponding face space was done using the eigenvectors corresponding to the eight largest eigenvalues.

The quality of a face detector was assessed by means of the distance between the pixel where it yielded the highest response and the pixel where it should have occurred.

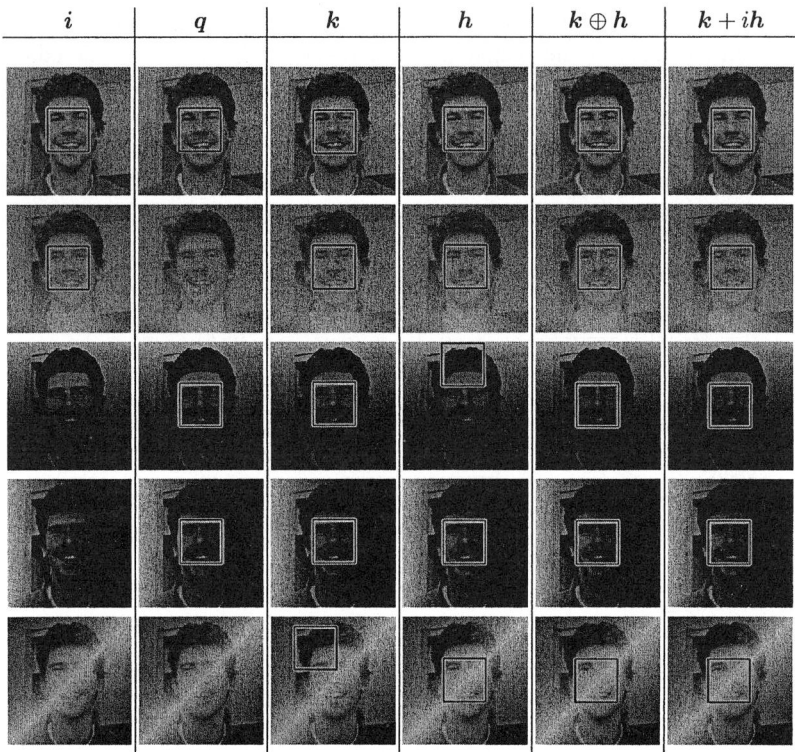

**Fig. 2.** Face detection examples under some of the artificial brightness distortions from our first series of experiments. Combined curvature features are most reliable in the case shown here.

To provide ground truth, the locations of the noses were labeled manually for all images in our test sets. Dividing the measured distance by the maximum possible distance to the nose yields the *deviation* $\delta \in [0, 1]$ to which we will refer for the rest of this discussion.

### 3.1 Semi Synthetic Data

The basis of our first test was formed by a set of 17 face images recorded under the same conditions as the training set. These images show 10 male and 7 female subjects; 6 of them are wearing glasses, 3 are bearded, one is of Asian ancestry the rest are Caucasian. Each test image was subject to 17 different intensity transformations, yielding a set of 289 face images. Examples of some of the distortions can be seen in Fig. 2.

Table 1(a) shows that (combined) curvature features perform better than the intensity based ones. The table summarizes the statistics gathered from the whole test set of 289 images. The first row lists the mean deviations $\mu(\delta)$ resulting from the tested features. The direct sum of curvatures has a one percent lead on the complex combination but face detection using only Mean curvature also performs well. Pure intensity based eigenfaces cannot compete given the kind of distortions in our test set. Eigenfaces from

**Table 1.** Experimental results: mean ($\mu$) and median (m) deviation in face detection (less is better)

| | $i$ | $q$ | $k$ | $h$ | $k \oplus h$ | $k + ih$ | | $i$ | $q$ | $k$ | $h$ | $k \oplus h$ | $k + ih$ |
|---|---|---|---|---|---|---|---|---|---|---|---|---|---|
| $\mu(\delta)$ | 0.51 | 0.25 | 0.29 | 0.20 | **0.17** | 0.18 | $\mu(\delta)$ | 0.72 | 0.29 | 0.16 | 0.14 | **0.09** | 0.13 |
| $\sigma^2(\delta)$ | 0.14 | 0.08 | 0.06 | 0.04 | 0.05 | 0.04 | $\sigma^2(\delta)$ | 0.07 | 0.15 | 0.03 | 0.03 | 0.02 | 0.02 |
| $m(\delta)$ | 0.52 | 0.06 | 0.33 | **0.04** | **0.04** | 0.05 | $m(\delta)$ | 0.83 | 0.03 | 0.05 | 0.03 | **0.02** | 0.08 |

(a) semi synthetic data    (b) real data

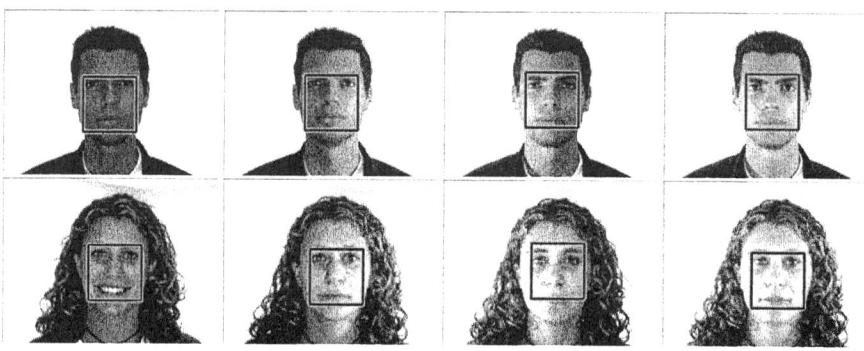

**Fig. 3.** Exemplary performance of the $k \oplus h$ feature under different lighting conditions

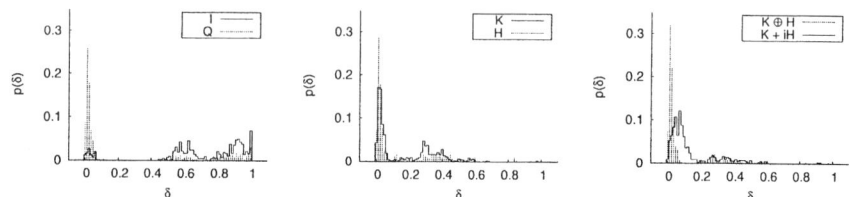

**Fig. 4.** Distributions of the deviation $\delta$ found in experiments with the AR face database

equalized intensity patches yield much better results but are outperformed by three out of four curvature based approaches. As Fig. 2 indicates, the precision in face detection may vary between the considered distortions. Since this behavior is also to be observed across different subjects, the mean might not be the most significant measure to characterize the overall performance of the tested detectors. In the lower most row, Tab. 1(a) thus lists the median deviations $m(\delta)$; they endorse our findings.

### 3.2 Real Data

In a second series of tests, we experimented with the AR face database [8] whose images show frontal view faces with different facial expressions under different lighting conditions (see Fig. 3). Again, (after scaling the images by 0.45 so that their size com-

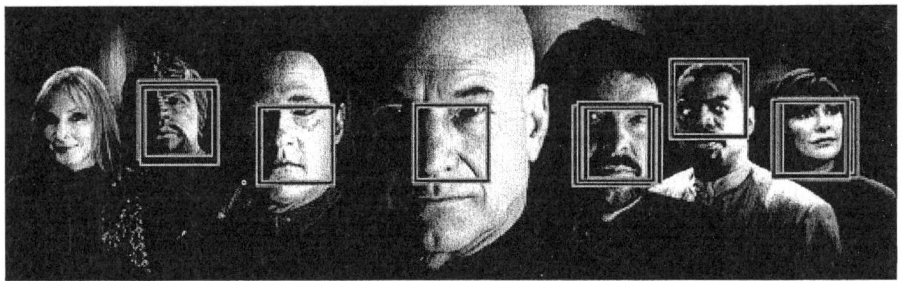

**Fig. 5.** The largest 10 local maxima in the $k \oplus h$ face response map for an image of extreme lighting conditions. Considering the size of the middle face, the corresponding response admittedly seems arbitrary. The other detection results, however, confirm our systematic experiments.

plied with our training set), the nose was labeled manually and the deviation $\delta$ was measured to assess our approach.

Table 1(b) summarizes our findings. Again, face detection by PCA of $k \oplus h$ vectors performs best; its mean deviation from the expected response location and the corresponding variance but also the median $m(\delta)$ are the smallest of all tested features. Figure 3 displays examples that illustrate this performance.

The plots of the distributions of the different deviations in Fig. 4 enable a more detailed analysis of the results. They document the complete breakdown of intensity based face detection and show sharp peaks in the vicinity of $\delta = 0$ for the histogram equalized intensity $q$, the Mean curvature $h$ as well as for the $k \oplus h$ feature. However, while the equalized intensity based approach also yields a notable number of responses for $\delta \in [0.5, 1.0]$, this is not quite as much the case for Mean curvature based face detection and even less so for the direct sum combination of Gaussian and Mean curvature. This observation is also reflected in the true positive and false positive classification rates we measured. Considering a 30 pixels radius around the manually labeled optimal response location acceptable, PCA on vectors $q$ yields a percentage of 67% true positives and 33% false positives on the AR face database. For PCA on $h$ and $k \oplus h$ features, we obtained 75% vs. 25% and 80% vs. 20%, respectively.

### 3.3 Discussion

Given the fact that all our results were obtained using an approach as simple as PCA trained on a small set of images of faces under ambient daylight, the above findings are remarkable. Curvature maps computed in $\mathbb{I}^3$ definitely provide a promising avenue to illumination insensitive face detection. Not only are these features able to cope with severe artificial illumination distortions but also perform well when applied to images taken under considerably different environmental lighting. Moreover, informal tests on images like the one shown in Fig. 5 revealed that even rather extreme conditions can be dealt with.

Concerning the different types of curvatures features or feature combinations that have been tested, the result is clear. Combining Gaussian and Mean curvature feature vectors in a direct sum yielded the best results in all our experiments. Appearance based face detection using the $k \oplus h$ feature produced useful and reliable results that hardly deviated from manually labeled locations.

## 4 Conclusion

In this paper, we tested Koenderink's proposal for a new image modeling paradigm. His idea to use a different geometric model than the physically incorrect Euclidean vector space $\mathbb{R}^3$ results in a representation of images that is invariant against several brightness transformations. Moreover, due to its degenerate metric this space comes along with remarkably simple expressions for features like Gaussian or Mean curvature.

Applying this idea to the problem of illumination insensitive face detection shows that curvature features computed in $\mathbb{I}^3$ indeed provide an auspicious but simple solution. Even an off the shelve appearance based method as simple as PCA does not require complex preprocessing or sophisticated tweaking to produce robust and reliable results under a wide range of lighting variations.

## References

1. Koenderink, J.J., van Doorn, A.J.: Image Processing Done Right. In: Proc. ECCV. Volume 2350 of LNCS., Springer (2002) 158–172
2. Hjelmås, E., Low, B.K.: Face Detection: A Survey. Comput. Vis. Image Underst. **83** (2001) 236–274
3. Yang, M.H., Kriegman, D., Ahuja, N.: Detecting Faces in Images: A Survey. IEEE Trans. Pattern Anal. Machine Intelli. **24** (2002) 34–58
4. Zhao, W., Chellappa, R., Phillips, P.J., Rosenfeld, A.: Face Recognition: A Literature Survey. ACM Comput. Surv. **35** (2003) 399–458
5. Sirovich, L., Kirby, M.: Low-dimensional procedure for the characterization of human faces. J. Opt. Soc. Am., A **4** (1987) 519–524
6. Turk, M.A., Pentland, A.P.: Eigenfaces for Recognition. J. Cogn. Neurosci. **3** (1991) 71–86
7. Li, J., Zhou, S., Shekhar, C.: A Comparison of Subspace Analysis for Face Recognition. In: Proc. ICASSP. Volume 3. (2003) 121–124
8. Martínez, A.M., Kak, A.: PCA versus LDA. IEEE Trans. Pattern Anal. and Machine Intelli. **23** (2001) 228–233
9. Chen, H.F., Belhumeur, P.N., Jacobs, D.W.: In Search of Illumination Invariants. In: Proc. CVPR. Volume 1. (2000) 254–261
10. Huang, Y., Lin, S., Li, S.Z., Lu, H., Shum, H.Y.: Face Alignment Under Variable Illumination. In: Proc. IEEE Int. Conf. on Automatic Face and Gesture Recognition. (2004) 85–90
11. Qing, L., Gao, S.S.W.: Eigen-Harmonics Faces: Face Recognition under Generic Lighting. In: Proc. IEEE Int. Conf. on Automatic Face and Gesture Recognition. (2004) 296–301
12. Gross, R., Baker, S., Matthews, I., Kanade, T.: Face Recognition Across Pose and Illumination. In Jain, A., Li, S., eds.: Handbook of Face Recognition. Springer (2004)
13. Gargesha, M., Panchanathan, S.: A hybrid technique for facial feature point detection. In: Proc. IEEE Southwest Symp. on Image Analysis and Interpretation. (1998) 134–139
14. Tanaka, H.T., Ikeda, M.: Curvature-based face surface recognition using spherical correlation–principal directions for curved object recognition. In: Proc. ICPR. Volume III. (1996) 638–642
15. http://www.techfak.uni-bielefeld.de/ags/ai/members/members.html (retrieved spring 2005)
16. Deriche, R.: Recursively Implementing the Gaussian and Its Derivatives. In: Proc. ICIP. (1992) 263–267

# Object Shape Extraction Based on the Piecewise Linear Skeletal Representation

Roman M. Palenichka and Marek B. Zaremba

Dept. of Computer Science and Engineering,
Université du Québec en Outaouais, Gatineau, Canada
{palenich, zaremba}@uqo.ca

**Abstract.** The goal of the skeletal shape extraction algorithm presented in this paper was to obtain a concise and robust description of planar shapes for object recognition and subsequent region segmentation. The solution of this problem is proposed in the form of a piecewise-linear skeletal representation of planar shapes, which is a very economical shape description, resistant to distortions and intensity changes. A vertex growing procedure – similar to that of pixel-by-pixel region growing – have been developed to obtain rapidly piecewise linear skeletons of gray-scale object regions without their segmentation. Simultaneously, the complete planar shape of the objects of interest is extracted by a locally-adaptive binarization performed locally at the skeleton vertex areas. The vertex extraction is implemented using a visual attention operator, which can measure the saliency level of image fragments and select vertices at the local maxima of this operator.

## 1 Introduction

Appearance-based solutions of many computer vision tasks rely mostly on object planar shape extraction and analysis. Object planar shape – also considered as an object support region on the image plane – is stable with respect to various changes of intensity and lighting conditions and can be made invariant to geometrical transformations of scaling and rotation. Concise, adequate, and stable to distortions representation of the object shape is essential because most object recognition algorithms are implemented as procedures for shape feature extraction and comparison with a reference shape [1, 2]. The approach based on shape skeletons is, in this context, efficient since it can represent in a very concise manner the topology of an object with several connected parts and shape details [3-6]. Such a description permits the complete morphological reconstruction of the planar shape provided local scale values (i.e., diameter values) are available in each skeleton point. The well-known contour-based representation as an alternative to the skeletal representation is less robust and requires a longer descriptive length on the average compared to the skeletal representation.

The classical skeletonization algorithms such as those based on an iterative (morphological) thinning and distance transformation extract complete shape skeletons but they are not robust to various shape distortions and noise [3, 4]. These methods are usually limited to process binary images only. Some multi-scale algorithmic generalizations to gray-scale image analysis are also proposed [5-7].

Their performance strongly depends on the knowledge of some additional parameters, which are sensitive to distortions and irregularities. Complete skeletal shape is usually redundant to describe shape in the majority of object recognition applications [1, 2]. More recently, several methods were developed to describe skeletal shapes in a piecewise-linear manner by skeleton vertices and their connections in the form of straight-line segments [8-10]. This is a very concise (although not precise) representation of skeletal shapes without using classical skeletonization algorithms. For example, a statistical method of principal curves was used to extract directly the skeletal description of point sets [8]. In their initial form the algorithms for drawing principal curves using piecewise-linear approximation are limited to simple curves or manifolds, and requires initial positioning of the skeleton vertices. Another piecewise-linear skeletonization algorithm involves unsupervised neural network methods, such as self-organizing maps [9]. The shape skeleton can be obtained from a data-driven minimal spanning tree topology of a self-organizing map. The method deteriorates significantly if the regions contain components of various local sizes. Another method for shape description uses local skeletal features in a limited number of salient locations [10].

In this paper, we present a novel algorithm to obtain a skeletal object description in gray-scale images and to execute adaptive binarization in the neighborhood of the skeleton vertices. The development of this shape extraction and segmentation method has the following objectives.

• Piecewise linear skeletal shape description is obtained directly from gray-scale images without intermediate image binarization.
• There is a possibility to obtain easily the complete planar shape (region of support) based on the extracted piecewise linear skeleton.
• The shape description has to be invariant to geometrical transformations such as translation, scaling, and rotation.
• The method has to be robust with respect to variable contrast, noise, and some local distortions (occlusions).

The underlying idea to extract vertices of piecewise-linear skeletons consists in using a visual attention operator, called multi-scale image relevance function (IRF), which takes its local salient maxima at the centers of the object of interest and its salient shape parts. Visual attention operators proved to be a time-effective solution to object localization problems since they allow focusing image analysis only on a few particular regions of interest containing potential objects of interest [11,12]. Such an attention operator, which is defined in the form of a multi-scale non-linear matched filter, was proposed earlier to extract local shape features for object description [10]. However, the previous algorithm is working well only on gray-scale images containing local shapes with high object-to-background contrast.

The current algorithm of skeletal shape extraction in based on an improved, contrast-invariant version of the IRF and sequential extraction of skeleton vertices. The piecewise-linear skeletonization is implemented as a vertex-growing algorithm, which allows to increase the sensitivity in low-contrast and noisy areas of local shapes. Finally, an adaptive binarization scheme is involved for the complete (pixel-by-pixel) shape extraction in the vertex neighbourhoods. Since the shape extraction algorithm is based of a morphological growing model, the description of this model is introduced first.

## 2 Morphological Modeling of Object Planar Shapes

In the current framework for shape description, an object planar shape is considered separately and independently from object intensity features. Such a separate treatment has certain advantages over the extraction of integrated shape features as descriptors of the image intensity surfaces because of the achieved invariance to transformation of translation, scaling and rotation and stability to some intensity changes and lighting conditions. Additionally, a few intensity and texture features can be used for object intensity description to represent intensity variations as a texture, especially in the case of large sizes of object support regions.

For the purpose of multi-scale shape modeling and extraction, a formal definition of a scale system is used [1]: a structuring element at scale $n$ of a *uniform scales system* is formed by the morphological dilation (denoted by $\oplus$), $S_n = S_{n-1} \oplus S_0$, $n=1, 2,...,M$, where ($M$+1) is the total number of scales and the initial structuring element $S_0$ defines the minimal scale and object resolution. The structuring elements have the same shape such as the disk shape (see example in Fig. 1a).

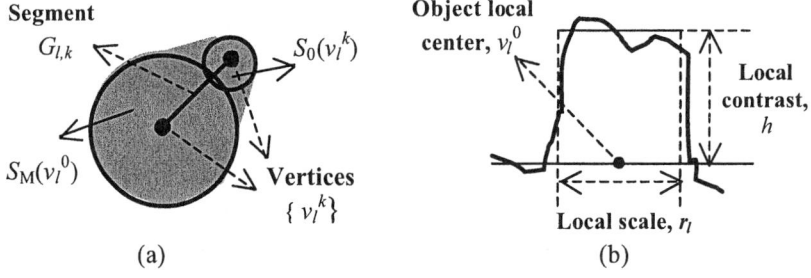

**Fig. 1.** Object shape and intensity modeling: (a) an example of the elementary cell used in the morphological shape modeling; (b) cross-section of the intensity model

Instead of using complete shape skeletons, a morphological piecewise-linear growing modeling is proposed. It includes, besides the structuring elements, an elementary cell model composed of two skeleton vertices, $v_l^0$ and $v_l^k$, connected by a straight line segment $G_{l,k}$ The growth of the elementary cell along the straight line segment $G_{l,k}$ can morphologically be described as follows (Fig. 1a) [1]:

$$E(v_l^0, v_l^k) = G_{l,k} \oplus S_m(v_l) = \bigcup_{v_l \in G_{l,k}} S_m(v_l), \qquad (2.1)$$

where $\oplus$ denotes the morphological dilation, $S_m(v_l)$ is a structuring element with variable size (radius $r_m$) as a function of point on the discrete straight line, $v_l \in G_{l,k}$. The value of $r_m$ is a linear combination of the scale sizes $r_0$ and $r_k$ at terminal vertices $v_l^0$ and $v_l^k$:

$$r_m = \frac{d(v_l^k, v_l)}{d(v_l^k, v_l^0)} \cdot r_0 + \frac{d(v_l^0, v_l)}{d(v_l^k, v_l^0)} \cdot r_k, \qquad (2.2)$$

where $d(.,.)$ is the Euclidean distance between two skeleton vertices on the image plane. A seed structuring element, $S(v_l^0)$, is first generated and centered at a given image skeleton vertex (seed point) $v_l^0$. A ring region $D(v_l^0)$ around $S(v_l^0)$ is determined and the second vertex is positioned within this ring. This determines the first elementary cell related to the current skeleton vertex. Given a vertex topological order $K$ – the largest possible number of skeleton segments – next $k$ vertices, $k=0,\ldots,K-1$, and elementary cells can be generated similarly within the region $D(v_l^0)$. All the elementary cells have common center vertex $v_l^0$. In fact, the union of $k$ elementary cells represents the object local planar shape at $l$th location. This procedure is applied recursively to all the vertices considering them as seed vertices.

This shape model is associated with an intensity model of the image fragment centered at $v_l^0$. The intensity modeling involves two dominant intensity levels, a smoothing linear filter, and additive noise model, which can also represent a textured intensity in order to describe image intensity locally and concisely (see Fig. 1b).

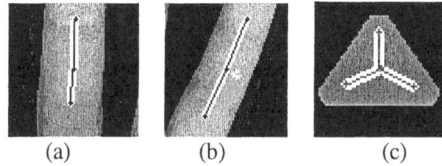

(a)         (b)         (c)

**Fig. 2.** Examples of salient image locations and extraction of skeleton vertices

## 3 Localization of Skeleton Vertices

Localization of piecewise-linear skeleton vertices is based on a fast computation of the multi-scale IRF and determination of its local salient maxima. The IRF is defined generically as a visual attention operator, which takes local maximal values at centers of salient image fragments containing objects of interest. At certain model-based conditions, the IRF maxima are positioned on object medial axes or at the centers of its shape parts, which are relevant to shape description (see Fig. 2). In order to address the aforementioned problems of skeletal shape extraction for object recognition and segmentation it is suggested to apply an improved version of a model-based IRF previously described in [10]. The positions of local maxima of the multi-scale IRF coincide with salient object locations in a region of interest $A$:

$$(i_f, j_f, \rho_f)_l = \arg \max_{(i,j) \in A} \max_m \{\Phi[(g(i,j), S_m], (i,j) \notin \Gamma_l\}, \qquad (3.1)$$

where $g(i,j)$ is the input gray-scale image, $\Phi[g(i,j), S_m]$ is a non-linear matched filter at $m$th scale, and $(i_f, j_f)_l$ are two coordinates of $l$th maximum, $\rho_f$ is the scale value at the maximum point. The region $\Gamma_l \subset A$ corresponds to the masking region, which excludes determined maximum points from further analysis.

Four basic conditions are considered in the explicit expression for $\Phi(g(i,j),S_m)$: 1) significant local contrast; 2) local shape symmetry; 3) local homogeneity of intensity; 4) specific scale range. The first condition is described by the absolute value for the local object-to-background contrast. The local homogeneity condition means that the intensity variance is relatively small in the object region. The intensity range means specific values for the object intensity in order to distinguish it from the background or other objects. The function expression for $\Phi(g(i,j),S_m)$ is obtained in the form of three saliency terms which evaluate the four basic saliency conditions in the image location $(i,j)$ [10].

The multi-scale IRF disclosed previously involves the shape symmetry condition only indirectly using circular symmetrical regions for the contrast estimation [10]. However, it is contrast sensitive and cannot work properly when extracting skeleton vertices of relatively low-contrast local shapes. Consequently, an explicit shape symmetry term is introduced, which evaluates the level of shape symmetry separately from the contrast estimate. The introduced shape symmetry term is computationally a matching distance between the current shape and a disk-shaped region centered at the same point and having the same scale.

Determination of each local maximum of the multi-scale IRF is immediately followed by the local scale estimation. The local scale is crucial to the skeletal shape extraction since it determines the object local size hence the object region around the current salient location. A so-called saliency hypothesis is tested first in each local maximum point: whether to accept the point $(i_f, j_f)$ or not as the next skeleton vertex [10].

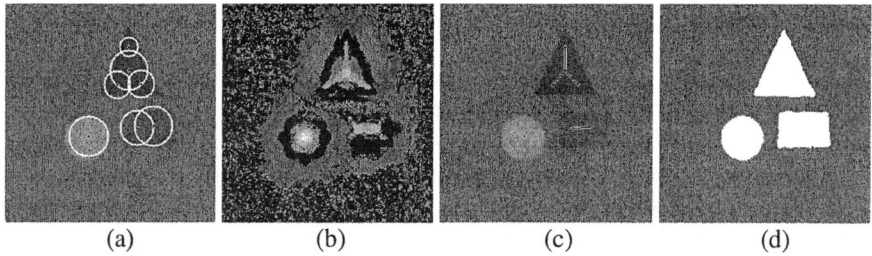

**Fig. 3.** Illustrative example of IRF calculation (b), piecewise-linear skeleton extraction (c) and complete shape determination (d) using medium scale range of the IRF. Found salient maxima and local scales are superimposed on the initial image in (a).

## 4 Piecewise-Linear Skeletonization by the Vertex Growing Algorithm

The extraction of skeletal shape features relies mostly on the intermediate results of IRF computation, (Eq. 3.1), and is computationally insignificant as compared to the computation of the multi-scale IRF. The proposed IRF approach provides at the same time a simple method to trace consecutively skeleton vertices in order to obtain a piecewise-linear skeletal representation of planar shapes. This can be done by analysing consecutive $K$ maxima of the IRF next to a given salient location $v_l^0$, where

$K$ is the maximal topological order of vertices. Such a procedure determines $K$ local skeleton vertices $\{v_l^k, k=1,\ldots,K\}$, which all are connected to the current (non-terminal) vertex $v_l^0$ according to the morphological model in Section 2. Given a neighborhood region $B(v_l^0)$ around the vertex $v_l^0$, the algorithm for the skeletal shape extraction starts from a seed vertex ($l=0$) and puts all extracted vertices into a non-terminal vertex stack.

*Step 0.* Find first (absolute) maximum of the IRF in the whole image plane and set it as the seed vertex with number $l=0$ and local vertex number $k=0$.

*Step 1.* Determine the location $v_l^k$ of the $k$th local maximum of IRF in the neighborhood region $B(v_l^0)$, which does not include all ($k$-1) previous IRF maxima.

*Step 2.* Test the saliency hypothesis with respect to $k$th local maximum. If the testing outcome is positive then go to *Step 3*, otherwise go to *Step 4*.

*Step 3.* Mask the neighborhood region of vertex $v_l^k$. If $k<K$ then $k<-k+1$ and go to *Step 1*, otherwise go to *Step 4*.

*Step 4.* Find in the stack of non-terminal vertices the first non-terminal vertex having number $l$. If not more untreated vertices then terminate the algorithm, otherwise set $k=0$ and go to *Step 1*.

One may observe that the proposed vertex growing algorithm represents at the same time a region growing procedure by entire sub-regions corresponding to neighbourhoods of newly extracted vertices at the IRF maxima. Moreover, such an algorithm builds a minimal spanning tree starting from the seed vertex since each new vertex is selected at a time and is located within the ring $B(v_l^0)$ with a preset minimal distance to the spanning tree under construction [9].

## 5 Locally-Adaptive Segmentation of Object Regions

The piecewise-linear skeletonization algorithm provides only an approximate representation of object planar shape since its performance is limited by the range of straight-line segments and scales. Consequently, the complete object shape can be reconstructed morphologically, but the precision is not as high as it can be requested. However, if an object recognition task requires the complete object shape then the IRF-based localization provides additionally a reliable object segmentation.

In object (region) segmentation, only the locally-adaptive threshold can solve the problem of intensity changes, variable lighting condition, and noise. Hence the proposed object skeletonization algorithm offers an advantage for two segmentation cases: it provides a reliable seed point (i.e., skeleton vertex) for a classical, pixel-by-pixel region growing procedure and it contributes to the local threshold determination if using a thresholding procedure [13]. As long as the IRF approach exhibits a good accuracy of vertex localization it provides a good estimate for the optimal threshold value in the current vertex $(i_f, j_f)$. The optimal threshold $t(i_f, j_f)$ for the binarization is determined by minimizing the segmentation error (object vs. background) as follows [13]:

$$t(i_f, j_f) = \frac{\tilde{h}}{2} + \frac{\tilde{\sigma}^2}{\tilde{h}} \cdot \ln \gamma, \qquad (5.1)$$

where $\tilde{h}$ is the estimated local contrast between the object and background intensities, $\gamma$ is the ratio of prior probabilities for the occurrence of background and object points, and $\tilde{\sigma}^2$ is the estimated noise variance.

## 6 Experimental Results

Since the performance of the developed algorithm, especially its localization precision, can be tested only with respect to the ground truth data some experiments were conducted with synthetic images with *a priori* known locations of skeleton vertices. Particular shape skeletons have been generated and test images with added noise have been created based on the underlying intensity model (Section 2). The position (two coordinates) and scale values of the skeleton vertices determined by salient maxima of the multi-scale IRF have been measured and compared with reference values to evaluate the accuracy. An example of synthetic image objects with known skeletons is shown in Fig. 3. Deliberately, an object (rectangle) with a low contrast-to-noise ratio was included in order to test the sensitivity of the new IRF algorithm. The results of accuracy testing are given in Table 1. The error was measured in pixel resolution relatively to the correct values of the skeleton vertices. Analysis of these data shows good accuracy and robustness of the proposed approach to vertex extraction.

**Table 1.** Measured accuracy of skeleton vertex extraction versus contrast-to-noise ratio

| Contrast-to-noise ratio | 2 | 4 | 8 | 16 | 32 |
|---|---|---|---|---|---|
| Localization error | 1.3 | 0.9 | 0.5 | 0 | 0 |
| Scale error | 3.1 | 1.8 | 0.2 | 0.1 | 0 |

The objective of the second kind of experiments was the evaluation of the algorithm performance in extracting skeletal shapes in digital angiography (medical imaging). The task was to extract piecewise-linear skeletons and complete (binary) shape of blood vessels in a specified scale range, i.e., vessel diameters. The proposed method was also compared with the skeletonization method using self-organizing maps [9] and the algorithm for extracting local shape features using the IRF approach [10]. The results obtained by these three different algorithms are shown in Fig. 4. The method of piecewise-linear skeletonization using self-organizing maps performed worse even when applied to the binary version of the input image and gave visible imprecision such as jaggedness of lines. Some shift of the skeleton lines for the object medial axes can also be observed. In this algorithm the extracted skeleton vertices are connected using the minimal spanning tree algorithm. The algorithm with local shape feature also includes the stage of complete shape reconstruction based on the mathematical morphology, Eq. (2.1) and Eq. (2.2). Results in Fig. 4 shows that the new vertex growing algorithm performed better for the skeleton extraction and complete shape extraction due to the locally-adaptive thresholding (Section 5). Figure 4 also contains images of the multi-scale IRF for these two methods.

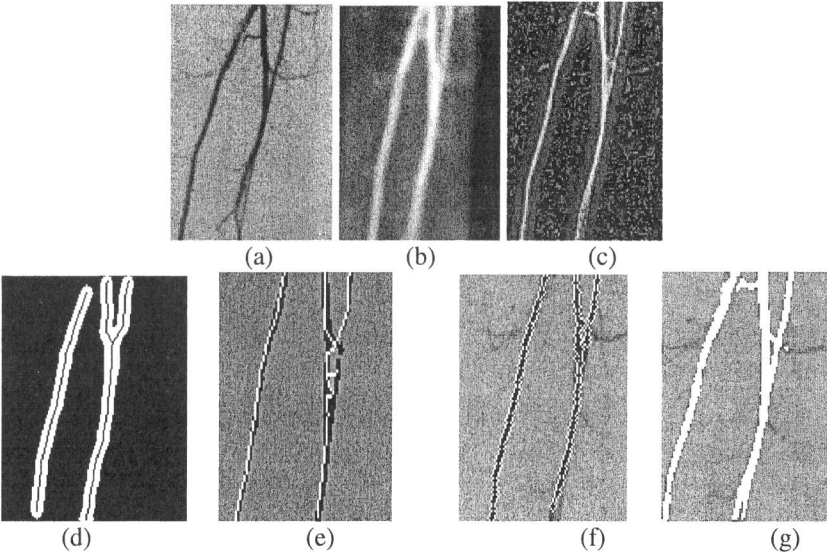

**Fig. 4.** Shape extraction of main blood vessels in digital angiography: (a) input image; (b) image of IRF without the use of shape symmetry term; (c) image of IRF with the explicit shape symmetry term; (d) skeletal shape in the selected region of interest using the algorithm of local shapes [10]; (e) skeletonization by the algorithm of self-organizing map [9]; (f) skeletonization using the proposed algorithm; (g) planar shape extracted by the locally-adaptive thresholding.

## 7 Conclusion

A method for extraction of piecewise-linear skeletons using a visual attention operator was developed. It is based on the determination of salient locations by the local maxima analysis of a modified version of the multi-scale image relevance function. The proposed concise description of local shapes has the following advantages in the object recognition context. It permits a robust shape extraction directly from gray-scale images in the presence of noise and under some local distortions. The complete planar shape of the objects of interest is extracted by a locally-adaptive binarization performed at the skeleton vertices.

## References

1. P. Maragos, "Pattern spectrum and multi-scale shape representation", *IEEE Trans. Pattern Analysis and Machine Intelligence*, Vol. 11, No. 7, pp. 701-717, 1989.
2. V. Conception and H. Wechsler, "Detection and localization of objects in time-varying imagery using attention, representation and memory pyramids", *Pattern Recognition*, Vol. 29, No. 9, pp. 1543-1557, 1996.
3. N. Blum and R.N. Nagel, "Shape description using weighted symmetric axis features", *Pattern Recognition*, Vol. 10, pp. 167-180, 1978.

4. Y. S. Chen and Y.T. Yu, "Thinning approaches for noisy digital patterns", *Pattern Recognition*, Vol. 29, No. 11, pp. 1847-1862, 1996.
5. G. Borgefors, "Distance transformation in digital images", *Vision, Graphics, and Image Processing,* Vol. 34, pp. 344-371, 1986.
6. G. Borgefors, G. Ramella, G. Sanniti di Baja, and S. Svenson, "On the multi-scale representation of 2D and 3D shapes", *Graphical Models and Image Processing,* Vol. 61, pp. 44-62, 1999.
7. C. Archelli and G. Ramella, "Sketching a grey-tone pattern from its distance transform," *Pattern Recognition,* Vol. 29, No. 12, pp. 2033-2045, 1996.
8. B. Kegl, *et al.*, "Learning and design of principal curves", *IEEE Trans. Pattern Analysis and Machine Intelligence,* Vol. 22, No. 3, pp. 281-297, 2000.
9. R. Singh, V. Cherkassky, and N. Papanikopoulos, "Self-organizing maps for the skeletonization of sparse shapes", *IEEE Trans. on Neural Networks*, Vol. 11, No. 1, pp. 241-248, 2000.
10. R. M. Palenichka, R. Missaoui, and M. B. Zaremba, "Extraction of skeletal shape features using a visual attention operator", *Proc. Int. Workshop S+SSPR2004*, LNCS, Vol. 3138, pp. 114-124, 2004.
11. T. Lindeberg, "Detecting salient blob-like image structures and their scale with a scale-space primal sketch: a method for focus of attention", *Int. Journal of Computer Vision*, Vol. 11, pp. 283-318, 1993.
12. L. Itti, C. Koch, and E. Niebur, "A model of saliency-based visual attention for rapid scene analysis", *IEEE Trans. Pattern Analysis and Machine Intelligence,* Vol. 20, No. 11, pp. 1254-1259, 1998.
13. P. K. Sahoo *et al.*, "A survey of thresholding techniques", *Computer Vision, Graphics and Image Process.,* Vol. 41, pp. 233-260, 1988.

# A Generic Shape Matching with Anchoring of Knowledge Primitives of Object Ontology

Dongil Han[1], Bum-Jae You[2], Yong Se Kim[3], and Il Hong Suh[4]

[1] Vision and Image Processing Lab., Sejong University
Seoul, Korea
dihan@sejong.ac.kr
[2] Intelligent Robotics Research Center
Korea Institute of Science and Technology
Seoul, Korea
ybj@kist.re.kr
[3] Creative Design and Intelligent Tutoring Systems Research Center
Sungkyunkwan University
Suwon, Korea
yskim@skku.edu
[4] Intelligence and Interaction Lab.
Hanyang University
Seoul, Korea
ihsuh@hanyang.ac.kr

**Abstract.** We have developed a generic ontology of objects, and a knowledge base of everyday physical objects. Objects are represented as assemblies of functional features and their spatial relations. Generic shape information of objects and features is stored using a partial boundary representation. Form-function reasoning is applied to deduce geometric shape elements from a feature's functions. We have also developed a generic geometric shape based object recognition method which uses many local features. The proposed recognition method considers the concept of ontology for representation of generic functions of objects. And the use of a general shape-function reasoning with context understanding enhances the performance of object recognition.

## 1 Introduction

To support a robot's interaction with a typical human environment requires a machine-understandable representation of objects, including their shapes, functions, and usages. Object recognition is supported by reasoning from each object's generic shape information. An object may have internal degrees of freedom, which means that its appearance and detailed geometry are highly variable, even though it fulfils the same function. Hence, many objects which have different shapes and geometry structures may be commonly known by the same name.

This condition can make model-based object recognition [1][2] extremely difficult because one may require either a classifier with a flexible boundary, or many different object models. Thus, for capturing and recognizing the object shape, function-based approach is introduced in [3]. The function models would capture a broad variation in allowed shape without reference to any specific geometric or structural plan. For this reason, function-based models seem to provide better support for "purposive" and "task-oriented" vision.

Previous research has explored the relationship between form and function for object recognition. The Generic Recognition Using Form and Function (GRUFF) system [4] represents objects as a set of functional elements (mostly planar surfaces), and spatial relations between elements. It performs generic object recognition by matching functional surfaces in the sensor input data to objects' definitions. It uses the Object Plus Unseen Space (OPUS) method to construct a partial 3D model from image and rangefinder data, but this has the drawback of sensitivity to varying image conditions.

Neumann et al. [5] performs context-based scene interpretation by modeling scenes as *aggregates*, where an aggregate is a set of entities and their spatial and temporal relations. They represent aggregates of scenes in description logic (DL), and match input models to scene definitions using the RACER DL reasoner [6]. However, their scene interpretation capability is beyond the current state-of-the-art in description logics, because a complete representation of the relations between entities exceeds the allowed expressiveness of RACER's DL.

## 2 Object Ontology

We adopt the ontology formalism in developing a generic ontology of objects. We use the standard OWL web ontology language, and the de facto standard Protégé ontology editor with OWL plugin [7]. Using this ontology, we have instantiated a knowledge base of ~300 objects for a typical indoor environment.

*A. Representation of objects*

Manufactured objects are typically assembled from multiple components, where each component contributes some specific functionality. Reflecting this, we adopt a hierarchical feature-based representation. An object is decomposed into a set of features and their spatial relationships, where a *feature* is a functionally significant subset of an object or another feature. Features are characterized by the functions they provide. Each feature can be further decomposed into more features.

*B. Spatial relations*

We define several spatial relations that frequently occur in everyday objects. For each spatial relation, we provide a definition that can be implemented as a (geometric) algorithm. For example, the ***above(A, B)*** relation is defined as: A is above B iff A's highest point is higher than B's highest point (with respect to the gravity direction), and A's lowest point is not lower than B's highest point.

*C. Form-function reasoning*

We characterize features using generic functions taken from function-based taxonomies for design [8][9]. While a feature is a 3D component, its functional elements, or *organs* [10], may correspond to subsets of its 3D shape. By applying form-function reasoning, we deduce geometric shape requirements for each functional element.

For example, a table's primary function is to limit the downward motion of many objects of any shape. The key feature for a table is a counter, which is typically a thin, rigid 3D slab. A counter's key organ is its top surface. To contact many objects implies many contact points, from which we deduce a planar surface. A table should also minimize the energy required to translate objects to different positions, which implies a horizontal orientation. Hence, we deduce a shape requirement of a *horizontal planar surface* for a counter's top surface.

## D. Geometric shape elements

We define a qualitative representation of geometric shape elements. A shape element has a geometric datum (usually a surface), which represents a generalized portion of a solid's boundary. Other constraints on the allowable orientation, curvature, and tolerance of a shape element are specified using a phrase structure.

## E. Representation of solids

A boundary representation (B-rep) is a 3D model that rigorously describes a solid by enumerating the topological elements of its boundary, including its faces, edges, and vertices. Other solid representations can be converted to B-rep, so a B-rep is a good candidate to be a generic solid representation.

On the other hand, an ontology of objects should also support generic representations of object families. This requires a capability to tolerate wide variations in specific geometry, while capturing the critical geometric relations only.

We adopt a *partial B-rep* scheme, in which a subset of a solid's boundary is fully specified, representing the critical geometric and topological relations only. Remaining portions of the boundary are abstracted away. Each solid has a bounding box data field, reflecting the principle that all real solid objects are bounded. Each feature class's shape information is then represented as a partial B-rep with 1 or more geometric shape elements.

# 3 Ontology-Based Object Recognition

A goal of this work is to design a vision-based context understanding system to enable a mobile robot to look for an object that it never seen before, in a place of first visit, where the object may be partially or completely obscured by other object. Such a visual context understanding system usually requires us to recognize place, objects, spatial and temporal relations, activities, and intentions.

In this paper, we describe the 2D object extractor. This module recognizes objects using two approaches. In the model-based approach, SIFT features [11]– [13] and edge features are directly matched to pre-computed vision feature-based models of objects. In the case that no vision feature models exist for an object, ontology-based object recognition proceeds as shown in Fig. 1.

- Local feature extraction obtains low-level vision feature information such as edges, lines, arcs, etc.
- The object ontology is queried for the object's feature decomposition and generic shape information, which includes geometric shape elements such as surfaces and curves, and spatial relations between features and shape elements.

- Low-level edge vision features are further processed to obtain mid-level vision features, such as rectangles. These are matched to the geometric shape elements to identify a set of candidate object features.
- For each object in the object ontology, check if all of its required features exist, and whether all spatial relations between its features are satisfied. This groups a set of features and spatial relations into a new instance of that object class.
- Repeat using only the unassigned shape elements in the scene data, until all input elements have been assigned to some object.

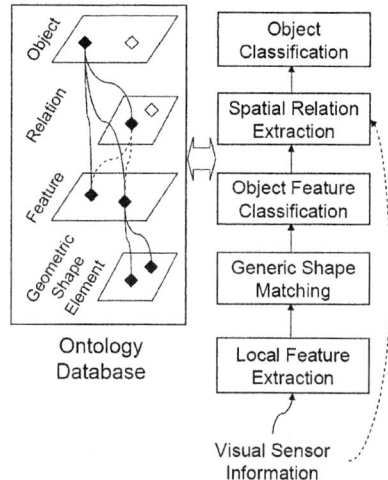

**Fig. 1.** Ontology-based object recognition scheme

A simplified subset of the ontology representation of a beam projector object is shown in Fig. 2.

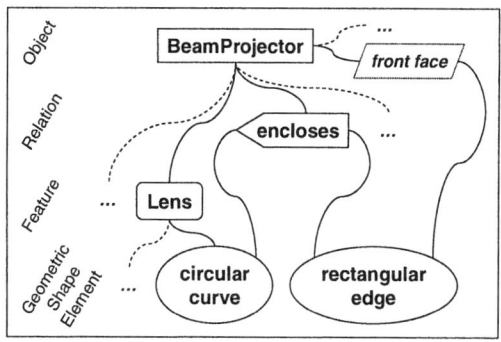

**Fig. 2.** Object decomposition of a beam projector (partial)

## 4 Experimental Results

To test this object recognition scheme, experiments were conducted on two kinds of beam projectors with different shapes and orientations, as shown in Fig. 3. First, edge information is extracted by using the canny edge detector, and it is further processed to generate the low-level image features such as connected line, arc, etc., as shown in Fig. 4. Circular edges are identified as shown in Fig. 5, and these are matched to the *circular curve* geometric shape element for a beam projector's lens feature. Similarly, rectangular edges are identified as shown in Fig. 6, and these are matched to the *rectangular edge* shape element for one face of a beam projector. In addition, the *encloses* spatial relation is checked, which rejects all rectangular edges that do not enclose any circular curve. The result of successful recognition of both beam projector objects is shown in Fig. 7.

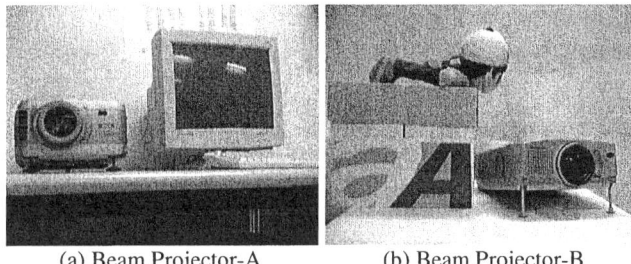

(a) Beam Projector-A    (b) Beam Projector-B

**Fig. 3.** Two test images

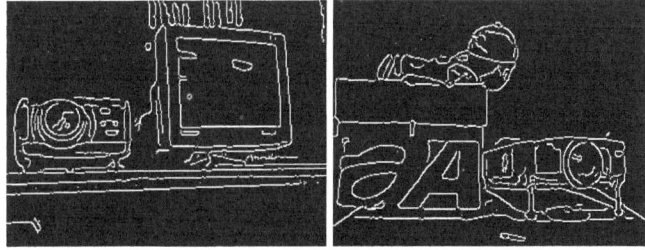

**Fig. 4.** Edge extraction and low-level image features

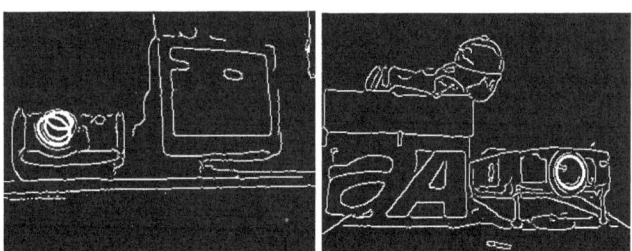

**Fig. 5.** Matching the *circular curve* geometric shape element

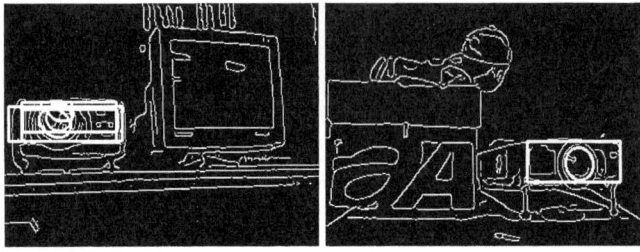

**Fig. 6.** Matching the *rectangular edge* geometric shape element and the *encloses* relation

**Fig. 7.** Successful recognition of both beam projectors

The performance of proposed ontology based recognition method is tested by comparing the model-based recognition system (Matrox MIL 7.5). As shown in Fig. 8 to Fig. 10, the several projector images are captured that have different size and orientation. The left images show the results of proposed recognition and the right images

**Fig. 8.** ontology (left) vs. model-based (right) recognition example

**Fig. 9.** ontology (left) vs. model-based (right) recognition example

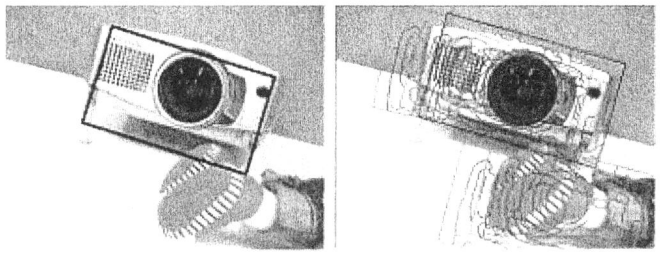

**Fig. 10.** ontology (left) vs. model-based (right) recognition example

**Table 1.** The comparison of maximum probability of presence of beam projector

| Max. Probability | Fig. 8. | Fig. 9. | Fig. 10. |
|---|---|---|---|
| Model based | 24.82% | 29.30% | 33.17% |
| Ontology based | 58.33% | 60.36% | 53.37% |

show the results of Matrox MIL 7.5. The Matrox MIL 7.5 shows the several matched results that the probability of recognition results exceeds the certain threshold level.

Table 1 shows the maximum probability of recognizing projector-B using the model-based recognition method and proposed method. In most cases, the proposed method shows better results and average performance of recognition result also shows better result.

The receiver operating characteristic (ROC) curves for the beam projector detectors are shown in Fig. 11. More than 60 test sample images are used in this experiment. The result of model-based beam projector detection method with Matrox MIL 7.5 is shown in Fig. 11-(b). The curve A in this figure shows the projector-A detection result with the model of projector-A. The curve B shows the projector-B detection result with the model of projector-A.

The curve A and B of Fig. 11-(a). show the projector-A and projector-B detection results with the proposed object recognition scheme.

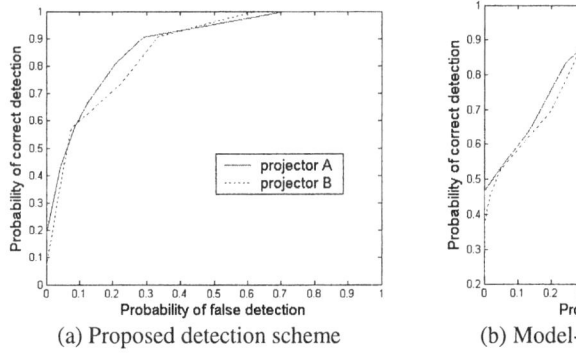

(a) Proposed detection scheme        (b) Model-based detection scheme

**Fig. 11.** The ROC curve comparison

## 5 Conclusion

We have developed a new object recognition scheme that combines generic shape information extraction and reasoning with function ontology for effective object recognition. The results of our research show that ontology based object recognition concept can be used to create a powerful object recognition scheme.

As a future work, we will include 3-D features such as surface patches, surface normal vectors for enhanced objection performance with more complex objects.

## Acknowledgments

This work is supported by KIST and Intelligent Robotics Development Program, one of the 21$^{st}$ Century Frontier R&D Programs funded by the Korea Ministry of Commerce, Industry and Energy.

## References

1. David A. Forsyth and J. Ponce: Computer Vision: A Modern Approach. in Prentice Hall, August, 2002.
2. R. Chin and C. Dyer: Model-based recognition in robot vision. in ACM Computing Surveys, vol. 18, no. 1, pp. 67-108. 1986.
3. L. Stark and K. Bowyer: Generic recognition through qualitative reasoning about 3-D shape and object function. in Proceedings of IEEE Conference on Computer Vision and Pattern Recognition, pp. 251-256. 1991.
4. Stark, L., and Bowyer, K.: Function-Based Generic Recognition for Multiple Object Categories. in Computer Vision, Graphics and Image Processing, Vol. 59, No. 1, pp. 1–21, Jan. 1994.
5. Neumann, B., and Möller, R.: On Scene Interpretation with Description Logics. in FBI-B-257/04 (Technical Report), Fachbereich Informatik, Universität Hamburg, 2004.
6. Haarslev, V., and Möller, R.: RACER System Description. in Proc. Int'l Joint Conf. on Automated Reasoning (IJCAR 2001), LNAI Vol. 2083, Springer, 2001, pp. 701–705.
7. Protégé, http://protege.stanford.edu.
8. Kirschman, C. F. and Fadel, G. M.: Classifying Functions for Mechanical Design. in Journal of Mechanical Design, Vol. 120, pp. 475–482, 1998.
9. Stone, R. B., and Wood, K. L.: Development of a Functional Basis for Design. in Proc. ASME Conf. on Design Theory and Methodology, Las Vegas, 1999.
10. Haudrum, J.: Creating the Basis for Process Selection in the Design Stage. in Ph.D. Thesis, Institute of Manufacturing Engineering, Technical University of Denmark, 1994.
11. D. Lowe: Distinctive image features from scale-invariant keypoints. in International Journal of Computer Vision, vol. 60, pp. 91-110, 2004.
12. S. Se, D. Lowe, and I. Little: Mobile Robot Localization and Mapping with Uncertainty using Scale-Invariant Visual Landmarks. in International Journal of Robotics Research, vol. 21, pp. 735-758, 2002.
13. S. Se, D. Lowe, and J. Little: Global localization using distinctive visual features. in International Conference on Intelligent Robots and Systems, pp. 226-231, 2002.

# Statistical Object Recognition Including Color Modeling

Marcin Grzegorzek* and Heinrich Niemann

Chair for Pattern Recognition,
University of Erlangen-Nuremberg,
Martensstr. 3, 91058 Erlangen, Germany
{grzegorz, niemann}@informatik.uni-erlangen.de

**Abstract.** In this paper an appearance-based statistical approach for localization and classification of 3-D objects in 2-D color images with real heterogeneous backgrounds is presented. The object feature extraction is done separately for the red, green, and blue channel. We compute six dimensional local feature vectors directly from pixel values in the images using wavelet multiresolution analysis. The first and second component of the feature vectors depend on the pixel values in the red channel, the third and fourth in the green channel, and fifth and sixth in the blue channel. Then we define an object area as a function of 3-D transformations and represent the feature vectors as probability density functions. In the recognition phase we use an algorithm based on maximum likelihood estimation for object localization and classification. Experiments made on a real data set with 39600 images compare the recognition rates for the new algorithm, which uses the color information of objects, with the results in the case of gray level images.

## 1 Introduction

For many tasks the localization and classification of objects in images is very useful, sometimes even necessary. Algorithms for automatic computational object recognition can be applied for example: to face classification [11], to localization of obstacles on the road with a camera mounted on a driving car, to service robotics [13], to handwriting recognition, and so on. There exist two main approaches for 3-D object recognition: based on results of a segmentation process [5], or directly on the object appearance [4]. The comparison of them can be found in [7]. The appearance-based methods compute feature vectors from pixel values in images without a previous segmentation process [8]. Some of them use only one global feature vector for the whole image (e.g. eigenspace approach [3]), others describe objects with more local features (e.g. neural networks [9]). Many recognition systems do not make use of the color information of objects. For some applications objects are distinguishable very well in the gray level

---

* This work was funded by the German Research Foundation (DFG) Graduate Research Center 3D Image Analysis and Synthesis.

space, for others the recognition algorithm with color modeling takes too much time compared to the improvement of the localization and classification rates. However, one can imagine situations, where two or more objects having totally different colors seem to look identical in gray level images. Their classification is very difficult, and it makes sense to use the color information of objects in this case. For some objects, which have different colors for different views, also the localization is easier in the color space.

In the present work we introduce the color modeling of objects, but in contrast to most approaches (e.g. [1]) we do not use histograms. Six dimensional local feature vectors are computed directly from pixel values (appearance-based approach) using wavelet multiresolution analysis [6] and modeled by density functions [10]. The first and second component of the feature vectors depend on the pixel values in the red channel, the third and fourth in the green channel, and fifth and sixth result from pixel values in the blue channel. The main advantage of the local feature vectors is that a local disturbance only affects the feature vectors in a small region around it. In contrast to this a global feature vector can change totally, if only one pixel in the image varies.

In Sect. 2 the training of statistical object models is presented. Beginning with the computation of the object density value, up to the algorithm for object localization and classification Sect. 3 describes the whole recognition phase. In Sect. 4 the recognition rates for the new algorithm with color modeling are compared with the results in the case of gray level images. Sect. 5 closes our contribution with conclusions.

## 2 Statistical Object Model

In order to learn a statistical object model $\mathcal{M}_\kappa$ for an object class $\Omega_\kappa$ we take training images of the object $\Omega_\kappa$ in known poses, compute feature vectors in these images (Sect. 2.1), define an object area (Sect. 2.2), and model the feature vectors by density functions (Sect. 2.3).

First we define a set of objects $\Omega = \{\Omega_1, \ldots, \Omega_\kappa, \ldots, \Omega_k\}$ and take training images of them on a dark background in known poses. The original training images are preprocessed by resizing them to RGB images sized $2^n \times 2^n$ pixels, where $n \in \{6, 7, 8, 9\}$. One image $\boldsymbol{f}_{\kappa,i}$ for each object class $\Omega_\kappa$ is used as a reference image. By pose of an object in the image $\boldsymbol{f}_{\kappa,j}$ we denote the 3-D transformation (translation and rotation) that maps the object in the reference image $\boldsymbol{f}_{\kappa,i}$ to the object in $\boldsymbol{f}_{\kappa,j}$. The 3-D transformation can be described by a translation $\boldsymbol{t} = (t_x, t_y, t_z)^\mathrm{T}$ and a rotation $\boldsymbol{\phi} = (\phi_x, \phi_y, \phi_z)^\mathrm{T}$. The $x$- and $y$-axes of the world coordinate system lie in the image plane, and the $z$ axis is orthographic to the image plane (Fig. 2). A rotation about the $x$- and $y$-axes as well as a translation along the $z$-axis (scaling) changes the size and appearance of the object in the image. These are the so called external transformation parameters ($t_{ext} = t_z$ and $\phi_{ext} = (\phi_x, \phi_y)^\mathrm{T}$). The remaining transformation parameters are called internal and do not change the object size and appearance. Up to the end of Sect. 2 the

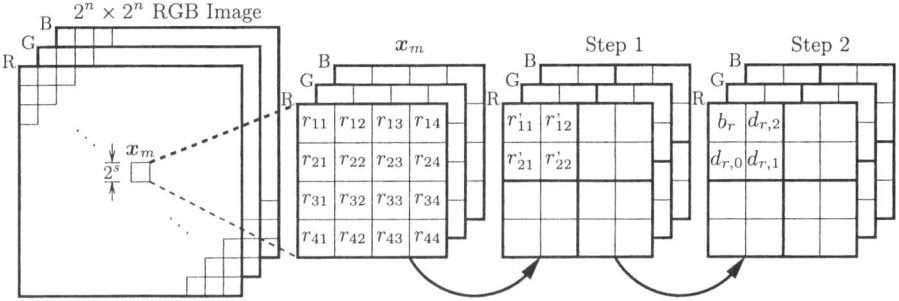

**Fig. 1.** Computation of a feature vector on a grid point $x_m$ for the scale $s = 2$. $r'_{ij}$ are calculated by horizontal and vertical low pass filtering of $r_{ij}$ and resolution reduction by factor 0.5. The final coefficients result from $r'_{ij}$ as follows: $b_r$ - low pass horizontal and low pass vertical, $d_{r,0}$ - low pass horizontal and high pass vertical, $d_{r,1}$ - high pass horizontal and high pass vertical, $d_{r,2}$ - high pass horizontal and low pass vertical.

number of the object class $\kappa$ is omitted, because the training of the statistical object model is identical for all object classes.

### 2.1 Feature Vectors

For the feature extraction we divide each preprocessed image $f$ into squares of size $2^s \times 2^s$ ($s \leq n$) pixels, and set in their centers grid points $x_m$. On all of these $2^{n-s} \times 2^{n-s}$ grid points six dimensional local feature vectors with the wavelet multiresolution analysis [6] are computed:

$$c_m = c(x_m) = (c_{m,r,1}, c_{m,r,2}, c_{m,g,1}, c_{m,g,2}, c_{m,b,1}, c_{m,b,2})^T \quad . \quad (1)$$

The choice of the wavelet transformation follows from the experimental results. The components $c_{m,r,1}$ and $c_{m,r,2}$ depend on the pixel values in the red channel, $c_{m,g,1}$ and $c_{m,g,2}$ in the green channel, and $c_{m,b,1}$ and $c_{m,b,2}$ in the blue channel. We explain their computation in detail only for the red channel $(c_{m,r,1}, c_{m,r,2})^T$, because for the other channels as well as for gray level images it is done in the same way. We perform $s$-times the wavelet multiresolution analysis for the red channel values in the local neighborhood of $x_m$ (neighborhood size: $2^s \times 2^s$ pixels) using Johnston 8-TAB wavelets [2]. The component $c_{m,r,1}$ of the feature vector $c_m$ is given by:

$$c_{m,r,1} = \ln |b_{r,s,m}| \quad , \quad (2)$$

and $c_{m,r,2}$ can be calculated with the equation:

$$c_{m,r,2} = \ln(|d_{r,0,s,m}| + |d_{r,1,s,m}| + |d_{r,2,s,m}|) \quad . \quad (3)$$

$b_{r,s,m}$ is the low pass coefficient and $d_{r,0...2,s,m}$ result from combinations of low pass and high pass filtering. An illustration of the feature vector computation for $s = 2$ can be seen in Fig. 1 (indices $m$ and $s$ are omitted). In Sect. 4.2 we compare the results for color and gray level images. In the case of gray level images two dimensional feature vectors $c_m = (c_{m,1}, c_{m,2})^\mathrm{T}$ computed according to (2) and (3) are used [10].

## 2.2 Object Area

For the object model we consider only those feature vectors that belong to the object and not to the background. For each feature vector $c_m$ in each external training pose $(\phi_{ext,t}, t_{ext,t})$ (for each training image) a discrete assignment function is defined:

$$\widehat{\xi}_m(\phi_{ext,t}, t_{ext,t}) = \begin{cases} 1, & \text{if } c_{m,\{r \vee g \vee b\},1}(\phi_{ext,t}, t_{ext,t}) \geq S_t \\ 0, & \text{otherwise} \end{cases} . \quad (4)$$

$S_t$ is chosen manually. If for all color channels the first feature vector coefficient $(c_{m,r,1}, c_{m,g,1}, c_{m,b,1})$ computed according to (2) is less than $S_t$, $c_m$ does not belong to the object. In the test images objects appear not only in the training poses, but also between them. In order to localize such objects we construct a continuous assignment function $\xi_m(\phi_{ext}, t_{ext})$ using values of $\widehat{\xi}_m(\phi_{ext,t}, t_{ext,t})$ by interpolation with trigonometric functions. The set of feature vectors belonging to the object for the given external pose $(\phi_{ext}, t_{ext})$ (called object area $O(\phi_{ext}, t_{ext})$) can now be determined with the following rule:

$$\xi_m(\phi_{ext}, t_{ext}) \geq S_O \Longrightarrow c_m(\phi_{ext}, t_{ext}) \in O(\phi_{ext}, t_{ext}) . \quad (5)$$

The threshold $S_O$ is also chosen manually. In the case of internal transformations the object area does not change the size and can be translated and rotated with these transformations. So, we can write the object area as a function of all transformation parameters: $O(\phi, t)$.

## 2.3 Density Functions of the Feature Vectors

All feature vectors computed in the training phase according to (1), (2), and (3) are interpreted as random variables. The object feature vectors are modeled with the normal distribution [10]. For each object feature vector we compute a mean value vector $\mu_m$ and standard deviation vector $\sigma_m$. The density of the object feature vector can be written as:

$$p(c_m) = p(c_m | \mu_m, \sigma_m, \phi, t) = \prod_{i \in \{r,g,b\}} \prod_{j=0}^{2} p(c_{m,i,j} | \mu_{m,i,j}, \sigma_{m,i,j}, \phi, t) . \quad (6)$$

The feature vectors, which belong to the background are modeled by an uniform distribution, and their density functions are constant $p(c_m) = p_b$.

## 3 Localization and Classification

After a corresponding object model $\mathcal{M}_\kappa$ was created for each object class $\Omega_\kappa$, we can localize and classify objects in test images. At the beginning each test image is preprocessed and feature vectors are computed according to (1), (2), and (3) with the same method as in the training phase (Sect. 2.1). Then we start our localization and classification algorithm based on the maximum likelihood estimation (Sect. 3.2), which maximizes the object density value (Sect. 3.1).

### 3.1 Object Density Value

In order to compute the object density value for the class $\Omega_\kappa$ in pose $(\boldsymbol{\phi}, \boldsymbol{t})$ for the given test image $\boldsymbol{f}$ we determine the set of feature vectors that belong to the object $C = \{c_1, c_2, \ldots, c_M\}$ (object area $O_\kappa(\boldsymbol{\phi}, \boldsymbol{t})$, Sect. 2.2) according to (5) and compute their values using equations (1), (2), and (3). Then we compare the calculated object feature vectors with the corresponding density functions (6) stored in the object model $\mathcal{M}_\kappa$ and determine density values for these vectors $(p(c_1), p(c_2), \ldots, p(c_M))$. The density value of object $\Omega_\kappa$ in pose $(\boldsymbol{\phi}, \boldsymbol{t})$ for the given test image $\boldsymbol{f}$ is given by:

$$p(C|\boldsymbol{B}_\kappa, \boldsymbol{\phi}, \boldsymbol{t}) = \prod_{i=0}^{M} \max\{p(c_i), p_b\} \quad . \tag{7}$$

$\boldsymbol{B}_\kappa$ comprehends the trained mean value vectors and standard deviation vectors from $\mathcal{M}_\kappa$ and $p_b$ is the background density value (Sect. 2.3).

### 3.2 Recognition Algorithm

The localization and classification algorithm is realized with maximum likelihood estimation [12] and can be described with the following equation:

$$(\widehat{\kappa}, \widehat{\boldsymbol{\phi}}, \widehat{\boldsymbol{t}}) = \underset{\kappa}{\operatorname{argmax}} \{\underset{(\boldsymbol{\phi}, \boldsymbol{t})}{\operatorname{argmax}} G(p(C|\boldsymbol{B}_\kappa, \boldsymbol{\phi}, \boldsymbol{t}))\} \quad . \tag{8}$$

$\widehat{\kappa}$ is the classification result and $(\widehat{\boldsymbol{\phi}}, \widehat{\boldsymbol{t}})$ is the localization result. First the object density (normalized by $G$) is maximized according to the pose parameters $(\boldsymbol{\phi}, \boldsymbol{t})$ and then to the class $\kappa$. The norm function $G$ is defined by:

$$G(p(C|\boldsymbol{B}_\kappa, \boldsymbol{\phi}, \boldsymbol{t})) = \sqrt[M]{p(C|\boldsymbol{B}_\kappa, \boldsymbol{\phi}, \boldsymbol{t})} \quad . \tag{9}$$

$M$ is the number of feature vectors belonging to the object area $O_\kappa(\boldsymbol{\phi}, \boldsymbol{t})$ (Sect. 3.1). This norm function reduces the dependency between the maximization result and the object area size.

## 4 Experiments and Results

We verified our approach on a 3D-REAL-ENV image data base (Sect. 4.1). The color modeling of objects brings the most profit in very heterogeneous environments compared to the algorithm for gray level images (Sect. 4.2).

**Fig. 2.** 10 object classes used for experiments. In the first row examples of test images with "more heterogeneous" backgrounds; from left: bank cup, toy fire engine, green puncher, siemens cup, nizoral bottle. In the second row examples of test images with "less heterogeneous" backgrounds; from left: toy passenger car, candy box, stapler, toy truck, white puncher. In the right upper corner the coordinate system for the object pose definition is shown.

### 4.1 Image Data Base

3D-REAL-ENV (Image Data Base for 3-D Object Recognition in Real World Environment) consists of 10 objects depicted in Fig. 2. The experiments were done using images of size 256 × 256 pixels. The pose of an object is defined with external rotations and internal translations $(\phi_x, \phi_y, t_x, t_y)^\mathrm{T}$ (Fig. 2). For the training we took 3360 images of each object with two different illuminations. The objects were put on a turntable ($0° \leq \phi_{table} < 360°$) and a robot arm with a camera was moved from horizontal to vertical ($0° \leq \phi_{arm} \leq 90°$). The angle between two adjacent training viewpoints amounts to 4.5°. For the tests 2000 images with homogeneous, 2000 images with "less heterogeneous", and 2000 with "more heterogeneous" backgrounds were taken. In the test images with "less heterogeneous" backgrounds the objects are easier to distinguish from the background than in the scenes with "more heterogeneous" backgrounds. The object poses and the illumination in the recognition phase are different from the training viewpoints and illuminations. For the test images with heterogeneous backgrounds we used more than 200 different backgrounds.

### 4.2 Localization and Classification Rates

We count a localization result as correct, if the error for the external rotations $(\phi_x, \phi_y)^\mathrm{T}$ is not larger than 15° and the error for the internal translations $(t_x, t_y)^\mathrm{T}$ is not larger than 10 pixels. The feature extraction for the experiments was made for the scale $s = 3$ of the wavelet multiresolution analysis (Sect. 2.1). Fig. 3 presents the recognition rates depending on the distance of the training views for test images with homogeneous, "less heterogeneous", and "more

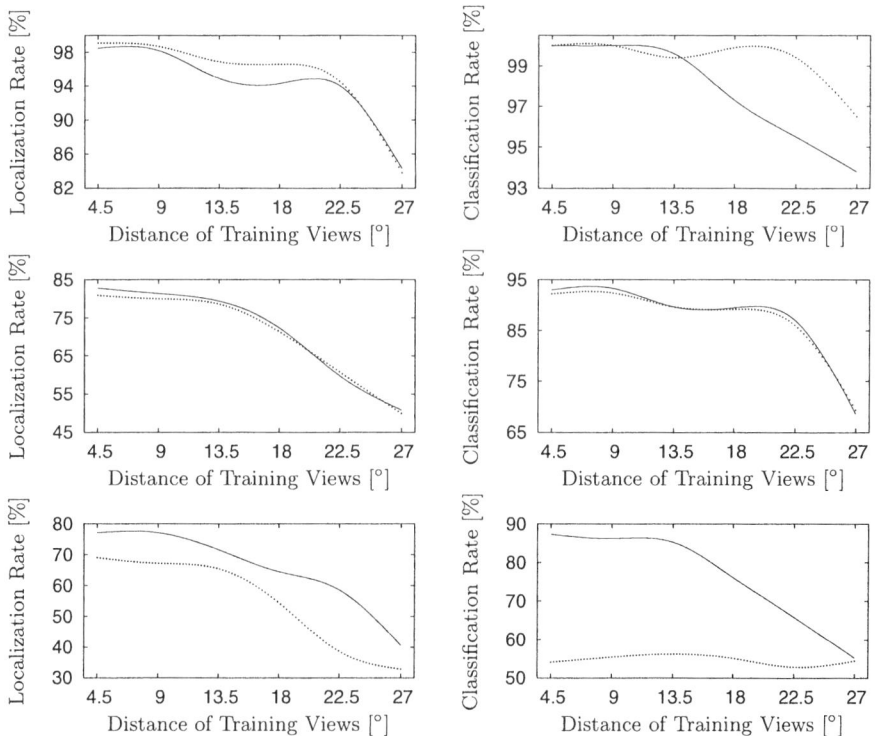

**Fig. 3.** Localization and classification rates depending on the distance of the training views for 2000 test images with homogeneous (first row), 2000 test images with "less heterogeneous" (second row), and 2000 test images with "more heterogeneous" backgrounds (third row). (— color images; ··· gray level images).

heterogeneous" backgrounds. Table 1 contains the recognition rates for 4.5° distance of training views. The color modeling brings the most improvement of the localization and classification rates for test images with "more heterogeneous" backgrounds. For scenes with homogeneous backgrounds the algorithm for gray level images works very well, and it is not necessary to use the color information of objects. Object localization and classification takes $3.6s$ in one gray level image, and $7s$ in one color image on Pentium 4, 2.66 MHz, 512 MB RAM.

## 5 Conclusions

In this article a powerful statistical appearance-based approach for 3-D object recognition in 2-D images with real heterogeneous backgrounds is presented. After feature extraction, which is done separately for the red, green, and blue channel, we define an assignment function, which assigns the features to the object or to the background, and statistically model them by density functions. In the recognition phase we use an algorithm based on the maximum likelihood es-

**Table 1.** Recognition rates for 4.5° distance of training views for 2000 test images with homogeneous, 2000 with "less heterogeneous", and 2000 with "more heterogeneous" backgrounds.

| Distance of Training Views 4.5° | Localization | | | Classification | | |
|---|---|---|---|---|---|---|
| | Hom. Back. | Less Het. Back. | More Het. Back. | Hom. Back. | Less Het. Back. | More Het. Back. |
| Color Images | 98.5% | 82.2% | 77.1% | 100% | 93.0% | 87.3% |
| Gray Level Images | 99.1% | 80.9% | 69.0% | 100% | 92.2% | 54.1% |

timation for localization and classification of objects. Results show that the color modeling brings a great improvement of the recognition rates in heterogeneous environments. On the other side we proved that for scenes with homogeneous backgrounds the use of gray level images is sufficient.

In the future we will try to obtain better recognition rates by transformation of the RGB images into other color spaces. We will also consider the case of multi-object scenes with context dependencies.

# References

1. P. Chang and J. Krumm. Object recognition with color cooccurrence histograms. In *IEEE Conference on Computer Vision and Pattern Recognition*, pages 498–504, Fort Collins, USA, June 1999. IEEE Computer Society.
2. C. Chui. *An Introduction to Wavelets*. Academic Press, San Diego, USA, 1992.
3. Ch. Gräßl, F. Deinzer, and H. Niemann. Continuous parametrization of normal distribution for improving the discrete statistical eigenspace approach for object recognition. In V. Krasnoproshin, S. Ablameyko, and J. Soldek, editors, *Pattern Recognition and Information Processing 03*, pages 73–77, Minsk, Belarus, Mai 2003.
4. R. Gross, I. Matthews, and S. Baker. Appearance-based face recognition and light-fields. *IEEE Transactions on Pattern Analysis and Machine Intelligence*, 26(4):449–465, April 2004.
5. J. Kerr and P. Compton. Toward generic model-based object recognition by knowledge acquisition and machine learning. In *Proceedings of the Eighteenth International Joint Conference on Artificial Intelligence*, pages 9–15, Acapulco, Mexico, August 2003.
6. S. Mallat. A theory for multiresolution signal decomposition: The wavelet representation. *IEEE Transactions on Pattern Analysis and Machine Intelligence*, 11(7):674–693, July 1989.
7. J. Mundy, A. Liu, N. Pillow, A. Zisserman, S. Abdallah, S. Utcke, S. Nayer, and C. Rothwell. An experimental comparison of appearance and geometric model based recognition. In J. Ponce, A. Zisserman, and M. Hebert, editors, *Object Representation for Computer Vision II*, pages 247–269, Cambridge, UK, April 1996. Springer Verlag.
8. H. Murase and S. K. Nayar. Visual learning and recognition of 3-d objects from appearance. *International Journal of Computer Vision*, 14(1):5–24, January 1995.
9. S. Park, J. Lee, and S. Kim. Content-based image classification using a neural network. *Pattern Recognition Letters*, 25(3):287–300, February 2004.

10. M. Reinhold. *Robuste, probabilistische, erscheinungsbasierte Objekterkennung.* Logos Verlag, Berlin, Germany, 2004.
11. D. Terzopoulos, L. Yuencheng, and M. Vasilescu. Model-based and image-based methods for facial image synthesis, analysis and recognition. In *Automatic Face and Gesture Recognition 2004*, pages 3–8, Seoul, Korea, Mai 2004.
12. A. R. Webb. *Statistical Pattern Recognition.* John Wiley & Sons Ltd, Chichester, England, 2002.
13. B. You, M. Hwangbo, S. Lee, S. Oh, Y. Kwon, and S. Lim. Development of a home service robot issac. In *Intelligent Robots and Systems 2003*, pages 2630–2635, Las Vegas, USA, October 2003.

# Determining Multiscale Image Feature Angles from Complex Wavelet Phases

Ryan Anderson, Nick Kingsbury, and Julien Fauqueur[*]

Signal Processing Group, Dept. of Engineering, University of Cambridge, UK

**Abstract.** In this paper, we introduce a new multiscale representation for 2-D images named the *Inter-Coefficient Product (ICP)*. The ICP is a decimated pyramid of complex values based on the Dual-Tree Complex Wavelet Transform (DT-CWT). The complex phases of its coefficients correspond to the angles of dominant directional features in their support regions. As a sparse representation of this information, the ICP is relatively simple to calculate and is a computationally efficient representation for subsequent analysis in computer vision activities or large data set analysis. Examples of ICP decomposition show its ability to provide an intuitive representation of multiscale features (such as edges and ridges). Its potential uses are then discussed.

## 1 Introduction

Wavelets, once used primarily for compression, have found new uses for image content analysis. The ability of the wavelet transform to isolate image energy concisely into spatial, directional, and scalar components have allowed it to characterize the multiscale profile of non-stationary signals, including 2-D images, very effectively. In particular, complex wavelets have shown a strong ability to consistently represent object structures in 2-D images for object recognition and computer vision activities.

In this paper, we explore methods of building upon the phase information of complex wavelets to yield intuitive image representations. To date, complex wavelet *magnitudes* have typically been used in place of real wavelets to improve the consistency of segmentation, denoising, etc. However, phase information, which indicates the offset of directional features within the support region of a wavelet coefficient, has found less application to date in analysis and coding applications (although stereo matching and motion estimation are two examples of its use). Recently, in [3], Romberg et al. have described a probabilistic model, the Geometric Hidden Markov Tree (GHMT), which uses phase as well as magnitude information to infer the angle and offset of contour segments in the vicinity of a complex wavelet coefficient. In this paper, we introduce a faster method to calculate the angle of directional energy in the vicinity of a coefficient. This method, which we have named the *Inter-Coefficient Product (ICP)*, may

---

[*] This work has been carried out with the support of the UK Data & Information Fusion Defence Technology Centre.

find use in large-scale image analysis or real-time computer vision, where computational complexity must be minimized. We introduce the ICP as a complement to another phase-based transform, the Interlevel Product (ILP) [1]. Upon describing the background of complex wavelets (section 2), we will develop the ICP transform in section 3 and show example ICP decompositions in section 4. We conclude in section 5 with a discussion of potential uses of the ICP and its relationship to the DT-CWT and the ILP.

## 2 The Dual-Tree Complex Wavelet Transform

Standard real wavelets, such as the Haar and Daubechies wavelets, suffer from *shift dependence*. Shift dependence implies that the decomposition of image energy between levels of a multiscalar decomposition can vary significantly, if the original image is shifted prior to decomposition. This variation limits the effectiveness of the real wavelet transform to consistently represent an image object at multiple scales.

Complex wavelets, including the linearly-separable Dual-Tree Complex Wavelet [2] have been created to address the problems of shift dependence. A complex wavelet is a set of two real wavelets with a 90° phase difference. For 2-D image analysis, the DT-CWT produces $d = 1\ldots 6$ directional subbands at approximately $\frac{\pi}{10}$, $\frac{\pi}{4}$, $\frac{2\pi}{5}$, $\frac{3\pi}{5}$, $\frac{3\pi}{4}$, and $\frac{9\pi}{10}$ (for convenience, these subbands are often labelled with equally-spaced angles of 15°, 45°, 75°, 105°, 135°, and 165° respectively). The impulse responses in each of these subbands are shown in figure 1. We note that the magnitude responses of each these subbands can be used to infer feature orientations. However, the lack of precision in these methods is the primary motivation for us to seek a superior representations through the use of complex phase information.

Figure 2 shows both the phase (fig. 2a) and magnitude (fig. 2b) responses of a DT-CWT coefficient to a shifting step response in 1-D. In particular, we

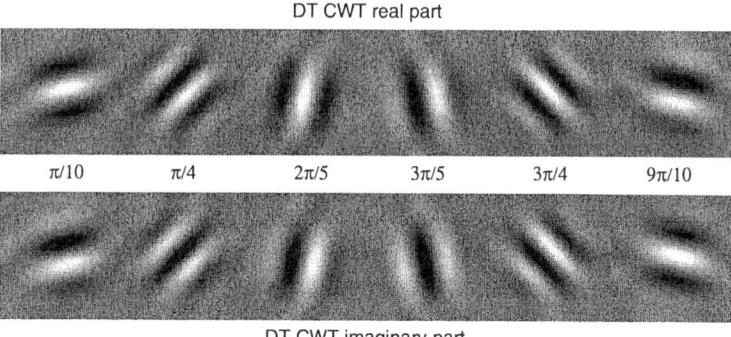

**Fig. 1.** The real and imaginary impulse responses of the DT-CWT for each of the six subbands

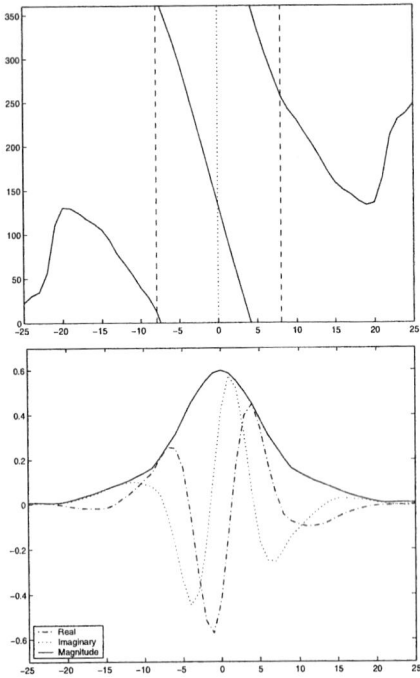

a) The complex phase of a decimated level 3 DT-CWT coefficient (located at the central dotted line), in the presence of a step edge at all possible offsets (the x axis). Note that when an edge or ridge occurs anywhere between the coefficient and its immediate neighbours (shown as the vertical dashed lines), the phase response is linear. This linearity will be used to infer the offset of the edge, relative to the coefficient location, at this scale.

b) The magnitude response of the same DT-CWT coefficient under the same conditions. The overall magnitude is calculated from real and imaginary components, as shown.

**Fig. 2.** Illustration in the 1-D case of the behaviour of the phase and magnitude of a DT-CWT coefficient (level 3, in this case) in the presence of a step edge, at the indicated $x$ coordinate, relative to the coefficient

observe that this phase response is consistently *linear* with respect to the feature offset, in the vicinity of the wavelet coefficient. If we define $D_W$ as the distance between adjacent coefficients, as indicated by the vertical lines in figure 2a, then we have experimentally determined the relationship between coefficient phase and feature offset to be $-4.49/D_W$ radians per unit length. With this ratio, we can convert DT-CWT phase to a spatial offset of an edge or impulse, or vice-versa.

In the 2-D case, the phase and magnitude relationships described above apply to edges and ridges oriented in the direction of the subband. The ratios for 2-D subbands differ from the 1-D example; for subbands 1, 3, 4, and 6, the ratio is $-4.49/\left(D_W \cos \frac{\pi}{10}\right)$ or $-4.72/D_W$ radians per unit length. For subbands 2 and 5, the ratio is $-4.49/\left(D_W \cos \frac{\pi}{4}\right)$ or $-6.35/D_W$ radians per unit length. for these 2-D cases, the *subband offset* of a feature is defined in the direction normal to the subband, as shown in figure 3.

## 3    The Inter-coefficient Product

In this section, we introduce the Inter-Coefficient Product (ICP). We begin in sections 3.1 and 3.2 by showing how the orientation of a 2-D feature (such as

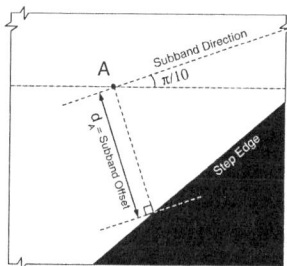

**Fig. 3.** Definition of the subband offset $d_A$ in the 2-D case between a coefficient location $A$ and a step edge

an edge or ridge) can be determined from the phase difference of two adjacent DT-CWT coefficients. This derivation leads us naturally to the definition of the ICP in section 3.3.

### 3.1 Determination of Feature Orientation from Neighbour Coefficients

Consider Figure 4, which shows a feature (a step edge, in this case) that spans the support regions of two horizontally adjacent DT-CWT coefficients at locations $A = (x, y)$ and $B = (x + 1, y)$, at some arbitrary level. This figure illustrates the trigonometric relationship between the angle of the feature and its subband offsets with respect to these coefficients.

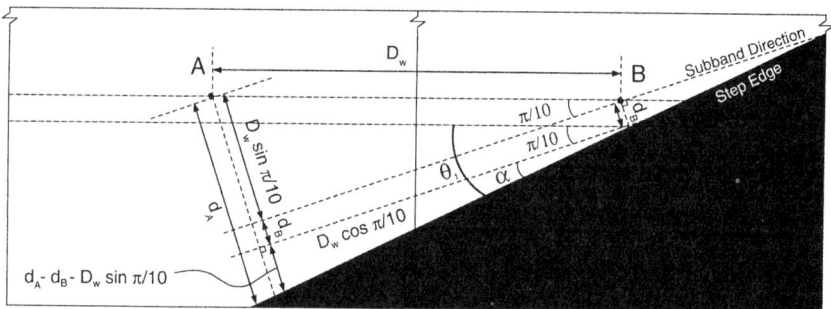

**Fig. 4.** Trigonometric relationship between the angle $\theta_1 = \alpha + \frac{\pi}{10}$ of a feature (step edge, in this case) and its subband offsets $d_A$ and $d_B$ to two horizontally adjacent $\frac{\pi}{10}$ subband DT-CWT coefficients located at $A=(x,y)$ and $B=(x+1,y)$

As this step edge is closest to the $d = 1$, $\frac{\pi}{10}$ subband, the DT-CWT coefficients $W_l(x, y, 1)$ and $W_l(x+1, y, 1)$ will correspondingly have large magnitudes in this subband only. From figure 4, we can see that the angle of the feature, $\theta_1$, can be calculated as

$$\theta_1 = \frac{\pi}{10} + \alpha = \frac{\pi}{10} + \tan^{-1}\frac{d_A - d_B - D_w \sin\frac{\pi}{10}}{D_w \cos\frac{\pi}{10}} \quad (1)$$

where $d_A$ and $d_B$ are the subband offsets of the edge to the two coefficients as defined in figure 3, using subband 1. These two offset lengths are equal to $\frac{D_w}{4.72}\angle W_l(x,y,1)$ and $\frac{D_w}{4.72}\angle W_l(x+1,y,1)$ respectively[1], according to our phase/offset relationships described at the end of section 2. Thus, we can rewrite Equation (1) as

$$\theta_1 = \frac{\pi}{10} + \tan^{-1}\frac{\frac{D_w}{4.72}\angle W_l(x,y,1) - \frac{D_w}{4.72}\angle W_l(x+1,y,1) - D_w \sin\frac{\pi}{10}}{D_w \cos\frac{\pi}{10}}$$

$$= \frac{\pi}{10} + \tan^{-1}\left[\frac{\angle W_l(x,y,1) - \angle W_l(x+1,y,1)}{4.72\cos\frac{\pi}{10}} - \tan\frac{\pi}{10}\right] \quad (2)$$

We note that for $-\frac{\pi}{5} < \alpha < \frac{\pi}{5}$, which is the approximate range of feature angles that will contribute to an individual subband, we can assume that $\alpha \approx \tan\alpha$. Applying this approximation twice to Equation (2), we can simplify this expression to

$$\theta_1 = \frac{\pi}{10} + \frac{\angle W_l(x,y,1) - \angle W_l(x+1,y,1)}{4.72\cos\frac{\pi}{10}} - \frac{\pi}{10} \quad (3)$$

$$\Rightarrow \theta_1 = \frac{1}{4.49}[\angle W_l(x,y,1) - \angle W_l(x+1,y,1)] \quad (4)$$

Thus, for subband 1, we merely divide the phase difference between two horizontally adjacent DT-CWT coefficients by 4.49 to obtain the angle of the dominant feature in their vicinity.

### 3.2 Feature Orientation Calculations for All Subbands

In the previous section example, we considered the $\frac{\pi}{10}$ subband ($d = 1$) given the orientation of our particular example of step edge. In the general case, to detect a feature at any orientation, the same type of calculation is achieved for all six subbands based on phase difference between appropriate neighbour DT-CWT coefficients: we compare horizontal neighbours for the $\frac{\pi}{10}$ and $\frac{9\pi}{10}$ subbands ($d = 1, 6$), vertical neighbours for the $\frac{2\pi}{5}$ and $\frac{3\pi}{5}$ subbands ($d = 3, 4$), and diagonal neighbours for the $\frac{\pi}{4}$ and $\frac{3\pi}{4}$ subbands ($d = 2, 5$). Thus six orientation angles are calculated $\theta_1, ..., \theta_6$, one for each subband. We have already determined $\theta_1$ (see Equation (4)).

By symmetry, the geometric relationship in the $\frac{\pi}{10}$ subband $d = 1$ can be equally applied to subbands $d = 3, 4$, and 6, where feature angles in subbands 3 and 4 are measured relative to the vertical axis. For these two subbands, therefore, we would therefore modify equation (4) to add $\frac{\pi}{2}$ to the angle. However, in the $\frac{\pi}{4}, \frac{3\pi}{4}$ subbands 2 and 5, the $W_l$ values possess a different relationship with the angles of dominant features with two diagonally adjacent coefficients.

---
[1] We denote the phase argument of a complex number $c$ as $\angle c = arg(c)$.

Using subband 2, the angle of the feature is related to coefficient offsets by the following simpler equation:

$$\theta_2 = \frac{\pi}{4} + \tan^{-1}\frac{d_A - d_B}{\sqrt{2}D_w} \tag{5}$$

Performing the same substitutions, assumptions, and simplifications as with our previous example, we establish the linear relationship between $\theta_2$ and the $W_l$ coefficient phases to be

$$\theta_2 = \frac{\pi}{4} + \frac{1}{8.98}[\angle W_l(x, y+1, 2) - \angle W_l(x+1, y, 2)] \tag{6}$$

As with the previous example, this relationship is identical for subband 5, except that $\frac{3\pi}{4}$ would be added to the phase of $\theta_5$ in the operation above.

## 3.3 Definition of ICP

In the previous section, we established the linear relationship formulae between a feature orientation and the difference of phase between adjacent DT-CWT complex coefficients. We calculate these phase differences by means of conjugate products of the adjacent pairs of DT-CWT coefficients as detailed in the previous section. The complex products are a natural way to represent the feature orientation (through the complex phase) and also the feature strength (through the complex magnitude). Thus, if we consider $W_l(x, y, d)$ to be the complex DT-CWT coefficient at spatial location $x, y$ (numbered from the top left corner), subband $d$, and level $l$, then we introduce the constant-phase complex values $W_{l\Delta}$:

$$\begin{aligned}
W_{l\Delta}(x, y, 1) &= W_l(x, y, 1) & &\times W_l(x+1, y, 1)^* \\
W_{l\Delta}(x, y, 2) &= W_l(x, y+1, 2) & &\times W_l(x+1, y, 2)^* \\
W_{l\Delta}(x, y, 3) &= W_l(x, y, 3) & &\times W_l(x, y+1, 3)^* \\
W_{l\Delta}(x, y, 4) &= W_l(x, y, 4)^* & &\times W_l(x, y+1, 4) \\
W_{l\Delta}(x, y, 5) &= W_l(x, y, 5)^* & &\times W_l(x+1, y+1, 5) \\
W_{l\Delta}(x, y, 6) &= W_l(x, y, 6)^* & &\times W_l(x+1, y, 6)
\end{aligned} \tag{7}$$

From this definition, the feature orientation $\theta_d$ calculated for each subband $d$ in the previous section, can be expressed with respect to $\angle W_{l\Delta}(x, y, d)$. For instance, from equation (4), $\theta_1 = \frac{1}{4.49}\angle W_{l\Delta}(x, y, 1)$.

The magnitudes of $W_{l\Delta}$ are the product of the magnitudes of the two adjacent DT-CWT coefficients, and the phases of $W_{l\Delta}$ are their shift-invariant phase differences. Note that we can divide the magnitudes of $W_{l\Delta}$ by $\sqrt{|W_{l\Delta}|}$ to mitigate the non-linear product effect of this operation.

Using the conjugate products $W_{l\Delta}$ and the expressions for feature orientations $\theta_d$, we now define the Inter-Coefficient Product.

**Definition 1 (Inter-coefficient Product).** *Given a DT-CWT decomposition of an image with coefficients $W_l(x, y, d)$ for levels $l$ and subbands $d = 1, ..., 6$, we* define the Inter-Coefficient Product (ICP) for each subband $d$, level $l$ and decimated location $(x, y)$ as the following set of complex coefficients $\{\psi_l(x, y, d), d = 1, ..., 6\}$:

$$\psi_l(x, y, 1) = \sqrt{|W_{l\Delta}(x, y, 1)|} \times e^{i(\frac{1}{4.49} \angle W_{l\Delta}(x, y, 1))}$$

$$\psi_l(x, y, 2) = \sqrt{|W_{l\Delta}(x, y, 2)|} \times e^{i(\frac{\pi}{4} + \frac{1}{8.98} \angle W_{l\Delta}(x, y, 2))}$$

$$\psi_l(x, y, 3) = \sqrt{|W_{l\Delta}(x, y, 3)|} \times e^{i(\frac{\pi}{2} + \frac{1}{4.49} \angle W_{l\Delta}(x, y, 3))}$$

$$\psi_l(x, y, 4) = \sqrt{|W_{l\Delta}(x, y, 4)|} \times e^{i(\frac{\pi}{2} + \frac{1}{4.49} \angle W_{l\Delta}(x, y, 4))}$$

$$\psi_l(x, y, 5) = \sqrt{|W_{l\Delta}(x, y, 5)|} \times e^{i(\frac{3\pi}{4} + \frac{1}{8.98} \angle W_{l\Delta}(x, y, 5))}$$

$$\psi_l(x, y, 6) = \sqrt{|W_{l\Delta}(x, y, 6)|} \times e^{i(\frac{1}{4.49} \angle W_{l\Delta}(x, y, 6))}$$

where $i = \sqrt{-1}$.

We will consider the contribution of a feature to the subband which is the closest to its orientation, since it is where the DT-CWT coefficient response is linear and the strongest. The coefficient magnitudes automatically reveal the dominant orientation of the feature across subbands.

At each location $(x, y)$ and each level $l$, the orientation of a potential feature (such as an edge or a ridge) in the vicinity of $(x, y)$ will be given by the phase of an ICP coefficient. The magnitude of the ICP coefficient will reflect the strength of this feature.

## 4 Results and Interpretation

Figure 5 shows an ICP decomposition for the "Lenna" image, for level $l=3$, $\frac{9\pi}{10}$ subband in figure 5a, and level $l=4$ (coarser), $\frac{\pi}{4}$ subband in figure 5b. When overlayed upon the original image, we can see the ability of the ICP to follow coarse and fine image contours.

If we shift the original image half the current subband coefficient spacing prior to ICP transform, we apply the worst possible offset in multiscale misalignment (described in [1]) that may occur if one was to compare two separate instances of an image object. Figure 6 shows this offset; note that, relative to figure 5b, the coefficients make small, predictable changes in direction and magnitude to reflect changing support regions, but dominant edge features in the image keep the coarse-level representation relatively invariant to multiscale misalignment, which shows the shift independence of ICP.

Note also that the ICP is a reversible transform; with all the ICP coefficients and the last row and column of DT-CWT coefficients, one can divide out all of the original DT-CWT coefficients one row/column at a time (and thence reconstruct the original image with a reverse DT-CWT transform). However, as the ICP itself acts in the manner of a differential operator, modifications to the ICP coefficients can propagate throughout the image, far beyond the support range of the original coefficient.

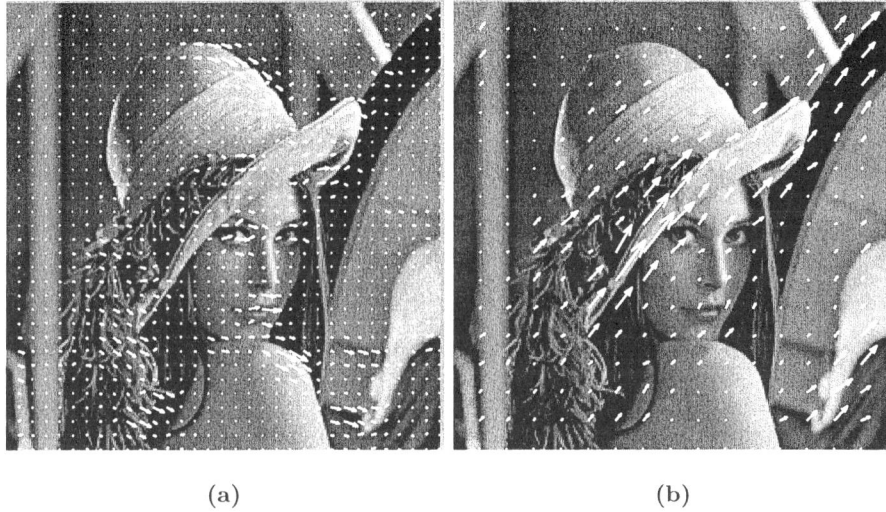

**Fig. 5.** ICP Coefficients for "Lenna" picture, at a) Level 3, Subband 6; and b) Level 4, Subband 2. Note the ability of the ICP to follow, for example, the fine edge of the top of the hat in a), and the coarse-scale $\frac{\pi}{4}$ rim of the hat on the left in b).

**Fig. 6.** ICP shift independence: the input image of figure 5b has been shifted by half a sample in each direction prior to ICP transform. Although this shift corresponds to the worst alignment case, we observe minor changes in the ICP coefficients.

## 5 Conclusions

The ICP transform extracts phase information from the DT-CWT transform into an intuitive, sparse format that reveals the orientation of directional features with finer precision than with the sole use of magnitudes of real or complex wavelets coefficients. The entire process from pixel domain to ICP domain is efficient to implement: the DT-CWT is linearly separable into row and column operations, and the subsequent ICP operation performs simple operations on decimated coefficients. Thus, we believe ICP coefficients to be appropriate for multiscale image processing activities such as contour tracking, registration, and rotation- and scale-invariant object recognition, in large images or real-time systems where computational complexity is a strong factor in system design.

In particular, we note that the ICP and the ILP [1] transforms complement one another very eloquently in the description of multiscale features. The ICP is highly informative as to small rotations and relatively insensitive to feature structure. By contrast, the ILP is indicative of the nature of the feature itself and is insensitive to small rotations. Between these two pyramidal image representation transforms, we can build a highly informative hybrid representation of image objects that can be detected at various scales and rotations. Our future research will pursue such models with these coefficients.

## References

1. R. Anderson, N. Kingsbury, and J. Fauqueur. Coarse level object recognition using interlevel products of complex wavelets. In *International Conference on Image Processing (ICIP)*, September 2005.
2. N.G. Kingsbury. Complex wavelets for shift invariant analysis and filtering of signals. *Journal of Applied and Computational Harmonic Analysis*, (3):234–253, 2001.
3. J. Romberg, M. Wakin, H. Choi, and R. Baraniuk. A Geometric Hidden Markov Tree Wavelet Model. In *SPIE Wavelets X*, San Diego, CA, August 2003.

# Cylinder Rotational Orientation Based on Circle Detection

Gabriel Thomas, John E. Kaye, Rajat Jayas, and Cam Kaye

University of Manitoba, Department of Electrical and Computer Engineering,
Winnipeg, Manitoba, Canada R3T 5V6
thomas@ee.umanitoba.ca

**Abstract.** The paper addresses the computer vision aspects of aligning a hydraulic cylinder prior to being hooked on a conveyer by a robotic arm. The robotic arm is programmed to assume the cylinder's clevis hole is perpendicular to the horizontal base of the stamping station; if the cylinder is not in this orientation, the arm will unsuccessfully attempt to hook the cylinder on the conveyor line, dropping it to the concrete floor. The approach is based on the use of the Hough transform for circle detection. A camera is mounted in a rotational orientation cradle and the different camera positions result in images in which the hole is seen as an ellipse that evolves to a circle as the correct angle is reached. The paper then discusses the effect of implementing circle detection on ellipses, and takes advantage of the count in the Hough parameter space that indicates the correct position. The approach has shown to be very efficient under the restrictions of positioning the cylinder in less than 35 seconds as well as achieving orientation errors less than +/- 5°.

## 1 Introduction and Motivation

In even the most precise automated assembly lines, there are times when moving objects or components are slightly out of alignment and attempts to continue production result in an arrest of the system. PAL Manufacturing (a division of Princess Auto Limited) uses an automated line to produce hydraulic cylinders for various industries. Prior to being hooked on a conveyer by a robotic arm for painting, each cylinder is placed on a stamping station, where the date and serial number is imprinted into the cylinder. Presently, the cylinder always reaches this station out of its proper orientation for stamping and pick-up, requiring shop floor personnel to manually rotate it. It is proposed that an automated computer vision system can be implemented for PAL Manufacturing in order to properly orient the cylinders without human intervention, thus reducing the time for cylinder production.

This paper describes the computer vision aspects of this project that is under development at the Department of Electrical and Computer Engineering, University of Manitoba. The solution is based on the use of the Hough transform for circle detection. Albeit most of the images taken from the cylinder at erroneous positions yield ellipses, it is shown that the maximum count on the accumulator cell for circle detection peaks at the right position which can act as a control signal indicating the correct orientation of the cylinder.

## 2 Description of the Computer Vision System

The system consists of a Rotational Orientation Cradle (ROC) – a mechanical apparatus (upon which a camera will be mounted) – that will physically seize and adjust the cylinder. Figure 1 shows the ROC already built for this project.

**Fig. 1.** Rotational orientation cradle. Cylinder can be seen on the left side.

Before stamping, each cylinder has a clevis welded on one end by a robotic welding machine; the cylinder is later hung onto the conveyor of thin-lined steel hooks by the hole(s) in this clevis. The robotic arm that will pick up the cylinders is programmed to assume the cylinder's clevis hole is perpendicular to the horizontal base of the stamping station; if the cylinder is not in this orientation and the process is allowed to continue, the arm will unsuccessfully attempt to hook the cylinder on the conveyor line, dropping it to the concrete floor. A picture of two types of cylinders to be analyzed is shown in Figure 2.

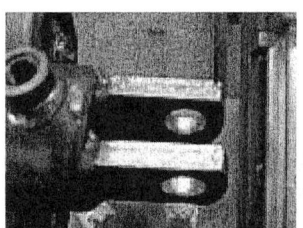

**Fig. 2.** Two types of cylinder clevises, both at incorrect positions

As the camera rotates around the cylinder (as instructed by a microcontroller), the system will have to distinguish between the orifice elliptical shape when viewed from an incorrect perspective, and its perfectly circular shape when viewed directly from the vertical. An example is illustrated in Figure 3.

When the correct orientation is found, the system will signal the microcontroller to halt rotation. The controller will then activate the ROC's pneumatic clamp, securing the cylinder in place (which is confirmed by a "clamp closed" limit switch), and then rotate the gripper and cylinder back to the correct vertical orientation. After the cylinder is stamped, the clamp will be released and the entire apparatus will retract from the cylinder to allow pick-up and hooking by the robotic arm.

The main task of determining the lateral position of the cylinder will be accomplished through the use of an infrared limit switch mounted on the ROC's gripper, triggered by the edge of the cylinder as the gripper moves towards it. The microcontroller will be pre-programmed with the relative distances of the holes from the edge of the clevis holes for each type of cylinder. This will give us the information of the location of the centre of the circle as well as one coordinate of the ellipse in the digital images.

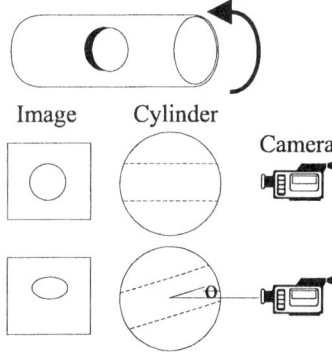

**Fig. 3.** The different shapes an orifice in a cylinder can take on the image

Despite the complexity of the system, its actual specifications boil down to the two major features summarized in Table 1. However, these requirements are deceptively simple, as their satisfaction involves applying constraints on all aspects of the system. For instance, the first time-based requirement includes the time elapsed for the motors to move laterally into position and rotate around the cylinder, the image transfer time and subsequent computation and decision time, and finally, the time taken to seize and rotate the cylinder. The rationale behind the second requirement (which will be measured manually) is a matter of physical necessity: if the system does not rotate the cylinder clevis into a vertical position (within 5 degrees), it cannot be hung on the conveyor hook.

**Table 1.** Orientation System Specifications

| Feature | Value or Range |
|---|---|
| Completion time per cylinder | **< 35 seconds** |
| Correct vertical orientation | **+/- 5°** |

## 3 The Use of Circle Detection on Ellipses

In order to understand what results can be obtained using the Hough transform for circle detection when an image consist of an ellipse, we must first ask what type of circles can be drawn that touches a single point in the ellipse.

### 3.1 Formation of an Ellipse Based on Circles

In 1797, Mascheroni proved that every geometric construction can be done with a movable compass alone. Mascheroni's results were published before by Mohr in 1672, and this geometric construction technique is now known as Mohr-Mascheroni's theorem. A very short proof can be found in [1].

In particular, an ellipse can be drawn using eight circles. The circles together with the ellipse formed are shown in Figure 4. Circle G in the figure is the one that touches the ellipse at a single point and its centre is always located at circle B (indicated by the arrow). As this centre moves along B, circle G changes its radius. The drawing on the right of this figure shows two different circles drawn in this way. There are two points in each left and right side of the ellipse that have the same circle with same radius and centre of location. This circle centre is the intersection of circle B with the major axis of the ellipse.

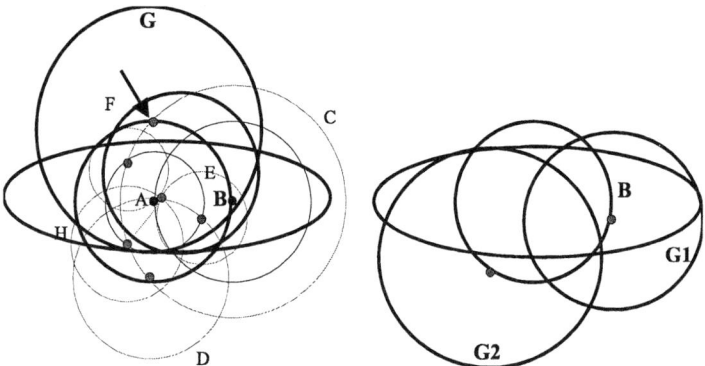

**Fig. 4.** Construction of an ellipse based on eight circles. The arrow indicates the centre of circle G. On the right, the two points indicate the centers of circles G2 and G1.

### 3.2 The Hough Transform

The Hough transform is used to detect pixels in a binary image that correspond to a curve of specified shape. Different type of shapes can be defined such as straight lines, circles, parabolas, hyperbolas or any other type of function of several parameters $f(x,b)$ where $b$ is the set of unknown parameters. For example, for a straight line $f(x_i, b) = ax_i + b$ in a binary image, there are two unknown parameters $b = \{a,b\}$. The algorithm consists of evaluating every pixel $(x_i,y_i)$ in the binary image that satisfy the equation $b = -ax_i + y_i$ for varying values of $a$ and $b$ and counting the points that intercept in this new parameter space [2]. The parameter space defined by $\{a,b\}$ is also referred to as the accumulator and for the case of a circle it has three parameters $\{h,k,a\}$ where $h$ and $k$ are the centre coordinates of the circle and $a$ its radius; and for the ellipse the parameter space consist of $\{h,k,a,b\}$ where as before, $h$ and $k$ are the centre coordinates for the ellipse case and $2a$, and $2b$ are the length of the horizontal axis and the length of the vertical axis respectively as shown in Figure 5. In our case, as depicted in Figure 5, the horizontal axis is always the major axis. The extra parameter for the ellipse and corresponding extra computations can be seen as a starting motivation towards favoring the choice of circle detection for computing the correct orientation of the cylinder.

Nevertheless, circle detection using the Hough transform takes many computations and different approaches have been suggested to improve the computational required time [3, 4]. The algorithm can also be generalized in order to detect non-analytic objects [5].

$$(x-h)^2 + (y-k)^2 = a^2 \qquad \frac{(x-h)^2}{a^2} + \frac{(y-k)^2}{b^2} = 1$$

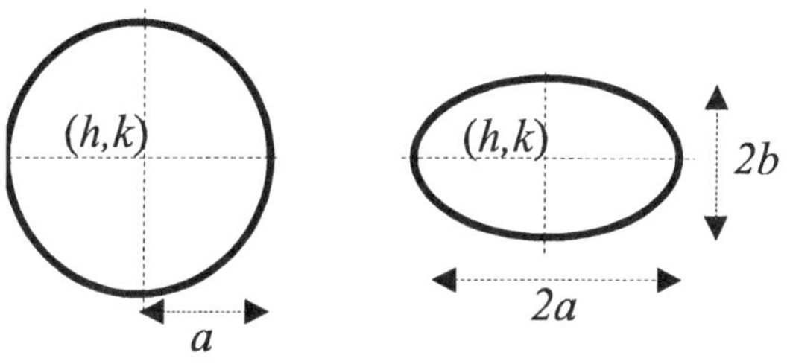

**Fig. 5.** Circle and ellipse and their equations

### 3.3 Detecting Circles in Ellipsoidal Traces

For a small piece of an arch in the ellipse, those pixels will contribute to counts in the accumulator of the Hough transform for circle detection at parameters equal to the radius of G (see Fig. 4) and the centre will be located along one of the arches of circle B contained within the ellipse. The normal of these pixels go from that point of the ellipse towards the point $\{h,k\}$ of G.

A series of ellipses were drawn with major axis equal to the diameter of a circle. All these shapes are depicted in Fig. 6. The Hough transform for circle detection was implemented and used in each of these shapes.

Figure 7 (a) shows the image of an ellipse that was used with the Hough circle detection algorithm. Parts (b) to (c) show the parameter space for three different radii values. The radius in (d) is greater than (c) which is greater than in (b). Because of the digitized curves, the count in the parameter space is the maximum for the biggest radius. That is, as a bigger circle is being fit in the ellipse, the Hough transform uses more pixels along the circle arch that touches the arch of the ellipse. Additionally, we can expect that as the ellipse in (a) approaches the circular shape, this count will increase and it will be maximum when it becomes a circle. We can also verify that the maximum count follows the circle centres along the arch in circle B in Figure 4.

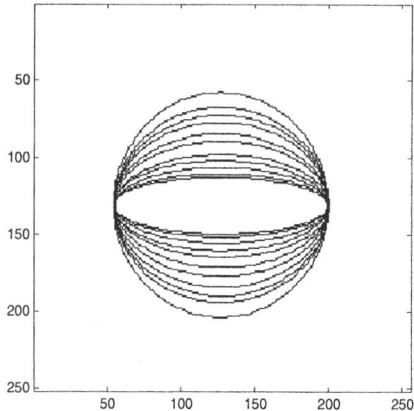

**Fig. 6.** Several ellipses contained in a circle

## 4 Results Obtained Using a Real Cylinder

In terms of the angle orientation accuracy needed for this project, the maximum accumulator count of the Hough transform occurs when the analyzed image is the one that has the cylinder at the correct position independently of any other variables.

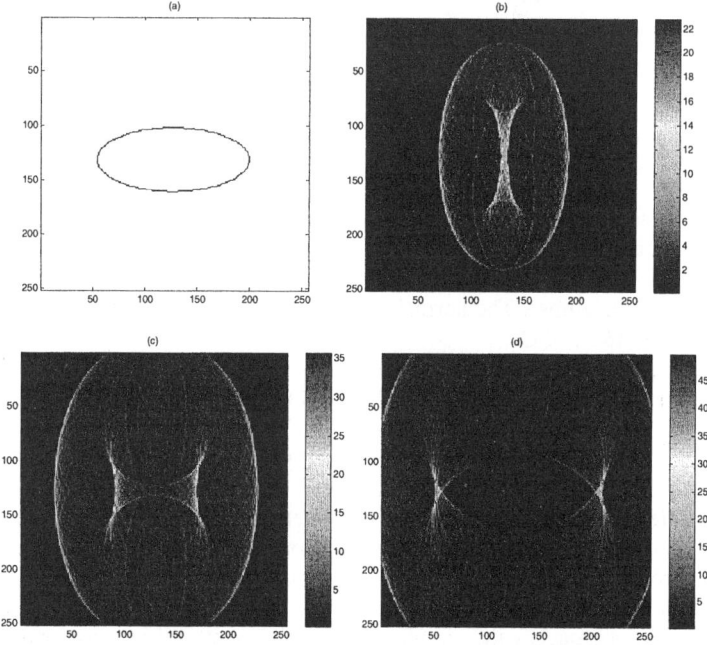

**Fig. 7.** (a) Image of ellipse used in this example. (b-d) Hough parameter space for three different increasing radii.

Therefore, the angle accuracy is just restricted to the task completion time. In the worst case scenario, the cylinder has to rotate 90°. If ±f is the restriction, no less than 90/f images must be analyzed. Thus, a time completion task can be specified by $t = 90(t_{cv} + t_r)/f$, where $t_{cv}$ is the time required by the proposed algorithm to analyzed each image and $t_r$ is the time taken to seize and rotate the cylinder as well as the other tasks not related to $t_{cv}$ as indicated in section 2.

A series of 16 images were taken with a cylinder at different orientations as shown in Figure 8. In this figure, the images correspond to image frames 4, 12 and 16 respectively. As can be seen, illumination of the scene is a factor that can help because reflections can help on the threshold operation performed prior to the Hough transform. The total number of pixels to be evaluated then reduces by selecting a higher threshold that will mostly select pixels around the orifice.

The Hough transform using circle detection was used in each of the image frames and the maximum count in the accumulator was computed and stored. Figure 9 shows the values obtained. Note how the plot peaks at image frame 12 which is the image of the cylinder at the correct orientation.

**Fig. 8.** Three different image frames showing the cylinder at different position

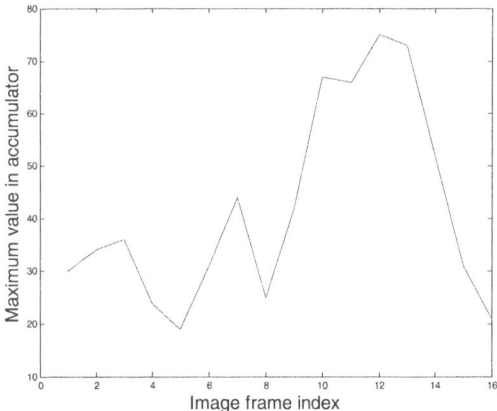

**Fig. 9.** Three different image frames showing the cylinder at different position

## 5 Conclusions

The use of the maximum values of the accumulator calculated using the Hough transform for circle detection in the type of problem discussed in this paper can be the control signal that indicates the correct position of the hydraulic cylinders under consideration. The robustness of the Hough transform is necessary in order to account for noise and external objects in the images. The precision of the correct orientation is limited only by the maximum time allowed for completion of the task. In this particular example, because the centre location of the circle imaged by the clevis at the correct orientation is known, the parameter space is reduced only to searches for different radii only. This has helped on the initial tests performed and the time constraints will be met for this project.

## References

1. Hugerbuhler, N.: A Short Elementary Proof of the Mohr-Mascheroni Theorem. American Mathematical Monthly Vol. 101, No. 8, (1994), 784—787
2. Gonzales R. C., and Woods R. E..: Digital Image Processing, Second Edition, Prentice Hall, New Jersey, (2002)
3. Nakanishi M., and Ogura T.: Real-time Line Extraction Using a Highly Parallel Hough Transform Board, IEEE Proceedings International Conference on Image Processing, Santa Barbara CA, USA, (1997).
4. Palmer P., Kittler J., and Petrou M.: Methods for Improving Line Parameter Accuracy in a Hough Transform Algorithm, IEE Colloquium on Hough Transforms, London UK, (1993)
5. Pui-Kin S., and Wan-Chi S., Object Recognition with a 2-D Hough Domain, IEEE International Symposium on Circuits and Systems, London UK, (1994)

# Lip Reading Based on Sampled Active Contour Model

Takeshi Saitoh and Ryosuke Konishi

Dept. of Electrical and Electronic Engineering, Tottori University,
4-101 Koyama, Tottori 680-8552, Japan
saitoh@ele.tottori-u.ac.jp

**Abstract.** This paper describes a model-based method for detecting lip region from image sequences. Our approach is by Sampled Active Contour Model (S-ACM). The original S-ACM has the problem which can't expand. To overcome this problem, we propose the elastic S-ACM. Moreover, based on the extracted lip contour, the effective delta radius features are fed to the word HMM. We recorded ten words that uses for the wheelchair control, and obtained a recognition rate of 89% with twelve features.

## 1 Introduction

The voice is the most natural communication way for man. Many studies have been done about voice recognition. However, the recognition rate decrease by a surrounding noise such as other's sound or voice. Therefore, the limitation such as putting the microphone near mouth is need. On the other hand, the image information of the lip shape is not influenced by the surrounding noise[1].

It is important to extract the efficient feature for lip reading. Basically, there are roughly two method to extract visual feature of the lip from image sequences, the image-based and the model-based method[2,3]. In this paper, we employ the latter method. Sampled Active Contour Model (called S-ACM) which is a dynamic power model[4] is applied to detect lip contour. However, this method has the problem which can't expand. This paper describes the modification for S-ACM, and propose an automatic lip detection method using S-ACM. Moreover, we define the effective feature to the lip reading. The lip reading that uses the word for the wheelchair control is tried in this paper.

This paper is organized as follows. The next section describes about S-ACM method. The automatic lip detection and lip reading method are in Section **3** and Section **4**, respectively. Experimental results are in Section **5**. Conclusion is in Section **6**.

## 2 Sampled Active Contour Model

There is a well-known method called "Snakes" by Kass et al.[5] which defines a contour as an energy minimizing problem. However, it is necessary to solve the minimization problem of each elasticity loop in Snakes, the real-time processing is difficult. On the other hand, Sampled Active Contour Model is proposed by Hashimoto et al.[4] is a method for control each point by local three forces. Sugahara et al.[6] modified S-ACM with adding new force the vibration.

## 2.1 Performance of S-ACM

Here we describe the essence of S-ACM. This is a method to determine a contour of target region based on control points. The characteristics of S-ACM is closed-loop of the polygon composed of contour point which work four forces shown in Figure 1.

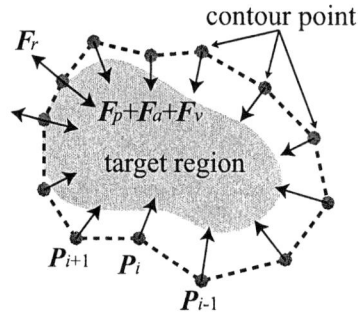

**Fig. 1.** Sampled Active Contour Model

These four force is a pressure $F_p$, attraction $F_a$, vibration $F_v$, and repulsion $F_r$. Pressure $F_p$ shown in Figure 2(a) is a force to work at the bisector direction of two neighboring control points. This force is a constant value. Attraction $F_a$ shown in Figure 2(b) is a force to work in proportion to the distance of two neighboring control points. Vibration $F_v$ shown in Figure 2(c) is a constant value, and works to vertical direction of resultant force $F_p + F_a$. The direction of $F_v$ is reverse in each loop. And, repulsion $F_r$ shown in Figure 2(d) is worked when the control point touches the object boundary, and, as a result, this force works to negative direction of other forces.

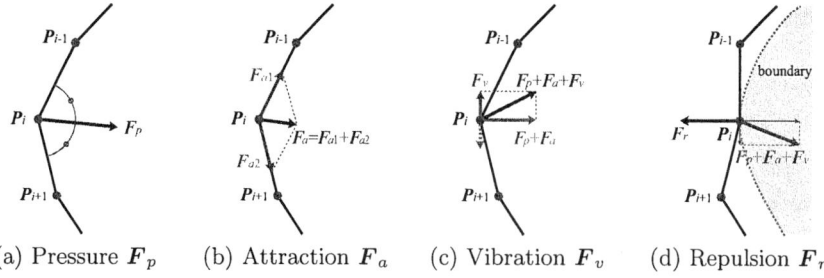

**Fig. 2.** Four forces to each control point

S-ACM is a method for applying to a binary image. This method also can add or delete control point like Snakes.

## 2.2 The Problem of Original S-ACM

The original S-ACM can only shrink or stop. Therefore, an initial control point should give a big one. Moreover, when it doesn't contact the object boundary, it enters into the object region, and the repulsion doesn't work. As the result, the shrinkage proceeds, and the contour becomes small.

Since we apply to the image sequence, a big initial contour is inconvenient. It takes a lot of time until contour point stop when such initial contour is given with each frame.

## 2.3 Proposal Method

Our idea is to consider an elastic S-ACM. The detail is as follows: when a control point is in background shown in Figure 3(a), conventional forces ($F_p$, $F_a$, and $F_v$) are worked. Oppositely, when a control point is in object region shown in Figure 3(b), pressure $F_p$ doesn't work and attraction $F_a$ works to opposite direction. As a result, an inside control point moves outside. By this improvement, it doesn't need to give a big initial contour, and the proceeding time is shortened.

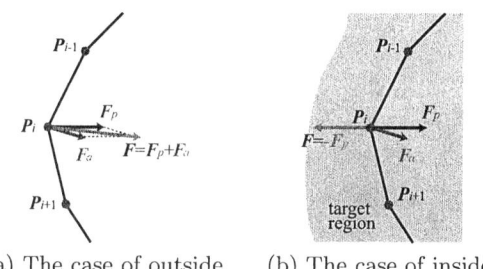

(a) The case of outside    (b) The case of inside

**Fig. 3.** Forces at outside and inside region

## 2.4 Comparison

A sample image of a curve region shown in Figure 4(a) is considered. A given initial contour where a right part of cross the target region is shown in Figure 4(b). Figure 4(c) and Figure 4(d) show the result of the original S-ACM and proposed method, respectively. Figure 4(c) is not satisfactory. This is because the right part of contour point could not move. On the contrary, Figure 4(d) obtained a correct contour.

Next consideration is a lip image shown in Figure 5(a). A given initial contour which is a oval shape is shown in Figure 4(b). Figure 4(c) and Figure 4(d) show the result of the original S-ACM and proposed method respectively. The extracted contour of Figure 4(c) is inside of the lip region. Figure 4(d) is obtained a correct contour.

These results show our method could move elasticity and detect an accurate contour.

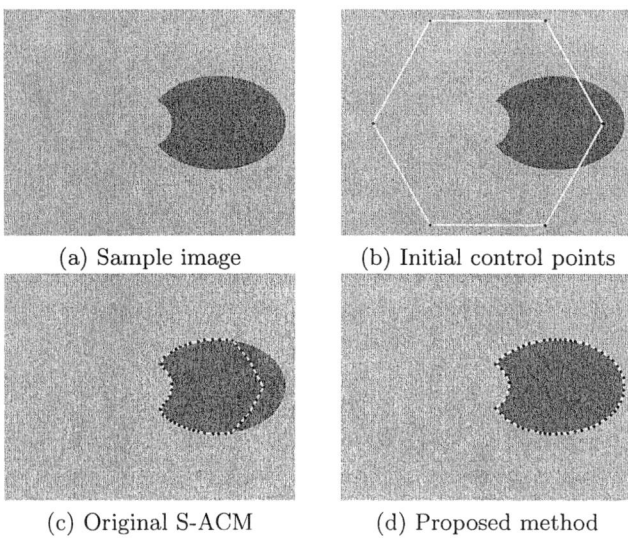

Fig. 4. Extracted results of sample image

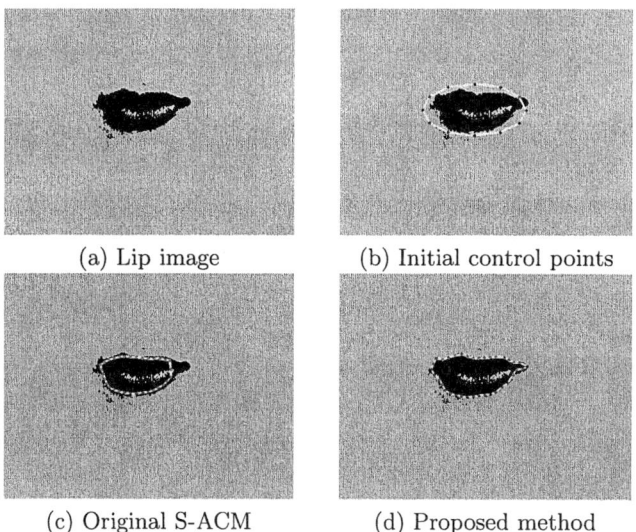

Fig. 5. Extracted results of lip image

## 3 Automatic Lip Detection

Our next problem is to extract a lip region from an image sequence without manually operation. It is convenient that the size and the position of lip are fixed. However, such information is unknown, since these are changeable when the person speaks.

Then, we first try to determine the lip location in the first frame, and detect an approximate box region called the Region Of Interest (ROI). Next, the binalization is applied in ROI. Finally, S-ACM is applied and detect a lip contour. Figure 6 shows the flowchart of the proposed automatic lip detection method. The detail of our method shows as follows.

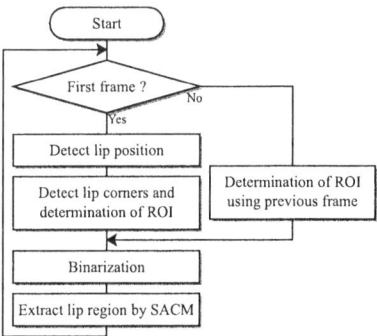

**Fig. 6.** Flowchart of automatic lip detection method

### 3.1 Base Point Detection

At first, we identify the base point from first frame as shown in Figure 7(b). For this task, we convert the original image into the block image to prevent wrong detection such as a pimple, and found most red block as the base point.

### 3.2 Set Up ROI

The top, bottom, left, and right position of lip are detected as ROI. Since S-ACM is a method to apply a binary image, it is desirable to obtain a correct binary image. Then, ROI where it touches the lip is set.

The edge image is obtained by sobel filter, and the lip joint is detected from the maximum edge distribution in the horizontal line as shown in Figure 7(c). After detected lip joint, the edge distribution of a vertical is calculated. Two positions $L'$ and $R'$ in which the distribution value becomes lower than the threshold from the center $C$ for right and left both sides are detected. These positions are related with left terminal point $L$ and right terminal point $R$ respectively. Moreover, from the joint line, the maximum distribution value for upper and lower both sides are detected as top terminal point $T$ and bottom terminal point $B$. These points are shown in Figure 7(d).

### 3.3 Binalization

Binalization is applied to the pixel in ROI. The image converts from RGB color space into xy color space, and the average color in the four corners of ROI (skin

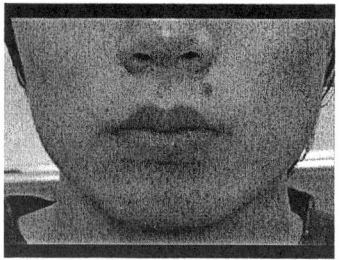
(a) Original image

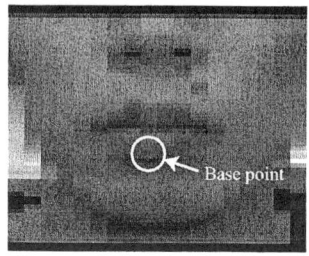
(b) Block image and detected base point

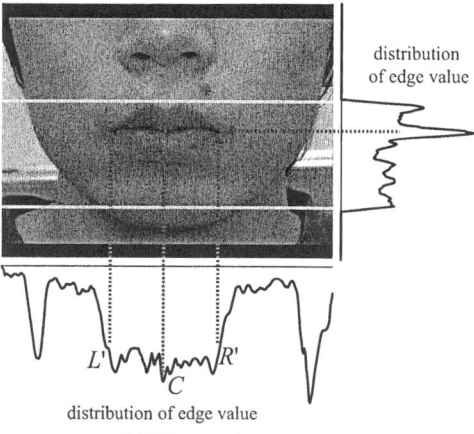
(c) Decide lip position

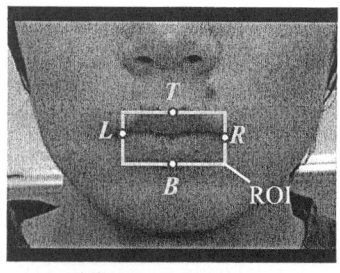
(d) Extracted ROI

(e) Binary image

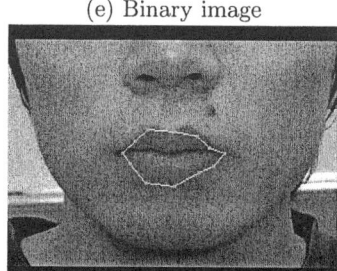

(f) Initial contour     (g) Detected lip region

**Fig. 7.** Lip detection

color) and the center (lip color) is calculated respectively. The pixel in ROI is classified into the lip or the skin which is similar color. Figure 7(e) shows the result of binalization.

### 3.4 Apply S-ACM

An initial contour of the oval shape that inside touches the ROI is set for the first frame. Given the initial contour is shown in Figure 7(f). Then, we apply the S-ACM. The extracted contour is shown in Figure 7(g). Though S-ACM can add or delete control point at any time, in this lip detection, the number of control point is fixed in relation to visual features.

### 3.5 For Other Frame

The initial contour for a frame except the first frame is given based on the extracted contour of previous frame.

## 4 Lip Reading

### 4.1 Detect Speech Period

For detected a lip contour sequence, the speech period is decided. In this paper, we set a condition to close his lip before and after the word utterance. Therefore, the speech period is obtained from observed lip shape.

### 4.2 Visual Features

The distance $r_i$ of control point $P_i$ and lip gravity $G$ is calculated shown in Figure 8. In addition, $\Delta r_i$ is calculated as a time change of $r_i$.

In our lip reading, the number of control point of S-ACM is fixed at twelve. Then, the number of $r_i$ and $\Delta r_i$ is twelve respectively.

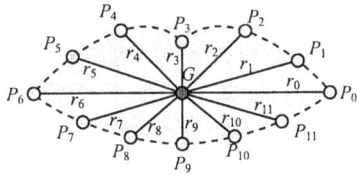

**Fig. 8.** Lip features

### 4.3 Recognition

The clustering by the k-means method is applied to the calculated feature, and these features are converted into the label sequences. Next, these are fed to the left-to-right type word HMM.

## 5 Experiments

Ten Japanese words ("zensin", "koutai", "tomare", "mae", "usiro", "usetu", "sasetu", "migi", "hidari", "hanten") for the wheelchair control were recognized. We recorded 50 times for each word (namely, we recorded 500 image sequences). The image size is 320 × 240 pixel and frame rate is 30 frame/sec. We set the number of cluster as 12, the number of state of HMM as 6, and the extracted control point of S-ACM as 12.

The automatic lip detection method was carried out 500 image sequences. It confirmed that our method obtained good result by observation visually. The average processing time of lip detection was 110 msec. per one frame on a DOS/V PC (CPU:Pentium IV 3.2GHz with 1GB main memory).

The recognition process was carried out with twelve radius features and twelve delta radius features. Out of 50 samples for each word, 40 samples are a training set and the remaining 10 samples are a recognition set. By varying 10 samples, the total number of recognition trials is 50 for each words. The average resulting recognition rates were 81% and 89%, respectively. This result indicates that the delta radius features are more effective for word recognition.

The next experiments were to determine which features among twelve control points are more effective for recognition. This process was carried out for four corner (left, right, top, and bottom) features, upper seven features, lower seven features, and left side seven features. These results are shown in Table 1. It found the most recognition rate was by twelve whole lip shape features.

Table 1. Recognition results

| features (number) | recognition rate [%] | | | | | | | | | | |
|---|---|---|---|---|---|---|---|---|---|---|---|
| | zensin | koutai | tomare | mae | usiro | usetu | sasetu | migi | hidari | hanten | average |
| radius | 90.0 | 90.0 | 90.0 | 76.0 | 72.0 | 64.0 | 86.0 | 86.0 | 78.0 | 82.0 | 81.4 |
| delta radius(12) | 90.0 | 96.0 | 98.0 | 82.0 | 80.0 | 84.0 | 96.0 | 78.0 | 94.0 | 92.0 | 89.0 |
| delta radius(four corner)(4) | 84.0 | 90.0 | 96.0 | 88.0 | 88.0 | 82.0 | 92.0 | 86.0 | 88.0 | 88.0 | 88.2 |
| delta radius(upper side)(7) | 86.0 | 94.0 | 94.0 | 76.0 | 84.0 | 76.0 | 92.0 | 92.0 | 92.0 | 92.0 | 87.8 |
| delta radius(lower side)(7) | 84.0 | 94.0 | 86.0 | 86.0 | 88.0 | 72.0 | 96.0 | 72.0 | 90.0 | 78.0 | 84.6 |
| delta radius(left side)(7) | 86.0 | 86.0 | 92.0 | 78.0 | 76.0 | 76.0 | 98.0 | 84.0 | 88.0 | 98.0 | 86.2 |

## 6 Conclusion

This paper has made some contributions. The first is modified S-ACM. The original S-ACM has the problem which can't expand, then we proposed an elastic S-ACM. The second is that we proposed the automatic extraction of lip region based on S-ACM. Moreover, the effective features were defined, and obtained 89% with twelve delta radius features.

In the future, we want to continue the experiment which the number of words increases.

# References

1. Iain Matthews, Timothy F. Cootes, J. Andrew Bangham, Stephen Cox, and Richard Harvey. Extraction of visual features for lipreading. *IEEE Transactions on Pattern Analysis and Machine Intelligence*, 24(2):198–213, Februnary 2002.
2. Jinyoung Kim, Joohun Lee, and Katsuhiko Shirai. An efficient lip-reading method robust to illumination variations. *IEICE*, E85-A(9):2164–2168, September 2002.
3. Juergen Luettin, Neil A. Thacker, and Steve W. Beet. Visual speech recognition using active shape models and hidden markov models. In *Proc. of ICASSP*, pages 817–820, 1996.
4. Masahiro Hashimoto, Hirotsugu Kinoshita, and Yoshinori Sakai. An object extraction method using sampled active contour model. *IEICE*, J77-D-II(11):2171–2178, 1994. written in Japanese.
5. Michael Kass, Andrew Witkin, and Demetri Terzopoulos. Snakes: Active contour models. *International Journal of Computer Vision*, 1:321–331, 1988.
6. Kazunori Sugahara, Toshimi Shinchi, and Ryosuke Konishi. Active contour model with vibration factor. *IEICE*, J80-D-II(12):3232–3235, 1997. written in Japanese.

# Fast Viseme Recognition for Talking Head Application

Mariusz Leszczynski[1], Władysław Skarbek[1], and Stanisław Badura[1]

Faculty of Electronics and Information Technology,
Warsaw University of Technology
W.Skarbek@ire.pw.edu.pl*

**Abstract.** Real time recognition of visual face appearances (visemes) which correspond to phonemes and their speech contexts is presented. We distinguish six major classes of visemes. Features are extracted in the form of normalized image texture. The normalization procedure uses barycentric coordinates in a mesh of triangles superimposed onto a reference facial image. The mesh itself is defined using a subset of FAP points conforming with MPEG-4 standard. The elaborated classifiers were designed by PCA subspace and LDA methods. It appears that the LDA classifier outperforms subspace technique. It is better than the best subspace PCA – in recognition rate by more than 13% times (97% versus 84%) and it is more than 10 times faster ($0.5ms$ versus $7ms$) and its time is neglected w.r.t. mouth image normalization time ($0.5ms$ versus $5ms$).

## 1 Introduction

This research has been conducted to support animation of human face model integrated with Polish speech generator.

With the increasing power of computer systems with respect of computing and transmission speed the *talking head application* exhibits the greater realism in both speech and dynamic visual face appearance (viseme), as well.

Except the performance of speech generator, the synchronization between the spoken content and facial *visual content,* is of high importance. The visual content should not only provide the time correspondence of face image and sound but also respect the semantic context of the speech, and the internal emotions of the speaker.

One of the important tasks in *talking head system* is the design of a correspondence table between visemes and phonemes (CTVP table). This correspondence is rather a relation of type *one to many* than a function. We can convert this relation to a mapping if we consider a *speech context* for the particular phoneme. In practice, it is enough to take into account three phonemes for such context, the current phoneme, the previous one, and the next one, to get a unique viseme to speech context.

---

* The work presented was developed within VISNET, a European Network of Excellence (http://www.visnet-noe.org), funded under the European Commission IST FP6 programme

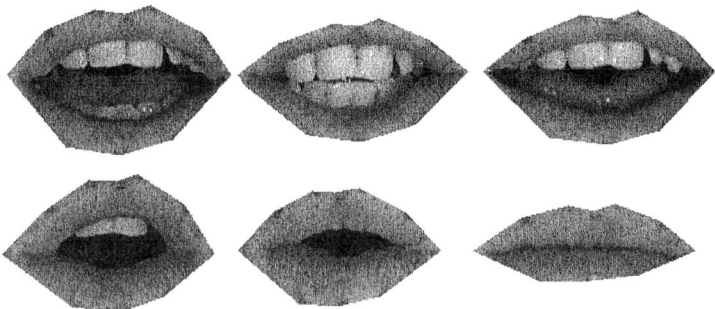

**Fig. 1.** Representative images for six major viseme classes – the 16 minor classes are obtained by discrimination between small, medium, and high degree of mouth opening within the first five major classes

In case of Polish speech patterns (the CORPORA database), the design of *phoneme context to viseme mapping* requires recording of video and audio material for more than 1000 seconds. Therefore we get more than 25000 visemes to be classified and assigned to recognized phonemes context. This cannot be implemented manually. Both, the automatic viseme classifier and phoneme classifier are necessary to complete the design of CTVP table.

For phoneme classifier we have used a speech recognition engine based on HTK toolkit (cf. [8]). As a side effect the speech recognition program produced the phoneme and diphone transcription labelled by time information. Having such timing we could segment the video sequence into phoneme related groups. From each group this video frame was selected for viseme classification which was closest in time to the middle of phoneme time interval, i.e. to the beginning of diphone interval. The recognized viseme class (cf. Fig.1) was joined to the phoneme context list. At the end from each phoneme list the class id was selected using the majority rule.

This work explains how the viseme classifier had been designed to support the creation of CTVP table. To this goal the performance of 80% could be sufficient. However, we are going to use our viseme classifier to animate the human head model on the basis of live video. Therefore the real time and the high performance of the classifier are the main objectives of our research.

Beside this introduction, the paper consists of five sections. In the section 2, image normalization by piecewise affine mapping is described. The section 3 includes the presentation of the subspace classifier using PCA approach. In the section 4 we discuss our implementation of LDA classifier based on two singular subspaces method. The last section shows comparative results for the two classifiers analyzed.

## 2  Image Normalization by Piecewise Affine Mapping

The realistic visual speech can be achieved by integrating the person specific face model with mouth model optionally augmented with the model of chin and cheeks. Using a triangle mesh (cf. Fig.2), we can cover those speech sensitive areas and try to get the model for at least two goals: viseme classification and mouth animation. In mesh approach we deal with variations of the mesh shape

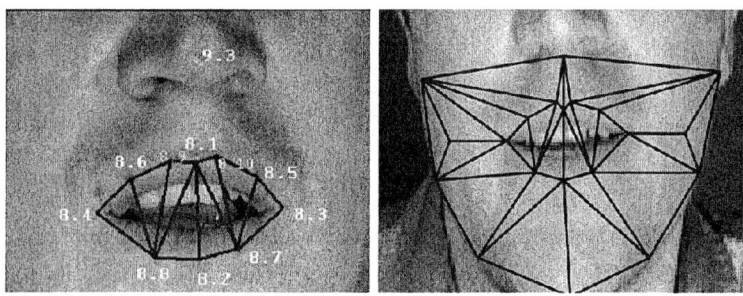

**Fig. 2.** Triangle mesh for mouth (left) and its neighbourhood (right) – on the left identifiers of MPEG-4 FAP points are depicted

and of the mesh texture (*appearance*). In order to make comparable two meshes we have to normalize them with respect to a reference mesh.

We perform the nonlinear normalization of the mesh by mapping each triangle in the current image onto the corresponding triangle in the reference image. Each local mapping is affine, but globally we obtain the mapping which is piecewise affine.

Let the $i$-th triangle $\Delta_i(P_0, P_1, P_2)$ in the reference mesh $\mathcal{M}$ be mapped by the affine mapping $A_i(P') = B_i P + t_i$ onto the triangle $\Delta'_i(P'_0, P'_1, P'_2)$ in the current mesh $\mathcal{M}'$, where $B_i$ is the square matrix, $t_i$ is the vector, $P \in \Delta_i$, $P' \in \Delta'_i$, $i = 1, \ldots, K$. Then we have the following properties:

1. The piecewise affine mappings $A_1, \ldots, A_K$ are *continuous mappings* of $\mathcal{M}$ onto $\mathcal{M}'$ in geometric space
2. If $P = \alpha_0 P_0 + \alpha_1 P_1 + \alpha_2 P_2$ has the barycentric coordinates $\alpha_0, \alpha_1, \alpha_2$ w.r.t the triangle $\Delta_i(P_0, P_1, P_2)$, then the point $A_i(P) = \alpha_0 P'_0 + \alpha_1 P'_1 + \alpha_2 P'_2$, i.e. it has *the same barycentric coordinates* with respect to the triangle $\Delta'_i(P'_0, P'_1, P'_2)$ :

$$A_i(P) = B_i P + t_i = B_i(\alpha_0 P_0 + \alpha_1 P_1 + \alpha_2 P_2) + (\alpha_0 P_0 + \alpha_1 P_1 + \alpha_2)t$$
$$= \alpha_0(B_i P_0 + t) + \alpha_1(B_i P_1 + t) + \alpha_2(B_i P_2 + t) = \alpha_0 P'_0 + \alpha_1 P'_1 + \alpha_2 P'_2$$

3. If $f' : \Delta'_i(P'_0, P'_1, P'_2) \to \mathcal{C}_{RGB}$ is the texture mapping in the current mesh then the mapping $f : \Delta_i(P_0, P_1, P_2) \to \mathcal{C}_{RGB}$ is defined by the barycentric coordinates for $i = 1, \ldots, K$ as follows:

$$f(P) = f(\alpha_0 P_0 + \alpha_1 P_1 + \alpha_2 P_2) \triangleq f'(\alpha_0 P'_0 + \alpha_1 P'_1 + \alpha_2 P'_2) \quad (1)$$

The above substitution transfers the texture from the current mesh onto the reference mesh with possible deformation of linear segments which intersect at least two triangles in the mesh.

We have used the texture mapping as described in point 3 above and despite the negative conclusion of the property 3 we observe no special visual degradation in the mapped texture on visemes (cf. Fig.3).

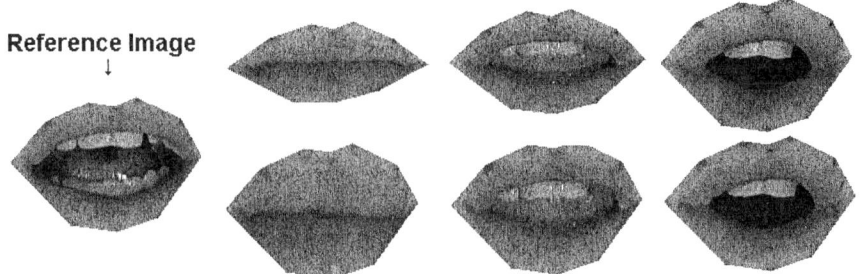

**Fig. 3.** Comparison of original mouth views with the normalized images with respect to the reference mouth (the leftmost image)

## 3  Subspace Method for Mouth Classification

Due to the robust normalization, all mouth classes can be now represented in one texture space of high dimensionality $N \approx 10^3$. Applying the Principal Component Analysis (PCA - cf. [4]) reduces this dimensionality significantly. However, the variability within the class using one PCA subspace for all classes is too high. Therefore we model each class with its own separate PCA subspace. This leads to the known subspace method of pattern recognition (cf. [5]).

In Fig.4 we show the dependence of subspace dimension $K_i(e)$ on percentage of signal energy $e$ represented by PCA subspaces obtained for six mouth appearance classes, $i = 1, \ldots, 6$.

Having PCA eigenvalues $\lambda_i^{(k)}$ for $i = 1, \ldots, 6$, and $k = 1, \ldots, N$, we compute $e_i$ as follows:

$$e_i(K) = \frac{\sum_{k=1}^{K} \lambda_i^{(k)}}{\sum_{k=1}^{N} \lambda_i^{(k)}} \cdot 100\% \qquad (2)$$

The classification of mouth texture $M \in \mathbb{R}^N$ by subspace method requires computing of reconstruction $M_i \in \mathbb{R}^N$ against each subspace $(\overline{M_i}, W_i)$, $\overline{M_i} \in \mathbb{R}^N$, $W_i \in \mathbb{R}^{N \times K_i}$ :

$$M_i = \overline{M_i} + W_i(W_i^t(M - \overline{M_i})), \ i = 1, \ldots, 6 \qquad (3)$$

Having reconstructions $M_i$ of mouth texture $M$, the subspace method selects the mouth class with minimum reconstruction error:

$$i_{opt} = \arg \min_{1 \leq i \leq 6} \|M - M_i\|^2 \qquad (4)$$

The time complexity for the subspace classification for $C$ classes, can be estimated from the above formulas to $O(NK + NC + N^2) = O(N^2)$.

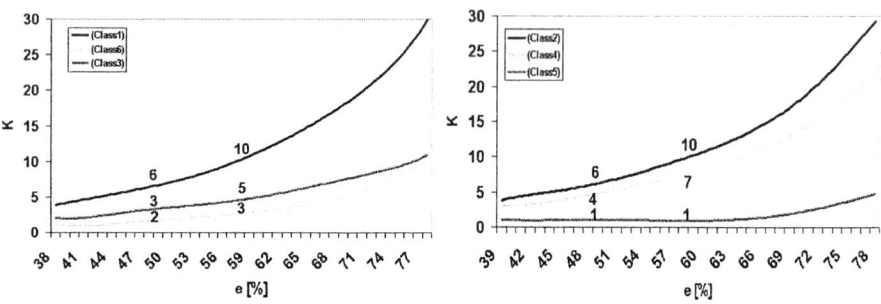

**Fig. 4.** Dependence of subspace dimension $K_i(e)$ on percentage of signal energy $e$ included in the $i$-th subspace, $i = 1, \ldots, 6$

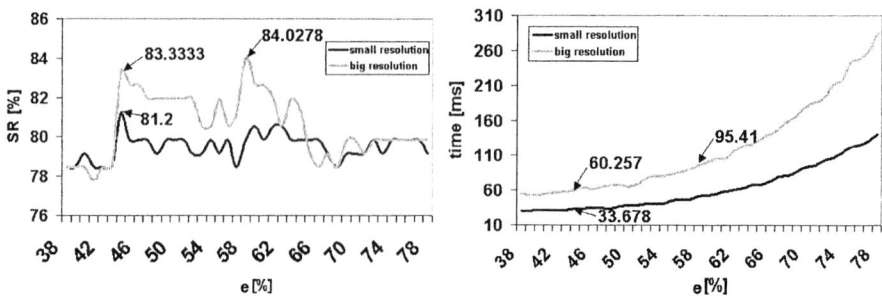

**Fig. 5.** Recognition rate (left graph) and time (right graph) for PCA classifier as a function of energy percentage $e$ included in each class subspace at big and small training images resolution

The subspace method does not require to have all classes modelled in one space. However, having classes in one space means that we avoid $C-1$ additional normalizations which take significant part of the algorithm's time.

## 4  LDA for Mouth Classification

The advantage of having all texture classes in common space $\mathbb{R}^N$ allows us to use the Linear Discriminant Analysis (LDA) to design the extremely fast classifier of linear complexity $O(N)$.

Before we reached LDA feature vector of dimension five, the general Fisher LDA criterium (cf. [2,6,7]) had been used for $K$ dimensional training feature vector $y_i = W^t x_i$, $x_i \in \mathbb{R}^N$, $i = 1, \ldots, L$, $y \in \mathbb{R}^K$, $W \in \mathbb{R}^{N \times K}$ :

$$W_{opt} = \arg\max \frac{\text{between class variance for } \{y_i\}}{\text{within class variance for } \{y_i\}} = \frac{tr(W^t S_b W)}{tr(W^t S_w W)} \quad (5)$$

where $S_b, S_w$ are the between and within class scatter matrices.

The above criterium has points of singularity if $W$ is arbitrary. Therefore Fisher imposed the following constraints on the domain of $W$ :

$$W^t S_w W = I, \ W \perp \ker(S_w) \qquad (6)$$

This leads us to the following steps to obtain the optimal $W$ described in details in [1] with two tuning parameters $q, r$ corresponding to steps where singular value approximation is performed (cf. [3])

1. Class mean shifting of the training sequence: $X = [x_1, \ldots, x_L]$;
2. Grand mean shifting for class means: $M = [m_1, \ldots, m_C]$;
3. Singular Value Approximation for $X$ with subspace dimension equal to $q$:

$$[U_q \Sigma_q] := sva(X, q); \ A_q = U_q \Sigma_q^{-1};$$

4. Whitening of columns in $M$ : $M = A_q^t M$;
5. Singular Value Approximation for $M$ with subspace dimension equal to $r$:

$$V_r := sva(M, q); \ W = A_q V_r;$$

6. Return W;

Fig.6 shows the expected behavior of recognition rate versus tuning parameters. The vector LDA features with maximum possible value $r = C - 1 = 5$ gives the best results. The LDA feature $y = W^t x$ for the texture vector $x$ is classified by the distance to LDA features $y_i = W^t x_i$ representing the mouth appearance classes, $i = 1, \ldots, 6$ :

$$i_{opt} = \arg \min_{1 \leq i \leq 6} \|y - y_i\|^2 \qquad (7)$$

## 5 Experimental Results

For the training of models for feature extraction 497 mouth image were selected with unbalanced distribution in the classes what corresponds to the distribution in the whole recorded video sequence:

$$L_1 = 127, \ L_2 = 123, \ L_3 = 42, L_4 = 89, L_5 = 37, \ L_6 = 79$$

For the testing stage, 152 frames were selected independently of training frames.

Dimensions $K_i$ of PCA subspaces were established using a common measure $e$ (cf. (2)):

$$e = e_i(K_i), \ i = 1, \ldots, 6$$

which specifies what fraction of signal energy (energy cover) included in the training set can be attributed to the given subspace. The Fig.5 (the left graph) shows how the recognition rate depends on this measure. The performance graphs show that the best results are obtained for high resolution training and testing frames.

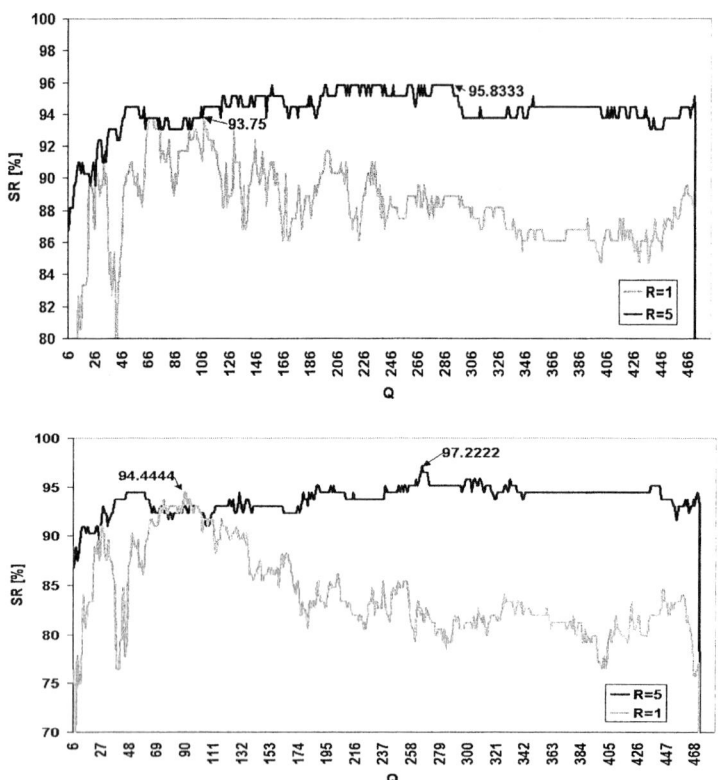

**Fig. 6.** Recognition rate versus LDA tuning parameter $q$ and $r = 1, 5$ : all elements (upper graph) and subsampled (lower graph) of texture vector are considered

However, the best result of 84% requires about three times more time for the recognition than slightly worse result (83.3%) at about 20% less of energy cover which also enables the real time recognition for video with $25 fps$. The time performance is referred to our algorithm implementation on PC Pentium IV, 3.2GHz.

For LDA, the best result (97.2% – cf. Fig.6) is achieved for lower resolution image with subsequent subsampling of texture vector. Since in case of LDA the extraction time is independent of $q$ we accept higher values of $q$ if the recognition rate is even slightly lower for low values of $q$.

It appears that mouth images which were wrongly classified are only from the class of slightly opened mouth with visible upper teeth, without visible tongue. They were confused with opened mouth, visible upper teeth and visible tongue. However, by eye view (the important measure in talking head application) the difference between such two images is not annoying while watching the mouth animation.

## 6 Conclusion

Real time recognition of visemes which correspond to phonemes and their speech contexts is presented. The piecewise affine mapping allowed us to define the texture vector indexed by barycentric coordinates. It appears that the classifier outperforms the subspace technique. It is better than the best subspace PCA – in recognition rate by more than 13% times (97% versus 84%) and it is more than 10 times faster ($0.5ms$ versus $7ms$) and its time is neglected w.r.t. mouth image normalization time ($0.5ms$ versus $5ms$). Moreover, LDA is better than PCA for each possible feature vector dimension $r = 1, \ldots, 5$.

Our recent experiments conducted on bigger testing database confirm superiority of LDA over PCA.

## References

1. Bober M., Kucharski K., and Skarbek W., Face Recognition by Fisher and Scatter Linear Discriminant Analysis, in Computer Analysis of Images and Patterns, eds. Petkov N., Westenberg M., Springer LNCS 2756, 638:645, 2003
2. Fukunaga K., Introduction to statistical pattern recognition (2nd ed). Academic Press, Boston, 1990
3. Golub G., Van Loan C., Matrix Computations. Baltimore: Johns Hopkins University Press, 1996
4. Jolliffe I.T., Principal Component Analysis. Springer, New York, 2002
5. Oja E., Subspace Methods of Pattern Recognition, Research Studies Press, England, 1983
6. Ripley B.D., Pattern Recognition and Neural Networks. Cambridge University Press, 1996
7. Swets D.L., Weng J., Using Discriminant Eigenfeatures for Image Retrieval, IEEE Trans. on PAMI, 18(8):831-837, August 1996
8. The Hidden Markov Model Toolkit (HTK) http://htk.eng.cam.ac.uk

# Image Analysis by Discrete Orthogonal Hahn Moments*

Jian Zhou[1], Huazhong Shu[1], Hongqing Zhu[1],
Christine Toumoulin[2], and Limin Luo[1]

[1] Lab of Image Science and Technology,
Department of Biological Science and Medical Engineering, Southeast University,
210096 Nanjing, China
zjseu@hotmail.com, {shu.list, hqzhu, luo.list}@seu.edu.cn
[2] Laboratoire Traitement du Signal et de l'Image,
INSERM - Université de Rennes 1, Campus de Beaulieu,
35042 Rennes Cedex, France
christine.toumoulin@univ-rennes1.fr

**Abstract.** Orthogonal moments are recognized as useful tools for object representation and image analysis. It has been shown that the recently developed discrete orthogonal moments have better performance than the conventional continuous orthogonal moments. In this paper, a new set of discrete orthogonal polynomials, namely Hahn polynomials, are introduced. The related Hahn moment functions defined on this orthogonal basis set are investigated and applied to image reconstruction. In experiments, the Hahn moments are compared with the other two discrete orthogonal moments: Chebyshev and Krawtchouk moments. The simulation results show that the Hahn moment-based reconstruction method is superior to the other two discrete orthogonal moment-based methods.

## 1 Introduction

Moments and functions of moments have been widely used in pattern recognition [1],[2], image analysis [3], [4], [5], object representation [6], edge detection [7], [8] and texture analysis [9]. Examples of moment-based feature descriptors include the geometric moments, rotational moments, orthogonal moments and complex moments.

Orthogonal moments defined in terms of a set of orthogonal basis are often preferred due greatly to its ability to represent images with the minimum amount of information redundancy. Moment-based image reconstruction was pioneered by Teague who noted that image can be reconstructed from a set of orthogonal moments [3]. Since then, successive studies on orthogonal moments such as Legendre moment and Zenike moments for image reconstruction have

---

* This work was supported by the National Basic Research Program of China under grant No. 2003CB716102 and the National Natural Science Foundation of China under grant No. 60272045.

been extensively addressed in [4] and [5]. However, these moments usually involve several major problems such as the numerical approximation of continuous integrals, coordinate space transformation, high computational costs and etc.

Recently, a set of discrete orthogonal moment functions based on discrete orthogonal polynomials, Chebyshev polynomials [10] and Krawtchouk polynomials [11] have been successfully introduced as alternatives to continuous orthogonal moments. The discrete orthogonal moments hold most of useful features embedded in the continuous orthogonal moments. Moreover, the implementation of discrete orthogonal moments does not require any numerical approximation since the basis set is orthogonal in the discrete domain of image coordinate space. Therefore, the accuracy of image reconstruction can be expectably better than the conventional continuous orthogonal moments.

In this paper, we will introduce a new set of discrete orthogonal moment functions which are characterized with the discrete orthogonal Hahn polynomials [12]. The resultant Hahn moment has most similar features to the Chebyshev and Krawtchouk moments, but it may outperform both the Chebyshev and Krawtchouk moments. The rest of paper is organized as follows: In Sect. 2, we introduce Hahn polynomials and the related Hahn moments, then briefly describe the computational aspects of the Hahn moments. In Sect. 3 we give out the experimental results. Finally, we conclude the paper.

## 2 Hahn Polynomials and Moments

### 2.1 Hahn Polynomials

For any integer $x \in [0, N-1]$ ($N$ is a given positive integer), Hahn polynomial of order $n$, $n = 0, 1, ..., N-1$, is defined as [12],

$$h_n^{(\mu,\nu)}(x, N) = (N+\nu-1)_n (N-1)_n \\ \times \sum_{k=0}^{n} (-1)^k \frac{(-n)_k (-x)_k (2N+\mu+\nu-n-1)_k}{(N+\nu-1)_k (N-1)_k} \frac{1}{k!}, \quad (1)$$

where $(a)_k = a \cdot (a+1) \cdots (a+k-1) = \frac{\Gamma(a+k)}{\Gamma(a)}$ is the Pochhammer symbol and $\mu, \nu$ ($\mu > -1, \nu > -1$) are adjustable parameters controlling the shape of polynomials. The discrete Hahn polynomials satisfy the following orthogonal condition:

$$\sum_{x=0}^{N-1} \rho(x) h_m^{(\mu,\nu)}(x, N) h_n^{(\mu,\nu)}(x, N) = d_n^2 \delta_{mn}, \quad 0 \le m, n \le N-1, \quad (2)$$

where $\delta_{mn}$ denotes the Dirac function, $\rho(x)$ is so-called weighting function which is given by

$$\rho(x) = \frac{1}{\Gamma(x+1)\Gamma(x+\mu+1)\Gamma(N+\nu-x)\Gamma(N-n-x)} \quad (3)$$

and the square norm $d_n^2$ has the following expression

$$d_n^2 = \frac{\Gamma(2N+\mu+\nu-n)}{(2N+\mu+\nu-2n-1)\Gamma(N+\mu+\nu-n)} \times \frac{1}{\Gamma(N+\mu-n)\Gamma(N+\nu-n)\Gamma(n+1)\Gamma(N-n)}. \quad (4)$$

To avoid numerical fluctuations in moment computation, we usually scale the Hahn polynomials by utilizing the square norm and the weighting function, i.e.,

$$\tilde{h}_n^{(\mu,\nu)}(x,N) = h_n^{(\mu,\nu)}(x,N)\sqrt{\frac{\rho(x)}{d_n^2}}, \quad n=0,1,...,N-1. \quad (5)$$

Therefore, the orthogonal property of normalized Hahn polynomials can be described as

$$\sum_{x=0}^{N-1} \tilde{h}_m^{(\mu,\nu)}(x,N)\tilde{h}_n^{(\mu,\nu)}(x,N) = \delta_{mn}, \quad 0 \le m,n \le N-1. \quad (6)$$

### 2.2 Hahn Moments of Image

Given a digitalized image $f(x,y)$ with size $N \times N$, the $(m+n)$th order of Hahn moment of image is

$$H_{mn} = \sum_{x=0}^{N-1}\sum_{y=0}^{N-1} f(x,y)\tilde{h}_m^{(\mu,\nu)}(x,N)\tilde{h}_n^{(\mu,\nu)}(y,N), \quad m,n=0,1,...,N-1. \quad (7)$$

Using (6), Eq.(7) leads to the following inverse moment transform

$$f(x,y) = \sum_{m=0}^{N-1}\sum_{n=0}^{N-1} H_{mn}\tilde{h}_m^{(\mu,\nu)}(x,N)\tilde{h}_n^{(\mu,\nu)}(y,N). \quad (8)$$

It indicates that the image can be completely reconstructed by calculating its discrete orthogonal moments up to order $2N-2$. This property makes the discrete orthogonal moments superior to the conventional continuous orthogonal moments. If moments are limited to an order $M$, we can approximate $f$ by $\hat{f}$

$$\hat{f}(x,y) = \sum_{m=0}^{M}\sum_{n=0}^{M} H_{m-n,n}\tilde{h}_{m-n}^{(\mu,\nu)}(x,N)\tilde{h}_n^{(\mu,\nu)}(y,N), \quad x,y=0,1,...,N-1. \quad (9)$$

### 2.3 Computational Aspects

Using (1) and (5), the zero-order and first-order normalized Hahn polynomials can be easily calculated, i.e.,

$$\tilde{h}_0^{(\mu,\nu)}(x,N) = \sqrt{\frac{\rho(x)}{d_0^2}}, \quad (10)$$

$$\tilde{h}_1^{(\mu,\nu)}(x,N) = \left\{(N+\nu-1)(N-1) - (2N+\mu+\nu-2)x\right\}\sqrt{\frac{\rho(x)}{d_1^2}}. \quad (11)$$

Higher orders polynomials can be deduced from the following recursive relations,

$$A\tilde{h}_n^{(\mu,\nu)}(x,N) = B\sqrt{\frac{d_{n-1}^2}{d_n^2}}\,\tilde{h}_{n-1}^{(\mu,\nu)}(x,N) + C\sqrt{\frac{d_{n-2}^2}{d_n^2}}\,\tilde{h}_{n-2}^{(\mu,\nu)}(x,N),$$
$$n = 2, 3, ..., N-1, \quad (12)$$

where

$$A = -\frac{n(2N+\mu+\nu-n)}{(2N+\mu+\nu-2n+1)(2N+\mu+\nu-2n)}, \quad (13)$$

$$B = x - \frac{2(N-1)+\nu-\mu}{4} - \frac{(\mu^2-\nu^2)(2N+\mu+\nu)}{4(2N+\mu+\nu-2n+2)(2N+\mu+\nu-2n)}, \quad (14)$$

$$C = \frac{(N-n+1)(N-n+\mu+1)(N-n+\nu+1)(N-n+\mu+\nu+1)}{(2N+\mu+\nu-2n+2)(2N+\mu+\nu-2n+1)}. \quad (15)$$

Equations (10)-(15) can be used to efficiently calculate the normalized Hahn moment of any order. Also the weighting function $\rho(x)$ can be solved by using the recursive relation with respect to $x$, i.e.,

$$\rho(x) = \frac{(N-x)(N+\nu-x)}{x(x+\mu)}\rho(x-1), \quad x = 1, 2, ..., N-1, \quad (16)$$

with

$$\rho(0) = \frac{1}{\Gamma(\mu+1)\Gamma(N+\nu)\Gamma(N-n)}. \quad (17)$$

To extract the image moment set $\{H_{mn}\}(0 \leq m, n \leq N-1)$, we can simply use the following matrix notation,

$$\mathbf{H} = \mathbf{H}_x^T\, \mathbf{f}\, \mathbf{H}_y \quad (18)$$

where $\mathbf{f}$ denotes the $N \times N$ image matrix and

$$\mathbf{H}_x = \left[\tilde{h}_0^{(\mu,\nu)}(x,N), \tilde{h}_1^{(\mu,\nu)}(x,N), \cdots, \tilde{h}_{N-1}^{(\mu,\nu)}(x,N)\right]^T,$$

$$\mathbf{H}_y = \left[\tilde{h}_0^{(\mu,\nu)}(y,N), \tilde{h}_1^{(\mu,\nu)}(y,N), \cdots, \tilde{h}_{N-1}^{(\mu,\nu)}(y,N)\right]^T$$

and

$$\tilde{h}_n^{(\mu,\nu)}(x,N) = \left[\tilde{h}_n^{(\mu,\nu)}(0,N), \tilde{h}_n^{(\mu,\nu)}(1,N), \cdots, \tilde{h}_n^{(\mu,\nu)}(N-1,N)\right]^T,$$
$$n = 0, 1, ..., N-1. \quad (19)$$

Similarly, the inverse reconstruction procedure can be represented as

$$\mathbf{f} = \mathbf{H}_x\, \mathbf{H}\, \mathbf{H}_y^T \quad (20)$$

**Fig. 1.** Test images. The left is binary image of Chinese character (size: 48 × 48) and the right is the standard gray image of Lena (size: 96 × 96).

To approximate the image with limited moments of order up to $M$, we need only to compute

$$\widetilde{\mathbf{H}}_x = \left[ \tilde{h}_0^{(\mu,\nu)}(x,N), \tilde{h}_1^{(\mu,\nu)}(x,N), \cdots, \tilde{h}_M^{(\mu,\nu)}(x,N) \right]^T,$$

$$\widetilde{\mathbf{H}}_y = \left[ \tilde{h}_0^{(\mu,\nu)}(y,N), \tilde{h}_1^{(\mu,\nu)}(y,N), \cdots, \tilde{h}_M^{(\mu,\nu)}(y,N) \right]^T$$

and then yield the moment matrix $\mathbf{H}$ using (18). The approximation of image, say $\hat{\mathbf{f}}$, can be solved by the analogous way as shown in (20).

Noticed that the normalized Hahn polynomials are unavoidably related to weighting function $\rho(x)$. For the case of image reconstruction, we usually expect that the Hahn polynomials are symmetric (odd or even) with respect to the center point $(x,y) = (N/2, N/2)$ (suppose $N$ is even). As a result, we require the same values for both $\mu$ and $\nu$. For the sake of simplicity, we choose $\mu = \nu = 0$.

## 3 Experimental Results

To evaluate the performance of image reconstruction using Hahn moments, we have selected several test images including the binary image and the gray level image (shown in Fig. 1). Reconstruction results are compared with those using Chebyshev and Krawtchouk moments. Noisy images are also considered to analyze the noise sensitivity of these different moment-based reconstruction methods.

The mean square error (MSE) is used as the fidelity criteria measuring the resemblance between the reconstructed images and the original one. It can be defined by

$$\text{MSE} = \frac{||\mathbf{f} - \mathbf{f}^*||^2}{||\mathbf{f}^*||^2} \quad (21)$$

where $||\cdot||$ is the standard Euclidean norm and $\mathbf{f}^*$ represents the original image vector and $\mathbf{f}$ the reconstructed image vector.

Fig. 2 shows reconstructions using three different discrete orthogonal moments and the corresponding MSE comparison through the reconstruction procedure is depicted in Fig. 3. We observe that the reconstruction based on Hahn

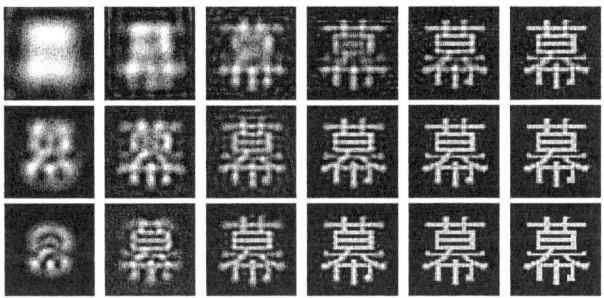

**Fig. 2.** Reconstructions using Chebyshev moments (first row), Krawtchouk moments (second row, $p = 0.5$ [11]) and Hahn moments (third row, $\mu = \nu = 0$). The orders from the left column to the right are 8, 16, 24, 32 and 47 respectively.

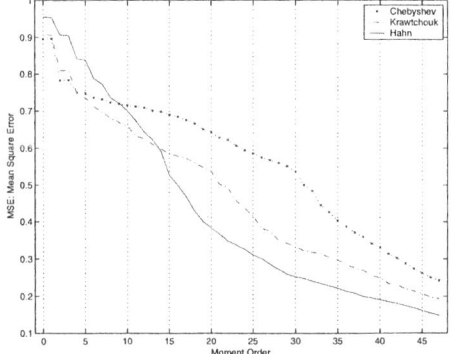

**Fig. 3.** Comparisons of the binary image reconstruction results

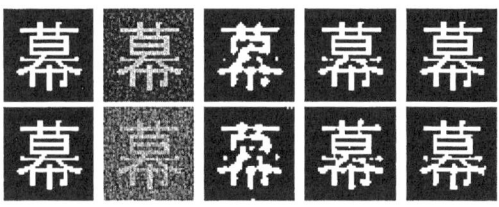

**Fig. 4.** Reconstructions using Gaussian noise-contaminated binary image where the maximum order is all fixed at 30. From left column to right column are: original images, noisy images, and reconstructions using Chebyshev, Krawtchouk ($p = 0.5$ [11]), Hahn moments ($\mu = \nu = 0$) respectively. The noise variance in the first row is 0.1 and the second row 0.3.

moment function may outperform the other two types of discrete orthogonal moments.

In Fig. 4, we test the noise robustness of different orthogonal moments. Gaussian noises with different variances have been added to the original binary image

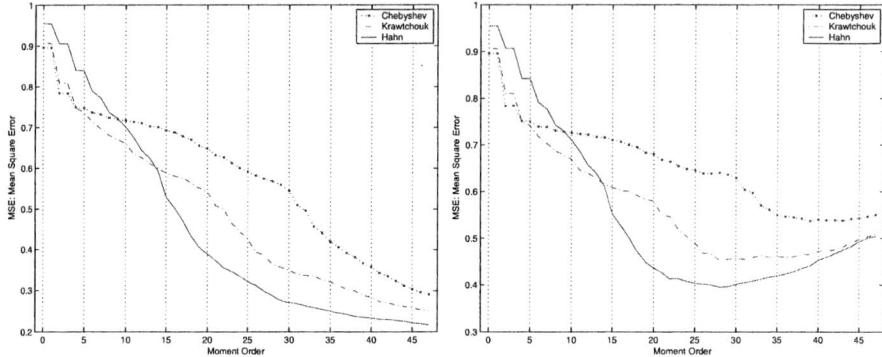

**Fig. 5.** Noisy binary image reconstruction MSE comparison where Gaussian noise with zero mean, variance: the left 0.1 and the right 0.3

(a) MSE: 0.1164   (b) MSE: 0.0830   (c) MSE: 0.0762

**Fig. 6.** Reconstructions of image Lena using (a) Chebyshev moments, (b) Krawtchouk moments ($p = 0.5$ [11]) and (c) Hahn moments ($\mu = \nu = 0$) respectively. Moments up to order 75 are used.

of Chinese character. All of the reconstructions have been normalized to binary values with the same threshold 0.5. The MSE's shown in Fig. 5 again indicate the better performance of Hahn moments even if the image is contaminated with slightly large variance Gaussian noise. In Fig. 5, we can see that the increasing order moment may inversely degrade the image when image signal-to-noise rate (SNR) is relatively low.

Fig. 6 shows the approximation of gray level image. Clearly, the Hahn moment based method can yield slightly lower MSE than the other two orthogonal moments. It may indicate the best performance of discrete orthogonal Hahn moments in image reconstruction.

## 4 Conclusions

In this paper, we have introduced a new set of discrete orthogonal polynomials, namely Hahn polynomials. The corresponding Hahn moment functions defined on this basis set were then investigated and applied to image reconstruction. In experimental studies, we have compared our Hahn moment based reconstruction method with the other two discrete orthogonal moments, Chebyshev and Krawtchok moments based method. The results have shown the best performance of Hahn moment based method.

## References

1. Lo, C. H., Don, H. S.: 3D moment forms: Their construction and application to object identification and positioning, IEEE Trans. Pattern Anal. Mach. Intell. **11** (1989), 1053–1064.
2. Flusser, J., Suk, T.: Pattern Recognition by affine moment invariants, Pattern Recognition, **26** (1993), 167–174.
3. Teague, M. R.: Image analysis via the general theory of moments, J. Opt. Soc. Am. **70** (1980), 920–930.
4. Teh, C. H., Chin, R. T.: On Image analysis by the method of moments, IEEE Trans. Pattern Anal. Mach. Intell. **10** (1988), 485–513.
5. Liao, S. X., Pawlak, M.: On image analysis by moments, IEEE Trans. Pattern Anal. Mach. Intell. **18** (1996), 254–266.
6. Papademetriou, R. C.: Reconstructing with moments, Proceedings of 11th International Conference, Pattern Recognition (1992) 476–480.
7. Luo, L. M., Hamitouche, C., Dilenseger, J. L., Coatrieux, J. L.: A moment-based three-dimensional edge operator, IEEE Trans. Biomed. Eng. **40** (1993), 693–703.
8. Luo, L. M., Xie, X. H., Bao, X. D.: A modified moment-based edge operator for rectangular pixel image, IEEE Trans. Circuits Systems Video Technol. **4** (1994), 552–554.
9. Tuceryan, M.: Moment-based texture segmentation, Pattern Recognition Lett. **15** (1994), 115–123.
10. Mukundan, R., Ong, S. H., Lee, P. A.: Image analysis by Tchebichef moments, IEEE Trans. Imag. Proc. **10(9)** (2001), 1357–1364.
11. Yap, P. T., Paramesran, R., Ong, S. H.: Image analysis by Krawtchouk moments, IEEE Trans. Imag. Proc. **12(11)** (2003), 1367–1377.
12. Nikiforov, A. F., Uvarov, V. B., Special functions of mathematical physics, Birkhäuser, Basel Boston, (1988).

# On Object Classification: Artificial vs. Natural

Minhwan Kim[1], Changmin Park[2], and Kyongmo Koo[1]

[1] Dept. of Computer Engineering, Pusan National Univ., Busan, Korea
{mhkim, kmkoo1}@pusan.ac.kr
[2] School of Multimedia Engineering, Youngsan Univ., Busan, Korea
cmpark@ysu.ac.kr

**Abstract.** Recently semantic classification of images is of great interest for image indexing applications. On the one hand, researchers in the field of content-based image retrieval are interested in object(s) of interest in an image, which is useful for representing the image. In this paper, we present a semantic classification method of the object(s) of interest into artificial/natural classes. We first show that dominant orientation features in Gabor filtering results of artificial objects are very useful for discriminating them from natural objects. Dominant orientations in artificial object images are not confined to horizontal and/or vertical directions, while those in artificial scene images tend to be greatly confined to them. Two classification measures are proposed; the sum of sector power differences in Fourier power spectrum and the energy of edge direction histogram. They show classification accuracy of 85.8% and 84.8% on a test with 2,600 object images, respectively.

## 1 Introduction

In content-based image retrieval (CBIR), images are automatically indexed by summarizing their visual contents, and are searched and matched usually based on low-level features such as color, texture, shape, and spatial layout. Usually a successful indexing of database images through appropriate classification greatly enhances the performance of CBIR systems by filtering out irrelevant images. On the one hand, we know that there is obvious semantic gap between what user-queries represent based on the low-level image features and what the users think. Therefore, many researchers try to develop semantic classification methods that can be effectively used for semantic indexing applications processing very large image databases. There are several semantic classification methods [1-3] that automatically classify scenes into general types such as indoor/outdoor or city/landscape. Especially, Oliva *et al.* [4] tried to classify scenery images into artificial and natural categories by using power spectrum templates.

On the one hand, many researchers believe that the key to effective CBIR performance lies in the ability to access images at the level of objects because users generally want to search for the images containing particular *object(s) of interest*. Thus several methods [5-8] that extract object(s) of interest from object images are studied. An object/non-object image classification method is also studied in [9].

There are few *object classification* methods; even though they believe that object-based systems are more effective in retrieving object images than image-based systems. The *image classification* methods [1-4] cannot be applied to object image classification. Park *et al.* [10] tried to classify object types to improve image retrieval performance, but their method classified unknown objects into only pre-defined specific classes such as cars, tanks, butterflies, etc.

In this paper, we present an object classification method into artificial or natural class. Automatic classification of an object image into such classes is a challenging problem, because it is not easy to find generic properties of each class and discriminating features between two classes. The object image is the image that contains an (artificial/natural) object with black background. The object is automatically extracted by the central object extraction method [8]. We first show that artificial object images tend to have dominant orientation(s) in their Gabor filtering results while natural object images do not. In artificial scene images, dominant orientations are greatly confined to horizontal and/or vertical directions, but those in artificial object images are not. Two classification measures are proposed, which represent existence of the dominant orientations well. One is the sum of sector power differences in Fourier power spectrum where occurrence of dominant orientations appears as well as in Gabor filtering results. The other is the energy of edge direction histogram [1], which has high value for the histograms having peaks but does not depend on location of the peaks.

## 2 Clustering Gabor Filtering Results of Object Images

### 2.1 Gabor Filtering and Gabor Energy Map

Given an object image (Fig. 1(a)), we pass it through a bank of 24 Gabor filters as shown in Fig. 1(b). The filter bank is similarly designed to the Gabor filter dictionary in [11]. The number of scales, the number of orientations, the lower and the upper center frequencies of interest are set by 4, 6, 0.1, and 0.4, respectively. The filtered image through the Gabor filter corresponding to $i$-th scale and $j$-th orientation is denoted by $f_{ij}$. The Gabor energy $e_{ij}$ for $f_{ij}$ is defined as the sum of magnitude squares of all complex pixel values in $f_{ij}$, as shown in Eq. 1. Fig. 1(c) shows a Gabor energy map $M$ for the object image in Fig. 1(a). The value of $M(i,j)$ is the Gabor energy $e_{ij}$.

$$e_{ij} = \sum\sum |f_{ij}(x, y)|^2 \qquad (1)$$

### 2.2 Clustering Gabor Feature Vectors

To find generic properties of artificial and natural object images, a clustering experiment is performed on 1,200 object images (600 artificial object images and 600 natural ones). A Gabor energy map for an object image can be considered as a 24-dimensional feature vector for the image. The K-means technique is used for clustering 1,200 Gabor feature vectors.

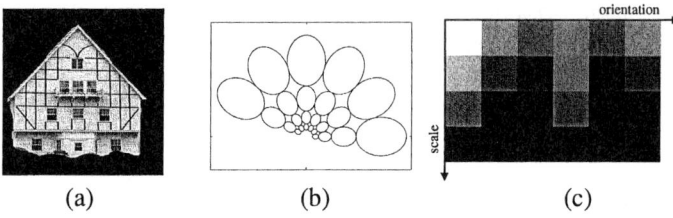

**Fig. 1.** An example of Gabor filtering and Gabor energy map: (a) an object image, (b) a Gabor filter bank designed with parameters, the number of scales = 4, the number of orientations = 6, the lower center frequency of interest = 0.1, and the upper center frequency of interest = 0.4, (c) a Gabor energy map for the object image in (a)

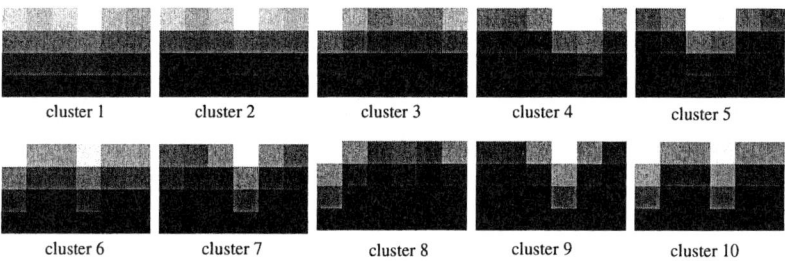

**Fig. 2.** Gabor energy maps for centroid vectors of the clusters that are determined by the K-means clustering algorithm with K = 10

Fig. 2 shows Gabor energy maps (GEMs) for cluster centroid vectors when K = 10 and the classification accuracy of the K-means technique is 82.6%. The first three GEMs represent characteristics of natural object class and the others that of artificial object class. We can see that there are relatively bright column stripe(s) in the GEMs of artificial object class. To show this phenomenon more clearly, Gabor orientation energy $E_j$ is computed by summing the Gabor energies $e_{ij}$ in corresponding orientation, as shown in Eq. 2. Then each Gabor orientation energy is drawn on the corresponding radiant axis of a radar chart as shown in Fig. 3.

$$E_j = \sum_{i=0}^{3} e_{ij} \qquad (2)$$

Fig. 3 shows ten radar charts corresponding to the GEMs in Fig. 2. Note that shapes of the radar charts for artificial object class are sharp-pointed. This shows that artificial object images tend to have dominant orientation(s) in their radar charts. However the dominant orientation(s) of artificial object images is not confined to horizontal and/or vertical directions as shown in Fig. 4, while that of artificial scene images tends to be greatly confined to them [4]. We can also see in Fig. 4 that the radar chart for natural object image (e.g. a pet dog) does not have any dominant orientation(s).

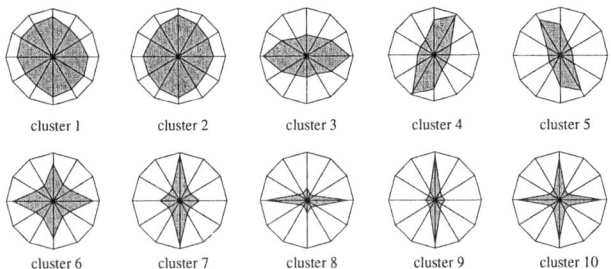

**Fig. 3.** Radar charts of Gabor orientation energy for the ten Gabor energy maps in Fig. 2. Shapes of the first three radar charts of natural object class tend to have round shapes, while those of artificial object class look sharp-pointed.

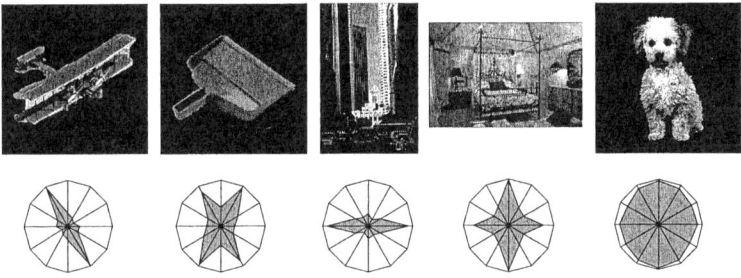

**Fig. 4.** This figure shows examples of several image types and their radar charts. The first two object images of artificial class shows oblique dominant orientations, while the artificial scene images (a city image and a bedroom image) have horizontal and/or vertical dominant orientations in their radar charts. The right-most image of natural object class does not any dominant orientation.

## 3 Classification of Artificial / Natural Object Images

### 3.1 Sum of Sector Power Difference

The dominant orientation discussed in section 2 can be considered as a texture feature of artificial object class images. This texture feature can be analyzed well in Fourier power spectrum by measuring the sector powers.

Let $F(u,v)$ be the discrete Fourier transform of an object image $f(x,y)$. The power spectrum $|F(u,v)|^2$ is defined by the magnitude of the spectral components squared. A sector power is measured by summing the power over range of corresponding sector. In this paper, six sectors are defined over half the power spectrum, as shown in Fig. 5(a). Very low frequency powers are excluded from computing the sector powers in order to make dominant orientations clear. The radar chart of sector power (Fig. 5(b)) for the plane image in Fig 4 is very similar to that of Gabor orientation energy as shown again in Fig. 5(c).

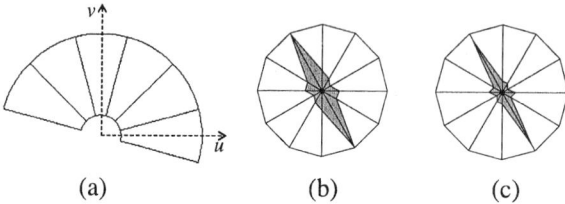

**Fig. 5.** Comparing a radar chart of sector power with that of Gabor orientation energy for the plane image in Fig. 4: (a) sector definition used in this paper, (b) the radar chart of sector power, (c) the radar chart of Gabor orientation energy

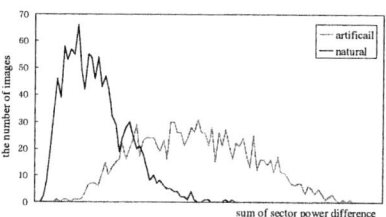

**Fig. 6.** Distribution of SSPDs (sum of sector power differences) for 1,300 artificial object images and 1,300 natural object images. The SSPDs for natural object images tend to have lower values than those for artificial object images.

Let the six sector powers be $SP_i$ ($i = 0,1,...,5$). The sum of sector power difference (SSPD) can be computed as in Eq. 3, which is very useful for representing existence of dominant orientations of any direction in the radar chart of sector power.

$$SSPD = \sum_{j=0}^{5} |SP_{(j+1) \bmod 6} - SP_j| \qquad (3)$$

The SSPD has a great value when there is abrupt change between neighboring sector powers. Thus SSPDs for artificial object images have greater values than those for natural object images. Fig. 6 shows distribution of the SSPDs for 1,300 artificial object images and 1,300 natural ones.

### 3.2 Energy of Edge Direction Histogram

The dominant orientation discussed in section 2 results mainly from occurrence of distinguishable line segments in boundary of an object and/or in internal region of the object. Thus, by finding the line segments, the dominant orientation can be analyzed in spatial domain as well as in spectral domain.

The edge direction histogram (EDH) [1] is a good tool for representing existence of the line segments. In this paper, edges are extracted by using the Canny edge detector [12] and a total of 45 bins are used to represent the edge directions (0°~180°) quantized at 4° interval. The EDH is normalized to compensate for different number of edge points and the energy of EDH is computed by summing squares of the count in each bin.

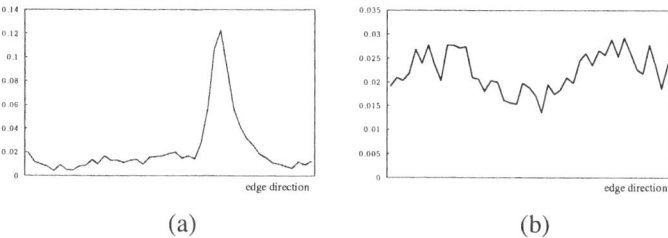

**Fig. 7.** Examples of edge direction histograms (EDHs) and their energies: (a) the EDH for the plane image in Fig. 4, (b) the EDH for the pet dog image in Fig. 4

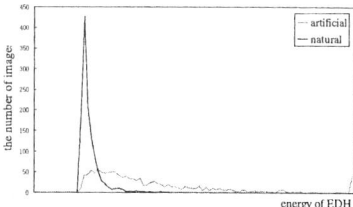

**Fig. 8.** Distribution of energy of EDHs for 1,300 artificial object images and 1,300 natural ones. Note that energy of EDH for natural object images tends to be smaller than that for artificial object image.

Fig. 7 shows the EDHs for the plane image and the pet dog image in Fig. 4. The former shows a peak corresponding to the dominant orientation in its radar chart of sector power, thereby having greater energy than the latter. Note that energy of EDH is not dependent on the direction of dominant orientations. Fig. 8 shows distribution of energy of EDHs for 1,300 artificial object images and 1,300 natural ones.

### 3.3 Classification of Object Images

In this paper, an unknown object image is classified into artificial class if its SSPD or its energy of EDH is greater than a classification threshold $t$. However, we cannot find a good classification threshold in Fig. 6 and 8 because two distribution curves are not clearly separated. Fig. 9 shows sensitivity of classification threshold for the SSPD. The threshold with lowest error rate will be selected as an optimal classification threshold in our experiments. Note that error rates near the optimal classification threshold vary slowly.

## 4 Experimental Results and Discussions

Two classification measures are evaluated on 2,600 object images (1,300 artificial object images and 1,300 natural ones) selected from the Corel Gallery photo-CD. To compensate for different object sizes, each object is scaled for longer one between its width and its height to be about 210 pixels and is centered in a (256 x 256) black background.

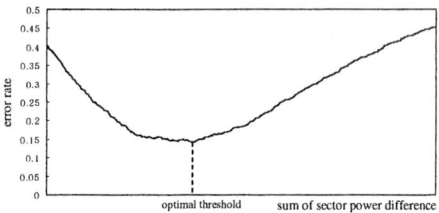

**Fig. 9.** This figure shows sensitivity of classification threshold for the SSPD (sum of sector power difference). Error rates near the optimal classification threshold vary slowly, so selection of a classification threshold is not sensitive.

Training object images (600 artificial object images and 600 natural ones) are randomly chosen from the 2,600 object images and the optimal classification threshold is selected as the threshold with the lowest error rate. Object classification is performed on the remaining object images. This procedure is repeated 30 times to reduce dependence of classification on the training set of object images. Average classification accuracies of the SSPD and the energy of EDH are 85.8% and 84.8%, respectively.

**Table 1.** Evaluation of the classification results for each classification method based on precision, recall, and F-measure

| | | SSPD Measure | Energy of EDH Measure |
|---|---|---|---|
| Artificial Object | Precision | 0.90 | 0.86 |
| | Recall | 0.80 | 0.84 |
| | F-measure | 0.85 | 0.85 |
| Natural Object | Precision | 0.82 | 0.84 |
| | Recall | 0.92 | 0.86 |
| | F-measure | 0.87 | 0.85 |

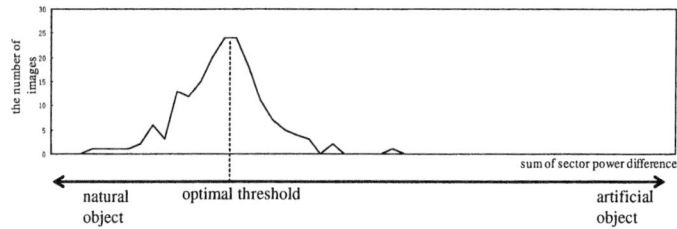

**Fig. 10.** Distribution of misclassified object images

Table 1 shows classification accuracy based on precision, recall and F-measure. We can see that both measures are not biased because all the F-measures are almost equal to. However, in the classification by the SSPD measure, precision of artificial object is higher than its recall, while precision of natural object is lower than its recall. This means that the number of artificial object images not having dominant orientations is larger than one of natural object images having dominant orientations. We also found that almost misclassification occurred near the optimal classification threshold (Fig. 10).

## 5 Conclusions

We first showed that the dominant orientation(s) of artificial object images in their radar charts of Gabor orientation energy was very useful for discriminating artificial object class from natural object class. Two classification measures, the sum of sector power differences in Fourier power spectrum and the energy of edge direction histogram, were proposed, which represented existence of the dominant orientations in any direction well. They showed classification accuracy of 85.8% and 84.8% respectively on a test with 2,600 object images. Our work can be applied to improving the performance of semantic-based image indexing.

## References

1. Vailaya, A., Jain, A.K., and Zhang, H.J.: On Image Classification: City Images vs. Landscape. Pattern Recognition. **31(12)** (1998) 1921-1936
2. Szummer, M., and Picard, R.W.: Indoor-Outdoor Image Classification. IEEE Int'l Workshop Content-Based Access Image Video Databases. (1998) 42-51
3. Vailaya, A., Figueiredo, M.A.T., Jain, A.K., and Zhang, H.J.: Image Classification for Content-Based Indexing. IEEE Trans. on Image Processing. **10(1)** (2001) 117-130
4. Oliva, A., Torralba, A.B., Gurin-Dugue, A., and Herault, J.: Global Semantic Classification of Scenes Using Power Spectrum Templates. Challenge of Image Retrieval (CIR99). Newcastle UK. (1999)
5. Osberger, W. and Maeder, A.J.: Automatic Identification of Perceptually Important Regions in an Image. IEEE Int'l Conf. on Pattern Recognition. (1998) 701-704
6. Huang, Q., Dom, B., Steels, D., Ashely, J., and Niblack, W.: Foreground / Background Segmentation of Color Images by Integration of Multiple Cues. Int'l Conf. on Image Processing. **1** (1995) 246-249
7. Serra, J.R. and Subirana, J.B.: Texture Frame Curves and Regions of Attention Using Adaptive Non-cartesian Networks. Pattern Recognition. **32** (1999) 503-515
8. Kim, S., Park, S., and Kim, M.: Central Object Extraction for Object-Based Image Retrieval. Int'l Conf. on Image and Video Retrieval (CIVR). (2003) 39-49
9. Kim, S., Park, S., and Kim, M.: Image Classification into Object / Non-object Classes. Int'l Conf. on Image and Video Retrieval (CIVR). (2004) 393-400
10. Park, S.B., Lee, J.W., and Kim, S.K.: Content-Based Image Classification Using a Neural Network. Pattern Recognition Letter. **25** (2004) 287-300
11. Manjunath, B.S. and Ma, W.Y.: Texture Features for Browsing and Retrieval of Image Data. IEEE Trans. on Pattern Analysis and Machine Intelligence. **18(8)** (1996) 837-842
12. Canny, J.: A Computational Approach to Edge Detection. IEEE Trans. on Pattern Analysis and Machine Intelligence. **8(6)** (1986) 679-698

# Recognition of Passports Using a Hybrid Intelligent System

Kwang-Baek Kim[1], Sungshin Kim[2], and Sang-An Ha[3]

[1] Dept. of Computer Engineering, Silla University, Busan 617-736, Korea
gbkim@silla.ac.kr
[2] Division of Electrical Engineering, Pusan National University, Busan 609-735, Korea
sskim@pusan.ac.kr
[3] Dept. of Environmental Engineering, Silla University, Busan 617-735, Korea
saha@silla.ac.kr

**Abstract.** This paper proposes a novel method for the recognition of passports based on the fuzzy binarization and the fuzzy RBF network. First, for the extraction of individual codes for recognizing, this paper targets code sequence blocks including individual codes by applying Sobel masking, horizontal smearing and a contour tracking algorithm on the passport image. Then the proposed method binarizes the extracted blocks using fuzzy binarization based on the trapezoid type membership function. Then, as the last step, individual codes are recovered and extracted from the binarized areas by applying CDM masking and vertical smearing. This paper also proposes an enhanced fuzzy RBF network that adapts the enhanced fuzzy ART network for the middle layer. This network is applied to the recognition of individual codes. The results of the experiments for performance evaluation on the real passport images showed that the proposed method has the better performance compared with other approaches.

## 1 Introduction

The immigration control system authorizes the immigration of travelers by means of passport inspections which includes the determination of forged passports, the search for a wanted criminal or a person disqualified for immigration, etc. The determination of forged passports plays an important role in the immigration control system, for which automatic and accurate processing is required because of the rapid increase of travelers. We propose a fuzzy image binarization method and a fuzzy RBF network, and by employing these methods, implement a novel system for the preprocessing phase for the determination of forged passports.

For extracting the individual codes from the passport image for recognizing, we extract the code sequence blocks including individual code using Sobel masking [1], horizontal smearing [2] and 4-directional contour tracking [3]. Then we extract the individual codes from the code sequence blocks using a novel fuzzy binarization algorithm, CDM masking [4] and vertical smearing. A novel fuzzy RBF network is proposed and applied for the recognition of extracted codes. The network constructs the middle layer using the enhanced fuzzy ART network for the adjustment of the weight of connections between the input layer and the middle layer. It supports the dynamical change of vigilance parameter, which makes it more efficient. The experiments for performance evaluation of the proposed fuzzy RBF network showed considerable improvement in learning performance and recognition rate.

## 2 Individual Code Extraction

The passport image consists of the three areas, the picture area in the top-left part, the user information area in the top-right part, and the user code area in the bottom part. For the recognition of passports, we extract the user codes from the passport image and digitalize the extracted codes.

### 2.1 Code Sequence Block Extraction

Fig.1 shows an example of passport image used for experiments in the paper. First, we extract the user code area, and next, extract the picture area to obtain the raw information from passport images.

The user code area in the bottom part of passport image has a white background and two code rows containing 44 codes. For extracting the individual codes from the passport image, first, we extract the code sequence blocks including the individual codes by using the feature that the user codes are arranged sequentially in the horizontal direction. The extraction procedure for code sequence blocks is as follows: First, Sobel masking is applied to the original image to generate an edge image [1]. By applying the horizontal smearing to the edge image, the adjacent edge blocks are combined into a large connected block. By successively applying contour tracking to the result of smearing process, a number of connected edge blocks are generated, and the ratio of width to height for all the blocks are calculated. Finally, the edge blocks with the maximum ratio are selected as code sequence blocks.

**Fig. 1.** An example of a passport image

Fig. 2 shows an edge image generated by applying Sobel masking to the image in Fig. 1. Fig. 3 shows the results generated by applying horizontal smearing to the edge image. We use 4-directional contour tracking to extract code sequence blocks from the results in Fig. 3.

The contour tracking extracts outlines of connected edge blocks by scanning and connecting the boundary pixels. This paper uses a $2 \times 2$ mask shown in Fig. 4 for the

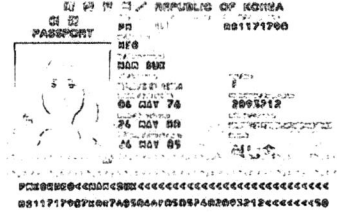

**Fig. 2.** Result of Sobel masking    **Fig. 3.** Result of horizontal smearing

4- directional contour tracking [3]. Contour tracking scans the smeared image from left to right and from top to bottom to find the boundary pixels of edge blocks. If a boundary pixel is found, the pixel is selected as the start position of tracking. The selected pixel is placed at the $x_k$ position of the 2×2 mask, and by examining the two pixels coming under the $a$ and $b$ positions and comparing with the conditions in Table 1, the next scanning direction of the mask is determined and the next boundary pixel being tracked is selected. The selected pixels coming under the $x_k$ position are connected into the contour of the edge block. By generating the outer rectangles including contours of edge blocks, and comparing the ration of width to height of the rectangles, the code sequence blocks with the maximum ration are extracted.

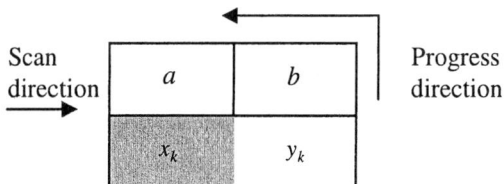

**Fig. 4.** 2x2 mask for 4-direction contour tracking

**Table 1.** Progress direction of $a$ and $b$ for 2×2 mask

|         | $a$ | $b$ | $x_k$ | $y_k$ |
|---------|-----|-----|-------|-------|
| Forward | 1   | 0   | $a$   | $b$   |
| Right   | 0   | 1   | $b$   | $y_k$ |
| Right   | 1   | 1   | $a$   | $x_k$ |
| Left    | 0   | 0   | $x_k$ | $a$   |

### 2.2 Individual Code Extraction

The individual codes are extracted by applying the proposed fuzzy binarization method and the CDM (Conditional Dilation Morphology) masking to the areas corresponding to code sequence blocks in the original passport image.

We propose a novel fuzzy binarization method based on the membership function of trapezoidal shape, which supports adaptive binarization for images with diversely shaped objects and various changes of intensity. Let $T$ be the mean value between the maximum value ($I_{Max}$) and the minimum value ($I_{Min}$) of intensity in the original grayscale image. Eq. 1 shows the relationship between the mean value $T$, $I_s$ and $I_e$. In the interval $[I_s, I_e]$ the degree of membership function of trapezoidal shape becomes 1.

$$I_s = \frac{T}{3}, \ I_e = I_s \times 2 \tag{1}$$

Hence, the membership function for the interval $[I_{Min}, I_{Max}]$ is formulated using Eq. 2 and it is used to calculate the degree of membership.

$$\begin{aligned} &if \ (I_{Min} < I \le I_s) \ then \ \mu(I) = \frac{1}{(I_s - I_{Min})} \times (I - I_s) + 1 \\ &if \ (I_s < I \le I_e) \ then \ \mu(I) = 1.0 \\ &if \ (I_e < I \le I_{Max}) \ then \ \mu(I) = \frac{1}{(I_{Max} - I_e)} \times (I - I_e) + 1 \end{aligned} \tag{2}$$

For each pixel in the passport image, the degree of membership is calculated using Eq. 2 and binarization is executed by applying $\alpha - cut$ to the degree of membership. Here, the $\alpha$ value used in the $\alpha - cut$ processing is given using Eq. 3 for the adaptive binarization of passport image.

$$\alpha = (T \times 2.02 - 75)/100 \tag{3}$$

That is, if the degree of membership of a pixel is greater than or equal to the $\alpha$ value, the intensity value of the pixel is set to 255. Otherwise, the intensity value is set to 0. We apply CDM masking to the result of binarization to recover the information loss caused by the low resolution of input. The CDM masking recover outer pixels of individual codes by executing only the dilation process without erosion and it is efficient in the images with low resolution [4]. Finally, we use vertical smearing and the horizontal projection to extract individual codes form the result of CDM masking. By projecting the vertical smeared areas in the horizontal direction, the horizontal coordinates of individual codes are calculated.

### 2.3 Picture Area Extraction

After individual codes are extracted, we extract the picture area containing the face using the start position of code sequence blocks and the characteristic that the vertical edge of picture area is greater than the horizontal edge, and the ratio of horizontal edge to vertical edge becomes approximately 3:4. As seen in Fig. 1 the picture area containing the face occupies 1/3 of the entire width of the passport page image, starting from its left edge, which matches with, left edge of the code sequence blocks. Hence, we select the start position for horizontal phase to matches with the code sequence block, and the end position is determined by scan which covers up to 1/3 of the width of the image.

Since, the Sobel masking makes the contour of picture more vivid by generating the thick edge, it is applied to the candidate area to extract edges. By generating the horizontal and vertical histograms in terms of the result of Sobel masking, the position method using only the Sobel masking and the histogram reduces the time required for face area extraction. Fig. 6(b) shows the passport page image along with the result of extraction of picture area containing the face. This data can now be sent to a face recognition system, which recognizes the face by matching with the passport database. The face recognition system can identify the person and provide name and other information from the passport database for validation of given passport.

## 3 Enhanced Fuzzy RBF Network for Recognition of Passports

We propose an enhanced fuzzy RBF network which constructs the middle layer using the enhanced fuzzy ART network for the recognition of extracted codes. In the traditional fuzzy ART network, the vigilance parameter determines the allowable degree of mismatch between any input pattern and stored patterns [5], [6]. Vigilance parameter is the inverse of degree of tolerance. A large value of vigilance parameter classifies an input pattern to a new category in spite of a little mismatch between the pattern and stored patterns. On the other hand a small value may allow the classification of the input pattern into an existing cluster in spite of a considerable mismatch. Moreover, because many applications of image recognition based on the fuzzy ART network assign an empirical value to the vigilance parameter, the success rate of recognition many deteriorate [7], [8]. To correct this defect, we propose an enhanced fuzzy ART network and apply it to the middle layer in a fuzzy RBF network.

The enhanced fuzzy ART network adjusts the vigilance parameter dynamically according to the homogeneity between the patterns using Yager's intersection operator, which is a fuzzy connection operator. The vigilance parameter is dynamically adjusted only in the case that the homogeneity between the saved pattern and the learning pattern is greater than or equal to the vigilance parameter. Also, the proposed fuzzy ART network adjusts the weight of connection for the learning patterns with the authorized homogeneity: Let $T^p$ and $T^{p*}$ be the target value of the learning pattern and the saved pattern respectively. If $T^p$ is equal to $T^{p*}$, the network decreases the vigilance parameter and adjusts the weight of connection between the input layer and the middle layer. Otherwise, the network increases the vigilance parameter and selects the next winner node.

The algorithm dynamically adjusts the vigilance parameter as follows:

$$if\ (T^p \neq T^{p*})\ then\ \rho(t+1)=1-\wedge\left(1,\left((1-\rho(t))^{-2}+(1-\rho(t-1))^{-2}\right)^{-1/2}\right) \quad (4)$$

$$else\ \rho(t+1)=1-\wedge\left(1,\left((1-\rho(t))^2+(1-\rho(t-1))^2\right)^{1/2}\right)$$

where $\rho$ is the vigilance parameter.

The authorization of homogeneity for the selected winner node is executed according to Eq. 5.

$$\frac{\|w_{j^*i} \wedge x_i^p\|}{\|x_i^p\|} < \rho \quad (5)$$

If output vector of the winner node is greater than or equal to the vigilance parameter, the homogeneity is authorized and the input pattern is classified to one of the existing clusters. Moreover, in this case, the weight of connection is adjusted according to Eq. 6 to reflect the homogeneity of the input pattern to the weight.

$$w_{ji}(t+1) = \beta \times (x_i^p \wedge w_{ji}(t)) + (1-\beta) \times w_{ji}(t) \quad (6)$$

where $\beta$ is the learning rate between 0 and 1. When the weight is adjusted in the traditional fuzzy ART network, $\beta$ is set to an empirical value. If a large value of $\beta$ is chosen, the success rate of recognition goes down since an information loss is caused by the increase in the number of cluster center updates. On the other hand, if the learning is performed with a small value of $\beta$, the information of the current learning pattern is unlikely to be reflected in the stored patterns and the number of clusters increases [9]. So, in the enhanced fuzzy ART network, the value of $\beta$ is dynamically adjusted based on the difference between the homogeneity of the learning pattern to the stored pattern and the vigilance parameter. The adjustment of $\beta$ is as follows:

$$\beta = \frac{1}{1-\rho} \times \left( \frac{\|w_{ji} \wedge x_i^p\|}{\|x_i^p\|} - \rho \right) \quad (7)$$

This paper enhances the fuzzy RBF network by applying the enhanced fuzzy ART algorithm to the middle layer, as shown in Fig. 5.

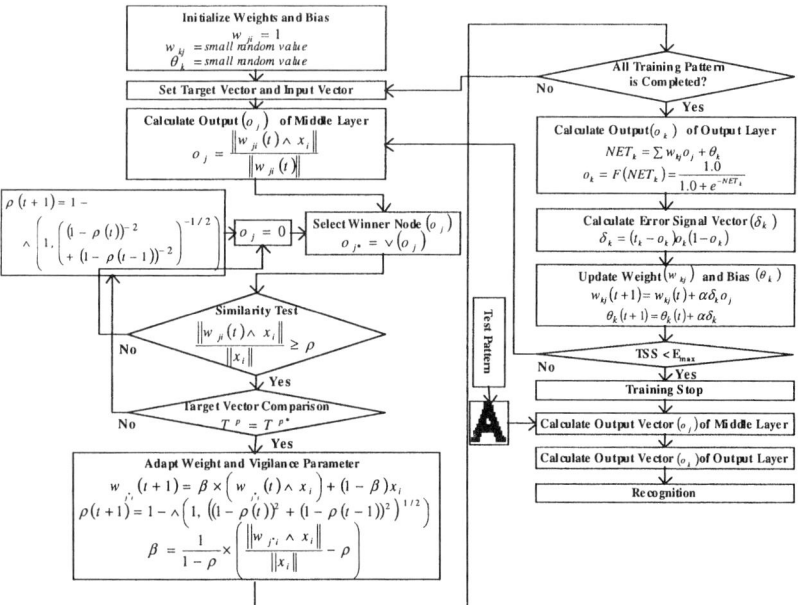

**Fig. 5.** Learning and recognition algorithm of the enhanced fuzzy RBF network

## 4 Performance Evaluation

For performance evaluation, we implemented the proposed algorithm and experimented on an IBM-compatible PC with Intel Pentium-IV 2GHz CPU and 256MB

RAM. And the 20's passport images of 600×437 pixel size were used in the experiments. Fig. 6 (a) shows the result of individual code extraction from the passport image in Fig. 1, and Fig. 6 (b) shows the result of picture area extraction. Fig. 7 shows the individual codes finally extracted by using fuzzy binarization and CDM masking.

(a) Example of individual code extraction    (b) Example of picture extraction

**Fig. 6.** Example of individual code and picture extraction

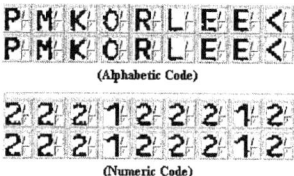

**Fig. 7.** Example of codes extracted by fuzzy binarization and CDM masking

Table 2 shows the number of code sequence blocks and individual codes extracted from the 20 passport images. The extracted individual codes contained 1140 alphabetic codes and 620 numeric codes. In the paper alphabetic codes and numeric ones were used separately in the learning and recognition experiments.

**Table 2.** Number of extracted for code sequence blocks and individual codes

|  | Code Sequence Blocks | Individual Codes |
|---|---|---|
| The number of extraction (success/target) | 40/40 | 1760/1760 |

**Table 3.** Comparison of the number of clusters between the fuzzy ART and the proposed fuzzy ART network

|  |  | Number of clusters / Number of patterns |
|---|---|---|
| Alphabetic Codes | Proposed Fuzzy ART | 48/1140 |
|  | Fuzzy ART | 303/1140 |
| Numeric Codes | Proposed Fuzzy ART | 14/620 |
|  | Fuzzy ART | 142/620 |

To evaluate the learning performance of the enhanced fuzzy ART network, this paper compared the number of clusters generated by the traditional fuzzy ART network and the enhanced fuzzy ART network in the learning experiments on individual codes.

**Table 4.** Result of learning and recognition by the proposed fuzzy RBF network

|  | The number of nodes in middle layer | The number of Epoch | The number of recognition |
|---|---|---|---|
| Alphabetic Codes | 40/40 | 4068 | 1140/1140 |
| Numeric Codes | 14/620 | 1527 | 620/620 |

Table 3 shows the result of the learning experiments. In the experiments, the vigilance parameters for the traditional fuzzy ART network were set to 0.9 and 0.85 for the alphabetic and the numeric codes respectively, and for the enhanced fuzzy ART network, the initial values of the vigilance parameter were set to 0.9 and 0.85 respectively. As shown in Table 3, the number of clusters in the enhanced fuzzy ART network was much lower than in the traditional fuzzy ART network, so we may know that the enhanced fuzzy ART network refines the classification of the homogenous patterns properly.Table 4 shows the results of the experiment involving enhanced fuzzy RBF network for the 20 passport images for recognition. In the experiment, the initial values of the vigilance parameter used for the creation and update of the nodes in the middle layer were set to 0.9 and 0.85 for the alphabetic and the numeric codes respectively. As shown in Table 4, the proposed fuzzy RBF network was able to successfully recognize all of the extracted individual codes.

In conclusion, the experiment for performance evaluation shows that the proposed fuzzy RBF network improves the learning performance and the success rate of recognition by supporting the dynamical change of the vigilance parameter and the adjustment of the weight of connection between the input layer and the middle layer.

## 5 Conclusion

Due to rapid increase of travelers globally, automatic and accurate processing of passports has become a necessity in order to avoid fraud and long waiting time for passengers. In this paper, we discuss an automated system for detection of forgeries in passports.

First, we proposed a novel method for the recognition of passports based on the fuzzy image binarization and the fuzzy RBF neural network. In the individual code extraction phase, we extracted the code sequence blocks including individual codes by using Sobel masking, horizontal smearing and the 4-directional contour tracking based on the $2 \times 2$ mask. Then we extracted the individual codes from the code sequence blocks by using the proposed fuzzy binarization, the CDM masking, and the vertical smearing. In this paper, an enhanced fuzzy RBF network was proposed and applied in the code recognition phase. This algorithm dynamically changes the vigilance parameter in order to improve the clustering performance. In the experiments for performance evaluation using 20 passport images, it was found that the enhanced fuzzy RBF network outperforms traditional approach.

In the future studies, we plan to implement a face authorization module, which can search many databases including driver licenses in order to detect the identity of the perpetrator.

## References

1. Jain,, A. K.: Fundamental of Digital Image Processing. Englewood Cliffs, New Jersey Prentice-Hall (1989)
2. Wang, K. Y., Casey, R. G. and Wahl, F. M. J.: Document analysis system, IBM J. Res. Develop. 26, No. 6. (1982) 647-656
3. Kim, K. B., Jang, S. W. and Kim, C. K.: Recognition of Car License Plate by Using Dynamical Thresholding Method and Enhanced Neural Networks. Lecture Note in Computer Science. LNCS 2756 (2003) 309-319
4. Gonzalez, R. C. and Wintz,, P.: Digital Image Processing. Addison-Wesley Publishing Company Inc., (1977)
5. Carpenter, G. A. and Grossberg, S.: Neural Networks for Vision and Image Processing. Massachusetts Institute of Technology, (1992)
6. Kim, K. B.: An Enhanced Fuzzy ART Algorithmm for the Effective Identifier Recognition from Shipping Container Image. Journal of the Korean Institute of Communication Science, Vol. 28, No. 5C, (2003) 486-492
7. Kothari, M. L., Madnami, S. and Segal, R.: Orthogonal Least Square Learning Algorithm Based Radial Basis Function Network Adaptive Power System Stabilizer. Proceedings of IEEE SMC, Vol. 1 (1997) 542-547
8. Kim, K. B., Kang, M. H. and Cha, E. Y.: A Fuzzy Self Organized Backpropagation using Nervous System Proceedings of IEEE SMC, Vol 5 (1997) 1457-1462
9. Kim, K. B. and Yun, H. W.: A Study on Recognition of Bronchgenic Cencer Cell using Fuzzy Neural Networks. Journal of Korea Society of Medical Informatics, Vol. 5, No. 1 (1999) 77-87

# Description of Digital Images by Region-Based Contour Trees

Shinobu Mizuta and Tetsuya Matsuda

Kyoto University, Kyoto 606-8501, Japan
smizuta@i.kyoto-u.ac.jp

**Abstract.** In analyzing the morphological information of objects in images, isosurfaces play important and application-independent roles. For continuous scalar field, Contour Trees have been used as a tool to select and visualize isosurfaces. However, the tree structure of contour trees is based on the critical points which does not exist in digital images. In this paper, we propose a tree structure of isosurfaces in digital images named Region-based Contour Tree. The proposed method describes a finite number of isosurfaces in digital images completely, without redundancy.

## 1 Introduction

With advances of imaging technology and improvements of computer power, the opportunities of using digital images are rapidly increasing. In the medical field, various types of digital images are used such as two-dimensional (2D) X-ray projection images, 3D X-ray computer tomography images, magnetic resonance images, and the temporal series of these images. The final goal of our research is to extract, analyze and display the morphological information of observed objects and relationship among them, from multidimensional digital images.

In analyzing the morphological information of objects in grayscale images, isosurfaces (isolines in 2D) play important and application-independent roles. In this paper, we focus on the relationship among isosurfaces in grayscale digital images. Isosurfaces of digital images can be defined as connected boundaries among pixels.

Max/Min Tree [1] is a tree structure to represent the transition of foreground/background connected components with changes of the threshold to binarize images. Watershed Lake Tree [3] is a related structure to Min Tree [4] for watershed image analysis. These tree structures can be considered as the structure of isosurfaces surrounding the connected components. However, these cannot represent some regions and surrounding isosurfaces. For example, Max Tree cannot represent holes inside connected components of foreground.

Inclusion Tree [5] to describe the relationship among closed isosurfaces can overcome the disadvantage of Max/Min Tree. Remarkable point of Inclusion Tree is the ability to describe the nesting relationship of shapes surrounded by closed isosurfaces. A problem of Inclusion Tree is that the structure cannot represent "open" isosurfaces connecting to the boundary to the outside of images. From the restriction of FOV (field of view), objects of interests and the surrounding isosurfaces are frequently cut at the boundaries of observed images.

"Contour Tree" (CT) [6] is a data structure to describe the relationship among isosurfaces in continuous scalar fields, based on the relationship between the critical points (local maxima, local minima and saddle points) where topological changes of isosurfaces occur by the changes of threshold (isovalue). The isosurfaces described by CT are not necessarily closed.

When digital images are represented as the set of pixels that have certain area, the critical points can be defined only with introducing additional assumptions. In constructing CT from digital images, this characteristic is a problem because some nodes of CT must correspond to the critical points. Asano proposed an idea of CT that could be applied to digital images [7], but the problem described above is not mentioned.

Our purpose here is to describe the relationship among isosurfaces in digital images to handle all the isosurfaces with minimum additional assumptions. When isosurfaces are defined as connected boundaries among pixels, a digital image consists of a finite number of isosurfaces. If the pixel values consist of limited integers that are widely used, the number of possible isosurfaces becomes much smaller.

In this paper, we propose a modified data structure of the conventional CT named Region-based Contour Tree (RBCT). RBCT describes the relationship among isosurfaces from the set of regions, without introducing additional assumptions to define critical points.

In the following sections, the scalar fields are assumed to be 2D. However, the procedures proposed in this paper can be applied to higher-dimensional fields directly.

## 2 Contour Trees for Continuous Scalar Fields

Contour Tree (CT) is a tree-structured graph, representing the transitions of isosurfaces (appearance, disappearance, join and split) in continuous scalar fields, with increase or decrease of the threshold (isovalue) of field value [6].

Figure 1 shows the outline of CT. Figure 1(a) represents a 2D scalar field, and $P$, $Q$, $R_1$, and $R_2$ are isosurfaces. $a,...,i$ denote critical points (local maxima, local minima and saddles) where the topological changes of isosurfaces occur.

Figure 1(b) is the CT corresponding to the scalar field (a). We define CT based on the references [8] [9] [10] as follows:

- CT is a tree-structured graph having nodes and arcs.
- A node of CT represents a critical point and the corresponding isosurface. Nodes and critical points satisfy one-to-one correspondence.
- An arc of CT links two nodes. The arc represents a region bounded by two isosurfaces corresponding to these two nodes. An arc and a region have a one-to-one relationship.

We call the nodes and arcs "supernodes" and "superarcs", respectively. In a region represented by a superarc, movement of an isosurface without topological change occurs with the increase or decrease of the threshold.

Additional nodes can be introduced on the superarcs to represent isosurfaces in the regions corresponding to the superarcs. The isosurfaces do not include any critical points. We call these nodes "regularnodes." "Nodes" consist of supernodes and regularnodes. We use the word "arcs" as the links between nodes. We call this type of CT Augumented Contour Tree (ACT) [10].

CT is a classical method, having a problem of the computational complexity for the construction. Recently, several groups have proposed efficient methods to construct CT [8][9][10][11][12].

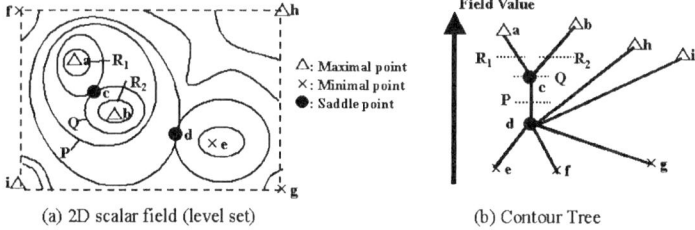

(a) 2D scalar field (level set)    (b) Contour Tree

**Fig. 1.** Contour Tree

## 3 Region-Based Contour Trees from Digital Images

In digital images, isosurfaces have different characteristics from those in continuous scalar fields. In this section, we propose a modified data structure of Contour Trees for digital images named Region-based Contour Trees.

### 3.1 Definition of Isosurfaces in Digital Images

In general, a digital image can be described as a set of pixels on the vertices of a multidimensional, rectangular mesh. The pixels have values of non-negative, finite integer.

A digital image can be binarized using a threshold of real value $t$. Here we denote $R_i(t)$ as the $i$-th region ($i = 1, 2, ...$) of connected pixels $\{p|V(p) \geq t\}$ and $S_j(t)$ as the $j$-th region ($i = 1, 2, ...$) of connected pixels $\{p|V(p) \leq t\}$, where $V(p)$ is a pixel value of pixel $p$. Using $R$ and $S$, an isosurface for threshold $t$ can be represented as a boundary of a pair of regions $[R_a(T), S_b(T-1)]$, where $T$ is the minimum integer value in $T \geq t$.

In binary images, ones of brighter or darker pixels are regarded as foreground, and the others become background. In order to avoid the contradiction between the connected regions of foreground/background, different types of connectivity are introduced. Generally, a combination of 8- and 4-connectivity for 2D images is used for foreground and background. In the following description, we deal with brighter $R_i(T)$ as a foreground region, with 8-connectivity of pixels.

## 3.2 Definition of the Transitions of Isosurfaces

When isosurfaces of a digital image are defined as boundaries among regions described above, the isosurfaces are discontinuously altered with the change of threshold. Because of the discontinuity, any critical points and corresponding isosurfaces do not appear during the change of threshold.

Here we define the transitions of isosurfaces in digital images by the set of isosurfaces before and after the transitions. We denote these sets of isosurfaces as $C^+(T)$ and $C^-(T)$ for a transition with the decrease of threshold from $t = T + \epsilon$ to $t = T$, where $\epsilon$ is a small positive value. These sets can be defined using the following conditions:

- All isosurfaces $C_i \in C^+(T)(i = 1, ..., M)$ are the boundaries between one region $S_1(T)$ and adjacent regions $R_i(T+1)$.
- All isosurfaces $C_j \in C^-(T)(j = 1, ..., N)$ are the boundaries between one region $R_1(T)$ and adjacent regions $S_j(T-1)$.
- $U(T) = \{p|V(p) = T\} = R_1(T) \cap S_1(T) \neq \phi$.

Figure 2 shows an example of the transitions. From the definition, the transitions can be classified as follows:

- appearance: $M = 0, N = 1$.
- disappearance: $M = 1, N = 0$.
- join: $M > 1, N = 1$.
- split: $M = 1, N > 1$.
- transition without topological change: $M = 1, N = 1$.

Other conditions of $M, N$ represent the combination of these transitions.

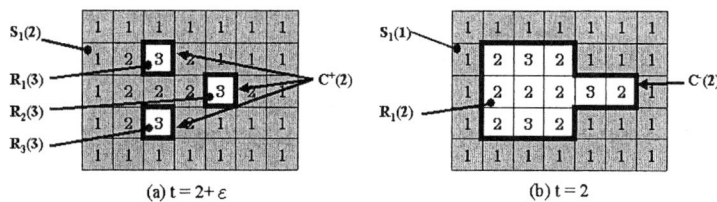

**Fig. 2.** A transition of isosurfaces (join with the decrease of threshold)

## 3.3 Region-Based Contour Trees

As described above, any critical points and corresponding isosurfaces do not appear in the change of isosurface. Therefore, the nodes of CT derived from a digital image cannot correspond to any critical point. The fact is against the definition of CT in section 2. Here we modify the definition of CT to describe digital images properly. The definition of the proposed CT having the structure of ACT is as follows:

- CT is a tree-structured graph having nodes and arcs.
- A supernode of CT represents a transition of isosurfaces involving topological changes, and the set of isosurfaces before and after the transition.
- A superarc of CT links two nodes. The arc represents a region bounded by two isosurfaces corresponding to these two nodes. An superarc and a region have a one-to-one relationship.
- A regularnode is on a superarc. The node represents a transition of isosurfaces in the region corresponding to the superarc. Nodes consist of supernodes and regularnodes. Arcs link nodes.

From the characteristics of isosurfaces in digital images, we can define:

- $n_i(i = 1, ..., X)$ : a node, and a transition of isosurfaces.
- $a_j(j = 1, ..., X-1)$ : an arc.
- $C(n_i) = \{C^+(n_i), C^-(n_i)\}$: a set of isosurfaces related to $n_i$.
- $U(n_i)$ : a set of pixels related to $n_i$.
- $V(n_i)$ : a field value that the pixels $U(n_i)$ have.
- $R(n_i)$ : a region of connected pixels including $U(n_i)$, having pixel value $t \geq V(n_i)$.
- $S(n_i)$ : a region of connected pixels including $U(n_i)$, having pixel value $t \leq V(n_i)$.

Here we can represent all the transitions of isosurfaces in a digital image by the set of nodes. Since any pixel in an image takes part in a transition of isosurfaces, each pixel is an element of $U(n_i)$ of exactly one node $n_i$.

If all the transitions of isosurfaces are represented by the nodes of CT, an arc $a_j$ which links $n_p$ and $n_q$ represents exactly one isosurface. If $V(n_p) > V(n_q)$ the isosurface for $a_j$ is the boundary between $R(n_p)$ and $S(n_q)$ where the threshold t is $V(n_p) \geq t > V(n_q)$. If the nodes represent all the transitions of isosurfaces, the arcs represent all the isosurfaces in the image. The arcs and isosurfaces satisfy one-to-one correspondence. Therefore, the arcs represent the isosurfaces completely, without any redundancy.

It can be considered that nodes of the proposed CT represent regions in an image, and the CT describes the structure of isosurfaces from the relationship among the regions. From this characteristic, we call the CT "Region-based Contour Tree (RBCT)." Figure 3 illustrates an example of RBCT. Figure 3(a) represents a digital image, and Figure 3(b) is the RBCT corresponding to (a).

Figure 4 shows the isosurfaces of Figure 3(a) by various methods. Here, bold and solid lines indicate the isosurfaces represented by these methods, and broken lines indicate the isosurfaces to be represented. The thin solid line is the boundary of outside image. As shown in this figure, conventional Max Tree or Inclusion Tree cannot represent several isosurfaces. On the other hand, RBCT can represent all isosurfaces.

## 3.4 Introducing the Isosurfaces Surrounding Whole Images

If necessary, we can represent the isosurface surrounding whole image, by setting the outside region of the image having pixel value $\psi$. If $\psi$ is smaller than the

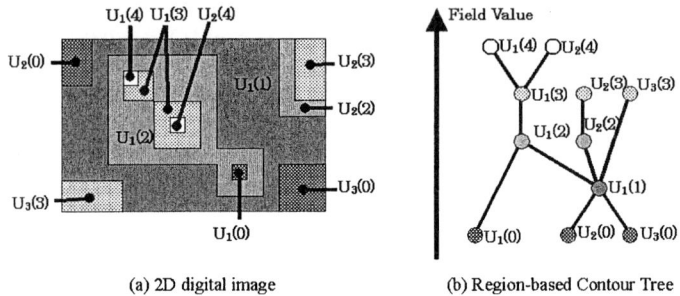

**Fig. 3.** Region-based Contour Tree

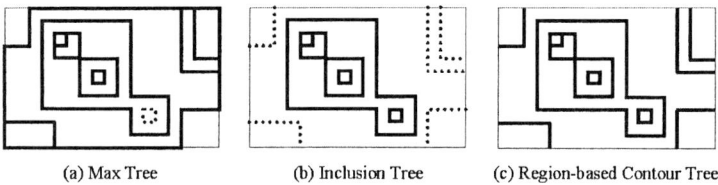

**Fig. 4.** Isosurfaces represented by various methods

minimum pixel value of the image on outside boundary (extremely $\psi = -\infty$) or larger than the maximum value (extremely $\psi = +\infty$), one closed isosurface surrounding whole image is extracted.

We can introduce this isosurface to RBCT as follows:

- Set a node which represents outside region of an image, having pixel value $\psi = -\infty(+\infty)$. We call the node "virtual node".
- Find a node $n_r$ where $U(n_r)$ includes the pixels on the outside boundary and $V(n_r)$ is the minimum (maximum) pixel value on the outside boundary if $\psi = -\infty(+\infty)$. We call the node "root node".
- Set an arc which links the virtual node and the root node. The arc represents the isosurface surrounding the whole image. We call the arc "root arc".

In this condition, all other isosurfaces are closed, and the resulting RBCT become an equivalent tree structure as Inclusion Tree [5] . The resulting isosurfaces change in response to the value of $\psi$ . Bold and solid lines of Figure 5 show the isosurfaces of Figure 3(a) for threshold $t$ that $2 \geq t > 1$, viewing the difference of isosurfaces with changes of the definition of virtual node.

### 3.5 Construction of Region-Based Contour Trees

RBCT can be constructed by modifying the method of Carr et al. [10] for continuous scalar fields. The outline of the procedure of their method is as follows:

- Represent a scalar field by a multidimensional mesh, where each vertex has field value.
- Sort the vertices of the mesh by field values in descending order.
- Construct a tree named Join Tree that represents the appearance, expansion and join of foreground regions with decreasing the threshold, by tracing the sorted vertices.
- Sort the vertices of the mesh by field values in ascending order.
- Construct a tree named Split Tree that represents the appearance, expansion and join of background regions with increasing the threshold (which also means the disappearance, contraction and split of the regions with decreasing the threshold), by tracing the sorted vertices.
- Combine Join Tree and Split Tree to represent both tree structure. Since these two trees have same number of nodes, the combination is easily processed.
- Merge the linked pairs of nodes if the correspondent pairs of vertices have the same field values.

In order to apply this method to construct RBCT, we deal with pixels of a digital image as the vertices of the mesh. To introduce the difference of connectivity of foreground/background regions, we used 8-connectivity to construct Join Tree and 4-connectivity for Split Tree. It is easily understood that Join Tree and Split Tree in the modified procedure for digital images are same as Max Tree and Min Tree [1][2], respectively.

In the procedures listed above, computational complexity to sort pixels is $O(N \log N)$ if heap-sort algorithm is used, where $N$ is the number of pixels. Since the pixel values are assumed to be finite integers here, counting-sort (bucket-sort) algorithm having the complexity $O(N)$ can be applied if the range of pixel values is not large (8 to 16 bit [2]). Computational complexities for other procedures in the list are $O(N)$ when the numbers of connectivity for foreground/background regions are treated as fixed, small-valued constants [10][2]. Spatial complexities of them are $O(N)$.

### 3.6 Experimental Result

In order to confirm that the proposed method works properly, we have carried out an experiment to extract RBCT from a digital image. Figure 6 shows the

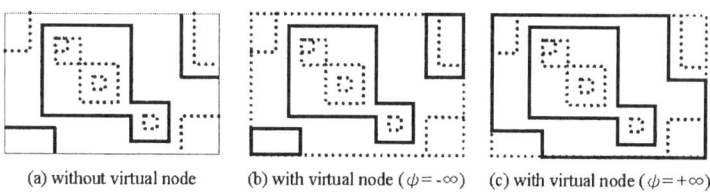

(a) without virtual node  (b) with virtual node ($\psi = -\infty$)  (c) with virtual node ($\psi = +\infty$)

**Fig. 5.** Difference of isosurfaces with changes of the definition of virtual node

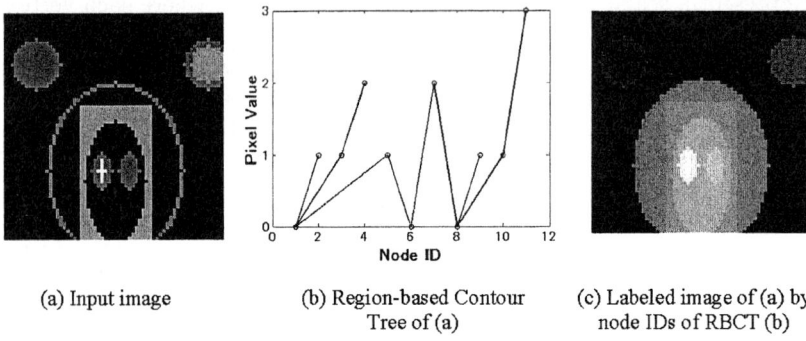

(a) Input image  (b) Region-based Contour Tree of (a)  (c) Labeled image of (a) by node IDs of RBCT (b)

**Fig. 6.** Experimental result

experimental result. Input image shown in Figure 6(a) is 64 × 64 pixel, 2-bit grayscale image. Figure 6(b) is the RBCT corresponding to (a). Figure 6(c) is a labeled image of (a) by the node IDs of RBCT (b).

## 4 Applications

### 4.1 Selection of Isosurfaces

For 3D images in paticular, selecting and visualizing isosurfaces corresponding to the objects of interest are fundamental and important procedures in analyzing morphological information of the objects. Thresholding procedure extracts not only the isosurface of interest but also other isosurfaces, such as those surrounding external noise area or internal holes (cavities in 3D) having the same isovalue. Since RBCT describes all isosurfaces in images, any isosurface can be extracted only by selecting the corresponding arc of the tree.

### 4.2 Image Segmentation

Selecting an isosurface from an image is equivalent procedure to divide the image into two regions. Here, the isosurface is not necessarily closed. If one of two regions represents an object of interest, this procedure can be considered as that for image segmentation. The segmented region using an isosurface is obviously connected, without holes (cavities).

Division of an image by an isosurface can be represented by using RBCT, as division of the tree structure into two subtrees by removing the arc corresponding to the isosurface.

Figure 7(a)(b)(c) illustrates an example of the image segmentation procedure. Figure 7(a) represents a digital image and Figure 7(b) is the RBCT corresponding to (a). By removing the arc corresponding to an open isosurface A, the RBCT is divided into two subtrees, where these two trees correspond to the regions. It can be seen that isosurface A divides image (a) into two sets of regions $\{U_1(0), U_1(2), U_1(3), U_1(4), U_2(4)\}$ and $\{U_2(0), U_1(1), U_2(2), U_2(3)\}$, while the corresponding arc in RBCT (b) divides the tree into two subtrees, where the two sets of nodes for these subtrees correspond to the sets of regions. Figure 7(c) is the segmented image of (a).

### 4.3 Image Filtering

Procedures to remove small regions in an image can be considered as those of image filtering for noise reduction. Max/Min Tree is used for morphological area filtering, where small foreground/background regions are removed, respectively [2]. A purpose to introduce Inclusion Tree is to suppress noise by removing small regions surrounded by closed isosurfaces [5].

After the image segmentation using RBCT described above, the segmented region can be removed. Figure 7(d) shows the result of region removal from image (a) using isosurface B. Using this procedure, image filtering to remove small regions can be carried out using both closed and open isosurfaces.

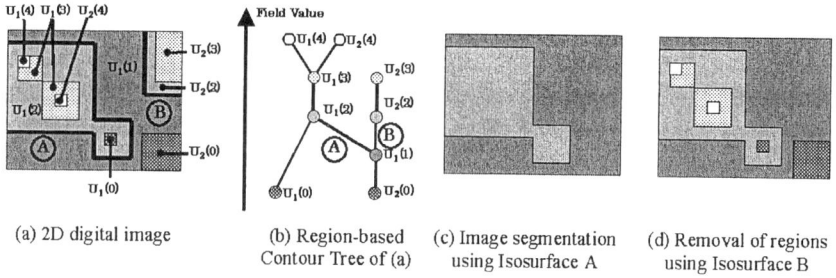

**Fig. 7.** Image processing using Region-based Contour Tree

## 5 Conclusion

In order to extract the relationship among isosurfaces in observed digital images, we have proposed a modified data structure of conventional CT named Region-based Contour Tree (RBCT). RBCT describes a finite number of isosurfaces in digital images completely, without redundancy. Our next step is to evaluate the efficiency of the procedure to construct RBCT, and to improve it.

**Acknouledgement.** A part of this research was supported by Grant-in-Aid for Scientific Research from Japan Society for the Promotion of Science, and also by Grant-in-Aid for Scientific Research from Ministry of Education, Culture, Sports, Science and Technology, Japan.

# References

1. P. Salembier, A. Oliveras, L. Garrido, Antiextensive connected operators for image and sequence processing, IEEE Trans. Image Processing, Vol.7, No.4, pp.555-570, 1998.
2. A. Meijster, H.F. Wilkinson, A comparison of algorithms for connected set openings and closings, IEEE Trans. Pattern Analysis and Machine Intelligence, Vol.24, No.4, pp.484-494, 2002.
3. M. Fisher, R. Aldrige, Hierarchical segmentation of images using a watershed scale-space trees, in: IEE Int. Conf. Image Processing and its Applications, pp.522-526, 1999.
4. FX. Huang, M. Fisher, Y. Zhu, From min tree to watershed lake tree: theory and implementation, in: Proc. ICIAR, pp.848-857, 2004.
5. P. Monasse, F. Guichard, Scale-space from a level lines tree, Journal of Visual Communication and Image Representation, Vol.11, pp.224-236, 2000.
6. R.W.Boyell, H. Ruston, Hybrid techniques for real-time radar simulation, IEEE Proceedings Fall Joint Computer Conference 63, pp.36-37, 1963.
7. T. Asano, Mathematical Sciences, No. 433, pp.34-40, July 1999 (in Japanese).
8. S.P. Tarasov, M.N. Vyalyi, Construction of contour trees in 3D in O(n log n) steps, in: Proceedings of the 14 th ACM Symposium on Computational Geometry, ACM, pp.68-75, 1998.
9. M. van Kreveld, R. van Oostrum, C.L. Bajaj, V. Pascucci, D.R. Schikore, Contour trees and small seed sets for isosurface traversal, in: Proceedings of the 13 th ACM Symposium on Computational Geometry, ACM, pp.212-220, 1997.
10. H. Carr, J. Snoeyink, U. Axen, Computing contour trees in all dimensions, Computational Geometry, Vol. 24, pp.73-94, 2003.
11. H. Carr, Topological Manipulation of Isosurfaces, PhD Thesis of The University of British Columbia, April 2004.
12. V. Pascucci, K. Cole-McLaughlin, Efficient Computation of the Topology of Level sets, Proc. IEEE Visualization 2002, pp.187-194, 2002.

# Compressing 2-D Shapes Using Concavity Trees

O. El Badawy[1] and M.S. Kamel[2]

[1] Dept. of Systems Design Engineering
[2] Dept. of Electrical and Computer Engineering.,
Pattern Analysis and Machine Intelligence Research Group,
University of Waterloo, Waterloo, Ontario, N2L 3G1, Canada

**Abstract.** Concavity trees have been known for quite some time as structural descriptors of 2-D shape; however, they haven't been explored further until recently. This paper shows how 2-D shapes can be concisely, but reversibly, represented during concavity tree extraction. The representation can be exact, or approximate to a pre-set degree. This is equivalent to a lossless, or lossy compression of the image containing the shape. This paper details the proposed technique and reports near-lossless compression ratios that are 150% better than the JBIG standard on a test set of binary silhouette images.

## 1 Introduction and Background

A *concavity tree* is a data structure used for describing non-convex two dimensional shapes. It was first introduced by Sklansky [1] and has since been further researched by others [2,3,4,5,6,7,8,9]. A concavity tree is a rooted tree in which the root represents the whole object whose shape is to be analysed/represented. The next level of the tree contains nodes that represent concavities along the boundary of that object. Each of the nodes on the following levels represents one of the concavities of its parent, *i.e.*, its meta-concavities. If an object or a concavity is itself convex, then the node representing it does not have any children. Figure 1 shows an example of a shape (a), its convex hull, concavities, and meta-concavities (b), and its corresponding concavity tree (c). The shape has *five* concavities as reflected in level *one* of the tree. The four leaf nodes in level *one* correspond to the highlighted triangular concavities shown in (d), whereas the non-leaf node corresponds to the (non-convex) concavity shown in (e). Similarly, the nodes in levels *two* and *three* correspond to the meta-concavities highlighted in (f) and (g), respectively. Typically, each node in a concavity tree stores information pertinent to the part of the object the node is describing (a feature vector for example), in addition to tree meta-data (like the level of the node; the height, number of nodes, and number of leaves in the subtree rooted at the node).

We recently proposed an efficient (in terms of space and time) contour-based algorithm for concavity tree extraction [9] and we showed how it surpasses other concavity tree extraction methods [6] in terms of speed and the accuracy of the

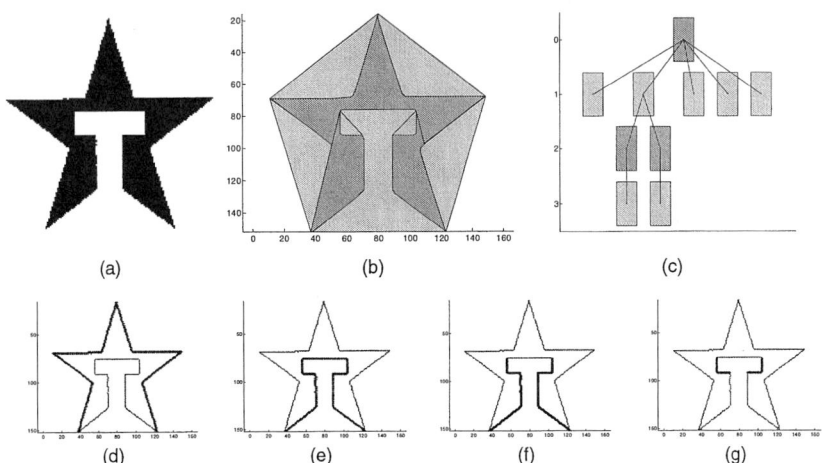

**Fig. 1.** An object (a), its convex hull and concavities (b), the corresponding concavity tree (c), and contour sections corresponding to concavities (d-g)

reconstructed image as a function of the number of nodes used in the reconstruction. In this paper, we explore the space efficiency of the method and compare it to the JBIG standard compression algorithm. With some modifications to the base algorithm, we are able to achieve near-lossless compression with ratios 150% better than that of JBIG, and a subjectively imperceptible error of around 0.006. The resulting compact representation is not the tree, but rather it is a sequence of vertices generated while the tree is extracted. The accuracy of the representation, and consequently the compression ratio, is controlled by specifying the minimum depth a concavity has to be in order to be taken into consideration. One direct advantage of this compressed representation is that the shape at hand can be analysed without the need to fully decompress the image. The resulting representation can as well be interpreted as a user-controlled polygonal approximation method whose degree of matching the original shape is also controlled by the same parameter as that controlling the compression ratio. The next section explains the methods while Section 3 discusses experimental results.

## 2  The Proposed Algorithm

Consider a 256x256 binary image containing a 128x128 black (filled) square, this image would have an uncompressed size of 8 KB (1 bpp). JBIG is able to losslessly compress it 80:1. We note however that if we only store the four corners of the square in a vector-graphics fashion (which is enough information to losslessly reconstruct it), we should achieve much higher ratios (around 800:1). The proposed method generalizes this concept to any binary image (but it is particularly suited to silhouettes images, single or multiple, with or without holes).

**Algorithm 1.** Concavity Tree Extraction and Compression

**Notation:**
  $I$ is the input image.
  $F$ is the set of foreground ("1") pixels (representing the shape in $I$).
  $B$ is the set of background ("0") pixels.
  $C$ is the contour of $F$.
  $T$ is a rooted tree (the concavity tree of the shape in $I$).
  $S$ is the output sequence.
  $N$ is a node in $T$.
**Require:** $I$ is bilevel, $F$ is 8-connected, and $B$ is 4-connected.
 1: $C \leftarrow$ contour of $F$
 2: $T, S = fCT(\ C\ )$
**Function** $T, S = fCT(\ C\ )$
 3:  $S \leftarrow []$ {Initialise sequence $S$}
 4:  $H \leftarrow$ convex hull of $C$
 5:  Re-arrange $H$ so that it is a subsequence of $C$
 6:  $T \leftarrow$ NIL
 7:  New $N$ {Instantiate a new tree node}
 8:  $N.\text{data} \leftarrow H$ {In addition to any features as necessary}
 9:  $T \leftarrow N$ {$T$ now points to $N$}
10:  **for** { each pair of consecutive points $p_1$ and $p_2$ in $H$ } **do**
11:    $C_2 \leftarrow$ subsequence of $C$ bounded between $p_1$ and $p_2$ {$C_2$ is a concave section along contour $C$}
12:    $S_2 \leftarrow []$
13:    **if** depth($C_2$) > *mindepth* **then**
14:      $T_2, S_2 = fCT(\ C_2\ )$
15:      $N.\text{newchild} \leftarrow T_2$ {$T$ has a new subtree $T_2$}
16:    **end if**
17:    $S \leftarrow S, p_1, S_2, p_2$ {such that no two consecutive elements are identical}
18:  **end for**

We focus on the case of an image containing a single object (no holes). The extension to multiple objects (with or without holes) is based on it (an example will be presented in Section 3; however, due to space constraints, the details are omitted). The main steps of the compression algorithm are shown in Algorithm 1. The input image $I$ is a binary image. The condition that the set of foreground pixels $F$ is 8-connected and the set of background pixels $B$ is 4-connected will ensure that there is only one object with no holes in $I$ (provided that $F$ does not intersect the boundary of $I$). The output of the algorithm is a sequence $S$ of pixels along the contour of $F$. $S$ is generated during the concavity tree extraction process. If, for example, $F$ is a rectangle, $S$ will be the clockwise (or anti-clockwise) sequence of the four corner pixels.

The algorithm basically computes the convex hull of $F$ and makes it the output sequence. It then iterates on each pair of consecutive vertices and inserts, between each pair in the sequence, all the resulting subsequences generated by recursively calling the main function on the section of the contour bounded between the two points at hand. The sequence is only updated if the vertex is

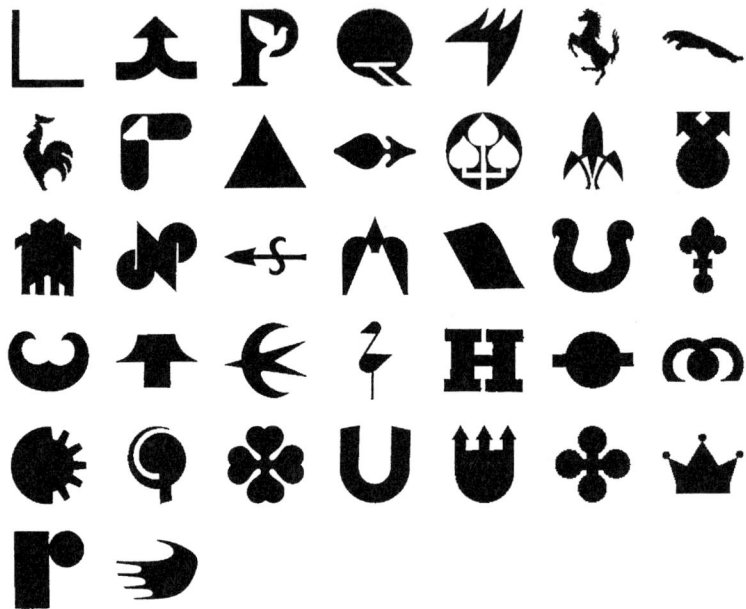

**Fig. 2.** Test set - originals

different from the one just before it. The number of rows and columns in the image as well as the sequence $S$ will be linearly stored on disk. (When the best bit-per-pixel resolution is used, it was found that RLE compression will result in no additional size reduction; an indication that the resulting file is quite compact and has a maximum entropy.)

The complexity of the algorithm is $O(nh)$ where $n$ is the number of contour pixels and $h$ is the height of the resulting tree. More details can be found in [9] with regard to the underlying base algorithm. (We note that the convex hull of a contour can be computed in $O(n)$.)

The reconstruction is done by a polygon filling algorithm applied to the resulting sequence of vertices $S$. Even though the pixels in $S$ are just a (usually small) subset of the pixels in $C$, they are *always* enough for an exact (lossless) reconstruction of the original set $F$. By controlling the parameter *mindepth* (line 13 of Algorithm 1), "shallow" concavities along $C$ can be ignored, consequently reducing the length of $S$, and therefore increasing the compression ratio. A *mindepth* value of *zero* will result in a lossless compression. A *mindepth* value of *one*, on the other hand, will result in a near-lossless compression with ratios that are usually much higher than the lossless case (for an $n \times n$ image, where approximately $32 < n < 256$).

The method also allows for shape information to be extracted, possibly for shape retrieval and matching purposes, from the compressed domain; that is, without the need to fully decompress the image. This can be done since the concavity tree of the shape can be easily extracted from the compressed domain,

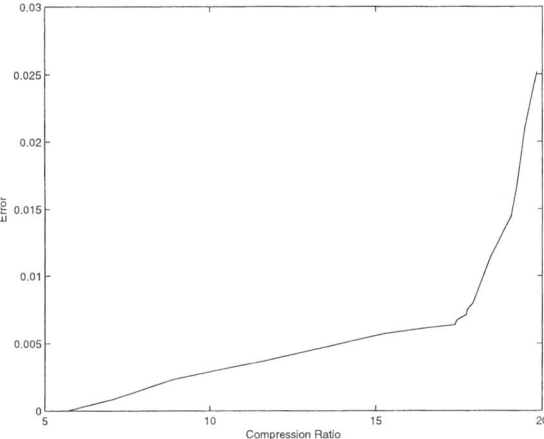

**Fig. 3.** Compression ratio versus error rate for the 37 images shown in Figure 2

without the need to reconstruct the image, and then find its contour(s), which can then be used for shape representation, matching, and retrieval as per [7,8], for example.

## 3 Experimental Results

We test the method on a set of 37 binary trademark images (see Figure 2) and compare the resulting compression ratio with that of JBIG. Figure 3 shows the plot of the reconstruction error as a function of the compression ratio averaged for the 37 images. The average compression ratio for JBIG for the 37 images was 11.5:1. For a lossless reconstruction, our method achieved a compression ratio of 5.7:1. However, with a near lossless reconstruction (examples are shown in Figures 4 and 5), the compression ratio averages 17.4:1. The average error was then 0.006. The method can simply be extended to multi-silhouette images, with or without holes, as shown in Figure 6. In addition, the resulting sequence of vertices that is used in the polygon filling operation can be used as a polygonal approximation of the object, either in the lossless or lossy case. Figure 7 shows some examples.

## 4 Summary and Conclusions

This paper presents a concise shape representation generated during the extraction of concavity trees. The representation is reversible and is equivalent to a lossless, near lossless, or lossy compression. When compared to the JBIG standard, compression ratios that are on average 150% better are obtained with a near-lossless error of 0.6%. The method is thus suitable for shape representation and matching in the compressed domain; polygonal approximation; and vector-based image compression.

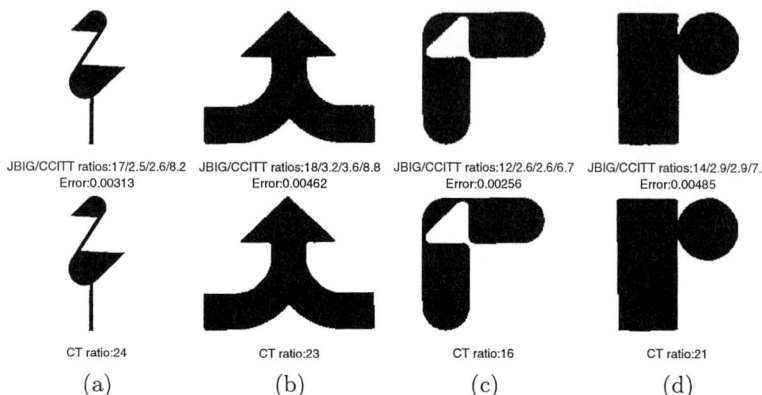

**Fig. 4.** Four examples of original (top) and compressed/reconstructed images (bottom). Note the almost imperceptible pixel error in the images in the bottom. JBIG as well as CCITT, group III, and group IV fax compression ratios are indicated below original. Concavity tree compression ratios are below.

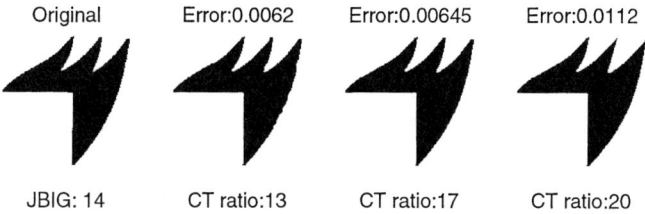

**Fig. 5.** This figure shows the effects of increasing the compression ratio for a given image. JBIG ratio is 14:1.

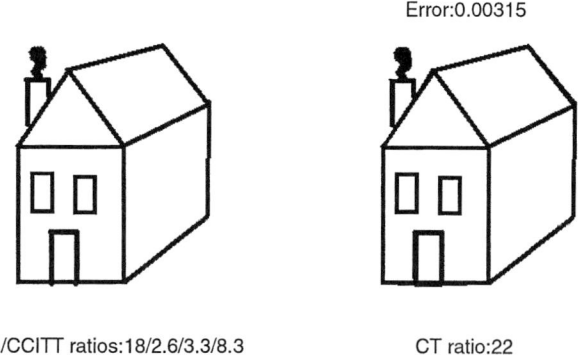

**Fig. 6.** Extensibility to multi-object shapes with holes

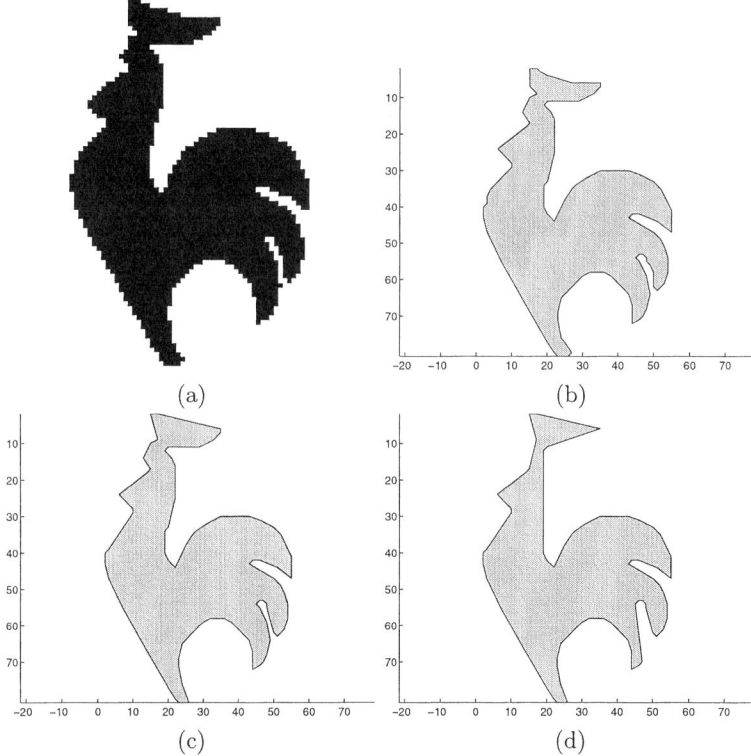

**Fig. 7.** The representation as a polygonal approximation of original (a) corresponding to a reconstruction error of 0.0058 (b), 0.008 (c), and 0.01 (d)

## References

1. Sklansky, J.: Measuring concavity on a rectangular mosaic. IEEE Transactions on Computers **C-21** (1972) 1355–1364
2. Batchelor, B.: Hierarchical shape description based upon convex hulls of concavities. Journal of Cybernetics **10** (1980) 205–210
3. Batchelor, B.: Shape descriptors for labeling concavity trees. Journal of Cybernetics **10** (1980) 233–237
4. Borgefors, G., Sanniti di Baja, G.: Methods for hierarchical analysis of concavities. In: Proceedings of the International Conference on Pattern Recognition. Volume 3. (1992) 171–175
5. Borgefors, G., Sanniti di Baja, G.: Analyzing nonconvex 2D and 3D patterns. Computer Vision and Image Understanding **63** (1996) 145–157
6. Xu, J.: Hierarchical representation of 2-D shapes using convex polygons: A morphological approach. Pattern Recognition Letters **18** (1997) 1009–1017
7. El Badawy, O., Kamel, M.: Shape retrieval using concavity trees. In: Proceedings of the International Conference on Pattern Recognition. Volume 3. (2004) 111–114

8. El Badawy, O., Kamel, M.: Matching concavity trees. In: Proceedings of the Joint IAPR International Workshops on Structural, Syntactic, and Statistical Pattern Recognition. (2004) 556–564
9. El Badawy, O., Kamel, M.: Hierarchical representation of 2-D shapes using convex polygons: a contour-based approach. Pattern Recognition Letters **26** (2005) 865–877

# Content-Based Image Retrieval Using Perceptual Shape Features

Mei Wu and Qigang Gao

Faculty of Computer Science, Dalhousie University, Halifax, NS B3H 1W5, Canada
{mwu, qggao}@cs.dal.ca

**Abstract.** A key issue of content-based image retrieval is exploring how to bridge the gap between the high-level semantics of an image and its lower-level properties, such as color, texture and edge. In this paper, we present a new method using perceptual edge features, called generic edge tokens (GET), as image shape content descriptors for CBIR. GETs represent basic types of perceptually distinguishable edge segments including both linear and nonlinear features, which are modeled as qualitative shape descriptors based on perceptual organization principles. In the method, an image is first transformed into GET map on the fly. The base GETs can be grouped into higher-level perceptual shape structures (PSS) as additional shape descriptors. Image content is represented statistically by perceptual feature histograms (PFHs) of GETs and PSSs. Similarity is evaluated by comparing the differences between the corresponding PFHs from two images. Experimental results are provided to demonstrate the potential of the proposed method.

## 1 Introduction

Content-based image retrieval (CBIR) is used to retrieve images from an archived database or the Web, based on analysis of image content and a user query. A major challenge of CBIR is to derive and represent meaningful semantics of and image from various lower-level features, such as color, texture and shape.

Most of the research in this domain have been dealing with the following three sub-areas: feature extraction, content representation and similarity measure. In the past few decades, various image features and extraction methods had been developed. The most commonly used features may be divided into following categories: color-based, such as color histograms and color moments [1]; texture-based, such as Tamura features [2] and wavelet transforms [3]; and shape-based, such as various Fourier descriptors [4] and moments [5]. In the area of image content representation, vector or histogram based methods are used [3] [1]. The methods for similarity measure include Minkowski distances, histogram intersection, Chi-square test, and information theory based measures [1].

The performance of most current systems is far from satisfactory. In contrast, the human vision system is incredibly powerful and flexible in evaluating content similarities between images. Clearly the mainstream CBIR techniques are not applying all the principles upon which human perception relies.

Hence, some researchers propose to use perceptual organization principles to model certain image features as perceived by humans. Perceptual features may be descriptive in nature and can be grouped by theories of human perception and cognition psychology [6]. Perceptual shape features, unlike color and texture features which rely on pixel-level computations, may be treated as meaningful entities that can incorporate with both local and global structural information. The combination of these two types of information can be used to interpret the semantics of the image. Perceptual grouping, as defined in theoretical psychology, may be used to model and merge small perceptual entities into larger ones, which may contain enhanced structural information. Some efforts have been made to apply this approach to CBIR. In [7], straight line features were used for grouping L-shape, U-shape and parallel lines for similarity measures. Bilodeau [8] proposed a parts-based model for object representation in which perceptual organization properties of proximity, similarity and parallelism were used for object segmentation.

In this paper, we will present a new edge-based feature model for simulating perceptual shape descriptors for CBIR, using generic edge tokens (GETs) [6]. GETs are base-level perceptual shape entities which are extracted on an ad hoc basis. GETs are then grouped into perceptual shape structures (PSS), including parallel pairs, and various junction patterns of GETs, which are higher-level features of image content. The GET and PSS features together form perceptual vocabularies for describing shape semantics. Image content is statistically represented by perceptual feature histograms (PFHs). Content similarity between two images is measured by comparing the corresponding PFHs.

The remaining sections of this paper are organized as follows. Section 2 introduces the generic model of GETs. Section 3 presents the content representation and similarity measures. Section 4 provides experimental results, system evaluation and comparison. Conclusion is drawn in Section 5.

## 2 Perceptual Features for CBIR

The base set of perceptual features for CBIR are generic edge tokens, i.e. GETs. Each GET represents a class of edge segments which satisfy the property definitions given in Figure 1. GETs can be grouped into higher-level shape structures based on perceptual organization principles. Perceptual organization is interesting because it helps discover the hidden structural information where constituent parts themselves can't express. Perceptual organization also makes this psychological property cognition process computationally implementable. Perceptual shape features in our system are made up by the following classes: base GETs, predominant GETs, parallel GETs and joint GETs.

### 2.1 Base GET Class

GETs are the minimum perceptual stable shape entities, first presented by Gao and Wong in [6]. Figure 1 (left) shows how an object shape or edge pattern is partitioned into GETs by a set of perceptual curve partitioning points (CPPs). GETs and CPPs are defined according to the monotonic changes of the generic curve geometry function and its first derivative function. Suppose a planar curve is expressed as $y = f(x)$, GETs are defined by the monotonic variations of $f(x)$ and $f'(x)$ binary functions, as is illustrated in Figure 1 (center). The eight classes of GETs are defined by the eight possible combinations of the two binary functions, shown in Figure 1 (right). Examples of GETs and CPPs extracted from an image can be found in Figure 2.

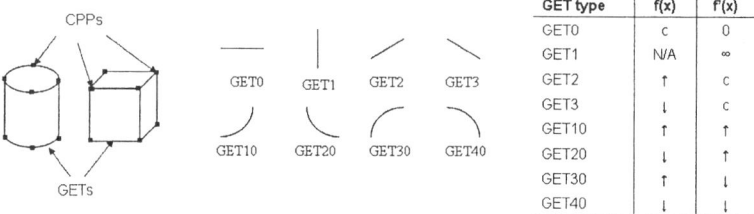

**Fig. 1.** Sample GETs and CPPs are shown in the left. In the center are eight GET types. The definition of 8 GET types are given in the right. ↑ stands for monotonic increase and ↓ stands for monotonic decrease.

**Fig. 2.** The image on the left is original image; the right is its GET and CPP map

### 2.2 Predominant GET

Predominant GET, or long GET (LGET), is used to extract from an image the most salient GETs, so as to best distinguish one image from another. In this work, supposing the mean and standard deviation of GET length in an individual image are $\mu$ and $\sigma$, predominant GETs are defined as those GETs whose length are greater than $\mu + \sigma$, assuming $\mu$ and $\sigma$ vary by image.

### 2.3 Parallel GET Pair

Parallel GET pairs (PGETs) are important perceptual features since many manmade objects have parallel edges, which can help distinguish images with manmade objects from natural scene images. Unlike other research relying on parallel lines, our parallel GETs include parallel curve features as well. Parallel curve segments are particular important for images containing curved objects, such as cars, which have more parallel curves than parallel lines because of their smooth metal surface. A commonly accepted parallel curve definition was given in [9]. It says that two curves are parallel if every normal to one curve is a normal to the other curve and the distance between where the normals cut the two curves is constant. However, it is computationally costly and unnecessary to strictly follow this definition for extracting parallel curves. Based on our GET model, parallel GET extraction process is illustrated in Figure 3 and explained below. First, nearby GET pairs sharing a same GET type are screened. Then for each GET pair, project both GET curves to the central line ($l$) of their chords ($l_1$ and $l_2$). If the overlap of the projection is longer than a pre-defined threshold (mean value of GET lengths, in our case), the overlapped curves are considered as a candidate PGET. A candidate PGET is truly parallel if they share a similar distance among $n$ pairs of points along curve. An empirical parallel confidence $pc$ is used to estimate the parallelism of PGET and defined as:

$$pc = 1 - \frac{max(dist_i) - min(dist_i)}{avg\_len} \qquad (1)$$

where $dist_i$ is the distance between the $i$th pair of points along curve, and $avg\_len$ is PGET's average curve length. A PGET example can be found in Figure 4 (upper right).

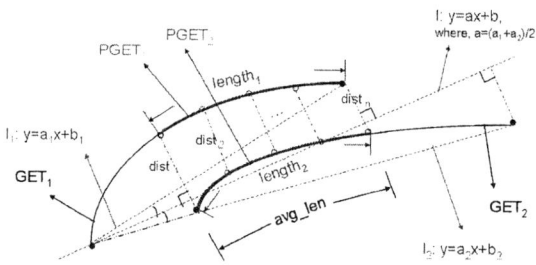

**Fig. 3.** Parallel GET extraction

## 2.4 Joint GET

Two adjacent GETs joint at a CPP and form a joint GET pattern (JGET). In our experiment, there are curve-curve, curve-line and line-line GET joint types. Figure 4 (lower right) shows detected line-line JGETs.

# 3 Image Content Representation and Similarity Measure

## 3.1 Feature Histogram Representation

Perceptual feature histograms (PFHs) are used to represent the statistical distributions of both GET features and perceptual shape structure (PSS) features.

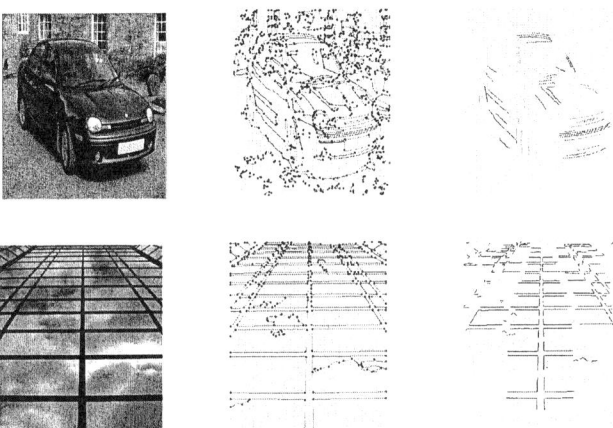

**Fig. 4.** The upper images, from left to right, are original image, GETs and detected PGETs; the lower images, from left to right, are original image, GETs and JGETs

In GET feature histogram, GET_type, GET_length and frequency percentage are used. In PSS histograms, features include PGET_type, parallel confidence, JGET_type, joint angle and frequency percentage.

Sturges' rule [10] is applied to determine the histogram bin number for GET attributes. According to Sturges' rule, the bin number is the integer number closest to: $1 + \log_2(M)$, $M$ is the number of observations. In our case, $M$ is for example the number of GETs detected in one image. Figure 5 is sample GET histograms of a flower image, representing the frequency distribution by GET_type and GET_length.

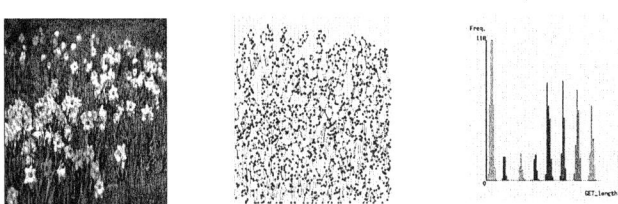

**Fig. 5.** Left: original image; center: GET map; right: GET histogram

### 3.2 Similarity Measure

The sum of weighted Euclidean distance of each PFH is used as the similarity measure. First a distance $d_{H_i}$, i.e., Euclidean distance, is calculated for each pair of corresponding histogram $H_i$ and $H_i^{'}$, $i = 1, 2, 3, 4$. Then the distance between two images is defined as:

$$Similarity = \sum_{i=1}^{4} w_i d_{H_i} \qquad (2)$$

The weighting coefficient $w_i$ is decided by decimal scaling normalization, where $w_i = 10^j$, $j$ is the largest number such that $|max(w_i * d_{H_i})| < 1$. In our experiment, the weights $w_i$ corresponding to GET, LGET, PGET and JGET histograms are 10, 1, 1, 10.

## 4 Experiments and Evaluation

We randomly selected 164 images from seven categories of a benchmark dataset [11]. Sample images are given in Figure 6.

**Fig. 6.** The test database has 164 images in 7 categories

Our evaluation is based on the method suggested by Müller et al. [12]. This evaluation method combines both numerical measures and graphical representation. The evaluation measurements are:

- $Rank_1$ and $\widetilde{Rank}$: are the rank of the first relevant image and the normalized average rank of all the relevant images retrieved:

$$\widetilde{Rank} = \frac{1}{NN_R}(\sum_{i=1}^{N_R} R_i - \frac{N_R(N_R-1)}{2})$$

where, N is the total image number, $N_R$ is the number of relevant images, $R_i$ is the rank of the $i$th relevant image.
- P(20), P(50), $P(N_R)$: the precision when the first 20, 50 and all relevant images are retrieved.
- $R_p(0.5)$ and R(100): the recall when the precision reaches 0.5 and when the first 100 images are retrieved.
- A recall-precision graph.

Since our test dataset is relatively small, the measures are scale down proportionally to the size of the dataset and the relevant images. For example, measure P(20) and P(50) are changed to P(10), and R(100) is changed to R(20). Our experiments are conducted on PFHs of (a) GETs only, (b) GETs and PSSs, and (c) GETs and weight-adaptive PSSs. The experimental results of $Rank_1$, $\widetilde{Rank}$ and $P(N_R)$ on these three tests are quite similar, with 1, 0.14 and 0.27 respectively. But $P(10)$, $R_p(0.5)$ and $R(20)$, which indicate how the first retrieved images are similar to the query images, vary by tests. An interesting observation can be made from Table 1 (a) and (b). When taking the P(10) as the main indicator of effectiveness, application of the PSS features increases the precisions for aircrafts and cars, but decreases the retrieval precisions of flower, tree and mountain images. This corresponds to the fact that many man-made objects have distinguishable parallel structures. Hence, in such cases, we further adjusting the weighting of PSS histograms. By increasing the weighting on man-made objects and decreasing the weighting of natural objects, an improved result is achieved as shown in $P(10)$ (c). Figure 7 shows sample results of two queries, using PFHs of both GET and weight-adaptive PSS.

**Table 1.** $P(10), R_p(0.5), R(20)$ comparison based on a) GETs only, b) GETs and PSSs, and c) GETs and weight-adaptive PSSs

|  | $P(10)$ | | | $R_p(0.5)$ | | | $R(20)$ | | |
| --- | --- | --- | --- | --- | --- | --- | --- | --- | --- |
|  | (a) | (b) | (c) | (a) | (b) | (c) | (a) | (b) | (c) |
| 04_25_1 (building) | 0.8 | 0.8 | 0.8 | 0.32 | 0.37 | 0.37 | 0.29 | 0.24 | 0.24 |
| 12_33_1 (flower) | 0.9 | 0.8 | 1 | 0.52 | 0.56 | 0.56 | 0.48 | 0.48 | 0.52 |
| 15_19_1 (tree) | 0.9 | 0.8 | 0.8 | 0.95 | 0.9 | 0.95 | 0.7 | 0.65 | 0.65 |
| 15_47_1 (mountain) | 0.8 | 0.7 | 0.9 | 0.71 | 0.82 | 0.79 | 0.46 | 0.39 | 0.46 |
| 20_20_1 (aircraft) | 0.6 | 0.8 | 0.8 | 0.38 | 0.46 | 0.5 | 0.38 | 0.42 | 0.5 |
| 2026_29_1 (ferry) | 0.9 | 0.9 | 0.9 | 1 | 1 | 1 | 0.92 | 0.92 | 0.92 |
| 29_06_1 (car) | 0.5 | 0.7 | 0.9 | 0.38 | 0.88 | 0.88 | 0.5 | 0.75 | 0.81 |
| Average | 0.77 | 0.79 | 0.87 | 0.61 | 0.71 | 0.72 | 0.53 | 0.55 | 0.59 |

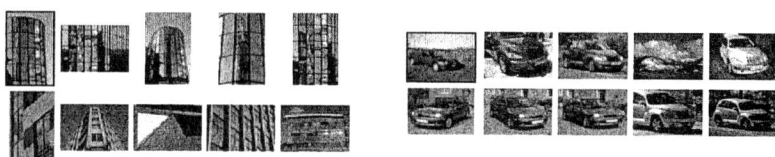

**Fig. 7.** Two samples of the top ten retrieved images. The upper left is the query.

## 5 Conclusions

In this paper, we present a set of novel perceptual edge features for CBIR. The experiments proved our hypothesis that the proposed GET features are useful for representing image as shape content descriptors. In addition to the base GETs, the high-level structures of GET groupings are also valuable for shape-based image content estimation. There are rich directions for future research in developing GET-based techniques which include the following: 1) Define various additional GET grouping structures. 2) Develop GET-based image representation schemes and similarity measure methods. 3) Investigate GET-based region grouping and texture representation methods. 4) Integrate GET features with colors.

# References

1. Siggelkow, S.: Feature histograms for content-based image retrieval. PhD thesis, Albert-Ludwigs-Universität Freiburg, Fakultät für Angewandte Wissenschaften, Germany (2002)
2. Tamura, H., Mori, S., Yamawaki, T.: Textural features corresponding to visual perception. IEEE Trans on Systems, Man and Cybernetics **8** (1978) 460–472
3. Chen, L., Lu, G., Zhang, D.: Effects of different gabor filters parameters on image retrieval by texture. In: Multimedia Modelling Conference, 2004. Proceedings. 10th International. (2004) 273–278
4. Zhang, D., Lu, G.: Shape-based image retrieval using generic fourier descriptor. SP:IC **17** (2002) 825–848
5. Kim, H., Kim, J.: A modified zernike moment shape descriptor invariant to translation, rotation and scale for similarity-based image retrieval. In: Multimedia and Expo, 2000 IEEE International Conference on. Volume 1. (2000) 307–310
6. Gao, Q., Wong, A.: Curve detection based on perceptual organization. Pattern Recognition **27** (1993) 1039–1046
7. Iqbal, Q., Aggarwal, J.: Perceptual grouping for image retrieval and classification. In: 3rd IEEE Computer Society Workshop on Perceptual Organization in Computer Vision (POCV01). (2001) 19.1–19.4
8. Bilodeau, G., Bergevin, R.: Plastique: Image retrieval based on cognitive theories. In: VI 2003. (2003) 292–298
9. of Mathematical, S., Computational Sciences, U.o.S.A.: More definitions for associated curves. http://www-groups.dcs.st-and.ac.uk/history/Curves/Definitions2.html (2005)
10. Sturges, H.: The choice of a class interval. Journal of the American Statistical Association **21** (1926) 65–66
11. Inc., F.: Free pictures. http://www.freefoto.com/ (2005)
12. Müller, H., Müller, W., Squire, D., Pun, T.: Performance evaluation in content-based image retrieval: Overview and proposals. Technical report, Computer Vision Group, Computing Science Center, University of Geneva (1999)

# Compressed Telesurveillance Video Database Retrieval Using Fuzzy Classification System

Samia F. Khelifi[1], M. Elarbi Boudihir[2], and Rachid Nourine[1]

[1] ICEPS Laboratory. Research Centre, Algeria
Samiafk@dammam.kfu.edu.sa, khelifisamia@lycos.com,
nourinerachid@lycos.com
[2] Dept. Computer Sciences and Information System, M. Ibn Saoud University, Er Riad, KSA
ELARBI@imamu.edu.sa

**Abstract.** This paper proposes a video retrieval system from compressed outdoor video surveillance databases. The aim is to extract moving objects from frames provided by MPEG video stream in order to classify them into predefined categories according to image-based properties, and then robustly index them. The principal idea is to combine between useful properties of metrical classification and the notion of temporal consistency. Fuzzy geometry classification is used in order to provide an efficient method to classify motion regions into three generic categories: pedestrian, vehicle and no identified object. The temporal consistency provides a robust classification to changes of objects appearance and occlusion of object motion. The classified motion regions are used as templates for metrical training algorithms and as keys for tree indexing technique.

## 1 Introduction

The large volume of images and videos pose a significant challenge for storage, retrieval and indexing the visual information from multimedia databases. Two approaches have been commonly used: a content indexing approach, where the index terms serve to encode the content of images; and a structural approach where images are represented as a hierarchy of regions, objects, and portions of objects. The content indexing approach is based on features such as colour, texture, shape and sketch extracted from an image, which essentially serve as the index. The structural approach is based on spatial relationships between objects or regions in a scene. In video indexing techniques using temporal features as keys, image sequences are indexed based on the motion properties of objects within the sequence. Temporal features allow the user to specify queries that involve the exact positions and trajectories of the objects in the shot. The survey of what has been achieved on the content-based image retrieval in the past few years and what are the potential research directions can be found in [Bru 99] [Hab 99] [Fer 98] [Gud 95] [Idr 97] [Smo 94] [Sch 00] [Tiz 97].

Many content-based image search systems have been developed for various applications in order to extract intrinsic image features suitable of automatic indexing and retrieval. These features are used to reduce the complexity of image comparisons and to improve the organisation of image database. Unfortunately, automatic retrieval of suitable features is very hard; it is usually only feasible for retrieval systems that incorporate a high degree of domain-specific knowledge about the type of image contents to be retrieved. In unconstrained images, the set of known object classes is not available. Also, use of the image search systems varies greatly. The knowledge of the image content can be used to index specific images in the database for purposes of rapid retrieval [Ike 01] [Nib 93] [Sch 00]. In this context, we developed a system for retrieval and indexing telesurveillance MPEG videos in relation to the dynamic content of image sequences. It includes a robust fuzzy inference system to classify motion regions into pedestrians, vehicles and no-identified objects.

## 2 System Overview

The system consists of five stages (figure 1). In the first stage (section 3), the digital video is segmented into elementary shots. In the second stage (section 4), all the moving objects are detected and segmented into motion regions. In the third stage (section 5), the principal idea is to exploit on one hand, the useful properties classification of fuzzy metrical classification in order to distinguish between types of motion regions, and on the other hand, the notion of temporal consistency in order to provide a robust classification against changes of objects appearance, occlusion, and cessation of object motion. In the fourth stage (section 6), once a motion region has been classified, it can be used as training template for the indexing and retrieval process.

## 3 Video Segmentation

The input data of the system consists of image sequences taken from outdoor video surveillance scenes. Video has both spatial and temporal dimensions and hence a good video index should capture the spatiotemporal contents of the scene. In order to achieve this, the first step in video indexing is to decompose a video sequence into shots. Video shots may be associated with key or representative frames that best represent the shot. Several shot detection algorithms on compressed and uncompressed video are presented in [Yeo 95, 96] [Shn 96] [Bru 99] [Idr 97].

We propose to use a unified approach for scene change detection in motion JPEG and MPEG. This algorithm is based on the use of only DC coefficients. First we have to construct DC frame $f_m^{DC}$ for every frame in the sequence. The DC coefficients in JPEG and I-frames in MPEG are obtained directly from each block. The DC coefficients for B- and P- frames are also estimated. The sum of the difference magnitude of the DC frames $f_m^{DC}$ and $f_n^{DC}$ is used as a measure of similarity between two frames.

$$D(f_m^{DC}, f_n^{DC}) = \sum_{i=1}^{X/8} \sum_{j=1}^{Y/8} \left| P(f_m^{DC}, I, i, j) - P(f_n^{DC}, I, i, j) \right| \qquad (1)$$

Where $P(f_m^{DC}, I, i, j)$ is the DC coefficient of block (i, j). A scene change from $f_m$ to $f_n$ is declared whenever $D(f_m^{DC}, f_n^{DC})$ exceeds a prespecified threshold.

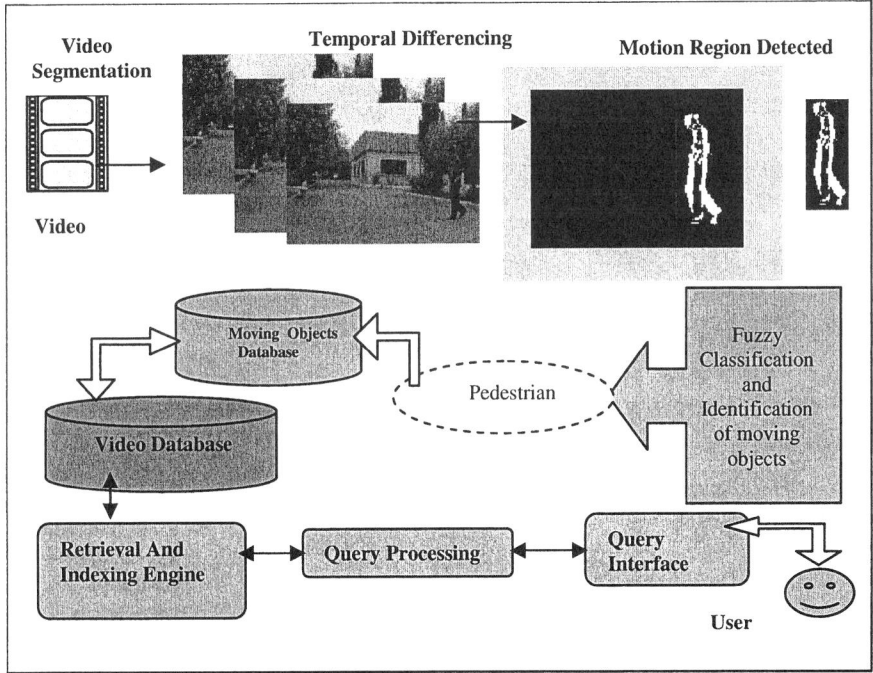

**Fig. 1.** The video retrieval system overview

Video shots may be associated with a key frame that best represents the shot and can later be used for the retrieval process. Let a shot represented by its first frame. Subsequent frames are then compared to the first frame, looking for a frame whose difference is above a given threshold $T_s$. If such a frame is found, it is considered as a key if it is followed by a continuous sequence of frames differing by at least $T_s$ from the previous key frame. Choosing those frames of a video shot as key frames is based on the observation that consecutive frames are often almost identical. In addition, the shot is usually characterized by the first few frames, before the camera begins to zoom or close-up. So in our application it is a sufficient choice.

## 4 Motion Region Detection

Then, all the moving objects must be accurately isolated from the background in order to be classified. Two methods are possible: temporal differencing (TD) and template correlation matching [Bre 97] [Bru 99] [Hua 83] [Kru 98] [Lip 98]. Both approaches have advantages and drawbacks. TD is impossible if there is a significant camera motion. It also fails if the target becomes occluded. On the other hand, the template correlation matching is not robust to changes in object size, orientation or even changing in light conditions. His use is most appropriate when the target size is small. So, the properties of these two methods are complementary. This is the motivation for combining TD and the notion of temporal consistency. The idea is to use TD to detect moving regions and apply temporal consistency algorithm to reduce misclassified motion regions.

Firstly each I frame of a shot is smoothed with the second derivative in time of the temporal Gaussian function. If $fn$ is the intensity of the $n^{th}$ I frame of the shot, then the absolute difference function $\Delta_n$ is:

$$\Delta_n = |f_n - f_{n-1}| \qquad (2)$$

The result of the difference is binarized in order to separate changed pixels from others. To do this, a threshold function is used and a motion image $M_n$ can be extracted.

$$M_n(u, v) = \begin{cases} f_n(u,v) & \text{if } \Delta_n(u,v) \geq T \\ 0 & \text{if } \Delta_n(u,v) < T \end{cases} \qquad (3)$$

Where $T$ is an appropriate threshold chosen after a several tests according to the exterior environment with different acquisition conditions [Khe 03].

To separate the regions of interest from the rest of image, binary statistical morphological operators (erosion and dilatation) are used. This allows decreasing the number of connected components. Then, the moving sections must be grouped into motion regions $R_n(i)$. This is done using a connected component criterion (figure 2). It allows to group different motion sections susceptible to be a part of the same region, or allows grouping the residual motion parts into one motion region. This propriety is useful to identify pedestrian who are not rigid and also useful in occultation of the moving object and other target.

## 5 Fuzzy Motion Region Classification System

The task of the system is to distinguish the cars from pedestrians from other moving and stationary objects like animals, trees, roads and buildings in the image sequences and identify them as vehicles, human or non-identified object. The principal idea is to

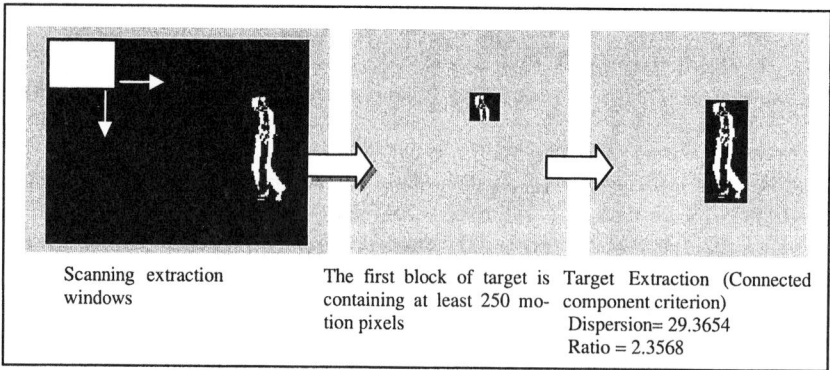

Fig. 2. Grouping moving objects into motion regions using a connected component criterion

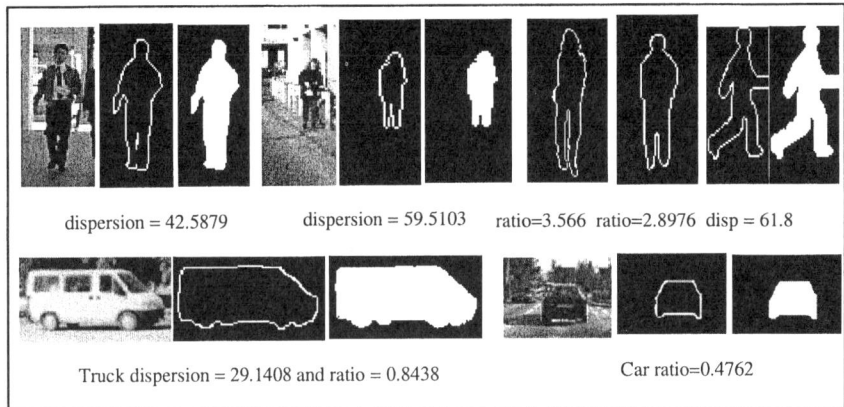

**Fig. 3.** Human and vehicles dispersion/ratio values calculated for some image of the learning database

exploit useful properties of fuzzy metrical classification in order to provide a robust method to classify motion regions. Indeed, the regions are not always crisply defined, it is sometimes more appropriate to regard them as fuzzy subsets of the image [Bar 92] [Bez 92] [Dzu 01] [Rud 94] [Tiz 97]. The motivation of the use of the geometry features is that is computationally inexpensive and invariant to lighting conditions. On the other hand, it is obvious that the human, with its small and more complex shape, will have larger dispersion than a vehicle (figure 3).

If we define an appropriate membership function μ for the object [Khe 04], the area *a* and the perimeter *p* of the object can be calculated as follows:

Area of fuzzy sets:

$$a(\mu) = \sum \mu \qquad (4)$$

Perimeter of a fuzzy set:

$$p(\mu) = \sum_{m=1}^{M} \sum_{n=1}^{N-1} |\mu_{mn} - \mu_{m,n+1}| + \sum_{n=1}^{N} \sum_{m=1}^{M-1} |\mu_{mn} - \mu_{m+1,n}| \qquad (5)$$

Where *M* and *N* are the dimensions of the image.

Based on the perimeter and the area, the dispersion and the ratio of a fuzzy set can be determined as follows:

$$Dispersion = \frac{(Perimetre)^2}{Area} \qquad (6)$$

$$Ratio = \frac{Length}{width} \qquad (7)$$

The classified motion regions are used as templates for metrical training algorithms (table 1). The fuzzy system is based on two entrances: the dispersion and the ratio of the motion regions, and three exits: one exit for human, one exit for the vehicles and one exit for no identified objects. For every entrance, we have two fuzzy sets: one for the category of humans and other for the category of vehicles [Khe 03].

**Table 1.** Results of the learning algorithm

| Class | Vehicle | Pedestrian |
|---|---|---|
| Dispersion | [17  45] | [23.2  125] |
| Dispersion Concentration | [20  30] | [30  60] |
| Ratio | [0.1  1.1] | [0.59  4.47] |
| Ratio Concentration | [0.2  0.7] | [1.9  3.2] |

The system leads good performances (98%) over databases of 270 examples where 116 are pedestrians, 124 are vehicles and the rest represent states that are no identified. The accuracy of the classification is largely independent of target size, appearance shape or speed. However, the main difficulty with metrical classification is that: when multiple humans close together, they can be misclassified as a vehicle according to the simple metric, if the target is very small, it tends to be rejected as no identified object, and a partly occluded vehicle may look like a human, or some background clutter may appear as a vehicle.

To overcome this problem, an additional hypothesis is used. The main idea is to record all potential motion regions $PR_n$ from the first frame of the shot. Each one of these potential regions must be observed along some frames of the shot to determine if they persist or not, and so decide to continue classifying them. To do this, for each new frame, each previous motion region $PR_{n-1}$ is matched to the spatially closest current motion region $R_n$ according to a mutual proximity rule. After this process, each previous potential motion region $PR_{n-1}$ whish have not been matched to current region are removed from the list of accepted motion regions. And any current motion region $R_n$ whish has not been matched is considered new potential region. The metric operators, dispersion and ratio of each frame, are used to update the classification hypothesis [Khe 04]. The most advantage of this method is that if an occluded object is misclassified it will be correctly classified with the passage of time. Another advantage is that the instable motions appearing at the background, such as leaves blowing in the wind, will be misclassified as no-identified regions.

## 6 Indexing and Retrieval

Indexing digital video, based on its content, can be carried out at several levels of abstraction, beginning with indices like the video program name to much lower level aspects of video like the specified motion objects and their locations of the video [Idr 97] [Ray 96].

The interactive retrieval system proposed in this paper includes a query interface sub-module and a query by content retrieval sub-module as shown in figure 1. To facilitate storage and retrieval in visual information systems, flexible data structures should be used. Structures such as R-tree family, R$^*$-tree, quad-tree, and grid file are commonly used. Each structure has its advantages and disadvantages; some have limited domains and some can be used concurrently with others. To achieve a fast retrieval speed and make the retrieval system truly robust, a quad-tree indexing technique is applied [Khe 03]. The goal of the system is to be able to retrieve a set of sequences, which have motion objects similar to that specified by the query. A database of moving objects is formed, where each object is indexed according to its descriptors that are defined in the section 4. Image indexing techniques are then applied on the reference frames.

## 7 Results

The system has been implemented at the intelligent control and electrical power systems laboratory ICEPS, Research Centre of Dr. D. Liabes University. SBA. Algeria. The system has been applied to large amounts of different video environments where human and vehicular activities are present. Fig. 4 shows some

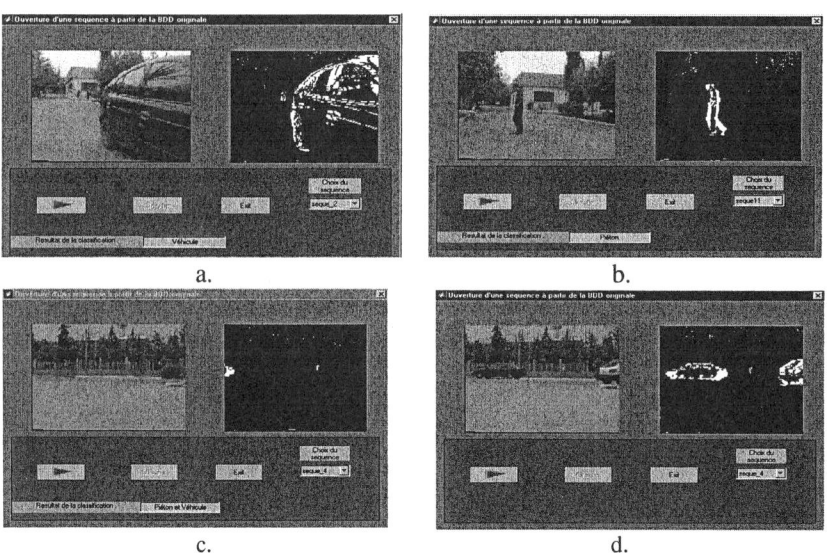

**Fig. 4.** Sequences from the ICEPS Laboratory Database automatically segmented and classified as vehicle regions (a), pedestrian regions (b), pedestrian and vehicles regions (c and d)

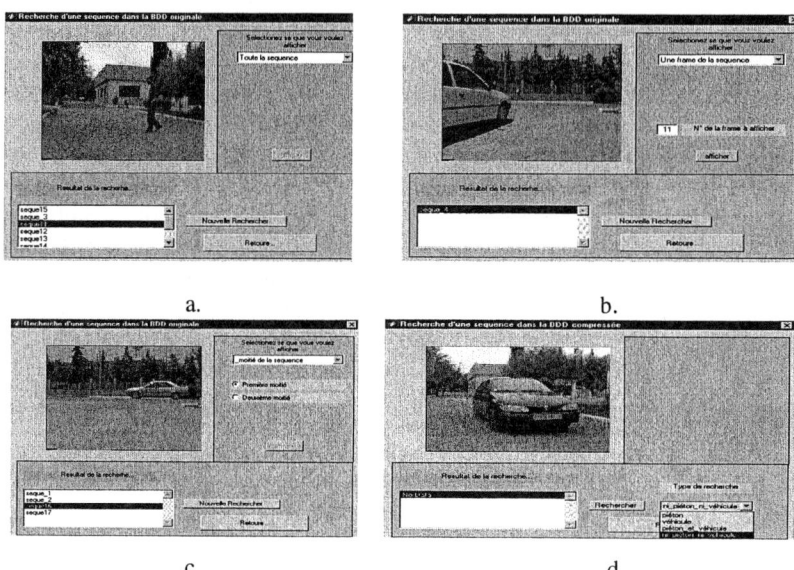

**Fig. 5.** Searching the sequences that contain mobile pedestrian (a), mobile vehicle and pedestrian (b). vehicle (c and d)

examples of target classification. For single targets, the system provides a robust classification. Note that trees blowing in the wind are completely rejected. Furthermore, the accuracy of the classification is largely independent of target size, appearance shape, speed, lighting conditions or viewpoint. It is also computationally inexpensive. However, when multiple humans close together for a long time, they can be misclassified as a vehicle according to the simple metric. Another limitation of the system is that if the target is very smal, less than 4x4 pixels, it tends to be rejected as no identified object. The main problem with vehicles recognition is that when, vehicle is partially occluded for long times, it could be rejected. Also, pedestrians tend to move in close groups that can be misclassified as vehicles according to the simple metric. Fig. 4 and 5 show some results of the system.

## 8 Conclusion

The work presented here is concerned with motion region detection, classification and indexing moving regions from MPEG surveillance video sequences. The first stage is to decompose the video sequences into shots saving unnecessary decompression. Then, a set of representative frames is selected. The representative frames of a shot are used to the image pre-processing stage in order to generate a collection of moving regions of interest. A robust fuzzy system is proposed to classify moving regions into predefined categories; humans and vehicles, according to image-based properties. Classification is based on simple rules whish are largely independent of appearance or

3D models. Consequently, the metrical classification whish is explored in this paper, is based purely on object's shape, and not on its image content. An additional hypothesis on temporal consistency is used to make the classification system robust to changes of objects appearance and occlusion of motion regions. However, some problems remain to solve: it is necessary to study the problem that when multiple humans close together and when a target is very small.

# References

[Bar 92] Bart K., 'Neural Networks and fuzzy Systems.' Prentice Hall. Englewood Cliffs.NJ. 1992.
[Bez 92] Bezdek J.C., 'On the relationship between neural networks, pattern recognition and intelligence', *Intenational Jornal of Approximate Reasonning,* Vol 6, p. 85-107, 1992.
[Bre 97] Bregler C., 'Learning and recognizing human dynamics in video sequences', *Proceeding of IEEE CVPR 97*, p. 568-574. 1997.
[Bru 99] Brunelli R., Mich O., Modena C. M., 'A survey on the automatic indexing of video data', *Jal. of visual communication and image representation,* Vol 10, p. 78-112, 1999.
[Dzu 01] Dzung L. Pham., 'Spatial models for fuzzy clustering', *Jal. Computer vision and image understanding*, Vol 84, p. 285-297, 2001.
[Fer 98] Ferman A. M., Murat Tekalp A., 'Efficient filtering and clustering methods for temporal video segmentation and visual summarization', *Jal. of visual communication and image representation,* 99(4), p. 336-351, 1998.
[Gud 95] Gudivada V. N., Raghvan V. V., 'Content-based image systems', *IEEE Comput,* 28(9), p.18-22, Sept. 1995.
[Hab 99] Habed A., 'Content-based access image and video libraries', Math-info department, Sherbrooke University, 1999.
[Idr 97] Idris F., Pandranathan S., 'Review of image and video indexing techniques', *Jal. of visual communication and image representation*, 8(2): 146-166, June 1997.
[Ike 01] Iketani A., Nagai A., Kuno Y., Shirai Y., 'Real time surveillance system detecting persons in complex scenes', Jal. of *Real time imaging*, Vol 7, p. 433-446, 2001.
[Khe 03] Khelifi S., Boudihir M. E., Nourine R.,'Fuzzy Classification System for outdoor Video Databases Retrieval'. *In proceeding of AICSSA'03.* IEEE Int. Conf. on Computer Systems and Applications. Gammart. Tunisia. 14-18 July 2003.
[Khe 04] Khelifi S., Boudihir M. E., Nourine R., 'Content-Based Video Database Retrieval Using Fuzzy Classification System'. *In proceeding of MediaNet'04. 2$^{nd}$ International Conference on Intelligent Access of Multimedia Documents on Internet.* Tozeur. Tunisia. 25-28 Nov. 2004.
[khe 04] Khelifi S., Boudihir M. E., Nourine R., 'Video Database Indexing: an Approach using Fuzzy Classification of Moving Objects in Outdoor Videos'. *In proc. of MCSEAI'04. 8$^{th}$ Maghrebian Conference on Software Engineering and Artificial Intelligence.* Sousse. Tinisia. p. 555-566. 9-12 May 2004.
[khe 04] Khelifi S., Boudihir M. E., Nourine R., 'Fuzzy Classification System for Telesurveillance Databases Retrieval and Indexing'. *In proceeding of International IEEE/APS Conference on Mechatronics and Robotics.* Aachen. Germany. p. 20-25. 13-15 Sep. 2004.
[Kru 98] Krüger S., 'Motion analysis and estimation using multi-resolution affine models', Thesis submitted at the university of Bristol, July 1998.
[Lip 98] Lipton A. J., Fujiyoshi H., Patil R. S., 'Moving target classification and tracking from real-time video', *Submitted to IEEE WACV 98*, 1998.

[Nib 93] Niblack W., 'The QBIC project: querying images by content using colour, texture, and shape. Storage and Retrieval for Image and Video Databases', *In proceedings of the SPIE. no 1908.* San Jose California SPIE, Bellingham, p.173-187, Feb. 1993.

[Ray 96] Raymond Ng., Sedighian A., 'Evaluating multi-dimensional indexing structures for images transformed by principals component analysis', *In Proc. SPIE Storage and retrieval for image and video databases,* 1996.

[Rud 94] Rudolf K., Gebhardt. J. and Klowonn. F., 'Fundations of fuzzy systems'. John Wiley and Sons Ltd. Chichester. 1994.

[Smo 94] Smoliar S. W., Zhang H. J., 'Content-based video indexing and retrieval', *In proceeding of IEEE Multimedia,* 1(2), p.62-72, Summer 1994.

[Sch 00] Schonfeld D., Lescu D., 'VORTEX: video retrieval and tracking from compressed multimedia databases- multiple object tracking from MPEG-2 bit stream', *Jal. of visual communication and image representation,* Vol.11, p. 154-182, 2000.

[Shn 96] Shneier M. and Abdel M. M., 'Exploiting the JPEG compression scheme for image retrieval', *In Proceeding in IEEE Trans. Patt. Anal. Mach. Intell.* 18(8), p. 849-853. August 1996.

[Tiz 97] Tizhoosh H., 'Fuzzy image processing', Springer, 1997.

[Yeo 95] Yeo B.-L. and Liu B. 'A unifiedapproach to temporal segmentation of motion JPEG and MPEG compressed videos', *In proceeding of the International Conference on Multimedia Computing and Systems,* p. 81-88, May 1995.

[Yeo 96] Yeo B.-L. and Liu B. 'Efficient processing of compressed images and video', Ph.D. thesis, Dept. Of Electrical Engineering, Princeton University, Jan. 1996.

# Machine-Learning-Based Image Categorization

Yutao Han and Xiaojun Qi

Computer Science Department, Utah State University, Logan, UT 84322-4205
{yhan, xqi}@cc.usu.edu

**Abstract.** In this paper, a novel and efficient automatic image categorization system is proposed. This system integrates the MIL-based and global-feature-based SVMs for categorization. The IPs (Instance Prototypes) are derived from the segmented regions by applying MIL on the training images from different categories. The IPs-based image features are further used as inputs to a set of SVMs to find the optimum hyperplanes for categorizing training images. Similarly, global image features, including color histogram and edge histogram, are fed into another set of SVMs. For each test image, two sets of image features are constructed and sent to the two respective sets of SVMs. The decision values from two sets of SVMs are finally incorporated to obtain the final categorization results. The empirical results demonstrate that the proposed system outperforms the peer systems in terms of both efficiency and accuracy.

## 1 Introduction

Automatic image categorization has become more and more important with the development of Internet and the growth in the size of image databases. Finding relevant images from Internet and a large size image database is not a trivial task if images are not annotated. Manual categorization is a possible solution, but it is time-consuming and subjective. As a result, many researchers have focused on automatic image categorization. A few existing systems are briefly reviewed here.

Huang et al. [1] categorize images by using a classification tree, which captures the spatial correlation of colors in an image. Chapelle et al. [2] apply SVMs on the global 16×16×16-bin HSV color histograms to categorize images. Smith and Li [3] classify images by applying a composite region template descriptor matrix on the spatial orderings of regions. Barnard and Forsyth [4] apply a hierarchical statistic model to generate keywords for classification based on semantically meaningful regions. Jeon et al. [5] use the cross media relevance model to predict the probability of generating a word given the regions in an image. Li and Wang [6] propose an ALIP system which uses the 2D multi-resolution hidden Markov model on features of image blocks for classification. Murphy et al. [7] build 4 graphical models to relate features of image blocks to objects and perform joint scene and object recognition.

Recently, MIL (Multiple Instance Learning) has been applied for automatic image categorization. Maron and Ratan [8] use the DD (Diverse Density) learning algorithm for natural scene classification. Zhang and Goldman [9] use EM-DD algorithm, which combines EM (Expectation Maximization) with DD, to achieve a fast and scalable categorization. Andrews et al. [10] propose an MI-SVM approach for categorization, where region-based image features are iteratively fed into SVMs until there are no updates in positive images. Chen and Wang [11] use the DD-SVM method, which combines EM-DD with SVMs for image categorization. Experimental results [10, 11] show that DD-SVM achieves the best categorization accuracy.

In spite of their successes, all these categorization systems have their shortcomings. Global-feature-based systems [1, 2] cannot precisely represent the semantics of an image, which corresponds to objects. Region-based systems [3-5] often break an object into several regions or put different objects into a single region due to inaccurate image segmentation. The block-based [6, 7] and MIL-based systems [8-11] have the similar problems as the region-based systems.

In this paper, we propose a novel machine-learning based approach, which combines MIL-based and global-feature-based SVMs, for image categorization. The MIL-based SVMs apply MIL on the segmented images to find the IPs (Instance Prototypes). The IPs-based image bag features are further used as inputs to a set of SVMs to find the optimum hyperplanes. To address the inaccurate segmentation issues, we create the global-feature-based SVMs, where MPEG-7 SCD (Scalable Color Descriptor) and the modified MPEG-7 EHD (Edge Histogram Descriptor) are used as the global features. For each test image, two sets of image features are constructed and sent to the two respective sets of SVMs. The decision values from two sets of SVMs are finally incorporated to obtain the final categorization results.

The remainder of the paper is organized as follows. Section 2 describes our proposed approach. Section 3 illustrates the experimental results. Section 4 draws conclusions.

## 2 Proposed Approach

### 2.1 MIL-Based SVMS

**Image Segmentation.** To segment an image into coherent regions, the image is first divided into non-overlapping blocks of size 2×2 and a color feature vector (i.e., the mean color of the block) is extracted for each block. The Luv color space is used because the perceptual color difference of the human visual system is proportional to the numerical difference in this space.

After obtaining the color features for all blocks, an unsupervised K-Means algorithm is used to cluster these color features. This segmentation process adaptively increases the number of regions $C$ (initially set as 2) until two termination criteria are satisfied. That is: (1) the total distance $D_i$ from each block to the corresponding cluster center in the $i^{th}$ iteration is less than $T_1$; or (2) the absolute difference between the total distances of the current and previous iterations (i.e., $|D_i - D_{i-1}|$) is less than $T_2$. These two thresholds are empirically chosen so reasonable segmentation can be achieved on all images in our test database.

Based on the segmentation results, the representative color feature $\vec{f}_j^c$ for each region $j$ is calculated by the mean of color features of all the blocks in region $j$. The representative texture feature $\vec{f}_j^t$ for each region $j$ is computed by the average energy in each high frequency band after 2-level wavelet decompositions. The wavelet transformation is applied to a "texture template" image obtained by keeping all the pixels in region $j$ intact and setting all the pixels outside region $j$ as white. The length of the feature vector for each region is 9 with 3 color features and 6 texture features.

**Multiple-Instance Learning (MIL).** MIL was originally studied by Dietterich et al. [12] in drug activity prediction and has recently received much attention in machine learning. In MIL, each image is a bag and its segmented regions are instances. Its objective is to find the commonalities in all positive images given a set of labeled images. The EM-DD [9] method solves this problem by finding the maximum *DD* value at point $t$ in the bag feature space:

$$DD(t) = \arg\max_t \prod_i^n \Pr(B_i, l_i \mid t) \qquad (1)$$

where $B_i$ is the $i^{th}$ bag, $l_i$ is the label of the $i^{th}$ bag, and $n$ is the total number of labeled bags. This maximum *DD* value indicates a higher probability that point $t$ fits better with the instances from positive bags than those from negative bags. The negative log transformation can be further used to simplify (1):

$$NLDD(t) = \arg\min_t \sum_{i=1}^n \left(-\log(\Pr(l_i \mid t, B_i))\right) = \arg\min_t \sum_{i=1}^n \left(-\log(1 - |l_i - Label(B_i \mid t)|)\right) \qquad (2)$$

where $Label(B_i \mid t) = \max_j \left\{ \exp\left[ -\sum_{d=1}^n (s_d (B_{ijd} - t_d))^2 \right] \right\}$, $B_{ij}$ is the $j^{th}$ instance of bag $i$, and $S_d$ refers to the feature weight on dimension $d$. That is, finding the maximum *DD* value in (1) is equivalent to finding the minimum *NLDD* value in (2).

The Quasi-Newton algorithm [13], a two-step gradient descent search, is able to find the point with the minimum *NLDD* value in (2). We start the search from every instance in all positive bags with the same initial weights to find its corresponding local minimum and associated weights. Unlike the DD and EM-DD methods, where the global minimum of all local minima represents the region of interests, our MIL-based method uses all the distinct local minima, called IPs, to create the image bag features. These IPs are selected from all local minima by the following two conditions: (1) they need to be far away from each other in the bag feature space; and (2) they need to have small *NLDD* values. Given IPs = $\{(x_k^*, w_k^*) : k = 1, \cdots, m\}$ where $x_k^*$'s are the IP's feature values, $w_k^*$'s are the IP's feature weights, and $m$ is the number of IPs, the bag feature $\phi(B_i)$ of image $i$ (i.e., bag $B_i$) is calculated as:

$$\phi(B_i) = \begin{bmatrix} \min_{j=1,\cdots,N_i} \|x_{ij} - x_1^*\|_{w_1^*} \\ \vdots \\ \min_{j=1,\cdots,N_i} \|x_{ij} - x_m^*\|_{w_m^*} \end{bmatrix} \qquad (3)$$

where $x_{ij}$ is the $j^{th}$ regional color and texture features of image $i$, $N_i$ is the number of segmented regions in image $i$, and $\|\ \|_{w^*}$ represents the weighted Euclidean distance.

**Support Vector Machines (SVMs).** SVMs have been successfully used in many applications and are adopted in our proposed system. A set of SVMs are used to train the bag features of all training images to find optimum hyperplanes, each of which separates training images in one category with the other categories by a maximal margin. That is, given $m$ training data $\{x_i, y_i\}$'s, where $x_i \in R^n, y_i \in \{-1,1\}$, SVMs need to solve the following optimization problem:

$$\min_{\omega,b,\xi} (\frac{1}{2}\omega^T\omega + C\sum_{i=1}^{l}\xi_i), \quad \text{Subject to} \quad y_i(\omega^T\phi(x_i)+b) > 1-\xi_i, \quad \xi_i > 0 \quad (4)$$

where $C$ is the penalty parameter of the error term and $K(x_i, y_i) = \phi(x_i)^T \phi(x_j)$ is the kernel function. The Gaussian radial basis function kernel are used in our system since they yield excellent results compared to linear and polynomial kernels [14].

Since the SVMs are designed for the binary classification, an appropriate multi-class method is needed to handle several classes as in image categorization. We use "one against the others" as it achieves comparable performance with a faster speed than "one against one". We further map the SVM outputs into probabilities [15] so that our system returns the likelihood of each category that an image may belong to.

## 2.2 Global-Feature-Based SVMs

Inaccurate image segmentation may make the MIL-based bag feature representation imprecise and therefore decrease the categorization accuracy. We add global-feature-based SVMs to address this problem. In order to compensate the limitations associated with the specific color space and the specific texture representation, we construct the global features in a different manner as used in creating the regional features. To this end, two MPEG-7 descriptors are adopted in our system.

The SCD is one of the four MPEG-7 normative color descriptors [16]. It uses the HSV color histograms to represent an image since the HSV color space provides an intuitive representation of color and approximates human's perception. We directly adopt the 64-bin SCD in our system.

The EHD is one of the three normative texture descriptors used in MPEG-7 [16], where five types of edges, namely, vertical, horizontal, 45° diagonal, 135° diagonal, and non-directional, have been used to represent the edge orientation in 16 non-overlapping subimages. Based on the EHD, we construct gEHD (global EHD) and sEHD (semi-global EHD) to address the rotation, scaling, and translation related issues. The gEHD represents the edge distribution for the entire image and has five bins. For the sEHD, we group connected subimages into 13 different clusters [16] and construct the EHD for each cluster. So the length of our modified EHD is 70 and the total length of our global feature is 134.

After the global features of all the training images are obtained, they are fed into another set of SVMs to find optimum hyperplanes to distinguish one category from the others. This set of SVMs is designed by the same approaches used in the MIL-based SVMs.

## 2.3 Fusion Approach

For each test image, two sets of image features (i.e., MIL-based features and global features) are generated and sent to two respective sets of SVMs. Let $y_1$ and $y_2$ respectively be the output vectors from the MIL-based and global-feature-based SVMs for a given test image. The final output vector $y$ is obtained by:

$$y = w * y_1 + (1-w) * y_2 \quad (5)$$

where $w$ determines the contribution from the MIL-based SVMs and is empirically set to be 0.5 as shown in Section 3.2. Once the integrated decision values are obtained, they are mapped to the probability values by the method introduced in [15].

## 3 Experimental Results

To date, we have tested our categorization algorithm on 2000 general-purpose images from COREL database. These images have 20 distinct categories with 100 images in each category. These categories contain different semantics including Africa, beach, buildings, buses, dinosaurs, elephants, flowers, horses, mountains, food, dogs, lizards, fashion, sunsets, cars, waterfalls, antiques, battle ships, skiing, and deserts.

### 3.1 Categorization Results

To measure the effectiveness of the proposed system, we randomly choose 50 images from each category as training images and the remaining 50 images are used as the testing images. We repeat the above procedure 5 times and calculate the average categorization accuracy for each category.

The proposed system is compared with DD-SVM [10] and our implemented HistSVM [3]. For the first 10 categories, the overall average categorization accuracy of HistSVM, DD-SVM, and our systems over 5 runs is 79.8%, 81.5%, and 88.2%, respectively. Our system performs 10.5% better than the HistSVM system in terms of the overall accuracy. In addition, the feature length of HistSVM system is 4096, which is about 20 times longer than ours. Our system also improves the accuracy by 8.2% over the DD-SVM system, which is 9 times slower than our system.

Fig. 1 plots the average categorization accuracy for each predefined image category of our proposed system, DD-SVM system, and HistSVM system. It clearly illustrates that the proposed system achieves the best average accuracy in most categories.

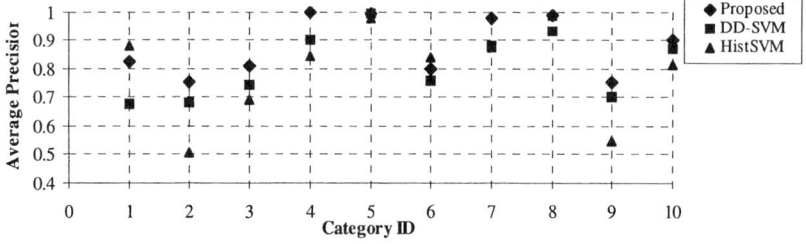

**Fig. 1.** Average categorization accuracy for each category by using three different methods

## 3.2 Validation of the Proposed Method

To verify the effectiveness of the proposed approach, the overall average categorization accuracy obtained by assigning different weights to the global-feature-based SVMs and the MIL-based SVMs is shown in Fig. 2, where G and R represent global and regional weight respectively. It clearly shows that our method (G:M = 0.5:0.5) achieves the best performance.

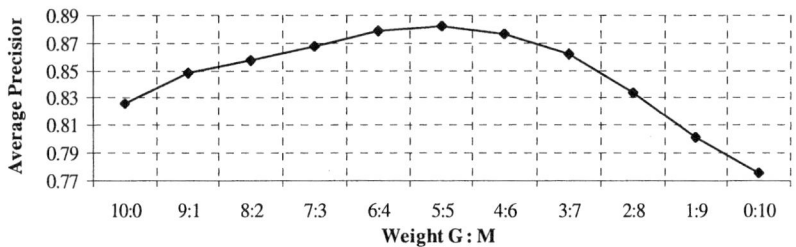

**Fig. 2.** Average categorization accuracy for different global and regional weights

It is observed that global-feature-based SVMs (i.e., G:R = 10:0) and MIL-based SVMs (i.e., G:R = 0:10) alone achieve the average accuracy of 82.6% and 77.6%, respectively. It clearly shows the effectiveness of the fusion approach as it improves the global and regional SVMs by 6.8% and 13.7% respectively. In addition, our global-feature-based SVMs system alone achieves better accuracy than both DD-SVM and HistSVM systems.

## 3.3 Sensitivity to the Number of Categories

The scalability of the method is tested by performing image categorization experiments over data sets with different numbers of categories. A total of 11 data sets are used in the experiments. The number of categories in a data set varies from 10 to 20. These data sets are arranged in the same manner as in [11] for fair comparisons. That is, the first 10 categories form the first data set; the first 11 categories form the second data set; etc. The average classification accuracy of our system and DD-SVM system by running 5 times on each of the 11 data sets is shown in Figure 3.

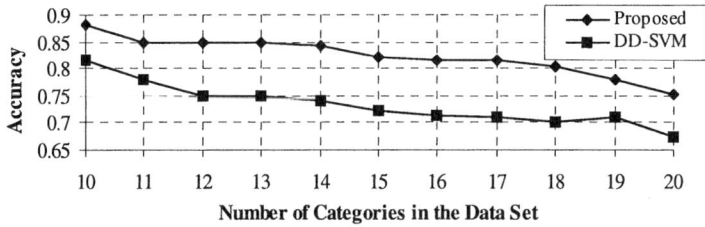

**Fig. 3.** Comparison of the two methods on the robustness to the number of categories

We observe a decrease in average categorization accuracy as the number of categories increases. When the number of categories becomes doubled (increasing from 10 to 20 categories), the average categorization accuracy of our proposed system and the DD-SVM system drops respectively from 88.2% to 75.3% and from 81.5% to 67.5%. However, our method outperforms DD-SVM consistently.

## 4 Conclusions

In this paper, we present an efficient and effective automatic image categorization system, which integrates MIL-based SVMs with global-feature-based SVMs. The main contributions are:

- EM-DD algorithm is used to find IP (Instance Prototypes) and the IP-based image bag features are further combined with SVMs to partly solve the problem of inaccurate image segmentation.
- Global-feature-based SVMs are integrated with MIL-based SVMs to further address the issues associated with inaccurate image segmentation, where global features are different from the regional features so that the limitations associated with specific color space and specific texture representation are also addressed.
- Multi-category SVMs are used to classify images by a set of confidence values for each possible category.

The proposed system has been validated by testing with 2000 general-purpose images with 20 distinct categories. The experimental results indicate that our system outperforms peer systems in the literature in terms of both accuracy and efficiency.

The proposed system can be easily integrated into the image retrieval system, where both categorized keywords and the query image(s) can be combined as the query. Furthermore, user's relevance feedback can be added to dynamically update the categorized images so that categorization accuracy can be further improved.

## References

1. Huang, J., Kumar, S., Zabih, R.: An automatic hierarchical image classification scheme. Proc. of 6th ACM Int'l Conf. on Multimedia (1998) 219-228
2. Chapelle, O., Haffner, P., Vapnik, V.: Support vector machines for histogram-based image classification. IEEE Trans. on Neural Networks 10(1999) 1055–1064
3. Smith, J. R., Li, C. S.: Image classification and querying using composite region templates. Int'l J. Computer Vision and Image Understanding 75(1999) 165-174
4. Barnard, K., Forsyth, D.: Learning the semantics of words and pictures. Proc. Int'l Conf. Computer Vision 2(2001) 408-415
5. Jeon, J., Lavrenko, V., Manmatha, R.: Automatic image annotation and retrieval using cross-media relevance models. Proc. 26th Intl. ACM SIGIR Conf. (2003) 119–126
6. Li, J., Wang, J. Z.: Automatic linguistic indexing of pictures by a statistical modeling approach. IEEE Trans. on PAMI 25(2003) 1075-1088
7. Murphy, K, Torralba, A., Freeman, W.: Using the forest to see the trees: a graphical model relating features, objects, and scenes. Advances in Neural Information Processing Systems, Vol. 16, Cambridge, MA, MIT Press (2004)

8. Maron O., Ratan, A. L.: Multiple-instance learning for natural scene classification. Proc. 15th Int'l Conf. Machine Learning (1998) 341-249
9. Zhang, Q., Goldman, S. A., Yu, W., Fritts, J.: Content-based image retrieval using multiple instance learning. Proc. 19th Int'l Conf. Machine Learning (2002) 682-689
10. Andrews, S., Tsochantaridis, I., Hofmann, T.: Support vector machines for multiple-instance learning. Advances in Neural Information Processing Systems 15, Cambridge, MA: MIT Press (2003)
11. Chen, Y., Wang, J. Z.: Image categorization by learning and reasoning with regions. Journal of Machine Learning Research 5(2004) 913-939
12. Dietterich, T. G., Lathrop, R. H. , Lozano-Perez, T., Solving the multiple-instance problem with axis-parallel rectangles. Artificial Intelligence 89(1997) 31-71
13. Press, S. A., Teukolsky, S. A., Vetterling, W. T., Flannery, B. P.: Numerical recipes in C: the art of scientific computing. Cambridge Univeristy Press, New York (1992)
14. Scholkopf, B., Sung, K., Burges, C., Girosi, F., Niyogi, P., Poggio, T., Vapnik, V., Comparing Support Vector Machines with Gaussian Kernels to Radial Basis Function Classifiers. MIT, A.I. Memo 1599 (1996)
15. Platt, J. C.: Probabilistic Output for Support Vector Machines and Comparisons to Regularized Likelihood Methods. In Bartlett, A., Schölkopf, P., Schuurmans, B. (eds.): Advances in Large Margin Classifiers. MIT Press Cambridge, MA (2000)
16. Manjunath, B. S., Salembier, P., Sikora, T.: Introduction to MPEG-7 Multimedia Content Description Interface. John Wiley & Sons (2002)

# Improving Shape-Based CBIR for Natural Image Content Using a Modified GFD

Yupeng Li[1], Matthew J. Kyan[2], and Ling Guan[1]

[1] Multimedia Research Laboratory, Ryerson University, Toronto, ON Canada
[2] School of Electrical & Information Engineering, University of Sydney, NSW Australia
{yli, mkyan, lguan}@ee.ryerson.ca

**Abstract.** We present a modified version of the Generic Fourier Descriptor (GFD) that operates on edge information within natural images from the COREL image database for the purpose of shape-based image retrieval. By incorporating an edge-texture characterization (ETC) measure, we reduce the complexity inherent in oversensitive edge maps typical of most gradient-based detectors that otherwise tend to contaminate the shape feature description. We find that the proposed techniques not only improve overall retrieval in terms of shape, but more importantly, provide for a more accurate similarity ranking of retrieved results, demonstrating greater consideration for dominant internal and external shape details.

## 1 Introduction

In Content Based Image Retrieval (CBIR), shape information is widely considered to play a key role in the characterization of scenes. Shape of itself however, is a difficult property to measure, and much work has been directed toward this effort. Recent descriptors proposed for capturing shape information, generally fall into two categories: contour-based methods (such as the popular fourier descriptor and its variants) and region-based methods (such as Zernike moments, Hu's geometric moments, etc). Due to the difficulty in measuring and assessing shape properties of natural images, the majority of CBIR work reported using shape information alone, tends to focus on simplified shape databases such as those of binary logos [1] and iconified/trademark graphics. In such collections, scenes often involve only a single object with a well defined shape, wherein a single class is often comprised of a set of images with only minor variations to the dominant shape, that whilst altered, remain well defined. In collections involving natural scenes however, such as those found in the well known COREL database, scenes are generally much more complex, involving many combinations of objects, of a variety of shapes and sizes that may or may not be embedded in equally complex backgrounds. Often shape information becomes contaminated by the mixture of content in a scene, rendering shape based retrieval results, relatively poor. In this work, we propose a modified region-based technique to better deal with CBIR applications in the domain of natural image databases.

One of the major problems in attempting to use the contour-based standard Fourier descriptor (FD) as a feature for assessing the similarity between images based on shape, lies in its dependence on the prior knowledge of boundary information. In particular, it assumes that for each image, we have an ordered description of the points that form the connected path responsible for a particular boundary. As such, when considering the boundary of regions of interest, some form of higher level segmentation becomes necessary. Unfortunately, even if such segmentation is available, it is often the case that multiple boundaries will occur within the image (either due to internal shape content or multiple regions of interest). In previous work [2], the FD has been applied to the description of edge information of natural images found in the COREL database, and has met with limited success in terms of shape identification.

In other work focusing on shape alone, Zernike moment descriptors (ZMD) have been proposed as a preferred technique over other region based techniques such as geometric moments (e.g. Hu's moments) [3]. Derived from a complex set of orthogonal polynomials over the unit disk, a more rotationally invariant description of shape information is achieved, independent of boundary information. Limitations exist in terms of computational complexity and a tendency to capture spatial moments in the radial directions rather than spectral features, thus spectral information is not captured evenly at each order resulting in loss of significant features useful for shape description [4].

As an alternative, a region-based 2D polar Fourier transform (PFT) attempts to better capture the spectral content of angular & radial information by transforming the polar description of an image into a rectangular image of radial vs. angular distribution of image intensities, upon which a standard 2D FT may be applied. This approach has been demonstrated to maintain rotational invariance in that a rotated shape generally yields a similar spectral definition. A generalized version of this technique (Generic Fourier Descriptor - GFD) was proposed in [4],[5]. Translation invariance was achieved by choosing the origin for polar space to be the centroid of the shape in question, thus all radial & angular content is then calculated from this origin. Scale invariance was achieved by normalizing the coefficients of each spectral component in the PFT (i.e. one for each combination of radius & angle, or each point in the rectangular mapped image of radius vs. angle), by its DC component, whilst the DC component itself was normalized by the mass or area over which the polar image was taken. This met with good results in simplified binary shape databases, although no real application to natural image data has been reported.

## 2 Modified Edge-Based GFD

In this current work, unlike that of [5], we consider the Canny edge description of natural image queries as input to a GFD inspired operator for shape description. Direct application of [5] might see a binary image formed from the original (either by thresholding or similar), such that a 'caricature' of the original could be utilized as input to the GFD. The problem with this is that the computation becomes quite extensive as more pixels need to be considered in the shape image. In addition, achieving a consistent thresholding for a natural image is not trivial as it is very sensitive to contrast, etc. By using an edge description we reduce the computational load (less pixels to consider in the polar mapping).

The GFD operator, as proposed by [5], involves first finding the polar description of the input edge image (mapped into a normal rectangular image format of radius vs. angle) with a 2D FT applied to this transformed image. The modified 2D FT is calculated as follows:

$$PFT(\rho,\phi) = \sum_r \sum_i f(r,\theta_i) \exp[j2\pi(\frac{r}{R}\rho + \frac{2\pi i}{T}\phi)] \ , \qquad (1)$$

where $(r,\theta)$ denote the polar coordinates in the image plane and $(\rho,\phi)$ denote the polar coordinates in the frequency plane. $0 \le r = [(x-x_c)^2 + (y-y_c)^2]^{1/2} < R$ and $\theta_i = i(2\pi/T)$; $(x_c, y_c)$ define the center of the shape; $0 \le \rho < R$, $0 \le \phi < T$, where $R$ and $T$ are the radial and angular resolutions. To get the GFD, we then normalize the PFT calculation as described previously, for more details see [4].

## 3 Ignoring Textured Regions Using ETC

Quite often, excessive textured regions contaminate the edge description of dominant objects in a scene. To remove the contaminating effect of over textured regions, we employ a further refinement in the shape image prior to extracting the shape description, by attempting to establish (and thus ignore) Canny responses resulting more from texture rather than more dominant edges. In this way, we attempt to supply a set of edges that better reflect the regional boundaries within an image rather than every intensity variation. The edge-texture characterization (ETC) approach introduced in [6] provides a fuzzy discrimination between edge & textured regions and is adopted in this work.

The principal of ETC is founded in examining the changes in variance occurring in a windowed local region when it is blurred by an averaging filter. In smooth regions the variance does not really change, however the response in textured versus edge images is quite marked. This is exploited in the ETC measure. Based on the size of the local window considered, the ratio $k = \overline{\sigma}/\overline{\sigma}'$ between the standard deviation $\overline{\sigma}$ of original versus $\overline{\sigma}'$ of blurred intensities, yields a measure of deviation due to the underlying nature of the image content in that region. A simple range of values captured by this measure can be attributed to a textured region, thus we can establish a regional mask over the textured regions so that they may be later ignored in the shape descriptor calculation. The equations of $\overline{\sigma}$ and $\overline{\sigma}'$ are defined as:

$$\overline{\sigma}^2 = \frac{1}{|N|} \sum_{(i,j) \in N} (x_{i,j} - \overline{x})^2 \qquad (2)$$

$$\overline{\sigma}'^2 = \frac{1}{|N|} \sum_{(i,j) \in N} (x'_{i,j} - \overline{x}')^2 \qquad (3)$$

In the equation (2) and (3), $N$ denotes a neighborhood set around the current pixel, $x_{i,j}$ denotes the gray level value of pixel $(i, j)$ in the set, and $x'_{i,j}$ is the corresponding smoothed gray level value under 5 X 5 averaging. $\bar{x}$ and $\bar{x'}$ are the mean of the gray level values of the original and smoothed variables in the neighborhood set. Most of the estimated $k$ values are restricted to the interval [0 5]. Experimental results show that the textured area of most images is located in the interval [2.1 5]. In order to extract the textured area from the image, we apply a morphological operation (erosion and dilation) to deal with the texture map extracted by ETC measurement and form a complete texture area, then we can mask and eliminate the texture area from the edge map extracted by Canny filter.

**Fig. 1.** (a) Original image; (b) Edge map; (c) Edge map (texture removed)

From fig.1(b), we see edge map of original image (Lenna) fig.1(a), extracted by the Canny filter, the edge map shows us that the feather texture of her hat produces an oversensitive edge response complicating the overall shape, fig.1(c) is the edge map after removing the textured part found with ETC and shows us the clear edge shape information.

## 4 Experimental Results

In order to test the retrieval performance of our proposed algorithm, we select three different shape descriptors: the standard Fourier Descriptor (FD), Modified Generic Fourier Descriptor (MGFD) and MGFD after removing texture part of edge map. Our simulations were carried out using a subset of the COREL image database consisting of 1000 natural color images (JPEG), from 10 classes that appeared to be more dominated by shape. Each class included 100 conceptually similar images.

Simulations were conducted to compare the retrieval effectiveness on this database when indexed with one of three alternative shape descriptors. The first used the lowest 50 coefficients from a standard FD (denoted FD) as a feature vector for each edge mapped image. The second feature vector is a set of 36 coefficients of the GFD, calculated for an equally distributed set of 4 radii and 9 angles (denoted MGFD). The third feature vector is the same as the second, however the GFD calculation is performed on the texture removed edge map of each image (denoted MGFD1). Each image in the database was then indexed with each of the three different feature vectors. In retrieval, similarity was measured using the Euclidean distance between the feature vector of a query image, and those of all other images in the database.

To measure general retrieval performance, statistical results were calculated by considering 10 different query images from each class (forming 100 queries in total). For each query, the first 16 most similar images were retrieved to evaluate the performance of the retrieval. The table 1 shows us the Retrieval Rate (the percentage of images in the 16 retrieved, belonging to the same class as the query image).

**Table 1.** Retrieval performance from three different sets of shape features

| Class | 1 | 2 | 3 | 4 | 5 | 6 | 7 | 8 | 9 | 10 | Average |
|---|---|---|---|---|---|---|---|---|---|---|---|
| FD(%) | 17.9 | 21.0 | 22.3 | 18.6 | 41.2 | 23.8 | 41.2 | 63.7 | 32.5 | 20.0 | 30.2 |
| MGFD(%) | 30.5 | 19.0 | 23.0 | 52.5 | 31.3 | 21.6 | 45.0 | 51.2 | 60.0 | 68.0 | 40.2 |
| MGFD1(%) | 31.6 | 22.5 | 22.0 | 62.5 | 30.0 | 22.0 | 43.0 | 55.0 | 68.7 | 69.5 | 42.6 |

Table 1 tells us that the retrieval results of most classes using the proposed MGFD and MGFD1 outperform results using FD. There were, however, a few classes demonstrating similar, but slightly worse performance. Such classes exhibit a much higher variation in shape between images considered of the same class conceptually, thus many images from different classes that have similar shape distribution are often confused. This generally highlights the limitations in using this performance measure to evaluate shape based results. This being said, the proposed MGFD1 method gives much better representation in the classes in which the images shape structure is more consistent across images, a factor especially evident in classes 4, 9 and 10, reflecting sets of rock formation, flag and aircraft images respectively.

Although the retrieval rate improves about 12 percent using MGFD1 over the standard FD approach. In most classes, the retrieval rate is similar to the edge mapped application of GFD (MGFD), with slight overall improvement. To effectively gauge each descriptor more intuitively, we look at some explicit visual results, and offer a more subjective view of their relative success, in terms of the shapes of images retrieved (regardless of class), and their ranking in terms of similarity to the query.

The left top first image in each of the following figures is the query image we selected. The order of similarity ranking is from left to right, top to bottom. In Fig. 2(a), FD only retrieves 3 flag images, whilst in Fig 2(b) The whole boundary shape of the flags (roughly rectangular due to the flags waving) as well as the internal Union Jack feature becomes significant. MGFD not only extracts a more accurate exterior boundary feature than FD, but also considers interior shape features, retrieving 8 flag images with a strong feature in the top left of the flag. In Fig 2(c), some of the more textured details in the flags are eliminated by the ETC consideration, thus only dominant edges (both internal and external) contribute to the search and improve the retrieval result. The proposed MGFD1 approach has the best performance, evident not only in a higher retrieval rate (10 flag images), but more importantly, in the set of Union Jack based flags dominating the *most* similar images, as opposed to the scattered flags found by the MGFD. This reflects a greater accuracy in the ranking of similar result images by the MGFD1.

**Fig. 2.** Flag query – CLASS 9 (a) FD top; (b) MGFD middle; (c) MGFD1 bottom

**Fig. 3.** Aircraft query – CLASS 10 (a) FD top; (b) MGFD middle; (c) MGFD1 bottom

In Fig. 3(a) FD only retrieves 3 aircraft images. Like the flags, the aircraft images exhibit some regularity in terms of shape, although this isn't captured effectively by FD. In Fig. 3(b) MGFD retrieves 9 aircraft images, but due to the influence of internal texture part, the fruit images (the $9^{th}$, $10^{th}$, $12^{th}$ and $16^{th}$ images) are retrieved falsely. Their apparent similarity may be in that the fruit is distributed in an elongated manner, yet internal textures are erratic and confuse the similarity matching.

In Fig. 3(c) MGFD1 removes the texture 'contamination' (the grass and internal part of the plane) and retrieves 13 aircraft images. Note also that the rock contour in the 15th retrieved image, where the shape somehow is similar to the straight body of the plane, with the kinking tail protruding upward at one end of the plane. This is similar to the contour in the rock formation.

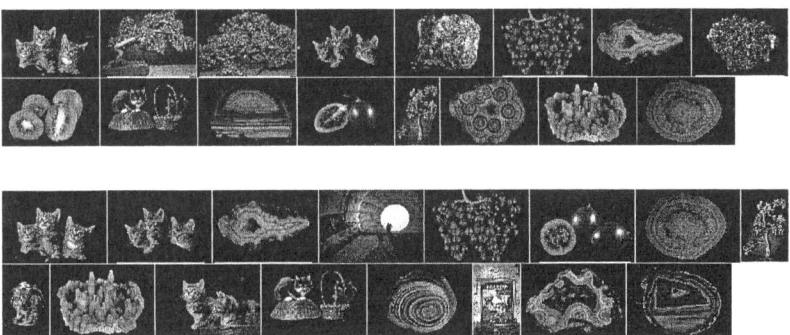

**Fig. 4.** Cat query – CLASS 3 (a) MGFD top; (b) MGFD1 bottom

**Fig. 5.** Fruit query – CLASS 1 (a) MGFD top; (b) MGFD1 bottom

In Fig. 4 the concept of a cat does not necessarily coincide with a consistent silhouette, in fact, in this class different numbers of cats may exist in some images. MGFD retrieves 3 cat images. The $4^{th}$ result, with 3 kittens is similar to the query. Likewise, the distribution in the tree images ($2^{nd}$ and $3^{rd}$), fruit ($9^{th}$) and rock formations ($7^{th}$, $15^{th}$) are more similar in terms of overall shape than the images with one cat. In the MGFD1 result, not only are 5 cat images retrieved, but the rank of the 3 kittens image is improved from $4^{th}$ to $2^{nd}$, (i.e. it is considered *most* similar to the query), as opposed to the MGFD result. In other queries from class 3 (not shown), MGFD occasionally yields a higher retrieval rate than MGFD1 (hence a slightly higher performance in Table 1). This is misleading however, as closer inspection reveals that images from the correct class may be retrieved by the MGFD method yet have a very different shape from the query. Also, some of the class images with different shape are often ranked as more similar to the query image than those intuitively closer in shape (using MGFD). The experimental results demonstrated that the MGFD1 approach achieves a better result as a shape feature. This effect should mean that if MGFD1 is combined with other features (colour, etc), we expect that the other features will help capture more images from the same class, allowing MGFD1 to sift out and rank the captured set more accurately.

In the same way, the fruit query of Fig. 5 (FD omitted), shows that the clustered balloons are considered to be similar to the clustered fruit objects. The MGFD1 result however, is still more accurate (same fruit ranked $4^{th}$ for MGFD1, $12^{th}$ for MGFD).

## 5 Conclusions

In this paper, we have proposed a modified generic Fourier descriptor (MGFD1) for image retrieval. Comparing with GFD, where the authors extracted the shape feature from the whole shape image in the MPEG-7 region shape database, if GFD is applied on natural image instead of binary trademark images, the computation will be very expensive because of high resolution and complicated shape information in natural images. GFD is not suitable for natural image retrieval. Our proposed MGFD1 overcame this drawback.

The PFT was applied to the Canny edge maps of images, thereby decreasing computational complexity. The MGFD1 shape feature improved average image retrieval rate (except where shape varied dramatically). In such cases however, the similarity rankings were more intuitive. It was argued that in the cases where retrieval rate was lower than that of MGFD, the ultimate performance of the system still showed improvement as images from the correct class, yet with different shape to the query, were rejected or ranked lower in terms of similarity to the query – reflecting an order that more closely fit the notion of shape. In the future, we will apply the MGFD1 method both in combination with other successful low level features to further improve overall retrieval rate for natural image databases, and in retrieval based on the more specific notion of ROI (Region of Interest), where it is expected that overall retrieval rate as well as accuracy will be improved.

## References

[1] A. Folkers and H. Samet, "Content-based image retrieval using Fourier descriptors on a logo database". *Proc. the 16th International Conference on Pattern Recognition.* Vol. 3, pp.521-524, Aug. 2002, Quebec City, Canada
[2] K.Jarrah, P. Muneesawang, I.Lee and L.Guan, "Minimizing human-machine interactions in automatic image retrieval". *Proc. Canadian Conference on Electrical and Computer Engineering.* Vol. 3, pp. 1589-1592 May 2004, Niagra Falls, Canada
[3] D. S. Zhang and G. Lu, "A comparative study of three region shape descriptors" DICTA 2002: *Digital Image Computing Techniques and Applications*, Jan. 2002, Melbourne, Australia
[4] D. S. Zhang, "Image retrieval based on shape". Chapter 5, 6 *PhD Thesis*, 2002.
[5] D. S. Zhang and G. Lu "Generic Fourier Descriptor for Shape-based Image Retrieval", *Proceedings of IEEE Int. Conf. On Multimedia and Expo.* Vol.1, pp. 425-428, Aug. 2002.
[6] H. S. Wong and L.Guan, "A neural learning approach for adaptive image restoration using a fuzzy model-based network architecture". *IEEE Transaction on Neural Networks.* Vol. 12, pp. 516-531. May 2001

# Probabilistic Similarity Measures in Image Databases with SVM Based Categorization and Relevance Feedback*

Md. Mahmudur Rahman[1], Prabir Bhattacharya[2], and Bipin C. Desai[1]

[1] Dept. of Computer Science, Concordia University, Canada
[2] Institute for Information Systems Engineering, Concordia University, Canada

**Abstract.** This paper demonstrates an approach to image retrieval by classifying images into different semantic categories and using probabilistic similarity measures. To reduce the semantic-gap based on low-level features, a relevance feedback mechanism is also added, which refines the query parameters to adjust the matching functions. First and second order statistical parameters (mean and covariance matrix) are pre-computed from the feature distributions of predefined categories on multivariate Gaussian assumption. Statistical similarity measure functions utilize these category specific parameters based on the online prediction of a multi-class support vector machine classifier. In relevance feedback, user selected positive or relevant images are used for calculating new query point and updating statistical parameters in each iteration. Whereas, most prominent relevant and non-relevant category specific information are utilized to modify the ranking of the final retrieved images. Experimental results on a generic image database with ground-truth or known categories are reported. Performances of several probabilistic distance measures are evaluated, which show the effectiveness of the proposed technique.

## 1 Introduction

Access to images based on low-level features (e.g., color, texture, shape, etc.), is commonly known as content-based image retrieval (CBIR). Last decade has witnessed an overwhelming research interest in CBIR systems with mainly three common functionalities: selection of appropriate image features in the form of feature vector, a distance based similarity matching function to compare query and target images in a database, and an indexing mechanism for efficient retrieval [13]. Early CBIR systems used low-level visual features without any semantic interpretation of images and as a result, contributed to the well known *semantic-gap* problem [6]. Therefore, new concepts are gaining popularity to improve image understanding and retrieval in the form of semantic image classification, adaptive similarity matching, and relevance feedback [6]. In a database whose

---
* This work was partially supported by grants from NSERC and ENCS Research Support.

semantic description is reasonably well defined and where category search is prefered (e.g., Personal photo collection, Medical images of different modalities etc.), it is possible to extract a set of low-level features to depict semantic content of each image by identifying its class assignment using a classifier and to find distinguishable feature distribution in each semantic categories. Thus, an image can be best characterized by exploiting information of feature distribution of its semantic category. Many early CBIR systems incorporated similarity matching functions (e.g., Euclidean, Manhattan, etc.) without paying enough attention about the underlying distribution of the feature space [11]. Similarity measures based on empirical estimates of the distributions of features have been proposed in recent years [11]. However, the comparison is most often based on point wise or statistics of the first order (mean vector) of the distribution [5].

This paper is primarily concerned with the appropriate choice of similarity matching functions based on the parameterization of underlying category specific distributions of feature space. A major contribution of this paper is to propose adaptive statistical similarity measure functions by utilizing a multi-class support vector machine (SVM) classifier and a relevance feedback (RF) mechanism. Training samples in the form of feature vectors of known categories are used to estimate the statistical parameters and train the SVM classifier by extrcting low-level features. We assume that, the distributions of the features in each category are multivariate Gaussian and based on this assumption, images are characterized with the first and second order statistical parameters. These category specific parameters are exploited by probabilistic distance measures based on the online SVM prediction. However, it is also impossible that the low-level features of the example image is just at the distribution center of a semantic class of images. Hence, we incorporate RF to allow user to refine the query parameters, which will adjust the matching functions and modify the ranking of finally retrieved images. Several objective comparison results of different distance measures, such as Mahalanobis, Bhattacharyya, KL divergence, and Symmetric KL divergence[8,10] are provided , which show the effectiveness of the proposed approach.

## 2 Parameter Estimation for Statistical Distance Measures

Statistical distance measure is the distance between two probability distributions, which captures correlations or variations between attributes of the feature vectors and provides bounds for probability of retrieval error of a two way classification problem. In this scheme query image $q$ and target image $t$ are assumed to be in different classes and their respective density as $p_q(x)$ and $p_t(x)$, both defined on $\mathbb{R}^d$. When these densities are multivariate normal, they can be approximated by mean vector $\mu$ and covariance matrix $C$ as $p_q(x) = N(x; \mu_q, C_q)$ & $p_t(x) = N(x; \mu_t, C_t)$, where,

$$N(x; \mu, C) = \frac{1}{\sqrt{(2\pi)d|C|}} \exp^{-\frac{1}{2}(x-\mu)^T C^{-1}(x-\mu)} \quad (1)$$

here, $\mathbf{x} \in \mathbb{R}^d$ and $|\cdot|$ is matrix determinant [8]. A popular measure of similarity between two Gaussian distributions is the Bhattacharyya distance, which is equivalent to an upper bound of the optimal Bayesian classification error probability [8] [10]. Bhattacharyya distance $D_B$ between query image $q$ and target image $t$ in the database is given by:

$$D_B = \frac{1}{8}(\mu_q - \mu_t)^T \left[\frac{(C_q + C_t)}{2}\right]^{-1}(\mu_q - \mu_t) + \frac{1}{2}\ln\frac{\left|\frac{(C_q+C_t)}{2}\right|}{\sqrt{|C_q||C_t|}} \quad (2)$$

where $\mu_q$ and $\mu_t$ are the mean vectors, and $C_q$ and $C_t$ are the covariance matrices of query image $q$ and target image $t$ respectively. Equation (2) is composed of two terms, the first one being the distance between mean vectors of images, while the second term gives the class separability due to the difference between class covariance matrices. When all classes have the same covariance matrices, the Bhattacharyya distance reduce to the Mahalanobis distance, a widely used similarity measure in CBIR literatures [5,8].

$$D_M = (\mu_q - \mu_t)^T C^{-1}(\mu_q - \mu_t) \quad (3)$$

However, if inclusion of both query and target covariance matrices is useful, Bhattacharyya distance will outperform Mahalanobis distance [5] as will be shown in results section. Another distance measure from information theory, Kullback-Leibler (KL) divergence or relative entropy [10] is regarded as a measure of the extent to which two probability density functions agree. Kullback-Leibler divergence is not symmetric and does not satisfy the triangle inequality. The Jeffrey-divergence (JD) or Symmetric KL divergence is the symmetric version of KL distance with respect to $p_q(\boldsymbol{x})$ and $p_t(\boldsymbol{x})$ [10].

Computing the above parametric based probabilistic distance measures requires estimation of $\mu$ and $C$. Suppose that there are $L$ different semantic categories in the database, each assumed to have a multivariate normal distribution with mean vector $\mu_i$ and covariance matrix $C_i$, for $i \in L$. However, the true values of $\mu$ and $C$ of each category usually are not known and must be estimated from a set of training samples $N$ [8]. We estimated the $\mu$ and $C$ of each category based on maximum likelihood approach as

$$\mu_i = \frac{1}{N_i}\sum_{j=1}^{N_i} \boldsymbol{x}_{i,j} \quad \& \quad C_i = \frac{1}{N_i - 1}\sum_{j=1}^{N_i}(\boldsymbol{x}_{i,j} - \mu_i)(\boldsymbol{x}_{i,j} - \mu_i)^T \quad (4)$$

where $\boldsymbol{x}_{i,j}$ is sample $j$ from category $i$, $N_i$ is the number of training samples from category $i$ and $N = (N_1 + N_2 + \ldots + N_L)$.

Similarity measure based on the above statistical parameters would perform better if the right categories for query and database images are predicted in real time. Hence, we utilize a multi-class support SVM classifier to predict the categories and based on the online prediction, similarity measure functions will be adjusted to accommodate category specific parameters. SVM is an emerging machine learning technology which has been successfully used in content based image retrieval [3]. Given training data $(x_1, \ldots, x_n)$ that are vectors in some space $x_i \in \mathbb{R}^n$ and their labels $(y_1, \ldots, y_n)$ where $y_i \in (+1, -1)^n$, the general form of the binary linear classification function is

$$g(x) = w \cdot x + b \quad (5)$$

where $x$ is an input vector, $w$ is a weight vector, and $b$ is a bias. The goal of SVM is to find the parameters $w$ and $b$ for the optimal hyper plane to maximize the geometric margin $\frac{2}{||w||}$ between the hyper planes. A number of methods have been proposed for the extension to multi-class problem essentially by solving many two-class problems and combining their predictions in various ways [3]. One technique, commonly known as *one-vs.-one* is to construct SVMs between all possible pairs of classes. During testing, each of the $L*(L-1)/2$ classifier votes for one class. The winning class is the one with the largest number of accumulated votes. It has particular advantage when applied to problems with limited samples in high dimensional spaces. We use this technique for the implementation of our multi-class SVM for online category prediction by using the LIBSVM software package [4].

## 3 Interactive Retrieval with Relevance Feedback

Users might have a different meaning of semantic description in mind or the prediction of the classifier might go wrong. In these cases, they have the option to interact with the system and refine the search process; using a technique commonly known as relevance feedback (RF) technique. RF is an iterative and/or supervised learning process used to improve the performance of information retrieval systems [9]. A number of techniques of RF have been proposed in the literatures[9,12], such as query point movement, feature re-weighting, active learning etc.. However, most of these are based on the fact that the user does not know the actual distribution of the images categories in the feature space and any hidden relation with similarity matching functions.

Our idea of relevance feedback is the following: user will provide the initial query image ($q_0$) to retrieve $K$ (fifteen) most similar images based on distance measures described in previous section. If user is not satisfied with the result, then system will allow him/her to select a set of relevant or positive images similar to the query image. It is assumed that, all the positive feedback images $Pos(q_i)$ at some particular iteration $i$ will belong to the user perceived semantic category and obey the Gaussian distribution to form a cluster in the feature space. We consider the rest of the images as negative or non-relevant $Neg(q_i)$ and they may belong to different semantic categories. The MindReader [12] retrieval system designed by Ishikawa et al. formulates a minimization problem on the parameter estimating process where the distance function is not necessarily aligned with the coordinate axis and allows for correlations between feature attributes. They proved that, when using positive feedback (scores) and the Mahalanobis distance, the optimal query point is a weighted average based on available set of good results. We have followed a similar approach to update the

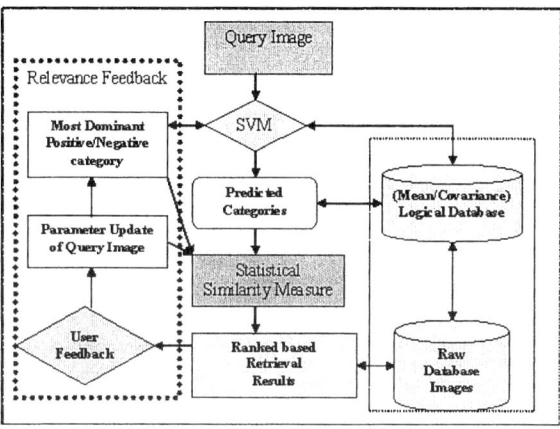

**Fig. 1.** Functional diagram of the proposed similarity matching technique

parameter of the query class based on the positive feedback images from the user, as our statistical distance measures are closely related to the distance measure they proposed. Let, $N_{\text{Pos}(q_i)}$ be the number of positive feedbacks to query image $q_i$ at iteration $i$ and $t_j \in \mathbb{R}^d$ be the feature vector that represents j-th image for $j \in N_{\text{Pos}(q_i)}$, then the new query point at iteration $i+1$ is estimated as $q_{i+1} = \frac{1}{N_{\text{Pos}(q_i)}} \sum_{j=1}^{N_{\text{Pos}(q_i)}} t_j$ as the mean vector of positive images and covariance matrix is estimated as $C_{q_{i+1}} = \frac{1}{N_{\text{Pos}(q_i)}-1} \sum_{j=1}^{N_{\text{Pos}(q_i)}} (t_j - q_{i+1})(t_j - q_{i+1})^T$. However, singularity issue will arise in covariance matrix estimation if fewer than $d+1$ training samples or positive images are available; thus would be the case for user feedback images. So, we add regularization to avoid singularity in matrices as follows[7]:

$$\hat{C_{q_{i+1}}} = \alpha C_{q_{i+1}} + (1-\alpha)I \quad (6)$$

for some $0 \leq \alpha \leq 1$ and $I$ is the $d \times d$ identity matrix. Hence, the proposed method is both a query point movement and parameter updating process. We have used another strategy to modify the ranking of the retrieved images. Based on the user feedbck of positive images, the multi-class SVM classifier will predict the closely related and most prevalent category of the query image by applying a voting rule in each iteration of feedback. We also consider the negative or non-relevant images to be those, which are not selected as relevant and are among the top 15 retrieved images in the previous iteration. From the non-relevant images, SVM also predict the most dominant negative category with the same voting rule. Let, SVM predicts $L_{\text{p}_i}$ and $L_{\text{n}_i}$ pre-defined different categories from $N_{\text{Pos}(q_i)}$ and $N_{\text{Neg}(q_i)}$ images respectively in iteration $i$. For each image, if it belongs to a particular predefined category based on SVM prediction, we increase the counter for that category or label. Using this approach the most dominant positive category is found by

$$L_{max} = max(C_{L_1}, \ldots, C_{L_{\text{p}_i}}) \quad (7)$$

where each $C_{L_i}, i \in (1,\ldots,p_i)$ is the occurence number(s) of a particular category and $(C_{L_1} + \ldots + C_{L_{p_i}}) = N_{\text{Pos}(q_i)}$. Similarly, most dominant negative category is found out from user perceived non-relevant images. Now for different distance measures in $i+1$ iteration, we reward those database images which belong to the most dominant positive category and punish the one in dominant negetive category. By rewarding, we mean that to decrease the distance measure value by a constant $\beta$ found experimentally and thereby increase the ranking and for punishing it goes the opposite way by increasing the values. Hence, if an image of a particular category in the database is close to many positive images of the same category then we will increase its ranking and do the opposite for images belong to most dominant negetive category. Figure 1, shows the block diagram of the proposed online probabilistic similarity matching technique and user interaction for image retrieval.

## 4 Experimental Setup and Results

For statistical parameter estimation and SVM training, we used a fully labeled database of generic images as training samples. However, for actual testing of similarity measure functions, we conducted our experiments on the whole database without any labeling but with known ground truth. Our entire generic database contains 3000 diverse images of natural scenery, people, animal, architecture, food, etc., which were taken from the Corel Photo Gallery. We experimentally selected 15 semantically different categories (Mountain, Beach, Flower, Architecture etc.) each with 100 images for generating the training samples. Now to estimate the parameters of the distributions and providing input to the SVM, feature vectors in the form of color and texture descriptors were extracted from each sample image. We extracted the first, second and third central moments of each color channel as proposed by Stricker and Orengo [14] for our color feature vector in HSV color space. Color moment descriptor is represented by a 9 dimensional color vector as $(\mu_h, \mu_s, \mu_v, \sigma_h, \sigma_s, \sigma_v, \gamma_h, \gamma_s, \gamma_v)$ here $\mu$, $\sigma$ and $\gamma$ are the mean, standard deviation and skewness of each color channel. We extracted texture features from the gray level co-occurrence matrix [2]. A gray level cooccurrence matrix is defined as a sample of the joint probability density of the gray levels of two pixels separated by a given displacement. Second order moments, such as energy, maximum probability, entropy, contrast and inverse difference moment were measured based on the gray level co-occurrence matrix [2]. A fifteen dimensional feature vector was formed for three different displacements or window sizes $(1 \times 1, 4 \times 4, 9 \times 9)$, with each consisting of a five dimensional feature vector. We normalized color and texture feature vectors and combine them to form a joint feature vector of 24 dimensions. For SVM training, we used radial basis kernel function $K(x_i, x_j) = \exp(-\gamma \|x_i - x_j\|^2), \gamma > 0$. After 10 fold cross validation, we found the best parameters $C = 15$ and $\gamma = .03$ with an accuracy of 81.23% in our current setting and finally trained the whole training set with these parameters. For relevance feedback, we added a regularization parameter of $\alpha = .75$ in the updated covariance matrices and we increased or decreased a

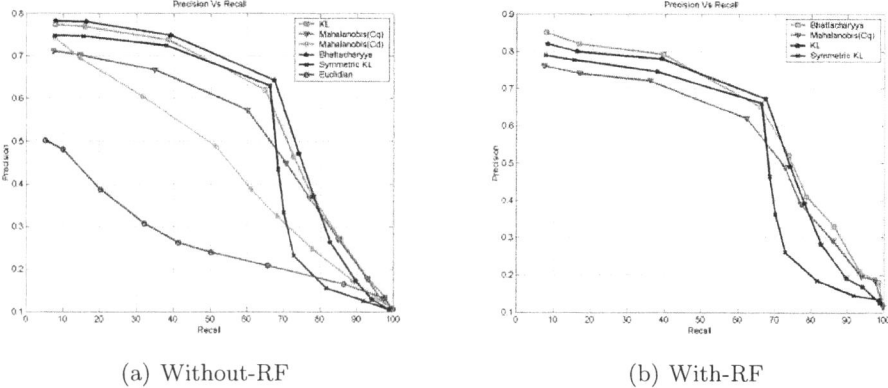

(a) Without-RF   (b) With-RF

**Fig. 2.** Precision-recall curves for similarity measures functions

distance measure value with a constant $\beta = .15$, which were found experimetally in the database consisting of the training images.

For performance evaluation, we selected a set of 10 bench mark queries for each category not included in the database and used *query-by-example* search method. For the similarity measure we compared the performances of Bhattacharyya, Mahalanobis, KL divergence and Symmetric KL distance measures along with most widely used Euclidean distance based on precision-recall metrics. We also evaluated the performances of the distance measures (except Euclidean and Mahalanobis with common covarinace matrix$(C_d)$), after the first three iterations of RF with the same set of 10 bench mark queries. Figure 2(a), presents precision-recall curves for different distance measures. It clearly shows that best performance was achieved by Bhattacharyya distance measure, whereas Euclidean distance performed very poorly. The result is expected as Euclidean distance does not take into account the correlations of its feature attributes. KL divergence and Symmetric KL divergence performed almost equally, whereas performence of Mahalanobis distance was somewhere in between Bhattacharyya and Euclidean distances. Based on this observation, we can conclude that distance measures which utilze both the covariances of query and database image categories performed better in our generic image database. Figure 2(b), presents precision-recall curves for the four statistical distance measures after the first three iterations of relevance feedback. It clearly shows that performances were improved for these distance measures, which justifies our proposed RF approach for query parameter updating and re-ranking of the retrieval results.

## 5 Conclusion

In this paper, we proposed a comparative statistical similarity matching technique based on image categorization and relevance feedback. Instead of comparing only the feature vectors of query and database images, we estimated the covariances of feature attributes in their category specific distributions and utilized it in various similarity measure functions. We also proposed a relevance feedback technique, which utilizes query shifting, parameter updating and re-ranking simultaneously. Performances of different probabilistic distance measures were evaluated in a generic image database with and without RF. Experimental results and retrieval performances are promising, although it is solely meant to illustrate the effectiveness of the probabilistic similarity measures and relevance feedback with simple low-level features.

## References

1. Aksoy, S., Haralick, R.M.: Probabilistic vs. geometric similarity measures for image retrieval., Proceedings. IEEE Conference on Computer Vision and Pattern Recognition,**2**(2000) 357–362
2. Aksoy, S., Haralick, R. M.: Texture Analysis in Machine Vision., Chapter Using Texture in Image Similarity and Retrieval,Series on Machine Perception and Artificial Intelligence., World Scientific (2000)
3. Chapelle, O., Haffner, P., Vapnik, V.: SVMs for histogram-based image classification.,IEEE Transaction on Neural Networks (1999)
4. Chang, C. C., Lin, C.J.: LIBSVM : a library for support vector machines., (2001) Software available at http://www.csie.ntu.edu.tw/ cjlin/libsvm
5. Comaniciu, D., Meer, P., Xu, K., Tyler D.: Retrieval Performance Improvement through Low Rank Corrections., In Workshop in Content-based Access to Image and Video Libraries, Fort Collins, Colorado, (1999) 50–54
6. Eakins John, P.: Towards Intelligent image retrieval., Pattern Recognition, **35** (2002) 3–14
7. Friedman,J.:Regularized Discriminant Analysis., Journal of American Statistical Association, **84** (2002) 165–175
8. Fukunaga,K.: Introduction to Statistical Pattern Recognition., Second ed. Academic Press, (1990)
9. Ishikawa, Y., Subramanya, R., Faloutsos, C.: MindReader: Querying Databases Through Multiple Examples.,24th International Conference on Very Large Databases, New York, (1998) 24–27
10. Kailath,T.: The divergence and Bhattacharyya distance measures in signal selection.,IEEE Trans. Commun. Technol, **COM-15**(1967) 52–60
11. Puzicha, J., Buhmann, J., Rubner, Y., Tomasi, C.: Empirical evaluation of dissimilarity measures for color and texture., Intern. Conf. on Computer Vision, (1999)
12. Rui, Y., Huang, T.S. : Relevance Feedback: A Power Tool for Interactive Content-Based Image Retrieval , IEEE Circuits Syst. Video Technol., **8** (1999)
13. Smeulder, A., Worring, M., Santini, S., Gupta, A., Jain, R.: Content-Based Image Retrieval at the End of the Early Years., IEEE Trans. on Pattern Anal. and Machine Intell., **22**, (2000) 1349–1380
14. Stricker, M., Orengo, M. : Similarity of color images: Storage and Retrieval for Image and Video Databases., SPIE, **2420** (1995)

# 3D Geometry Reconstruction from a Stereoscopic Video Sequence

A. Salgado and J. Sánchez

Departamento de Informática y Sistemas,
Universidad de Las Palmas de G.C.,
35017, Las Palmas de G.C., Spain
{a2652, jsanchez}@dis.ulpgc.es,
http://serdis.dis.ulpgc.es/~jsanchez

**Abstract.** The aim of this work is to propose a method for recovering the 3D geometry of a video sequence taken from a pair of stereo cameras. The cameras are rigidly situated in a fixed position and there are some objects which are moving in front of them. Our method estimates the displacements of objects and the 3D structure of the scene. We establish a temporal constraint that relates the computation of the optical flow and the estimation of disparity maps. We use an energy minimisation approach that yields a system of partial differential equations (PDE) which is solved by means of a gradient descent technique.

## 1 Introduction

In this paper we present a new method for the reconstruction of the 3D geometry of a scene from a stereoscopic video sequence. There are two video–cameras pointing to the same scene and recording frames at the same time. These two cameras are situated in a fixed position and always looking at the same direction. There are some objects in front of the cameras that are moving. We suppose that the stereo rig is weakly calibrated – the fundamental matrix is known–. We also suppose that the objects could undergo large displacements.

For every stereoscopic pair of images in the sequence we may compute a disparity map independently from the others, so we would obtain a set of independent disparity maps. The problem with this is that, in general, the continuity of the solution is not preserved and it is very sensitive to the presence of noise. If we want to overcome this problem then we have to relate the estimation of disparity maps during the sequence. One way to do this is to compute the displacement of objects on both video–cameras and use this information to constraint the computation of the disparity maps in time.

The aim of our method is both to estimate the optical flow for the two cameras and to constraint the computation of disparity maps by introducing the information of optical flows. We propose an energy–based method to estimate a set of dense disparity maps. We introduce the so–called fundamental matrix [3], [5], [4] in the equations and also compute the optical flows related with both cameras.

In order to deal with large displacements, we use a multigrid approach in where the solutions at lower scales are used as initial approximation for upper scales. At the end of the process we obtain three sets of dense matching functions – the disparity maps associated with the stereoscopic system and the optical flows for the left and right cameras, respectively.

This work is a continuation of previous works on optical flow [2] and disparity map estimation [1]. These two methods were also based on energy minimization techniques and showed to be reliable and accurate.

The paper is organized as follows: In Sect. 2 we explain several concepts on optical flow estimation and the geometry associated to a static stereoscopic system. In Sect. 3 the method is explained. In Sect. 5 there are some numerical experiences with synthetic sequences. Finally the conclusions with a summary of the most important contributions of this work are in Sect. 6.

## 2 Background

The optical flow is the apparent motion of pixels between images. Under the Lambertian assumption that corresponding pixels have equal grey values, the determination of the optical flow comes down to finding a function $\mathbf{h}(\mathbf{x}) = (u(\mathbf{x}), v(\mathbf{x}))^t$ that complies with (1).

In our case we have two video-cameras so we may determine the optical flow for each one. Looking at Fig. 1, we represent by $\mathbf{h}_{i,l}(\mathbf{x})$ the optical flow for the left camera and by $\mathbf{h}_{i,r}(\mathbf{x})$ the optical flow for the right one. The subindex $i$

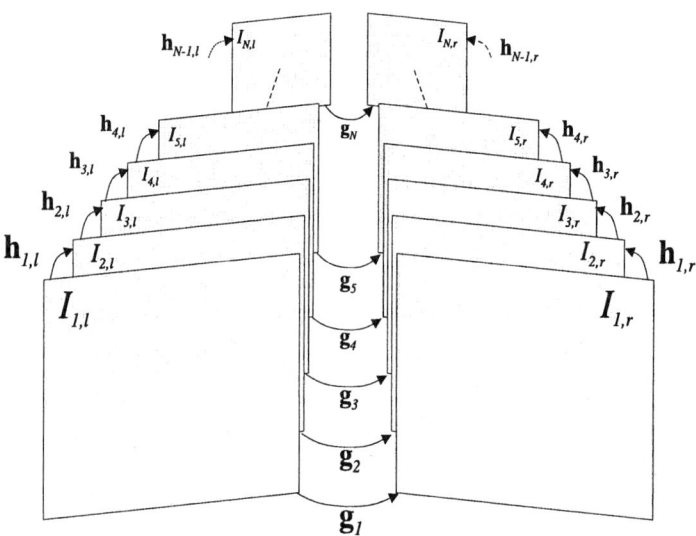

**Fig. 1.** We note by $I_{i,l}(\mathbf{x})$ the images taken from the left camera and by $I_{i,r}(\mathbf{x})$ the ones from the right camera. $\mathbf{h}_{i,l}(\mathbf{x})$ and $\mathbf{h}_{i,r}(\mathbf{x})$ are the optical flows for both cameras and $\mathbf{g}_i(\mathbf{x})$ is the matching function computed between every stereoscopic pair.

stands for the temporal estimation of optical flows between two consecutives frames, $l$ for the left video-camera and $r$ for the right one.

Then the optical flow constraint equation may be expressed as

$$I_{i,l}(\mathbf{x}) \simeq I_{i+1,l}\left(\mathbf{x} + \mathbf{h}_{i,l}(\mathbf{x})\right)$$
$$I_{i,r}(\mathbf{x}) \simeq I_{i+1,r}\left(\mathbf{x} + \mathbf{h}_{i,r}(\mathbf{x})\right)$$

for the left and right cameras respectively. $I_{i,l}(\mathbf{x})$ is the image captured by the left video-camera at instant $i$ and $\mathbf{x} = (x,y)$ is the coordinate for the pixels on the image. $I_{i,r}(\mathbf{x})$ is the correspondent for the right video-camera.

Regarding the stereoscopic system we know that at every instant both cameras are related. We may compute the optical flow within a frame from the left image into the right one. This kind of optical flow is constraint by a geometrical relation that is called the epipolar geometry. We will call this optical flow the stereo flow to note that the flow is undergoing the influence of the epipolar geometry.

The epipolar constraint equation $\mathbf{m}'^t \mathbf{F} \mathbf{m} = 0$ states that two corresponding points, $\mathbf{m} = (\mathbf{x}, 1) = (x, y, 1)$ and $\mathbf{m}'^t = (\mathbf{x}, 1) = (x, y, 1)$, on the two images are related by the Fundamental Matrix, $\mathbf{F}$ [4], [5]. This allows us to estimate the stereo flow only along certain lines like:

$$a(\mathbf{x}) = f_{11}x + f_{12}y + f_{13}$$
$$b(\mathbf{x}) = f_{21}x + f_{22}y + f_{23}$$
$$c(\mathbf{x}) = f_{31}x + f_{32}y + f_{33}$$

In Fig. 1 we name this stereo flow as $\mathbf{g}_i(\mathbf{x}) = (u_{i,s}(\mathbf{x}), v_{i,s}(\mathbf{x}))^t$. The stereo flow depends on a scalar function $\lambda(\mathbf{x})$ and on the epipolar geometry in the following way

$$u_{i,s}(\mathbf{x}) = \frac{-\lambda_i(\mathbf{x})b(\mathbf{x})}{\sqrt{a^2(\mathbf{x})+b^2(\mathbf{x})}} - \frac{a(\mathbf{x})x+b(\mathbf{x})y+c(\mathbf{x})}{a^2(\mathbf{x})+b^2(\mathbf{x})} a(\mathbf{x})$$
$$v_{i,s}(\mathbf{x}) = \frac{\lambda_i(\mathbf{x})a(\mathbf{x})}{\sqrt{a^2(\mathbf{x})+b^2(\mathbf{x})}} - \frac{a(\mathbf{x})x+b(\mathbf{x})y+c(\mathbf{x})}{a^2(\mathbf{x})+b^2(\mathbf{x})} b(\mathbf{x})$$

More details about this parameterization could be read in paper [1]. The stereo flow constraint equation is

$$I_{i,l}(\mathbf{x}) \simeq I_{i,r}\left(\mathbf{x} + \mathbf{g}_i(\mathbf{x})\right) \tag{1}$$

Regarding Fig. 2 it is easy to note that for any two consecutive frames on the sequence we may establish a relation between the optical and the stereo flows as

$$\mathbf{h}_{i,l}(\mathbf{x}) + \mathbf{g}_{i+1}(\mathbf{x} + \mathbf{h}_{i,l}(\mathbf{x})) \equiv \mathbf{g}_i(\mathbf{x}) + \mathbf{h}_{i,r}(\mathbf{x} + \mathbf{g}_i(\mathbf{x})) \tag{2}$$

The path of the vectorial functions $\mathbf{h}_{i,l}$ and $\mathbf{g}_{i+1}$ should provide the same result as following the path $\mathbf{g}_i$ and $\mathbf{h}_{i,r}$. Therefore, we have to find out the functions that fulfill this constraint. This temporal constraint relates all the unknowns of our problem and represents a feature that is desirable to keep.

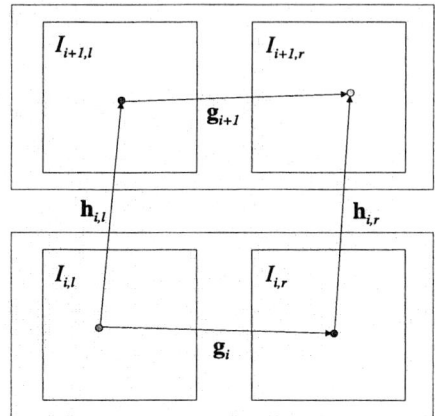

**Fig. 2.** Temporal constraint $\mathbf{h}_{i,l}(\mathbf{x}) + \mathbf{g}_{i+1}(\mathbf{x} + \mathbf{h}_{i,l}(\mathbf{x})) \equiv \mathbf{g}_i(\mathbf{x}) + \mathbf{h}_{i,r}(\mathbf{x} + \mathbf{g}_i(\mathbf{x}))$

## 3 The Method

The aim of our method is to estimate the stereo and optical flows for the video sequence. The unknowns for the stereo flow are given by the $\mathbf{g}_i$ vectorial functions and thanks to the epipolar geometry it is equivalent to computing the scalar functions $\lambda_i, i = 1,..N$. The unknowns for the optical flows are $\mathbf{h}_{j,l}$ and $\mathbf{h}_{j,r}, j = 1,..N-1$. These two ones are also vectorial functions and their components are $\mathbf{h}_{j,l} = (u_{j,l}, v_{j,l})$ and $\mathbf{h}_{j,r} = (u_{j,r}, v_{j,r})$.

The variational approach proposed is given by the following energy functional:

$$E(\lambda_i, \mathbf{h}_{j,l}, \mathbf{h}_{j,r}) = E_s(\lambda_i) + E_{o_l}(\mathbf{h}_{i,l}) + E_{o_r}(\mathbf{h}_{i,r}) + E_c(\lambda_i, \mathbf{h}_{i,l}, \mathbf{h}_{i,r}) \quad (3)$$

with $E_s(\lambda_i)$ the energy corresponding to the stereo flow estimation, $E_{o_l}(\mathbf{h}_{i,l})$ and $E_{o_r}(\mathbf{h}_{i,r})$ the energies for the computation of the optical flows for the left and right video-cameras respectively, and $E_c(\lambda_i, \mathbf{h}_{i,l}, \mathbf{h}_{i,r})$ is the energy that relates the three unknowns as it is remarked on Fig. 2.

The energy functional for the disparity map estimation is

$$E_s(\lambda_i) = \sum_{i=1}^{N} \left( \int_\Omega (I_{i,l}(\mathbf{x}) - I_{i,r}(\mathbf{x} + \mathbf{g}(\lambda_i(\mathbf{x}))))^2 \, dx \, dy \right.$$
$$\left. + \alpha \int_\Omega \nabla \lambda_i(\mathbf{x})^t \mathbf{D}(\nabla I_{i,l}) \nabla \lambda_i(\mathbf{x}) dx \, dy \right)$$

This energy is similar to the one explained in [1]. The main difference is that in this case there is a family of stereoscopic pair of images and we have introduced an addition to include all the frames. The first term of this energy is the data term and refers to the stereo flow constraint equation (1). The second is the regularizing term that makes it possible to find a unique and smooth solution.

The optical flow energies are

$$E_{o_l}(\mathbf{h}_{i,l}) = \sum_{i=1}^{N-1} \left( \int_\Omega (I_{i,l}(\mathbf{x}) - I_{i+1,l}(\mathbf{x} + \mathbf{h}_{i,l}(\mathbf{x})))^2 \, dx \, dy \right.$$
$$\left. + \alpha \int_\Omega \text{trace} \left( (\nabla \mathbf{h}_{i,l}(\mathbf{x}))^t \, \mathbf{D}(\nabla I_{i,l}) \nabla \mathbf{h}_{i,l}(\mathbf{x}) \right) dx \, dy \right)$$

for the left camera and

$$E_{o_r}(\mathbf{h}_{i,r}) = \sum_{i=1}^{N-1} \left( \int_\Omega (I_{i,r}(\mathbf{x}) - I_{i+1,r}(\mathbf{x} + \mathbf{h}_{i,r}(\mathbf{x})))^2 \, dx \, dy \right.$$
$$\left. + \alpha \int_\Omega \text{trace} \left( (\nabla \mathbf{h}_{i,r}(\mathbf{x}))^t \, \mathbf{D}(\nabla I_{i,r}) \nabla \mathbf{h}_{i,r}(\mathbf{x}) \right) dx \, dy \right)$$

for the right one. These two energies are similar to the one explained in paper [2]. We have also introduced a summation. Note that the range of the addition is from 1 to $N-1$ since the optical flow cannot be computed for the last frame.

In these equations $\alpha$ is a constant and $\mathbf{D}(\nabla I)$ is a projection matrix perpendicular to $\nabla I$. This matrix was first introduced by Nagel and Enkelmann [7].

$$\mathbf{D}(\nabla I) = \frac{1}{\|\nabla I\|^2 + 2v^2} \left( \nabla I_\perp \nabla I_\perp^t + v^2 \mathbf{Id} \right) \quad (4)$$

$\nabla I_\perp$ is the vector orthogonal to the gradient and is given by $\nabla I_\perp = \left( -I_y \; I_x \right)^t$. This is a projection matrix on the direction perpendicular to the gradient and thus on the contour direction.

The last part of the energy arise from the relation between the optical and stereo flows. Regarding Fig. 2 we may relate them as

$$E_c(\lambda_i, \mathbf{h}_{i,l}, \mathbf{h}_{i,r}) = \beta \sum_{i=1}^{N-1} \int_\Omega \Phi \left( \|\mathbf{h}_{i,l}(\mathbf{x}) + \mathbf{g}_{i+1}(\mathbf{x} + \mathbf{h}_{i,l}(\mathbf{x})) \right.$$
$$\left. - \mathbf{g}_i(\mathbf{x}) - \mathbf{h}_{i,r}(\mathbf{x} + \mathbf{g}_i(\mathbf{x}))\|^2 \right) dx \, dy$$

This equation impose a constraint for consecutive frames. In this equation $\gamma$ is a constant and $\Phi(.)$ is a function like

$$\Phi(s) = \rho \left( 1 - e^{\frac{-s}{\rho}} \right)$$

Intuitively it acts like a force that attracts two corresponding points in the $I_{i+1,r}$ image. In most of cases if we follow the two paths we have to arrive to the same point, but it is not going to occur unless we force it.

## 4 Energy Minimization

When we minimize the energy functional we obtain the associated Euler-Lagrange equations. In this case we have a system of equations corresponding to the three unknowns $\lambda_i, h_{i,l}$ and $h_{i,r}$. Then we embed these equations into a gradient descent method and we obtain a system of time varying partial differential equations. If we introduce some variables to simplify the equations $B := \frac{-b(\mathbf{x})}{\sqrt{a^2(\mathbf{x})+b^2(\mathbf{x})}}$, $A := \frac{a(\mathbf{x})}{\sqrt{a^2(\mathbf{x})+b^2(\mathbf{x})}}$, $Ca := -\frac{a(\mathbf{x})x+b(\mathbf{x})y+c(\mathbf{x})}{a^2(\mathbf{x})+b^2(\mathbf{x})}a(\mathbf{x})$ and $Cb := -\frac{a(\mathbf{x})x+b(\mathbf{x})y+c(\mathbf{x})}{a^2(\mathbf{x})+b^2(\mathbf{x})}b(\mathbf{x})$ so the stereo flow is simplified to $u_{i,s} = B\lambda_i + Ca$ and $v_{i,s} = A\lambda_i + Cb$, then the gradient descent equation for the stereo flow is

$$\frac{\partial \lambda_i}{\partial t} = \alpha \operatorname{div}\left(\mathbf{D}\left(\nabla I_{i,l}\right) \nabla \lambda_i\right) + \left(I_{i,l} - I_{i,r}^{\lambda_i}\right)\left(AI_{i,r,y}^{\lambda_i} + BI_{i,r,x}^{\lambda_i}\right)$$

$$+\beta \Phi_i' \begin{pmatrix} u_{i,l} + u_{i+1,s}^{\mathbf{h}_{i,l}} - B\lambda_i - Ca - u_{i,r}^{\mathbf{g}_i} \\ v_{i,l} + v_{i+1,s}^{\mathbf{h}_{i,l}} - A\lambda_i - Cb - v_{i,r}^{\mathbf{g}_i} \end{pmatrix}^t \begin{pmatrix} 1 + u_{i,r,x}^{\mathbf{g}_i} & u_{i,r,y}^{\mathbf{g}_i} \\ v_{i,r,x}^{\mathbf{g}_i} & 1 + v_{i,r,y}^{\mathbf{g}_i} \end{pmatrix} \begin{pmatrix} B \\ A \end{pmatrix}$$

Considering the left optical flow, the gradient descent equations are

$$\frac{\partial u_{i,l}}{\partial t} = \alpha \operatorname{div}\left(\mathbf{D}\left(\nabla I_{i,l}\right) \nabla u_{i,l}\right) + \left(I_{i,l} - I_{i+1,l}^{\mathbf{h}_{i,l}}\right) I_{i+1,l,x}^{\mathbf{h}_{i,l}}$$

$$-\beta \Phi_i' \begin{pmatrix} u_{i,l} + u_{i+1,s}^{\mathbf{h}_{i,l}} - B\lambda_i - Ca - u_{i,r}^{\mathbf{g}_i} \\ v_{i,l} + v_{i+1,s}^{\mathbf{h}_{i,l}} - A\lambda_i - Cb - v_{i,r}^{\mathbf{g}_i} \end{pmatrix}^t \begin{pmatrix} 1 + u_{i+1,s,x}^{\mathbf{h}_{i,l}} \\ u_{i+1,s,y}^{\mathbf{h}_{i,l}} \end{pmatrix}$$

$$\frac{\partial v_{i,l}}{\partial t} = \alpha \operatorname{div}\left(\mathbf{D}\left(\nabla I_{i,l}\right) \nabla v_{i,l}\right) + \left(I_{i,l} - I_{i+1,l}^{\mathbf{h}_{i,l}}\right) I_{i+1,l,y}^{\mathbf{h}_{i,l}}$$

$$-\beta \Phi_i' \begin{pmatrix} u_{i,l} + u_{i+1,s}^{\mathbf{h}_{i,l}} - B\lambda_i - Ca - u_{i,r}^{\mathbf{g}_i} \\ v_{i,l} + v_{i+1,s}^{\mathbf{h}_{i,l}} - A\lambda_i - Cb - v_{i,r}^{\mathbf{g}_i} \end{pmatrix}^t \begin{pmatrix} v_{i+1,s,x}^{\mathbf{h}_{i,l}} \\ 1 + v_{i+1,s,y}^{\mathbf{h}_{i,l}} \end{pmatrix}$$

For the right optical flow we have

$$\frac{\partial u_{i,r}}{\partial t} = \alpha \operatorname{div}\left(\mathbf{D}\left(\nabla I_{i,r}\right) \nabla u_{i,r}\right) + \left(I_{i,r} - I_{i+1,r}^{\mathbf{h}_{i,r}}\right) I_{i+1,r,x}^{\mathbf{h}_{i,r}}$$

$$\frac{\partial v_{i,r}}{\partial t} = \alpha \operatorname{div}\left(\mathbf{D}\left(\nabla I_{i,r}\right) \nabla v_{i,r}\right) + \left(I_{i,r} - I_{i+1,r}^{\mathbf{h}_{i,r}}\right) I_{i+1,r,y}^{\mathbf{h}_{i,r}}$$

In order to overcome the problem of large displacements, we embed our method into a multi-resolution framework. We start with a large initial scale $n_0$ which yields the smallest image size. Then we compute the stereo and optical flows for this scale using the gradient equations of the previous section. In the following scale we use them as initial approximation. We repeat this process for several scales and finish when we reach the final scale – the original sized images.

## 5 Experimental Results

In Fig. 3 we show a synthetic sequence of a cylinder which is moving horizontally from the right border to the left one. The epipolar lines are also horizontal which means that the projective planes of the cameras are situated in a common plane and their focus are displaced horizontally.

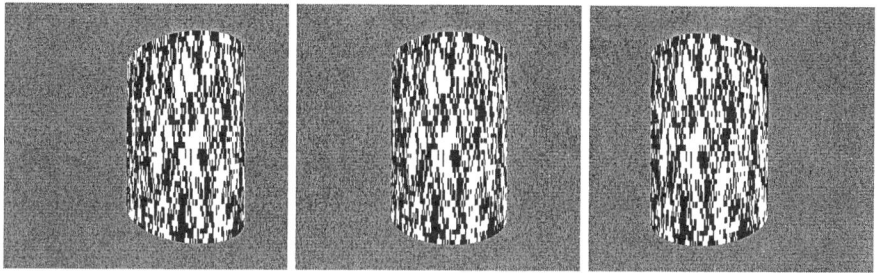

**Fig. 3.** Images of the cylinder sequence

In Fig. 4 we show the dense disparity maps associated with the previous images. The average euclidean error for these maps are about 0,2. The value of $\alpha = 0,7$ and $\beta = 3x10^{-3}$.

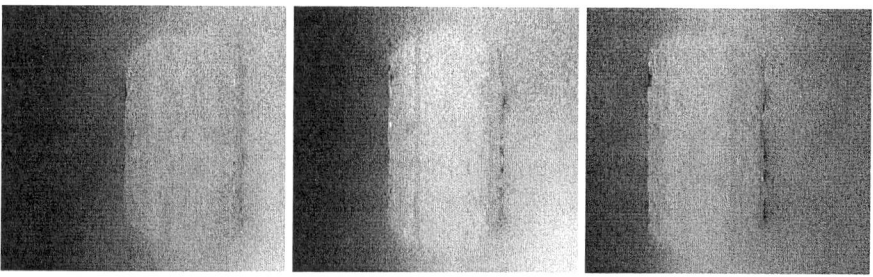

**Fig. 4.** Disparity maps corresponding to the images in Fig. 3

## 6  Conclusions

In this paper we have proposed a novel method for the estimation of dense disparity maps from a stereoscopic video sequence. The method that we have proposed stablishes a unified framework to deal with optical flow estimation and stereo flow computation in continuous stereo video. We have extended some well studied stereoscopic and optical flow techniques for pair of images to a sequence of images. In order to have a consistent solution we have introduced a temporal constraint between the stereo and the optical flows. We obtain dense solutions thanks to a variational formulation and to deal with large displacements we have introduced a pyramidal approach.

## Acknowledgements

This paper has been partly funded by the spanish Ministry of Science and Technology and FEDER through the research project TIC2003-08957, and by the

Consejería de Educación Cultura y Deportes of the Canary Islands Government through the research project PI2002/193.

# References

1. Alvarez, L., Deriche, R., Sánchez, J., and Weickert, J.: Dense disparity map estimation respecting image derivatives: a PDE and scale-space based approach. Journal of Visual Communication and Image Representation **13** (2002) 3–21. Also published as Inria Research Report n$^o$ 3874
2. Alvarez, L., Weickert, J., and Sánchez, J.: Reliable Estimation of Dense Optical Flow Fields with Large Displacements. International Journal of Computer Vision, Vol. **39**, **1** (2000) 41–56. An extended version maybe be found at Technical Report n$^o$2 del Instituto Universitario de Ciencias y Tecnologías Cibernéticas
3. Faugeras, O.: Three-Dimensional Computer Vision: A Geometric Viewpoint. MIT Press (1993)
4. Faugeras, O., and Luong, Q., and Papadopoulo, T.: The Geometry of Multiple Images. Mit Press (2001)
5. Hartley, R. and Zisserman, A.: Multiple View Geometry in Computer Vision. Cambridge University Press (2000)
6. T. Kanade, "A Video-Rate Stereo Machine for 3D Reconstruction," Proc. of International Workshop on Stereoscopic 3D Display Technologies and Applications '95, 1995.
7. H. H. Nagel and W. Enkelmann: An Investigation of Smoothness Constraints for the Estimation of Displacements Vector Fields from Image Sequences. IEEE Trans. Pattern Anal. Mach. Intell. 8, 565–593, 1986
8. Perona, P. and Malik, J.: Scale-Space and Edge Detection Using Anisotropic Diffusion. IEEE Transactions on Pattern Analysis and Machine Intelligence **12** (1990) 429–439
9. Li Zhang, Brian Curless, and Steven M. Seitz. Spacetime Stereo: Shape Recovery for Dynamic Scenes. In Proceedings of IEEE Computer Society, Conference on Computer Vision and Pattern Recognition (CVPR), Madison, WI, June, 2003, pp. 367-374

# Three-Dimensional Planar Profile Registration in 3D Scanning

João Filipe Ferreira and Jorge Dias

Institute of Systems and Robotics,
University of Coimbra, Portugal
{jfilipe, jorge}@isr.uc.pt

**Abstract.** Three-dimensional planar profile sampling of surfaces is a very common method of structural recovery in 3D scanning. In handheld 3D scanners, this has scarcely ever been taken into account resulting in poor precision ratings. Therefore, in this text we will describe a novel use of the profiling geometrical context to derive an intuitive and physically meaningful approach on solving the 3D profile registration problem. We will finish by describing the global optimisation algorithm and by showing experimental results achieved with a 3D scanner prototype comprising a camera, a laser-plane projector and a pose sensor.

## 1 Introduction

Most three-dimensional recovery and reconstruction systems, commonly known as 3D scanners, acquire samples of object surfaces on a three-dimensional scene so as to achieve their goal. Examples of devices resorting to this methodology are laser range finders, scanners using structured light projection, ultrasound systems, stereoscopic systems (photogrammetry), to name but a few.

Although some of these systems instantly sample complete surface patches from the object, others require a sweep of the three-dimensional scene in order to sample large sets of curvilinear profiles. More precisely, these profiles belong to planes which are projected in space in a controlled fashion in order to perform the sweep — these planes may be formed by light projection, laser projection, ultrasound projection, etc.

### 1.1 Brief Overview of Registration in 3D Scanning

Most of the research conducted regarding 3D registration has relied on the fact that large sets of points sampled from a surface from *each viewpoint* can be trusted as being accurately *locally registered* inside that set. As a result, integration can be achieved through registration of several overlapping surface patches resulting from those point-sets [1,2].

However, there is also an important group of scanners that can only trustingly yield sets of points locally registered as belonging to curvilinear planar patches. These are the main subjects of our study, and examples of these devices belong to one of the most cutting-edge and also challenging groups of 3D scanners of today: the *handheld 3D scanners*.

## 1.2 Overview of Profile Registration

There is one main difficulty regarding the 3D registration process that implies a big loss in redundancy when considering scanners that can only scan point-sets of one planar profile at a time: each profile can only be registered with other profiles that *intersect it* inside the bounds of the visible surface of the scanned object [3].

This means that it is only possible to register **crossing profiles** as opposed to overlapping surface patches and that the feature space is reduced to their intersection points. Let us assume for now that this issue has been taken care of so that intersecting profiles have been matched together. Then, one preliminary solution to the 3D registration problem for a particular profile with its set of intersecting profiles, down the line of well-known algorithms such as ICP (Iterative Closest Point), could be given by the following equation (*cf* [1,3])

$$e = \sum_{i=1}^{N} \left\| {}^W\mathbf{T}_{C_n} \mathbf{P}_{ni} - {}^W\mathbf{T}_{C_i} \mathbf{P}''_{in} \right\|^2,$$

$$\mathbf{P}''_{in} = \mathbf{P} \vert \min_{\mathbf{P} \in p_i} \left\| {}^W\mathbf{T}_{C_n} \mathbf{P}_{ni} - {}^W\mathbf{T}_{C_i} \mathbf{P} \right\| \tag{1}$$

where $\{C\}$ represents the local referential corresponding to the sampling sensor (usually a camera), $\{W\}$ represents the global integrating referential and $e$ is the error function to be minimised in a least-square sense. This function represents the sum of squares of euclidian distances between the elements of each pair, index $i$, of correspondent intersection points. These pairs consist of the intersection points $\mathbf{P}_{ni}$, taken from the considered profile $p_n$ at point of view $n$, for which the transformation ${}^W\mathbf{T}_{C_n}$ is to be estimated so as to achieve registration, and points $\mathbf{P}''_{in}$ from the intersecting profiles $p_i$ at point of view $i$ (paired with transformations ${}^W\mathbf{T}_{C_i}$, assumed given), taken to be correspondent through matching based on the minimum euclidian distance.

Studies have been made by Hébert and Rioux, as shown in [3], that attempt to solve the local registration problem by profiting from the profiling geometry indirectly through the use of the properties of the plane which is tangent to the scanned surface so as to match points between crossing profiles.

Our solution, described in the following text, directly exploits the benefits of the profiling geometry to achieve better point correspondence, using the knowledge that intersection points between profiles also belong to the lines of intersection of crossing profile planes.

## 2 Local Optimisation for 3D Profile Registration

In the following subsections, the main contribution of our work is presented, which is twofold: a novel approach to profile matching and point correspondence, and a powerful formulation and solution of the local optimisation problem.

## 2.1 Profile Matching and Point Correspondence

In figure 1, a hypothetical (since all the true positions/orientations of all entities are assumed known) scan situation is shown, consisting of a projected plane $\Pi_3^n$ of radiant energy[1] (be it light, ultrasound or of any other kind of energy propagating with a similar geometric model) crossing two other planes, $\Pi_3^i$ and $\Pi_3^j$, all of which crossing an undulating surface creating profiles. Here we can clearly observe the redundancy achieved by taking advantage of its geometry, since we are considering several different entities that intersect at the same registration points: two planes, one line and two profiles for each of these points.

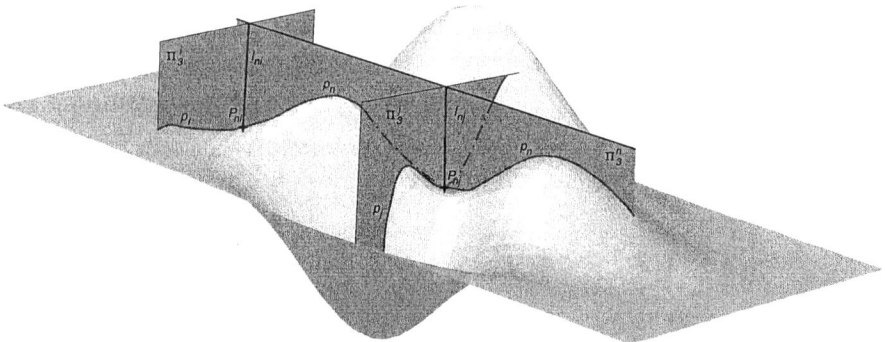

**Fig. 1.** Plane registration. One plane can be seen crossed by two other planes; their intersection lines, their corresponding profiles and the profiles' intersection points are also shown.

We propose that each light plane intersection line referred to point of view $i$ and denoted as $l_{in}$ can be used as a search line to determine which points belonging to profile $p_i$ correspond to other points belonging to profile $p_n$ in a reference point of view $n$.

The mathematical formalisation of 3D registration of a profile performed in this manner would thus be stated as

$$e = \sum_{i=1}^{N} \left\| {}^W\mathbf{T}_{C_n} \mathbf{P}_{ni} - {}^W\mathbf{T}_{C_i} \mathbf{P}'_{in} \right\|^2,$$

$$\begin{cases} \mathbf{P}'_{in} = l_{in} \cap p_i \\ l_{in} = {}^{C_i}\Pi_3^n \cap {}^{C_i}\Pi_3^i \end{cases} \qquad (2)$$

where all entities have the same meanings as in equation (1), with the exception of $\mathbf{P}'_{in}$, which represents the correspondent point in profile $p_i$ taken using search

---

[1] Subscript "3" appears due to the fact that the planes usually present the third restriction in triangulation based systems — see [4].

line $l_{in}$, which is the result of the intersection between ${}^{C_i}\mathbf{\Pi}_3^n$, the plane taken from point of view $n$, and ${}^{C_i}\mathbf{\Pi}_3^i$, the plane taken from point of view $i$, both referred to $\{C_i\}$.

## 2.2 Local Optimisation Methodology

The minimisation of the error function given by equation (2) is referred to as *local optimisation*. This particular part of the 3D registration process has been studied thoroughly in the past — it relates to the popular *absolute orientation estimation problem*, which also has applications in photogrammetry, object motion analysis, determining the hand-eye transform and pose estimation [5].

An overall study of the performances of the most popular closed-form methods proposed by several authors was done in [5]. Four major algorithms are compared in this work and it makes clear that most of them achieve similar results under realistic conditions. However, the first three methods are solutions built on top of different formulations of the *Procrustes problem* where rotation is estimated first, then translation, which for obvious reasons implies error propagation and compounding — the implications of error propagation using these types of formulations were studied in [6]. With this in mind, we have decided on using Michael Walker's solution, described in [7], which uses an elegant formulation, resorting to dual quaternions to provide a linear least-square method to solve simultaneously for rotation and translation, avoiding in this way error compounding.

According to this method, the equation that represents the transformation $\mathbf{T}$ that takes point $\mathbf{P}_{ni}$ into coinciding with its match $\mathbf{P}_{in}$ is

$$\mathring{\mathbf{p}}_{in} = \mathbf{W}(\mathring{\mathbf{q}})^T \mathbf{Q}(\mathring{\mathbf{q}}) \mathring{\mathbf{p}}_{ni} + \mathbf{W}(\mathring{\mathbf{q}})^T \mathring{\mathbf{q}}' \quad (3)$$

where $\mathring{\mathbf{q}} = [q_1, q_2, q_3, q_4]^T$ (representing rotation) and $\mathring{\mathbf{q}}' = [q_1', q_2', q_3', q_4']^T$ (representing translation) are the real and dual parts, respectively, of the dual unit quaternion $\breve{\mathbf{q}}$ corresponding to the screw motion related to ${}^W\mathbf{T}_{C_n}$, and $\mathring{\mathbf{p}}_{ni}$ and $\mathring{\mathbf{p}}_{in}$ are the purely imaginary quaternions corresponding to $\mathbf{P}_{ni}$ and $\mathbf{P}_{in}$, respectively (for in-depth information regarding dual quaternions and the kinematic notion of a screw, please refer to [8]).

In addition we have the following auxiliary matrices:

$$\mathbf{K}(\mathring{\mathbf{q}}) = \begin{bmatrix} 0 & -q_3 & q_2 \\ q_3 & 0 & -q_1 \\ -q_2 & q_1 & 0 \end{bmatrix}, \mathbf{Q}(\mathring{\mathbf{q}}) = \begin{bmatrix} q_4 \mathbf{I} + \mathbf{K}(\mathring{\mathbf{q}}) & \mathring{\mathbf{q}} \\ -\mathring{\mathbf{q}}^T & q_4 \end{bmatrix}, \mathbf{W}(\mathring{\mathbf{q}}) = \begin{bmatrix} q_4 \mathbf{I} - \mathbf{K}(\mathring{\mathbf{q}}) & \mathring{\mathbf{q}} \\ -\mathring{\mathbf{q}}^T & q_4 \end{bmatrix}$$

Re-writing equation (2) according to [7] and considering $\tilde{\mathbf{p}}_{in}$, corresponding to $\tilde{\mathbf{P}}_{in} = {}^W\mathbf{T}_{C_i} \mathbf{P}'_{in}$, and $\mathring{\mathbf{p}}_{in}$ resulting from equation (3), gives

$$e = \sum_{i=1}^{N} \beta_i \left\| \mathring{\mathbf{p}}_{in} - \tilde{\mathring{\mathbf{p}}}_{in} \right\|^2,$$

$$\begin{cases} \tilde{\mathbf{P}}_{in} = {}^W\mathbf{T}_{C_i} \mathbf{P}'_{in} \mapsto \tilde{\mathring{\mathbf{p}}}_{in} \\ \mathbf{P}'_{in} = l_{in} \cap p_i \\ l_{in} = {}^{C_i}\Pi_3^n \cap {}^{C_i}\Pi_3^i \end{cases} \quad (4)$$

where $\beta_i$ are constant positive weighting factors that may be used to reflect data reliability [7,5].

Using dual quaternion properties and equation (3), one may expand the squared norm as [7]

$$\left\| \mathring{\mathbf{p}}_{in} - \tilde{\mathring{\mathbf{p}}}_{in} \right\|^2 = \mathring{\mathbf{q}}'^T \mathring{\mathbf{q}}' + 2\mathring{\mathbf{q}}'^T \left( \mathbf{W}(\mathring{\mathbf{p}}_{ni}) - \mathbf{Q}(\tilde{\mathring{\mathbf{p}}}_{in}) \right) \mathring{\mathbf{q}} - 2\mathring{\mathbf{q}}^T \mathbf{Q}(\tilde{\mathring{\mathbf{p}}}_{in})^T \mathbf{W}(\mathring{\mathbf{p}}_{ni}) \mathring{\mathbf{q}}$$
$$+ \left( (\mathring{\mathbf{p}}_{ni})^T \mathring{\mathbf{p}}_{ni} + (\tilde{\mathring{\mathbf{p}}}_{in})^T \tilde{\mathring{\mathbf{p}}}_{in} \right) \quad (5)$$

Thus, the error function can be written as a quadratic function of $\mathring{\mathbf{q}}$ and $\mathring{\mathbf{q}}'$ [7]

$$e = \mathring{\mathbf{q}}^T \mathbf{C}_1 \mathring{\mathbf{q}} + \mathring{\mathbf{q}}'^T \mathbf{C}_2 \mathring{\mathbf{q}}' + \mathring{\mathbf{q}}'^T \mathbf{C}_2 \mathring{\mathbf{q}} + K \quad (6)$$

where

$$\mathbf{C}_1 = -2 \sum_{i=1}^{N} \beta_i \mathbf{Q}(\tilde{\mathring{\mathbf{p}}}_{in})^T \mathbf{W}(\mathring{\mathbf{p}}_{ni})$$

$$\mathbf{C}_2 = \left( \sum_{i=1}^{N} \beta_i \right) \mathbf{I}$$

$$\mathbf{C}_3 = 2 \sum_{i=1}^{N} \beta_i \left( \mathbf{W}(\mathring{\mathbf{p}}_{ni}) - \mathbf{Q}(\tilde{\mathring{\mathbf{p}}}_{in}) \right)$$

$$K = \sum_{i=1}^{N} \beta_i \left( (\mathring{\mathbf{p}}_{ni})^T \mathring{\mathbf{p}}_{ni} + (\tilde{\mathring{\mathbf{p}}}_{in})^T \tilde{\mathring{\mathbf{p}}}_{in} \right) \quad (7)$$

Using unit norm condition of the dual unit quaternion $\check{\mathbf{q}}$, which in terms of its real and dual parts implies $\mathring{\mathbf{q}}^T \mathring{\mathbf{q}} = 1$ and $\mathring{\mathbf{q}}'^T \mathring{\mathbf{q}} = 0$, Walker et al. use Lagrange multipliers (see [9]) to prove that the solution for $\mathring{\mathbf{q}}$ is the eigenvector of [7]

$$\mathbf{A} = \frac{1}{2} \left( \mathbf{C}_3^T (\mathbf{C}_2 + \mathbf{C}_2^T)^{-1} \mathbf{C}_3 - \mathbf{C}_1 - \mathbf{C}_1^T \right) \quad (8)$$

corresponding to its largest positive eigenvalue. The solution for the dual part is easily shown to be $\mathring{\mathbf{q}}' = -(\mathbf{C}_2 + \mathbf{C}_2^T)^{-1} \mathbf{C}_3 \mathring{\mathbf{q}}$ [7].

## 3  The 3D Planar Profile Registration Algorithm

The global algorithm for three-dimensional profile registration can be described as the successive iteration of the steps described in the text that follows, using prior knowledge of the approximate attitude of each radiant energy plane (as said in section 2.1, this can be light, ultrasound, etc.) as an initial value source for transformation estimates.

At iteration $t$ all $\mathbf{T}_n(t), n = 1..m$ for a total of $m$ profiles are estimated as follows:

1. Firstly, sets of all other energy planes which are known to cross each referential energy plane inside surface bounds are grouped. Planes which are not intersected may be eliminated as lacking information, if wanted.
2. Next, each set of intersecting planes is processed by reference plane, and points belonging both to the reference plane and to each corresponding crossing plane which are closest to the intersection line estimates are determined and matched per intersection line. Correspondences are validated if distances between matched points are lower than a threshold.
3. Equation (4) is solved as described earlier so as to determine $\mathbf{T}_n(t)$. To this end, transformations $^W\mathbf{T}_{C_i}$ corresponding to iteration $t - 1$ are used. The weights $\beta_i$ are computed resorting to two unit and scale independent measures: the so-called *Tanimoto measure or distance* (similarity or proximity measure) between two 3D points $\mathbf{x}$ and $\mathbf{y}$ given by [10,11]

$$S_T(\mathbf{x}, \mathbf{y}) = \frac{\mathbf{x}^T \mathbf{y}}{\|\mathbf{x}\|^2 + \|\mathbf{y}\|^2 - \mathbf{x}^T \mathbf{y}} = \frac{1}{1 + \frac{(\mathbf{x}-\mathbf{y})^T(\mathbf{x}-\mathbf{y})}{\mathbf{x}^T \mathbf{y}}} \qquad (9)$$

which is noticeably inversely proportional to the squared euclidean distance between the points divided by its correlation, and is thus normalised; the normalised orthogonality, measure between two crossing planes (i.e. crossing planes which are "more" orthogonal yield more important correspondences) with normals $\hat{\mathbf{n}}$ and $\hat{\mathbf{m}}$, respectively, given by

$$O(\hat{\mathbf{n}}, \hat{\mathbf{m}}) = 1 - \hat{\mathbf{n}} \cdot \hat{\mathbf{m}} \qquad (10)$$

Hence, $\beta_i = S_T^j \cdot O^k$, was used, where $j$ and $k$ may be chosen empirically, given the characteristics and average performance ratings of the scanner.
4. Finally, the global correspondence error given by the sum of distances between points is computed — if less than a chosen error threshold, the algorithm is considered as having converged and is stopped; otherwise, the algorithm proceeds to the next iteration. Another stopping condition is met if all $\mathbf{T}_n(t)$ approximate the identity matrix.

## 4  Results and Discussion

Figure 2 on the next page shows the handheld 3D laser scanner prototype which was used to scan a mannequin for the experimental application of the 3D planar

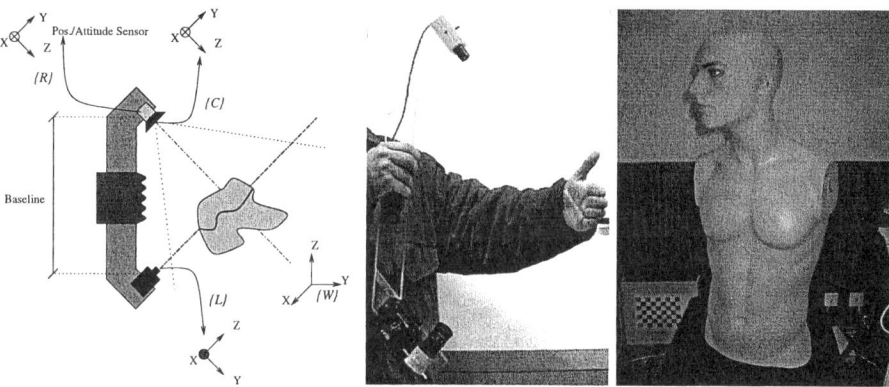

**Fig. 2.** The Tele-3D handheld scanner's schematics and photo on the left and the mannequin test subject on the right. The Tele-3D is a triangulation-based laser scanner with a camera, a laser-plane projector and a pose sensor mounted on a boomerang-shaped acrylic structure.

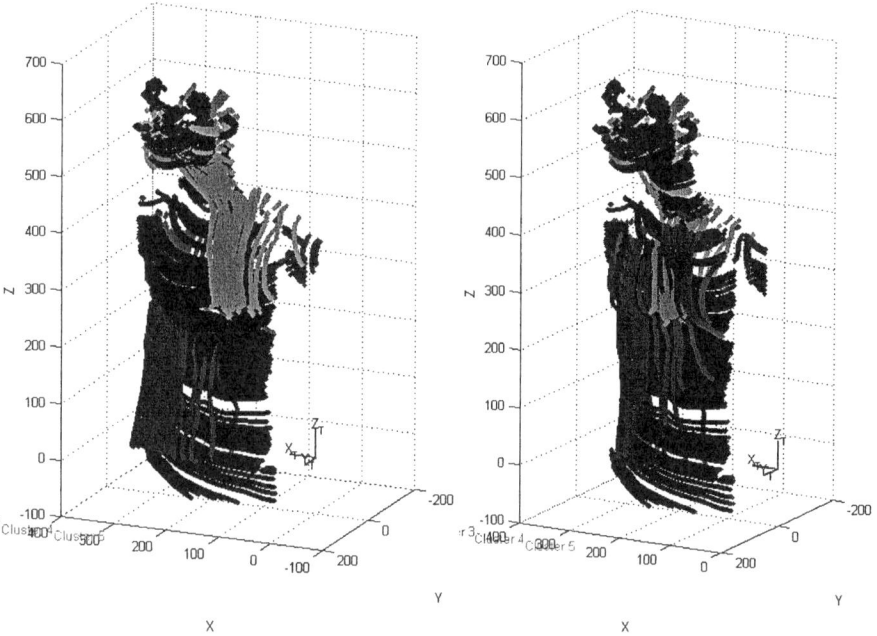

**Fig. 3.** 3D planar profile registration — on the left, pre-integration using the pose sensor readings to obtain initial values for transformations is shown; on the right, the final result using our method is presented. Profiles with clearly different orientations were clustered and represented with different colours so as to improve visualisation of the results.

profile registration algorithm. This system was set up using proprietary calibration algorithms[2], which produced estimates for triangulation errors per profile of 2.6 mm and for pose orientation and position readings of 2.7° and 12.6 mm, respectively [4]. Considering the magnitude of these error estimates, especially the latter, good performance for the registration algorithm was paramount.

On figure 3 on the preceding page, the results yielded before (using the pose sensor readings to obtain initial values for transformations) and after the registration/integration process are shown [4]. The success of the proposed registration algorithm can be clearly seen by the reasonable re-orientation of the profiles yielded with its application.

# References

1. Chen, Y., Medioni, G.: Object Modelling by Registration of Multiple Range Images. Image and Vision Computing **10** (1992) 145–155
2. Rusinkiewicz, S., Levoy, M.: Efficient variants of the ICP algorithm. In: Proceedings of the Third Intl. Conf. on 3D Digital Imaging and Modeling. (2001) 145–152
3. Hébert, P., Rioux, M.: Toward a hand-held laser range scanner: Integrating observation-based motion compensation. In: Proceedings of IS&T/SPIE's 10th Annual Symposium on Electronic Imaging (Photonics West); Conference 3313: Three-Dimensional Image Capture and Applications, San Jose, Ca, USA (1998)
4. Ferreira, J.: Tele-3d: Um scanner para registo tridimensional de objectos. Master's thesis, Department of Electrical Engineering and Computer Science, University of Coimbra, Portugal (2004)
5. Eggert, D.W., Lorusso, A., Fisher, R.B.: Estimating 3-D rigid body transformations: a comparison of four major algorithms. Machine Vision and Applications (1997) 272–290
6. Dorst, L.: First order error propagation of the procrustes method for 3-d attitude estimation. In: IEEE Transactions on Pattern Analysis and Machine Intelligence. Volume 27. (2005) 221–229
7. Walker, M.W., Shao, L., Volz, R.A.: Estimating 3-D Location Parameters Using Dual Number Quaternions. CVGIP: Image Understanding **54** (1991) 358–367
8. Daniilidis, K.: Hand-Eye Calibration Using Dual Quaternions. International Journal of Robotics Research (1998)
9. Rao, S.S.: 12. In: Applied Numerical Methods for Engineers and Scientists. Prentice Hall (2002) 899–902 Sections 12.4.3/12.4.4 — Function of Several Variables with Equality Constraints/Mixed Equality and Inequality Constraints.
10. Tanimoto, T.T.: An elementary mathematical. Technical report, IBM (1959) As cited by [11].
11. Scott, S., Cao, L.: Topic clustering basic (1999) CSCE 970: Pattern Recognition Spring Semester.

---

[2] For more details concerning the Tele-3D scanner and its calibration algorithms, please refer to [4] and http://paloma.isr.uc.pt/www/Tele3DWeb.

# Text-Pose Estimation in 3D Using Edge-Direction Distributions

Marius Bulacu and Lambert Schomaker

AI Institute, Groningen University, The Netherlands
{bulacu, schomaker}@ai.rug.nl

**Abstract.** This paper presents a method for estimating the orientation of planar text surfaces using the edge-direction distribution (EDD) extracted from the image as input to a neural network. We consider canonical rotations and we developed a mathematical model to analyze how the EDD changes with the rotation angle under orthographic projection. In order to improve performance and solve quadrant ambiguities, we adopt an active-vision approach by considering a pair of images (instead of only one) with a slight rotation difference between them. We then use the difference between the two EDDs as input to the network. Starting with camera-captured front-parallel images with text, we apply single-axis synthetic rotations to verify the validity of the EDD transform model and to train and test the network. The presented text-pose estimation method is intended to provide navigation guidance to a mobile robot capable of reading the textual content encountered in its environment.

## 1 Introduction

Our main research effort is concentrated on developing a vision system for an autonomous robot that will be able to find and read text. This paper focuses on the problem of text-pose estimation and we propose a method to compute the orientation of the text surface with respect to the viewing axis of the camera mounted on the robot. Once this information is known, the robot can be maneuvered to obtain a front-parallel view of the text, which, in principle, would give the best final OCR result.

Camera-based text reading in 3D space is a more defiant problem than classical optical character recognition (OCR) used for processing scanned documents. Two major aspects are different and play a very important role: the text areas must be first found in the image because text may be anywhere in the scene (text detection) and, secondly, the orientation of the text surface with respect to the camera viewing axis needs to be inferred (pose estimation) as it will be different from case to case.

We built a connected-component-based text-detector that exploits edge, color and morphological information to find candidate text regions from scene images [1]. Though far from perfect, we assume, in the rest of the paper, that text detection is solved.

After text detection, the orientation of the text surface must be determined. A very effective solution to text-pose estimation is based on finding vanishing points of text lines [2,3]. This type of knowledge-based approach has to impose restrictions on text layout and the search for vanishing points is computationally expensive.

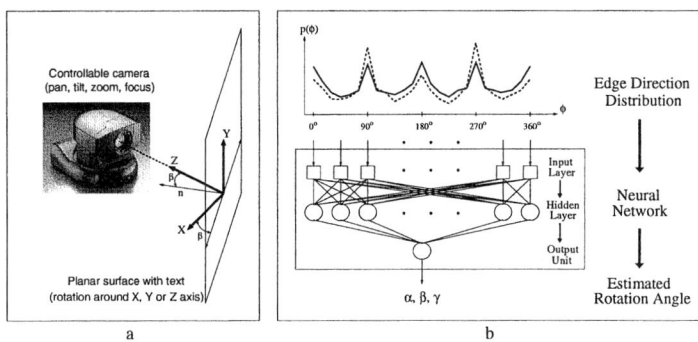

**Fig. 1.** a) Experimental setup. b) Text-pose estimation method. The neural network has one input unit for every EDD bin. The rotation angle is given by the output unit.

In contrast, we assume a different approach that can best be described as a simple shape-from-texture model. Determining the orientation (pose) and curvature (shape) of 3D surfaces from image texture information is a core vision problem. The proposed solutions make assumptions regarding the texture (isotropic [4] or homogeneous [5]) and type of image projection (perspective [6] or orthographic [7]). These general shape-from-texture algorithms rely on differential distortions in the local spatial frequency spectra of neighboring image patches. However, text texture does not have texels, it is homogeneous only in a stochastic sense and also, as we shall see, strongly directional, being a difficult candidate for the classical shape-from-texture algorithms.

We adopt a simplified, but more robust, feature-based method to solve the problem of text-pose estimation. The feature that we shall use is the angular distribution of directions in the text region extracted from the edges. This distribution changes systematically with the rotation angle and we develop a mathematical model to describe this trend. We then show how the rotation angle of the text surface can be recovered back from the *edge-direction distribution* (EDD) using a feed-forward neural network. We assume that text lies on a planar surface and we consider only single axis rotations. In this case, the general shape-from-texture problem reduces to determining the slant angle (the angle between the normal and the viewing axis Z) for rotations around the X and Y axes. We impose these constraints in order to obtain a basic module working on the robot in real-time, rather than a broad and generic solution. Because robot motion is confined to the horizontal plane, only the rotation angle ($\beta$) of text around the vertical axis (Y) can be used for repositioning (see fig. 1a).

## 2 Extraction of the Edge-Direction Distribution

The probability distribution of edge directions in the text area is extracted following a classical edge-detection method. Two orthogonal Sobel kernels $S_x$ and $S_y$ are convolved with the image $I$ (in eq. 1, $\otimes$ represents the convolution operator). The responses $G_x$ and $G_y$ represent the strengths of the local gradients along the x and y directions. We compute the orientation angle $\phi'$ of the gradient vector measured from the horizontal (gradient phase). A correction of 90 degrees is then applied to go from gradient-direction ($\phi'$) to edge-direction ($\phi$), which is a more intuitive measure.

$$G_x = S_x \otimes I, \ G_y = S_y \otimes I, \ \phi' = arctan(\frac{G_y}{G_x}), \ \phi = \phi' + \frac{\pi}{2} \quad (1)$$

As the convolution runs over the image, we build an angle histogram of the edge-directions by counting the pixels where the gradient surpasses a chosen threshold. In the end, the edge-direction histogram is normalized to a probability distribution $p(\phi)$.

## 3 Text Rotation in 3D and Transform Model for the EDD

In this section, we analyze how the EDD changes with the rotation angle. We shall consider canonical rotations of a planar text surface under orthographic projection.

**Rotation Around X Axis**

Consider a needle OA of length $l_0$ initially contained in the front-parallel plane XOY and oriented at angle $\phi_0$ from to the horizontal. We rotate it by angle $\alpha \in (-90°, +90°)$ around X axis to the new position OA' and then we project it back onto the front-parallel plane to OB (see fig. 2a). The projection OB will

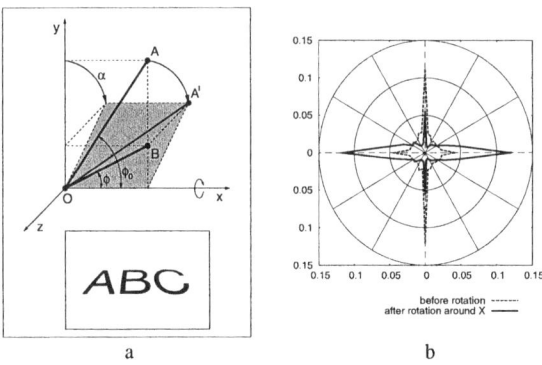

**Fig. 2.** a) Text rotation around X axis, b) EDD change after rotation around X by 50°

be of length $l$ ($l < l_0$) and oriented at angle $\phi$ ($\phi < \phi_0$) from the horizontal. The projection equations are:

$$l_x = l\,cos\phi = l_0\,cos\phi_0, \quad l_y = l\,sin\phi = l_0\,sin\phi_0\,cos\alpha \qquad (2)$$

Forward and backward relations for needle length and orientation are:

$$l = l_0\,\sqrt{1 - sin^2\phi_0\,sin^2\alpha}, \quad l_0 = l\,\frac{\sqrt{1 - cos^2\phi\,sin^2\alpha}}{cos\alpha} \qquad (3)$$

$$\phi = arctan(tan\phi_0\,cos\alpha), \quad \phi_0 = arctan(\frac{tan\phi}{cos\alpha}) \qquad (4)$$

The initial needle OA and its projection OB will appear at rescaled dimensions in the image. If we consider that the needle actually stands for a small edge fragment, we can now describe how the text EDD changes from the initial $p_0(\phi_0)$ to $p_\alpha(\phi)$ after rotation. Two elements need to be taken into account: the length change $l_0 \rightarrow l$ and the angle change $\phi_0 \rightarrow \phi$. We express the new distribution as:

$$h(\phi) = p_0(\phi_0)\,\frac{l}{l_0}\,\frac{d\phi_0}{d\phi} \qquad (5)$$

where $h(\phi)$ are some intermediary values. A renormalization of these values is necessary in order to obtain a proper final probability distribution that adds up to 1.

Therefore, the EDD transform model that we propose is:

$$p_\alpha(\phi) = \frac{h_\alpha(\phi)}{\sum_\phi h_\alpha(\phi)}, \quad h_\alpha(\phi) = \frac{cos^2\alpha}{(1 - cos^2\phi\,sin^2\alpha)^{\frac{3}{2}}}\,p_0(arctan(\frac{tan\phi}{cos\alpha})) \qquad (6)$$

In eq. 6, the intermediary values $h$ undergo renormalization. The expression for $h$ is obtained from eq. 5 after evaluating the lengths ratio and the angle derivative.

Unfortunately, the model cannot be formally developed beyond this point, making the numerical analysis our only option. This is the reason why we formulate eq. 6 using discrete sums. The EDD $p_\alpha(\phi)$ corresponding to rotated text cannot be expressed in closed form as a function of the rotation angle $\alpha$ and the base EDD $p_0(\phi_0)$ corresponding to front-parallel text.

Qualitatively, after rotation around X axis, text appears compressed vertically. This foreshortening effect is reflected in the EDD (fig. 2b): the horizontal component of the distribution increases at the expense of the vertical one. The changes in EDD are more pronounced at larger angles and this makes possible recovering the rotation angle $\alpha$.

### Rotation Around Y Axis

We apply a similar analysis considering a rotation of angle $\beta \in (-90°, +90°)$ around Y axis (see fig. 3a). The projection equations are:

$$l_x = l\,cos\phi = l_0\,cos\phi_0\,cos\beta, \quad l_y = l\,sin\phi = l_0\,sin\phi_0 \qquad (7)$$

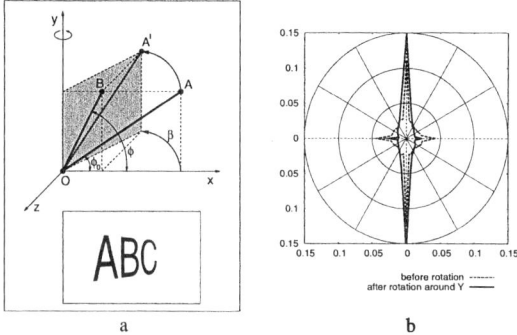

**Fig. 3.** a) Text rotation around Y axis, b) EDD change after rotation around Y by 50°

Forward and backward relations for needle length and orientation are:

$$l = l_0 \sqrt{1 - cos^2\phi_0 \, sin^2\beta}, \quad l_0 = l \frac{\sqrt{1 - sin^2\phi \, sin^2\beta}}{cos\beta} \tag{8}$$

$$\phi = arctan(\frac{tan\phi_0}{cos\beta}), \quad \phi_0 = arctan(tan\phi \, cos\beta) \tag{9}$$

Applying eq. 5, the EDD transform model becomes:

$$p_\beta(\phi) = \frac{h_\beta(\phi)}{\sum_\phi h_\beta(\phi)}, \quad h_\beta(\phi) = \frac{cos^2\beta}{(1 - sin^2\phi \, sin^2\beta)^{\frac{3}{2}}} p_0(arctan(tan\phi \, cos\beta)) \tag{10}$$

where $h$ are intermediary values that undergo renormalization.

Here again, $p_\beta(\phi)$ (corresponding to rotated text) cannot be expressed in closed form as a function of the rotation angle $\beta$ and the base EDD $p_0(\phi_0)$ (corresponding to front-parallel text).

Qualitatively, after rotation around Y axis, text appears compressed horizontally. This foreshortening effect is reflected in the EDD (fig. 3b): the vertical component of the distribution increases at the expense of the horizontal one. The rotation angle $\beta$ can be recovered because the changes in EDD are more pronounced at larger angles.

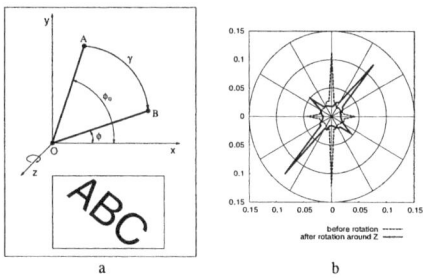

**Fig. 4.** a) Text rotation around Z axis, b) EDD change after rotation around Z by 40°

**Rotation Around Z Axis**

In this case, text rotation by angle $\gamma \in (0°, 360°)$ simply results in a rotation of the EDD (considered in polar form) by the same angle (see fig. 4):

$$\phi = \phi_0 + \gamma, \quad l = l_0, \quad p_\gamma(\phi) = p_0(\phi - \gamma) \tag{11}$$

## 4 Text-Pose Estimation Method

First we attempted to recover the rotation angle using multilinear regression and obtained correlation coefficients larger than 0.85 between the cosine squared of the rotation angle and the probability values in the EDD. But an obvious and more appropriate choice is to use a neural network to extract the nonlinear inverse relationship between the EDD and the rotation angle. The ground-truth data needed to train and test the network is obtained using synthetic rotations starting from front-parallel views.

However, in trying to recover the rotation angle directly from the EDD, two problems appear: font-dependence of the base EDD and quadrant ambiguity.

An important underlying assumptions is that the base EDD corresponding to the front-parallel view is almost the same for all machine-print text. Otherwise, a change in the EDD due to font will be wrongly interpreted as a rotation. This assumption is not true: the EDD is actually different for different fonts. We very successfully exploited this fact in solving the problem of identifying people based on their handwriting [8].

The second problem is quadrant ambiguity for rotations around X and Y: under orthographic projection, text looks the same under rotation of $+\alpha$ and $-\alpha$ ($+\beta$ and $-\beta$). The EDD cannot distinguish between the two situations and this can also be confirmed by observing that the functions depending on the rotation angle appearing in equations 6 and 10 are even. For eliminating this problem, the idea is to consider in the analysis two images rather a single one, the second image being rotated at a fixed small angle $\delta$ from to the first. In one quadrant, the second image will be closer to the front-parallel view than the first. In the other quadrant, the situation will be reversed. This will be clearly reflected in the difference between the EDDs extracted from the two images and the neural network will learn it from the training data. Using the difference between two EDDs diminishes also the font-dependence problem. The robot, therefore, will need - for rotations around Y axis - to make a small exploratory movement, always to the same side (e.g. to the right) in order to alleviate the ambiguity.

For rotations around Z axis the quadrant ambiguity cannot be eliminated. While usually the vertical component of text is stronger than the horizontal one in machine-print, this difference is not reliable enough to obtain accurate predictions based on it. The EDD is almost symmetric to rotations of 90° around Z axis and consequently our solution can only encompass one quadrant. In this case, two images are not needed, the EDD from a single image suffices to determine the rotation angle.

## 5 Results

We used a Sony Evi D-31 PAL controllable camera to collect 165 images containing text in front-parallel view (gray-scale, 8 bits/pixel, 748x556 resolution). We strived to obtain sufficient variability in the dataset: 10 different fonts, appearing at different sizes in the images, from a single word to a whole paragraph per image. Single-axis synthetic rotations are applied to these images using our own custom-built rotation engine. The number of bins in the EDD was set to $N = 36$. This was found to give a sufficiently fine description of text texture ($10°$/bin).

First we verify the validity of our EDD transform model and then we train a neural network to predict the rotation angle and evaluate its performance.

**Verification of the Theoretical Model**

From every image in the dataset, we extract the base EDD corresponding to the front-parallel view. We then randomly select a rotation angle and we theoretically compute (using equations 6, 10, 11) what the EDD should be for the rotated image (forward transform). We then apply the rotation on the image and we directly extract the EDD corresponding to the new pose. We compare the theoretically predicted EDD with the empirically extracted EDD to check the validity of our formal model. An appropriate similarity measure between the two EDDs is Bhattacharyya distance: the distance varies between 0 and 1 and we express it in percentages to have an intuitive measure. If the distance is null, the two distributions are identical.

We applied 400 random rotations on every image around each axis. The average distance is around 1% (see table 1) and in fig. 5a we show its dependence on the rotation angle. For rotations around X and Y axes, the error increases with the rotation angle. At larger angles, text is so compressed that letters

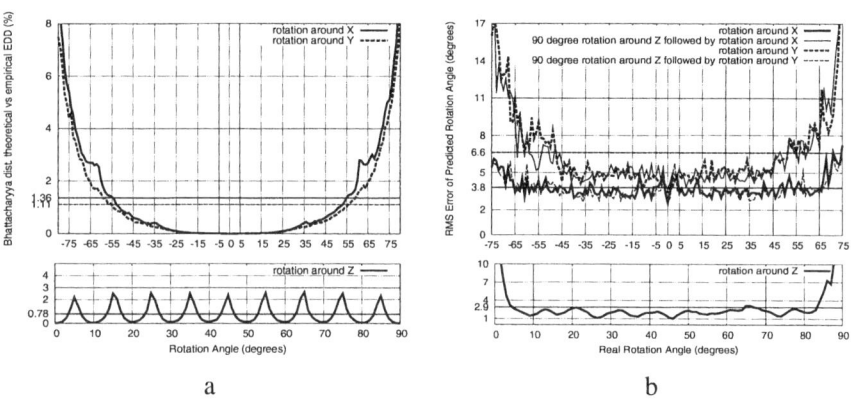

**Fig. 5.** a) Verification of theoretical model: Bhattacharyya distance between theoretical and measured EDDs (in percentages). b) Prediction results: angular error (in degrees). Horizontal lines represent average values (from table 1).

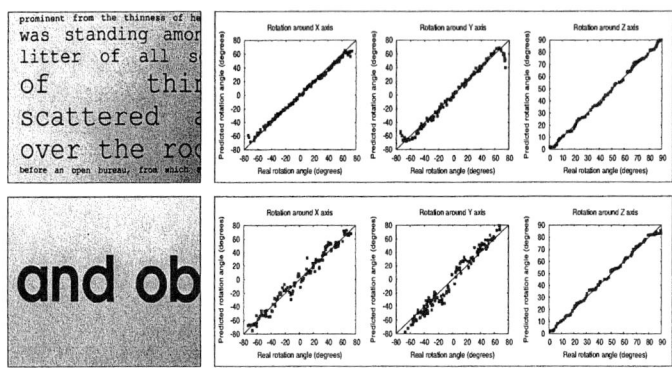

**Fig. 6.** Typical performance: "good" example up, "bad" example down. Angular predictions are given for rotations around X, Y, Z from left to right panel. Ideally all the experimental points would be placed exactly on the diagonal for perfect predictions.

fuse together in a single lump and our mathematical model no longer correctly describes the changes in the EDD. For rotations around Z, the error is small and does not have a systematic trend, but we can observe a sampling artifact: the error shows an oscillatory behavior as the probability flows from one bin to another of the EDD.

### Evaluation of the Angle Prediction Method

For predicting the rotation angle from the EDD (inverse transform), we use a standard feed-forward neural network (3 layers, fully connected, nonlinear transfer functions in the hidden layer). The network architecture is 36x10x1 (see fig. 1b).

From the start, we split the data into 100 images for training and 65 for testing. Every image is then rotated 400 times at random angles (40000 training examples, 26000 testing examples). For rotations around X and Y, two rotated images are in fact generated with a slight pose difference between them $\delta = 10°$. The network is trained to predict the rotation angle (e.g. of the second image) using the difference between the two EDDs. For rotations around Z, a single EDD is used with rotations limited to one quadrant. Fig. 6 shows how the method performs on two typical examples.

On the test data, we compute the root mean square (RMS) error between the predicted and the real rotation angle. The average angular prediction error is given in table 1. The method demonstrates good performance (3° - 7° angular error). In fig. 5b we show the dependence of the angular error on the rotation angle. As expected, it can be observed again that the error increases at larger angles for rotations around X and Y axes. Another interesting observation is that the prediction error for rotations around Y axis is larger than that for rotations around X axis. So we performed the following simple test: we first rotated all the images by 90° around Z and subsequently we applied all the regular analysis. The angular error for rotations around X axis snaps into the

**Table 1.** Correlation between theoretical model and empirical data (column 2). Overall angle prediction error (column 3).

| Rotation around | Theoretical Model Error (percentages) | Angle Prediction Error (degrees) |
|---|---|---|
| X axis (pitch) | 1.36% | 3.8° |
| Y axis (yaw) | 1.11% | 6.6° |
| Z axis (roll) | 0.78% | 2.9° |

range of errors for rotations around Y axis and the reverse (see fig.5b), proving to be an inherent property of the data. The explanation is that the vertical component of text is more reliable than the horizontal one and, as it is most affected by rotations around X axis, the prediction is more accurate in this case. Unfortunately, rotations around Y axis represent the case of most interest for our robotic application.

For rotations around Z axis, we can observe that for angles $\gamma$ close to 0° and 90° the error increases as confusion appears (especially for uppercase characters) between the vertical and the horizontal components, which are the most prominent in the EDD. This is the reason why we opted for a single quadrant solution for this type of rotation.

The method becomes unreliable for small characters (less than 20 pixels in height or width) as the EDD cannot be consistently extracted. We found that the method works well if more than 10 characters are present in the image (see fig. 6). In a qualitative evaluation, we found that the proposed method works also on-line in combination with our controllable camera. The neural network, trained and tested off-line on synthetic rotations, estimates reasonably well text-pose during on-line operation under real rotations. The errors are, nevertheless, relatively larger. We found that Greek fonts can be handled too by the same neural network. It is important to note at this point that the proposed algorithm is lightweight, on average 70 msec being necessary on a 3.0 GHz processor to extract the EDDs from 2 images and run the neural network on their difference to predict the rotation angle. Therefore, using the robot's ability to make small exploratory movements seems like an attractive idea for solving the pose-estimation problem. We treated here only canonical rotations. The method can be directly extended to two-axis rotations. We have not addressed free three-axis rotations. The proposed texture-based method for text-pose estimation does not impose constraints on text layout. It works even when text lines are not present or they are very short.

## 6 Conclusions

We presented a method for estimating the orientation of planar text surfaces using the edge-direction distribution (EDD) in combination with a neural network. We considered single-axis rotations and we developed a mathematical model to analyze how the EDD changes with the rotation angle under orthographic projection. We numerically verified the validity of our underlying mathematical model. In order to solve the quadrant ambiguity and improve performance, for rotations around X and Y axes, we consider a pair of images with a slight rotation difference between them. The change in the EDD is extracted and sent to a feed-forward neural network that predicts the text rotation angle. The method has been tested off-line with single-axis synthetic rotations and shows good performance. Though limited in scope, the text-pose estimation method proposed here is elegant, quite simple and very fast. Further work will be directed at integrating this pose estimation method within a complete robotic reading system.

# References

1. Ezaki, N., Bulacu, M., Schomaker, L.: Text detection from natural scene images: Towards a system for visually impaired persons. In: Proc. of 17th Int. Conf. on Pattern Recognition (ICPR 2004), Cambridge, UK, IEEE CS (2004) 683–686
2. Clark, P., Mirmehdi, M.: On the recovery of oriented documents from single images. In: Proc. of ACIVS 2002, Ghent, Belgium (2002) 190–197
3. Myers, G.K., Bolles, R.C., Luong, Q.T., Herson, J.A.: Recognition of text in 3-d scenes. In: Proc. of 4th Symposium on Document Image Understanding Technology, Columbia, Maryland , USA (2001)
4. Garding, J.: Shape from texture and contour by weak isotropy. J. of Artificial Intelligence **64** (1993) 243–297
5. Malik, J., Rosenholtz, R.: Computing local surface orientation and shape from texture for curved surfaces. Int. J. Computer Vision **23** (1997) 149–168
6. Clerc, M., Mallat, S.: Shape from texture and shading with wavelets. Dynamical Systems, Control, Coding, Computer Vision, Progress in Systems and Control Theory **25** (1999) 393–417
7. Super, B.J., Bovik, A.C.: Shape from texture using local spectral moments. IEEE Trans on PAMI **17** (1995) 333–343
8. Schomaker, L., Bulacu, M.: Automatic writer identification using connected-component contours and edge-based features of uppercase western script. IEEE Trans on PAMI **26** (2004) 787–798

# A Neural Network-Based Algorithm for $3D$ Multispectral Scanning Applied to Multimedia

Alamin Mansouri[1], Alexandra Lathuiliere[2], Franck S. Marzani[1],
Yvon Voisin[2], and Pierre Gouton[1]

[1] Le2i, UMR CNRS 5158, Université de Bourgogne, Aile des sciences de l'ingénieur,
BP 47870 21078 Dijon CEDEX, France
{alamin.mansouri, franck.marzani, pgouton}@u-bourgogne.fr
[2] Le2i, UMR CNRS 5158, Université de Bourgogne, IUT du Creusot, 12 rue de la fonderie, 71200 Le Creusot, France
{a.lathuiliere, y.voisin}@iutlecreusot.u-bourgogne.fr

**Abstract.** We describe a new stereoscopic system based on a multispectral camera and an $LCD$-Projector. The novel concept we want to show consists in the use of multispectral information for $3D$-scenes reconstruction. Each $3D$ point is linked to a curve representing the spectral reflectance. This latter is a physical representation of the matter and presents the advantage over color information, which is perceptual, that it is independent from both illuminant and observer. We first present an easy methodology to geometrically and spectrally calibrate such a system. We then describe an algorithm for recovering $3D$ coordinates based on triangulation and an algorithm for reflectance curves reconstruction based on neural networks. The results are encouraging, they confirm the feasibility of such a system and in the same time enable some *multimedia* applications like simulating illumination change.

## 1 Introduction

In the field of $3D$ object reconstruction and metrology, vision-based systems are becoming increasingly prevalent, including, for example, industrial applications. In particular, within the framework of applications whose scene has a significant volume, they seem preferable to techniques based on interferometry or the watered effect, techniques which mainly measure nanometer order depths.

Vision systems can be divided into two categories: passive or active vision. The passive systems use several sensors, cameras for example, to acquire the scene. The method used to give position and depth information is based on the matching of the points between images in order to reconstruct by triangulation their position in $3D$. The problem with such methods is in the detection and matching of the characteristic points. The last is non trivial for two reasons: firstly, the camera's point of view can make a same scene zone appear differently in various images; secondly, some visible parts in one image can be blacked in another. Moreover, very small textured objects become very difficult to analyze because of the lack of characteristic points appearing on their surface. Active systems replace one of the cameras of a passive system with a device which projects a structured light onto the scene. This light creates a kind of texture on the scene surface that a camera can then acquire. If it is supposed that this system is geometrically calibrated, the position and the depth of the scene points, as illuminated by the projected pattern, can be calculated. Many types of structured light have already been studied. The interested reader can refer to the Battle article [1] in which one can find state of the art techniques.

Within this framework, the use of systems made up of a camera and an $LCD$ projector has emerged [2]. Currently, projector-camera systems use a grey level or RGB camera [3]. The main interest of color is to be able to differentiate geometrically similar patterns by color coding. Color coding also allows an easier matching of the points. Moreover, color data available in the acquired image gives the color of the object surface's reconstructed points present in a scene. However, this knowledge can be strongly skewed because of the limited number of color channels (three) within classical $RGB$ camera. The concept that we wish to describe in this article is based on the use of a multispectral camera built with interference filters. In this case, a reflectance spectrum can be associated with each $3D$ reconstructed point. A multispectral image is an image made up of several monochannel images of the same scene. In each image we have data about a specific wavelength according to the used interference filter. Such an imaging technique is becoming more and more interesting because of its great application potential. It is especially useful for the resolution of applied problems requiring an analysis of the spectral field, for example remote sensing, medical imagery, cosmetic products, high quality colors reproduction, etc. [4]. The system that we developed is described in Section 2. Before using it to analyze a scene, calibration is necessary, as described in Section 3. The term calibration is used for both the geometrical calibration of the stereoscopic system and the spectral characterization of the camera. Geometrical calibration consists of determining the intrinsic and extrinsic parameters of the camera and the $LCD$ projector. The spectral calibration consists on the determination of the spectral sensitivity of each channel of the system. This characterization is based on a spectral model of acquisition. Treatment of acquired images permits scene reconstruction at the geometrical and at the spectral level. This is described in Section 4. It is followed by a discussion and presentation of results in Section 5. Lastly, the Conclusion completes this article.

## 2 System Description

Firstly, we developed a low cost [5] multispectral imaging system. It is designed to be portable and flexible, and is composed of a simple monochromatic $CCD$-based camera, a standard photographic lens, seven interference filters, a $PC$ calculator, and $C$ software developed especially for this system. A motorized wheel is placed in front of the camera/lens system. The wheel has eight holes accepting seven filters and one hole empty, in order to make an acquisition without filter. Such a multispectral camera can reproduce the color with more precision

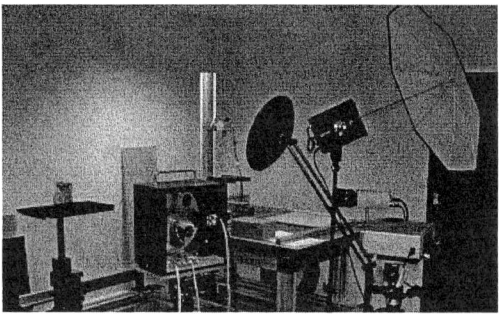

**Fig. 1.** The proposed $3D$ multispectral scanner

than a traditional RGB camera since it is less affected by metamerism [6]. The complete $3D$ multispectral scanner system that we propose is composed of the camera detailed above and an $LCD$ projector. We chose an angle ranging between 35° and 40° between the camera sight axis and that the $LCD$ projector one, which is the best compromise [7]. In addition to the luminosity, the $LCD$ projector depth-of-field and optical characteristics are important in the choice of an $LCD$ projector. A study that we carried out showed that an $LCD$ projector could be described by a pinhole type model [8]. In sum, the results presented in this article are based on a scene located at approximately $2m$ from the multispectral camera and $LCD$ projector, with an area of $50cm$ per $50cm$, and a depth of approximately $20cm$ ('Fig. 1').

## 3 Calibration

Before any acquisition, spectral and geometrical calibration is necessary. Once done, several acquisitions and reconstructions can be carried out without having to recompute these calibration parameters. In geometrical calibration, the only constraint is not to modify the geometrical configuration of the stereoscopic pair. As for the spectral characterization, it is necessary to preserve the camera acquisition parameters and not to modify the scene illuminant.

According to a spectral model of the acquisition chain, the signal $d_k$ observed from the camera output, relative to channel $k$ ($k$=1...7), is given by Equation (1):

$$d_k = \int_{\lambda_{min}}^{\lambda_{max}} I(\lambda) r(\lambda) c(\lambda) t_k(\lambda) o(\lambda) d\lambda + \eta_k \quad (1)$$

where $I(\lambda)$ is the spectral radiance of the illuminant, $r(\lambda)$ is the spectral reflectance of the surface, $c(\lambda)$ is the camera spectral sensitivity, $t_k(\lambda)$ is spectral transmittance according to the filter number $k$, $o(\lambda)$ is the transfer function of optics, and $\eta_k$ expresses the spectral noise of the $k^{th}$ filter.

In order to faithfully attain the spectral reflectance, a set of radiometric calibrations must be done. The interested reader can refer to the following article [9]. Preprocessing and noise reduction finished, we can spectrally characterize the system. The goal is to determine its spectral sensitivity for each channel according to the spectral model of Equation (1). This spectral model is based on a linear $opto-electronic$ transfer function assumption. This assumption generally holds when noise is reduced and makes Equation (1) as a simple multiplication of spectra contained wavelength by wavelength in vectors. By sampling out of $N$ regular intervals the spectrum range in which we work, we can rewrite Equation (1) in matrix notation. Thus, Equation (1) becomes:

$$d_k = \mathbf{r}(\lambda)^T \mathbf{S}_k(\lambda) \qquad (2)$$

where $\mathbf{S}_k(\lambda) = [S_k(\lambda_1)S_k(\lambda_2)...S_k(\lambda_N)]^T$ and $\mathbf{r}(\lambda) = [r(\lambda_1)r(\lambda_2)...r(\lambda_N)]^T$ are respectively the vectors containing the spectral sensitivity of the acquisition system relating to the channel $k$, and spectral reflectances. $^T$ is the transpose operator. We search to characterize the spectral response of the system by finding the operator $\mathbf{S} = [S_1(\lambda)S_2(\lambda)...S_7(\lambda)]^T$. To do this, we scanned the Macbeth chart using a $MinoltaCS-1000$ spectrophotometer and we acquired a multispectral image of this chart. The results is a set of corresponding pairs $(\mathbf{d}_p, \mathbf{r}_p)$, for $p=1,...,24$, where $\mathbf{d}_p$ is a vector of dimension $k=7$ containing the camera output and $\mathbf{r}_p$ is a vector of dimension $N$ representing the spectral reflectances of the $p^{th}$ patch. By observing the camera output responses, we can estimate the system response to known theoretical reflectances in the input. This stage is called learning because we use a neural network to invert the Equation (2). Specifically, we use a linear neural network associative memories [10]. The use of linear operator is justified by the fact that we supposed a linear $opto-electronic$ transfer function and since the noise have been reduced in the pre-processing stage.

We chose a global solution which consists of calibrating the stereoscopic system set. This weak calibration method does not require any object of known size and can thus be carried out very easily. Both the camera and the projector are modeled by a pinhole model [8]. Let $\mathbf{M} = (X\ Y\ Z\ 1)^T$ be the $3D$ point homogeneous coordinates in the reference frame of the scene, let $\mathbf{m} = (u\ v\ 1)^T$ be those of its projection in an image and expressed in pixels, then we can write:

$$\mathbf{m} = f(\mathbf{k}, \mathbf{d}, \mathbf{E}, \mathbf{h}, \mathbf{M}) \qquad (3)$$

where $\mathbf{k}$ is a vector of length 4 containing the intrinsic parameters: $(u0, v0)^T$ optical center coordinates and $du$, $dv$, pixel size in the two directions. $\mathbf{E}$ size $[3\star 3]$ and $h$ size $[3\star 1]$ are respectively $3D$ rotation, and $3D$ translation between the world and camera reference frames. $\mathbf{d}$ is the polynomial coefficients vector of the radial distortions which are most significant. Thus, the system calibration is similar to that of a standard stereoscopic system composed of two cameras. The only difference is based in the fact that the $3D$ characteristic points are not physically on an object but emitted by the $LCD$ projector. Thus, we created an image pattern. It is made up of $n$ luminous points on a dark background.

This pattern is projected by the $LCD$ projector on a support with an unspecified position, and then it is acquired by the multispectral camera without filter. With the same pattern, this operation is repeated for $q$ positions of this support. 'Equation (3)' can be written for the camera and for the $LCD$ projector. $\mathbf{m}_p$ is the point of the pattern projected on the support in $\mathbf{M}$ and $\mathbf{m}_c$ its projection in the image. We have 26 unknown factors for the whole 25, camera and $LCD$ projector. The establishment of the calibration parameters needs the minimization of the sum of the following equations:

$$\|\mathbf{m}_p - f(\mathbf{k}_p, \mathbf{d}_p, \mathbf{E}_p, \mathbf{h}_p, \mathbf{M})\|^2 + \|\mathbf{m}_c - f(\mathbf{k}_c, \mathbf{d}_c, \mathbf{E}_c, \mathbf{h}_c, \mathbf{M})\|^2 \qquad (4)$$

for each $n * p$ points. This overdetermined problem is nonlinear and we solved it by $Levenberg - Marquardt$ optimization method.

## 4 Reconstruction

The two calibration stages finished, it is now possible to acquire as many scenes as we wish as long as the acquisition configuration remains unchanged. It suffices to put the object to be reconstructed in the calibrated work volume. Then, a multispectral image of the scene is acquired without light projection by the $LCD$ projector. This image will thereafter allow, during the spectral reconstructing detailed in paragraph 4.2., correlating a reflectance spectrum to each $3D$ point reconstructed of the scene. Then, a set of monochannel images is acquired without filter. For each one, the $LCD$ projector emits a sufficiently intense luminous vertical line so that it appears on the surface of the scene and thus on the images. The line is shifted pixel by pixel between the images.

### 4.1 Geometrical Reconstruction

The camera and the $LCD$ projector being placed at the same height and approximately at the same distance front the scene, the projection of a vertical line allows a precise $3D$ reconstruction. Because the distortion parameters of the $LCD$ are weak, we supposed them negligible. That is why $2D$ line in the $LCD$ projector image plan describes, in space, a $3D$ plan. We can calculate the equation of this plan of sight with a $2D$ line, the optical center of the $LCD$ projector and its geometrical calibration parameters in world reference frame. Let us note that the origin of this reference frame is located at the farthest plan of the work volume, in the top, right of the scene. We analyze each horizontal line for each image. The coordinates of the pixel with the maximum value are extracted. After distortion correction, a $3D$ line is expressed in the world reference frame. This line of sight goes through the pixel detected and the optical center of the camera. We can finally calculate the intersection of the luminous plan and the line of sight. A $3D$ point expressed in the world reference is so processed from each horizontal profile of each image. Geometrical reconstruction allows us to obtain the $3D$ position of the different parts of the luminous pattern on the scene by using triangulation afterwards the spectral reconstruction associates a spectral reflectance to each of them.

## 4.2 Spectral Reconstruction

The spectral characteristics **S** of the multispectral system are henceforth known. The estimate of a reflectance spectrum $\tilde{\mathbf{r}}$ in each pixel of an acquired scene with this system is thus possible. The vector $\mathbf{d} = [d_1 d_2 ... d_7]^T$ containing the responses for the 7 filters is given by Equation (2). The second step is the reconstruction. Since all weighted synapses are gathered in the matrix **S**, the reconstruction is fast and easy: the estimated spectral reflectance in each pixel of a scene is equal to a product between the operator **S** and the camera response contained in **d**.

During the training, the memory may learn only few samples among possible stimuli. The memory stops learning when it ceases to mistake any more. So, it may place the discriminating function too much close to the boundaries of the samples with which it was trained. If we test it on new samples, the memory may badly generalize its training. To overcome this problem, we use associative memories with a rule of training which consists on continuously modifying the strengths of the weight matrix. In doing so, the memory becomes more efficient for generalization. Furthermore, this algorithm is low time consuming in the reconstruction stage since it is forward matrices multiplication.

## 5 Results and Discussion

In order to evaluate the $3D$ reconstruction error, we compared the results of our scanning method with those coming from the $Minolta\ VIVID$ 910 'Fig. 2.c' professional scanner. In order to visualize the $3D$ reconstructed cloud of points 'Fig. 2.a', and in general to handle the $3D$ data, we used $3D$ visualization software. Our geometrical reconstruction gives a weak number of points. The triangulation algorithms contained in the software are not appropriate for this case 'Fig. 2.b'. That is why the aspect of reconstructed surface is granular on this figure. The software used enables us to compare a dot cloud with a scanned surface. We found that 99% of the values are between $-0.8$ and $0.8mm$. On this figure, it is seen very clearly that the strong errors are on the edges of the object and on the level of the strong curves. The scanning method that we used involves such errors because we have only one camera and thus a weak in-depth precision when scanning away from the camera axis. On other hand, the use of the multispectral camera enables us to go up with the spectral reflectance of scene surfaces. This information can be attached to each $3D$ reconstructed point. It is a valuable information because it represents a physical property which depends neither on the illuminant nor on the subjectivity of human vision. In order to validate the reconstruction of the spectral reflectance by the suggested method, we made a comparison, for a set of pixels, between the measured spectrum using the spectrophotometer and the one reconstructed from the otput of the multispectral camera. We calculated the frequently used Goodness-of-Fit Coefficient $(GFC)$ as criterion given by the formula:

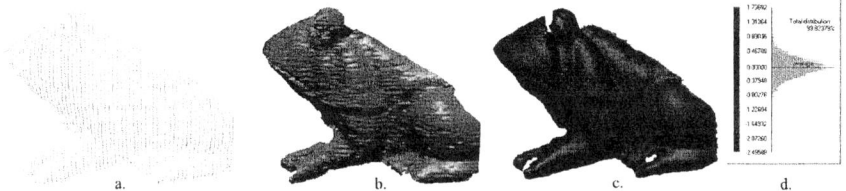

**Fig. 2.** *a.* Dots cloud obtained by $3D$ reconstruction, *b.* Triangulated surface, *c.* Surface obtained with the scanner, and *d.* the distance card between *b.* and *c.*

$$GFC = \frac{\left|\sum_{j} R_m(\lambda_j) R_r(\lambda_j)\right|}{\left(\left|\sum_{j} [R_m(\lambda_j)]^2\right|\right)^{1/2} \left(\sum_{j} [R_r(\lambda_j)]^2\right)^{1/2}} \quad (5)$$

where $R_m(\lambda_j)$ is the value of the measured spectrum with the spectrophotometer at the wavelength $\lambda_j$, and $R_r(\lambda_j)$ represents that related to the reconstructed spectrum at the wavelength $\lambda_j$. Within the meaning of this criterion, the results are very satisfactory. The reconstructed spectrum shows few errors compared to that obtained by the spectrophotometer. We note an average error of the $GFC$ equal to 1.8% for a standard deviation of 0.7%. Once we have the reconstructed $3D$ scene, each $3D$ point thus sees associated spectral reflectance. So, we have a $3D$ *spectral scene*. In order to visualize it, we choose an illuminant and associate a chromatic $RGB$ triplet to each point. Note that we are able to simulate and visualize the scene such as it will be with any illuminant. In order to emphasize this point, the 'Fig. 3' presents two $3D$ *spectral scene* visualized with two different illuminants and finally projected in $RGB$ space. This can be interesting for some multimedia applications, e.g for three-dimensional artwork objects for virtual museum. Thus, we show the method feasibility that aims at the development of a $3D$ multispectral scanner for multimedia applications.

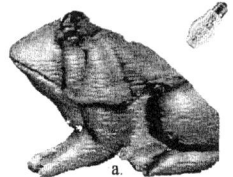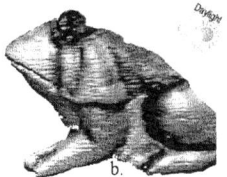

**Fig. 3.** Projection of the $3D$ *spectral scene* in $RGB$ color space after simulation of illuminant change, *a.* scene appearance under the $CIE$ $A$ illuminant, and *b.* scene appearance under the $CIE$ $D65$ illuminant (daylight)

## 6 Conclusion

We have just presented an active stereovision system based on an $LCD$ projector and a camera. The characteristic of the latter is that it is a multispectral one. The main contribution of the multispectral concept comes back to the possibility of reconstructing and associating a reflectance spectrum for each $3D$ point. It produces much more relevant information of the scene points than during the use of color camera. The results presented proved the feasibility of such a system that we named "$3D$ *multispectral scanner*". Measured errors at the geometrical and spectral level, remain relatively weak. Our current work consists of simultaneously generating and emitting several luminous patterns. The goal is to decrease the number of acquisitions while preserving a dense scene reconstruction.

## References

1. J. Battle, J. Mouaddib, and J. Salvi, Recent Progress in Coded Structured Light as a Technique to Solve the Correspondence Problem: a Survey, *Pattern recognition*, **31**(7), 963-982, 1998.
2. S. Rusinkiewicz, O. all-Holt, M. Levoy, Real-Time $3D$ Model Acquisition, *ACM Trans. On Graphics*, Siggraph 2002.
3. T. Jaeggli, T.P. Koninckx, L. Van Gool, Online $3D$ Acquisition and Model Integration, In *IEEE international workshop on projector-camera systems (in conjunction with ICCV 2003)*, France, October 2003.
4. J.Y. Hardeberg, *Acquisition and reproduction of colour images: colorimetric and multispectral approaches*, dissertation.com, Parkland, Florida, USA, 2001.
5. A. Mansouri, F.S. Marzani, J.Y. Hardeberg, P. Gouton, Optical calibration of a multispectral imaging system based on interference filters, *Optical Engineering*, **44**(2), February 2005.
6. S. Tominaga, Spectral imaging by multichannel camera, *Journal of Electronic Imaging*, **8**(4), October 1999.
7. S. Woo, A. Dipanda, F. Marzani, Y. Voisin, Determination of an optimal configuration for a direct correspondance in an active stereovision system, In Proc. of $2^{nd}$ *IASTED INT. Conf. VIIP*, Espagne, 596-601, 2002.
8. A. Lathuiliere, F.S. Marzani, Y. Voisin, Modélisation d'un projecteur vidéo suivant le modèle du sténopé dans le cadre d'un système de stéréovision active, In Proc. of *4ème colloque francophone, Contrôles et Mesures Optique pour l'Industrie*, France, 17-21 novembre, 27-32, 2003.
9. A. Mansouri, F.S. Marzani, P. Gouton, Development of a protocol for CCD calibration: application to a multispectral imaging system, *International Journal of Robotics and Automation*, Acta Press, **20** (2), pp. 94-100, 2005.
10. A. Mansouri, M. Sanchez, F.S. Marzani, P. Gouton, Spectral Reflectance Estimation From Multispectral Images using Neural Networks, In Proc. of *Physics in Signal and Image Processing (PSIP)*, Toulouse, France, January 2005.

# A Novel Stereo Matching Method for Wide Disparity Range Detection

Dongil Han[1] and Dae-Hwan Hwang[2]

[1] Vision and Image Processing Lab.
Sejong University, Seoul, Korea
dihan@sejong.ac.kr
[2] Embedded H/W Component Research Team,
Electronics and Telecommunications Research Institute,
Daejeon, Korea
hdh@etri.re.kr

**Abstract.** This paper describes a real-time stereo depth measurement image processing system. This system uses Xilinx Virtex-II Series XC2V3000 FPGA and generates 8-bit sub-pixel disparities on 640 by 480 resolution images at video rate (60 frames/sec) with maximum disparity ranges of up to 128 pixels. The implemented stereo matching algorithm finds a minimum of window-based sum of absolute difference (SAD) operation. And the preprocessing, scale transformation and final stage compensation technique are adopted for maximizing the wide disparity range detection. The proposed vision system is suitable for real-time range estimation and robot navigation applications.

## 1 Introduction

Robots have been mostly used in industrial environment, but modern developments of household robot-cleaner suggest the necessity of household robots as becoming in reality. Most industrial robots have been used for factory automation that perform simple and iterative tasks at high speed, whereas household robots need various interfaces with a man while moving in indoor environment like a household robot-cleaner does.

Robots activate in indoor environment using various sensors such as vision, laser, ultrasonic sensor, or voice sensor to detect indoor circumstance. Especially robot's routing plan and collision avoidance need three-dimensional information of robot's surrounding environment. This can be obtained by using a stereo vision camera which provides a general and huge amount of 3-D information. But this computation is too big to solve in real-time with the existing microprocessor when using a stereo vision camera for capturing 3-D image information.

High-level computer vision tasks, such as robot navigation and collision avoidance, require 3-D depth information about the surrounding environment at video rate. Current general-purpose microprocessors are too slow to perform stereo vision at video rate. For example, it takes several seconds to execute a medium-sized stereo vision algorithm for a single pair of images on a 1 GHz general-purpose microprocessor.

To overcome this limitation, designers in the last decade have built re-programmable chips called FPGAs(Field-Programmable Gate Arrays) hardware systems to accelerate the performance of the vision systems. These devices consist of programmable logic gates and routing that can be re-configured to implement essentially any hardware function. Hardware implementations allow one to exploit the parallelism that usually exists in image processing and vision algorithms, and to build systems to perform specific calculations very quickly compared to software.

A number of methods for finding depth information in video-rate have been reported. Especially, multi-baseline stereo theory is developed and the video-rate stereo machine has the capability of generating a dense depth map of 256x240 pixels at the frame rate of 30 frames/sec in [1]. The developed stereo machine is applied to two applications: virtualized reality and z keying.

Jeong and Oh [2] present a VLSI architecture and implementation for a highly parallel trellis-based stereo matching algorithm which obtains disparity and depth information from a pair of images and has a complexity of $O(N^2)$ for N pixel scan lines and $O(N)$ operations can be performed in parallel. But, the overall system can only achieve 4 frames/s for 320 by 240 pixel images with live image capture due to PCI bus usage by other PC components, and due to inefficient PCI implementation by the PC hardware and operating system.

A multi-resolution, multi-orientation phase based technique called Local Weighted Phase-Correlation is introduced in [3]. And recently, researchers at Tyzx [4] introduce the DeepSea stereo vision system which makes the use of high speed 3-D images practical in many application domains. That system is based on the DeepSea processor which implements the Census stereo algorithm and computes absolute depth based on simultaneously captured left and right images with high frame rates, low latency, and low power.

But, the stereo matching systems mentioned above have narrow detectable disparity range and also have difficulties in household mobile robot applications. In this paper, we adopted the image scaling transformation and SAD(Sum of Absolute Difference) based stereo matching, barrel shifting and final compensation processing for wide disparity measurement range. And this paper also describes the implementation of a stereo matching algorithm in hardware on FPGAs which has maximum disparity measurement ranges by comparing the existing hardware systems [1~4].

## 2 Stereo Matching Algorithm

Many researchers have been devoted to solving the stereo matching problems [1~7] and some good results have been obtained. However, most methods have a computational complexity or structure that is not suitable for real time operation. For this reason, in spite of the rapid progress of VLSI technology, only a few real-time stereo vision systems have been built so far. Some of the significant systems are summarized in Table 1.

**Table 1.** Comparison of stereo systems

| System(year) | Frames/sec | Image size | Max. disparity |
|---|---|---|---|
| CMU(1996)[1] | 30 | 200x200 | 60 |
| Postech(2001)[2] | 30 | 340x340 | NA |
| Toronto(2003)[3] | 30 | 720x480 | 20 |
| TYZX(2004)[4] | 200 | 512x512 | 52 |

Our goal is to construct an inexpensive and truly portable stereo vision system which can be used in household mobile robot. A mobile robot in indoor environment can interact with humans and other household products. In that case, the stereo vision system in mobile robot must detect objects in near position.

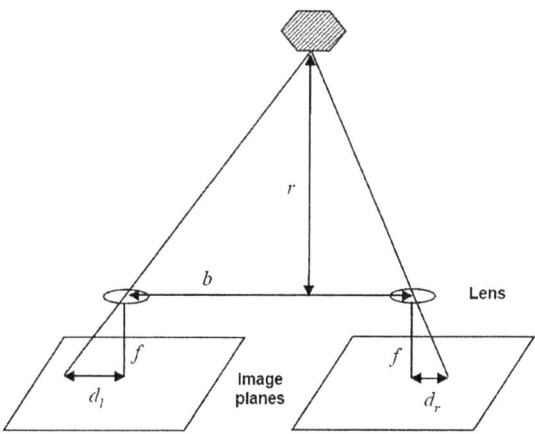

**Fig. 1.** A stereo vision geometry

As shown in figure 1, let's consider a typical stereo matching system. Suppose that a typical 1/3" monochrome CMOS camera with focal length f = 7.4 mm and effective image area: 4.86 mm x 3.64 mm with image resolution of 640 x 480. The equation for the distance to the object is:

$$r = f \frac{b}{d} \qquad (1)$$

where $d$ = observed disparity and can be calculated by $d_l - d_r$, $f$ = focal length of camera, and $b$ = camera displacement.

In above situation, a stereo vision system with 32 pixels of maximum disparity search range cannot detect depth information of objects which are located in closer than 1,827 mm. A household mobile robot must detect an object at the distance of around 500 mm. In that case, 128 pixels of maximum disparity search range are required. Thus, although, some of the previous systems have good matching performance, the wide disparity range requirements make them unsuitable for household mobile robot applications.

Figure 2 shows the block diagram of proposed real-time stereo matching system. In preprocessing block, various image processing functions are used in order to make stereo matching easy. Each processing block is designed to be bypassed fundamentally. The preprocessing block removes image noise and adjusts image levels when brightness levels or contrasts of input images from the two cameras are unequal.

The scale transform block changes image resolution dependent on the given maximum disparity range. When taking a measurement of the disparity range using a real robot applied with stereo matching system using vision, the same point of objects exists with big disparities between left image and right image as the robot and objects get closer. In this case the hardware complexity increases very sharply for calculating the wide range correlation between two images. For example, even though the simple window based SAD operation is used, the existing FPGAs have difficulties in including the required logics for implementing the stereo matching with maximum disparity range of 128 pixels.

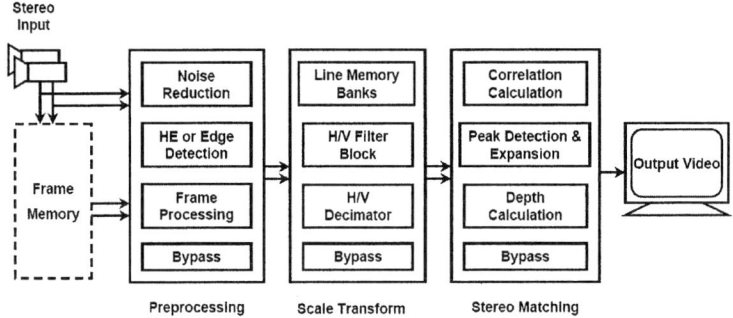

**Fig. 2.** The overall system block diagram

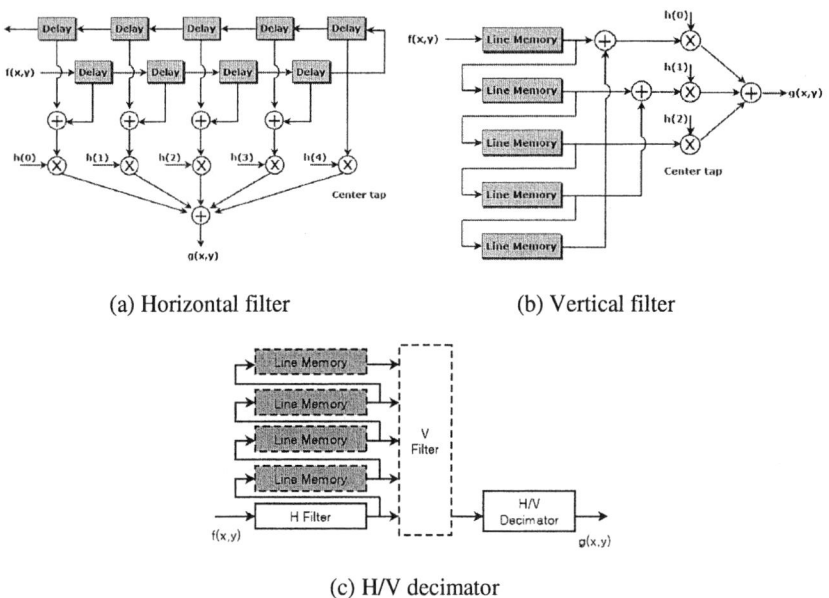

**Fig. 3.** Scale transform

Therefore, before measuring the pixel disparity of two images, the resolution of original image should be reduced first. This approach would expand the maximum value of disparity range easily, and this eventually solves the problem that mentioned earlier. Before decrease image resolution, low pass filtering is essential to prevent aliasing. Figure 3 shows the scale transform block diagram. When decreasing image resolution, both horizontal and vertical direction could be decreased, but it is possible to perform stereo matching efficiently if even only resolution of horizontal direction is decreased.

Figure 4 shows a detailed diagram of stereo matching block. This block estimates depth information between camera and objects using data of similarity between left and right image. Similarity measure of left and right images can be solved in various ways and here we used SAD(Sum of Absolute Difference) to detect minimum disparity value.

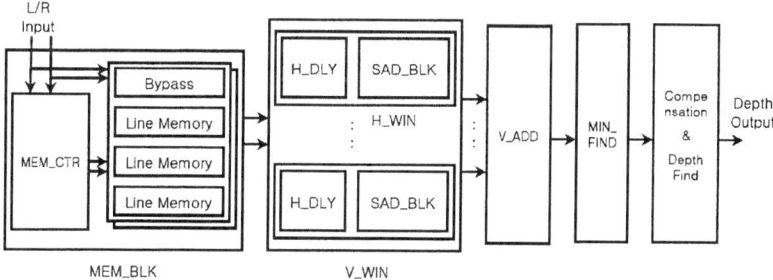

**Fig. 4.** Stereo matching system block diagram

To compute SAD in real time, each left and right image use several line memories as shown in figure 4. We can compute SAD by using 3 line memories for each left and right image when vertical window size is 4. Line memory control block stores input images to line memory and reads stored images from line memories at the same time when a new input scan line image goes to the SAD block. The SAD operation in a window size $W$ is given by following equation.

$$f_{SAD}(x,y,d) = \sum_{i \in W} \sum_{j \in W} |I_l(x+i+d, y+j) - I_r(x+i, y+j)| \qquad (2)$$

where $I_l$ and $I_r$ are intensity values in the left and right images respectively.

The horizontal delay block (H_DLY), which performs pixel delay for window operation, gives that result to SAD computation block. Such operation is processed in parallel by number of horizontal lines of window. After that, the vertical direction add block (V_ADD) adds all of SAD values which are computed in horizontal direction. And then, we can extract SAD values between all windows for each disparity value. This block also provides SAD values of right image disparity upon left image by delaying vertical direction SAD value.

A pixel where the SAD value has its minimum is called a matched pixel. To find a matched pixel, the minimum detecting block computes a minimum value of SAD for each disparity when left image and right image are centered. The disparity computed from SAD block of figure 4 can be obtained with reduced resolution according to the decreasing in horizontal image resolution in scale transform block. Therefore revising in compensation block will be performed finally. That is, this block computes the maximum disparity value which has good precision after barrel shifting the output image pixels using the disparity values and computing SAD of neighbor sections for the last, and we can get disparity value with higher precision than pixel value.

## 3 Experimental Results

The proposed hardware architecture is firstly simulated in C. The simulation includes the pre-processing, scale transform, stereo matching and compensation. Figure 5 shows an example of image scaling. The vertical or horizontal filtering is an essential part of image size reduction and as shown in figure 5 (b) and figure 5 (c), if the proper filtering is not included, the aliased image disables the correct stereo matching. The proposed hardware architecture is implemented in VHDL and the VHDL simulation shows the same result compared to the C simulation. Figure 6 shows the output examples of stereo matching and figure 7 shows a snap shot of VHDL simulation window.

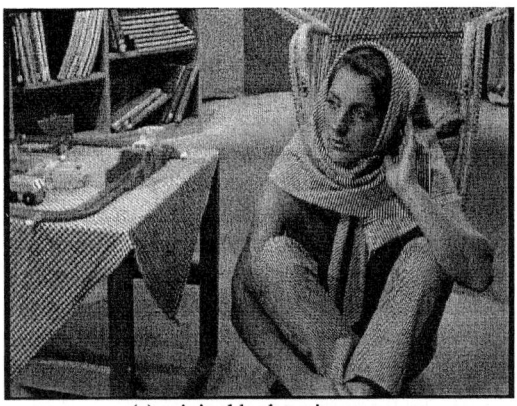

(a) original barbara image

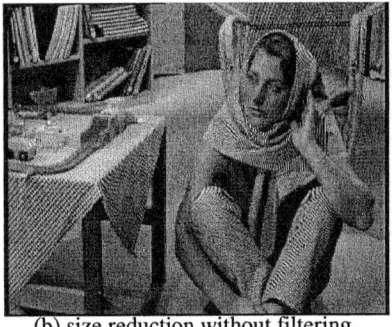 

(b) size reduction without filtering  (c) size reduction with filtering

**Fig. 5.** Size reduction example

Finally, the proposed hardware architecture is implemented in FPGA. Figure 8 shows the developed stereo vision system. We used 640x480 resolution and frame rates of 60 fps, 1/3" CMOS stereo camera, and the full logic is tested with Xilinx Virtex-II Series XC2V3000. The operation frequency of the proposed system is faster than 50 MHz and generates depth information on VGA resolution images in real-time. The total memory and logic gates for implementing the proposed stereo matching block with wide disparity range are described in table 2.

**Table 2.** Memory and logic gates for implementing the stereo matching block

| Mem_Ctr | Line Mem. | V_WIN | V_ADD | Min_Find |
|---|---|---|---|---|
| 9,708 | 223,049 | 663,240 | 129,774 | 34,484 |

**Fig. 6.** Output disparity map examples

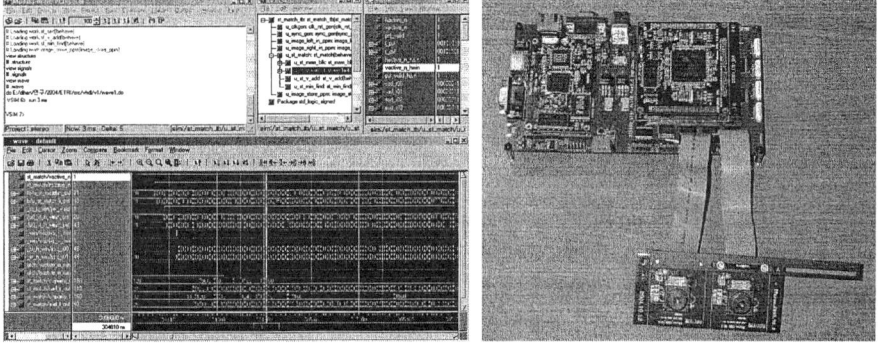

**Fig. 7.** A snapshot of VHDL window   **Fig. 8.** The developed stereo matching system

## 4 Conclusion

We have described a real-time stereo matching system which detects depth information data using stereo camera. The proposed vision system uses Xilinx XC2V3000 FPGA and generates 8-bit sub-pixel disparities on 640 by 480 resolution images at video rate with maximum disparity ranges up to 128 pixels.

The proposed real-time stereo matching system is designed to detect higher disparity ranges and can be installed to household mobile robots. And with simple modifications, the detectable disparity range can be increased with ease.

As a future work, we will include test result with in a real household mobile robot environment. The camera rectification is also an important problem and future work will include this function in FPGA.

## Acknowledgments

This work is supported by ETRI and Intelligent Robotics Development Program, one of the 21st Century Frontier R&D Programs funded by the Korea Ministry of Commerce, Industry and Energy. The hardware verification tools are support by the NEXTEYE Co., Ltd and the IC Design Education Center.

## References

1. Takeo Kanade, Atsushi Yoshida, Kazuo Oda, Hiroshi Kano and Masaya Tanaka: A Stereo Machine for Video-rate Dense Depth Mapping and Its New Applications. in Proceedings of IEEE Computer Society Conference on Computer Vision and Pattern Recognition, pp. 196 – 220, 18-20 June 1996.
2. Hong Jeong and Yuns Oh: A Parallel Real Time Implementation of Stereo Matching. in Proceedings of 15th International Symposium on Parallel and Distributed Processing, pp. 23-27, April 2001.
3. Ahmad Darabiha, Jonathan Rose and W. James MacLean: Video-Rate Stereo Depth Measurement on Programmable Hardware. in Proceedings of IEEE Computer Society Conference on Computer Vision and Pattern Recognition, 2003. vol. 1, pp. I203-I210, June 2003.
4. John I. Woodfill, Gaile Gordon and Ron Buck: Tyzx DeepSea High Speed Stereo Vision System. in Proceedings of IEEE Computer Society Workshop on Real Time 3-D Sensors and Their Use, Conference on Computer Vision and Pattern Recognition, June 2004.
5. A. Koschan and V. Rodehorst: Towards Real-Time Stereo Employing Parallel Algorithms For Edge-Based And Dense Stereo Matching. in Proceedings of Computer Architecture for Maching Perception, pp. 233-241, Sept. 1995.
6. Olga Veksler: Stereo Correspondence with Compact Windows via Minimum Ratio Cycle. in IEEE Trans. Pattern Anal. Machine Intell., vol. 24, no. 12, pp. 1654-1660, 2002.
7. R. Sastry, N. Ranganathan and R. C. Jain: VLSI Architecture for High-Speed Range Estimation. in IEEE Trans. Pattern Anal. Machine Intell., vol. 17, no. 9, pp. 894-899, 1995

# Three-Dimensional Structure Detection from Anisotropic Alpha-Shapes

Sébastien Bougleux[1], Mahmoud Melkemi[2], and Abderrahim Elmoataz[3]

[1] GREYC CNRS UMR 6072, ENSICAEN,
6 Bd du Maréchal Juin, 14050 Caen Cedex, France
sebastien.bougleux@greyc.ensicaen.fr
[2] LMIA, équipe MAGE, 4 rue des Frères Lumière,
68093 Mulhouse Cedex, France
mahmoud.melkemi@uha.fr
[3] LUSAC, Site Universitaire, BP 78,
50130 Cherbourg-Octeville, France
abder.elmoataz@greyc.ensicaen.fr

**Abstract.** We present an application of a family of affine diagrams to the detection of three-dimensional sampled structures embedded in a perturbated background. This family of diagrams is an extension of the Voronoi diagram, namely the anisotropic diagrams. These diagrams are defined by using a parameterized distance whose unit ball is an ellipsoidal one. The parameters, upon which depends this distance, control the elongation and the orientation of the associated ellipsoidal ball. Based on these diagrams, we define the three-dimensional anisotropic $\alpha$-shape concept. This concept is an extension of the Euclidean one, it allows us to detect structures, as straight lines and planes, in a given direction. The detection of a more general polyhedral structure is obtained by merging several anisotropic $\alpha$-shapes, computed for different orientations.

## 1 Introduction

The Voronoi diagram and its dual Delaunay triangulation are one of the most significant concepts in computational geometry, they allow to design efficient algorithms to solve proximity problems in many application areas, such as pattern recognition, image processing, computer graphics, clustering or scientific visualization. Historically, they were defined for a set of points and the Euclidean distance. Without being exhaustive, they were extended to other geometric elements such as segments, circles and polygons. Also, they were generalized by using other distances like $L_1$, $L_\infty$ [1] and power distance [2]. A more general family of diagrams, called affine diagrams [3], is defined for a set of points and a distance such that the equidistant set of points from two points is an hyper-plane. A detailed study of some affine diagrams and other extensions of the Voronoi diagram are presented with their applications in [4].

In the context of computational morphology, which aim is to extract a shape from the input data by means of computational geometrical structures [5], we study the problem of detecting linear structures as straight lines, planes and polyhedral patterns, from a set of points. The existing methods, based on neighborhood graph analysis and related to the Voronoi diagram, are especially conceived for set of points having certain density conditions [4]. When patterns are curves or surfaces, these conditions can be established explicitly. This solves the problem of structure detection in several situations. However, they are unsuited when patterns are represented by low density set of points, embedded into a perturbated background. This is explained by the fact that these methods are conceptually based on density analysis and do not integrate the morphological aspect of a pattern to detect. To deal with these cases, we propose a method which combines an anisotropic analysis and the morphological aspect of the patterns to extract from the data. The analysis based on the anisotropy is employed to detect linear structures from a two-dimensional set of points [6]. It is also used to reconstruct parts of surfaces by local interpolation [7]. Recently, anisotropic meshes has been built using curved anisotropic Voronoi diagrams [8].

The method we develop concerns the extraction of polyhedral structures from a three-dimensional set of points, even if these structures are embedded in a perturbated background. The detection of the suitable patterns is formalized by a particular family of affine diagrams, namely the anisotropic diagrams. Intuitively, these diagrams are generated using ellipsoidal balls. The morphological aspect of the pattern to detect is represented by a parameter $Q$, measuring the orientation and the elongation of the ellipsoidal balls. For a fixed parameter $Q$ and a fixed value $\alpha$, we compute from the anisotropic diagram, a three-dimensional anisotropic $\alpha$-shape of the set of points, which is an extension of the Euclidean one [9]. The anisotropic $\alpha$-shape detects, in the chosen direction, the existing linear structures with some non-significant ones. These non-significant structures, due to the interaction of the background points, are removed by a filtering algorithm. More generally, polyhedral structures can be extracted following these steps : first, we compute a spectrum of anisotropic $\alpha$-shapes ; second, we remove non-significant structures from each shape of the computed spectrum ; third, we merge the shapes of the filtered spectrum to get the adequate polyhedral structure.

In this article, we first introduce several geometrical concepts related to the $\alpha$-shapes. Then we present the anisotropic concepts and its application to the detection of sampled polyhedral structures.

## 2 Related Geometrical Concepts

### 2.1 The Voronoi Diagram and the Delaunay Triangulation

Let $P = \{p_1, \ldots, p_n\}$ be a finite three-dimensional set of points. Let $d_2(p,q)$ be the Euclidean distance between two points $p$ and $q$. The Voronoi cell $V(p_i, P)$ of $p_i \in P$ is the set of points $p \in \mathbb{R}^3$ such that $d(p, p_i) \leq d(p, p_j)$, for all $p_j \in P$. The Voronoi diagram of $P$, denoted by $V(P)$, is the set of the Voronoi cells $V(p_i, P)$, for $i = 1, \ldots, n$. From a morphological point of view, $V(P)$ is generated using a unit ball as a structuring element.

Two points are neighbors in $V(P)$ if the intersection of their cells is not empty. The graph obtained by connecting the points of $P$ to their neighbors is the dual of $V(P)$, called the Delaunay triangulation of $P$ and noted $D(P)$. Recall that a $k$-simplex, noted $s(T)$, is a polytope which vertices $T$ are $k+1$ affinely independent points. In 3-dimensions, a 0-simplex is a vertex, a 1-simplex is an edge, a 2-simplex is a triangle and a 3-simplex is a tetrahedron. Then $D(P)$ is a set of $k$-simplicies, $0 \leq k \leq 3$, circumscribed to the boundary of an open ball which is empty of points of $P$. Each $k$-simplex $s(T)$ of $D(P)$ is the dual of the intersection of the $k+1$ cells $V(p_i, P)$, $p_i \in T$.

## 2.2 Euclidean $\alpha$-Shapes

Let $b(\alpha)$, $0 < \alpha < +\infty$, be an open ball of radius $\alpha$, $b(\alpha)$ is a point if $\alpha = 0$ and an half-space if $\alpha = +\infty$. The $\alpha$-shape of $P$, denoted by $F_\alpha(P)$, is the set of $k$-simplicies $s(T)$, $k = 1, 2$ and $T \subset P$, such that there exists an open ball $b(\alpha)$ with $b(\alpha) \cap P = \emptyset$ and $T \subset \partial b(\alpha) \cap P$, where $\partial b(\alpha)$ is the boundary of $b(\alpha)$. The $\alpha$-shape of $P$ is a sub-graph of the Delaunay triangulation of $P$ [9]. For $k = 1$ or 2, a $k$-simplex $s$ of $D(P)$ is an element of $F_\alpha(P)$ if and only if $\alpha_{min}(s) < \alpha < \alpha_{max}(s)$, where $\alpha_{min}(s)$ and $\alpha_{max}(s)$ are two positive real numbers that can be computed from $V(P)$. Indeed, $\alpha_{min}(s)$ corresponds to the minimum distance from a vertex of $s$ to the Voronoi dual element of $s$. And $\alpha_{max}(s)$ corresponds to the maximum distance.

By varying the value $\alpha$ from $+\infty$ to 0, the $\alpha$-shape of $P$ catch different levels of detail. When $\alpha = +\infty$, the $\alpha$-shape is the convex hull of $P$. As $\alpha$ decreases, cavities and holes are reflected. And when $\alpha = 0$, then the $\alpha$-shape is the set $P$.

## 3 Anisotropic Concepts

### 3.1 Global Anisotropy

Let $R = (u_1, u_2, u_3)$ be a rotation matrix and $E$ be a scaling matrix with $1/e_i$ on its diagonal, where $e_i \geq 1$ for $i = 1, 2, 3$. In the next, the notation $A^t$ represents the transpose matrix of the matrix $A$. Then the anisotropy is formalized by a $3 \times 3$ metric tensor, denoted by $M = RER^t$, commonly used in anisotropic mesh generation [8] and scene analysis [10]. By definition, $M$ is a positive definite matrix that can be written as $M = Q^t Q$, where :

$$Q = \begin{pmatrix} 1/\sqrt{e_1} & 1 & 1 \\ 1 & 1/\sqrt{e_2} & 1 \\ 1 & 1 & 1/\sqrt{e_3} \end{pmatrix} R^t.$$

In the next, the matrix $Q$ identifies the anisotropy. Using the anisotropy, the distance between two points of $\mathbb{R}^3$ is defined by :

$$d_Q(p, q) = \sqrt{(p-q)^t M(p-q)} = \sqrt{(Q(p-q))^t Q(p-q)}. \tag{1}$$

It can be viewed as performing a non-uniform scaling along the axes of a rotated orthogonal system on $p$ and $q$ before taking the Euclidean distance. Let $\tau$ be the transformation such that $\tau(p) = Qp$, for all $p \in \mathbb{R}^3$. Then from equality (1) we have:

$$d_Q(p,q) = d_2(\tau(p), \tau(q)). \tag{2}$$

Balls associated to the distance $d_Q$ are ellipsoidal balls. Their direction axes are given by $R$ and their elongation ratio along these axes by $E$. Let $b_Q(p,r)$ be an open ellipsoidal ball, centered at $p$, bounded by the ellipsoid $\partial b_Q(p,r)$ of radius $r > 0$. Then the semi-axes of $b_Q(p,r)$ are $r.\sqrt{e_i}$, for $i = 1, 2, 3$.

### 3.2 The Anisotropic Diagrams and Triangulations Based on the Distance $d_Q$

For a fixed anisotropy $Q$, let $V_Q(p_i, P)$ be the anisotropic cell of $p_i \in P$. It is the set of points $p \in \mathbb{R}^3$ such that $d_Q(p, p_i) \leq d_Q(p, p_j)$, for all $p_j \in P$. Based on the distance $d_Q$, the equidistant set of points between two points is a plane. It follows that the union of the anisotropic cells defines an affine diagram [3]. We call it the anisotropic diagram of $P$ and we note it $V_Q(P)$. From a morphological point of view, $V_Q(P)$ is generated by ellipsoidal balls that have both the same orientation and the same elongation ratio.

The dual of $V_Q(P)$, obtained by connecting the points of $P$ to their neighbors, is the anisotropic triangulation of $P$, which we note $D_Q(P)$. It defines a set of $k$-simplicies $s(T)$, $0 \leq k \leq 3$, such that $s(T)$ is the dual of the intersection of the $(k+1)$ anisotropic cells $V_Q(p_i, P)$, for all $p_i \in T$.

The anisotropic diagram and triangulation are extensions of the Voronoi diagram and the Delaunay triangulation. When $E$ represents the identity matrix of $\mathbb{R}^3$, the ellipsoidal balls become balls, thus $V_Q(P)$ becomes $V(P)$ and $D_Q(P)$ becomes $D(P)$.

### 3.3 The Anisotropic $\alpha$-Shapes Based on the Distance $d_Q$

Let $b_Q(\alpha)$, $0 < \alpha < +\infty$, be an open ellipsoidal ball of radius $\alpha$, $b_Q(\alpha)$ is a point if $\alpha = 0$ and an half-space if $\alpha = +\infty$. Let $F_{k,\alpha,Q}(P)$ be the set of $k$-simplicies $s(T)$, $T \subset P$, such that $b(\alpha) \cap P = \emptyset$ and $T \subset \partial b_Q(\alpha) \cap P$, where $\partial b_Q(\alpha)$ is the boundary of $b_Q(\alpha)$. We define the anisotropic $\alpha$-shape of $P$ as the union of the sets $F_{1,\alpha,Q}(P)$ and $F_{2,\alpha,Q}(P)$, and we note it $F_{\alpha,Q}(P)$. For a given $\alpha$ and through different values of $Q$, the family of anisotropic $\alpha$-shapes extends the Euclidean ones. When $E$ is equal to the identity matrix of $\mathbb{R}^3$, $b_Q(\alpha)$ becomes $b(\alpha)$, and then $F_{\alpha,Q}(P)$ becomes $F_\alpha(P)$. Moreover, the anisotropic $\alpha$-shapes are sub-graphs of the anisotropic triangulations. So they are linked to the anisotropic diagram.

Recall that $\tau$ is the transformation represented by the matrix $Q$. Let $\tau^{-1}$ be the inverse of $\tau$ and let $\tau(P)$ be the set of points $\tau(p_i)$, for all $p_i \in P$. Let $s(T)$ be a $k$-simplex of vertices $T = \{p_0, \ldots, p_k\}$. Then $s(\tau(T))$ represents the simplex of vertices $\tau(T) = \{\tau(p_0), \ldots, \tau(p_k)\}$. The anisotropic concepts are related to the Euclidean ones by the transformation $\tau$ : (1) $v$ is a point of $V(\tau(p_i), \tau(P))$ if and only if $\tau^{-1}(v)$ is a point of $V_Q(p_i, P)$. (2) For $\alpha \in \mathbb{R}^+$, $s(T)$ is a simplex of

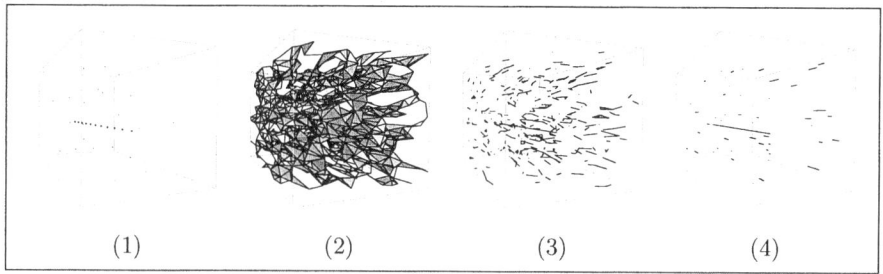

**Fig. 1.** Anisotropic $\alpha$-shapes of (1) a sampled line (11 points) embedded in a random perturbated background (1000 points). $R = Id_{\mathbb{R}^3}$ and $e_1 = e_2 = 1$. (2) $F_{25,Q}$ with $\sqrt{e_3} = 4$. (3) $F_{15,Q}$ with $\sqrt{e_3} = 6$. (4) $F_{8,Q}$ with $\sqrt{e_3} = 8$.

$F_{\alpha,Q}(P)$ if and only if $s(\tau(T))$ is a simplex of $F_\alpha(\tau(P))$. These relations prove that the anisotropic $\alpha$-shapes can be computed from the Euclidean ones. For a given anisotropy $Q$ and a value of $\alpha$, the algorithm works in two steps to compute $F_{\alpha,Q}(P)$. First, $V(\tau(P))$ and its dual $D(\tau(P))$ are computed. And second, for each simplex $s(\tau(T))$ of $D(\tau(P))$, if $s(\tau(T))$ is a simplex of $F_\alpha(\tau(P))$, then $s(T)$ is retained as a simplex of $F_{\alpha,Q}(P)$.

## 4 Detection of Structures

### 4.1 Detection of Structures in a Given Direction

The anisotropic $\alpha$-shapes detect structures, like straight lines and planes. Recall that $Q$ is computed from a scaling matrix $E$ and a rotation matrix $R$. The parameters $\alpha$, $E$ and $R$ control the shape and the orientation of the ellipsoidal ball. For a fixed orientation $R$, when $\alpha$ decreases from a fixed large value and particular values of $E$ increase from 1, the shape of the ellipsoidal ball varies from the ball to finer elongated balls. Similarly, the behavior of the anisotropic $\alpha$-shape is as follows : it detects global structures as the convex hull of the set of points. Then finer and localized structures appear gradually in the direction given by $R$. This behavior is illustrated in the Fig. 1 and the Fig. 2. The example of the Fig. 1 shows four $\alpha$-shapes of a set of points. This set corresponds to the samples of a straight line embedded in a perturbated background (Fig. 1(1)). The Euclidean $\alpha$-shapes cannot detect the straight line. This is due to the interaction of the sampled points with their background neighbors. When the balls are replaced by ellipsoidal ones, the anisotropic $\alpha$-shape reflects linear structures. Those of the Fig. 1(2,3) are non-significants. An adequate choice of the parameters $\alpha$ and $E$ is illustrated in the Fig. 1(4), where the suitable linear structure is detected, with some non-significant ones. The same behavior is observed with planar structures (Fig. 2).

Let $\{p_i, p_{i+1}, \ldots, p_j\} \subseteq P$ be a set of ordered points on a straight linear structure $L$ having orientation $R$. Suppose that the Euclidean distance between two successive sampled points is constant. Also suppose that no background

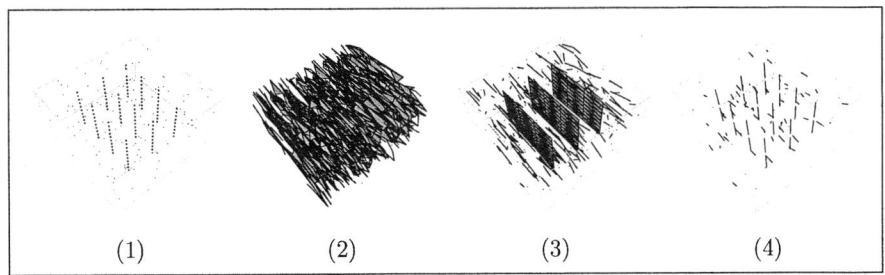

**Fig. 2.** Anisotropic $\alpha$-shapes (1) sampled planes (120 points) embedded in a random perturbated background (1500 points). $R = Id_{\mathbb{R}^3}$ (2) $F_{10,Q}$ with $\sqrt{e_2} = 2$, $\sqrt{e_3} = 4$, $e_1 = 1$. (3) $F_{5,Q}$ with $\sqrt{e_2} = 4$ and $\sqrt{e_3} = 12$. (4) $F_{1.5,Q}$ with $\sqrt{e_2} = 7$ and $\sqrt{e_3} = 16$.

points lie on $L : d_2(p, L) \neq 0$ for all $p \in P - \{p_i, \ldots, p_j\}$. Then, there exists a pair $(\alpha, E)$ such that the line segment $[p_{i+l}, p_{i+l+1}]$ is a 1-simplex of $F_{1,\alpha,Q}(P)$, for all $l = 0, \ldots, j - i - 1$. In the same way, let $P_L \subseteq P$ be a set of points regularly sampled on a planar structure $L$ having orientation $R$. Suppose that for all $p \in P - P_L$, $d_2(p, L) \neq 0$. Then there exists a pair $(\alpha, E)$ such that $L$ is detected by $F_{2,\alpha,Q}(P)$. In other terms, when a linear or planar structure is regularly sampled, there exists an anisotropic $\alpha$-shape such that the linear structure is detected. This behavior is illustrated in the Fig. 1(4) and the Fig. 2(3).

### 4.2 Removing Non-significant Structures

For an adequate choice of the pair of parameters $(\alpha, Q)$, the anisotropic $\alpha$-shape also detects several structures that do not fit with the suitable structures (Fig. 1(4) and Fig. 2(3)). These structures, characterized by a low number of connected points, are called non-significants. To delete them, the sets $F_{k,\alpha,Q}(P)$ are filtered by analyzing their connected components. Formally, a $k$-simplex is $h$-connected if it is incident to $h$ $(k+1)$-simplicies. For a fixed value $k$ (1 or 2), a set of $k$-simplicies $\{s_i, s_{i+1}, \ldots, s_j\}$ is a path of length $l$ in $F_{k,\alpha,Q}(P)$ if and only if the four following properties are verified :

(1) $s_z$ is a $k$-simplex of $F_{k,\alpha,Q}(P)$ such that $s_z \cap s_{z+1} \neq \emptyset$, for all $z = i, \ldots, j-1$
(2) for all $(k-1)$-simplex $s \subset s_z$, $s$ is 1-connected or 2-connected
(3) there exists no $k$-simplex $s$ in $F_{k,\alpha,Q}(P)$ such that $\{s_i, \ldots, s_j\} \cup s$ verifies the properties (1) and (2)
(4) the number of elements of the path is $l$.

The property (1) guarantees that the path represents a connex structure. The property (2) ensures that the path has no ramifications. And the properties (3) and (4) ensure that the length $l$ of the path is maximal. A path is non-significant in $F_{k,\alpha,Q}(P)$ if and only if the length of the path is less than a fixed threshold $t$. To delete the non-significant paths, the algorithm is the following : for $l = 1, \ldots, t$, the non-significant paths of length $l$, and the simplicies that become 0-connected, are iteratively deleted. The action of the filter is illustrated in the Fig. 3 for $k = 1$

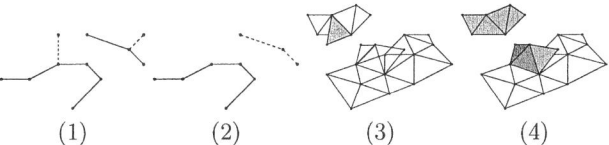

**Fig. 3.** Steps of the filter for $F_{1,\alpha,Q}(P)$ with (1) $t = 1$ and (2) $t = 2$ where dashed segments are deleted ; and for $F_{2,\alpha,Q}(P)$ with (3) $t = 1$ and (4) $t = 3, 4$ where grey triangles are deleted

and 2. The filter can remove two kinds of non-significant structure : artifacts on the boundary of a structure and small connex structures.

### 4.3 Detection of Polyhedral Structures

Let $\{R_1, \ldots, R_l\}$ be a finite set of distinct rotation matrices that decomposes $\mathbb{R}^3$ in $l$ orientations. For fixed values of $k$, $\alpha$ and $E$, the set $\{R_1, \ldots, R_l\}$ represents the spectrum of the family $\{F_{k,\alpha,Q}(P)\}$, where $Q$ is represented by $R_i$ and $E$, $1 \leq i \leq l$. This family of graphs is suitable to detect dot pattern having a polyhedral shape. In this way, we propose an algorithm which works in three main steps. Its input data are the points of $P$, the matrices $E$ and $\{R_1, \ldots, R_l\}$, the value of $\alpha$ and the filter threshold $t$. The algorithm is as follows :

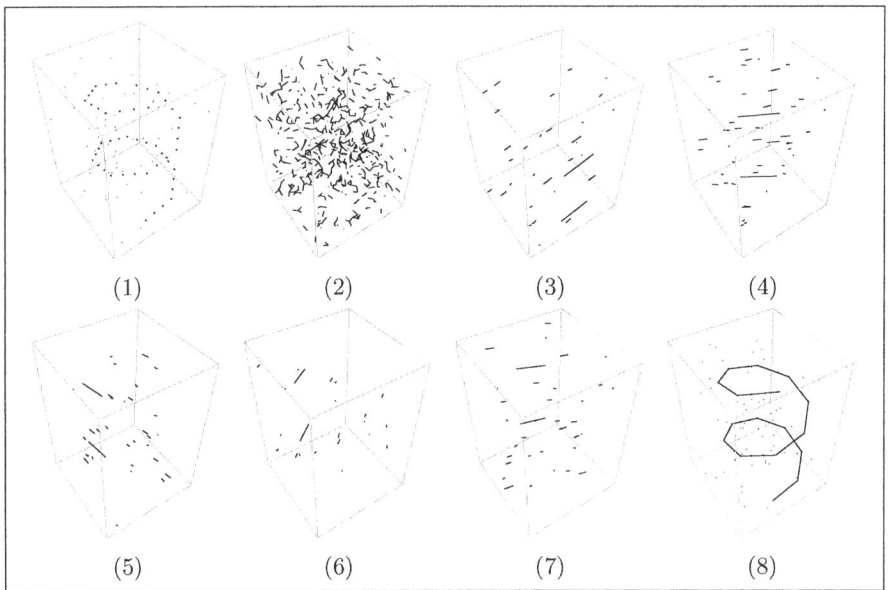

**Fig. 4.** Polyhedral structure detection using $F_{1,\alpha,Q}(P)$. (1) a sampled polyhedral structure (50 points) in a random perturbated background (1500 points). (2) shows that Euclidean $\alpha$-shapes are not suitable to detect the line. (3) to (7) are some $F_{1,\alpha,Q}(P)$ before the filtering procedure. (8) Union of the $F_{1,\alpha,Q}(P)$ after the filtering procedure.

(1) For $1 \leq i \leq l$, the $F_{k,\alpha,Q}(P)$ are computed.
(2) For $1 \leq i \leq l$, the $F_{k,\alpha,Q}(P)$ are filtered according to $t$.
(3) The resultant graph is the union of the filtered $F_{k,\alpha,Q}(P)$ for $1 \leq i \leq l$.

The detection of a polyhedral structure is illustrated in the Fig. 4.

## 5 Conclusion

In this article we have shown the adequacy of a family of graphs to detect regularities in a three-dimensional set of points. This family is a set of anisotropic $\alpha$-shapes that extend the Euclidean ones. Each anisotropic $\alpha$-shape, generated by an ellipsoidal ball as a structuring element, is suitable to detect straight linear or planar structures in a perturbated background. The elongation and the orientation of the ellipsoidal ball, compensate the low density of the sampled structures in the background and ensure the detection of these structures. From an algorithmic point of view, the anisotropic $\alpha$-shape can be computed efficiently from the Euclidean Voronoi diagram.

The ongoing work is to construct extensions based on more complex structuring elements than ball and ellipsoidal balls. These extensions will be employed to detect patterns which are more complex than the polyhedral structures, such as curved lines or surfaces. One of the possible applications is the detection of structures in unorganized set of points collected from range scanners.

## References

1. Lee D.T. and Wong C.K.: Voronoi diagrams in $L_1$ ($L_\infty$) metrics with 2-dimensional storage applications. SIAM J. Comput., Vol. 9, (1980) 200–211
2. Aurenhammer F.: Power diagrams : properties, algorithms and applications. SIAM J. Comput., Vol. 16 (1987) 78–96
3. Aurenhammer F. and Imai H.: Geometric relations among Voronoi diagrams. Geometriae Dedicata Vol. 27 (1988) 65–75
4. Goodman J.E. and O'Rourke J.: Handbook of Discrete and Computational Geometry. 2nd Ed., Chapman and Hall (2004)
5. Toussaint G.T.: Pattern Recognition and Geometrical Complexity. In Proc. Int. Conf. on Pattern Recognition, (December 1980) 1324–1347
6. Melkemi M. and Djebali M.: Elliptic diagrams: application to patterns detection from a finite set of points. Pattern Recognition Letters, Vol. 22(8) (2001) 835–844
7. Teichmann M. and Capps M.: Surface reconstruction with anisotropic density-scaled alpha shapes. In VIS'98 : Proc. of the conference on Visualization, IEEE Computer Society Press (1998) 67–72
8. Labelle F. and Shewchuk J.R.: Anisotropic voronoi diagrams and guaranteed-quality anisotropic mesh generation. In SCG '03 : Proc. of the 9th Annual Symposium on Computational Geometry, San Diego, ACM Press (2003) 191–200
9. Edelsbrunner H. and Mücke E.P.: Three-Dimensional Alpha Shapes. ACM Transactions on Graphics, Vol. 13(1) (1994) 43–72
10. Duda R.O., Hart P.E. and Stork D.G.: Pattern Classification. 2nd Ed., Wiley-Interscience (2000)

# A Morphological Edge Detector for Gray-Level Image Thresholding

Bin Chen[1], Lei He[2], and Ping Liu[1]

[1] Chengdu Institute of Computer Applications, Chinese Academy of Sciences,
Chengdu, Sichuan, P.R. China 610041
`bchen@casit.com.cn`
[2] Information Technology Department, Armstrong Atlantic State University,
Savannah, Georgia, USA 31419
`helei@mail.armstrong.edu`

**Abstract.** A morphological edge detector for robust real time image segmentation is proposed in this paper. Different from traditional thresholding methods that determine the threshold based on image gray level distribution, our method derives the threshold from object boundary point gray values and the boundary points are detected in the image using the proposed morphological edge detector. Firstly, the morphological edge detector is applied to compute the image morphological gradients. Then from the resultant image morphological gradient histogram, the object boundary points can be selected, which have higher gradient values than those of points within the object and background. The threshold is finally determined from the object boundary point gray values. Thus noise points inside the object and background are avoided in threshold computation. Experimental results on currency image segmentation for real time printing quality inspection are rather encouraging.

## 1 Introduction

Image segmentation plays an important role in image understanding and computer vision. For most image segmentation methods, such as thresholding, region growing, random field, deformable contours, etc., they can be roughly classified into two categories [1]: one is based on the measure of point homogeneity within objects, which is region-based segmentation method; The other is based on the measure of contrast on the border of objects, which is edge-based segmentation method. As one of the most commonly used classes, thresholding approaches are usually region-based and they are applied to convert the gray-scale image to a binary one, which usually contains the objects of interest and the background or, more generally, two classes in the image. A plethora of thresholding methods [2-13] and their performance evaluations on different applications [14-17] have been proposed in past several decades, which can be approximately classified into six categories: histogram shape-based, clustering-based, entropy-based, image attribute-based, spatial-based and local characteristics-based approaches.

In general, histogram shape-based approaches [2,3] analyze the shape properties of the image gray level histogram to find the threshold for the object and background separation, such as the peaks, valleys and curvatures of the histogram. Clustering-based approaches use certain algorithms, such as mean square [4] or fuzzy clustering [5], to group the image points into two clusters according to their gray values. Entropy-based approaches exploit the entropy of the gray level distribution in an image for thresholding, such as maximization of the entropy of the thresholded image [6] or minimization of the cross-entropy between the original image and the output binary image [7]. Image attribute-based approaches determine the threshold by searching some attribute quality or measure of similarity between the original and the binarized images, such as gray level moments [8], edge coincidence [9], etc. Spatial methods select the threshold by using not only gray value distribution but also the spatial relationship of pixels in a neighborhood, for example, in the form of correlation functions [10] or cooccurrence probabilities [11]. Local characteristics-based methods [12,13] adjust threshold value on each pixel according to the local image characteristics like range, variance, or contrast. These methods are usually either sensitive to image noises or complex in algorithm computation, which is not suitable for our real time image segmentation applications. Moreover, most of the existing thresholding approaches are region-based image segmentation methods. These methods consider only the point gray value homogeneity distributions, while the contrast information between the object and the background is not utilized. In this paper, we propose a new thresholding method based on the object boundary gray value distribution. Firstly, we define a novel morphological edge detector to select the object boundary points in image. Then the gray values of the object boundary point are used to derive the optimal threshold. Therefore, the proposed method is an edge-based image segmentation method that avoids the noise effects within the object and background.

The rest of this paper is organized as follows. Section 2 gives the definition of the morphological edge detector, based on which Section 3 proposes an adaptive algorithm, together with the algorithm computation complexity analysis, to determine the optimum image gray level threshold. An experimental comparison of different approaches on real time currency image thresholding is provided in Section 4. Section 5 draws the conclusions.

## 2 Morphological Edge Detector

Morphology techniques have been extensively applied in image processing, such as filtering, pruning, and shape representations [1]. Traditional morphological operations like opening and closing can be applied to filter out image noises. They are based on the combination of two fundamental operations: dilation and erosion, which are defined in terms of the union (or intersection) of an image with a translated shape (structuring element). In our thresholding method, we propose a new morphological object edge detector based on the morphology erosion and dilation operators, which is efficient to remove the image noise for object boundary searching.

First, we define two structuring elements as shown in Fig. 1: the static structuring element (SSE) $B_0(i, j)$ and the dynamic structuring element (DSE) $B_1(i, j)$, $i=\{-1,0,1\}$, $j=\{-1,0,1\}$.

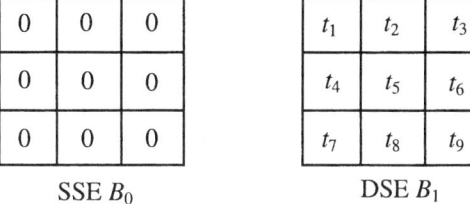

**Fig. 1.** Static (*SSE*) and dynamic (*DSE*) structuring element

The variable values in $B_1$ are determined by the 3 by 3 neighborhood of an image pixel $(x, y)$. The $t_k$ ($k=1,...,9$) is set to be 0 when the corresponding image pixel has the maximum or minimum value within the neighborhood. Otherwise the $t_k$ has value 1. Two examples are shown in Fig. 2. Given a gray-scale image $I$ and a 3 by 3 structuring element $s(i,j)$, $i,j=\{-1,0,1\}$, the morphology erosion ($\ominus$) and dilation ($\oplus$) operators for the gray-scale image are defined as [1]:

$$I \ominus s(x, y) = \min\{I(x+i, y+j) - s(i, j)\} \qquad (1)$$

$$I \oplus s(x, y) = \max\{I(x-i, y-j) + s(i, j)\} \qquad (2)$$

Based on the above definitions, we define the morphological edge detector as:

$$MG = |(I \times B_1) \oplus B_0 - (I \times B_1) \ominus B_0|, \qquad (3)$$

where $(I \times B_1)$ is implemented by multiplying the gray values of pixels in the neighborhood with their corresponding DSE $B_1$ variables $t_k$. It can be seen that $B_1$ performs as a "mask" to filter out the noise points which has the maximum or minimum values in the neighborhood of pixel $(x, y)$. Due to the connectivity of edge points in image, the gradient information can still be computed correctly after the removal of the two noise points. Here $B_0$ is to specify the effective range (3x3) of the morphological operations with all elements being set to zero. The elements can be set to special values as different weights for particular applications.

| 4 | 9 | 4 |
|---|---|---|
| 3 | 3 | 3 |
| 2 | 2 | 2 |

| 1 | 0 | 1 |
|---|---|---|
| 1 | 1 | 1 |
| 0 | 1 | 1 |

| 4 | 4 | 4 |
|---|---|---|
| 3 | 3 | 3 |
| 2 | 2 | 2 |

| 0 | 1 | 1 |
|---|---|---|
| 1 | 1 | 1 |
| 0 | 1 | 1 |

(a) Noise neighborhood    (b) *DSE* of (a)    (c) Normal neighborhood    (d) *DSE* of (c)

**Fig. 2.** Two examples to illustrate the morphological edge detector

Here we use two examples to demonstrate the noise robustness of the *MG* operator. Given two neighborhoods as shown in Fig. 2(a) and (c), the first one includes a noise point and the second does not. The points with maximum and minimum gray values are bolded in the neighborhoods. The corresponding DSEs ($B_1$) are shown in Fig. 2(b) and (d), respectively. The *MG* operator computes the morphological gradient values as 2 for both cases, while the traditional gradient calculator usually generates different values due to the noise points. Moreover, the *MG* operator can detect the gradient from all directions, i.e., it is an isotropic operator.

## 3 Thresholding Algorithm

As described in the first section, current thresholding methods focus on the image gray value statistics analysis, such as histogram, image attribute and entropy, etc. In practice, most of images contain noisy points that prevent an accurate segmentation by a simple thresholding approach. Many researchers proposed different methods to overcome or reduce the image noise effects, such as spatial-based or local characteristics-based algorithms. However, the computational complexity increased much in these advanced approaches, which are not suitable for real time machine vision applications. This paper proposes a new algorithm that utilizes the gray level contrast information provided by object boundary points to determine the correct threshold for image segmentation. In this section, the analysis on image morphological gradient histogram is firstly given for object boundary points selection. Then the image threshold determination algorithm is described, followed by the algorithm computation complexity analysis.

### 3.1 Morphological Gradient Histogram Analysis

Given an image, the morphological edge detector is applied to compute the image morphological gradients and derive the morphological gradient histogram. As indicated in Section 2, the proposed morphological gradients are computed after noise removal by using the DSE mask. Thus the morphological gradient histogram is reliable to determine the real object boundary points. Two sample images, together with their morphological gradient images and histograms are shown in Fig. 3. It can be seen that their histogram shapes are analogous, which in fact can be taken as a model according to the observations from the morphological gradient histograms of a large set (over a half million) of images. Therefore, we assume that the shape of an image morphological gradient histogram can be described as the curve in Fig. 4. If an input image has a large amount of edge points, we expect a "fat tail" at the right side of the gradient histogram shape, i.e., there are many high gradient points in the image, as shown in Fig. 3(c). On the other hand, if an input image has a small number of edge points, we expect a "thin tail" in the gradient histogram shape, i.e., there are only a few high gradient points in the image, as shown in Fig. 3(f). Thus the purpose here is to find a threshold in the morphological gradient histogram to correctly separate the images points with high and low gradient values. The image points with morphological gradient values higher than the threshold will be considered as the object boundary points, while other image points with morphological gradient values smaller than the threshold are from the interior of object and background.

From the probability theory, the mean and the standard deviation of a distribution are the most important statistical measurements to specify a pattern. Here the mean

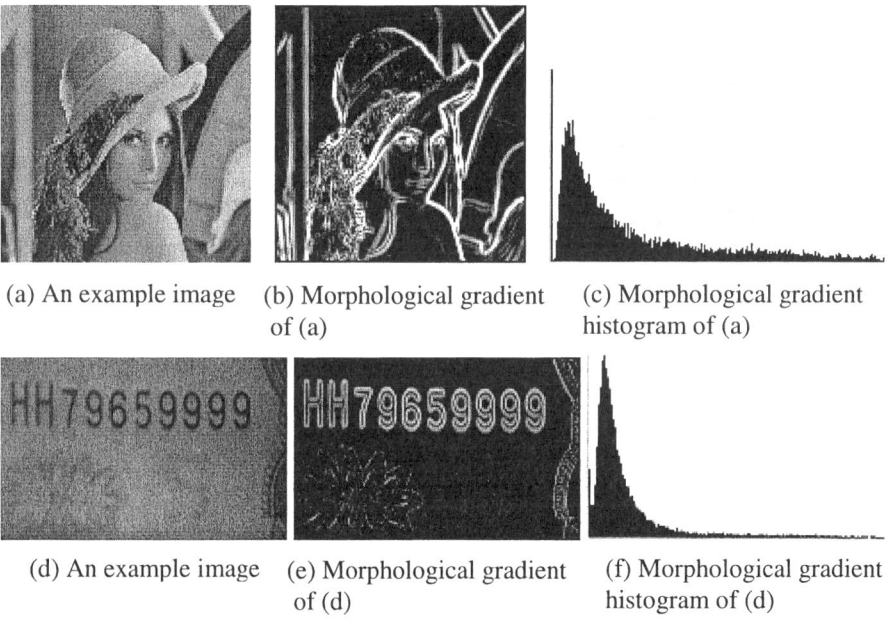

(a) An example image  (b) Morphological gradient of (a)  (c) Morphological gradient histogram of (a)

(d) An example image  (e) Morphological gradient of (d)  (f) Morphological gradient histogram of (d)

**Fig. 3.** Two examples to illustrate the morphological gradient histogram model

and the standard deviation of the image morphological gradients are used to determine the object boundary points. In Fig. 4, A is the mean of the image morphological gradients and B = A+D. D represents the standard deviation of the image morphological gradients and it characterizes the image texture complexity. Thus B can be used as the gradient threshold to differentiate the object boundary points and the object and background interior points because the former always have larger gradient values than the later in our application. The image points with gradient values MG≥B are considered as the object boundary points, while the other image points with MG<B are object and background points.

**Fig. 4.** Morphological gradient histogram model

### 3.2 Proposed Algorithm and Computation Complexity

The complete thresholding algorithm for image segmentation is described as:

(1). Apply the morphological edge detector *MG* to compute the image morphological gradients;

(2). Compute the mean and standard deviation of the image morphological gradients;
(3). Select object boundary points in image using the gradient threshold, which is the summation of the mean and standard deviation of the image morphological gradients;
(4). Average the gray values of the object boundary points to obtain the threshold for image segmentation.

The computation complexity of our algorithm is O(N), with N corresponding to the image size. In practice, it takes around 1ms for a Pentium IV (1GHz) to process a grayscale image of size 512×512. Thus the algorithm is suitable for real time image segmentation applications.

## 4 Experiments

In this section, two examples taken in different conditions are used to illustrate the proposed algorithm robustness on image noises by comparing its thresholding results with those of several other traditional methods: histogram shape-based method [2], clustering-based method [4], entropy-based method [6], image attribute-based method [8], spatial method [10] and local characteristics-based method [12].

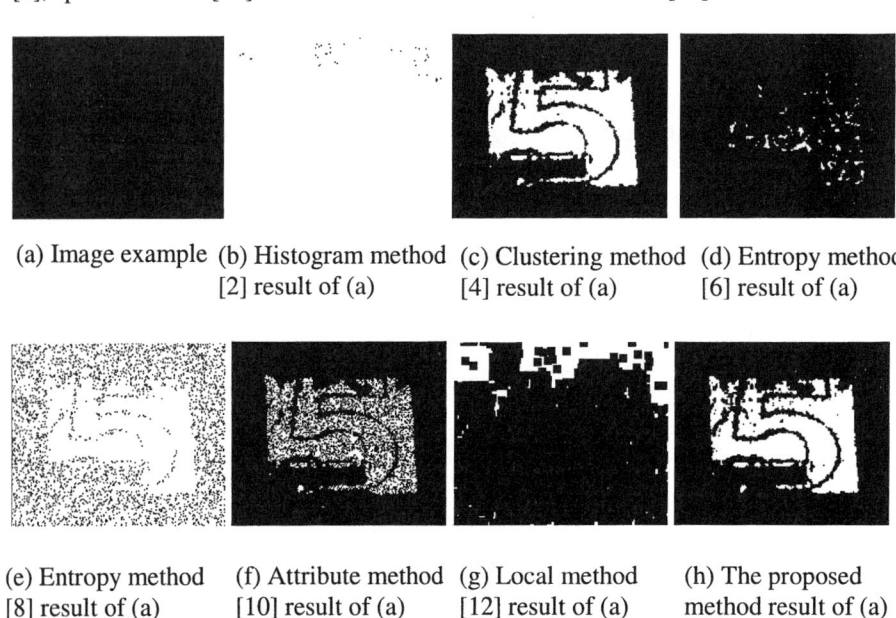

(a) Image example  (b) Histogram method [2] result of (a)  (c) Clustering method [4] result of (a)  (d) Entropy method [6] result of (a)

(e) Entropy method [8] result of (a)  (f) Attribute method [10] result of (a)  (g) Local method [12] result of (a)  (h) The proposed method result of (a)

**Fig. 5.** An example of thresholding results comparison

Fig. 5 presents a rather difficult case: a dark image has very low contrast between object and background. The segmentation results by different methods are illustrated, from which it can be seen that the morphology-based method has better performance than most of the other methods. Most of the object boundary points can be correctly determined in this difficult example by our method. Fig. 6 compares the thresholding results by different methods on an input image with complicated background. It can be seen that the proposed method is the best to extract the object boundary after thresholding. Moreover, the time complexities of the proposed algorithm on these two images are around 0.5ms, while other methods took around 5ms to 10ms. The proposed method has superior performances in both segmentation accuracy and speed compared with the other methods.

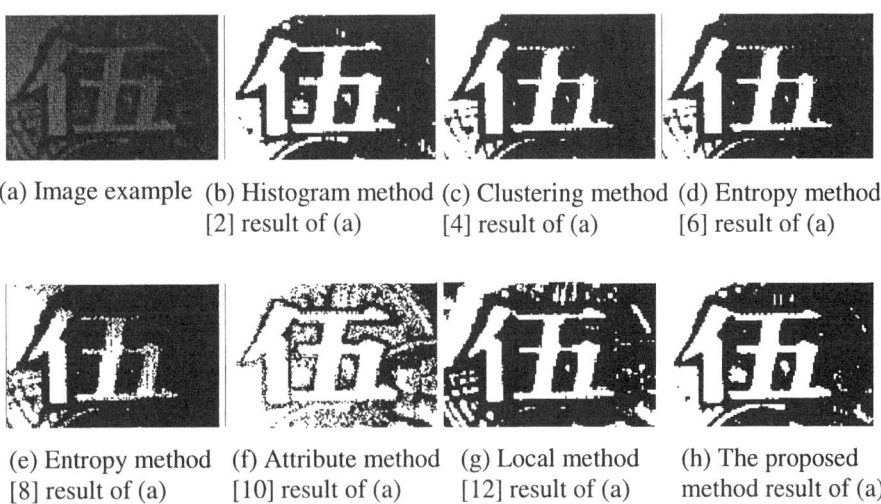

(a) Image example  (b) Histogram method [2] result of (a)  (c) Clustering method [4] result of (a)  (d) Entropy method [6] result of (a)

(e) Entropy method [8] result of (a)  (f) Attribute method [10] result of (a)  (g) Local method [12] result of (a)  (h) The proposed method result of (a)

**Fig. 6.** An example of thresholding results comparison

Currently the algorithm has been widely applied on fifty-five banknote inspection systems in China for real time image segmentation. The segmentation error is less than 0.03% for around a half million real time currency images. The segmentation error is determined by the following quality inspection process using template matching [18] between the segmented objects and different templates.

## 5 Conclusions

This paper presents a novel morphology-based thresholding approach for real time image segmentation. The proposed algorithm is an edge-based method, which determines the threshold according to the gray levels of object boundary points in image. A morphological edge detector is firstly defined and applied on the input image to compute the image morphological gradients. Then the object boundary points can be determined from the morphological gradient statistics analysis, with the elimination of the noise point effects. Finally the optimum image threshold is derived from the object boundary point gray level distributions. The successful field application of the algorithm in a variety of currency image segmentation for real time printing quality inspection demonstrates the capability and potential of this new approach.

## References

1. Gonzalez, R.C., Woods R.E.: Digital Image Processing. 2nd edn. Prentice Hall (2002)
2. Rosenfeld, A., Torre, P. De la: Histogram Concavity Analysis As an Aid in Threshold Selection," IEEE Trans. Syst. Man Cybern. 13 (1983) 231-235
3. Guo, R., Pandit, S.M.: Automatic Threshold Selection Based on Histogram Modes and a Discriminant Criterion. Mach. Vision Appl. 10 (1998) 331–338
4. Otsu, N.: A Threshold Selection Method From Gray Level Histograms. IEEE Trans. Syst. Man Cybern. 9 (1979) 62–66
5. Jawahar, C.V., Biswas, Ray, A.K.: Investigations on Fuzzy Thresholding Based on Fuzzy Clustering. Pattern Recognition 30 (1997) 1605–1613
6. Kapur, J.N., Sahoo, P.K., Wong, A.K.C.: A New Method for Gray-level Picture Thresholding Using the Entropy of the Histogram. CVGIP: Graph. Models Image Process. 29 (1985) 273–285
7. Pal, N.R.: On Minimum Cross-entropy Thresholding. Pattern Recognition 29 (1996) 575–580
8. Tsai, W.H.: Moment-preserving Thresholding: A New Approach. CVGIP: Graph. Models Image Process. 29 (1985) 373–393
9. Venkatesh, S., Rosin, P.L.: Dynamic Threshold Determination by Local and Global Edge Evaluation. CVGIP: Graph. Models Image Process. 57 (1995) 146–160
10. Beghdadi, A., Negrate, A.L., Lesegno, P.V. De: Entropic Thresholding Using a Block Source Model. Graph. Models Image Process. 57 (1995) 197-205
11. Lie, W.N.: An Efficient Threshold-evaluation Algorithm for Image Segmentation Based on Spatial Gray Level Cooccurrences. Signal Process. 33 (1993) 121–126
12. Bernsen, J.: Dynamic Thresholding of Gray Level Images. Proc. Intl. Conf. Patt. Recog. (ICPR 1986) 1251-1255
13. Kamel, M., Zhao, A.: Extraction of Binary Character/Graphics Images From Grayscale Document Images. CVGIP: Graph. Models Image Process. 55 (1993) 203–217
14. Le, S.U., Chung, S.Y., Park, R.H.: A Comparative Performance Study of Several Global Thresholding Techniques for Segmentation. CVGIP: Graph. Models Image Process. 52 (1990) 171–190
15. Sahoo, P.K., Soltani, S., Wong, A.K.C., Chen, Y.: A Survey of Thresholding Techniques. Comput. Graph. Image Process. 41 (1988) 233-260
16. Glasbey, C.A.: An Analysis of Histogram-based Thresholding Algorithms. CVGIP: Graph. Models Image Process. 55 (1993) 532-537
17. Sezgin, M., Sankur, B.: Survey Over Image Thresholding Techniques and Quantitative Performance Evaluation. J. Electronic Imaging 13 (2004) 146-165
18. Chen, B., He, L.: Fuzzy Template Matching for Printing Character Inspection. WSEAS Trans. Circuits and Sys. 3 (2004) 575-580

# Vector Morphological Operators for Colour Images

Valérie De Witte, Stefan Schulte, Mike Nachtegael, Dietrich Van der Weken, and Etienne E. Kerre

Ghent University,
Department of Applied Mathematics and Computer Science,
Fuzziness and Uncertainty Modelling Research Unit,
Krijgslaan 281 (Building S9), B-9000 Gent, Belgium
Valerie.DeWitte@UGent.be
http://www.fuzzy.ugent.be

**Abstract.** In this paper we extend the basic morphological operators dilation and erosion for grey-scale images based on the threshold approach, umbra approach and fuzzy set theory to colour images. This is realised by treating colours as vectors and defining a new vector ordering so that new colour morphological operators are presented. Here we only discuss colours represented in the RGB colour space. The colour space RGB becomes together with the new ordering and associated minimum and maximum operators a complete chain. All this can be extended to the colour spaces HSV and L*a*b*. Experimental results show that our method provides an improvement on the component-based approach of morphological operators applied to colour images. The colours in the colour images are preserved, that is, no new colours are introduced.

## 1 Introduction

Mathematical morphology is used in many applications in image processing such as granulometry, pattern recognition, image segmentation, image filtering, etc. Different colour morphological approaches have already been introduced, a.o. [1], [2], [3], [4] and [5]. In this work we will present a new vector-based approach for the extension of mathematical morphology to colour images. First we discuss the component-based approach of morphology to colour images. Thereafter we describe our new developed vector-based approach. In section 3 we introduce a vector ordering for colours represented in the RGB colour space. With this ordering new maximum and minimum operators are proposed in section 4. We then define the binary operations addition (+), subtraction (−) and multiplication (∗) between a colour and a shade of grey to obtain useful vector morphological operators for colour images (section 5). Not only the t- and u-morphological operators (threshold and umbra approach) are extended to colours but also the fuzzy morphological operators. Finally, in section 6 some experimental results are shown, where we have compared our new approach with the well known component-based approach.

## 2 Basic Notions

### 2.1 Modelling of Images

Digital images are often represented by a two-dimensional array, where a pair $(i,j)$ denotes a position in the image, called pixel. Mathematically, a 2-dimensional grey-scale image can be represented as a mapping from a universe $X$ of pixels (usually $X$ is a bounded and finite subset of the real plane $\mathbb{R}^2$, in practice it will even be a subset of $\mathbb{Z}^2$) to the universe of grey-values $[0,1]$, where 0 corresponds to black, 1 to white and in between we have all shades of grey.

### 2.2 Fuzzy Sets

A fuzzy set $F$ in a universe $X$ is a $X - [0,1]$ mapping, where for all $x$ in $X$, $F(x)$ denotes the degree in which $x$ belongs to the fuzzy set $F$. Further on we will need the extension of the binary logical operators conjunction ($\wedge$) and implication ($\Rightarrow$) to fuzzy logic, where these operators are called conjunctors and implicators. The most popular conjunctors $\mathcal{C}$ on $[0,1]$ are the triangular norms minimum $T_M$, algebraic product $T_P$ and Lukasiewicz triangular norm $T_W$; the most popular implicators $\mathcal{I}$ on $[0,1]$ are the Kleene-Dienes implicator $I_{KD}$, the Reichenbach implicator $I_R$ and the Lukasiewicz implicator $I_W$ given by

| conjunctor | implicator |
|---|---|
| $T_M(a,b) = \min(a,b)$ | $I_{KD}(a,b) = \max(1-a,b)$ |
| $T_P(a,b) = a.b$ | $I_R(a,b) = 1 - a + a.b$ |
| $T_W(a,b) = \max(0, a+b-1)$ | $I_W(a,b) = \min(1, 1-a+b)$ |

An extensive study of fuzzy sets can be found in [6].

### 2.3 Binary Morphology, Grey-Scale Morphology Based on the Threshold Approach and on the Umbra Approach

For a detailed study of binary and grey-scale morphology we refer to [7], [8], [9].

### 2.4 Fuzzy Mathematical Morphology

Consider a grey-scale image $A$ and a grey-scale structuring element $B$. Because grey-scale images can be modelled as $\mathbb{R}^n - [0,1]$ mappings (usually $n = 2$), we can identify grey-scale images with fuzzy sets and extend binary morphology to grey-scale morphology using fuzzy set theory. The translation $T_y(B)$ of $B$ by a vector $y \in \mathbb{R}^n$ is then defined by $T_y(B)(x) = B(x-y)$, $\forall x \in \mathbb{R}^n$ and the support $d_A$ of $A$ is defined as the set $d_A = \{x \in \mathbb{R}^n \mid A(x) > 0\}$.

**Definition 1.** *Let $A$ be a grey-scale image and $B$ a grey-scale structuring element, $\mathcal{C}$ a conjunctor on $[0,1]$ and $\mathcal{I}$ an implicator on $[0,1]$. The fuzzy dilation $D_\mathcal{C}(A,B)$ and the fuzzy erosion $E_\mathcal{I}(A,B)$ are the fuzzy sets defined by*

$$D_{\mathcal{C}}(A,B)(y) = \sup_{x \in T_y(d_B) \cap d_A} \mathcal{C}(B(x-y), A(x)) \text{ for } y \in \mathbb{R}^n,$$
$$E_{\mathcal{I}}(A,B)(y) = \inf_{x \in T_y(d_B)} \mathcal{I}(B(x-y), A(x)) \text{ for } y \in \mathbb{R}^n.$$

More information about fuzzy mathematical morphology can be found in [10], [11], [12], [13].

### 2.5 Colour Morphology

Colour images are represented as mappings from a universe $X$ of pixels to a "colour interval" that can be for example the product interval $[0,1] \times [0,1] \times [0,1]$ (RGB). Colour images can be modelled using different colour spaces; here we will only consider the RGB colour space. More information about colour spaces can be found in [14], [15]. Mathematical morphology can be naturally extended to colour images by processing the morphological operators on each of the colour components separately. A major disadvantage of this approach is that the existing correlations between the different colour components are not taken into account and this often leads to disturbing artefacts, that is, colours that are not presented in the original colour image appear. Another approach is to treat the colour at each pixel in a colour image as a vector. Because we need the concept of a supremum and infimum to define basic vector morphological operators, we first have to define an ordering between colours in RGB.

## 3 New Vector Ordering in the RGB Colour Space

A colour in the RGB colour space is obtained by adding the three colours red, green and blue in different combinations. Therefore a colour can be defined as a vector in the three-dimensional RGB colour space, which can be represented as a unit cube using a Cartesian coordinate scheme. This way every point in the cube represents a vector (colour). The grey-scale spectrum is characterised by the line between the black top $Bl$ with coordinates $(0,0,0)$ and the white top $Wh$ $(1,1,1)$.

On the RGB cube we observe that colours lying close to black are 'dark' colours while colours lying close to white are 'light' colours, so we can order the colour vectors with respect to their distance to black and white as follows:

1. To determine which of two colours is ranked lowest, colours are first ordered from vectors with smallest distance to black to vectors with largest distance to black. The smaller the distance to black, the lower the colour is ranked. This way the RGB cube is sliced into different parts of spheres around the black top. Colours that are part of the same sphere (around the black top) are then ordered according to their distance with respect to white, from colours with largest distance to white to colours with smallest distance to white. So we will 'cut' the spheres around the black top with spheres with the white top as centre. Those colours closest to white are farthest away from black and vice versa.

2. Here we use a similar technique as in the previous point 1. If we want to know which one of two colours is ranked highest in the RGB colour space, we look at the distance with respect to white. The colour with the smallest distance to white is ordered higher than the other colour. If the distance to white is equal, so if both colours lie on the same sphere around the white top, we select that colour lying farthest from black. Again, the RGB cube is sliced into parts of spheres, but now first towards the white top and then towards the black top.

3. Finally there are colours that have the same distance to the black top and the same distance to the white top, and thus lie on a circle (as profile of two spheres) in the RGB cube. Colours lying on such a circle are ranked equally.

This leads us to a new ordering $\leq_{RGB}$ of vectors in the RGB colour space. If we consider two colours $c(r_c, g_c, b_c)$ and $c'(r_{c'}, g_{c'}, b_{c'})$ in the RGB cube, we get:

$$c <_{RGB} c' \Leftrightarrow d(c, Bl) < d(c', Bl) \text{ or}$$
$$\quad \text{if } (d(c, Bl) = d(c', Bl)) \text{ then } (d(c, Wh) > d(c', Wh))$$
$$c >_{RGB} c' \Leftrightarrow d(c, Wh) < d(c', Wh) \text{ or}$$
$$\quad \text{if } (d(c, Wh) = d(c', Wh)) \text{ then } (d(c, Bl) > d(c', Bl))$$
$$c =_{RGB} c' \Leftrightarrow (d(c, Bl) = d(c', Bl)) \text{ and } (d(c, Wh) = d(c', Wh)),$$

with $d$ the Euclidean distance, i.e. $d(c, Bl) = \sqrt{(r_c - 0)^2 + (g_c - 0)^2 + (b_c - 0)^2}$.

## 4 Definition of New Maximum and Minimum

Based on this vector ordering in the RGB colour space, we can define new minimum and maximum operators. Consider a set $S$ of $n$ colours $c_1(r_1, g_1, b_1), \ldots, c_n(r_n, g_n, b_n)$ in RGB, with $r_\alpha, g_\alpha, b_\alpha \in [0, 1]$ for $\alpha = 1, \ldots, n$. We then define the minimum $\wedge$ of $S$, $\wedge S = \wedge \{c_1, c_2, \ldots, c_n\}$ using the following approach:

if $(\exists!\alpha)(d(c_\alpha, Bl) = \min(d(c_1, Bl), \ldots, d(c_n, Bl)))$ then $\wedge S = c_\alpha$
else if $(\exists!\alpha)(d(c_\alpha, Bl) = \min(d(c_1, Bl), \ldots, d(c_n, Bl))$ and $d(c_\alpha, Wh) = \max(d(c_1, Wh), \ldots, d(c_n, Wh)))$ then $\wedge S = c_\alpha$
else if $(\exists!\alpha)(d(c_\alpha, Bl) = \min(d(c_1, Bl), \ldots, d(c_n, Bl)), d(c_\alpha, Wh) = \max(d(c_1, Wh), \ldots, d(c_n, Wh))$ and $r_\alpha = min(r_1, \ldots, r_n))$ then $\wedge S = c_\alpha$
else if $(\exists!\alpha)(d(c_\alpha, Bl) = \min(d(c_1, Bl), \ldots, d(c_n, Bl)), d(c_\alpha, Wh) = \max(d(c_1, Wh), \ldots, d(c_n, Wh)), r_\alpha = min(r_1, \ldots, r_n)$ and $g_\alpha = \min(g_1, \ldots, g_n))$ then $\wedge S = c_\alpha$
else if $(\exists!\alpha)(d(c_\alpha, Bl) = \min(d(c_1, Bl), \ldots, d(c_n, Bl)), d(c_\alpha, Wh) = \max(d(c_1, Wh), \ldots, d(c_n, Wh)), r_\alpha = min(r_1, \ldots, r_n), g_\alpha = \min(g_1, \ldots, g_n)$ and $b_\alpha = \min(b_1, \ldots, b_n))$ then $\wedge S = c_\alpha$,

where $1 \leq \alpha \leq n$.

Analogously we define the maximum of $S$, $\vee S = \vee \{c_1, c_2, \ldots, c_n\}$, where we first look at the white top and secondly at the black top.

After the first two steps in the determination of the minimum or maximum of a set of colours, there may still be colours lying on the profile of two spheres, a circle, in the RGB cube. In this case we look at the red colour component $R$ of these remaining colours: the colour with the smallest $R$-value is the minimum, the colour with the largest $R$-value is the maximum. If two or more colours of $S$ have the same minimum (resp. maximum) $R$-value, we look at the green colour component $G$ of these colours. The smallest $G$-value gives us the minimum, the greatest $G$-value the maximum. Finally if there still remain colours with the same minimum (resp. maximum) $G$-value, we consider the blue colour component, where the smallest $B$-value will determine the minimum, the greatest $B$-value the maximum.

We want to notice here that the last three steps in the determination of minimum and maximum of a set of colours in the RGB colour space are a bit artificial, because the three colour components $R$, $G$ and $B$ are equally important. But in practical applications of morphological operators to colour images, maximum and minimum are usually already obtained after the second step. And if not, in other words, if we get more than one colour for the minimum or maximum after the first two steps, these obtained colours are equally ranked, and then we really have to choose one.

It is easy to verify that the RGB colour space with the above defined ordering of colours and associated minimum and maximum operators is a complete chain, with least element $(0,0,0)$ and greatest element $(1,1,1)$. Also important to mention is that the minimum and maximum operators are vector preserving: minimum or maximum of a set $S$ of colours in the colour space RGB is a colour contained in the set $S$, so no new colours are created.

## 5 New Vector Morphological Operators for Colour Images

To apply the umbra and fuzzy morphological operators to colour images, we also have to define the operators $+$ and $-$ between two colours, where the ordering, minimum and maximum are defined as before. If $c(r_c, g_c, b_c)$ is a colour and $c'(r_{c'}, g_{c'}, b_{c'})$ a shade of grey (thus $r_{c'} = g_{c'} = b_{c'}$) in RGB, we define the complement $1 - c$ or $co(c)$ of $c$, the sum $c + c'$ of $c$ and $c'$, and the difference $c - c'$ of $c'$ from $c$ as:

$$(co(c))(x,y,z) = 1_{RGB} - c \text{ with } x \stackrel{def}{=} 1 - r_c, y \stackrel{def}{=} 1 - g_c, z \stackrel{def}{=} 1 - b_c;$$

$$(c + c')(x,y,z) \text{ with } x \stackrel{def}{=} (r_c + r_{c'})/2, y \stackrel{def}{=} (g_c + g_{c'})/2, z \stackrel{def}{=} (b_c + b_{c'})/2;$$

$$(c - c')(x,y,z) \stackrel{def}{=} c + co(c') = c + (1_{RGB} - c'), \text{ with } x = (r_c + (1 - r_{c'}))/2,\\ y = (g_c + (1 - g_{c'}))/2, z = (b_c + (1 - b_{c'}))/2.$$

For the fuzzy mathematical morphological operators we also need the operation multiplication ($*$) between two colours. As 3-dimensional structuring element in

RGB we can and will take a symmetric grey-scale structuring element of the form (all three colour components R, G and B are equally important)

$$B = \begin{pmatrix} c_{B_1} & c_{B_{11}} & c_{B_1} \\ c_{B_{11}} & 1 & c_{B_{11}} \\ c_{B_1} & c_{B_{11}} & c_{B_1} \end{pmatrix} \times \begin{pmatrix} c_{B_1} & c_{B_{11}} & c_{B_1} \\ c_{B_{11}} & 1 & c_{B_{11}} \\ c_{B_1} & c_{B_{11}} & c_{B_1} \end{pmatrix} \times \begin{pmatrix} c_{B_1} & c_{B_{11}} & c_{B_1} \\ c_{B_{11}} & 1 & c_{B_{11}} \\ c_{B_1} & c_{B_{11}} & c_{B_1} \end{pmatrix}$$

to give a certain weight, thus a certain grade of importance, to each colour in the window we observe. So we define the product $*$ of a colour $c(r_c, g_c, b_c)$ and a shade of grey $c_B(r_{c_B}, g_{c_B}, b_{c_B})$ of the chosen structuring element $B$ as

$$(c * c_B)(x, y, z) \text{ with } x \stackrel{def}{=} r_c * r_{c_B}, y \stackrel{def}{=} g_c * g_{c_B}, z \stackrel{def}{=} b_c * b_{c_B},$$

where $r_{c_B} = g_{c_B} = b_{c_B} \in \{c_{B_1}, c_{B_{11}}, 1\}$.

## 6 Experimental Results

Consider a colour image $C$, modelled in the RGB colour space, and a grey-scale structuring element $B_{RGB}$. For the extension of the grey-scale morphological operators to vector morphological operators for colour images we can apply two methods:

1. we only work with distances
2. we work with distances and mixture of colours.

1. In the first method we calculate the maximum and/or minimum of the set of colours contained in the considered $m \times m$ window (we choose $m = 3$) in our image around a central colour pixel $y$ and the maximum and/or minimum of the grey-values in the chosen structuring element. Secondly we add, subtract or multiply the two obtained distances in each colour pixel in our window and determine the maximum or minimum of these $m * m$ values. So the dilation and erosion are the original colours (in the original image) of the pixels where this maximum, resp. minimum is reached.

2. In contrast to the previous applied method we can also first mix the colours of our window around a central pixel $y$ (addition, subtraction and multiplication) and then determine the maximum or minimum of this new set of colours, using distances. Again, the dilation and erosion are the original colours of the obtained maximum and/or minimum pixel.

Finally in our experimental results we have compared the new vector morphological operators with the component-based approach. We have used different test images in our experiments (the well known Tulips, Trees and Lena images). Fig. 1 shows the Lena image, where the fuzzy dilation and erosion for the conjunctor-implicator pair $(C, \mathcal{I}) = (T_W, I_W)$ are illustrated. Notice that because the dilation is a supremum operator, this operator will suppress dark colours and intensify light colours: objects/areas in the image that have a dark colour become smaller while objects/areas that have a light colour become larger. The erosion

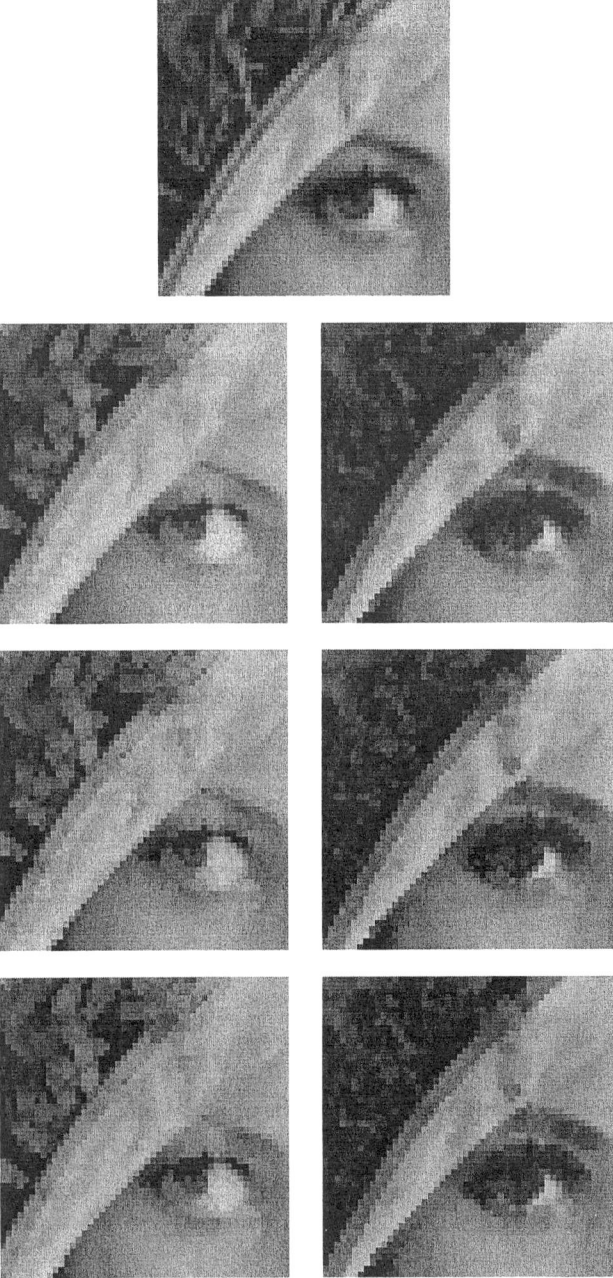

**Fig. 1.** Fuzzy morphological operators for $(\mathcal{C}, \mathcal{I}) = (T_W, I_W)$ in the RGB colour space: at the top: original image, left column: the dilations $D_{T_W}(A, B')$ and right column: the erosions $E_{I_W}(A, B')$: from top to bottom: the component-based approach and our new approach, method 1 and 2

on the other hand is an infimum operator so that light colours are suppressed and dark colours intensified. The choice of the structuring element has of course a great influence on the result and will obviously depend on the application. We have also tried different structuring elements, in Fig. 1 the following structuring element is used (scaled to $[0, 255]$)

$$B' = \begin{pmatrix} 155 & 235 & 155 \\ 235 & \underline{255} & 235 \\ 155 & 235 & 155 \end{pmatrix} \times \begin{pmatrix} 155 & 235 & 155 \\ 235 & \underline{255} & 235 \\ 155 & 235 & 155 \end{pmatrix} \times \begin{pmatrix} 155 & 235 & 155 \\ 235 & \underline{255} & 235 \\ 155 & 235 & 155 \end{pmatrix}.$$

We may conclude that our new method provides more beautiful results than those obtained by the component-based approach. Firstly, one great advantage is that the colours are preserved and thus no new colours appear in the images after applying the new vector morphological operators to it. Secondly, more details from the original colour image are preserved, and thus visible. On the other hand visual observation shows that there still may appear some artefacts.

We have assessed the resultant images objectively. We have even done experiments with several similarity measures [16] and these experiments have shown that the loose of quality is lowest with our vector ordering approach.

**Remark:** We have already extended the above vector ordering approach for colours to the HSV and L*a*b* colour space [17].

## 7 Conclusion

In this paper we have presented a new vector ordering procedure for morphological processing of colour images based on fuzzy sets, umbra and thresholding techniques. The problem of looking for a vector ordering for colour or multivariate morphological image processing is not new and is being developed since the early 90's. What is new here is the used approach, namely through the umbra approach and fuzzy set theory. As future work we will compare our approach with previous morphological approaches that have already solved the problem of not creating new colours. Currently we are setting up an experiment regarding the psycho visual behaviour of similarity measures, and this can also be useful for the evaluation of morphological operators.

**Acknowledgement.** This research was financially supported by the GOA-project 12.0515.03 of Ghent University.

## References

1. Talbot, H., Evans, C., Jones, R.: Complete Ordering and Multivariate Mathematical Morphology: Algorithms and Applications, Mathematical Morphology and Its Applications to Image and Signal Processing, Kluwer Academic Press, Amsterdam (1998) 27–34

2. Hanbury, A., Serra, J.: Morphological Operators on the Unit Circle, IEEE Transactions on Image Processing, Vol. 10, No. 12, USA, (2001) 1842–1850
3. Hanbury, A., Serra, J.: Mathematical Morphology in the HLS Colour Space, Proceedings of the 12th British Machine Vision Conference, United Kingdom, (2001) 451–460
4. Hanbury, A., Serra, J.: Mathematical Morphology in the CIELAB Space, Image Analysis and Stereology, Vol. 21, No. 3, Slovenia, (2002) 201–206
5. Louverdis, G., Vardavoulia, M.I., Andreadis, I., Tsalides, Ph.: A New Approach to Morphological Color Image Processing, Pattern Recognition, Vol. 35, USA, (2002) 1733–1741
6. Kerre, E. E.: Fuzzy sets and approximate reasoning, Xian Jiaotong University Press, Softcover (1998)
7. Heijmans, H. J.A.M., Ronse, C.: The Algebraic Basis of Mathematical Morphology, Part1: Dilations and Erosions, Computer Vision, Graphics and Image Processing, Vol. 50, (1990) 245–295
8. Ronse, C., Heijmans, H. J.A.M.: The Algebraic Basis of Mathematical Morphology, Part2: Openings and Closings, Computer Vision, Graphics and Image Processing, Vol. 54, (1991) 74–97
9. Heijmans, H. J.A.M.: Morphological Image Operators, Advances in Electronics and Electron Physics, Academic Press, Inc., London (1994)
10. De Baets, B., Kerre, E. E., Gupta, M. M.: The Fundamentals of Fuzzy Mathematical Morphology Part 1: Basic Concepts, International Journal of General Systems, Vol. 23, (1995) 155–171
11. Baets, M., Kerre, E. E., Gupta, M.M.: The Fundamentals of Fuzzy Mathematical Morphology Part 2: Idempotence, Convexity and Decomposition, International Journal of General Systems, Vol. 23, (1995) 307–322
12. De Baets, B.: Fuzzy Morphology: a Logical Approach, Uncertainty Analysis in Engineering and Sciences: Fuzzy Logic, Statistics, and Neural Network Approach, Kluwer Academic Press, Boston (1997) 53–67
13. Nachtegael, M., Kerre, E. E.: Classical and fuzzy approaches towards mathematical morphology, Fuzzy Techniques in Image Processing, Series Studies in Fuzziness and Soft Computing, Physica Verlag, Heidelberg (2000) 3–57
14. Sangwine, S. J., Horne, R.E.N.: The Colour Image Processing Handbook, Chapman & Hall, London (1998)
15. Sharma, G.: Digital Color Imaging Handbook, CRC Press, Boca Raton (2003)
16. Van der Weken, D., Nachtegael, M., Kerre, E. E.: Using Similarity Measures and Homogeneity for the Comparison of Images, Image and Vision Computing, Vol. 22, (2004) 695–702
17. De Witte, V.: Colour preserving morphological operators for image processing, Internal Research Report, Fuzziness and Uncertainty Modelling Research Unit, Ghent University (2005)

# Decomposition of 3D Convex Structuring Element in Morphological Operation for Parallel Processing Architectures*

Syng-Yup Ohn

Hankuk Aviation University,
Department of Computer and Information Engineering,
Seoul, Korea
syohn@hau.ac.kr

**Abstract.** Morphological operations with 3D images require a huge amount of computation. The decomposition of structuring elements used in the morphological operations such as dilation and erosion greatly reduces the amount of computation. This paper presents a new method for the decomposition of a 3D convex structuring element into a set of basis convex structuring elements. Furthermore, the decomposition method is applied to the neighborhood decomposition, in which each basis is one of the combinations of the origin voxel and its 26 neighborhood voxels. First, we derived the set of decomposition conditions on the lengths of the original and the basis convex structuring elements, and then the decomposition problem is converted into a linear integer optimization problem. The objective of the optimization is to minimize a cost function representing the optimal criterion of the parallel processing computer architecture on which the operation is performed. Thus, our method can be used to obtain the different optimal decompositions minimizing the amount of computation for different parallel processing computer architectures.

**Keywords:** mathematical morphology, dilation, erosion, structuring element, decomposition, convex polyhedron.

## 1 Introduction

Mathematical morphology provides powerful tools in the fields of image processing and computer vision. The basic operations of mathematical morphology are dilation and erosion, which stems from Minkowski addition and subtraction. An image processing task can be achieved by arranging dilation and erosion operations as well as set operations suitably for the goal of the task. The structuring elements used in dilation and erosion operations play the important role of the probe to detect and extract the geometrical characteristics of an input image, and one should choose the structuring element with the size and shape appropriate for the purpose of the operation[1], [2]. If a large structuring element is decomposed into a set of smaller structuring ele-

---

* This research was supported by the Internet Information Retrieval Research Center(IRC) in Hankuk Aviation University. IRC is a Regional Research Center of Kyounggi Province, designated by ITEP and Ministry of Commerce, Industry and Energy.

ments, the dilation of an image by the original structuring element can be achieved by a sequence of the dilation operations using the set of smaller structuring elements[3]. Generally, such a decomposition reduces the amount of computation required to perform dilation.

Due to their regularity and simplicity, morphological operations are often implemented on parallel processing architectures or VLSI for fast processing of images [6], [7]. Most parallel processing architectures are designed to efficiently perform local window operations within a window size of 3×3, and for pipelined architectures such as Cytocomputer, the size of the local window is restricted to 3×3[8]. Thus, the neighborhood decomposition of a structuring element, in which every component structuring element is a neighborhood structuring element consisting of a subset of the origin and its neighborhood pixels, is an important issue.

The decomposition of 2D structuring elements was first investigated by Zhuang and Haralick[4]. Xu[8] and Park[9] developed the methods to decompose a 2D convex- structuring element into a set of neighborhood structuring elements. Convex structuring elements are often used in morphological image processing because of its good geometrical characteristics[8].

3D mathematical morphology is shown to be effective in the areas of medical image processing and shape analysis[10]. Also, numerous 3D parallel image processors have been proposed and implemented for fast processing of 3D images. As in the 2D case, it is desirable and often inevitable to decompose 3D structuring elements for effective and efficient computations of 3D morphological operations. Much research efforts are concentrated on the 2D decomposition problems. However, 3D decomposition problems are yet to be explored. Furthermore, the amount of 3D image data is generally much larger than that of 2D image data, and the fast image operations are indispensable.

In this paper, we present the conditions for decomposition of a digital convex polyhedron into a set of basis digital convex polyhedra and propose a new technique for the neighborhood decomposition of 3D convex structuring elements. The structuring elements in a neighborhood decomposition are neighborhood structuring elements, each of which is a subset of a set consisting of the origin voxel and its 26 neighborhood voxels.

Generally, the optimal decompositions of a structuring element are different for different computer architectures. Since different parallel processing machines exploit different modes of parallelism, one should choose the decomposition which provides a feasible implementation, yet, requiring the minimum amount of computation on a particular parallel processing architecture. In this paper, we defined cost function, which represents the total amount of computation or time required to perform a sequence of dilations by the structuring elements in a decomposition. By minimizing the cost functions representing the different optimal criteria for different architectures or computing environments, the optimal decompositions for different cases can be obtained.

This paper is organized as follows. In Section 2, the terminologies and notations on 3D digital geometry are provided, and a digital convex polyhedron which is also a 3D convex structuring element is defined. In Section 3, we present the conditions for the decomposition of a digital convex polyhedron into the set of basis convex polyhedra. In Section 4, we propose the new technique for the neighborhood decomposition of

3D convex structuring element and show an example decomposition. Finally, Section 5 presents our conclusion

## 2 Preliminaries

In this section, the geometrical terms on 3D Euclidean space are introduced, and their 3D digital counterparts are analogously defined. In the following, $E^3$ is the 3D Euclidean space, and $Z^3$ is the 3D digital space in which each component of the position vector of a point is an integer. $Z^3$ is the 3D image space in which an image is represented as a set of the voxels in the volume occupied by objects.

### 2.1 Notations on 3D Euclidean Geometry

3D Euclidean hyperplane H normal to non-zero vector **d** and translation $t$ is the set of points **x** such that $\mathbf{d}\,\mathbf{x} = t$. H divides the entire 3D Euclidean space into two half spaces. The set of points in H and the half space in the direction of -**d** forms the closed half space L with outward normal **d** and translation $t$. L is the set of points $\mathbf{x} \in E^3$ such that $\mathbf{d}\,\mathbf{x} \le t$. If closed convex set $K \subset E^3$ exists only in L and $H \cap K \ne \emptyset$, then H is called a supporting hyperplane of K with outward normal **d**, and L is called the supporting half space of K with outward normal **d**. The closed bounded set K is called a convex polyhedron if it can be represented as the intersection of the set of closed half spaces.

### 2.2 Notations on 3D Digital Geometry and Definition of Digital Convex Polyhedron

The geometrical terms on 3D digital space is defined as follows. First, we define 26 principal directions, each of which is a non-zero 3D vector consisting of 3 components having the values of 1, -1, or 0, and they are denoted as $\mathbf{d}_i$, $i = 1, \ldots, 26$. Furthermore, the principal directions are categorized into type 1, 2, and 3 depending on the number of non-zero components in the vectors representing principal directions. For example, principal direction (1, 0, 0) is type 1, and (1, 0, -1) is type 2.

The digital hyperplane normal to principal direction $\mathbf{d}_i$ and translation $t \in Z$ is the set of digital points in analogous Euclidean hyperplane. The digital hyperplane is the set of points $\mathbf{x} \in Z^3$ such that $\mathbf{d}_i\,\mathbf{x} = t$. Note that a digital hyperplane sweeps the whole digital space while $t \in Z$ varies from minus infinity to plus infinity. Also, the digital half space with outward normal principal direction $\mathbf{d}_i$ and translation $t \in Z$ is the set of digital points in analogous Euclidean half space. Similarly, digital supporting half space and hyperplane are the sets of points in the analogous Euclidean counterparts.

3D chain code directions are defined on each of 26 hyperplanes with outward normal $\mathbf{d}_i$. 8, 6, and 4 chain code directions are defined on type 1, 2, and 3 hyperplanes, and they are ordered in clockwise sense by their orientations. See Fig. 1 for the examples of the chain code directions. The $j$ th chain code directions on the hyperplane with outward normal $\mathbf{d}_i$ are denoted as $D_{(i,j)}$.

The digital face of a set of points $S \subset Z^3$ with outward normal principal direction $\mathbf{d}_i$, denoted as $F(S, \mathbf{d}_i)$, is the set of the points shared by both S and the digital supporting hyperplane of S with outward normal $\mathbf{d}_i$. The digital half spaces, hyperplanes, and faces are also categorized into type 1, 2, and 3 depending on their outward normal principal directions.

The set of digital points $P \subset Z^3$ is called a digital convex polyhedron (DCPH), which is also a 3D convex structuring element, if P satisfies the following two conditions.

*i*) P is the intersection of 26 digital half spaces with outward normal principal direction $\mathbf{d}_i = 1, \ldots, 26$

*ii*) The boundary of each face of P, $F(P, \mathbf{d}_i)$, where $i = 1, \ldots, 26$, can be represented with a chain code in the form of

$$D_{(i,1)}^{l_1} D_{(i,2)}^{l_2} \ldots D_{(i,m)}^{l_m}, \tag{1}$$

where $l_j$ represents the number of repetition of chain code $D_{(i,j)}$ and $m$ depends on $i$.

Fig. 1 shows an example of a DCPH. In the figure, each set of the voxels covered by one of polygons A, B, and C forms a faces. The principal directions of the faces shown are $\mathbf{d}_1 = (0, 0, 1)$, $\mathbf{d}_{13} = (1, 0, -1)$, and $\mathbf{d}_{19} = (1, 1, 1)$. The face denoted as A/B/C is an example of type 1/2/3 faces. The set of arrows on each face represents the chain code directions on the face. The chain code directions are denoted as $D_{(i,1)}$, $D_{(i,2)}, \ldots, D_{(i,m)}$ in a clockwise sense starting with the directions marked with *. The number of chain code directions defined on type 1/2/3 face is 8/4/6.

Since a DCPH is the intersection of 26 digital supporting half space, it is bounded by 26 digital supporting hyperplane and enclosed by 26 faces. The face with outward normal principal direction $\mathbf{d}_i$ of DCPH P, represented as $F(P, \mathbf{d}_i)$, is a digital convex polygon on the supporting hyperplane of the DCPH with outward normal $\mathbf{d}_i$. A line segment or a vertex can be regarded as a degenerate form of a face.

The *j*th edge of the face with outward normal principal direction $\mathbf{d}_i$ on DCPH, denoted as $E(P, \mathbf{d}_i, j)$, is the set of points corresponding to the chain code run of $D_{(i,j)}$ in the boundary chain code of the face including the starting and ending points of the chain code run. Furthermore, $|E(P, \mathbf{d}_i, j)|$ denotes the length of digital edge $E(P, \mathbf{d}_i, j)$. i.e. $|E(P, \mathbf{d}_i, j)| = l_j$, where $D_{(i,1)}^{l_1} D_{(i,2)}^{l_2} \ldots D_{(i,j)}^{l_j} \ldots D_{(i,m)}^{l_m}$ is the chain code representation of the boundary of P.

## 3 Decompositions of 3D Digital Convex Polyhedrons

In this section, decomposition condition of a DCPH is derived. First, the condition for a DCPH to be decomposed into two basis DCPH's is derived in terms of their faces, each of which in turn forms a digital convex polygon. Then the relationships of the faces are further converted into the relationships on the lengths of edges in each face. We ignore the positions of DCPH's in the discussion of decomposition and only consider the shapes of DCPH's. The considerations on the position will be added later.

### 3.1 Decomposition Condition of Digital Convex Polyhedron

Suppose $P = Q \oplus R$, where P, Q, and R are DCPH's. Consider the *i* th face of P and the *i* th faces of Q and R, where the *i* th face of DCPH A denotes the face of A outward normal $d_i$. If we further suppose that the $i$ th face of Q consists of the subset of the points on the hyperplane with outward normal principal direction $d_i$ with translation $t_q$, then the points $\mathbf{u}$ on the face satisfies $d_i \mathbf{u} = t_q$, where $\mathbf{u} = (x_u, y_u, z_u)$ denotes a digital point. Similarly, for the points $\mathbf{v}$ on the $i$ th face of R, $d_i \mathbf{v} = t_r$. Since the dilation of two sets are defined as the set of the vector sums between the elements from each sets, the dilation of the $i$ th faces of Q and R consists of only the points $\mathbf{w}$ such that $d_i \mathbf{w} = t_q + t_r$. Furthermore, $d_i \mathbf{x} \leq t_q + t_r$ for the points $\mathbf{x} \in Q \oplus R$, and the dilation of the $i$ th faces of Q and R is on the supporting hyperplane with outward normal principal direction $d_i$ and translation $t_q + t_r$, Therefore, the $i$ th face of Q $\oplus$ R is equivalent to the $i$ th face of P, and

$$F(P, d_i) = F(Q, d_i) \oplus F(R, d_i) \tag{2}$$

for $i = 1, \ldots, 26$.

(2) is only a necessary condition for decomposition. It is not a sufficient condition since the dilations of some combinations of DCPH's result in the images shaped like a DCPH but with holes inside.

Since each face of a DCPH forms a digital convex polygon on a hyperplane, the condition for $F(P, d_i)$ to be decomposed into $F(Q, d_i)$ and $F(R, d_i)$ can be represented in terms of the lengths of the edges of the faces as follows.

$$|E(P, d_i, j)| = |E(Q, d_i, j)| + |E(R, d_i, j)| \tag{3}$$

for $j = 1, \ldots, m$ and $m$ depends on $i$. The decomposition condition for a convex polygon to be decomposed into two basis convex polygon can be proved similarly to the case of a convex polyhedron. In [8] and [9], such decomposition condition is exploited to decompose 2D convex structuring elements. In case of type 1 faces, the dilation of the two images shaped as diagonal line segments in different directions results in a rhombus shaped image with holes inside and such an image can not be a face of a DCPH. The condition to prevent the decomposition with the combination of only diagonal line segments in different orientations is added in the case of type 1 faces.

## 4 Decomposition of Convex Structuring Element into Neighborhood Structuring Elements

### 4.1 Decomposition of Convex Structuring Elements into a Set of Bases

The decomposition condition of a DCPH can be extended to a linear combination form. The condition for DCPH P to be decomposed into the combination of $a_1$ $Q_1$'s, $a_2$ $Q_2$'s, ..., $a_n$ $Q_n$'s such as

$$P = a_1 Q_1 \oplus a_2 Q_2 \oplus \ldots \oplus a_n Q_n, \tag{4}$$

where P, $Q_1$, $Q_2$, ..., and $Q_k$ are DCPH's, and $a_k Q_k$ represents $a_k$-fold dilation of $Q_k$, is

$$|E(P, d_i, j)| = a_1 |E(Q_1, d_i, j)| + a_2 |E(Q_2, d_i, j)| + \ldots + a_n |E(Q_n, d_i, j)| \tag{5}$$

for $i = 1, \ldots, 26$, and $j = 1, \ldots, m$, and $m = 8, 4, 6$ each for $\mathbf{d}_i$ of type 1, 2, 3 directions. Also, in the case of type 1 principal directions, the condition to prevent the decomposition with the combination of only diagonal line segment shaped images in different orientations is added in the case of type 1 faces. The above condition is called boundary condition for decomposition.

However, the dilations of some combinations of DCPH's result in convex shaped volumes with holes inside. For example, the dilation of two DCPH's each consisting of the set of the points on a hyperplane with outward normal principal directions (1, 1, 1) and (1, -1, 1) does not results in a DCPH but a convex shaped volume with holes inside. To prevent such a combination in a decomposition, a condition on the connectivity of voxels is added as follows. First, a DCPH is defined to be f-connected if two of the voxels in the DCPH share a face. Then the connectivity condition is that at least one f-connected DCPH should be included in the decomposition of an f-connected DCPH. For an f-connected DCPH, the boundary condition along with the connectivity condition serves as necessary and sufficient conditions for the DCPH to be composed into a set of basis DCPH's in terms of shape only. For a DCPH which is not f-connected, the connectivity condition is not necessary.

Finally, the positions of DCPH's in a decomposition is considered. Suppose A, B, and C to be the sets of 3D digital points such that $C = A \oplus B$. Then $\min_x(C) = \min_x(A) + \min_x(B)$, where $\min_x(C)$ denotes the minimum $x$-coordinate of the volume occupied by C, and similarly for $y$- and $z$-coordinates. Thus, if $P = a_1Q_1 \oplus a_2Q_2 \oplus \ldots \oplus a_nQ_n$, then $\min_x(P) = a_1\min_x(Q_1) + a_2\min_x(Q_2) + \ldots + a_n\min_x(Q_n)$, and similarly for $y$- and $z$-coordinates.

The boundary, position, and edge conditions are the necessary and sufficient conditions for decomposition. The $n$-tuple $(a_1, a_2, \ldots, a_n)$ which satisfies the three conditions determines a decomposition of DCPH P into the set of bases $\{Q_1, Q_2, \ldots, Q_n\}$, and the solution space of the $n$-tuples satisfying the three conditions contains all the possible decompositions of P into the set of bases.

### 4.2 Neighborhood Decomposition of 3D Convex Structuring Elements and Cost Function

The decomposition conditions for DCPH presented in the above can be immediately applied to the decomposition of a 3D convex structuring element into a set of 3D neighborhood structuring elements. A neighborhood structuring element is a 3D convex structuring element which can be contained in the window of size 3×3×3 centered on the origin. There are altogether 16,678 neighborhood structuring elements ($B_1$, $B_2 \ldots, B_{16678}$).

A cost function which represents the total processing cost or time required to perform the sequence of dilation operations with structuring elements of $a_1 Q_1$'s, $a_2 Q_2$'s, $\ldots, a_n Q_n$'s can be formulated as

$$\sum_{k=1}^{n} a_k c_k, \qquad (6)$$

where $c_k$ is the processing cost to perform a dilation operation with structuring element $Q_k$ with an input image. Generally, it is reasonable to assign a constant cost to each structuring element since the processing time for a dilation operation does not depend on the contents of an input image but on the size of the input image. A cost function can be used to represent the optimal criterion of decomposition for particular computer architecture on which the dilation is performed. The optimal decomposition for particular computer architecture is the one that minimizes the computation time or cost to perform dilation on the computer architecture, and different optimal decompositions can be obtained for different machine architectures.

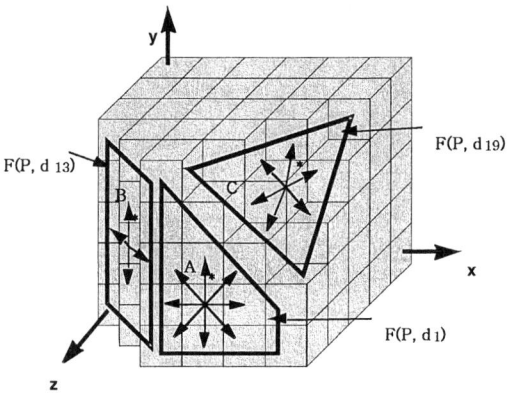

**Fig. 1.** Example DCPH P and chain code directions on some faces. Each set of the voxels covered by one of polygons A, B, and C forms a faces.

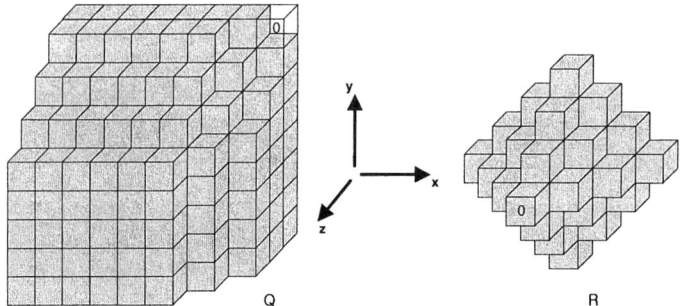

**Fig. 2.** Example DCPH Q and R. The arrows represent x, y, z directions and the volxels marked with 0 represent the origins.

Cyto type 3D parallel processors are expected to have the capability to perform a local operation within a 3×3×3 cube window in one step. In this case, the cost of every local basis structuring element is the same; therefore, let $c_k = 1$ for each $k$.

In a 3D parallel array architecture, a dilation can be performed by translating and ORing an input image. Such an architecture has the capability that it can shift a whole image to a neighboring position in one step in a parallel fashion. For such an architecture, the cost to perform a dilation operation with a structuring element is the number of required shifts of input image, and $c_k$ is the number of shifts of an input image required to perform a dilation operation with $Q_k$. The number of shifts depends on the topology of the connection among the processing elements in the array.

The solution $n$-tuple that minimizes a cost function and satisfies the three decomposition condition at the same time can be found by linear integer programming technique[11]. The objective function to be minimized is a cost function representing the optimal criterion of a computer architecture on which a dilation is performed. The constraints of the linear integer programming are the set of linear integer equations generated by the three decomposition conditions involving the original structuring element and the set of basis.

### 4.3 Decomposition Examples

Table 4 shows the decomposition results of the 3D convex structuring elements shown in Fig.1 and 2. 3D neighborhood structuring elements in the decompositions are listed in Table 1, 2 and 3. Also, in Table 4, the costs for performing dilations with the sequence of the structuring elements in the optimal neighborhood decompositions are compared to the costs with the original structuring elements.

**Table 1.** Neighborhood structuring elements used for the optimal neighborhood decomposition of P in Fig. 1. Each matrix shows a slice of a structuring element on a plane $z = i$. The y/x - coordinate of the first row/column of each matrix is 1, the second 0, and the third -1.

|  | $B_{17}$ | $B_{34}$ | $B_{44}$ | $B_{190}$ | $B_{480}$ | $B_{2019}$ | $B_{3938}$ |
|---|---|---|---|---|---|---|---|
| plane $z = 1$ | 0 0 0<br>0 0 0<br>0 0 0 | 0 0 0<br>0 0 0<br>0 0 0 | 0 0 0<br>0 1 0<br>0 0 0 | 0 0 0<br>0 0 1<br>0 0 0 | 0 1 0<br>0 1 1<br>0 0 0 | 0 0 1<br>0 0 0<br>0 0 0 | 0 0 1<br>0 0 1<br>0 0 1 |
| plane $z = 0$ | 0 0 0<br>0 0 1<br>0 0 0 | 0 1 0<br>0 1 0<br>0 0 0 | 0 0 0<br>1 1 0<br>0 0 0 | 0 0 0<br>0 1 1<br>0 0 0 | 0 1 1<br>0 1 1<br>0 0 0 | 0 1 1<br>0 0 0<br>0 0 0 | 0 1 1<br>0 1 1<br>0 1 1 |
| plane $z = -1$ | 0 0 0<br>0 0 0<br>0 0 0 | 0 0 0<br>0 0 0<br>0 0 0 | 0 0 0<br>0 0 0<br>0 0 0 | 0 0 0<br>0 0 0<br>0 0 0 | 0 0 0<br>0 0 0<br>0 0 0 | 0 0 0<br>0 0 0<br>0 0 0 | 0 0 0<br>0 0 0<br>0 0 0 |

**Table 2.** Neighborhood structuring elements used for the optimal neighborhood decomposition of Q in Fig. 2

|  | $B_0$ | $B_{88}$ | $B_{1646}$ |
|---|---|---|---|
| plane $z = 1$ | 0 0 0<br>0 0 0<br>0 0 0 | 0 0 0<br>0 1 0<br>0 0 0 | 0 0 0<br>0 0 0<br>0 0 0 |
| plane $z = 0$ | 0 0 0<br>0 0 0<br>0 0 0 | 0 1 0<br>1 1 1<br>0 1 0 | 0 0 0<br>0 1 0<br>0 0 0 |
| plane $z = -1$ | 0 0 0<br>0 1 0<br>0 0 0 | 0 0 0<br>0 0 0<br>0 0 0 | 0 1 0<br>1 1 1<br>0 1 0 |

**Table 3.** Neighborhood structuring elements used for the optimal neighborhood decomposition of R in Fig. 2

|  | $B_2$ | $B_8$ | $B_{30}$ | $B_{36}$ | $B_{42}$ | $B_{60}$ | $B_{68}$ |
|---|---|---|---|---|---|---|---|
| plane $z = 1$ | 0 0 0<br>0 0 0<br>0 0 0 | 0 0 0<br>0 0 0<br>0 0 0 | 0 0 0<br>0 0 0<br>0 0 0 | 0 0 0<br>0 1 0<br>0 0 0 | 0 0 0<br>0 0 0<br>0 0 0 | 0 0 0<br>0 1 0<br>0 0 0 | 0 0 0<br>0 1 0<br>0 0 0 |
| plane $z = 0$ | 0 0 0<br>0 0 0<br>0 1 0 | 0 0 0<br>1 0 0<br>0 0 0 | 0 0 0<br>0 1 0<br>0 1 0 | 0 1 0<br>0 1 0<br>0 0 0 | 0 0 0<br>1 1 0<br>0 0 0 | 0 0 0<br>0 1 1<br>0 0 0 | 0 1 0<br>0 1 1<br>0 0 0 |
| plane $z = -1$ | 0 0 0<br>0 0 0<br>0 0 0 | 0 0 0<br>0 0 0<br>0 0 0 | 0 0 0<br>0 0 0<br>0 0 0 | 0 0 0<br>0 0 0<br>0 0 0 | 0 0 0<br>0 0 0<br>0 0 0 | 0 0 0<br>0 0 0<br>0 0 0 | 0 0 0<br>0 0 0<br>0 0 0 |
|  | $B_{147}$ | $B_{154}$ | $B_{9641}$ | $B_{9646}$ | $B_{9730}$ | $B_{10409}$ |  |
| plane $z = 1$ | 0 0 0<br>0 0 0<br>0 0 0 | 0 0 0<br>0 0 0<br>0 0 0 | 0 0 0<br>1 0 0<br>1 0 0 | 0 0 0<br>1 0 0<br>1 0 0 | 0 0 0<br>0 0 0<br>1 1 0 | 0 0 0<br>0 0 0<br>1 1 1 |  |
| plane $z = 0$ | 0 0 0<br>0 0 0<br>1 0 0 | 0 0 0<br>1 1 0<br>1 1 0 | 0 0 0<br>1 1 0<br>1 1 0 | 1 0 0<br>1 1 0<br>1 1 0 | 0 0 0<br>1 1 0<br>1 1 0 | 0 0 0<br>1 1 1<br>1 1 1 |  |
| plane $z = -1$ | 0 0 0<br>0 0 0<br>0 0 0 | 0 0 0<br>0 0 0<br>0 0 0 | 0 0 0<br>0 0 0<br>0 0 0 | 0 0 0<br>0 0 0<br>0 0 0 | 0 0 0<br>0 0 0<br>0 0 0 | 0 0 0<br>0 0 0<br>0 0 0 |  |

**Table 4.** Optimal neighborhood decompositions of P, Q, R and the costs of performing dilation

|  | Type of Architecture | Optimal Decomposition | Original | Decomposition |
|---|---|---|---|---|
| P | Cytocomputer | $3B_{480} \oplus B_{2019} \oplus B_{3938}$ | NA | 5 stages |
|  | Parallel Array Processor | $2B_{17} \oplus 2B_{34} \oplus 2B_{44} \oplus 3B_{480}$ | 1350 shifts | 35 shifts |
| Q | Cytocomputer | $3B_{1646}$ | NA | 3 stages |
|  | Parallel Array Processor | $3B_0 \oplus 3B_{88}$ | 186 shifts | 18 shifts |
| R | Cytocomputer | $B_{147} \oplus 2B_{154} \oplus B_{9641} \oplus B_{9646} \oplus B_{9730} \oplus B_{10409}$ | NA | 7 stages |
|  | Parallel Array Processor | $3B_2 \oplus 2B_8 \oplus 4B_{30} \oplus 2B_{36} \oplus 5B_{42} \oplus B_{60} \oplus B_{68}$ | 2358 shifts | 23 shifts |

## 5 Conclusion

In this paper, a new method to decompose 3D convex structuring element used in morphological operation is proposed. First, the decomposition condition for digital convex polyhedron is derived in terms of the length of edges of original and basis convex polyhedrons. The condition is applied to the decomposition of a convex structuring element into a set of neighborhood structuring elements. Furthermore, we defined cost function to represent the different optimal criteria on the decomposition for different parallel computer architectures. The optimal decompositions, which satisfy the decomposition condition and minimize the cost function at the same time, can be found by linear integer programming. Thanks to the cost function, our method can be used to obtain different optimal neighborhood decompositions for different cases.

# References

1. Serra, J.: Introduction to Mathematical Morphology. Computer Vision, Graphics and Image Processing 35 (1986) 285-305
2. Serra, J.: Image Analysis and Mathematical Morphology. Academic Press London(1982)
3. Haralick, R. M., Sternberg, S.R., Zhuang, X.: Image Analysis Using Mathematical Morphology. IEEE Trans. on PAMI 9 (1987) 532-550
4. Zhuang, X., Haralick, R. M.: Morphological Structuring Element Decomposition. Computer Vision, Graphics and Image Processing 35 (1986) 370-382
5. Dadda, L.; Parallel algorithms and architectures for CPUs and dedicated processors: development and trends Algorithms and Architectures for Parallel Processing ICAPP 95 vol. 2 (1995) 939 - 948
6. Svolos, A.I.; Konstantopoulos, C.G.; Kaklamanis, C.: Efficient Binary Morphological Algorithms on a Massively Parallel Processor. International Parallel and Distributed Processing Symposium 2000 Proceedings (2000) 281 - 286
7. York, G., Managuli, R., Kim, Y.: Fast Binary and Grayscale Mathematical Morphology on VLIW. Proc. Of SPIE: Real-Time Imaging IV (1999) 45–55
8. Levialdi, S.: Computer Architectures for Image Analysis. 9th International Conference on Pattern Recognition vol.2 (1988) 1148 - 1158
9. Xu, J.: Decomposition of Convex Polygonal Morphological Structuring Elements into Neighborhood Subsets. IEEE Trans. on PAMI 13 (1991) 153-162.
10. Park, H., Chin, R.T,: Optimal Decomposition of Convex Morphological Structuring Elements for 4-connected Parallel Array Processors. IEEE Trans. on PAMI 16 (1994) 304-313
11. Aykac, D., Hoffman, E.A., McLennan, G., Reinhardt, J.M.: Segmentation and analysis of the human airway tree from three-dimensional X-ray CT images., IEEE Transactions on Medical Imaging **22** (2003) 940 - 950
12. Syslo, M. M., Deo, N., Kowalik, J. S.: Discrete Optimization Algorithms. Prentice Hall Englewood Cliff (1983)

# Soft-Switching Adaptive Technique of Impulsive Noise Removal in Color Images

Bogdan Smolka[1,*] and Konstantinos N. Plataniotis[2]

[1] Silesian University of Technology, Department of Automatic Control,
Akademicka 16 Str, 44-100 Gliwice, Poland
bsmolka@ia.polsl.gliwice.pl
[2] The Edward S. Rogers Sr. Department of Electrical and Computer Engineering, University of Toronto, 10 King's College Road, Toronto ON, M5S 3G4, Canada

**Abstract.** In this paper a novel class of filters designed for the removal of impulsive noise in color images is presented. The proposed filter family is based on the kernel function which regulates the noise suppression properties of the proposed filtering scheme. The comparison of the new filtering method with standard techniques used for impulsive noise removal indicates superior noise removal capabilities and excellent structure preserving properties.

## 1 Introduction

During image *formation, acquisition, storage* and *transmission* many types of distorsions limit the quality of digital images. Transmission errors, periodic or random motion of the camera system during exposure, electronic instability of the image signal, electromagnetic interferences from natural or man-made sources, sensor malfunctions, optic imperfections, electronics interference or aging of the storage material all disturb the image quality.

In many practical situations, images are corrupted by the so called *impulsive noise* caused mainly either by faulty image sensors or due to transmission errors. In this paper we address the problem of impulsive noise removal in color images and propose an efficient technique capable of removing the impulsive noise and preserving important image features.

## 2 Vector Median Based Filters

Mathematically, a $N_1 \times N_2$ multichannel image is a mapping $\mathbb{Z}^l \rightarrow \mathbb{Z}^m$ representing a two-dimensional matrix of three-component samples (pixels), $\mathbf{x}_i = (x_{i1}, x_{i2}, \ldots, x_{im}) \in \mathbb{Z}^l$, where $l$ is the image domain dimension and $m$ denotes the number of channels, (in the case of standard color images, parameters $l$ and $m$ are equal to 2 and 3, respectively). Components $x_{ik}$, for $k = 1, 2, \ldots, m$ and $i = 1, 2, \ldots, N$, $N = N_1 \cdot N_2$, represent the color channel values quantified into the integer domain, [1].

---

[*] This research has been supported by the KBN grant 4T11F01824.

The majority of the nonlinear, multichannel filters are based on the ordering of vectors in a sliding filter window. The output of these filters is defined as the lowest ranked vector according to a specific vector ordering technique, [2,3].

Let the color images be represented in the commonly used RGB color space and let $\mathbf{x}_1, \mathbf{x}_2, \ldots, \mathbf{x}_n$ be $n$ samples from the sliding filter window $W$, with $\mathbf{x}_1$ being the central pixel in $W$. Each of the $\mathbf{x}_i$ is an $m$-dimensional vector. The goal of the vector ordering is to arrange the set of $n$ vectors $\{\mathbf{x}_1, \mathbf{x}_2, \ldots, \mathbf{x}_n\}$ belonging to $W$ using some sorting criterion.

In [3,4] the ordering based on the cumulative distance function has been proposed: $R(\mathbf{x}_i) = \sum_{j=1}^{n} \rho(\mathbf{x}_i, \mathbf{x}_j)$, where $\rho(\mathbf{x}_i, \mathbf{x}_j)$ is a function of the distance among $\mathbf{x}_i$ and $\mathbf{x}_j$. The increasing ordering of the scalar quantities $\{R_1, \ldots, R_n\}$ generates the ordered set of vectors $\{\mathbf{x}_{(1)}, \mathbf{x}_{(2)}, \ldots, \mathbf{x}_{(n)}\}$.

One of the most important noise reduction filter is the vector median, [2]. Given a set $W$ of $n$ vectors, the vector median of the set is defined as $\mathbf{x}_{(1)} \in W$ satisfying $\sum_j \|\mathbf{x}_{(1)} - x_j\| \leq \sum_j \|\mathbf{x}_i - \mathbf{x}_j\|$.

The orientation difference between two vectors can also be used as their dissimilarity measure. This so-called vector angle criterion is used by the *Basic Directional Filter* (BDF), to remove vectors with atypical directions, [5]. Other techniques like the *Directional Distance Filter* DDF, [5,6,7,8] and their modifications, [9,10,16] combine the distance and angular criteria to achieve better noise suppression results,.

## 3 Proposed Filtering Design

The well known local statistic filters constitute a class of linear minimum mean squared error estimators, based on the non-stationarity of the signal and the noise model, [11,12]. These filters make use of the local mean and the variance of the input set $W$ and define the filter output for the gray-scale images as

$$y_i = \hat{x}_i + \alpha(x_i - \hat{x}_i) = \alpha x_i + (1 - \alpha)\hat{x}_i, \tag{1}$$

where $\hat{x}_i$ is the arithmetic mean of the image pixels belonging to the filter window $W$ centered at pixel position $i$ and $\alpha$ is a filter parameter usually estimated through, [13]

$$\alpha = \frac{\sigma_x^2}{\sigma_n^2 + \sigma_x^2}, \quad \hat{x}_i = \frac{1}{n}\sum_{k=1}^{n} x_k, \quad \nu^2 = \frac{1}{n}\sum_{k=1}^{n}(x_k - \hat{x}_i)^2, x_k \in W, \tag{2}$$

$$\sigma_x^2 = \max\{0, \nu^2 - \sigma_n^2\}, \quad \alpha = \max\{0, 1 - \sigma_n^2/\nu^2\}, \tag{3}$$

where $\nu^2$ is the local variance calculated from the samples in the filter window and $\sigma_n^2$ is the estimate of the variance of the noise process. If $\nu \gg \sigma_n$, then $\alpha \approx 1$ and practically no changes are introduced. When $\nu < \sigma_n$, then $\alpha = 0$ and the central pixel is replaced with the local mean. In this way, the filter smooths with the local mean, when the noise is not very intensive and leaves the pixel value unchanged when a strong signal activity is detected. The major drawback of this filter is that it **fails to remove impulses** and leaves noise in the vicinity of high gradient image features.

Equation (1) can be rewritten using the notation $x_i = x_1$, [13] as

$$y_1 = \alpha x_i + (1-\alpha)\hat{x}_i = \alpha x_1 + (1-\alpha)\hat{x}_1 = (1-\alpha)(\psi_1 x_1 + x_2 + \ldots + x_n)/n, \quad (4)$$

with $\psi_1 = (1-\alpha+n\alpha)/(1-\alpha)$ and in this way the local statistic filter (1) is reduced to the *central weighted average*, with a weighting coefficient $\psi_1$.

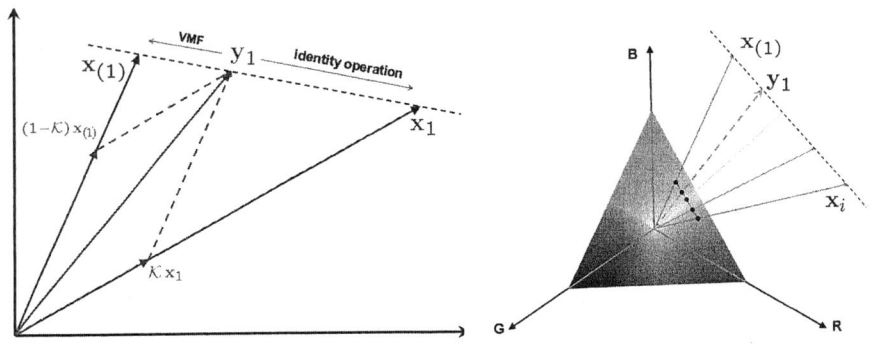

**Fig. 1.** Vector $\mathbf{y}_i$ lies on the line connecting the vector $\mathbf{x}_i$ and $\mathbf{x}_{(1)}$ in the RGB space

**Table 1.** Kernel functions, $(x = \langle -1, 1\rangle, h = \langle 0, \infty\rangle, [f(x)]^+ = f(x)$ for $x \geq 0$ and $0$ if $x < 0$) used for the construction of the proposed filter (**a**) and its efficiency in comparison with VMF, BDF and DDF, (**b**)

a)

| Kernel | $K(x)$ | $\mathcal{K}(x) = \gamma_h K(x)$ |
|---|---|---|
| (L) | $e^{-\lvert\frac{x}{h}\rvert}$ | $\frac{1}{2h} e^{-\lvert\frac{x}{h}\rvert}$ |
| (G) | $e^{-\frac{x^2}{2h^2}}$ | $\frac{1}{\sqrt{2\pi}h} e^{-\frac{x^2}{2h^2}}$ |
| (C) | $\frac{1}{1+\frac{x^2}{h^2}}$ | $\frac{1}{\pi h}\frac{1}{1+\frac{x^2}{h^2}}$ |
| (T) | $[1-\lvert\frac{x}{h}\rvert]^+$ | $\left[\frac{h(1-\lvert\frac{x}{h}\rvert)}{2h-1}\right]^+$ |
| (E) | $[1-\frac{x^2}{h^2}]^+$ | $\left[\frac{3h^2(1-\frac{x^2}{h^2})}{6h^2-2}\right]^+$ |

b)

| Filtering efficiency, (PSNR, [dB] LENA) | | | | | | |
|---|---|---|---|---|---|---|
| Noise | $p=1\%$ | | $p=3\%$ | | $p=5\%$ | |
| Kernel | $h_{\text{opt}}$ | $h_{\text{est}}$ | $h_{\text{opt}}$ | $h_{\text{est}}$ | $h_{\text{opt}}$ | $h_{\text{est}}$ |
| L | 40.75 | 40.70 | 37.92 | 37.90 | 36.38 | 36.35 |
| G | 39.22 | 39.22 | 36.96 | 36.95 | 35.68 | 35.67 |
| C | 39.65 | 39.39 | 37.11 | 37.03 | 35.72 | 35.67 |
| T | 40.46 | 40.45 | 37.76 | 37.76 | 36.27 | 36.27 |
| E | 40.87 | 40.81 | 37.96 | 37.94 | 36.39 | 36.34 |
| VMF | 33.33 | | 32.94 | | 32.58 | |
| DDF | 32.90 | | 32.72 | | 32.25 | |
| BDF | 32.04 | | 31.81 | | 31.14 | |

The structure of the new filter called *Kernel based VMF* (KVMF) is similar to the presented above approach. However, as our aim is to construct a filter capable of removing impulsive noise, instead of the mean value, the VMF output is utilized and the noise intensity estimation mechanism is accomplished through the similarity function, which can be viewed as kernel function, known from the nonparametric probability density estimation, (Tab. 1a).

In this way, the proposed technique is a **compromise** between the VMF and the identity operation. When an impulse is present, then it is detected by the kernel $\mathcal{K} = f(\|\mathbf{x}_1 - \mathbf{x}_{(1)}\|)$, which is a function of the distance between the central pixel $\mathbf{x}_i = \mathbf{x}_1$ and the vector median $\mathbf{x}_{(1)}$, and the output $\mathbf{y}_i$ is close to the VMF. If the central pixel is not disturbed by the noise process then the kernel function is close to 1 and the output is near to the original value $\mathbf{x}_1$. If the central pixel in $W$ $\mathbf{x}_i$ is denoted as $\mathbf{x}_1$ and the vector norm as $\|\cdot\|$, then

$$\mathbf{y}_i = \mathbf{x}_{(1)} + \mathcal{K}\left(\mathbf{x}_1, \mathbf{x}_{(1)}\right) \cdot \left(\mathbf{x}_1 - \mathbf{x}_{(1)}\right) = \mathcal{K}\mathbf{x}_1 + (1-\mathcal{K})\mathbf{x}_{(1)}, \quad (5)$$

where $\mathcal{K} = f\left(\|\mathbf{x}_1 - \mathbf{x}_{(1)}\|\right)$, which is quite similar to (1).

If $\{\mathbf{x}_{(1)}, \mathbf{x}_{(2)}, \ldots, \mathbf{x}_i, \ldots, \mathbf{x}_{(n)}\}$ denotes the ordered set of pixels in $W$, then the weighted structure corresponding to (4) is $\{(1-\mathcal{K})\mathbf{x}_{(1)}, \ldots, \mathcal{K}\mathbf{x}_1, \ldots, \mathbf{x}_{(n)}\}$.

It is interesting to observe that the filter output $\mathbf{y}_i$ lies on the line joining the vectors $\mathbf{x}_i$ ($\mathbf{x}_1$) and $\mathbf{x}_{(1)}$ and depending on the value of the kernel $\mathcal{K}$ it slides from the identity operation and the vector median, (Fig. 1).

The proposed structure can be seen as a modification of the known techniques used for the suppression of the Gaussian noise. In the proposed technique we replace the mean of the pixels in $W$ with the vector median and such an approach proves to be capable of removing strong impulsive noise while preserving important image features like edges, corners and texture.

## 4  Experimental Results

The noise modelling and evaluation of the efficiency of noise removal methods using the widely used test images allows the objective comparison of the noisy, restored and original images.

In this paper we assume a simple *salt & pepper* noise model, [3,6,14]

$$\mathbf{x}_i = \begin{cases} \{v_{i_1}, o_{i_2}, o_{i_3}\}, \text{ with probability } p, \\ \{o_{i_1}, v_{i_2}, o_{i_3}\}, \text{ with probability } p, \\ \{o_{i_1}, o_{i_2}, v_{i_3}\}, \text{ with probability } p, \end{cases} \quad (6)$$

where $\mathbf{x}_i$ represents the pixel in the corrupted image, $\mathbf{o}_i = \{o_{i_1}, o_{i_2}, o_{i_3}\}$ represents the original sample and $v_{i_1}, v_{i_2}, v_{i_3}$ are random, uncorrelated variables taking the value 0 or 250, with equal probability. The impulsive noise suppression efficiency was measured using the commonly used PSNR image quality measure

$$PSNR = 20\log_{10}\left(\frac{255}{\sqrt{MSE}}\right), \quad MSE = \frac{\sum_{i=1}^{N}\sum_{k=1}^{m}(x_{ik} - o_{ik})^2}{Nm}. \quad (7)$$

The efficiency of the proposed filtering approach is summarized in Tab. 1 and also presented in Fig. 2. As can be seen the dependence on the kind of the kernel function is not, as expected, very strong. However, the main problem is to find an adaptive optimal bandwidth parameter $h$, as the proper setting of the bandwidth guarantees good performance of the proposed filtering design.

The experimentally found *rule of thumb* for the value of $h$ called $h_{est}$ is: $h_{est} = \gamma_1/\sqrt{\hat{\sigma}}$, where $\hat{\sigma}$ is the mean value of the approximation of variance, [15] calculated using the whole image: $\hat{\sigma}^2 = \sum_{i=1}^{N}(x_i - \hat{x}_i)^2/8N^2$ or randomly selected image pixels and $\gamma_1$ is the coefficient taken from Tab. 1.

The comparison of the efficiency of the proposed scheme in terms of PSNR for the optimal values of $h$ and estimated by the developed *rule of thumb* is shown in Tab. 1 and Fig. 4. In the corner of the Fig. 4 the magnified part of the plot shows the excellent performance of the proposed bandwidth estimator. The dotted lines represent the best possible PSNR values and the continuous line show the PSNR obtained with the proposed estimation of the kernel bandwidth. Practically the $h_{est}$ yields the best possible impulsive noise attenuation, (see also the comparison in Tab. 1).

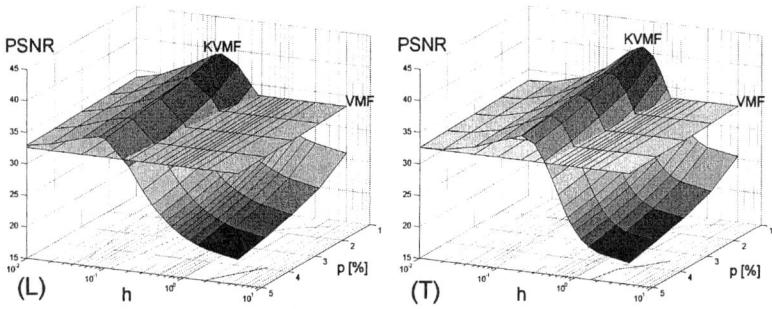

**Fig. 2.** Dependence of the PSNR on the $h$ parameter for the KVMF with the L and T kernels in comparison with the VMV for $p$ ranging from 1% to 5%, (*LENA* image)

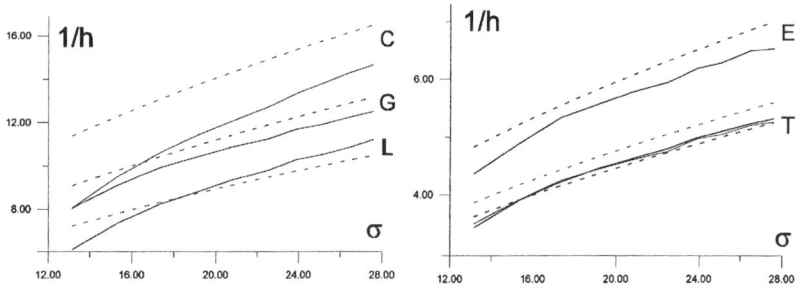

**Fig. 3.** Comparison of the estimated, (dashed line) and optimal bandwidth, (solid line) as functions of the noise intensity expressed through $\sigma$ for the *LENA* image

The illustrative examples depicted in Fig. 6 show that the proposed filter efficiently removes the impulses and preserves edges and small image details. Additionally due to its smoothing nature it is also able to suppress slightly the Gaussian noise present in natural images, (see Fig. 5).

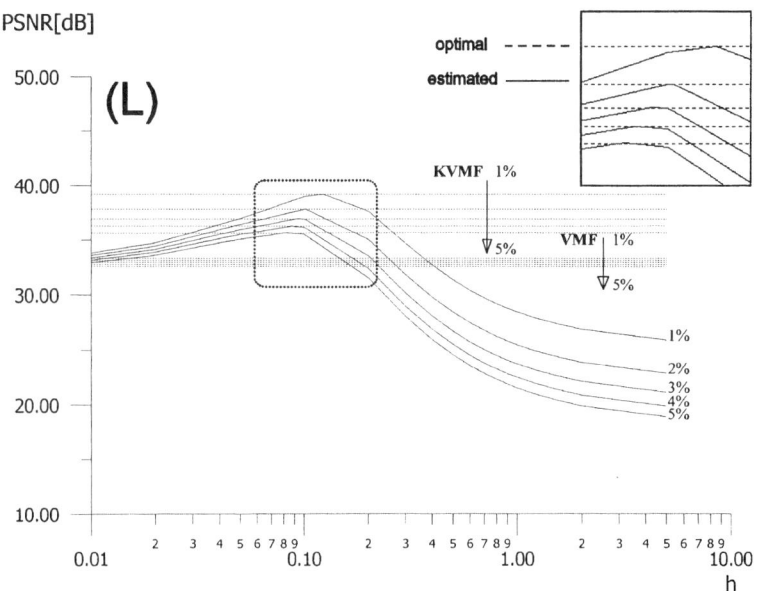

**Fig. 4.** Dependence of the PSNR on the $h$ parameter of the L kernel, for $p = 1 - 5\%$ in comparison with the standard VMF, (*LENA* image). The dotted lines indicate the optimal, (best possible) values of PSNR achievable by the KVMF filter and the VMF and the continuous line presents the achieved PSNR using the $h_{est}$ bandwidth.

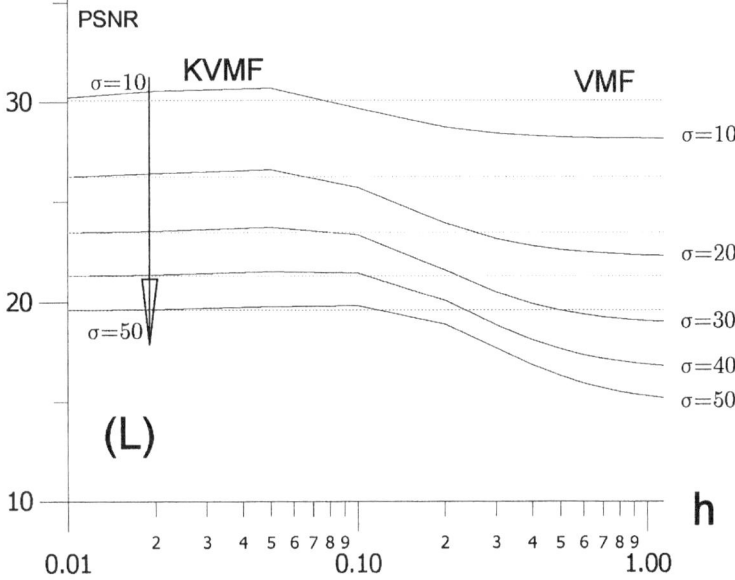

**Fig. 5.** Dependence of PSNR on the $h$ parameter of the L kernel, for the Gaussian noise of $\sigma = 10 - 50$, (solid line) in comparison with the VMF, (dotted line)

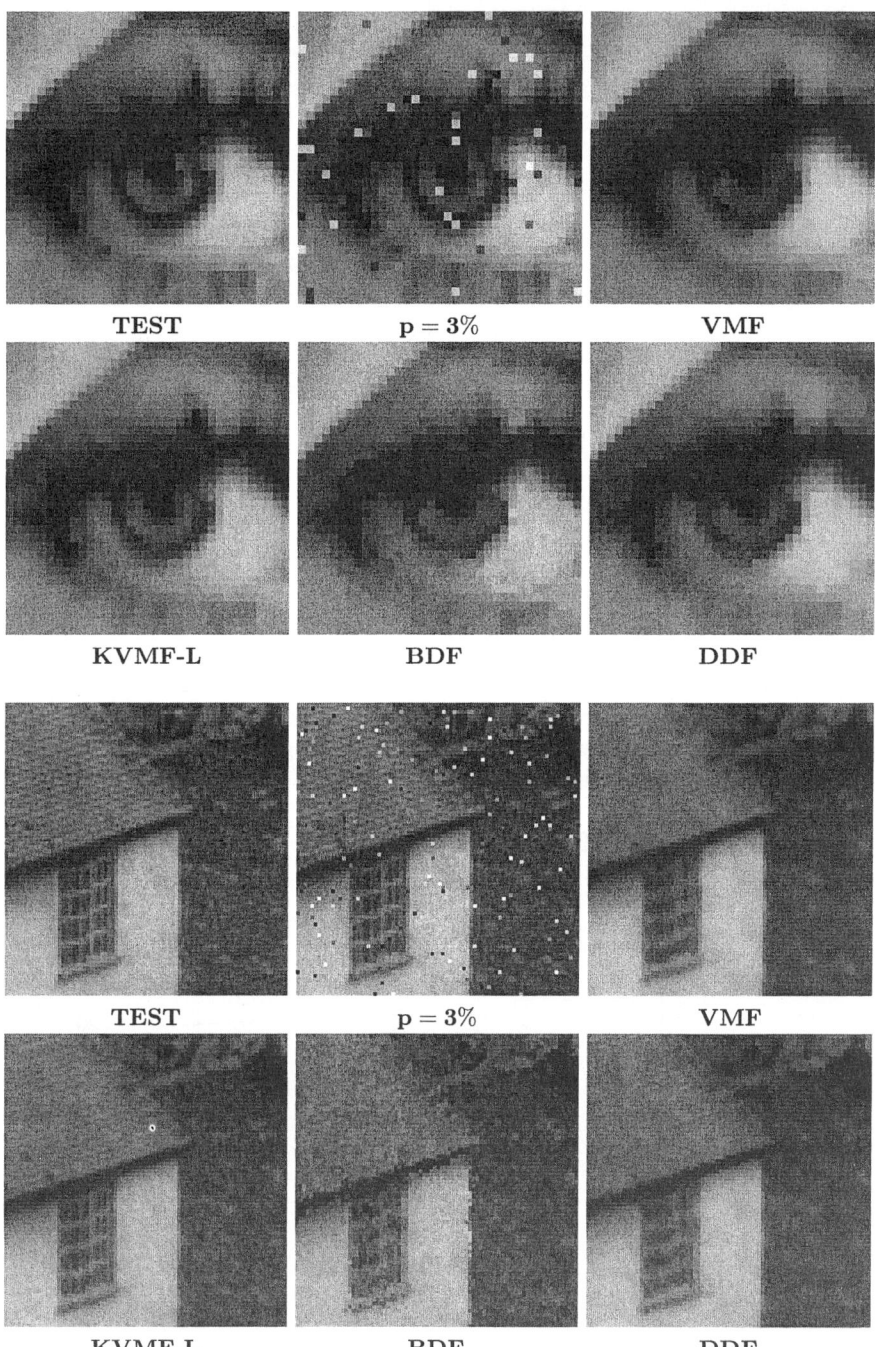

**Fig. 6.** Comparison of the filtering efficiency of the proposed filter with the Laplace kernel (KVMF-L) with the VMF, BDF and DDF methods

## 5 Conclusion

In the paper an adaptive soft-switching scheme based on the vector median and similarity function has been presented. The proposed filtering structure is superior to the standard filtering schemes and can be applied for the removal of impulsive noise in natural images. It is relatively fast and the proposed bandwidth estimator enables automatic filtering independent of noise intensity.

## References

1. Lukac R.: Adaptive Color Image Filtering Based on Center-Weighted Vector Directional Filters. Multidimensional Systems and Signal Processing, Vol. 15, No. 2, (2004) 169-196
2. Astola, J., Haavisto, P., Neuvo, Y.: Vector Median Filters. Proc. of IEEE, Vol. 78, No. 4, (1990) 678-689,
3. Pitas, I., Tsakalides, P.: Multivariate Ordering in Color Image Processing. IEEE Trans. on Circuits and Systems for Video Technology, Vol. 1, No. 3, (1991) 247-256
4. Tang, K., Astola, J., Neuvo, Y.: Nonlinear Multivariate Image Filtering Techniques. IEEE Trans. on Image Processing, Vol. 4, (1995) 788-798
5. Trahanias, P.E., Venetsanopoulos, A.N.: Vector Directional Filters: a New Class of Multichannel Image Processing Filters. IEEE Trans. on Image Processing, Vol. 2, No. 4, (1993) 528-534
6. Plataniotis, K.N., Venetsanopoulos, A.N.: Color Image Processing and Applications. Springer Verlag, (2000)
7. Lukac, R.: Optimised Directional Distance Filter. Machine Graphics and Vision, Vol. 11, No. 2-3, (2002) 311-326
8. Lukac R.: Vector LUM Smoothers as Impulse Detector for Color Images. Proc. of European Conference on Circuit Theory and Design, (ECCTD'01) in Espoo, Finland, August 28-31, III, (2001) 137-140
9. Smolka, B., Plataniotis, K.N., Chydzinski, A., Szczepanski, M., Venetsanopulos, A.N., Wojciechowski, K.: Self-Adaptive Algorithm of Impulsive Noise Reduction in Color Images. Pattern Recognition, Vol. 35, (2002) 1771-1784
10. Smolka, B., Lukac, R., Chydzinski, A., Plataniotis, K.N., Wojciechowski, K.: Fast Adaptive Similarity Based Impulsive Noise Reduction Filter. Real-Time Imaging, Vol. 9, No. 4, (2003) 261-276
11. Lee, J.S.: Digital Image Enhancement and Noise Filtering by use of Local Statistics. IEEE Trans. on PAMI, Vol. 2, No. 2, (1980) 165-168
12. Kuan, D.T., Sawchuk, A.A., Strand, T.C., Chavel, P.: Adaptive Noise Smoothing Filter for Images with Signal-Dependent Noise. IEEE Trans. on PAMI, Vol. 7, No. 2, (1985) 165-177
13. Sun, T., Gabbouj, M., Neuvo, Y.: Adaptive L-Filters with Applications in Signal and Image Processing. Signal Processing, Vol. 38, (1994) 331-344
14. Smolka, B., Plataniotis, K.N., Venetsanopoulos, A.N., Nonlinear Techniques for Color Image Processing. In: Nonlinear Signal and Image Processing: Theory, Methods, and Applications, CRC Press, (2004) 445-505
15. Lukac, R.: Adaptive Vector Median Filtering. Pattern Recognition Letters, Vol. 24, No. 12, (2003) 1889-1899
16. Lukac, R., Fischer, V., Motyl, G., Drutarovsky, M.: Adaptive Video Filtering Framework. International Journal of Imaging Systems and Technology, Vol. 14, No. 6, (2004) 223-237

# Color Indexing by Nonparametric Statistics

Ian Fraser[1] and Michael Greenspan[1,2]

[1] School of Computing
[2] Dept. Electrical and Computer Engineering,
Queen's University, Kingston, Ontario, Canada
michael.greenspan@queensu.ca

**Abstract.** A method for color indexing is proposed that is based upon nonparametric statistical techniques. Nonparametrics compare the ordinal rankings of sample populations, and maintain their significance when the underlying populations are not Normally distributed. The method differs from previous approaches to color indexing, in that it does not involve histogramming. Principal component analysis is performed to extract the three orthogonal axes of maximum dispersion for a given color signature. These axes are then used to select Lipschitz embeddings to generate sets of scalars that combine all color channel information. These scalar sets are compared against a ranked database of such scalars using the Moses test for variance. On the resulting top matches, the Wilcoxon test of central tendency is applied to yield the best overall match.

The method has been tested extensively on a number of image databases, and has been compared against eight standard histogram methods using four color space transformations. The tests have shown its performance to be competitive with, and in certain cases superior to, the best histogram methods. The technique also shows a greater robustness to noise than all histogram methods, with a noise robustness comparable to that of the more expensive Variable Kernel Density method.

## 1 Introduction

The use of histograms to compare and index images based upon their color content was first proposed by Ballard and Swain [10]. Histogramming is conceptually straightforward and enhancements have aimed to improve robustness, particularly to illumination changes, by empirically comparing the effects of different combinations of color space mappings and histogram similarity metrics. In [4] several invariant color models such as normalized rgb and Hue are proposed to improve robustness to illumination effects. Color constancy has also been proposed for illumination invariance [3]. Several comparision metrics such as Earth Mover's Distance, Jessen Divergence and Kolmogorov-Smirnov Distance, etc., are tested in [9].

We propose an alternative to histograms for color indexing that is based upon nonparametric statistical methods (*Nonparametrics*). Nonparametrics are an elegant class of technique that assume very little about the underlying population. In particular, a Gaussian distribution is not assumed, nor for that matter is any

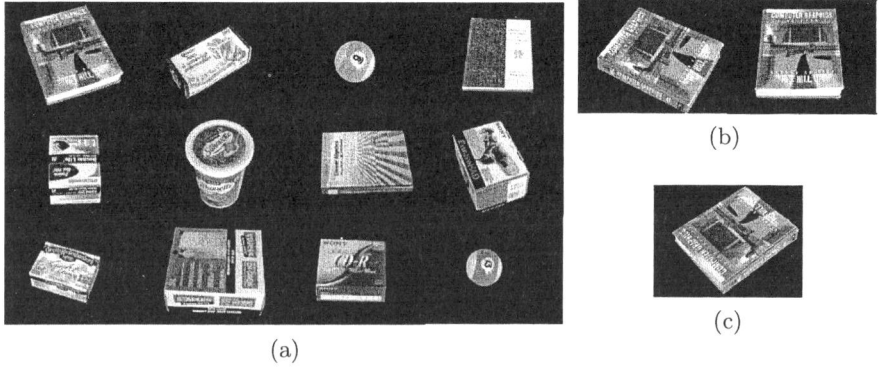

**Fig. 1.** Database Images: a) 1 of 3 database images of each object, b) remaining 2 database images for top left object, c) test image for top left object

other parametric form. This becomes important when comparing color values, which can be arbitrarily distributed throughout the color space. Nonparametrics use ordinal rankings to infer statistical properties from two sample distributions. Ranking techniques have been previously applied to provide robustness in visual correlation [1], by ranking the correlation windows and applying a distance metric to the resulting rank matrices. While histograms themselves are considered a nonparametric representation, to our knowledge nonparmetric statistical ranking methods have not previously been applied to color comparisons.

## 2 Nonparametrics

The goal of Nonparametrics is to draw inferences from test statistics derived from an ordinal ranking of the sample populations under comparison. Even if the underlying populations are not normally distributed, their rank statistics will be predictable if the two populations are similar. Nonparametric counterparts exist for most classical statistical tests, such as the Student $t$-test and the $F$-test.

The Wilcoxon Rank Sum test is the nonparametric alternative to the two sample $t$-test. If the samples are drawn from the same population, then they will be similar, and this is examined by jointly ranking them. If the sum of the ranks of the first sample population is significantly larger or smaller than that of the second, then there is evidence to reject the hypothesis that the samples follow the same distribution.

Let the two respective sample populations be denoted as $\mathbf{X} = \{X_i\}_1^m$ and $\mathbf{Y} = \{Y_i\}_1^n$, and let $\mathbf{Z} = \mathbf{X} \cup \mathbf{Y} = \{Z_i\}_1^{m+n}$ be ordered such that $Z_i \leq Z_j \iff i < j$. The quantities $R_X$ and $R_Y$ are then defined as the sum of the ranks of $\mathbf{Z}$ whose elements originated from $\mathbf{X}$ or $\mathbf{Y}$ respectively, i.e., $R_X = \Sigma_{i=1}^{m+n}(i \mid Z_i \in \mathbf{X})$. The test statistic is then defined as $W = (R_X - \mu)/\sigma$, where $\mu$ and $\sigma$ are the respective mean and standard deviation of all ranks in $\mathbf{Z}$. When there are no ties in the ranks (i.e., no two $Z_i$ are identical) the expressions for $\mu$ and $\sigma$ are derived from combinatorics [7] as $\mu = n(m+n+1)/2$ and $\sigma = [mn(m+n+1)/12]^{1/2}$.

When ties exist, a correction factor is subtracted from $\sigma$ to compensate for the expected reduction in variance.

Whereas the Wilcoxon is a measure of central tendency, the Moses Ranklike Test uses similar concepts to compare the relative dispersion of two populations, and is analogous to the $F$-test. The Moses randomly partitions the data from each of $\mathbf{X}$ and $\mathbf{Y}$ into groupings of size $k$. In the case where $k$ unevenly divides the number of observations, any leftovers are discarded. The variance is then found for each of the resulting groupings. This set of variances for the groupings of the sample populations forms two new distributions, i.e., $\mathbf{C}$ for $\mathbf{X}$ and $\mathbf{D}$ for $\mathbf{Y}$. The distribution $\mathbf{C}$ is calculated from the $m'$ groupings of $\mathbf{X}$ as follows. Define $C_1, \ldots, C_{m'}$ by $C_i = \sum_{s=1}^{k}(X_{is} - \overline{X_i})^2, i = 1, \ldots, m'$, where $\overline{X_i}$ is the mean of the $i^{th}$ grouping. Similarly, $\mathbf{D}$ is calculated from the $n'$ groupings of $\mathbf{Y}$. The Moses Ranklike test ends by applying the Wilcoxon to $\mathbf{C}$ and $\mathbf{D}$. One downside to the Moses test is the random grouping of the data. It is possible for two separate tests to be run on the same data with different results. This is accepted by an adjustment to the significance level of the test.

## 3 Application to Color Indexing

We apply Nonparametrics to image data by considering each pixel as a single independant sample. The assumptions behind Nonparametrics are less stringent than their classical counterparts, but it is assumed that the underlying population is continuous. This assumption is significant because the probability of two samples with identical values in a continuous population is small, whereas in a discrete population duplicates are more likely. A complication therefore arises when many pixels have the same value. Identical values produce ties in the subsequent rankings, and the test statistics require some accomodation to maintain significance when ties occur. The treatment of ties has itself been a topic of separate investigation for Nonparametrics in general [8] and the Wilcoxon in particular [2]. When both the sample population sizes and the number of ties are large, the performance of the test statistic degrades [8].

In the case of image data, the number of ties can be large. The color space contains at most $256^3$ possible values, which may be smaller than the number of pixels in a large image. Even for smaller images, many objects tend to have large regions over which the changes in color are small. As an example, the top left image in Fig.1(a) contains 320,961 foreground pixels. The largest single grouping of ties is 6,448 pixels (2%), and only 89,476 (28%) of the pixel values are distinct.

### 3.1 Color Space Embedding

A straightforward application of Nonparametrics would for each image produce a separate ranking for each color channel. The similarities of the separate color channels could then be compared using the Wilcoxon and Moses, and the results combined into a single similarity measure. There are two problems with this approach, the first being that simple transpositions of channel values cannot be discriminated. A mostly red image, for example, might be deemed similar to a mostly blue image. The second problem is that a single channel is limited to a small set of possible values, typically 256. All but the tiniest of images will therefore produce many ties in each channel ranking.

The use of Lipschitz embeddings effectively circumvents these difficulties [6]. An embedding $e$ is a reference point inserted at a specific location in space. The value of a pixel $p$ is then taken as $\|p-e\|$, where $\|.\|$ is the $L_2$ metric. This measure has the benefit of encoding all color channel information into a single scalar value, which reduces the occurence of ties. Discrimination can be increased by using multiple embeddings and combining the results from the separate tests.

The selection of embedding locations affects the quality of the results. An arbitrary selection, such as chosing $e_1, e_2, e_3$ to lie at the maximal values along each axis is simple, though not necessarily optimal. Principal component analysis (PCA) provides information to select embeddings tailored to a particular color distribution.

The quality of an embedding $e$ can be characterised by the number of different points $p_i$, $p_j$ where $\|p_i - e\| = \|p_j - e\|$. The fewer such points exist, the less ambigious the embedding. The set of possible points that are equidistant from $e$ form the surface of a sphere with a radius of $\|p - e\|$. Any datapoints that lie on the surface of the sphere will be considered as the same point by the embedding, even though the points may represent different colors. An embedding location selected in the center of a point cloud will thus have a high probability of having several datapoints in this state of ambiguity. Alternately, if it were selected to lie outside the point cloud, the probability of equidistant datapoints will be reduced. Discrimination can be further improved by choosing a location aligned with the major axis of dispersion of the point cloud, thereby minimizing the size of the arc that a sphere centered at $e$ cuts in the cloud.

To align the embedding point with the data set, PCA is performed to establish the three orthogonal vectors associated with the axes of maximum dispersion in the data. Along each principal component, $e$ is chosen to be outside the bounding box of the color data. The resulting axes and embedding locations $e_1, e_2, e_3$ for an example dataset in RGB space are shown in Fig. 2.

Instead of using the Euclidean distance, the projected distance is used for the scalar value to further reduce the level of embedding ambiguity. Each point $p$ is projected onto the principal component $v_j$ so that $p$ becomes $p^j$. The distance function is then $\|p^j - e\|$. The arc defining the ambiguous points for a given distance is reduced to a straight line perpendicular to the principal component $v_j$.

This process has two effects. It increases the descriptive power of the embeddings, and it also reduces the number of tied values. The effective dynamic range is increased from 256 levels to a near continuous range along each of the three eigenvectors. The object in the top-left image of Fig. 1(a) originally contained only 28% distinct values. After the 3 sets of embeddings are calculated, the number of distinct values is increased to 43% and the largest group of ties is reduced from 6,448 (2%) to 1,850 (0.6%).

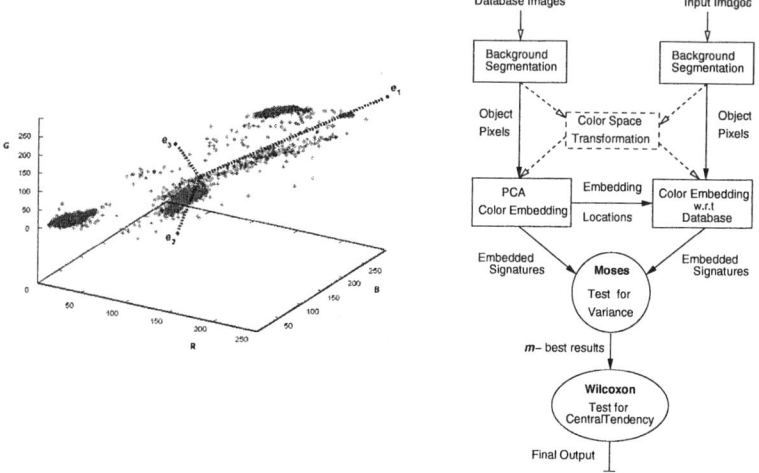

**Fig. 2.** Principal Axes and Embeddings     **Fig. 3.** The NECRIS algorithm

## 4 Experimentation

A process flow diagram of our method, which we call Nonparametric Embeddings for Color Recognition and Indexing Systems (*NECRIS*), is illustrated in Fig. 3. To evaluate NECRIS, the following histogram metrics [9,10] were implemented and their performance was compared: Earth Movers Distance (EMD), Bhattacharya Distance (BD), $L_2$-Norm ($L_2$), Kullback-Liebler Divergence (K-L), Jessen Divergence (JD), Kolmogorov-Smirnov (K-S), Chi-Squared statistic ($\chi^2$), and Histogram Intersection (HI). Standard histogram construction techniques were used with the bin size set at the maximum color resolution for a total of 256 bins per channel. It has also been shown that the choice of color space representation can affect performance, especially when illumination varies [4]. The four color spaces tested here were described by [4]: RGB, normalized rgb (rgb), $C_1C_2C_3$, and $I_1I_2I_3$.

There are 3 distinct performance measures used in these experiments to compare the various methods. The first is *accuracy*, which measures the percentage of trials where the method matches the correct database object with the test object. The second is *recall*, which is the ratio of correctly matched instances of an object to the total number of instances of the same object available in the database. The final performance measure is the *percentile ranking*. For $R$ possible ranks and $N$ input objects, let $r_i$ denote the rank of the correctly matching database object to the input object $i$. If the best match is the correct object, then $r_i = 1$. Conversely if the correct object is the worst match, then $r_i = R$. The average percentile ranking $\bar{r}$ is given by [5] as $\bar{r} = \frac{1}{N}\sum_{i=1}^{N}\frac{R-r_i}{R-1}$.

The 9 methods were compared for each of the 4 color spaces on several image databases, the first of which was the Swain and Ballard database [10] which consists of 68 household items. Each object was placed on a black background

**Table 1.** Accuracy and (Percentile Ranking) for Swain & Ballard Database

| Metric | RGB | rgb | $c_1c_2c_3$ | $l_1l_2l_3$ |
|---|---|---|---|---|
| EMD | .30 (.935) | .33 (.943) | .47 (.962) | .37 (.904) |
| BD | .70 (.981) | **.93** (.993) | .83 (.989) | **.67** (.988) |
| $L_2$ | .57 (.957) | .73 (.988) | .70 (.987) | .47 (.955) |
| K-L | .43 (.944) | .30 (.902) | .17 (.874) | .37 (.972) |
| JD | .60 (.946) | .87 (.993) | .67 (.984) | .63 (.986) |
| K-S | .37 (.931) | .43 (.957) | .47 (.952) | .33 (.887) |
| $\chi^2$ | .67 (.977) | **.93** (.993) | **.87** (.990) | **.67 (.989)** |
| HI | .63 (.974) | **.93** (.995) | .83 (**.991**) | .63 (.987) |
| NECRIS | **.77 (.988)** | .80 (**.996**) | .77 (.988) | .57 (.966) |

**Table 2.** Accuracy (Acc), Recall (Rec), Av. Percentile Ranking(%) for Recall Database

| | RGB | | | | rgb | | | | $c_1c_2c_3$ | | | | $l_1l_2l_3$ | | |
|---|---|---|---|---|---|---|---|---|---|---|---|---|---|---|---|
| Metric | Acc | Rec | % | Metric | Acc | Rec | % | Metric | Acc | Rec | % | Metric | Acc | Rec | % |
| EMD | 1 | .83 | 1 | EMD | 1 | .83 | 1 | EMD | .92 | .83 | .99 | EMD | 1 | .78 | 1 |
| BD | 1 | .94 | 1 | BD | 1 | 1 | 1 | BD | 1 | .94 | 1 | BD | 1 | .83 | 1 |
| $L_2$ | 1 | .92 | 1 | $L_2$ | 1 | .92 | 1 | $L_2$ | .92 | .78 | .98 | $L_2$ | .92 | .81 | .99 |
| K-L | 1 | .92 | 1 | K-L | 1 | .89 | 1 | K-L | .92 | .89 | .99 | K-L | 1 | .89 | 1 |
| JD | 1 | .92 | 1 | JD | .92 | .94 | 1 | JD | .92 | .83 | .98 | JD | 1 | .86 | 1 |
| K-S | .92 | .94 | .99 | K-S | 1 | .78 | 1 | K-S | .92 | .72 | 1 | K-S | .92 | .67 | .98 |
| $\chi^2$ | 1 | .94 | 1 | $\chi^2$ | 1 | 1 | 1 | $\chi^2$ | 1 | .94 | 1 | $\chi^2$ | 1 | .86 | 1 |
| HI | 1 | 92 | 1 | HI | 1 | 1 | 1 | HI | .92 | .94 | 1 | HI | 1 | .86 | 1 |
| NECRIS | 1 | .89 | 1 | NECRIS | 1 | 1 | 1 | NECRIS | 1 | .94 | 1 | NECRIS | .92 | .72 | 1 |

to facilitate background subtraction. An additional 30 images of the objects were acquired in random poses to serve as test images.

The results of the experiment on the Swain and Ballard database are tabulated in Table 1. Recall is not included as there was only 1 instance of every test object in the database, and so in this case recall is equivalent to accuracy. In the RGB color space NECRIS outperformed all the histogram metrics with an average percentile ranking of 98.8% and an indexing accuracy of 77%. The normalized $rgb$ color space raised the accuracy of the best histogram methods significantly to 93%. NECRIS outperformed all of the histogram methods in $rgb$ in terms of percentile ranking at 99.6%. In the other two color spaces HI, BD and $\chi^2$ show strong performance over NECRIS and the other comparison metrics.

An additional database was collected using a similar methodology as [10]. Twelve objects were taken in 3 poses each against a black background. The images were acquired using a consumer level digital camera (Fuji FinePix6800Z). A separate set of test images were acquired for each object with slightly different scales and rotations. Fig.1a) illustrates 1 of the 3 database images acquired for each of the 12 objects. Fig.1b) shows the remaining 2 database images for the top left object of part a), and Fig.1c) shows the test image for this object.

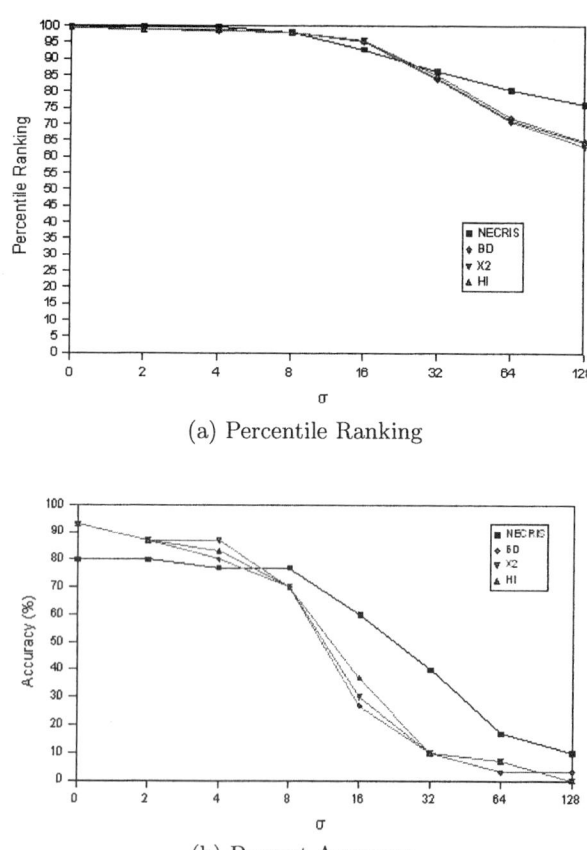

**Fig. 4.** Performance Degradation Under Added Noise

The accuracy, recall, and percentile ranking for all combinations of color space and similarity measure are listed in Table 2. NECRIS performed well with an accuracy of 100% though with a recall of 89% with the RGB color space. In $rgb$ and $c_1c_2c_3$, NECRIS tied for best performance with the best histogram metrics. The $rgb$ color space yielded perfect accuracy and recall for NECRIS, HI, $\chi^2$ and BD. In $I_1I_2I_3$, of the three methods that did not obtain 100% accuracy, NECRIS scored the highest average percentile ranking (99.8%) and the lowest recall (72%).

To compare noise immunity, a similar methodology was used as [5]. Zero mean Gaussian noise was added along all 3 channels for every input image in the Swain and Ballard database. Following [5], the level of noise was selected as $\sigma \in \{2, 4, 8, 16, 32, 64, 128\}$. The best 3 histogram metrics from the previous test (BD, $\chi^2$, and HI). were run on this data. The color space selected for this experiment was $rg$ as used by [5].

The degradation in accuracy and average percentile ranking are shown graphically in Figs. 4(a) and (b) respectively. NECRIS shows superior noise immunity over the best histogram methods. This is especially noticeable in the accuracy metric. Fig. 4(b) shows that the accuracy of NECRIS outperforms all histogram methods for noise levels $\sigma > 8$, and is accurate to 10% at $\sigma=128$, where the best histogram result is only 3%. The average percentile ranking of NECRIS is generally higher for each level of noise, with the exception of $\sigma=16$. Most importantly, the performance of NECRIS degrades more gracefully than all tested histogram methods as the noise level increases. At the extreme($\sigma=128$), NECRIS shows an improvement of $> 10\%$ which is favorable compared to the Kernel Density Estimation method for a similar experiment in the same $rg$ color space [5].

## 5 Conclusions

The proposed NECRIS method shows comparable results with the best histogram metrics, in some cases outperforming all histogram methods. NECRIS also shows a natural noise immunity that is not present in histogram techniques. Without any special consideration, NECRIS shows a strong immunity under simulated conditions and is comparable to the method proposed by Gevers and Stokman [5]. NECRIS also does not suffer from the increase in complexity that hinders the Kernel Density Estimation technique.

The time complexity of the NECRIS method is $\mathbf{O}(n)$, as are most of the Histogram metrics. The preprocessing stage of NECRIS is $\mathbf{O}(n \log n)$, although this can be done offline for the database images. NECRIS also tends to be more space efficient than histogramming, requiring only a small number of lists of ranks, one for each embedding. By comparison, histograms are $K$-dimensional data structures for $K$ color channels, and therefore can be large. It is a common technique in histogramming to reduce the color resolution along each channel in order to save space, albeit possibly at the cost of reducing accuracy.

In future work, NECRIS can be improved by removing the random component of the Moses Ranklike test. Further work will evaluate how NECRIS can be applied to color constancy techniques [3].

## References

1. D. Bhat and S. Nayar. Ordinal measures for visual correspondence. In *Proc. CVPR*, pages 351–357, 1996.
2. W. J. Buhler. The treatment of ties in the wilcoxon test. *The Annals of Mathematical Statistics*, 38(2):519–522, April 1967.
3. B. V. Funt and G. D. Finlayson. Color constant color indexing, May 1995.
4. T. Gevers and A. W. Smeulders. Color-based object recognition. *Patt. Rec.*, 32:453–464, March 1999.
5. T. Gevers and H. Stokman. Robust histogram construction from color invariants for object recognition. *IEEE Transactions on Pattern Analysis and Machine Intelligence*, 26(1):113–118, January 2004.
6. G. Hjaltason and H. Samet. Properties of embedding methods for similarity searching in metric spaces. *Trans. PAMI*, 25(5):530–550, May 2003.

7. Hollander and Wolfe. *Nonparametric Statistical Methods*. John Wiley and Sons, Inc., 1973.
8. J. Putter. The treatment of ties in some nonparametric tests. *The Annals of Mathematical Statistics*, 26(3):368–386, September 1955.
9. Puzicha, Buhmann, Rubner, and Tomasi. Empirical evaluation of dissimilarity measures for color and texture. In *Proc. ICCV*, pages 1165–1172, 1999.
10. M. J. Swain and D. H. Ballard. Color indexing. *Int. Jour. Comp. Vis.*, 1(7):11–32, 1991.

# High Order Extrapolation Using Taylor Series for Color Filter Array Demosaicing

J.S. Jimmy Li and Sharmil Randhawa

GPO Box 2100, Adelaide, Australia 5001,
School of Informatics and Engineering, Flinders University
{Jimmy.Li, Sharmil.Randhawa}@flinders.edu.au

**Abstract.** A novel noniterative extrapolation method based on Taylor series approximation is proposed for color filter array demosaicing. New extrapolation equations are derived for the estimation of the green plane with higher accuracy by including higher order terms of the Taylor series. Our proposed method avoids interpolation across an edge and thus reduces errors in the demosaiced image. It has been shown that our method outperforms other techniques in image quality measures, especially around edges.

## 1 Introduction

Color filter array demosaicing refers to determining the missing color values at each pixel when a single-sensor digital camera is used for color image capture. The most common array used is the Bayer [1] color filter array as seen in Fig. 2, where the green color is sampled at twice the rate of the red and blue values. This is due to the peak sensitivity of the human visual system which lies in the green spectrum [1].

In this paper, we introduce a noniterative extrapolation method to recover missing color pixels. It differs from others in that we extrapolate rather than interpolate to recover missing color information. Our method is divided into two stages. In the first stage, a higher order extrapolation of the green plane is carried out to approximate four possible estimates with high accuracies. New equations have been derived to produce these highly accurate estimates.

The second stage serves to select the best estimate out of the possible four choices, using a classifier instead of a linear combiner. Other demosaicing methods [6],[8] determine the missing color values by combining weighted estimates from corresponding directions. Inaccurate estimation of weightings will produce artifacts which manifest themselves in the demosaiced output.

The remainder of the paper is organized as follows. Section 2 details the extrapolation method. Section 3 presents the experimental results, and compares this method with other existing methods, with the conclusion in Section 4.

## 2 Demosaicing Using Taylor Series Extrapolation

In the first stage of our proposed method, we approximate the green plane using Taylor series, by including higher-order terms. Similar techniques are used in the red/blue plane extrapolation.

### 2.1 Stage 1 - Green Plane Extrapolation

The green plane is extrapolated first as it contains the most samples, twice as many as the red or blue samples. The approximation is carried out using Taylor series [7] as follows:

$$g(x) = \sum_{m=0}^{\infty} \frac{g^{(m)}(a)}{m!} (x-a)^m . \tag{1}$$

Suppose we want to estimate the green value at position x ($G_x$) at which only the blue value ($B_x$) is known. Let's consider the one-dimensional case with an edge boundary on the right-hand side of $B_x$, as shown in Fig. 1. To meet the requirements for the assumptions used in the evaluation of the Taylor series coefficients, we extrapolate the green value pixel at position x along the edge from pixels on the left-hand side of it.

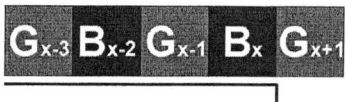

**Fig. 1.** 1D Bayer Pattern and Edge Boundary on the RHS of Bx

$$g(x) = g(x-1) + g'(x-1) + \frac{1}{2!}g''(x-1) + \ldots + \frac{1}{n!}g^{(n)}(x-1) + \ldots , \tag{2}$$

where g(x) is the value of a green pixel at location x. For first order approximations, we assume that:

$$g^{(n)}(x-1) = 0 \; for \; n \geq 2 , \tag{3}$$

and using the central difference approximation for first order differentiation:

$$g'(x) = \frac{g(x) - g(x-2)}{2} = \frac{\overline{G}_x - \overline{G}_{x-2}}{2} , \tag{4}$$

where $\overline{G}_x$ and $\overline{G}_{x-2}$ are the missing green pixel values at position x and x-2 respectively. Using forward and backward difference approximations may produce different results.

Based on the assumption that the green and red/blue pixel values are well correlated with constant offsets [4] along an edge:

$$\overline{G}_x - B_x = G_{x-1} - \overline{B}_{x-1} = \overline{G}_{x-2} - B_{x-2} . \tag{5}$$

From (5):
$$\overline{G}_x - \overline{G}_{x-2} = B_x - B_{x-2}. \tag{6}$$

Substituting (6) into (4):
$$g'(x-1) = \frac{B_x - B_{x-2}}{2}, \tag{7}$$

Hence by (2) and (3),
$$\widehat{G}_x = G_{x-1} + \frac{1}{2}(B_x - B_{x-2}), \tag{8}$$

where $\widehat{G}_x$ is the estimated green value at position x. By using Taylor series, we have derived the same equation (8) as given by Lu and Tan [8].

We can improve the accuracy of the green plane approximation by including the next higher order term, i.e. $g''(x-1)$, into the equation. For second order approximation, we assume the third and higher order derivatives are negligible:
$$g^{(n)}(x-1) = 0 \; for \; n \geq 3, \tag{9}$$

then (2) can be approximated as:
$$\widehat{G}_x = G_{x-1} + g'(x-1) + \frac{1}{2}g''(x-1). \tag{10}$$

By applying central difference approximation for $g''(x-1)$, we obtain
$$g''(x-1) = \frac{g'(x) - g'(x-2)}{2}. \tag{11}$$

Hence (10) can be modified to:
$$\widehat{G}_x = G_{x-1} + g'(x-1) + \frac{1}{4}(g'(x) - g'(x-2)). \tag{12}$$

By (9), this implies that
$$g^{(3)}(x-1) = g''(x-\frac{1}{2}) - g''(x-\frac{3}{2}) = 0. \tag{13}$$

Therefore,
$$g'(x) = 2g'(x-1) - g'(x-2). \tag{14}$$

Substituting (14) into (12)
$$\widehat{G}_x = G_{x-1} + \frac{3}{2}g'(x-1) - \frac{1}{2}g'(x-2). \tag{15}$$

Applying the central difference approximation,
$$g'(x-1) = \frac{g(x) - g(x-2)}{2} = \frac{\overline{G}_x - \overline{G}_{x-2}}{2}, \tag{16}$$

and
$$g'(x-2) = \frac{g(x-1) - g(x-3)}{2} = \frac{G_{x-1} - G_{x-3}}{2}. \quad (17)$$

Substituting (16) and (17) into (12) gives:

$$\widehat{G}_x = G_{x-1} + \frac{3}{4}(\overline{G}_x - \overline{G}_{x-2}) - \frac{1}{4}(G_{x-1} - G_{x-3}). \quad (18)$$

Hence using (6), (18) becomes:

$$\widehat{G}_x = G_{x-1} + \frac{3}{4}(B_x - B_{x-2}) - \frac{1}{4}(G_{x-1} - G_{x-3}). \quad (19)$$

Now $\widehat{G}_x$ can be determined by all known color values in the Bayer pattern. For a 2D image, we can obtain the extrapolated values for the other three directions, top, bottom and right directions similarly.

**Fig. 2.** An 8x8 window of the Bayer pattern

Fig. 2 shows an 8 x 8 window of a Bayer array neighbourhood, where the index (i,j) of each color is given by the row and column location. Consider the case where we want to determine the missing green value $\overline{G}_{45}$. It can be selected from a list of $\left\{\widehat{G}^T_{45}, \widehat{G}^L_{45}, \widehat{G}^R_{45}, \widehat{G}^B_{45}\right\}$ where T, L, R and B indicate the top, left, right and bottom directions from which the estimates are extrapolated w.r.t. (19).

$$\widehat{G}^T_{45} = G_{35} + \frac{3}{4}(B_{45} - B_{25}) - \frac{1}{4}(G_{35} - G_{15}),$$

$$\widehat{G}^L_{45} = G_{44} + \frac{3}{4}(B_{45} - B_{43}) - \frac{1}{4}(G_{44} - G_{42}),$$

$$\widehat{G}_{45}^{R} = G_{46} + \frac{3}{4}(B_{45} - B_{47}) - \frac{1}{4}(G_{46} - G_{48}),$$
$$\widehat{G}_{45}^{B} = G_{55} + \frac{3}{4}(B_{45} - B_{65}) - \frac{1}{4}(G_{55} - G_{75}). \quad (20)$$

(19) and (20) are new extrapolation equations derived for better approximation of the green plane. By including the second-order terms, a higher accuracy is introduced into the estimates of the missing values in the green plane.

Regardless of the orientation of an edge, at least one of the four estimates will be an accurate estimate of the missing green color. To illustrate the above mentioned concept, we use the pixels in the original image to pick one of the four estimates based on the minimum mean square error criterion. Fig. 3(a) and (b) show the original and the ideal selector output. These two images are visually indistinguishable from each other and this indicates clearly that the selected output is a very good approximation of the original. This confirms the presence of a highly accurate estimate within the four extrapolated choices.

In most cases, higher order approximation is required for the green plane only, and first order approximation is sufficient for the red and blue planes. (21) and (22) are the equations for determining the red pixel value at a blue and green position respectively. Equations are similar for the blue plane.

$$\widehat{R}_{45}^{TL} = R_{34} + (\widehat{G}_{45} - \widehat{G}_{34}),$$
$$\widehat{R}_{45}^{TR} = R_{36} + (\widehat{G}_{45} - \widehat{G}_{36}),$$
$$\widehat{R}_{45}^{BL} = R_{54} + (\widehat{G}_{45} - \widehat{G}_{54}),$$
$$\widehat{R}_{45}^{BR} = R_{56} + (\widehat{G}_{45} - \widehat{G}_{56}). \quad (21)$$

$$\widehat{R}_{44}^{T} = R_{34} + (G_{44} - \widehat{G}_{34}),$$
$$\widehat{R}_{44}^{L} = R_{43} + (G_{44} - \widehat{G}_{43}),$$
$$\widehat{R}_{44}^{R} = R_{45} + (G_{44} - \widehat{G}_{45}),$$
$$\widehat{R}_{44}^{B} = R_{54} + (G_{44} - \widehat{G}_{54}). \quad (22)$$

## 2.2 Stage 2 - Classifier

As one of the four estimates gives an accurate value, a classifier instead of a linear combiner is needed to select one of the four directed samples. Since a linear combiner, as used in other methods [6],[8], will blur an edge, our classifier will preserve sharp edges better.

In our classification process, an orientation matrix for every pixel is produced using the CFA image input. This is used to indicate the possible orientation of an edge for that pixel.

At a red/blue pixel, e.g. $B_{45}$, we define the vertical gradient and horizontal gradient as:

$$V = |G_{35} - G_{55}|, \quad H = |G_{44} - G_{46}|. \quad (23)$$

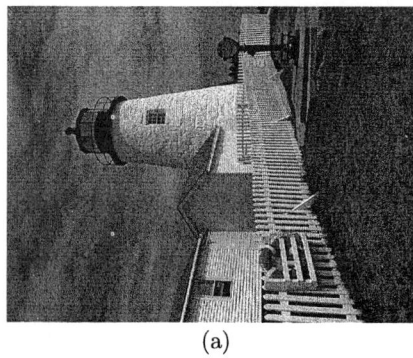 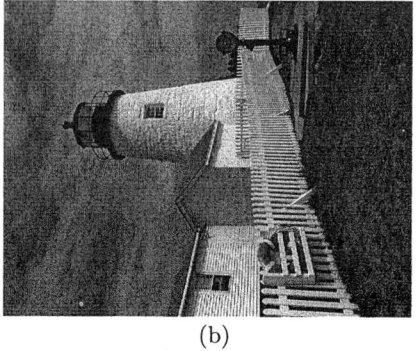

**Fig. 3.** The Original Lighthouse image (a) and the Ideal Selector output (b)

At a green pixel, e.g. $G_{44}$, the vertical and horizontal gradients are defined as:

$$V = |R_{34} - R_{54}|, \; H = |B_{43} - B_{45}|. \qquad (24)$$

A logical function is used to produce an orientation matrix for the whole color filter array image:

$$f(V < H) = \begin{cases} 1, \, if \, V < H \\ 0, \, otherwise \end{cases}. \qquad (25)$$

A '1' in the orientation matrix indicates that a possible vertical edge exists at that position.

The orientation matrix is used to indicate the orientation of edges in images, and the underlying assumption made is that the neighborhood orientation must be aligned in a direction along an edge. False indication of edges due to noise will be removed by a smoothing filter. Experimental results indicate that a simple standard 2D median filter will suffice for the application.

In order to avoid blurring an edge, an odd window width for the median filtering is preferred. The orientation matrix is used to reject one sample before we apply median filtering. If it is a '1' in the orientation matrix, a possible vertical edge exists and hence one of the two estimates in the horizontal direction will be rejected. Similarly for a '0' in the orientation matrix, we reject an estimate in the vertical direction. The one, out of the two, to be rejected has the greatest difference in magnitude from the median of the four extrapolated estimates.

## 3 Experimental Results

The picket-fence region of the lighthouse image was used to assess the edge-preserving performance of our method and compare it with other methods. This is a challenging area for many demosaicing methods because of the presence of many edges close together. Table 1 lists the image quality performance measures,

**Table 1.** Image Quality Performance Measures - MSE, MAE and NCD. Measures with red, green and blue color planes listed as rows.

| Method | MSE | MAE | NCD |
|---|---|---|---|
| | 47.41 | 29.50 | |
| Bilinear | 23.81 | 14.20 | 0.2337 |
| | 45.69 | 28.26 | |
| | 31.97 | 19.92 | |
| Freeman [3] | 13.98 | 6.60 | 0.1813 |
| | 32.07 | 20.14 | |
| | 30.00 | 19.16 | |
| Kimmel [6] | 23.81 | 14.16 | 0.1959 |
| | 33.70 | 21.47 | |
| | 22.00 | 12.15 | |
| Hamilton [5] | 10.80 | 3.45 | 0.0846 |
| | 20.52 | 11.05 | |
| | 12.54 | 6.74 | |
| Lu&Tan [8] | 8.36 | 3.95 | 0.0576 |
| | 11.96 | 6.19 | |
| | 12.85 | 6.82 | |
| Gunturk [4] | 7.24 | 2.72 | 0.0487 |
| | 11.09 | 5.45 | |
| | 12.29 | 7.74 | |
| Plataniotis [10] | 8.77 | 4.31 | 0.0435 |
| | 11.79 | 7.28 | |
| | 6.17 | 2.92 | |
| Proposed Method | 4.66 | 1.75 | 0.0123 |
| | 5.39 | 2.38 | |
| | 2.20 | 1.05 | |
| Ideal Selector | 2.89 | 1.18 | 0.0048 |
| | 1.79 | 0.96 | |

mean square error (MSE), mean absolute error (MAE) and normalized color difference (NCD)[9], of the various demosaicing methods [3],[6],[5],[8],[4],[10]. Fig. 4 shows that our method is visually superior to other demosaicing methods. It is clear that our proposed method outperforms all other methods in this region. For the ideal selector as mentioned in 2.1, it gives us an error value which is an order of magnitude below the other methods. This indicates that the higher order approximation method gives a high accuracy output.

## 4 Conclusion

A new demosaicing method is presented that preserves edge information by extrapolating from the same side of an edge. New equations are proposed for the estimation of the green plane with higher accuracy by including higher order terms based on Taylor series approximation. The underlying idea behind the proposed method is that the desired output for a missing color pixel can be found

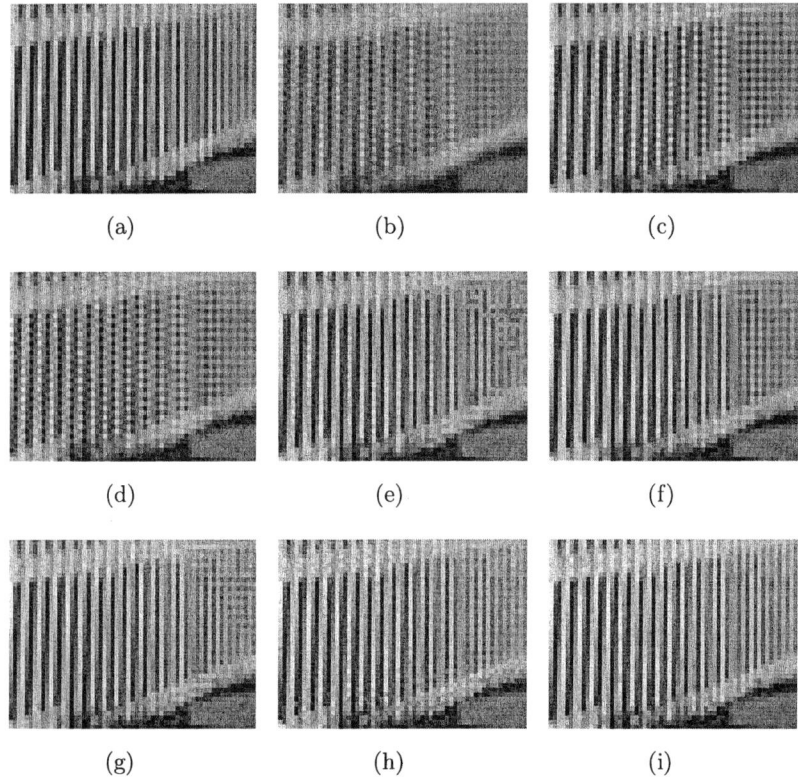

**Fig. 4.** Picket fence region of (a) the original Lighthouse image and the demosaiced output images using (b) Bilinear interpolation, (c) Freeman, (d) Kimmel, (e) Hamilton, (f) Lu&Tan, (g) Gunturk, (h) Plataniotis and (i) our proposed method

in one of four estimates extrapolated in four different directions. A classifier is used to select the appropriate estimate. The results from this method are superior both visually and quantitatively to those from other methods.

## References

1. Bayer, B.E.: Color Imaging Array. U.S. Patent 3 971 065, (1976)
2. Cok, D.R.: Signal Processing Method and Apparatus for Producing Interpolated Chrominance Values in a Sampled Color Image Signal. U.S. Patent 4,642,678, (1987)
3. Freeman, W.T.: Median Filter for Reconstructing Missing Color Samples. U.S. Patent 4,724,395, (1988)
4. Gunturk, B.K., Altunbasak, Y., Mersereau, R.M.: Color Plane Interpolation Using Alternation Projections. IEEE Transactions on Image Processing 11 (2002) 997-1013
5. Hamilton Jr., J. F., Adams Jr., J.E.: Adaptive Color Plan Interpolation in Single Sensor Color Electronic Camera. U.S. Patent 5 629 734, (1997)

6. Kimmel, R.: Demosaicing: Image Reconstruction from Color CCD Samples. IEEE Transactions on Image Processing 8 (1999) 1221-1228
7. Kreyszig, E.: Advanced Engineering Mathematics. Wiley, 1999
8. Lu, W., Tan, Y.-P. :Color Filter Array Demosaicking: New Method and Performance Measures. IEEE Transactions on Image Processing 12 (2003) 1194-1210
9. Plataniotis, K.N., Venetsanopoulos, A.N.: Color Image Processing and Applications, Springer Verlag, 2000
10. Plataniotis K.N., Lukac R. An Efficient Demosaicing Approach with a Global Control of Correction Steps. IEEE International Conference on Acoustics, Speech, and Signal Processing Proceedings (2004) III 469-472

# Adaptive Colorimetric Characterization of Digital Camera with White Balance

Soo-Wook Jang, Eun-Su Kim, Sung-Hak Lee, and Kyu-Ik Sohng

School of Electronic Engineering and Computer Science,
Kyungpook National University 1370, Sankyug-Dong,
Buk-Gu, Daegu, 702-701, Korea
{jjang, saeloum, shark2, kisohng}@ee.knu.ac.kr

**Abstract.** A camera is an effective tool in capturing images for colorimetric use. However, the $RGB$ signals generated by different cameras are not equal for the same scene. Therefore, cameras are characterized based on a CIE standard colorimetric observer. This paper proposes a new method for obtaining camera transfer matrices under different white balances using a 3×3 camera transfer matrix under a specific white balance point. As such, the proposed methods enables a camera transfer matrix under any other white balance to be obtained using the colorimetric coordinates for the phosphor primaries derived from a 3×3 linear transfer matrix under a certain white balance point. Experimental results confirmed that the proposed method produced a 3×3 linear transfer matrix under any other white balance with a reasonable degree of accuracy compared with the transfer matrix obtained by the conventional method.

## 1 Introduction

A color camera is a powerful acquisition tool in image processing and color communication. However, the $RGB$ signals generated by a camera are generally device-dependent, i.e., different cameras produce different $RGB$ responses to the tristmulus $XYZ$ for the same scene. Furthermore, such $RGB$ signals are not colorimetric, as they do not directly correspond to device-independent tristimulus values based on CIE color-matching functions (CMFs). The reason for this is that the spectral sensitivity of the color sensors used in cameras does not correspond to device-independent tristimulus values based on CIE CMFs [1]. Plus, the spectral sensitivity of the sensors used in different cameras varies significantly from one another. Therefore, a transform that defines a mapping between camera $RGB$ signals and a device-independent color space, such as $XYZ$ or CIE$LAB$, is essential for high-fidelity color reproduction.

The transform derivation process is known as camera characterization [2]. Colorimetric characterization methods can be divided into two general categories: spectral sensitivity based and color target based. With spectral sensitivity-based characterization [3], the camera spectral sensitivity needs to be measured using specialized apparatus, such as a monochromator and radiance meter. Meanwhile, color target-based characterization [4]-[8] only requires a known target, making it more practical. Plus, polynomial regression is usually adopted for model derivation. Yet, a camera has a different colorimetric characterization according to the white balance established by the photographing conditions. Therefore, tedious experiments are required to obtain a camera transfer matrix under various white balance points for the same camera [2].

Accordingly, the current paper proposes a new method for obtaining camera characterization under different white balances using a camera transfer matrix under a specific white balance point. Experimental results confirm that the proposed method can produce a 3×3 linear transfer matrix under any other white balance with a reasonable degree of accuracy when compared with the transfer matrix obtained by the conventional method.

## 2 Conventional Colorimetric Characterization of Digital Camera

Colorimetric characterization methods can be divided into two general categories: (a) spectral sensitivity based and (b) color target based. With spectral sensitivity-based characterization, the camera spectral sensitivity needs to be measured using specialized apparatus, such as a monochromator and radiance meter. A relationship needs to be found between the camera spectral sensitivity and CIE CMFs. This relationship can then be used to transform the camera $RGB$ values into $XYZ$ values. As such, the basic concept of color target-based characterization is to use a reference target that contains a certain number of color samples. These color samples are then imaged by a camera and measured by a spectrophotometer to obtain the $RGB$ values and their corresponding $XYZ$ values. Methods such as three-dimensional lookup tables with interpolation and extrapolation [4]-[6], least squares polynomial modeling [7], and neural networks [8] are typically used to derive the transformation between the camera $RGB$ values and the $XYZ$ values. However, color target-based characterization is more widely used, as it only requires a known target, which makes it more practical. Plus, polynomial regression is adopted for model derivation.

Device characterization by polynomial regression with least squares fitting has already been adequately explained by many other researchers [2], [9], [10]. In particular, Hong et al. [2] studied camera characterization using variable polynomial regression with least squares fitting and found that camera characterization accuracy is reliable when the number of training samples is over 60.

However, as previously mentioned, a camera will have a different colorimetric camera characterization according to the white balance established by the photographing conditions. Therefore, tedious experiments are needed to obtain a camera transfer matrix using over 60 training samples under various white balance points for the same camera. Also, the training samples must be uniformly spread within the camera's color gamut. Therefore, a simple and soft method is required for the characterization of a commercial camera. As such, this paper proposes a new method for obtaining camera characterization matrices under different white balances using a camera characterization matrix under a specific white balance point.

## 3 Proposed Colorimetric Characterization of Digital Camera

### 3.1 Colorimetric Characterization of Ideal Color Camera

The intension of an ideal color camera is to provide $RGB$ channel voltages suitable for a display with specified primary chromaticity coordinates and a specified reference white. As such, the $RGB$ channel voltages required for the camera to produce perfect color fidelity with a specified set of display primaries and normalizing white illuminant can be calculated for a linear system as follows [11], [12]:

$$[R\ G\ B]^T = \mathbf{K}^{-1} \cdot \mathbf{x_p}^{-1} \cdot [X\ Y\ Z]^T \tag{1}$$

$$\mathbf{K} = \begin{bmatrix} K_R & 0 & 0 \\ 0 & K_G & 0 \\ 0 & 0 & K_B \end{bmatrix}, \quad \mathbf{x_p} = \begin{bmatrix} x_R & x_G & x_B \\ y_R & y_G & y_B \\ z_R & z_G & z_B \end{bmatrix} \tag{2}$$

$$[K_R\ K_G\ K_B]^T = \frac{1}{y_W} \cdot \mathbf{x_p}^{-1} \cdot [x_W\ y_W\ z_W]^T \tag{3}$$

$\mathbf{x_p}$ represents the phosphor primaries chromaticity coordinate matrix, and $[x_W\ y_W\ z_W]^T$ represents the reference white illuminant chromaticity coordinate matrix. Matrix $\mathbf{K}$ can be determined by requiring that the output be the desired normalizing white illuminant for equal channel voltages.

### 3.2 Proposed Adaptive Colorimetric Characterization of Digital Camera with the White Balance

This paper proposes a new method for obtaining a camera transfer matrix under different white balances using a 3×3 camera transfer matrix under a specific white balance point. A flowchart of the proposed method is shown in Fig. 1.

The camera characterization is determined as the product of the phosphor primaries chromaticity coordinate matrix and tristimulus constant matrix, as shown in Eq. (1). Here, the tristimulus constant matrix $\mathbf{K}$ is changed according to a change in the camera white balance point. Therefore, once the phosphor primaries chromaticity and reference white point of the camera are estimated, a camera characterization matrix can be easily obtained under any other white balance.

Thus, to obtain a camera transfer matrix under any other white balance according to the proposed method, the 3×3 linear transfer matrix under a specific white balance point is assumed to be equal to Eq. (1). Thereafter, the proposed method obtains the phosphor primaries chromaticity and reference white point of the camera as follows: First, $R=1$ and $G=B=0$ are substituted in Eq. (1) to estimate the **R** phosphor primary chromaticity coordinates. The **G** and **B** phosphor primaries chromaticity coordinates are also estimated in the same way. Second, $R=G=B=1$ is substituted to estimate the reference white chromaticity coordinates. Here, the value 1 means the normalized maximum $RGB$ camera output. Third, the tristimulus constant matrix $\mathbf{K}$ can be calculated using the colorimetric coordinates estimated for the phosphor primaries and reference white point.

Therefore, a camera transfer matrix under any other white balance can be obtained using the estimated phosphor primaries chromaticity coordinate matrix and tristimulus constant matrix.

$$X = x_R K_R, \quad Y = y_R K_R, \quad Z = z_R K_R \tag{4}$$

$$T = X + Y + Z = x_R K_{Rc} + y_R K_{Rc} + z_R K_{Rc}$$
$$= (x_R + y_R + z_R) K_{Rc} = K_{Rc} \tag{5}$$

$$x = \frac{X}{T} = x_R, \quad y = \frac{Y}{T} = y_R, \quad z = \frac{Z}{T} = z_R \tag{6}$$

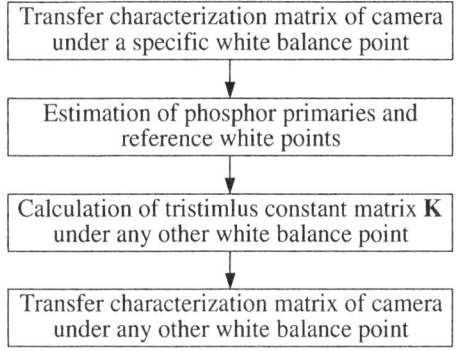

**Fig. 1.** Flowchart of the proposed colorimetric characterization according to white balance

## 4 Experiments and Results

To assess the performance of the proposed colorimetric characterization of cameras, experiments were conducted using 4 kinds of reference white and a Sony DVCAM DSR200. The test color samples consisted of GretagMacbeth ColorChecker's colors and 59 free colors that covered a large color gamut in $XYZ$ color space. The test color samples were displayed on a Sony G500 monitor and the camera $RGB$ values for each test color sample calculated by averaging the $RGB$ values of 80% of the pixels in the sample, excluding the boundary pixels.

**Table 1.** Camera transfer characterization matrices resulting from polynomial regression with least squares fitting under each reference white

| Reference White | $\mathbf{M}_{RGB}$ | | | $\mathbf{M}_{GIM}$ | | |
|---|---|---|---|---|---|---|
| $D_{65}$ | 0.6135 | 0.2584 | 0.1748 | 0.5750 | 0.2240 | 0.1663 |
| | 0.3131 | 0.6915 | 0.0764 | 0.2837 | 0.6589 | 0.0765 |
| | 0.0306 | 0.1188 | 1.0330 | 0.0088 | 0.1099 | 1.0046 |
| 5800 K | 0.7662 | 0.2550 | 0.1801 | 0.7633 | 0.2284 | 0.1630 |
| | 0.3960 | 0.6709 | 0.0774 | 0.3915 | 0.6594 | 0.0648 |
| | 0.0394 | 0.1156 | 1.0600 | 0.0452 | 0.1144 | 1.0345 |
| 3200 K | 1.4392 | 0.2946 | 0.1032 | 1.2577 | 0.2403 | 0.1578 |
| | 0.7361 | 0.7645 | 0.0469 | 0.6220 | 0.7181 | 0.0988 |
| | 0.0825 | 0.1110 | 0.6296 | 0.0283 | 0.0861 | 0.6483 |
| A | 1.1718 | 0.2580 | 0.0652 | 1.0148 | 0.2189 | 0.0925 |
| | 0.5996 | 0.6938 | 0.0301 | 0.4912 | 0.6663 | 0.0565 |
| | 0.0592 | 0.0671 | 0.3832 | −0.0120 | 0.0596 | 0.3898 |

**Table 2.** Chromaticity coordinates for phosphor primaries estimated using proposed method

| Estimated Phosphor Primaries | $\mathbf{M}_{RGB}$ | | | $\mathbf{M}_{GIM}$ | | |
|---|---|---|---|---|---|---|
| | R | G | B | R | G | B |
| $x$ | 0.6410 | 0.2418 | 0.1361 | 0.6628 | 0.2256 | 0.1333 |
| $y$ | 0.3271 | 0.6471 | 0.0595 | 0.3271 | 0.6637 | 0.0613 |
| $z$ | 0.0320 | 0.1111 | 0.8045 | 0.0101 | 0.1107 | 0.8205 |

**Table 3.** Estimated transfer characterization matrices under each reference white based on chromaticity coordinates for phosphor primaries obtained when using $M_{RGB}$ and $M_{GIM}$

| Reference White | By Phosphor Primaries Obtained by $\mathbf{M}_{RGB}$ | | | By Phosphor Primaries Obtained by $\mathbf{M}_{GIM}$ | | |
|---|---|---|---|---|---|---|
| 5800 K | 0.8014 | 0.2706 | 0.1918 | 0.6727 | 0.2022 | 0.1593 |
| | 0.4089 | 0.7241 | 0.0838 | 0.3319 | 0.5948 | 0.0733 |
| | 0.0400 | 0.1244 | 1.1337 | 0.0103 | 0.0993 | 0.9619 |
| 3200 K | 1.2587 | 0.2728 | 0.0940 | 0.8948 | 0.1788 | 0.0709 |
| | 0.6423 | 0.7301 | 0.0411 | 0.4415 | 0.5259 | 0.0326 |
| | 0.0628 | 0.1254 | 0.5559 | 0.0137 | 0.0878 | 0.4280 |
| A | 1.0122 | 0.2463 | 0.0438 | 1.0264 | 0.2264 | 0.0489 |
| | 0.5165 | 0.6592 | 0.0191 | 0.5065 | 0.6660 | 0.0225 |
| | 0.0505 | 0.1132 | 0.2587 | −0.0157 | 0.1111 | 0.2955 |

**Table 4.** Chromaticity errors for tristimulus values obtained when using proposed and conventional method

| Reference White | Estimated Transfer Matrix | $x_m - x_c$ | $y_m - y_c$ | $\Delta u'v'$ | $\Delta E^*_{uv}$ |
|---|---|---|---|---|---|
| 5800 K | $\mathbf{M}_{RGB}$ | 0.0076 | 0.0043 | 0.0061 | 6.84 |
| | $\mathbf{M}_{RGB\_5800\,K}$ | 0.0059 | 0.0043 | 0.0066 | 6.74 |
| | $\mathbf{M}_{GIM}$ | 0.0066 | 0.0053 | 0.0072 | 5.22 |
| | $\mathbf{M}_{GIM\_5800\,K}$ | 0.0096 | 0.0050 | 0.0084 | 10.20 |
| 3200 K | $\mathbf{M}_{RGB}$ | 0.0098 | 0.0100 | 0.0113 | 1.050 |
| | $\mathbf{M}_{RGB\_5800\,K}$ | 0.0082 | 0.0075 | 0.0091 | 7.74 |
| | $\mathbf{M}_{GIM}$ | 0.0091 | 0.0063 | 0.0166 | 7.27 |
| | $\mathbf{M}_{GIM\_5800\,K}$ | 0.0137 | 0.0087 | 0.0136 | 9.07 |
| A | $\mathbf{M}_{RGB}$ | 0.0082 | 0.0104 | 0.0105 | 11.30 |
| | $\mathbf{M}_{RGB\_5800\,K}$ | 0.0152 | 0.0124 | 0.0068 | 18.80 |
| | $\mathbf{M}_{GIM}$ | 0.0079 | 0.0059 | 0.0149 | 7.33 |
| | $\mathbf{M}_{GIM\_5800\,K}$ | 0.0115 | 0.0094 | 0.0093 | 14.20 |

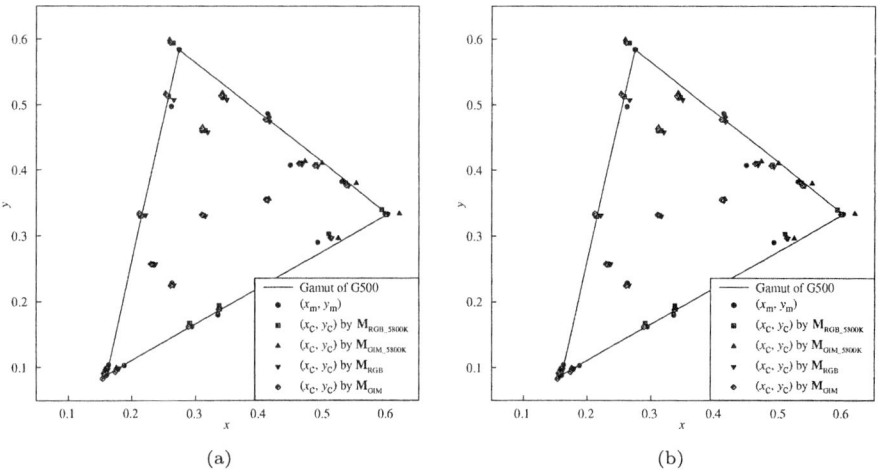

**Fig. 2.** The $xy$ coordinates $(x_m, y_m)$ measured by the $xy$ coordinates $(x_c, y_c)$ calculated using estimated transfer matrix. (a) A and (b) 5800 K.

First, 2 kinds of 3×3 transfer matrix were obtained according to a conventional camera characterization method using variable polynomial regression with least squares fitting, where $\mathbf{M}_{RGB}$ was generated by least squares fitting the camera $RGB$ values to $XYZ$ values using red, green, and blue samples, while $\mathbf{M}_{GIM}$ was generated by least squares fitting the camera $RGB$ values to $XYZ$ values using all test samples. The camera transfer matrixes $\mathbf{M}_{RGB}$ and $\mathbf{M}_{GIM}$ under each reference white are shown in Table 1. Although the two transfer matrixes were unequal, they did show a similar tendency.

Second, the chromaticity coordinates for the phosphor primaries were estimated using the camera transfer matrix under white balance point $D_{65}$. The estimated chromaticity coordinates for the phosphor primaries are shown Table 2.

Third, camera transfer matrixes under any other white balance were calculated using the estimated chromaticity coordinates for the phosphor primaries and each reference white point. Table 3 shows the estimated transfer matrixes under each reference white when using the proposed method.

Finally, the performance of the camera transfer matrix was compared when using the proposed method and conventional method under each reference white. Table 4 shows the chromaticity errors of the tristimulus obtained when using the proposed method and conventional method. Here, $\mathbf{M}_{RGB\_5800K}$, $\mathbf{M}_{RGB\_3200K}$, and $\mathbf{M}_{RGB\_A}$ mean the estimated transfer matrix when using the chromaticity coordinates for the phosphor primaries obtained by $\mathbf{M}_{RGB}$. Also, $\mathbf{M}_{GIM\_5800K}$, $\mathbf{M}_{GIM\_3200K}$, and $\mathbf{M}_{GIM\_A}$ mean the estimated transfer matrix when using the chromaticity coordinates for the phosphor primaries obtained by $\mathbf{M}_{GIM}$. In Table 4, the chromaticity errors $\triangle E_{xy}$ and $\triangle E_{uv}^*$ as regards the average of the estimated transfer matrix when using the proposed method were similar to those when using the conventional method under each reference white.

In the experimental results, we confirmed that the maximum chromaticity error between the proposed method and the conventional method is 0.017 in a $u'v'$ chromaticity coordinates. It is known that two separated color patches can usually be distinguished with a $\triangle u'v' \geq 0.04$ [13], [14]. Therefore, the prediction errors of the proposed method are excellent because this errors are smaller than the threshold value that two separated color patches can be distinguished. It was also confirmed that $\mathbf{M}_{RGB}$ was more efficient than $\mathbf{M}_{GIM}$ as the transfer matrix to obtain the chromaticity coordinates for the phosphor primaries and reference white. The $xy$ coordinates measured by a spectroradiometer MINOLTA CS1000 were compared with the $xy$ coordinates calculated by the estimated transfer matrix. Fig. 2 shows the measured and calculated $xy$ coordinates for the test color samples, where the performance of the $3\times 3$ transfer matrix estimated using the proposed method was better than that of the conventional method.

## 5 Conclusions

This paper proposed a new method for obtaining camera characterization matrices under different white balances based on a camera characterization matrix under a specific white balance point. First, the transfer matrix is obtained through a conventional method using variable polynomial regression with least squares fitting under white balance point $D_{65}$. Second, the chromaticity coordinates for the phosphor primaries are then estimated from the camera transfer matrix. By calculating the change in the tristimulus constant matrix $\mathbf{K}$ according to a change in the camera white balance point, a camera transfer matrix under any other white balance can be obtained. Experimental results confirmed that the proposed method enabled a 3×3 linear transfer matrix under any other white balance to be produced with a reasonable degree of accuracy when compared with the matrices resulting from the conventional method. Accordingly, the proposed method is a simple and soft solution for obtaining commercial camera characterization without the need for tedious experiments using over 60 training samples under various white balance points for the same camera.

# References

[1] CIE Pub. 15.2. Colorimetry, 2nd Ed., CIE Central Bureau, Vienna, (1986)
[2] G. Hong, M.R. Luo, and P.A. Rhodes: A study of digital camera colorimetric characterization based on polynomial modeling. J. Color Res. and App., Vol. 26, No. 1, (2001) 76-84
[3] R.S. Berns and M.J. Shyu: Colorimetric characterization of a desk-top drum scanner using a spectral model. J. Electronic Imag., Vol. 4, (1995) 360-372
[4] S. Suzuki, T. Kusunoki, and M. Mori: Color characteristic design for color scanners. Applied Optics, Vol. 29, (1990) 5187-5192
[5] P. C. Hung: Colorimetric calibration in electronic imaging devices using a look-up tables model and interpolations. J. Electronic Imag., Vol. 2, No. 1, (1993) 53-61
[6] P. C. Hung: Colorimetric calibration for scanners and media. Proc. SPIE, Vol. 1448, (1991) 164-174
[7] H. R. Kang: Color scanner calibration. J. Imaging Sci. and Tech., Vol. 36, (1992) 162-170
[8] H. R. Kang and P.G. Anderson: Neural network application to the color scanner and printer calibration. J. Electronic Imag., Vol. 1, (1992) 125-134
[9] H. R. Kang: The color technology for electronic imaging devices. SPIE, (1997)
[10] T. Johnson: Methods for characterizing color scanners and digital cameras. Displays, Vol. 16, (1996) 183-191
[11] K. B. Benson and J. C. Whitaker: Television Engineering Handbook, McGraw-Hill, (1992)
[12] C. Bailey Neal: Television colorimetry for receiver engineers. IEEE Trans. BTR, Vol. BTR-19, (1973) 149-162
[13] R. W. G. Hunt: The Reproduction of Colour in Photography, Printing & Television. Fountain Press, England, (1987) 177-196
[14] VESA Display Metrology Committee: Flat Panel Display Measurements Standard. VESA, (2001) 115

# A New Color Constancy Algorithm Based on the Histogram of Feasible Mappings*

Jaume Vergés–Llahí and Alberto Sanfeliu

Institut de Robòtica i Informàtica Industrial,
Technological Park of Barcelona, U Building
{jverges, asanfeliu}@iri.upc.edu

**Abstract.** Color is an important cue both in machine vision and image processing applications, despite its dependence upon illumination changes. We propose a color constancy algorithm that estimates both the set and the likelihood of feasible color mappings in respect to their frequency and effectiveness. The best among this set is selected to rendered back image colors as seen under a canonical light. Experiments were done to evaluate its performance compared to Finlayson's 2D gamut–mapping algorithm, outperforming it. Our approach is a helpful alternative wherever illumination is poorly known since it employs only image data.

**Keywords:** Color, color mappings, color constancy, color histograms.

## 1 Introduction

In a number of applications from machine vision to multimedia or even mobile robotics, it is important that the recorded colors remain constant under changes in the scene illumination. Hence, a preliminary step when using color must be to remove the distracting effects of such a variation. This problem is usually referred to as *color constancy*, i.e., the stability of surface color appearance under varying illumination. Part of the difficulty is its entanglement with other confounding phenomena such as object shape, viewing and illumination geometry, besides changes in the nature of light and the reflectance properties of surfaces.

Generally, color constancy (CC) is understood as the recovery of *descriptors* for the surfaces in a scene as they would be seen under a canonical illuminant. This is similar to recover an estimate of the illumination color from an image under an unknown light, since it is relatively straightforward to map image colors back to illuminant independent descriptors [1]. Therefore, *finding a mapping between colors or the color of the scene illuminant are equivalent problems*.

Some algorithms followed such a path, specially those related to the *gamut–mapping* approach [2,3,4,5]. Recently, the trend has slightly changed to make a guess on the illumination, as in *color–by–correlation* [1] or *color–voting* [6], rather than attempting to recover only one estimate. A measure of the *likelihood* that each of a set of feasible candidates was the scene illuminant is set out instead, which is afterwards used to render the image back into the canonical illuminant.

---

* Sup. by the Spanish Min. of Edu. & Sci. under proj. TIC2003-09291 & DPI2004-5414.

Some difficulties arise among the approaches above. The main one for us is the dependence on the fact that *all* possible colors under a canonic illuminant be available *a priori*. Besides, while gamut–mapping employs a selection strategy blind to any information about the likelihood of a particular mapping, color–by–correlation can only chose an illumination out of a discrete set of lights known a priori. Real–world applications usually do not fit such requirements.

Hence, in this paper we propose a new color constancy algorithm that can be used in tasks with little knowledge on the scene illumination. Our algorithm computes the histogram of the feasible maps and recovers one to changes image colors as if seen under a canonic light only using a canonic image picturing a similar scene. The performance of this algorithm is compared to that of the Finlayson's 2D gamut–mapping, outperforming it and obtaining similar figures to those of the color–by–correlation approach.

## 2 The Color Constancy Algorithm

The goal of this algorithm is to recover an image as seen under some canonic illumination. This algorithm gives to each feasible color mapping a particular likelihood related to its *frequency* and *performance*. The frequency is estimated from the histogram of feasible mappings, while the performance evaluates how close colors are rendered to those in the canonic set. The combined measure is used afterwards to select the best color mapping. Hereafter, we describe the basis of our algorithm along with its elements, namely, likelihood function, color coordinates, color change model, and mapping estimation and selection.

Let $\mathcal{I}_c$ and $\mathcal{I}_a$ be the *canonic* and the *actual* images, respectively, picturing similar scenes under two different lights. The algorithm only employs image raw data and no segmentation is needed. Our aim is to find the likeliest color transformation T mapping colors of image $\mathcal{I}_a$ as close to those of $\mathcal{I}_c$ as possible. We note as $\mathcal{I} \subset \mathbb{R}^d$ a set of colors, where $d$ is the color space dimension. Its origin can be either a specified color gamut or an image. The color histogram of $\mathcal{I}$ is noted as $\mathcal{H}_\mathcal{I}$. If a mapping T $\in$ <T> is applied to each color in $\mathcal{I}$, a transformed set T($\mathcal{I}$) is obtained. <T> is the set of *feasible color mappings*. Analogously, T($\mathcal{H}_\mathcal{I}$) represents the transformation of the histogram $\mathcal{H}_\mathcal{I}$ by the map T.

In general, given two color sets, $\mathcal{I}_a$ and $\mathcal{I}_c$, a *model of color change* consists in a mapping T $\in$ <T> so that

$$\text{T}: \mathcal{I}_a \longrightarrow \mathcal{I}_c \\ s \longmapsto \text{T}(s) = q \tag{1}$$

where $s \in \mathcal{S}$ and $q \in \mathcal{Q}$ are *corresponding* colors. The set of feasible maps is <T>= {T = $\Delta(\mathcal{S}, \mathcal{Q})$ | $\forall \mathcal{S} \subset \mathcal{I}_a$ and $\forall \mathcal{Q} \subset \mathcal{I}_c$} and $\Delta$ is a *mapping estimation scheme* computing a map T out of two corresponding sets $\mathcal{S}$ and $\mathcal{Q}$.

### 2.1 Likelihood Function

The color constancy algorithm must select the likeliest transformation $\hat{\text{T}}$ from the set <T> accordingly to a likelihood function $\mathcal{L}_\Delta(\text{T} \mid \mathcal{I}_a, \mathcal{I}_c)$ as

$$\hat{T} = \underset{T \in <T>}{\operatorname{argmax}} \{\mathcal{L}_\Delta(T \mid \mathcal{I}_a, \mathcal{I}_c)\} \tag{2}$$

Any likelihood $\mathcal{L}_\Delta$ is related to a probability function Pr as $\mathcal{L}_\Delta(T \mid \mathcal{I}_a, \mathcal{I}_c) = log(\Pr(T \mid \mathcal{I}_a, \mathcal{I}_c))$, noting that the map maximizing $\mathcal{L}_\Delta(T \mid \mathcal{I}_a, \mathcal{I}_c)$ also maximizes $\Pr(T \mid \mathcal{I}_a, \mathcal{I}_c)$), and *vice versa*. Hence, we must first get a value for the probability of any mapping T. As an estimate of $\Pr(T \mid \mathcal{I}_a, \mathcal{I}_c)$ we use the *histogram* of the set of feasible mappings, noted as $\mathcal{H}_{<T>}$. In order to compute frequencies we employ colors in the sets $\mathcal{I}_a$ and $\mathcal{I}_c$, as well as the mapping estimator $\Delta$. The point is that the likelier a mapping is, the more frequent it should be in the histogram $\mathcal{H}_{<T>}$, and the other way round.

Nonetheless, a particular mapping T can be produced from different groups of colors. Thus, it is useful to define the set of all pairs $(\mathcal{S}, \mathcal{Q})$ giving rise to a certain map T from the estimator $\Delta$, i.e., $\Delta^{-1}(T) = \{(\mathcal{S}, \mathcal{Q}) \in 2^{\mathcal{I}_a} \times 2^{\mathcal{I}_c} \mid \Delta(\mathcal{S}, \mathcal{Q}) = T\}$, where $2^{\mathcal{I}}$ stands for the set of all subsets of $\mathcal{I}$. Therefore, the set $\Delta^{-1}(T)$ is equivalent to T and can be taken instead of it since $\Delta^{-1}(T) = \Delta^{-1}(T') \Leftrightarrow T = T'$. Hence, it is true that $\Pr(T \mid \mathcal{I}_a, \mathcal{I}_c) = \Pr(\Delta^{-1}(T) \mid \mathcal{I}_a, \mathcal{I}_c)$.

In practice, $\Delta^{-1}(T)$ can be thought as a finite disjoint union of singletons $\{(\mathcal{S}, \mathcal{Q})\}$, being each set a combination of colors from sets $\mathcal{I}_a$ and $\mathcal{I}_c$, respectively. Besides, to compute $\Pr((\mathcal{S}, \mathcal{Q}) \mid \mathcal{I}_a, \mathcal{I}_c)$ we must only remind that each $\{(\mathcal{S}, \mathcal{Q})\}$ is formed by two independent sets, namely, $\mathcal{S} \subset \mathcal{I}_a$ and $\mathcal{Q} \subset \mathcal{I}_c$. Therefore,

$$\Pr((\mathcal{S}, \mathcal{Q}) \mid \mathcal{I}_a, \mathcal{I}_c) = \Pr(\mathcal{S} \mid \mathcal{I}_a) \cdot \Pr(\mathcal{Q} \mid \mathcal{I}_c) \tag{3}$$

Then, we get that

$$\Pr(T \mid \mathcal{I}_a, \mathcal{I}_c)) = \sum_{\forall (\mathcal{S}, \mathcal{Q}) \in \Delta^{-1}(T)} \Pr(\mathcal{S} \mid \mathcal{I}_a) \cdot \Pr(\mathcal{Q} \mid \mathcal{I}_c) \tag{4}$$

that is, frequency of a mapping T in the histogram of feasible mappings $\mathcal{H}_{<T>}$ is computed adding the product of frequencies corresponding to all the pairs $\mathcal{S}$ and $\mathcal{Q}$ giving rise to the mapping T by means of the mapping estimator $\Delta$.

$\Pr(\mathcal{S} \mid \mathcal{I}_a)$ and $\Pr(\mathcal{Q} \mid \mathcal{I}_c)$ are approximated by the frequency of the corresponding bins in histograms $\mathcal{H}_{\mathcal{I}_a}$ and $\mathcal{H}_{\mathcal{I}_c}$. In case $\mathcal{S} = \{s\}$, it is straightforward that $\Pr(\mathcal{S} \mid \mathcal{I}) \approx \mathcal{H}_{\mathcal{I}}(s)$. Hence, in general, if $\mathcal{S} = \{s_i\}_{i=1,\ldots,n}$, the probability of the set under the hypothesis of independence of colors is

$$\Pr(\mathcal{S} \mid \mathcal{I}) \approx \prod_{i=1}^{n} \mathcal{H}_{\mathcal{I}}(s_i) \tag{5}$$

On the other hand, usually some spurious peaks appear in $\mathcal{H}_{<T>}$, which might mislead the algorithm. To improve the robustness of Eq. (4), a measure of similarity between the transformed set $T(\mathcal{I}_a)$ and the canonic set $\mathcal{I}_c$ is taken into account, evaluating the efficiency of a particular mapping T. We use the Swain & Ballard intersection–measure between histograms defined in [7] as

$$\cap(\mathcal{H}_1, \mathcal{H}_2) = \sum_k \min\{\mathcal{H}_1(k), \mathcal{H}_2(k)\} \in [0, 1] \tag{6}$$

The advantages of such a measure are that it is very fast to compute if compared to other matching functions. Besides, if the histograms are sparse and colors equally probable, it is a robust way of comparing images [7]. This step helps in practice to eliminate outlier mappings among candidates.

As a consequence, we finally define our likelihood function by joining the probability of a mapping and its performance in a single expression as follows

$$\mathcal{L}_\Delta(T \mid \mathcal{I}_a, \mathcal{I}_c) = log(\cap(T(\mathcal{H}_{\mathcal{I}_a}), \mathcal{H}_{\mathcal{I}_c})) \cdot \Pr(T \mid \mathcal{I}_a, \mathcal{I}_c)), \quad \forall T \in <T> \quad (7)$$

where $T(\mathcal{H}_{\mathcal{I}_a})$ is the transformation of $\mathcal{H}_{\mathcal{I}_a}$ by a mapping T and $\Pr(T \mid \mathcal{I}_a, \mathcal{I}_c))$ is the frequency of T in the histogram $\mathcal{H}_{<T>}$ computed with Eq. (4).

## 2.2 Color Coordinates

Colors can be represented as vectors in $\mathbb{R}^d$. In our case, to alleviate problems with specularities or shape and to reduce at the same time the computational burden, we use the *perspective color coordinates* $(r, g) = (R/B, G/B)$ proposed by Finlayson in [3]. Finlayson and Hordley also proved in [8] for these coordinates that the set of feasible mappings computed in a $3D$ space and projected into a $2D$ space afterward is the same as the one directly computed in a $2D$ space.

## 2.3 Color Change Model

It is been stated that any color change could be described using a homogeneous linear relation [2]. Thus, the mapping T is specified in coordinates as follows

$$\begin{aligned} T: \mathcal{I}_a &\longrightarrow \mathcal{I}_c \\ s &\longmapsto T(s) = \mathbf{T}\, s^t = \mathbf{q}^t \end{aligned} \quad (8)$$

A reasonable tradeoff between simplicity and performance is attained employing a *diagonal model* [2,1,3]. This model assumes color sensors are completely uncorrelated and any change in the light falling into them equates to independently scaling each channel, that is, $\mathbf{T} = diag(t_1, \ldots, t_d)$. Equivalently, $\mathbf{T}$ can be expressed as a vector $\mathbf{t} = (t_1, \ldots, t_d) \in \mathbb{R}^d$, so that, $\mathbf{T} = \mathbf{t}\,\mathbf{I}_d$. This is the model used in this paper, despite the color constancy algorithm also works with any other more complete model, involving more computational time as a result.

## 2.4 Mapping Estimation

Formally, the mapping estimator $\Delta$ is a function computing a mapping $T \in <T>$ from two sets $\mathcal{S} = \{s_i\}_{i=1,\ldots,n} \subset \mathcal{I}_a$ and $\mathcal{Q} = \{q_i\}_{i=1,\ldots,n} \subset \mathcal{I}_c$, i.e.,

$$\begin{aligned} \Delta: 2^{\mathcal{I}_a} \times 2^{\mathcal{I}_c} &\longrightarrow <T> \\ (\mathcal{S}, \mathcal{Q}) &\longmapsto \Delta(\mathcal{S}, \mathcal{Q}) = T \end{aligned} \quad (9)$$

A mapping T can be expressed as a matrix $\mathbf{T}$ so that $q = T(s)$ is equivalent to $\mathbf{T}\,s^t = \mathbf{q}^t$. In general, it is not possible to find a matrix $\mathbf{T}$ out of just a pair of corresponding vectors **s** and **q**, since we need, at least, as many linearly independent pairs as the space dimension $d$. Taking advantage of the nature of **T** and two sets of $n \geq d$ one–to–one corresponding vectors, namely, $\{\mathbf{s}_i\}_{i=1,\ldots,n}$ and $\{\mathbf{q}_i\}_{i=1,\ldots,n}$, it is true that $\mathbf{T}\,(\mathbf{s}_1^t \mid \cdots \mid \mathbf{s}_n^t) = (\mathbf{q}_1^t \mid \cdots \mid \mathbf{q}_n^t)$.

If $\mathbf{S} = (\mathbf{s}_1^t \mid \cdots \mid \mathbf{s}_n^t) \in \mathcal{M}_{d \times n}(\mathbb{R})$ and $\mathbf{Q} = (\mathbf{q}_1^t \mid \cdots \mid \mathbf{q}_n^t) \in \mathcal{M}_{d \times n}(\mathbb{R})$ are introduced by joining vectors columnwise, finding a matrix **T** consists in solving the linear system $\mathbf{Q} = \mathbf{T}\mathbf{S}$, where **T** is the unknown. The usual method to solve this system is by a SVD to compute pseudo–inverse $\mathbf{S}^+$. Therefore, the version of Eq. (9) in coordinates is

$$\begin{aligned}\Delta \colon \mathcal{M}_{d \times n}(\mathbb{R}) \times \mathcal{M}_{d \times n}(\mathbb{R}) &\longrightarrow \mathcal{M}_d(\mathbb{R}) \\ (\mathbf{S},\mathbf{Q}) &\longmapsto \Delta(\mathbf{S},\mathbf{Q}) = \mathbf{Q}\,\mathbf{S}^+ = \mathbf{T}\end{aligned} \qquad (10)$$

In case the diagonal model is used, the above function is greatly simplified

$$\begin{aligned}\Delta \colon \mathbb{R}^d \times \mathbb{R}^d &\longrightarrow \mathbb{R}^d \\ (\mathbf{s},\mathbf{q}) &\longmapsto \Delta(\mathbf{s},\mathbf{q}) = \left(\tfrac{q_1}{s_1},\ldots,\tfrac{q_d}{s_d}\right)^t = \mathbf{t}\end{aligned} \qquad (11)$$

The method for carrying out the mapping computations between two color sets consists in first computing the histograms of both sets and applying the estimator $\Delta$ to every possible pair of color sets. Colors in $\mathcal{S}$ need not to be really in a correspondence with those in $\mathcal{Q}$, since *all* possible combinations are checked. Nevertheless, in a real case some heuristic are necessary to speed up the process. In our case, only the colors with nonzero frequency are considered, which reduces the amount of computations to less than $O\left(p^2\right)$, where $p \ll n$ is the number of histogram bins and $n$ the number of colors in a set.

### 2.5 Mapping Selection

In addition to Eq. (2), other heuristics can be useful to improve the results

**Max:** As said in Eq. (2), the mapping with the highest likelihood is selected.
**Mean:** Mean among the candidates, after weighting them by their likelihood.
**CMax:** The same as in **Max**, after constraining the set of feasible illuminants, as proposed by Finlayson.
**CMean:** The same as in **Mean**, after constraining the illuminant set.
**CM:** The center of mass of the convex hull from the set of feasible mappings.

## 3 Experiments and Results

We show now the performance of our color constancy algorithm compared to that of Finlayson's 2D gamut mapping. To that goal, the database[1] considered consisting in a set of 220 images from 20 objects viewed under 11 illuminants.

---
[1] http://www.cs.sfu.ca/~color/data/objects_under_different_lights/index.html

Basically, these are images (Fig. 1) of single colorful objects in a black background to avoid interreflections. The pose of the objects varied every time lights were changed. Additionally, authors took care of analyzing the lights used to produce the images, quite helpful in building the set of feasible illuminants.

A canonic image of the scene is employed as the reference for colors. Experiments carried out basically consists in computing a distance between colors from each scene and those of the canonic one before and after the CC stage to measure the amount of reduction in color dissimilarity. This is done for the two algorithms and one canonic image per set. The more the processed images resemble to the canonic, the greater the color dissimilarity reduction. Each algorithm has various selection heuristics. Our algorithm used $CM$, $Mean$, $Max$, $CMean$, and $CMax$, as explained in Section 2.5. In Finlayson's 2D–GM we employed the center of mass ($FinCM$), the mean ($FinMean$), and the 3D mean proposed by Hordley and Finlayson in [8] ($FinHord$), all constrained by the set of lights.

(a)  (b)

**Fig. 1.** Sets of some objects under all light variation: (a) rollups, (b) book

Two measures of color dissimilarity were applied to estimate the performance of the two CC methods, namely, the Swain & Ballard difference [7] and a RMS error. The first accounts for the difference between the canonic and the processed color histograms. Here, an extra result ($True$) is obtained using the maps from the true lights in the database. Instead, RMSE compares two images obtained from each actual image after transforming it with the *true* mapping and the one from the particular CC algorithm. The canonic image is useless here because RMSE is pixelwise and objects were moved from one image to another.

The results are summarized in Fig. 2 through Fig. 5. Plots in Fig. 2 and Fig. 3 show the results corresponding to the S&B distance, while Fig. 4 and Fig. 5 illustrate those using the RMSE distance. These graphics consist in three plots each: mean, median, and a distribution boxplot[2], where colors represents versions of the algorithms. Additionally, the numerical values for the mean distances and the percent reduction of the color dissimilarity are accounted in Table 1 (Finlayson's 2D–GM) and Table 2 (our CC algorithm), where *No CC* correspond to the distance between images before any CC is carried out.

First of all, when considering the performance of our algorithm, we state the results from the Finlayson's 2D–GM – 0.27 (RMSE) – are comparable to those in

---

[2] A boxplot is a statistic descriptive tool showing, at once, a distribution of values.

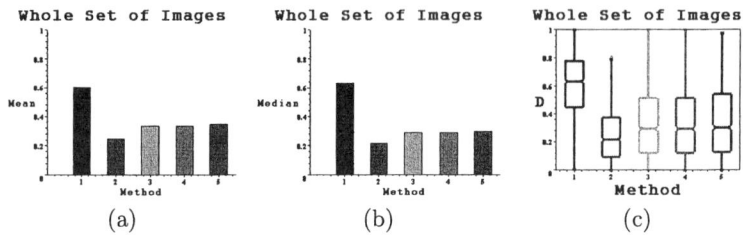

**Fig. 2.** Results using S&B and Finlayson's 2D–GM. Blue: *No CC*. Red: *True*. Green: *FinCM*. Magenta: *FinMean*. Violet: *FinHord*. (a) Mean, (b) median, and (c) boxplot.

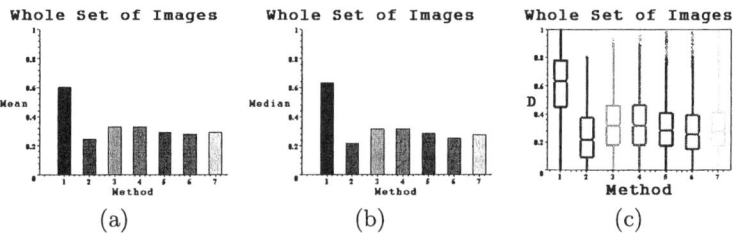

**Fig. 3.** Results using S&B and our algorithm. Blue: *No CC*. Red: *True*. Green: *CM*. Magenta: *Mean*. Violet: *Max*. Orange: *CMean*. Yellow: *CMax*. (a) Mean, (b) median, and (c) boxplot.

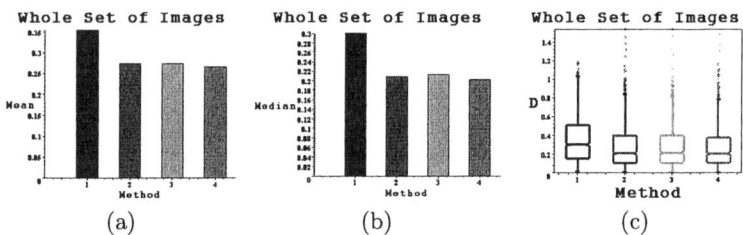

**Fig. 4.** Results using RMSE and Finlayson's 2D–GM. Blue: *No CC*. Red: *FinCM*. Green: *FinMean*. Magenta: *FinHord*. (a) Mean, (b) median, and (c) boxplot.

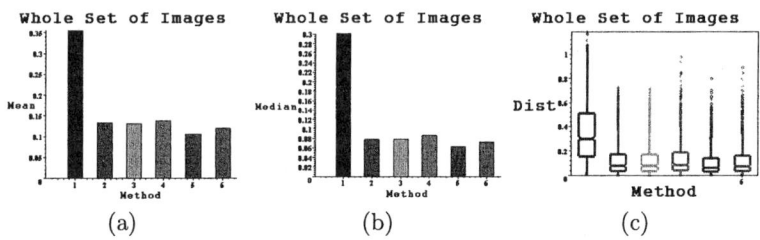

**Fig. 5.** Results using RMSE and our algorithm. Blue: *No CC*. Red: *CM*. Green: *Mean*. Magenta: *Max*. Violet: *CMean*. Orange: *CMax*. (a) Mean, (b) median, and (c) boxplot.

Table 1. Results using Finalyson's 2D–GM algorithm

| Finalyson's 2D-GM | | FinCM | FinMean | FinHord | No CC | True |
|---|---|---|---|---|---|---|
| S&B | Mean Dist. | 0.3367 | 0.3357 | 0.3464 | **0.6036** | 0.2488 |
| | % Red. | 44.22 | 44.38 | 42.61 | ~ | **58.78** |
| RMSE | Mean Dist. | 0.2732 | 0.2738 | 0.2655 | **0.3559** | |
| | % Red. | 23.24 | 23.07 | 25.40 | ~ | |

Table 2. Results using our color constancy algorithm

| Our CC alg. | | CM | Mean | Max | CMean | CMax | No CC | True |
|---|---|---|---|---|---|---|---|---|
| S&B | Mean Dist. | 0.3301 | 0.3301 | 0.2956 | 0.2805 | 0.2945 | **0.6036** | 0.2488 |
| | % Red. | 45.31 | 45.31 | 51.03 | 53.53 | 51.21 | ~ | **58.78** |
| RMSE | Mean Dist. | 0.1330 | 0.1313 | 0.1382 | 0.1060 | 0.1200 | **0.3559** | |
| | % Red. | 62.63 | 63.11 | 61.17 | 70.32 | 66.28 | ~ | |

[1] – 0.21 (RMSE) –. In Table 1 and 2 it is shown that with the S&B distance the Finlayson's 2D–GM best result is achieved with $FinMean$ (44.38%), whereas for our algorithm the best result is obtained with $CMean$ (53.53%), which is pretty close to the figure from the true lights mappings (58.78%). In respect to the RMSE results, figures obtained for our algorithm (70.32%) are definitely better than those of Finlayson's 2D–GM (25.40%) and totally comparable to the best CC algorithm so far, namely, color–by–correlation [1] – 0.11 (RMSE) –, which is fairly a good result since our approach works with less information.

## 4 Conclusions

This paper describes a new color constancy algorithm. This is based on the computation of the histogram of feasible maps between two light conditions and selecting the best mapping on the base of a likelihood measure for each mapping encompassing both its frequency and effectiveness. Experiments were done to evaluate the performance of our algorithm in comparison to that of Finlayson's 2D–GM, outperforming it and attaining similar results to those of the color–by–correlation scheme. Our algorithm works with only a canonic image as a reference and resulting maps are not restricted to a discrete set of feasible ones. Besides using less information than other methods, it is a useful alternative in tasks where little knowledge on the illumination is at hand.

## References

1. Finlayson, G., Hordley, S., Hubel, P.: Colour by correlation: A simple, unifying framework for colour constancy. IEEE Trans. on Pattern Analysis and Machine Intelligence **23** (2001) 1209–1221
2. Forsyth, D.: A novel algorithm for color constancy. Int. Journal of Computer Vision **5** (1990) 5–36

3. Finlayson, G.: Color in perspective. IEEE Trans. on Pattern Analysis and Machine Intelligence **18** (1996) 1034–1038
4. Barnard, K., Cardei, V., Funt, B.: A comparison of computational colour constancy algorithms: Part one: Methodology and experiments with synthesized data. IEEE Trans. on Image Processing **11** (2002) 972–983
5. Barnard, K., Martin, L., Coath, A., Funt, B.: A comparison of computational colour constancy algorithms: Part two: Experiments with image data. IEEE Trans. on Image Processing **11** (2002) 985–996
6. Sapiro, G.: Color and illuminant voting. IEEE Trans. on Pattern Analysis and Machine Intelligence **21** (1999) 1210–1215
7. Swain, M., Ballard, D.: Indexing via color histograms. In: Proc. Int. Conf. on Computer Vision. (1990) 390–393
8. Finlayson, G., Hordley, S.: Improving gamut mapping color constancy. IEEE Trans. on Image Processing **9** (2000) 1774–1783

# A Comparative Study of Skin-Color Models

Juwei Lu, Qian Gu*, K.N. Plataniotis, and Jie Wang

Bell Canada Multimedia Laboratory, The Edward S. Rogers Sr.,
Department of Electrical and Computer Engineering,
University of Toronto, Canada M5S 3G4

**Abstract.** In this paper, we report the results of a comparative study on skin-color models generally used for facial region location. These include two 2D Gaussian models developed in normalized RGB and HSV color spaces respectively, a 1D lookup table model of hue histogram, and an adaptive 3D threshold box model. Also, we present a new model - called "adaptive hue lookup table". The model is developed by introducing the so-called "Continuously Adaptive Mean Shift" (Camshift) technique into a traditional hue lookup table method. With the introduction of Camshift, the lookup table is able to adaptively adjust its parameters to fit the illumination conditions of different test images. In the experiments reported here, we compare the proposed method with the four typical skin-color filters in the scenarios of different human races and illuminations. The obtained results indicate that the proposed method reaches the best balance between false detection and detect rate.

## 1 Introduction

Automatic location of facial region is an important first step in face recognition/tracking systems. Its reliability has a major influence on the performance and usability of entire face recognition/tracking systems. Numerous solutions to the problem have been presented. Generally, they can be roughly classified into two classes [1]: (1) gray-level based methods and (2) color-based methods. Among the gray-level based methods, most are based on template matching techniques [2]. The input image is windowed (with varying window sizes) from location to location, and the sub-image in the window is classified as face or non-face. Although accurate in terms of detect rate, most of them are highly complicated and time-costing, which are major reasons why the kind of methods are not typically used in real-time tasks. Also, they are sensitive to facial variations due to view-points, scales, rotations and illuminations.

The color-based methods are normally based on various skin-color filters and region segmentation techniques [3,4]. This kind of methods have many advantages compared to the gray-level based methods. First, processing color is much faster than doing template matching. Second, color models are scale/orientation/rotion invariant. These properties are particularly important for a real-time

---

* Ms Qian Gu performed the work while at School of Electrical and Electronic Engineering, Nanyang Technological University, Singapore, 639798.

face/human tracking system. Successful applications of color-based algorithms include some state-of-the-art face/human tracking systems, such as Pfinder [5] and Yang's face tracker [6]. In this work, we first study the properties of various skin-color filters, which are typically used for face detection tasks. Then, a new model - called "adaptive hue lookup table" (AH-LT) is developed. By introducing the so-called Camshift technique [7], the AH-LT model is able to take advantages of the available color information, and adaptively update its thresholds for different input images to identify skin-color. In the experiment reported here, we compare the AH-LT model with four typical skin-color filters in the scenarios of different human races and illuminations. The AH-LT model shows promising results.

## 2 Skin-Color Models

### 2.1 2D Gaussian Model in RGB Color Space (RG-GM)

In the RGB color space, a triple of $[R, G, B]$ represents not only color but also brightness. A typical way to separate chromatic colors or *pure* colors $(r, g)$ from brightness is to apply a normalization process [8],

$$r = R/(R+G+B), \quad g = G/(R+G+B) \quad (1)$$

Eq.1 defines a mapping from $\mathbb{R}^3$ to $\mathbb{R}^2$, and the color blue is redundant after the normalization due to $r+g+b=1$. It is found by Yang *et al.* [6] that the human skin-color distribution tends to cluster in a small region in the $(r,g)$ space, although in reality skin-colors of different people appear to vary over a wide range. These variations are generally believed to be mainly caused by brightness or intensity. Thus, the skin-color distribution can be represented exactly by a 2D Gaussian model $N(u, \Sigma^2)$ where $u = (\bar{r}, \bar{g})^T$,

$$\bar{r} = \frac{1}{N}\sum_{i=1}^{N} r_i, \quad \bar{g} = \frac{1}{N}\sum_{i=1}^{N} g_i, \quad \Sigma = \begin{bmatrix} \sigma_{rr} & \sigma_{rg} \\ \sigma_{gr} & \sigma_{gg} \end{bmatrix}, \quad (2)$$

$N$ is the number of the training pixels. Fig.1:Left shows the skin-color distribution of a set of training samples, which are collected from different racial people. For simplicity, we call the model "RG-GM" hereafter. A successful application of RG-GM is Yang's face tracker [6].

### 2.2 2D Gaussian Model in HSV Color Space (HS-GM)

Compared to RG-GM, a better way to extract chromatic colors seems to transform color representation from the $(R, G, B)$ space to the $(H, S, V)$ space, where $H$ denotes Hue distinguishing pure colors such as red, green, purple and yellow, $S$ denotes Saturation referring to how far color is from a gray of equal intensity, and $V$ denotes Value embodying the lightness or intensity. Compared with the $(R, G, B)$ color space, the $(H, S, V)$ space embodies the artist's ideas of

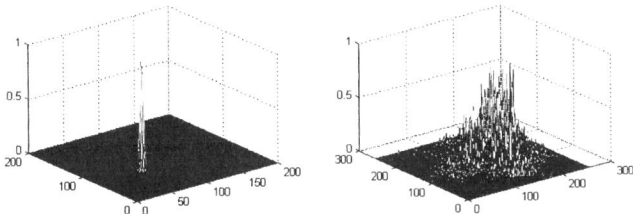

**Fig. 1.** The skin color distributions in the normalized $(r,g)$ space (Left), and the $(h_x, h_y)$ space (Right), respectively

tint, shade and tone. Unlike the normalization of $(R, G, B)$, the mapping from $(R, G, B)$ to $(H, S, V)$ is nonlinear. Research studies indicate that HSV-based models outperform RGB-based models in skin pixel classification [3,7].

Similar to the normalized RGB space, observations show the human skin-color distribution also tends to cluster in a small region in the HSV space [9]. As such, we can model the skin-color distribution using a 2D Gaussian Model of $(H, S)$ components. It is well-known that $H$ represents angle and $S$ represents distance. In order to combine the two variables with different units, we can derive a pair of new variables $(h_x, h_y)$ from $(H, S)$ to represent color pixels, where $h_x = S \cdot \cos(H)$, and $h_y = S \cdot \sin(H)$. Then, the skin-color distribution can be modeled by a 2D Gaussian distribution: $N(\mu, K)$ with

$$\mu = \frac{1}{N} \sum_{n=1}^{N} H_n, \quad K = \frac{1}{N} \sum_{n=1}^{N} (H_n - \mu)(H_n - \mu)^T \quad (3)$$

where $H_n = \left[h_x^{(n)}, h_y^{(n)}\right]^T$, and $\left(h_x^{(n)} h_y^{(n)}\right)$ denotes the $n$th pixel. The model has been applied into extraction of hand region [9]. For simplicity, we call it HS-GM hereafter. Fig.1:Right shows the distribution of a set of training skin-color pixels used in our experiments.

### 2.3 1D Lookup Table Based on Hue Histogram (H-LT)

Some researchers [7] found that saturation is also influenced by lightness. Thereby, a simple but efficient model is derived only from the histogram of the $H$ (hue) component. In this method, a hue histogram of the training skin-color pixels is first built. Then, the histogram is smoothed by a Gaussian low-pass filer. The values in each bin are further normalized to the range $[0, 1]$. The obtained histogram is called hue lookup table (H-LT hereafter). The values in the H-LT cells reflect the likelihood that the corresponding color is classified to the skin color. Fig.2 shows the hue histogram used in our experiments.

### 2.4 Adaptive Hue Lookup Table Model (AH-LT)

Often it is found to be insufficient to use only hue information for skin-color classification in practical applications [4]. In order to improve the performance,

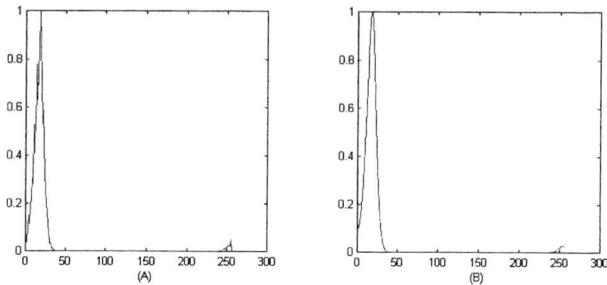

**Fig. 2.** (A): Original hue histogram, (B): Smoothed hue histogram

it is important to integrate saturation and value information into the skin-color models. However, since the saturation and value of skin-color often vary with illumination conditions, the models have to be able to adaptively update their decision boundaries on $(S, V)$ according to the illumination conditions of the input images. To this end, Cho et al. [10] presented an adaptive 3D threshold box model (3D-TBox) in the HSV color space. The 3D box is constructed by 6 thresholds, i.e. upper and lower thresholds of $H$, $S$ and $V$ respectively. All the pixels whose $(h, s, v)$ fall in the box are identified as skin-color pixels. In the model, the thresholds of hue is considered to be stable and fixed, while those of saturation and value are adaptively updated when a new image is tested. The update is implemented by a simple search procedure of gravity center. We found that the updating algorithm can be improved using an efficient alternative method - called "Continuously Adaptive Mean Shift Algorithm" (Camshift), which is based on the Meanshift technique [11]. Also, it seems to be not a good way to classify skin color using a pair of *hard* hue thresholds. An obviously better alternative is the *soft* H-LT model.

Based on the above two points, an improved model - called "Adaptive Hue Lookup Table Model" (AH-LT) is proposed here. The AH-LT model integrates Camshift, H-LT and the adaptive scheme of 3D-TBox together. The advantages of such a combination will be demonstrated in our experiments. The detail procedure of how the AH-LT model works can be divided into two steps: offline and online. In the offline learning step, we firstly build the H-LT model from a set of given skin-color pixels. Then, the initial upper and lower thresholds for $S$, $V$ are chosen manually by observing the skin color distributions of training sample images that are obtained under various illumination conditions. In order to compare our method with the 3D-TBox as fair as possible, we use the same initial threshold values for $S$ and $V$ as [10].

In the online test step, we first go through the input image using H-LT to find all skin-color pixel candidates. The threshold for the likelihood is set to 0.3 in our experiments. Then, we find the distribution of the skin-color pixel candidates in the $(S, V)$ space by constructing a 2D $(S, V)$ histogram of these candidates. All the values in the 2D histogram is linearly normalized to the range $[0, 1]$. Thus, we can obtain a likelihood $p(s_i, v_i) \in [0, 1]$ for any candidate pixel from the normalized histogram or lookup table. Since $(S,V)$ of skin-color often shift with variation of lightness conditions, we have to adaptively update the thresholds of $(S,V)$ for different test images. This can be done by finding the mode of the probability distribution $p(s_i, v_i)$ using the Camshift algorithm [7].

Since the Camshift algorithm is derived from the Meanshift [11], it is necessary to introduce the Meanshift prior to the Camshift. The Meanshift is a non-parametric technique that climbs the gradient of a probability distribution to find the nearest dominant mode (peak). The procedure to calculate the Meanshift algorithm is given as follows:

1. Set size and location of initial search window $W_0$.
2. Compute the mean location in the search window. Let $M_{00}$, $M_{10}$ and $M_{01}$ denote the zero-th and first moments for $(s,v)$. These moments can be found by $M_{00} = \sum_{(s,v)\in W_i} p(s,v)$, $M_{10} = \sum_{(s,v)\in W_i} s \cdot p(s,v)$, and $M_{01} = \sum_{(s,v)\in W_i} v \cdot p(s,v)$, where $W_i$ denotes current search window. Then we have the mean location $(s_c, v_c)$, where $s_c = M_{10}/M_{00}$ and $v_c = M_{01}/M_{00}$.
3. Center the search window at the mean location computed in Step 2.
4. Repeat Step 2 and 3 until convergence..

A shortcoming of the Meanshift algorithm is that the size of the search window cannot be updated, but it is overcomed in the Camshift algorithm. The complete procedure to update the thresholds of $(S,V)$ using Camshift is given as follows:

1. Set size and location of initial search window $W_0$ (as shown in [10]).
2. Do Meanshift as above.
3. Update the search window size. Let $M_{20}$ and $M_{02}$ denote the second moments, and we have

$$M_{20} = \sum_{(s,v)\in W_i} s^2 \cdot p(s,v), \quad M_{02} = \sum_{(s,v)\in W_i} v^2 \cdot p(s,v). \quad (4)$$

Then the length and width of the probability distribution "blob" can be found as in [12]. Let $a = \frac{M_{20}}{M_{00}} - s_c^2$, $b = 2\left(\frac{M_{11}}{M_{00}} - s_c \cdot v_c\right)$, and $c = \frac{M_{02}}{M_{00}} - v_c^2$. We have the length and width of the new search window,

$$l = \sqrt{(a+c+\sqrt{b^2+(a-c)^2})/2}, \quad w = \sqrt{(a+c-\sqrt{b^2+(a-c)^2})/2}. \quad (5)$$

4. Repeat Steps 2 and 3 until convergence. The final search window gives new thresholds of $(S,V)$.

An assumption behind AH-LT is that the areas of real skin-color regions are comparable to (or larger than) the areas of those regions similar to skin-color. Otherwise, the Camshift may converge to the largest false skin-color region. Fig.3 show an example obtained by AH-LT. The initial detect result without threshold updating is shown in Fig.3(B), where some parts of the clothes were detected as well as the face region. However, one can see that most of false detects has been removed in Fig.3(C), after the threshold values of $(S,V)$ are updated accordingly.

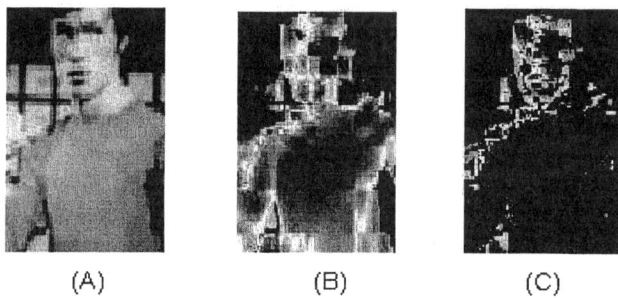

**Fig. 3.** An skin-color detect example using AH-LT. (a): Input image; (b): Result obtained with the initial threshold values recommended in [10]; (c): Result obtained with the updated threshold values.

## 3 Experimental Results

In the experiments, a set of human images were collected from the Internet. They are partitioned into two sets: training set and test set with no overlapping between the two. Skin-color pixels are cut manually from the training images to form a set of skin-color samples, which contain a total of 56279 pixels. The testing set contains 200 images, consisting of different racial people (Asian, African and Caucasian). Since the images were taken and digitized under various conditions, it can be said that no special illuminations or other constraints are imposed on the test images. Two experiments are implemented for the evaluation. One is designed to compare performance of the five skin color filters for different racial people. To this end, the testing set is manually partitioned into three groups according to races of people in the images. Another is designed to compare performance of the skin-color filters in different illuminations. In this experiment, according to the illumination variations of the skin regions in the images, we partition the test set to four groups: normal (161), reddish (13), bright (17) and dark (9). The five skin-color filters are applied in the two experiments, and the obtained results are shown in Table 1, where we define a detect if at least half of the true skin-color regions are found in a given test image.

In the first experiment, there are 88 images of Asian, 12 of African and 100 of Caucasian in the test set. From Table 1(Races), it can be seen that there are not significant difference in terms of detect rate among the three groups for each skin-color model. This demonstrates the observation by Yang et al. [6], that is, human skin colors tend to cluster into a small region in a color space. Also, not surprisingly, the HSV-based models (HS-GM, H-LT, 3D-TBox and AH-LT) are overall superior to the RGB-based model (RG-GM) in all the three groups. This result is consistent with our analysis in previous sections.

In the second experiment, it can be seen from Table 1(Illuminations) that RG-GM has the lowest detect rate among the five models. Specifically, it is difficult for RG-GM to detect the reddish or too dark skin-color regions. For example, only 2 out of 13 reddish images and 1 out of 9 dark images are detected by the

**Table 1.** Detect rates (%) of the five skin-color models in different experimental conditions of race and illumination

| Algs. | Illuminations | | | | | Races | | |
|---|---|---|---|---|---|---|---|---|
| | Normal | Reddish | Bright | Dark | Overall | Asian | African | Caucasian |
| RG-GM | 80.1 | 18.2 | 100 | 11.1 | 74.5 | 78.4 | 83.3 | 73 |
| HS-GM | 82 | 92.3 | 64.7 | 88.9 | 81.5 | 79.5 | 91.7 | 82 |
| H-LT | 93.8 | 92.3 | 100 | 100 | 94.5 | 93.2 | 91.7 | 96 |
| 3D-TBox | 85.7 | 76.9 | 82.4 | 100 | 85.5 | 84.1 | 91.7 | 89 |
| AH-LT | 90 | 76.9 | 94.1 | 100 | 90 | 87.5 | 91.7 | 92 |

method. This shows that the RGB-based models are rather sensitive to variations of illumination, because the saturation component influenced by illumination is not separated. Similar observations are also found by Bradski et al. [7].

In Table 1, the overall detect rate of HS-GM is 81.5%. This result is higher than that of RG-GM, but lower than those of the other three models. It failed when the skin-color regions are too bright. Although H-LT obtained the highest detect rate among the five models, it is found that its false alarm is much higher than AH-LT. One reason is that H-LT cannot adaptively update its parameters for the specific illumination conditions in different images. In contrast with H-LT, saturation and value can be appropriately adjusted in the AH-LT approach to fit the requirements of different inputs. As a result, some false detects can be removed and skin-color regions can be more accurately extracted as shown in Fig.3. Therefore, we have reasons to believe that the AH-LT method embodies a better trade-off between detect rate and false alarm.

## 4 Conclusion

In this paper, a new skin-color model is introduced by combining several commonly used techniques, such as the hue lookup table, the continuously adaptive mean shift, and the adaptive update of thresholds. Also, a comparative study between the proposed method and four traditional methods is carried out in various experimental settings such as races and illuminations. The obtained results indicate that the proposed AH-LT method is a promising solution to balance the tradeoff of detection rate and false alarm. Due to low computational costs and insensitivity to most facial variations such as view-points, scale, rotation and expressions, we expect that the AH-LT method can be used as an important pre-processing step in a real-time face location/tracking system.

Following the work presented here, there are several interesting topics to be conducted in the future. First, many of existing color-based methods use Gaussian models to approximate the skin-color distributions. However, it has been found that the practical distributions in the color spaces are much more complicated than Gaussian. Thus, it seems to be a better solution to map the color spaces to a feature space, where the assumption is closer to be true. Such a mapping can be implemented by using a kernel technique such as [13]. Furthermore, more sophisticated pattern recognition techniques, such as discriminant analysis used in face recognition [14,15,16] can be applied in the feature spaces to enhance the separability between the two classes, skin and non-skin pixels.

# References

1. Li, S.Z., Lu, J.: Face detection, alignment and recognition. In Medioni, G., Kang, S.B., eds.: EMERGING TOPICS IN COMPUTER VISION. Prentice-Hall, Upper Saddle River, New Jersey, ISBN: 0-13-101366-1 (2004)
2. Yang, M.H., Kriegman, D.J., Ahuja, N.: Detecting faces in images: A survey. IEEE Transactions on Pattern Analysis and Machine Intelligence 24 (2002) 34–58
3. B., Z., B., S., , F., Q.: Comparison of five color models in skin pixel classification. In: Proc. International Workshop on Recognition, Analysis, and Tracking of Faces and Gestures in Real-Time Systems, Corfu, Greece (1999) 58–63
4. Phung, S.L., Bouzerdoum, A., Chai, D.: Skin segmentation using color pixel classification: Analysis and comparison. IEEE Transactions on Pattern Analysis and Machine Intelligence 27 (2005) 148–154
5. Wren, C., Azarbayejani, A., Darrell, T., Pentland, A.: Pfinder: real-time tracking of the human body. In: Proc. SPIE. Volume 2615. (1996) 89–98
6. Yang, J., Waibel, A.: Tracking human faces in real-time. Technical report (CMU-CS-95-210), Carnegie Mellon University (1995)
7. Bradski, G.R.: Computer vision face tracking for use in a perceptual user interface. Intel Technology Journal (1998)
8. Wyszecki, G., Styles, W.: Color Science: Concepts and Methods, Quantitative Data and Formulae. 2 edn. John Wiley and Sons, Inc., New York (1982)
9. S., T., A., K., T., W., Y., M., M., I.: Extraction of hand region and specification of finger tips from color image. In: Proc. of International Conference on Virtual Systems and MultiMedia. (1997)
10. Cho, K.M., Jang, J.H., Hong, K.S.: Adaptive skin-color filter. Pattern Recognition 34 (2001) 1067–1073
11. Comaniciu, D., Meer, P.: Mean shift analysis and applications. In: Proc. IEEE Int'l Conf. Comp. Vis., Kerkyra, Greece (1999) 1197–1203
12. Freeman, W., Tanaka, K., J.Ohta, Kyuma, K.: Computer vision for computer games. In: Int. Conf On Automatic Face and Gesture Recognition. (1996) 100–105
13. Lu, J., Plataniotis, K., Venetsanopoulos, A., Wang, J.: An efficient kernel discriminant analysis method. to appear in Pattern Recognition (2005)
14. Lu, J., Plataniotis, K., Venetsanopoulos, A.: Face recognition using LDA based algorithms. IEEE Transactions on Neural Networks 14 (2003) 195–200
15. Lu, J., Plataniotis, K., Venetsanopoulos, A.: Face recognition using kernel direct discriminant analysis algorithms. IEEE Transactions on Neural Networks 14 (2003) 117–126
16. Lu, J., Plataniotis, K., Venetsanopoulos, A.: Regularization studies of linear discriminant analysis in small sample size scenarios with application to face recognition. Pattern Recognition Letter 26 (2005) 181–191

# Hermite Filter-Based Texture Analysis with Application to Handwriting Document Indexing

Carlos Joel Rivero-Moreno, Stéphane Bres, and Véronique Eglin

LIRIS, UMR 5205 CNRS, Lab. d'InfoRmatique en Images et Systèmes d'information,
INSA de Lyon, Bât. Jules Verne, 17 av. Jean Capelle, Villeurbanne Cedex, 69621 France
{carlos.rivero-moreno, stephane.bres,
veronique.eglin}@liris.cnrs.fr

**Abstract.** We present a texture analysis approach for texture image indexing based on Gabor-like Hermite filters, which are steered versions of discrete Hermite filters. Hermite filters are the backbone of the Hermite transform, which is a polynomial transform and a good model of the human visual system. Experimental results show that our filters have better performance than Gabor filters. The texture analysis system is then applied to handwriting document indexing. For that doing, handwriting documents are decomposed into local frequencies through the presented filter bank and, using this decomposition, we analyze the visual aspect of handwritings to compute similarity measures. A direct application is the management of document databases, allowing to find documents coming from the same author or to classify documents containing handwritings that have similar visual aspect. The current results are very promising and show that it is possible to characterize handwritten drawings without any a priori graphemes segmentation.

## 1 Introduction

In this paper we present an image texture indexing system [11] [4] based on extracted features by filtering the textured images [9] [1]. We focus on the multi-channel filtering (MCF) approach. It is inspired by the MCF theory for processing visual information in the early stages of the human visual system (HVS) [1], where receptive field profiles (RFPs) of the visual cortex can be modeled as a set of independent channels, each one with a particular orientation and frequency tuning. It then involves the decomposition of an input image into multiple features images by filtering. Each such an image captures textural features occurring in a narrow band of spatial frequency and orientation. Among the MCF models having the above properties, Gabor filters [7] have been widely used in texture feature extraction [9] [1] and image indexing and retrieval [11]. Another model corresponds to Hermite filters of the Hermite transform [6] that agree with the Gaussian derivative model of the HVS [12]. It has also been shown that Hermite and Gabor filters are equivalent models of RFPs of the HVS [10]. However, Hermite filters have some advantages over Gabor ones, like being an orthogonal basis and filter separability which allows efficient implementation. Despite these advantages, Hermite filters are not used as much as Gabor filters for texture feature extraction. In previous investigations we have found that cartesian Hermite filters perform less texture discrimination than Gabor filters. Hence, in order to improve texture discrimination, we present the Gabor-like Hermite filters, which are a modified version of steered Hermite filters [3].

The goal of our texture analysis system is the indexing of ancient manuscripts or handwriting documents from a texture viewpoint. Therefore, we apply the proposed Gabor-like Hermite filter bank to extract texture features. Our purpose here is to characterize precisely a handwriting document whatever its author is and to classify it into visual writers families. Our approach considers handwritings as special drawings that create a specific texture, which will be subsequently analyzed by considering orientations at different scales. Orientations extracted by the proposed filter bank are considered as sufficiently relevant perceptual features to characterize the special texture of handwritten drawings. The Gabor-like Hermite filter bank is a model that leads to the development of an original method of handwriting classification by the computation of handwriting signatures and similarity measures that reveal their "visual textural aspects".

## 2 Gabor-Like Hermite Filter Bank

### 2.1 Cartesian Hermite Filters

Hermite filters $d_{n-m,m}(x,y)$ decompose a localized signal $l_v(x-p, y-q) = v^2(x-p, y-q)\, l(x,y)$ by a Gaussian window $v(x,y)$ with spread $\sigma$ and unit energy, into a set of Hermite orthogonal polynomials $H_{n-m,m}(x/\sigma, y/\sigma)$. Coefficients $l_{n-m,m}(p,q)$ at lattice positions $(p,q) \in P$ are then derived from the signal $l(x,y)$ by convolving with the Hermite filters. These filters are equal to Gaussian derivatives where $n-m$ and $m$ are respectively the derivative orders in $x$- and $y$-directions, for $n=0,\ldots,D$ and $m=0,\ldots,n$. Thus, the two parameters of Hermite filters are the maximum derivative order $D$ (or polynomial degree) and the scale $\sigma$. Hermite filters are separable both in spatial and polar coordinates, so they can be implemented very efficiently. Thus, $d_{n-m,m}(x,y) = d_{n-m}(x)\, d_m(y)$, where each 1-D filter is:

$$d_n(x) = \left((-1)^n / (\sqrt{2^n \cdot n!} \sqrt{\pi}\sigma)\right) H_n(x/\sigma) e^{-x^2/\sigma^2}. \tag{1}$$

where Hermite polynomials $H_n(x)$, which are orthogonal with respect to the weighting function $exp(-x^2)$, are defined by Rodrigues' formula [5] as:

$$H_n(x) = (-1)^n e^{x^2} \frac{d^n}{dx^n} e^{-x^2}. \tag{2}$$

In the frequency domain, these filters are Gaussian-like band-pass filters with extreme value for $(\omega\sigma)^2 = 2n$ [10], and hence filters of increasing order analyze successively higher frequencies in the signal.

### 2.2 Krawtchouk Filters

Krawtchouk filters are the discrete equivalent of Hermite filters. They are equal to Krawtchouk polynomials multiplied by a binomial window $v^2(x) = C_N^x / 2^N$, which is the discrete counterpart of a Gaussian window. These polynomials are orthonormal with respect to this window and they are defined as [5]:

$$K_n(x) = \frac{1}{\sqrt{C_N^n}} \sum_{\tau=0}^{n} (-1)^{n-\tau} C_{N-x}^{n-\tau} C_x^{\tau} \ . \qquad (3)$$

for $x=0,\ldots,N$ and $n=0,\ldots,D$ with $D \leq N$.

It can be shown that the Krawtchouk filters of length $N$ approximates the Hermite filters of spread $\sigma = \sqrt{N/2}$. In order to achieve fast computations, we present a normalized recurrence relation to compute these filters:

$$K_{n+1}(x) = \frac{1}{\sqrt{(N-n)(n+1)}} \left[ (2x-N)K_n(x) - \sqrt{n(N-n+1)} K_{n-1}(x) \right] \ . \qquad (4)$$

for $n \geq 1$ and with initial conditions $K_0(x) = 1$, $K_1(x) = \frac{2}{\sqrt{N}} \left( x - \frac{N}{2} \right)$.

### 2.3 Steered Hermite Filters

In order to have a MCF approach based on Hermite filters, they must be adapted to orientation selectivity and multi-scale selection. For doing this, we apply their property of steerability [3]. The resulting filters then may be interpreted as directional derivatives of a Gaussian (i.e. the low-pass kernel).

Rotated versions of a filter of order $n$ can be constructed by taking linear combinations of the filter of order $n$. The Fourier transform of Hermite filters $d_{n-m,m}(x,y)$ can be expressed in polar coordinates ($\omega_x = \omega \cos\theta$, $\omega_y = \omega \sin\theta$) as $\hat{d}_{n-m,m}(\omega_x, \omega_y) = \hat{d}_n(\omega) \alpha_{n-m,m}(\theta)$ where $\hat{d}_n(\omega)$, which expresses radial frequency selectivity, is the 1-D Fourier transform of the $n$th Gaussian derivative in (1) but with radial coordinate $r$ instead of $x$. The cartesian angular functions of order $n$ for $m=0,\ldots,n$, are given as

$$\alpha_{n-m,m}(\theta) = \sqrt{C_n^m} \cos^{n-m}\theta \cdot \sin^m\theta \ . \qquad (5)$$

which express the directional selectivity of the filter.

Steered coefficients $l_n(\theta)$ resulting of filtering the signal $l(x,y)$ with these steered filters can be directly obtained by steering the cartesian Hermite coefficients $l_{n-m,m}$ as:

$$l_n(\theta) = \sum_{m=0}^{n} l_{n-m,m} \cdot \alpha_{n-m,m}(\theta) \ . \qquad (6)$$

### 2.4 Gabor-Like Hermite Filters

In order to turn the steered Hermite filters into a MCF bank, we construct a multi-scale representation that fulfils the desired constraints in the frequency domain, which are mainly the number of scales $S$ (radial frequencies $\omega_0$) and the number of orientations $R$ in the filter bank. Since previous works have been done essentially with

Gabor filters, we have then adopted a similar multi-channel design. Moreover, both Hermite and Gabor filters are similar models of the RFPs of the HVS [10]. For these reasons, we have named the resulting filters as Gabor-like Hermite filters. The strategy design in the frequency domain is the same as that presented in [11]. It is to ensure that the half peak magnitude supports of the filter responses in the frequency spectrum touch each other. Let $g(x,y)$ be a Gabor-like Hermite filter. Then, its scaled and oriented versions $g_{s,r}(x,y)$ are given by:

$$g_{s,r}(x,y) = a^{-s} g(x',y') \quad , \quad a > 1 \quad , \quad s, r \in \mathbb{N} \; ,$$

$$x' = a^{-s}(x\cos\theta + y\sin\theta) \; , \; y' = a^{-s}(-x\sin\theta + y\cos\theta) \; . \tag{7}$$

where $\theta = r\pi/R$, $r=0,\ldots,R-1$, $s=0,\ldots,S-1$. The scale factor $a^{-s}$ in (7) is meant to ensure that the energy is independent of scale $s$. Let $\sigma_x$ and $\sigma_u$ be, respectively, the spatial and frequency spreads of a 1-D Hermite filter as defined in (1) which has radial frequency selectivity $\omega_0$. Let $f_l$ and $f_h$ denote the lower and upper normalized center frequencies (between 0 and ½) of interest for the MCF bank. Then, for each scale, parameters $a$, $\sigma_x$, $\sigma_u$, and $\omega_0$ of each channel are computed as:

$$\omega_0 = 2\pi f_0 \; , \; \sigma_x = 1/(2\pi\sigma_u) \; , \; f_0 = a^{-s} f_h \; ,$$

$$a = (f_h / f_l)^{\frac{1}{S-1}} \; , \; \sigma_u = \frac{(a-1)f_0}{(a+1)\sqrt{2\ln 2}} \; . \tag{8}$$

Gabor-like Hermite filters already have zero mean (null DC). The (discrete) Krawtchouk filters are linked to Hermite filters by these parameters as:

$$N = \left[2\sigma_x^2\right] \quad \text{and} \quad D = \left\lceil (\sigma_x \omega_0)^2 / 2 \right\rceil \; . \tag{9}$$

where $[\cdot]$ rounds to the nearest integer whereas $\lceil \cdot \rceil$ does it too but towards infinity. Notice that for each scale there is a set of parameters $(N,D)$.

## 3 Texture Feature Extraction and Indexing

The Gabor-like Hermite MCF-bank presented in the previous section is applied to decompose a given textured image into a set of filtered images that represent the image information at different frequencies and at different orientations. Therefore, each of the channel outputs of the filter bank can be considered as one component of a texture feature vector of dimension $S \cdot R$. Thus, there are as much feature vectors as pixels in the image. For our application, we chose $S = 4$ scales and $R = 6$ orientations, which results in a bank of 24 filters. There is then an important dimensionality increasing which is $S \cdot R = 24$ times the original image size. Dimensionality reduction is thus an important goal in image indexing techniques, since one needs to store such indexes. Parametric texture models use combinations of parameters to characterize textures [8]. We only keep parameters which describe well the essential structure of texture. For this purpose, we have tested different combinations of parameters and we have found that the best results, for texture indexing, are obtained for only considering the spatial auto-correlation of coefficients of each subband. Since auto-correlations imply a spatial lag from the central pixel in both x- and y-directions, we have then fixed it to $M=7$ as in [8]. It then represents, for each of the subbands, a dimensionality reduction which goes from the image size to $(M^2+1)/2$ parameters, since the spatial correlation is symmetric. It yields $S \cdot R \cdot (M^2+1)/2 = 600$ parameters, which is a significant dimensionality reduction. These parameters represent structures in images (e.g., edges, bars, corners).

## 4 Experimental Results on Textured Images

In this study, texture under consideration are either gray-scale or luminance-based. We have made our experiments on a well-known set of images by Brodatz [2]. The texture database consists of 112 different texture images where each one has an image with size of 640x640 pixels. Each of the images is divided into 9 256x256 overlapping subimages, thus creating a database of 1008 images. We have then applied the texture feature extraction approach described in the previous section to every subimage in the database. The resulting feature vectors were saved as texture image indexes. Thus, one has a texture-based retrieval system in which distances between the query pattern and patterns in the database are computed. We have used as distance $1-|\rho|$, where $\rho$ is a normalized correlation coefficient in $[-1;1]$. In the ideal case all the top 9 retrievals, which have the lowest distance to the query, are from the same large image. We have measured the performance of the indexing system in terms of the average retrieval rate, which is defined as the average percentage number of patterns belonging to the same image as the query pattern in the top 9 matches (*average recall*).

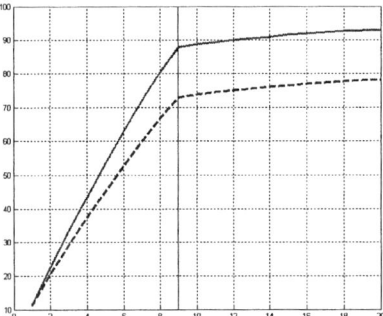

**Fig. 1.** Percentage retrieval performance (average recall) versus retrieved images. (*solid line*): Gabor-like Hemite filters, (*dashed line*): Gabor filters.

The average retrieval rate (retrieval efficiency) according to the number of top matches considered is about 88% for the top 9 retrievals (see figure 1) when Gabor-like Hermite filters are used. On the other hand, it is about 73% for the top 9 retrievals when Gabor filters are used. Therefore, a better performance is achieved with our proposed filter bank. It means that, in average, about one texture among the 9 most relevant ones is apparently not well classified.

## 5 Handwriting Document Indexing

A handwriting document can be viewed as special drawings that create a specific texture with particular orientation and scale that depend on the document's author. Thus, handwriting documents can be considered as textured images. The database we want to process contains historical handwriting documents. We assume that the images in the database are not significantly degraded by the presence of strong artefacts in their backgrounds so that a relevant handwriting characterization could be achieved. This characterization that rely on the shape of the handwriting lines is performed using the texture analysis system presented in the previous sections. By this way, the orientation and scale selectivity of the Gabor-like Hermite filter bank let a manuscript orientation and scale be extracted. Similarly to the case of general textures, we have chosen $S=4$ scales and $R=6$ orientations. Therefore, there are 24 oriented filters and for each pixel in the image each of these 24 filters will give a response that characterize a given orientation at a given scale. In this case, the scale determines the size of the pixel neighborhood. Since we are only interested in handwriting analysis, we only keep responses on pixels identified as handwriting lines so that the background is left out. Therefore, we have a 24-valued vector for each handwriting line pixel. All these vectors can be represented as a cluster in a 24-dimension space, and this cluster is a good characterization of the analyzed handwriting. Unfortunately, we cannot use these clusters as signatures, because of the data size they need on storage. Too big signatures take too much place in databases and too much computation time for comparison, and similarity evaluation during the retrieval step. That is the reason why we wanted to reduce those cluster-signatures to something as small as possible with a minimal information loss. We choose to keep geometrical information of the clusters, like the main axis, after a Principal Component Analysis (ACP) -like step. The signature for a given handwriting document is then the 24 normalized eigenvectors and the 24 corresponding eigenvalues of the covariance matrix computed from the orientation vector cluster. This is small enough for our needs, and the results we obtain show that this signature gives a good characterization of handwritings. With the signature of every document in the database, we only need to define a distance between these signatures to introduce the similarity notion in the database. Similarity leads to indexing which is the goal we want to reach.

### 5.1 Similarity Computation

Our signatures are made of 24 normalized eigenvectors $V_i$ and the 24 corresponding eigenvalues $L_i$. $L_{i0}$ quantifies the importance of the vector $V_{i0}$ in the shape of the cluster. The distance we choose to define uses both information of vectors $V_i$ and values $L_i$ in a linear combination. Thus, the distance $D(H_i, H_j)$ between the handwriting $H_i$ and the handwriting $H_j$ can be expressed as:

$$D(H_i, H_j) = \sum_{n=1}^{24} \left| L_i.V_i(n) - L_j.V_j(n) \right| . \tag{10}$$

This distance is symmetrical, which is a good property to assure coherent results during multiple comparisons of document databases.

### 5.2 Practical Results and Evaluation on Handwriting Documents

We have tested the whole system on our personal database composed of documents coming from different authors but mainly patrimonial handwritings documents. Most of the time, we have full pages of the same author and for evaluation purposes these pages are divided into smaller images, 9 per page. Then, most pages give us 9 images from the same author, containing what we can suppose to be similar handwritings. This is how we build our "ground truth": images coming from the same original page image should look the same and have similar handwritings. It is difficult to complete this ground truth with similarities between different author's handwritings because of the subjective judgment involved in such estimation.

**Fig. 2.** Examples of images coming from the same authors (*one author per row*)

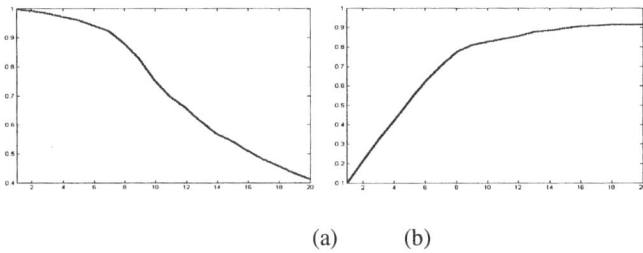

(a)    (b)

**Fig. 3.** (*a*) Precision and (*b*) recall curves computed on the entire database containing more than 1400 handwriting documents

The figure 2 gives some examples of images coming from the same original page. Our database contains 1438 images coming from 189 different authors, in different languages and alphabets. The results we obtain are really promising because, according to our ground truth, a given request has, in the ten first better answers (documents with the higher similarity or equivalently the smaller distance), in average more than 83% of correct responses; see the recall curve on the figure 3. This is an average value computed on the documents that have 9 similar images in the database. These precision and recall curves are a common way to show the efficiency of an indexing system. They have been computed using the 20 first responses. Let's remember that we only have 9 images for each handwriting document. That is the reason why the precision decreases strongly after the 9$^{th}$ response.

## 6 Conclusion

We have presented a new filter bank for efficient texture feature extraction: the Gabor-like Hermite filter bank, which is a multi-scale decomposition of steered discrete Hermite filters. Efficient indexing has been achieved by a powerful dimensionality reduction, which is based on spatial auto-correlations of all multi-channel outputs. We have showed that our method is suitable for texture indexing purposes since the only available information is that resulting from our filter bank. Thus, these filters characterize well enough texture. This work is a response to scientific problems of historical handwritten corpus digitalization. It deals with handwriting document indexation and is applied here to a multi-language and multi-alphabet corpus. We propose here a biological inspired approach for handwriting characterization and corpus indexing. The developed perception based model lies on the Hermite frequency decomposition for image indexing. The current results of handwriting document classification with Hermite-based orientation features are very promising. We are currently working on an enlarged database (with recent digitalization within a European project) and in consequence we are statistically evaluating the minimal required images sizes that guaranty the writer identification and a valuable image indexing.

## References

1. Bovik, A.C., Clark, M., W Geisler,.S.: Multichannel Texture Analysis using Localized Spatial Filters. IEEE Trans. Pattern Analysis Mach. Intell. Vol. 12 (1990) 55-73
2. Brodatz, P.: Textures: A Photographic Album for Artists and Designers. New York: Dover. (1966)
3. van Dijk, A.M., Martens, J.-B.: Image Representation and Compression with Steered Hermite Transforms. Signal Processing. Vol. 56 (1997) 1-16
4. Huang, P.W., Dai, S.K.: Image Retrieval by Texture Similarity. Pattern Recognition. Vol. 36 (2003) 665-679
5. Koekoek, R., Swarttouw, R.F.: The Askey-scheme of Hypergeometric Orthogonal Polynomials and its q-Analogue. Delft University of Technology, Faculty of Information Technology and Systems, Department of Technical Mathematics and Informatics. Report 98-17 (1998)

6. Martens, J.-B.: The Hermite Transform – Theory. IEEE Trans. Acoust., Speech, Signal Processing. Vol. 38 **9** (1990) 1595-1606
7. Porat, M., Zeevi, Y.Y.: The Generalized Gabor Scheme of Image Representation in Biological and Machine Vision. IEEE Trans. Pattern Analysis Mach. Intell. Vol. 10 (1988) 452-468
8. Portilla, J., Simoncelli, E.P.: A Parametric Texture Model based on Joint Statistics of Complex Wavelet Coefficients. Int. Journal Computer Vision. Vol. 40 (2000) 49-71
9. Randen, T., Husøy, J.H.: Filtering for Texture Classification: A Comparative Study. IEEE Trans. Pattern Analysis Mach. Intell. Vol. 21 (1999) 291-310
10. Rivero-Moreno, C.J., Bres, S.: Conditions of Similarity between Hermite and Gabor Filters as Models of the Human Visual System. In: Petkov, N., Westenberg, M.A. (eds.): Computer Analysis of Images and Patterns. Lectures Notes in Computer Science, Vol. 2756. Springer-Verlag, Berlin Heidelberg (2003) 762-769
11. Wu, P., Manjunath, B.S., Newsam, S., Shin, H.D.: A Texture Descriptor for Browsing and Similarity Retrieval. Signal Processing: Image Communication. Vol. 16 **1,2** (2000) 33-43
12. Young, R.A., Lesperance, R.M., Meyer, W.W.: The Gaussian Derivative Model for Spatial-Temporal Vision: I. Cortical Model. Spatial Vision. Vol. 14 **3,4** (2001) 261-319

# Rotation-Invariant Texture Classification Using Steerable Gabor Filter Bank

Wumo Pan[1,2], T.D. Bui[1], and C.Y. Suen[2]

[1] Dept. Computer Science and Software Engineering, Concordia University,
1455 De Maisonneuve Blvd. West,
Montreal, Quebec, Canada H3G 1M8
{wumo_pan, bui}@cs.concordia.ca
[2] Centre for Pattern Recognition and Machine Intelligence, Concordia University,
1455 de Maisonneuve Blvd. West, Suite GM-606,
Montréal, Québec, Canada H3G 1M8
suen@cenparmi.concordia.ca

**Abstract.** An efficient rotation invariant feature extraction technique for texture classification based on Gabor multi-channel filtering is proposed. In this technique, Gabor function is approximated by a set of steerable basis functions, which results in a significant saving in the computation cost. The classification of 15 classes of Brodatz textures are considered in our experiments. Results show that up to 40% of computation can be saved compared with traditional Gabor multi-channel filtering method. In the mean time, almost the same high texture classification correct rate can be achieved.

## 1 Introduction

Texture classification is a topic investigated by many researchers during the past decades. It plays an important role in many applications such as remote sensing, robot vision, document image processing, medical imaging and content based image retrieval. One important issue in texture classification is the extraction of features which can adequately characterize the textures under consideration. Furthermore, it is desirable in some applications that these texture features be invariant under certain transformations, such as rotation, scaling and translation, and be insensitive to the variations of the pose and illumination. Many approaches for texture features extraction have been proposed in literature, including the co-occurrence matrix [1], Gabor filtering technique [2–6], wavelet theory [7–9, 13], stochastic models [10-12], and fractal model [14].

Among the proposed methods, multi-channel filtering technique using Gabor functions has drawn much attention. Studies on the human visual system have suggested that its processing of pictorial information involves transforming it into a local spatial/frequency representation [15], which can be computationally simulated by convolving the input image with a bank of filters with tuned frequencies and orientations. Gabor filters have been widely applied in such simulation since they have tunable orientations, radial frequency bandwidths and center frequencies. Furthermore, they optimally achieve joint resolution in the space and in the frequency domain.

Despite all these advantages, Gabor function based multi-channel filtering technique could be quite time consuming, especially when rotation-invariant features are needed. In that case, the sample rate of the orientation interval (usually [0, π)) at each fixed central frequency has to be dense enough. For example, a sample rate of 16 was used in [3] in script identification application. This drawback could become a bottleneck for the multi-channel filtering technique to be used in real applications.

In this paper, we propose an efficient rotation-invariant feature extraction technique for texture classification, which is an extension to a commonly used Gabor function based multi-channel filtering model. In this model, Gabor filters with the same central frequency but different orientations are only rotated versions of each other. Therefore, these filters can be efficiently approximated using the steerable basis functions discussed in [16-19]. The effectiveness of the proposed method has already been observed in our previous work where the problem of language identification from printed documents was considered [25].

This paper is organized as follows: in section 2, we introduce a commonly used Gabor function based multi-channel filtering configuration. Based on this configuration, rotation invariant features are extracted. In section 3, steerable filter theory is introduced and we explain how this theory can be applied to design an efficient feature extraction method. To demonstrate the validity of the new feature extraction method, classification of 15 Brodatz textures is investigated and the results are given in section 4. Section 5 concludes this paper.

## 2 Rotation Invariant Feature Extraction

### 2.1 Gabor Function Based Multi-channel Filtering Model

Gabor filters are complex sinusoidal gratings modulated by 2-D Gaussian functions in the space domain, and shifted Gaussian functions in the frequency domain. They can be configured to have various shapes, bandwidths, orientations and center frequencies. For the sake of convenience, we assume in this research that these filters can be defined as [26]

$$h(x, y; F, \phi) = g(r_x(x, y, \phi), r_y(x, y, \phi)) \cdot \exp(2\pi j F r_x(x, y, \phi)) \quad (1)$$

where $r_x(x, y, \phi) = x\cos\phi + y\sin\phi$, $r_y(x, y, \phi) = -x\sin\phi + y\cos\phi$. F is the radial frequency, $\phi$ stands for the orientation and

$$g(x, y) = (\frac{1}{2\pi\lambda\sigma^2}) \cdot \exp(-\frac{(x/\lambda)^2 + y^2}{2\sigma^2}) \quad (2)$$

with $\sigma$ being the scale parameter, which determines the channel bandwidth, and $\lambda$ being the aspect ratio. The frequency response of (1) is

$$H(u, v; F, \phi) = \exp\{-2\pi\sigma^2[(r_u(u, v, \phi) - F)^2 \lambda^2 + r_v(u, v, \phi)^2]\} \quad (3)$$

with $r_u(u, v, \phi) = u\cos\phi + v\sin\phi$, $r_v(u, v, \phi) = -u\sin\phi + v\cos\phi$. What we need to do in applying Gabor function based multi-channel filtering technique is to configure the channel parameters F, $\phi$, $\sigma$, and $\lambda$. However, just a few values of these free parameters can result in a large set of filters. To make it easier, we assume that $\lambda$ be the same for all Gabor filters and $\sigma$ be chosen to be inversely proportional to the central frequencies of the channels [20]. For filters with the same central frequency, $\sigma$ will be the same.

## 2.2 Rotation Invariant Features

Each input image is first filtered by the Gabor filters in the filter bank. Then, we calculate the mean and standard deviation of the filtered image, which are denoted as m(F, $\phi$) and s(F, $\phi$) respectively.

For a given radial frequency, the rotation of the input image would only result in a shift in $\phi$ of both m(F, $\phi$) and s(F, $\phi$), and the amplitude of the 1-D Fourier transform in $\phi$ of these two quantities would remain invariant. Therefore, we can obtain rotation invariant features by taking 1-D Fourier transform in $\phi$ of both m(F, $\phi$) and s(F, $\phi$). In this research, only the amplitudes of the first 5 coefficients of the DFT are selected as features. Similar features may also be found in [3, 21].

## 3 Feature Extraction via Steerable Gabor Filters

The above mentioned feature extraction mechanism can be extremely time consuming. Therefore, a more efficient feature extraction method is absolutely desirable.

From formula (3), we can observe that the Gabor filters at a fixed central frequency (hence fixed $\sigma$) in the filter bank are actually the rotated version of one filter, let's say, the filter with $\phi = 0°$. This observation suggests that the theory of steerable filters can be applied to reduce the high computational cost of multi-channel filtering technique.

### 3.1 Steerable Filter

The concept of steerability was first proposed by Freeman and Adelson in [16] and was further discussed by others in [17, 18, 19]. Here, we are interested in the transform of rotation. A function $f(x,y) : R^2 \to C$ is steerable with respect to rotation if:

$$f^\theta(x, y) = \sum_{j=1}^{M} k_j(\theta) \varphi_j(x, y) \qquad (4)$$

here $f^\theta(x, y)$ is the rotated version (by an angle $\theta$) of $f(x, y)$. { $\varphi_j(x, y)$ }($j = 1, ..., M$) are the base functions which are independent of the rotation angle $\theta$. { $k_j(\theta)$ }($j = 1, ..., M$) are called the steering functions of $f$ associated with the base functions { $\varphi_j(x, y)$ } and depend solely on $\theta$.

It is well known that convolution is a linear operation. Therefore, if a filter is steerable with respect to rotation, the filter output of a rotated version of this filter can be obtained by linearly combining the filter outputs of its associated basis functions, or specifically,

$$f^{\theta}(x,y) * I(x,y) = \sum_{j=1}^{M} k_j(\theta) \cdot [\varphi_j(x,y) * I(x,y)] \quad (5)$$

where $I(x,y)$ is the image to be filtered.

If M is smaller than the number of orientation samples we need, we can save some computations. If M is not so small, or even if no finite M can be found in formula (4), as the case of Gabor filter with non-zero shift in frequency domain [19], we still can find a way to approximate the exact Gabor filters without significant lost in classification performance.

### 3.2 Steerable Approximations of Gabor Filters

Perona [17] proposed a singular value decomposition (SVD) based method to compute the least-squares optimal set of basis functions. With a given tolerable amount of error, this method also gives the minimum number of basis functions.

Perona's method works as follows: Let $G$ be a matrix whose columns are the transformed replicas of a discretely sampled function f. Thus, each column in $G$ corresponds to a specific sample of the parameter space over which the function is to be steered and each row in $G$ corresponds to a specific sample of the function's domain. The SVD decomposes the matrix $G$ into a product of three matrices:

$$G = \begin{bmatrix} \vdots & & \vdots \\ f^{\theta_1} & \cdots & f^{\theta_p} \\ \vdots & & \vdots \end{bmatrix} = U_G S_G V_G^T = U_G W_G \quad (6)$$

where $U_G^T U_G = I, V_G^T V_G = I$, and $\theta_1, \ldots, \theta_p$ are the angles of rotation. $S_G$ is a diagonal matrix of non-negative singular values, in decreasing order of magnitude. It can be shown that the first $n$ columns of $U_G$ represent the optimal, least-squares set of basis functions needed to steer f. The first $n$ rows of the matrix $W_G$ give the weights of the linear combination needed to steer f.

An approximation function $D(n)$ as a measurement of the degree of approximation of the leading $n$ basis functions given by SVD can be defined as:

$$D(n) = \frac{[\sum_{i=1}^{n} s_G^2(i)]^{\frac{1}{2}}}{[\sum_{i=1}^{p} s_G^2(i)]^{\frac{1}{2}}} \quad (7)$$

where $s_G^2(i) = S_G^2(i,i)$ and $n = 1, \ldots, p$. $D(n)$ is normalized to [0, 1]. As an example, Fig. 1 shows the approximation function $D(n)$ for the basis functions of the Gabor filter spectrum in formula (3) with $F = 16$, $\lambda = 1$, $p = 16$ while Fig. 2 shows these basis functions. We can see that the first 8 basis functions actually account for 99% of the total square norm. The other 8 basis functions have little contribution and thus can be ignored when synthesizing the Gabor filter according to formula (5).

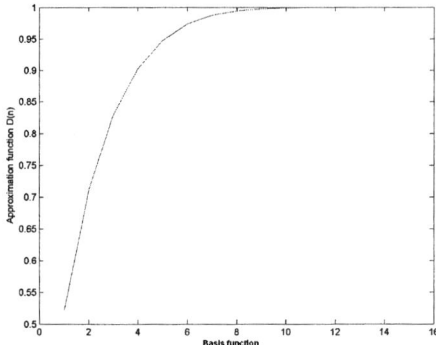

**Fig. 1.** Plot of the approximation function $D(n)$

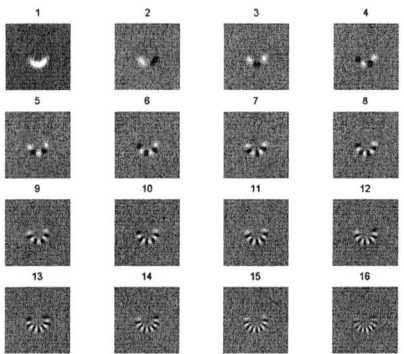

**Fig. 2.** Basis functions to steer the Gabor Spectrum function (3) with F = 16, $\lambda = 1$, $p = 16$. The basis functions are arranged in descending order of the magnitude of their singular values from left to right and from top to bottom. Image has been rescaled for better visibility.

### 3.3 Fast Feature Extraction Using Basis Functions

Feature extraction using exact Gabor filters has already been discussed in section 2. Here we show in pseudo-code how to extract features from these synthesized filter outputs.

Initialize a desired approximation level $\tau$ between 0 and 1;
*For* each needed central frequency F in current application *Do*

- Calculate the $p$ rotated replicas of the discretized Gabor spectrum function H(u, v; F, 0) based on formula (3);
- Re-arrange each replica into a column vector and build the matrix $G$;
- Do SVD of $G$;
- Find $n$ such that $n$ is the minimum positive number satisfying $D(n) \geq \tau$;

- Use the first $n$ columns of $U_G$ as basis functions, re-arrange each column back into a square matrix and do image filtering;
- Use the first $n$ rows of $W_G$ as weights and synthesize the original $p$ filter outputs using formula (5);
- Extract features as described in section 2.

*End For*

## 4 Experimental Results

In this research, 15 textures are selected from the Brodatz album [22] to evaluate the performance of the rotation-invariant features extracted using our method. These texture samples are shown in Fig. 3. We follow the experiment configuration used in [23]. The training set for each class was composed by textures at angles 0°, 30°, 45°, 60°. For each angle, 30 non-overlapping gray level image blocks of dimension 64×64 pixels are considered. Test set for each class is obtained from images at angle 0°, 70°, 90°, 120° and 150°. For each angle, 20 non-overlapping gray level image blocks with size 128×128 are selected.

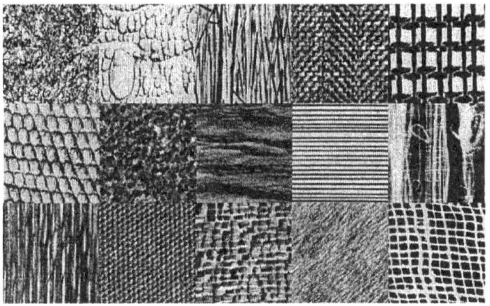

**Fig. 3.** Texture samples. From left to right. First row: D9 (Grass lawn), D10 (Crocodile skin), D15 (Straw), D17 (Herringbone weave), D20 (French canvas). Second row: D22 (Reptile skin), D29 (Beach sand), D37 (Water), D49 (Wood grain), D51 (Raffia woven). Third row: D68 (Wood grain), D77 (Cotton canvas), D84 (Raffia), D93 (Fur), D103 (Loose burlap).

The parameters for the filter bank are chosen as follows: two central frequencies are considered: F = 16, 32. An orientation sample interval of 11.25° is used. The aspect ration $\lambda$ is set to 1. 20 features are extracted here. The approximation level is set to $D(n) = 97.5\%$. For Gabor filters with central frequency 16, 7 basis functions are used. For Gabor filters with central frequency 32, 12 basis functions are used. In total, we can save 40% of image filtering operations.

The Bayes classifier [24] is applied for texture classification in this experiment. It is the optimum one when the texture features are assumed to have a Gaussian distribution. Table 1 gives the percentages of the correct classifications using the proposed steerable Gabor filtering method (SG), exact Gabor based multi-channel filtering method (GM) and the moment invariant (MI) method proposed in [23].

**Table 1.** Percentages of correct classification for rotated texture samples using Steerable Gabor filtering method (SG), extact Gabor based multi-channel filtering method (GM) and the moment invariant (MI) method [23]

| Texture | 20° | | | 70° | | | 90° | | | 120° | | | 150° | | |
|---|---|---|---|---|---|---|---|---|---|---|---|---|---|---|---|
| | (SG) | (GM) | (MI) | (SG) | (GM) | (MI) | (SG) | (GM) | (MI) | (SG) | (GM) | (MI) | (SG) | (GM) | (MI) |
| D9 | 100.0 | 100.0 | 80 | 88.9 | 88.9 | 80 | 100.0 | 100.0 | 75 | 94.4 | 94.4 | 80 | 94.4 | 94.4 | 80 |
| D10 | 100.0 | 100.0 | 90 | 100.0 | 100.0 | 80 | 100.0 | 100.0 | 70 | 100.0 | 100.0 | 90 | 100.0 | 100.0 | 80 |
| D15 | 100.0 | 100.0 | 70 | 100.0 | 100.0 | 90 | 100.0 | 100.0 | 75 | 100.0 | 100.0 | 75 | 100.0 | 100.0 | 80 |
| D17 | 100.0 | 100.0 | 100 | 100.0 | 100.0 | 90 | 100.0 | 100.0 | 95 | 100.0 | 100.0 | 95 | 100.0 | 100.0 | 85 |
| D20 | 100.0 | 100.0 | 100 | 100.0 | 100.0 | 100 | 100.0 | 100.0 | 100 | 88.9 | 100.0 | 95 | 94.4 | 100.0 | 85 |
| D22 | 100.0 | 100.0 | 65 | 100.0 | 100.0 | 85 | 100.0 | 100.0 | 90 | 100.0 | 100.0 | 90 | 100.0 | 100.0 | 70 |
| D29 | 100.0 | 100.0 | 95 | 94.4 | 100.0 | 90 | 95.0 | 95.0 | 90 | 94.4 | 94.4 | 95 | 94.4 | 94.4 | 95 |
| D37 | 88.9 | 88.9 | 95 | 94.4 | 94.4 | 95 | 100.0 | 100.0 | 95 | 94.4 | 94.4 | 80 | 94.4 | 94.4 | 80 |
| D49 | 72.2 | 100.0 | 80 | 100.0 | 100.0 | 85 | 0.0 | 25.0 | 85 | 44.4 | 61.1 | 70 | 100.0 | 100.0 | 70 |
| D51 | 100.0 | 100.0 | 90 | 100.0 | 100.0 | 90 | 100.0 | 100.0 | 95 | 100.0 | 100.0 | 80 | 100.0 | 100.0 | 80 |
| D68 | 94.4 | 88.9 | 90 | 94.4 | 94.4 | 80 | 100.0 | 100.0 | 85 | 100.0 | 100.0 | 95 | 100.0 | 100.0 | 95 |
| D77 | 100.0 | 100.0 | 85 | 100.0 | 100.0 | 70 | 100.0 | 100.0 | 95 | 88.9 | 77.8 | 90 | 50.0 | 50.0 | 90 |
| D84 | 100.0 | 100.0 | 85 | 100.0 | 100.0 | 85 | 100.0 | 100.0 | 80 | 94.4 | 100.0 | 75 | 100.0 | 100.0 | 80 |
| D93 | 100.0 | 94.4 | 75 | 88.9 | 88.9 | 85 | 100.0 | 100.0 | 85 | 94.4 | 94.4 | 70 | 94.4 | 94.4 | 80 |
| D103 | 100.0 | 100.0 | 75 | 100.0 | 100.0 | 75 | 100.0 | 100.0 | 85 | 100.0 | 100.0 | 80 | 100.0 | 100.0 | 80 |
| Average | 97 | 98.1 | 85 | 97.4 | 97.8 | 85.3 | 93 | 94.67 | 86.7 | 93 | 94.4 | 84 | 94.8 | 95.2 | 82 |

In several cases, steerable Gabor approximation would outperform the exact Gabor filtering. The reason why this can happen will be investigated in the future. However, one possible reason is due to the insufficient data.

## 5 Conclusion

We proposed an efficient rotation invariant feature extraction technique for texture classification. This technique adopts the framework of Gabor function based multi-channel filtering. However, Gabor filters with the same central frequency in this framework are approximated by a finite set of steerable basis functions. By doing so, we can save some image filtering operations. The experimental results show that we can save up to 40% of computation with almost the same texture classification correct rate.

## References

1. R. M. Haralik, K. Shanmugam, and I. Dinstein, "Textural features for image classification," IEEE Trans. Syst., Man, Cybern., vol. SMC-3, pp. 610–621, 1973.
2. A. K. Jain and F. Farrokhnia, "Unsupervised texture segmentation using Gabor filters," Pattern Recognit., vol. 24, no. 12, pp. 1167–1185, 1991.
3. T. N. Tan, "Rotation Invariant Texture Features and Their Use in Automatic Script Identification," IEEE Trans. Pattern Anal. Machine Intell., vol. 20, no. 7, pp. 751-756, 1998.
4. A. C. Bovik, M. Clark, and W. S. Geisler, "Multichannel texture analysis using localized spatial filters," IEEE Trans. Pattern Anal. Machine Intell., vol. 12, no. 1, pp. 55–73, 1990.
5. A. Teuner, O. Pichler, and B. J. Hostica, "Unsupervised texture segmentation of images using tuned matched Gabor filters," IEEE Trans. Image Processing, vol. 4, no. 6, pp. 863–870, June 1995.

6. B. S. Manjunath and W. Y. Ma, "Texture features for browsing and retrieval of image data," IEEE Trans. Pattern Anal. Machine Intell., vol. 18, no. 8, pp. 837–842, 1996.
7. M. Unser, "Texture Classification and Segmentation Using Wavelet Frames," IEEE Trans. Image Processing, vol. 4, pp. 1,549-1,560, 1995.
8. G. Van de Wouwer, P. Scheunders, and D. Van Dyck, "Statistical texture characterization from discrete wavelet representation," IEEE Trans. Image Processing, vol. 8, no. 4, pp. 592–598, 1999.
9. Minh N. Do and Martin Vetterli, "Rotation Invariant Texture Characterization and Retrieval Using Steerable Wavelet-Domain Hidden Markov Models," IEEE Trans. On Multimedia, vol. 4, no. 4, pp. 517-527, 2002.
10. B. S. Manjunath and W. Y. Ma, "Texture features for browsing and retrieval of image data," IEEE Trans. Pattern Anal. Machine Intell., vol. 18, no. 8, pp. 837–842, 1996.
11. G. R. Cross and A. K. Jain, "Markov random field texture models," IEEE Trans. Pattern Anal. Machine Intell., vol. 5, no. 1, pp. 25–39, 1983.
12. R. Chellappa and S. Chatterjee, "Classification of texture using Gaussian Markov random fields," IEEE Trans. Acoust., Speech, Signal Processing, vol. 33, no. 4, pp. 959–963, 1985.
13. G. M. Haley and B. S. Manjunath, "Rotation-invariant texture classification using a complete space-frequency model," IEEE Trans. Image Processing, vol. 8, no. 2, pp. 255–269, 1999.
14. L. M. Kaplan, "Extended fractal analysis for texture classification and segmentation," IEEE Trans. Image Processing, vol. 8, no. 11, pp. 1572–1585, 1999.
15. F.W. Campbell and J. G. Robson, "Application of Fourier analysis to the visibility of gratings," J. Physiol. (Lond.), vol. 197, pp. 551–566, 1968.
16. W. Freeman and E. Adelson. "The design and use of steerable filters," IEEE Trans. Pattern Analysis and Machine Intelligence, vol. 13, no. 9 pp. 891-906, 1991.
17. P. Perona, "Deformable Kernels for Early Vision," IEEE Trans. Pattern Analysis and Machine Intelligence, vol. 17, no. 5, pp. 488-499, 1995.
18. E. Simoncelli, W. Freeman, E. Adelson, and D. Heeger. "Shiftable multiscale transforms." IEEE Trans. Information Theory, vol. 38, no. 2, pp. 587-607, 1992.
19. P.C. Teo and Y. Hel-Or, "Design of Multi-Parameter Steerable Functions Using Cascade-Basis Reduction," IEEE Trans. Pattern Analysis and Machine Intelligence, vol. 21, no. 6, pp. 552-556, 1999.
20. T.N. Tan, "Texture Feature Extraction via Cortical Channel Modeling," Proc. 11th Int'l Conf. Pattern Recognition, vol. III, pp. 607-610, 1992.
21. G.M. Haley, B.S Manjunath, "Rotation-invariant texture classification using modified Gabor filters," Proc. Int'l Conf. Image Processing, vol. I, pp. 262 – 265, 1995.
22. T. Brodatz, Textures: A Photographic Album for Artists and Designers. New York: Dover, 1966.
23. P. Campisi, A. Neri, G. Panci and G. Scarano, "Robust Rotation-Invariant Texture Classification Using a Model Based Approach," IEEE Trans. Image Processing, Vol. 13, no. 6, pp. 782-791, 2004.
24. S. Theodoridis and K. Koutroumbas, Pattern Recognition. New York: Academic, 1999.
25. Wumo Pan, C. Y. Suen, and T. D. Bui, "Scripts identification using Steerable Gabor Filters," submitted to ICDAR'05.
26. A.C. Bovik, M. Clark and W.S. Geisler, "Multichannel Texture Analysis Using Localized Spatial Filters." IEEE Trans. On Pattern Recognition and Machine Intelligence, vol. 12, no. 1, pp. 55-73, 1990.

# Multiresolution Histograms for SVM-Based Texture Classification

Srinivas Andra and Yongjun Wu

ECSE Department, Rensselaer Polytechnic Institute, Troy, NY 12180, USA

**Abstract.** Multiresolution histograms have been recently proposed as robust and efficient features for texture classification. In this paper, we evaluate the performance of multiresolution histograms for texture classification using support vector machines (SVMs). We observe that the dimensionality of multiresolution histograms can be greatly reduced with a Laplacian pyramidal decomposition. With an appropriate kernel, we show that SVMs significantly improve the performance of multiresolution histograms compared to the previously used nearest-neighbor (NN) classifiers on a texture classification problem involving Brodatz textures. Experimental results indicate that multiresolution histograms in conjunction with SVMs are also robust to noise.

## 1 Introduction

Texture classification is important in many applications, such as object recognition, image segmentation, content-based image retrieval and scene understanding. Two major steps involved in texture classification are feature extraction and classification method. Numerous features have been proposed for use in texture classification, which are categorized into statistical, geometrical, model-based and signal processing methods [1]. Many classifiers have been used in conjunction with texture features, e.g., nearest-neighbor classifiers, Fisher linear discriminants, neural networks and support vector machines as summarized in [2].

Multiresolution histograms have been recently proposed as robust and efficient features for texture classification [3]. Multiresolution histograms have many desirable properties, such as ease of computation, invariance to rigid motions, and robustness to noise. The relatively high dimensionality of multiresolution histograms as compared to other texture features, however, requires the use of a classifier that does not seriously suffer from the *curse of dimensionality* [4]. Support vector machines (SVMs) gained a great deal of attention in the recent years due to their good generalization ability on high-dimensional data [5,6]. SVMs therefore make a natural choice to deal with multiresolution histograms.

In this work, we evaluate the performance of multiresolution histograms using SVMs. We observe that the effective dimensionality of multiresolution histograms can be greatly reduced using a Laplacian pyramid. With an appropriately tuned Laplacian RBF kernel, we show that SVMs improve the classification performance of multiresolution histograms significantly compared to the previously used NN classifiers. We also experimentally demonstrate that this improvement in classification performance is robust to noise.

The organization of the paper is as follows. Brief introductions to both multiresolution histograms and SVMs are provided in Sections 2 and 3, respectively. Section 4 presents the reasons for considering SVMs for multiresolution histograms and a method to reduce the dimensionality of multiresolution histograms. Section 5 presents experimental results on Brodatz textures, and Section 6 concludes the paper.

## 2 Multiresolution Histograms

Multiresolution histogram is the set of histograms of an image at multiple scales [3]. The multiscale decomposition of an image can be computed via Gaussian or Laplacian pyramids [7]. Unlike a single image histogram, the multiresolution histogram encodes spatial information in an image while retaining many desirable properties of the single image histogram, such as ease of computation and invariance to rigid motions. Two dissimilar images having identical histograms do not have identical multiresolution histograms since the image histograms at lower resolutions are affected by spatial image information. This notion can be formalized via generalized Fisher information measures [3,8].

The generalized Fisher information measures are directly related to the image spatial variation or *sharpness*. For an image $I$ of unit $L_1$ norm, the generalized Fisher information measure, as a function of a continuous parameter $q$, is given by

$$J_q(I) = \int_D |\nabla I(\mathbf{x})/I(\mathbf{x})|^2 \, I^q(\mathbf{x}) \, d^2x, \tag{1}$$

where the sharpness of the image $I$ at a pixel $\mathbf{x}$ is given by $|\nabla I(\mathbf{x})/I(\mathbf{x})|^2$. With $q = 1$, the average sharpness $J_1$ is the Fisher information.

The generalized Fisher information is also related to the rates of change of histogram densities with image resolution. This relation can be obtained from the Tsallis generalized entropy which can be expressed as a linear transformation of the histogram. The Tsallis generalized entropy $S_q$ of an image histogram with unit $L_1$ norm and density $h_j$ at intensity $v_j$ is given by

$$S_q = \sum_{j=0}^{m-1} \left( \frac{v_j - v_j^q}{q - 1} \right) h_j, \tag{2}$$

and is a function of continuous parameter $q$. Here $m$ is the number of bins in the histogram. For $q = 1$, the Tsallis generalized entropy reduces to the familiar Shannon entropy.

The resolution of an image can be decreased by using a Gaussian filter $G(l) = \frac{1}{2\pi l \sigma^2} \exp\left(-\frac{x^2+y^2}{2l\sigma^2}\right)$, with resolution $l$. Let $\tilde{h}_j$ denote the histogram density at intensity $v_j$ and $\tilde{S}_q$ the Tsallis generalized entropy of the filtered image $I * G(l)$.

The generalized Fisher information measure of the image $I$ is related to the rate at which the Tsallis generalized entropy changes as

$$J_q(I) = \frac{\sigma^2}{2}\frac{d\tilde{S}_q}{dl} = \frac{\sigma^2}{2}\sum_{j=0}^{m-1}\left(\frac{v_j - v_j^q}{q-1}\right)\frac{d\tilde{h}_j}{dl}, \qquad (3)$$

where we used the expression (2). Thus the generalized Fisher information measure, which is a closed-form functional of an image (refer to (1)), can also be expressed in terms of rates of change of histogram densities. This formally establishes the connection between the image spatial variation and the rates of change of histogram densities.

We outline the steps involved in extracting the multiresolution histogram features [3]: (i) construct the multiscale decomposition of an image via Gaussian or Laplacian pyramids, (ii) compute the histograms of the image at different resolutions at a chosen bin width and normalize all to have unit $L_1$ norm, (iii) convert the histograms into cumulative histograms, (iv) subtract the adjacent cumulative histograms to obtain the difference histograms and concatenate the difference histograms to form the feature vector. The step (iv) gives the rate of change of histogram densities with image resolution. The cumulative histograms are used because they capture the dependence between bins corresponding to similar intensities, whereas the original histograms assume that different intensity bins are independent [9].

## 3 Support Vector Machines

In this section, we briefly review SVMs for binary classification [5]. Given a set of training examples $\{(\mathbf{x}_i, y_i), i = 1,\ldots,l\}$, where $\mathbf{x}_i$ are the patterns (e.g., vectors in Euclidean space $\mathbb{R}^n$), and $y_i \in \{\pm 1\}$ are the binary labels, a binary SVM constructs a maximum margin hyperplane in a very high-dimensional space (can be an infinite dimensional space) known as *feature space* $\mathcal{F}$, while at the same time minimizing the training error. The feature space is obtained by transforming the input space, $\mathbb{R}^n$, via a nonlinear map $\phi : \mathbb{R}^n \to \mathcal{F}$. The feature space is usually of a much higher dimension than the input space.

Cover's theorem [10] states that patterns that are nonlinearly separable in the input space $\mathbb{R}^n$ become linearly separable in the feature space $\mathcal{F}$ with high probability provided the dimensionality of the feature space is sufficiently high. The maximum margin hyperplane, $\mathbf{w}^T\phi(\mathbf{x}) + b = 0$, therefore constructs a nonlinear decision surface in the input space (also called nonlinear SVM). It can be obtained by solving the following primal optimization problem:

$$\min_{\mathbf{w},b,\boldsymbol{\xi}} \quad \frac{1}{2}\|\mathbf{w}\|^2 + C\sum_{i=1}^{l}\xi_i, \qquad (4)$$

$$\text{subject to} \quad y_i(\mathbf{w}^T\phi(\mathbf{x}_i) + b) \geq 1 - \xi_i, \qquad (5)$$

$$\text{and} \quad \xi_i \geq 0, \quad i = 1,\ldots,l \qquad (6)$$

where $\xi_i$ are the penalty terms associated with patterns $\phi(\mathbf{x}_i)$, and $C$ is a constant that determines the trade-off between the training error and the margin width. The normal vector to the hyperplane can be found by forming the Lagrangian function and is given by $\mathbf{w} = \sum_1^l \alpha_i y_i \phi(\mathbf{x}_i)$, where $\alpha_i$ are the Lagrange multipliers corresponding to the constraints (5); $\mathbf{w}$ is thus determined only by those patterns that have non-zero Lagrange multipliers. These patterns are called *support vectors*. The $\alpha_i$ can be obtained by solving the corresponding dual optimization problem:

$$\max_{\alpha_i} \sum_{i=1}^{l} \alpha_i - \frac{1}{2} \sum_{i,j=1}^{l} \alpha_i \alpha_j k(\mathbf{x}_i, \mathbf{x}_j), \qquad (7)$$

$$\text{subject to } \sum_{i=1}^{l} \alpha_i y_i = 0, \qquad (8)$$

$$\text{and } 0 \leq \alpha_i \leq C, \quad i = 1, \ldots, l \qquad (9)$$

where inner products in the feature space are replaced by a kernel function, $k(\mathbf{x}_i, \mathbf{x}_j) \equiv \phi(\mathbf{x}_i)^T \phi(\mathbf{x}_j)$, evaluated at input patterns $\mathbf{x}_i$ and $\mathbf{x}_j$. Thus the dual optimization problem depends only on inner products in the feature space.

The decision function of the SVM also depends only on the inner products: $f(\mathbf{x}) = \text{sgn}\left(\mathbf{w}^T \phi(\mathbf{x}) + b\right)$ and can therefore be expressed in terms of kernel functions as $f(\mathbf{x}) = \text{sgn}(\sum_{i=1}^{l} \alpha_i y_i k(\mathbf{x}_i, \mathbf{x}) + b)$. The SVM solution therefore does not require any explicit feature space mapping as long as the inner products in the feature space can be efficiently computed. This can be accomplished by choosing a symmetric positive definite kernel or a Mercer kernel $k(\mathbf{x}_i, \mathbf{x}_j)$, for which Mercer's theorem [6] implies the existence of a mapping $\phi$ such that $k(\mathbf{x}_i, \mathbf{x}_j) = \phi(\mathbf{x}_i)^T \phi(\mathbf{x}_j)$. Therefore, without considering the mapping $\phi$ explicitly, a nonlinear SVM can be constructed with an appropriate Mercer kernel; see [6] for choices of a Mercer kernel and further details.

## 4 Learning SVMs with Multiresolution Histograms

We investigate the suitability of SVMs for texture classification using multiresolution histograms. The distance between two histogram feature vectors is usually computed using $L_1$ distance since it gives equal importance to all densities [11]. Other norms give higher (e.g., $L_2$ norm) or lower (sublinear norms) importance to higher bin counts, and vice versa. In the absence of any prior information, the histogram is best represented by the $L_1$ norm.

An SVM with a Laplacian RBF kernel ($k(\mathbf{x}, \mathbf{y}) = \exp(-\sum_i |x_i - y_i|/2\sigma^2)$) computes the similarity between feature vectors using the $L_1$ norm. Furthermore, the Laplacian RBF kernel is a Mercer kernel which ensures that the *feature space* hyperplane has maximum margin [5]. This implies that Laplacian RBF kernels perform better on histograms compared to other kernels. Previous work using SVMs with Laplacian RBF kernels on histograms reported excellent results [12,13]. SVMs offer good performance on high-dimensional data with small training sample size [5,12], which is typically the case with multiresolution histograms. It is therefore expected that SVMs with Laplacian RBF kernel perform well on multiresolution histograms.

The dimensionality of multiresolution histograms can be reduced using Laplacian pyramids without affecting the classification performance. This is possible because successive images in a Laplacian pyramid are detail images (also signed) with most pixel intensity values near zero. This results in sparse histograms resembling Gaussian densities with low variance centered near zero [7]. Consequently, the cumulative histograms of an image at different resolutions have similar values at tails, where the tails represent high intensity values of either sign. The difference histogram features corresponding to these tails tend to be zero, which is not necessarily the case with Gaussian pyramids. If a given feature has the same value, zero in this case, for all the training samples, it can be removed with no effect on the classification results. In other words, the training samples lie in a lower dimensional subspace of a space of their original dimensionality and can discriminate (classify) test patterns only along these feature dimensions.

## 5 Experiments

We evaluate the performance of multiresolution histogram features using SVMs on Brodatz textures. In [3], authors use $L_1$ distance to match multiresolution histograms. This is identical to a one nearest-neighbor classifier (1–NN) using $L_1$ distance. We demonstrate that the performance of multiresolution histograms can be significantly improved by SVMs and it is also robust to noise. This improvement is significant particularly when the training sample size of the classifier is small (as a fraction of the total samples).

### 5.1 Data

We experimented with 30 natural textures selected from Brodatz album[1] [14]. A few sample textures are shown in Figure 1. The texture images are of size 640 × 640 with 256 gray levels. We divided each texture image into 100 non-overlapping subimages (samples) of size 64 × 64. Each texture class thus has a total of 100 samples. In all our experiments, the training set comprises 10% (10) and the test set the remaining 90% (90) of the total samples of a texture class. The test errors reported are averaged over 20 runs, where each time the 100 samples of each texture class are randomly split into 10 training samples and 90 test samples.

### 5.2 Experimental Setup

We extracted the multiresolution histogram features as described in Section 2. The multiscale decomposition of subimages was computed using a Laplacian

---
[1] Available at http://www.ux.his.no/~tranden/brodatz.html

**Fig. 1.** Sample textures from the Brodatz texture database

pyramid. The number of levels in the pyramid was set to 5, and the number of histogram bins to 64. We did not subsample the images at lower resolutions to avoid the problem of estimating histograms with too few pixels (with subsampling, the lowest resolution image is of size $4 \times 4$). Features generated with these parameter settings yielded the best results on both SVMs and NN classifiers. The dimensionality of the feature vector is 256 obtained by concatenating the four difference histograms of 64 bins, calculated by taking the adjacent differences of the five cumulative histograms. The effective feature dimensionality, however, is approximately 90 after removing all the zero features from the training set as described in Section 4. The exact (number of) features removed depends on the random partitioning of the total samples into training and test sets. The training samples were normalized so that all the features are in the range $[0, 1]$.

We have described SVMs for binary classification in Section 3. Multiclass classification problem using SVMs is usually solved by training several binary SVMs. We used *one-vs-all* classification scheme in which one binary SVM is trained for each texture class to separate it from the rest [15]. We set the constant $C = 100$ (refer to (4)). We tried both polynomial and radial basis function (RBF) kernels for SVMs. The parameter $\sigma$ of the RBF kernel was tuned manually for the best classification results. For the NN classifiers, a value of $k = 1$ (1–NN) yielded the best results.

### 5.3 Experimental Results

The classification results of both SVMs and 1–NN classifiers on noiseless and noisy Brodatz texture samples are summarized in Table 1. The error rates shown in the third column were obtaining by adding white Gaussian noise of standard deviation 10 (on intensity scale [0,255]) to all the samples in the database. On both noiseless and noisy textures, SVMs clearly outperform the 1–NN classifiers. As expected, both SVMs and 1–NN classifiers perform best with $L_1$ metric. The SVM with Laplacian RBF kernel performs best on both noiseless and noisy texture samples (error rates 1.44% and 1.79%, respectively), while the 1–NN classifier with $L_2$ metric performs worst (error rates 4.11% and 4.58%, respectively). The SVM with Laplacian RBF kernel performs almost twice as better as 1–NN classifier with $L_1$ metric. In general SVMs with Laplacian or Gaussian RBF kernels perform better than 1–NN classifiers. We observed a similar trend in the results when the fraction of total samples used for training is increased to 25%. As can be seen from Table 1, the classification performance of SVMs remains reasonably robust in the presence of noise. It is interesting to note that the

**Table 1.** Error rates (E.r.) of SVMs with different kernels, and 1–NN classifiers with different metrics on noiseless and noisy Brodatz textures. The error rates are averaged over 20 runs.

| SVMs (Kernel type) | E.r (%) (noiseless) | E.r. (%) (noisy) |
|---|---|---|
| Polynomial (degree = 5) | 2.93 | 3.26 |
| Polynomial (degree = 6) | 2.89 | 3.26 |
| Polynomial (degree = 7) | 2.92 | 3.25 |
| Gaussian RBF ($\sigma = 2$) | 2.30 | 2.54 |
| Gaussian RBF ($\sigma = 3$) | 2.26 | 2.57 |
| Gaussian RBF ($\sigma = 4$) | 2.49 | 2.77 |
| Laplacian RBF ($\sigma = 5$) | 1.56 | 1.79 |
| Laplacian RBF ($\sigma = 5.5$) | **1.44** | **1.79** |
| Laplacian RBF ($\sigma = 6$) | 1.75 | 1.92 |
| 1-NN Classifiers (Metric type) | E.r. (%) (noiseless) | E.r. (%) (noisy) |
| $L_1$ distance | 2.86 | 3.68 |
| $L_2$ distance | 4.11 | 4.58 |

error rates of SVMs with Laplacian or Gaussian RBF kernels on noisy samples are lower than those of 1–NN classifiers on noiseless samples.

## 6 Conclusion

We evaluated the performance of multiresolution histograms using SVMs. We verified that the dimensionality of multiresolution histograms can be reduced significantly using a Laplacian pyramid. We also showed that the classification performance of multiresolution histograms on Brodatz textures can be improved significantly using SVMs with a Laplacian RBF kernel compared to the previously used 1–NN classifier. We also demonstrated the robustness of SVM classification performance in the presence of noise.

## References

1. Tuceryan, M., Jain, A.K.: Texture analysis. In: Handbook of Pattern Recognition & Computer Vision, (World Scientific, Singapore, 1993) 235–276
2. Li, S., Kwok, J.T., Zhu, H., Wang, Y.: Texture classification using the support vector machines. Pattern Recognition **36** (2003) 2883–2893
3. Hadjidemetriou, E., Grossberg, M.D., Nayar, S.K.: Multiresolution histograms and their use for recognition. IEEE Trans. Pattern Anal. Mach. Intell. **26** (2004) 831–847
4. Duda, R.O., Hart, P.E., Stork, D.G.: Pattern Classification. John Wiley and Sons, New York (2000)

5. Vapnik, V.: Statistical Learning Theory. Wiley, New York (1998)
6. Schölkopf, B., Smola, A.J.: Learning with Kernels. MIT Press (2002)
7. Burt, P.J., Adelson, E.H.: The Laplacian pyramid as a compact image code. IEEE Trans. Commun. **31** (1983) 532–540
8. Plastino, A., Plastino, A., Miller, H.: Tsallis nonextensive thermostatistics and Fisher's information measure. Physica A **235** (1997) 577–588
9. Stricker, M., Orengo, M.: Similarity of color images. In: Storage and Retrieval for Image and Video Databases (SPIE). (1995) 381–392
10. Cover, T.M.: Geometrical and statistical properties of systems of linear inequalities with applications in pattern recognition. IEEE Trans. Elect. Comp. **14** (1965) 326–334
11. Izenman, A.J.: Recent developments in nonparametric density estimation. J. Amer. Statist. Assoc. **86** (1991) 205–224
12. Chapelle, O., Haffner, P., Vapnik, V.: SVMs for histogram-based image classification. IEEE Trans. Neural Networks **10** (1999) 1055–1064
13. Barla, A., Odone, F., Verri, A.: Histogram intersection kernel for image classification. In: IEEE Proc. ICIP. Volume 2. (2003) 513–516
14. Brodatz, P.: Textures: a photographic album for artists and designers. Dover Publications, New York (1966)
15. Rifkin, R.M., Klautau, A.: In defense of one-vs-all classification. J. Mach. Learn. Res. **5** (2004) 101–141

# Texture Classification Based on the Fractal Performance of the Moment Feature Images

Guitao Cao[1], Pengfei Shi[1], and Bing Hu[2]

[1] Institute of Image Processing and Pattern Recognition, Shanghai Jiaotong University,
Shanghai 200030, China
{maggie, pfshi}@sjtu.edu.cn
[2] Department of Ultrasound in Medicine, Shanghai Sixth Hospital, Shanghai Jiaotong University, Shanghai 200233, China
binghuzz@263.net

**Abstract.** Texture classification plays an important role in identifying objects. The fractal properties based on moment feature images for texture classification are investigated in this paper. The two-order moments of the image in small windows are used as feature images whose fractal dimensions are then computed and employed to classify the textures using support vector machines (SVMs). Experiments on several Brodatz nature images and four in-vivo B-mode ultrasound liver images demonstrate the effectiveness of the proposed algorithm.

## 1 Introduction

Texture classification is conventionally divided into two stages: first, textures in an image are differentiated and then their representations for further classification are developed. Secondly, appropriate classifier is selected to operate on the above representations and then discriminate the texture features associated with different texture classes.

Various algorithms that perform texture analysis, such as statistical, model-based, and signal processing algorithms, have been developed in the past. The statistical algorithms include gray level co-occurrence matrix (GLCM) [1, 2], autocorrelation function analysis [3], and texture Spectrum [4]. Model-based algorithms include statistical modeling such as Markov random fields (MRF) [5] and fractal based modeling [6, 7]. Moment, as one of signal processing algorithms, has often been utilized previously for characterizing texture [8, 9].

In this paper, an algorithm is developed to obtain texture features from the fractal dimensions of the feature images, which are computed by the moments of the image in local regions. The moments of a two-dimensional function is defined and the computation of fractal dimensions from the moment feature images is derived in Section 2. In Section 3, the support vector machines (SVMs) that uses the obtained features to classify the texture images is presented. Section 4 gives experimental results, and conclusions are then followed in Section 5. In this study, two performance indices are employed to evaluate the classification rate. One is the polynomial kernel degree of SVMs and the other is the size of the local subimages for fractal dimension estimation. The proposed algorithm is tested using several Brodatz and in-vivo B-mode ultrasound liver images.

## 2 Features Extraction

The moments alone are not sufficient to obtain good texture features in certain images. However, their distribution would be different for different textures. One solution suggested by Caelli [10] is to introduce a nonlinear transducer that maps moments to texture features. Coggins and Jain [11], on the other hand, use the absolute deviation of their feature vectors from the mean. Tuceryan [12] has chosen to use the hyperbolic tangent function as their nonlinear transducer which is logistic in shape. In this paper two-order moments of the original are introduced as the feature images and their corresponding fractal dimensions are computed for the classification.

### 2.1 Moments

The moments of an image are used to compute texture features. The $(p+q)th$ order moment [13] of a function with two variables $f(x,y)$ with respect to the origin (0,0) is defined as:

$$m_{pq} = \int_{-\infty}^{\infty}\int_{-\infty}^{\infty} f(x,y) x^p y^q dxdy, \tag{1}$$

where $p+q = 0,1,2,\cdots$.

Tuceryan [12] took the image intensity as a function with two variables, $f(x,y)$, and calculated the two order moments of each pixel in the image, which were interpreted as a convolution of the image with a mask. The set of values for each moment over the entire image can be regarded as a new feature images. Fig.1 shows the masks corresponding to the moments up to the second order with a window size of three.

$$m_{00} = \begin{bmatrix} 1 & 1 & 1 \\ 1 & 1 & 1 \\ 1 & 1 & 1 \end{bmatrix} \quad m_{10} = \begin{bmatrix} -1 & -1 & -1 \\ 0 & 0 & 0 \\ 1 & 1 & 1 \end{bmatrix} \quad m_{01} = \begin{bmatrix} -1 & 0 & 1 \\ -1 & 0 & 1 \\ -1 & 0 & 1 \end{bmatrix}$$

$$m_{20} = \begin{bmatrix} 1 & 1 & 1 \\ 0 & 0 & 0 \\ 1 & 1 & 1 \end{bmatrix} \quad m_{11} = \begin{bmatrix} 1 & 0 & -1 \\ 0 & 0 & 0 \\ -1 & 0 & 1 \end{bmatrix} \quad m_{02} = \begin{bmatrix} 1 & 0 & 1 \\ 1 & 0 & 1 \\ 1 & 0 & 1 \end{bmatrix}$$

**Fig. 1.** The masks corresponding to the moments up to the second order with a window size of three

In our experiments, subimages are selected randomly from each original image and their corresponding feature images M1, M2, M3, M4, M5, and M6 are derived from $m_{00}, m_{10}, m_{01}, m_{20}, m_{11}$, and $m_{02}$, respectively. And then the fractal dimensions of the moment feature images can be computed to classify the texture.

### 2.2 Fractal Dimension

Fractal is a term introduced by Mandelbrot to describe the shape and appearance of objects that have the property of self-similarity. Among various approaches for estimating fractal dimension (FD) in an image, the differential box counting (DBC) algorithm, which can cover a wide dynamic range with high computing efficiency, is adopted herein [15].

Assume that an image with $M \times M$ pixels has been scaled down to that of $s \times s$ pixels($s$ is an integer, and $1 < s \leq M/2$), and the scale ratio $r$ becomes $s/M$. Subsequently, the image is considered as a three-dimensional space with $(x, y)$ indicating the two-dimensional position and the third coordinate denoting intensity. The $(x, y)$ space is partitioned into grids of size of $s \times s$, and on each grid there is a column of boxes of size of $s \times s \times h$. If the total number of gray-levels is $G$, denote $[G/h] = [M/s]$. Let the minimum and the maximum gray-level of the image in the $(i, j)$th grid both fall in the box number $k$ and $l$, as illustrated in Fig.2.

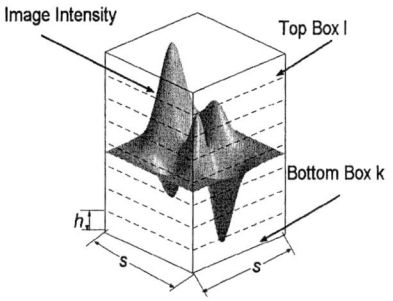

**Fig. 2.** Determination of $n_r(i, j)$

So,

$$n_r(i, j) = l - k + 1, \qquad (2)$$

where, $n_r(i, j)$ is the contribution of $N_r$ in the $(i, j)$th grid. By taking the contributions from all grids of the image, it gives as follows.

$$N_r = \sum_{i,j} n_r(i, j), \qquad (3)$$

where, $N_r$ is for different $r$ (i.e., different $s$). And then, the fractal dimension $D_f$ can be estimated by using the least-square linear fitting of $log(N_r)$ versus $log(1/r)$.

The success of the texture classification by fractal performance algorithm greatly depends on how well it can model the underlying statistical distribution of data. The two-order moments can give six different feature images for each image, so it is more accurate than single original image.

## 3 Support Vector Machines (SVMs)

The features extracted by the preceding algorithm are used for classification. From Bayes classifiers to neural networks, there are many choices for an appropriate classifier. Among them, Support Vector Machines (SVMs) is a good candidate due to their ability to transform the learning task to the quadratic programming problem in high-dimensional spaces [16].

Usually, an SVM constructs a binary classifier from a set of two-class labeled patterns called training examples. Given the training data set $(x_i, y_i)$ (where $x_i \in R^N, i = 1, \cdots, l$ is the N-dimensional input feature, $l$ is the number of training samples, and $y_i \in \{+1, -1\}$ is the class label), the SVM selects the optimal separating hyperplane as follows:

$$f(x) = \mathrm{sgn}(\sum_{i=1}^{l} y_i \alpha_i x_i \cdot x + b), \qquad (4)$$

Where, the points from the data set that fall closest to the separating hyperplane are called support vectors. The coefficients $\alpha_i$ and b can be determined by solving the large-scale quadratic programming problem:

$$W(\alpha) = \sum_{i=1}^{l} \alpha_i - \frac{1}{2} \sum_{i,j=1}^{l} \alpha_i \alpha_j y_i y_j (x_i \cdot x_j), \qquad (5)$$

Where, $W(\alpha)$ is subject to the constraints:

$$\sum_{i=1}^{l} \alpha_i y_i = 0, 0 \leq \alpha_i \leq C \ for \quad i = 1, \cdots, l. \qquad (6)$$

The parameter $C$ can be regarded as the regularization parameter and be selected by the user. A larger $C$ corresponds to assigning a higher penalty to the training errors. Under certain conditions, the computational intensive mapping process can be reduced with an appropriate kernel function $K$ such that the decision function becomes:

$$f(x) = \mathrm{sgn}(\sum_{i=1}^{l} y_i \alpha_i K(x_i, x) + b). \qquad (7)$$

In this paper, polynomial kernel function is used as:

$$K(x_i, x_j) = (\gamma x_i \cdot x_j + c)^d, \gamma > 0, \qquad (8)$$

where $\gamma = 1$, $c=1$, and $d$ is the degree of the polynomial kernel in our experiments.

SVM is originally developed for two-class problems, however, it can be extended to multi-texture classification by adopting the one-against-others decomposition algorithm.

## 4 Experiments

The proposed classification algorithm has been tested on both nature images and some in-vivo B-mode ultrasound liver images. Fig.3 shows six nature images with 512×512 pixels, D9 (Grass), D15 (Straw), D19 (Woolen cloth), D29 (Beach sand),

D68 (Wood grain), and D84 (Raffia), are from Brodatz album, http://sipi.usc.edu/services/database/database.cgi?volume=textures.

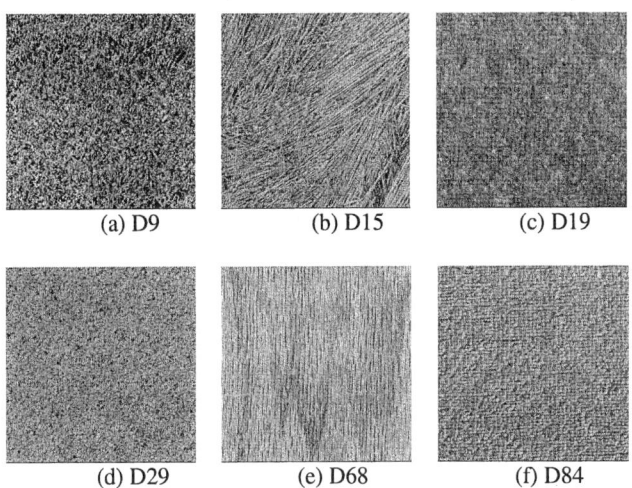

**Fig. 3.** Nature images from the Brodatz album: (a) D9 (Grass), (b) D15 (Straw), (c) D19 (Woolen cloth), (d) D29 (Beach sand), (e) D68 (Wood grain), and (f) D84 (Raffia)

In our experiments, 40 subimages were randomly selected in every original image, and their corresponding fractal dimensions of feature images are computed separately, so there is a total of 240 patterns for training and classification. The entire sample set is randomly divided into two groups: set A (120 samples) and set B (120 samples), and set A is always used as training set to evaluate the performance of the classifier. Two different sample set are used as test set to obtain the correct classification rate (CCR) using the proposed SVM algorithm with polynomial degree 1 through 9. The CCRs are tested by set A, the same as the training set, are shown in Fig.4. Then, set B is used as test set (see Fig.5). It can be seen from Fig.5 that the CCRs for subimage with a size of 256×256 can reach 100% when the polynomial degree is higher than 3.

In order to investigate the influence of the size of the subimage, the CCRs for different subimages, such as 128×128, 64×64, 32×32,16×16, and 8×8 pixels, are all taken into considered. It is obviously that the CCRs can be greatly improved by using the same training and test set (set A), which are larger than 95% when the polynomial degree is higher than 4. Even the size of the subimage is smaller than 64, the CCRs are still satisfactory. However, the CCRs decrease rapidly if different training and test set are applied as shown in Fig.5.

Meanwhile, Fig.5 indicates that the size of subimages is the key factor in determining the texture patterns compared to the polynomial degree. The CCRs achieved by set B are basically the same for the same subimage, but decrease sharply with the sizes of subimage reduce. So it is preferable to choose suitable size of subimage for the texture classification.

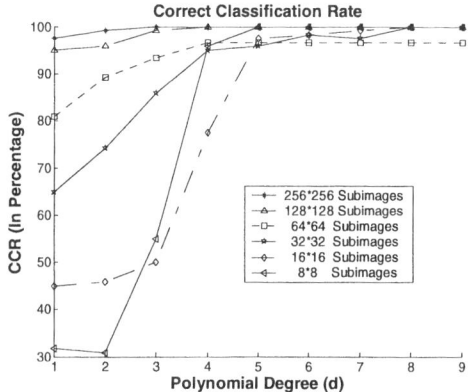

**Fig. 4.** CCRs (in percentage) of Brodatz nature images tested by set A for Polynomial degree 1 through 9 with different size of subimages (256×256, 128×128, 64×64, 32×32, 16×16, and 8×8 pixels)

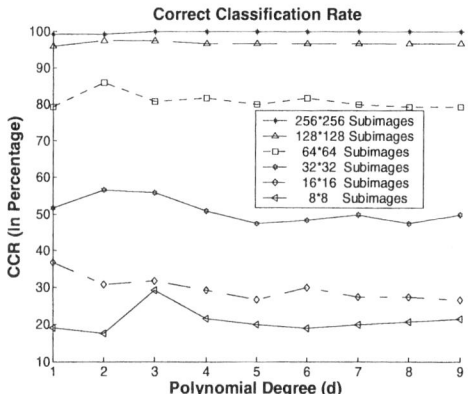

**Fig. 5.** CCRs (in percentage) of Brodatz nature images tested by set B for Polynomial degree 1 through 9 with different size of subimages (256×256, 128×128, 64×64, 32×32, 16×16, and 8×8 pixels)

In addition, the proposed texture classification algorithm is applied to solve practical problems including identifying four types of B-mode ultrasound liver images, i.e. healthy, fatty, fibrosis and cirrhosis, as shown in Fig.6. There are four in-vivo ultrasound images with 400×400 pixels for each type of liver, and 10 samples with 64×64 pixels are chosen from each type of image, in which only the liver parenchyma is left without major blood vessels, acoustic shadowing, or any type of distortion. The entire sample set is also divided into two groups: set A (80 samples) and set B (80 samples), and set A is always regarded as the training set. The CCRs tested by set A and B are shown in Fig.7, respectively. It is clearly that the CCRs are satisfactory for the same training and test set, and the CCR of 88.75% can be achieved when polynomial degree is 5. But the CCRs are very poor tested by set B. This implies that this algorithm for the in-vivo liver disease identification should be tested by the same training and test samples.

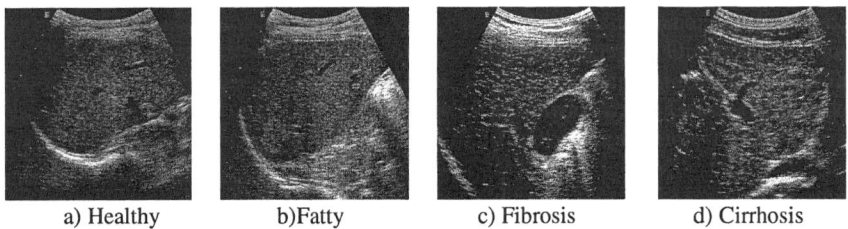

a) Healthy    b)Fatty    c) Fibrosis    d) Cirrhosis

**Fig. 6.** Four types of B-mode liver images: a)Healthy b) Fatty c) Fibrosis d) Cirrhosis liver

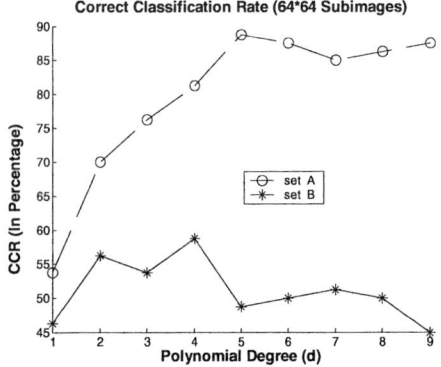

**Fig. 7.** CCRs (in percentage) of four types of B-mode liver images by SVMs for Polynomial degree 1 through 9 and tested by two different test sets: set A and set B

## 5 Conclusions

In this paper, a texture classification algorithm is developed based on the fractal performance of the moment feature images, which is tested by using several nature images and four types of in-vivo ultrasound liver images. The classification rate with different subimage sizes and different polynomial degrees are compared in Fig.4 and Fig.5. The results show that the fractal dimensions obtained by moment feature images can reflect the textural properties of images.

There are more works on this study need to be done in the future. First, the size of the window within which the fractal dimensions are calculated can be regarded as a scale parameter. This can be verified by the fact that the CCR corresponds to the size of the fractal window. Second, the selection of the fractal window to derive the texture features from the moment feature images is also not done automatically. In such case, the window should cover enough texture elements expressing meaningful features. Finally, the general purpose of SVMs algorithm requires that the polynomial degree is provided artificially. In this experiment polynomial degrees from 1 to 9 are tested, and it shows that the polynomial degree 4~6 can provide good performance in classifying texture pairs.

# References

1. Haralick RM, Shanugam K, Dinstein I, Texture features for image classification. IEEE Trans. on Systems, Man and Cybernetics, 1973, 3, pp:610-621.
2. L. S. Davis, M. Clearman, and J. K. Aggarwal, An empirical evaluation of generalized co-occurrence matrices, IEEE Trans. Pattern Analysis and Machine Intelligence, 1981,PAMI-3, pp: 214–221.
3. J.S. Weszka, C.R. Dryer, and A. Rosenfeld, A comparative study of texture measures for terrain classification, IEEE Trans. on Systems, Man and Cybernetics, 1976, Vol.SMC-6, pp: 269-285.
4. He DC, Wang L, Texture unit, texture spectrum and texture analysis. IEEE Trans. on Geoscience. Remote Sensing, 1990, 28, pp:509-512.
5. Chellappa, R. and S. Chatterjee, Classification of textures using Gaussian Markov Random Fields, IEEE Trans. on Acoustic, Speech, and Signal Processing, 1985, ASSP-33, pp: 959-963.
6. B.B.Chaudhuri and Nirupam Sarkar, Texture segmentation using fractal dimension, IEEE Trans. on Pattern Analysis and Machine Intelligence, Jan.1995, vol.17, No.1, pp: 72-77.
7. Nirupam Sarkar and B.B. Chauhuri, An efficient differential Box-counting approach to compute fractal dimension of image, IEEE Trans. on Pattern Analysis and Machine Intelligence, Jun. 1994, vol.24, No.1, pp: 115-120.
8. K. I. Laws, Textured Image Segmentation. Ph.D. Thesis, University of Southern California, 1980.
9. M. Tuceryan and A. K. Jain. Texture segmentation using Voronoi polygons. IEEE Trans. on Pattern Analysis and Machine Intelligence, Feb. 1990, PAMI-12, pp: 211 – 216.
10. T. Caelli and M. N. Oguztoreli. Some tasks and signal dependent rules for spatial vision. Spatial Vision, 1987, 2, pp: 295 – 315.
11. J. M. Coggins and A. K. Jain. A spatial filtering approach to texture analysis. Pattern Recognition Letters, 1985, 3, pp: 195–203.
12. Mihran Tuceryan, Moment based texture segmentation. Pattern Recognition Letters, July 1994, vol. 15, pp: 659-668.
13. M. K. Hu. Visual pattern recognition by moment invariants. IEEE Trans. on Information Theory, 1962, IT-8, pp: 179–187.
14. A. K. Jain, Fundamentals of Digital Image Processing. Prentice Hall, Englewood Cliffs, New Jersey, 1989.
15. N. Sarkar and B. B. Chaudhuri. An efficient differential box-counting approach to compute fractal dimension of image. IEEE Trans. on Systems, Man and Cybernetics, Jan. 1994, 24, pp: 115–120.
16. Burges CJC. A tutorial on support vector machines for pattern recognition. Data Mining Knowledge Discovery. 1998;2, pp: 955–974.

# Mapping Local Image Deformations into Depth

Stephen Benoit and Frank P. Ferrie

Department of Electrical and Computer Engineering,
and the Centre for Intelligent Machines
McGill University, Montréal, Canada

**Abstract.** The paper presents a 2 frame structure-from-motion algorithm that operates by mapping local changes (image deformations) into estimates of time-to-collision (TTC). For constant velocity motion of the camera in a stationary scene, time-to-collision amounts to coarse depth data - useful for navigation and qualitative scene understanding. The theory is supported by a set of experiments demonstrating accurate TTC recovery from video sequence data acquired by a mobile robot.

## 1 Introduction

Recovery of structure from motion has been examined from a variety of approaches, mainly feature point extraction and correspondence[5,7] or computing dense optical flow[6,8,1]. Typically, the Fundamental Matrix framework or a global motion model is used to solve for global motion after which the relative 3-D positions of points of interest in the scene can be computed[9,11]. Appearance-based methods have been mostly discarded for structure from motion because much of the shape and motion information are so confounded that they cannot be recovered separately or locally[3]. Soatto proved that perspective is non-linear, therefore no coordinate system will linearize perspective effects[10]. However, in [2] we showed that some useful structure and motion information could indeed be directly recovered, namely time-to-collision (TTC) and heading information. In this paper we present a practical, two-frame algorithm for recovering TTC and experimental results showing how it can be used to recover a qualitative 3-D scene description from video sequences acquired by a mobile robot.

## 2 Theory

The key result from [2] is that useful shape and motion information can be extracted from the analysis of local image deformations along 1-D neighbourhoods. The set-up is shown in Figure 1. Each oriented, rectangular window corresponds to the image of of a cross-section of a 3-D surface, essentially a *normal section* in the context of differential geometry[4]. There is a precise relationship between the structure and motion of this cross-section and deformations of two corresponding 1-D windows, $(x_a, y_a, \theta_i, t_0)$ and $(x_a, y_a, \theta_i, t_1)$ (Figure 1), that is made explicit for particular choice of image formation model.

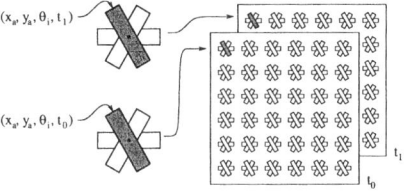

**Fig. 1.** Oriented slits at image coordinates $(x_a, y_a)$ at multiple orientations $\theta_i$ cover the image plane at instants $t_0$ and $t_1$

The image formation model we use, i.e., the *forward-model*, is shown schematically in Figure 2. The mapping from cross-section to image is defined by the perspective camera model shown in Figure 2a, and the motion and structure model relating 3-D change to appearance is shown in Figure 2b, the latter comprising 5 parameters, $\mathbf{m} = (\Omega, \delta, \eta, \beta, k)$. Referring to Figure 2b, the 3-D cross-section is characterized by a curvature $K$, a normal vector $\mathbf{N}$ and distance from the viewpoint, $d$. Distance $d$ scales all lengths of the diagram, so it is factored out to a canonical representation with unit distance between first viewpoint $VP$ and the fixation point on the surface 0. The surface normal vector $\mathbf{N}$ at 0 is encoded by the angle $\eta$ with respect to the first view axis $VP - 0$. The curvature of the canonical surface, the reciprocal of the radius of the circular approximation to the surface, becomes $k = Kd$.

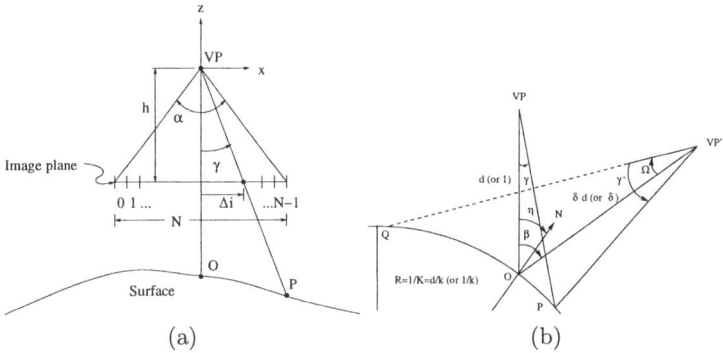

**Fig. 2.** (a) The 1-D camera model. (b) Motion and structure model for a surface cross-section

The motion model is chosen to minimize image deformation due to translation, defining the second viewpoint $VP'$ at a given distance $\delta$ at an angle $\beta$ from the first view axis $VP - 0$. $VP'$ is fixated on point $Q$ on the surface, a view rotation $\Omega$ away from the first fixation point 0. Collectively, the camera and shape and motion models are sufficient to describe the forward mapping of a 3-D contour, parameterized by orientation, $\eta$, and curvature, $k$, onto a 1-D image slit, $\mathcal{I}$, and then onto a corresponding image slit, $\mathcal{I}'$ via translation, $\Omega$, change in distance to viewer, $\delta$, and change in viewpoint direction, $\beta$. Details are given in [2].

Solution of the inverse problem involves recovery of $\mathbf{m}$ given two 1-D windows, $\mathcal{I}$ and $\mathcal{I}'$. Here an appearance-based approach is used. For the experiments presented in this paper, the parameter space $\mathbf{m}$ is quantized into 21 levels for $\Omega$ and $\delta$ respectively, and 5 levels each for $\eta$, $\beta$, and $k$. This follows from [2] - only $\Omega$ and $\delta$ are recoverable, but fortunately these parameters are sufficient to recover TTC. For each of the 55,125 instances of $\mathbf{m}_i$, we create corresponding window pairs, $\mathcal{I}_i$ and $\mathcal{I}'_i$, by applying the forward model shown earlier in Figure 2.

Let $\mathcal{I}_i$ and $\mathcal{I}'_i$ be represented by $n \times 1$ vectors such that $\mathcal{I}_i = \mathbf{H}_i \mathcal{I}'_i$, where $\mathbf{H}_i$ is an $n \times n$ matrix that encodes the bi-directional mapping from $\mathcal{I}_i$ to $\mathcal{I}'_i$ and vice-versa. We refer to this as a *correspondence matrix*, and it is relatively straightforward to determine given $\mathcal{I}_i$ and $\mathcal{I}'_i$. A practical procedure for computing $\mathbf{H}_i$ is given in [2]. To minimize the effects of intensity variations between frames, before computing $\mathbf{H}_i$, $\mathcal{I}_i$ and $\mathcal{I}'_i$ are first normalized as $\tilde{\mathcal{I}}_i, \tilde{\mathcal{I}}'_i$ for a zero mean intensity and a contrast of 1 by finding the image's brightness $\mu_{\mathcal{I}}$ and contrast $\Delta_{\mathcal{I}}$.

$$\mu_{\mathcal{I}} \triangleq \frac{\sum_i \mathcal{I}_i + \sum_i \mathcal{I}'_i}{2N},$$

$$\Delta_{\mathcal{I}} \triangleq \frac{\max_i(|\mathcal{I}_i - \mu_{\mathcal{I}}|, |\mathcal{I}'_i - \mu_{\mathcal{I}}|)}{\mu_{\mathcal{I}}} \subset (0,1),$$

$$\tilde{\mathcal{I}} = \frac{\mathcal{I} - \mu_{\mathcal{I}}}{\mu_{\mathcal{I}} \Delta_{\mathcal{I}}}, \tilde{\mathcal{I}}' = \frac{\mathcal{I}' - \mu_{\mathcal{I}}}{\mu_{\mathcal{I}} \Delta_{\mathcal{I}}}. \quad (1)$$

Another key result from [2] concerns the singular value decomposition (SVD) of $\mathbf{H}_i$. Let $\mathbf{U}_i$ and $\mathbf{V}_i$ be left and right matrices respectively of the SVD of $\mathbf{H}_i$, and let $\mathbf{U}_{\mathbf{k}i}$ and $\mathbf{V}_{\mathbf{k}i}$ be their corresponding $k^{th}$ order approximations. The latter correspond to the first $k$ columns of $\mathbf{U}_i$ and $\mathbf{V}_i$ respectively sorted by singular values. Now let feature vector $\hat{w}_i$ represent the image vectors $\tilde{\mathcal{I}}$ and $\tilde{\mathcal{I}}'$ as follows:

$$\hat{w}_i = \left[ \mathbf{U}_{\mathbf{k}i}^T / \sqrt{2} \vdots \mathbf{V}_{\mathbf{k}i}^T / \sqrt{2} \right] \begin{bmatrix} \tilde{\mathcal{I}} \\ \cdots \\ \tilde{\mathcal{I}}' \end{bmatrix}, \quad (2)$$

where $\tilde{\mathcal{I}}$ and $\tilde{\mathcal{I}}'$ are a pair of inputs for which we wish to test $\mathbf{H}_i$. The feature vector $\hat{w}_i$ is now the best parameterization for the image pair assuming deformation $\mathbf{H}_i$. The residual error can be computed by projecting the feature vector back into the image space. If the assumed deformation $\mathbf{H}_i$ is sufficiently close to the scene geometry, then residual signal error $r_i$, the difference between the original image signal and the reconstructed image signal will be low,

$$r_i = \left( \begin{bmatrix} \tilde{\mathcal{I}} \\ \cdots \\ \tilde{\mathcal{I}}' \end{bmatrix} - \begin{bmatrix} \mathbf{U}_{\mathbf{k}i} \\ \cdots \\ \mathbf{V}_{\mathbf{k}i} \end{bmatrix} \hat{w}_i \right) \Big/ \left\| \begin{bmatrix} \tilde{\mathcal{I}} \\ \cdots \\ \tilde{\mathcal{I}}' \end{bmatrix} \right\|. \quad (3)$$

The likelihood of correspondence $\mathbf{H}_i$ given evidence $(\tilde{\mathcal{I}}, \tilde{\mathcal{I}}')$ can be expressed as a function $\mathcal{L}\left(\mathbf{H}_i | \tilde{\mathcal{I}}, \tilde{\mathcal{I}}'\right)$,

$$\mathcal{L}\left(\mathbf{H}_i | \tilde{\mathcal{I}}, \tilde{\mathcal{I}}'\right) \triangleq e^{-\|r_i\|} \subset (0, 1] . \qquad (4)$$

The uncertainty of the maximum likelihood choice can be expressed as the entropy $h$ of the likelihoods for all the different hypotheses,

$$h_i = \frac{-\sum_{i=1}^{n} \mathcal{L}\left(\mathbf{H}_i | \tilde{\mathcal{I}}, \tilde{\mathcal{I}}'\right) \log\left(\mathcal{L}\left(\mathbf{H}_i | \tilde{\mathcal{I}}, \tilde{\mathcal{I}}'\right)\right)}{\log(n)} \subset (0, 1] . \qquad (5)$$

## 3 Implementation

In practice, the computational complexity of searching for $\mathbf{H}_i$ is quite managable [2]. Only $\Omega$ and $\delta$ are observable, so $\eta$, $\beta$, and $k$ can be marginalized out by averaging the 125 matrices associated with each $\Omega,\delta$ pair. This reduces the search space to 441 distinct $\mathbf{H}_i$. $\Omega$ can be found independently by marginalizing $\delta$, but $\delta$ must be determined jointly with $\Omega$. The net result is that $\mathbf{H}_i$ can be found with a maximum of $21+21 = 42$ matches, in each of $n$ image orientations ($n = 6$ in this paper), for each $i \times j$ neighbourhood of the input image pair.

Time-to-collision is carried by the $\delta$ parameter, which indicates the ratio of the distance between the new viewpoint to the surface over the distance between the old viewpoint to the surface,

$$\delta = \frac{\|VP' - O\|}{\|VP - O\|} . \qquad (6)$$

The time between observations, $\Delta t$, is known beforehand. Assuming that the camera's motion relative to the scene will continue at constant velocity, one can estimate how much time will elapse before the camera reaches the point on the surface it is looking at and heading toward,

$$T = \Delta t \left(\frac{\delta}{1-\delta}\right) . \qquad (7)$$

Recovering $\Omega$ and $\delta$ locally in forward time can be augmented by recovering $\Omega'$ and $\delta'$ by reversing the sequence of the images. A direct method of computing the time to collision $\tilde{T}$ between two images, using both forward and reverse information, separated by a delay of $\Delta t$ is to average the two contributions,

$$\tilde{T} = \frac{\Delta t}{2}\left(\frac{\delta}{1-\delta} + \frac{1}{\delta' - 1}\right) . \qquad (8)$$

Taking contributions from different orientations into account, and weighting by their respective uncertainties (5), we obtain a more robust estimate of TTC,

$$\tilde{T} = \frac{\Delta t}{2n} \sum_{\theta=1}^{n} \left(\frac{\delta_\theta h_\theta}{1 - \delta_\theta h_\theta} + \frac{1}{\delta'_\theta h'_\theta - 1}\right) . \qquad (9)$$

## 4 Experiments

The forward model shown earlier in Figure 2 is used to produce correspondence matrices $\mathbf{H}_i$ indexed by $\Omega$ and $\delta$ as outlined in Section 2. The range of values for each parameter in experiments are summarized in Table 1.

**Table 1.** Parameters of structure from motion model. $N$ and $\alpha$ are known constants.

| Symbol | Values | Description |
|---|---|---|
| $\Omega$ | $-4.0°$ | translate left 32/64 pixels |
|  | $0°$ | no change |
|  | $+4.0°$ | translate right 32/64 pixels |
| $\delta$ | 0.80 | zoom in 20% |
|  | 1.0 | no change |
|  | 1.25 | zoom out 25% |
| $\eta$ | $-45°$ | normal pointing 45° left of $VP$ |
|  | $0°$ | normal pointing toward $VP$ |
|  | $+45°$ | normal pointing 45° right of $VP$ |
| $\beta$ | $-10°$ | $VP'$ moves to left of $VP$ |
|  | $0°$ | $VP'$ stays in line with $VP$ |
|  | $+10°$ | $VP'$ moves to right of $VP$ |
| $k$ | -4 | concave surface |
|  | 0 | flat surface |
|  | +4 | convex surface |

Applying SVD to each of the $\mathbf{H}_i$ yields corresponding $\mathbf{U}_{ki}, \mathbf{V}_{ki}$ pairs. These detectors, some of which are shown in Figure 3, are automatically synthesized to optimally recognise the distance-to-viewer change while remaining insensitive to other surface motions.

The one-time offline training, i.e. constructing the 441 64×64 correspondence matrices and their detectors by Singular Value Decomposition, required less than 90 seconds on an Intel Pentium 4 2660 MHz workstation.

The video test sequence was obtained by a video camera on a mobile robot as it travelled along a linear trajectory through a room, taking images at known positions in a fixed direction, looking in the direction of travel. The first and last images of the 11 frame sequence are shown in Figure 4.

The robot's position advances 20cm between each image, hence a velocity of 20cm per unit of time $\Delta t$. The map of maximum likelihood $\hat{\delta}$ and the map of time to collision $T$ were computed over a grid of 48×36 slits at 6 orientations and are rendered in Figure 5. Computation time on an Intel Pentium 4 2660 MHz workstation was approximately 90 seconds per image frame pair using an exhaustive search. In a practical implementation, the redundancy in the detectors would be reduced using linear combinations of Principal Components, potentially reducing computation time by a factor of 10. Using a sparser sampling of the image plane would further reduce the computation time closer to real time.

One significant observation is that although the floor tile pattern expands closer to the camera due to perspective and the texture of the floor is moving

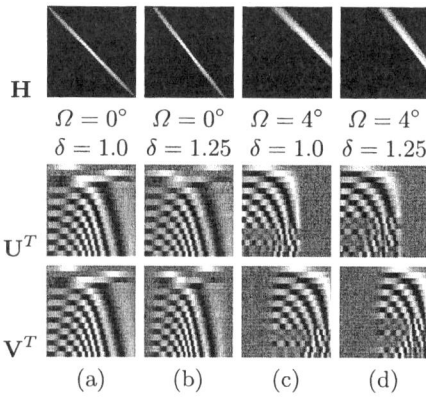

**Fig. 3.** Correspondence Matrices for some motions. For each **H**, black indicates 0, white represents 1. $\mathbf{H}_{ij}$ (row $i$, column $j$) indicates the amount of correspondence between $\mathcal{I}_i$ and $\mathcal{I}'_j$. For $\mathbf{U}^T$ and $\mathbf{V}^T$, black indicates -1 and white represents +1. Each row of $\mathbf{U}^T$ is a distorted sinusoid to be applied to $\mathcal{I}$ and the the same row in $\mathbf{V}^T$ is the corresponding distorted sinusoid for $\mathcal{I}'$.

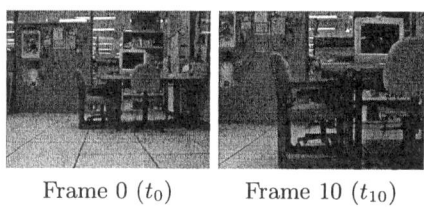

Frame 0 ($t_0$)     Frame 10 ($t_{10}$)

**Fig. 4.** Lab1 sequence, source images

toward the robot, the floor is heading *underneath* the camera and does not appear to be on a collision course with the camera. Because the camera line of sight is parallel to the floor, the algorithm has effectively classified the floor motion as maintaining constant distance from the camera, and thus not an obstacle. The algorithm performs a literal figure-ground separation, and the obstacle blobs are at least qualitatively useful for identifying the location of the nearest obstacles in the image. Next, the quantitative estimates are examined.

Note that in Figure 5, there are holes in the time map between the table and chair legs, where the back wall is beyond the detector's range. The chair near the center of the image started 400cm from the camera, and by the eleventh frame is 200cm from the camera. The chair has a large opening in it, letting a view of the background through. The image slits are based on a model of a continuous surface, so some uncertainty in the maximum likelihood estimates in this situation is unavoidable. The usefulness of the estimates can be shown in Figure 6, comparing the mean of the estimated time to collision of the region around that chair to ground truth from actual measurements.

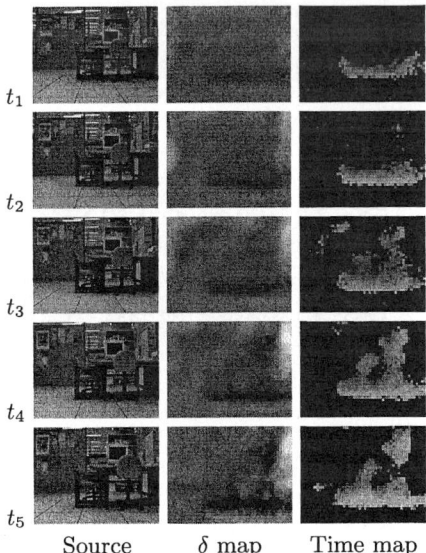

**Fig. 5.** Results from Lab1 sequence. For the $\delta$ map, $\delta = 0.8$ (rapid approach) is rendered as black, $\delta = 1.0$ (no depth change) is middle gray and $\delta = 1.25$ (rapid retreat) is white. The time map indicates proximity (either about to touch or recently touched) as brightness. Dark patches are more than 25 units of time away, either in the future or the past.

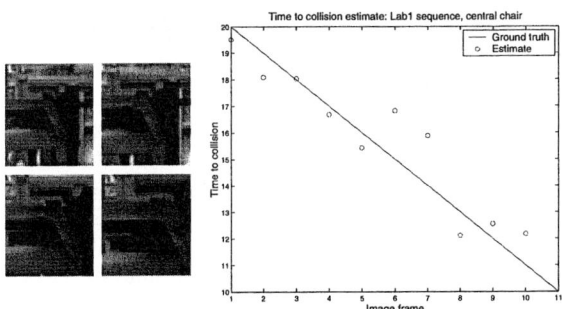

**Fig. 6.** Neighborhood of central chair in Lab1 sequence. Image patches from frames 0, 3, 6, and 9 (left to right, top to bottom) are shown at left. At right, the mean time to collision with this patch, shown as small circles are compared with the ground truth (line).

## 5 Conclusions

A time to collision or contact map provides a form of figure-ground separation that may be more informative to mobile robotics than instantaneous range images of similar resolution: it not only provides the instantaneous location of obstacles in the image plane, it also offers a prediction of their future locations. Distance to an obstacle is not the only factor to consider when ranking its importance to navigation. For example, an obstacle 1m away but maintaining its distance from the mobile robot is not significant, but an obstacle 20m away approaching at 2m/sec is critical.

As an added feature of the method proposed in this paper, the floor is naturally ignored in the case when the camera's line of sight is parallel to the floor, a task that is more difficult to achieve using optical flow methods.

The 1-D image slit surface model is often violated along various orientations at different locations in the image plane during the experiment (narrow features such as table legs, poor texture), and as a result, the maximum likelihood estimate at those orientations and locations are given higher uncertainties. Pooling together estimates from other, more confident orientations in the neighborhood leads to group estimates that are more robust to gauge time to collision.

# References

1. J. Barron and R. Eagleson. Motion and structure from time-varying optical flow. In *Vision Interface*, pages 104–111, May 1995.
2. S. Benoit and F. P. Ferrie. Towards direct recovery of shape and motion parameters from image sequences. In *Proceedings of ICCV*, pages 1395–1402, Nice, France, October 2003.
3. D. DiFranco and S. Kang. Is appearance-based structure from motion viable? In *2nd International Conference on 3-D Digital Imaging and Modeling*, Ottawa, Canada, Oct. 1999.
4. M. do Carmo. *Differential Geometry of Curves and Surfaces*. Prentice-Hall, Inc., Englewood Cliffs,New Jersey, 1976.
5. B. Krse, N. Vlassis, R. Bunschoten, and Y. Motomura. Feature selection for appearance-based robot localization. In *Proceedings 2000 RWC Symposium*, 2000.
6. H. Liu, R. Chellappa, and A. Rosenfeld. Accurate dense optical flow estimation using adaptive structure tensors and a parametric model. In *Intl. Conf. Pattern Recognition 2002*, pages I: 291–294, 2002.
7. J. Oliensis. Direct multi–frame structure from motion for hand–held cameras. In *ICPR Vol. I*, pages 889–895, 2000.
8. S. Roy and I. J. Cox. Motion without structure. In *13th Int. Conference on Pattern Recognition, Vol. I*, pages 728–734, Vienna, Austria, August 1996. IEEE.
9. S. Soatto and P. Perona. Dynamic visual motion estimation from subspace constraints. Technical Report CIT-CDS 94-006, California Institute of Technology, Pasadena, CA, Jan. 1994.
10. S. Soatto and P. Perona. On the exact linearization of structure from motion. Technical Report CIT-CDS 94-011, California Institute of Technology, Pasadena, CA, May 1994.
11. C. Tomasi. Input redundancy and output observability in the analysis of visual motion. In *Proc. Sixth Symposium on Robotics Research*, pages 213–222. MIT Press, 1993.

# Motion Segmentation Using a K-Nearest-Neighbor-Based Fusion Procedure of Spatial and Temporal Label Cues

Pierre-Marc Jodoin and Max Mignotte

Université de Montréal,
Département d'Informatique et de Recherche Opérationnelle (DIRO),
P.O. Box 6128, Studio Centre-Ville, Montréal, Québec, H3C 3J7
{jodoinp, mignotte}@iro.umontreal.ca

**Abstract.** Traditional motion segmentation techniques generally depend on a pre-estimated optical flow. Unfortunately, the lack of precision over edges of most popular motion estimation methods makes them unsuited to recover the exact shape of moving objects. In this contribution, we present an original motion segmentation technique using a $K$-nearest-neighbor-based fusion of spatial and temporal label cues. Our fusion model takes as input a spatial segmentation of a still image and an estimated version of the motion label field. It minimizes an energy function made of spatial and temporal label cues extracted from the two input fields. The algorithm proposed is intuitive, simple to implement and remains sufficiently general to be applied to other segmentation problems. Furthermore, the method doesn't depend on the estimation of any threshold or any weighting function between the spatial and temporal energy terms, as is sometimes required by energy-based segmentation models. Experiments on synthetic and real image sequences indicate that the proposed method is robust and accurate.

## 1 Introduction

Motion segmentation is one of the most studied research areas in computer vision. It refers to the general task of labeling image regions that contain uniform displacement. Consequently, motion segmentation has often be related to motion estimation. Actually, a common way to segment an image sequence is to estimate an optical flow field and then segment it into a set of regions with uniform displacement. Such an approach is sometimes called *motion-based* [1] since segmentation is performed on the basis of displacement vectors only. This kind of segmentation is rather easy to implement and generates more accurate results than say, an $8 \times 8$ block classification-segmentation procedure. However, motion-based approaches are known to depend on the accuracy of an optical flow field which isn't reliable over textureless and/or occluded areas. Consequently, motion-based algorithms are doomed to return imprecise results, especially around edges of moving objects.

To help motion segmentation converge toward more precise solutions (i.e., solutions in which the contour of segmented regions fit the silhouette of the moving objects), some include spatial constraints to the segmentation process. These constraints are often edges or regions extracted from one or more image frames. Motion segmentation approaches with spatial constraints are often called *spatio-temporal techniques*. These techniques are generally slower than motion-based approaches, but generate more precise segmentation results.

The approach we propose is based on a $K$-nearest-neighbor-based fusion procedure that mixes spatial and temporal data taken from two input label fields. The first one is a *spatial segmentation* which contains regions of uniform brightness while the second label field is an estimated version of the *motion label field* we will search to refine. The two segmentation maps are obtained with an unsupervised Markovian procedure. Our fusion method works with an iterative optimization algorithm called ICM (Iterative Conditional Mode) [2] whose mode (the maximum local energy for each site at each iteration) is obtained with a $K$-nearest neighbor algorithm. The result returned by our fusion model is a label field that exhibits uniform regions in the sense of brightness and motion.

The rest of the paper is organized as follows. In Section 2, we present some motion segmentation techniques recently proposed by the computer vision community before section 3 describes the proposed technique. The Markovian method we use to generate the two input label fields is discussed in Section 4 while the overall algorithm we proposed is summarized in section 5. Section 6 presents results produced by our method while concluding remarks are presented in Section 7.

## 2 Previous Work

A great number of papers have been published in motion segmentation during the past two decades [1,3]. Among the most popular *motion-based* approaches are the ones using parametric motion models [1]. The goal of these motion segmentation methods is to jointly estimate motion models and their associate motion regions. To this end, the motion regions and the motion model parameters are generally estimated in two steps [4] that are iterated until convergence. The first step consists in estimating the motion model parameters according to a pre-estimated optical flow field and the current motion label field [5,6]. By opposition, the second step consists in estimating new motion regions while the motion models are kept unchanged. Tekalp [7,8] summarizes these two steps with his *Maximum Likelihood* (ML) and *Maximum a Posteriori* (MAP) procedures. The difference between the former and the latter is the use of an *a priori* energy function that helps smoothing the resulting motion label field.

To our knowledge, Murray and Buxton [9] were the first to embed motion segmentation in a statistical framework using a Markov random field (MRF) model and a Bayesian criterion (a MAP criterion). Their technique uses quadratic motion models and represents the segmentation field with a Gibbs distribution whose energy is optimized with a Simulated Annealing (SA) algorithm. A few years later, Bouthemy and Francois [4] presented a motion-based segmentation approach relying on 2D affine models, used to detect moving objects in a scene observed by a moving camera. As for Murray and Buxton's method [9], they proposed a model based on a MAP criterion but include a temporal link between successive partitions to ensure temporal coherence. Bouthemy and Francois uses an ICM optimization to find the solution.

Other authors use motion segmentation to separate the scene into *moving layers* [10]. A well known iterative approach is the one proposed by Wang and Adelson [11]. The algorithm starts by estimating an optical flow field and subdivides the current frame into a predetermined number of square blocks. Affine motion models are then fitted over each block to get an initial set of motion models. Since the number of initial models is larger then the number of layers, the models are merged together with a $K$-means clustering method. Some layers can be split afterward to preserve spatial coherency.

Others have proposed segmentation models based on multiple features, such as brightness and motion. They are often refereed to as *spatio-temporal* segmentation techniques. In this context, Black [12] presented an incremental approach with constraint on intensity and motion while accounting for discontinuity. Its approach is based on a MRF and minimizes a three- term energy function using a stochastic relaxation technique. Altunbasak *et al.* [13] presented a motion segmentation approach working at a region level. As a first step, they independently compute a motion-based partition and a color-based partition. Assuming that color regions are more accurate than the motion regions, a region-based motion segmentation is performed, whereby all sites contained in a color region are assigned a single motion label. Bergen and Meyer [14] show how to use a still image segmentation combined with robust regression to eliminate error due to occlusion. This technique computes depth cues on the basis of motion estimation error.

Finally, a recent paper proposed by Khan and Shah [15] presents a MAP framework that softly blends color, position and motion cues to extract motion layers. Each cue has its own probability density function (PDF). These PDF are combined together with feature weights that give more or less importance to a cue depending on some defined observations.

## 3 Our Method

Our motion segmentation procedure takes as input two label fields. The first one is a spatial partition of a frame at time $t$ ($I^t$) while the second one is an estimated version of the motion partition (cf. Fig.1). In our application, these two label fields –called respectively $r$ and $x^{[0]}$– are estimated separately with an unsupervised Markovian procedure (although any other valid segmentation approaches would do the trick). The Markovian framework used in this paper is presented in Section 4.

Once $r$ and $x^{[0]}$ have been computed, they are fed to a $K$-nearest-neighbor-based fusion procedure. This procedure –which is the core of our contribution– blends together spatial and temporal label cues to generate a partition with uniform regions in the sense of brightness *and* motion. In other words, this fusion procedure optimizes an energy function made of spatial and motion label terms extracted from the two input label fields. Details on this function and the optimization procedure are presented in Section 5.

Compared to previous methods, our approach has legitimate advantages. To start off with, our solution is unsupervised and, as opposed to [11] and [15], doesn't depend on any threshold or weighting function that might change from one sequence to another. Secondly, our method is stable and doesn't generates unexpected results when its parameters are tweaked. For example, as opposed to [13] that needs an accurate spatial partition, our method reacts well when $r$ and/or $x^{[0]}$ lacks precision. Finally, our method is simple to implement and remains sufficiently general to be applied to other segmentation problems.

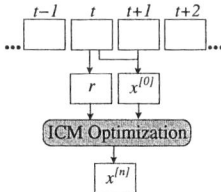

**Fig. 1.** Schematic representation of our approach. From two frames at times $t-1$ and $t$, a spatial and a motion label field ($r$ and $x^{[0]}$) are estimated. These label fields are then fed to the $K$-nearest neighbor fusion procedure (ICM optimization) that returns a partition ($x^{[n]}$) in which regions are uniform in the sense of brightness and motion.

## 4 Markovian Segmentation

Given $Z = \{X, Y\}$, a pair of random fields where $X = \{x_s, s \in S\}$ and $Y = \{y_s, s \in S\}$, represent respectively the label field and observation field defined on $S = \{s = (i, j)\}$, a 2D lattice of $N$ sites. Here, $Y$ (an image frame $I^t$ or a vector field $v$) is known *a priori* whereas $X$ has to be estimated. Each $x_s$ takes a value in $\Gamma = \{1, \ldots, m\}$, where $m$ corresponds to the number of classes of the segmentation map while $y_s$ is a vector made of real elements.

Segmentation can be viewed as a statistical labeling problem, i.e., a problem where each observation vector $y_s$ needs to be associated to the *best* class $x_s \in \Gamma$. Thus, inferring a label field can be seen as an optimization problem that searches for *the best* $x$ in the sense of a given statistical criterion. Among the available statistical criterion, the *Maximum a posteriori* states that a label field $x$ is *optimal* according to $y$ when it maximizes the *a posteriori* PDF $P(x|y)$. In this way, $x$ is optimal whenever $x = \arg \max_x P(x|y)$ [2].

Because $P(x|y)$ is often complex and/or undefined, it is common to assume that $X$ and $Y$ are MRFs. In this way, this posterior distribution can be defined by a Gibbs distribution of the form $P(X|Y) \propto \exp -U(X, Y)$ where $U(X, Y)$ is an *energy* function [2]. From Bayes theorem [16], the a posteriori distribution can be represented as $P(X|Y) \propto \exp\{-(U_1(X,Y) + U_2(X))\}$ where $U_1$ and $U_2$ are the likelihood and prior energy functions.

By assuming independence between each random variable $\boldsymbol{Y}_s$ (i.e., $P(Y|X) = \prod_{s \in S} P(\boldsymbol{Y}_s|X_s)$), the corresponding posterior energy to be minimized is

$$U(X,Y) = \sum_{s \in S} \bigg( \underbrace{\Psi_s(x_s, \boldsymbol{y}_s)}_{U_1(x_s, y_s)} + \underbrace{\sum_{<s,t>} \beta\big[1 - \delta_{x_s, x_t}\big]}_{U_2(x_s)} \bigg), \qquad (1)$$

where $U_2$ is an isotropic Potts model. Here, $\delta_{a,b}$ is the Kronecker function (returns 1 if $a = b$ and 0 elsewhere), $\beta$ is a constant, $<s,t>$ is the set of binary *cliques* that includes $s$, and $\Psi_s(x_s, \boldsymbol{y}_s) = -\ln P(\boldsymbol{y}_s|x_s)$. Notice that the cliques are defined on a second-order neighborhood.

The conditional distribution $P(\boldsymbol{y}_s|x_s)$ models the distribution of the observed data $\boldsymbol{y}_s$ given a class $x_s$. In this paper, this distribution is modeled with a Normal law which depends on the two parameters $(\boldsymbol{\mu}_{x_s}, \Sigma_{x_s})$. Since there are $m$ different classes, there are $m$ different Normal laws and a total of $2m$ parameters $\Phi = [(\mu_1, \sigma_1), \ldots, (\mu_m, \sigma_m)]$. Because these parameters are initially unknown, they have to be estimated. To this end, we resort to an iterative method called Iterated Conditional Estimation (ICE) [17].

**Markovian Spatial Segmentation.** The spatial label field $r$ is obtained by segmenting image frame $I^t$ with a Markovian procedure based on the the framework presented in the previous Section. Here, $I^t$ stands for the observation field $y$ while $\boldsymbol{y}_s$ is a singleton that takes its value in $\{0, \ldots, 255\}$. For RGB color images, the brightness of each site is obtained by simply computing the average value of the three channels, i.e. $y_s = (I^t_{s_r} + I^t_{s_g} + I^t_{s_b})/3$.

**Markovian Motion Segmentation.** The second label field fed to the optimization procedure is a motion-based partition called $x^{[0]}$. Although this partition could be obtained with any method presented in Section 2, we decided to use an unsupervised statistical Markovian procedure. Here, an optical flow field $v$ computed with an iterative version [18] of Simoncelli *et al.*'s algorithm [19] stands for the observation field $y$. Every element $\boldsymbol{y}_s$ is thus a two-dimensional real vector. For every sequence we have tested, $v$ was computed with a two-level pyramid and an integration window of size $7 \times 7$ [18].

## 5   $K$-Nearest-Neighbor-Based Fusion

Once $r$ and $x^{[0]}$ have been estimated, they are fed to the $K$-nearest-neighbor-based fusion approach as shown in Fig.1. This procedure seeks a motion label field $x$ made of regions uniform in the sense of brightness ($r$) and motion ($x^{[0]}$). To this end, the fusion procedure was designed as a global spatio-temporal optimizer minimizing the following energy function:

$$E(r, x) = \sum_s V(r_s, x_s), \qquad (2)$$

where $V(r_s, x_s)$ is a local energy term and $r_s$ and $x_s$ are assumed to be independent. This energy term returns a low value when the neighborhood surrounding $s$ (called $\eta_s$) is spatially and temporally uniform. To measure the *degree of uniformity* of a neighborhood $\eta_s$, the local energy term uses two potential functions applied on every site $t \in \eta_s$

$$V(r_s, x_s) = -\sum_{t \in \eta_s} \delta_{r_t, r_s} \delta_{x_t, x_s}. \tag{3}$$

Here, $\eta_s$ is a square integration window of size $L \times L$ centered on $s$ and $\delta$ is the Kronecker delta function. $V(.)$ works in a similar way the well known $K$-nearest neighbor algorithm does [16]. For a given site $s$ and its neighborhood $\eta_s$, $V(r_s, x_s)$ counts the number of sites $t \in \eta_s$ that are simultaneously in spatial region $r_s$ and part of motion class $x_s$. In this way, the class $x_s \in \Gamma$ that occurs the most often within region $\eta_s$ is the one with the smallest energy. The way $V(.)$ works is illustrated in Fig.2. In image $r$, site $\alpha$ is part of the black class (which is a section of the vehicle) but has the *immobile* label in $x^{[0]}$. When looking at every site in $\eta_\alpha$ *part of the black section of the vehicle in* $r$, we see there is a majority of sites with *mobile* label in $x^{[0]}$. In other words, within the $K$-nearest neighbors around site $s$ with a black label in $r$, there is a majority of *mobile* sites. For this reason, $V(r_\alpha, \text{mobile}) < V(r_\alpha, \text{immobile})$ and thus, $\alpha$ is assigned a *mobile* label in the resulting motion field $x^{[n]}$. The system works in a similar way for site $\beta$.

Since there are no analytical solutions to $x = \arg\max_{x'} E(r, x')$, we resort to a classical iterative ICM [2] technique whose mode (the maximum local energy

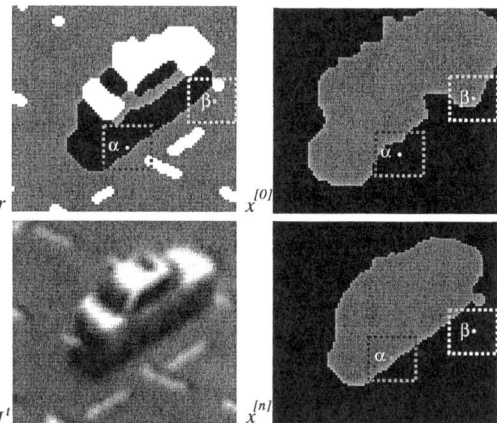

**Fig. 2.** Zoom on *Karlsruhe* sequence. Top left is label field $r$ and top right is motion label field $x^{[0]}$. The motion label field contains two classes which can be understood as the "mobile" and "immobile" classes. Bottom left is the image frame at time $t$ while bottom right shows the motion label field after the $n^{\text{th}}$ iteration. Note how $x^{[n]}$'s region silhouette is well localized as compared to $x^{[0]}$'s.

```
┌─────────────────────────────────────────────────────────────┐
│            K-Nearest-Neighbor-Based Fusion Procedure        │
│            ─────────────────────────────────────────        │
│                                                             │
│   $I^t$        Image frame at time $t$                      │
│   $v$          Vector field between $I^t$ and $I^{t-1}$     │
│   $r$          Spatial segmentation of $I^t$                │
│   $x^{[k]}$    Motion label field after $k^{\text{th}}$ iteration │
│   $\eta_s$     Window of size $L{\times}L$ centered at site $s$ │
│   $\delta_{a,b}$  Kronecker delta                           │
│   $m,m'$       Number of motion/spatial classes             │
│                                                             │
│   1. Initialization                                         │
│   $v \leftarrow$ optical flow between $I^t$ and $I^{t-1}$   │
│   $x^{[0]} \leftarrow$ segmentation of $v$ in $m$ classes   │
│   $r \leftarrow$ segmentation of image $I^t$ in $m'$ classes │
│   $i \leftarrow 0$                                          │
│                                                             │
│   2. ICM Optimization (Fusion)                              │
│   do                                                        │
│   │  $i \leftarrow i+1$                                     │
│   │  for each site $s \in S$ do                             │
│   │  │  for each class $x_c \in \Gamma$ do                  │
│   │  │  │  $V(r_s, x_c) \leftarrow \sum_{t \in \eta_s} \delta_{r_t, r_s} \delta_{x_c, x_t^{[i-1]}}$ │
│   │  │  $x_s^{[i]} \leftarrow \arg\min_{x_c \in \Gamma} V(r_s, x_c)$ │
│   │  while $x^{[i-1]} \neq x^{[i]}$                         │
└─────────────────────────────────────────────────────────────┘
```

**Algorithm 1.** Our spatio-temporal motion segmentation algorithm based on a $K$-nearest neighbor algorithm

for each site at each iteration) is defined by local energy function $V(r_s, x_s)$. The complete algorithm of our method is presented in Algo. 1.

## 6 Experimental Results

To validate our algorithm, we have segmented sequences representing different challenges. Some sequences are real while others are synthetic. The latter come with perfect ground-truth image $g$ and with various degrees of difficulty. The tests presented aim at validating how stable and robust our algorithm is with respect to the window size $L \times L$ and to the precision of the spatial partition $r$.

At first, we built two synthetic sequences with different textures that are more or less easy to segment spatially. As shown in Fig.4, the sequences allow a well-defined spatial partition $r$, a medium and a badly defined partition $r$. In the badly defined partitions (cf. last column of Fig.3), the objects edges in $r$ are barely

**Fig. 3.** Sequences *Karlsruhe*, *Taxi*, *Tennis*, *Trevor White*, *SequenceA*, and *SequenceB*. *SequenceA* and *SequenceB* are synthetic sequences with respectively a *precise* and an *imprecise* spatial partition $r$. The first row presents frames at time $t$, the second row spatial partitions $r$ and the last two rows the motion label fields $x^{[0]}$ and $x^{[n]}$ superposed to $I^t$. Notice that $x^{[0]}$ is visually similar to the results returned by Tekalp MAP algorithm [7,8].

recognizable. To measure how precise our algorithm is as compared to groundtruth image $g$, we have computed the percentage of bad matching pixels [20], i.e.,

$$B = \frac{1}{N_S} \sum_{s \in S} (1 - \delta_{x_s, g_s}) \qquad (4)$$

where $N_S$ is the number of sites in $S$ and $\delta_{x_s, g_s}$ is the Kronecker delta function.

In Fig.4, we compare our results to the ones obtained with methods close to ours. The first method is Tekalp's MAP [7,8] which is a motion-based Markovian approach using affine motion models. The results return by this method are visually similar to $x^{[0]}$ (c.f. third row of Fig. 3). The second method is Altunbasak et al.'s [13] region-based approach which relies on a pre-estimated segmentation map $r$. As shown in Fig.4, their method is more sensitive to the precision of $r$. These results underline the fact that our algorithm reacts smoothly to a change of its parameters $L$ and $r$. It is thus stable and doesn't generate unexpected results especially when segmented regions in $r$ don't exhibit precise edges.

As for the real sequences, we superposed the motion label fields $x^{[0]}$ and $x^{[n]}$ with image $I^t$ to illustrate how precise the results are. Results are shown in Fig.3. From left to right, sequences were segmented with respectively three, three, four, six, four, and three motion classes. We can see that in most cases,

|  | Partition r | MAP | Alt. | $x^{[0]}$ | 3 × 3 | 7 × 7 | 11 × 11 | 21 × 21 | 31 × 31 |
|---|---|---|---|---|---|---|---|---|---|
| Sequence A | precise | 15.7 | 0.8 | 13.2 | 13.1 | 5.0 | 1.9 | 1.0 | 0.9 |
| | mediocre | 12.5 | 12.5 | 10.8 | 10.7 | 5.4 | 4.0 | 4.2 | 5.3 |
| | imprecise | 6.0 | 25.5 | 8.1 | 8.1 | 5.4 | 5.3 | 8.3 | 9.3 |

|  | Partition r | MAP | Alt. | $x^{[0]}$ | 3 × 3 | 7 × 7 | 11 × 11 | 21 × 21 | 31 × 31 |
|---|---|---|---|---|---|---|---|---|---|
| Sequence B | precise | 11.1 | 0.4 | 6.2 | 2.9 | 0.4 | 0.4 | 0.4 | 0.5 |
| | mediocre | 11.6 | 8.9 | 6.7 | 3.3 | 0.7 | 0.8 | 0.9 | 1.3 |
| | imprecise | 12.4 | 42.6 | 5.2 | 3.3 | 2.0 | 2.6 | 2.7 | 5.4 |

**Fig. 4.** Percentage of bad matching pixels computed with three different versions of two synthetic image sequences. From left to right: results obtained with Tekalp's MAP algorithm [7,8], Altunbasak et al. [13], our unsupervised statistical Markovian algorithm and results obtained with our fusion algorithm. The five rightmost columns measure the effect of the window size ($L \times L$). The quality of the spatial partition r is ranked from *precise* to *imprecise* depending on how well objects have been segmented (see second row of Fig.3).

the segmentation map returned by our algorithm is more accurate than the ones with no fusion procedure.

## 7 Discussion

In this paper, we have considered the issue of segmenting an image sequence based on spatial and motion cues. The core of our method is a $K$-nearest-neighbor-based fusion between a spatial partition $r$ and a temporal partition $x^{[0]}$. The two fields are blended together by an ICM optimization procedure that minimizes an energy function made of a spatio-temporal potential function. This function works in a similar way the $K$-nearest neighbor algorithm does.

Although a spatio-temporal segmentation based on pre-estimated label fields might appears as a step backward when compared to methods such as Black's [12] or Khan and Shaw's [15] (that minimize one large spatio-temporal energy function) it has legitimate advantages. To start off with, these methods rely heavily on weighting functions and/or on weighting coefficients that give more or less influence to the temporal data vs the spatial data. A bad choice of these parameters can resolve in a bad segmentation. Also, because these parameters generally depend on the sequence content, they have to be re-estimated when used on new sequences. Unfortunately, tweaking these weighting factors isn't trivial, especially when their number is large (such as 8 for Black's [12]). Furthermore, large energy functions (the ones with many energy terms and/or defined over multidimensional data) are generally less stable than smaller ones and thus need sometimes to be implemented along with a stochastic (and slow) optimization procedure such as simulated annealing.

The point with our method is to alleviate these problems by minimizing individually the spatial and temporal energy functions before to blend it together.

Our method can thus be seen as a divide-and-conquer approach that doesn't rely on weighting factors. It uses short energy functions that can be minimized with a deterministic optimization procedure which converges faster than stochastic solutions. This makes the solution stable and tractable. Furthermore, we believe our fusion method is trivial to implement and, since it processes every pixels independently, it could be efficiently implemented on parallel hardware.

Results obtained on real and synthetic image sequences shows that our algorithm is stable and precise. It reacts well to a change of its parameters and/or to a poorly estimated spatial label field $r$. In the future, we look forward to extend this method to other vision problems such as stereovision, motion detection and motion estimation.

# References

1. Zhang D. and Lu G. Segmentation of moving objects in image sequence: A review. *Circuits, Systems and Signal Process.*, 20(2):143–183, 2001.
2. Besag J. On the statistical analysis of dirty pictures. *J. Roy. Stat. Soc.*, 48(3):259–302, 1986.
3. Megret R. and DeMenthon D. A survey of spatio-temporal grouping techniques. Technical report, University of Maryland, College Park, 2002.
4. Bouthemy P. and Lalande P. Recovery of moving object masks in an image sequence using local spatiotemporal contextual information. *Optical Engineering*, 32(6):1205–1212, 1993.
5. J.-M. Odobez and P. Bouthemy. Robust multiresolution estimation of parametric motion models. *Journal of Visual Communication and Image Representation*, 6(4):348–365, 1995.
6. Stiller C. and Konrad J. Estimating motion in image sequences: A tutorial on modeling and computation of 2d motion. *IEEE Signal Process. Mag.*, 16:70–91, 1999.
7. A. Murat Tekalp. *Digital video processing.* Prentice-Hall, Inc., 1995.
8. Bovik A., editor. *Handbook of Image and Video Processing.* pub-ACADEMIC, 2000.
9. Murray D. and Buxton B. Scene segmentation from visual motion using global optimization. *IEEE Trans. Pattern Anal. Machine Intell.*, 9(2):220–228, 1987.
10. Darrell T. and Pentland A. Cooperative robust estimation using layers of support. *IEEE Trans. Pattern Anal. Mach. Intell.*, 17(5):474–487, 1995.
11. Wang J. and Adelson E. Representing moving images with layers. *The IEEE Trans. on Image Proces. Sp. Issue: Image Seq. Comp.*, 3(5):625–638, September 1994.
12. Black M. Combining intensity and motion for incremental segmentation and tracking over long image sequences. In *Proc. of the Sec. European Conf. on Compt. Vis.*, pages 485–493, 1992.
13. Altunbasak Y., Eren P., and Tekalp M. Region-based parametric motion segmentation using color information. *Graph. Models Image Process.*, 60(1):13–23, 1998.
14. Bergen L. and Meyer F. A novel approach to depth ordering in monocular image sequences. In *Proc. of CVPR*, pages 536–541, 2000.
15. Khan S. and Shah M. Object based segmentation of video color, motion and spatial information. In *Proc. of CVPR*, pages 746–751, 2001.

16. Bishop C. *Neural Networks for Pattern Recognition*. Oxford University Press, 1996.
17. Pieczynski W. Statistical image segmentation. *Machine Graphics and Vision*, 1(1):261–268, 1992.
18. Bouguet J.-Y. Pyramidal implementation of the lucas kanade feature tracker: Description of the algorithm. Technical report, Intel Corporation, 1999.
19. Simoncelli E., Adelson E., and Heeger D. Probability distributions of optical flow. In *Proc. of CVPR.*, pages 310–315, 1991.
20. Scharstein D., Szeliski R., and Zabih R. A taxonomy and evaluation of dense two-frame stereo correspondence algorithms. In *Proc. of the IEEE Workshop on Stereo and Multi-Baseline Vision*, 2001.

# 2D Shape Measurement of Multiple Moving Objects by GMM Background Modeling and Optical Flow

Dongxiang Zhou[1,2] and Hong Zhang[1]

[1] CIMS, Computing Science Dept., University of Alberta, Alberta, Canada T6G-2E8
{dxzhou, zhang}@cs.ualberta.ca
[2] JCISS, School of Electronic Science and Engineering, National University of Defense Technology, ChangSha, China 410073
dxzhou@nudt.edu.cn

**Abstract.** In mineral processing industry, it is often useful to be able to obtain statistical information about the size distribution of ore fragments that move relatively to a static but noisy background. In this paper, we introduce a novel approach to estimate the 2D shapes of multiple moving objects in noisy background. Our approach combines adaptive Gaussian mixture model (GMM) for background subtraction and optical flow methods supported by temporal differencing in order to achieve robust and accurate extraction of the shapes of moving objects. The algorithm works well for image sequences having many moving objects with different sizes as demonstrated by experimental results on real image sequences.

## 1 Introduction

In the mineral processing industry, there is often the need to determine the size distribution of crushed ore fragments in order to optimize the performance of ore sizing equipments. Optical techniques have been widely used to provide this capability. In some of the applications, video sequences are available as the ore fragments move at high speed relatively to a static but noisy background. In such cases it is possible to apply motion segmentation techniques in image processing to determine the size distribution of the ore fragments. In this paper, we present one such algorithm that combines three existing common motion segmentation techniques, namely temporal differencing, background subtraction, and optical flow [1][2][3], in order to reliably and accurately calculate the ore size distribution of multiple moving ore particles.

Temporal differencing, or change detection based on frame difference [4][5][6], attempts to detect moving regions by making use of the difference of consecutive frames (two or three) in a video sequence. This method is highly adaptive to dynamic environments, but generally does a poor job of extracting the complete shapes of certain types of moving objects [2].

Background subtraction is a commonly used technique for segmenting objects of interest in static scenes [7][8][9]. It attempts to detect moving regions by subtracting the observed image from an estimated reference background image. The pixels where the difference is above a threshold are classified as foreground or the objects of interest. The Mixture of Gaussians (MoG) method has enjoyed tremendous popularity for background modeling since it was first proposed by Friedman and Russell [10]. Stauffer [11] presented an adaptive background mixture model by a mixture of $K$ Gaussian distributions ($K$ is a small number from 3 to 5). The method is stable and robust. The background subtraction technique works well at identifying moving objects, but it requires an accurate reference image and is usually sensitive to changes in illumination condition, background trembling and so on.

Optical Flow methods refer to grouping those optical flow vectors that are associated with the same motion or structure [12][13][14][15]. It can be used to detect independently moving objects even in the presence of camera motion. In theory, this is an ideal way to solve the segmentation problem; however, motion field usually appears quite noisy in real images and optical flow estimation involves only local computation [16]. Therefore, its accuracy is limited and segmentation from it generally does not detect the exact contours of the objects. Moreover, most optical flow computation methods are computationally complex and sensitive to noise.

The analysis of the above three different segmentation methods reveals that temporal differencing is good at providing initial coarse motion areas. Background subtraction can provide the most complete feature data. Optical flow technique has an advantage at detecting movement or the velocities of objects from an image sequence. We will demonstrate in this paper a new segmentation algorithm that combines these three techniques in order to arrive at a solution to our problem. Specifically, we use a GMM-based background subtraction algorithm to aggressively classify pixels that are likely moving in an image. The resulting image is then filtered by a mask image generated with a combined optical flow and temporal differencing algorithm to remove noisy false positives. The last step also overcomes the well-known difficulty with optical flow in detecting exact object boundaries.

The rest of the paper will be organized as follows. Section 2 outlines the algorithm. Section 3 presents background subtraction using Gaussian mixture model. Section 4 describes optical flow computation by coarse-to-fine strategy and fusion with temporal differencing. Section 5 analyzes our experimental results. Finally section 6 presents our conclusions.

## 2 Outline of the Algorithm

The flowchart of our algorithm is shown in Fig. 1. The algorithm consists of background subtraction, optical flow computation, temporal differencing and data fusion. Stauffer and Grimson's method [11] is used for background subtraction, which uses a mixture of normal distributions to model a multimodal background sequence. Pixel values that do not fit the background distributions are considered as foreground. For the task of optical flow computation, we adopt Lucas-Kanade method [17] which can quickly provide dense optical flow information, but only works well for small displacement. So we use Bergen et al.'s hierarchical framework and parametric model methodology [18] to allow estimation of a wide range of displacements. One of the drawbacks of such a scheme, however, is the inaccurate estimate of motion boundaries due to the use of image gradients and fixed support regions. In order to solve the problem, temporal differencing is considered as a support technique. Otsu's algorithm [19] is chosen to determine this change. Specifically, those pixels whose intensity differences are bigger than the Otsu threshold are considered as moving regions, and only the pixels within these regions retain the velocities of optical flow. In the data fusion step, we only consider those foreground objects as moving rejects, where the amplitude and direction of the optical flow are within the ranges of consideration.

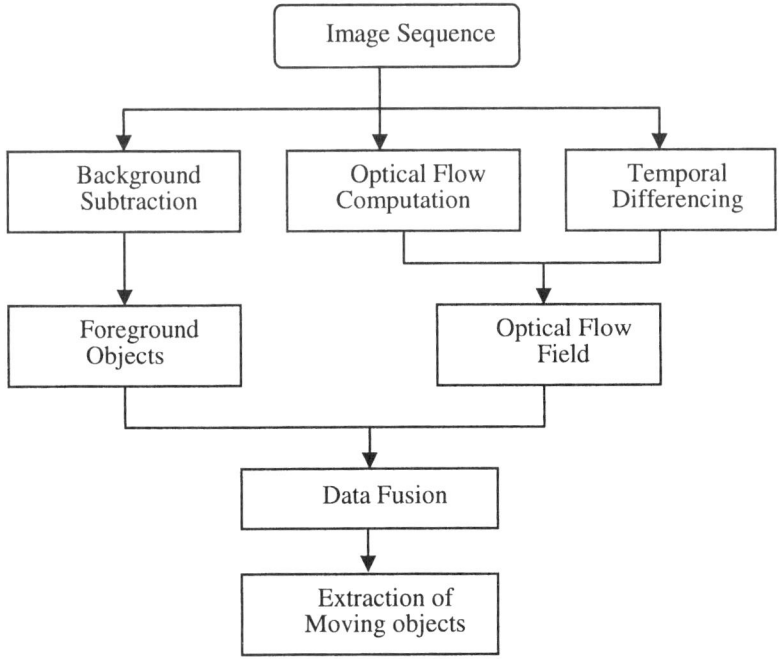

**Fig. 1.** The block diagram of the algorithm

## 3 Background Subtraction by MoG

Background subtraction is a particularly popular method for motion segmentation, especially under those situations with a relatively static background. The numerous approaches to this problem differ in the type of the background model and the procedure used to update the background model. Gaussian background models are among the most robust available. Stauffer and Grimson generalized this model by allowing for multiple Gaussian distributions per pixel to account for multimodal backgrounds.

Each pixel in the scene is modeled by a mixture of $K$ Gaussian distributions. The probability that a certain pixel has intensity $x_t$ at time $t$ is estimated as:

$$P(x_t) = \sum_{i=1}^{K} \omega_i * \eta(x_t, \mu_i, \Sigma_i) \qquad (1)$$

where $\omega_i$ is the weight, $\mu_i$ is the mean, $\Sigma_i = \sigma_i^2$ is the covariance for the $i^{th}$ distribution, and $\eta$ is a Gaussian probability density function:

$$\eta(x_t, \mu, \Sigma) = \frac{1}{(2\pi)^{\frac{1}{2}}|\Sigma|^{\frac{1}{2}}} e^{-\frac{1}{2}(x_t-\mu)^T \Sigma^{-1}(x_t-\mu)} \qquad (2)$$

The $i^{th}$ Gaussian component is updated as follows:

$$\begin{cases} \omega_{i,t} = (1-M_{i,t})\omega_{i,t-1} + (\omega_{i,t-1}+\alpha)M_{i,t} \\ \mu_t = (1-M_{i,t})\mu_{t-1} + ((1-\rho)\mu_{t-1}+\rho x_t)M_{i,t} \\ \sigma_t = (1-M_{i,t})\sigma_{t-1} + ((1-\rho)\sigma_{t-1}+\rho|x_t-\mu_t|)M_{i,t} \\ \rho = \alpha\eta(x_t, \mu_i, \Sigma_i) \end{cases} \qquad (3)$$

where $\alpha$ is the learning rate, set to be 0.05 in our algorithm. $\rho$ is the learning factor for adapting current distributions, set to be constant 0.005. $M_{i,t}$ is defined as follows:

$$M_{i,t} = \begin{cases} 1: & \text{if } w_i \text{ is the matched Gaussian component} \\ 0: & \text{otherwise} \end{cases} \qquad (4)$$

After the updates, the weights $\omega_i$ are renormalized.

The $K$ distributions are ordered based on $\omega_i/\sigma_i$ and the first $B$ distributions are used as a model of the background of the scene where $B$ is estimated as:

$$B = \arg\min\left(\sum_{i=1}^{b} \omega_i > T\right) \qquad (5)$$

The threshold $T$ is the minimum fraction of the background model. Background subtraction is performed by marking any pixel that is more than $\lambda$ (1.0~1.5 in our experiments) standard deviation away from any of the $B$ distribution as a foreground pixel.

## 4 Optical Flow Computation

There are many methods of computing optical flow. The most common are matching, gradient and filter based approaches. A recent study by Barron *et al.* suggests that Lucas-Kanade's gradient-based method is among the most accurate and computationally efficient methods for optical flow estimation [20]. In addition, the gradient solution can produce sub-pixel displacement estimates. However, this technique can only be applied for small displacements. In our application, the displacements of moving objects between consecutive frames are more than 15 pixels. Therefore, a hierarchical coarse-to-fine warping technique proposed by Bergen [18] is adopted to handle large displacements in our algorithm, as is illustrated in Fig. 2. It consists of four parts: (i) pyramid construction, (ii) motion estimation, (iii) image warping, and (iv) coarse-to-fine refinement.

A Gaussian pyramid is built for both source (at time $t-1$) and target images (at time $t$), which provides a range of coarse to fine views of the image. Initial motion is estimated at the coarsest level where the pixel displacements are small, so that the optical flow constraint equation becomes applicable. At the next finer level, the image at time $t-1$ is warped towards the image at time $t$ using the current motion estimate.

The motion parameters are refined at this level and the process continues until the finest level.

With the coarse-to-fine method described above, rough optical fields can be obtained. In order to acquire accurate boundaries of moving objects, we apply the temporal differencing technique to correct motion estimates. Otsu's global threshold algorithm is used to detect change for the frame differencing image. Based on this threshold, the differencing image is classified into moving and static regions, and only moving regions retain the displacements computed before. Thus, relatively accurate optical flow fields are produced. In addition, in our particular case, since the moving objects are darker than the usually background, we need only consider positive change. Moreover, in order to handle the case when an object moves to a position previously occupied by a smaller object and creating an interior hole after change detection, we apply a simple fill-hole operation in a post-processing step.

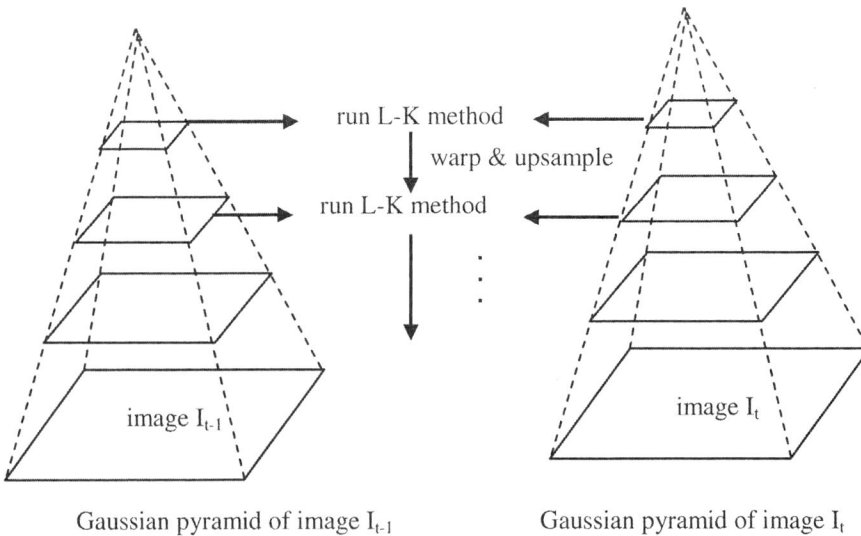

**Fig. 2.** Coarse-to-fine optical flow estimation

## 5 Experimental Results

This section demonstrates the performance of our proposed algorithms on an image sequence. Figure 3 shows the experimental results. The sequence shown here is 640×480 images. The top row displays the images at frame 100,150 and 200 respectively. The second row shows the results of background subtraction by mixture Gaussian model. We can see clearly that there are many noise points caused by trembling of the background. The third row is the results of optical flow fields computed by combining hierarchical coarse-to-fine optical flow estimation and change detection. The results show that almost all the moving objects can be detected but with poor boundaries. The bottom row is the final segmentation results by fusing the data from

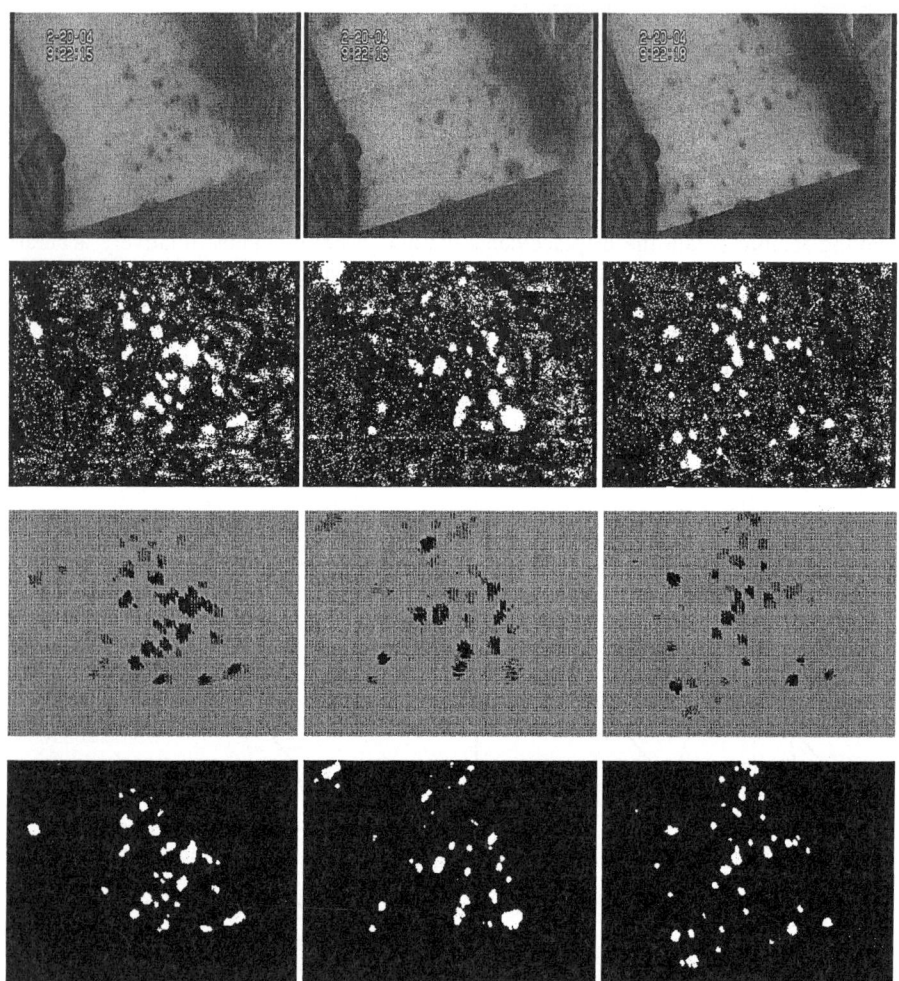

**Fig. 3.** Sample frames and segmentation results

background subtraction and optical flow fields. It is clear seen that almost all the moving rejects with different sizes are successfully detected and the accurate boundaries can be extracted.

## 6 Conclusions

This paper has shown a novel method for efficiently combining background subtraction, optical flow and temporal differencing methods, which is useful in environments where many moving objects with different sizes existed. In particular, the method leads to very precisely located boundaries.

The approach had satisfactory performance on real image sequence and the technique is stable enough to support real applications.

# References

1. Kanade T. et al.: Advances in cooperative multi-sensor video surveillance. Proc. of DARPA Image Understanding Workshop, Morgan Kaufmann, November (1998) 3-24
2. Collins R.T. et al.: A system for video surveillance and monitoring. Technical report, CMU-RI-TR-00-12, Robotics Institute, Carnegie Mellon University, May ( 2000)
3. Wang L., Hu W., Tan T.: Recent development in human motion analysis. Pattern Recognition. Vol. 36, No.3 (2003) 585-601
4. Bergen J. R. et al.: A three frame algorithm for estimating two-component image motion. IEEE Trans. On Pattern Analysis and Machine Intelligence. Vol. 14, no. 9, (1992)886-896
5. Radke R. et al.: Image change detection algorithms: a systematic survey. IEEE Transactions on Image Processing. Vol. 14, No. 3 (2005)294-307
6. Miller O. et al.: Automatic adaptive segmentation of moving objects based on spatial-temporal information. Proc. of VIIth Digital Image Computing: Techniques and Applications. Sydney. (2003)1007-1016, 10-12
7. Chien S., Ma S., Chen L.: Efficient moving object segmentation algorithm using background registration technique. IEEE Trans. On circuits and systems for video technology. Vol. 12, No. 7 (2002) 577-586
8. McIvor A. M.: Background subtraction techniques. In Prof. of Image and Vision Computing. Auckland, New Zealand (2000)
9. Cheung S. C., Kamath C.: Robust techniques for background subtraction in urban traffic video. Video Communications and Image Processing. SPIE Electronic Imaging, San Jose, UCRL-JC-153846, UCRL-CONE-200706 (2004)
10. Friedman N., Russell S.: Image segmentation in video sequences: a probabilistic approach. In Proceedings of the Thirteenth Annual Conference on Uncertainty in Artificial Intelligence. Morgan Kaufmann Publishers, Inc., San Francisco, CA, (1997) 175-181
11. Stauffer C., Grimson W.: Adaptive background models for real-time tracking. Proc. of IEEE CS Conf. on Computer Vision and Pattern Recognition. Vol. 2 (1999) 246-252
12. 12.T. Hirai et al: Detection of small moving objects by optical flow. In 11th International Conference on Pattern Recognitio. Vol. II, the Hague, Netherlands (1992) 474-478
13. Huang Y. et al.: Optical flow field segmentation and motion estimation using a robust genetic partitioning algorithm. IEEE Trans. On Pattern Analysis and Machine Intelligence. Vol. 17, no. 12 (1995) 1177-1190
14. Bors A. G., Pitas I.: Optical flow estimation and moving object segmentation based on RBF network. IEEE Trans. On Image Processing, Vol. 7, no. 5 (1998) 693-702
15. Chunke Y., Oe S.: A new gradient-based optical flow method and its application to motion segmentation. 26th Annual Conference of the IEEE Industrial Electronics Society. Vol. 2 (2000) 1225-1230
16. Dufaux F., Moscheni F., Lippman A.: Spatio-temporal segmentation based on motion and static segmentation. In Proc. of Second IEEE Int. Conf. of Image Processing. Washington (1995) 306-309
17. Lucas B.D., Kanade T.: An iterative image registration technique with application to stereo vision. In Proc. of Image Understanding Workshop. (1981) 121-130
18. Bergen J. R. et al: Hierarchical Model-Based Motion Estimation. ECCV (1992) 237-252
19. Otsu N.: A Threshold Selection Method from Gray-Scale Histogram. IEEE Trans. Systems, Man, and Cybernetic. Vol. 8 (1978) 62-66
20. Barron J. L., Fleet D. J., Beauchemin S.S.: Performance of optical flow techniques. International Journal of Computer Vision. Vol. 12, No. 1 (1994) 43-77

# Dynamic Water Motion Analysis and Rendering

Yunjun Zhang

University of Central Florida,
Orlando, Florida 32826

**Abstract.** In this paper, we present a novel approach for analyzing the dynamic water motion and transforming the motion in natural scenes to non-photorealistic 2D cartoons. We limit the domain of the original water sequences containing only water surfaces with shallow relief, (the heights of the water wave are relatively small compared to the wave lengths) and one parallel light source. Within this constrained domain, we first automatically rectify the water wave sequence from a generic pose to orthogonal view direction. Then we clearly reveal the relationship between the rectified frames and the surface normal maps. Finally, as an application, a non-photorealistic rendering step is applied to transform the water motion to new cartoon sequences. several results are shown in the paper to demonstrate the quality and widely usability of this novel approach.

## 1 Introduction

How to analyze dynamic water motion and render the motion in cartoon videos vividly remains as a hard topic in computer vision and computer graphics communities for years. In this paper, we focus on water sequences containing only water surfaces with shallow relief, (the heights of the water wave are relatively small compared to the wave lengths) and there is only one parallel light source with an illumination direction close to the normal of the water wave tangent plane. Within this constrained domain, we first automatically rectify the water wave sequence from a generic pose to orthogonal view direction. Then we clearly reveal the relationship between the rectified frames and the surface normal maps (derived from the height map). Finally a non-photorealistic rendering step is applied to transform the water motion to a cartoon sequence.

### 1.1 Related Work

There has been a growing interest in computer vision communities focusing on the research of dynamic motion [1,2,3,4,5,6,7].

The dynamic texture concept was first defined by Soatto *et al.*[2], who studied the motion dynamics explicitly using moving average, auto-regression model, which was inspired by [3]. It was also shown to be useful for segmentation, controlled video synthesis, and recognition. Szummer and Picard [3] applied a spatio-temporal auto-regressive approach(STAR) to model the dynamic texture. This method calculates the regression coefficients directly from the image intensity value.

Another research direction introduced by Schödl *et al.* [8] presents a "video segmentation" like technique called "video texture". This technique was used to synthesize seamless looping videos based on a proper segmentation of the input. No model was actually constructed, therefore it is impossible to retarget the motion with the input to a new sequence with different appearance.

Recently, some researcher worked on extracting physical based coefficients from the dynamic motion of the scene [9]. These methods show the potential advantage of being able to retarget pure motion to new synthesized sequences, though may have not been explored clearly.

Retargeting approaches for image and video can be separated into two classes: style retargeting and motion retargeting. The style retargeting was started by [10], in which the drawing style of an image is simply retargeted to another image based on texture examplar correspondence. Drori *et al.* [11] extended the work to extrapolate the novel styles for a given image based on bilinear models [12]. Although these methods achieve good style retargetting result, it can not be directly used to retarget motion. The global motion exacting and retargeting has been a well studied problem [13]. Bregler *et al.* [14] retarget the global and non-rigid motion extracted from characters in commercial cartoon to new 2D or 3D cartoons. Fitzgibbon [7] registers the stochastic scene by the global motion.

### 1.2 Overview

Our contributions in this paper include an automatic approach to rectify the water wave sequence, a clear explanation of the relationship between the rectified frames and the water surface normal. Also, to the best of our knowledge, our non-photorealistic rendering method for water waves is the first of its kind.

This paper is organized as follows: Section 2 explains the automatic rectification and clearly describes the relation between image and water surface normals. Section 3 gives the non-photorealistic rendering method and several results are shown in Section 4.

## 2 Video-Based Analysis

### 2.1 Automatic Projective Rectification

Most existing water wave analysis and illumination analysis methods [15,16,17] require that the input image or video is viewed orthogonally to avoid the projective distortions. For an input image it is relatively easy to fulfil the requirement by taking the picture from a airplane. However, to take a top-view water wave video with a fixed camera is almost imposable. Therefore, the requirement of an orthogonal viewing direction dramatically reduce the available video sources for these analysis methods.

Given a water wave sequence by fixed camera taken from a generic viewing direction, ideally our aim is to remove the projective distortion by transforming the frames to an orthogonal viewing direction to the extent that the similarity properties can be recovered for measurement. If we can find at least four pairs of corespondent points, and the points in the orthogonal view appropriately exhibit their 3D space geometric information, (if the points form a rectangle in 3D space, they should forms a rectangle in the rectified frames) we can easily calculate the $3 \times 3$ homography $M_H$ for the rectification. As we know that a homography has four more degree of freedom than a similarity, which is a transformation including only rotation, translation and isotropic scaling, we only need to constrain four degree of freedom to recover the orthogonal views. (the metric properties are up to an isotropic factor $s$). However, it is almost impossible to find the line at infinity and two vanishing points in a water wave sequence automatically, neither even manually. We design an iterative method to correct 2 degree of freedom for the rectification. Therefore, the rectified frames have two different scaler factors $s_1, s_2$ along two orthogonal directions.

Assuming the water wave sequence has a relatively noticeable wave propagation, and the wave is taken parallel to one of the coordinate axis (not losing generality, we select axis $x$). In this case, vanishing point along the waves is much farther than the vanishing point of the moving direction. Under this assumption, the rectification problem can be reduced to align the moving directions to parallel lines.

A location motion scale (LMS) is defined as the summation of the energy of local motion flow in a neighborhood area.

$$LMS = \sum_{(x,y) \in A} \frac{v_x^2 + u_y^2}{|A|} \quad (1)$$

LMS defines the strength of the dynamic motion projected on the image plane. For a top-view isotropic water wave sequence, the values of LMS for different locations should be very close. Based on this, we define our rectification method as below:

1. Pick four initial points $P_1, P_2$ and $P_3, P_4$ on two water waves respectively, therefore $P_1 P_2$ and $P_3 P_4$ are parallel. Set $LMS_{smallest}$ as $LMS$ of the original image. Set step length as $\Delta$.
2. Locate the four correspondent points $Q_i, i = 1..4$ in orthogonal viewing plane, which form a parallelogram.
3. Calculate the homography $M_H$ between $P_i$ and $Q_i$, and rectify the water frame based on $M_H$.
4. Calculate $LMS$ for the rectified image, defined as $LMS_{current}$. If $LMS_{current} < LMS_{smallest}$, $LMS_{smallest} = LMS_{current}$, $P_2 = P_2 + \Delta \frac{P_1 P_2}{||P_1 P_2||}$||; otherwise, $\Delta = -\Delta, P_2 = P_2 + \Delta \frac{P_1 P_2}{||P_1 P_2||}$||.
5. If $|LMS_{current} - LMS_{smallest}| > \delta$ goto 3, else end.

Fig. 1 explains this algorithm and gives a rectified result and the related optical flow plot.

## 2.2 Water Surface Normal

In Section 1 we give a constraint on the illumination direction to be near orthogonal to the water surface plane. Though it appears rather restrictive, it is much easier to acquire than an orthogonal viewing direction, and we demonstrate a clear relationship between a rectified water surface plane and a surface normal map.

If the rectified water surface can be presented by Lambertian model, the image intensities depend only on the angle between the surface normal at each pixel location

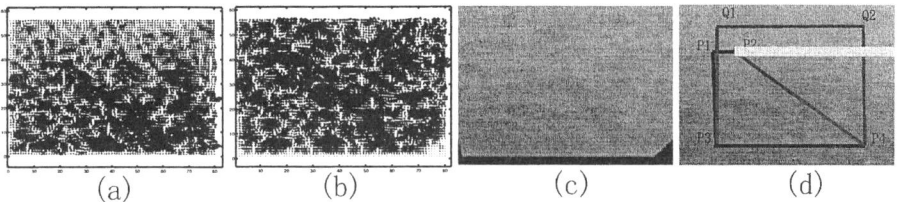

**Fig. 1.** (a): the optical flow field based on the original frame. (c)(b):the rectified frame and the correspondent flow field, notice that the (b) is much more isotropic than (a). (d): The explanation of our rectification method. $Q_3, Q_4$ share the same location with $P_3, P_4$. The location of $P_2$ can be adjusted in the yellow thick line segment.

and the illumination's direction. Based on this model and a constant albedo, the image intensities can be presented by

$$I(x,y) = \frac{\alpha}{\sqrt{1+H}}[\sin\theta - \cos\theta(h_x \cos\phi + h_y \sin\phi)] \qquad (2)$$

where $\alpha$ is a coefficient defined by the surface albedo, $\theta$ and $\phi$ are the illumination's elevation and azimuthal angle, respectively. $h(x,y)$ is the surface height at location $(x,y)$, with $H = h_x^2 + h_y^2$. When the elevation angle closes to 90 degree, equation 2 can be simplified as

$$I \approx \frac{\alpha}{\sqrt{1+H}} \qquad (3)$$

Under shallow relief assumption, $H << 1$. We then Applying a first order Tylor series expansion to equation 3,

$$I \approx \alpha(1 - \frac{1}{2}H) \qquad (4)$$

Therefore, it is clear that following our constraints, the image intensities of the rectified images are inversely proportional to $H$, and can not be affected by the direction of surface normal in $XY$ plane. Hence, we can directly use the rectified color intensity image to substitute the surface normals for non-photorealistic rendering purpose.

## 3 Non-photorealistic Rendering Application

Mostly, 2D cartoon artists draw dynamic motions, *eg.*, water waves and fire flames, in a way that mimics the plausible motion of the original natural phenomena. An efficient way to achieve this goal is to only preserve the dynamic motion in the cartoon but to ignore the photometric properties of the original video. Keeping this in mind, we design a simple, but effective approach to retarget the dynamic water motion to a stroke-based 2D cartoon. We turn back to examine the visual appearance within the dynamic motion of water waves, and discover that mostly our eyes are attracted by the moving leading boundaries between dark and bright regions. These boundaries turn out to be curves which roughly maintain their color intensity along the temporal direction.

Assuming a Lambertian image formation model, having similar image intensity is a necessary condition of having similar surface normal vectors. A set of water surface locations in a neighborhood area can reflect the same light intensity if the angles between their surface normals and the illumination direction are the same based on equation 4. Therefore, giving one abstract stroke $S_{i,j}$ in the cartoon frame $F_i$ corresponding to the color intensity, finding an updated stroke $S_{i+1,j}$ in frame $F_{i+1}$ can be defined as finding a stroke $S'_{i+1,j}$, on which every correspondent location with $S_{i,j}$ has similar color intensity in $I(p,i)$ and $I(p', i+1)$.

The photometric model represents a stroke-based hand drawn image $I_c$ by a collection of $N$ strokes $S_{0,j}$, $j = 1, 2, ... N$, where $S_{0,j} = \{p_{0,j,m} = (x_m, y_m) : m = 1, ..., n_j, i = 0\}$. For any time instance, $i$, the corresponding collection of strokes $S_{i,j}$ is obtained by minimizing:

$$S_{i,j} = \arg\min_{p_{i,j,m}} \sum_{m=1}^{n_j} (I(p_{i,j,m}, i) - I(p_{i,j,m}, i-1))^2$$

The above minimization can be achieved by applying a optical flow calculation. Then we get a displacement vector $(u_{i,j,m}, v_{i,j,m})$ for each $p_{i,j,m}$. An intuitive way to obtain $S_{i,j}$ can be:

$$p_{i,j,m} = p_{i-1,j,m} + [u_{i,j,m}, v_{i,j,m}],$$

However, this calculation ignores a very important factor in cartoon animation: stroke connectivity. optical flow results do not grantee the connectivity of the generated stroke. By examining some of the basic physical rules, we present a very simple, but effective method to maintain the connectivity of the strokes.

Due to the fact that a set of forces acting on a object for translational motion is equivalent to a proper force acting on the centroid of the object, we constrain our stroke model to have solid connections between consecutive nodes. Therefore, the distance $L$ between the nodes can not be changed by external forces. Not losing generality, we denote $S_{i,j}$ as $S$ and $p_{i,j,m}$ as $p_m$. Firstly, we find the centroid of $S$ by ordering $S$ in a consecutive manner, and pick the median point $p_c$ in it. The location of $p_c$ in time $i+1$ will be defined by the displacement vector $u_c, v_c$. Secondly, the two tails in $S$ from $p_c$ are treated equally. Here, we only show the updating of the right tail. The left tail has a similar solution. Giving the right tail, $C_R = \{p_c, p_{c+1}, p_{c+2}, ... p_{end}\}$, we define a constrain tail, $C' = \{p_c + [u_c, v_c], ..., p_{end} + [u_{end}, v_{end}]\}$.

For simplicity and clearness, we define a discrete version of the length calculation along curve $C'$ starting at $p'_c$ and ending at $p'_end$ as

$$\mathbf{L(c,end)} = \sum_{i=c}^{end-1} ||p'_i - p'_{i+1}||$$

The resultant connected tail $C''$ is computed by

$$p''_i = \arg_{p''_i}(\mathbf{L(c,i)} == (i-c)l)$$

where $l$ is the unit length between two consecutive nodes.

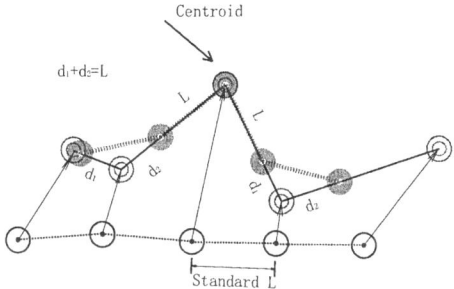

**Fig. 2.** This figure explains our approach to maintain the connectivity of synthesized strokes. Initially, the distances between all adjacent points are the same, standard L. After finding the point offset, a constraint stroke is located along all the double-circled points. The centroid is directly updated by the offset, whilst all other points are stretched along the potential stroke by constraining the distance between the adjacent points along potential stroke as standard L.

The cartoon sequences we generate here are parallel to $XY$ plane. In general, the water region in a cartoon scene can be constrained to a plane $P$. Therefore, there exist a projective transformation between plane $XY$ and plane $P$. In our case, users can roughly specify the plane $P$ in the cartoon scene with respect to that a cartoon video. This does not require a perfect correctness of the geometric relations in the scene.

## 4 Results

We have tested our methods on synthesized and real water wave sequences. The program runs on a Desktop PC with a P4 2.8gHz CPU, 512 MB memory.

Fig. 3 shows the non-photorealistic rendering results of a synthesized water sequence. it is first been tested without the connectivity constraint. The result clearly shows that the strokes are broken down to points due to the offset updating. After applying the connectivity constraint, we can get much better results as shown in the bottom row of Fig. 3.

Fig. 4 shows two synthesized cartoon videos generated from the same water videos with different initial hand-drawn images. The mountain in the background is converted from a real image to have a hand-drawn appearance. Two stroke-based images are drawn by hand with different styles. Two different projective transformations are applied to the images for matching their correspondent backgrounds. Each of them is driven by the same set of water sequence, whilst, it is clear to see that they present dramatically differences in those two image sets. This best demonstrates the advantage and flexibility of our method.

## 5 Conclusion and Future Work

We present a novel approach in this paper to analyze dynamic water motion, and an efficient non-photorealistic rendering method to retarget the motion onto 2D cartoons. This

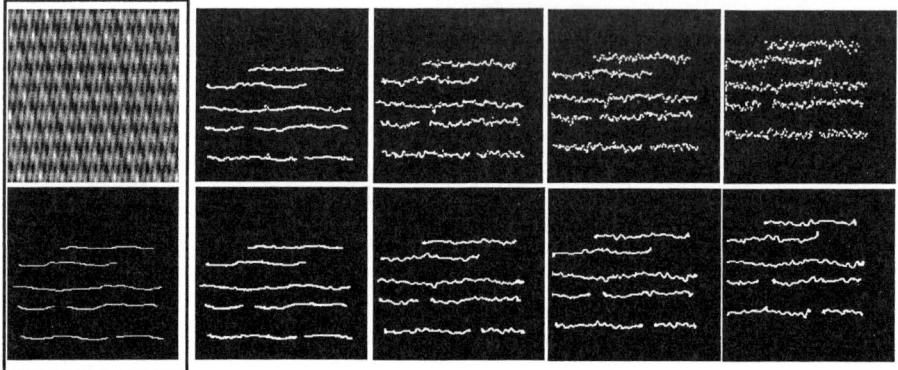

**Fig. 3.** Top row, image 1: One selected image for the synthesized top view water waves sequence. Bottom row, image 1: The initial hand-draw stroke image. Top row, image 2 to 5: Rendering result without the connectivity constraint. Bottom row, image 2 to 5: Rendering result with the connectivity constraint.

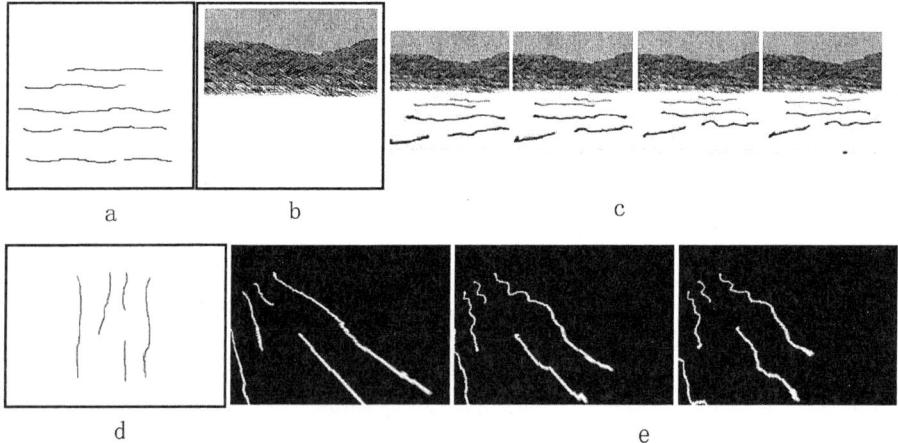

**Fig. 4.** These results are derived from the same input rectified water wave sequence. (a) Same stroke image from the previous result. (b) A hand-draw style background. (c) Four selected frames from the rendered cartoon based on stroke map (a). (d) Another stroke map. (e) Three selected frames from the rendered result.

work shows some promising results and it is easy to implement. The proposed method is non-generative, therefore the rendering length is bounded by the temporal dimension of the input video. However, due to the fact that the location motions are directly calculated from the videos sequences, the resulting models capture more realistic dynamic motion than other parametric models. Thus, the extracted model has wide usage like motion retargeting or mixed reality.

In the future, we will explore the possibility to generate non-parametric model for natural fire flames and other natrual dynamic motions.

# References

1. Yung-Yu Chuang, Dan B Goldman, Brian Curless, David H Salesin, and Richard Szeliski, "Animating pictures with stochastic motion textures," in *UW CSE Technical Report*, 2002.
2. G. Doretto and S. Soatto, "Editable dynamic textures," in *CVPR*, 2003.
3. M. Szummer and R.W. Picard, "Temporal texture modeling," in *ICIP*, 1996.
4. Y. Wang and S. Zhu, "Modeling textured motion : Particle,wave and sketch," in *ICCV*, 2003.
5. Neill W. Campbell, Colin Dalton, David Gibson, and Barry Thomas, "Practical generation of video textures using the auto-regressive process," in *BMVC*, 2002.
6. G. Doretto, A. Chiuso, S. Soatto, and Y.N. Wu, "Dynamic textures," *IJCV*, 2003.
7. A. W. Fitzgibbon, "Stochastic rigidity: Image registration for nowhere-static scenes," in *ICCV*, 2001.
8. Arno Schödl, Richard Szeliski, David H. Salesin, and Irfan Essa, "Video textures," in *Siggraph*, 2000.
9. Sun M., Jepson A., and Fiume E., "Video input driven animation (vida)," in *ICCV*, 2003.
10. Aaron Hertzmann, Charles E. Jacobs, Nuria Oliver, Brian Curless, and David H. Salesin, "Image analogies," in *SIGGRAPH*, 2001.
11. I. Drori, D. Cohen-Or, and H. Yeshurun, "Example-based style synthesis," in *CVPR*, 2003.
12. William T. Freeman and Joshua B. Tenenbaum, "Learning bilinear models for two-factor problems in vision.," in *CVPR*, 1997.
13. S. Mann and R. Picard, "Video orbits of the projective group: a new perspective on image mosaicing," *Technical Report 338, MIT Technical Report*, 1995.
14. C. Bregler, L. Loeb, E. Chuang, and H Deshpande, "Turning to the masters: Motion capturing cartoons," in *SIGGRAPH*, 2002.
15. J. J. Koenderink and S. C. Pont, "Irradiation direction from texture," *Optical Society of America Journal*, 2003.
16. M. Varma and A. Zisserman, "Estimating illumination direction from textured images," in *CVPR*, 2004.
17. S. Thon and D. Ghazanfarpour, "Ocean waves synthesis and animation using real world information," *Computers and Graphics*, 2002.

# A Fast Real-Time Skin Detector for Video Sequences

Farhad Dadgostar[1] and Abdolhossein Sarrafzadeh[2]

[1,2] Institute of Information and Mathematical Sciences, Massey University,
Private Bag 102 904, North Shore Mail Centre, Albany,
Auckland, New Zealand
{F.Dadgostar, H.A.Sarrafzadeh}@massey.ac.nz
http://www.massey.ac.nz/~fdadgost
http://ngits.massey.ac.nz

**Abstract.** Skin detection has been employed in various applications including face and hand tracking, and retrieving people in video databases. However most of the currently available algorithms are either based on static features of the skin color, or require a significant amount of computation. Moreover, skin detection algorithms are not robust enough to deal with real-world conditions, such as background noise, change of intensity and lighting effects. This situation can be improved by using dynamic features of the skin color in a sequence of images. This article proposes a skin detection algorithm based on in-motion pixels of the image. The membership measurement function for recognizing skin/non skin is based on the Hue histogram of skin pixels that adapts itself to the user's skin color, in each frame. This algorithm has demonstrated significant improvement in comparison to the static skin detection algorithms.

## 1 Introduction

Hand, head, and body tracking has become an important research topics in HCI, during the last decade. Moreover, the applications are not limited to HCI, and have many other usages, like animation creation, virtual reality, disability support, performance measurement, and movement analysis.

In research literature there are many studies on vision-based body tracking, detection and recognition. For many applications factors, such as availability of hardware and real-time operation are considered the most important characteristics. There are two significant approaches for body-parts tracking: pattern recognition (e.g. using neural networks or statistical analysis) which usually are used for face detection [1], and segmentation (e.g. skin color segmentation); are used for hand tracking and gesture recognition [2].

This paper presents a real-time approach for skin segmentation based on motion features of a video sequence. The system is reliably operable in a wide range of office environments, and it is robust with typical environment lighting and un-calibrated camera. The proposed system, needs an initial training with a small number of samples of segmented skin colors. It retrains and adapts itself to the user's skin color while he/she is using the system.

## 2 Research Background

Skin color segmentation has shown promising results for hand/face detection and tracking [3-5]. Different color spaces, including RGB, ICrCb, HSV, HSI, HS and IUV color spaces have been used for this purpose [6-9]. The main idea in these approaches is using a set of training data (usually images in which skin region was manually segmented), finding a connected region in color space, and using the result as a color skin probability density function. Research shows the best results are achieved by using RGB, HS, and Hue color spaces [2, 10]. Obviously, storing RGB training data requires a large amount of memory space, and because of the nature of RGB color space, a classifier based on it is very sensitive to the intensity of pixels. For covering different intensities, a bigger region in RGB space is required, which results in more false detections and less accuracy in the final results. Moreover, a smaller region in RGB color space also results a weaker classifier.

HS [8] and Hue [8, 10, 11] as other color spaces have been used successfully in color skin segmentation. The interesting feature of Hue factor for skin color is its similarity even for different races. Research shows that probability density function in distribution of Hue factor is a single connected region that is almost Gaussian [2], and what is different for different races, is the Saturation factor [10].

Bradski [10] has used this method to find the centre of mass of the skin pixels for face detection of the computer user. Kolsch and Turk [12] have used a similar approach for detecting a group of features they called "flocks of features", for hand tracking. Ruiz-del-Solar and Verschae [13] have used this technique together with a fuzzy approach for calculating the membership degree of a pixel to the color skin set based on its probability density and its neighbors' probability density. Imagawa, Lu and Igi [5] have used a mixed approach based on locating the face using non-invariant features and estimating the color probability density function for segmenting hands.

All of these methods except the last one can not dynamically adapt themselves to the change of color skin features like slight histogram shifting, due to change of lighting, environmental noises, or the effect of the color of objects that are similar to skin color. For instance, the hue factor of wood, is similar to skin color, and using it as indicated in Bradski [10], the filtered image will be like figure 1-b. It is obvious that tracking the face, because of the noise (wood color) is almost impossible. On the other hand, our observations show that the peak, including position and height, and width of the training histogram are dependent on the image grabbing hardware, and therefore the best results for a static (separate training and detection) algorithm can only be achieved by using the same hardware.

**Fig. 1.** (a) Original Image, (b) Filtered image based on thresholding Hue factor of skin color extracted from training data, (c) Hue histogram of the training data

Using the histogram as a probability density function, as mentioned in [13], and calculating membership probability to skin color based on neighborhood pixels, can reduce the number of morphological operations, that are required for noise removal. However the assumption that the skin color of the current user has the highest probability in the probability density function is not always reliable. Figure 2 presents a filtered image based on probability density of pixels; lighter pixels have highest probability in the training data and darker pixels have the lowest probability. In this condition, the segment that belongs to the skin color of the user is almost darker than the segment that belongs to the surface of the table. Therefore using the work of Ruiz-del-Solar and Verschae [13] not only doesn't improve the results but also decreases the accuracy of the color skin filter.

The idea introduced in [5], because of the retraining and adapting to the color space that is used in the image, is more robust. However, in comparison to other methods, it requires a significant amount of computation for face detection. In addition, most of the fast face tracking techniques [1] are not robust to changes like rotation or to situations where a complete frontal view of the face is not presented.

**Fig. 2.** In some conditions probability density of the skin color of the user is lower than some of the unwanted regions like wood color

## 3 Design Discussion

Based on the discussion and the results of other research work discussed in the previous section, we believe that using Hue factor for skin segmentation could be one of the fastest methods for implementing a skin detector. Because it requires few CPU instructions per pixel, it is a good candidate for real-time skin detection. In addition, it is reliable for ideal conditions (e.g. special applications, or using a blue background - Figure 3).

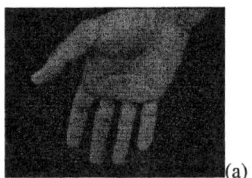 

**Fig. 3.** (a) Original image, (b) Filtered image using Hue threshold

Moreover, retraining the skin detector in a sequence of images improves this method for real-time video processing and finding skin color. Our method for improving the skin detector is explained in the following paragraph.

### 3.1 Underlying Assumptions

We should note that in this study, our primary assumption has been that the computer user is sitting in front of the camera; that is, a simple image grabbing device like a web cam, as input source of the incoming frames to skin detector (Figure 4). The camera is in a fixed position, and the user is the only moving object in front of the camera.

**Fig. 4.** Testing environment

### 3.2 Image Grabbing

The image grabbing device was a Dragonfly camera based on Sony CCD, connected to a Pentium4 PC using an IEEE 1349 connection, with a maximum frame-rate of 30 fps. Each frame was a raw RGB image, size 640x480. The software was a C++ program developed using Visual Studio.Net™. A function converted RGB values to HSI values, ranging from zero to 255.

### 3.3 Training and Calculating Initial Thresholds

For training, we used about 20 colored images (approximately 3200000 skin color pixels) of hands in which the skin region had been manually segmented. Half of these images were recorded using our image-grabbing device, and the other half acquired from the Internet. Using this data, a histogram for Hue factor was calculated and the lower and upper bound of the threshold were specified such that 90% of the pixels inside the histogram were covered.

## 4 The Algorithm

Using just constant thresholding in practice is not sufficient for skin detection and in some cases not practical (Figure 1). On the other hand, our observations show that manually changing the lower and upper bounds of the threshold can significantly improve the results. Based on the observations, and the assumption that the computer user is the only moving object in front of the camera, we used motion features of the image for re-evaluating the training histogram and recalculating the thresholds.

In the first step, simple subtraction of two sequential frames is used as measurement for motion detection. Although this technique is not reliable for recognizing a moving object, but it requires little memory space (one frame) and a small number of operations per pixel (integer subtraction). This makes it suitable for real-time applications. In this technique, the pixels that have a different value other than their value in the previous frame are considered changed pixels. Changed pixels can potentially belong to a moving object.

In a real application, this technique has two main problems. The first problem is that the noise in CCD cameras can cause some sparse falsely-detected pixels. This effect can easily be eliminated, using simple morphological operations. Another problem is that a moving object in a 2D image fills the space that in the previous frame was the background, and the background fills the pixels that previously were the object. Thus, we have two sets of pixels; one set belongs to the object, and the other set belongs to the background. We solved this problem by ignoring those pixels that can not pass through the primary filter for skin color detection. Therefore the probability of detecting some parts of the skin will be higher than non-skin (Figure 5).

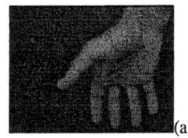  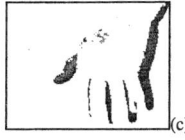

**Fig. 5.** A moving hand: (a) Original image, (b) In-motion pixels of the frame, filtered using Hue threshold (c) Mapping the result to the original image

In the next step, the pixels that are considered as moving pixels belonging to the user's skin are used for retraining the detector. In this article we have used a histogram of Hue factor as the base for calculating low ($T_L$) and high ($T_U$) thresholds for filtering the image. From the motion detection frame (Figure 4-c), another histogram is extracted, and the second histogram is added to the original histogram using the following equation:

$H_{n+1} = (1-A)*H_n + A*H_M$
$H_{n+1}$ *is the new histogram for skin detection (for the next frame)*
$H_n$ *is the histogram for skin detection in the current frame*
$H_M$ *is the histogram of the in-motion pixels of the skin color (Figure 4-c)*
*And A, is the weight for merging two histograms.*

Empirical results show that a value between 0.02 - 0.05 brings the best output for the final skin detector. For each frame, thresholds of the Hue factor are recalculated such that they cover 90% of the area of the new histogram. The filter for each frame could be described as follows.

$$f(I) = \begin{cases} true & if \quad T_L(H_n) \leq I \leq T_U(H_n) \\ false & else \end{cases}$$

*I is the Hue factor for each pixel*
*$H_n$ is the Hue histogram for the skin color*
*$T_L$ is the calculated lower threshold for histogram $H_n$*
*$T_U$ is the calculated upper threshold for the histogram $H_n$.*

## 5 Results

Filtering the input image using the described method significantly improves the performance of the detector, by increasing the ratio of positive to false detections while still keeping the ratio of positive detections to actual pixels high (Figure 6).

In the initial frames, the performance of the adaptive and non-adaptive filter is the same. In Figure 6-b, the surface of the table creates false detection, as the number of its pixels is approximately bigger than positive recognition (face area). It is obvious that using morphological operations can not remove this kind of noise (Figure 6-c).

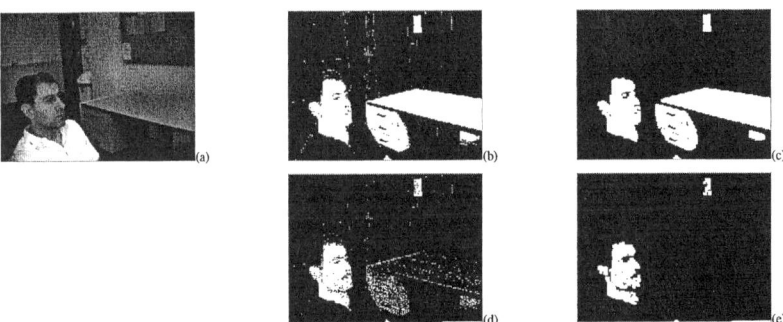

**Fig. 6.** (a) Original Image, (b) filtered image using non-adaptive threshold, (c) After doing morphological operations Erode/Dilate on [b], (d) filtered image using adaptive threshold, (e) After doing morphological operations Erode/Dilate on [d].

Using the proposed algorithm, while the user is interacting with the computer (using mouse, keyboard, and sometimes slight changes in head pos), the system captures the movements and retrains itself based on the user's skin color. Figure 6-d is the output of the adaptive filter after approximately 2 minutes of using the application. The unwanted detection (table, in this image), was almost eliminated, and the ratio of positive/false detections has increased dramatically.

The system, together with color skin tracking, retrains itself based on new data gathered from moving pixels. It also recalculates the lower and upper thresholds for filtering the next frame. Figure 7 represents changes in lower and upper thresholds through time.

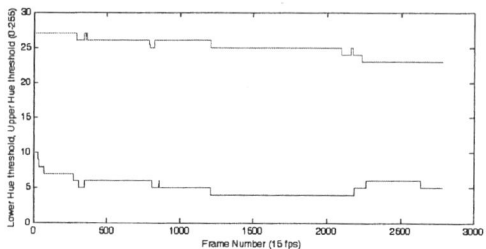

**Fig. 7.** Changes in lower threshold and upper threshold between frames 0 and 2791

We have used this technique for face tracking of the computer user (Figure 8). The application is robust against environmental noise like lighting condition, noise caused by fluorescent lights, changes in intensity level caused by automatic gain control in digital cameras, and background noise. The performance of the system is less than 20 milliseconds per frame, on a P4 2.2GHz PC, for an RGB image size 640x480 with non-optimized C++ code.

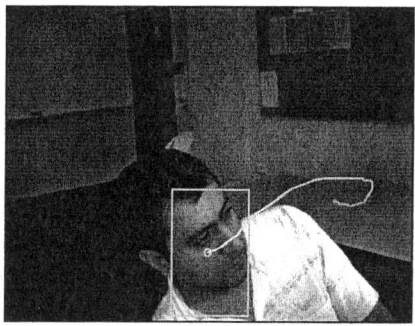

**Fig. 8.** Face tracking using the proposed algorithm

## References

1. Viola, P. and M.J. Jones, *Robust Real-Time Face Detection.* International Journal of Computer Vision, 2004. **57**(2): p. 137-154.
2. Sigal, L., S. Sclaroff, and V. Athitsos, *Skin Color-Based Video Segmentation under Time-Varying Illumination.* IEEE Transactions on Pattern Analysis and Machine Inteligence, 2004. **26**(7): p. 863-877.
3. Bretzner, L., I. Laptev, and T. Lindeberg. *Hand Gesture Recognition using Multi-Scale Colour Features, Hierarchical Models and Particle Filtering.* in *Fifth IEEE International Conference on Automatic Face and Gesture Recognition.* 2002: IEEE Computer Society.
4. Corradini, A. and H.M. Gross. *Camera-based gesture recognition for robot control.* in *IEEE-INNS-ENNS International Joint Conference on Neural Networks, IJCNN.* 2000. Como, Italy.

5. Imagawa, K., S. Lu, and S. Igi, *Color-Based Hands Tracking System for Sign Language Recognition*, in *Proceedings of the 3rd. International Conference on Face and Gesture Recognition*. 1998, IEEE Computer Society. p. 462.
6. Butler, D., S. Sridharan, and V. Chandran. *Chromatic colour spaces for skin detection using GMMs.* in *Proceedings of the IEEE International Conference on Acoustics, Speech, and Signal Processing, ICASSP*. 2002.
7. Srisuk, S. and W. Kurutach. *A new robust face detection in color images.* in *Proceedings of the Fifth IEEE International Conference on Automatic Face and Gesture Recognition*. 2002.
8. Zhu, Q., et al. *Adaptive learning of an accurate skin-color model.* in *Proceedings. Sixth IEEE International Conference on Automatic Face and Gesture Recognition*. 2004.
9. Chen, L., et al. *A skin detector based on neural network.* in *IEEE International Conference on Communications, Circuits and Systems*. 2002.
10. Bradski, G.R., *Computer Vision Face Tracking For Use in a Perceptual User Interface.* Intel Technology Journal, 1998.
11. Shin, M.C., K.I. Chang, and L.V. Tsap. *Does colorspace transformation make any difference on skin detection?* in *Proceedings. Sixth IEEE Workshop on Applications of Computer Vision (WACV)*. 2002.
12. Kolsch, M. and M. Turk. *Fast 2D Hand Tracking with Flocks of Features and Multi-Cue Integration.* in *Conference on Computer Vision and Pattern Recognition Workshop (CVPRW'04)*. 2004. Washington, D.C., USA.
13. Ruiz-del-Solar, J. and R. Verschae. *Skin detection using neighbourhood information.* in *Proceedings of the Sixth IEEE International Conference on Automatic Face and Gesture Recognition*. 2004.

# Efficient Moving Object Segmentation Algorithm for Illumination Change in Surveillance System

Tae-Yeon Jung, Ju-Young Kim, and Duk-Gyoo Kim

School of Electronic Engineering and Computer Science,
Kyungpook National University, 1370, Sankyug-Dong,
Buk-Gu, Daegu, 702-701, Korea
{jty, alteir, dgkim}@ee.knu.ac.kr

**Abstract.** An efficient algorithm to segment the moving object is very important in the surveillance system. In general, the change detection by comparing brightness value is a good and simple method, but it shows a poor performance under illumination change. Therefore, we propose the segmentation algorithm to extract effectively the object in spite of the illumination change. There are three modes to extract the object, the criteria of mode selection are both available background existence and illumination change. Then the object is finally obtained by using projection and the morphological operator in post-processing. Furthermore, the double binary method using the similarity of brightness value and spatial proximity is used to obtain more edge information. A good segmentation performance is demonstrated by the simulation result.

## 1 Introduction

Video segmentation, which emphasizes partitioning the video frames to semantically meaningful object and background, has become an important issue in the content-based video coding. The conventional video segmentation can be roughly divided into the two categories; one utilizes the spatial homogeneity and the other uses the change detection from temporal information. The segmentation techniques based on the spatial homogeneity simplify an image by using morphological filters, and then decide the region boundary [1], [2]. The motion vector of each region is calculated and regions with similar motion are merged together to form the final object region. However, this has the drawback that the computation complexity is very high. The other segmentation techniques extract the moving objects by using a change detection mask from the consecutive frames [3]-[6]. This algorithm is more efficient than previous category because it is the motion that distinguishes a moving object from background.

In general, the motion detection is usually utilized as an image segmentation technique especially where the background is stationary. The object segmentation technique just using the difference of brightness value is a simple scheme, however, it has difficulty in extracting an accurate object region under the variable illumination condition. The object segmentation based on the edge information is quite efficient for the variable illumination conditions, on the contrary, is more sensitive to noise.

Kim et al. obtained the object by partitioning an object into the moving region and the still region [5]. The moving region includes any motion in current frame, which is obtained from the edge map of the difference in successive images. The still region is obtained by the comparison of the edge of previous object and the current frame edge. If the previous object is not correct, then the current object is extracted wrongly because still region with errors has wrong effect to get the current object. Chien et al. generate the reliable background information by using the accumulated frame difference information, and then, extract the object region by comparing the current frame with the constructed background image [6]. However, this algorithm is not considered in case that the illumination is changed suddenly.

This paper presents an efficient algorithm to extract the moving object even if illumination change occurs in the remote surveillance systems. The information of previous object is not utilized for extraction of object and the background frame is updated on occasion of illumination change. There are three modes to extract the object under varying circumstances. The first mode uses the difference between the background and the current frame while the available background frame exists. With a moment of illumination change the second mode is applied. The object edge can be extracted eliminating the background edge from the current frame edge. In last mode the object is extracted using both the difference of the successive frames and the background removal method, simultaneously the background generation process makes steady progress until new background frame is achieved. The final object can be obtained by using projection and the morphological operator. Furthermore, the double binary method using the similarity of brightness value and the spatial proximity is used to achieve the better performance of extraction.

## 2 Proposed Algorithm

In the video surveillance system, the camera is fixed and background remains unchanged before the illumination change. Therefore, to consider the situation on illumination change, we propose the separate extraction methods. In this paper, the block diagram of the proposed method is shown in Fig. 1. The block diagram has the three modes according to the circumstances. The extraction mode should be adaptively selected in consideration of both the illumination change and the existence of reliable background frame. And the all extraction mode extracts the binary frame efficiently by using the double binary. In the end, the final object can be extracted by using projection and the morphological operator on the binary frame.

### 2.1 Decision for Illumination Change

This paper proposes the separate processing modes based on illumination change. Thus each mode requires the criterion for illumination change. The reminder except for the object region in the current frame is used to determinate the

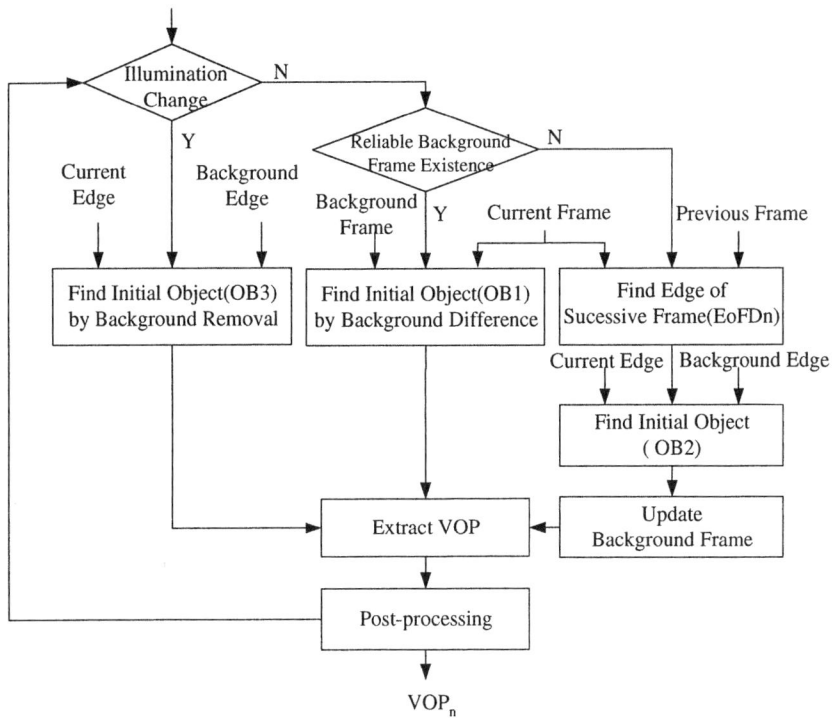

**Fig. 1.** The blockdiagram of proposed algoritm

criteria for illumination change. If the mean of brightness value in the reminder is higher than the threshold, we assume that the illumination change is occurred.

## 2.2 The Extraction Mode

**Background Difference.** In this mode, the initial object is extracted from the difference between the background and the current frame. This background difference method shows a good performance as well as a little computation complexity for extraction. The frame difference is obtained through the absolute value of the difference between the background and the current frame. In this case, the frame difference has a lot of background noises. This drawback can be overcome using edge information. Then, the edge information of the background difference performed by using the canny operator becomes the robust edge information for the noises. This method efficiently extracts the shape information of object in video sequences having lots of noise in the stationary background. The edge of difference $OE1_n$ is defined as follow:

$$OE1_n = \Phi|C_n - B| = \theta(\nabla G * |C_n - B|) \qquad (1)$$

$C_n$ and $B$ are the current and the background frame respectively. The represents the canny edge detection [7], which is accomplished by performing a gradient operation on the Gaussian convoluted image $G*I$. The $OE1_n$ denotes the spatial edge information of the initial object in this step.

**Background Removal.** As the illumination suddenly is changed, the background difference method can't generate the reliable initial object. Therefore, we use the current frame edge and the background edge both of which have less sensitiveness in the illumination change. In this mode, the initial object is constructed by eliminating the background edge from the current frame edge. After calculating the edge of current and background frame with the canny operator individually, we obtain the $DoE_n$ of difference.

The searching region is limited to minimize the influence of the background noise. In order to obtain a searching region, a morphological dilation operator can be applied to the previous moving object. The process obtaining the initial object is defined as

$$OE3_n(i,j) = \begin{cases} 1, & \text{if } ((DoEn(i,j) > T_r) \quad and \quad (FEn(i,j) > Tc)) \\ 0, & \text{otherwise} \end{cases} \quad (2)$$

where $DoE_n(i,j)$ is the frame difference which obtained both from the background and the current frame, $FE_n(i,j)$ is the current edge frame. $T_r$ is the threshold value for removing the edge points of background frame among those of current frame, indicating 10 in simulation. $T_c$ is the threshold value from Otus' binary algorithm.

**Frame Difference.** This sub-section describes the extracting method of the object when the brightness of the background region is not changed and the reliable background frame is not generated. The process of generating background makes steady progress through registering the elements of the background in each frame. If the reliable background frame is constructed finally, the background difference method is performed to obtain the initial object. In this mode, both the motion of the object and the current edge are used in order to extract the exact motion of object. The edge of the frame difference is defined as

$$EoFD_n = \Phi|F_n - F_{n-1}| \quad (3)$$

where $F_n$ and $F_{n-1}$ are the current and the previous frame respectively. This result frame has boundary of the object that happens to the object motion. We select the pointer that the position of the $EoFD_n(i,j)$ is equal to the position of the current frame edge $FE_n$. Thus, this pointers, $EP_n$, contain the only information having any motion in the current frame. Moreover this mode is used the background removal method for the sufficient edge information. The acquired edge of an object is defined as follows:

$$OE2_n(i,j) = \begin{cases} 1, & \text{if } ((EP_n(i,j) > 0) \quad or \quad (OE3_n(i,j) > 0)) \\ 0, & \text{otherwise} \end{cases} \quad (4)$$

A process for generating the new background frame is described as follows. The pixels belong to the object in previous frame and the pixels having high difference in value should be removed. The removed pixels are defined as

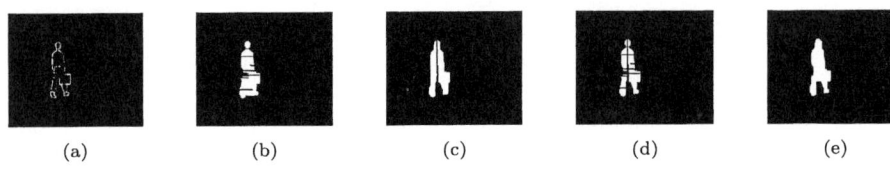

**Fig. 2.** VOP Extraction process. (a) binary edge image, (b) horizontal element image, (c) vertical element image, (d) logical AND of horizontal and vertical candidate image, and (e) image after morphological operation.

$$\nabla(i,j) = \begin{cases} 1, & \text{if } ((DCP_n(i,j) > T) \quad or \quad (DOR_{n-1}(i,j))) \\ 0, & \text{otherwise} \end{cases} \quad (5)$$

where is the excluded pixels in the background generation process, $DCP_n(i,j)$ is the difference value in the successive frames and $DOR_{n-1}(i,j)$ is the pixels which belong to the previous object. And $T$ is the calculated threshold value by using the Otus' algorithm. In this mode, the background generation process makes steady progress in each frame. The residual pixels except for excluded ones are to be dealt with candidate pixels of the background frame and used for generating the new background frame. The candidate pixels are continuously accumulated during several frames. Thus, the completed background frame is defined as

$$B_{New}(i,j) = \frac{1}{M} \sum_{k=N}^{N+M} F_k(i,j) \quad (6)$$

where $B_{New}(i,j)$ is the brightness value of the new background frame and $F_k(i,j)$ denotes the brightness values during continuous frames. $M$ is the number of the accumulated frames, indicating 15 in this simulation. $N$ denotes the beginning frame number to be accumulated. The pixels to be satisfy equation (6) during 15 frames become to represent the background element for the new background.

### 2.3 Double-Thresholding

Thresholding for the difference from two input frames is the basic concept of the change detection for binary. However, since the circumstance and characteristics of video sequences differ significantly, the quality of the segmentation results depends strongly on background noise, object motion, reliable and consistent object information is very difficult to obtain. So the reformed double-thresholding method is more robust and efficient in frame difference. The proposed double-thresholding method using the similarity of brightness and spatial proximity may include more edge information. Any pixel is connected to its eight neighbors. Therefore brightness of the neighbor pixels may affect the decision for binary operation. The threshold value ($T_{high}$) is calculated by using Otsu' algorithm, $T_{low}$ becomes 2/3 times $T_{high}$. And the difference of two threshold values is used to calculate weighted value of neighbor pixel. If the sum of the weighted value and brightness value of targeting pixel is higher than $T_{high}$, the targeting pixel is classified into the object pixel. Otherwise, the targeting pixel is classified into background pixel.

For the pixel elements that tend to have the possibility of becoming the object pixel, we include the object pixel for more edge information. Thus, the proposed method can obtain more edge information and detect efficiently the object pixels.

### 2.4 VOP Extraction

To extract the VOP of frame, the extracting the VOP stage has to perform a morphological operation on the initial object, because the initial object has the only the edge information of object. Both the horizontal and the vertical candidates are declared to be the region inside the first and last edge points in each row and column line. Fig. 2 shows the result image through the morphological operation. After finding both horizontal and vertical candidates of VOP, the intersection regions through the AND operation are further processed by the morphological operation. Morphological operation applied to the VOP extraction uses the closing-operator that has $9 \times 19$ element in size. Post-processing for eliminating sharp peaks and small islands use the opening operator that has $5 \times 7$ element in size [8].

## 3 Experimental Results

The proposed algorithm was applied to the standard MPEG-4 test sequences 'Hall monitor' as well as the video sequence captured in the laboratory. In CIF format 300 frames of 'Hall monitor' and 628 frames of sequences captured by Sony DCR-TRV310 handycam were used. The error rate of the object is adopted to evaluate the objective quality[6] for the proposed algorithm. The error rate is defined as the following equation:

$$Error\ Rate = \frac{Error\ Pixel\ Count}{Frame\ Size} \quad (7)$$

where the error pixel count represents the number of the pixels of which the extracted binary object is different from the reference binary object.

In order to clarify the performance of the proposed algorithm even at the various lightness circumstances, brightness is added artificially from the frame 38 to 300 of 'Hall monitor'. Additional brightness value corresponding to the illumination change is 50 at the luminous body. The amplitude of an additional brightness value is gradually decreased to 20 while getting away from the luminous body. In the Fig. 3 and Fig. 4, the illumination change has existed from the frame 38 to 300 and the luminous body located at the top left in frame. Fig. 3 shows the result under illumination change in the test sequence 'Hall monitor'.

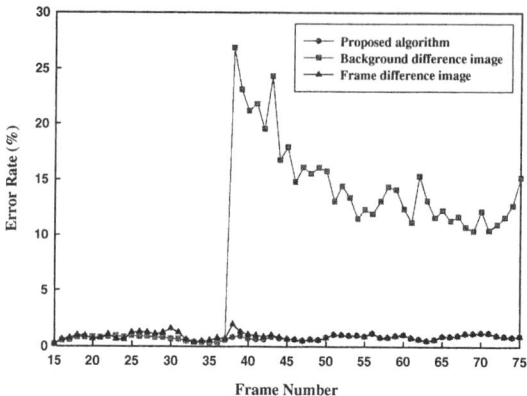

**Fig. 3.** The comparison result of the separate methods

**Fig. 4.** The result frame for 'Hall monitor' (a) frame 34, (b) frame 38, (c) frame 217, and (d) frame 291

The error rate has been degraded abruptly from the fame 38 in the background difference method, and shows bad result on the frame 38 in case only frame difference method is used. However, the proposed algorithm shows continuously the low error rate, the result represents the robust segmentation for illumination change. Fig. 4 (a) shows the result by the background difference method and (b) shows the result by the background removal method at the moment of illumination change. Fig. 4 (c) shows the result by the frame difference method and (d) shows the result by background difference method because the reliable background frame has accomplished at the frame 269. Fig. 5 shows the result frame is extracted from the test sequences having the changed brightness from the frame 150 to the 628. The test sequences represents the situation of sudden illumination change such as the passenger may turn off the lighting fixtures.

## 4 Conclusions

In this paper, we propose an efficient moving object segmentation algorithm for a surveillance system. Three separate modes for considering situation such as illumination change are used to extract the object. The background difference mode among them has less computation complexity and shows good results

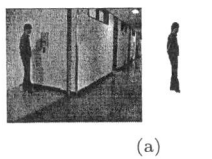   

(a)   (b)   (c)

**Fig. 5.** The result frame for test sequences (a) frame 149, (b) frame 150, and (c) frame 566

under non-illumination change. If the illumination may change, the edge information, insusceptible to the effect of brightness, is used for extracting the object. The process of generating background is used to construct a reliable background frame after illumination change. And the double binary method considering the influence of neighboring pixels may obtain more information about the object region. Our experimental results demonstrate that the proposed method is able to extract successfully a moving object from video sequence in spite of illumination change.

## References

[1] D. Wang: Unsupervised video segmentation based on watershed and temporal tracking. IEEE Trans. Circuits Syst. Video Technol., vol. 8, (1998) 539-546
[2] J.C. Choi, S.-W. Lee, and R. Mester: Spatio-temporal video segmentation using a joint similarity measure. IEEE Trans. Circuits Syst. Video Technol., vol. 7, (1997) 279-286
[3] A. Neri, S. Colonnese, G. Russo, P. Talone: Automatic moving object and background separation. Signal Processing, vol. 66, no. 2, (1998) 219-232
[4] J. Guo, J. W Kim, and C-C. J. Kuo: Fast and accurate moving object extraction technique for MPEG-4 object-based video coding. SPIE, vol. 3653, (1999) 1210-1221
[5] C. G. Kim and J. N. Hwang: Fast and automatic video object segmentation and tracking for content-based applications. IEEE Trans. on Circuits and Systems for Video Technology, vol. 12, no. 2, (2002) 122-129
[6] S. Y. Chien, S. Y. Ma, and L. G. Chen: Efficient moving object segmentation algorithm using background registration technology. IEEE Trans. on Circuits and Systems for Video Technology, vol. 12, no. 7, (2002) 577-586
[7] J. F. Canny: A computational approach to edge detection. IEEE Trans. Pattern Anal. Machine Intell., vol. PAMI-6, (1986) 679-698
[8] L. G. Shapiro and G. C. Stockman, Computer Vision, NJ Prentice-Hall, 2001

# Maintaining Trajectories of Salient Objects for Robust Visual Tracking

Filiz Bunyak and S.R. Subramanya

Department of Computer Science,
University of Missouri-Rolla, Rolla MO 65409, USA

**Abstract.** This paper presents a robust approach to track multiple objects for low resolution, far-field visual surveillance applications. Multiple moving objects are detected by utilizing an adaptive background model and tracked by resolving the correspondence between their trajectory segments using proximity and appearance similarity measures. A new confidence measure is assigned to each possible match between objects and this information is maintained by a graph structure. This graph is utilized to prune and refine the trajectories. Kalman filter is used to handle discontinuities and occlusions. Proposed approach handles problems such as spurious objects, fragmentation, shadow, clutter and occlusions.

## 1 Introduction

Success of many recent computer vision applications such as traffic monitoring, visual event recognition for intelligent surveillance systems, human-computer interaction etc. depends on reliable tracking and analysis of moving objects in image sequences. Typically, tracking process involves a cycle of feature extraction, prediction, data association, and update. Tracking research in computer vision generally concentrates on segmentation of the objects to be tracked, association measures, and appearance models. As association strategy, generally simple association methods such as nearest neighbor match is used. In [1], each moving object is represented by a token consistent of its center position and size. Data association is done by nearest neighbor association. In case of occlusion, velocity, size, and intensity features are used to validate the data association. In [2], temporal matching is based on support map and bounding box. In order to track people through occlusions and grouping, person's color distribution is modeled using color histograms or mixture models. In [3], elliptic shape masks, texture templates, and foreground probability templates; in [4], a RGB color model which shows the appearance of each pixel of an object and a probability mask; in [5], gray-textural appearance and shape information are used to track objects. In [6], correspondence of connected components between frames is accomplished using multiple hypothesis tracking which incorporates position and size. While computer vision research generally relies on appearance models, research in target tracking concentrates on assignment strategies such as SNF (strongest neighbor filter), NNF (nearest neighbor filter), PDA (probabilistic data association), JPDA (joint probabilistic data association), and MHT (multiple hypothesis tracking) ([7,8,9]).

In high resolution videos, tracking can be performed using simple data association techniques, since complex object appearance models can be obtained. But in low resolution surveillance videos, the number of pixels supporting an object is too few to obtain a complex color, shape or texture appearance model. Therefore better association and filtering strategies are required for reliable multiple object tracking. In this paper, we present a detection based multiple-object tracking method. Objects are matched based on their proximities and appearances. Goodness of the matches are measured with a new confidence measure. Instead of a simple association strategy, delayed decision enabled by multi-hypothesis testing is used. Trajectories are pruned and refined in different stages of the process. Proposed approach is robust to imperfections in moving object detection such as spurious objects, fragmentation, shadow, clutter and occlusions. Figure 1 shows outline of the system.

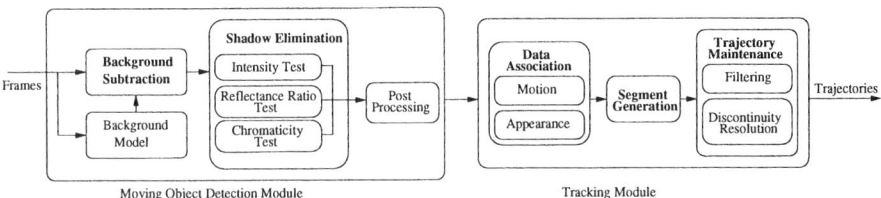

**Fig. 1.** Outline of the system

## 2 Moving Object Detection and Shadow Elimination

To obtain moving objects, we use the mixture of Gaussians (MoG) approach described in [6] because of its adaptive and multi-modal nature. The recent history of each pixel is modeled by a mixture of $k$ Gaussian distributions and RGB color vector of each new pixel is assigned to a Gaussian. Then the distributions are labeled as foreground or background based on their $weight/\sigma$ ratio. This process results in a background model and a binary foreground mask. Moving cast shadows cause serious problems in this process because they can easily be misclassified as foreground. This misclassification may lead to drastic changes in the shapes of objects or merging of multiple objects. In order to improve the performance of moving object detection, we formulated a shadow detection algorithm based on a combination of photometric invariants reflectance ratio and normalized color. The details of this algorithm is presented in [10]. Another problem in moving object detection is the sudden illumination changes such as the ones due to cloud movements. Mixture of Gaussians method can adapt to gradual changes, but can not cope with sudden changes. These changes alter the appearance of the background pixels suddenly and result in a drastic increase in the number of false detections. Misdetections due to cast shadows and sudden illumination changes are both due to the changes in the illumination component of the pixel color. Since our shadow detection algorithm relied only on spatial and spectral information and not on a priori information on scene geometry or object model, we were able to modify it to cope with the sudden illumination changes. We removed the intensity test, because unlike shadows, illumination changes may darken or lighten the background, and relaxed the compactness constraint of shadow regions. Figure 2 shows shadow and sudden illumination detection results.

**Fig. 2.** Results after shadow and sudden illumination change detection superimposed on original. Left: moving objects and shadows. Right: moving objects and sudden changes.

## 3 Tracking

Tracking module receives shadow corrected foreground masks and identifies connected foreground regions in a frame. To overcome fragmentation and to remove spurious objects, regions whose bounding boxes overlap are merged into a single object, and regions with areas smaller than a threshold are eliminated. Obtained region information is arranged into a graph structure we call *ObjectGraph*. Data association module matches objects in $frame(t)$ to objects in $frame(t-1)$. *ObjectGraph* is updated by linking nodes corresponding to objects in $frame(t)$ to the nodes corresponding to objects in $frame(t-1)$. Match confidence value is attached to each link. Segment generation module traces the links on *ObjectGraph* and generates trajectory segments. These segments are organized into a data structure called *SegmentList*. *SegmentList* is refined by filtering spurious segments, and joining temporarily disconnected segments. Trajectories are formed by linking these refined segments.

### 3.1 Data Association

Data association (correspondence analysis) matches objects in the current frame to the objects in the previous frame. Matching is done based on proximity and appearance similarity of the objects. For each $frame(t)$, a match matrix $Match$ and a confidence matrix $Conf$ are computed. $Match(i,j)$ indicates whether the $i^{th}$ object in $frame(t)$ corresponds to the $j^{th}$ object in $frame(t-1)$, $Conf(i,j)$ denotes the confidence in $Match(i,j)$. Possible matches are kept to be pruned gradually, as more information becomes available. Besides one-to-one matches, this scheme supports many-to-one, one-to-many, many-to-many, one-to-none, none-to-one matches that may result from fragmentation, occlusion, entering, exiting objects or group behaviors.

Proximity is measured in terms of $L_2$ distance between the centroids of the objects. For appearance model, we use color features. To measure color (dis)similarity, for each object, an RGB color histogram is computed. $N$ RGB color vectors, corresponding to $N$ peaks in the histogram are selected as color descriptors of an object. Color dissimilarity $D_{color}$ (Eq. 1) between two objects $O_A$ and $O_B$ is computed as the weighted sum of the peak color distances. In Eq. 1, $L_2(O_A(i), O_B(j^*))$ denotes the distance of the $i^{th}$ peak color in $O_A$ to its best matched peak $j^*$ in $O_B$ and $P_X(k)$ denotes the number of pixels in the object $X$ that have the $k^{th}$ peak color.

$$D_{color}(O_A, O_B) = \sum_i \left( \frac{L_2(O_A(i), O_B(j^*))}{MaxDist_{Color}} \times \frac{min(P_A(i), P_B(j^*))}{min(\sum(P_A), \sum(P_B))} \right) \quad (1)$$

At this level, unfeasible matches with distances above a threshold are eliminated. For color similarity, an absolute threshold called maximum match distance $MMD_{color}$ is used. For proximity measure, absolute and relative gatings are applied. Absolute gating uses an absolute threshold $MMD_{centroid}$ set for the system based on the image resolution and average size of the objects. Relative gating is used to compensate for the distortions of the perspective projection (objects closer to the camera are seen larger and appear to be moving faster). Objects' heights are used to approximate their distances from the camera. Relative thresholds for horizontal and vertical displacement (Eq. 2) are computed as a function of the object's height and camera's approximate tilt angle $\alpha$.

$$MMD_x^{centroid} = f(height_{obj}) \quad MMD_y^{centroid} = f(height_{obj}) \times cos(\alpha) \quad (2)$$

We compute the confidence value of a match not only based on similarity and proximity of the objects that are matched, but also based on availability and goodness of other possible matches. Similarity confidence (Eq. 3) is a measure of how similar the matched objects are.

$$Conf_{sim}(i, j) = 1 - \frac{D(i,j)}{MaxDist} \quad (3)$$

Separation confidence (Eq. 4) is a measure of how distinct the match is. It measures the competition between all possible matches for the current object. The measure favors matches without competitors and matches with competitors having higher distances. In Eq. 4, $j^*$ denotes the closest competitor in terms of distance.

$$Conf_{sep}(i,j) = \begin{cases} 1, \text{no closest competitor} \\ 0.5 - \frac{D(i,j) - D(i,j^*)}{2 \times max(D(i,j), D(i,j^*))}, \text{otherwise} \end{cases} \quad (4)$$

Similarity and separation confidence measures are computed for both color based and centroid based matching. Total similarity and total separation confidence values are computed as weighted sums of color based and centroid based confidence values. Similarity and separation confidence values are further combined into a single confidence value $Conf_{Match}$ by a weighted sum. Matches whose confidence values are below an absolute confidence threshold (absolute pruning) and matches whose confidences values are below a percentage of the highest confidence value (relative pruning) are eliminated from the possible match list.

### 3.2 Segment Generation and Trajectory Maintenance

Segment generation module processes the *ObjectGraph* and extracts object trajectories. Nodes of *ObjectGraph* are classified into nine types: *single, source, source-split, sink, inner, split, sink-merge, merge, merge-split*, based on the number of parent and child nodes. *Trajectory segments*, a linked list of inner nodes (nodes that have one single parent and one single child), starting with a source or split type node and ending with a merge or sink type node, are identified and organized into a data structure called *SegmentList*. Extracted segments are labeled. Each segment without a parent is given a new label. Segments that have parents inherit their parents' labels. If parents' labels are inconsistent, smaller label (older segment) is kept and a flag is set indicating the inconsistency. Trajectory segments are first filtered to remove spurious segments, then discontinuity resolution is performed to join temporarily disconnected trajectory segments. Finally, trajectories are formed by linking segments sharing the same label.

**Trajectory Segment Filtering:** Moving object detection process results in many spurious objects due to various sources such as noise, fragmentation, shadows, illumination changes (i.e. cloud movements), reflections from specular surfaces (i.e. car windows), periodic movements (i.e. moving tree branches) etc. Use of a multi-modal moving object detection scheme, such as mixture of Gaussians used in this work eliminates some of the artifacts caused by repetitive motion in the background. Shadow elimination module eliminates most of the moving cast shadows. And filtering done before data association filters out small spurious regions. The remaining artifacts that can not be totally removed by image or object level processing produce spurious trajectories. At segment level, we use heuristics based on temporal and spatial consistency, to filter out trajectories.

*Temporal Consistency:* Segments resulting from temporarily fragmented parts of an object or uneliminated cast shadows tend to cause short segments that split from or merge to a longer trajectory segment. Temporal consistency prunes these segments. In order not to remove possible segments of an occluded trajectory, filtering of the short disconnected segments are delayed until after discontinuity resolution.

*Spatio-temporal Cluster Check:* Repetitive motion of the background (i.e. moving tree branches or their cast shadows), and spectral reflections (i.e. reflections from car windows) tend to produce temporally consistent and spatially clustered segments. We measure degree of spatio-temporal clustering with Average-Displacement-Length ratio $ADLR$ (Eq. 5) and with Diagonal-Length ratio $DLR$

(Eq. 6). Trajectory segments whose $ADLR$ or $DLR$ are below a threshold are filtered out.

$$ADLR = \frac{\sum_{i=2}^{n} \frac{\sqrt{(x_i - x_1)^2}}{i-1}}{\sum_{i=2}^{n} \sqrt{(x_i - x_{i-1})^2}} \qquad (5)$$

$$DLR = \frac{\sqrt{(Max(x_{i,1}) - Min(x_{i,1}))^2 + (Max(x_{i,2}) - Min(x_{i,2}))^2}}{\sum_{i=2}^{n} \sqrt{(x_i - x_{i-1})^2}} \qquad (6)$$

**Discontinuity Resolution:** Discontinuities in trajectories are caused by temporarily undetected objects, due to low contrast, partial or total occlusion; or by incorrect pruning in data association, due to significant change in appearance or size caused by partial occlusion or fragmentation. To resolve discontinuities, source and sink locations where the objects are expected to appear and disappear are defined. Segments dissappearing unexpectedly (at a non-sink location) and segments appearing unexpectedly (at a non-source location) are identified as possible start and end points of discontinuities. A match matrix *MatchSeg* is formed to match disappearing segments to appearing segments. Possible matches are first filtered based on temporal consistency. $Seg_{App}$ (appearing segment) is expected to start within $\Delta T$ frames from when $Seg_{Dis}$ (disappearing segment) ends. If the time constraint is satisfied, Kalman filter is used to predict future positions of the disappearing segments, and past positions of the appearing segments. Direction and position consistencies are checked on the matched disappearing & appearing segments, and the predicted segment joining them. If the direction and position consistencies are satisfied color similarity is checked. In case of multiple possible matches for a single disappearing segment, among the possible matches, appearing segment starting earliest is selected. In case of multiple possible matches for an appearing segment, disappearing segment that ends latest is selected. The matched disappearing and appearing segments are linked. Appearing segment inherits disappearing segment's label, and propagates this new label to its children segments.

## 4 Experimental Results

The proposed approach is tested on several outdoor sequences recorded by two different cameras in different resolutions under varying lighting conditions. Figure 3 shows visual results, table 1 gives numerical results for the sequences walk-in, ups, and people2. The major difficulty in the walk-in sequence is strong shadow. Beside moving cast shadows, there are static and self shadows. Some of the moving cast shadows that could not be eliminated cause small split and merge segments. Self shadow of the person walking on the left, combined with static shadow of the wall causes fragmentation and spurious segments. Two trees and a light pole in the scene causes occlusions.

The major problems in the ups sequence are perspective distortion, cast shadows of the tree branches, and dynamic occlusion on the road (top right corner

**Fig. 3.** Top to bottom: walk-in, ups, and people2 sequences. Left to right: trajectory segments before pruning, trajectory segments after pruning, trajectories after discontinuity resolution and final filtering. Red lines indicate resolved discontinuities.

**Table 1.** Numerical results for the sequences walk-in, ups, and people2. (SC:Scene Complexity, OC:OCclusion source, PD:Perspective Distortion, $N_S^{all}$, $N_S^{pruned}$: Number of Segments before and after filtering, $N_T^{final}$: Number of trajectories after discontinuity resolution and filtering, $N_T^{Ground}$: Number of trajectories in the ground truth, FN, FP, FM: Number of missed, misdetected, mismatched segments.)

|  | SC | OC | PD | $N_S^{all}$ | $N_S^{filtered}$ | $N_T^{final}$ | $N_T^{Ground}$ | FN:FP:FM |
|---|---|---|---|---|---|---|---|---|
| walk-in | low | low | low | 19 | 7 | 4 | 4 | 0:0:0 |
| ups | med | med | med | 413 | 38 | 13 | 13 | 0:0:1 |
| people2 | high | high | high | 174 | 31 | 9 | 9 | 1:0:1 |

of the image). The field of view extends toward the horizon, so the variations in object sizes and displacements are high, which makes filtering challenging. Towards the end of the sequence a strong wind moves the tree branches close to the camera. Their cast shadows on the ground plane cause large spurious objects, which results in many spurious segments.

The major problems in people2 sequence are perspective distortion, non-linear trajectories, occlusions, and reflections from the car windows. In people2, pedestrians walk around the cars in a parking lot, so the trajectories are quite non-linear and occluded by the cars. Both cloud and object movements cause reflections on the car windows, which in result cause many spurious segments.

These segments can not be filtered simply based on their lengths, since the cars are close to the camera these segments are quite long.

As seen in figure 3 and table 1, we obtained promising results. Both mismatches (one in ups sequence, one in people2 sequence) happen far from the camera. The mismatch in people2 sequence happens between two pedestrians behind the cars and with similar appearances. The sequences will be available at http://www.umr.edu/~bunyak/tracking.

## 5 Conclusion

In this paper, we propose a detection-based tracking method and various filtering and pruning approaches to obtain robust trajectories in low resolution, far-field visual surveillance videos. Segmentation and tracking modules do not need initialization or training. Use of multi-hypothesis approach as assignment strategy and the proposed confidence measures enable the system to delay the decisions until further levels of processing. Various filtering and pruning approaches, applied at different levels of processing, eliminate spurious objects and trajectories. Trajectories are further refined by resolving discontinuities utilizing Kalman filter and color similarity. This approach results in robust trajectory information, which we will utilize later for automated annotation of simple visual events.

## References

1. Jung, Y., Lee, K., Ho, Y.: Content-based event retrieval using semantic scene interpretation for automated traffic surveillance. IEEE Trans. on Intell. Transportation Systems **2** (2001) 151–163
2. McKenna, S., Jabri, S., Duric, Z., Rosenfeld, A., Wechsler, H.: Tracking groups of people. Computer Vision and Image Understanding: CVIU **80** (2000) 42–56
3. Zhao, T., Nevatia, R.: Tracking multiple humans in complex situations. IEEE Trans. on Patt. Anal. and Mach. Intell. **26** (2004) 1208–1221
4. Senior, A., Hampapur, A., Tian, Y.L., Brown, L., Pankantiand, S., Bolle, R.: Appearance models for occlusion handling. In: Second International workshop on Performance Eval. of Tracking and Surv. Sys. (2001)
5. Haritaoglu, I., Harwood, D., Davis, L.: W4: real-time surveillance of people and their activities. IEEE Trans. on Patt. Anal. and Mach. Intell. **22** (2000)
6. Stauffer, C., Grimson, W.: Adaptive background mixture models for real-time tracking. In: IEEE Conf. on Computer Vision and Pattern Recognition. (1999) 246–252
7. Cox, I.: A review of statistical data association techniques for motion correspondence. Intl. Journal of Computer Vision **10** (1993) 53–66
8. Rasmussen, C., Hager, G.: Probabilistic data association methods for tracking complex visual objects. IEEE Trans. on Patt. Anal. and Mach. Intell. **23** (2001) 560–576
9. Kirubarajan, T., Bar-Shalom, Y.: Probabilistic data association techniques for target tracking in clutter. Proceedings of the IEEE **92** (2004) 536 – 557
10. Bunyak, F., Ersoy, I., Subramanya, S.: Shadow detection by combined photometric invariants for improved foreground segmentation. In: IEEE Workshop on Applications of Computer Vision, WACV2005. (2005) 510–515

# Real Time Head Tracking via Camera Saccade and Shape-Fitting

Jason Z. Zhang[1], Ye Lu[2], and Q.M. Jonathan Wu[3]

[1] Micro-technology and Sensing Group, Institute for Fuel Cell Innovation,
National Research Council of Canada, Vancouver, B.C. V6T 1W5 Canada
jason.zhang@nrc-cnrc.gc.ca
[2] Vision and Media Laboratory, School of Computing Science,
Simon Fraser University, Burnaby, B.C. V5A 1S6 Canada
yel@cs.sfu.ca
[3] Department of Electrical and Computer Engineering,
University of Windsor, Ontario N9B 3P4 Canada
jwu@uwindsor.ca

**Abstract.** This paper presents a system that tracks human heads in real-time under unconstrained environments where target occlusion, varying illumination, and cluttered backgrounds exist. Tracking is formulated as an active visual servo problem based on the integration of a saccade and a smooth pursuit processes. The head is modelled as an ellipse computed from the color clusters of candidate targets using a robust least square ellipse fitting algorithm. The Farnsworth Perceptually Uniform Color Model is employed to represent the color information of the visual objects. Kalman filtering is applied to the head ellipse to track the evolution of the position, size, and orientation of the target such that the occlusion of objects with similar color and shape as those of the target are effectively accommodated. Experiments with tracking scenarios demonstrate the effectiveness of the system.

## 1 Introduction

Head tracking is an important issue for automatic human tracking in unconstrained environments. Human tracking has widely been investigated in robotic vision, active vision, automatic surveillance, telepresence and interactive environments [9,7], facial feature tracking and analysis [10], 3D head modelling [3], and video coding [13]. Because of its rigid shape and constrained motion, a human head reveals reliable positional information for surveillance and monitoring of people. Moreover, dimensional and orientational information of a head can reliably be extracted by fitting the head to a parameterized shape, suggesting a new approach to a wide range of applications from content-oriented video coding and retrieving to metric visual measurements and active vision control.

Previous work on head tracking was reported in [4,5,10]. However, problems such as occlusion in the presence of multiple targets with similar colors, integration of the tracking algorithm with active camera movement, and occlusion and distraction by multiple targets were not adequately addressed in the work.

In this paper, we propose a cost-effective human head tracking system based on a single pan/tilt camera and implemented using a low cost PC. The head tracker is implemented by integrating the peripheral and foveated motion vision strategies. The target head is initially located by clustering the candidate pixels with colors similar to the facial skin and hair of a template of the target, manually determined in an image before the tracking process begins. The color images are represented in a *perceptually uniform color space* (PUCS). The tracking system is comprised of a foveation module and a precaution module.

## 2 Head Modelling

Methods for modelling a human head can be classified into two categories: 2D models and 3D models. With 2D models, a head is represented by a rectangular region [4] or an elliptical area [2]. For the 3D case, on the other hand, ellipsoids [1] and cylinders [3] are the representative shapes to model the head. In this work, we represent a head with an ellipse for the following reasons: First, our tracking method is performed within a 2D domain (image), regardless of arbitrary 3D movements of the target. Second, an ellipse is a compact form to formulate the positions, dimensions, and orientations of the moving head. Finally, it is easier to fit candidate pixels to an ellipse.

### 2.1 Perceptually Uniform Color Space

Despite the color representation systems used in computer vision and image processing, e.g. RGB, YUV and HSV, the *Perceptually Uniform Color Space* (PUCS) proposed by Farnsworth [12] is important for the application of color object detection/tracking. In PUCS, the MacAdam ellipses [8] that represent the chromatic discrimination of the human visual system in the CIE 1931 XYZ color system become circles with approximately the same radius ([12], page 311). With this feature, the chromatic difference perceived by a human viewer is represented in an isotropic metric. That is, any pair of colors with an equal distance in the color representation system corresponds to a similar subjective color difference perceived by human viewers, which implies that objects represented in the PUCS can metrically be discriminated as a human being perceives colors.

To represent an image pixel in PUCS, the RGB components of the pixel in our digital image are first transformed into the CIE 1931 XYZ format as follows ([12], page 139):

$$\left.\begin{array}{l} x = \frac{1}{s}(0.49000r + 0.31000g + 0.20000b) \\ y = \frac{1}{s}(0.17697r + 0.81240g + 0.01063b) \\ z = \frac{1}{s}(0.00000r + 0.01000g + 0.99000b) \end{array}\right\} \quad (1)$$

where

$$\left.\begin{array}{l} s = 0.66697r + 1.13240g + 1.20063b, \\ r = \frac{R}{R+G+B} \\ g = \frac{G}{R+G+B} \\ b = \frac{B}{R+G+B} \end{array}\right\} \quad (2)$$

In Eqs. (1) and (2), $R, G, B$ are the quantized trisitimulus values of the pixel in the range $[0, 255]$ and $(x, y)$ describes the chromaticity of the pixel. The luminance of the stimulus from pixel $Y$ is represented in $R, G, B$, as follows:

$$Y = 0.298839R + 0.586811G + 0.114350B \tag{3}$$

The chromaticity $(x, y)$ is then transformed into the pair $(u_f, v_f)$ in PUCS using Farnsworth's nonlinear transformation [11]. The values of a visible color $(u_f, v_f)$ are in the range $[0, 91] \times [0, 139]$.

### 2.2 Head Representation

We represent a head using a bimodal model in a simpler manner. The bimodal model of a template head is constructed with a two-step procedure. First, from a sample image in which the target head appears, we manually select two patches $F$ and $H$ which represent a representative facial skin region and a hair region, respectively. Let $x_i^f = (u_i^f, v_i^f)$ be a point in $F$ represented in the PUCS chromaticity. Construct a 2D histogram $H_f$ with $92 \times 140$ bins from $\{x_i^f\}_{i=1\cdots n}$, where $n$ is the number of the pixels in $F$. Second, find $B^*$, the bin with the most pixel counts. Let $b^*$ be the index of $B^*$ corresponding to the most likely color of the facial skin $c_f = (u_f, v_f)$. To classify image pixels, the following criterion is applied: $\forall x_i^f = (u_i^f, v_i^f)^\top, x_i^f \in F$ and is registered as a facial skin candidate pixel if and only if:

$$|u_i^f - u_f| \leq u_{tf} \text{ and } |v_i^f - v_f| \leq v_{tf}$$

where $u_{tf}$ and $v_{tf}$ are thresholds that are determined as $u_{tf} = \sigma_u$, $v_{tf} = \sigma_v$. $\sigma_u$ and $\sigma_v$ are the standard deviations of the $u$ and $v$ components of the chromatic variables $\{x_i^f\}$ in $H_f$.

The hair region is registered in a similar way as a facial region. However, since the estimated chromaticity is usually unstable in dark hairs, the luminance $Y$ in Eq. (3) is utilized together with the chromatic information to form hair pixel identification criteria as follows:

$$|u_i^f - u_h| \leq u_{th}, \ |v_i^f - v_h| \leq v_{th}, \text{ and } |Y_i - Y_h| \leq Y_{th}$$

where $(u_h, v_h) = c_h$ is the most likely value for chromaticity of the hair, $Y_h$ the luminance of the hair, and $u_{th}, v_{th}, Y_{th}$ are thresholds, which are empirically determined as

$$u_{tf} = 1.5 \times \sigma_u, \ v_{tf} = 1.5 \times \sigma_v, \text{ and } Y_{tf} = 3.0 \times \sigma_Y$$

Experiments show that the empirical coefficients in the thresholds are robust to the variation of environment.

Automatic determination of the color templates can only be achieved as long as a reliable facial color detection algorithm is available. However, since the scenarios are unconstrained in lighting condition, diversity of target colors, occlusion, and so on, it is not an easy task to implement such a reliable facial color detection algorithm.

With these parameters, the head candidate pixels with either the facial skin color or the hair color are clustered into candidate blobs according to the following procedure:

1. Starting with any candidate pixel $p_i = (x_i, y_i)$, where $(x_i, y_i)$ is the coordinates of $x_i$ in the image grid system, let $S_k$ be a set such that $S_k$ is registered as $S_k \ni p_i$.
2. For $p_j \in N(p_i) = \{(x-1, y), (x+1, y), (x, y-1), (x, y+1)\}$, where $p_j$ is the coordinates of $x_j$, register $S_k$ so that $S_k \ni p_j$, if either $x_j \in F$ or $x_j \in H$.
3. Repeat Step 2 until $S_k$ cannot be registered with any candidate points in the image.
4. Repeat Steps 1 through 3 until no new sets of candidate points can be formed in the image.

With the clustering method, an image is segmented into blobs that refer to candidate head regions and background regions. In the presence of noise and false targets which are of similar color information as the real target, false head blobs may be obtained. In this case, the head cannot be distinguished from the false targets unless other discrimination criteria are applied.

### 2.3 Elliptic Fitting

For a given contour point set $C$, we fit the data in $C$ to an ellipse with which we can model the head with the parameters such that the position, orientation, and shape of the head can explicitly be represented. In this research, we apply least-squares based minimization to the ellipse fitting task. The minimization is constrained by an algebraic ellipse condition $4ac - b^2 = 1$ resulting in a robust and efficient solution [6].

Figure 1 illustrates examples of fitting head blob contours using the algorithm. We observed that the algorithm works well with various sizes, angles, and distributions of scattered data. In each case, the procedure correctly obtained the positions and dimensions of the head.

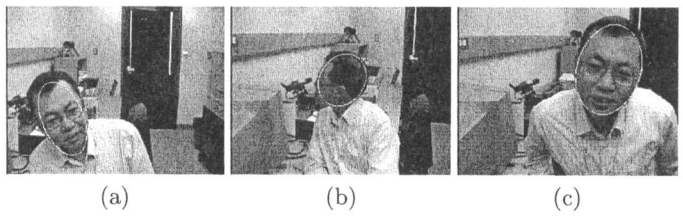

**Fig. 1.** Head blobs of different sizes and orientations are tracked by ellipses

## 2.4 Ellipse Modelling

A head is modelled as an ellipse $E$ obtained through the elliptical fitting process. Five parameters of the ellipse are adopted in the model: center coordinates $\boldsymbol{x}_c = (x_c, y_c)$, lengths of the minor and the major axes $l_m, l_M$, and yaw angle $\alpha$. The ellipse $E$ is represented as $E = \{x_c, y_c, l_m, l_M, \alpha\}$. When incorporated into a target filtering process, the model allows adaptive updates of the position, shape, and orientation of the target being tracked. With these advantages, the model is superior to previous elliptical head models. In Birchfield [2], the size, aspect ratio, and the orientation of the model ellipse of a head remain fixed regardless the constant changes in the information of the target in a tracking scenario. In Comaniciu, et al. [5], the orientation of the ellipse is also fixed. The ellipse is updated with limited size options during a tracking process. An adaptive scale mechanism is implemented through a complex multi-bandwidth search process.

## 3 Head Tracking

A robust head tracker in unconstrained environments needs to possess two distinguishable functional components. The first is a bottom-up process which deals with target representation (or modelling) and localization. The second is implemented with signal filtering and data fusion functions that reveal the dynamics of the targets, derive a priori probabilities of the scene from observations, and evaluate hypotheses. Active tracking has an additional functional component that is implemented with foveo-peripheral sensing and oculomotor mechanisms, such as saccade and pursuit processes. How the three components are combined determines the properties and performance of the tracker. Section 2 addresses our approach for implementing the first component. This section will discuss the last two components.

Kalman filtering is employed to implement the data fusion component of the head tracker and thereby ensure robustness in the presence of occlusion and cluttered background. The parameters of the ellipse $E$ are the state of the tracking system. The five components of the state vector are estimated using five independent Kalman filters with each of the filters assigned to one parameter. A constant-velocity dynamic model driven by white noise is utilized in the filters for $x_c, y_c, l_m$, and $l_M$, whereas a Ornstein-Uhlenbeck velocity model with white noise is applied to the rotation angle $\alpha$. Such assumptions are made based on the following considerations.

The head tracker works in an active tracking framework with a sensing scheme involving foveation and peripheral vision mechanisms. The two vision functions work cooperatively depending on the location of the target. The foveation function is active when the target lies in the foveal area predefined in images, whereas the peripheral vision function takes over the control of the system only when the target moves out of the foveal area. The active head tracker is implemented as a *visual fixation* process that localizes the target in an image, and maintains and tracks the target within the fovea. The visual fixation process is supported by saccade and pursuit processes that switch between foveation and

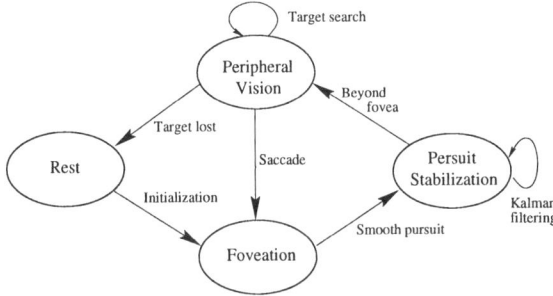

**Fig. 2.** State transitions in the visual fixation process

peripheral vision states. The fixation process can be described graphically by the state transition diagram illustrated in Figure 2.

## 4 Experimental Results

The proposed head-tracking system was applied to real scenarios demonstrating good performance in various aspects. The tracking computations were performed in video images with a 320 × 240 pixels and 24 bit RGB color depth. The system performs real-time foveal pursuit using the first model (30 frames/second), whereas only semi real-time tracking speed is achieved with the second foveal pursuit model due to latches in the serial communication between the computer and the camera and the mechanics of the camera pan/tilt platform.

The video clip in Figure 3 demonstrates the bimodal color registration method. The ellipses correctly remain on the head while the color distribution of the target zone changes constantly as the person is turning about 180 degrees.

The effectiveness of the system in combatting the interference from similar targets is shown in Figure 4. There are two scenarios of occlusion in the video

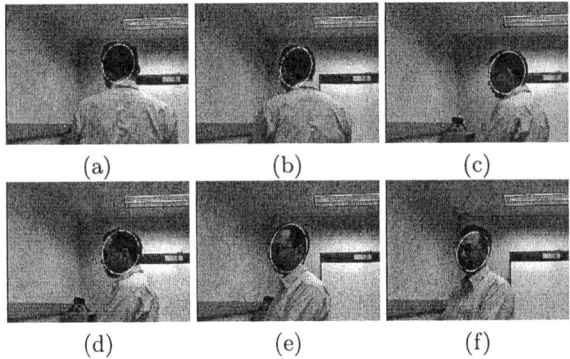

**Fig. 3.** Bimodal color model in the head tracking

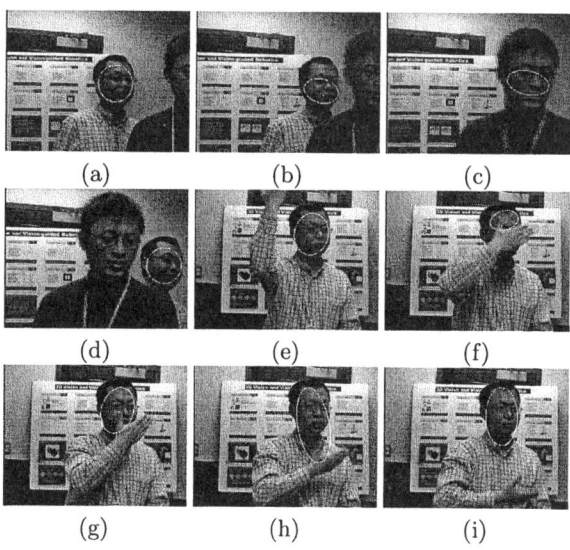

**Fig. 4.** Tracking in presence of occlusion

clip. In the first scenario illustrated in Figure 4 (a) - (d), the camera tracks the target correctly as he walks behind another person with a similar head color distribution. In Figure 4 (c), the focus of the camera temporarily stays on the second person's face when the target is completely occluded. The focus of the camera returns onto the real target after the target appears again in the view in Figure 4 (d), indicating that the tracker predicted target positions correctly. The system's effectiveness of resisting other interference is demonstrated in the second occlusion scenario shown in Figure 4 (e) - (i). Although the hand has similar colors as the facial color, the system maintains its attention on the facial area during the occlusion process.

Malfunction of the system exists in some situations. For example, when the background has similar color as the target's facial skin or hair, the system might be allured to false targets. This problem could be tackled by introducing more comprehensive criteria for target motion detection in the algorithm.

## 5  Conclusions

A head tracking system has been described and implemented for unconstrained environments. The system works in an active tracking framework that integrates foveo-peripheral sensing and color ellipse head fitting. The system can track a head within the foveal area in real time, and it performs peripheral target localization when the target moves to the periphery of the view.

Foveo-peripheral sensing is implemented with combined saccade and smooth pursuit processes. With the sensing scheme, the system detects a head in images by fitting candidate color blob contours to an ellipse. The centroid, size, and orientation are state variables that are estimated during the tracking process using Kalman filters. The head blob is obtained by registering candidate pixels represented in the Perceptually Uniform Color Space and clustering the registered pixels. The target is pursued smoothly within the fovea of the camera and recaptured quickly by a saccade process. The system provides a reliable and cost-efficient solution to visual tracking applications.

## References

1. S. Basu, I. Essa, and A. Pentland. "Motion Regularization for Model-Based Head Tracking," *Proc. 13th IEEE Int'l Conf. on Pattern Recognition,* pp. 611-616, 1996.
2. S. Birchfield, "Elliptical head tracking using intensity gradients and color histograms," *Proc. IEEE Conf. on Computer Vision and Pattern Recognition,* pp. 232-237, 1998.
3. M. La Cascia, S. Sclaroff, and V. Athitsos, "Fast, reliable head tracking under varying illumination: An approach based on registration of texture-mapped 3D models," *IEEE Trans. on Pattern Analysis and Machine Intelligence,* vol. 22, no. 4, pp. 322-336, 2000.
4. D. Comaniciu and V. Ramesh, "Robust detection and tracking of human faces with an active camera," *Proc. 3rd IEEE Computer Soc. Int'l. Workshop on Visual Surveillance,* pp. 11-18, 2000.
5. D. Comaniciu, V. Ramesh, and P. Meer, "Kernel-based object tracking," *IEEE Trans. on Pattern Analysis and Machine Intelligence,* vol. 25, no. 5, pp. 564-577, 2003.
6. D. Fitzgibbon, M. Filu, and R. Fisher, "Direct least square fitting of ellipses," *IEEE Trans. on Pattern Analysis and Machine Intelligence,* vol. 21, no. 5, pp. 476-480, 1999.
7. J. Heuring and D. W. Murray, "Modeling and copying human head movements," *IEEE Trans. on Robotics and Automation,* vol. 15, no. 6, pp. 1095-1108, 1999.
8. A. Kaarna, T. Kuparinen, and P. Toivanen, "Chromaticity difference from surfaces defined from MacAdam ellipse," *Proc. European Conf. on Color in Graphics, Image and Vision,* 2002.
9. L. Morency, A. Rahimi, N. Checka, and T. Darrell, "Fast stereo-based head tracking for interactive environments," *Proc. IEEE Int'l. Conf. on Automatic Face and Gesture Recognition,* 2002.
10. N. Oliver, A. Pentland, and F. Bérard, "LAFTER: A real-time lips and face tracker with facial expression recognition," *Pattern Recognition,* vol. 33, no. 8, pp. 1369-1382, 2000.
11. H. Wu, Q. Chen and M. Yachida, "Face detection from color images using a fuzzy pattern matching method," *IEEE Trans. on Pattern Analysis and Machine Intelligence,* vol. 21, no. 6, pp. 557-563, 1999.
12. G. Wyszechi and W. S. Stiles, *Color Science: Concept and Methods, Quantitative Data and Formulae,* 2nd Edition. New York: John Wiley & Sons, Inc., 1982.
13. J. Xu, L. Po, and C. Cheung, "Adaptive motion tracking block matching algorithms for video coding," *IEEE Trans. on Circuits and Systems for Video Technology,* vol. 9, no. 7, pp. 1025-1029, 1999.

# A Novel Tracking Framework Using Kalman Filtering and Elastic Matching

Xingzhi Luo and Suchendra M. Bhandarkar

Department of Computer Science, The University of Georgia,
Athens, Georgia, 30602-7404, USA

**Abstract.** A novel region-based multiple object tracking framework based on Kalman filtering and elastic matching is proposed. The proposed Kalman filtering-elastic matching model is general in two significant ways. First, it is suitable for tracking of both, rigid and elastic objects. Second, it is suitable for tracking using both, fixed cameras and moving cameras since the method does not rely on background subtraction. The elastic matching algorithm exploits both the spectral features and structural features of the tracked objects, making it more robust and general in the context of object tracking. The proposed tracking framework can be viewed as a generalized Kalman filter where the elastic matching algorithm is used to measure the velocity field which is then approximated using B-spline surfaces. The control points of the B-spline surfaces are directly used as the tracking variables in a grid-based Kalman filtering model. The limitations of the Gaussian distribution assumption in the Kalman filter are overcome by the large capture range of the elastic matching algorithm. The B-spline approximation of the velocity field is used to update the spectral features of the tracked objects in the grid-based Kalman filter model. The dynamic nature of these spectral features are subsequently used to reason about occlusion. Experimental results on tracking of multiple objects in real-time video are presented.

## 1 Introduction and Background

Multiple object tracking is challenging in several aspects. The first challenge arises from mutual occlusion between objects. When occlusion occurs, some objects are partially or totally invisible. This makes it hard to accurately localize the position of the occluded object and track the occluded object continuously. The second challenge is the formulation of a good object model. A good object model should be able to capture the most important and relevant information about the object and facilitate fast and reliable tracking. The ability to deal with occlusion depends, to a great extent, on the object model. The third challenge is to be able to accurately predict the object position and update the prediction via accurate localization. The fourth challenge is to meet the real time constraints of most tracking applications in the real world. Fast and accurate object localization over time is the ultimate objective of a tracking system.

Generally speaking, there exist three broad categories of object models in the context of tracking: contour-based models [1], [5], [8], [9], region-based models [2], [3], [4], and feature point-based models [10], [12]. The contour-based model does not encode any color or edge information within the interior of the object. The contour information by itself is not enough to handle general instances of occlusion. In the absence of any spectral information, feature point-based tracking methods are easily distracted by noisy feature points in the background and are, by their very nature, limited to objects rich in feature points. A region-based object model is more suitable when occlusion is present since it encodes the spectral information.

Occlusion handling is another important issue that arises in multiple object tracking systems and is closely intertwined with the choice of the object model. In the case of contour-based models, the robustness of the occlusion reasoning is highly dependent on the quality of object segmentation and typically, only simple cases are well handled [8]. Region-based object models that rely primarily on color/gray level histograms of the moving regions are not well suited to handle occlusion since no object shape information is available. Correspondence-based schemes [3] for occlusion handling typically compute only a statistical probability that a pixel of a given color belongs to a specific object which does not ensure accurate object localization.

Object position estimation/prediction is also an important issue in multiple object tracking. An accurate estimation of the new location of the tracked object, provides a good starting point for the tracking system. Some tracking systems do not rely on estimation, instead, the results of matching and correspondence analysis are used to determine the new position of the tracked object [3], [10]. However, since moving objects typically exhibit spatial coherence, position prediction is both, feasible and computationally advantageous. The Kalman filter is a popular technique used to predict the position(s) of the tracked object(s) on account of its computational simplicity [8], [9]. Also, the Kalman filtering algorithm is computationally less intensive than the particle filter. It is for the above reasons that the Kalman filter is used in our tracking algorithm.

## 2 Overview of the Approach

In this paper, a region-based model that combines the Kalman filtering algorithm with elastic matching is proposed for multiple object tracking. Each object is modeled as a network of grids. The color information and the feature points are extracted for each grid. The object contour and the object shape information are automatically encoded within the grid network. The Kalman filtering algorithm is used as the velocity prediction model on account of its simplicity. The velocity fields of the tracked objects are represented using B-spline surfaces. One of the advantages of the proposed model is that the tracked object can possess different velocity (or displacement) vectors in the different image regions that comprise the tracked object. This permits tracking of both rigid and elastic objects. Another advantage of the proposed model is that the approximation of the object contour as a convex contour or by a combination of several elliptical contours as done in [8] is not necessary. Highly elastic objects such as fish can be easily modeled and tracked using the proposed method.

The elastic matching algorithm is used to accurately localize the tracked objects in the proposed model. Elastic matching has been used widely for deformable object recognition [6]. In this paper, elastic matching is shown to be potentially well suited for tracking of deformable objects. In the event of inaccurate prediction by the Kalman filtering algorithm, the elastic matching algorithm can still guide the tracking towards the optimal solution, thus overcoming the limitations of the Gaussian distribution assumption in the Kalman filtering algorithm. Another advantage of elastic matching is that the tracking results are not dependent on the accuracy of the background subtraction used to extract the moving objects. This makes it possible to track moving objects with a moving camera.

The rest of the paper is organized as follows. The overall tracking model is described in Sections 3 and the three sub-models, i.e., the object model, the prediction model and the velocity measurement model are described in Section 3.1, 3.2 and 3.3 respectively. Section 4 describes the occlusion reasoning algorithm in detail. Section 5 presents experimental results for the proposed tracking scheme on video data from indoor and outdoor scenes. Section 6 concludes the paper with direction for future research.

## 3 The Proposed Tracking Model

The proposed tracking model is composed of three sub-models: the *object model*, the *velocity estimation model* and the *velocity measurement model*. The *object model* defines the features for object representation and the tracking parameters. The features used in the object model incorporate both color (spectral) and edge (structural) information of the tracked objects. The *velocity estimation model* uses a canonical Kalman filtering algorithm. B-spline surfaces are used to approximate the object velocity field considering that the velocity in the image plane could potentially vary at different pixels belonging to the same object. For example, when a person bows or starts to run, the upper and lower portions of the person's body may undergo different displacements. The control points of the B-spline surfaces are used as estimation variables in the Kalman filtering algorithm. The B-spline surface approximation smoothes the velocity field obtained via elastic matching, resulting in a velocity field that more closely approximates the real world motion. Using B-spline surface approximation also allows for a finite number of tracking variables to be used in the Kalman filtering algorithm. A detailed description of the B-spline surface approximation algorithm can be found in [13]. The *velocity measurement model* uses a generalized elastic matching algorithm to measure the velocity of each grid in a region-based object model that is represented by a collection of non-overlapping grids. The overall tracking framework is shown in Figure 1. The Kalman filtering algorithm is used to estimate/predict the velocities of the control points on the B-spline surfaces. The estimated control point positions are used to compute the grid velocities, which are then used to initialize the elastic matching algorithm. The elastic matching algorithm determines the new locations of the tracked objects by seeking to optimize an energy function defined over the velocity field. The B-spline surface control points are updated using the velocity field computed by the elastic matching algorithm. The updated B-spline surface control points in turn are used to update the Kalman filter parameters. The details of the proposed tracking scheme are provided in the following subsections.

### 3.1 The Object Model

Given an image frame $F(t)$, non-overlapping grid cells of size $l \times l$ pixels are imposed on $F(t)$ and the relevant features extracted for each grid cell. The parameter $l$ controls

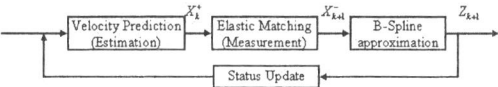

**Fig. 1.** The proposed tracking model

the granularity of the object model. Let $F_G(t)$ denote the grid image at time $t$, i.e. the set of all grid cells at time $t$. An object $O(i)$ is modeled as a set of grid cells $O(i) = \{G, G_B\}$, where $G = \{g_k\}$ is the set of grid cells that belong to the object and $G_B$ is the set of grid cells that contain the boundary points. Note that $G \subset F_G(t)$ and $G_B \subseteq G$. The boundary grid cells $G_B$ are used to localize the boundary of the tracked object. Henceforth we refer to each grid cell as a grid for the sake of convenience.

Each grid $g_k$ has several attributes given by $g_k = \{X, \xi, c\}$ where $X = (x, y)$ is the location of grid $g_k$, $\xi = (\xi^x, \xi^y)$ is the velocity of grid $g_k$ and $c$ is the vector of extracted features for grid $g_k$. Note that each grid has its own velocity vector. B-spline surfaces are used to approximate the velocity field of each object. Color and edge features are extracted for each grid and denoted by the feature vector $c = \{c_i^c, c_i^e\}$, where $c^c$ is the color feature vector and $c^e$ is the set of corner pixels associated with the grid.

Given an RGB color image, three new color channels are computed. The three new color channels are a linear combination of the original RGB channels and are given by $I_1 = (R+G+B)/3, I_2 = R-B, I_3 = 2G-R-B$. These three new color channels are more stable to changes in illumination than the original RGB channels [7]. The channel $I_1$ denotes the image intensity or luminance whereas channels $I_2$ and $I_3$ denote roughly orthogonal color components. For each grid, the color features are the spatial average of each color channel computed over all the pixels within the grid. The color feature for a grid is denoted by $c^c = \{i_1, \sigma_1, i_2, \sigma_2, i_3, \sigma_3\}$ where $i_k$ is the spatial average of color channel $k$ computed over all pixels of the corresponding grid in the current image frame and $\sigma_k$ is the standard deviation of $i_k$ along the temporal dimension. When there is insufficient temporal information for a grid, $\sigma_k$ is initialized to a default value of $\sigma_k^0$. ABOVE. An online occlusion reasoning scheme, detailed in Section 4, is used to update the aforementioned parameters for each grid.

The Harris corner detector [11] is used to extract the corner points. The corner feature for a grid is represented by a set of corner points $c^e = \{c_i^e\}$. If the grid size is small (i.e. 5 × 5), very few or no corner points are detected within the grid resulting in the absence of any structural information for that grid. Hence in our experiments, the corner points associated with a grid are deemed to be those that are detected within a window that is larger than the grid size and centered within the grid. Thus, corner points from the neighboring grids are included within the set of corner points associated with a given grid.

The similarity between two grids is quantified by the distance between their associated features. The distance between two color feature vectors is considered to be the Euclidean distance $d(c_1^c, c_2^c) = \|c_1^c - c_2^c\|^2$ whereas the distance between two sets of corner points $A$ and $B$ is the Hausdorff distance $H(A, B)$ [10]. Given the feature vectors associated with two grids $g$ and $g'$, their feature distance is evaluated as $d(c_g, c_{g'}) = d(c_g^c, c_{g'}^c) + \beta H(c_g^e, c_{g'}^e)$, where $\beta$ is a predetermined constant.

## 3.2 Velocity Estimation Model

A Kalman filter is used to estimate/predict the velocity field of an object. Note that the term velocity field, in our case, actually denotes the control point values resulting from the B-spline surface approximation of the velocity field. The canonical Kalman filter used in this paper can be described using the following equations:

$$\hat{\xi}_{k+1}^- = \hat{\xi}_k^+ + q_k \quad (1)$$

$$Z_k = \hat{\xi}_k^- + v_k \quad (2)$$

where $\xi$ is the estimated/predicted velocity field. and $Z_k$ is the actually measured velocity field. Equation (1) represents the prior estimation of $\xi$ whereas equation (2) describes the linear relation between the estimated $\xi$ and the actually measured velocity field $Z_k$. Variables $q_k$ and $v_k$ represent random noise in the prior estimation and actual measurement of the velocity field respectively. Both $q_k$ and $v_k$ are modeled as Gaussian white noise with distributions $\mathcal{N}(0, Q)$ and $\mathcal{N}(0, R)$ respectively, where $Q$ and $R$ are the corresponding covariance matrices.

## 3.3 Velocity Measurement Model

The Kalman filtering algorithm results in an estimation of the velocities for the control points of an object velocity field, which are used to calculate the velocity (displacement) of each grid from one frame to the next. The estimated displacement of each grid is used to initialize the elastic matching algorithm. The elastic matching algorithm searches for the corresponding location of the tracked object in the new image frame. Given the set of grids $G$ belonging to an object at time $t-1$, where $G \subset F_G(t-1)$, the elastic matching can be viewed as a procedure to determine a mapping $f : G \mapsto G'$ where $G' \subset F_G(t)$ is a set of corresponding grids in the new image frame such that: (i) for each $g \in G$, there exists $g' \in G'$ such that $g' = f(g)$, and (ii) the following energy function is minimized:

$$E(f) = \sum_{g \in G} o_g d(c_g, c_{g'}) + \lambda \sum_{(g_1, g_2) \in G} [(X_{g_1} - X_{g_2}) - (X_{g'_1} - X_{g'_2})]^2 \quad (3)$$

In equation (3), $o_g$ denotes the occlusion assumption for grid $g$: $o_g = 0$ if grid $g$ is occluded, otherwise $o_g = 1$; $g'_1 = f(g_1)$; $g'_2 = f(g_2)$; $d(c_g, c_{g'})$ is the distance between grids $g$ and $g'$ (Section 3.1); $X_{g_k}$ is the location of grid $g_k$; and $c_g$ denotes the feature vector associated with grid $g$. The first summation in equation (3) represents the contribution to the energy function arising from the dissimilarity between the feature vectors associated with grids $g$ and $g'$. This summation is minimized when the feature vectors associated with grids $g$ and $g' = f(g)$ are similar. The second summation in equation (3) represents the contribution to the energy function arising from the difference in mutual distance between corresponding grid pairs which can be viewed as a measure of object shape distortion. This summation is minimized when the object shape distortion between successive frames is minimized.

By constraining the grid pairs $(g_1, g_2)$ to be neighbors, the computational complexity of the second summation in equation (3) can be significantly reduced and the energy function simplified. The simplified energy function can be written as $E(f) = \sum_{g \in G} E(g)_{g \mapsto g'}$, in which

$$E(g)_{g \mapsto g'} = o_g d(c_g, c_{g'}) + \lambda \sum_{g_i \in O(g)} \|X_{g_i} - X_g - (X_{g'_i} - X_{g'})\|^2 \quad (4)$$

Note that $E(g)_{g \mapsto g'}$ is the contribution of the mapping $g \mapsto g'$ to the energy function $E(f)$. Given an initial matching $G \mapsto G'$, an iterative local search is performed to minimize the energy function $E(f)$.

Given grids $g$ and $g'$ (where $g \mapsto g'$), we search for a grid $g''$ in $O(g')$ (the neighborhood of $g'$), to see whether the alternative mapping $g \mapsto g''$ can result in a lower value of the energy function. If $g'$ is replaced by $g''$, the overall change in the energy function is localized to grid $g$ and its neighboring grids $g_i \in O(g)$. The contribution of the mapping $g \mapsto g''$ to the energy function can be evaluated as:

$$E(g)_{g \mapsto g''} = o_g d(c_g, c_{g''}) + \lambda \sum_{g_i \in O(g)} \|X_{g_i} - X_g - (X_{g'_i} - X_{g''})\|^2 \quad (5)$$

The overall change in the energy can be evaluated as:

$$\Delta E(f)_{g' \to g''} = E(g)_{g \mapsto g''} - E(g)_{g \mapsto g'} = \sum_{g_i \in O(G)} (E(g_i)_{g \mapsto g''} - E(g_i)_{g \mapsto g'}) \quad (6)$$

The iterative algorithm outlined below is used to minimize the total energy $E(f)$. Given the estimated velocity field computed using equation (1), the initial displacement of each grid is computed and used to initialize the following algorithm for elastic matching:

(1) For each grid $g$ determine its initial matching grid $g'$ as predicted by the Kalman filter.
(2) Compute the initial energy $E(g)_{g \mapsto g'}$ for each pair $(g, g')$ using equation (4).
(3) For each grid $g$ and its matching grid $g'$, compute $\Delta E(f)_{g \to g''}$ for all $g'' \in O(g')$. If there exists a $g'' \in O(g')$ such that $\Delta E(f)_{g \to g''} < 0$ and $\Delta E(f)_{g \to g''}$ is the minimum amongst all $g'' \in O(g')$, then replace $g'$ with $g''$ as the mapping grid of $g$.
(4) Repeat step 3 until there is no change in the mapping $f$.

## 4 Object Parameter Updating and Occlusion Reasoning

After computation of the B-spline surface fit to the 2-D velocity field, the grid mapping is recomputed based on the B-spline surface representation. Suppose there are $n$ objects at time $t - 1$, where object $i$ is associated with a corresponding grid set $G_i^{t-1}$, $i = 1, ..., n$. By mapping $G_i^{t-1}$ to grid image $F_G$ at time $t$, the corresponding grid set $G_i^t$ can be recomputed such that for each grid in $G_i^t$, there is a corresponding grid in $G_i^{t-1}$.

In a multiple object tracking scenario, occlusion reasoning is invoked if several grids from different objects correspond to a single grid $g_i^t$. The occlusion analysis is based on the estimation of the conditional probabilities that the grid corresponds to each of the several objects. The grid is deemed to correspond to the object for which the conditional probability is maximized.

Suppose grid $g^t$ at time $t$ corresponds to $m$ grids $g_{k_i}^{t-1}$ at time $t-1$, where $0 \leq i < m$ and $0 \leq k_i < n$. Let $g_{k_i}^{t-1}$ be a grid associated with object $k_i$, that is $g_{k_i}^{t-1} \in G_{k_i}^{t-1}$. We assume that the color feature vector for each object $k_i$ at time $t$ exhibits a normal distribution $\mathcal{N}(c_{k_i}^{c,t-1}, \sigma_{k_i}^{t-1})$ with mean $c_{k_i}^{c,t-1}$ and standard deviation $\sigma_{k_i}^{t-1}$. The conditional probability that $g^t$ is the corresponding grid of object $k_i$ at time $t$ is $p(g^t|G_{k_i}^{t-1}) = \mathcal{N}(c^{c,t}|c_{k_i}^{c,t-1}, \sigma_{k_i}^{t-1})$. The grid $g^t$ is labeled as $k_i$ if the conditional probability $p(g^t|G_{k_i}^{t-1})$ is a maximum over all possible objects. However, this simple approach could result in incorrect labeling due to noise and inherent inaccuracies in the object model. To minimize such labeling errors, we exploit spatial coherence. For every grid labeled using the above procedure, we check its eight neighbors; if five or more of the eight neighboring grids have the same label $k_i$, we change the label of this grid to $k_i$. The occlusion parameter $o_{g_{k_i}}$ is set to 1 and $o_{g_{k_j}}$ is set to 0, where $0 \leq j < m$ and $j \neq i$.

After the grids within the confusion area are classified, the parameters of each non-occluded grid are updated. If the color feature of grid $g$ is $c^{c,t-1}$ with standard deviation $\sigma^{t-1}$ at time $t-1$, and the observed color feature at time $t$ is $c^{c',t}$ then the grid parameters are updated as $c^{c,t} = c^{c,t-1} + \rho(c^{c',t} - c^{c,t-1})$ and $(\sigma^t)^2 = (\sigma^{t-1})^2 + \rho[(c^{c',t}, -c^{c,t-1})(c^{c',t} - c^{c,t})^T - (\sigma^{t-1})^2]$ where $\rho = \alpha \mathcal{N}(c^{c',t}|c^{c,t-1}, \sigma^{t-1})$.

## 5 Experimental Results

The proposed tracking algorithm has been applied to various tracking scenarios. Figure 2(a) shows the snapshots of the tracking of a person bowing to reach the keyboard on the table. The dots in the figure represent the grids in the object model and hence the object shape. The tracking result shows that the proposed scheme can adapt to changes in the object shape. The set of video frames in Figure 2(b) show the results of simultaneous tracking of three persons in an indoor video taken with a static camera. All the three persons are continuously tracked and the tracking scheme is shown to be robust and resilient to occlusion. Videos depicting the above results and various other tracking results can be viewed at http://www.cs.uga.edu/~xingzhi/research/elastic/index.html.

(a) Object deformation  (b) Object occlusion

**Fig. 2.** Tracking under conditions of object deformation and occlusion

## 6 Conclusions

A novel multiple object tracking scheme based on Kalman filtering and elastic matching is proposed in this paper. The proposed scheme provides a general framework for tracking of both rigid and elastic objects. It can be viewed as a generalized Kalman filter where elastic matching is used to measure the velocity field which is then approximated (and smoothed) using B-spline surfaces. Control points of the B-spline surfaces are used directly as tracking variables in the Kalman filter. The limitation of the Gaussian distribution assumption in the Kalman filter is overcome by the large capture range of the elastic matching algorithm which can correct for the prediction errors made by the Kalman filter. The B-spline surfaces are used to update the grid-based object color features. The adaptation of the object color features is subsequently used in occlusion reasoning. Since the proposed tracking method does not rely on background subtraction, it is suitable for object tracking in dynamic scenes captured using both, a static camera and a moving camera.

## References

1. P. Li, T. Zhang and A.E.C.Pece, Visual contour tracking based on particle filters, *Img. Vis. Comput.*, Vol. 21, 2003, pp. 111-123.
2. M. Isard and J. MacCormick, BraMBLe: A Bayesian Multiple-Blob Tracker, *Proc. ICCV*, Vancouver, Canada, Vol. 2, July 2001, pp. 34-41.
3. S.J. McKenna, S. Jabri, Z. Duric, A. Rosenfeld and H. Wechsler, Tracking Groups of People, *CVIU*, Vol. 80, 2000, pp. 42-56.
4. K. Nummiaro, E. Koller-Meier and L.V. Gool, An adaptive color-based particle filter, *Img. Vis. Comput.*, Vol. 21, No. 1, 2003, pp. 99-110.
5. A. Blake, R. Curwen and A. Zisserman, A framework for spatio-temporal control in the tracking of visual contours, *IJCV*, Vol. 11, No. 2, 1993, pp. 127-145.
6. M. Lades, J. Vorbruggen, J. Buhmann, J. Lange, C.V.D. Malburg and R. Wurtz, Distortion Invariant Object Recognition in the Dynamic Link Architecture, *IEEE Trans. Comp.*, Vol. 42, No. 3, 1992, pp. 300-311.
7. M. Pietikainen, T. Maenpaa and J. Virtola, Color Texture Classification with Color Histogram and Local Binary Patterns, *Proc. 2nd Intl. Wkshp. Texture Anal. Synth.*, Copenhagen, UK, June 2002, pp. 109-112.
8. D. Koller, J.W. Weber and J. Malik, Robust Multiple Car Tracking with Occlusion Reasoning, *Proc. ECCV*, Stockholm, Sweden, 1994, pp. 189-196.
9. D. Terzopoulos and R. Szeliski, Tracking with Kalman Snakes, in *Active Vision*, MIT Press, Cambridge, MA, USA, 1993, pp. 3-20.
10. W.J.Rucklidge, Locating Objects Using the Hausdorff Distance, *Proc. ICCV*, Cambridge, MA, June, 1995, pp. 457-464.
11. C. Harris and M. Stephens, A Combined Corner And Edge Detector, *Proc. The Fourth Alvey Vision Conference*, Manchester, UK, 1988, pp. 147-151.
12. S. Malik, G. Roth and C. McDonald, Robust Corner Tracking for Real-Time Augmented Reality, *Proc. Vision Interface*, Calgary, Alberta, Cananda, May, 2002, pp. 399-406.
13. X. Huang, N. Paragios and D.N. Metaxas, Establishing Local Correspondences towards Compact Representations of Anatomical Structures, *6th Intl. Conf. MICCAI*, Montreal, Canada, November 2003, pp. 926-934.

# Singularity Detection and Consistent 3D Arm Tracking Using Monocular Videos

Feng Guo[1] and Gang Qian[1,2]

[1] Department of Electrical Engineering
[2] Arts, Media and Engineering Program,
Arizona State University, Tempe, AZ,85287, USA
{feng.guo, gang.qian}@asu.edu

**Abstract.** Singular (unobservable) movements pose major challenges for consistent 3D human arm tracking using monocular image sequences. In this paper, we present an efficient and robust method for the detection and tracking recovery from one of the singular movements: rotation about humerus with outstretched arm. In our approach using a particle filter for 3D arm tracking, movement constraints (i.e. range of arm joint angles) are not enforced in particle generation. Instead, singularity detection is achieved by looking for particles with joint angles violating these constraints. Once such a singular movement has been detected, inverse kinematics method is used to recover correct arm tracking by transferring invalid particles from unconstrained movement parameter space into valid constrained space. Experimental results have demonstrated the efficacy of our approach in terms of explicit singularity detection, fast recovery of tracking and small number of particles.

## 1 Introduction

3D arm tracking from monocular videos is one of the active research areas in human motion analysis. Due to the broad spectrum of applications, it has received much attention recently. Although arms are relatively simple articulated body parts, robust 3D tracking using a monocular video still poses a challenge.

In addition to general tracking challenges, such as cluttered background, (self-)occlusion, the existence of singular arm movements makes the problem even harder to solve [2]. Several 2D approaches [1,2] have been proposed to solve some of the 3D singularities, which are no longer singular in 2D approaches. However there are 3D singular movements which stay singular for 2D approaches, e.g. rotation about humerus with outstretched arm. In the presence of this type singular arm movements, the image observation such as image edges of the arm does not constrain the rotation of the upper arm. Particle filter has been applied in human motion tracking widely. While the standard particle filter uses multiple particles to sample the posterior distribution of the state space, it suffers from the problem of high dimensionality, which causes sample depletion in most of the state space. As a result, when a singular movement occurs, it is easy to lose track. Recovering lost tracking is difficult. Therefore particle filter requires a large number of particles to thoroughly sample the high dimensional state space effectively. There are several strategies for improving the efficiency of the samples. [3,4] use learned dynamical model to introduce constraints. [6,5] design efficient stochastic estimators for large state spaces. [7] exploits gradient-based search strategies to find local and global minimum structure.

However, to effectively handle singular movement, explicit steps need to be taken. In this paper, we present an efficient and robust method for the detection and tracking recovery from such singular movements, namely rotation about humerus with outstretched arm. The proposed method deploys the unconstrained samples to keep track of the arm in the image and transfers physically invalid samples to valid state space using inverse kinematics.

## 2  3D Arm Tracking Using a Particle Filter

In our tracking approach, the upper arm and forearm are modeled as truncated cones which are connected by the elbow joint. The state vector given by $\mathbf{X}_t = [\varphi_x, \varphi_y, \varphi_z, \varphi_e, T_x, T_y, T_z]^T$. It contains global configuration of the arm $[\varphi_x, \varphi_y, \varphi_z]$ and $[T_x, T_y, T_z]$ which respectively represent the rotation angles and translation of the upper arm coordinate system with the camera coordinate system. $\varphi_e$ is the relative rotation angle of forearm with upper arm.

The 3D arm model can be projected on image plane to generate predicted edges using joint angle samples. Here the method discussed in [8] is explored to obtain four straight lines as the projection edges.

A second order auto regressive process is used to model the dynamics. The dynamic equation is:

$$\begin{bmatrix} \mathbf{X}_t \\ \dot{\mathbf{X}}_t \end{bmatrix} = F \begin{bmatrix} \mathbf{X}_{t-1} \\ \dot{\mathbf{X}}_{t-1} \end{bmatrix} + V_t \tag{1}$$

where $\mathbf{X}_t$ is the state vector and $\dot{\mathbf{X}}_t$ is the velocity of the state vector. $F$ is dynamic matrix, process noise matrix is $V_t = [\mathbf{0}, v_i \mathbf{1}]^T$, where $v_i$ is angle velocity $\dot{x}_i$, following a Gaussian random variable with distribution $N(0, \sigma_i^2)$.

The likelihood based on arm configuration is $p_{image}(z_t|x_t^{(i)})$. Both the edge orientation and intensity of the detected edges are used to compute image likelihood. For one projection line, a set of independent normal lines are generated to measure the likelihood of detected edge points, as shown in Figure 1. Along each normal line, the detected edge points are located and the corresponding orientations are calculated. If the difference between edge orientation of the point

**Fig. 1.** Edge matching process

and the orientation of projected contour is less than a preselected threshold, the point is set as edge candidates. This will reduce the clutter noise from the image background. The resulting likelihood function is multi-modal. We combine the distance measure with edge intensity measure. Let $K$ be the number of peaks. For each peak, the distance similarity measure is given by:

$$p(z_k|c) = e^{-\frac{f^2(d_k;\mu)}{2\sigma^2}} \quad k = 1 \cdots K \quad (2)$$

where $f(d_k;\mu) = min(d(z_k,c),\mu)$, $d(z_k,c)$ is the distance of point $k$ to the projected contour $c$, $\mu$ controls the clutter-resistance of the tracker, $\sigma^2$ is the variance of model and input edge disparity.In these $K$ candidates, the relative weight of each candidate point can be obtained as $\pi_k = \frac{I_k}{N_m}, k = 1,\cdots,K$, where $I_k$ is the edge intensity value and $N_m$ is the normalization factor. Given the clutter probability, for each normal line $l$, the combined likelihood is obtained by

$$p^l(z_t|x_t^i) = \sum_{k=1}^{K} \pi_k p(z_k|c) + U(1 - \sum_{k=1}^{K} \pi_k) \quad (3)$$

where $U$ is uniform distribution,$1 - \sum_{k=1}^{K} \pi_k$ is background clutter probability,here we choose 0.05. The overall likelihood is

$$p_{image}(z_t|x_t^i) = \prod_{l=1}^{L} p^l(z_t|x_t^i) \quad (4)$$

where $L$ is the number of normal lines.

## 3 Singular Movement Detection and Tracking Recovery Through Physically Invalid Samples

In this section, we present an algorithm to explicitly detect the presence of one of the major singular movements: rotation about humerus with outstretched arm, and to recover tracking from such singular movements. This type of movements is singular because the projection lines of the arm are not affected by $\varphi_x$, rotation about humerus with outstretched arm, i.e., different $\varphi_x$ will create very similar edges in the image.

In [9], the Condensation algorithm was used to successfully track an arm through this kinematic singularity. However, in our experiments, we have found out that for Condensation algorithm to successfully track arm through such a singular movement, specific models of dynamic noises for each angle are needed. For example, dynamic noise with large covariance is needed for $\varphi_x$, to cover the gap in $\varphi_x$ before and after the singular movement. However, such movement-specified models are not suitable for general movements, since it will increase local uncertainty and will cause more ambiguity. Furthermore, even in the case of using this specific movement to handle such singular movement, the singularity detection is not straightforward. From the tracking results, it's hard to tell when a singular movement occurs and how long it lasts. These information might be useful for particular applications, e.g. in rehabilitation of stroke patients, when such a movement needs to be done during therapy and the patient's performance needed to be monitored. A large number of particles are needed to cover the necessary neighborhood in the state space when large dynamic noise is used. It consequently increases the computational intensity and makes real-time implementation difficult.

Anatomical kinematic constraints limit the joint movements. In traditional particle filter-based articulate limb tracking algorithms, these constraints are enforced to generate physically valid samples. For example, in [9], at regions close to the endstop (angle limits) in the valid state space, the state velocity was reversed proportionally to a reversal coefficient drawn from a uniform distribution. Thus all the samples are physically valid, i.e. within the possible state space defined by the physical anatomical limits. However, at the same time, as we will explain below, it also prohibits tracking recovery from singular movements.

Consider the scenario mentioned above, where $\varphi_x$ slowly changed with arm outstretched. Assume that $\varphi_x$ changed from one position to the others, namely from $\varphi_{x(a)}$ to $\varphi_{x(b)}$. Let the gap be $\Delta\varphi_x = \varphi_{x(b)} - \varphi_{x(a)}$ during the tracking. Assume that $\varphi_x$ is relatively large, say 60 degree. Since the change of $\varphi_x$ is unobservable in the image, nearly all entries in current samples corresponding to $\varphi_x$ will be far away from $\varphi_{x(b)}$, the true rotation angle when small dynamic noise is applied to $\varphi_x$. With the above anatomical constraints enforced in sample generation, the corresponding $\varphi_x$ in samples are way off from the ground truth. Consequently, tracking will fail right after the arm moves out of such a singularity. One way to solve this problem is to allow the existence of *physically-invalid samples* which can correctly track the arm profiles on the image plane and then transfer these invalid samples back to valid sample space later. Hence, tracking can be successfully recovered after singular movements. We apply this "unconstrained+transfer" strategy to our framework.

In our approach, we use the joint angle limits in a way similar to the one presented in [3], except that there is no hard upper bound applied in sample generation for the elbow angle $\varphi_e$. The physical range of $\varphi_e$ is $[\varphi_{e,min}, \pi]$, where $\varphi_{e,min}$ here is chosen as 15 degrees. When there is a predicted sample, with $\varphi_e$ out of this physical range, it will not be corrected immediately. Instead, these invalid samples will be utilized to keep track of the arm profiles on the image plane and the forearm distal point (i.e. the wrist) in the 3D space.

Once a physically-invalid sample has been used to track the arm, it then can be mapped or transferred back to the valid joint angle space. This step of sample transfer is done through inverse kinematics. First, forward kinematics is used to obtain the 3D position of shoulder, elbow and wrist from kinematic chain using the joint angle configuration in the invalid sample, since the 3D shape of the arm is known and modelled using connected truncated cones.

With these joints positions and rotation of initial position with respect to the camera coordinate system, similar to [10], we can infer the actual joint angles from the inverse kinematics, as shown in Figure 2.

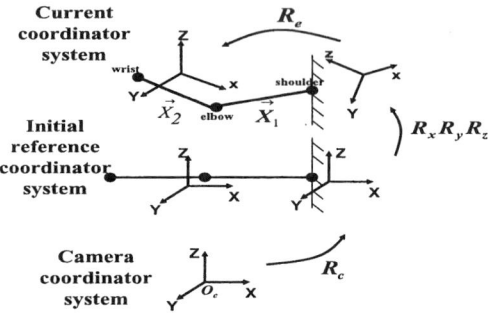

**Fig. 2.** Mapping using inverse kinematics

The elbow angle is the dot product of vector of $\vec{x}_1$ and $\vec{x}_2$, which are normalized vector along local $x$ axes direction. It should satisfy the inequality $\varphi_e > \Psi_{min}$. The rotation angle $\varphi_x$ of upper arm can be obtained using inverse kinematics. To calculate the shoulder rotation angles, we use a simple Euclidean coordinate transformation. Given previous coordinate rotation with initial reference system, we know vector $\vec{x}$ in camera coordinate system as $\vec{x}_1$ and current coordinate system as $[1 \ 0 \ 0]^T$. We can calculate the rotation for this vector from these two systems to previous coordinate system. And we can obtain the rotation angles $\varphi_y$ and $\varphi_z$. Different from [10] is that we only get one angle value for elbow angle and upper arm bone rotation angle. This is because we have joint constraints to set the angle in specific range.

Since singular movements are being handled explicitly in our approach in terms of the transfer of invalid samples into valid joint angle space, the probability of singularity can be computed directly. At time $t$, the probability of singularity $P_s(t)$ is given by

$$P_s(t) = \frac{\sum_{j \in T} w_t^j}{\sum_{i=1}^{N} w_t^i} \quad (5)$$

where $N$ is the total sample number and $T = \{j : x_t^j \text{ is mapped into valid space at time } t\}$.

## 4 Experimental Results

The current implementation is developed in C++ using a Pentium 4 3.0GHz PC running Windows XP. No optimization is attempted. The system runs at 5 frames/sec with 640 × 480 color image for 48 normal lines and 1000 samples. The video camera has been calibrated beforehand and the initial fit of the model to the first frame is done manually. The system tracks the right upper arm and forearm.

The proposed approach has been tested against the basic Condensation algorithm [9] using several video sequences.

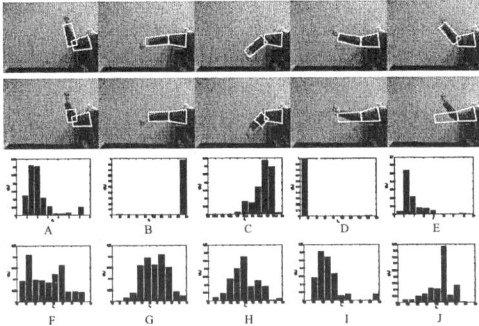

**Fig. 3.** Arm tracking with singular movement. The first row shows the tracking results using the proposed our approach and the second row shows the result using the basic Condensation algorithm. The third row is empirical posterior distribution of $\varphi_x$ using the proposed approach and forth row is results from the basic Condensation algorithm.

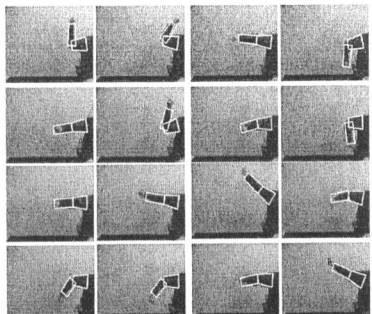 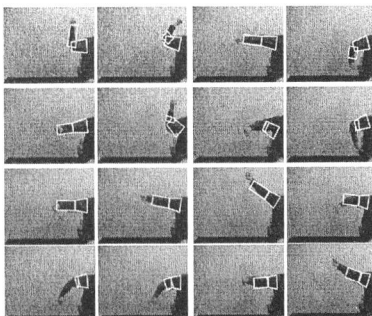

**Fig. 4.** (Left): Arm movements tracking results using the proposed approach with inverse kinematics mapping with 800 samples. (Right): Arm movements tracking using the Condensation algorithm with 1200 samples.

The first sequence has 500 frames. This sequence contains the singular movement discussed in this paper. Both approaches used 500 motion samples. As shown by figures in the first row of Figure 3, the proposed approach successfully tracked arm movements when the arm rotated with the elbow angle moving away from the singularity. However the basic Condensation algorithm tracked the first singularity but lost another one (the second row of Figure 3). Corresponding to the each image, empirical posterior distributions of $\varphi_x$ obtained using both approaches are shown in third and forth row in Figure 3. It can be seen that the $\varphi_x$ estimates obtained using our approach have less uncertainty than those from the Condensation algorithm when the arm moves out of singularity.

Figure 4 shows the tracking results using another sequence of 700 frames involving more complicated arm movement with several singular movement segments. Our approach(left part) can track the movements using only 800 samples,

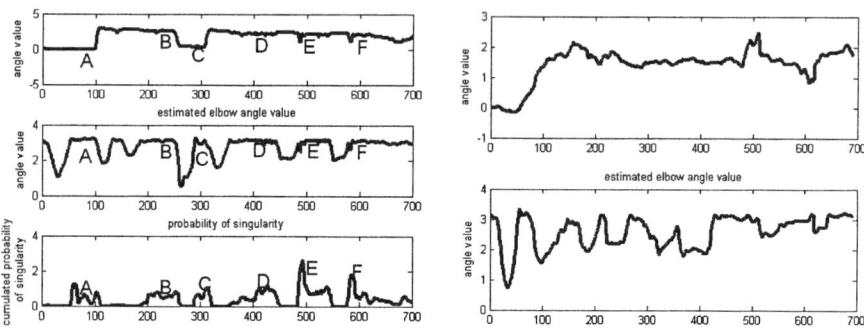

**Fig. 5.** (Left): The MMSE estimates of $\varphi_x$, $\varphi_e$ and cumulated probability of singularity obtained using our method. The top plot shows the estimates of $\varphi_x$, the middle one $\varphi_e$ and lower one cumulated probability of singularity. (Right):The MMSE estimates of $\varphi_x$ and $\varphi_e$ obtained using the Condensation. The first plot is the estimate of $\varphi_x$ and second one $\varphi_e$.

while basic Condensation (right part)will fail for some singularities and also has more ambiguities even with 1200 samples and increased noise for $\varphi_x$.

Figures 5 shows the minimum mean square error (MMSE) estimates (the mean of the empirical posterior distribution) of $\varphi_x$ and $\varphi_e$ using the two approaches. In addition, the third row of left part gives the cumulated probability of singularity of the movement. It is the sum of instantaneous probability of singularity over a window. Here we use window size $s = 10$ frames. We can observe that the shoulder angle $\varphi_x$ changes quickly near the singularity in our method(left). While for Condensation algorithm, the shoulder angle $\varphi_x$ changes gradually(right).

The accurate detection of the presence of singular movement is of great importance, as mentioned above, e.g. in rehabilitation of stroke patients. Using Condensation algorithms, one can only roughly tell its presence by looking for movement segments with outstretched arm ($\varphi_e$ close to $\pi$) and changing $\varphi_x$ in the estimates. It is not quantitative and not accurate either. In our approach, the probability of singularity can be computed by looking at the weights of transferred invalid samples. Moreover, during a singular movement, one expects the invalid samples transferred gradually over a period of time. Therefore, the continuous nonzero value of probability of singularity in a small window strongly indicated the presence of singularity. The cumulated probability of singularity over this window is the probability of singularity of this movement segment. In this sequence, there are totally six singular movements, indicated by segments"A", "B", "C", "D", "E", and "F" in Figure 5 left part. They in turn correspond to left part images in Figure 4. "A" relates to the first row, "B" the left two images of the second row, "C" the right two images of the second row, "D" the left two images of the third row, "E" the right two images of the third row and "F" the last row. In the computed cumulated probability of singularity, we see that these singular movement segments are all related to continuous nonzero regions.

## 5 Conclusion

We have presented an efficient and robust for the detection of arm tracking recovery from one of the singular movements: rotation about humerus. In our approach using a particle filter for 3D arm tracking, movement constraints (i.e. range of arm joint angles) are not enforced in particle generation. Instead, singularity detection is achieved by looking for particles with joint angles violating these constraints. Once such a singular movement has been detected, inverse kinematics method is used to recover correct arm tracking by transferring invalid particles from unconstrained movement parameter space into valid constrained space. Experimental results have demonstrated the efficacy of our approach in terms of explicit singularity detection, fast recovery of tracking and small number of particles.

## References

1. S.X.Ju,M.J.Black,and Y.Yacoob, "Cardboard people: A parameterized model of articulated motion," *2nd Int. Conf. on Automatic Face- and Gesture-Recognition*, pp.38-44, Killington, VT, Oct 1996.
2. James M.Rehg, Daniel D.Morris and Takeo Kanade, "Ambiguities in visual tracking of articulated objects using two- and three-dimensional models," *The International Journal of Robotics Research*, Vol.22, No.6, Jun 2003,pp.393 - 418.
3. H.Sidenbladh, M.Black and D.Fleet, "Stochastic Tracking of 3D Human Figures Using 2D Image Motion," *In ECCV*, 2000
4. H.Sidenbladh, M.Black and L.Sigal., "Implicit Probabilistic Models of Human Motion for Synthesis and Tracking," *In ECCV*, 2002
5. J. Deutscher, A.Blake and I.Reid., "Articulated Body Motion Capture by Annealed Particle Filtering,", *CVPR* Vol.2, pp.126-133, 2000
6. J.MacCormick, M.Isard., " Partitioned Sampling,Articulated Objectes and Interface-quality Hand Tracking," *ECCV*,Vol.2,pp.3-19, 2000
7. C. Sminchisescu and B.Triggs.,"Covariance Scaled Sampling for Monocular 3D Body Tracking," *CVPR*, Vol.1, pp.447-454, 2001
8. B. Stenger, *Model-Based Hand Tracking Using A Hierarchical Bayesian Filter* University of Cambridge, St. Johns College, 2004
9. J.Deutscher, B.North, B.Bascle and A.Blake, "Tracking through Singularities and Discontinuities by Random Sampling," *ICCV*,pp.1144-1149, 1999
10. C. Sminchisescu and B.Triggs.,"Kinematic Jump Processes for Monocular 3D Human Tracking" *CVPR*, Vol.1, pp.69-77, 2003

# Predictive Estimation Method to Track Occluded Multiple Objects Using Joint Probabilistic Data Association Filter

Heungkyu Lee[1] and Hanseok Ko[2]

[1] Dept. of Visual Information Processing,
[2] Dept. of Electronics and Computer Engineering,
Korea University, Seoul, Korea
hklee@ispl.korea.ac.kr, hsko@korea.ac.kr

**Abstract.** In multi-target visual tracking, tracking failure due to miss-association can often arise from the presence of occlusions between targets. To cope with this problem, we propose the predictive estimation method that iterates occlusion prediction and occlusion status update using occlusion activity detection by utilizing joint probabilistic data association filter in order to track each target before, during and after occlusion. First, the tracking system predicts the position of a target, and occlusion activity detection is performed at the predicted position to examine if an occlusion activity is enabled. Second, the tracking system re-computes positions of occluded targets and updates them if an occlusion activity is enabled. Robustness of multi-target tracking using predictive estimation method is demonstrated with representative simulations.

## 1 Introduction

In automatic visual object tracking such as autonomous vehicle navigation, human interface, traffic monitoring, and surveillance [1], it is desirable to track multiple objects simultaneously, while their motion is continuously analyzed [2][3][4]. Especially, the visual surveillance of human activity requires complex tracking algorithms because of the unpredictable situations, which occur whenever multiple peoples are moving, stopping, and interacting with each other. Human actions within the field of view have no consistent rules concerning their movement. When multiple peoples are interacting with each other, a variety of events can occur such as occlusion, partial occlusion or short-time stopping. However, Some tracking algorithms have a weakness according to the given specific situation such as occlusions between targets.

To overcome the weakness in occlusion time, following issues can be considered. First, the prediction about the occlusion activity of moving blobs should be done to predict occlusion occurrence and to associate them with real targets respectively. Second, the decision logic that identifies an occluded object should be supported with high reliability. For associating an occluded target, partial information can be used by inspecting the overlapping region of occluded object in the predicted position.

Thus, we propose the predictive estimation method that iterates prediction and update procedures of target position information by utilizing joint probabilistic data association (JPDA) filter to track each target before, during and after occlusion [5][6]. First, the tracking system predicts the position of a target and occlusion activity detection is performed at the predicted position to examine if an occlusion activity is enabled. Second, the tracking system re-computes positions of occluded targets and updates them if an occlusion activity is enabled. In previous work [5], the limitation of some multi-target tracking algorithm using the JPDA is not specified in occlusion time because they does not refer necessary condition for constructing the validation matrix in JPDA filter. This assumes that a moving blob can have only one source, and no more than one moving blob can originate from one person [6]. Thus, accurate position of each object even in the occlusion time should be recomputed. To do this, our proposed occlusion predictor enables to re-compute the semi-accurate position at the predicted position. In addition, general Kalman tracking algorithm has only an iterative innovation and prediction procedure to pursue a target trajectory, while we perform the occlusion reasoning procedure by comparing region occupancy in predicted position as an extra task with iterative innovation and prediction.

The content of this paper is as follows. In Section 2, we propose predictive estimation method to track multi-targets reliably using joint probabilistic data association filter. In Section 3, we show the result and analysis of multi-target tracking using the proposed method. Finally, concluding remarks are presented in Section 4.

## 2  Predictive Estimation to Track Multi-targets

We assume that we found the moving blobs from image sequences, and performed data alignment in image coordinates. In addition, it is important for any data representation to contain a measure of the quality of data. If a sensor is operating reasonably well, it is expected that the acquired data will be within the explicit accuracy bounds. For doing this, we present a set of minimum bounding rectangles (MBR) employing "object range" and "validation region", as a means to represent the position, size and region of a target as feature vectors for describing the accuracy bound and range.

### 2.1  Track Initialization

Prior to tracking using selected features for preceded processes, a track initialization step is necessary while the object's kinematics model needs to be determined [6]. In order to model the kinematics of moving objects, representative parameters and expressions are defined as follows. Let $o = [o_1, o_2, ..., o_M]$ denote the set of objects to track, $\varphi$ denotes the movement directions for object $o_i$ and $x=[\ x_i\ ,\ y_i\ ]^T$ denote the vector of points of center corresponding to $o_i$, with $v = [\ \dot{x}_i, \dot{y}_i\ ]^T$, where $\dot{x}_i$ and $\dot{y}_i$ denote the derivative of $x_i$ and $y_i$ with respect to $t$, respectively. The Kanade-Lucas tracking equation (1) is differentiated with respect to time $t$ as follows.

$$\mathbf{v} = G^{-1}e \quad , \quad \dot{\mathbf{v}} = \frac{d\mathbf{v}}{dt} = -G^{-1}(\Sigma \mathbf{v} + u^e) \tag{1}$$

where $G = \int_W gg^T \omega dA$, $e = \int_W (I(\mathbf{x},t) - I(\mathbf{x},t+\tau))g\omega dA$, $\Sigma = \frac{d}{dt}G$, $u^e = \frac{d}{dt}e$

The movement directions among features of the object are also computed using motion vectors extracted by the optical flow method. To obtain the movement directions of objects, we first compute the direction of motion vector for each pixel located in the area of the object. The direction $\varphi$ of the vector is defined as follows:

$$\varphi(rad) = angle(\frac{v_y}{v_x}) \qquad 0 \leq \varphi < 2\pi \tag{2}$$

$$= \{\varphi \mid \sin\varphi = v_y/\|\mathbf{v}\|\} \cap \{\varphi \mid \cos\varphi = v_x/\|\mathbf{v}\|\} \cap \{\varphi \mid \tan\varphi = v_y/v_x\}$$

where $v_x$ and $v_y$ are motion vectors in moving objects for x and y direction respectively, and $\|\mathbf{v}\| = \sqrt{v_x^2 + v_y^2}$. From Equation (2) of direction $\varphi$, we know $\dot{x} = \|\mathbf{v}\|\cos\varphi$ and $\dot{y} = \|\mathbf{v}\|\sin\varphi$. The equations are differentiated with respect to $t$ as follows.

$$\frac{d}{dt}\varphi = -\frac{1}{\|\mathbf{v}\|\sin\varphi}\ddot{x} = \frac{1}{\|\mathbf{v}\|\cos\varphi}\ddot{y} = \frac{1}{2\|\mathbf{v}\|}(\frac{1}{\cos\varphi}\ddot{y} - \frac{1}{\sin\varphi}\ddot{x}) \tag{3}$$

Using Equations (2) and (3), the proposed system model is given by

$$\dot{s} = \Psi s + \Pi u^e + v \qquad v \sim N(0,Q) \tag{4}$$

$$\Psi = \begin{bmatrix} O_{2\times 2} & I_2 & O_{2\times 2} & O_{2\times 1} \\ O_{2\times 2} & -G^{-1}\Sigma & O_{2\times 2} & O_{2\times 1} \\ O_{2\times 2} & O_{2\times 2} & O_{2\times 2} & O_{2\times 1} \\ O_{1\times 2} & O_{1\times 2} & \frac{1}{2\|\mathbf{v}\|}[-\csc\varphi \quad \sec\varphi] & 0 \end{bmatrix}, \Pi = \begin{bmatrix} O_{2\times 2} \\ -G^{-1}I_2 \\ O_{2\times 2} \\ O_{1\times 2} \end{bmatrix} \tag{5}$$

where $O_{m \times n}$ is an $m \times n$ zero matrix, $I_m$ is an $m \times m$ identity matrix and $s = [x^T, v^T, a^T\ \varphi]^T$ denote the system state, which is composed of center points, velocity, acceleration and direction of moving object. In the proposed method, the acceleration component in state vector is included to cope with maneuvering of object. The model assumes random acceleration with covariance $Q$, which accounts for changes in image velocity. As the eigenvalues of $Q$ become larger, old measurements are given relatively low weight in the adjustment of state. This allows the system to adapt to changes in the object velocity. Since time interval $\Delta t$ between one frame and next is very small, it is assumed that $F$ is constant over the $(t_k, t_{k+1})$ interval of interest. The state transition matrix is simply given by

$$F_k = e^{\Psi \Delta t} = \begin{bmatrix} I_2 & I_2\Delta t & \frac{\Delta t^2}{2}I_2 & O_{2\times 1} \\ O_{2\times 2} & I_2 - G^{-1}\Sigma\Delta t & O_{2\times 2} & O_{2\times 1} \\ O_{2\times 2} & O_{2\times 2} & I_2 & O_{2\times 1} \\ O_{1\times 2} & O_{1\times 2} & \frac{\Delta t}{2\|\mathbf{v}\|}[-\csc\varphi \quad \sec\varphi] & 1 \end{bmatrix} \tag{6}$$

Let $z = [z_1, z_2, ..., z_M]$ and $z_i$ denote the measurement vector for object $o_i$. In the proposed model, center points and movement directions for each object are treated as system measurements. The measurement vector satisfies:

$$z_i = Hs + w \quad w \sim N(0, R) \tag{7}$$

$$H = \begin{bmatrix} 1 & 0 & 0 & 0 & 0 & 0 & 0 \\ 0 & 1 & 0 & 0 & 0 & 0 & 0 \\ 0 & 0 & 0 & 0 & 0 & 0 & 1 \end{bmatrix}$$

where matrix $H$ connects the relationship between $z_i$ and $s$. After all, the object kinematics model is determined by setting the appropriate parameters.

### 2.2 Predictive Estimation Using Occlusion Activity Detection

The purpose of occlusion activity detection is to provide the current status of occlusion between objects, which are just labeled blobs of a blob detection level. According to the occlusion status, a countermeasure to reliably track can be applied. We assumed that occluded objects from the first time have not appeared, and the objects are non-rigid. The predictive estimation procedure is as follows.

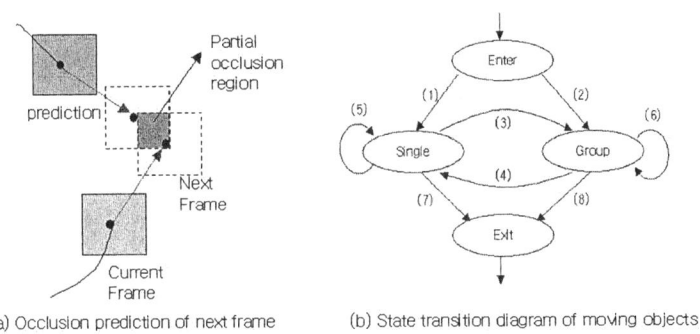

(a) Occlusion prediction of next frame  (b) State transition diagram of moving objects

**Fig. 1.** Occlusion prediction method using predicted position information

### - STEP 1: Occlusion Prediction Stage

This step predicts the next positions (centroids) of blobs employing the Kalman prediction model used in JPDAF [6] as in (a) of Figure 1:

$$\widehat{X}(k+1/k) = F(k)\widehat{X}(k/k) + u(k) \tag{8}$$

where $X(k+1/k)$ is the state vector at time $k+1$ given cumulative measurements to time $k$, $F(k)$ is a transition matrix, and $u(k)$ is a sequence of zero-mean, white Gaussian process noise. Using the predicted position computed at equation (8), we can determine the redundancy of objects within the field of view using the intersection measure. The decision of the occlusion is computed by comparing if or not there is an overlapping region between the validation regions, $MBR_i$ in the predicted center points as follows.

$$F_{oc} \begin{cases} 1 & \text{if } (MBR_i \cap MBR_j) \neq \phi \\ 0 & \text{otherwise} \end{cases}, \text{ where } i, j = 1,...,m \qquad (9)$$

where $F_{oc}$ is an occlusion alarm flag, the subscript $i$ and $j$ are the index of the detected target at the current frame, and $m$ is a number of a target. If a redundant region has occurred at the predicted position, the probability of occlusion occurrence in the next step will be increased. Therefore, the occlusion alarm flag is set to 1.

(a) occluded people; example 1

(b) Validation region using occlusion reasoning; result of (a)

(c) occluded people; example 2

(d) Validation region using occlusion reasoning; result of (c)

**Fig. 2.** Validation region using occlusion reasoning

**- STEP 2: Update Stage of Occlusion Status**

In the current frame, the occlusion status is updated to decide the occlusion occurrence. The first time, the size of the labeled blobs is verified whether they are contained within the validation region or not. If the size of labeled blobs is contained within the validation region, the occlusion status flag is disabled. Otherwise, the occlusion alarm flag is set to 1, we can conclude that the occlusion has occurred at the region, and the occlusion status is enabled. At this time, from the predicted center points of the previous step, we apply the predicted position to the system and predicted MBR is recomputed as in Figure 2. Then, the Kalman gain is computed and the measurement equation is updated. In addition, the process transition mode is changed as in (b) of Figure 1.

### 2.3 Data Association Between Moving Blobs and Real Targets

Similarly to the PDA algorithm, the JPDA algorithm computes the probabilities of association of only the latest set of measurements $Z(k)$ to the various targets [6]. The key to the JPDA algorithm is the evaluation of the conditional probabilities of the following joint association events pertaining to the current time k.

$$\Theta = \bigcap_{j=1}^{m_k} \theta_{jt_j} \quad (10)$$

where $\theta_{jt}$ is measurement $j$ originated from target $t$ ($j=1,...,M_k$, $t=0,...,T$) and $m$ is a number of a target and subscript $k$ is the current time. We employ the process state transition model to differently cope with occlusion status according to the state transition mode as in (b) of Figure 1. (1) A specific target enters into the scene. (2) Multiple targets enter into the scene. (3) A specific target is moving and forms a group with other targets, or just moves beside other targets or obstacles. (4) A specific target within the group leaves a group. (5) A specific target continues to move alone, or stops moving and then starts to move again. (6) Multiple targets in a group continue to move and interact between them, or stop interacting and then start to move again. (7) (8) A specific target or a group leaves a scene. The events of (1), (4), (5), and (7) can be tracked using general Kalman tracking. In addition, the events of (2), (3), (6) and (8) can be tracked reliably using predictive estimation method.

Figure 3 shows the final tracking flow incorporating the state transition model. It performs predictive estimation steps using occlusion prediction and update by utilizing the Kalman filter.

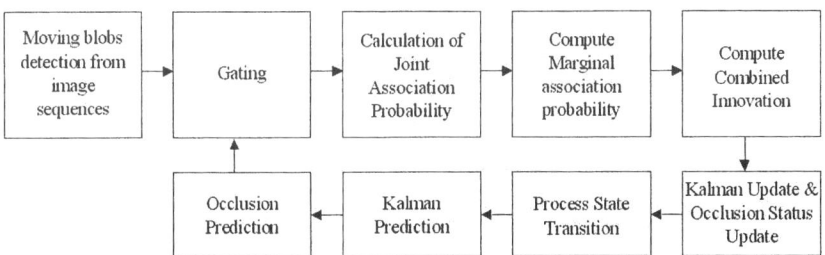

**Fig. 3.** Flow of multi-target tracking using JPDA

## 3 Experimental Results

The tracking scheme was tested on real image sequences to assess its capabilities for tracking multiple moving targets (two people) in complex road scenes. Two different road scenes with increasing complexity were considered. This system is more efficient to multiple tracking under problems of tracking adjacent, overlapped targets and crossing targets than those related to the system described in [2][3] and [4]. This system addresses the problem of occlusions in tracking multiple 3-D objects in a known environment by employing predictive estimation and data association. It is used to solve the problem of tracking adjacent, overlapped targets and crossing targets.

Obtained images were sampled at video rate : example 1 (total 640 frames, 15 frames per seconds, and its size is 240×320) and example 2 (total 570 frames, 15 frames per seconds, and its size is 240×320) which is a gray level image. In the initial value of the JPDA algorithm to track multi-targets in Figure 4, the process noise variance = 10 and the measurement noise variance = 25 are used. The initial position value of two people are set to A(17, 60), B(254,147) and A(16,115), B(108,215) in Cartesian coordinates. The object A moved from the left-bottom to the right-top, and the object B moved from the right-center to the left-center in example 1. In example 2, the object A moved from left to right and the object B moved from top to bottom. An occlusion state is maintained for 34, 24 frames. We assumed that we knew the size of a target to track within field of view. Assumed size of target is set with the following parameters: validation region is (100 pixel, 60~150 pixel) in example 1. In example 2, validation region is (100~120 pixel, 60~170 pixel).

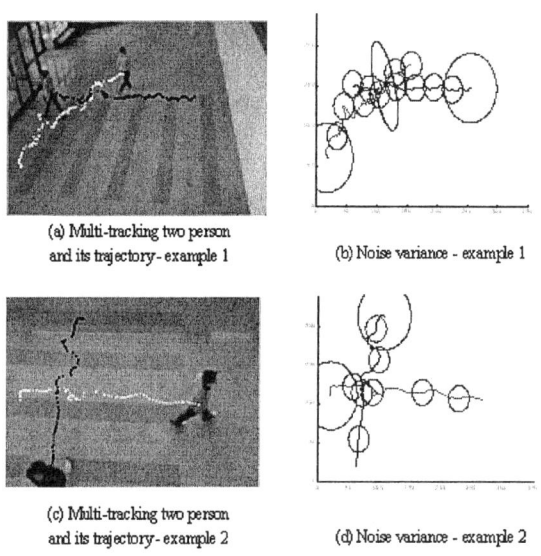

(a) Multi-tracking two person and its trajectory - example 1

(b) Noise variance - example 1

(c) Multi-tracking two person and its trajectory - example 2

(d) Noise variance - example 2

**Fig 4.** Multi-target tracking of two persons using JPDAF: (a) and (c) show the trajectories of tracking two people. (b) and (d) show ellipses to represent noise variance.

Robustness has been evaluated mainly in terms of location accuracy and error rate of feature extraction and capability to track under occlusion in complex load scenes. The table 1 is an error rate that extracted blobs are not targets within field of view. It is computed as

$$\varepsilon = \frac{1}{N} \sum_{k=1}^{N} \frac{|N_f - N_0|}{N_0} \quad (11)$$

where $N$ is number of frames, $N_f$ is number of extracted feature sets at frame $k$, and $N_0$ is number of moving objects at frame $k$.

**Table 1.** Simulation results of test image sequences

| Error Rate($\varepsilon$) | Error Rate of Feature Extraction | | |
|---|---|---|---|
| | Data association is only applied. | Predictive Estimation without data association is applied | Predictive Estimation with data association is applied. |
| Example 1 | 42.8549 | 15.8805 | 0.7862 |
| Example 2 | 14.2241 | 6.5621 | 0.4241 |

The result of blob decision through gating and occlusion reasoning has a smallest error rate. When occlusion activity is enabled, coupled objects are isolated using predictive estimation and each of the position of the two objects is re-computed. The computed position value is inputted to the state measurement equation within a JPDA algorithm, and then proposed system tracked two people reliably.

## 4 Conclusions

In this paper, we proposed the predictive estimation method using occlusion predictor and the JPDA filter to remedy occlusion problems and to associate the relationship between moving blobs and real targets. When using the JPDA filter for multi-target tracking, the necessary condition for constructing the validation matrix should be satisfied. This filter assumes that a moving blob can have only one source, and no more than one moving blob can originate from one person. Thus, accurate position of each object even in the occlusion time should be recomputed. To do this, our proposed occlusion predictor enabled to re-compute the semi-accurate position at the predicted position. In addition, general Kalman tracking algorithm has only an iterative innovation and prediction procedure to pursue a target trajectory, while we performed the occlusion reasoning procedure by comparing region occupancy in predicted position as an extra task with iterative innovation and prediction procedure.

## Acknowledgements

This work was supported by grant No. 10012805 from the Korea Institute of Industrial Technology Evaluation & Planning Foundation.

## References

[1] Haritaoglu, I, Harwood, D, Davis, L.S, "Hydra: multiple people detection and tracking using silhouettes" Visual Surveillance, Second IEEE Workshop on, pp 6 -13, June 1999.
[2] S. J. McKenna, S. jabri and Z. Duric, A. Rosenfeld, H. Wechsler "Tracking Groups of people", Computer Vision and Image Understanding, pp42-56, 2000.
[3] Wenmiao Lu, Yap-Peng Tan, "A color histogram based people tracking system", Circuits and Systems, The 2001 IEEE International Symposium on , pp 137 -140, May 2001.

[4] Romer Rosales and Stan Sclaroff, "3D Trajectory Recovery for Tracking Multiple Objects and Trajectory Guided Recognition of Actions", In Proc of IEEE on Computer Vision and Pattern Recognition, June 1999.
[5] Rasmussen, C, Hager, G.D, "Joint probabilistic techniques for tracking multi-part objects", Computer Vision and Pattern Recognition, Proceedings. IEEE Computer Society Conference on, pp 16 -21, June 1998.
[6] Y. Bar-Shalom and X. R. Li, Multitarget-multisensor tracking: principles and techniques, YBS Press, 1995.

# A Model-Based Hematopoietic Stem Cell Tracker

Nezamoddin N. Kachouie[1], Paul Fieguth[1], John Ramunas[2], and Eric Jervis[2]

[1] Department of Systems Design Engineering,
[2] Department of Chemical Engineering,
University of Waterloo, Waterloo, Canada
nnezamod@engmail.uwaterloo.ca, pfieguth@uwaterloo.ca,
johnramunas@yahoo.com, ejervis@cape.uwaterloo.ca
http://ocho.uwaterloo.ca

**Abstract.** A better understanding of cell behavior is very important in drug and disease research. Cell size, shape, and motility may play a key role in stem-cell specialization or cancer development. However the traditional method of inferring these values manually is such an onerous task that automated methods of cell tracking and segmentation are in high demand. Image cytometry is a practical approach to measure and extract cell properties from large volumes of microscopic cell images. As an important application of image cytometry, this paper presents a probabilistic model based cell tracking method to locate and associate HSCs in phase contrast microscopic images. The proposed cell tracker has been successfully applied to track HSCs based on the most probable identified cell locations and probabilistic data association.

## 1 Introduction

One of the most important and common tasks for biomedical researchers is cell tracking, which continues to be undertaken manually. Researchers visually perform cell motion analysis and observe cell movement or changes in cell shape for hours to discover when, where and how fast a cell moves, splits or dies. This task is tedious and painful due to the often corrupted or blurred images, the presence of clutter, fixing eyes for a long time, and repeating the same task for different cell types. Furthermore, with the extent of cell imaging data ever increasing, manual tracking becomes progressively impractical. As a result, automated cell tracking systems are mandatory to further advance the study of biological cells. Such a tracking system will require automatic object tracking, usually under challenging conditions

A variety of semi-automatic or automatic methods have been proposed to segment cell boundaries [1,2,3]. These methods include thresholding, watershed, nearest neighborhood graphs, mean shift procedure and deformable models. Overall, these can be divided into three major categories: *boundary based*, *region based*, and *thresholding*.

Markiewicz et al [4] have used watershed for the segmentation of bone marrow cells. Thresholding methods have been used by Wu [5] and Glasbey [6]. Different

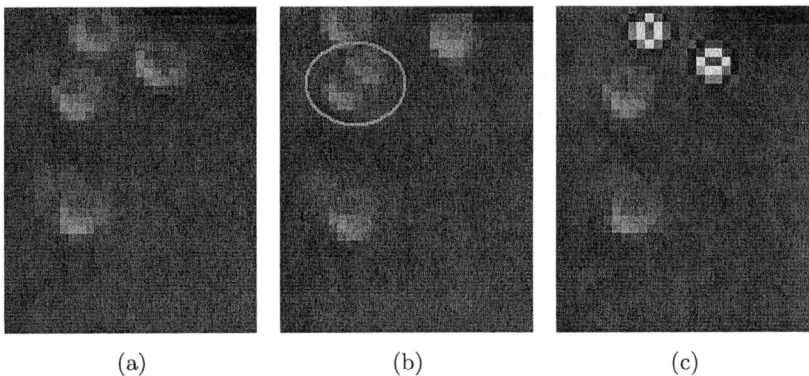

**Fig. 1.** (a) Phase contrast microscope image. (b) A mature cell is splitting. (c) Cell model superimposed on original HSC image.

techniques have been used for choosing a suitable threshold, such as calculating the image variance to separate the cell from the background [5], assuming the intensity of the background to be uniform with a low variance while cell intensity variance is high. Comaniciu et al [7] proposed a mean shift procedure method for cell image segmentation for diagnostic pathology. Geusebroek et al [8] introduced a method based on Nearest Neighbor Graphs to segment the cell clusters. Meas-Yedid et al [9] proposed a method to quantify the deformation of cells using snakes.

Due to the large number of cell types having different features such as shape, size, motility, and proliferation rate, designing a universal cell tracking system is impractical. In this paper, we focus on Hematopoietic Stem Cells (HSCs), which proliferate and differentiate to different blood cell types continuously during their lifetime, and are of substantial interest in gene therapy, cancer, and stem-cell research. A novel cell tracking system is developed based on a probabilistic cell model which effectively detect cells and a joint probabilistic data association which associate detected cells over time.

## 2 Proposed Model-Based Cell Tracking

As a crucial step towards fully automatic cell tracking, an effective cell localization/segmentation method is needed. To keep cells alive and dynamically active, light exposure must be controlled during their life cycle. The limited light exposure and cell transparency both contribute to the very low contrast, moreover most of the cell staining techniques which are used to increase the contrast between cell areas and background undesirably stain different parts of a tissue unevenly, causing inhomogeneity. Fortunately the HSCs in our study have a fairly regular shape and brightness pattern. Hence, a segmentation method which exploits this useful information should be able to perform better than simple thresholding.

## 2.1 Cell Image Model

HSCs must be prepared befor imaging. HSC sample preparation is a two stage process:

1. Extract and process mouse bone marrow.
2. Process and culture the HSCs.

After preparation HSCs are imaged using manual focusing through a 5X phase contrast objective using a digital camera (Sony XCD-900). Images are acquired every three minutes. When a cell division is observed, the progeny are imaged at higher magnification using a 40X DIC objective. A typical HSC phase contrast image is depicted in Fig. 1.

From Fig. 1 we observe that HSCs can be characterized as an approximately circular object with a dark interior and a bright boundary. During splitting, a mature cell is divided to give birth to two new cells, as marked by a circle in Fig. 1(b). The radius of these new cells is slightly smaller than that of their parent. The phase contrast imaging technique leads to an asymmetric cell boundary, one side dark and the other side bright. So rather than a heuristic thresholding approach, the specific, consistent cell attributes observed should allow us to formulate a far more specific model, essentially a matched filter, to be more robust to noise and low contrast. We propose to consider the following criteria: *Cell size*, *Boundary brightness*, *Interior brightness*, and *Boundary uniformity or symmetry*. These criteria are combined to formulate the probability of a cell in image $I_k$ at location $(x_c, y_c)$ and radius $r$

$$P(x_c, y_c, r | I_k) = P_{cb}(\bar{B}(x_c, y_c, r)) \cdot P_{ic}(\bar{B}(x_c, y_c, \frac{r}{2})) \cdot P_{cdf}(D(cdf(B))) \quad (1)$$

where the meanings of the individual terms $P_{cb}$, $P_{ic}$ and $P_{cdf}$ will be elaborated in the following sections.

## 2.2 Probability of Cell Boundary $P_{cb}$

As depicted in Fig. 1(c), to model a dark region surrounded by a bright boundary, the proposed cell model consists of two concentric circles, with the radius of the internal circle being half of that of the external one. The external circle represents the bright boundary while the internal one represents the dark region inside a cell. Assuming $(x_c, y_c)$ and $r$ as center coordinates and radius of the exterior circle respectively, the continuous circle is discretized spatially as

$$|(x_i - x_c)^2 + (y_i - y_c)^2 - r^2| \leq \epsilon^2, \quad (2)$$

where $(x_i, y_i)$ are coordinates of circle boundary pixels and $\epsilon$ is half a pixel. Function $B_i(x_c, y_c, r)$, which is a vector returning the intensity of all boundary pixels, is defined as

$$B_i(x_c, y_c, r) = \{I(x_i, y_i), |(x_i - x_c)^2 + (y_i - y_c)^2 - r^2| \\ \leq \epsilon^2 \text{ and } i = 1, 2, ..., N\}, \quad (3)$$

where $N$ is the total number of pixels located on the cell boundary. In our implementation, a rotation angle of 20° is adopted, and the total number of boundary pixels ($N$) is equal to 18. The probability of cell boundary $P_{cb}$ is assumed to be Gaussian with mean $\mu_{cb}$ and variance $\sigma_{cb}^2$

$$P_{cb}(\bar{B}(x_c, y_c, r)) \sim N(\mu_{cb}, \sigma_{cb}^2), \tag{4}$$

where $\bar{B}(x_c, y_c, r)$ is the average cell boundary intensity

$$\bar{B}(x_c, y_c, r) = \frac{\sum_{i=1}^{N} B_i(x_c, y_c, r)}{N}. \tag{5}$$

### 2.3 Probability of Cell Interior $P_{ic}$

The interior dark region of a cell is represented by the internal circle in the proposed model. Assuming $(x_c, y_c)$ and $\frac{r}{2}$ as center coordinates and radius of the interior circle, it is discretized as

$$|(x_i - x_c)^2 + (y_i - y_c)^2 - \frac{r^2}{2}| \leq \epsilon^2. \tag{6}$$

The probability of dark region inside the cell $P_{ic}$ is assumed to be another Gaussian distribution with mean $\mu_{ic}$ and variance $\sigma_{ic}^2$

$$P_{ic}(\bar{B}(x_c, y_c, \frac{r}{2})) \sim N(\mu_{ic}, \sigma_{ic}^2), \tag{7}$$

where $\bar{B}(x_c, y_c, \frac{r}{2})$ is the average intensity of cell interior region.

### 2.4 Probability of Uniformity of Cell Boundary $P_{cdf}$

Despite having an asymmetric boundary, both dark and bright sides of the cell boundary maintain almost uniform intensities. To maximize the likelihood of cell detection, an empirical cumulative density function (CDF) is calculated to discriminate uniform background from the cell boundary. The CDF on cell boundary pixel intensities is computed by

$$cdf_n(\bar{B}(x_c, y_c, r)) = \frac{\sum_{i=1}^{n} B_i(x_c, y_c, r)}{N \cdot \bar{B}(x_c, y_c, r)}, \quad n \in 1:N \tag{8}$$

A distance function $D(cdf)$ is defined to find the maximum non uniformity of cell boundary, i.e., the maximum cumulative distance of cell boundary intensities from local mean:

$$D(cdf) = \max_{n \in [1:N]} |cdf_n - \frac{n}{N}| \tag{9}$$

An exponential function $P_{cdf}(D)$ is used to penalize the non uniformity in cell boundary:

$$P_{cdf}(D) = \exp\{-2 \cdot N \cdot D(cdf)\} \tag{10}$$

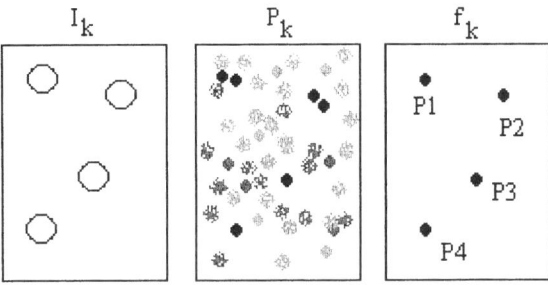

**Fig. 2.** Measurement hypothesis for frame $k$ which is generated based on image frame $k$ ($I_k$) by thresholding the local maxima map

### 2.5 HSC Tracking

A joint probabilistic data association (JPDA) method is proposed to solve the object tracking problem. A probability map is obtained by applying the cell model to the microscope image. The measurements are inferred from the input microscope image by finding the local maxima in the probability map and thresholding the local maxima map. As depicted in Fig. 2 the local maxima which are at least $\delta D$ apart in the probability map $P_k$ are located and the generated local maxima map is thresholded to obtain a set $S_{\tau h}$ of local maxima which are $\delta D$ apart and are greater than a threshold $\tau_h$

$$S_{\tau_h} = \begin{cases} \text{Location}: & x_{k,1}^h, \ x_{k,2}^h, \ ..., \ x_{k,q}^h \\ \text{Probability}: & P_k(x_{k,1}^h), \ P_k(x_{k,2}^h), \ ..., \ P_k(x_{k,q}^h) \end{cases}$$

This set is considered as HSC centre candidates. To track the HSCs over time, each detected cell in the current frame must be associated to the proper one in the previous frame as depicted in Fig. 3. To achieve this goal a distance matrix $D$ is generated to determine the validation gate of each cell as

$$D = \{d_{j,i}, \ j \in [1, M_{k-1}] \ and \ i \in [1, M_k]\} \quad (11)$$

where $M_{k-1}$, the number of rows is equal to the number of cells in previous frame $k-1$ and $M_k$, the number of columns is equal to the number of detected cells in the frame $k$. Each element $d_{j,i}$ shows the euclidian distance between detected cell $j$ in frame $k$ and identified cell $i$ in frame $k-1$.

The displacement of HSCs over time can be considered as a random walk, hence a probabilistic validation gate is obtained by considering a Gaussian motion. A Gaussian function $N(0, \sigma)$

$$Pd_{j,i} \sim N(0, \sigma) = \frac{1}{\sqrt{2\pi}} \exp\left(-\frac{d_{j,i}^2}{\sigma^2}\right) \quad (12)$$

is applied on the distance matrix to obtain a Gaussian probability distance matrix. Each element $P_{j,i}$ of this matrix shows the probability of associating

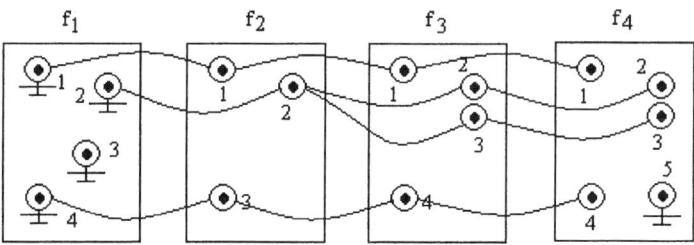

**Fig. 3.** Cell centre association over time

detected cell $j$ in frame $k$ to identified cell $i$ in frame $k-1$ and is higher if they have smaller distance.

To associate the cell centers, a zero scan joint probabilistic data association is considered as

$$P(f_k|\ f_{k-1}) = \prod_{j \in [1, M_{k-1}]} max(P_{j,i}, P_F) \cdot \prod_N max(P_{j,i}, P_F) \cdot \prod_{\sim F \cap N} P_{age} \quad (13)$$

where $P_F$ is probability of false alarm and is assumed as a constant, $P_{age}$ is age penalty which means cell split may not occur sooner than a minimum age, $S =\sim F \cap N$ is the set of splitted cells, $F$ and $N$ are

$$F : \{i|\ i \in \{False\ alarm\}\}$$
$$N : \{i|\ i \in \{New\ detected\ objects\}\} \quad (14)$$

## 3 Results

By applying our proposed model based tracking method to the phase contrast microscopic images, first a probability map of cell centers is obtained for each frame. To further identify the cell centers, the probability map is thresholded and local maxima are located. Eventually the detected cell centers are associated based on proposed JPDA method.

Fig. 4(a) shows the detected cell centers which is obtained by applying the proposed probabilistic cell model, locating the local maxima in the probability map and thresholding the local maxima map. Results obtained by applying the proposed tracking method are depicted in Fig. 4(b). As can be observed from Fig. 4(b), by applying our probabilistic model based tracking to depicted HSC image sequence, it is able to identify and associate all cell centers correctly not only in the non splitting case but also in the more challenging splitting case. Color coding is used to high light associated cell centers such that different colors show the association of cell centers over time.

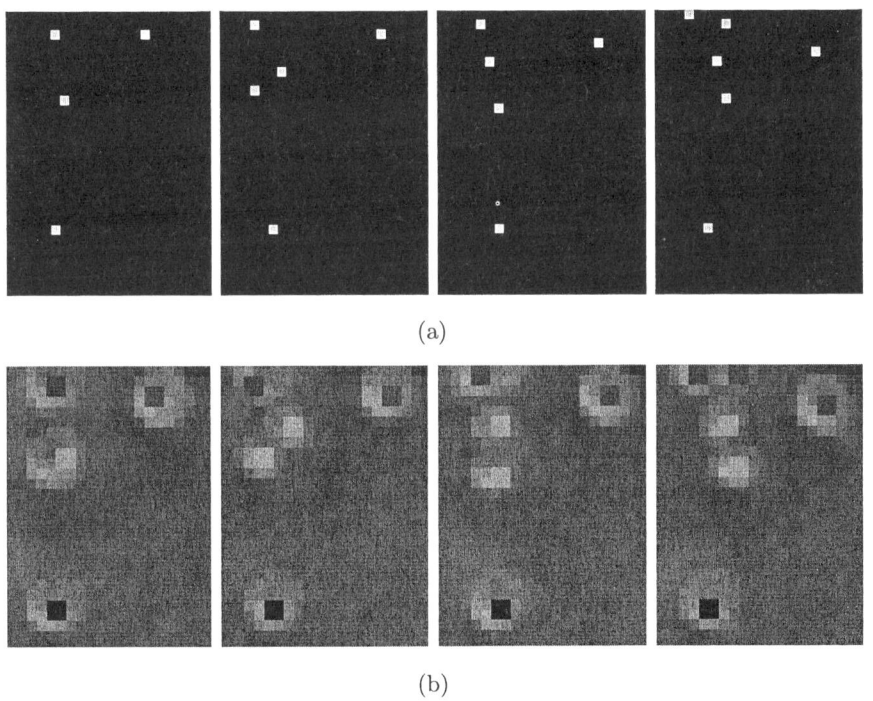

**Fig. 4.** (a) Detection of non splitting and splitting cell centers. (b) Associated cell centers superimposed on original HSC image such that each color shows a different cell track over time (from left to right).

## 4 Conclusions and Discussions

The fields of bioinformatics and biotechnology rely on the collection, processing and analysis of a huge number of bio-cellular images, including cell features such as cell size, shape, and motility. This paper presents a probabilistic model based cell tracking method to locate and associate HSCs in phase contrast microscopic images. Our statistical cell model, which is constructed after carefully observing HSCs in typical image sequences, captures the key properties of HSCs. By matching the image data with the cell model, a probability map of cell centers is generated for each frame. Cell centers are located by further thresholding the probability map and locating the local maxima. Cell association is accomplished based on a joint probabilistic data association in which random walk is considered to model the cell motion. It can be seen from the previous section that such a probabilistic model- based cell tracking method has produced very promising results.

Our future work includes further improving the cell model to more accurately reflect unique properties of the cells under different conditions and to fuse information from adjacent image frames to make the method more robust to noise and clutters. Designing a parametric cell shape with more degrees of freedom has also been considered as future work to adapt the proposed model to other cell types.

## Acknowledgements

This research has been performed in close cooperation with Cancer Research Laboratory (CRL) of University of British Columbia (UBC). We would like to thank researchers in CRL-UBC for providing HSC samples for this research.

## References

1. I. Bauman, R. Nenninger, H. Harms, H. Zwierzina, K.Wilms, A. Feller, V. Meulen, and H. Muller-Hermelink, "Image analysis detects lineage-specific morphologic markers in leukemia blast cells," American Journal of Clinical Pathology 105(1), pp. 23–30, 1995.
2. D. Comaniciu, D. Foran, and P. Meer, "Shape-based image indexing and retrieval for diagnostic pathology," in Int'l Conf. on Pattern Recognition, pp. 902–904, 1998.
3. E. Campo and E. J. E, "Mantle cell lymphoma," Arch. Pathology Lab. Med. 120(1), pp. 12–14, 1996.
4. T. Markiewicz, S. Osowski, L. Moszczyski, and R. Satat1, "Myelogenous leukemia cell image preprocessing for feature generation," in 5th International Workshop on Computational Methods in Electrical Engineering, pp. 70–73, 2003.
5. K. Wu, D. Gauthier, and M. Levine, "Live cell image segmentation," IEEE Transactions on Biomedical Engineering 42(1), pp. 1–12, 1995.
6. C. Glasbey, "An analysis of histogram-based thresholding algorithm," Graphical Models and Image Processing 55(6), pp. 532–537, 1993.
7. D. Comaniciu and P. Meer, "Cell image segmentation for diagnostic pathology," Advanced algorithmic approaches to medical image segmentation: State-of-the-art applications in cardiology, neurology, mammography and pathology , pp. 541–558, 2001.
8. J. Geusebroek, A. Smeulders, and F. Cornelissen, "Segmentation of cell clusters by nearest neighbour graphs," in Proceedings of the third annual conference of the Advanced School for Computing and Imaging, pp. 248–252, 1997.
9. V. Meas-Yedid, F. Cloppet, A. Roumier, A. Alcover, J.-C. Olivo-Marin, and G. Sta- mon, "Quantitative microscopic image analysis by active contours," in VI 2001 Vision Interface Annual Conference - Medical Applications, 2001.

# Carotid Artery Ultrasound Image Segmentation Using Fuzzy Region Growing

Amr R. Abdel-Dayem and Mahmoud R. El-Sakka, Senior Member, IEEE

Computer Science Department,
University of Western Ontario, London, Ontario, Canada
{amr, elsakka}@csd.uwo.ca

**Abstract.** In this paper, we propose a new scheme for extracting the contour of the carotid artery using ultrasound images. Starting from a user defined seed point within the artery, the scheme uses the fuzzy region growing algorithm to create a fuzzy connectedness map for the image. Then, the fuzzy connectedness map is thresholded using a threshold selection mechanism to segment the area inside the artery. Experimental results demonstrated the efficiency of the proposed scheme in segmenting carotid artery ultrasound images, and it is insensitive to the seed point location, as long as it is located inside the artery.

## 1 Introduction

According to the heart and stroke foundation of Canada, stroke is the fourth leading cause of death in Canada, where approximately 16,000 Canadians die from stroke every year. Vascular plaque, a consequence of atherosclerosis, results in an accumulation of lipids, cholesterol, smooth muscle cells, calcifications and other tissues within the arterial wall. It reduces the blood flow within the artery and may completely block it. As plaque builds up, it can become either stable or unstable layers. Unstable plaque layers in a carotid artery can be a life-threatening condition. If a plaque ruptures small solid components (emboli) from the plaque drift with the blood stream into the brain. This may cause a stroke. Early detection of unstable plaque plays an important role in preventing serious strokes.

Currently, carotid angiography is the standard diagnostic technique to detect carotid artery stenosis and the plaque morphology on artery walls. This technique involves injecting patients with an X-ray dye. Then, the carotid artery is examined using X-ray imaging. However, carotid angiography is an invasive technique. It is uncomfortable for patients and has some risk factors, including allergic reaction to the injected dye, kidney failure and the exposure to X-ray radiation.

Ultrasound imaging provides an attractive tool for carotid artery examination. The main drawback of ultrasound imaging is the poor quality of the produced images. It takes considerable effort from radiologists to extract significant information about carotid artery contours and the possible existence of plaque layers that may exist. This task requires a highly skilled radiologist. Furthermore, manual extraction of carotid artery contours generates a result that is not reproducible. Hence, a computer aided diagnostic (CAD) technique for segmenting carotid artery contours is highly needed.

Mao et al. [1] proposed a scheme for extracting the carotid artery walls from ultrasound images. The scheme uses a deformable model to approximate the artery wall. The user has to specify a seed point inside the artery. The initial contour shape is estimated from the image entropy map. However, the result accuracy depends, to a large extent, on the appropriate estimation of the initial contour. Furthermore, the deformable model takes a considerable amount of time to approach the equilibrium state. It is worth mentioning that the equilibrium state of a deformable model does not guarantee the optimal state or contour shape.

Abolmaesumi et al. [2] proposed a scheme for tracking the center and the walls of the carotid artery in real-time. The scheme uses an improved star algorithm with temporal and spatial Kalman filters. The major drawback of this scheme is the estimation of the weight factors used by Kalman filters. In the proposed scheme, these factors are estimated from the probability distribution function of the boundary points. In practice, this distribution is usually unknown.

Da-chuan et al. [3] proposed a method for automatic detection of intimal and adventitial layers of the common carotid artery wall in ultrasound images using a snake model. The proposed method modified the Cohen's snake [4] by adding spatial criteria to obtain the contour with a global maximum cost function. The proposed snake model was compared with a ziplock snake [5] and was found to give superior performance. However, the computational time for the proposed model was significantly high. It took a long amount of time for the snake to reach the optimum shape.

Hamou et al. [6] proposed a segmentation scheme for carotid artery ultrasound images. The scheme is based on Canny edge detector [7]. The scheme requires three parameters. The first parameter is the standard deviation of the Gaussian smoothing kernel used to smooth the image before applying edge detection process. The second and the third parameters are upper and lower bound thresholds to mask out the insignificant edges from the generated edge map. The authors empirically tuned these parameters, based on their own database of images. This makes the proposed scheme cumbersome when used with images from different databases.

Abdel-Dayem et al. [8] proposed a new scheme for carotid artery contour extraction. The proposed scheme uses a uniform quantizer to cluster the image pixels into three major classes. These classes approximate the area inside the artery, the artery wall and the surrounding tissues. A morphological edge extractor is used to extract the edges between these three classes. The system incorporates a pre-processing stage to enhance the image quality and to reduce the effect of the speckle noise in ultrasound images. A post-processing stage is used to enhance the extracted contours. This scheme can accurately outline the carotid artery walls. However, it cannot differentiate between relevant objects with small intensity variations within the artery tissues. Moreover, it is more sensitive to noise.

Abdel-Dayem et al. [9] used the watershed segmentation scheme [10] to segment the carotid artery ultrasound images. Watershed segmentation schemes usually produce over-segmented images. Hence, a region merging stage is used to merge neighbouring regions based on the difference on their average pixel intensity. A single global threshold is needed during the region merging process. If this threshold is properly tuned, the proposed scheme produces accurate segmentation results.

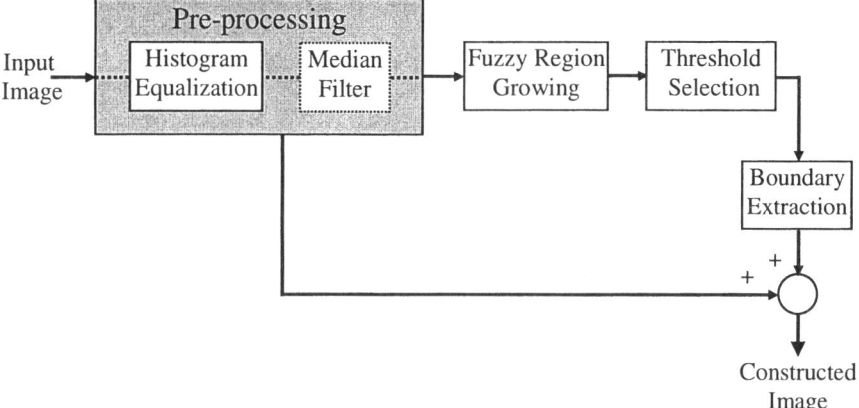

Fig. 1. The block diagram of the proposed scheme

Fuzzy-based segmentation techniques are powerful in segmenting objects with diffused and not well-defined boundaries. Hence, these techniques can be used effectively to segment ultrasound images. In this paper, we proposed a novel scheme for extracting the contours of the carotid artery in ultrasound images. The proposed scheme is based on the fuzzy connectedness principle, where the fuzzy connectedness map is calculated starting from a seed point within the artery. This map is thresholded to segment the area inside the artery. The threshold is chosen, based on the histogram of the fuzzy connectedness map.

The rest of this paper is organized as follows. Section 2 describes the proposed scheme in details. Section 3 presents the results. Finally, Section 4 offers the conclusions of this paper.

## 2 The Proposed Solution

We propose a novel scheme for segmenting carotid artery ultrasound images. The proposed scheme consists of four major stages. These stages are pre-processing, fuzzy region growing, threshold selection and finally boundary extraction stage. Fig. 1 shows the block diagram of the proposed method. In the following subsections, a detailed description of each stage is introduced.

### 2.1 The Pre-processing Stage

Ultrasound images suffer from several drawbacks. One of these drawbacks is the presence of random speckle noises, caused by the interference of the reflected ultrasound waves. Another sever problem is that ultrasound images have relatively low contrast. These factors severely degrade any automated processing and analysis of the images. Hence, it is crucial to enhance the image quality prior to any further processing. In this stage we try to overcome these problems by performing two pre-processing steps. The first is a histogram equalization step [11] to increase the dynamic range of the image gray levels. In the second step, the histogram equalized

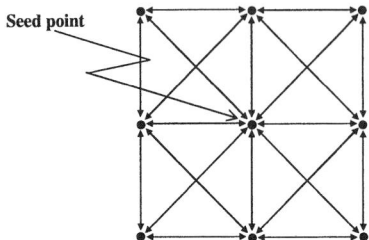

**Fig. 2.** The 20 pairs of adjacent pixels used to calculate $\mu_i$ and $\sigma_i$ of Equation 2

image is filtered using a median filter to reduce the amount of the speckle noise in the image. It was empirically found that a 3×3 median filter is suitable for the removal of most of the speckle noise without affecting the quality of the edges in the image.

### 2.2 The Fuzzy Region Growing Stage

The concept of fuzzy connectedness is an efficient tool for segmenting objects with diffused and not-well defined boundaries [12][13][14]. It uses the idea of "hanging together" image pixels or *spatial image elements* (spels). In digital images, the image is considered as a grid; in which each pixel is connected to its adjacent pixels by a link. The strength of a link is determined based on a certain fuzzy spel affinity. The selection of the fuzzy spel affinity reflects our confidence that a pair of spels belong to same object. There are several ways to define the fuzzy spel affinity [15][16]. A chain is a sequence of consecutive links that connects two pixels together. The strength of a chain is determined by the minimum link strength among the links forming the given chain. The fuzzy connectedness between any pair of pixels in the image is determined by the strongest chain connecting them. In the fuzzy region growing algorithm, a seed pixel is selected within the object of interest. The fuzzy connectedness between the seed pixel and every pixel in the image is calculated. This step produces a fuzzy connectedness map. Then, the object of interest can be segmented by thresholding this map.

Using the image obtained from the previous enhancement stage, the fuzzy connectedness map is calculated. The user is asked to select a seed pixel that belongs to the object of interest. The seed pixel with its 8-connected neighbouring pixels provides 20 pairs of adjacent pixels as shown in Fig. 2. From these 20 pairs the following parameters are calculated:

- $\mu_1$ and $\sigma_1$ are the mean and the standard deviation of $f(a) + f(b)$.
- $\mu_2$ and $\sigma_2$ are the mean and the standard deviation of $|f(a) - f(b)|$.

where $f(a)$ and $f(b)$ are the intensity of two adjacent pixels $a$ and $b$. We use the fuzzy spel affinity $\Psi(a,b)$ defined as follows:

$$\psi(a,b) = \frac{g_1(f(a)+f(b)) + g_2(|f(a)-f(b)|)}{2} \quad (1)$$

where $a$ and $b$ are two adjacent pixels and

```
Module Name  Fuzzy Region Growing
Input     Image I and Seed Pixel P_ij
Output    Fuzzy connectedness map FM of image I
Description
Variable
    Stack:    S
    Pixel:    CP   /* current pixel*/
    Pixel:    Q    /* temporary pixel*/
Begin
Step1  /*Initialization step */
    Initialize_stack (S)  /*stack initialization */
    Push pixel P_ij into the stack S
    Set FM(P_ij) ← 1 and set FM(x) ← 0 for all x ≠ P_ij
    Calculate the parameters μ_1, σ_1, μ_2 and σ_2 for P_ij
Step2
    Repeat
        Pop pixel CP from the stack S
            For every pixel Q in the eight-connectivity
                    neighborhood of the current pixel (CP) Do
                Begin
                    If min{FM(CP), Ψ(CP,Q)}> FM(Q)
                    Begin
                        Push pixel Q into the stack S
                        Set FM(Q) ← min{FM(CP), Ψ(CP,Q)}
                    End
                End
    Until the stack S is empty
Step3
        Return the fuzzy connectedness map FM
End
```

**Fig. 3.** The Fuzzy Region Growing algorithm

$$g_i(x) = e^{-\frac{(x-\mu_i)^2}{2\sigma_i^2}} \quad for \ i = 1,2 \qquad (2)$$

The fuzzy region growing algorithm is implemented following the dynamic programming model proposed in [12]. A summary of this algorithm is shown in Fig. 3. The algorithm starts by setting the fuzzy connectedness of the seed pixel to one and all other members to zero. Then, the algorithm computes the connectivity of the eight neighbouring pixels. The condition in step 2 of the algorithm checks if the current chain between the seed pixel and the current pixel is stronger than the previously detected chains. If this condition is satisfied, the fuzzy connectedness of this pixel is updated and the pixel is added to the stack for further processing. This process continues until the stack becomes empty. This map will be used during the next stage to segment the area inside the carotid artery. More efficient implementations of this algorithm, based on greedy algorithms and Dijkstra's Algorithm, can be found in [13]. However, this is irrelevant to the main idea of this paper.

## 2.3 The Threshold Selection Stage

The objective of this stage is to find a suitable threshold to be applied to the fuzzy connectedness map. We propose a threshold selection scheme based on the analysis of

```
Module Name  Threshold Selection
Input    Fuzzy connectedness map FM
Output   Threshold value t*
Description
Variable
   Integer:  Histogram[MAX_Connectedness_LEVEL]
   Integer:  Area  /* segmented area size*/
   Integer:  t
   Float:    Percentage_Difference[MAX_Connectedness_LEVEL]
Begin
Step1 /* Convert the fuzzy connectedness map to discrete values */
    Multiply every element of FM by 255
    Round every element of FM to the nearest integer value
Step2 /*Initialization step */
    Generate the Histogram of FM
    Set t ← MAX_Connectednes_LEVEL
    Set Area ← Histogram[t]
    Set Percentage_Difference [t] ← 0
Step3 /* Find the rate of change for all threshold values*/
    Repeat
        Decrement the threshold t
        Set Percentage_Difference [t] ← Histogram[t]/Area
        Set Area ← Area + Histogram[t]
    Until t=0
Step4 /* find the optimal threshold*/
    Return t* such that Percentage_Difference[t*] is maximum
End
```

**Fig. 4.** The threshold selection algorithm

the histogram of the fuzzy connectedness map. This map contains real values in the range from zero to one. In order to build the histogram of the fuzzy connectedness map, it is necessary to discretize its individual elements. Hence, we multiply the map elements by a large integer number (in our case, we chose 255 so that we can visualize the map as a gray image) and then round the results to the nearest integer values. The threshold selection process starts by a threshold value equals to the maximum level in the discretized fuzzy connectedness map. The algorithm calculates the area of the segmented region using this threshold by counting the number of pixels that have connectedness values greater than or equal to this threshold. Then, the threshold is iteratively decreased by one and the new area is calculated. At each step, the percentage difference of the segmented area is calculated according to Equation (3).

$$Percentage\ difference\ of\ segmented\ area = \frac{Area_{t-1} - Area_t}{Area_t} \qquad (3)$$

where, $Area_t$ is the area of the segmented region using threshold $t$.

This process continues for all intensity levels in the map. The threshold is selected to be the one that corresponds to the maximum percentage difference. This threshold represents the point at which parts of the background start to merge with the object of interest. Fig. 4 shows a summary of the threshold selection algorithm.

## 2.4 The Boundary Extraction Stage

The objective of this stage is to extract the boundaries of the segmented regions. Various edge detection schemes can be used for this purpose [11]. In our system, we use a morphological-based contour extraction mechanism [11], [17]. First, the segmented image is morphologically eroded using a 3×3 rounded square structuring element. Then, the eroded image is subtracted from the segmented image to obtain the boundary of the segmented region, which represents the artery wall. Finally, the extracted contour is superimposed on the histogram equalized image.

## 3 Results

The test images used in this research were obtained using an ultrasound acquisition system (Ultramark 9 HDI US machine and L10-5 linear array transducer). The output is digitized with a video frame grabber before saving it. These images include patients with different ages and different degrees of plaque layers. Fig. 5(a) shows one of the original ultrasound images that are used as an input to our system. Fig. 5(b) shows the output after the histogram equalization step. Fig. 5(c) shows the output after applying the median filter where the amount of noise is reduced. Fig. 5(d) shows the fuzzy connectedness map (after multiplying it by 255) for the image shown in Fig. 5(c). The map shows that the area inside the artery appears as a bright region, while getting darker near the arterial walls. Fig. 5(e) shows the segmented image after applying the threshold on the fuzzy connectedness map shown in Fig. 5(d). Fig. 5(f) shows the final output of the proposed scheme. For clarity, we magnify the region of interest for both the histogram equalized image in Fig. 5(g) and the final image in Fig. 5(h).

Since, the seed point represents the only input from the user, it is crucial to analyze the proposed scheme sensitivity to the seed point selection. For this analysis, we used a set of *forty four* images. For each image, five seed points were randomly selected *inside the artery*. The artery region was segmented for each selected seed point. These segmented binary images were added up to produce a grayscale image that demonstrates the overlapping areas between segmented regions generated by the five seed points. Fig. 6(a-e) show the five segmented areas for the test case shown in Fig. 5, whereas Fig. 6(f) shows the summation image. The *percentage overlap* between segmented areas (the number of pixels having a value of 5 over all non-zero pixels) is 88.23% for this test case.

The statistical analysis over the entire *forty four* images revealed that, on average, the proposed scheme achieved a *percentage overlap* equal to 88.8%. Hence, we can conclude that the proposed scheme is less sensitive to the selected seed point.

## 4 Conclusions

In this paper, we proposed a novel scheme for carotid artery segmentation. The scheme is based on fuzzy region growing and thresholding techniques. The proposed scheme requires minimal user interaction. Only one seed point is needed to start the

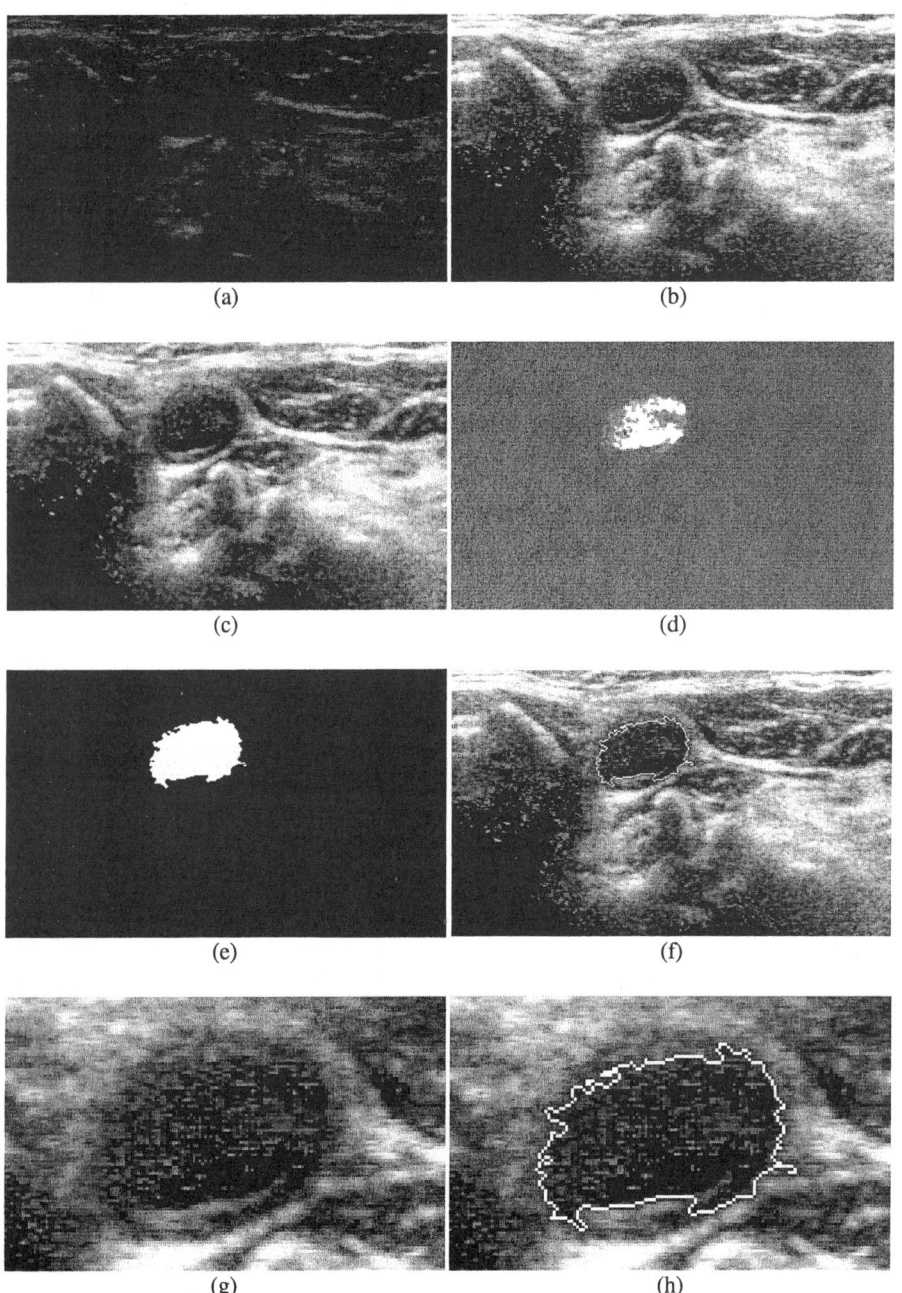

**Fig. 5.** Experimental results: (a) Original ultrasound image; (b) The image after applying the histogram equalization step; (c) The histogram equalized image after applying a 3×3 median filter; (d) The Fuzzy Connectedness Map (after multiplying it by 255) for the image shown in (c); (e) The segmented image using the calculated threshold; (f) The final result of the proposed scheme; (g) The original region of interest; (h) The region of interest with the extracted contour

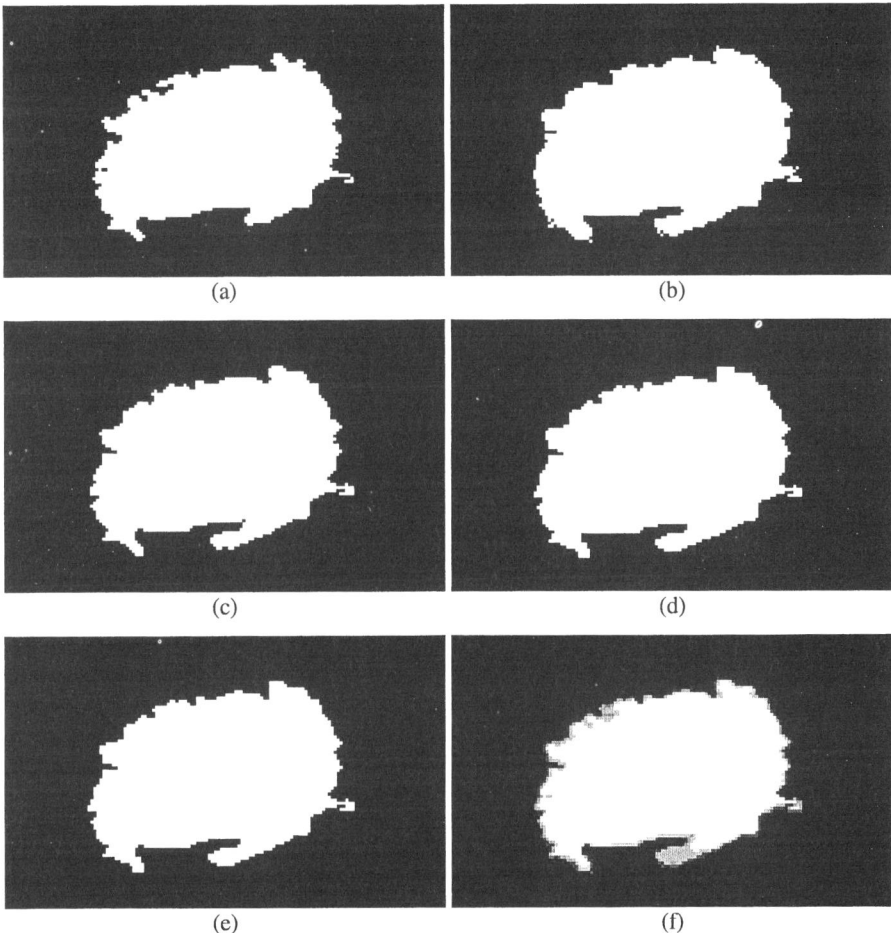

**Fig. 6.** Experimental results using different seed points: (a)(b)(c)(d) and (e) are the segmented areas (multiplied by 255) using different seed points for the case shown in Fig. 5; (f) the summation image (scaled from 0 to 255) for (a) to (e) cases

fuzzy region growing process. All other parameters are calculated based on the image under consideration. Experimental results over a set of sample images showed that the proposed scheme provides a good estimation of the carotid artery contours, and it is insensitive to the seed point location, as long as it is located inside the artery.

## Acknowledgements

The authors would like to thank The Robarts Research Institute at the University of Western Ontario for providing us with the ultrasound images that were used to test the proposed scheme.

## References

1. F. Mao, J. Gill, D. Downey, and A. Fenster, "Segmentation of carotid artery in ultrasound images", Proceedings of the 22nd IEEE Annual International Conference on Engineering in Medicine and Biology Society, Vol. 3, pp.1734-1737, July 2000.
2. P. Abolmaesumi, M. Sirouspour, and S. Salcudean, "Real-time extraction of carotid artery contours from ultrasound images", Proceedings of the 13th IEEE Symposium on Computer-Based Medical Systems, pp.181-186, June 2000.
3. C. Da-chuan, A. Schmidt-Trucksass, C. Kuo-Sheng, M. Sandrock, P. Qin, and H. Burkhardt, "Automatic detection of the intimal and the adventitial layers of the common carotid artery wall in ultrasound B-mode images using snakes", Proceedings of the International Conference on Image Analysis and Processing, pp. 452 – 457, September 1999.
4. L. Cohen, "On active contour models and balloons", Computer Vision, Graphics, and Image Processing: Image Understanding, Vol. 53, No. 2, pp. 211-218, 1991.
5. W. Neuenschwander, P. Fua, L. Iverson, G. Szekely, and O. Kubler, "Ziplock snake", International Journal of Computer Vision, Vol. 25, No. 3, pp. 191-201, 1997.
6. A. Hamou and M. El-Sakka, "A novel segmentation technique for carotid ultrasound images", Proceedings of the IEEE International Conference on Acoustics, Speech and Signal Processing, Vol. 3, pp. 521-424, May 2004.
7. J. Canny, "Computational Approach To Edge Detection", IEEE Transactions on Pattern Analysis and Machine Intelligence, Vol. 8, No. 6, Nov 1986, pp. 679-698.
8. A. Abdel-Dayem and M. El-Sakka, "A novel morphological-based carotid artery contour extraction", Proceedings of the Canadian Conference on Electrical and Computer Engineering, Vol. 2, pp. 1873-1876, May 2004.
9. A. Abdel-Dayem and M. El-Sakka, "Watershed segmentation for carotid artery ultrasound images", Proceedings of the IEEE International Conference on Computer Systems and Applications, Jan 2005.
10. L. Vincent and P. Soille, "Watersheds in digital spaces: an efficient algorithm based on immersion simulations", IEEE Transactions on Pattern Analysis and Machine Intelligence, Vol. 13, No. 6, pp. 583-598, June 1991.
11. G. Gonzalez and E. Woods, "Digital image processing", Second Edition, Prentice Hall, 2002.
12. J. Upupa and S. Samarasekera, "Fuzzy connectedness and object definition: theory, algorithms, and applications in image segmentation", Graphical Models and Image Processing, Vol. 58, No. 3, pp. 246-261, 1996.
13. B. Carvalho, C. Gau, G. Herman and T. Kong, "Algorithms for fuzzy segmentation", Pattern Analysis and Applications, Vol. 2, pp. 73-81, 1999.
14. J. Udupa, L. Wei, S. Samarasekera, Y. Miki, and M. Buchem, and R. Grossman, "Multiple sclerosis lesion quantification using fuzzy-connectedness principles", IEEE Transactions on Medical Imaging, Vol. 16, No 5, pp. 598 609, Oct. 1997.
15. S. Pal and D. Majunder, "Fuzzy mathematical approach to pattern recognition", New Delhi, India: Wiley, 1986.
16. A. Kandel, "Fuzzy techniques in pattern recognition", New York: Wiley, 1982.
17. E. Dargherty and R. Lotufo, "Hands–on morphological image processing", The society of Photo-Optical Instrumentation Engineers, 2003.

# Vector Median Root Signals Determination for cDNA Microarray Image Segmentation

Rastislav Lukac and Konstantinos N. Plataniotis

The Edward S. Rogers Sr. Dept. of Electrical and Computer Engineering,
University of Toronto, 10 King's College Road, Toronto, M5S 3G4, Canada
{lukacr, kostas}@dsp.utoronto.ca
http://www.dsp.utoronto.ca/~lukacr

**Abstract.** This paper presents a new cDNA microarray image segmentation framework. The framework uses robust vector median filtering to generate a root sigLnal which is an image obtained from the input by repeatedly filtering it until no more changes occur. During the convergence to the root signal, the framework classifies the cDNA image data as either microarray spots or image background, and ideally separates the regular spots from the background. Thus, the obtained root signal represents the segmented microarray image. In addition, the framework excellently removes noise present in the cDNA microarray images and normalizes spots' intensities.

## 1 Introduction

Complementary Deoxyribonucleic Acid (cDNA) microarray technology is a powerful tool used to extract and interpret genomic information [1]-[5]. It has found applications in gene and drug discovery, toxicological research, and diagnosis of cancer, diabetes and genetic diseases [1],[2]. During the cDNA microarray experiment, Ribonucleic Acid (RNA) from both control and experimental sample are isolated and converted into cDNAs by the so-called reverse transcription process [6], and the obtained cDNAs are labelled with fluorescent probes, usually Cy3 for the control and Cy5 for the experimental channel [7]. After hybridization, heating and washing, a specialized scanner is used to acquire cDNA microarrays at the ~ 540 nm (Green) for the control (Cy3) and ~ 630 nm (Red) for the experimental channel (Cy5) respectively [2],[7]. The scanning procedure produces a Red-Green image (*Fig.1*) which is a multichannel vector signal which can be represented, for storing or visualization purposes, as the RGB color image with a zero blue component [2],[8],[9].

The objective of the microarray experiment is to measure the abundance of hybridized RNA and analyze the gene expression activity in the recorded samples [6],[8]. Based on a simple coloration concept, the observance of non-fluorescent black spots in the microarray image denotes no binding of RNA while the occurrence of red, green, or yellow spots suggests that RNA sequences from the experimental, control, or combined population of cells contribute to the abundance. Since strong noise and various impairments are present in cDNA microarray images, image processing is used prior the analysis step.

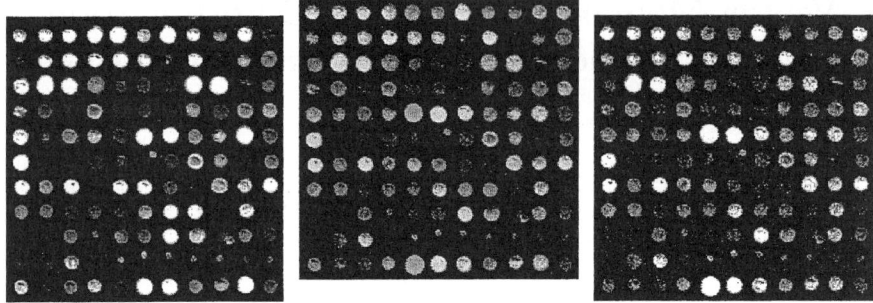

**Fig. 1.** Typical cDNA microarray image (middle) with the decomposed Red (left) and Green (right) channels

## 2  cDNA Microarray Imaging Basics

Let us consider, a $K_1 \times K_2$ Red-Green (RG) image $\mathbf{x} : Z^2 \to Z^2$ representing a two-dimensional matrix of two-component samples $\mathbf{x}_{(r,s)} = [x_{(r,s)1}, x_{(r,s)2}]$ with $r = 1, 2, ..., K_1$ and $s = 1, 2, ..., K_2$ denoting the image rows and columns, respectively. The component $x_{(r,s)1}$ indicates the R channel while $x_{(r,s)2}$ indicates the G channel. The two channels are combined to form the cDNA vector $\mathbf{x}_{(r,s)}$ in a two-dimensional vector space [8],[9].

cDNA microarray images (*Fig.1*) suffer from noise introduced during image formation which is a complicated, nonlinear process influenced by many factors [2]. Therefore, image processing is necessary in order to eliminate processing errors from propagating further down the processing pipeline to the gene expression analysis tasks [1],[8]. The acquired cDNA signal $\mathbf{x}_{(r,s)} = [x_{(r,s)1}, x_{(r,s)2}]$ can be expressed as follows [9]:

$$\mathbf{x}_{(r,s)} = \mathbf{o}_{(r,s)} + \mathbf{v}_{(r,s)} \tag{1}$$

where $\mathbf{o}_{(r,s)} = [o_{(r,s)1}, o_{(r,s)2}]$ represents the original, noise-free cDNA signal while $\mathbf{v}_{(r,s)} = [v_{(r,s)1}, v_{(r,s)2}]$ is used to denote the various image impairments introduced during image formation. The vectorial samples $\mathbf{v}_{(r,s)}$ are considered random in nature and can be modelled through the additive noise model [7]. The noise signal $\mathbf{v}_{(r,s)}$ is considered either impulsive in nature or it can be modelled as mixed noise (white additive Gaussian noise followed by impulsive noise) [2],[8].

Each acquired cDNA sample $\mathbf{x}_{(r,s)}$ is uniquely determined by its magnitude $M_{(r,s)} = \|\mathbf{x}_{(r,s)}\| = \sqrt{(x_{(r,s)1})^2 + (x_{(r,s)2})^2}$ and direction $D_{(r,s)} = \frac{1}{\|\mathbf{x}_{(r,s)}\|}\mathbf{x}_{(r,s)} = \frac{1}{M_{(r,s)}}\mathbf{x}_{(r,s)}$ in the vector space [2]. Due to the various image impairments, such as those attributed to [10],[11]: i) variations in the image background, ii) variations in the spot sizes and positions, iii) artifacts caused by laser light reflection and dust on the glass slide, and iv) photon and electronic noise introduced during scanning, the cDNA vector fields exhibit considerable variations in intensity (*Fig.1*) [2],[8].

## 3 Root Signals Based Segmentation Framework

The proposed cDNA image segmentation framework uses uniformity in the characteristics of the cDNA vectors as the base for segmentation [2]. Since the noisy samples deviate from other samples in a given data population [8], the determination of the outlying cDNA vectors is of a paramount importance. Due to the vectorial nature of the cDNA microarray image, the microarray image processing operator should process the cDNA image data as the set of vectors. The most popular vector processing techniques, such as those listed in [9], operate over magnitude or direction of cDNA vectors, or combine both magnitude and directional characteristics to ensure proper processing of vectors within the localized image area. Such solutions have been used to denoise and enhance cDNA microarray image, and detect spots' edges [8],[11],[12].

In this work, we use the vector processing concepts to build a unique segmentation framework. The framework employs the vector processing operator to produce a root signal which represents a segmented microarray image. As it is demonstrated in [2], by employing various vector processing operators the framework offers solutions which differ in their design philosophy, characteristics, and performance. To demonstrate the suitability of the proposed framework, the well-known vector median filter (VMF) [13] will be used in the sequence.

### 3.1 Vector Median Filter

The most popular vector operators such as the VMF are based on the theory of order-statistics [9],[14]. Since outliers are associated with the maximum extremes of aggregated distances to other input vectors in the sliding window, the output of the ordering-based vector filters is the lowest ranked vector in a predefined sliding window. Such an approach makes the processing operators robust to noise and various impairments present in cDNA microarray images.

The VMF operates over samples $\mathbf{x}_{(i,j)}$ localized within a sliding window $W_{(r,s)} = \{\mathbf{x}_{(i,j)}; (i,j) \in \zeta = \{(r-1, s-1), (r-1, s), ..., (r+1, s+1)\}\}$. The filtering procedure replaces the sample $\mathbf{x}_{(r,s)}$ placed in the window center through a function $\mathbf{y}_{(r,s)} = f(W_{(r,s)})$ applied to a local neighborhood area $W_{(r,s)}$:

$$\mathbf{y}_{(r,s)} = \min_{\mathbf{x}_{(i,j)} \in W_{(r,s)}} \arg \sum_{(g,h) \in \zeta} \left\| \mathbf{x}_{(i,j)} - \mathbf{x}_{(g,h)} \right\|_L \qquad (2)$$

This window operator slides over the entire image, for $r = 1, 2, ..., K_1$ and $s = 1, 2, ..., K_2$, to cover all the pixels in the microarray image [9]. In the expression above the term $\left\| \mathbf{x}_{(i,j)} - \mathbf{x}_{(g,h)} \right\|_L$ represents the $L$-metric (Minkowski metric [14],[15]) used to quantify the distance between two cDNA vectors $\mathbf{x}_{(i,j)}$ and $\mathbf{x}_{(g,h)}$:

$$\left\| \mathbf{x}_i - \mathbf{x}_j \right\|_L = \left( \sum_{k=1}^{m} |x_{ik} - x_{jk}|^L \right)^{\frac{1}{L}} \qquad (3)$$

where $L$ denotes the norm parameter, e.g. the city-block distance ($L = 1$) or considered here Euclidean distance ($L = 2$).

## 3.2 Root Signals

The VMF produces root signals if $\mathbf{y}_{(r,s)} = \mathbf{x}_{(r,s)}$, i.e. the filter output $\mathbf{y}_{(r,s)}$ is identical to a multichannel signal located at the reference window position $(r, s)$. Due to the localized nature of cDNA image features, the analysis of the root signals necessitates the definition of the following basic cDNA image structures which can be observed in the processing window $W_{(r,s)}$, [2],[16]: i) a multichannel constant region is a neighborhood formed by identical, in terms of both magnitude and direction, cDNA image vectors, ii) a multichannel cDNA step edge is a multichannel constant region followed by another multichannel constant region, iii) a multichannel impulse is a cDNA image vector which significantly deviates from a surrounding multichannel constant region, and iv) multichannel oscillation is a sequence of cDNA vectors which is not part of a constant region, an edge, or an impulse. The consideration of the structures defined above is essential in the proposed segmentation framework since the root signals consist solely of constant neighborhoods (background and spots) and edges (step transitions between spots and background) [2]. In order to obtain a root, defined over a cDNA microarray image, the elimination of impulses and oscillations (data variations) is an essential step.

Due to the low-pass nature of the smoothing operator, the utilization of the VMF (as well as some other robust vector filters) in a unique cascade cycle [2]: i) eliminates redundant information such as impulses and noise-like variations in the sample population, ii) converges to VMF roots (signals invariant to further processing by the VMF operator) that retain the spatial and spectral characteristics of the input cDNA image, and iii) produces a root signal which represents a segmented cDNA image. Since the VMF response to any input signal is uniquely defined in (2) with the VMF output $\mathbf{y}_{(r,s)} \in W_{(r,s)}$, the root signal [2]:

$$\mathbf{x}_{(r,s)} = f\left(W_{(r,s)}\right) \quad (4)$$

can be obtained by filtering repeatedly with a VMF operator any finite-length cDNA signal.

Assuming that $\mathbf{y}^n_{(r,s)}$ is a vector in the image $\mathbf{y}^n$ obtained after filtering $n$ times the input cDNA image $\mathbf{x}$, the convergence to a root signal can be expressed as a function of the difference between two successive filtering results [2],[17]:

$$\gamma = \left\| \mathbf{y}^n, \mathbf{y}^{n-1} \right\|_L \quad (5)$$

where $\mathbf{y}^0 = \mathbf{x}$ denotes the (input) cDNA microarray image which undergoes segmentation. The proposed segmentation procedure is completed when $\gamma = 0$ indicating that there are no changes in the filtered signal and that the root signal has been reached. Alternatively, the segmentation process can be stopped for $\gamma$ smaller that a user defined threshold. When the stopping condition is satisfied, the value of $n-1$ denotes the iteration for which the root signal has been reached.

The VMF root signal based procedure divides an image into different regions that are homogeneous with respect to its magnitude characteristics. Since pixels with the same magnitude characteristics constitute meaningful regions, such as the spots present in a cDNA microarray image, the problem reduces to pixel classification defined as follows [2]:

$$\mathbf{x}_{(r,s)} \in \mathbf{x} \to \{F, B\} \qquad (6)$$

where disjoint sets $F$ and $B$ denote the foreground and background cDNA vectors $\mathbf{x}_{(r,s)}$ in the microarray image $\mathbf{x}$, respectively. The foreground is constituted by microarray spots, typically of a circular shape of 150-200 cDNA vectors $\mathbf{x}_{(r,s)}$. A gap between spots or alternatively the presence of cDNA vectors residing outside spots areas constitute the background. By extracting the spots from the microarray image $\mathbf{x}$, the background can be viewed as a homogeneous region, while the essential foreground should remain heterogonous as a result of the variable spots' coloration [2]. The use of the VMF operator makes the vectors within individual spots uniform and removes noisy foreground information.

It is argued in [2] that the root signal convergence process performs morphological operations such as various compositions of erosion and dilatation operations defined over $W_{(r,s)}$, which is considered as the structuring element. By employing the robust filter, the proposed segmentation procedure removes "positive" noise (impairments present in background have magnitude larger than the desired background samples) similarly to morphological erosion or opening. At the same time, the procedure removes negative noise (cDNA vectors which are, in terms of amplitude of their components, smaller than neighboring vectors, and holes which have been created by cDNA vectors of zero-like magnitude) similarly to morphological dilatation or closing. In addition, the procedure removes any high-frequency impairments such as outliers in the cDNA image data population, and any small signal structures such as irregular spots or holes present in the microarray spots, performing thus erosion/opening or dilatation/closing operations.

The replacement of the window center $\mathbf{y}_{(r,s)}^{n-1}$ with the statistically most similar, to the cDNA samples within $W_{(r,s)}$, vector $\mathbf{y}_{(r,s)}^{n}$: i) produces an image which has normalized intensity in both the background and the spot locations, ii) enhances the difference between foreground and background information [2],[8]. As it is suggested in [2], the root-signal based segmentation procedure can be completed by performing thresholding operations over the magnitude of the root signal in order to remove residual irregular (small) spots and idealize the background in the segmented microarray image.

## 4 Experimental Results

In order to demonstrate the performance of the proposed segmentation framework, we used a number of cDNA microarray images, such as those shown in *Fig.1* and *Fig.2a*. The images have been captured using laser microscope scanners and vary in both complexity and noise appearance. The proposed method is compared, in terms of performance, against other segmentation techniques such as the clustering based segmentation technique and the morphological approach.

*Fig.2* shows the input cDNA microarray image and the corresponding segmented images. As it can be seen in *Fig.2a*, the input cDNA image contains various foreground and background impairments, which usually affect the performance of the processing and analysis techniques. Visual inspection of the

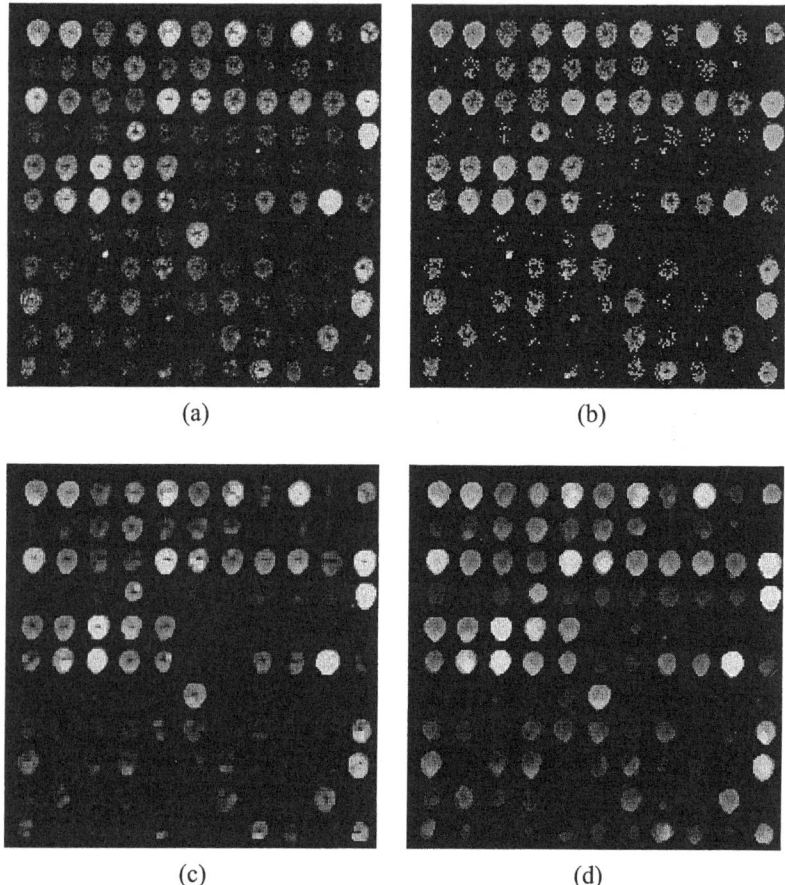

**Fig. 2.** Experimental results: (a) input cDNA microarray image, (b)-(d) segmented images obtained using (b) clustering technique, (c) morphological approach, (d) VMF root-signals based framework

image shown in *Fig.2b* reveals that the clustering approach is sensitive to noise. *Fig.2c* shows that the morphological approach delivers better performance, although it does not completely eliminate the holes present in the spots while at the same time enhances irregular spots in various image locations. However, the best results are obtained using the proposed solution. *Fig.2d* clearly shows that the proposed method removes noise, preserves the coloration of the spots and readily separates the foreground information from the background.

## 5 Conclusion

This paper presented a root-signal based concept for cDNA microarray image segmentation. A popular vector median filter was employed here to demonstrate the concept of the proposed framework by producing a root signal which is invariant to further processing with the same type of the filtering operator. The achieved root signal represents a segmented microarray image which exhibits enhanced spot information and data normalization.

## References

1. Zhang, X.Y., Chen, F., Zhang, Y.T., Agner, S.G., Akay, M., Lu, Z.H., Waye, M.M.Y., Tsui, S.K.W.: Signal processing techniques in genomic engineering. Proceedings of the IEEE **90** (2002) 1822-1833
2. Lukac, R., Plataniotis, K.N.: cDNA microarray image segmentation using root signals. Pattern Recognition, Special Issue on Bioinformatics, submitted (2005)
3. Arena, P., Bucolo, M., Fortuna, L., Occhipinty, L.: Cellular neural networks for real-time DNA microarray analysis. IEEE Engineering in Medicine and Biology **21** (2002) 17–25
4. Dopazo, J.: Microarray data processing and analysis. In Microarray Data Analysis II, ed. SM Lin and KF Johnson, Kluwer Academic (2002) 43–63
5. Eisen, M.B., Brown, P.O.: DNA arrays for analysis of gene expression. Methods in Enzymology **303** (1999) 179–205
6. Whitchurch, A.K.: Gene expression microarrays. IEEE Potentials **21** (2002) 30–34
7. Nagarajan, R.: Intensity-based segmentation of microarrays images. IEEE Transactions on Medical Imaging **22** (2003) 882–889.
8. Lukac, R., Plataniotis, K.N., Smolka, B., Venetsanopoulos, A.N.: A multichannel order-statistic technique for cDNA microarray image processing. IEEE Transactions on Nanobioscience **3** (2004) 272–285
9. Lukac, R., Smolka, B., Martin, K., Plataniotis, K.N., Venetsanopulos, A.N.: Vector filtering for color imaging. IEEE Signal Processing Magazine; Special Issue on Color Image Processing **22** (2005) 74–86
10. Wang, X.H., Istepian, R.S.H., Song, Y.H.: Microarray image enhancement using stationary wavelet transform. IEEE Trans. Nanobioscience **2** (2003) 184–189
11. Lukac, R., Plataniotis, K.N., Smolka, B., Venetsanopoulos, A.N.: cDNA microarray image processing using fuzzy vector filtering framework. Journal of Fuzzy Sets and Systems: Spec. Iss. Fuzzy Sets and Systems in Bioinformatics **152** (2005) 17–35
12. Lukac, R., Plataniotis, K.N., Smolka, B., Venetsanopoulos, A.N.: An automated multichannel procedure for cDNA microarray image processing. Lecture Notes in Computer Science **3212** (2004) 1–8
13. Astola, J., Haavisto, P., Neuvo, Y.: Vector median filters. Proceedings of the IEEE **78** (1990) 678–689
14. Lukac, R.: Adaptive vector median filtering. Pattern Recognition Letters **24** (2003) 1889–1899
15. Duda, R.O., Hart, P.E., Stork, D.G.: Pattern Classification and Scene Analysis. John Wiley, 2nd Edition, (2000)
16. Tang, K., Astola, J., Neuvo, Y.: Multichannel edge enhancement in color image processing. IEEE Trans. Circuits & Systems for Videotechnology **4** (1994) 468-479
17. Burian, A., Kuosmanen, P.: Tuning the smoothness of the recursive median filters. IEEE Transactions on Signal Processing **50** (2002) 1631–1639

# A New Method for DNA Microarray Image Segmentation

Luis Rueda[1] and Li Qin[2]

[1] School of Computer Science, University of Windsor
401 Sunset Ave., Windsor, ON N9B 3P4, Canada
lrueda@uwindsor.ca
[2] IBM Canada Ltd.
3600 Steeles Ave. East, Markham, ON, Canada
liqin@ca.ibm.com

**Abstract.** One of the key issues in microarray analysis is to extract quantitative information from the spots, which represents gene expression levels in the experiments. The process of identifying the spots and separating the foreground from the background is known as microarray image segmentation. In this paper, we propose a new approach to microarray image segmentation, which we called the *adaptive ellipse method*, and shows various advantages when compared to the adaptive circle method. Our experiments on real-life microarray images show that adaptive ellipse is capable of extracting information from the images, which is ignored by the traditional adaptive circle method, and hence showing more flexibility.

## 1 Introduction

The analysis of DNA microarray gene expression data involves two main steps [11]. The first step is image quantitation, i.e. the extraction of gene expression data. The second step is gene expression data analysis, in which after the ratios of the intensities are obtained, various methods can be applied to cluster the genes into different functional groups based on the ratios retrieved in the first step. Microarray image quantitation involves various steps, including addressing or gridding, segmentation or background separation, and normalization. The success of the subsequent steps in the analysis resort mainly in how efficient the initial stages, gridding and segmentation, are conducted.

To deal with the microarray image segmentation problem, many approaches have been proposed. Fixed circle segmentation, a traditional technique that was first used in ScanAlyze [4], assigns the same diameter and shape (circle) to all spots. GenePix [5] and ScanArray Express [6] also provide the option for fixed circle method. A method that was proposed to avoid the drawback of fixed circle is the adaptive circle segmentation technique and can be found in GenePix, ScanAlyze, ScanArray Express, Imagene, and Dapple [1]. Seeded region growing (SRG) has been successfully applied to image segmentation in general, and has recently been introduced in microarray image processing [13].

Another technique that has been successfully used in microarray image segmentation is the histogram-based approach. Using histograms to classify a pixel into either foreground or background is a simple and intuitive idea. Chen *et al.* introduced a method that uses a circular target mask to cover all the foreground pixels, and computes a threshold using Mann-Whitney test [2].

Clustering has also been used in microarray image segmentation, showing some advantages when applied to microarray image segmentation, since they are not restricted to a particular shape and size for the spots [9,10,12]. Although they produce irregular-shaped spots, clustering-based methods are prone to include noisy pixels in the foreground regions, producing incorrect quantitation measures for the spots in such cases.

In this paper, we present a novel fixed-shaped spot segmentation method, which we call the *adaptive ellipse method*. Due to the fact that most of the spots in a microarray have the form of circles or ellipses (in the most general case), this method utilizes the process of diagonalization [8]. Our empirical results show that the adaptive ellipse method produces quite good results compared to the adaptive circle method, and can be applied to a much wider range of microarray images. In fact, the adaptive circle method can be seen as a particular case of the adaptive ellipse approach.

## 2 Adaptive Ellipse Method

The method that we introduce in this section can be seen as a generalization of the adaptive circle technique. We first describe the process of diagonalization, which is crucial in our method, and then the remaining details of the approach.

Diagonalization is the process of transforming a $d$-dimensional normally distributed random vector, $x \sim N(\mu, \Sigma)$, where $\mu$ is the mean vector and $\Sigma$ is the covariance matrix, into a new normally distributed random vector $z \sim N(\mu_z, I)$, where $I$ is the identity matrix. This is achieved by means of two linear transformations: an orthonormal and a whitening transformation [8]. After applying diagonalization, the normally distributed data with arbitrary mean and covariance matrix is transformed into a distribution in which the covariance is the identity matrix.

Diagonalization involves two steps. For a normally distributed random vector $x \sim N(\mu, \Sigma)$, first, the following orthornormal linear transformation transforms $x$ into another random vector $y = \Phi^t x$, where $\Phi$ is a $d \times d$ orthogonal matrix that contains the $d$ eigenvectors of $\Sigma$, namely $\phi_1 \ldots \phi_d$. After this step, the underlying covariance matrix, $\Lambda$, for $y$ is diagonal, where the diagonal elements of $\Lambda$ are the corresponding eigenvalues of $\Sigma$, $\lambda_1 \ldots \lambda_d$. The next step is the whitening transformation, which transforms $y$ into a new random vector $z = \Lambda^{-1/2} y$, whose covariance is the identity matrix. Since $z$ is normally distributed, its elements (random variables) are independent and uncorrelated, and their variances are equal to unity.

In our method, we use the diagonalization transformation to obtain new pixel coordinates for a given spot, where the pixel intensities after normalized yield a histogram that approximates the probability density function of a two-dimensional normally distributed random vector with the identity as the covariance matrix. Once the transformation has taken place, the radius that determines the "edge" to separate foreground from background has to be obtained. For this, we propose a new procedure, since traditional image processing techniques, such as the Laplacian transform, cannot be applied due to the fact that, after the transformation, the pixel coordinates become real numbers. The details of the steps involved in our approach are discussed below.

### 2.1 Parameter Estimation

We consider the spot region in terms of two sources: one containing the pixel coordinates, namely $X = \{x_{ij} | i = 1\ldots m, j = 1\ldots n\}$, where $x_{ij}$ is the coordinate of the $(ij)^{th}$ pixel, and the other containing the pixel intensities, namely $I = \{I_{ij} | i = 1\ldots m, j = 1\ldots n\}$. We assume that each element, $x_{ij}$, occurs $I_{ij}$ times in a sample dataset, and hence conforming a dataset $\mathbf{D}$ that contains $x_{ij}$, $I_{ij}$ times. Thus, assuming that the underlying random vector obeys the normal distribution $x \sim N(\mu, \Sigma)$, $\mu$ is estimated using the following expression:

$$\mu = \frac{1}{\Sigma_{i=1}^{m} \Sigma_{j=1}^{n} I_{ij}} \Sigma_{i=1}^{m} \Sigma_{j=1}^{n} I_{ij} x_{ij} . \tag{1}$$

On the other hand, the covariance matrix $\Sigma$ is estimated as follows:

$$\Sigma = \frac{\Sigma_{i=1}^{m} \Sigma_{j=1}^{n} I_{ij} (x_{ij} - \mu)(x_{ij} - \mu)^t}{\Sigma_{i=1}^{m} \Sigma_{j=1}^{n} I_{ij}} . \tag{2}$$

Thus, the parameters of the underlying normally distributed random vector have been estimated, and hence the next steps, which are discussed below, are applied.

### 2.2 Diagonalization

After the two parameters, $\mu$ and $\Sigma$, of the underlying random vector $x$ are estimated, the next step is to apply diagonalization, based on the eigenvalues and eigenvectors of $\Sigma$, $\Lambda$ and $\Phi$ respectively. Since diagonalization is applied to the original random vector, $x$, the corresponding pixel coordinates have to be transformed to the new space by applying the following linear transformation: $z = \Lambda^{-1/2} \Phi^t x$. This result can be verified by estimating $\mu'$ and $\Sigma'$ in the new distribution: the mean obtained using the transformed points is the same as the mean obtained using the points in the original distribution, and $\Sigma'$ is the identity matrix. After the diagonalization process, the dataset is transformed into a new space, where the data points with the same probability have the same Mahalanobis distance in the original space, while they lie on a circle in the transformed space. Fig. 1 shows a typical case in which the spot takes the shape of an ellipse in the original space. After the diagonalization process is applied, the coordinates of the pixels are real (not necessarily integer) numbers, as can be observed in the plot on the right hand side of the figure. For example, the pixel coordinates, which in the original space are [1,1], result in [-0.4139, 0.4934] in the transformed space.

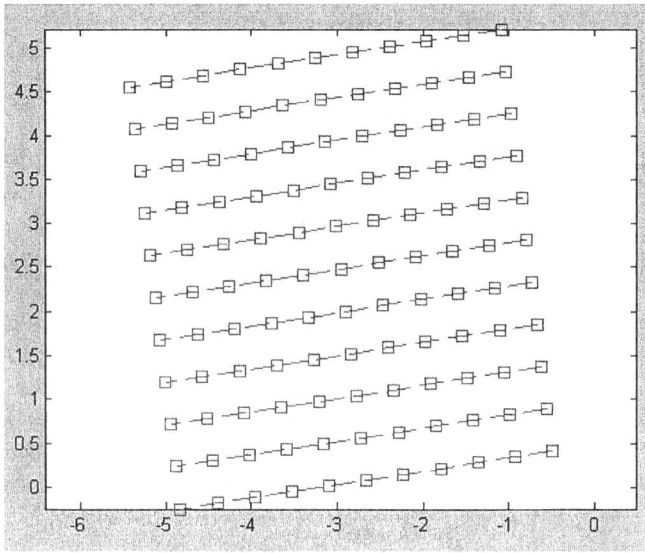

**Fig. 1.** Change of coordinates after diagonalization. The left image shows a sample spot(Spot No. 12 of 1230c1G/R microarray image) that has an elliptic shape. The right hand side shows the coordinates of each pixel in the transformated space.

## 2.3 Computing the Radius

Once the points (pixel coordinates) in the transformed space are obtained, the aim is to compute the radius that determines the edge that separates the spot from the background region. As pointed out earlier, the pixel coordinates, in most of the cases, become real numbers, and so it is not possible to apply traditional edge detection techniques, such as the Laplacian transform. We adopt, instead, a statistical method to compute the radius of the foreground region. First, we use the Mann-Whitney test to estimate a threshold. A more detailed discussion of Mann-Whitney test can be found in [3]. Pixels from the predefined positions, i.e. the four corners and four middle-points in the edges of the spot region, are chosen, namely $y_1, y_2, \ldots, y_8$. The pixels from the other region of the spot are sorted and the lowest 8 pixels are chosen as $x_1, x_2, \ldots, x_8$. We need a parameter to compute the rank-sum statistic, namely W. If the null hypothesis is not rejected, the pixel with the lowest intensity is discarded from the target set, and the next lowest intensity pixel is chosen from the remaining pixels. The process is repeated until the null hypothesis is rejected. The lowest intensity of the eight pixels is then the threshold that determines the radius for the spot. The pixels whose intensities are above the threshold are considered to be foreground pixels. In the next stage, we sort all the pixels by their distance to the spot center, $\mu$, in an increasing order. Starting from the smallest distance pixel, we count the number of foreground pixels and background pixels for the next $2n+1$ pixels. The foreground and background pixels are grouped according to the threshold obtained in the Mann-Whitney test. The process stops when the majority in the testing set are background pixels. Otherwise, we move the starting pixel to the next one in the sorted pixels and use the next $2n+1$ pixels. The average distance of the $2n+1$ pixels is the radius that defines the foreground region. All the pixels whose distance to the spot center, $\mu$, is smaller than the radius are labeled "foreground", otherwise they are assigned to the background. In our implementation, we set the size of the testing set to three pixels. A formal implementation of the algorithm for the adaptive ellipse method can be found in [7].

## 3 Experimental Results

In order to evaluate the adaptive ellipse method proposed in this paper, we performed some simulations on real-life microarray images obtained from the ApoA1 data[1], and compared our results with the well-known adaptive circle method. In our experiments, the significance level was set to 0.01. This value has been found to yield good results in most of our experiments. The programs have been implemented in Matlab, and the source code is listed as an appendix in [7].

Fig. 2 (a) shows the result of the adaptive ellipse method and the adaptive circle method for some spots drawn from the 1230c1G/R microarray image. For those ellipse-shaped spots, we observe that the adaptive ellipse method generates a foreground region that is closer to the original spot in both shape and size than adaptive circle method. Consider spot No. 49, for example. The foreground region generated by the adaptive ellipse method has the form of an ellipse, while the foreground region generated by the adaptive circle looks like a circle. The same situation occurs as in spot No. 65, but in this case, the axes of the resulting ellipse are not coincident with the coordinates of the system.

Fig. 2 (b), on the other hand, shows the comparison of the two methods for some spots whose shape is similar to a circle. Because the circle is a particular case of the ellipse, the adaptive ellipse method also works well for circular spots. We observe that these two methods generate almost identical results for these spots.

Based on the above observations, we conclude that the adaptive ellipse method generates better results when dealing with spots that have the shape of an ellipse. Meanwhile, it generates results as good as the adaptive circle method when dealing with circular spots. In general, the adaptive ellipse method is suitable for a wider range of spots, and generates better results. This argument could be shown theoretically, and is observed in the experiments below. The former constitutes an open problem, and proposes a future avenue for research.

We also provide a numerical comparison; the measurement that we adopt for the comparison is the intensity of the foreground region for each spot, and the number of pixels belonging to that region. The results are shown in Table 1. The first column for each method contains the number of pixels in the foreground

---

[1] Apo A1 microarray data website. Terry Speed's Microarray Data Analysis Group Page. http://www.stat.berkeley.edu/users/terry/zarray/Html/apodata.html

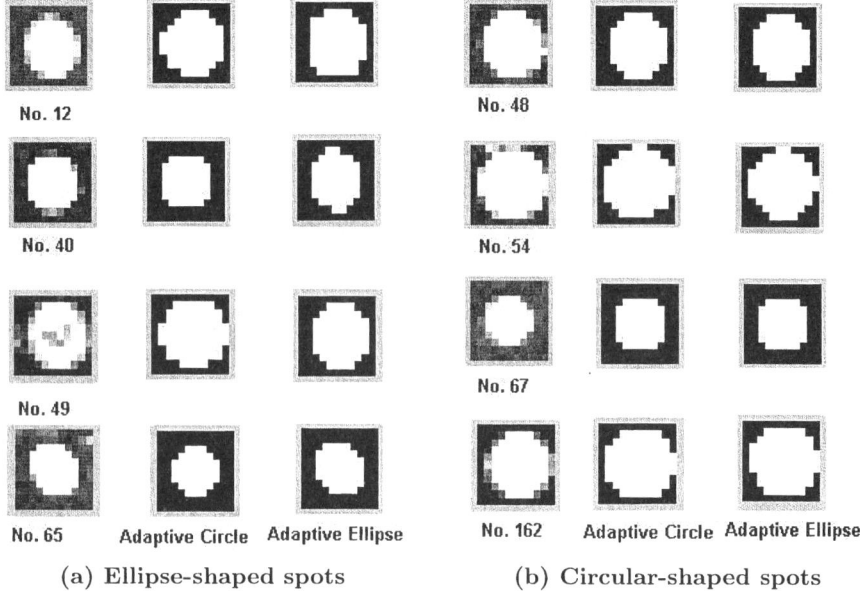

**Fig. 2.** Different results obtained from the adaptive circle and adaptive ellipse methods for spots taken from 1230c1G/R microarray image

region, $N_{fg}$, and the second column represents the total spot foreground intensity of the green channel, $I_{fg}$. In the first two columns, we notice that the average foreground intensity generated by adaptive ellipse is higher than adaptive circle, in most of the cases. Meanwhile the number of pixels generated by the former is approximately in the same range as the latter, but slightly larger. This can be easily justified by the fact that adaptive ellipse finds a foreground region that represents the spot foreground better, which means that it includes more foreground pixels and fewer background pixels than the adaptive circle method. Thus, it results in higher foreground intensity even though it contains more pixels in general. In our experiments, seven out of the nine images result in higher foreground intensity.

In order to enhance the quality of our assessment about the experiments, we compare the number of "hits", i.e. the number of the pixels that are incorrectly labeled by the two algorithms. Because there are no standard solutions for microarray image segmentation and classifying the pixels manually is still subjective and error-prone, we choose a histogram-based algorithm as the reference method to classify the pixels into foreground and background. Then, we apply the two methods to the same spots, and count the number of hits. The spots are obtained randomly from image 1230c1G/R of the Apo A1 dataset. Table 2 shows the results. We observe that, in most of the cases, the adaptive ellipse method generates fewer hits, which implies that it generates a foreground region that is more similar to that of the histogram-based approach.

**Table 1.** Comparison of Adaptive Circle method and adaptive ellipse method for a batch of images from the ApoA1 dataset, where the first sub-grid of each image is analyzed

|  | Adaptive Circle | | | Adaptive Ellipse | | |
| --- | --- | --- | --- | --- | --- | --- |
|  | $N_{fg}$ | $I_{fg}$ | $I_{bg}$ | $N_{fg}$ | $I_{fg}$ | $I_{bg}$ |
| 1230c1G | 28.24 | 3,652 | 846 | 28.34 | 3,670 | 843 |
| 1230c2G | 25.36 | 4,301 | 1,120 | 25.80 | 4,314 | 1,123 |
| 1230c3G | 28.17 | 4,178 | 595 | 28.29 | 4,181 | 592 |
| 1230c4G | 24.37 | 3,248 | 818 | 24.57 | 3,235 | 816 |
| 1230c5G | 26.88 | 2,914 | 459 | 26.91 | 2,961 | 459 |
| 1230ko1G | 33.86 | 2,018 | 396 | 33.81 | 2,022 | 387 |
| 1230ko2G | 20.69 | 2,353 | 532 | 20.54 | 2,373 | 531 |
| 1230ko3G | 29.05 | 2,884 | 577 | 28.85 | 2,902 | 576 |
| 1230ko4G | 24.56 | 2,735 | 564 | 24.64 | 2,729 | 563 |

**Table 2.** Comparison of adaptive circle and adaptive ellipse with a histogram-based approach

|  | File | Hits (adaptive circle) | | | Hits (adaptive ellipse) | | |
| --- | --- | --- | --- | --- | --- | --- | --- |
| Spot Number → |  | 12 | 24 | 36 | 12 | 24 | 36 |
|  | 1230c1 | 29 | 8 | 7 | 25 | 8 | 7 |
|  | 1230c2 | 48 | 22 | 24 | 47 | 21 | 24 |
|  | 1230c3 | 12 | 12 | 11 | 9 | 14 | 9 |
|  | 1230c4 | 36 | 13 | 17 | 36 | 10 | 16 |
|  | 1230c5 | 21 | 17 | 23 | 18 | 15 | 23 |
|  | 1230ko1 | 11 | 18 | 9 | 14 | 18 | 9 |
|  | 1230ko2 | 29 | 41 | 19 | 29 | 41 | 19 |
|  | 1230ko3 | 15 | 17 | 15 | 15 | 18 | 15 |
|  | 1230ko4 | 17 | 16 | 25 | 17 | 16 | 25 |
| Total → |  | Adaptive circle: 532 | | | Adaptive ellipse: 518 | | |

## 4 Conclusions

We have introduced a new microarray image segmentation method, which we call the *adaptive ellipse method*. The advantage of this method is that it results in a foreground region that better represents the actual spots, and can be used for a wider range of microarray images than the traditional adaptive circle method. We view each spot in the microarray image from another perspective: the intensities of the spot region conform a histogram that is used to approximate the probability density function of a bivariate normal distribution. This enable us to extract statistical information from the images that is typically ignored by the traditional adaptive circle method, and hence showing more flexibility.

The empirical results on DNA microarray images drawn from the Apo A1 dataset show that the adaptive ellipse method can reveal the true shape of the spots, and works better than the adaptive circle method. We have shown the superiority of adaptive ellipse over adaptive circle both visually and numerically.

The adaptive ellipse method, which generates quite satisfying results, still has room for improvements. After the dataset is transformed to the new distribution, various methods can be applied to obtain the radius that defines the foreground region. A possible approach is to compute the slope of the probability density function for each pixel, and then find the radius that generates the largest slope average. This problem constitutes a possible avenue for future research. More work can also be done in more elaborated experiments to seek for better parameters of the present approach in finding the foreground radius.

*Acknowledgements.* This research work has been partially supported by NSERC, the Natural Sciences and Engineering Research Council of Canada, CFI, the Canadian Foundation for Innovation, and OIT, the Ontario Innovation Trust.

# References

1. J. Buhler, T. Ideker, and D. Haynor. Dapple: Improved Techniques for Finding Sports on DNA Microarrays. Technical Report UWTR 2000-08-05, University of Washington, 2000.
2. Y. Chen, E. Dougherty, and M. Bittner. Ratio-based Decision and the Quantitative Analysis of cDNA Microarray Images. *Journal of Biomedical Optics*, 2:364–374, 1997.
3. E.R. Dougherty. *Probability and statistics for the engineering, computing, and physical sciences.* Prentice-Hall, Englewood Cliffs, NJ, 1990.
4. M. Eisen. *ScanAlyze User's Manual.* M. Eisen, 1999.
5. Axon Instruments. *Genepix 4000A: User's Manual.* Axon Instruments Inc., 1999.
6. GSI Lumonics. *QuantArray Analsyis Software: Operator's Manual.* 1999.
7. L. Qin. New Machine-learning-based Techniques for DNA Microarray Image Segmentation. Master's thesis, School of Computer Science, University of Windsor, Canada, 2004. Electronically available at http://www.cs.uwindsor.ca/~lrueda/papers/LiThesis.pdf.
8. L. Rueda and B. J. Oommen. On Optimal Pairwise Linear Classifiers for Normal Distributions: The Two-Dimensional Case. *IEEE Transactions on Pattern Analysis and Machine Intelligence*, 24(2):274–280, 2002.
9. L. Rueda and L. Qin. An Improved Clustering-based Approach for DNA Microarray Image Segmentation. In *Proc. of the International Conference on Image Analysis and Recognition*, pages 17–24, Porto, Portugal, 2004.
10. L. Rueda and L. Qin. An Unsupervised Learning Scheme for DNA Microarray Image Spot Detection. In *Proc. of the First International Conference on Complex Medical Engineering*, pages 996–1000, Takamatsu, Japan, 2005.
11. M. Schena. *Microarray Analysis.* John Wiley & Sons, 2002.
12. H. Wu and H. Yan. Microarray Image processing Based on Clustering and Morphological Analysis. In *Proc. of the First Asia Pacific Bioinformatics Conference*, pages 111–118, Adelaide, Australia, 2003.
13. Y. Yang, M. Buckley, S. Dudoit, and T. Speed. Comparison of Methods for Image Analysis on cDNA Microarray Data. *Journal of Computational and Graphical Statistics*, 11:108–136, 2002.

# Comparative Pixel-Level Exudate Recognition in Colour Retinal Images

Alireza Osareh[1], Bita Shadgar[1], and Richard Markham[2]

[1] Department of Computer Science, Shahid Chamran University, Ahwaz, Iran
{Osareh, Shadgar}@cs.bris.ac.uk
[2] Bristol Eye Hospital, Bristol, BS1 2LX, U.K
markham@gifford.co.uk
http://www.cs.bris.ac.uk/~osareh
http://www.cs.bris.ac.uk/~shadgar

**Abstract.** Retinal exudates are typically manifested as spatially random yellow/white patches of varying sizes and shapes. They are a visible sign of retinal diseases such as diabetic retinopathy. Following some key preprocessing steps, colour retinal image pixels are classified to exudate and non-exudate classes. $K$ nearest neighbour, Gaussian quadratic and Gaussian mixture model classifiers are investigated within the pixel-level exudate recognition framework. A Gaussian mixture model-based classifier demonstrated the best classification performance with 89.2% *sensitivity* and 81.0% *predictivity* in terms of pixel-level accuracy and 92.5% *sensitivity* and 81.4% *specificity* in terms of image-based accuracy.

## 1 Introduction

Diabetic retinopathy is a severe and widely spread eye disease which can be regarded as manifestation of diabetes on the retina. Intraretinal hard exudates are a visible sign of diabetic retinopathy and also a marker for the presence of co-existent retinal oedema. If present in the macular area, oedema and exudates are a major cause of visual loss in the non-proliferative forms of diabetic retinopathy. Exudates are associated with patches of vascular damage with leakage and typically manifested as spatially random yellow patches of varying sizes and shapes [1]. Currently, there is an increasing interest for setting up systems and algorithms that can screen a large number of people for sight threatening diseases, such as diabetic retinopathy and then provide an automated detection of the disease.

In this paper we report the benefits of developing an automated decision support system for the purpose of detecting and classifying exudate pathologies of diabetic retinopathy. $K$ nearest neighbour (*KNN*), Gaussian quadratic (*GQ*) and Gaussian mixture model (*GMM*) classifiers are exploited towards a binary pixel-level classification task. The expectation-maximisation algorithm is applied to determine the *GMM* parameters and the optimum number of mixture model components is decided based on the minimum description length criterion. Finally, to assess the efficiency of our pixel-level exudate recognition scheme in terms of image-based accuracy, an unseen set of images are classified using the optimum *GMM* classifier.

Sinthanayothin [2] identified exudates in greylevel images based on a recursive region growing technique. The sensitivity and specificity reported was 88.5% and

99.7%, however, these measurements were based on 10x10 windows where each window was considered as an exudates or a non-exudate region. The reported *sensitivity* and *specificity* only represent an approximate accuracy of exudates recognition, because any particular 10x10 window may be only partially affected by exudates. Gardner et al. [3] used a neural network to identify the exudates in greylevel images. The authors reported a *sensitivity* of 93.1%. Again, this figure is the result of their identification of exudates by classifying regular regions of size 20x20 pixels rather than a pixel-level classification. This involved training their network on patches that were 'bad' if one or more pixels in the 20x20 patch were exudates or 'good' if no pixels were affected.

One novelty of our proposed method here is that we locate exudates at pixel-level rather than estimate for regions. The colour retinal images are automatically analysed in terms of pixel-level and image-based diagnostic accuracies and an assessment of the level of retinopathy is derived. This paper is organised as follows. Section 2 briefly outlines our image pre-processing steps. In Section 3, *KNN*, *GQ*, and *GMM* classifiers will be compared in how they perform in classifying the image pixels to exudates and non-exudates. Section 4 reports on the application of the *GMM* pixel-level classifier towards an image-based classification scheme. The paper is concluded in Section 5.

## 2 Preprocessing

We used 142 colour retinal images obtained from a Canon CR6-45 non-mydriatic camera with a 45° field of view. This consisted of 75 images for training and testing our classifiers in the pixel-level classification stage. The remaining 67 images were employed to investigate the image-based diagnostic accuracy of our system. The image resolution was 760x570 at 24bit RGB.

Typically, there is wide variation in the colour of the fundus from different patients, related to race and iris colour. The first step is therefore to normalise the images across the set [4]. We selected a particular image as a reference and used histogram specification to modify the values of each image in the dataset such that its frequency histogram matched the reference image distribution (Figure 1(c)). The contrast of retinal images is not sufficient due to the intrinsic attributes of lesions. Thus, in the next step, the contrast between exudates and the retina background was enhanced using a local contrast enhancement method (Figure 1(d)).

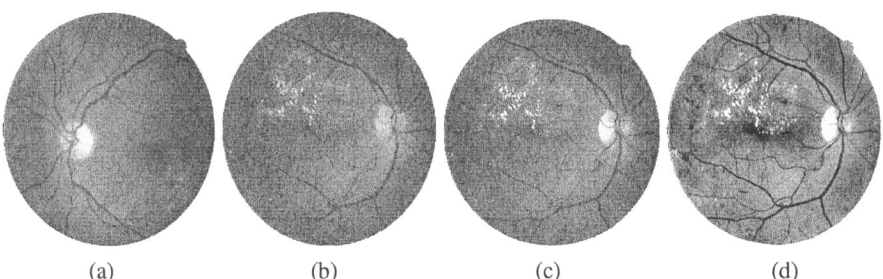

**Fig. 1.** Colour normalisation and contrast enhancement: (a) reference image, (b) typical retinal image (including exudates), (c) colour normalised version, (d) after contrast enhancement

## 3 Pixel-Level Exudate Recognition

Pixel classification can be performed based on non-contextual or contextual pixel labelling. Non-contextual labeling methods have an intrinsic limitation, as they do not take the spatial relationship of the pixels into account [5]. Here, for each image pixel $x_0$ a feature vector consisting of multi-spectral values of pixels in a defined neighbourhood $N(x_0)$ were used as a feature representation. An odd-sized square window was centered on each underlying pixel $x_0$ in the dataset. Then the L$uv$ colour components (this colour space was found the most appropriate space for our analysis) of the pixels in the window composed into the feature vector of $x_0$.

The selection of a colour space for image processing is application dependent. To select the most suitable colour space for our pixel-based classification approach, we conducted a quantitative analysis and applied a metric to evaluate the performance of various colour spaces. This metric [6] estimated the class separability of our exudate and non-exudate pixel classes in different colour spaces and was measured using within-class and between-class scatter matrices. After within-class ($S_w$) and between-class ($S_b$) matrices are measured the following metric $J$ can be obtained:

$$J = trace\left(\frac{S_b}{S_w}\right) \quad (1)$$

A higher value of $J$ indicates that the classes are more separated while the members within each class are closer to each other. We have experimented with different colour spaces and found that the L$uv$ colour space is the most appropriate space for our retinal image analysis (Table 1). Thus, we chose this colour space to carry out our pixel-level classification task.

Table 1. Comparative analysis of different colour spaces

| Colour Space | YIQ | RGB | HSL | HSI | Lab | Luv |
|---|---|---|---|---|---|---|
| $J$ | 2.20 | 2.25 | 2.64 | 2.81 | 3.32 | **3.67** |

There might be no constraint on the neighbourhood window size $N$ in theory, but it was assumed that most contextual information was presented in a small neighbourhood of the $x_0$ pixel. Here, to determine the optimal window size, we examined various pixel patch sizes, i.e. 1x1, 3x3, 5x5 and 7x7. To construct learning datasets of exudate and non-exudate (including cotton-wool spots, red lesions, blood vessels and background) pixels, a consultant ophthalmologist manually segmented 75 pre-proceed images and marked the exudate lesions. An almost balanced learning dataset of exudates and non-exudates was then established to eliminate any possible bias towards either of the two classes. This representative learning dataset comprised of 62501 exudate and 63046 non-exudate pixels.

To model the exudate and non-exudate probability density function, we chose one very commonly used classifier, for every type of probability density estimation approaches, i.e. non-parametric *KNN*, parametric *GQ*, and semi-parametric *GMM*.

Each classifier was trained and tested against our four pixel datasets (1x1, 3x3, 5x5, and 7x7).

In *KNN* classification, the number of neighbours, i.e. *K* needs to be pre-defined. Here, we experimented with different *K* values ranging from 1 to 7 (*K* was chosen to be odd to avoid ties), to find the optimum value with lowest misclassification error rate. Table 2 summarises the best overall performances accomplished using *KNN* classifiers. As can be seen, these classifiers achieved good generalisation ability, with a best overall performance of 90.26% against 5x5 pixel patch size dataset. In this case, the correct classification rates for exudate and non-exudate classes were 88.92% and 91.60% respectively.

The Gaussian distribution is one of the most generally used density estimators. According to Bayes' theorem, the posterior probability is written as:

$$P(C_i \mid x) = \frac{p(x \mid C_i) P(C_i)}{p(x)} \quad (2)$$

The likelihood function $p(x|C_i)$ was defined in terms of exudates and non-exudates class mean and covariance matrix. $P(C_i)$ was a priori probability denoting the probability that a pixel (exudate or non-exudate) occurs in the entire set of pixels. The posterior probability measured the probability of the pixel belonging to either the exudates ($C_{Exu}$) or non-exudates ($C_{Non}$) class once we have observed the feature vector *x*. Here, the class attached to each feature vector *x* was selected based on a maximum a posterior (MAP) rule. Table 2 illustrates the overall performances achieved using *GQ* classifiers. The best obtained overall classification accuracy was 88.24% comprising of 89.14% and 87.34% correct classification rates for exudates and non-exudates respectively.

**Table 2.** The best overall pixel-level classification performances

| Pixel-level dataset | Classifier | | |
|---|---|---|---|
| | KNN | GQ | GMM |
| 1x1 | 84.29% (K=7) | 82.25% | 85.13% |
| 3x3 | 86.85% (K=5) | 86.15% | 92.35% |
| 5x5 | **90.26% (K=5)** | **88.24%** | **96.49%** |
| 7x7 | 89.87% (K=5) | 87.58% | 96.32% |

A disadvantage of parametric density estimation techniques is their lack of flexibility when compared with non-parametric methods. Although single Gaussian density estimation models can be set up easily, they are restricted in their ability to efficiently estimate more complex distributions [7]. *GMMs* combine much of the flexibility of non-parametric methods with certain amounts of the analytical advantages of parametric approaches. Basically, in a mixture model distribution, the data is represented as a linear combination of component densities in the form:

$$p(x_i) = \sum_{k=1}^{K} p(x_i \mid w_k; \Theta_k) P(w_k) \qquad (3)$$

where $K$ represents the number of components and each component is defined by $w_k$ and parameterised by $\Theta_k$ (mean vector and covariance matrix). The coefficient $P(w_k)$ is called the mixing parameter. We benefited from the theory behind these models and used a separate mixture of Gaussians to estimate the class densities $p(x|C_i,\Theta)$ of exudates and non-exudates as follows:

$$p(x \mid C_i, \Theta) = \sum_{k=1}^{K_i} \frac{P(w_k)}{(2\pi)^{\frac{d}{2}} \det(\Sigma_k)^{\frac{1}{2}}} \exp\left\{-\frac{1}{2}(x-\mu_k)^T \Sigma_k^{-1}(x-\mu_k)\right\} \qquad (4)$$

where $\mu_k$ and $\Sigma_k$ represent the mean and covariance of the *kth* component of the mixture density of class $C_i$. $K_i$ denotes the numbers of components in class $i$ and $C_i$ refers to either the exudates or non-exudates class. Having estimated the likelihood functions of these two classes the posterior probabilities were obtained. The decision about the affiliation of each new feature vector $x$ was then taken by applying the MAP rule. We assumed a full covariance matrix for each component, since these types of matrices have higher flexibility in estimating the underlying distributions.

To determine the parameters of a *GMM* and fit a model to the data expectation maximisation algorithm was utilised. This algorithm started by making some initial guess for the parameters of the model and then iteratively modified these parameters and decreased an error function until a minimum was reached. The parameters were initialised using a *K*-means clustering algorithm. The *K*-means algorithm partition the feature space into *K* clusters. To apply *K*-means algorithm, the number of clusters, i.e. *K* (or equivalently the number of components) needs to be known. Choosing too few components produces a model that cannot accurately model the distributions. With an increasing number of components, the probability that the model fits the dataset better will be increased, but the model also loses its capability to generalise well.

Here, the appropriate number of components was chosen by repeating the density model estimation and evaluating minimum description length criteria [8]. We obtained the optimum mixture model of each exudate and non-exudate pixel-level dataset separately by varying the number of components within a range of 1 to 20. The optimum number of *GMM* components for exudate and non-exudate datasets were found equal to 7 and 9 (for 1x1 dataset), 10 and 11 (for 3x3 dataset), 15 and 17 (for 5x5 dataset), 19 and 23 (for 7x7 dataset) respectively. It is evident that by increasing the pixel patch size the model complexity was also raised and necessitated a higher number of components for effective density estimation.

Table 2 summarises the overall performances achieved using *GMMs*. Typically, the performance of a classifier improves up to a certain point as additional features are added, and then deteriorates. This can be seen in Table 2, as performances continued to improve when the patch size was increased up to 5. At this point all classifiers achieved their best results. However, by increasing the pixel patch size more, i.e., to 7, the accuracies were decreased.

In many situations, such as our application, it is valuable to obtain a 2D or 3D projection of the original multivariate data for visual examination. Here, principal component analysis was applied to the pixel dataset that achieved the highest classification accuracy, i.e. our 5x5 dataset. The first two exudate principal modes contained 62.4% of the total variance, i.e. 49.7% + 12.7%. Similarly, the first two non-exudate principal modes represent 53.2% of the total variance (38.0% + 15.2%).

Figure 2 shows the response of the exudates 5x5 pixel dataset to the first two principal modes where the optimum number of *GMM* components was found equal to 9 using minimum description length criteria. The yellow marks in this figure demonstrate the final locations of Gaussian component mean values, which were found initially by *K*-means and then expectation maximisation algorithms. On the other hand, this figure shows the estimation of mixture components and their centres as elliptical contours of equal probability in the direction of their eigenvectors and a diameter of twice the square root of the corresponding eigenvalues.

The *GMM* classifiers performed better than the other two classifiers and provided the best results irrespective of the choice of pixel patch size. The best *GMM* classifier demonstrated an overall performance equal to 96.49%, based on the 5x5 pixel-level dataset (Table 2). In this case, the correct classification rates for exudates and non-exudates were 96.15% and 96.83% respectively. Therefore, this *GMM* classifier was utilized to classify the pixels of a new set of images.

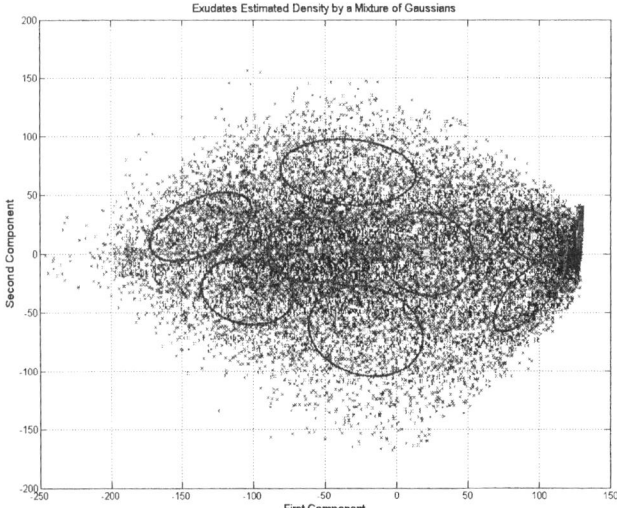

**Fig. 2.** *GMM* density estimation for the first two principal modes of exudate pixels (schematic of the estimated density)

## 4 Application of Pixel Level Exudate Recognition on Whole Retinal Image

The performance of a medical diagnosis system is best described in terms of *sensitivity* and *specificity*. The *sensitivity* gives the percentage of correctly classified abnormal cases while the *specificity* defines the percentage of correctly classified normal cases. Classification of the whole retinal image pixels was required to work on an imbalanced dataset of exudate and non-exudate pixels where the number of *true negatives (TN)* was much higher than the *false positives (FPs)*. The *specificity* measure was mostly near 100% and did not represent an informative measurement. Thus, we used the *predictivity* measure, which is the probability that a pixel classified as exudate is really an exudate. This was defined as:

$$predictivity = \frac{TP}{TP + FP} \quad (5)$$

where *TP* refers to the *true positive*. In real applications, such as ours, there is no previous knowledge of actual prior probabilities of exudates and non-exudates. For example, the underlying test image can be either a normal image with no exudate, or an abnormal severe retinopathy image with a significant number of exudate pixels. Thus, to accomplish an efficient image classification process and control the balance between *sensitivity* and *predictivity*, we constructed a series of classifiers by varying the prior probability ratio of exudates to non-exudates using a decision threshold T. For instance, a threshold value equal to 0.8 sets the exudates' prior probability to 0.8 and non-exudates' prior probability equal to 0.2 (i.e. 1-T). Figure 3 shows an abnormal image that has been classified using the *GMM* classifier. The original image and its ground-truth are shown in Figures 3 (a, b). The corresponding classification results for T values of 0.3, 0.5 and 0.7 are illustrated in Figure 3 (c, e, g).

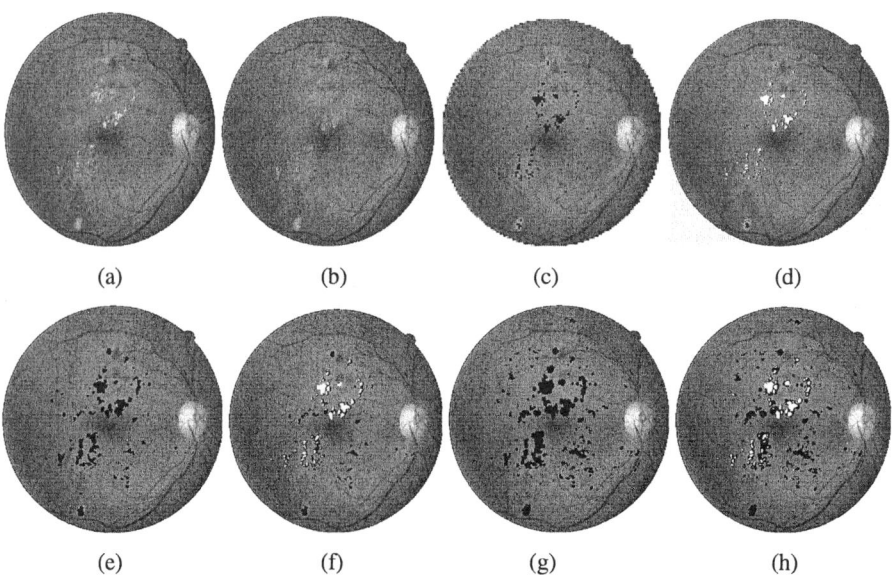

**Fig. 3.** Pixel-level exudate recognition application on a retinal image using different ratio of exudate and non-exudate prior probabilities. The identified exudates are shown in blue and *TPs* in white. (a) Original image, (b) Ground-truth, (c) T = 0.3, (d) Superposition of (b) and (c), (e) T = 0.5, (f) Superposition of (b) and (e), (g) T = 0.7, (h) Superposition of (b) and (g).

By increasing the threshold value and assigning higher prior probabilities to the exudates, the number of *TPs* was increased while at the same time the *false negatives* (*FNs*) were decreased. Thus, the *sensitivity* measure was enhanced. Indeed, by increasing the threshold value another reverse trend was noticed, where the *FPs* also begin to intensify, which leads to a decrease in *predictivity*. The trade-off between *sensitivity* and *predictivity* measures (choice of T) needs to be appropriately balanced according to the diagnostic strategy. We considered a new set of 40 abnormal images and then each image was separately classified with different T values.

The overall pixel-level classification performance was obtained based on the average of all images' *sensitivities* and *predictivities* values. Table 3, summarises some of these averaged *sensitivity-predictivity* values. As is evident, the threshold values which provided the highest average of *sensitivity* and *predictivity* values were 0.40 and 0.45. An important issue in choosing the threshold is ensuring that our classifier does not have a very high *sensitivity* for exudate detection; otherwise it can wrongly classify the normal images as abnormal. Therefore, to assess the efficiency of our proposed exudate recognition scheme in terms of image-based accuracy, we set the threshold T equal to 0.45 and classified the whole set of 67 retinal images (40 abnormal and 27 normal) using the optimum *GMM* classifier. Then a final decision was made as to whether each image had some evidence of retinopathy.

When we manually analysed the system's decision on normal images we found that in most cases when a normal image had been wrongly identified as abnormal not many *FP* pixels had been detected. To improve the image-based *specificity* of the system without sacrificing the *sensitivity*, a threshold value was defined. Based on this threshold, each classified abnormal image with less than 50 identified exudate pixels in size was considered normal. This threshold was determined in agreement with our experiments and our consultant clinician. The *GMM* classifier could identify abnormal images with 92.5% *sensitivity* (correct identification of 37 abnormal images out of 40), while it correctly classified 81.4% (correct identification of 22 normal images out of 27) of the normal images (the *specificity*).

**Table 3.** Pixel-level accuracy in terms of *sensitivity-prodictivity* criteria

| T | Sensitivity | Predictivity |
|---|---|---|
| 0.30 | 80.3 | 88.3 |
| 0.40 | **87.2** | **83.0** |
| 0.45 | **89.2** | **81.0** |
| 0.50 | 90.4 | 79.5 |
| 0.85 | 94.5 | 57.6 |

# 5 Conclusions

This paper has reported work undertaken to investigate the use of three well-known statistical classifiers, i.e. *KNN*, *GQ* and *GMM* for pixel-level exudate recognition. It was found that the *GMM* classifiers performed better than the other two classifiers.

*KNN* classifiers could outperform the *GQs* but the latter were much quicker to develop. An acceptable trade-off between the system's *sensitivity* and *predictivity* was achieved by inspecting different ratios of exudate and non-exudate prior probabilities. The proposed scheme achieved 92.5% *sensitivity* and 81.4% *specificity* in terms of image-based classification accuracy. It also illustrated 89.2% *sensitivity* and 81.0% *predictivity* in terms of pixel-level accuracy. The results demonstrated here indicate that automated diagnosis of exudative retinopathy based on colour retinal images can be very successful.

## References

[1] I. Ghafour, D. Allan, W. Foulds, "Common cause of blindness and visual handicap in the west of Scotland", *British Journal of Ophthalmology*, Vol 67, pp. 209-213, 1983.
[2] C. Sinthanayothin, "Image analysis for automatic diagnosis of diabetic retinopathy," *PhD Thesis*, King's College, London, 1999.
[3] G. Gardner, D. Keating, T. Williamson, et al, "Automatic detection of diabetic retinopathy using an artificial neural network: a screening tool" *British Journal of Ophthalmology*, Vol 86, pp. 940-944, 1996.
[4] A. Osareh, M. Mirmehdi, B. Thomas, R. Markham "Classification and localisation of diabetic-related eye disease", *Proc $7^{th}$ European Conference on Computer Vision*, pp. 502-516, 2002.
[5] J. Kittler, J. Foglein, "Contextual classification of multispectral pixel data", *Image and Vision Computing*, Vol 2 (1), pp. 13-29, 1984.
[6] K. Fukunaga, *Statistical pattern recognition*, Academic Press, 1990.
[7] C. Bishop, *Neural networks for pattern recognition*, Oxford University Press, Oxford, 1995.
[8] J. Rissanen,"A universal prior for integers and estimation by minimum description length", *Annals of Statistics*, Vol 11, pp. 415-431, 1983.

# Artificial Life Feature Selection Techniques for Prostate Cancer Diagnosis Using TRUS Images

S.S. Mohamed[1], A.M. Youssef[2], E.F. El-Saadany[1], and M.M.A. Salama[1]

[1] Department of Electrical and Computer Engineering,
University of Waterloo, Ontario, Canada
(smohamed, ehab, msalama)@hivolt.uwaterloo.ca
[2] Concordia Institute for Information Systems Engineering,
Concordia University, Montréal, Quebec, Canada
youssef@ciise.concordia.ca

**Abstract.** This paper presents two novel feature selection techniques for the purpose of prostate tissue characterization based on Trans-rectal Ultrasound (TRUS) images. First, suspected cancerous regions of interest (ROIs) are identified from the segmented TRUS images using Gabor filters. Next, second and higher order statistical texture features are constructed for these ROIs. Furthermore, a representative feature subset with the best discriminatory power among the constructed features is selected using two artificial life techniques: the Particle Swarm Optimization (PSO) and the Ant Colony Optimization (ACO). Both the PSO and ACO are tailored to fit the binary nature of the feature selection problem. The results are compared to the results obtained using the Genetic Algorithm (GA) feature selection approach. When Support Vector Machine (SVM) classifier is applied for the purpose of tissue characterization, the features obtained using the PSO and ACO outperforms the features obtained using the GA, i.e., they are capable of discriminating between suspicious cancerous and non-cancerous in a better accuracy. The obtained results demonstrate excellent tissue characterization with 83.3% sensitivity, 100% specificity and 94% overall accuracy.

## 1 Introduction

Prostate cancer is the highest-incidence cancer and the second leading cancer killer in men. It is only curable at an early stage; therefore, early detection is highly recommended [1]. Different types of diagnosis such as the Prostatic Specific Antigen (PSA) value, family history, age, race, prostate volume, as well as Digital Rectal Examination (DRE) lack reliability and therefore, are not sufficient for accurate diagnosis. Depending on these results, the doctor usually refers the patient to the next common diagnostic stage which is using Trans-rectal Ultrasound (TRUS) imaging system. Based on the radiologist scrutiny to the TRUS image a biopsy operation might follow [2]. The radiologist experience plays an important role in identifying the biopsy locations.

TRUS provides information about the size and shape of the prostate; it is also used for identifying different gland zones. TRUS is considered the dominant imaging modality for diagnosis of Prostatism as well as detection and staging of prostate cancer. However, TRUS is still deficient in early and accurate detection of tumours due to the low quality and noise characteristics of the TRUS images. The only way for recognizing the suspicious zones is with the aid of expert radiologist, which makes this process time consuming and operator dependent. Therefore, mimicking the expert radiologist decision is recommended as an assistive method for newer radiologists. This is achieved by the means of Computer Aided Diagnosis (CAD).

CAD of prostate cancer is a developing field where several aspects can be tackled. A typical CAD system consists of a segmentation stage, region of interest identification, feature construction, feature selection and classification. The work in this paper is focuses on ROI identification, feature extraction and selection where the selected features are then tested by a classifier that is capable of dealing with the noisy and distorted features of the TRUS images.

The first phase in CAD diagnosis from TRUS images is *segmentation* where the prostate boundaries are being detected from the TRUS image, a step that leads to determining the volume of the gland. Lots of research has been done in this area using different methods such as statistical shape model [3], super ellipses [4] and wavelet analysis [5] which makes it well established.

The second important phase is *ROI identification*, which deals with highlighting the most probable cancerous regions in the gland, a step that is usually achieved by an expert radiologist. This step is crucial as studying the whole image is computationally demanding. Moreover, choosing the incorrect ROIs results in misleading features that might lead to inaccurate medical decisions. A promising ROI identification method using Gabor multi-resolution analysis was proposed and applied to TRUS images in [6].

The next stage is *feature construction* where different statistical and spectral features are constructed from the identified ROIs. The features used in this paper include second order as well as higher order statistical features. The obtained features might have some redundancy or correlation; therefore, selection among features is necessary in order obtain a highly representative feature set [7]. Several methods can be used for feature selection. These methods can be categorized into classifier independent and classifier dependent feature selection. For the classifier independent feature selection, features are ranked according to the information content of each feature. While in the classifier dependent, a pre-specified classifier is used and the features that lead to the best classification results are selected.

Mutual Information Feature Selection (MIFS), as a classifier independent algorithm, was applied to TRUS images features in [8] and leads to excellent results, however, on the expense of the computational effort. This paper focuses on classifier dependant feature selection algorithms. These methods are Particle Swarm Optimization (PSO) and Ant Colony Optimization (ACO). The results of these two artificial life techniques are then compared to the Genetic Algorithm (GA) based feature selection.

The ultimate goal of this work is to mimic the radiologist's decision which is achieved using several consecutive stages that are highlighted in figure 1. The first stage is ROI identification using Gabor filters; the second stage is extracting statistical features from the identified ROIs. The third phase is a classifier based feature selection based on GA, PSO or ACO. The results obtained are compared to the doctor's diagnosis.

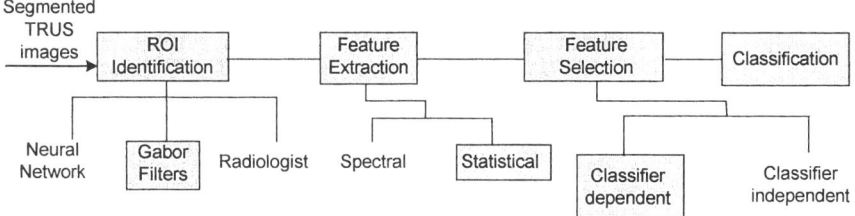

**Fig. 1.** Prostate Cancer Diagnosis from TRUS images

## 2 ROI Identification

ROI segmentation is a vital stage for TRUS image feature extraction for the purpose of prostate cancer diagnosis and it is usually performed by the aid of an expert radiologist. With the goal of assisting radiologist's decision and getting accurate rapid results, there is a great need for an automated ROI segmentation algorithm. Multi-resolution filtering is an excellent method for texture investigation, which is achieved by using Gabor multi-resolution analysis that is able to segment the image according to the frequency response of the pixels. The pixels that have similar response will be assigned to the same cluster. The Gabor function was chosen for this application for its high

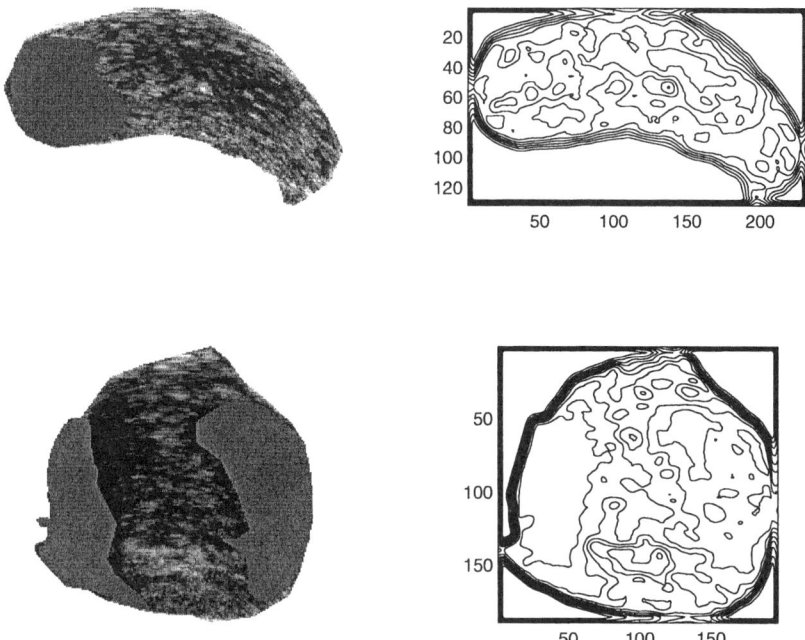

**Fig. 2.** Two different TRUS professionally segmented images and the corresponding ROIs

localization in both the spatial frequency domain as well as the spatial domain. The Gabor function in the spatial domain is a Gaussian modulated sinusoid, while in the spatial-frequency domain the Gabor function becomes two shifted Gaussians at the location of the modulating frequency. This method is applied in this paper and a sample of the segmented images and the original TRUS images is shown in figure 2.

## 3 Texture Feature Construction

Texture is used to describe the local spatial variations in image brightness which is related to image properties such as coarseness, and regularity. This is achieved by performing numerical manipulation of digitized images to get quantitative measurements. Texture analysis can potentially expand the visual skills of the expert eye by extracting image features that are relevant to diagnostic problem and not necessarily visually extractable. Statistical approaches represent texture with features that depend on relationships between the grey levels of the image. It is very helpful to know that different tissues have different textures. Benign tumors are described as regular masses with homogenous internal echoes, while carcinomas are masses with fuzzy borders and heterogenous internal echoes. In this work statistical texture features of identified ROIs are constructed. Statistical texture features proved its high recognition ability in ultrasound images. These features has been used for fetal lung maturity [9], liver tissue characterization [10], prostate cancer recognition [8] as well as some other applications. Second and higher order statistical features are used in this work where different texture features are constructed from the identified regions of interest of the TRUS images.

### 3.1 Second Order Statistics

The second order statistical features are considered crucial as the human visual system is capable of identifying different textures only if their second order statistics are different. However, textures which differ in higher-order statistics but have the same first- and second-order statistics cannot be recognized spontaneously by the human visual system. These features were used earlier for fetal lung maturity, liver tissue characterization, as well as prostate cancer diagnosis [8, 9, 10]. The two sets of second order statistical features used in this work are the Grey Level Difference Matrix (GLDM) and the Grey Level Difference Vector (GLDV). A set of nine features are constructed using GLDM and GLDV and the details of both methods are explained in [8].

### 3.2 Higher Order Statistics

With the relative immaturity of CAD applied to TRUS images, it would be unsuitable to think about the image analysis only using second-order statistical techniques. Moreover, as textures differing in third or higher-order statistics escape the capabilities of the human perceptual system, it is expected that considering higher-order analysis of TRUS images will give good results. Two higher order statistical algorithms are adopted and applied for the first time to the TRUS images in this work which are the Neighborhood Grey Tone Difference Matrix (NGTDM) and the Grey Tone Run Length Matrix

GTRLM where nine features are extracted from both matrices. The details and mathematical formulation of these methods are explained in [11,12] respectively.

- **Neighborhood Grey Tone Difference Matrix NGTDM**

NGTDM features are the properties, that might be used to discriminate between different textural patterns, include coarseness, contrast, complexity, busyness (fineness), shape, directionality and texture strength. In this approach the $i^{th}$ entry in NGTDM is a summation of the differences between all pixels with grey-tone $i$ and the average value of their surrounding neighbors. NGTDM applied in this work used a square region of five pixels as the neighborhood size. If $i$ is the grey-level at $(x,y)$ then the average grey-level over the square neighborhood centered at $(x,y)$ is given by:

$$A_i = A(x,y) = \frac{1}{W-1} \sum_{m=-d}^{d} \sum_{n=-d}^{d} i(x+n, y+m), \qquad (1)$$

Where $(m,n) \neq (0,0)$, $d$ specifies the neighborhood size and $W = (2d+1)^2$ it follows that the $i^{th}$ entry in the NGTDM is given as:

$$s(i) = \begin{cases} \sum |i - A_i|, & \text{for } i \in N_i \text{ if } N_i \neq 0 \\ 0, & \text{Otherwise.} \end{cases} \qquad (2)$$

Five texture features are constructed from the NGTDM which are: coarseness, contrast, busyness and complexity. The details of these features is explained in [11].

- **Grey Tone Run Length Matrix GTRLM**

GTRLM calculates the run length of a specific image grey-tone in a direction α within a textured ROI. A run is a set of successive pixels having the same or similar intensities along a specified direction. The considered pixels have to be linearly adjacent in the direction α. The run length is the number of pixels enclosed within the run. The number of runs with grey-tone $i$ of run length $j$ in some α direction is denoted by $R(\alpha) = [r'(i,j|\alpha)]$. Five features are computed from the GTRLM which are: short run emphasis, long run emphasis, grey tone distribution, run length distribution and run percentage. The mathematical formulation of these features is explained in [12].

## 4 Feature Selection

The output of the previous stage is a feature vector that is composed of GLDV, GLDM, NGTDM and GTRLM features. This feature vector is applied to a classifier that should identify some classes (e.g., cancerous and non-cancerous). This feature vector might have some redundant and correlated features (curse of dimensionality) which is the main motivation for using the feature selection techniques.

The principle of feature selection decides on a subset of features, which preserve most of the information needed for pattern classification [7]. An optimal set is a subset of features, which forfeit none of the information needed for classification and results in no increase in the minimum probability of error, when a decision rule is applied in both the observation and the subset space. The Feature Selection algorithms used in this paper are classifier dependant FS methods. This means that the possible feature subsets are obtained and the classifier performance is tested for each subset and finally the best discriminatory feature subset is chosen.

### 4.1 Particle Swarm Optimization (PSO)

PSO [13, 14, 15] is a new population based stochastic optimization technique inspired by social behavior of bird flocking or fish schooling. Each particle is treated as a point in a $2^n$ dimensional space where $n$ denote the total number of features. Let $v_{ij}$ and $p_{ij}$ denote the $j^{th}$ component of the $i^{th}$ particle velocity $v_i$ and position $p_i$ respectively.

We define the fitness of each particle as the recognition accuracy corresponding to the features selected by this particle using a pre-specified classifier (in this work, we use Support Vector Machine classifier.)

The algorithm described in here is a slightly modified version of the PSO algorithm to fit the binary nature of the feature selection problem.

The system is initialized with a group of random particles with $0 \le p_{i,j} \le 1$, and then searches for optima by updating generations. In each iteration, each particle position is updated by following two "best" particles. The first one (denoted by *pbest*) is the best fitness it has achieved so far. The fitness value is also stored. Another "best" value that is tracked by the particle swarm optimizer is the best value (denoted by *gbest*), obtained so far by any particle in the population.

After finding the two best values, the particle updates its velocity and positions with following equations

$$v_{i,j} = v_{i,j} + c_1 r_1 (pbest_{i,j} - p_{i,j}) + c_2 r_2 (gbest_{i,j} - p_{i,j}), \quad (3)$$

$$v_{i,j} = 2\sigma(v_{i,j}) - 1, \quad (4)$$

$$p_{i,j} = f_i(p_{i,j} + v_{i,j}), \quad (5)$$

Where $1 \le r_1, r_2 \le 0$ are uniformly distributed random variables, $c_1, c_2$ are learning factors and $\sigma(x)$ is the sigmoid function given by

$$\sigma(x) = \frac{1}{1 + \exp(-\alpha x)} \quad (6)$$

$f_i = (T(p_{i,0}), T(p_{i,1}), ... T(p_{i,2^n-1}))$ where

$$T(x) = \begin{cases} 1, & x \ge 0.5, \\ 0, & x < 0.5. \end{cases} \quad (7)$$

The output of the above adopted algorithm is a vector composed of ones that correspond to the selected features and zeros that correspond to the rejected features.

## 4.2 ANT Colony Optimization

ANT Colony Optimization [16] is another heuristic optimization method for solving optimization problems which borrows ideas from biological ants. Experiments with real ants showed that ants go from the nest to the food source and backwards then, after a while, the ants prefer the shortest path from the nest to the food source. The ants communicate indirectly by laying pheromone trails and following trails with higher pheromone. Naturally, larger amount of pheromone will accumulate on the shorter paths to good food sources because larger number of ants will cross it back and forth per unit time as compared to longer paths.

The originally proposed ANT colony optimization algorithm fits naturally in optimization problems corresponding to the selection of optimum permutation (such as the traveling sales person problem), i.e., we can apply it for the feature selection problem if we fixed the size of the subset of features to be chosen.

In here, we present a simple algorithm that borrows ideas from the ANT colony but doesn't have the above constraint, i.e., we don't have to pre-determine the size of the optimal feature subset.

The system is initialized with a group of ants moving across a full binary tree of depth $n$ and $2^n$ leaves. Each leaf corresponds to one of the possible $2^n$ feature subsets. The root of the tree corresponds to the nest of the ants and the accuracy of the classifier based on the feature subset associated with each leaf corresponds to the amount of food found at the food source.

The algorithm proceeds by iterating through the following three basic steps:

- Construct a solution for all ants: At each node, each ant has to make a (statistical) decision whether to follow the right path or the left path. At the first iteration, all the ants will move randomly. However, on subsequent iterations, the ants' choices will be influenced by the intensity of the pheromone trails left by preceding ants. A higher level of pheromone on the right path gives an ant a stronger stimulus and thus a higher probability to turn right and vice versa. Let $Pher_l(R)$ and $Pher_l(L)$ denote the value of the pheromone accumulated at the right edge and the left edge of a given node at the $l^{th}$ level of the tree. Then the ants' behavior equivalent to having each ant choosing a uniformly distributed random variable $0 \leq r \leq 1$ and choosing to follow the right edge at the $l^{th}$ level of the tree if $r \geq \dfrac{Pher_l(L)}{Pher_l(R)+Pher_l(L)}$, and to follow the left edge otherwise.
- Do a global pheromone update: For our problem, this step is also different than the one proposed in the original ANT colony optimization algorithm. Instead of updating the pheromone along the visited arcs only, we update all the corresponding $2^{l-1}$ arcs at $l^{th}$ level of the tree. The amount of pheromone laid by each ant corresponds to the amount of food (i.e., the classifier accuracy) that the ant finds at the leaf of the tree at the end of the path followed by this ant.
- Evaporate pheromone: After each iteration, a portion of the pheromone of the edge is evaporated according to a local updating rule, such that the probability of the selection of that edge by other ants decreases. This

prevents construction of similar paths by the set of ants and increases the diversity of the system. The rate of evaporation provides a compromise between the rate of convergence and reliability of convergence. Fast evaporation causes the search algorithm to be stuck at local optima, while slow evaporation lowers the rate of convergence. After enough iteration of the algorithm, the pheromone of the good edges which are used in constructing of low-cost paths will increase and the pheromone of the other edges will evaporate. Thus, in the higher iterations the probability of constructing low-cost paths increases.

As in the PSO method the accuracy criterion is based on SVM classifier.

## 5 Classification

Support Vector Machines are known to be a leading method for solving non-linear classification problems [8]. SVM depends mainly on pre-processing the data to represent patterns in a higher dimensionality space, usually much higher than the original feature space. This is achieved with a suitable non-linear mapping $\Phi(.)$ to a sufficiently high dimension [8]. Data from two classes are always separated by a hyper-plane. In binary classification, the task is to find a function $\Phi(.)$ that separates the two classes by learning from a set of samples. The hyperplane is selected so that it maximizes the margin between the two classes. The vectors (samples) defining the hyperplane are the most difficult patterns to classify and are called Support Vectors.

Each of the four feature sets as well as the selected feature subsets using the feature selection algorithms above are examined using the Support Vector Machine classifier.

## 6 Results and Discussion

The constructed feature sets are separately tested using the SVM classifier. The results are shown in table 1 where cancer and non-cancer attributes represents the suspicious cancerous cases and the non-suspicious cancerous cases according to the radiologist opinion. A set of 96 regions were used in this study where 80 regions were used as training set and a set of 16 regions were used as the test set. The following parameters are used to evaluate these feature:

*Accuracy:* 1 - probability of misclassification
*False Negative:* probability of classifying a cancerous prostate as a normal prostate.
*False Positive:* probability of classifying a cancerous prostate as a normal prostate.
*Sensitivity:* 1 - false negative rate
*Specificity:* 1 - false positive rate

Specificity, sensitivity and accuracy are the measures used to test different feature sets applied in this work. The table shows that the classification accuracy obtained using second order statistics is much better than that obtained accuracy using the higher order statistics. It is expected to obtain this kind of result due to the fact that the main target is to mimic the expert radiologist, whose classification accuracy is bounded by the human vision capabilities that is limited to the second order statistics. It is also clear that the GLDV features obtained better results than the GLDM features which show that the GLDM features have redundant information that is confusing the classifier.

Table 1. Classification results using the constructed feature sets

| | | Cancer | Non-cancer |
|---|---|---|---|
| **GLDM** | cancer | 5 | 1 |
| | Non-cancer | 1 | 9 |
| 83.33% Sensitivity; 90% Specificity; 87.75% Accuracy | | | |
| | | Cancer | Non-cancer |
| **GLDV** | cancer | 5 | 1 |
| | Non-cancer | 0 | 10 |
| 83.33% Sensitivity; 100% Specificity; 93.75% Accuracy | | | |
| | | Cancer | Non-cancer |
| **GTRLM** | cancer | 4 | 2 |
| | Non-cancer | 2 | 8 |
| Sensitivity = 66.67%; Specificity 90%; 81.25% Accuracy | | | |
| | | Cancer | Non-cancer |
| **NGTDM** | cancer | 4 | 2 |
| | Non-cancer | 2 | 8 |
| Sensitivity = 66.67%; Specificity 80%; 75% Accuracy | | | |

The constructed feature sets are combined together to form a feature set that includes GLDM, GLDV, NGTDM and GTRLM features. The proposed feature selection algorithms are then applied to the obtained feature set. Genetic algorithms [16] have been used for the past decade for feature selection applications. A basic binary GA feature selection is used in this work for the purpose of comparison with the results obtained using the above two techniques. The classification results show that the GA obtained the least classification accuracy with 83.33% sensitivity; 90% specificity and 87.75% accuracy where the PSO and ACO obtained a better classification results with 83.33% sensitivity; 100% specificity and 93.75% accuracy.

Table 2. Classification results using the selected feature sets

| | | Cancer | Non-cancer |
|---|---|---|---|
| **GA** | Cancer | 5 | 1 |
| | Non-cancer | 1 | 9 |
| 83.33% Sensitivity; 90% Specificity; 87.75% Accuracy | | | |
| | | cancer | Non-cancer |
| **PSO** | cancer | 5 | 1 |
| | Non-cancer | 0 | 10 |
| 83.33% Sensitivity; 100% Specificity; 93.75% Accuracy | | | |
| | | cancer | Non-cancer |
| **ACO** | cancer | 5 | 1 |
| | Non-cancer | 0 | 10 |
| 83.33% Sensitivity; 100% Specificity; 93.75% Accuracy | | | |

# 7 Conclusions

Two novel feature selection algorithms were applied for accurate feature selection for the purpose of prostate cancer diagnosis using TRUS images. ROIs were identified from the segmented prostate TRUS images using Gabor multi-resolution analysis leading to accurate identified regions. Second and higher order statistical texture features such as GLDM, GLDV, NGTDM and GTRLM were constructed from these automatically segmented regions. Moreover, a feature subset representing the most salient and uncorrelated features was generated utilizing three different artificial life techniques where the well established GA is compared to both the PSO and the ACO. Finally these features were used for tissue characterization using SVM algorithm. The obtained results revealed the out performance of the ACO and the PSO compared to the basic binary GA. The sensitivity was 83.3% for all three feature selection methods and the specificity was 90% for GA and 100 % for the PSO and ACO. Moreover, it is observed that the selected features using both the PSO and the ACO were from the second order statistical features which prove that the system is limited with the human visual system and cannot go beyond what the HVS can recognize. This shows a great radiologist mimicking capability of the proposed system.

# References

1. Scardino, PT., "Early detection of prostate cancer". ; Urol Clin North Am. 1989 Nov; 16(4) Pages: 635-55.
2. Scheipers, U., Lorenz, A., Pesavento, A., Ermert, H., Sommerfeld, H., Garcia-Schurmann, M., Kuhne, K., Senge, T. and Philippou, S "Ultrasonic multifeature tissue characterization for the early detection of prostate cancer", IEEE Ultrasonics Symposium, Volume: 2 , 7-10 Oct. 2001 Pages: 1265 -1268 vol.2
3. Dinggang S., Yiqiang Z. and Davatzikos, C."Segmentation of prostate boundaries from ultrasound images using statistical shape model" IEEE Transactions on Medical Imaging, Volume: 22 , Issue: 4 , April 2003 Pages:539 – 551
4. Lixin G., Pathak, S.D., Haynor, D.R., Cho, P.S. and Yongmin K, "Parametric shape modeling using deformable super ellipses for prostate segmentation", IEEE Transactions on Medical Imaging, Volume: 23, Issue: 3, March 2004 Pages:340 – 349
5. Chiu, B., Freeman, G., Salama, M.M.A. and Fenster, A., "Prostate segmentation algorithm using dyadic wavelet transform and discrete dynamic contour", Physics in Medicine and Biology, Vol. 49, No.20, pp. 4943-4960.
6. Mohamed, S.S., Salama, M.M.A., Kamel, M. and Rizkalla, K. "Region of interest based prostate tissue characterization using least square support vector machine LS-VSM", Proceedings of ICIAR, Lecture Notes in Computer Science, Vol. 3212, pp. 51-58,
7. R. Duda, P. Hart, D. Stork, "Pattern Classification", John Wiley and Sons.2001
8. S.S. Mohamed, M.M. Salama "Computer Aided diagnosis for Prostate cancer using Support Vector Machine" medical imaging conference 2005, California, SPIE.
9. Bhanu, K.N.; Ramakrishnan, A.G.; Suresh, S. and Chow, T.W.P.; "Fetal lung maturity analysis using ultrasound image features" Information Technology in Biomedicine, IEEE Transactions on , Volume: 6 , Issue: 1 , March 2002 Pages:38 – 45

10. Chung-Ming W.; Yung-Chang C. and Hsieh, K; "Texture features for classification of ultrasonic liver images". Medical Imaging, IEEE Transactions on, Volume: 11 Issue: 2, June 1992 Page(s): 141 –152
11. Amadasun, M. and King, R., "Textural features corresponding to textural properties", IEEE Transactions on Systems, Man, and Cybernetics, vol. 19, no. 5, pp. 1264-1274, September 1989.
12. Galloway, M. M. "Texture analysis using gray-level run lengths", Computer Graphics and Image Processing, vol. 4, pp. 172-179, June 1975.
13. Kennedy J. and Eberhart, R. " Particle Swarm Optimization", Proc. IEEE, Int Conf. Neural Network, pp 1942-1948, 1995
14. "Special Issue on Particle Swarm Optimization", IEEE Transactions on Evolutionary Computation publication information, Volume: 8, Issue: 3, June 2004.
15. Eberhart R.C. and Shi, Y. "Comparison between genetic algorithms and particle swarm optimization" Proc. IEEE international conference on evolutionary Comp. pp 611-616, May 1998
16. Dorigo, M. Maniezzo, V. and Colorni, A. "The ant system: optimization by a colony of cooperating agents", IEEE Transactions on Systems, Man, and Cybernetics-Part B 26(1) (1996), pp. 29–41.
17. Goldberg, D. "Genetic algorithms in search, optimization and machine learning", Reading, MA: Addison, Wesley.

# A Border Irregularity Measure Using a Modified Conditional Entropy Method as a Malignant Melanoma Predictor

Benjamin S. Aribisala and Ela Claridge

School of Computer Sciences,
The University or Birmingham,
Birmingham B15 2TT, U.K.
{B.S.Aribisala, E.Claridge}@cs.bham.ac.uk

**Abstract.** In the diagnosis of malignant melanoma, a skin cancer, the degree of irregularity along the skin lesion border is an important diagnostic factor. This paper presents a new measure of border irregularity based on conditional entropy. The measure was tested on 98 skin lesions of which 16 were malignant melanoma. The ROC analysis showed that the measure is 70% sensitive and 84% specific in discriminating the malignant and benign lesions. These results compare favourably with other measures and indicate that conditional entropy captures some distinguishing features in the boundary of malignant lesions.

## 1 Introduction

Melanoma is a malignant tumour of melanocytes. The tumour initially starts from the epidermis and if not detected and removed early it invades the dermis. The patient's survival rate is inversely proportional to the depth of the tumour. Early detection of melanoma is the most important factor affecting the survival of a patient.

Malignant melanoma can be characterised by shape, edge, colour and surface texture of the lesion. The border irregularity of pigmented skin lesions is one of the most significant diagnostic factors in clinical diagnosis of melanoma [6,7].

It has been empirically discovered that clinicians have difficulties in visually assessing border irregularity of skin lesion outlines and that their assessments are not invariant to reflection and rotation [7,4]. Much research on quantitative measures of irregularity has been carried out to overcome these shortcomings [7]. The most common approaches include the Compactness Index (e.g. [13]), Fractal Dimension and Structural Fractal Dimension (e.g.[4]), measures based on radial distance (e.g. [12]), Sigma Ratio and Indentation Irregularity Index (III) [11]. III is the most successful algorithm to date for classifying skin lesions on the basis of their border irregularity.

The term *"Irregularity"* is contextual and can express different meanings. If irregularity is to be quantified, it is necessary first to develop its formal definition, or at least provide its formal description. Five attributes of irregularity have been proposed [8]. One of these attributes which is of interest here is unpredictability. The elements of a sequence corresponding to a regular shape or pattern are predictable, whereas in an irregular shape or sequence they cannot be easily predicted. That is, the extent to which a sequence can be predicted may suggest its degree of irregularity.

This paper presents a new measure of border irregularity based on conditional entropy. In contrast to the existing measures, the proposed measure is based on a formal criterion of irregularity outlined above. A prior knowledge of some points along the border of a normal skin lesion can be used to predict more points along the same border with high degree of certainty, whereas predictions for abnormal skin lesions will have reduced certainty leading to high value of entropy. That is conditional entropy increases with the degree of unpredictability.

Section 2 presents a brief description of the entropy while section 3 presents the proposed method of computing conditional entropy. Section 4 describes the experimental data while section 5 describes the experiments. Results and discussion are presented in section 6. Finally, section 7 presents the conclusion.

## 2 Entropy

Entropy can be described as a measure of information, the degree of uncertainty or unpredictability of a system or sequence. Entropy is directly proportional to unpredictability. That is, a sequence which is highly unpredictable (or random) has higher entropy than an easily predictable sequence. The original entropy (equation (1)) called the Shannon's entropy was designed by Claude Shannon in 1948 [2]. The wide range of applications of entropy has motivated different modifications to Shannon's entropy. Some of its modifications are Renyi's entropy [3], mutual information, conditional entropy and joint entropy [5]. Here we are interested in conditional entropy but first provide some background related to joint entropy.

$$H(x) = - \sum_{x \in X} P_r(x) log_2 P_r(x) \quad (1)$$

Let X and Y be random variables such that $x \in X$ and $y \in Y$ and let $P_r(x)$ be the probability of a particular value x. The joint entropy H(X, Y) (equation (2)) of X and Y measures the unpredictability associated with the joint probability $P_r(x,y)$ of X and Y while the conditional entropy of Y given X denoted H(Y/X) (equation(3)) measures the unpredictability associated with the conditional probability $P_r(y/x)$ of Y given X. Since H(X)$\geq$ 0, equation (4) implies that conditioning reduces entropy.

$$H(X,Y) = - \sum_{x \in X} \sum_{y \in Y} P_r(x,y) log_2 P_r(x,y) \quad (2)$$

$$H(Y/X) = - \sum_{x \in X} \sum_{y \in Y} P_r(x,y) log_2 P_r(y/x) \quad (3)$$

$$H(X,Y) = H(X) + H(Y/X) \tag{4}$$

Entropy has two major problems. First, it is not sensitive to the relative position of elements in a sequence, e.g. a periodic sequence 10101010101010101010 and a random sequence 110100111011001011 have the same entropy. This is due to the fact that entropy is computed by counting the number of elements of the sequence that belong to each distinct category of a sequence determined by the value of the bin size r. This constitutes a weakness of any entropy based measure (such as conditional entropy and joint entropy), most especially in pattern recognition and classification problems where the relative position of elements of a signal is important. Secondly, the value of entropy is strictly dependent on the bin size. A wrong choice may lead to a wrong and misleading result. We investigated these problems and proposed a new technique of computing conditional entropy. This was implemented on both simulated and real data. Simulated data was used to investigate the relationship between the proposed conditional entropy and the amount of noise level in a signal while the real data was used for characterisation of malignancy in pigmented skin lesions.

## 3 Computing Conditional Entropy

Conditional entropy can be computed using equation (3). This implies that two sequences are needed for its computation, X and Y. We describe equation (3) as a *sequence based conditional entropy* (SBCE) because H(Y/X) is computed by computing the entropy of sequence Y based on the knowledge of sequence X (note that we can have more than two random variables in which case the conditional entropy of one variable can depend on two or more variables). The sequence based entropy is not a good measure of irregularity because it is independent on the relative positions of the elements of a sequence (see section 2). Here we propose a new type of conditional entropy which depends on the relative positions of elements of a sequence, we call it "*element based conditional entropy*" (EBCE).

Let $X = x_1, x_2, ..., x_n$ be a random sequence of length n. We define the *element based conditional entropy* of a sequence X, denoted $H_e(X)$, as the overall conditional entropy of successive elements of X based on the preceding elements (equation (5)). The EBCE is similar to the SBCE but they have two major differences. The first difference is that unlike the SBCE, the EBCE is sensitive to the relative positions of elements of X. Secondly the EBCE can be computed for just one sequence while the sequence based conditional entropy is designed for at least two sequences.

$$H_e(X) = -\sum_{t=m}^{t=n} P_r(x_t, (x_{t-1}, ..., x_{t-m+1})) log P_r(x_t/(x_{t-1}, x_{t-2}, ..., x_{t-m+1})) \tag{5}$$

where n is the length of X and m is the length of different subsequences of X. The case for m=2 is represented in equation (6).

$$H_e(X) = -\sum_{t=2}^{t=n} P_r(x_t, x_{t-1}) log P_r(x_t/x_{t-1}) \qquad (6)$$

Like other entropy based measures $H_e$ is directly proportional to unpredictability and $H_e$ of a regular sequence is 0. Like other entropy based measures, $H_e$ is also strictly dependent on the bin size r.

The computation of EBCE using equation (5) requires a good choice of m, the bin size r and a good definition of the conditionality variable

$$q_t = (x_t/(x_{t-1}, x_{t-2}, ..., x_{t-m+1})) \qquad (7)$$

We have investigated different ways of defining $q_t$ using different choices of m and r. Here we present the definition that gave us the best result. We use $H_e^r(m_0 \to m_f)$ to denote EBCE for fixed r and variable m where $m_0$ and $m_f$ are the minimum and maximum m such that $2 \leq m \leq n$, n is the sequence length. $\coprod_{i=1}^{i=n-m+1}\{x_i x_{i+1} x_{i+2}...x_{i+m-1}\}$ will be used to denote a set of all subsequences of X.

Let S be a set of all subsequences of X each of length m (see equation(9)). $H_e^r(m_0 \to m_f)$ can be computed by defining $q_t$ as the difference between the last and the first element of each subsequence (see equation (8))

$$q_t = (x_t/(x_{t-1}, x_{t-2}, ..., x_{t-m+1})) = (x_t - x_{t-m+1}) \qquad (8)$$

$$S = \coprod_{i=1}^{i=n-m+1} \{x_i x_{i+1} x_{i+2}...x_{i+m-1}\} \qquad (9)$$

For example if $X = \{x_1, x_2, x_3, x_4, x_5\}$ and $q_t$ is computed for m=3, using equation (9) $S = \{x_1 x_2 x_3, x_2 x_3 x_4, x_3 x_4 x_5\}$ and $q_3 = \{x_3 - x_1, x_4 - x_2, x_5 - x_3\}$.

## 4 Data Description

Medical experts regard a skin lesion that is nearly circular or elliptical in overall shape as more likely to be normal than not [4]. In view of this we have taken the ellipse to be a shape model for a normal skin lesion and to represent the most regular instance of the lesion shape. Figure (1) shows examples of real lesion outlines, (a) regular and (b) irregular. Thus if we assume prior knowledge of a regular (normal) skin lesion, points along its border can be predicted with high certainty whereas prediction for irregular skin lesions will have relatively reduced certainty. That is irregularity increases with unpredictability, hence we frame irregularity as unpredictability.

The lesion border data is represented as a sequence of (1D) radial coordinates in a polar coordinate system centred at the centre of gravity of the lesion. The coordinates constitute a sequence $O = O_1, O_2, ..., O_M$ where $O_i$, i=1, ..., M is an ith boundary point.

In a polar coordinate system the radial coordinates of an ellipse can be represented by a sine function. In view of this the simulated data is composed of

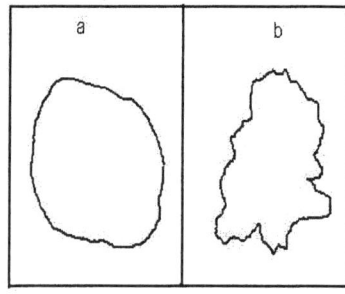

**Fig. 1.** Lesion Outline samples:(a) regular, (b) irregular

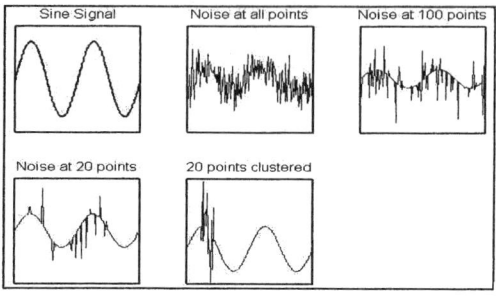

**Fig. 2.** Simulated data

sine signals each of length 200 with random noise added at different points. The data was grouped into 5 categories with each category having 50 sequences. The first category is a set of 50 sine signals. These 50 signals were used to generate the remaining four categories by adding Gaussian random noise (with standard deviation ranging from 1 to 10) at all points, at 100 randomly selected points, at 20 randomly selected points, and at 20 randomly selected points but clustered together (See Figure (2) for some examples of these signals). The sine signals without noise represent "*normal*" skin lesions while those with noise represent irregular skin lesions with the amount of noise suggestive of the degree of irregularity. The conditional entropy for all the simulated and the real data was computed using the proposed method. Our hypothesis is that conditional entropy increases with the degree of irregularity.

## 5  Experiments

Simulated data consisted of 250 sine signals with different amount of noise. The real data represented 98 skin lesion of which 16 were histologically confirmed cases of melanoma [9]. The radial coordinates corresponding to lesion boundary were extracted using a boundary modelling technique [1]. The data was normalised by subtracting the mean and dividing by standard deviation to make it scale invariant. Using equations(8, 9 and 5), EBCE was computed for both the simulated and the real data. The value of r was set to r=0.01*SD (SD is the standard deviation of each sequence) and m = 2 to n was used. It was observed that in both cases $H_e^r(m_0 \rightarrow m_f)$ increased exponentially with increase in m (see Figures 3a and 3b). To determine the degree of irregularity $H_e^r(m_0 \rightarrow m_f)$ for each sequence was fitted using an exponential fit and the exponential parameter $H_e^\mu(i)$ was estimated. Additionally the standard deviation $H_e^\sigma(i)$ and the slope $H_e^{slope}(i)$ (i is the lesion number) of each $H_e^r(m_0 \rightarrow m_f)$ with respect to r was computed.

To assess the discriminatory power of EBCE in characterisation of malignancy of pigmented skin lesion the ROC analysis was performed for all the three proposed estimators of irregularity: $H_e^\mu$, $H_e^\sigma$ and $H_e^{slope}$.

## 5.1 Experimental Survey

One interesting question, not answered through the above experiments, was whether any of the computed measures for real data corresponds to the human perception of the border irregularity in the skin lesions. To this end an experimental survey was carried out. 20 skin lesion outlines randomly selected from the full data set were given to 23 subjects, none of whom had medical training. The subjects were asked to rank the outlines based on their degree of irregularity. The level of agreement among the subjects was evaluated using rank correlation $r_s$ based on Kendall coefficient of concordance W [10]. The value of $r_s$ ranges from 0 (no agreement) to 1 (perfect agreement).

To test a "default" hypothesis, that irregularity simply depends on the magnitude of variations along the boundary, the standard deviation was computed for all the lesion outlines before normalisation.

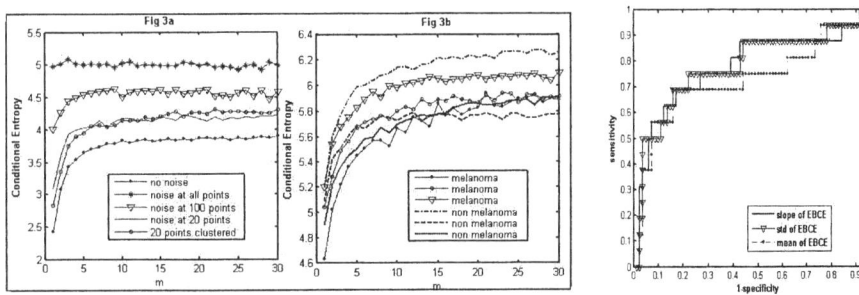

**Fig. 3.** Conditional Entropy    **Fig. 4.** ROC Curve

The Spearman coefficient of correlation was determined for each of the proposed irregularity estimators ($H_e^\mu, H_e^\sigma, H_e^{slope}$), the visual assessment (using the average ranking from the 23 subjects), and the standard deviation for the selected 20 lesions. Finally, the relationship between all estimators was examined using multiple linear regression analysis.

## 6 Results and Discussion

Figures (3a and 3b) show that EBCE increases exponentially as m increases in both the simulated and real data. This is a good result because intuitively increase in m increases the elements of each subsequence hence the probability of each element decreases which leads to reduction in the degree of predictability. Additionally $H_e^\mu$ and $H_e^\sigma$ increase with noise level in the simulated data while $H_e^{slope}$ decreases with noise level. These suggest that all the three statistics are potentially useful estimators of noise levels of a signal. Since the noise level is an indicator of the level of unpredictability, it can hence be proposed that all the three statistics are potentially useful measures of degree of unpredictability of signals.

The ROC analysis of $H_e^\mu$ as a melanoma classifier showed 68% sensitivity and 84% specificity, $H_e^\sigma$ gave 70% sensitivity and 82% specificity while $H_e^{slope}$ gave 70% sensitivity and 84% specificity. Figure 4 shows the ROC plots for all the three statistics. These results show that EBCE can be used to measure the degree of unpredictability of a signal and that boundary sequences corresponding to abnormal lesions have high level of unpredictability (i.e. more irregular) when assessed using $H_e^{slope}$. Hence we propose the use of $H_e^{slope}$ as a measure of irregularity.

In a way of illustration, the value of $H_e^{slope}$ for the regular lesion in figure 1(a) is 0.03 and for the irregular lesion in figure 1(b) it is 0.01 on the scale where 0.06 corresponds to the most regular shape and 0.001 to the most irregular shape.

In the experiments examining the perception of irregularity, the coefficient of concordance W was 0.886, indicating good agreement between all 23 subjects. The assessment of irregularity by the subjects correlated moderately well with both the EBCE ($H_e^{slope}$) measure (Spearman correlation coefficient of 0.55) and standard deviation (0.466). Correlation was very good between the EBCE irregularity measure and standard deviation of the real data (0.87). The multiple linear regression analysis for all three tests showed good correspondence (0.51). These results suggest that humans have similar way of assessing shape irregularity, and that the human notion of irregularity is similar to the assessment by the indicators investigated here. The strong correlation between the EBCE measure and the standard deviation suggest that the conditional entropy based measure is good at measuring the variation along the lesion border.

We have compared the result of the proposed measure with one of the best published melanoma predictors based on irregularity, the Indentation Irregularity Index (III) [9]. The comparison used the area under the ROC curve, which is a global measure commonly used to assess the overall predictive power of classification schemes. The III computed for a superset of the set of lesions used in our experiments has the area under ROC curve of 0.73 [9], whereas the EBCE gave area of 0.76. This indicates that the conditional entropy based measure has a greater discriminatory power than the III index.

## 7 Conclusion

In this paper we have proposed a new measure of border irregularity based on conditional entropy. This measure has been devised to quantify lack of predictability. We have demonstrated that abnormality of skin lesion can be described using irregularity along the skin lesion border. Given some prior knowledge of a normal skin lesion, points along its border can be predicted with high degree of certainty whereas prediction for abnormal skin lesion will have reduced certainty leading to high value of entropy. That is entropy increases with the degree of irregularity.

The ROC analysis of the conditional entropy based measure as a malignancy predictor gave 70% sensitivity and 84% specificity. This result shows that the conditional entropy based measure captures some distinguishing features in the boundary of malignant lesions and thus can contribute to lesion classification.

# References

1. Claridge, E. and Orun, A.: Modelling of Edge Profiles in Pigmented Skin Lesions. Medical Image Understanding and Analysis (2002) 53-55
2. Shannon, C.E.: A Mathematical Theory of Communication. Bell Systems Technical Journal **27** (July and Oct.1948) 379 - 423 and 623 - 656
3. Renyi, A.: On Measures of entropy and Information. In Proc. Fourth Berkeley Symposium, Math., Stat. Prob., Berkeley, University of Carnifornia Press.**1** (1961)
4. Claridge, E. and Hall, P.N. and Keefe, M. and Allen, J.P.: Shape Analysis for Classification of Malignant Melanoma. J. Biomed. Eng. **14** (1992) 229-234
5. Cover, T.M.and Thomas J.A.: Elements of Information Theory. John Wiley and Sons, New York (1991)
6. Keefe, M. and Dick, D and Wakeel, R.: A Study of the Value of the Seven Point Checklist in Distinguishing Benign Pigmented Lesions From Melanoma. Clin. and Exp. Derm. **15** (1990) 167 - 171
7. Morris-Smith, J. D.: Characterisation of the Appearance of Pigmented Skin Lesions. The University of Birmingham, U.K. (1996)
8. Aribisala, B.S.: Computing Irregularity for Features in Medical Images. Technical Report, The University of Birmingham, U.K. (May 2003)
9. Lee, T. K. and Claridge, E.: Predictive Power of Irregular Border Shapes for Malignant Melanoma. Skin Research and Technology (2005)
10. Hays, W.: *Statistics*, Chap. 19. Holt, Rinehart and Winston (1988)
11. Lee, T. K. and McLean, D. I. and Atkins, M. S.: Irregularity index: A new border irregularity measure for cutaneous melanocytic lesions. Med. Img. Analysis **7** (2003) 47-64
12. Gutkowicz-Krushin, D. and Elbaum, M. and Szwaykowski, P. and Kopf, A. W.: Can early malignant melanoma be differentiated from atypical melanocytic nevus by in vivo techniques ? Skin Research and Technology **3** (1997) 15-22
13. Stoecker, W.V. and Moss, R. H. and Ercal, F. and Umbaugh, S.E.: Nondermatoscopic digital imaging of pigmented lesions. Skin Res. and Tech. **1** (1995) 7-16

# Automatic Hepatic Tumor Segmentation Using Composite Hypotheses

Kyung-Sik Seo

MOMED Company,
Chosun University, Gwangju, Korea
nmsu2@hanmail.net

**Abstract.** This paper proposes an automatic hepatic tumor segmentation method of a computed tomography (CT) image using composite hypotheses. The liver structure is first segmented using histogram transformation, multi-modal threshold, maximum a posteriori decision, and binary morphological filtering. Hepatic vessels are removed from the liver because hepatic vessels are not related to tumor segmentation. In order to find an optimal threshold, composite hypotheses and minimum total probability error are used. Then a hepatic tumor is segmented by using the optimal threshold value. In order to test the proposed method, 272 slices from 10 patients were selected. Experimental results show that the proposed method is very useful for diagnosis of the normal and abnormal liver.

## 1 Introduction

Liver cancer, which is the fifth most common cancer, is more serious in areas of western and central Africa and eastern and southeastern Asia [1]. The average incidence of liver cancer in these areas is 20 per 100,000, and liver cancer is the third highest death cause from cancer [1]. In Korea, the incidence of liver cancer is quite high at 19% for males and 7% for females [2]. New cases of liver cancer in the Seoul area have an approximate rate per year of 34.1 for males and 11.5 for females per 100,000 people [2]. In order to improve the curability of liver cancer, early detection is critical. Liver cancer, like other cancers, manifests itself with abnormal cells, conglomerated growth, and tumor formation. If the hepatic tumor is detected early, treatment and curing of a patient may be easy, and human life can be prolonged.

Liver segmentation using CT images has been vigorously performed because CT is a very conventional and non-invasive technique. Bae et al. [3] used priori information about liver morphology and image processing techniques such as gray-level thresholding, Gaussian smoothing, mathematical morphology techniques, and B-splines. Gao et al. [4] developed automatic liver segmentation using a global histogram, morphologic operations, and the parametrically deformable contour model. Park et al. [5] built a probabilistic atlas of the brain and extended abdominal segmentation including the liver, kidneys, and spinal cord. Tsai [6] proposed an alternative segmentation method using an artificial neural network to classify each pixel into three categories. Also, Husain et al. [7] used neural networks for feature-based recognition of liver region. Seo et al. [8] presents efficient liver segmentation based on the spine.

However, most previous research has been concentrated on only liver segmentation and volume construction. In this paper, a simple automatic hepatic tumor segmentation method using composite hypotheses (CH) is proposed. An automatic hepatic tumor segmentation method is presented in the following section. Experiments and analysis of results are described in the next section. Finally, the conclusion will be drawn in the last section.

## 2 Hepatic Tumor Segmentation

In this section, an automatic hepatic tumor segmentation method is presented. A liver structure is first segmented and then vessels in the liver are removed. Optimal threshold (OT) is found by composite hypotheses (CH) and minimum total probability error (MTPE). A region of interest (ROI) of a hepatic tumor is segmented and estimated.

### 2.1 Liver Segmentation

The first important work to segment a hepatic tumor is to segment a liver boundary. The ROI of the liver is extracted using histogram transformation such as convolution and scaling [9, 8]. Multi-modal threshold based on piecewise linear interpolation is performed to find the range of the ROI [10, 8]. Then the ROI is selected by maximum a posteriori decision [11, 8]. In order to eliminate other abdominal organs such as the heart and right kidney, binary morphological (BM) filtering is performed by dilation, erosion, and filling [8, 12, 13, 14]. Fig. 1(a) shows an abnormal CT image with a tumor. Fig. 1(b) shows the ROI of the liver. Also, Fig. 1(c) shows the segmented liver image using BM filtering.

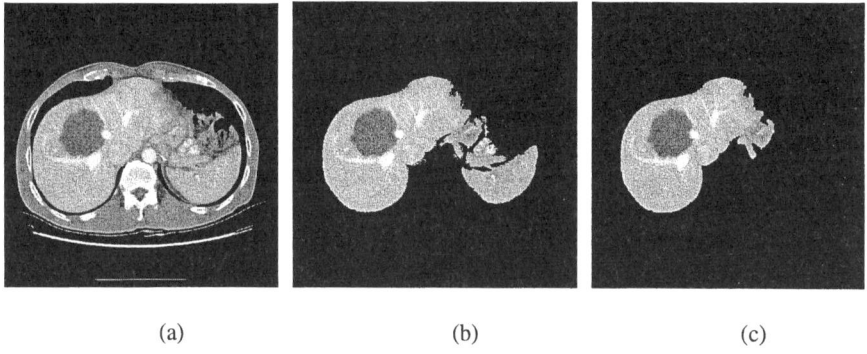

(a)             (b)             (c)

**Fig. 1.** Liver segmentation: (a) CT image, (b) ROI of the liver, (c) liver image segmented by BM filtering

## 2.2 Vessel Elimination

The liver image with a tumor obtained by BM filtering consists of the pure liver, tumor, and vessels. As vessels of the liver have no influence on tumor segmentation, vessels are eliminated from the liver. Histogram transformation for better histogram threshold is first performed to reduce histogram noises. Then the left and right valleys, called object ranges, are calculated using a piecewise linear interpolation method [10]. The vessel range is located in the rightmost side of the histogram because pixel values are higher than other objects. Therefore, the vessel range is decided easily. Fig. 2(a) shows the liver image after vessel elimination.

## 2.3 Composite Hypotheses

After eliminating vessels, the histogram has only two peaks, and the liver image consists of the pure liver and tumor region. Therefore, the gray-level value thresholding two regions is easily calculated by using bi-modal threshold method. However, it is not known this threshold value is optimal. In order to find the OT value, $T_{optimal}$, composite hypotheses with a random parameter are used [11]. The composite hypotheses are given as

$$PL: x \sim p(x \mid a, PL) \text{ where } p_A(a) \text{ is known.} \quad (1)$$

$$Tumor: x \sim p(x \mid b, Tumor) \text{ where } p_B(b) \text{ is known} \quad (2)$$

where *PL* and *Tumor* are pure liver and tumor parts known to be Gaussian, each with known variances, $\sigma_{PL}$ and $\sigma_{Tumor}$, and unknown random means of A and B.

Thus given probability density functions such as $p(x \mid a, PL)$, $p(x \mid b, Tumor)$, $p_A(a)$, and $p_B(b)$ are formulated by

$$p(x \mid a, PL) = \frac{1}{\sqrt{2\pi}\sigma_{PL}} \exp\left\{-\frac{(x-a)^2}{2\sigma_{PL}^2}\right\} \quad (3)$$

$$p(x \mid b, Tumor) = \frac{1}{\sqrt{2\pi}\sigma_{Tumor}} \exp\left\{-\frac{(x-b)^2}{2\sigma_{Tumor}^2}\right\} \quad (4)$$

$$p_A(a) = \frac{1}{\sqrt{2\pi}\tilde{\sigma}_a} \exp\left\{-\frac{(a-\tilde{\mu}_a)^2}{2\tilde{\sigma}_a^2}\right\} \quad (5)$$

$$p_B(b) = \frac{1}{\sqrt{2\pi}\tilde{\sigma}_b} \exp\left\{-\frac{(b-\tilde{\mu}_b)^2}{2\tilde{\sigma}_b^2}\right\} \quad (6)$$

where $\tilde{\mu}_a$ and $\tilde{\mu}_b$ are small different means from means of A and B and $\tilde{\sigma}_a^2$ and $\tilde{\sigma}_b^2$ are small different variances from variances of A and B.

Using two formulas given as

$$p(x|PL) = \int_{-\infty}^{\infty} p(x|a,PL) p_A(a) da \qquad (7)$$

$$p(x|Tumor) = \int_{-\infty}^{\infty} p(x|b,Tumor) p_B(b) db, \qquad (8)$$

joint probability densities are calculated by

$$p(x|PL) = \int_{-\infty}^{\infty} \frac{1}{\sqrt{2\pi}\sigma_{PL}} \exp\left\{-\frac{(x-a)^2}{2\sigma_{PL}^2}\right\} \frac{1}{\sqrt{2\pi}\tilde{\sigma}_a} \exp\left\{-\frac{(a-\tilde{\mu}_a)^2}{2\tilde{\sigma}_a^2}\right\} da \qquad (9)$$

$$p(x|Tumor) = \int_{-\infty}^{\infty} \frac{1}{\sqrt{2\pi}\sigma_{Tumor}} \exp\left\{-\frac{(x-b)^2}{2\sigma_{Tumor}^2}\right\} \frac{1}{\sqrt{2\pi}\tilde{\sigma}_b} \exp\left\{-\frac{(b-\tilde{\mu}_b)^2}{2\tilde{\sigma}_b^2}\right\} db \qquad (10)$$

$p(x|PL)$ is simplified by

$$p(x|PL) = \frac{1}{\sqrt{2\pi(\sigma_{PL}^2 + \tilde{\sigma}_a^2)}} \exp\left\{-\frac{(x-\tilde{\mu}_a)^2}{2(\sigma_{PL}^2 + \tilde{\sigma}_a^2)}\right\} \qquad (11)$$

where a mean is $\tilde{\mu}_a$ and a variance is $\sigma_{PL}^2 + \tilde{\sigma}_a^2$. Also, $p(x|Tumor)$ is simplified by

$$p(x|Tumor) = \frac{1}{\sqrt{2\pi(\sigma_{Tumor}^2 + \tilde{\sigma}_b^2)}} \exp\left\{-\frac{(x-\tilde{\mu}_b)^2}{2(\sigma_{Tumor}^2 + \tilde{\sigma}_b^2)}\right\} \qquad (12)$$

where a mean is $\tilde{\mu}_b$ and a variance is $\sigma_{Tumor}^2 + \tilde{\sigma}_b^2$. The conditional mixture probability density (CMPD) is formulated by

$$p(x) = P_{PL} p(x|PL) + P_T p(x|Tumor). \qquad (13)$$

The $T_{optimal}$ is found by calculating the minimum total probability error (MTPE), $E(T)$, defined as [11]

$$E(T) = P_{PL} \int_{-\infty}^{T} p(x \mid PL)dx + P_T \int_{T}^{\infty} p(x \mid Tumor)dx . \tag{14}$$

where $T$ is the threshold value. Then the $T_{optimal}$ is selected by the threshold value calculating the minimum TPE. Fig. 2(b) shows the segmented tumor using $T_{optimal}$.

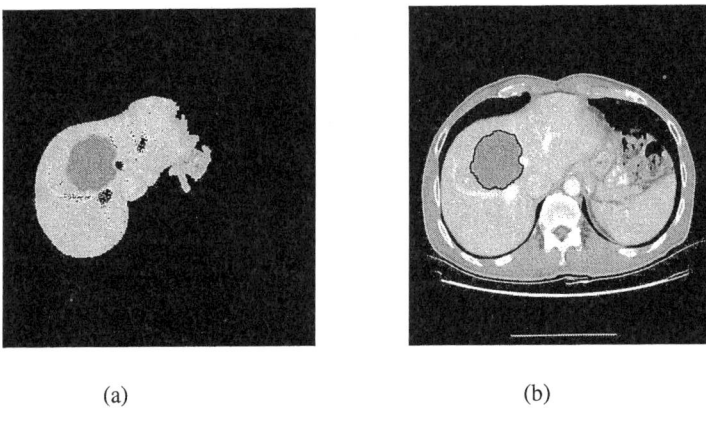

(a)             (b)

**Fig. 2.** Tumor segmentation: (a) liver image after hepatic vessel elimination, (b) segmented tumor using the optimal threshold value

## 3 Experiments and Analysis

CT images to be used in this research were provided by Chonnam National University Hospital in Kwangju, Korea. The CT scans were obtained by using a LightSpeed Qx/i, which was produced by GE Medical Systems. Scanning was performed with intravenous contrast enhancement. Also, the scanning parameters used a tube current of 230 mAs and 120 kVp, a 30 cm field of view, 5 mm collimation and a table speed of 15 mm/sec (pitch factor, 1:3).

Ten patients were selected for testing the new proposed method to segregate a hepatic tumor. Five people had normal livers and the other five people had abnormal livers. 272 total slices from ten patients were used. One radiologist took part in this research in order to evaluate liver status. Fig. 3 shows examples of segmented tumors. Table 1 shows the data of evaluated slices followed by slice numbers, true negative (TN), false positive (FP), false negative (FN), and true positive (TP) [15].

As the evaluation measure, sensitivity, specificity, and accuracy were calculated. As sensitivity represents the fraction of patients with disease who test positive, sensitivity is defined as

$$Sensitivity = \frac{TP}{TP + FN} . \tag{15}$$

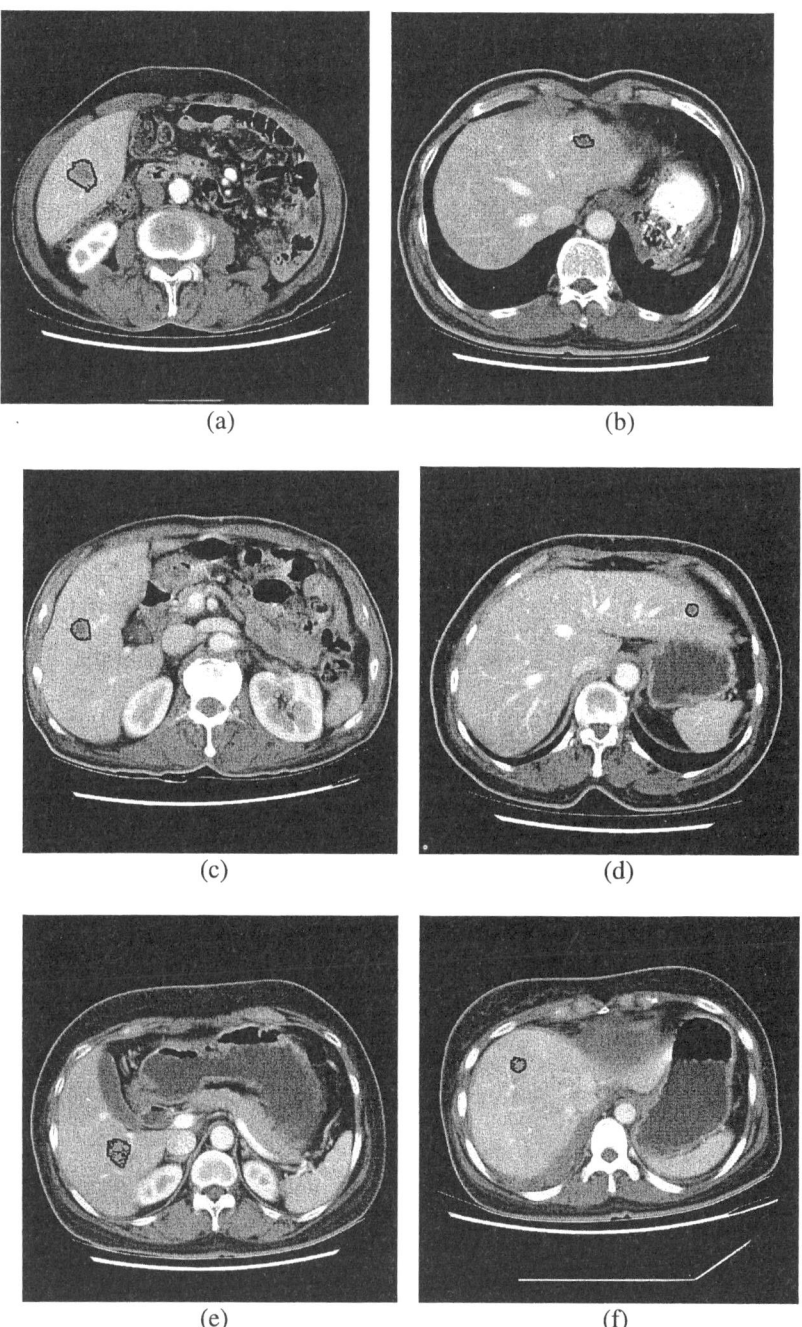

**Fig. 3.** Examples of tumor segmentation

**Table 1.** Data of evaluated slices

| PATIENTS | SLICES TAKEN | FREQUENCY OF TN | FREQUENCY OF FP | FREQUENCY OF FN | FREQUENCY OF TP |
|---|---|---|---|---|---|
| PAT. 01 | 33 | 30 | 3 | 0 | 0 |
| PAT. 02 | 31 | 30 | 1 | 0 | 0 |
| PAT. 03 | 24 | 21 | 3 | 0 | 0 |
| PAT. 04 | 26 | 25 | 1 | 0 | 0 |
| PAT. 05 | 28 | 28 | 0 | 0 | 0 |
| PAT. 06 | 34 | 30 | 2 | 1 | 1 |
| PAT. 07 | 23 | 21 | 1 | 0 | 1 |
| PAT. 08 | 23 | 19 | 3 | 0 | 1 |
| PAT. 09 | 26 | 16 | 0 | 3 | 7 |
| PAT. 10 | 24 | 17 | 4 | 2 | 1 |
| TOTAL NUM. | 272 | 237 | 18 | 6 | 11 |

As specificity represents the fraction of patients without disease who test negative, specificity is defined as

$$Specificity = \frac{TN}{TN + FP}. \quad (16)$$

Also, accuracy is defined as

$$Accuracy = \frac{TP + TN}{TP + TN + FP + FN}. \quad (17)$$

In this research, we had 0.6471 of sensitivity, 0.9294 of specificity, and 0.9118 of accuracy. These results show the proposed method is very useful for diagnosis of the normal liver. Values of FP and FN are high for tumors located in the left portal branch and tumors with a diameter less than 2 cm.

## 4 Conclusions

In this paper, an automatic hepatic tumor segmentation method using composite hypotheses was proposed. The liver structure was first segmented in order to remove other abdominal organs. Hepatic vessels were removed from the liver because hepatic vessels were not related to tumor segmentation. Then optimal threshold was calculated by composite hypotheses and minimum total probability error. Finally, a hepatic tumor was segmented using the optimal threshold value. In order to evaluate the proposed method, 272 slices from 10 patients were selected. From the evaluation results, we had 0.6471 of sensitivity, 0.9294 of specificity, and 0.9118 of accuracy.

These results show that the proposed method is very useful for diagnosis of normal and abnormal livers. In the future, algorithms for reducing false positives of the left portal branch will be developed.

## References

1. Parkin, D. M.: Global cancer statistics in the year 2000. Lancet Oncology, Vol. 2. (2001) 533-54
2. Lee H.: Liver cancer. The Korean Society of Gastroenterology, Seoul Korea (2001)
3. Bae, K. T., Giger, M. L., Chen, C. T., Kahn, Jr. C. E.: Automatic segmentation of liver structure in CT images. Med. Phys.,Vol. 20. (1993) 71-78
4. Gao, L., Heath, D. G., Kuszyk, B. S., Fishman, E. K.: Automatic liver segmentation technique for three-dimensional visualization of CT data. Radiology, Vol. 201. (1996) 359-364
5. Park, H., Bland, P. H., Meyer, C. R.: Construction of an abdominal probabilistic atlas and its application in segmentation. IEEE Trans. Med. Imag., Vol. 22. No. 4. (2003) 483- 492
6. Tsai, D.: Automatic segmentation of liver structure in CT images using a neural network. IEICE Trans. Fundamentals, Vol. E77-A. No. 11, (1994) 1892-1895
7. Husain, S. A., Shigeru, E.: Use of neural networks for feature based recognition of liver region on CT images. Neural Networks for Sig Proc.-Proceedings of the IEEE Work., Vol.2. (2000) 831-840
8. Seo, K., Ludeman, L. C., Park S., Park, J.: Efficient liver segmentation based on the spine. LNCS, Vol. 3261. (2004) 400-409
9. Orfanidis, S. J.: Introduction to signal processing. Prentice Hall, Upper Saddle River NJ (1996)
10. Schilling, R. J., Harris, S. L.: Applied numerical methods for engineers. Brooks/Cole Publishing Com., Pacific Grove CA (2000)
11. Ludeman, L. C.: Random processes: filtering, estimation, and detection. Wiley & Sons Inc., Hoboken NJ (2003)
12. Gonzalez, R. C., Woods, R. E.: Digital image processing. Prentice Hall, Upper Saddle River NJ (2002)
13. Shapiro, L. G., Stockman, G. C.: Computer vision. Prentice-Hall, Upper Saddle River NJ (2001)
14. Parker, J.R.: Algorithms for image processing and computer vision. Wiley Computer Publishing, New York (1997)
15. Rangayyan R.M.: Biomedical signal analysis. Wiley, New York NY (2002)

# Automated Snake Initialization for the Segmentation of the Prostate in Ultrasound Images

S. Rahnamayan[1], H.R. Tizhoosh[2], and M.M.A. Salama[3]

[1,2] Department of Systems Design Engineering
[3] Department of Electrical and Computer Engineering
[1,2,3] Medical Instrument Analysis and Machine Intelligence Research Group,
University of Waterloo, Waterloo, Ontario, Canada
shahryar@pami.uwaterloo.ca, tizhoosh@uwaterloo.ca,
msalama@hivolt1.uwaterloo.ca

**Abstract.** Segmentation is a crucial task in medical image processing. Snakes or Active Contour Models (ACM) are valuable tools to segment images. However, they need a good initialization, which is usually provided manually by an expert. In order to achieve a reliable automation of prostate segmentation in ultrasound images, morphological techniques have been used in this work to automatically generate the initial snake. The accuracy of the proposed approach is verified by testing several images. The automated segmentation of the prostate can be done in the majority of the cases without user interaction.

**Keywords:** Seed Points; Initial Snake; Ultrasound; Prostate; Mathematical Morphology; Active Contour Model.

## 1 Introduction

Prostate cancer is a common disease for men; early detection can be helpful for effective treatment. Ultrasound imaging is a common imaging technique which is used for prostate cancer detection. On the other hand, segmentation is one of the main tasks for medical image processing. Snakes or Active Contour Models (ACM) are valuable tools to segment images [1,2] because they can guarantee smoothness and continuity of boundaries with small segmentation error [3]. However, snakes suffer from some weaknesses. For instance, they depend on the assistance of the user to initialize the snake in the vicinity of the target tissue [4, 8]. Although this assistance is sometime acceptable but it is generally an obstacle preventing a reliable and full automation of the segmentation process.

In this paper, we propose a new technique that will enable us to overcome the aforementioned drawback. By applying mathematical morphology, initial snake is generated automatically leading to a fully automated prostate segmentation. Morphological filtering and conditional erosion are used to find a portion inside the prostate. The method can be generalized to any algorithm, which needs seed point(s) to start. By testing with 111 images, the success rate of correctly finding specific zones of prostate is 84.68%. By this achievement, the fully automated segmentation of the prostate can be achieved in the most of cases without any user interaction.

The paper is organized as follows: In section 2, a brief overview of binary mathematical morphology is given. In section 3, the proposed approach is introduced. Section 4 and 5 deliver the experimental results and the discussion. Finally, in section 6 the work is concluded.

## 2 Binary Mathematical Morphology(MM)

Mathematical morphology was developed based on works by Serra and Matheron [9,10,11]. Morphology is a shape-based approach to image processing. The value of each pixel in the output image is based on a comparison of the corresponding pixels in the input image with the structuring element(SE). The MM techniques provide remarkable tools for image filtering [12], object extraction, and edge detection [13]. Dilation, erosion, opening, and closing are fundamental operators of mathematical morphology. Dilation expands the boundaries of the object; erosion, as a dual operation to dilation, shrinks the boundaries of the object. Objects and connections between them can be eliminated by opening with suitable structuring elements. Closing removes small holes on the foreground, which are smaller than the chosen SE. Combination of closing and opening is also known as morphological filtering [14].

## 3 Proposed Approach

The proposed approach to automated snake initialization has several steps according to the diagram in Fig. 1. The individual steps of the proposed approach are discussed in the following subsections.

### 3.1 Thresholding

Since the binary morphology is being used in this approach, the gray level images should be converted to a binary image. Otsu method has been applied to threshold the image [15]. This method calculates a threshold to minimize the intra-class variance of the black and white pixels in the histogram.

A test image (Fig.2.a) and its thresholded version (Fig.2.b) are shown in Fig.2. In order to have the prostate as foreground and other tissues as background in the image, the thresholded image is inverted (Fig.2.c).

### 3.2 Morphological Filtering

In this stage white pixels in the background and black pixels in the foreground which are smaller than selected structuring element are removed in two steps,

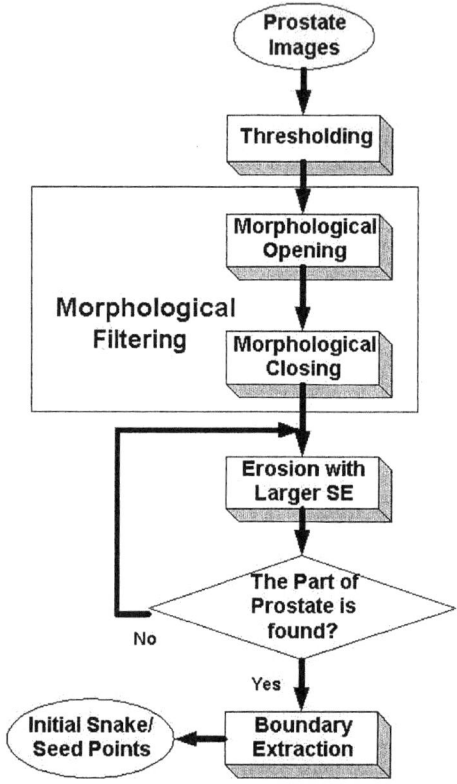

**Fig. 1.** The individual steps of the proposed approach

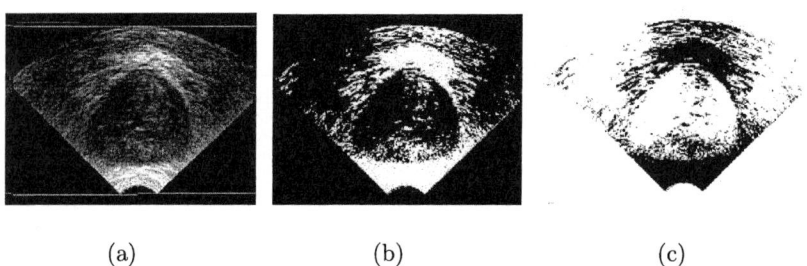

**Fig. 2.** Thresholding of ultrasound image by Otsu method: (a) original image, (b) thresholded by Otsu method, (c) after inversion

opening and closing. The structuring element (SE) used for filtering is defined as a disk shape with diameter of 2 pixels, as follows:

$$SE = \begin{bmatrix} 0 & 0 & 1 & 0 & 0 \\ 0 & 1 & 1 & 1 & 0 \\ 1 & 1 & 1 & 1 & 1 \\ 0 & 1 & 1 & 1 & 0 \\ 0 & 0 & 1 & 0 & 0 \end{bmatrix}. \tag{1}$$

First, the opening step removes small islands (noisy points) and makes contours smoother. Fig.3.a shows the result of opening on the inverted binary image.

The closing step smoothes contours and removes small holes. Fig.3.b shows result of closing on opened image which is the final result of morphological filtering.

(a) (b)

**Fig. 3.** Result of morphological filtering: (a) opening and (b) closing

### 3.3 Conditional Erosion

Erosion contracts the foreground boundary and eliminates holes on the background. Because it assigns the smallest neighborhood pixel value defined by SE to each pixel. The conditional erosion is defined by:

$$E_k = (A \ominus B_k), \qquad (2)$$

where $E_k$ is the $k^{th}$ resulted image of erosion and $B_k$ is the $k^{th}$ disk shaped structuring element with diameter of $5 + 2(k-1)$ pixels.

The condition to stop this erosion process is the remaining one object inside of the solid background. The objects are labeled and counted in each step to verify this condition.

The erosion is repeated with a two pixel larger SE in each iteration until one object remains inside of the solid background. This object, with high probability, should be a part of the prostate because the prostate obviously is the largest object in this kind of medical images. Some results for the conditional erosion are illustrated in Fig.4.

### 3.4 Initial Snake/Seed Points Extraction

After finding a part inside the prostate, the boundary of the detected region can be determined as follows:

$$Bound_{Int}(A) = A - (A \ominus B). \qquad (3)$$

The object boundaries in the image are detected by the subtraction of the eroded image from the original image. A sample result is shown in Fig.5. This boundary, which is completely inside the prostate, can be used by active contour models as the initial snake for prostate segmentation.

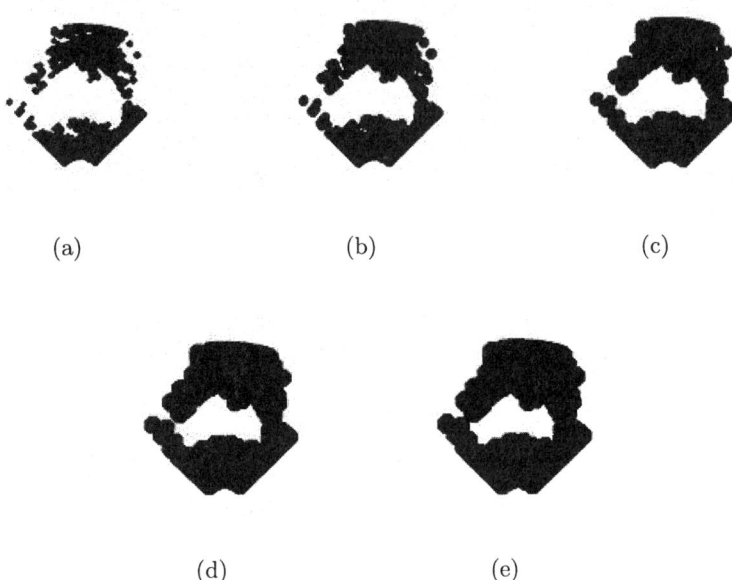

**Fig. 4.** Some selected results of conditional erosion: (a),(b),(c),(d) and (e) are eroded images after 1, 3, 5, 7, and 9 iterations, respectively

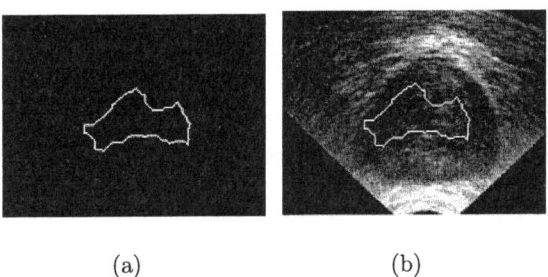

**Fig. 5.** (a) Initial snake resulted by applying internal boundary detection approach. (b) the resulted snake is completely inside of the prostate, and can be used as an initial snake for final prostate segmentation.

## 4 Experimental Results

The approach has been tested by 111 low quality prostate ultrasound images. In 94 cases, the initial snake has been found inside the prostate, In 17 cases, however, it failed to extract an inner portion of the prostate. Hence, the total success rate of the approach is 84.68%. The results of applying the proposed approach to two images to find the initial snake inside of the prostate are shown in Fig.6.

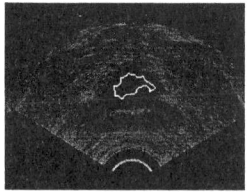 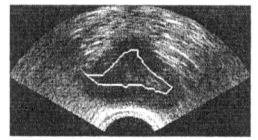

**Fig. 6.** The final results of applying the proposed approach to find the initial snake; as seen, the extracted initials are totally inside the prostates and ready to be used by active contour models

Failures can be categorized in two groups: 1) finding a wrong region (8 cases; 7.21%), which means the snake is not totally inside the prostate and 2) finding no region (9 cases; 8.11%); which both kind of errors are caused because of very low quality of captured images. Preprocessing prior to thresholding might decrease the failure rate.

## 5 Discussion

The main part of our approach after thresholding and morphological filtering, removing noise from the image foreground and background, is based on the conditional erosion. In fact we assumed that the largest object in the image is the prostate. This assumption is generally reasonable and can be supported by empirical knowledge. By applying conditional erosion we can assume that the last remaining object is (a part of) the prostate.

In the majority of the cases (84.68%) the result was what we expected but the algorithm failed also for some cases (15.32%).

Two factors caused those failed results. The first reason for failure was the existence of a shadowy region in the image, which was larger/darker/smoother than the prostate, an unusual case in this kind of images. This caused the prostate to erode earlier than the shadowy region. In fact, the shadowy region is mistaken with the prostate. An example for this case is given in Fig.7. The region enclosed by thicker line is the mentioned shadowy region. The wrong result found is marked by thinner line which is inside of that. About 47.06% of the failed cases were caused by this problem.

It seems possible to overcome this kind of problem by applying different (e.g. larger) structuring element for region outside of prostate. In fact applying adaptive structuring elements could solve this problem. Having images with higher quality could be much helpful as well.

The second reason for the failure was a complete erosion of all objects at the same time such that no specific region could be identified as the prostate. This happens when in the last step of the erosion all remaining objects are smaller than SE. About 52.94% of failing cases were caused by this phenomenon. This problem can probably be overcome by applying adaptive SE as well. For instance, one could make the SE smaller when only a small number of objects remain.

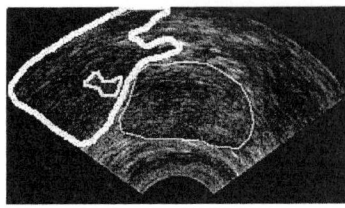

**Fig. 7.** An example of finding wrong result due to existence of larger adjacent shadowy region

## 6 Conclusion

The work in this paper aimed at automatic initialization of a snake or seed points inside the prostate in ultrasound images. The success rate of the proposed technique is 84.68% which can be improved by increasing the image quality. In fact, this work represents a possibility achieving a fully automated segmentation by snakes or active contour models. The proposed approach in this paper can eliminate user interaction to define initial snake for the segmentation of the prostate in ultrasound images.

Future objectives are directed towards adaptive thresholding and adaptive erosion. The role of thresholding in this project is essential. Conditional erosion is the main part of the method, and finding wrong result or no result has occurred in this stage. According to our experiments, it seems that we should apply the different erosion operations for the background and foreground. This means different structuring elements should be incorporated to erode the prostate region and non-prostate region differently.

**Acknowledgements.** Special thanks to Robarts Research Institute, London, Ontario for preparing and providing database of prostate ultrasound images. This project has been supported partially by a CIHR strategic training fellowship.

## References

1. M. Kass, A. Witkin, D. Terzopoulos: Active Contour Models, First International Conference on Computer Vision (1987) 259-268
2. G. Sullivan, A. Worrall, R. Hockney, K. Baker: Active Countours In Medical Image Processing Using a Networked SIMD Array Processor, First British Machine Vision Conference (1990) 395-400
3. G. Hamarneh: Towards Intelligent Deformable Models for Medical Image Analysis, Thesis submitted to Department of Signals and Systems, Chalmers University of Technology, Gteborg, Sweden (2001)
4. J. Ivins and J. Porrill: Active region models for segmenting medical images, Proceedings. ICIP-94., IEEE International Conference , Vol. 2 , (1994) 227-231
5. J.G. Snel, H.W. Venema, C.A. Grimbergen: Detection of the carpal bone contours from 3-D MR images of the wrist using a planar radial scale-space snake, IEEE Transactions on Medical Imaging, Vol. 17 , Issue 6, (1998) 1063-1072

6. G. Hamarneh, A. Chodorowski, T. Gustavsson: Active contour models: application to oral lesion detection in color images, IEEE International Conference on Systems and Cybernetics , Vol. 4, (2000) 2458-2463
7. S.D. Fenster and J.R. Kender, Sectored snakes: evaluating learned-energy segmentations, IEEE Transactions on Pattern Analysis and Machine Intelligence, Vol. 23, Issue 9, (2001) 1028-1034
8. Xie Xianghua and M. Mirmehdi, RAGS: region-aided geometric snake, IEEE Transactions on Image Processing, Vol. 13, Issue 5, (2004) 640-652
9. J.Serra: Image analysis and mathematical morphology, Academic Press Inc. (1982)
10. G. Matheron: Random Sets and Integral Geometry, Wiley, New York (1975), ISBN: 0-471-57621-2.
11. S.R. Sternberg: Grayscale morphology, Computer Vision Graphics and Image Processing, Vol. 35, (1986) 333-355
12. S. Rahnamayan, H.R. Tizhoosh, M.M.A. Salama: Learning Image Filtering from a Gold Sample Based on Genetic Optimization of Morphological Processing, Proc. of 7th Int. Conf. on Adaptive and Natural Computing Algorithms, Springer-Verlag (Vienna), Coimbra, Portugal (2005) 478-481
13. J. Serra and P. Soille, eds.: Mathematical Morphology and Its applications to Image Processing, Kluwer Academic Publishers, Dordrecht (1994)
14. Rafael C. Gonzalez and Richard E. Woods: Digital Image Processing, Prentice Hall, Second Edition (2002) 519-566
15. N. Otsu: A Threshold Selection Method from Gray-Level Histograms, IEEE Transactions on Systems and Cybernetics, Vol. 9, No. 1, (1979) 62-66

# Bayesian Differentiation of Multi-scale Line-Structures for Model-Free Instrument Segmentation in Thoracoscopic Images

Luke Windisch[1], Farida Cheriet[1,2], and Guy Grimard[2]

[1] Ecole Polytechnique de Montreal, C.P. 6079, 53851 succ. Centre-ville,
Montreal, Canada H3C 3A7
{first.last}@polytml.ca
[2] Department of Orthopaedics, Sainte Justine Hospital,
Montreal, Canada
guy_grimard@ssss.gouv.qc.ca

**Abstract.** A reliable method to segment instruments in endoscope images is required as part of an enhanced reality system for minimally invasive surgery of the spine. Numerous characteristics of these images make typical intensity or model constraints for segmentation impractical. Rather, line-structure concepts are used to exploit the high length-to-diameter ratio expected of surgical instruments. A Bayesian selection scheme is proposed, and is shown to reliably differentiate these target objects from other line-like background structures.

## 1 Introduction

The risks associated with exposing the interior of a patient's body during spinal surgery can be mitigated by minimally invasive techniques, under which a surgeon inserts instruments through a number of small incisions and views the surgical site via video from an endoscope, a monocular camera with integrated light source (fig. 1). Compared to conventional surgeries that fully expose the surgical site, patient risk and costly in-hospital recovery periods are reduced.

Unfortunately, adoption of these procedures has been slowed by the considerable difficulties faced by surgeons, who lose depth perception since the surgical site is viewed indirectly via the monocular endoscope. Moreover, contextual depth cues are few, as the proximity of the endoscope to the objects being imaged creates a narrow field-of-view (FOV), on order of 5-cm or less. Ultimately, the long training needed to gain comfort and expertise working with such a difficult view of the surgical site has limited the spread of this approach.

An enhanced reality surgical system to integrate 3D preoperative patient models with the endoscope video stream would help solve the problems of depth and context loss. Central to the success of this system is automatic recalibration of the extrinsic and intrinsic endoscope parameters, which may vary throughout the surgery due to camera motion and manual focusing. The extrinsic parameters of the endoscope are updated in real time by using an optical tracking system. However, updating the intrinsic parameters requires tracking features that can be easily and automatically detected from the image sequence. It is difficult to determine whether changes in features such as intensity arise due to camera or instrument movements, thus we only consider corners and others instrument features that represent precise 3D points on instruments. Relative camera and instrument movements reported by the optical tracking system can then be used to give real-world context to the image-based movements of the identified features so that the intrinsic camera parameters can be updated. Actually identifying these instrument features is complicated by several difficulties, the first of which are the characteristics of endoscope images themselves (see fig. 2):

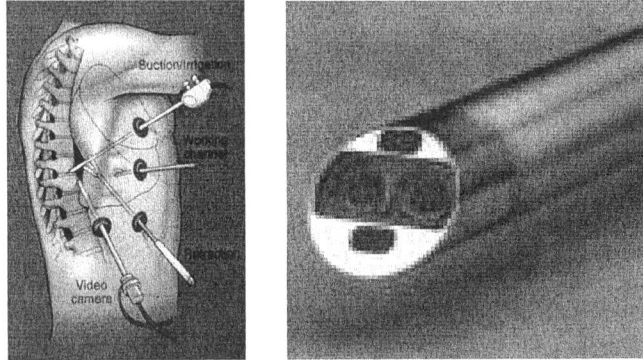

**Fig. 1.** Left—A typical set-up for a minimally invasive surgery (source: www.spineuniverse. com); Right—An endoscope tip, showing the integrated lens and light source (source: www.intuitivesurgical.com)

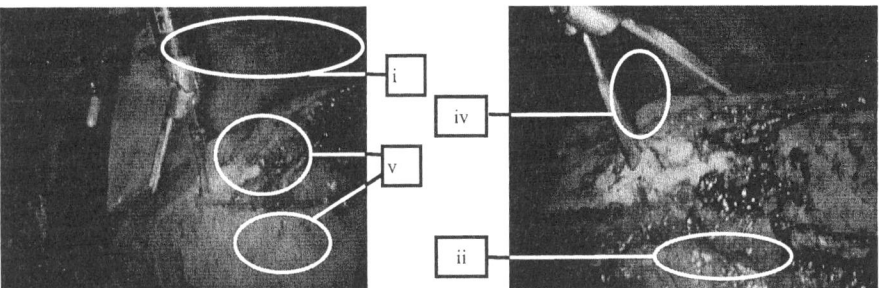

**Fig. 2.** Two images of the same instrument. Numbered areas correspond to the list of problems above. Note that due to endoscope movement, only the prongs of the instrument are visible in the second image.

  i. Rapid intensity fall-off with radial distance from the image center;
  ii. Strong specular reflections from metallic instruments and moist tissues, which change unpredictably under endoscope and instrument movements;

iii. Large changes in the appearance of objects due to motion and focusing of the endoscope;
iv. Blood, exposed tissue, and steam at the surgical site that blur and occlude boundaries; and
v. Cut or exposed tissues, which cause strong variations in background textures and colours.

A second complication arises from smooth instrument surfaces, which offer only a sparse set of features that are difficult to isolate from background features – a stringent detection criterion to suppress background may also too strongly prune the instrument features. Zhang and Payandeh solved this problem by affixing artificial markers to the instruments [1]; however, such features are not immune to noise, occlusion, poor lighting, or wash-out from specular reflections. More importantly, artificial markers complicate the sterilization of instruments, and we would like to move towards a tracking method that operates with instruments "as is." Accordingly, the preferred approach is to use as large a set of natural instrument features as possible. To do so, background features must be distinguished from instrument features, and this demands a viable scheme to segment instruments from the image.

Segmentation algorithms are typically constrained by metrics that are intensity-based [2, 3], region-based [4, 5], or object-model based [6]. Unfortunately, many of the image characteristics outlined above make such constraints unreliable or impractical for our context. Instead, motivated by recent work by Chen and Amini [7], we have approached segmentation using the concept of line-structures, which exhibit a significant length-to-width ratio, a property common to instruments for minimally invasive surgery.

In Section 2 we present a novel multi-scale, line-structure-based scheme to effectively distinguish between line-responses arising from instruments and from background objects. Results are presented in section 3. The discussion of section 4 summarizes the advantages of the segmentation scheme.

## 2 Multi-scale Line-Structure Segmentation

A line-structure has an extended length compared to its width (a high 'length-to-width ratio'), and the intensity profile of the image of such an object will show only slight variation along, relative to across, its longitudinal direction. Numerous line-detector operators have been developed to exploit this property [7, 8, 9]. Often, the scales and orientations of line-structures in an image are unknown, requiring the detection operator to be applied at several scales and orientations to identify the best line object at a point $\mathbf{x} = (x_1, x_2)$.

### 2.1 Line-Structure Detection with the Hessian Matrix

A popular detector, proposed by Lorenz et al. [9], is based on a Hessian matrix analysis. The characteristics of line-object intensity profiles imply that the second derivative across a line-structure should be large compared to along it. Accordingly, an eigen-analysis of the Hessian matrix $H_\mathbf{x}$ can be used to identify line-structures by looking for points with $|\lambda_1| \gg |\lambda_2|$ and having a high line response given by:

$$R(\sigma,\mathbf{x})_{2D} = \sigma^{\gamma} \cdot \lambda_1(\sigma,\mathbf{x}) \quad (1)$$

where the scale, $\sigma$, is the standard deviation of a smoothing Gaussian kernel, $\gamma > 0$, and $\sigma^{\gamma}$ compensates for the decrease in the response due to increased smoothing at higher scales. Detection proceeds in three steps: First, an image is blurred with a Gaussian kernel at several scales. Then, each image point $\mathbf{x}$ is assigned the extremum value of (1) across all scales, as well as the scale at which the extremum occurred. Finally non-maximum suppression of the set of responses (1) generates skeletons centered along the image's line-objects (note that a second function must be used with (1) to distinguish lines from step edges).

**Problems with Current Detection Methods**

Detection schemes like this have been shown to work very well for problems like vessel-tree extraction from 2D images and 3D volumes [7, 9], where the objects of interest have good contrast against relatively homogeneous backgrounds. Unfortunately, segmentation is complicated by the complex backgrounds of endoscope images. In certain cases, background objects such as veins are themselves line-objects. Current detection methods implicitly assume that any local extrema arising from a function such as (1) correspond to the objects to be segmented; the possibility of non-target line-structures is not considered, and line-responses arising from these objects cannot be differentiated. This problem is illustrated in fig. 3(a), where the skeletons extracted by the previously described detection scheme based on (1) have been superimposed on the original endoscope image. These skeletons all encode scale information and thus represent the final segmentation of the image. Clearly, the presence of blood vessels is problematic – our objective is to segment only instruments.

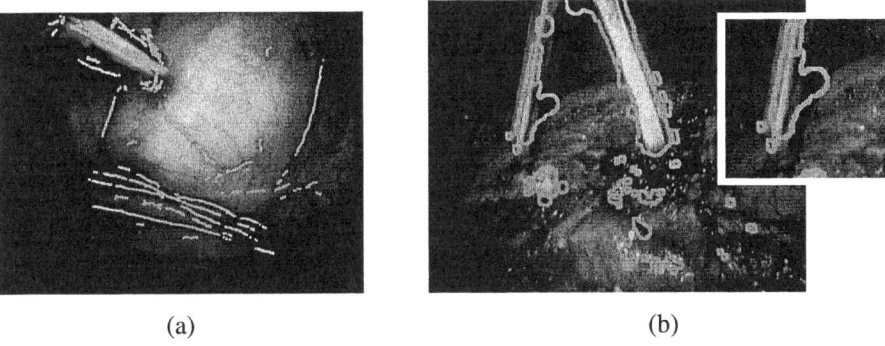

(a)          (b)

**Fig. 3.** Current line-object detection methods applied to endoscope images. In (a), skeletons corresponding to the instrument and background objects (veins) cannot be differentiated. In (b), responses to background texture have led to isolated patches of segmented background, and have also resulted in inaccurate representations of instrument shape and size, as seen in the over-segmentation of the of the lower-left instrument prong (enlarged in image inset).

While the results in fig. 3(a) are clearly sub-optimal, the background skeletons at least correspond to real line-objects. In 3(b), the image background does not contain any line-objects, but the highly variable texture still gives rise to extrema in the response given by (1). This introduces two difficulties: First, for the same reasons just mentioned, these extrema cannot be distinguished by current methods, leading to isolated regions of incorrectly segmented background.

Second, skeletons corresponding to actual instruments can be quickly led astray of true object shapes, especially when instrument contrast is weak. Consider the lower left prong of the instrument, which has been enlarged in the image inset. At the extreme lower tip of the prong the instrument exhibits good contrast and the segmentation corresponds well with the actual shape. However, a problem quickly develops as the segmentation follows the prong upwards: the contrast towards the right instrument edge falls, while a significant edge in the background tissue develops. The response (1) to the intensity profile between this tissue and the left instrument edge is stronger than to the profile between the left and right instrument edges, and the non-maximum suppression scheme keeps only the response at the higher scale. Thus the skeleton is led astray of the true instrument shape and encodes too-high scale information, resulting in over-segmentation.

## 2.2 Modified Scale-Specific Line-Structure Detection

A first step towards successfully applying line-object concepts to endoscope images involves making the initial detection process more robust to the problems of weak instrument contrast in the presence of background textures. To increase robustness, we modify the line-structure detection process by applying non-maximum suppression to the responses (1) obtained at a *specific* scale, rather than to the set of across-scale extrema of (1). Numerous scales are still processed, but we now have a set of skeletons at each scale.

Limiting the extraction to individual scales reflects the observation that most line objects exhibit a high degree of parallelism between their occluding boundaries, so that the object scale in an image should vary little along its length. By restricting the extraction in this way, textures in the background at higher scales are less likely to lead the skeleton astray of the true object shape.

Two problems remain: combining the skeletons from different scales, and identifying which skeletons correspond to instruments. While previous detection schemes used extracted skeletons as the final segmentation result, the skeletons in our scheme are simply a comprehensive set of *candidate* instruments. We now apply highly general assumptions to develop a Bayesian framework to distinguish which candidate skeletons to keep.

## 2.3 Bayesian Identification of Instruments

After the extraction step, each skeleton will have a scale and length. This information can be used to identify instrument skeletons by considering that instrumentation used in minimally invasive procedures must be narrow enough (small scale) to fit through the small incisions on a patient's body while long enough to reach the surgical site. We embed these characteristics into a Bayesian expression for the probability that a skeleton corresponds to an instrument, given the skeleton's observed scale $\sigma$ and length $l$:

$$P(Inst|\sigma,l) = \frac{P(\sigma,l|Inst)P(Inst)}{P(\sigma,l)}. \qquad (2)$$

The left term in the numerator of the right-hand side of (2) represents the likelihood of a skeleton having the observed length and scale, assuming the skeleton corresponds to an instrument. The right term in the numerator reflects any *a piori* information regarding instruments in endoscope images. The denominator can be ignored, leaving only the terms in the numerator to be defined more rigorously.

**Likelihood Term**
The long-but-thin characteristic of instruments implies that corresponding skeletons should have a high length-to-width ratio, and that the first term in the numerator of the right-hand side of (2) should assign higher probabilities to skeletons accordingly. However, skeletons with high ratios are more likely at smaller scales – as an instrument gets near the camera, its image scale will necessarily increase while its visible length will simultaneously decrease. Therefore, any scheme that assigns probabilities to skeletons by looking for high ratios should allow for lower ratios at higher scales. The following non-linear weighting is applied to each skeleton, which assigns a weight on [0 1) and is plotted in fig. 4:

$$P(\sigma,l|Inst) = \frac{1}{2} + \frac{1}{\pi}\operatorname{atan}\left\{\alpha_\sigma\left(l - \beta_\sigma\right)\right\} - P(\sigma=0, l=0|Inst). \qquad (3)$$

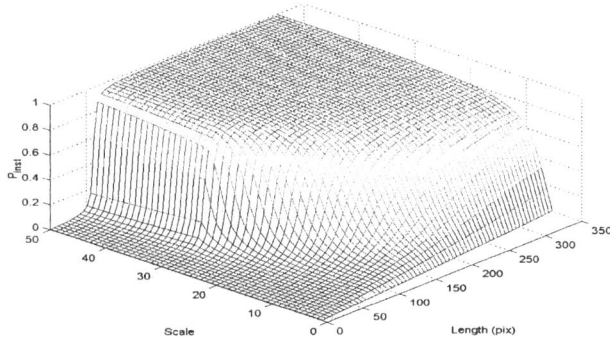

**Fig. 4.** The likelihood given by (3) plotted against length and scale. For the 320x240 images presented later, the parameters in (4) were: $l_{min}=60$, $\sigma_{max}=40$, $l_{max}=240$ and $\sigma_{min}=2$.

The shape of this functional is controlled as follows:

- $\beta$, a function of scale, positions the half-maximum point of (3) at the minimum length a skeleton must achieve before it can be considered a potential instrument. $\beta$ varies inversely with scale:

$$\beta(\sigma) = \begin{cases} l_{min} & \text{if } \sigma > \sigma_h \\ \exp\left\{-\dfrac{\sigma - \sigma_l}{\eta}\right\} \cdot l_{max} & \text{if } \sigma_h \geq \sigma \geq \sigma_l \\ l_{max} & \text{if } \sigma < \sigma_l \end{cases} \qquad (4)$$

$\eta$ controls the sharpness of the transition of $\beta$ from high to low scales, and is specified according to: i) $\sigma_h$, the (high) scale at which it is reasonable to assume an instrument may give rise to a skeleton only $l_{min}$ pixels long; and, ii) $\sigma_l$, the smallest scale at which skeletons corresponding to instruments are expected, which may be up to $l_{max}$ long. To be as general as possible, these parameters are set once to cover the extreme cases of instrument length and scale that might arise in any endoscope image due to camera motion and focusing. For the results presented later with 320x240 images, $l_{min}$=60, $\sigma_h$=40, $l_{max}$=240 and $\sigma_l$=2 were used. These values set the half-maximum of (3) at a line ratio of only ~1.5 at higher scales, and at 100 or more for smaller scales.

- $\alpha$ determines the slope of the transition through the half-maximum. For most endoscope images, textures and tissues that generate longer skeletons are more common at lower scales. By extension, skeletons that correspond to background textures and exceed the $l_{min}$ threshold in (4) are unlikely at higher scales, so we can allow a sharper transition to the high probability asymptote of (3) as the object scale increases:

$$\alpha(\sigma) = \dfrac{\sigma}{\beta_\sigma}. \qquad (5)$$

- The last term on the right hand side of (3) simply enforces $P(\sigma, l \mid Inst) = 0$ for a zero-length chain.

**Prior Term**

The likelihood term just described cannot be guaranteed to suppress all non-instrument skeletons: at lower scales especially, long background objects may still exist with a length over the threshold assigned in (4). To increase the probability of isolating only instruments we observe that, regardless of the scale at which instruments appear in an image due to varying distances from the endoscope, they are typically physically larger than other highly line-like background objects such as veins. This characteristic is embedded in the following *a priori* term:

$$P(Inst) = \dfrac{\sigma_{skel}}{\sigma_{max}}, \qquad (6)$$

where $\sigma_{skel}$ is the scale of the extracted skeleton, and $\sigma_{max}$ is the maximum scale of all line objects detected.

## 2.4 Final Identification

It is important to note that we do not use (2) as a *maximum a posteriori* detector of instruments, since we have no knowledge about the number of instruments that will be visible in an image. Instead, we keep those skeletons in the image that have an *a posteriori* probability greater than 0.5. This value gives us reasonable confidence that the skeletons we retain correspond to instruments: while long line-objects such as veins may receive a high weighting from the likelihood term in (3) they are unlikely to be selected as an instrument unless they also have a large scale relative to other objects.

## 3 Results and Discussion

All segmentation results were obtained running non-optimized MATLAB code on a 512-MB P4 IBM PC. Parameters for detection using (2) are given in section 2, and were the same for all images. Segmentation results for the two endoscope images previously considered in fig. 3 are shown in fig. 5(a) and (b).

Segmentation of fig. 5(a) is complicated not only by having to differentiate background line-objects from instruments as previously discussed, but also by the instrument's proximity to the endoscope, which makes it appear short and wide. This problem is addressed by the likelihood term in (3), which is sensitive to the fact that shorter objects are common at higher scales. Removing the background structures is handled by the *a priori* term in (6), which takes a greater value for the instrument due to its higher scale.

Image 5(b) is of the same instrument shown in fig. 3(b). This image illustrates again the utility of the likelihood term in (3), which helps suppress the numerous small, isolated background textures. Further, the scale-specific skeleton extraction described in section 2.2 has helped ensure the final segmentation more closely reflects the true instrument shape.

In 5(c), endoscope and instrument movements have created a dramatically different view of the instrument from 5(b). Changes in appearance like this are common in our application, and would be difficult to handle with current model-based segmentation techniques; a comprehensive set of *a priori* models to guide segmentation is intractable, even using PCA approaches. Our scheme robustly identifies the target regions without any prior knowledge of the *specific* instrument; only extended length relative to width is assumed.

Finally, in fig. 6 we have compared our method to segmentation results obtained using the Gradient Vector Flow (GVF) approach for Snakes [10]. The images in (a) and (b) serve to underscore some of our introductory comments about difficulties applying existing segmentation metrics to endoscope images (see discussion of fig. 2). In (a), the GVF segmenting contour was initialized to the interior of the instrument region, and eventually stabilized on the boundaries of the strong reflection on the instrument surface. In (b), the contour was initialized to a region outside the instrument, and the evolution was stopped after 150 iterations because the result was unacceptable – the contour had leaked over the real instrument boundary (a part of which has been superimposed in the image for clarity). The problem here is the strong dependence of the contour evolution on intensity/edge content in the image; the real instrument edge is weak, and evolution was only constrained by the apparent edge caused by the reflection. The general shape measures we have embedded in our Bayesian line-object scheme are more stable indicators of instruments in endoscope images, and results of our method applied to the same image are shown in (c). As in (a), the instrument is still under-segmented, but our method is more robust in general. Specifically, as 6(a) and (b) indicate, results with other methods can depend strongly on specifics of the implementation such as the initial location of the segmenting contour. They may also leave unresolved the interpretation of the segmented regions. In contrast, all the results shown using our method were obtained with an identical implementation, and unlike in 6(a), the interpretation of the final segmentation in all cases is automatically provided.

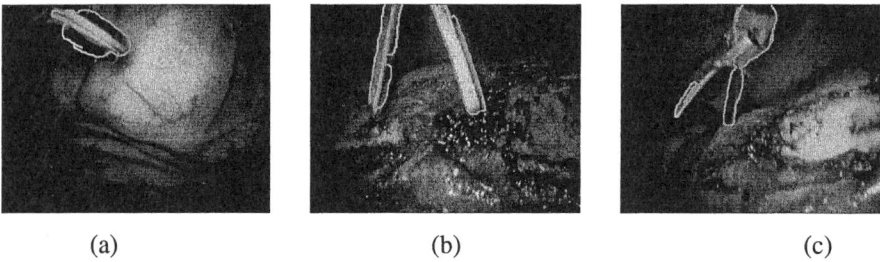

(a) (b) (c)

**Fig. 5.** Results obtained with our proposed segmentation scheme using parameters given in section 2. Results in (a) and (b) can be directly compared with those in fig. 3. The result in (c), while sub-optimal, illustrates that our method is highly robust to changes in instrument shape – the instrument is the same as that in (b).

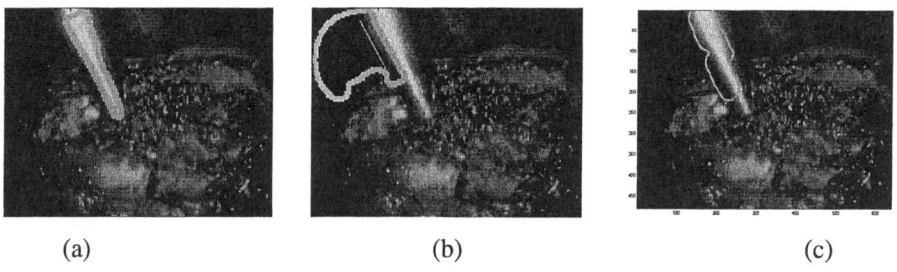

(a) (b) (c)

**Fig. 6.** Segmentation results obtained with a Snake-based contour approach are shown in (a) and (b), where the segmenting contour was initialized inside and outside the instrument, respectively. Segmentation of the same image obtained with our method is shown in (c). The segmentation in (b) has mistakenly included part of the instrument in the background. Moreover, unlike our method, neither of the results in (a) or (b) provide an interpretation of the final segmentation.

At this time, a persistent problem with our method tends to be under-segmentation. This is particularly notable in images 5(c) and 6(c). Work is currently under way to automatically identify and remove the strong reflections on the instrument surfaces and should improve results: with these reflections diminished, the intensity profiles will be closer to ideal, and the response in (1) will be more stable.

Under-segmentation problems also result in part from a deliberate choice we have made. If a we are to rely on natural instrument features for the overall tracking and calibration objective, it is better to under-segment an image than over-segment; we must have confidence that any features identified in the segmented regions correspond to an instrument rather than background. Accordingly, we have set up the Bayesian detection scheme to be strict, and consequently, some skeletons corresponding to instruments are suppressed. For instance, in fig. 5(c), the prior probability term in (6) has caused the loss of a skeleton corresponding to the bright reflection on the left instrument prong since the skeleton encodes a very small scale compared to the upper portion of the instrument.

To conclude these discussions, it is important to reiterate why we do not circumvent the segmentation issue altogether and meet our calibration objective by simply tracking a set of artificial markers attached to the instruments. Natural instrument features such as corners are consistent with an instrument's structure at a much higher-level compared to artificial markers, and tracking these natural, high-level features is expected to create a more robust method overall. Additionally, this approach does not impose any extra procedures on the surgical teams that will ultimately use the application. An intensive validation using a large number of images is currently in progress to evaluate the precision of our approach compared to existing methods.

## 4 Conclusions

Endoscope images provide a particularly challenging set of obstacles for segmentation. Camera motion, inconsistent intensity, variable colour information, and uncertain contrast all hamper traditional segmentation approaches: while certain algorithms may perform well with one image, these constantly changing characteristics can render them ineffective on others. These problems demand segmentation approaches based on more stable aspects of the images. One constant, regardless of camera position, lighting, or background appearance, is the general shape of the target instruments themselves. Their long and narrow structures point towards the use of line-structure concepts; however, previous line-structure segmentation schemes do not transfer well to these images. In particular, changing contrast characteristics mean that responses similar to (1), which depend strongly on intensity, are unreliable. In our method, we have dramatically reduced the dependence of line-structure segmentation on the actual response magnitude. Instead, we have incorporated line-structure ideas into a Bayesian framework that allows us to extract many line-objects while still remaining confident we will isolate the ones that correspond to instruments. This flexibility affords greater independence from, and adaptability to, the changing properties typical of endoscope images.

At the cost of under-segmentation, we have shown the results of the method to reliably isolate only instrument regions in the image. In other contexts where over-segmentation is not as critical a concern, the Bayesian selection criteria can be loosened accordingly. This speaks to a particular advantage of our approach: integration of line-structures into Bayesian concepts, which are highly adaptable to myriad problems, should help extend the use of line-structure concepts to more challenging images than those with good contrast or homogeneous backgrounds.

## Acknowledgements

Financial support for this project was provided by the Natural Sciences and Engineering Research Council of Canada and the MENTOR-CIHR program for research into spinal deformities.

## References

[1] X. Zhang and S. Payandeh, Application of Visual Tracking for Robot Assisted Laparoscopic Surgery, *J. Robotic Systems*, 19(7), 315-328, 2002.
[2] V. Caselles, R. Kimmel and G. Sapiro, Geodesic Active Contours, *Int. J. Computer Vision*, 22(1), 61-79, 1997.
[3] M. Leventon, O. Faugeras, E. Grimson, and W. Wells, Level Set Based Segmentation with Intensity and Curvature Priors, *Mathematical Methods in Biomedical Image Analysis 2000*.
[4] T. Chan and L. Vese, Active Contours Without Edges, *IEEE Trans Image Pro*, 10(2), 266-277, 2001.
[5] X. Xie and M. Mirmehdi, RAGS: Region-Aided Geometric Snake, *IEEE Trans Image Pro*, 13(5), 640-652, 2004.
[6] M. Leventon, W. Grimson, O. Faugeras, Statistical Shape Influence in Geodesic Active Contours, *Comp. Vision and Patt. Recon. (CVPR)*, 2000.
[7] J. Chen and A. Amini, Quantifying 3-D Vascular Structures in MRA Images Using Hybrid PDE and Geometric Deformable Models, *IEEE Trans Medical Imaging*, 23(10), 1251-1262, 2004.
[8] T. Koller, G. Gerig, G. Szekely and D. Dettwiler, Multiscale Detection of Curvilinear Structures in 2-D and 3-D Image Data, *IEEE Proc. $5^{th}$ Int'l. Conf. Comp. Vision*, 864-869, 1995.
[9] C. Lorenz, I.-C. Carlsen, T. Buzug, C. Fassnacht and J. Weese, Multi-scale Line Segmentation with Automatic Estimation of Width, Contrast and Tangential Direction in 2D and 3D Medical Images, *Proc. $1^{st}$ Int'l Joint Conf. CVRMed and MRCAS (CVRMed/MRCAS '97)*, 233-242, 1997.
[10] C. Xu and J. L. Prince, ``Snakes, Shapes, and Gradient Vector Flow,'' *IEEE Transactions on Image Processing*, 7(3), 359-369, 1998.

# Segmentation of Ultrasonic Images of the Carotid

Rui Rocha[1,2,3], Aurélio Campilho[1,2], and Jorge Silva[1,2]

[1] INEB - Instituto de Engenharia Biomédica, Laboratório de Sinal e Imagem Biomédica
[2] Universidade do Porto, Faculdade de Engenharia, Dep. Eng. Electrotécnica e de Computadores
[3] Instituto Politécnico do Porto, Instituto Superior de Engenharia, Dep. Matemática
Porto - Portugal

**Abstract.** A new algorithm for an effective and automatic segmentation of the carotid wall in ultrasonic images is proposed. It combines the speed of thresholding algorithms with the accuracy, flexibility and robustness of a successful geometric active contour model which incorporates an optimal image segmentation model in a level set framework. Due to the multiphase nature of these images, a sequential minimum cross entropy thresholding is used to get a first approximation of the segments, reducing the problem to a two phase segmentation. This thresholding solution is then used as a starting point for a two phase piecewise constant version of a geometric active contour model to reduce noise, smooth contours, improve their position accuracy and close eventual gaps in the carotid wall.

## 1 Introduction and Motivations

The diagnosis of atherosclerosis, i.e., the presence of plaque in artery walls, is one of the most important medical exams for prevention of cardiovascular events, like myocardial infarction and stroke. The intima-media thickness of the common carotid artery can be viewed as a descriptive general index of individual atherosclerosis. Since the carotid is a superficial artery and of easy access, it is quite suited for medical imaging using ultrasonography technology, which is greatly desirable because of its low cost and small risk to the patient [1]. This explains the great interest and effort, manifested by scientific community in the last decade, in the development of algorithms for the segmentation of carotid ultrasonic images. Even more attractive is the idea of using recent advances in ultrasound acquisition technology, for 3D medical imaging, to reconstruct a 3D surface model of the carotid walls from sequences of 2D ultrasonic images [1]. The 3D surface representation would allow a more friendly and powerful manipulation of the artery data, as well as a better diagnosis. Unfortunately, automatic segmentation of ultrasonic medical images is extremely difficult, due to their complexity and to several degrading phenomena inherent to this type of image acquisition technology. Some of these degrading factors are [1,2]: speckle noise, occlusions, low contrast and movement artifacts. As a result, these images are noisy, some parts of the edges may be missing, producing gaps in organ boundaries (like the carotid wall), and their structure is so complex that it is difficult to interpret even for a human eye. As a consequence, a manual segmentation of these images, performed by an experienced medical doctor, is the usual adopted procedure (see, for instance, [3,4]), which is a tedious and time consuming task and tends to give subjective results.

We propose a new effective and automatic algorithm to perform segmentation of the carotid wall in ultrasonic images. The procedure starts with a specially conceived sequential thresholding, using a minimum cross entropy (MCE) algorithm [5,6], which separates, reasonably well, the lumen (carotid interior, with blood) from the soft tissues involving the carotid. The thresholding is very fast and the resulting binary image is a good approximation to the desired segmentation (the extraction of the lumen), but it isn't capable, on its own, to deal with heavy noise or wall gaps. To overcome this, a second processing stage, involving a two phase piecewise constant geometric active contour [7,8], is applied to the image, taking advantage of the information inherited from the thresholding: the binary image is used for the contour initialization and some parameters of the active contour are defined as a function of the threshold obtained in the first stage. With a very fast convergence, the active contour cleans the noise, smooths contours, improves their position accuracy and closes eventual carotid wall gaps.

The outline of the paper is as follows. Next section is a brief presentation of previous work in this area, most promising trends and main difficulties. Section 3 introduces the Chan-Vese two phase piecewise constant geometric active contour [7,8]. The proposed algorithm is described in some detail in section 4. Results validating our algorithm are presented in section 5 and the paper ends with some conclusions in section 6.

## 2 Previous Work

Since the first attempt to (semi-)automatically detect the carotid boundaries in ultrasonic images [9], numerous investigators worldwide have tried to find better approaches to this problem. A brief summary of this work can be found in [10,11]. As pointed out in [11], a direct comparison of these approaches is still pending. Nevertheless, the approaches based on active contours [11,12,13,14] seem to be the most powerful and promising, although generally with some limitations, like manual initialization or gradient dependence. Another very interesting approach for images severely degraded by noise and occlusions is the shape-based segmentation [15], which has shown some success and may be very useful for segmentation of images acquired with ultrasonography. Unfortunately, due to possible presence of plaque and to the arbitrary angle of pulse incidence (essential for 3D surface reconstruction, for instance), our ultrasonic images have a very high variability of shapes of the carotid walls, which constitutes a serious and discouraging problem for these models. In this context, the ideal segmentation model for carotid ultrasonic images should be very flexible and include some sort of an elastic force to deal with noise and eventual gaps along the carotid walls.

Thresholding techniques are incapable of solving the problem of wall gaps and there is usually some remaining noise that needs to be removed. Experiments have shown that an anisotropic diffusion [16] after the thresholding is enough to clean the noise and smooth irregularities in the boundaries, but not enough to eliminate the gaps. This requires a more powerful technique like an active contour with an elastic force. In previous active contour algorithms [11,12,13], it is common the need for a manual initialization of contours near or inside the carotid boundary, and propagation forces are usually based on gradients. In the first case, the algorithm is not completely automatic, because it needs human intervention in each individual image. This is even more discouraging if the final aim is to create a 3D model of the carotid wall. On the other hand, gradient-based active contours are greatly unadvisable when dealing with images with high levels of noise or occlusions. In fact, if the noise is strong, it may cause the stopping of the contour at false edges. And if there are contours with weak gradient or even without gradient ('cognitive contours'), the active contour will not stop at these points. The Chan-Vese two phase piecewise constant active contour model [7] solves both of these problems. It is robust to the initial position of the active contour (unlike the multiphase version), and the propagation force for the contour is not based on gradients, thus giving it the ability to detect cognitive contours. Moreover, it is very accurate, it has the ability to automatically detect interior contours and it is embedded in a level set framework [17,18].

## 3 Active Contour Models

The Chan-Vese two phase piecewise constant segmentation model, recently introduced in [7,8], is the chosen active contour, for its potential and flexibility, as discussed in section 2. This active contour belongs to a family of level set formulations of the well-known image segmentation variational model of Mumford and Shah [19].

In Chan-Vese active contours, the number of implicit functions in the model is given by $m = \log_2(n)$, where $n$ is the number of phases in the image to segment. Thus, for a two phase image, only one implicit function is needed. The level set formulation for the Euler-Lagrange equation of the Chan-Vese two phase piecewise constant model is [7,8]:

$$\frac{\partial \phi}{\partial t} = \delta_\epsilon(\phi) \left[ \mu \text{div}\left(\frac{\nabla \phi}{|\nabla \phi|}\right) - \lambda_1(u_0 - c_1)^2 + \lambda_2(u_0 - c_2)^2 \right] \quad (1)$$

$$c_1(\phi) = \frac{\int_\Omega u_0(x,y) H_\epsilon(\phi(t,x,y)) dx dy}{\int_\Omega H_\epsilon(\phi(t,x,y)) dx dy} \quad (2)$$

$$c_2(\phi) = \frac{\int_\Omega u_0(x,y)(1 - H_\epsilon(\phi(t,x,y))) dx dy}{\int_\Omega (1 - H_\epsilon(\phi(t,x,y))) dx dy} \quad (3)$$

where $\mu, \lambda_1$ and $\lambda_2$ are fixed parameters, $u_0 : \Omega \to \mathbb{R}$ is the original image function, $\Omega \subset \mathbb{R}^2$ is open and bounded, $\phi : \Omega \to \mathbb{R}$ is a Lipschitz continuous function with its zero level set representing the active contour that separates the image regions defined by $\{(x,y) \in \Omega : \phi(x,y) > 0\}$ and $\{(x,y) \in \Omega : \phi(x,y) < 0\}$, $H_\epsilon$ and $\delta_\epsilon = H'_\epsilon$ are $C^1$ approximations and regularizations of the Heaviside function $H$ and Delta function $\delta$. A more complete and detailed description of this active contour model may be found in [7,8].

## 4 Proposed Hybrid Model

We have conceived an algorithm for carotid lumen extraction in ultrasonic images, consisting of two image processing stages, in the following sequence:

1. A new multiphase thresholding scheme, for carotid ultrasonic images, computes an optimal threshold, $T_{\text{opt}}$, for the separation of the lumen phase from the other phases in the gray-scale image, $I$. This is described in subsection 4.1.
2. The gray-scale image, $I$, is then processed by a modified version of Chan-Vese two phase piecewise constant active contour, which defines its intensity constants, $c_1$ and $c_2$, as functions of the threshold, $T_{\text{opt}}$, obtained in the first stage. These functions are chosen to preserve the intensity classification threshold between phases, while allowing the active contour to use its elastic properties and image spatial information to reduce noise, smooth contours and close eventual carotid wall gaps, left from the first stage. This is described in section 4.2.

### 4.1 Sequential MCE Thresholding

A set of selected thresholding algorithms, chosen for their success or special interest for ultrasonic image segmentation, were tested in carotid ultrasonic images. These comparative tests showed that MCE produced the best results. Considering also that MCE criterion is the best choice when no assumption is made about the populations' distributions or their size and variance [5], this is the best choice for the problem in hand.

The MCE algorithm was designed for images with only two phases, with bimodal histograms. Since carotid ultrasonic images are multiphase, a single MCE iteration is not enough to isolate the lumen. Since the phase of interest, corresponding to the lumen, is the darkest one, a straightforward way to adapt this algorithm to these multiphase images is as follows. In the first iteration, the MCE algorithm is used to divide the original image into two regions. In the second iteration, the darkest region produced by the first iteration is further subdivided into another pair of regions, and so on, until a certain stopping criterion is satisfied. At the end of each iteration, only two regions are of interest: the region with intensities below the last threshold and the region with all other intensities. This is the *sequential MCE thresholding*. To select a reliable stopping criterion, a set of evolution curves were computed for several different measures of the pair of regions defined by the threshold at each iteration. Two of these measures turned out to be useful: the standard-deviation, $\sigma$, and the total contour length, $L$, of the darkest region for each iteration. These curves showed that the desired segmentation was systematically obtained when $\sigma < 0.01$, except for a small set of more degraded images which had significant blood echo. Two segmentation examples with this iterative algorithm, using only $\sigma$ as stopping criterion, are presented in Fig. 1.

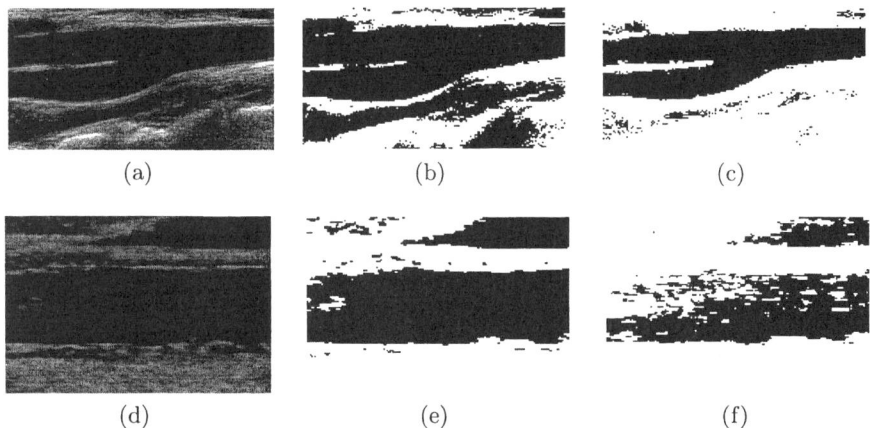

**Fig. 1.** Sequential MCE with stopping criterion based only on $\sigma$: a) Carotid A; b) Carotid A after first threshold; c) Carotid A after last threshold; d) Carotid B; e) Carotid B after first threshold; f) Carotid B after last threshold

As we can see in Fig. 1 (f), in images with some blood echo there is a tendency to misclassify these blood spots as soft tissue. This typically results in new islands of white regions inside the lumen, which sometimes fuse with the carotid wall. Of course, this type of echo, when present, is weak. Thus, it is only detected at the end of the iterative procedure. If the detection of these new white regions happens, as it seems, only after the desired threshold, this misclassification brings an increase in the total length of interface boundaries. A simple and effective way to avoid this under-thresholding is to stop iterations and discard the last one whenever a new thresholding produces an increase in the total interface length. The evolution of $L$ as a function of iterations for carotid A and carotid B can be seen in Fig. 2 (a) and Fig. 2 (b), respectively. For carotid A, $L$ never increases and $\sigma$ falls below 0.01 in the third iteration. In this case, $T_{opt}$ becomes the third threshold obtained for the image. The result is the binary image in Fig. 1 (c). On the other hand, for carotid B, $L$ increases between the first and the second iterations. Thus, for carotid B, the sequential MCE algorithm sets $T_{opt}$ as the first threshold, discarding the second. This gives the binary image in Fig. 1 (e) as the final thresholding segmentation.

If, in any case, these false tissue regions appear for the desired threshold or a previous one, this means the image is too degraded and it might be preferable to discard the image altogether, depending on the degree of degradation. Otherwise,

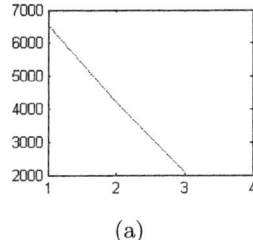 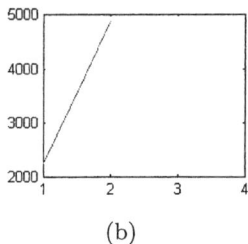

**Fig. 2.** Evolution of $L$: a) $L$ vs Iterations for Carotid A; b) $L$ vs Iterations for carotid B

we will be stuck with this over-segmentation of the lumen, since, in this case, there is no automatic and universal way to distinguish between soft tissue echo and blood echo, specially when considering the possible presence of plaque.

Next, a summary of the proposed sequential MCE thresholding algorithm is presented:

1. Compute MCE threshold, $T$, for the entire gray-scale image, $I$.
2. Compute standard-deviation, $\sigma$, for pixels of $I$ with intensity $\leq T$.
3. If $\sigma < 0.01$, then set $T_{opt} = T$ and stop iterations.
4. Initialize $L_{new}$ with the total interface length for threshold, $T$. Set $T_{new} = T$.
5. Set $T_{old} = T_{new}$ and $L_{old} = L_{new}$.
6. Compute a new MCE threshold, $T_{new}$, for pixels of $I$ with intensity $\leq T_{old}$.
7. Compute new total interface length, $L_{new}$, for current threshold, $T_{new}$.
8. If $L_{new} > L_{old}$, then set $T_{opt} = T_{old}$ and stop iterations.
9. Compute standard-deviation, $\sigma$, for pixels of $I$ with intensity $\leq T_{new}$.
10. If $\sigma < 0.01$, then set $T_{opt} = T_{new}$ and stop iterations, else goto step 5.

### 4.2 Chan-Vese Active Contour with Fixed Intensity Constants

The MCE sequential thresholding isn't capable, on its own, to deal with heavy noise or wall gaps. To overcome this, the threshold $T_{opt}$ is passed to a second processing stage, which applies a two phase piecewise constant geometric active contour to the gray-scale image, $I$, but taking advantage of the information inherited from the thresholding. The number of iterations necessary for the active contour convergence is significantly reduced by initializing the active contour with the approximation to lumen edges given by the thresholding stage. To reduce the multiphase problem to a two phase case, we propose to fix the intensity constants as $c_1 = 2T_{opt}$ for the higher phase and $c_2 = 0$ for the other one, instead of updating them as in the original Chan-Vese model, where their value is assumed to be unknown. This way, the elastic active contour is not used to estimate the intensities of each phase, which are already known from the thresholding. It just uses its elastic properties and the image spatial information to clean the noise, smooth contours, improve their position accuracy and close eventual carotid wall gaps.

## 5 Results

The parameters used for the Chan-Vese model were: $\mu = 0.025 \times 255^2$, $\lambda_1 = \lambda_2 = 1$, $\Delta x = \Delta y = 1$, $\epsilon = \Delta x$ and $\Delta t = 0.1\Delta x$. The value of parameter $\mu$, which is proportional to the elastic strength of the contour, was empirically determined as a good compromise between maximum noise removal and minimum loss of image details. Since the image gray level scale used is $0 \ldots 255$, the factor $255^2$ present in parameter $\mu$ is necessary to keep unity consistence in the level set equation. The values used for the other parameters are the ones proposed in [7,8]. The numerical scheme used in this work was the semi-implicit scheme proposed by Chan and Vese in [7,8] for the two phase piecewise constant model, with the Euler-Lagrange equation given by (1). To improve efficiency, part of the code used in this work was implemented as a C function, which is called from Matlab. This is the case of the semi-implicit updating scheme for the implicit function of the level set equation. Before the initialization of the active contour in the second stage, small black segments, left by the first stage, were automatically removed to improve efficiency even more, avoiding eventual delays in the active contour convergence due to segments without interest. The removal of these small black segments is done using a labeling function from Matlab and requires very little CPU time. The cleaning procedure is not applied to white segments, to prevent the aggravation of eventual gaps along the carotid wall. The implicit function is then initialized as a signed distance function with the contours of the cleaned binary image as its zero level set. Figure 3 shows the results of the application of the proposed hybrid algorithm to carotids A and B of Fig. 1. These results clearly illustrate the effectiveness of our model for the segmentation of this type of images.

Although the second stage (active contour) is much more time consuming than the first one (thresholding), the hybrid algorithm formed by the combination of these two stages is still a very fast and effective algorithm when compared to other alternatives, like multiphase active contours [8,20]. In fact, we have confirmed in our tests that the four phase piecewise constant model [8,20] requires significantly more CPU time to converge than our model. Moreover, it fails to correctly detect the carotid lumen boundary, sometimes leaving large gaps in the carotid walls, which means an 8 phase version (at least) should be used, and, therefore, an additional increase in the computational effort.

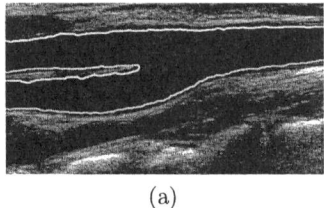
(a)

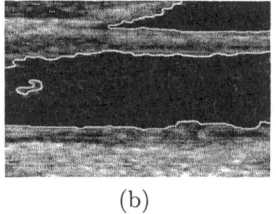
(b)

**Fig. 3.** Chan-Vese 2 phase with fixed constants, $c_1$ and $c_2$, after sequential MCE: a) Carotid A with contour; b) Carotid B with contour

## 6 Conclusions

Ultrasonic images of the carotid pose a great challenge to automatic segmentation, due to their complexity. A new algorithm for the segmentation of these images was introduced, consisting of two image processing stages, which combine a new MCE-based thresholding multiphase scheme with a modified version of the Chan-Vese two phase piecewise constant active contour model. Instead of dynamically updating the phase intensity parameters, as in the original Chan-Vese model, we have defined them as functions of the threshold obtained in the first stage. This way we were able to reduce a multiphase problem to a two phase one and drastically speed up the active contour convergence. The results obtained confirm the effectiveness and efficiency of the proposed hybrid algorithm for the lumen extraction in carotid ultrasonic images. This algorithm was specifically designed to extract a single phase of interest from a multiphase image (or both phases of a biphase image), and proved to be a good alternative when thresholding algorithms or active contours give unsatisfactory results on their own. Of course, it may be applied to other types of images. But, if these images are not so complex as the ones considered in this work, the multiphase model presented in [20] could be a better choice, specially if several phases are of interest.

## Acknowledgments

The authors would like to thank Dr. Vasco Gama and colleges, from the Cardiology Department of Centro Hospitalar de Vila Nova de Gaia, Portugal, for providing most part of the set of ultrasonic images used in this work.

## References

1. Gee, A., Prager, R., Treece, G., Berman, L.: Engineering a freehand 3D ultrasound system. Pattern Recogn. Lett. **24** (2003) 757–777
2. Sonka, M., Liang, W., Stefancik, R., Stolpen, A.: Handbook of Medical Imaging: Medical Image Processing and Analysis. Volume 2. SPIE (2000)
3. Christodoulou, C.I., Pattichis, C.S., Pantziaris, M., Nicolaides, A.: Texture based classification of atherosclerotic carotid plaques. IEEE Trans. Med. Imaging **22** (2003) 902–912
4. Barratt, D., Ariff, B., Humphries, K., Thom, S., Hughes, A.: Reconstruction and quantification of the carotid artery bifurcation from 3-d ultrasound images. IEEE Trans. Med. Imaging **23** (2004) 567–583
5. Li, C., Lee, C.: Minimum cross entropy thresholding. Pattern Recogn. **26** (1993) 617–625
6. Brink, A., Pendock, N.: Minimum cross-entropy threshold selection. Pattern Recogn. **29** (1996) 179–188
7. Chan, T., Vese, L.: Active contours without edges. IEEE Trans. on Image Processing **10** (2001) 266–277
8. Vese, L.A., Chan, T.F.: A multiphase level set framework for image segmentation using the Mumford and Shah model. Int. J. Comput. Vision **50** (2002) 271–293

9. Touboul, P., Prati, P., abd V. Adrai, P.Y.S., Thibout, E., Ducimetiere, P.: Use of monitoring software to improve the measurement of carotid wall thickness by B-mode imaging. J. Hypertension **10** (1992) 37–41
10. Liang, Q., Wendelhag, I., Wikstrand, J., Gustavsson, T.: A multiscale dynamic programming procedure for boundary detection in ultrasound artery images. IEEE Trans. Med. Imaging **19** (2000) 127–142
11. Schmidt-Trucksass, A., Cheng, D., Sandrock, M., Schulte-Monting, J., Rauramaa, R., Huonker, M., Burkhardt, H.: Computerized analysing system using the active contour in ultrasound measurement of carotid artery intima-media thickness. Clinical Physiology **5** (2001) 561–569
12. Cheng, D., Schmidt-Trucksass, A., Cheng, K., Sandrock, M., Pu, Q., Burkhardt, H.: Automatic detection of the intimal and the adventitial layers of the common carotid artery wall in ultrasound B-mode images using snakes. In: International Conference on Image Analysis and Processing, B. Werner (1999) 452–457
13. Cheng, D., Schmidt-Trucksass, A., Cheng, K., Burkhardt, H.: Using snakes to detect the intimal and adventitial layers of the common carotid artery wall in sonographic images. Computer Methods and Programs in Biomedicine **67** (2002) 27–37
14. Baillard, C., Barillot, C., Bouthemy, P.: Robust adaptive segmentation of 3D medical images with level sets. Technical report, IRISA, Campus Universitaire de Beaulieu, France (2000)
15. Tsai, A., Yezzi, A.J., III, W.M.W., Tempany, C., Tucker, D., Fan, A., Grimson, W.E.L., Willsky, A.S.: A shape-based approach to the segmentation of medical imagery using level sets. IEEE Trans. Med. Imaging **22** (2003) 137–154
16. Perona, P., Malik, J.: Scale-space and edge detection using anisotropic diffusion. IEEE Trans. Pattern Anal. Mach. Intell. **12** (1990) 629–639
17. Sethian, J.A.: Level Set Methods and Fast Marching Methods. Cambridge University Press (1999)
18. Osher, S., Fedkiw, R.: Level Set Methods and Dynamic Implicit Surfaces. Springer-Verlag. New York (2003)
19. Mumford, D., Shah, J.: Optimal approximations by piecewise smooth functions and associated variational problems. Communications on Pure and Applied Mathematics **42** (1989) 577–685
20. Gao, S., Bui, T.D.: Image segmentation and selective smoothing by using the Mumford-Shah model. (To be published in) IEEE Trans. on Image Processing (2005)

# Genetic Model-Based Segmentation of Chest X-Ray Images Using Free Form Deformations

Carlos Vinhais[1,2] and Aurélio Campilho[1,3]

[1] INEB - Instituto de Engenharia Biomédica, Laboratório de Sinal e Imagem Biomédica, Campus da FEUP, Rua Roberto Frias, s/n, 4200-465 Porto, Portugal
[2] ISEP - Instituto Superior de Engenharia do Porto, Departamento de Física, Porto, Portugal
cav@isep.ipp.pt
[3] Universidade do Porto, Faculdade de Engenharia, Departamento de Engenharia Electrotécnica e Computadores, Porto, Portugal
campilho@fe.up.pt

**Abstract.** A method is proposed to segment digital posterior-anterior chest X-ray images. The segmentation is achieved through the registration of a deformable prior model, describing the anatomical structures of interest, to the X-ray image. The deformation of the model is performed using a deformation grid. A coarse matching of the model is done using anatomical landmarks automatically extracted from the image, and maps of oriented edges are used to guide the deformation process, optimized with a probabilistic genetic algorithm. The method is applied to extract the ribcage and delineate the mediastinum and diaphragms. The segmentation is needed for defining the lungs region, used in computer-aided diagnosis systems.

**Keywords:** Gabor Filters, Free Form Deformation, Genetic Algorithms, Model-based Image Segmentation.

## 1 Introduction

The automatic delineation of anatomical structures of interest in digital X-ray chest images provides useful information required in computer-aided diagnosis (CAD) schemes. For instance, the ribcage boundary represents a convenient reference frame of human thorax for locating such structures. In chest radiography, CAD schemes have been developed for automated detection of abnormalities, such pulmonary nodules [1] or cardiomegaly [2]. An overview of the literature on lung field segmentation, rib detection and methods for selection of nodule candidates can be found in [3]. The accurate segmentation of anatomical structures in chest X-ray images is still an open problem and manual extraction is often considered as the most reliable technique.

We present an automatic technique for segmenting anatomical structures in posterior-anterior (PA) chest X-ray images, based on the matching of a geometrical deformable model, that represents the structures of interest to be segmented, to the X-ray input image. The proposed method relies on a registration process as described in Sec. 2. Anatomical landmarks are initially extracted by processing the input image and are used to coarsely align the geometric model to the image. The deformation of the model, described in Sect. 2.2, is performed using Free Form Deformation (FFD) by minimizing an energy term derived from oriented response maps, defined in Sect. 2.3 by means of Gabor filtering. The model-based segmentation is then considered as an optimization problem solved with a genetic algorithm (GA), presented in Sect. 3, carefully designed to preserve the shape of the model during deformation. Finally, we present some results and draw conclusions.

## 2 Materials and Methods

The aim of this work is to automatically segment anatomical structures in PA chest X-ray images starting from a deformable geometrical model. The prior model used represents the contour of the projected area of the lungs, non obscured by overlying cardiac, mediastinal and subdiaphragmatic structures.

### 2.1 Geometrical Model

We describe the geometric prior model as a labelled set of vertices $V_n^* = (x_n^*, y_n^*)$ in a system of coordinates $OXY$ centered in the image plane, as shown in Fig. 1. The construction of the model is based on a general technique, known as *Point Distribution Model* [4]: a mean shape, or *prototype*, is obtained from statistical analysis of manually traced contours in a training set of X-ray images, where each labelled vertice $V_n^*$ represents the same part of the undeformed contour.

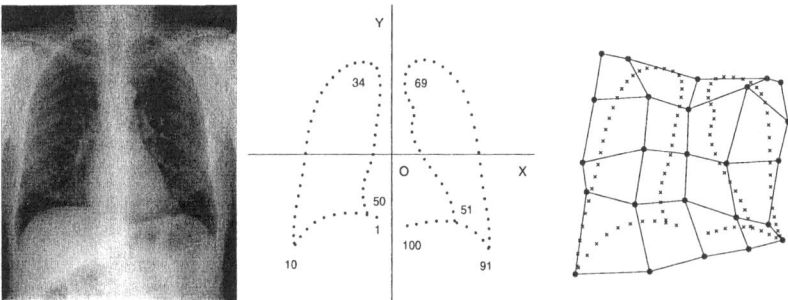

**Fig. 1.** PA chest X-ray image (*left*), geometrical model (*middle*) and its deformation using a 5 × 5 FFD grid of control points randomly displaced (*rigth*)

This parametrization is used to represent the model into five different sections. The correspondence between anatomical structures and the model is easily accomplished by defining each section of the model as a different subset $S$ of the labelled vertices $V_n^*$ as follow: the subset $S_{rib} = V_{11-34,69-90}^*$ represents the thoracic cage or ribcage (see Fig. 1), $S_{med,R} = V_{35-50}^*$ and $S_{med,L} = V_{51-68}^*$ are associated with the right and left boundaries of the mediastinum, respectively, and $S_{diaph,R} = V_{1-10}^*$ and $S_{diaph,L} = V_{91-100}^*$ represent the boundaries of the right and left diaphragm, respectively. The purpose of this model representation will be explained in Sec. 3.

## 2.2 Model Deformation

The deformation of the prior model is accomplished using Free Form Deformation (FFD), a popular deformation technique in computer graphics [5]. The FFD is controlled by a rectangular deformation grid, of size $N_x \times N_y$, that surrounds the model (or just a portion of it), and is defined by the lattice of control points $L_{ij}^* = (x_{ij}^*, y_{ij}^*)$ ($i \in [1, N_x]$, $j \in [1, N_y]$).

When one or more points $L_{ij}^*$ of the grid are moved to new positions, $L_{ij}$, the model is deformed correspondingly. The local coordinates $(s_n^*, t_n^*)$, $s_n^*, t_n^* \in [0, 1]$, of each vertice $V_n^*$ in the model point set are first computed with respect to the undisplaced FFD grid, and the new position $V_n$ of each vertice, after moving the control points, can be calculated using a bivariate tensor product:

$$V_n = \sum_{i=0}^{N_x-1} \sum_{j=0}^{N_y-1} B_{i,N_x}(s_n^*) \cdot B_{j,N_y}(t_n^*) \cdot L_{ij}, \qquad (1)$$

where $B_{i,N}(s)$ is the Bernstein polynomial blending function of degree $N$, defined as

$$B_{i,N}(s) = \frac{N!}{i!(N-i)!} \cdot s^i \cdot (1-s)^{N-i}. \qquad (2)$$

The deformation of the model using FFD is illustrated in Fig. 1, using a $5 \times 5$ grid of a lattice of control points, randomly displaced from their original positions. Bilinear interpolation could be used as well to establish the relation between the displacement of the grid points and the vertices to be deformed.

## 2.3 Oriented Maps

Compared to other medical image modalities such computer tomography or magnetic resonance, edges are more difficult to extract from X-ray projections images. We decide to enhance the edges of the structures of interest to be delineated in the PA X-ray image, using Gabor filters [6] in analogy with the processing of stimuli by simple cells present in the human visual cortex. A receptive field function of such a cell, $g_{\lambda,\sigma,\theta,\phi}(x, y)$, centered in the origin, can be represented by a linear Gabor filter:

$$g_{\lambda,\sigma,\theta,\phi}(x, y) = \exp^{-\frac{\tilde{x}^2 + \gamma^2 \tilde{y}^2}{2\sigma^2}} \cos\left(\frac{2\pi \tilde{x}}{\lambda} + \phi\right), \qquad (3)$$

where

$$\begin{array}{l} \tilde{x} = x\cos\theta + y\sin\theta \\ \tilde{y} = -x\sin\theta + y\cos\theta \end{array}. \qquad (4)$$

and $\gamma = 0.5$ is a constant, called the spatial aspect ratio, that determines the ellipticity of the receptive field of the simple cell. The value of the ratio $\sigma/\lambda$ is considered as in [7] to be 0.56, where $1/\lambda$ is the spatial frequency of the cosine factor. We choose the standard deviation, $\sigma$, of the Gaussian factor (see Eq. 3) to be a free parameter to fix. The value of $\sigma$ is imposed by the width of the edges we want to enhance. The phase offset $\phi$, $\phi \in (-\pi, \pi]$ determines the symmetry of the filter with respect to the origin. For $\phi = 0, \pi$, it is a symmetric or even function. For $\phi = -\frac{\pi}{2}, \frac{\pi}{2}$, the filter is antisymmetric or odd. The parameter $\theta$, $\theta \in [0, \pi)$ in Eq. 4 determines the preferred orientation of a simple cell.

We assume that the positive spatial response $R_{\theta,\phi}(x,y)$ of a simple cell to the X-ray input intensity distribution $I(x,y)$, with a receptive field (selective) orientation $\theta$, is given by:

$$R_{\theta,\phi}(x,y) = \begin{cases} r_{\theta,\phi}(x,y), & r_{\theta,\phi}(x,y) > 0 \\ 0, & r_{\theta,\phi}(x,y) \leq 0 \end{cases}, \quad (5)$$

where the filtered image $r_{\theta,\phi}(x,y)$ is computed by convolution:

$$r_{\theta,\phi}(x,y) = I(x,y) \otimes g_{\theta,\phi}(x,y). \quad (6)$$

Based on the columnar organization of cortical simple cells [8], the input image is filtered with a bank of Gabor filters, and *oriented maps* $R_{\theta,\phi}(x,y)$ can be defined for a number $N_\theta$ of different equally spaced orientations:

$$\theta_k = \frac{k-1}{N_\theta} \cdot \pi, \quad k = 1, \cdots, N_\theta. \quad (7)$$

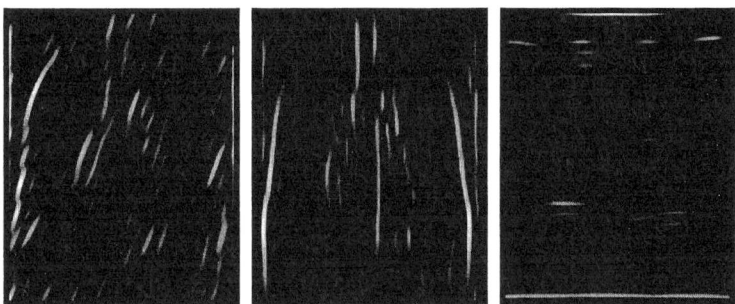

**Fig. 2.** Orientated maps $R_{\theta,\phi}(x,y)$ of PA X-ray image of Fig. 1, for $\theta = \frac{3\pi}{8}$, $\phi = 0$ (*left*), $\theta = \frac{\pi}{2}$, $\phi = 0$ (*middle*) and $\theta = 0$, $\phi = -\frac{\pi}{2}$ (*rigth*)

Examples of oriented maps $R_{\theta,\phi}(x,y)$, for different orientations and phase offset values, are shown in Fig. 2.

Once the oriented maps have been computed, we can define an energy function, $E$, describing the mismatch between such enhanced edges and the vertices of the deformed model. The definition of such function, based on the idea that boundaries of given orientation in the model have to mach with similarly oriented edges enhanced by the processing of the X-ray image, is given by

$$E = 1 - \frac{1}{N_v} \cdot \sum_{n=1}^{N_v} R_{\theta_k, \phi(n)}(x_n, y_n), \qquad (8)$$

where $N_v$ is the number of vertices defining the model, $(x_n, y_n)$ are the coordinates of the vertice $V_n$, and $\theta_k$ is the angle, given by Eq. 7, closest to the normal of the contour model at the vertice $V_n$. Because symmetrical Gabor filters cannot be used to discriminate between light-to-dark and dark-to-light transitions, different values of the phase offset $\phi$ of the orientation maps have to be considered. The energy is computed taking into account the subsets of vertices $S$, defined in Sect. 2.1, considering the following rules: $\phi(n) = 0$ if $V_n \in S_{rib}$, $\phi(n) = \frac{\pi}{2}$ if $V_n \in \{S_{med,R} \cup S_{diaph,R}\}$, and $\phi(n) = -\frac{\pi}{2}$ if $V_n \in \{S_{med,L} \cup S_{diaph,L}\}$.

The registration of the geometric model to the X-ray image relies on its deformation, using FFD, in order to match the salient edges of the oriented maps, used to guide the model deformation considering the energy defined in Eq. 8 as a registration function to judge the goodness of the fit. The matching process is then considered as an optimization problem as explained in the next section.

## 3 Model Registration

The registration of the deformable model to the X-ray image relies on its deformation and consists on the minimization of the energy defined by Eq. 8. For this purpose, a sequential displacement of each control point of the FFD grid, independently of all others, can be considered [9]. In this work, an optimization strategy based on genetic algorithms (GA) [10] is adopted to solve this problem, where Eq. 8 is used as the fitness function.

GA starts with an initial set or *population* of probable solutions, referred to as *chromosomes*. Each chromosome **C** is an ordered list of the control points (*genes*) $L_{ij}$ of a displaced FFD grid that deforms the model as explained in Sec. 2.2. In each iteration of the algorithm, GA searches for the best chromosome (optimal position of the grid points) that minimize the fitness function.

As a first step of the registration process, anatomical landmarks corresponding to the center of the thorax, at the aortic arc level, and the center of the upper lobes of each lung are automatically extracted from the processing of the input image with a LoG filter, using a high standard deviation of 50 pixels. These large scale anatomy features (see Fig. 4) are used to perform a coarse alignment of each chromosome (undisplaced FFD grids) of the initial population of the GA with the X-ray image. Because PA chest X-ray images have symmetry axis nearly-vertical, these initial chromosomes are randomly rotated in the image plane, with standard deviation of 3°. The goal function (Eq. 8) is then evaluated for every chromosome in the population.

We adopt a GA in its probabilistic form [11], where a weighted mean of the best chromosomes is computed according to:

$$\mathbf{C}_{mean} = \frac{1}{\sum_{c=1}^{N}(1-E_c)} \cdot \sum_{c=1}^{N}(1-E_c)\cdot \mathbf{C}_c. \qquad (9)$$

where $N$ is the fixed number of chromosomes considered to compute the mean configuration and $E_c$ is the fitness value of the chromosome $\mathbf{C}_c$.

In each iteration, new chromosomes are generated by randomly displacing the control points of the FFD grid represented by the mean chromosome $\mathbf{C}_{mean}$. Three mutation operators are defined for this purpose. They consists of vertical random displacement of all the points, symmetrical displacement of external points and random displacement of internal points of the FFD grid, as illustrated in Fig. 3. All these random displacements are accomplished using a standard deviation $\sigma_m$ pixels and only one operator is applied to produce a new chromosome. Each operator is designed to increase the diversity in the population, and to constrain the allowable deformations of the geometrical model.

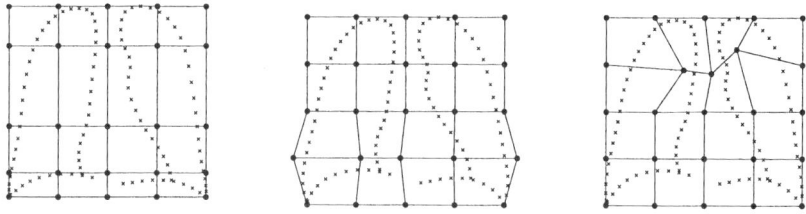

**Fig. 3.** Mutation operators applied to a 5 × 5 FFD lattice of control points: vertical displacement of all points (*left*), symmetrical displacement of external points (*middle*) and random displacement of internal points (*rigth*)

The fitness function is now evaluated for the new chromosomes, and the best chromosomes in the combined pool of current and new chromosomes are kept for the next generation. The stopping criteria is defined in terms of the maximum number of iterations of the GA.

## 4 Results

The proposed method has been tested on several PA chest X-ray images. The orientation maps were generated using $N_\theta = 8$ orientations, for a pair of quadrature Gabor filters, with $\phi = 0, -\frac{\pi}{2}$, and $\sigma = 10$ pixels. We assumed that a FFD grid of constant size 5 × 5 should allow enough degrees of freedom for a good match of the model.

The number of chromosomes in the beginning and end of each generation was $N = 25$, and the number of new chromosomes created in each generation was 50. The value $\sigma_m = 10$ pixels was used for all the mutation operators. Segmentation results for some digital chest X-ray images are shown in Fig. 4. 100 iterations of the GA were enough to reach convergence in all the tested images.

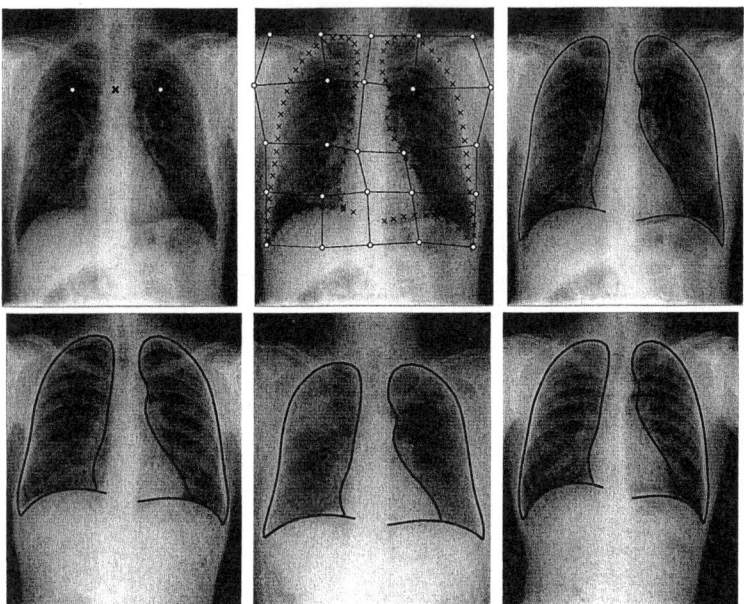

**Fig. 4.** *First row*: Extracted landmarks, displaced FFD grid and corresponding deformed model matched to X-ray image of Fig. 1; *Second row*: Segmentation results of the proposed method for other images of the database

## 5 Conclusions

We have described a method for segmenting PA chest X-ray images based on the global minimization of an energy function, defined from oriented maps of enhanced edges of the image.

The search algorithm is implemented by using a probabilistic genetic algorithm, avoiding an exhaustive search for the best transformation of the image. The choice of a probabilistic GA relies on its ability of stabilizing the population. This property is useful for the regularization of the geometrical model deformation. The mutation operators of this algorithm have been defined to preserve the knowledge of the geometrical model. In this work, the symmetry exhibited by PA chest X-ray images has been exploited, and can be included in the definition of the fitness function as an additional term. The initial population of the GA can be generated at random, but a robust extraction of anatomical landmarks is required to properly initialize the registration process.

The method has been tested using a FFD lattice of control points of constant size to deform the model. The method is suitable to be used in a global to local or multi-resolution approach. The preliminary results obtained so far, although not yet validated in a large set of images, make the method attractive. The method herein presented has been worked out in two dimensions, although extension to three dimensions will be considered in a near future.

# References

1. M. Carreira, D. Cabello, M. Penedo, and A. Mosquera, "Computer-Aided Diagnoses: Automatic Detection of Lung Nodules," *Medical Physics*, vol. 25 (10), pp. 1998–2006, 1998.
2. N. Nakaromi, K. Doi, H. MacMahon, Y. Sasaki, and S. M. Montner, "Effect on heart-size parameters computed from digital chest radiographs on detection of cardiomegaly: Potencial usefulness for computer-aided diagnosis," *Inv. Radiology*, vol. 26, pp. 546–550, 1991.
3. B. van Ginneken, B. H. Romeny, and M. A. Viergever, "Computer-aided Diagnosis in Chest Radiography: A survey," *IEEE Trans. on Medical Imaging*, vol. 20 (12), pp. 1228–1241, 2001.
4. T. E. Cootes, A. Hill, C. J. Taylor, and J. Haslam, "The Use of Active Shape Models for Locating Structures in Medical Images," *Image and Vision Computing*, vol. 12 (6), pp. 355–366, 1994.
5. T. W. Sederberg and S. R. Parry, "Free-Form Deformation of Solid Geometric Models," *ACM SIGGRAPH Computer Graphics*, vol. 20 (4), pp. 151–160, 1986.
6. D. J. Field, "Relations between the statistics of natural images and the response properties of cortical cells," *J. Opt. Soc. Am. A*, vol. 4 (12), pp. 2379–2394, 1987.
7. N. Petkov and P. Kruizinga, "Computational models of visual neurons specialised in the detection of periodic and aperiodic oriented visual stimuli: bar and grating cells," *Biol. Cybern.*, vol. 76, pp. 83–96, 1997.
8. M. B. Carpenter, *Core Text of Neuroanatomy*. 4th ed., 1991.
9. J. Lotjonen, I. Magnin, J. Nenonen, and T. Katila, "Reconstruction of 3-D Geometry Using 2-D Profiles and a Geometric Prior Model," *IEEE Trans. on Medical Imaging*, vol. 18 (10), pp. 992–1002, 1999.
10. D. E. Goldberg, *Genetic Algorithms in Search, Optimization and Machine Learning*. 1989.
11. Y. Gofman and N. Kiryati, "Detecting Symmetry in Grey Level Images: the Global Optimization Approach," *International Journal of Computer Vision (IJCV)*, vol. 29, pp. 29–45, 1998.

# Suppression of Stripe Artifacts in Mammograms Using Weighted Median Filtering

Michael Wirth and Dennis Nikitenko

Department of Computing and Information Science, University of Guelph,
Guelph, Ontario Canada N1G 2W1
{mwirth, dnikiten}@uoguelph.ca
http://www.uoguelph.ca/~mwirth

**Abstract.** X-ray images, such as mammograms, often contain high-intensity radiopaque artifacts in the form of horizontal or vertical stripes, often the result of the digitization process. These artifacts can contribute to difficulties in segmentation and enhancement algorithms. This paper presents an algorithm to suppress stripe artifacts based on weighted median filtering and shows how it affects post-processing segmentation.

## 1 Introduction

Many existing Computer Aided Detection (CADe) systems work by processing analog film mammograms acquired through digitization. Such mammograms often contain radiopaque artifacts in the form of identification labels, opaque markers, and wedges in the unexposed air-background (non-breast) region. Although a multitude of papers deal with tasks such as mammogram segmentation [1], very little work has been done in the realm of pre-processing relating to the suppression of background artifacts. The primary motivation for removing such artifacts from mammograms is too lessen their effect on subsequent processing algorithms. Artifacts can be defined as false features that can significantly hinder the automated interpretation of the images.

A recent article examined the effectiveness of removing such artifacts from the background region of a mammogram prior to processing tasks such as segmentation [2]. One of the caveats of this algorithm was the presence of stripe artifacts in the background, often overlapping the breast region in such a manner that they could not be effectively removed. Fig. 1 shows an example of a stripe artifact overlapping the breast region.

The effect of these stripes was made apparent during testing of a breast region segmentation algorithm using fuzzy reasoning [3]. Testing of the algorithm on 322 mammograms from the MIAS mammogram resulted in eight failures. Of those, in five of these mammograms (1.55%) the failure was attributable to the presence of vertical strip artifacts. Fig. 2 shows the effect of a vertical stripe artifact on the segmentation algorithm.

This paper proposes an automated approach for suppressing stripe artifacts from mammograms based on the use of a simple weighted median filter.

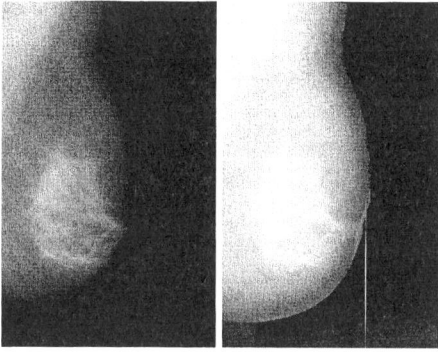

**Fig. 1.** Examples of stripe artifacts (left-to-right): (i) Mammogram after artifact suppression; (ii) LOG-accentuated form of (i) containing a residual "stripe" artifact

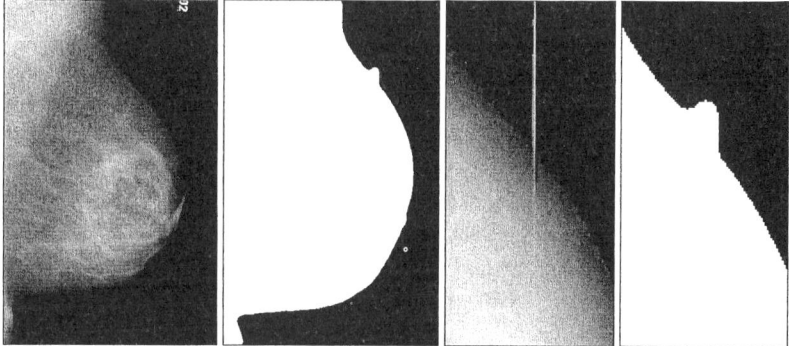

**Fig. 2.** Effect of strip artifacts on segmentation (MIAS 138.l). (i) Original, (ii) Segmented mask, (iii) LOG-accentuated ROI of (i), (iv) Corresponding ROI of (ii).

## 2 Mammogram Artifacts

There are two distinct regions in a mammogram: the exposed breast region and the unexposed air-background region. Visual assessment often results in the identification of radiopaque artifacts in the form of identification labels, opaque markers, and wedges in this background region. While the human visual system can easily ignore such artifacts during interpretation, a computerized system must first identify and classify features within a mammogram before it can decide whether or not to eliminate them from the interpretation process. There are three main advantages to performing artifact suppression in mammograms. In the first instance it facilities lossless compression by making the background region more homogeneous. This is significant with large images where the background region comprises in excess of 50% of the image. Secondly, a mammogram whose artifacts have been suppressed shows an improved "visual quality". For example the histogram of a processed image provides a better representation of the range of intensities found in the breast region.

Thirdly, the removal of radiopaque artifacts from mammograms lessens their effect on subsequent processing algorithms [4]. For example, accurate segmentation of the breast region is an important phase in the computerized analysis of mammograms. It allows the search for abnormalities to be limited to the breast region of a mammogram without undue influence from the background. One of the problems with precise segmentation of the breast region is that the existence of artifacts (e.g. a label overlapping the breast region) often results in a nonuniform background region which may cause a segmentation algorithm to fail. Artifacts may also unduly influence algorithms which rely on the intensity distribution of mammograms such as similarity-measure based mammogram registration, or contrast enhancement. Van Engeland et al. [5] cite that excluding the background region in mammograms leads to improvement in the registration of temporal mammograms. Stripe artifacts in mammograms are visible as lines of bright intensity, oriented more or less vertically.

## 3 Stripe Suppression

A stripe is a local extremum of intensity along the x-axis of an image. Detection and suppression is complicated by the fact that they often overlay the breast region, and hence can be quite subtle in appearance. The objective of suppressing vertical artifacts is two-fold. If they exist in the background region of a mammogram, the application of an appropriate filter could lessen their effect in the context of direct post-processing. Alternatively, if they exist in both the background and breast region, they could be suppressed for the purpose of improving the visual acuity of the image. There is little previous work dealing with the removal of such artifacts, the closest related to the detection and removal of line scratches in motion picture films [6].

### 3.1 Weighted Median Filter

The algorithm relies on the application of a filter to aid stripe suppression, in this case the *weighted median* (WM) filter, first introduced by Brownrigg [7] in 1984. The WM filter uses a two-dimensional mask, $M$, of size $n$, containing coefficients which are used to weight a neighborhood in an image (See Fig.3). The action of the filter at point $(p,q)$ of image $I_m$ is to take $M(i,j)$ copies of $I_m(p+i, q+j)$ for $i,j = -n,\ldots,n$. The values are sorted into ascending order and the median is determined. The resulting enhanced image is denoted $I_e$.

| 2 | 0 | 2 | 0 | 2 |
|---|---|---|---|---|
| 0 | 0 | 0 | 0 | 0 |
| 2 | 0 | 4 | 0 | 2 |
| 0 | 0 | 0 | 0 | 0 |
| 2 | 0 | 2 | 0 | 2 |

**Fig. 3.** Mask for the weighted median filter

The weighted median filter is used for two purposes: (i) to help determine the locality of the stripe artifacts, and (ii) to help in the restoration process.

### 3.2 Stripe Extraction

After the filter is applied, a post-processing segmentation algorithm can be applied directly, or the region representing the stripe artifacts can be restored. To achieve the latter, we first subtract the processed image from the original, yielding a difference image containing the stripe artifacts. A morphological filter, opening by reconstruction [8] is then performed using a vertical structuring element (SE) to restore the vertical objects. The length of the SE used has been set to 10% the height of the image. To isolate the vertical objects, a binary image is created by computing the regional maxima of the restored image, according to connectivity defined by a vertical SE. A regional maximum is a flat zone not surrounded by flat zones of higher gray values, where a flat zone is a connected-component of an image with the same pixel values [9]. The objects within the binary image are then expanded using morphological dilation in combination with a vertical SE to create a binary *stripe mask* image, $I_{mask}$, from which the stripe artifacts can be restored.

### 3.3 Stripe Restoration

The final stage consists of post-processing the detected artifacts to restore or reconstruct the corrupted pixels of the identified stripe region. In this form of the algorithm, where the emphasis is on removing stripe artifacts from the background region, and hence their subsequent effect on segmentation algorithms, we use a restoration algorithm based on polynomial interpolation. The background region of a mammogram normally occupies a band of low intensity values on a closed interval. Polynomial interpolation is well suited to reconstructing homogeneous regions. For each object pixel $(i, j)$ in the *stripe mask* image, a corresponding 5×5 region is extracted from both $I_e$, $I_m$ and $I_{mask}$. To create the surface to model, for every "live" pixel in $I_{mask}$ (pixel value=1) select the corresponding pixel from the enhanced image $I_e$. All other pixels are not stripe pixels and are selected from $I_m$. The effect of this blended surface are shown in Fig. 4. A simple interpolation model based on a cubic polynomial is then used to approximate the "missing" pixel.

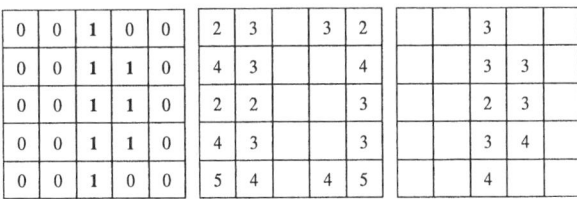

**Fig. 4.** Stripe restoration (left-to-right) (i) Region extracted from the *stripe mask* showing "live" pixels; (ii) $I_m$, and (iii) $I_e$, showing corresponding pixels used for the surface modeling

## 4 Experimental Results

The MIAS mammogram database [10] contains 34 images which contain some form of vertical stripe artifact. Of those 26 also contain significant background artifacts in the form of identification labels, opaque markers, and wedges. The mammograms were first cleansed of these artifacts using the algorithm described in [11]. Visual inspection of the results show that the algorithm was successful in suppressing the majority of stripe artifacts in the mammograms. The few instances where their were residual stripes occurred in regions where the stripes overlaid the breast region. This could be solved by improving the restoration algorithm used, however this must be balanced with making extensive changes to the breast region. For instance Joyeux et al. [6] augment the low-pass filter which is in the form of a cubic polynomial with a high-pass reconstruction technique based on Fourier series.

Two examples of results are shown in Fig. 5 and 6. The mammogram in Fig. 5 contains multiple vertical stripes, both overlaid on the breast region and the background region of the mammogram. Two of the stripes are quite distinct, the remaining are more subtle in appearance. Fig 5(iii) shows the extent of the stripe artifacts, and Fig. 5(iv) a LOG-accentuated form of the restored "live" pixels from the stripe mask. The mammogram shown in Fig. 6 contains both a single stripe artifact overlying the breast region and both a label artifact and radiopaque marker in the background region. The artifact suppression algorithm [11] is first used to remove the latter artifacts before the stripe algorithm begins (Fig. 6(ii)). Fig. 6(iv) shows the stripe artifact, and Fig. 6(v) a LOG-accentuated form of the restored "live" pixels from the stripe mask.

To illustrate the effect of this algorithm on post-processing, we have extracted the breast region of the mammograms using a fuzzy-reasoning based algorithm [3]. Of the 34 mammograms containing vertical stripe artifacts, 21 are apparent enough to cause difficulties for the algorithm, not always sufficient to cause the algorithm to fail, but often enough to cause under-segmentation or discontinuities in the breast contour. Consider the example shown in Fig.7 representing a case of under-segmentation. Fig. 7(ii) shows the result of the segmentation algorithm with the

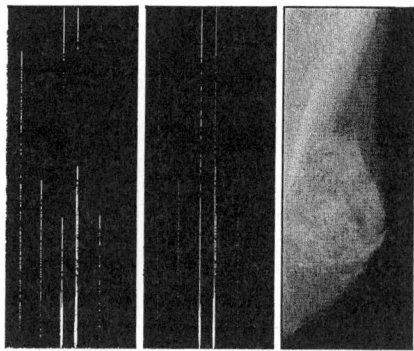

**Fig. 5.** Experiment 1: MIAS (093.l) with multiple stripes (left-to right) (i) Original image; (ii) Median-weighted image, (iii) Binary mask of stripe artifacts, (iv) LOG-accentuated restoration template, (v) Image with stripes suppressed

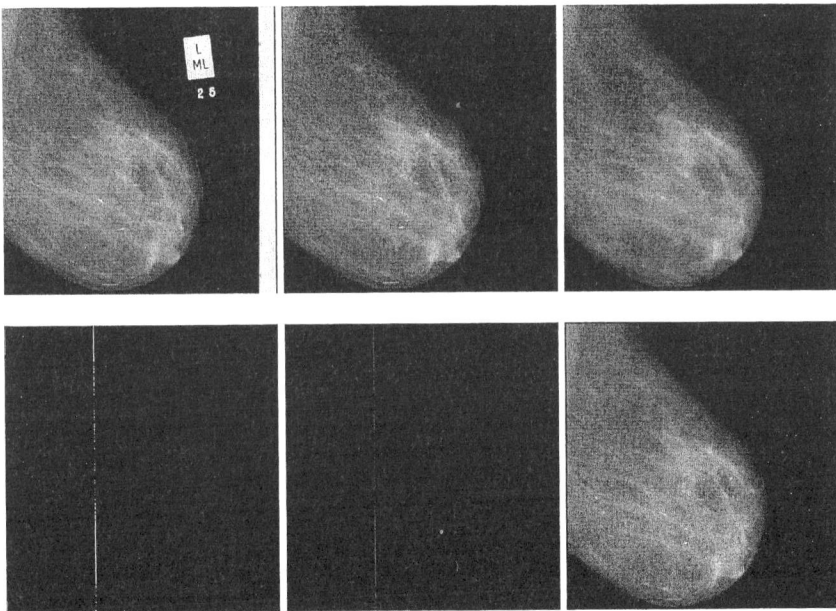

**Fig. 6.** Experiment 2: MIAS (074.l) with single stripe overlying the breast region (left-to-right) (i) Original image; (ii) Artifact-suppressed image; (iii) Median-weighted image, (iv) Binary mask of stripe artifacts, (v) LOG-accentuated restoration template, (vi) Image with stripes suppressed

artifacts removed, but the stripe nonetheless present. The effect on the lower portion of the mammogram is to incorporate part of the background to the left of the stripe into the breast region. The metrics for this particular image change from CM=1.0, CR=0.91, to CM=1.0, CR= 0.97, resulting in.

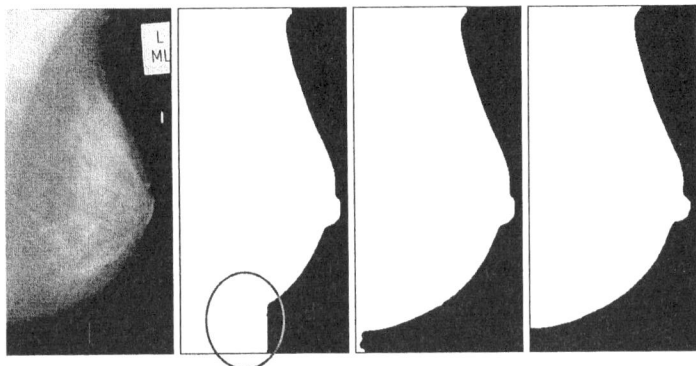

**Fig. 7.** Example of post-processing segmentation (under-segmentation) (left-to-right) (i) Original mammogram (MIAS 99.l); (ii) Segmentation with no stripe suppression, (iii) Segmentation with stripe suppression; (iv) Ground truth image

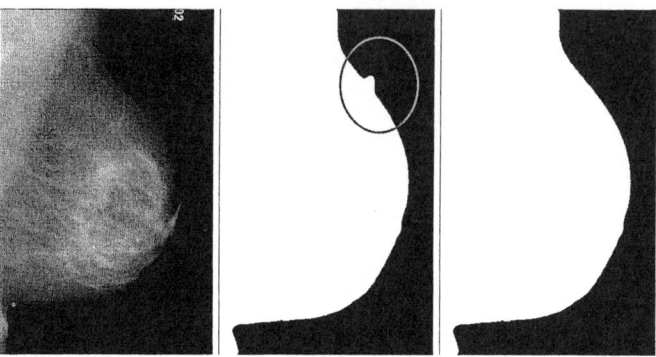

**Fig. 8.** Example of post-processing segmentation (contour discontinuity) (left-to-right) (i) Original mammogram (MIAS 138.l); (ii) Segmentation with no stripe suppression, (iii) Segmentation with stripe suppression

The second example, shown in Fig.8 shows the effect of the algorithm on removing stripe artifacts which result in contour discontinuities. Here the algorithm has suppressed the stripe artifact sufficiently to allow the segmentation algorithm to extract the breast region without any effects along the edge of the contour. There is no significant change in the metrics, CM=1.0, CR=0.99. All 21 mammograms showed improvement with respect to the segmentation accuracy achieved.

## 5 Conclusion

We have proposed a simple algorithm to suppress the presence of stripe artifacts in mammograms. The nature of the algorithm is such that it could easily be adapted to deal with horizontal stripe artifacts, or indeed scratch artifacts which exist in mediums such as historic photographs or films. Ongoing work will look at a more precise methodology of restoring the region containing the artifacts

## References

1. Chandrasekhar, R., Attikiouzel, Y.: Segmenting the breast border and nipple on mammograms. Australian Journal of Intelligent Information Processing Systems. 6 (2000) 24-29
2. Wirth, M., Lyon, J., Nikitenko, D.: Removing radiopaque artifacts from mammograms using area morphology. SPIE Medical Imaging: Image Processing. SPIE. San Diego. 5370 (2004) 1042-1053
3. Wirth, M., Nikitenko, D., Lyon, J.: Segmentation of the breast region in mammograms using a rule-based fuzzy reasoning algorithm. ICGST International Journal on Graphics, Vision and Image Processing. 2 (2005) 45-54
4. Pieka, E., McNitt-gray, M.F., Huang, H.K.: Computer-assisted phalanheal analysis in skeletal age assessment. IEEE Trans. on Medical Imaging. 10 (1991) 616-620

5. van Engeland, S., Snoeren, P., Hendriks, J., Karssemeijer, N.: A comparison of methods for mammogram registration. IEEE Trans. on Medical Imaging. 22 (2003) 1436-1444
6. Joyeux, L., Buisson, O., Besserer, B., Boukir, S.: Detection and removal of line scratches in motion picture films. International Conference on Computer Vision and Pattern Recognition, Fort Collins, Colorado. (1999) 548-553
7. Brownrigg, D.R.K.: The weighted median filter. Comm. of the ACM. 27 (1984) 807-818.
8. Vincent, L.: Morphological grayscale reconstruction in image analysis: Application and efficient algorithms. IEEE Trans. on Image Processing. 2 (1993) 176-201.
9. Dougherty, E.R., Lotufo, R.A..: Hands-on Morphological Image Processing. SPIE Press. Bellingham, Washington (2003)
10. Suckling, J., Parker, J., Dance, D.R., Astley, S., Hutt, I., Boggis, C.R.M., Ricketts, I., Stamatakis, E., Cerneaz, N., Kok, S.-L., Taylor, P., Betal, D., Savage, J.: The Mammographic Image Analysis Society Digital Mammogram Database. Int. Workshop on Digital Mammography, York, England (1994) 375-378.
11. Wirth, M., Lyon, J.: Suppression of background artifacts in mammograms using morphological image processing. (2005) under review.

# Feature Extraction for Classification of Thin-Layer Chromatography Images

António V. Sousa[1,2], Ana Maria Mendonça[1,4], Aurélio Campilho[1,4], Rui Aguiar[3], and C. Sá Miranda[3]

[1] Instituto de Engenharia Biomédica
Rua Roberto Frias, 4200-465 Porto, Portugal
[2] Instituto Superior de Engenharia do Porto
Rua Dr. António Bernardino de Almeida 431, 4200-072 Porto, Portugal
ats@isep.ipp.pt
[3] Instituto de Biologia Molecular e Celular
Rua do Campo Alegre, 823, 4150-180 Porto – Portugal
[4] Faculdade de Engenharia da Universidade do Porto
Rua Roberto Frias, 4200-465 Porto, Portugal
{amendon, campilho}@fe.up.pt

**Abstract.** Thin-Layer Chromatography images are used to detect and identify the presence of specific oligosaccharides, expressed by the existence, at different positions, of bands in the gel image. 1D gaussian deconvolution, commonly used for band detection, does not produce good results due to the large curvature observed in the bands. To overcome this uncertainty on the band position, we propose a novel feature extraction methodology that allows an accurate modeling of curved bands. The features are used to classify the data into two different classes, to differentiate normal from pathologic cases. The paper presents the developed methodology together with the analysis and discussion of the results.

## 1 Introduction

The separation of materials based on Thin-Layer Chromatography (TLC) is used as a mean for the diagnosis of lysosomal pathologies that can be identified in the patient's urine. This analysis results are influenced by the salinity of the samples, which are very variable from patient to patient. Even for the same person, urine samples obtained at distinct time instants present different salinities, as a consequence of the ingested amount of liquids.

In a chromatographic analysis the salinity of the sample affects the shape and location of the bands, and these effects are dependent on the sample concentration. The processes for urine desalinization are not always successful in solving this problem, as it was verified in many results.

Several methodologies proposed in the literature for chromatographic image analysis do not account for this problem [1-3]. In fact, 1D gaussian deconvolution, commonly used for band detection, does not produce good results due to the large curvature observed in the bands. To overcome the uncertainty on position of bands, we propose a novel feature extraction methodology that allows accurate modeling of curved bands. The extracted features are used to classify the data into two different classes, to differentiate normal from pathologic cases.

Section 2 presents briefly the method developed by the authors for initial band location. The problems associated with band curvature are discussed in section 3, where some solutions are also proposed. In section 4, we present some results for the 2-class classification problem, using the new features extracted from the image data. Finally, some conclusions are discussed in section 5.

## 2 Detection of Lanes and Bands

In a previous paper [4], we proposed a method for band detection based on the analysis of the lane mean intensity profile. This method can be concisely described in two steps. In the first step, the lane mean intensity profile is extracted just considering a narrow central slice of the image. This profile is processed in order to estimate the corresponding baseline, which is afterwards subtracted from the original data, aiming at producing a signal where the local maxima are associated with possible band positions. In the second step, features that characterize the bands are extracted. For this purpose, it is assumed that the signal is a mixture of gaussian curves, such that each individual component corresponds to a band. The separation and characterization of these curves was performed using two different approaches: EM-algorithm and Trust-Region nonlinear least square method. The parameters of the gaussian curves were subsequently used for the classification phase: the band position is the mean value of the curve, the band width is calculated as four times the standard deviation, and the band area is obtained from the mixture coefficient of the corresponding gaussian in the mixture.

When the bands present an ellipsoidal shape, 1D analysis is adequate. However, this is not the case when the bands present a parabolic shape, demanding a different approach that takes into account this deformation.

Figure 1 presents four TLC lanes related with the same disease. The first three lanes show illustrative examples, and the last one is a typical pattern of this particular disease. The two lanes represented in the top of the figure correspond to chromatographic analyses of the urine of one patient, both obtained from the same sample. The first lane corresponds to normal urine, while the second one shows the chromatographic result using desalinized urine.

The comparison of the two separation results allows some comments, namely that:

- some bands disappeared with the desalinization process, causing a loss of relevant information;
- some bands have parabolic shape in the normal lanes and linear shape in the desalinized lanes;
- in the same lane, bands can present different curvatures.

From the first observation it is possible to conclude that the desalinization process may not be a good practice as it introduces distortions that will negatively affect the classification process.

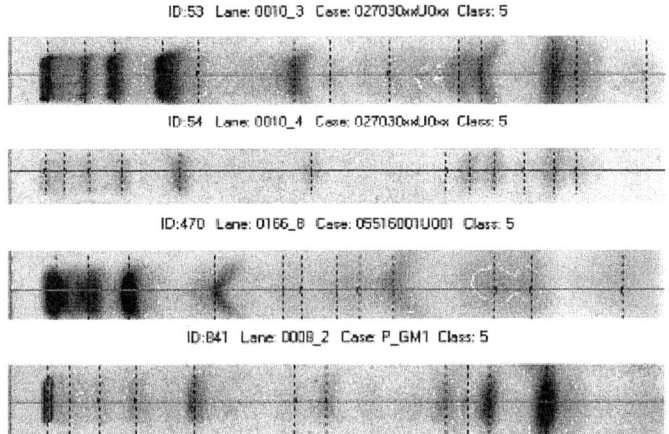

**Fig. 1.** Results of chromatographic separation for patients with the same disease. The band positions estimated by the algorithm are represented by dashed lines.

After the application of the original band separation algorithm described before, an accentuated variability in the position of the characteristic bands for the same class was noticed. This fact can be observed when comparing the band positions estimated by the algorithm for the third lane with the other three examples. The principal reason for the incorrect localization of the bands is that the estimation based on the analysis of a 1D profile is unable to cope with the accentuated curvature, as the extraction of curvature derived information demands a 2D analysis methodology.

The identification of this problem lead us to the conclusion that the information obtained from the 1D profile is insufficient to characterize a band, and also that the information related with the curvature is an essential aid for the classification phase.

## 3 Band Characterization

The image analysis methodology developed to solve the characterization problems raised by the presence of curved bands on TLC image lanes is described in the following sections. With this goal in mind, 2D information is obtained based on the analysis of several parallel 1D profiles. The individual results are grouped together and a set of band features are derived.

### 3.1 Band Shape Characterization

In the lanes with desalinized or low saline concentration urine, bands present an ellipsoidal shape with its major axis perpendicular to the development direction of the chromatographic separation process. However, if the saline concentration is high, the bands usually present curved shapes, similar to those observed in figure 1.

This shape can be thought as a result of a deformation, where the major axis acquires a parabolic profile.

Based on the assumption of a parabolic deformation, our main interest is the determination and characterization of the profile associated with every band resulting from the separation of Gaussian components.

Let us consider an orthonormal axis system defined by the lane central axis, with origin on the initial lane position (position of the first band of the lane). The axis scale is defined using the position of lactose as unitary distance reference. Figure 2 illustrates the axis system for that particular lane. The reference lane of the image, with the lactose position used for setting the scale unit, is also represented in the same figure.

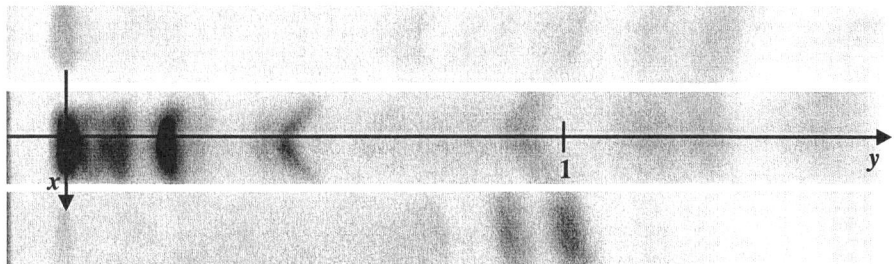

**Fig. 2.** TLC lanes examples: top- normal class; middle – abnormal class; bottom – lactose reference. Lane axis system is marked on the middle lane.

For each band, we look for a profile given by

$$y = ax^2 + bx + c \qquad (1)$$

where $a$ and $c$ are, respectively, the curvature and central position parameters of each band. In an ideal symmetric band, the value of $b$ is null; if the band has an ellipsoidal shape, then the parameter $a$ is also zero.

In what concerns the estimation of the band position feature for classification purposes, the basic idea is that the $c$ value, which corresponds to the initial band position estimated by the original algorithm, is not the correct solution. Instead, a "corrected" band position, derived from the band parabolic profile, must be calculated and used as a feature for classification.

### 3.2 Parameter Estimation

For estimating the parameters of the approximation parabola we need to obtain 2D information from the lane region where the band is located. 2D analysis for this kind of images has already been suggested by some authors, as a solution for the band detection problem [1-2], as well as for a better characterization of bands [3]. However, none of these approaches consider the determination of band profiles.

When the lane is divided into several strips parallel to the lane central axis, from each of these strips a 1D profile similar to the central one can be obtained. After the analysis of these parallel profiles using the local maxima position detection, a specific band is expected to be represented by a local maximum in each of these parallel profiles. As a consequence, some sets of points correspond to effective bands, while others are mainly noise.

The results of strip analysis are illustrated in figure 3, where the detected maxima are marked. A visual observation of these results allows the identification of several coherent sets of points associated with bands, but most of the points located on the right part of the figure are essentially erroneous detection results.

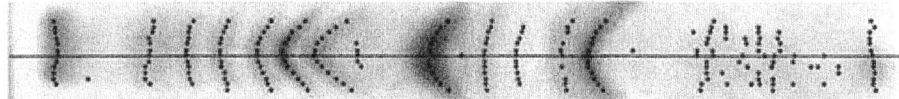

**Fig. 3.** Marks of the estimated locations of the bands, and representation of the lane central line

The next step is the assignment of the initial set of unclassified pixels to one or more bands, using a sequential clustering process. The grouping starts with the separation of all detected points into two different sets, corresponding, respectively, to the points above (top set) and bellow (bottom set) the central line. From each of these sets, subgroups are generated containing the pixels belonging to the same band. For this purpose, each subgroup is initialized with the points at the farthest distance from the central line; the inclusion of new points is a subgroup is controlled by the distance between the pixel being currently analyzed and the most recently included one. For each subgroup, this procedure is iterated until the distance between the current candidate to inclusion and the point previously included is below a predefined threshold. This limit was calculated considering that, on adjacent strips of ideal ellipsoidal shape bands, the distance between the two local maxima is the strip width as these points are vertically aligned; for curved bands, the distance threshold is calculated assuming a maximal vertical misalignment of 60 degrees. When a point cannot be included in none of the already created subgroups, a new subgroup is constituted.

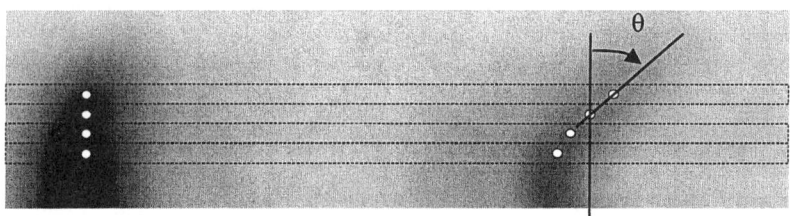

**Fig. 4.** Schematic representation of the process for including local maxima into subgroups

A schematic representation of the process for point inclusion is shown in figure 4. In this figure, strips are marked with dashed lines, and $\theta$ is the angle that measures the vertical misalignment.

A band is defined by the union of the closest two subgroups, one from the top set and the other from the bottom set. The criteria used for this purpose is the vertical distance between the subgroup centroids. After the conclusion of this union step, the subgroups that could not be associated with an existing band are once again verified.

If some intense local maxima are found, it is assumed that they belong to an undetected band and the subgroup is also considered.

For the identified bands, profile characterization is obtained by quadratic regression using the associated sets of local maxima.

Several considerations are taken into account to determine the final values of the parabolic parameters associated with each band:

- if the curvature (parameter $a$) is negative, this parameter is set to zero;
- the calculated value for $b$ is ignored and set to zero.

As a final result, only $a$ and $c$ values are considered for the band feature set. All the other characteristics such as the width, height, and area delimited by the band, are extracted using the method described in section 2. The goodness of fit was evaluated by the coefficient of determination, $r^2$ [9]. Figure 5 shows the final approximation curves for the local maxima detected in the image of figure 3.

**Fig. 5.** Approximation of band profiles by parabolic functions. For the bands 3 to 12, the coefficient of determination range is [0.76; 0.98].

## 4 Feature Extraction and Classification

The main problem to be addressed is the extraction of a feature set for complete band characterization. For every band in the lanes, the following features are measured: width, area (both determined by the method described in section 2), and the coefficients from the parabolic profile. The basic idea is to combine these two last values, in order to generate a "corrected" band position.

A "corrected" band position is defined from equation (1) as the $y$-value for a specific $x$-value. Aiming at determining the ideal $x$-value for establishing the best "corrected" band position feature, we have decided to evaluate the influence of $x$ on the classification results for different values of $x$. In the defined axis system (fig. 2), the $x$ variable can take values in the $[-0.1, +0.1]$ interval.

Our problem follows a typical supervised learning approach. Two classifiers based on parametric learning, linear ($ldc$) and quadratic ($qdc$), were selected. Two other classifiers, without parametric learning, were also used: the K-Nearest Neighbour Classifier ($knn$) with different values for $K$, and the Parzen density classifier ($pdc$) with maximum likelihood estimation for the smoothing parameter [5].

The dataset consists in 88 lanes, 49 classified as normal and 39 as abnormal. The abnormal group contains three different diseases.

For classification purposes, only four bands per lane are used. The classifier is able to select the positions of the four bands to be analyzed, by comparison with four reference positions. Three of these reference positions correspond to the three pathological cases under study, while the forth is taken from the normal set. For each abnormal case, the reference corresponds to the position of the band that best characterizes the disease, as mentioned in [6-8]. The reference associated with normal lanes takes a value slightly greater than 1 (position of the lactose band), taking into account the typical distribution of band positions in normal cases (see figure 2).

The dataset was divided into two groups: a training set with 50% of the samples randomly selected, and, a test set with the remaining samples. The training set was used for a dimensionality reduction through principal components analysis. The main conclusion was that, to preserve a significant fraction of the total variance, only 6 components are necessary.

As aforementioned, the extracted features, as a function of $x$ to calculate the "corrected" band position, were evaluated with the four classifiers: *ldc*, *qdc*, *knn* and *pdc*. The classification results are presented graphically in figure 6.

For all classifiers, the results show an increasing classification performance when the band position feature is a "corrected" value approximately defined near the two end points of the parabolic profile. This result is consistent with the visual observation of the two top lanes of figure 1, as a better agreement between bands position can be achieved if, for the curved bands on the top lane, the "corrected" positions are considered.

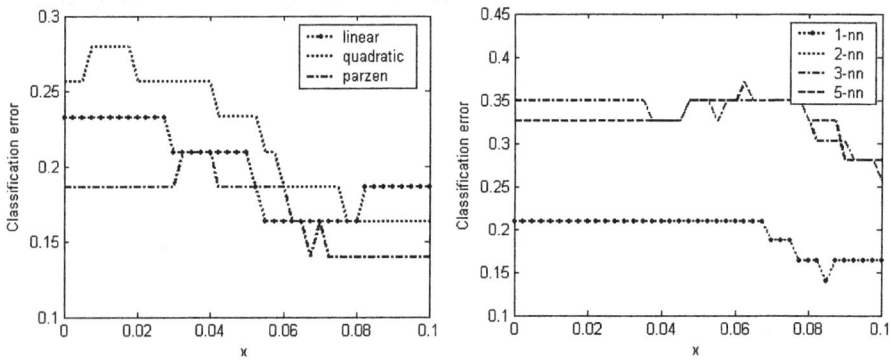

**Fig. 6.** Classification performance using different values for "corrected" band position feature: left -*ldc*, *qdc* and *pdc*; right – *knn* for different values of *k*

After the analysis of the classification results shown in figure 6, the value $x=0.08$ was selected for obtaining the "corrected" band position feature. Table 1 presents the classification matrices for the *ldc* and *pdc* classifiers, obtained with these particular set of features.

Almost all normal cases in the test set were correctly classified (only a misclassified case was reported for the *pdc* classifier). However, the classification error is still high for the abnormal class. A possible justification for these facts is the predominance, for normal cases, of the bands in the lane area to the right of lactose, while the selected three diseases present bands along the whole chromatogram. In fact, the use of a single band for disease/normal class characterization is probably not sufficient in this situation, and an approach based on the band distribution pattern should be followed instead.

**Table 1.** Classification matrices for the linear (left matrix) and parzen classifiers (rigth matrix). The classification errors are 16% and 14% respectively.

| True Labels | Estimated 1 | Estimated 2 | Totals | True Labels | Estimated 1 | Estimated 2 | Totals |
|---|---|---|---|---|---|---|---|
| 1 | 24 | 0 | 24 | 1 | 23 | 1 | 24 |
| 2 | 7 | 12 | 19 | 2 | 5 | 14 | 19 |
| Totals | 31 | 12 | 43 | Totals | 28 | 15 | 43 |

## 5 Conclusions and Future Work

In this paper, a novel methodology for the characterization of bands in Thin-Layer Chromatographic images is proposed. The new features extracted allow an accurate modeling of the curved bands that normally are present when normal urine samples are used on the chromatographic separation process. These features are utilized to classify data into two different classes, to differentiate normal from pathologic cases. The results show that the classifiers have better performance when the curvature of the bands is used to correct the initial band position.

As future work, a new approach based on a band distribution pattern should be tried for abnormal/normal class characterization.

## References

1. Bajla, I., Holländer, I., Burg, K. - *Improvement of Electrophoretic Gel Image Analysis* - M. S. R, V.1, N.1, (2001)
2. Ye, X., Suen, C., Cheriet, M., Wang, E. - *A Recent Development in Image Analysis of Electrophoresis Gels* - Vision Interface 99, Canada (1999)
3. Shadle, S., Allen, D., Guo, H., Pogozelski, W., Bashkin, J., Tullius, T. - *Quantitative analysis of electrophoresis data: novel curve fitting methodology and its application to the determination of a protein-DNA binding constant* - Nucleic Acids Research, Vol. 25, No. 4, (1997)
4. Sousa, A., Aguiar, R., Mendonça, A. M., Campilho, A. - *Automatic Lane and Band Detection in Images of Thin Layer Chromatography* – Springer Lecture Notes on Computer Science, LNCS 3212, pp. 372-380 ( 2004)
5. Heijden, F., Duin, R., Ridder, D., Tax, D. – *Classification, Parameter Estimation and State Estimation* – John Wiley and Sons, England (2004)
6. Sewell, A. - *Urinary Oligosaccharides. Techniques in Diagnostic Human Biochemical Genetics* - Willey-Liss, Inc. (1991) 219-231
7. Thomas, G. - *Disorders of Glycoprotein Degradation. α-Mannosidosis, β-Mannosidosis, Fucosidosis and Sialidosis. Disorders of Glycoprotein Degradation* - (Chap. 140)
8. Durant, G., Seta, N. - *Protein Glycosylation and Diseases: Blood and Urinary Oligosaccharides as Markers for Diagnosis and Therapeutic Monitoring* - Clinical Chemistry 46:6 – pp 795-805 (2000)
9. Marques de Sá, J. - *Applied Statistics using SPSS, STATISTICA and MATLAB* – Springer Verlag, (2003).

# A New Approach to Automatically Detecting Grids in DNA Microarray Images

Luis Rueda and Vidya Vidyadharan

School of Computer Science, University of Windsor,
401 Sunset Ave., Windsor, ON N9B 3P4, Canada
lrueda@uwindsor.ca

**Abstract.** Image and statistical analysis are two important aspects of microarray technology. Of these, gridding is necessary to accurately identify the location of each spot while extracting spot intensities from the microarray images and automating this procedure permits high-throughput analysis. In this paper, an automatic gridding and spot quantification technique is proposed, which takes a microarray image (or a sub-grid) as input, and makes no assumptions about the size of the spots, and number of rows and columns in the grid. The proposed method is based on a weighted energy maximization algorithm that utilizes three different energy functions. The method has been found to effectively detect the grids on microarray images drawn from databases from GEO, Stanford genomic laboratories and on some images obtained from private repositories.

## 1 Introduction

Microarrays, widely recognized as the next revolution in molecular biology, enables scientists to analyze genes, proteins and other biological molecules on a genomic scale [2,8]. Image processing and analysis is an important aspect of microarray experiments, one which have a potentially large impact on the identification of differentially expressed genes. Image processing for microarray images includes three tasks: spot gridding, segmentation and information extraction. In the analysis of microarray experiments gridding techniques based on distribution of pixel intensities play an important role, since automizing this process leads to high throughput analysis, including segmentation [7], normalization, and clustering [2]. Rougly speaking, gridding consists of determining the spot locations in a microarray image (typically, in a sub-grid). The problem that we consider in this paper takes a matrix of pixel intensities (or a sub-grid) as input and makes the following assumptions: (1) number of rows of spots unknown, (2) number of columns of spots unknown, (3) boundaries of the sub grid known, and (4) size of the spot unknown. It can be stated more formally as follows.

Consider an image (matrix) $A = \{a_{ij}\}, i = 1, ...., n$ and $j = 1, ...., m$, where $a_{ij} \in [0, p]$, and $p$ is the maximum pixel intensity (usually 65,536 in a TIFF image). The aim is to obtain a matrix $G$ (grid) where $G = \{g_{ij}\}, i = 1, ...., n$ and $j = 1, ...., m$, $g_{ij} = 0$ or $g_{ij} = 1$ (a binary image), where 0 means that $g_{ij}$ belongs to the grid. This image could be thought of as a "free-form grid". However, in order to strictly use the definition of a "grid", our aim is to obtain vectors **v** and **h**, $\mathbf{v} = [v_1, ...v_n]$, $\mathbf{h} = [h_1, ...h_n]$, where $v_i \in [1, m]$ and $h_j \in [1, n]$. Informally speaking, the latter implies that the grid is composed of lines (not necessarily equally-spaced), which are parallel to the vertical axis or the horizontal axis.

Most of the previous approaches have used different application specific constraints, making some assumptions of the above-mentioned parameters, and proceeding in a semiautomatic manner. These parameters are not always available, and have to be specified by the user. For example, when the size of the spots is not known, the user needs to manually count the number of pixels in order to estimate the appropriate size. Approaches that need this kind of information available include Markov random fields (MRF), which is a well known approach that applies different application specific constraints and heuristic criteria [5]. Another gridding method is the mathematical morphological model, which represents the image as a function and applies erosion operators and morphological filters to transform it to other images resulting in shrinkage and area opening of the image and which further helps in removing peaks and ridges from the topological surface of the images [1,6]. Jain [3], Katzer [4], and Stienfath's [10] models are integrated systems for microarray gridding and quantitative analysis. They impose different kinds of restrictions on the print layout or materials used. Stienfath's model requires filter arrays with radioactive label different from glass arrays. Jain's model requires the rows and columns of all grid to be strictly aligned. Katzer's model requires gaps between the grids and most of the other existing approaches do not aim at solving the problem automatically.

In this paper, we propose a new energy maximization based approach for automatic gridding of microarray images. The method that we propose relaxes three assumptions made by traditional techniques, and is shown to be very accurate in standard microarray databases.

## 2 A Weighted Energy Maximization Approach

Our approach to find the grid lines in microarray images is based on a series of steps, which involve weighted energy maximization functions. We separate the problems into two parts. First we find the spot size (or spot width) using $r$ arbitrary pixels in the microarray images using four different modules, and one of three weighted energy functions. Then, we capture every spot in the microarray image using the spot size and a recursive estimator to correct the spot size, and by finding the local maxima within the range of spot width. The weighted energy functions are described below, while the algorithm involved in the proposed method are discussed in the next section.

The energy function takes a sub-image (a matrix of pixel intensities) as input. It computes the energy of the sub-image by weighting each pixel based on a parametric probabilistic distribution, where the underlying random variable is the distance from the center of the sub-image to the corresponding pixel. In our approach, we propose to use three different parametric distributions, namely uniform, exponential, and normal.

Consider a sub-image, $B = \{b_{ij}\}$, where $i = 1, \ldots, n_b, j = 1, \ldots, m_b$, $b_{ij} \in [o, p]$, $p$ is the maximum pixel intensity, and $\mathbf{x}_{ij} = [x_{ij}, y_{ij}]$ represent the coordinates of the pixels. Note that $\mathbf{x}$ represents the relative position in $B$. The different functions are described below.

1. **Uniform energy function:** Assuming that the weights for the pixels are assigned by means of a bivariate uniform distribution, e.g. they are all equally weighted, the energy for $B$ is computed as follows:

$$E = \sum_{i=1}^{n_b} \sum_{j=1}^{m_b} b_{ij}, \qquad (1)$$

2. **Exponential energy function:** For this function, we first estimate the mean of the distribution as $\mathbf{c} = [n/2, m/2]$. The distance from each pixel $\mathbf{x}_{ij}$ to the center is then computed as $d_{ij} = [(\mathbf{c} - \mathbf{x})^t (\mathbf{c} - \mathbf{x})]$. Then, assuming that $d_{ij}$ is an exponential random variable, the weighted energy is computed as follows:

$$E = \sum_{i=1}^{n_b} \sum_{j=1}^{m_b} b_{ij} \lambda e^{-\lambda d_{ij}}, \qquad (2)$$

where $\lambda$ is the parameter to the distribution.

3. **Normal energy function:** Assuming that the weighting function is given by a bivariate normal distribution, whose mean is $\mathbf{c}$, and whose covariance is $\Sigma = \begin{bmatrix} \sigma^2 & 0 \\ 0 & \sigma^2 \end{bmatrix}$, the energy is computed as follows:

$$E = \sum_{i=1}^{n_b} \sum_{j=1}^{m_b} b_{ij} \frac{1}{2\pi |\Sigma|^{\frac{1}{2}}} e^{-\frac{1}{2}(\mathbf{x}_{ij} - \mathbf{c})^t \Sigma^{-1} (\mathbf{x}_{ij} - \mathbf{c})}, \qquad (3)$$

Thus, the only parameter needed is the variance of the distribution, $\sigma^2$.

## 2.1 Gridding Algorithms

The first module involved in our method is the local maximum energy spot algorithm, which takes a sub-grid, $A$, a starting pixel, $\mathbf{p}$, a step size, $s$, a "scanning" range, $g$, and finds the maximum energy sub-matrix of size $n_n \times n_b$. The procedure that formalizes this algorithm is shown in Algorithm **Local_Maximum_Energy_Spot**. The algorithm proceeds by scanning a "portion" of the sub-grid, at arbitrary positions which are $s$ pixels apart. Once the maximum energy is found at these arbitrary positions, the energy is maximized, locally, by a "greedy" procedure.

The second module proceeds by scanning the image horizontally to the left and then to the right. The aim is to find the positions of the "peaks" of energy along the horizontal line. The procedure that implements this algorithm can be found in [11]. This procedure receives (as input) a starting pixel that is obtained from the greedy procedure discussed above, $\mathbf{p} = [h, v]$, and the sub-grid $A$. It returns an array that contains the positions of the peaks along the horizontal line. The scanning to the right of $h$ is done in a similar manner, and can also be found in [11].

The vertical spot detection algorithm is similar to the horizontal one described above, except that the former scans to the top and bottom of $A$, starting from $v$. The output of the algorithm is a vector, $\mathbf{v}$, which contains the positions of the energy peaks. The formal algorithm can also be found in [11].

### 2.1.1 Capturing All Spot Centers

Once the peaks with maximum energy have been found for the horizontal and vertical line, for the $r$ selected points, the aim is now to find all the spots in the microarray image (or sub-grid). To achieve this, we first estimate the spot width by computing the difference between the positions of the peaks, which are stored in $\mathbf{h}_{peak}$ (or equivalently for $\mathbf{v}_{peak}$). Thus, an estimate of the spot width mean is computed as follows:

$$\hat{\mu}_i = \frac{1}{|\mathbf{h}_{peak}|} \sum_{j=1}^{|\mathbf{h}_{peak}|-1} \mathbf{h}_{peak}[j] - \mathbf{h}_{peak}[j+1] \qquad (4)$$

This is done for all $r$ spots selected, obtaining one set of means for the horizontal array, and another for the vertical array. Using the resulting means, we then compute the *mean of the means* (for the vertical array is similar), as follows:

$$\hat{\mu}_h = \frac{1}{r} \sum_{j=1}^{r} \hat{\mu}_j \qquad (5)$$

Using this mean, we find all "potential" spot centers as follows. Starting from the initial pixel, $\mathbf{p} = [h, v]$, move horizontally to the left (and to the right) $\hat{\mu}_h$ pixels, and find the maximum local energy, which is at pixel $\mathbf{p}_{max}$, and update $\hat{\mu}_h$ recursively as follows:

$$\hat{\mu}_h = \frac{r}{r+i}\hat{\mu}_h + h_{i-1} - h_{max} \qquad (6)$$

Once a row is exhausted, the pointer is moved vertically using $\hat{\mu}_v$, and updating it recursively as in (6). As a result, the "potential" spot centers are obtained and stored in a matrix, $C = \{\mathbf{c}_{ij}\}$, where $\mathbf{c}_{ij} = [x_{ij}, y_{ij}]$, $i = 1, \ldots, n_c, j = 1, \ldots, m_c$.

Using these potential spot centers, the aim now is to find the actual spot centers, and subsequently the corresponding grid. To achieve this, we construct a histogram for all the horizontal positions in $C$, $x_{ij}$ (and another histogram for all the vertical positions, $y_{ij}$), by counting the number of occurrences of $i$, $i = 1, \ldots, n$, in $C$. The corresponding histogram for a sample microarray image (a sub-grid) is depicted in Figure 1. The peaks observed in the figure denote the most likely positions for the columns (rows) of spots. Once this histogram is constructed, the column (and row) lines are found by starting from the maximum

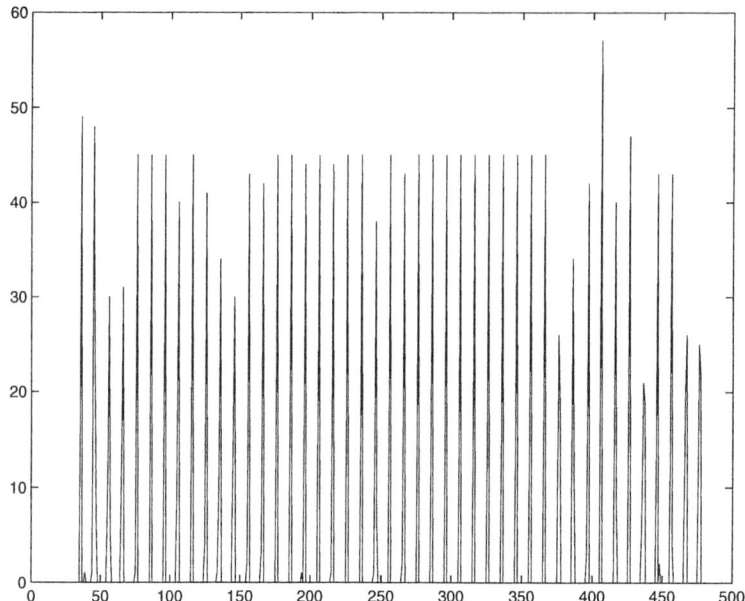

**Fig. 1.** The histogram for the peaks obtained while traversing (horizontally left) an image from the SMD database

peak in the histogram, moving $\hat{\mu}_h$ (which has been computed in (6)) pixels, and finding a local maxima (a peak in the histogram). The estimate for the spot width can be adaptively updated at this point, by keeping the running estimate. This process is repeated until all the peaks are exhausted. The formal algorithm that implements the procedure to find the grid columns and rows can be found in [11]. It is not difficult to see (observing Figure 1) that finding the "peaks" of the histogram is a straightforward task, once the potential spot centers are given. It is, however, difficult to predict where the spot centers are, when the image is rotated or the grids are distorted. This is a problem that we are currently investigating.

## 3  Experimental Results

To perform the tests we collected the raw data (original microarray images) from the cancer database from GEO[1], and yeast cell cycle microarray images from Stanford microarray database (SMD) [9].

We have analyzed the efficiency of our method using the uniform energy function, where $g = 40$, and $n_b = m_b = 10$, by means of a numerical analysis. The results have been obtained for images from SMD and GEO, and are shown

---

[1] Electronically available at ftp://ftp.ncbi.nih.gov/pub/geo/data/geo_raw_data/samples/

**Table 1.** Resulting accuracy for the proposed gridding method applied to microarray images drawn from the Stanford dataset

| Image | Sub-grid | NS | NS_R | NS_M | Accuracy | NP_M | Error |
|---|---|---|---|---|---|---|---|
| EE-channel 1 | 2 | 1828 | 1816 | 12 | 99.34 | 21 | 0.046 |
| EE-channel 2 | 2 | 1837 | 1823 | 14 | 99.24 | 30 | 0.071 |
| EE-channel 2 | 2 | 1886 | 1835 | 51 | 97.30 | 78 | 0.172 |
| cdc-channel1 | 3 | 2022 | 2008 | 15 | 99.32 | 32 | 0.083 |
| cdc-channel2 | 2 | 2039 | 2017 | 24 | 98.91 | 45 | 0.116 |
| EE-channel 1 | 3 | 1837 | 1823 | 14 | 99.24 | 38 | 0.067 |
| EE-channel 2 | 3 | 1828 | 1816 | 21 | 99.34 | 54 | 0.118 |
| EE-channel 2 | 4 | 1872 | 1811 | 61 | 96.74 | 126 | 0.269 |
| PE-channel 1 | 4 | 1904 | 1852 | 52 | 97.27 | 75 | 0.127 |
| EE-channel 2 | 3 | 1881 | 1823 | 58 | 96.91 | 119 | 0.263 |
| Average | | | | | 98.36 | | 0.133 |

**Table 2.** Accuracy in spot detection and pixel inclusion for the proposed method on microarray images drawn from the GEO dataset

| Image | Sub-grid | NS | NS_R | NS_M | Accuracy | NP_M | Error |
|---|---|---|---|---|---|---|---|
| GSM17163 | 2 | 340 | 340 | 0 | 100.00 | 0 | 0.000 |
| GSM17186 | 5 | 380 | 380 | 0 | 100.00 | 0 | 0.000 |
| GSM17137 | 5 | 377 | 373 | 4 | 98.94 | 5 | 0.040 |
| GSM17192 | 5 | 422 | 422 | 0 | 100.00 | 0 | 0.000 |
| GSM17190 | 16 | 354 | 354 | 0 | 100.00 | 0 | 0.000 |
| GSM17192 | 13 | 410 | 410 | 0 | 100.00 | 0 | 0.000 |
| GSM17186 | 12 | 147 | 140 | 7 | 95.24 | 21 | 0.446 |
| GSM17192 | 6 | 405 | 405 | 0 | 100.00 | 0 | 0.000 |
| GSM17193 | 4 | 429 | 426 | 3 | 99.30 | 5 | 0.035 |
| GSM17137 | 2 | 424 | 420 | 4 | 99.06 | 7 | 0.050 |
| Average | | | | | 99.25 | | 0.057 |

in Tables 1 and 2 respectively. The second column shows the sub-grid number used in the experiment. The third column contains the number of spots in the sub-grid, NS. The fourth column contains the number of "recognized" spots. The fifth column displays the number of spots which are not *entirely* contained in the grid cell, or which are misplaced, NS_M. The percentage of spots (Accuracy) that are correctly placed inside the grid cell is shown in the sixth column. The total number of pixels, which are misplaced, NP_M, is displayed in the seventh column. The eight column contains the percentage of pixels (Error) which are not included in the grid cell.

From the tables, we observe that the proposed method is quite accurate in finding the grids for the microarray images tested. In both databases, SMD and GEO, the percentage of spots which are correctly placed in their corresponding grid cells is very high, exceeding 98%. Note that in this case, we are counting the

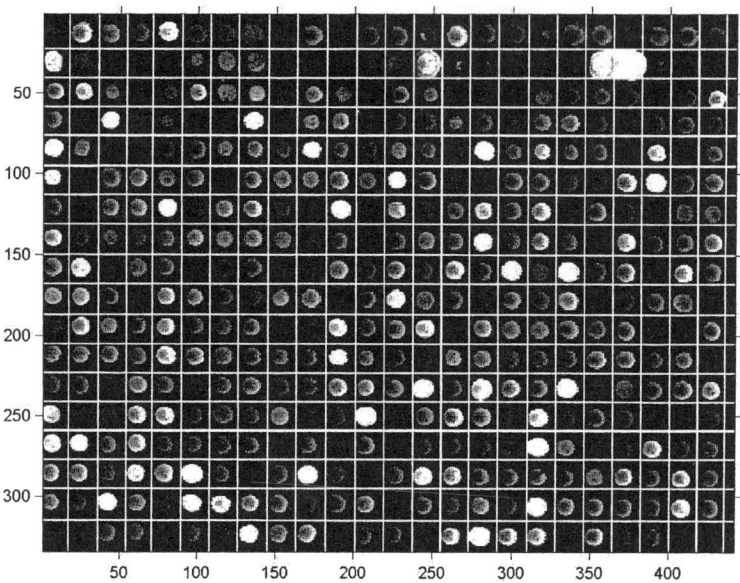

**Fig. 2.** The resulting grid for an image (GSM17137, grid 9) which was drawn from the GEO database

number of spots which contain *all* their pixels in the corresponding cell, while those that contain *at least* one pixel outside the cell are counted as *misplaced*. Regarding the number of pixels which fall *outside* the grid cell, we also observe that the proposed method is quite efficient, yielding, on the average, around 1% and 0.5% for SMD and GEO respectively. In most of the images, the accuracy is exactly (or nearly) 100%, while in a couple of images the percentage is below 95%, which indicates that these images contain a relatively high amount of noise. To visually observe the accuracy of the proposed method, in Figure 2 we show the resulting grid, and the corresponding image (sub-grid 9) from image GSM17137. The figure corroborates the accuracy of the proposed method in obtaining the grid 100% accurately, despite the image contains noise and many spots with low intensity.

## 4 Conclusion

In this paper, we propose a gridding approach, which is different from the existing techniques, as we make no assumptions about the spot size, rows and columns of the spots in the image or grids in the microarray image.

We have visually demonstrated that our approach is quite accurate in obtaining the grid for microarray images drawn from standard databases. In the numerical comparison, the accuracy of our method has been found to be almost 100%, when counting the number of spots which are *completely* enclosed in a grid cell, and the number of pixels which belong to the spot, and are enclosed in the cell too.

As a result of our study, we recommend that some additional work be done in this area. In this paper, we only consider those sub-girds which have no rotations. Although this is not the case always, in some case the images become rotated after the spots are printed on the glass chip. This problem, which is quite complicated, is currently being investigated. Also, additional testing on other datasets, and using other energy functions are topics to investigate.

*Acknowledgements.* This research work has been partially supported by NSERC, the Natural Sciences and Engineering Research Council of Canada, CFI, the Canadian Foundation for Innovation, and OIT, the Ontario Innovation Trust.

## References

1. J. Angulo and J. Serra, Automatic Analysis of DNA Microarray Images Using Mathematical Morphology *Bioinformatics*, vol. 19(5), pp. 553-562, 2003.
2. S. Drăghici *Data Analysis Tools for DNA Microarrays*. Chapman and Hall/CRC, 2003.
3. A. Jain, T. Tokuyasu, A. Snijders, R. Segraves, D. Albertson, and D. Pinkel, Fully Automatic Quantification of Microarray Image Data. *Genome Res.*, 12(2):325332, 2002.
4. M. Katzer, F. Kummert, and G. Sagerer. Automatische Auswertung von Mikroarraybildern. *Proc. of Workshop Bildverarbeitung für die Medizin*, Leipzig, Germany, 2002.
5. M. Katzer, F. Kummert and G. Sagerer, A Markov Random Field Model of Microarray Gridding In *Proceedings of the 2003 ACM Symposium on Applied Computing*, pp. 72-77, 2003.
6. A. Liew, H. Yan, and M. Yang. Robust Adaptive Spot Segmentation of DNA Microarray Images. *Pattern Recognition*, 36(5):152-155, 2003.
7. L. Rueda and L. Qin. An Improved Clustering-based Approach for DNA Microarray Image Segmentation In *Proceedings of the 2004 International Conference on Image Analysis and Recognition*, pp. 17-24, 2004.
8. M. Schena *Microarray Analysis*. Wiley-Liss, 2002.
9. G. Sherlock, T. Hernandez-Boussard, A. Kasarskis, G. Binkley, J. Matese, S. Dwight, M. Kaloper, S. Weng, H. Jin, C. Ball, M. B. Eisen, P. T. Spellman, P. O. Brown, D. Botstein, and J. M. Cherry. The Stanford Microarray Database. *Nucleic Acids Research*, (29):152155, 2001.
10. M. Steinfath, W. Wruck, and H. Seidel. Automated Image Analysis for Array Hybridization Experiments. *Bioinformatics*, 2001, Vol. 17, T. 7, S. 634-641, 2001.
11. V. Vidyadharan Automatic Gridding of DNA Microarray Images M.Sc. Thesis, School of Computer Science, University of Windsor, Canada, 2004. Electronically available at http://www.cs.uwindsor.ca/~lrueda/papers/VidyaThesis.pdf.

# Ultrafast Technique of Impulsive Noise Removal with Application to Microarray Image Denoising

Bogdan Smolka[1,*] and Konstantinos N. Plataniotis[2]

[1] Silesian University of Technology, Department of Automatic Control,
Akademicka 16 Str, 44-100 Gliwice, Poland
bsmolka@ia.polsl.gliwice.pl

[2] The Edward S. Rogers Sr. Department of Electrical and Computer Engineering,
University of Toronto, 10 King's College Road, Toronto ON, M5S 3G4, Canada

**Abstract.** In this paper a novel approach to the impulsive noise removal in color images is presented. The proposed technique employs the switching scheme based on the impulse detection mechanism using the so called *peer group* concept. Compared to the vector median filter, the proposed technique consistently yields better results in suppressing both the random-valued and fixed-valued impulsive noise. The main advantage of the proposed noise detection framework is its enormous computational speed, which enables efficient filtering of large images in real-time applications. The proposed filtering scheme has been successfully applied to the denoising of the cDNA microarray images. Experimental results proved that the new filter is capable of removing efficiently the impulses present in multichannel images, while preserving their textural features.

## 1 Introduction

In this paper a novel approach to the detection and removal of impulsive noise in color images is presented. The main advantage of the described technique is its simplicity and enormous computational speed. The proposed method is using the well known vector median filter for the suppression of the detected noise, however different techniques can be used for the denoising of the previously detected impulses.

The cDNA microarray is a popular and effective method for simultaneous assaying the expression of large numbers of genes and is perfectly suited for the comparison of gene expression in different populations of cells. A microarray is a collection of spots containing DNA, deposited on the surface of a glass slide. Each of the spots contains multiple copies of a single DNA sequence.

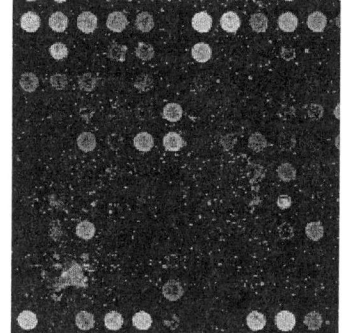

**Fig. 1.** Two-channel image of the cDNA microarray

---

* This research has been supported by the KBN grant 4T11F01824.

The probes are tagged with fluorescent reporter molecules, which emit detectable light when stimulated by laser. The emitted light is captured by a detector, which records the light intensity. When the laser scans the entire slide, a large array image containing thousands of spots is produced. The fluorescent intensities for each of the two dyes are measured separately, producing a two-channel image, (Figs. 1, 8).

The intensities provided by the array image can be quantified by measuring the average or integrated intensities of the spots. However, the evaluation of microarray images is a difficult task as the natural fluorescence of the glass slide and non-specifically bounded DNA or dye molecules add a substantial noise floor to the microarray image. To make the task even more challenging, the microarrays are also afflicted with discrete image artifacts, such as highly fluorescent dust particles, unattached dye, salt deposits from evaporated solvents, fibers and various airborne debris. So, the task of microarray image enhancement and especially the removal of artifacts is of paramount importance, [1].

## 2 Impulsive Noise Removal

The majority of the nonlinear, multichannel filters are based on the ordering of vectors in a sliding filter window. The output of these filters is defined as the lowest ranked vector according to a specific vector ordering technique.

Let the color images be represented in the RGB color space and let $\mathbf{x}_1$, $\mathbf{x}_2$, ..., $\mathbf{x}_n$ be $n$ samples from the sliding filter window $W$. Each of the $\mathbf{x}_i$ is an $\mu$-dimensional multichannel vector, (in our case $\mu = 3$). The goal of the vector ordering is to arrange the set of $n$ vectors $\{\mathbf{x}_1, \mathbf{x}_2, \ldots, \mathbf{x}_n\}$ belonging to $W$ using some sorting criterion.

The ordering based on the cumulative distance function $R(\mathbf{x}_i)$ is usually defined as: $R(\mathbf{x}_i) = \sum_{j=1}^{n} \rho(\mathbf{x}_i, \mathbf{x}_j)$, where $\rho(\mathbf{x}_i, \mathbf{x}_j)$ is a function of the distance among $\mathbf{x}_i$ and $\mathbf{x}_j$. The ordering of the scalar quantities according to $R(\mathbf{x}_i)$ generates the ordered set of vectors, [2,3].

One of the most important noise reduction filters is the vector median. In the case of gray scale images, given a set $W$ containing $n$ samples, the median of the set is defined as $x_{(1)} \in W$ such that $\sum_j \left| x_{(1)} - x_j \right| \leq \sum_j \left| x_i - x_j \right|$, $\forall\, x_i, x_j \in W$. Median filters exhibit good noise reduction capabilities, and outperform simple nonadaptive linear filters in preserving signal discontinuities.

As in many applications the signal is multidimensional, in [4] the *Vector Median Filter* (VMF) was introduced, by generalizing the scalar median definition using a suitable vector norm denoted as $\|\cdot\|$. Given a set $W$ of $n$ vectors, the vector median of the set is defined as $\mathbf{x}_{(1)} \in W$ satisfying

$$\sum_j \left\| \mathbf{x}_{(1)} - \mathbf{x}_j \right\| \leq \sum_j \left\| \mathbf{x}_i - \mathbf{x}_j \right\|, \quad \forall\ \mathbf{x}_i, \mathbf{x}_j \in W. \tag{1}$$

## 3 Proposed Noise Detection Algorithm

The main objective of the noise reduction algorithms is to suppress noise, while preserving important image features like edges, corners or texture.

Over the years various impulsive noise reduction algorithms have been proposed, [5,6,7]. The main drawback of many standard filters is the fact that they fail to distinguish between the original uncorrupted pixels and pixels affected by the noise process, which leads to poor visual quality of the restored images.

This is also a serious drawback of the very popular Vector Median Filter. It is quite easy to notice that the VMF offers good performance in the removal of impulsive noise, but at the same time it introduces unnecessary changes to the pixels not corrupted by the noise process, which leads to extensive image blurring, destruction of image texture and even artifacts like artificial streaks. This behavior of the VMF can be easily observed in Fig. 2d in which the the black pixels indicate those image pixels that were changed by the VMF algorithm. The test image was distorted by 5% random valued impulsive noise and the VMF replaced 80.7% of the image pixels.

Let us now modify the concept of the *peer group* introduced in [8] and extensively used in various filtering designs, mostly under the name of *extended spatial neighborhood*, [9].

The *peer group* $\mathcal{P}(\mathbf{x}_i, m, d)$, in this paper will denote the set of $m$ neighbors $\mathbf{x}_j$ of the central pixel of $W$, which satisfy he following condition: $\|\mathbf{x}_i - \mathbf{x}_j\| \leq d$, $\mathbf{x}_j \in W, \mathbf{x}_j \neq \mathbf{x}_i$. In other words, the peer group $\mathcal{P}$ *associated* with the central pixel $\mathbf{x}_i$ of $W$ is a set of $m$ pixels which are in neighborhood relation with $\mathbf{x}_i$, whose distance to the central pixel is not exceeding $d$, (Fig. 3).

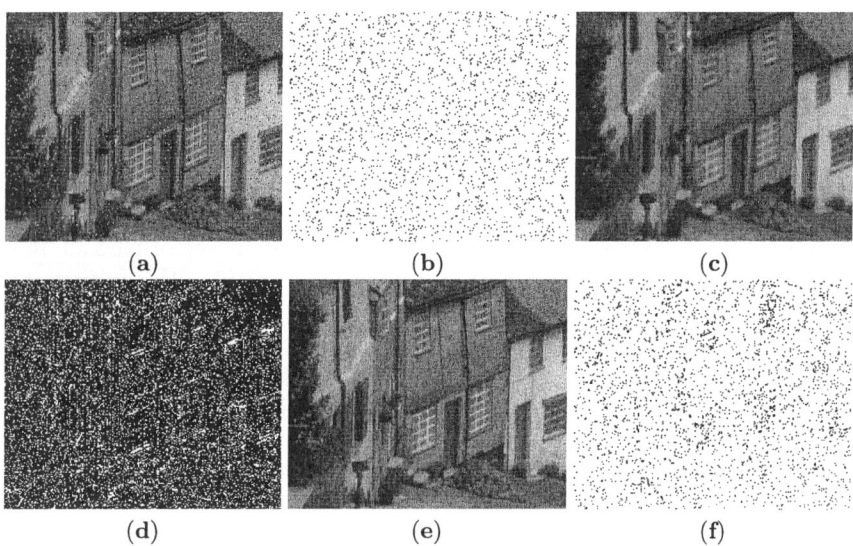

**Fig. 2.** Illustration of the efficiency of the new filtering design: a) test image GOLD-HILL contaminated by random valued impulsive noise of $p = 5\%$, b) black dots show the pixels disturbed by noise, c) image restored with VMF, d) difference between the original and the VMF output, e) new filter output, ($m = 3, d = 50$) and besides the corresponding residual image f)

The proposed impulsive noise detection algorithm works as follows: if there exists a peer group $\mathcal{P}(\mathbf{x}_i, m, d)$, which means that at least $m$ neighbors of $\mathbf{x}_i$ satisfy the *closeness* condition, then the pixel $\mathbf{x}_i$ is treated as not corrupted by noise, otherwise it is declared to be noisy and can be filtered with any efficient noise reduction algorithm.

As the output is switched between the identity and a filtering operation, various filtering designs can be used instead of the VMF, [5]. In this paper we have chosen the VMF mainly to demonstrate the efficiency and extremely low computational effort of the proposed noise detection framework.

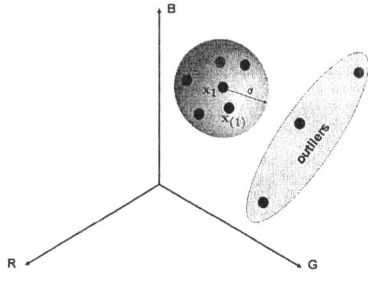

**Fig. 3.** The concept of the *peer group* centered at $\mathbf{x}_1$, ($m = 5$)

The low computational complexity stems from the fact that when the peer group parameter $m$ is low, for example $m = 2$, then if the algorithm finds two pixels, which are close enough to the central pixel under consideration, the pixel $\mathbf{x}_i$ is declared as noise-free and the sliding window moves to the adjacent pixel. Very often only a few calculations of the distances $\|\mathbf{x}_i - \mathbf{x}_j\|$, $\mathbf{x}_j \in W$ are needed to classify the pixel as undisturbed by noise. The minimal number of calculation of the distances needed to classify the pixel is thus equal to $m$ and the maximal number of distances is $n - m$, where $n$ is the number of pixels contained in the filtering window $W$. The number of distances needed for the detection of impulses is extremely low when compared with the number of distances needed by the VMF algorithm which is equal to $n(n-1)/2$.

## 4 Simulation Results

In many practical situations, images are corrupted by noise caused either by faulty image sensors or due to transmission errors resulting from man-made phenomena such as ignition transients in the vicinity of the receivers or even natural phenomena such as lightning in the atmosphere.

The impulsive noise is often generated by bit errors, especially during the scanning or transmission over noisy information channels. In this paper the noisy signal is modelled as $\mathbf{x}_i = \{x_{i1}, x_{i2}, x_{i3}\}$, where $x_{ik} = v_{ik}$ with probability $\pi$ and $o_{ik}$ (original, undisturbed value) with probability $1 - \pi$, and the contamination component $v_{ik}$ is a random variable. We will assume two models, which will be called impulsive *salt & pepper* or *fixed-valued* noise, when $v_{ik} = \{0, 255\}$ and impulsive *uniform* or *random-valued* noise, when $v_{ik} \in [0, 255]$. It can be noticed that the first model is a special case of the *uniform* noise, as this noise can take on only two values 0 or 255 with the same probability, assuming 8-Bit per channel, color image representation.

In both noise models the contamination of the color image components is uncorrelated, and the overall contamination rate is $p = 1 - (1 - \pi)^3$. For the measurement of the restoration quality the commonly used *Root Mean Square*

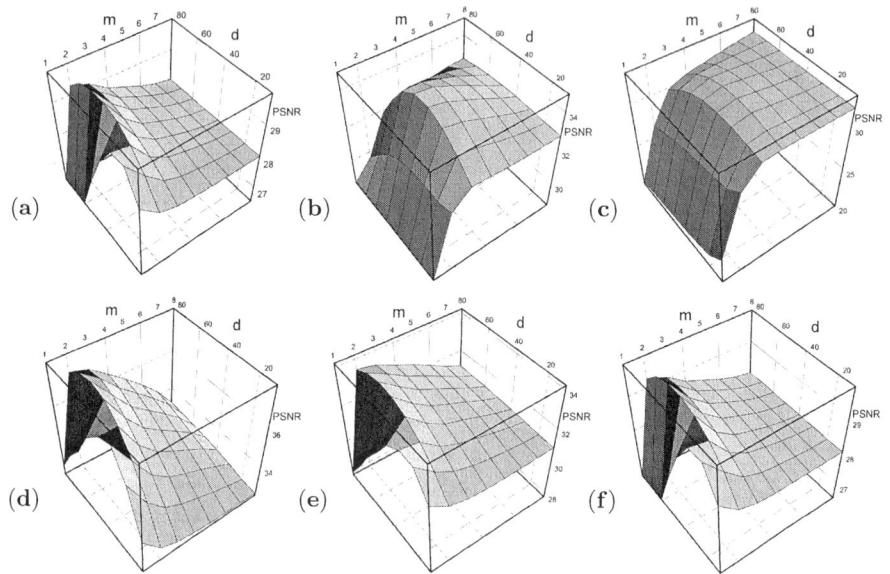

**Fig. 4.** Dependence of the PSNR on parameters $m$, $d$ for the LENA image contaminated by *salt & pepper* (**a-c**) and *uniform* (**d-f**) impulsive noise for $p = 10, 20, 30\%$

*Error* (RMSE) expressed through the *Peak Signal to Noise Ratio* (PSNR) was used, as the RMSE is a good measure of the efficiency of impulsive noise suppression. The PSNR is defined as

$$PSNR = 20 \log_{10}\left(\frac{255}{\sqrt{MSE}}\right), \; MSE = \frac{\sum\limits_{i=1}^{N}\sum\limits_{k=1}^{\mu}(x_{ik} - o_{ik})^2}{N\mu}, \tag{2}$$

where $N$ is the total number of image pixels, and $x_{ik}$, $o_{ik}$ denote the $k$-th component of the noisy image pixel channel and its original, undisturbed value at a pixel position $i$, respectively.

The parameters $m$ and $d$ provide control over the performance of the impulsive noise detection process. For its assessment a series of simulations on natural images was performed.

With regard to the parameter $m$ of the peer group $\mathcal{P}$ the simulation results show that when the contamination intensity is low, good results are achieved for $m = 2$ in case of both the fixed valued and impulsive noise, (Figs. 4 a,d). For higher noise probability $p$, the images contaminated by fixed valued impulsive noise require $m = 3$, (Figs. 4 b,c). Surprisingly, good results are achieved for $m = 2$, when the images are contaminated by random valued noise, (Figs. 4 e,f). As the filtering results are not very sensitive to the choice of $m$, we used $m = 3$ for the comparisons with the VMF.

The experiments conducted on a broad variety of natural color images have shown, [10,11] that the parameter $d$ should be equal to about 50, (Fig. 6) as such a setting guarantees good performance of the proposed switching scheme, independently on the image characteristics, noise model and contamination intensity.

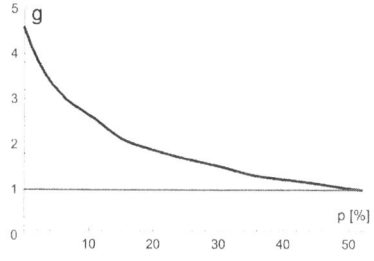

The main advantage of the proposed noise detection technique is its enormous computational speed. The comparison with the VMF, presented in Fig. 5 shows that the new technique is for low contamination intensities 2-4 times faster than the VMF.

The efficiency of the proposed technique can be observed in Fig. 7, in which zoomed parts of the test color images were distorted by uniform impulsive noise and restored with VMF and with the new filter. As can be observed the incorporated switching scheme enables the preservation of edges and fine image details. This behavior is also confirmed in Fig. 2 f,g, which shows that the new filter rejects the impulses and replaces only a small fraction of the undisturbed pixels, (in this example the contamination intensity was $p = 5\%$ and only 6.7% of the pixels were replaced by the VMF).

**Fig. 5.** Filtering efficiency of the proposed noise removal algorithm in comparison with the VMF for *salt & pepper* noise for LENA image with $d = 50$ and $m = 3$

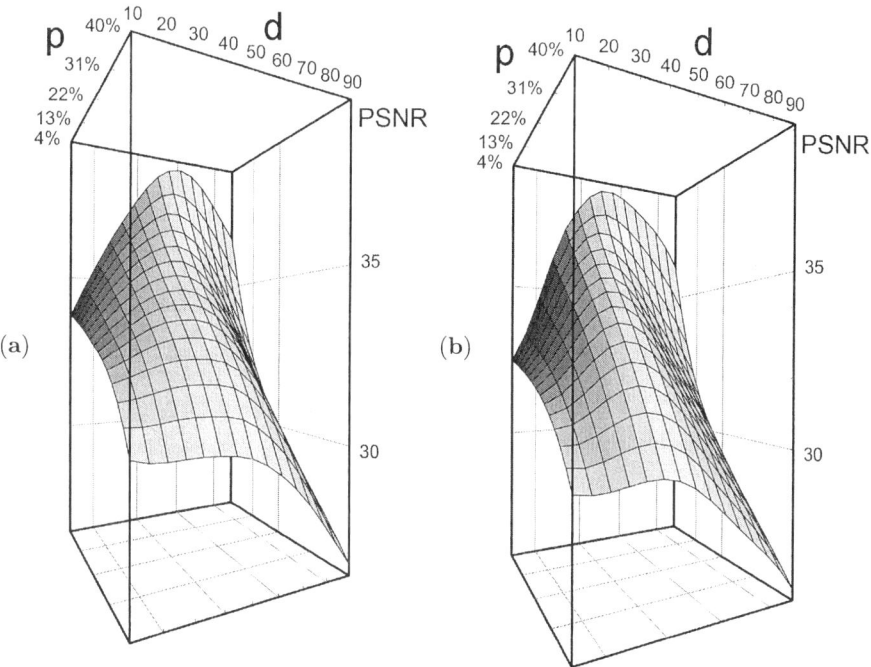

**Fig. 6.** Dependence of PSNR on parameters $d$ and $p$ for the test images LENA corrupted by *salt & pepper* (a) and *uniform* (b) impulsive noise for $m = 3$

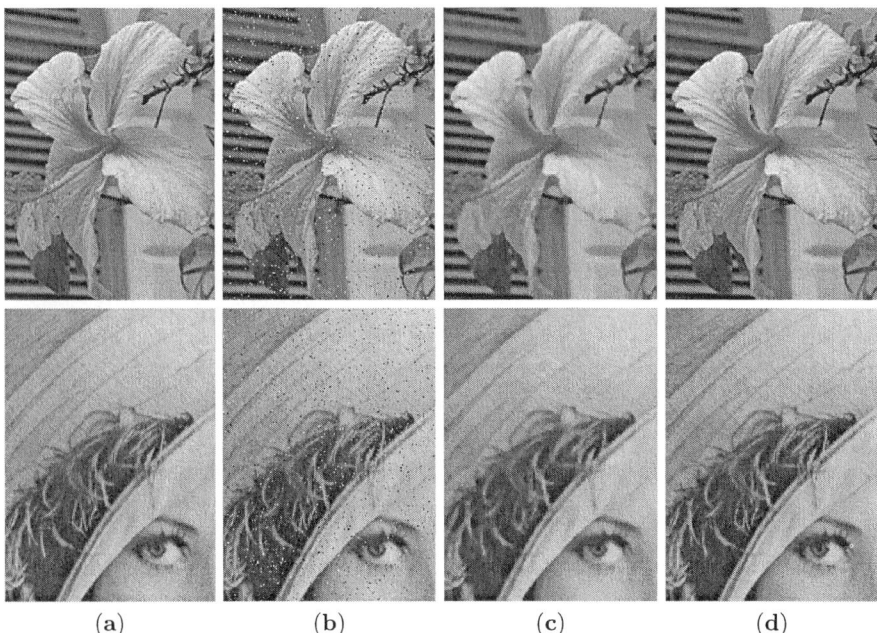

**Fig. 7.** Illustrative examples of the filtering efficiency: **a)** zoomed parts of the color test images, **b)** images contaminated by 5% *uniform* noise, **c)** restoration achieved with the VMF, **d)** filtering results achieved using the new noise detection technique

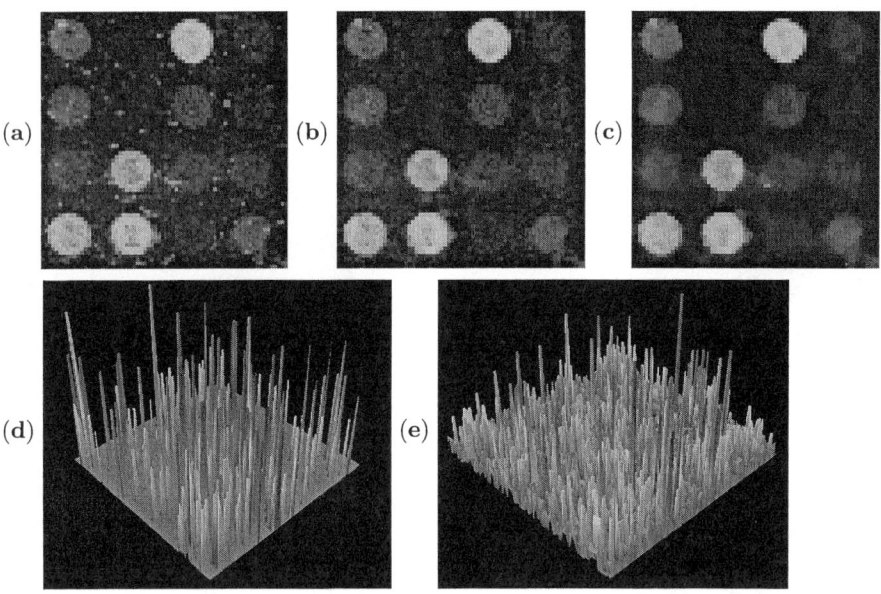

**Fig. 8.** Filtering efficiency on the cDNA images: **a)** noisy image, **b)** restored with the new technique, **c)** restored with VMF, **d)** visualization of the difference between the noisy image and its restored version corresponding to the new filter, **e)** error images corresponding to VMF, (see also Fig. 2)

The good performance of the proposed switching scheme can be also observed in Fig. 8, which depicts the results of impulsive noise suppression in cDNA microarrays. It can be noticed that the proposed filter removes the spikes only, while preserving the textural information needed for the assessment of the spots intensity. This behavior enables better evaluation of the spots intensities as the impulsive noise is efficiently removed and does not affect the measurements of the mean spot's intensity. Additionally the removal of impulses and small clusters enables further filtering of the Gaussian noise with fast linear techniques.

## 5 Conclusion

In this paper a new approach to the problem of impulsive noise detection and removal in color images has been presented. The main advantage of the proposed technique is its extraordinary high computational speed, which makes it attractive for real-time applications and denoising of very large images, like the cDNA microarrays. The noise detection scheme has been coupled in this paper with the vector median filter, however the computational speed can be further increased when employing a less computationally demanding noise removal algorithm.

## References

1. Lukac, R., Plataniotis, K.N., Smolka, B., Venetsanopoulos, A.N.: A Multichannel Order-Statistic Technique for cDNA Microarray Image Processing. IEEE Transactions on Nanobioscience, Vol. 3, No. 4, (2004) 272-285
2. Lukac, R., Smolka, B., Martin, K., Plataniotis, K.N., Venetsanopoulos, A.N.: Vector Filtering for Color Imaging. IEEE Signal Processing Magazine, Special Issue on Color Image Processing, Vol. 22, No. 1, (2005) 74-86
3. Lukac, R.: Adaptive Vector Median Filtering. Pattern Recognition Letters. Vol. 24, No. 12, (2003) 1889-1899
4. Astola, J., Haavisto, P., Neuvo, Y.: Vector Median Filters. Proceedings of the IEEE, Vol. 78, (1990) 678-689
5. Plataniotis, K.N., Venetsanopoulos, A.N.: Color Image Processing and Applications. Springer Verlag, (2000)
6. Lukac, R.: Color Image Filtering by Vector Directional Order-Statistics. Pattern Recognition and Image Analysis, Vol. 12, No. 3, (2002) 279-285
7. Lukac, R.: Vector LUM Smoothers as Impulse Detector for Color Images. Proceedings of European Conference on Circuit Theory and Design (ECCTD'01) in Espoo, Finland, August 28-31, III, (2001) 137-140.
8. Kenney, C., Deng, Y., Manjunath, B.S., Hewer, G.: Peer Group Image Enhancement. IEEE Trans. Image Processing, Vol. 10, No. 2, (2001) 326-334
9. Kober, V., Mozerov, M., Alvarez-Borrego, J: Nonlinear Filters with Spatially-Connected Neighborhoods. Optical Engineering, Vol. 40, No. 6, (2001) 971-983,
10. Smolka, B., Plataniotis, K.N., Chydzinski, A., Szczepanski, M., Venetsanopulos, A.N., Wojciechowski, K.: Self-Adaptive Algorithm of Impulsive Noise Reduction in Color Images. Pattern Recognition, Vol. 35, (2002) 1771-1784
11. Smolka, B., Lukac, R., Chydzinski, A., Plataniotis, K.N., Wojciechowski, K.: Fast Adapive Similarity Based Impulsive Noise Reduction Filter. Real-Time Imaging, Vol. 9, No. 4, (2003) 261-276

# Detection of Microcalcification Clusters in Mammograms Using a Difference of Optimized Gaussian Filters

Samuel Oporto-Díaz[1], Rolando Hernández-Cisneros[2], and Hugo Terashima-Marín[2]

[1] Universidad Nacional de Ingeniería, FIIS
Av. Túpac Amaru 210 Rímac, Lima, Peru
soporto@aurigacorp.com.pe
[2] Tecnológico de Monterrey, Campus Monterrey, Centro de Sistemas Inteligentes,
Av. Eugenio Garza Sada 2501, Monterrey, N.L. Mexico
{A00766380, terashima}@itesm.mx

**Abstract.** Since microcalcification clusters are primary indicators of malignant types of breast cancer, its detection is important to prevent and treat the disease. This paper proposes a method for detection of microcalcification clusters in mammograms using sequential Difference of Gaussian filters (DoG). In a first stage, fifteen DoG filters are applied sequentially to extract the potential regions, and later, these regions are classified using the following features: absolute contrast, standard deviation of the gray level of the microcalcification and a moment of contour sequence (asymmetry coefficient). Once the microcalcifications are detected, two approaches for clustering are compared. In the first one, several microcalcification clusters are detected in each mammogram. In the other, all microcalcifications are considered in a single cluster. We demonstrate that the diagnosis based on the detection of several microcalcification clusters in a mammogram is more efficient than considering a single cluster including all the microcalcifications in the image.

## 1 Introduction

Breast cancer is one of the main causes of death in women and early diagnosis is an important means to reduce the mortality rate. Mammography is one of the most common techniques for breast cancer diagnosis, and microcalcifications are one type of objects that can be detected in a mammogram. Microcalcifications are calcium accumulations of 0.1 mm to 2 mm wide, and they are indicators of the presence of breast cancer. Microcalcification clusters are groups of three or more microcalcifications that may appear in areas smaller than 1 cm$^2$, and have a high probability of becoming a malignant lesion.

Nevertheless, the predictive value of mammograms is relatively low, compared to biopsy. The causes of this low sensitivity [5] are the low contrast between the cancerous tissue and the normal parenchymal tissue, the small size of microcalcifications and possible deficiencies in the image digitalization process. The sensitivity may be improved having each mammogram be checked by two or more radiologists, with the consequence of making the process inefficient by reducing the individual productivity of each specialist. A viable alternative is replacing one of the radiologists by a computer system, giving a second opinion [2], [13].

Several methods have been proposed for detection of microcalcifications in mammograms, like wavelets, fractal models, support vector machines, mathematical morphology, bayesian image analysis models, high order statistic, fuzzy logic, etc. The use of a Difference of Gaussian Filters (DoG) for detection of potential microcalcifications has been addressed by Dengler et al. [4] and Ochoa [11]. In this work, we developed a procedure that applies a sequence of Difference of Gaussian Filters (DoG), in order to maximize the amount of detected probable individual microcalcifications in the mammogram (signals), which are later classified by an artificial neural network (ANN) in order to detect real microcalcifications. Later, microcalcification clusters are identified. Additionally, the hypothesis to be tested states that the diagnosis accuracy of the mammograms is higher if it is based on the diagnosis of every microcalcification cluster detected in the mammogram, instead of considering of all the microcalcifications in the mammogram as a single cluster.

The rest of this document is organized as follows: in the second section, the proposed procedure is described in detail. In the third section, the experimental results are shown and discussed, and finally, in the fourth section, the conclusions are presented, and some comments about future work are also mentioned.

## 2 Methods

The mammographic images used in this project were provided by The Mammographic Image Analysis Society [12]. The MIAS database contains 322 images, and only 25 of them contain microcalcifications. Among these 25 images, 13 cases are diagnosed as malignant and 12 as benign. The size of all images is 1024x1024 pixels, digitized at 8 bits. Several related works have used this same database [3], [6], [7], [10].

The proposed solution model is shown in Figure 1. The general procedure receives a digital mammogram (I) as an input, and it is conformed by five stages: pre-processing, detection of potential microcalcifications (signals), classification of signals into real microcalcifications, detection of microcalcification clusters and classification of microcalcification clusters into benigns and malignants.

### 2.1 Pre-processing

The main objective of this stage is to eliminate those elements in the image that could interfere in the process of identifying microcalcifications. A secondary goal is to reduce the work area only to the relevant region that exactly contains the breast. The procedure receives the original image as an input. First, a median filter is applied in order to eliminate the background noise; second, a binary image is created from the filtered image, where each pixel represents a 16x16 window centered in the corresponding pixel from the original image. If the gray

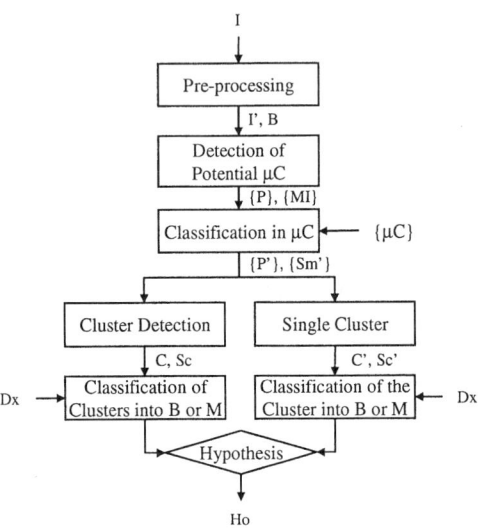

**Fig. 1.** Proposed Model for Hypothesis Testing

average level of the window is below certain threshold (established empirically, after visually analyzing the histograms of average gray level for several window sizes), a zero value is placed in the binary image; otherwise, a unitary value is placed. Third, an automatic cropping procedure is applied in order to delete the background marks and the isolated regions, so the image will contain only the region of interest. The result is a smaller image, with less noise.

### 2.2 Detection of Potential Microcalcifications (Signals)

This stage has the aim of detecting the mass centers of the potential microcalcifications in the image (signals). The pre-processed image of the previous stage is the input of this procedure. The optimized difference of two gaussian filters (DoG) is used for enhancing those regions containing bright points. A gaussian filter is obtained from a gaussian distribution, and when it is applied to an image, eliminates high frequency noise, acting like a smoothening filter. A DoG filter is built from two simple gaussian filters. These two smoothening filters must have different variances. When two obtained images after applying each filter separately are subtracted, an image containing only the desired frequency range is obtained. The DoG filter is obtained from the difference of two gaussian functions, as follows: it is shown in equation 1, where $x$ and $y$ are the coordinates of a pixel in the image, $k$ is the height of the function and $\sigma_1$ and $\sigma_2$ are the standard deviations of the two gaussian filters that construct the DoG filter.

$$DoG(x,y) = k_1 e^{(x^2+y^2)/2\sigma_1^2} - k_2 e^{(x^2+y^2)/2\sigma_2^2} \qquad (1)$$

The resultant image after applying a DoG filter is globally binarized, using a threshold. In Figure 2, an example of the application of a DoG filter is shown.

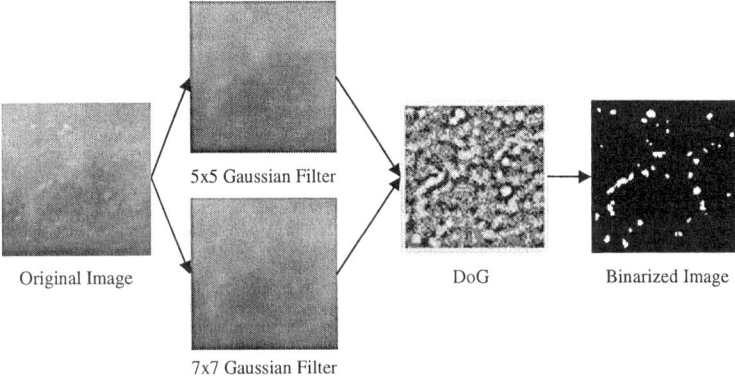

**Fig. 2.** Example of application of a DoG filter (5x5, 7x7)

A region-labeling algorithm allows the identification of each one of the points. Then, a segmentation algorithm extracts small 9x9 windows, containing the region of interest whose centroid corresponds to the point centroid. The size of the windows is adequate for containing the signals, given that at the current resolution, their area is 5x5 pixels in average.

Three selection methods are applied in order to transform a point into a signal. The first one performs selection according to the region area, the second one according to the gray level and the third one according to the gray gradient. The result is a list of signals represented by their centroids. In order to detect the greater possible amount of points, six gaussian filters of sizes 5x5, 7x7, 9x9, 11x11, 13x13 and 15x15 are combined, two at a time, to construct 15 DoG filters that are applied sequentially. Each one of the 15 DoG filters was applied 51 times, varying the binarization threshold in the interval $[0, 5]$ in increments of 0.1. The points obtained by applying each filter are added to the points obtained by the previous one, deleting the repeated points. The same procedure is repeated with the points obtained by the remaining DoG filters. All of these points are passed later to the three selection procedures.

### 2.3 Classification of Signals into Real Microcalcifications

The objective of this stage is to identify if an obtained signal corresponds to an individual microcalcification or not. With this in mind, a set of features are extracted from the signal, related to their contrast and shape. From each signal, 47 features are extracted: seven related to contrast, seven related to background contrast, three related to relative contrast, 20 related to shape, six related to the moments of the contour sequence and the first four Hu invariants.

There is not an a priori criteria to determine what features should be used for classification purposes, so the features pass through two feature selection processes [8]: the first one attempts to delete the features that present high correlation with other features, and the second one uses a derivation of the forward sequential search algorithm, which is a sub-optimal search algorithm.

The algorithm decides what feature must be added depending of the information gain that it provides, finally resulting in a subset of features that minimize the error of the classificator. After the two selection processes, only three features were selected and used for classification (absolute contrast, standard deviation of the gray level and the third moment of contour sequence).

A back-propagation neural network is used to classify each signal and to obtain those signals that correspond to real microcalcifications. The number of inputs for the neural network is three, equal to the number of selected features. According to Kolmogorov's theorem [9], and considering the number of inputs as $n = 6$, three layers were considered. The hidden layer contains $2n + 1 = 7$ neurons, and the output layer has only one neuron. The transfer function of each neuron is the sigmoid hyperbolic tangent function, and the error is measured with the mean square error function.

Even before the detection of microcalcification clusters, the global performance of the neural network at the classification of individual microcalcifications was 85%, confirmed by experts, and related to the application of the DoG filters in sequence. After the individual microcalcifications were detected, they had to be grouped in clusters. Two clustering procedures were proposed for comparison: a) Detection of microcalcification groups that can form clusters. In a single mammogram, one or more clusters can be identified; and b) Consideration of all the microcalcifications in a mammogram as part of a single cluster [1].

## 2.4 Detection of Microcalcification Clusters

During this stage, the microcalcification clusters are identified. The algorithm tries to locate those microcalcification clusters occupying regions where the quantity of microcalcifications per $cm^2$ is higher. The microcalcifications forming a cluster are later labeled. From each cluster, a cluster feature set is extracted.

There is an additional clustering procedure that considers all the microcalcifications identified in the mammogram as members of a unique cluster. From each cluster, 30 features are extracted: six related to the shape of the cluster, six related to the area of microcalcifications and 10 related to the contrast of the microcalcifications. The same two feature selection procedures mentioned earlier are also included in this stage. Only three cluster features were selected for the classification process (minimum diameter, minimum radius and average radius).

## 2.5 Classification of Microcalcification Clusters into Benigns and Malignants

This stage has the objective of classifying each cluster in one of two classes: benign or malignant. This information is provided by the MIAS database. The classificator used in this stage is also a backpropagation neural network with three layers, again considering Kolgomorov's Theorem [9]. The performance measure for this classificator is the success rate.

Finally, the performances provided by both classification processes (detection of microcalcification clusters and single clustering) are compared.

## 3 Results

In order to demonstrate the proposed hypothesis in this work, an experiment was prepared for evaluating two treatments applied to two datasets, and identify if these treatments have some influence in the results or the variations are random.

Two data groups were prepared. From each data group, the following features were extracted: minimum diameter, minimum radius, and average radius. The first data group ($G_{MC}$) corresponds to 40 identified microcalcification clusters, using the density technique and a radius of 100 pixels. Each microcalcification cluster has a diagnosis provided by the MIAS database. The second data group ($G_{SC}$) corresponds to the 22 unique, single clusters obtained by considering all the microcalcifications in a mammogram as members of a single cluster. Each single cluster (mammogram) has a diagnosis provided by the MIAS database.

Table 1 presents the obtained performances (proportion of correctly diagnosed mammograms) after 25 runs of each neural network (treatment). We can observe that both means (0.91 for $G_{MC}$ and 0.89 for $G_{SC}$) indicate very good and similar performances by both treatments, and a statistical test should be applied in order to know if there is a significant difference between them. If the mean of $G_{MC}$ is significantly greater than the mean of $G_{SC}$, it would mean that considering one or more microcalcification clusters in a mammogram leads to a more accurate diagnosis than considering all the microcalcifications as members of a single cluster, thus confirmating the hypothesis of this work. The following hypotheses were formulated:

1. $H_1$: There is a significant difference between the means of $G_{MC}$ and $G_{SC}$.
2. $H_0$: There is no significant difference between the means of $G_{MC}$ and $G_{SC}$.

The F test was used to validate or discard the hypothesis $H_0$, and the probability is 95%. $F_{calculated}$ is 4.82, and $F_{table(0.48)}$ is 3.01. $F_{calculated}$ is greater than $F_{table(0.48)}$, so $H_0$ is rejected and we can conclude that there is a significant difference between the means of $G_{MC}$ and $G_{SC}$, and the hypothesis of this research is confirmed.

**Table 1.** Obtained performances (proportion of correctly diagnosed mammograms) after 25 runs of each neural network (treatment)

| N | $G_{MC}$ | $G_{SC}$ | N | $G_{MC}$ | $G_{SC}$ | N | $G_{MC}$ | $G_{SC}$ |
|---|---|---|---|---|---|---|---|---|
| 1 | 0.98 | 1.00 | 10 | 0.85 | 0.82 | 19 | 0.90 | 0.86 |
| 2 | 0.93 | 0.91 | 11 | 0.95 | 0.91 | 20 | 0.88 | 0.86 |
| 3 | 0.98 | 0.95 | 12 | 0.95 | 0.91 | 21 | 0.95 | 0.91 |
| 4 | 0.90 | 0.86 | 13 | 0.90 | 0.86 | 22 | 0.90 | 0.86 |
| 5 | 0.85 | 0.82 | 14 | 0.88 | 0.82 | 23 | 0.90 | 0.86 |
| 6 | 0.95 | 0.91 | 15 | 0.93 | 0.91 | 24 | 0.95 | 0.95 |
| 7 | 0.93 | 0.91 | 16 | 0.93 | 0.91 | 25 | 0.88 | 0.86 |
| 8 | 0.95 | 0.91 | 17 | 0.90 | 0.86 | mean | 0.91 | 0.89 |
| 9 | 0.83 | 0.82 | 18 | 0.95 | 0.91 | STD | 0.04 | 0.05 |

## 4 Conclusions and Future Work

It is not possible to use a single DoG filter and a unique binarization threshold that maximizes the number of potential microcalcifications detected in a mammogram, because it would identify only some frequency ranges. The use of multiple DoG filters with different relations $\sigma_1/\sigma_2$ and different binarization thresholds solves this problem, because more ranges of frequencies are analyzed. The global performance achieved at the classification of individual microcalcifications was 85%, confirmed by experts, and related to the application of the DoG filters in sequence.

The three features extracted from individual microcalcifications that maximize the rate of true positives and the success rate simultaneously are: absolute contrast, gray standard deviation of a microcalcification, and a moment of contour sequence (asymmetry coeficient). Contrast properties provide more information than shape properties for the classification of signals into microcalcifications. The performance achieved for classifying signals into microcalcifications are 70.8% for true-positives and 85.7% for all the examples. Despite the performance in the classification of individual microcalcifications is not commonly reported in literature, we consider that the performance obtained by the proposed method (sequence of DoG filters) is reasonably good. On the other hand, shape properties provide more information than contrast properties when microcalcification clusters are classified. In this case, the features that provide better results for maximizing the success rate of the classificator are minimum diameter, minimum radius, and average radius, all of them shape properties. The performance achieved at diagnosing a microcalcification cluster is 91%. After analyzing the result of the experiments, the main conclusion of this work is that diagnosing a mammogram based on one or more microcalcification clusters in the image provides better results than always considering all the microcalcifications in the image as a single and unique cluster.

Several subjects were not solved nor implemented for this research, and they are proposed as future work. It could be useful to use other mammography databases, and test how different resolutions could affect system effectiveness. The size of the gaussian filters could be adapted depending on the size of the microcalcifications to be detected and the resolution of images. The correspondence between the spatial frequency of the image and the relation $\sigma_1/\sigma_2$ has to be thoroughly studied. Different features could be extracted from the microcalcifications in the images and tested also. Enhancements on the architecture or training methods for the neural network, or even other approaches for classification could be proposed. Finally, it would be recommendable to study the obtained results using ROC curves, for comparison with other works.

## Acknowledgments

This project was developed at the Instituto Tecnológico y de Estudios Superiores de Monterrey (ITESM), thanks to the support of the National Council of Science and Technology of Mexico (CONACYT).

# References

1. Aghdasi, F., Ward, R. K., Palcic, B.: Classification of mammographic microcalcifications clusters. In Proc. of the CCECE, Vancouver, BC, Canada (2003) 1196–1199
2. Anttinen, I., Pamilo, M., Soiva, M., Roiha, M.: Double reading of mammography screening films: one radiologist or two? Clin. Radiol. **48** (1993) 414–421
3. Chandrasekhar, R., Attikiouzel, Y.: Digitization regime as a cause for variation in algorithm performance across two mammogram databases. Technical Report 99/05, Centre for Intelligent Information Processing Systems, Department of Electrical and Electronic Engineering, The University of Western Australia (1999)
4. Dengler, J., Behrens, S., Desaga, J. F.: Segmentation of microcalcifications in mammograms. IEEE Trans. Med. Imaging **12**(4) (1993) 634–642
5. Ganott, M. A., Harris, K. M., Klaman, H. M., Keeling, T. L.: Analysis of false-negative cancer cases identified with a mammography audit. The Breast Journal **5**(3) (1999) 166–175
6. Gulsrud, T. O.: Analysis of mammographic microcalcifications using a computationally efficient filter bank. Technical Report, Department of Electrical and Computer Engineering, Stavanger University College (2001)
7. Hong, B.-W., Brady, M.: Segmentation of mammograms in topographic approach. In IEE International Conference on Visual Information Engineering, Guildford, UK (2003)
8. Kozlov, A., Koller, D.: Nonuniform dynamic discretization in hybrid networks. In Proceedings of the 13th Annual Conference of Uncertainty in AI (UAI), Providence, Rhode Island (2003) 314–325
9. Kurkova, V.: Kolmogorov's theorem. In: Arbib, M. A. (ed.): The handbook of brain theory and neural networks. MIT Press, Cambridge, Massachusetts (1995) 501–502
10. Li, S., Hara, T., Hatanaka, Y., Fujita, H., Endo, T., Iwase, T.: Performance evaluation of a CAD system for detecting masses on mammograms by using the MIAS database. Medical Imaging and Information Science **18**(3) (2001) 144–153
11. Ochoa, E. M.: Clustered microcalcification detection using optimized difference of gaussians. Master Thesis, Air Force Institute of Technology, Wright-Patterson Air Force Base (1996)
12. Suckling, J., Parker, J., Dance, D., Astley, S., Hutt, I., Boggis, C., Ricketts, I., Stamatakis, E., Cerneaz, N., Kok, S., Taylor, P., Betal, D., Savage, J.: The Mammographic Images Analysis Society digital mammogram database. Exerpta Medica International Congress Series **1069** (1994) 375-378. http://www.wiau.man.ac.uk/services/MIAS/MIASweb.html
13. Thurfjell, E. L., Lernevall, K. A., Taube, A. A. S.: Benefit of independent double reading in a population-based mammography screening program. Radiology **191** (1994) 241–244

# A Narrow-Band Level-Set Method with Dynamic Velocity for Neural Stem Cell Cluster Segmentation

Nezamoddin N. Kachouie and Paul Fieguth

Department of Systems Design Engineering,
University of Waterloo, Waterloo, Canada
nnezamod@engmail.uwaterloo.ca
pfieguth@uwaterloo.ca
http://www.ocho.uwaterloo.ca

**Abstract.** Neural Stem Cells (NSCs) have a remarkable capacity to proliferate and differentiate to other cell types. This ability to differentiate to desirable phenotypes has motivated clinical interests, hence the interest here to segment Neural Stem Cell (NSC) clusters to locate the NSC clusters over time in a sequence of frames, and in turn to perform NSC cluster motion analysis. However the manual segmentation of such data is a tedious task. Thus, due to the increasing amount of cell data being collected, automated cell segmentation methods are highly desired. In this paper a novel level set based segmentation method is proposed to accomplish this segmentation. The method is initialization insensitive, making it an appropriate solution for automated segmentation systems. The proposed segmentation method has been successfully applied to NSC cluster segmentation.

## 1 Introduction

Neural Stem Cells (NSCs) as building blocks of the brain can proliferate and differentiate into all neural phenotypes. Progress in the analysis of NSC functional properties is required for development of clinically applicable procedures for stem cell transplantation and for the treatment of various incurable diseases. NSC can be used to repair damaged neuro-degenerative processes such as Alzheimer and to repair brain injuries such as stroke.

Due to the universal attributes of NSCs, there has been great interest to develop a practical automated approach to measure and extract NSCs properties from microscopic cell images and track individual cells over time. To accomplish this task the NSC clusters must first be segmented. In practice, due to the presence of clutter, corrupted and blurred images, manual cell segmentation is a tedious task. An automated cell segmentation system may eliminate the onerous process of manual cell segmentation, extracting cell features from microscopic images.

Several methods have been developed for region segmentation such as region growing, watershed and thresholding methods [2, 5]. Recently researchers have

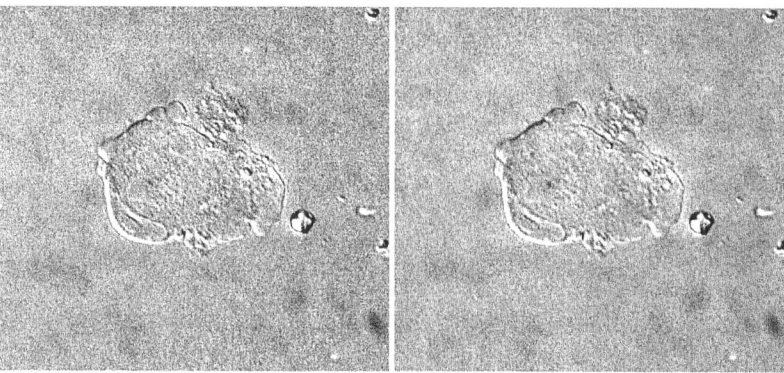

**Fig. 1.** (Left) Noisy NSC cluster image, (Right) Denoised image using BayesShrink Wavelet denoising

been more interested in deformable partitioning methods based on Partial Differential Equations (PDEs), as in deformable region segmentation by employing methods of snakes and level sets [6,7,8] In this paper a PDE-based cell segmentation method is presented to segment NSC Clusters.

## 2 Background: Level Set Method

Level sets were first introduced by Osher, Sethien and Malladi [6,7,9] for shape recovery. This framework supports problems from fluid mechanics to image processing [6], with image processing applications including segmentation, denoising, and restoration. The initial position of an interface is considered as the zero level set of a higher-dimensional surface. Implicitly representing the curve by the zero level set of a function has some major benefits in comparison with the explicit definition and evolution of the interface. These benefits can be summarized as topology independence and numerical stability to handle singularities. Since each level set surface has a uniform spacing and is defined over a discrete grid, all derivatives can be computed using finite difference approximations, hence the problem of discretizing doesn't occur with the level set representation, though it is an important concern with an explicit representation of the interface in other deformable models such as snakes.

Let $\wp(t)$ be a simple time dependent closed curve which is considered as the zero level set of a higher dimensional function $\Phi(x, y, t)$ [6,7,9]:

$$\wp(t) = \{(x, y) | \Phi(x, y, t) = 0\} \quad (1)$$

To initialize the interface, let the level set function $\Phi(x, y, t)$ be consider as a signed distance function:

$$\Phi(x, y, t) = z(x, y) \quad (2)$$

where $z(x, y)$ is the distance from the closest point on the interface $\wp(t)$ to the point $(x, y)$ such that if the point is inside the interface the distance is negative, for the points outside the curve, the distance $z$ is positive and it is equal to zero for all the points lie on the interface:

$$\wp(t) = \{(x,y)|z(x,y) = 0\} \quad (3)$$

Having $\Phi(x,y,t) = 0$, for each point on the interface, the chain rule can be used to derive

$$\Phi_t + \nabla\Phi(x,y,t).(x,y)' = 0 \quad (4)$$

Let $N$ be the outward normal:

$$\hat{N} = \frac{\nabla\Phi}{|\nabla\Phi|} \quad (5)$$

The velocity function $F$ is in the same direction with outward normal direction and we have

$$(x,y)' = F\hat{N} = F\frac{\nabla\Phi}{|\nabla\Phi|} \quad (6)$$

which yields the evolution equation of the interface as

$$\Phi_t + F|\nabla\Phi| = 0 \quad (7)$$

where, $\Phi(x,y,t=0)$ is known. By using the numerical solutions of hyperbolic conservation laws (7) can be approximated. The approximation may be obtained by defining a discrete grid in $x-y$ domain and replacing the temporal and spatial derivatives by finite differences. Assume $(j,k)$ as the grid points and define a uniform spacing between the grid points, $\Phi_{jk}^k$ is the approximate solution for $\Phi(j,k,h\Delta t)$ in time step $h\Delta t$:

$$\frac{\Phi_{jk}^{k+1} - \Phi_{jk}^k}{\Delta t} + F|\nabla_{jk}\Phi_{jk}^k| = 0 \quad (8)$$

Here the forward difference is used to define the finite difference. The curvature of the interface at each point can be calculated using the divergence of the unit normal vector:

$$\aleph = \nabla.\frac{\nabla\Phi}{|\nabla\Phi|} = \left\{\frac{\Phi_{xx}\Phi_y^2 - 2\Phi_x\Phi_y\Phi_{xy} + \Phi_{yy}\Phi_x^2}{(\Phi_x^2 + \Phi_y^2)^{\frac{3}{2}}}\right\} \quad (9)$$

## 3 Materials

NSC samples must be extracted and processed before imaging. NSC sample preparation is two stage process consisting of

1. The extraction of NSCs from the mice, and
2. The processing and culturing of NSCs.

An NSC phase contrast image is depicted in Fig. 1. The cells were imaged using manual focusing through a 5X phase contrast objective using a digital camera (Sony XCD-900) connected to a PC computer by an IEEE 1394 connector. Images were acquired every three minutes. When a cell division was observed, the progeny were imaged at higher magnification using a 40X DIC objective.

## 4 Methods

Employing the level sets for NSC cluster boundary detection, (7) must be solved. To find a solution for (7), considering the Hamilton-Jacobi equation:

$$\Re(q) = F\sqrt{q^2} = f|q| \qquad (10)$$

Thus (7) can be written as

$$\Phi_t + \Re(\nabla\Phi) = 0 \qquad (11)$$

Let $\nabla\Phi = q$; using the hyperbolic conservation law we can conclude that

$$q_t + \nabla\Re(q) = 0 \qquad (12)$$

By discretizing, this equation can be solved as

$$\Phi_{jk}^{k+1} = \Phi_{jk}^k - \Delta t \Re(\nabla\Phi) \qquad (13)$$

where $\nabla\Phi$ is computed using finite differences. Let the velocity function be [6]

$$F = V_g(V_0 - \eta\aleph) \qquad (14)$$

where $\aleph$ and $\eta$ are curvature and curvature coefficients respectively, $V_0$ is a constant velocity coefficient and $V_g$ is gradient based velocity term, we will have

$$\Phi_t + V_g(V_0 - \eta\aleph)|\nabla\Phi| = 0 \qquad (15)$$

As the most important part of the solution, an appropriate velocity function $F$ based on the application (an automatic segmentation system) and nature of phase contrast microscopic NSC images must be designed. The evolving interface must converge toward a cluster boundary and stop in its vicinity. $F$ can be determined based on the specific features of the object such as the object's gray level intensity, its texture, specific shape, etc. Since cell clusters and the background have almost the same gray level intensities, the first and second order statistics of the cluster's intensity are not useful terms to be considered for velocity function definition. To segment the cluster boundary, texture information can be used to define the velocity function. A bank of Gabor filters was considered to derive the velocity function, but to achieve valuable texture features by Gabor filter bank a minimum number of four orientations and four radial frequencies are required that reach the number of extracted textured images to 16 for every single frame. Although this is a very moderate number of filtered images, the computational burden is too expensive for this approach to be considered as an applicable solution for a large number of images over time. Based on the cell cluster image properties, different velocity functions were considered and designed. The following approach uses a dynamic velocity function which satisfies the systems requirement and produces the best results according to the segmentation accuracy and time spent:

$\phi = \phi_{initalize}$
$V_I = |\nabla B(D_\beta[I])|$
$V_{\phi_{nb}} = |\nabla B(D_\beta[I]_{\phi_{nb}})|$
do
{

    $if\ (\mu\{V_{\phi_{nb}}\} > \mu\{V_I\})\ then$
        $\phi^{k+1} = \phi^k + \Delta t\{|\nabla\phi|(\epsilon\aleph + 1)\}$
    $else$
        $\phi^{k+1} = \phi^k + \Delta t\{$
        $|\nabla\phi|(\epsilon\aleph - \exp(-\alpha|\nabla B(D_\beta[I])|))\}$

    $V_{\phi_{nb}^{k+1}} = |\nabla B(D_\beta[I]_{\phi_{nb}^{k+1}})|$
}
$while(\phi^{k+1} \neq \phi^k)$

BayesShrink Wavelet Denoising [10,11] ($D_\beta[I]$) is used to denoise cell image $I$ and $B(D_\beta[I])$ is blurred version of the denoised image which is obtained using a Gaussian filter. Subscript ($nb$) shows that the gradient is calculated on a narrow band close to the zero level set. The mean $\mu$ of the gradient is computed over the image and on the narrow band of the zero level set as well. An important attribute of this velocity function is that it changes based on the location of interface and ensures that the zero level set is attracted toward the boundaries (edge locations) and stops in the vicinity of edges. In the proposed method, in each iteration the mean of gradient over a narrow band close to the zero level set ($\mu\{V_{\phi_{nb}}\}$) is computed. Level set deformations are based on its curvature as long as ($\mu\{V_{\phi_{nb}}\} > \mu\{V_I\}$) is satisfied. As soon as the zero level set contour passes the boundary of the cell cluster, ($\mu\{V_{\phi_{nb}}\} > \mu\{V_I\}$) is not valid anymore and the level set deforms based on gradient speed function ($exp(-\alpha|\nabla B(D_\beta[I])|)$) and its curvature. The deformations will continue until the zero level set stops on the boundary of the NSC cluster.

## 5 Results and Conclusions

Fig. 2 shows the the deformations of the level set toward cell cluster boundary. The circular initialized curve is depicted, followed by the interface after 20, 30, 40, 50 and 60 iterations in which the interface is deforming based on its curvature. After 70 iterations, Fig. 3, where the mean gradient of the narrow band level set is not anymore greater than the mean gradient of the image, the interface begins to shrink toward the cell cluster boundary with a velocity which has two terms. The first is a gradient-based term and the second curvature-based. As depicted in Fig. 4, the interface is converging to the cell cluster boundary in which the major velocity term is the gradient based function.

In this paper a novel level set method was presented for Embryonic Stem Cell cluster segmentation in Phase Contrast microscopy images. The proposed

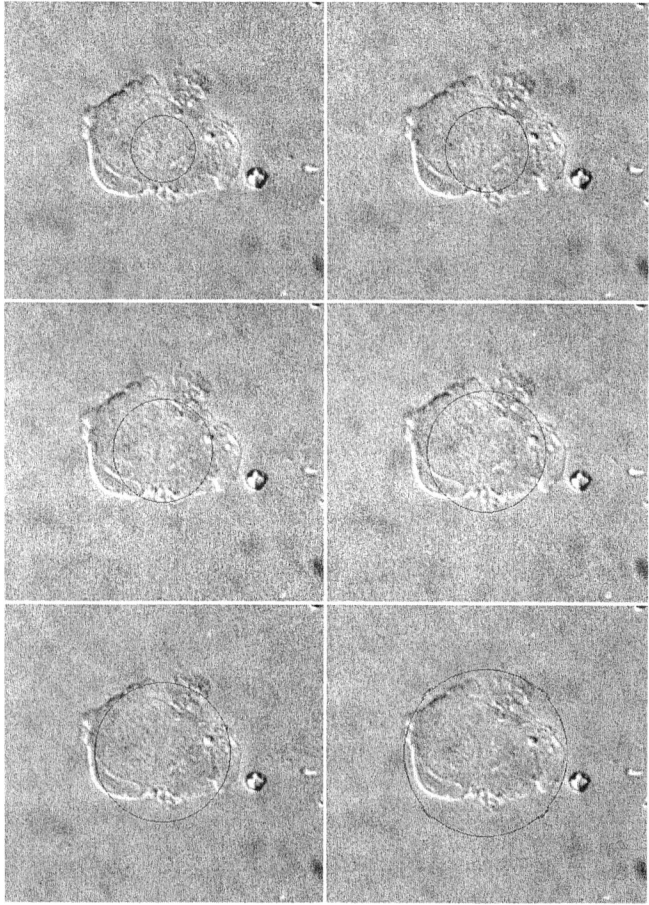

**Fig. 2.** The initialized curve (top left) and curvature based deformations after 20, 30, 40, 50 and 60 iterations

method is initialization insensitive and dynamically deforms toward cell cluster boundary. Hence it is an appropriate solution for automated segmentation systems. The proposed method is applied to NSC cluster image sequences and promising results are produced. Future work is to adapt the model to other cell types in the same category, extended in the form of coupled level sets with adaptive motion functions.

## Acknowledgements

We would like to thank Dr. Eric Jervis and John Ramunas from the Chemical Engineering Department of the University of Waterloo for providing microscopic images for this research and their valuable comments on NSC biology, and Dr. Leo J. Lee for his valuable discussions on cell modelling.

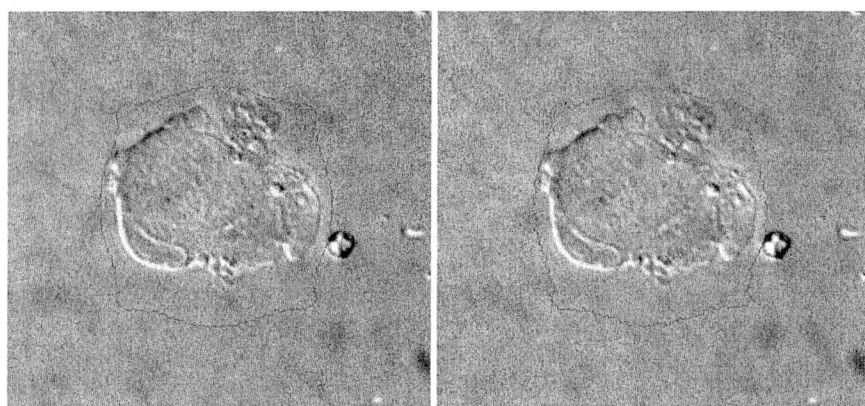

**Fig. 3.** Curvature based velocity function (left column) turns to gradient based velocity function (right column)

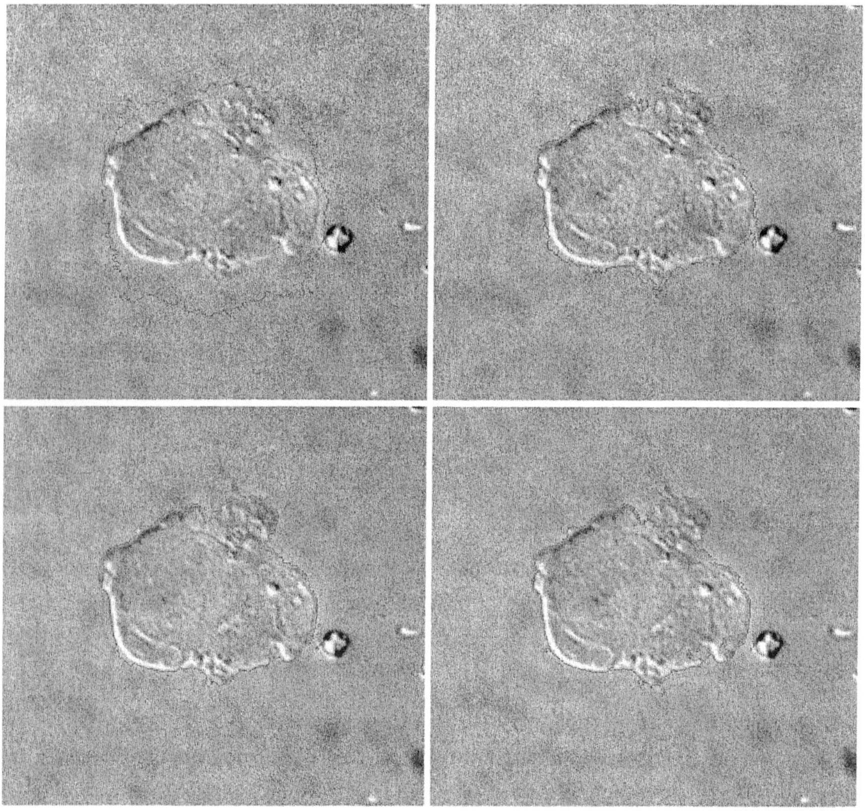

**Fig. 4.** Deforming curve based on gradient based velocity: First row and second row show the interface after 100, 200, 300 and 400 iterations where the cell boundary is completely segmented by the interface

# References

1. G. Nistor, M. Totoiu, N. Haque, M. Carpenter, and H. Keirstead, "Human embryonic stem cells differentiate into oligodendrocytes in high purity and myelinate after spinal cord transplantation," *GLIA* **49**(3), pp. 385–396, 2004.
2. K. Wu, D. Gauthier, and M. Levine, "Live cell image segmentation," *IEEE Transactions on Biomedical Engineering* **42**(1), pp. 1–12, 1995.
3. J. Geusebroek, A. Smeulders, and F. Cornelissen, "Segmentation of cell clusters by nearest neighbour graphs," in *Proceedings of the third annual conference of the Advanced School for Computing and Imaging*, pp. 248–252, 1997.
4. T. Markiewicz, S. Osowski, L. Moszczyski, and R. Satat1, "Myelogenous leukemia cell image preprocessing for feature generation," in *5th International Workshop on Computational Methods in Electrical Engineering*, pp. 70–73, 2003.
5. D. Comaniciu and P. Meer, "Cell image segmentation for diagnostic pathology," *Advanced algorithmic approaches to medical image segmentation: State-of-the-art applications in cardiology, neurology, mammography and pathology* , pp. 541–558, 2001.
6. S. J. Osher and R. P. Fedkiw, *Level Set Methods and Dynamic Implicit Surfaces*, Springer, 2002.
7. J. Sethian, *Level Set Methods and Fast Marching Methods Evolving Interfaces in Computational Geometry, Fluid Mechanics, Computer Vision and Materials Science*, Cambridge University Press, 1999.
8. J. A. Yezzi, S. Kichenassamy, A. Kumar, P. Olver, and A. Tannenbaum, "A geometric snake model for segmentation of medical imagery," *IEEE Tran. on Medical Imaging* **16**(2), pp. 199–209, 1997.
9. R. Malladi, J. A. Sethian, and B. C. Vemuri, "Shape modeling with front propagation: A level set approach," *IEEE Transactions on PAMI* **27**(2), pp. 158–175, 1995.
10. D. L. Donoho and I. M. Johnstone, "Denoising by soft thresholding," *IEEE Tran. on Inf. Theory,* **41**, pp. 613–627, 1997.
11. S. G. Chang, B. Yu, and M. Vetterli, "Adaptive wavelet thresholding for image denoising and compression," *IEEE Trans. on Image Processing,* **9**(9), pp. 1532–1546, 2000.

# Multi-dimensional Color Histograms for Segmentation of Wounds in Images

Marina Kolesnik[*] and Ales Fexa

Fraunhofer Institute for Media Communication, Schloss Birlinghoven,
D-53754 Sankt-Augustin, Germany
marina.kolesnik@imk.fraunhofer.de

**Abstract.** The work investigates the use of multi dimensional histograms for segmentation of images of chronic wounds. We employ a Support Vector Machine (SVM) classifier for automatic extraction of wound region from an image. We show that the SVM classifier can generalize well on the difficult wound segmentation problem using only 3-D dimensional color histograms. We also show that color histograms of higher dimensions provide a better cue for robust separation of classes in the feature space. A key condition for the successful segmentation is an efficient sampling of multi-dimensional histograms. We propose a multi-dimensional histogram sampling technique for generation of input feature vectors for the SVM classifier. We compare the performance of the multi-dimensional histogram sampling with several existing techniques for quantization of 3-D color space. Our experimental results indicate that different sampling techniques used for the generation of input feature vectors may increase the performance of wound segmentation by about 25%.

## 1 Introduction

Chronic skin wounds affect many people and take a long time to heal. Systematic measurement of the physical dimensions of a chronic wound is an excellent way to record the progress of healing. Normal practice of wound care includes weekly check-up of a patient at which an image of wound is acquired. A clinician draws a contour around the wound and assesses its size by comparing contours in subsequent images. This is a time consuming and subjective process. The work here attempts at developing an automatic procedure for *automatic segmentation* of wound region in wound images.

Even for restricted instances of wound image segmentation, the use of simple features is not sufficient for reliable differentiation of image pixels onto different classes. An efficient separation of classes can be achieved if features are derived from various histograms counted in a local neighborhood of image pixels [1]. Further improvement is obtained if multiple local histograms are linked together thus resulting into a single multi-dimensional histogram. Feature space generated by a sampling of such multi-dimensional histogram provides most efficient local description of image pixels.

---

[*] Corresponding author.

Several methods for the histogram sampling have been suggested in the literature. Chapelle et al. [2] downsize the original color range with 255 bins down to 16 bins. This reduces the size of any 3-dimensional color histogram to $16^3$=4096. Experiments with a smaller number of bins have produced worse image classification, whereas a larger number of bins have not been tested on the ground of limited computational resources. Pietikäinen et al. [3] apply a more advanced approach by dividing each color dimension into $N$ bins with an equal number of entrees. They confirm that best classification accuracy is obtained using the sampling into 16x16x16 bins. This kind of sampling was found to be efficient for wound segmentation [4]. However, both methods sampled each color dimension independently, which cannot be fully justified because it does not take into account the inherent dependency of different color dimensions in natural objects.

In this work we employ 3-D color histograms to generate a set of features, which are then used as input to the Support Vector Machine Classifier (SVM) [5], [6]. We show that a single histogram of higher dimensions provides a better description of pixels of one class than a collection of several 1-D histograms. Also, the role of different sampling techniques cannot be underestimated. Our experiments indicate that different sampling techniques make a profound impact on the quality of wound segmentation.

The paper is organized in six sections. We start by introducing the multi-dimensional *Histogram Sampling* (Section 2). We proceed by describing SVM[light] implementation classifier and generation of input feature vectors. (Section 3). Next, we look at performance of the SVM classifier by conducting experiments when using a single 3-D color histogram versus three 1-D histograms, and different sampling techniques (Section 4). Discussion of segmentation results concludes the paper (Section 5).

## 2 Histogram Sampling

We distinguish between the 3-D color space and a higher dimensional feature space, which consists of feature vectors attributed to image pixels. The *Histogram Sampling* as introduced [3] uses a normalized 1-D histogram $M$ of an image, or an averaged histogram of a set of images, and samples it into a number of $L$ bins, each one constituting an equal fraction of pixels *1/L*:

$$\sum_{k=l-1}^{l} M(k) = \frac{1}{L}$$

for all bins *l=1,...,L*. Note that such a sampling automatically gives a denser bin distribution for those histogram parts with larger number of elements thus providing an optimal sampling of histogram entries into bins.

Let $H$ be a local histogram $H$ computed in a neighborhood of pixel *(i,j)*. Next, $H$ is sampled into the same set of bins, $L$. A number of histogram elements falling into each bin defines one feature per bin. Thus, elements falling into first *L-1* bins (the last bin is excluded as dependent on the previous ones) define *L-1* features, which, when taken together, form a point in the *(L-1)*-dimensional feature space. The point coordinates define a feature vector associated with the pixel *(i,j)*. Fig. 1a shows an example of the *Histogram Sampling*.

An extension of *Histogram Sampling* for the case of multi dimensional histogram is built upon recursive sampling. Consider 3-D color space in which $M$ being a 3-D image histogram. Let $M_I$ be a selected image histogram of one color dimension. Next, $M_I$ is being sampled into $L$ equal sized bins. Elements $E_l$ of $M_I$, falling into each bin, $l$, form a set of entries for the computation of 1-D histogram of next color dimension. Let histogram $M_{II}$ be generated. Next, $M_{II}$ is sampled into $L$ equal sized bins, too. The process of sampling is repeated recursively for all bins and three dimensions of the color space. It generates a total number of $L^3$ bins which gives rise to a set of $L^3$-$1$ features. These features form a feature vector attributed to a central pixel of window used for the computation of local histogram. The multi-dimensional *Histogram Sampling* can be easily extended to a general case of $N$-dimensional histogram in which case a set of $L^N$-$1$ features would be generated. Fig. 1b illustrates the *Histogram Sampling* in case of two dimensions.

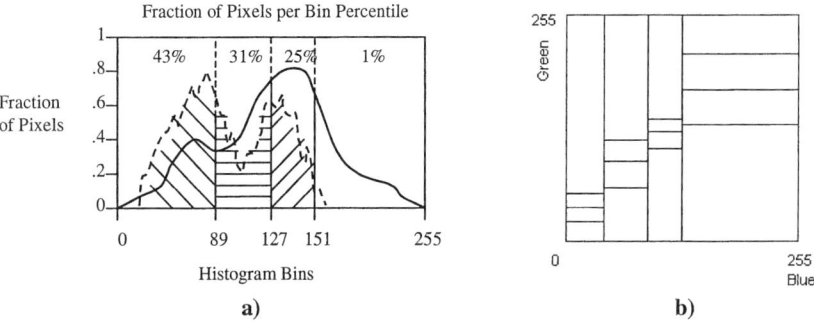

**Fig. 1. a)** Histogram Sampling into four bins. The image histogram (solid line) is sampled into four equal sized bins. The local histogram (dashed line) is sampled into same four bins. The Histogram Sampling defines three features indicating a fraction of entries falling into three first bins: 43%; 31% and 25% in our example. **b)** Schematic illustration of the multi-dimensional Histogram Sampling in case of two dimensions. Blue and Green channels are used for the generation of 15 color-based features.

## 3 SVM-Based Wound Segmentation in the Color Feature Space

SVM is an approach for supervised classification of data into two classes [6]. In this work we use SVM$^{light}$ - implementation of the SVM classifier available for research application at http://svmlight.joachims.org/ [7]. SVM classification is performed in two stages. The aim of the first, *training stage,* is to find an *optimal separating hyperplane* which divides the set of test examples into two classes. Note that each test example has to bear a label of either class. During the second, *classification stage,* each input point is attributed a label according to the side this point appears with respect to the hyperplane. A more detailed account of SVM's is out of the scope of this paper and here we will only discuss those aspects of the Training and Classification Stage, which are specific for wound segmentation.

Input to the SVM$^{light}$ is a set of feature vectors attributed to selected image pixels. We use manually segmented images of wounds to compose a *training set* of feature vectors attributed to pixels of wound and non-wound class. Our experiments suggest that a balanced contribution of feature vectors from two classes improves the quality of classification. We therefore select an approximately equal number of evenly distributed pixels from across the wound and non-wound regions for the generation of input for the training stage.

SVM$^{light}$ offers three optional kernels such as linear, polynomial and radial one. In our experiments the radial kernel performed best followed by the polynomial and linear one. These results are consistent with earlier experiments on image classification [8].

The choice of feature space is crucial for the performance of the SVM classifier. In a "good" feature space, input elements originating from either wound or skin class, would form two volume clusters, which are widely separated from each other and easy to classify. In spite of the fact, that the color histogram technique is a very simple method, it has shown good results for image indexing and segmentation [1]. Below we investigate the impact of two factors on the performance of the SVM classifier: 1) the use of three 1-D color histograms versus a single 3-D color histogram for the generation of input feature vectors and 2) different quantization techniques employed in the histogram sampling.

### 3.1 Computation of Feature Vectors

A training set of input feature vectors for the case of $N$ wound images and 3-D color histogram is obtained as follows. For every image, about 2000 evenly distributed pixels are selected from the wound region and approximately the same number from outside of the wound region. This gives rise to a set of about 4000 pixels for each image. Pixels from image background are counted as belonging to "not a wound class". Pixels from a boundary region around the wound of about 12 pixels wide are not selected so as to exclude a confusing mixed wound/skin region. A 3-D color histogram is computed for every image using the selected pixels. A *3-D average histogram* is generated by summing up all the 3-D color histograms and dividing the sum by the number of images, $N$. This *average histogram* is sampled into 64 bins using the multi-dimensional *Histogram Sampling*.

The ordering of color dimensions in the RGB space used for the recursive sampling depends on the level of differentiation between wound and skin provided by these dimensions: color dimensions with higher differentiation are sampled first. This resulted into the blue/green/ red-ordering of dimensions for the recursive sampling.

Computation of feature vectors for SVM segmentation utilizes the bins resulted from the *Histogram Sampling* of the *average histogram*. Computation of feature vectors for each pixel of an image to be segmented takes the following steps: 1) Generation of 3-D *local histogram* in a local window of about 75x75 pixels; 2) Sampling the *local histogram* into 64 bins resulted from the sampling of the *average histogram*; 3) Composing a 63-element feature vector out of entries of the *local histogram* falling into the first 63 bins.

## 4 Experiments and Results

We present several experimental trials each one testing a specific way of computation of input feature vectors. Six images of different wound types were used for the training of the SVM in each experimental trial. Each of these images was then segmented using the trained SVM. As required by the training, the images were manually segmented onto a wound and "non wound" region.

The quality of segmentation in each trial was measured by counting an average rate of erroneously classified pixels as follows. Let $W_m$ be a number of wound pixels and let $S_m$ be a number of "non-wound" pixels in a manually classified image. Similarly, let $W_c$ and $S_c$ be a number of pixels classified as wound and "non-wound" in a computer-segmented image, respectively. Error rate for misclassified wound pixels is given by the normalized intersection of the manual wound segment and the computer-generated non-wound segment:

$$E_{wound} = (W_m \cap S_c)/W_m$$

where $\cap$ denotes the intersection of two sets. Similarly, the error rate for misclassified "non-wound" pixels is given by the normalized intersection of the manually defined non-wound segment and the computer-generated wound segment:

$$E_{skin} = (S_m \cap W_c)/S_m$$

Full classification error is then given by the sum of the above error rates:

$$Error = (E_{wound} + E_{skin})/2$$

### 4.1 Single Multi-dimensional Histogram Versus Multiple 1-D Histograms

A series of experiments tested the quality of segmentation when sampling 1) three 1-D histograms and 2) a single 3-D color histogram. In the first experimental trial each 1-D histogram was sampled into 22 bins generating 63 input features per pixel. In the second trial each dimension of the 3-D color histogram was sampled into 4 bins giving rise to 63 features. The generated features were firstly used for the training of the SVM classifier on six wound images and, after that, for the segmentation of each one of these six images, independently. All other segmentation parameters used by the SVM classifier were kept identical in all experiments.

Segmentation results in Table 1 display a convincing advantage in the performance of the SVM classifier for the case of 3-D color histogram over a corresponding collection of three 1-D histograms. We extent this conclusion to a more general statement: a better performance of multi-dimensional histogram can be explained by the fact that the sampling in the 3-D color space indeed exploits the inherent dependency of color dimensions usually shown by complex natural objects. This is especially true for the human skin. Light remitted from skin is a complete spectrum. Consequently, the 3-D color histogram is a gross approximation of the true remitted light. The composition of the spectrum for the skin depends on the mixture of scatters and absorbers in the skin, each one of these affecting each primary dimension of the spectrum. This results into correlation of R, G and B parts of the RGB histogram, which is exploited by the multi-dimensional Histogram Sampling.

**Table 1.** The error percentile, *Error,* of erroneously classified pixels resulted from the segmentation of six images. Input feature vectors are generated by the independent sampling of 1-D histograms (column 3 x 1-D), and the sampling of 3-D color histograms (column 3-D).

| Image | 3 x 1-D | 3-D |
|---|---|---|
| 1 | 0.63 | 0.36 |
| 2 | 1.74 | 1.46 |
| 3 | 1.25 | 1.38 |
| 4 | 2.41 | 1.93 |
| 5 | 1.86 | 1.56 |
| 6 | 0.61 | 0.47 |
| Average | 1.42 | 1.19 |

### 4.2 Comparison of Different Sampling Techniques

In order to perform an independent testing of the multi-dimensional *Histogram Sampling* technique, we have conducted a series of experiments in which other quantization methods were involved. Five sampling techniques have been tested:

1. *Independent Sampling* (IS) performs independent sampling of each color histogram into $N$ bins with an equal number of histogram entrees [4].
2. *Learning Vector Quantization* (LVQ) performs the quantization of unlabeled data vectors into a smaller set of codebook vectors. Each data vector is then represented by its nearest codebook vector. An initial set of random codebook vectors is trained so as to minimize the error of misclassification of data vectors. We use an optimized LVQ1 training algorithm [10] for the quantization of 3-D histogram.
3. *Vector Quantizer Design* (LBG-VQ) [9] is a lossy data compression method based on the principle of block coding. The reason of applying the LBG-VQ for the sampling of 3-D histogram is similar to the motivation of any image compression algorithm, namely, the need to downsize an original dataset by extracting most important information while leaving out the rest. We use the LBG-VQ algorithm for the coding of wound images. Code vectors characterizing image pixels are used for generation of input features: each image pixel is attributed a feature vector that gives a fraction of occurrences of coding vectors in a local window. 63 coding vectors used by the LVG-VQ compression give rise to a same number of 63 features composing the elements of a feature vector.
4. *Random Density Estimation* (RDE) employs the *Voronoi Diagram* which, in our case, is a partition of color space into Voronoi cells, each of which consists of elements closer to one particular object than to any others. The advantage of RDE is that the shape of Voronoi cells varies with the density of elements of the 3-D color histogram. Because most of the histogram elements are concentrated within an ellipsoid of revolution around the axis R=G=B, one would expect that flexibly shaped Voronoi cells could "better" partition the area within the ellipsoid than the square-shaped bins of the *Histogram Sampling*. The following iterative procedure was used: 1) Select $N$ *(N=250)* random color vectors out of the elements of 3-D color histogram; 2) Construct the Voronoi Diagram using the selected color vectors; 3) Compute a

number of histogram elements falling into each Voronoi cell; 4) Delete a color vector with the smallest number of histogram elements contained in its Voronoi cell; 5) Update the Voronoi Diagram down to $N-1$ cells; Step 4 and Step 5 were repeated until a required number of cells $N$ (in our case $N=64$) is obtained.

5. *Histogram Sampling (HS)* is the multi-dimensional *Histogram Sampling* technique (Section 3) applied to the 3-D color histogram.

**Table 2.** Average segmentation error for the different sampling techniques. The average error is computed over six wound images.

| IS | LVQ | LBQ-VQ | RDE | HS |
|---|---|---|---|---|
| 1.42 | 7.86 | 1.35 | 1.12 | 1.19 |

Table 2 shows how average error of segmentation of six wound images is affected by the use of the above sampling techniques. As evidenced by the error values, the RDE sampling provides the lowest rate of misclassified pixels. This can be explained by the fact that the Histogram Sampling based on the Voronoi Diagram provides an optimal partitioning of elements of the 3-D color histogram.

### 4.3 Examples of Wound Segmentation

The capability of SVM classifier to segment a wound was tested with numerous images. Here we show the result of segmentation of three test images from the sequence of six ones used in the previous experiments. Input feature vectors were obtained by the sampling of 3-D color histograms. Examples of segmentation in Fig. 2 show that the SVM-classifier produces a fairly reliable segmentation of wound tissue despite of large variations in brightness of skin and quite a different appearance of wounds.

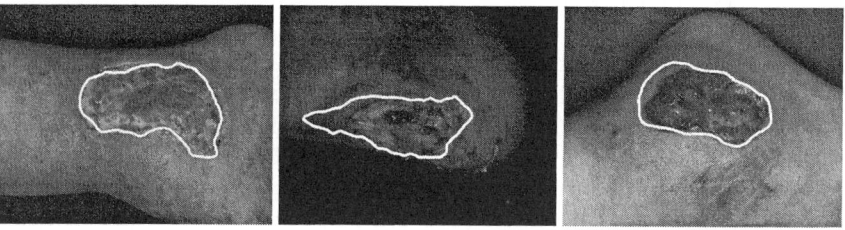

**Fig. 2.** Three examples of wound segmentation. 63 input features were computed locally in the window of 95 pixels. The SVM classifier employed the polynomial kernel. Corresponding error rates for misclassified pixels are given in Table 1, images 1, 4 and 6, column 3-D.

## 5 Conclusion and Future Work

The *Histogram Sampling* technique generates the efficient set of feature vectors, which, when inputted into the SVM-classifier, enable the reliable segmentation of wound region in images. The generalized multi-dimensional *Histogram Sampling* of 3-D color histograms further improves the discrimination of feature vectors.

Processing time needed for the SVM training depends linearly on the number of input feature vectors (i.e. of the number of training images), but also, on their "quality" in terms of how well these can be separated into two classes. For about 2000 feature vectors from the wound class and the same amount from outside the wound region, the observed training time is of the order of 2 minutes (Pentium, 1000 MHz). If, however, the training feature vectors are not widely separated in the feature space, the convergence of searching for the support vector may become problematic.

Our experimental results indicate that the sampling of 3-D color histogram generates input features with a better discrimination than those ones obtained by the independent sampling of 1-D histograms: the quality of wound segmentation in our experiments was improved by as much as 20%-30%. It is therefore always advantageous to employ the single 3-D color histogram for the generation of input feature vectors used by the SVM for wound segmentation. Experiments with different quantization techniques have lead to an unexpected result. Although the Learning Vector Quantization technique provide a "better" partitioning of multi-dimensional feature space in a sense that cell distribution is related to a density of space elements, the quality of wound segmentation is significantly worse. Also surprisingly, the rate of misclassified pixels resulted from the Voronoi Diagram sampling is comparable with the error rate when the multi-dimensional *Histogram Sampling* is used.

More words are to be said with regard to 3-D color histograms. Despite of their simplicity, 3-D color histograms provide an efficient cue for the description of different image objects, which are in our case, of course, wounds. Color histograms are invariant to translation and rotation and change only slowly under change of angle of view and scale. As a result, *Histogram Sampling* generates image features, which are fairly invariant to small variations in brightness and scale. The multi-dimensional Histogram Sampling is therefore provides best cumulative measure characterizing image objects locally. Note that the 3-D color histogram can be easily extended to higher dimensions by adding other discreet distributions related, for instance, to texture. Applying the *Histogram Sampling* to the extended multi-dimensional histogram would certainly generate highly efficient local description of image pixels.

A less optimistic conclusion of this work is this one: however robust and good the SVM segmentation is, it cannot produce a wound contour which is as fine as the manual one drawn by a clinician. It seems that there should be an additional and independent mechanism that complements region segmentation on a final stage of contour generation. The aim of our future research will be aimed at the fusion of two processing methods -the SVM segmentation and wound contour detection.

# References

1. Swain, M.J., Ballard, D.H.: Color Indexing. International Journal of Computer Vision, 7:1 (1991) 11-32.
2. Chapelle, O., Haffner, P., and Vapnik, V.: SVMs for histogram-based image classification ", IEEE Trans. on Neural Networks, 9 (1999)
3. Pietikäinen, O., Nieminen, S., Marszalec, E., and Ojala T: Accurate Color Discrimination with Classification based on Feature Distributions. *Proc. of the Inter. Conference on Pattern Recognition (ICPR'96)*, (1996) 833-838.

4. Kolesnik, M., Fexa, A.: Segmentation of wounds in the combined color-texture feature space. *Proc. of SPIE Medical Imaging 2004: Image Processing,* 16-19 Feb. 2004, San Diego, CA, 549-556.
5. Vapnik, V.: The Nature of Statistical Learning Theory. Springer, New York (1995)
6. Vapnik, V.: Statistical Learning Theory. John Wiley, New York (1998)
7. Joachims, T.: Making large-Scale SVM Learning Practical. In Advances in Kernel Methods - Support Vector Learning, B. Schölkopf and C. Burges and A. Smola (eds.), MIT Press, (1999)
8. Schölkopf, B., Sung, K., Burges, C., Girosi, F., Niogi, P., Poggio, T., Vapnik, V.: Comparing support vector machines with gaussian kernels to radial basis function classifiers. A.I. Memo. No. 1599, MIT (1996)
9. Linde, Y., Buzo, A., Gray, R., M.: An Algorithm for Vector Quantizer Design, *IEEE Transaction on Communications*, pp. 702-710, January (1980)
10. Kohonen, T., Kangas, J., Laaksonen, J., Torkola, K.: LVQ_PAK: A program package for the correct application of Learning Vector Quantization algorithms, *Proc. of the Inter. Conference on Neural Networks,* Baltimore, (1992) 1725-1730.

# Robust Face Recognition from Images with Varying Pose

Jae-Young Choi[1], Murlikrishna Viswanathan[2], Taeg-Keun Whangbo[2],
Young-Gyu Yang[2], and Nak-Bin Kim[2]

[1] Dept. of Computer Science, University of California,
Los Angeles
`jaeyoung@ cs.ucla.edu`
[2] Dept. of Computer Science, Kyungwon University
`{murli, tkwhangbo, ykyang, nbkim}@kyungwon.ac.kr`

**Abstract.** Recognition of faces under varied poses has been a challenging area of research due to the complex dispersion of poses in feature space when compared to that of frontal faces. This paper presents a novel and robust pose-invariant face recognition method in order to improvise over existing face recognition techniques. First, we apply the TSL color model for detecting facial region and estimate the direction of face using facial features. The estimated pose vector is decomposed into X-Y-Z axes. Second, the input face is mapped by a deformable template using these vectors and the 3D *CANDIDE* face model. Finally, the mapped face is transformed to the frontal face which appropriates for face recognition by the estimated pose vector. Through the experiments, we come to validate the application of face detection model and the method for estimating facial poses. Moreover, the tests show that recognition rate is greatly boosted through the normalization of the poses.

## 1 Introduction

Face Recognition including fingerprint, iris, and voice recognition is a significant aspect of identity verification systems due to the fact that these methods are far more accurate and effective than other techniques. Thus research in this area, especially face recognition, has gained prominence with results being spontaneously incorporated into application systems. In this paper we focus on the issues in face recognition. Since most studies in this field have employed full frontal facial photos the rate of recognition has been lower than that of the fingerprint and iris based techniques in the real-world due to the effects of illumination and variation of facial poses [1]. Additionally, the rate of recognition for a face varies depending on the pose.

In order to overcome the insufficiency of the existing facial recognition methods, this paper proposes a pose-invariant face recognition system. Assessing and analyzing the ever-changing facial poses (external feature) we transform the face into a normalized form that can also be recognized by the existing face recognition systems. This approach boosts the accuracy of facial recognition and substantially reduces the FAR (False Acceptance Rate) and FRR (False Rejection Rate).

## 2 Face Detection and Pose Estimation Using Geometrical Relationship

Tint-Saturation-Luminance (TSL) color model has been known to be efficient in extracting facial region on image since its T-S space is classified densely and independent from illumination [2]. Sometimes, however, T-S color model detects spurious regions when the background has a similarity with the facial color. In this case, we find the final facial region using labeling.

Irregular illumination sometimes causes different facial colors, and these are classified as a different region [3, 4]. In this paper following process is applied for reducing illumination effects: first, analyze effects of brightness according to angle of face, second, compensate value of intensity for effected region, and lastly, detect facial color.

Facial poses are then calculated using the relative position of facial features: two eyes, and mouth. Generally, geometrical and template-based techniques use edge detection methods in pre-processing while detecting facial features since most facial features are horizontal shapes. However, facial features may not be horizontal shapes when input faces are angularly dispersed. Facial features in this paper are detected using their geometric relationship such as the line connecting two ends of the mouth being parallel to the line connecting the centers of two eyes and the length of two lines are almost same, etc.

Provided the facial features (two eyes, mouth) are detected correctly, connecting the center of each feature makes a triangle. With the exact frontal pose, the center of the triangle coincides with the center of the facial region. As the pose varies, there is the offset between two centers, a direction vector. As Figure (1) indicates, the direction of vector $v$ gives indication of facial pose; the length of vector is shift offset from center of facial region. We can estimate the values of yaw and tilt after analyzing this vector. $A(x_1, y_1)$ is the gravity center of the facial region and $B(x_1, y_1)$ is the midpoint of the triangle made by facial features. It is possible to decompose $v = \overrightarrow{AB}$ into $v_{yaw}$ and $v_{tilt}$ using Eqn. (1)-(3). The formulas (1)-(3) are represented in degrees. In addition, $half_{face\_width}$ and $half_{face\_height}$ imply a radius of major and minor axis on the momentum of facial region, respectively.

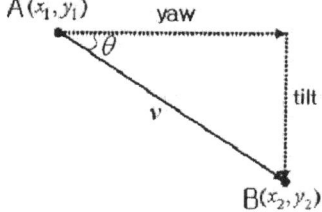

**Fig. 1.** Analyzing vector for estimation of angle

$$\angle v_{yaw} = \frac{v \cdot \cos\theta}{half_{face\_width}} \cdot 90 \quad , where \quad \theta = \arctan\left(\frac{|y_2 - y_1|}{|x_2 - x_1|}\right) \tag{1}$$

$$\angle v_{tilt} = \frac{v \cdot \sin \theta}{half_{face\_height}} \cdot 90 \qquad (2)$$

$$\angle roll_{face} = \arctan\left(\frac{|y_{R_{eye}} - y_{L_{eye}}|}{|x_{R_{eye}} - x_{L_{eye}}|}\right) \times 180 / \pi \qquad (3)$$

## 3 Synthesizing Deformable Face and Normalizing Poses

This paper uses the *CANDIDE*-3 3D wire frame model for input face mapping [6]. The process of pose normalization finds additional features including facial features for mapping the 3D wire frame model with the input image. The mapped face is normalized by transformation of texture using inverse value of the estimated pose vector for frontal face.

### 3.1 Mapping Input Image to Facial Model Using Extracted Features

This paper uses template matching for finding facial features since it is known to be more accurate than other geometrical techniques and although it is a slower technique the speed of searching can be increased if positions of eye, nose, and mouth are roughly acquainted [7]. However, a problem with template matching is that the mask has to be similar with the object. And in our case the need to match a proper mask to image in real time becomes difficult as the input data has varying poses thus requiring many templates. Therefore, this study suggests a deformable template which transforms one template mask to special template by estimated geometrical value in advance (as in Fig. 3).

Mapping implies overlapping between input image and facial model using extracted features. In this case, we use additional features of face in order to map more accurately as in Fig 2.

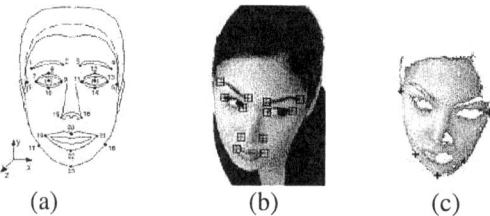

(a)        (b)        (c)

**Fig. 2.** Facial features for mapping. (a) Total features, (b) Features by deformable template, (c) Features by facial region we detected previous

Three dimensions decompose rotation $\Re = R(r_x, r_y, r_z)$ into rotation of x-axis, y-axis, and z-axis. We use the homogeneous form in rotation and translation. Moreover, scale vectors use equal transformation matrix to apply different scales to x, y, and z-axis respectively. So we can deform a model through calculating parameters

$P = [r_x, r_y, r_z, s, t_x, t_y, \sigma]^T$ using Eqn. (4)-(5) where $\overline{g}$ is original model, $\sigma$ is parameter for shape, $S$ is shape, $t$ is translation matrix, $R$ is rotation, and $s$ is scale.

$$g = sR(\overline{g} + \sigma S) + t \quad (4)$$

$$\min \left\| g - f_{features} \right\|^2 \quad (5)$$

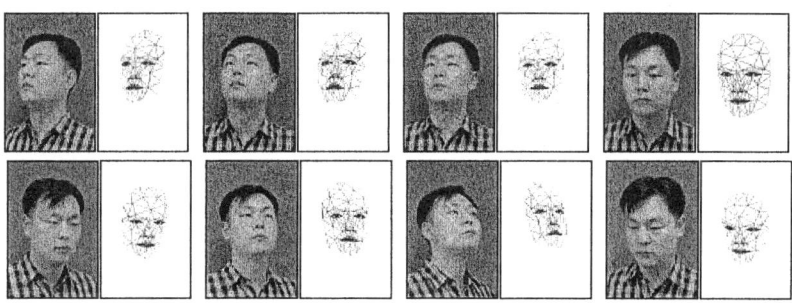

**Fig. 3.** Deformation of facial model using estimated angle

### 3.2 Transforming Input Face to Frontal Face

Facial template consists of a phase model and texture. Therefore, total transformation of the facial template synthesizes a new model by transforming the coordinates of points and the textures of the triangle which comprises of these points. Generally, the pixel coordinates are always integers. But, in our approach, sometimes the coordinates of transformed texture can be non-integral. In this case we use a reverse direction warping which interpolate the points using adjacent four points before translation [8].

The example of this process is presented in Fig. 4. The original template is deformed by estimated pose vector and mapped on to the input face. The texture is then transformed to normal value as shown in Fig. 4(f). The pose of the eyes is not rectified as it is not essential.

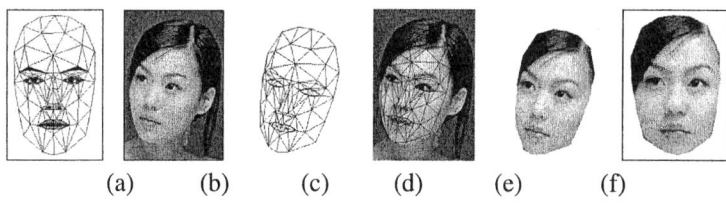

(a)    (b)    (c)    (d)    (e)    (f)

**Fig. 4.** Face mapping and pose normalization. (a) Original template, (b) Input image, (c) Deformation of template, (d) Mapping frame, (e) Mapping texture, (f) Pose normalization by transformation.

## 4 Empirical Analysis

Fig. 6 outlines the experimental framework and process. The experimentation consists of two processes; Ex1 is face recognition without compensation while Ex2 is with compensating pose. Fig. 5 presents a sampling of input faces from a total of 45 used in the empirical analysis.

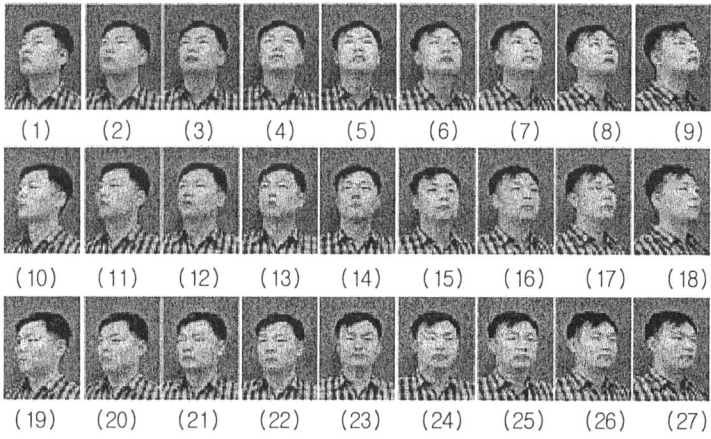

**Fig. 5.** A variety of poses

Principle Component Analysis (PCA) is used for comparing the two processes Ex1 and Ex2, and we analyze the Euclidean distance for rate of recognition [9,10]. For PCA, the face of ten people is used as learning data as shown in Fig. 7 [11].

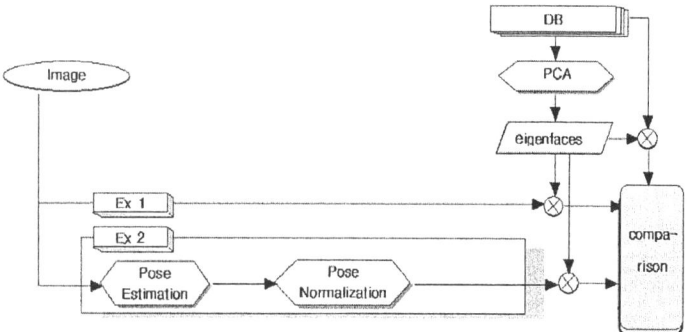

**Fig. 6.** Flowchart of face recognition experiment

This paper measures Euclidean distance error $\varepsilon_k$ for each component between the normalized and DB faces using Eqn. (6) where $f_k$ represents the learning faces and $f_i$, the input faces. In these experiments the hair is also eliminated for an accurate measurement of face like in Fig. 8.

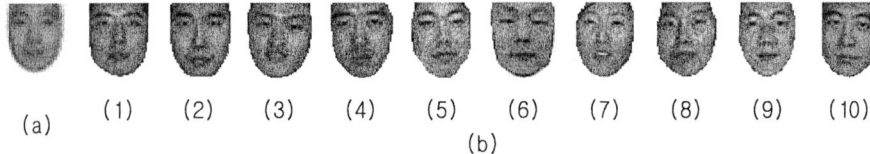

**Fig. 7.** Face examples for PCA; (a) Mean face, (b) Learning faces

**Fig. 8.** Examples of extracting facial region for PCA

$$\varepsilon_k = \|y_i - y_k\|$$
$$y_k = \Omega^T * f_k, \qquad y_i = \Omega^T * f_i, \tag{6}$$

### 4.1 Results and Analysis

Fig. 9 shows estimated angle of input images from Fig. 5 using our proposed method. There is no bar where it fails calculation of angle. The reason of failure implies that it is difficult to extract the opposite eye if the angle of yaw is large.

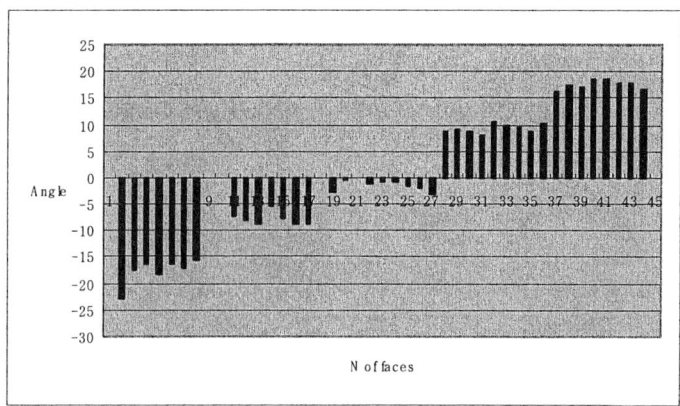

**Fig. 9.** Angle of face through estimated poses (tilt)

Almost of facial models are transformed in the same direction. However, as we can observe from Fig. 3, the error is large when the pose is upward facing. This is due to the ambiguity between the jaw and forehead region. The estimated pose value is used to normalize face as well as map input face to facial model such as Fig. 10.

In case that the angle of face is large, the mirroring process is needed due to the lack of facial information the region that is located on the other side of camera view [11]. For the mirroring process the visible half of face detected by the camera is duplicated and put it on the other side lacking information after transformation (see Fig. 10).

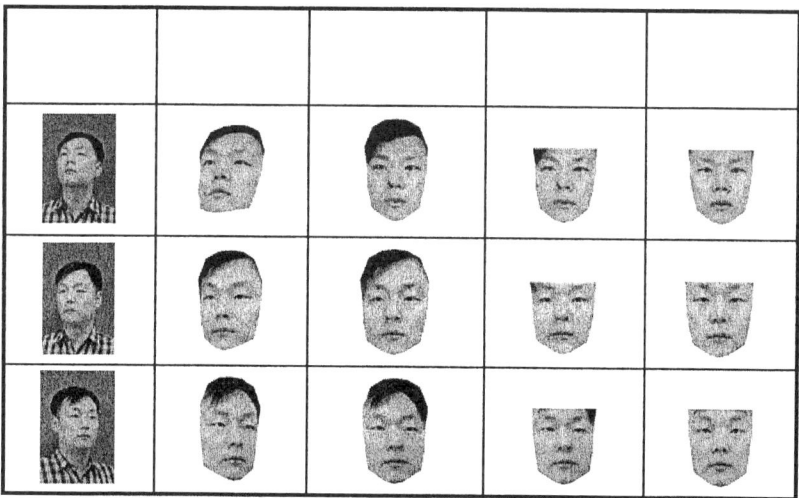

**Fig. 10.** Examples of facial pose normalization

We test input faces shown in Fig. 5 using the two processes Ex1 and Ex2 as depicted in Fig. 6. The result of test is shown in Fig. 11. The graph represents the distance values of PCA coefficients between input images before and after normalization. The lower the distance value, the higher is accuracy of face recognition. Naturally, when the angle of face is close to the center the distance error measured is small and the more a face points downward the larger the distance error.

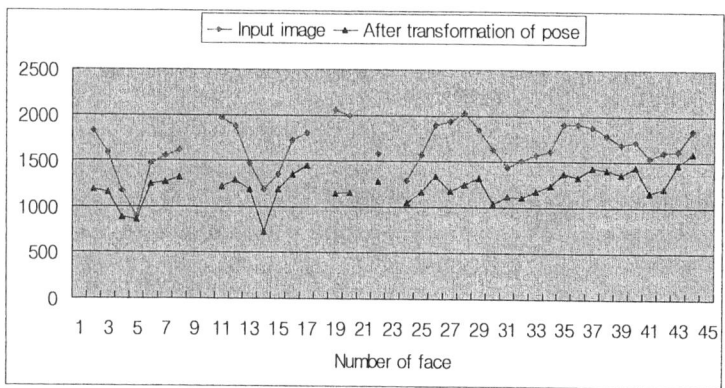

**Fig. 11.** Difference of principle vector from normalized face

Fig. 12 presents the result of recognition where the x-axis and y-axis of graph imply the number of faces in Fig. 5 and Fig. 7, respectively. No. 6 on the y-axis is a face that we want to detect. After normalization, more input faces on x-axis are recognized as a No. 6 on the y-axis.

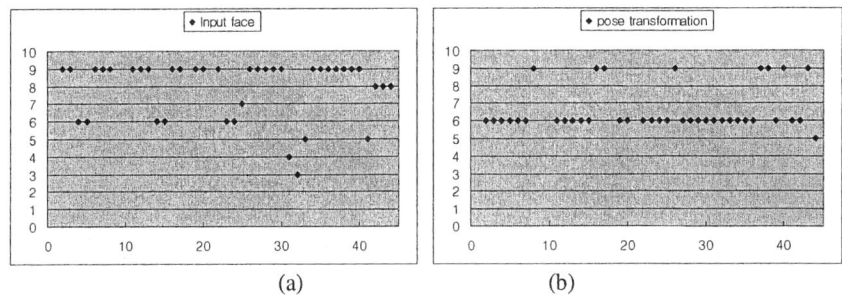

**Fig. 12.** Results of recognition; (a) Before normalization, (b) After normalization

To judge the accuracy of face recognition we use minimum Euclidean distance between input face in Fig.5 and learning face in Fig. 7. Although face recognition generally uses a threshold value for reducing FAR(false acceptance rate), in our case a face satisfying a minimum distance is considered as similar for reducing FRR(false rejection rate) because it just confirms the recognition. Fig. 13 shows a proportion of results from Fig.12. Face No. 6 is our target face and its rate of recognition can be seen to increase from 13% to 76%.

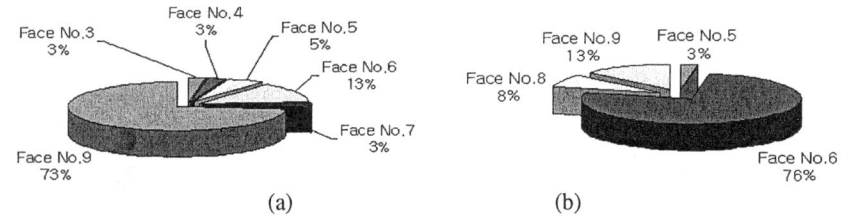

**Fig. 13.** Improvements in recognition rate - (a) Before normalization, (b) After normalization

## 5 Conclusion

In general, varying facial poses create problems with acquisition, analysis, and recognition. Thus most studies showing plausible performance are restricted to frontal face and normalized face without rotation. In order to overcome this insufficiency of existing face recognition methods this paper proposes a novel pose-invariant face recognition system by using a normalized algorithm in preprocessing.

Numerous tests have been experimented categorically to evaluate proposed algorithm and many facial images which have various poses, and used to experiment on normalization. Through the experiments, we come to validate the rationale of our face detection model and method for estimating facial poses. Moreover, the tests show that recognition rate is greatly boosted through the normalization of poses by 76%. The accuracy is improved six-fold than prior to pose transformation. In the future we would like to solve problems associated with distortion by large angles and design a facial model that it is optimized to warp the facial features.

## References

[1] G. Yongsheng, "Face recognition using line edge map," IEEE Trans. on Pattern Analysis and Machine Intelligence, vol. 24, no. 6, pp. 764-779, 2002.
[2] J. C. Terrillon and S. Akamatsu, "Comparative performance of different chrominance spaces for color segmentation and detection of human faces in complex scene images," Proc. of the 4th IEEE Int'l Conf. on Automatic Face and Gesture Recognition, pp. 54-60, 2000.
[3] H. Yao and W. Gao, "Face locating and tracking method based on chroma transform in color images," Proc. Int'l Conf. on Signal Processing, vol. 2, pp. 1367-1371, 2000.
[4] K. K. Sung and T. Poggio, "Example based learning for view-based human face detection," IEEE Trans. on Pattern Recognition and Machine Intelligence, vol. 20, pp. 39-51, 1998.
[5] J. Ahlberg, "Model-based Coding : Extraction, Coding, and Evaluation of Face Model Parameters," Dissertations, Dept. of Electrical Engineering, Linköping University, Sweden, 2002.
[6] R. Brunelli and T. Poggio, "Face Recognition: Features versus Templates," IEEE Trans. on Pattern Analysis and Machine Intelligence, vol. 15, no 10, pp. 1042-1052, 1993.
[7] D. J. Beymer, "Pose-Invariant Face Recognition Using Real and Virtual Views," Ph.D. Thesis, Massachusetts Institute of Technology, Cambridge, MA, 1995.
[8] M. Turk and A. Pentland, "Eigenfaces for face recognition," Journal of Cognitive Neuroscience, vol. 3, no. 1, pp. 71-86, 1991.
[9] A. M. Martinez and A. C. Kak, "PCA versus LDA," IEEE Trans. on Pattern Analysis and Machine Intelligence, vol. 23, no. 2, pp. 228-233, 2001.
[10] V. I. Belhumeur, J. P. Hespanha, and D. J. Kriegman, "Eigenfaces vs. fisherfaces : Recognition using class specific linear projection," IEEE Trans. on Pattern Analysis and Machine Intelligence, vol. 19, no. 7, pp. 711-720, 1997.
[11] S. H. Hwang, J. Y. Choi, N. B. Kim, "A Study on Face Reconstruction using Coefficients Estimation of Eigen-Face," Proc. of Korean Society for Internet Information, vol. 4, no. 1, pp. 505-509, 2003.

# Feature Extraction Used for Face Localization Based on Skin Color

Juan José de Dios[1] and Narciso García[2]

[1] E. U. Politécnica, Universidad de Castilla-La Mancha,
Cuenca, Spain
`JuanJose.deDios@uclm.es`
[2] E.T.S. Ing. Telecomunicación, Universidad Politécnica de Madrid,
Madrid, Spain
`narciso@gti.ssr.upm.es`

**Abstract.** This paper presents a morphological- and color-based method for face localization in color images. Basically, it uses a skin-color segmentation technique in a novel color space, YCg'Cr', and the application of the shape information and the location of the facial features to the definition of a face model. First, a color-based segmentation technique detects the skin regions inside the image, and then, a combination of morphological operators and algorithms is used for completing the segmentation masks. At last, the feature extraction lets define a model based on the best-fit ellipse determined by the position of the eyes and mouth inside the image. Finally, the detection mask based on this ellipse is used for locating the face in the image under test.

## 1 Introduction

Recently, research activities have been increased in the image analysis and processing areas, due to new applications where object segmentation and recognition in color images is required. The achieved results in the face detection process depend on the complexity of the image and its application [1]. Several face segmentation techniques which work with a normalized face have been proposed in the last years, but some of them require that its location is previously known [2].

The main advantage of using face detection schemes based on color information is that it can be segmented independently on its size and position within the image. Considering that people with different skin color have major differences in their intensity than in its chrominance, and that human skin color is concentrated in a small region of the color space, color can been considered as a distinguishing and effective parameter for face detection [3-4].

Nevertheless, the classification into skin and non-skin regions will fail if faces are partially detected or there are skin-like objects in the background of the image, so faces are not correctly detected [3]. Color-based segmentation can be combined with other techniques in order to improve the segmentation results, so that the undetected areas may be added to the detected face [4].

Different color spaces, such as RGB, HSV or YCbCr, and pixel-based skin detection methods have been proposed for the individual classification of the pixels in an image as skin or non-skin, independently on its neighbors [4-6]. Color spaces with separated luminance and chrominance components, like the last two, seem to be more appropriate for face detection [5]. Based on YCbCr, two new color spaces, YCgCr and YCg'Cr', a transformed space of the first one were specifically defined for face detection [7].

A new technique for face localization is presented in this paper. It is based on the combination of a chrominance segmentation scheme in the YCg'Cr' color space and the use of the facial shape information and the extraction of the face features for determining its position.

First, a pixel-based color segmentation algorithm is used, then pixels are grouped in order to determine skin regions which are completed by means of morphological techniques, and, at last, the detection of the face inside the image is performed using the position of the eyes and the mouth. Finally, the application of an elliptical model based on the extracted features is used for the face localization.

## 2 YCg'Cr' Color Space

The YCgCr and YCg'Cr' color spaces were specifically proposed for analysis applications, mainly for face segmentation [7]. YCgCr is based on YCbCr, but it differs on the use of the Cg color component instead of Cb. While the color spaces used in television systems (YUV, YCbCr) use the biggest color differences: (R-Y) and (B-Y), as they are transmission oriented, the YCgCr color space uses the smallest color difference (G-Y) instead of (B-Y).

Besides, skin detection can be performed ignoring the luminance coordinate, as skin tone is more controlled by the chrominance than luminance components [6]. Then, the color analysis is simplified by reducing the space dimensionality, defining a color model in the chrominance plane. Skin color is concentrated in a small region of the chrominance plane, so the simplest color model used for classifying each pixel as skin or non-skin is based on the definition of a boundary box [5]. Therefore, a skin-like pixel is determined when both of its color components are within the individual ranges defined by the maximum and minimum thresholds of each coordinate of the chrominance plane.

Face regions are extracted from a set of training images acquired by different sources (digital cameras, scanned photographs, software edited images, etc.) under different lighting conditions, and are used for defining the maximum and minimum thresholds that constitute the boundary box.

The transformed color space, YCg'Cr', is based on the skin color distribution in the Cg-Cr plane, and basically consists of a 30° clockwise rotation of the Cg and Cr axes, so the color pixel segmentation will be performed in the new chrominance plane, Cg'-Cr', represented in Figure 1.

The vertical axis, Cr', is defined in the direction of the line that connects the Red and Cyan colors in the Cg-Cr plane, where most of the skin pixels were distributed. (see Figure 1). The other axis, Cg', is perpendicular to Cr'. The center of coordinates needs to be recalculated to (128,128), and the new axes range is [0, 255]. So, the transformed color space, YCg'Cr', is defined by the following equations [7]:

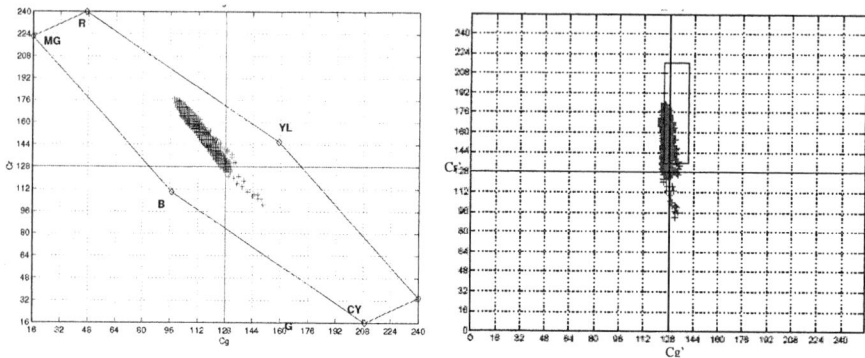

**Fig. 1.** Skin color pixels in the Cg-Cr (left) and Cg'-Cr' (right) planes

$$Cg' = Cg * \cos 30° + Cr * \sin 30° - 48 . \quad (1)$$

$$Cr' = - Cg * \sin 30° + Cr * \cos 30° + 80 . \quad (2)$$

The maximum and minimum values of Cg' (Cgmin', Cgmax') and Cr' (Crmin', Crmax') that constitute the boundary box were computed for each face region manually extracted during the training process for every individual image. They were characterized as Gaussian distributions, obtaining their statistics: mean, minimum, maximum, etc. for each Cg' and Cr' threshold.

The skin color representation of an individual image in the YCg'Cr' space, concentrated in a small area of the chrominance plane and distributed along the vertical axis is shown in Figure 1.

## 3 Color-Based Segmentation

Different decision regions defined by the thresholds for Cg' and Cr' calculated using their statistics: mean, minimum, maximum, centroids, modified-mean (Cg'- ½(Cg'mean-Cg'min) , Cr' + ½(Cr'max -Cr'mean)), minimum for Cg' and maximum for Cr', etc. were tested in order to find the set that provides the best segmentation results with the training images.

Two types of decision regions: maximum ([125,140] for Cg' and [136,217] for Cr') and modified-mean thresholds ([119,131] and [128,199] for Cg' and Cr') provided the best results. The skin region is better detected using the first set of thresholds, while the segmented region is bigger in the second case, as the eyes and the hair are detected too [7].

For face detection purposes, it has been considered that the segmentation results achieved by means of the maximum set of thresholds are better, as only the skin-like pixels are detected.

Similar tests were performed using a set of portrait-like images (AR face database [8]) with homogeneous background and different lighting conditions. Human faces with different types of facial expressions, such as neutral or smiling, objects occluding the faces (like a pair of sunglasses or a scarf), and also several combinations of them have been tested.

**Fig. 2.** Detection masks for Cg' (left ), Cr' (center) and both of them (right), using maximum thresholds

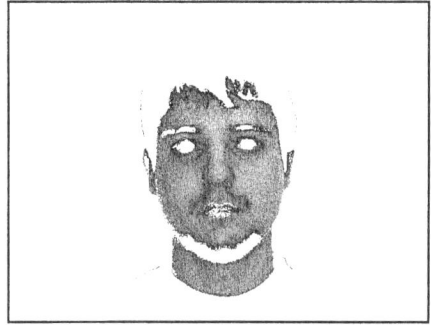

**Fig. 3.** Color-based segmented face using maximum thresholds in the YCg'Cr' color space

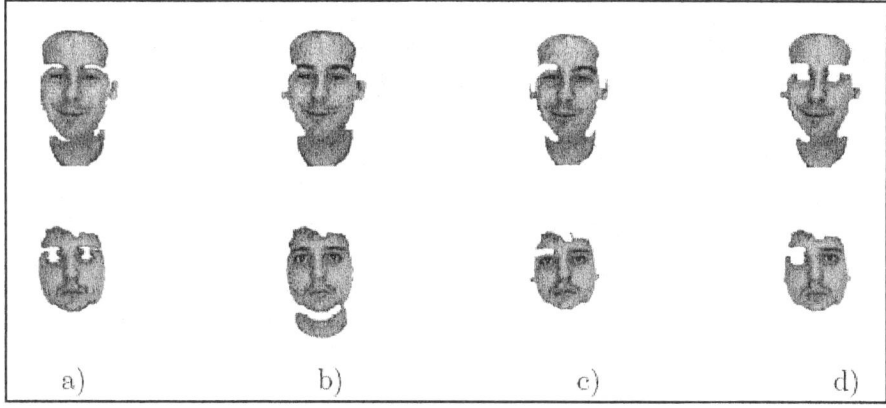

**Fig. 4.** Segmented faces after using morphological operators: a) opening, b) opening + closing, c) erosion + closing, and d) erosion + closing + opening

The detection masks obtained by applying the maximum thresholds to one of these images for each of the color components and both of them are represented in Figure 2. The face region has been correctly detected, as the eyes, the hair and also the clothes have been eliminated during the color segmentation, as it can be seen on the detected face represented in Figure 3, obtained by the application of the final chrominance mask depicted in the last image in Figure 2.

It will only be necessary to separate the neck from the face region in the image, as it has been considered part of the skin area.

## 4 Morphological-Based Segmentation

The segmentation process presented in the previous section should be continued in order to detect the whole faces by completing the color-based segmentation masks with the use of other techniques, such as morphological ones.

For this purpose, two different morphological algorithms were implemented: first, a connected components method for selecting the bigger size region in order to consider it as a face candidate, and, second, a hole-filling technique for completing the segmentation mask, adding the undetected regions inside it, such as the eyes, the eyebrows, and the mouth.

Those techniques which provided the best segmented faces after applying individual or combinations of morphological operators will be presented in this section. First, the segmentation results achieved by the only application of the opening morphological operator are represented in Figure 4a) after using the two algorithms for selecting the face region and hole-filling.

Second, the combination of several morphological operators is considered: opening + closing, erosion + closing, and erosion + closing + opening. They are also represented in Figure 4, after applying the two morphological algorithms. The results achieved in the four cases are different, as either both or none of the eyes and also the neck can be considered as part of the face region, depending on the set of operators used for the segmentation process.

As can be seen in the examples depicted in Figure 4, not only the face region is segmented at this phase of the process, and it is necessary to complete the face region and eliminate some elements that are not part of it, like the neck. In some of the images under test, other head components that have been detected as face candidates, such as the hair, should also be separated from the face candidate, using the feature characteristics and an elliptical model of the face, as it will be presented in the next section.

## 5 Face Detection

This new phase of the detection process will basically consist of the implementation of a face model based on the location of the eyes and mouth features that will allow the definition of the best-fit ellipse adapted to the face contour, in order to separate the face region from the neck and hair areas.

This procedure will be described in this section. First, the detection of the eyes and mouth position inside the face region segmented in the previous section will be presented.

### 5.1 Feature Extraction

In the feature extraction step, based on the holes detection inside the face candidate region, the segmentation mask before applying the region-filling algorithm will be used, as only the bigger area should be selected. After considering all the morphological operators described in the previous section, the results achieved using the mask obtained in the case of the application of the erosion + closing operators to most of the images under test were better for this purpose.

The localization of the position of the eyes and the mouth was obtained applying the connected components algorithm to the inverse mask of the region considered as face candidate. To avoid the incorrect consideration as eyes of either the eyebrows or the nose, due to its similarirty, a previous dilation operation is applied for reducing the size of the holes inside the face. According to the size of the image, a circular structuring element of radius 7 was used in this morphological operation.

Before applying this algorithm to the feature extraction process, the image is split up into three: the upper left, the upper right and the bottom areas for detecting the left and right eyes and the mouth, respectively. Then, the detected regions are classified according to its size, considering as eyes and mouth areas those which have a minimum size of 250 and 145 pixels, respectively. The achieved results can be refined by including in the classification step other criteria such as the symmetric position of the eyes inside the face.

The so-located areas corresponding to these features (left and right eyes and mouth) are represented in Figure 5 for the faces depicted in Figure 4c).

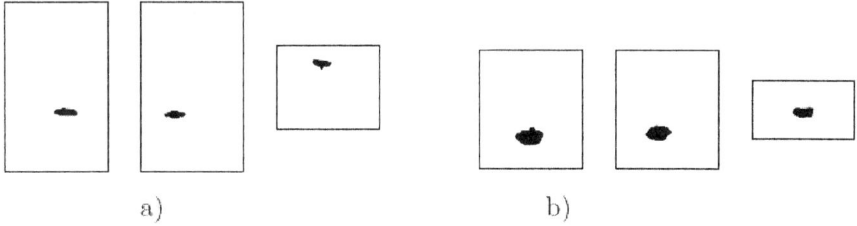

**Fig. 5.** Left, right eye and mouth located areas for the men in Figure 4c)

### 5.2 Best-Fit Ellipse Model

Based on the feature regions extracted in the previous section, a simple model can be defined for representing the face by means of an ellipse fitted at the face contour, as it is represented in Figure 6a).

This model has been defined for characterizing the best-fit ellipse inside the limiting rectangle, considering the center of coordinates in the middle point of the line that connects both eyes. The four parameters that will define this ellipse are: a) the upper left corner point (O), b) its minor axis, c) its major axis, and d) its orientation, defined by the angle formed between the X axis and the horizontal line.

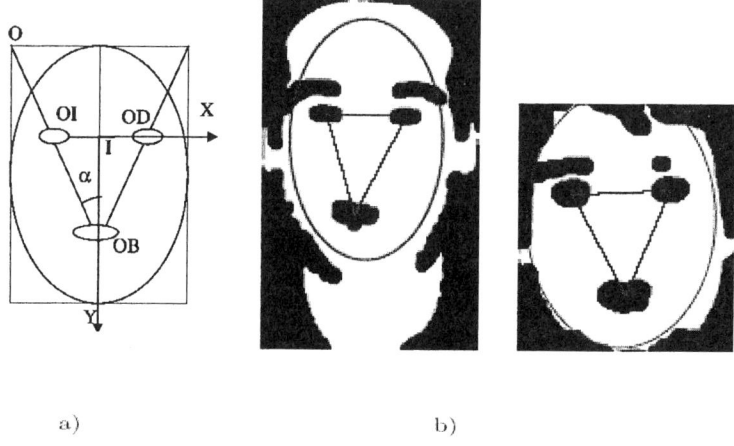

a)  b)

**Fig. 6.** a) Face model and b) best-fit ellipses located for the men in Figure 4c)

For determining the best-fit ellipse based on the features previously extracted the following distances should be calculated: first, between both eyes, d(OI-OD); second, between the left eye and the mouth, d(OI-OB); and third, between the eyes line and the mouth, d(I-OB). The parameters that define the rectangle: origin (O), width (w) and height (h) are calculated according to the following equations:

$$d(O-OB) = \frac{d(OI-OB)}{K} \; ; \; w = \frac{d(OI-OD)}{K_m} \; ; \; h = \frac{d(I-OB)}{K_M} . \qquad (3)$$

where the K factors are experimentally obtained (K=0.5, $K_m$=0.52 and $K_M$=0.4).

The best-fit ellipses thus obtained inside the detection masks are represented in Figure 6b). Based on the location of the eyes and mouth, a new segmentation method can be implemented using this ellipse.

**Fig. 7.** Detected faces applying the proposed method to the men images in Figure 4c)

The final segmentation mask is obtained by representing the best-fit ellipse in the previous mask, taking into account its orientation, which is the angle formed by the eyes and the horizontal axis. The detected faces using this final mask based on the best-fit ellipse are represented in Figure 7.

## 6 Conclusions

A new method for face detection has been proposed in this paper. It is based on a combined technique using the skin-color segmentation in the YCg'Cr' color space and also the facial features position for defining a face model based in the best-fit ellipse determined by them.

The final segmentation mask for the face localization is obtained considering the contour and orientation of this ellipse. Our future work will consist of improving the face localization method and the parameters used for the feature extraction and the face model presented in this paper in order to refine the segmentation results.

## References

1. M. Abdel-Mottaleb, A. Elgammal, "Face detection in complex environments from color images", Proc. of the IEEE Int. Conf. on Image Proc. ICIP'99, pp 622-626, Kobe, Oct. 1999.
2. L. Torres, J.Y. Reutter, L. Lorente, "The importance of the color information in face recognition", Proc. of the IEEE Int. Conf. on Image Proc. ICIP'99, pp 627-631, Kobe, Oct. 1999.
3. M.H. Yang, N. Ahuja, "Detecting Human Faces in Color Images", Proceedings of the 1998 IEEE International Conf. on Image Processing ICIP'98, pp. 127-139, Chicago, Oct. 1998.
4. M-H. Yang, D. J. Kriegman, N. Ahuja, "Detecting Faces in Images: A Survey", IEEE Transactions on Pattern Analysis and Machine Intelligence, 24, pp. 34-58, January 2002.
5. J-C. Terrillon, M.N. Shirazi, H. Fukamachi, S. Akamatsu, "Comparative performance of different skin chrominance models and chrominance spaces for the automatic detection of human faces in color images", Proc. of the 4th IEEE Int. Conf. on Aut. Face and Gest. Recogn. FG'00, pp. 54-63, March 2000.
6. V. Vezhnevets, V. Sazonov, A. Andreeva, "A Survey on Pixel-Based Skin Color Detection Techniques", Graphicon-2003, Moscow, Russia, Sept. 2003.
7. J.J. de Dios, N. García, "Fast Face Segmentation In Component Color Space", Proc. of the IEEE Int. Conf. on Image Processing ICIP'04, Singapore, Oct. 2004.
8. A.M. Martinez and R. Benavente, "The AR face database", CVC Tech. Report #24, 1998.

# Rotation-Invariant Facial Feature Detection Using Gabor Wavelet and Entropy

Ehsan Fazl Ersi and John S. Zelek

Department of System Design Engineering,
University of Waterloo, Waterloo, Ontario, Canada N2L 3G1
{efazlers, jzelek}@uwaterloo.ca

**Abstract.** A novel technique for facial feature detection in images of frontal faces is presented. We use a set of Gabor wavelet coefficients in different orientations and frequencies to analyze and describe facial features. However, due to the lack of sufficient local structures for describing facial features, Gabor wavelets can not perfectly capture the wide range of possible variations in the appearance of facial features, and thus can give many false positive (and sometimes false negative) responses. We show that the performance of such a feature detector can be significantly improved by using the local entropy of features. Complex regions in a face image, such as the eye, exhibit unpredictable local intensity and hence high entropy. Our method is robust against image rotation, varying brightness, varying contrast and a certain amount of scaling.

## 1 Introduction

Detection of facial features (eyes, nose, mouth corners and etc.) plays an important role in many facial image interpretation tasks such as face verification, face tracking, face expression recognition and 3D face modeling. Generally, there are two types of information available for facial feature detection [4]: (i) local texture around a given feature, for example, the pixel values in a small region around an eye, and (ii) the geometric configuration of a given set of facial features, e.g. both eyes, nose, mouth and etc. Many different methods for modeling these types of information have been proposed. In [4] a method for facial feature detection was proposed which utilizes the successful Viola and Jones face detection method [5], combined with the statistical shape models of Dryden and Mardia [6]. In [10], the authors discussed a face localization and feature detection system which employs morphological filtering and blob coloring to generate hypothesis about eye locations followed by the use of deformable templates and the Hough transform to confirm theses hypotheses. In [11], Yang et al. proposed a hierarchical three level knowledge-based system for locating human faces and facial features in relatively complex backgrounds. Chang et al. [12] proposed a color segmentation and thresholding algorithm to pinpoint the eyes, nostrils and mouth in color head images. In [7] an efficient method was proposed for eye detection that used iris geometries to determine the region candidates which possibly contain the eye, and then the symmetry, for selecting the couple of eyes. In addition, active contour models were employed in [13] to capture the eyebrows, nostrils and face.

Our method uses the Gabor wavelet for describing and analyzing facial features. The Gabor wavelet has been widely used in image processing, pattern recognition and computer vision and there have been some successes in using Gabor filters for facial feature extraction [1, 2, 3]. Wiskott et al. [1] and Liao et al. [2] used a Gabor Jet, which is a set of convolution coefficients for kernels of different orientations and frequencies at one image pixel [1], to represent a facial feature. In both approaches a graph-like data structure called a Face Bunch Graph (FBG), is derived from training samples to describe facial features and to cover the wide range of possible variations in the appearance of facial features. The average of FBG is used in order to find the approximate position of each facial feature and then FBG is used without averaging to refine the approximate position. In a similar but faster and simpler approach, Feris et. al. [3] used a two stage hierarchy of Gabor wavelet networks. The first stage localizes the whole face and the second stage searches for individual features. The approximate shape of the face, predicted from the first stage, is used to guide the feature detection.

Although the overall performances of all these three approaches are satisfactory, there are two limitations: (i) if the actual position of a facial feature is not close enough to the approximated determined position, it will be located at a wrong point; and (ii) detecting a particular facial feature necessitates the presence of a whole face image and other facial features; which may decrease the efficiency of the system and increase the processing time. A natural extension of these approaches for overcoming the above limitations is to ignore the use of a global models (e.g. FBG in [1, 2]) and use only the description of local structures (in our case, Gabor Jets) for finding and localizing each facial feature. Although this extension can solve the above two problems, it results in a more serious problem: due to the lack of sufficient local structures for describing facial features, Gabor Jets can not perfectly cover the wide range of possible variations in the appearance of facial features, and thus can give many false positive (and sometimes false negative) responses.

Our method combines the Gabor Jet with the entropy of the local image intensities to increase both the reliability and overall accuracy of the feature detection system. The entropy of local attributes measures the predictability of a region with respect to an assumed model of simplicity [9]. In the case of entropy for pixel intensities, the model of simplicity corresponds to a piecewise constant region. For example the PDF (Probability Distribution Function) of intensities (an intensity histogram in our system) is peaked in the cheek region, which indicates that most of these pixels are highly predictable and hence entropy is low. However, the PDF in the eye region is flatter, which indicates that pixel values are highly unpredictable and this corresponds to high entropy. Another reason for applying entropy is its robustness against image rotation, if it is computed in circular image regions (instead of rectangular regions). Further, to make the Gabor Jets invariant to image rotation, we assign an orientation to each pixel and then compute the Gabor Jet at that point within a circular window and relative to the assigned orientation. In the following sections, we describe the approach in more details, and demonstrate the results of application to the ORL face dataset (14).

## 2 Facial Feature Extraction

In our system, each image pixel is described by a set of complex-valued Gabor wavelet coefficients (Gabor Jet), and the entropy of local image properties. However, before describing each image pixel, we assign an orientation to the pixel and then perform all processing tasks within a circular window and relative to that orientation, in order to achieve invariance to image rotation. This section provides a detailed explanation of the different steps of the method.

### 2.1 Orientation Assignment

In most of the orientation assignment approaches reported in the literature, three general methods are used for computing the principal orientation [16]: (i) gradient orientation at a center pixel location, (ii) a peak in the orientation histogram of the local region, and (iii) orientation of the eigenvector of the second moment matrix of the local region. Following the satisfactory results of the orientation invariant descriptors of Lowe [17] (which is based on (ii)), we use a similar approach, with some slight changes, for assigning a local orientation.

For each image pixel, $I(x,y)$, the gradient magnitude, $m(x,y)$, and orientation, $\theta(x,y)$, is precomputed using pixel differences:

$$m(x,y) = \sqrt{(I(x+1,y) - I(x-1,y))^2 + (I(x,y+1) - I(x,y-1))^2} \qquad (1)$$

$$\theta(x,y) = \tan^{-1}((I(x,y+1) - I(x,y-1))/(I(x+1,y) - I(x-1,y))) \qquad (2)$$

At each particular image pixel, an orientation histogram is formed from the gradient orientations of that pixel and its neighbors within a circular window of radius $s$ (in our experiments $s = 11$). The value of $s$ was chosen particular for the feature sizes in our test set, a more general solution would be to search scale space as is done in [17]. The orientation histogram has 36 bins covering the 360 degree range of orientations. Each sample, $\theta(x,y)$, added to the histogram is weighted by $m(x,y) \times G(x,y,\sigma)$, where $G(x,y,\sigma)$ is Gaussian function at $(x,y)$ with $\sigma = 1.5 \times s$. The highest peak in the orientation histogram, as well as any other local peak which is within 80% of the highest peak [17], correspond to dominant directions of the local gradients. In our experiments nearly 90% of pixels are assigned single orientation.

### 2.2 Gabor Wavelets

Gabor wavelets are biologically motivated convolution kernels in the shape of plane waves, restricted by a Gaussian envelope function [1]. The general form for a 2D Gabor wavelet is presented in equation 3.

$$\Psi(\vec{r}) = \frac{k^2}{\sigma^2} \exp\left(-\frac{k^2 r^2}{2\sigma^2}\right) \times \left[\exp(i\vec{k}\vec{r}) - \exp\left(-\frac{\sigma^2}{2}\right)\right] \qquad (3)$$

In the above equation, $\sigma$ is a parameter to control the scale of the Gaussian (in our experiments $\sigma = \pi$) and $\vec{k}$ is a 2D wave vector which its magnitude and angle determine respectively the scale and the orientation of the Gabor kernel.

A set of convolution coefficients for kernels of varying orientation and frequencies at one image pixel, form a Gabor Jet. A Gabor Jet describes a small patch of grey values in an image around a given pixel. We chose 16 Gabor kernels in 8 orientations (as suggested in [1]), varying in increments of $\pi/8$ from 0 to $7\pi/8$, and in 2 scales (the third and fifth scales suggested in [1]) in which $|\vec{k}| = \pi/4$ and $|\vec{k}| = \pi/8$. Since the phase of the Gabor coefficients varies so quickly with location, it could cause severe problems for matching [1] and therefore we ignore it.

## 2.3 Local Entropy

Facial features are unpredictable complex regions, located in nearly uniform distributed areas such as the skin (for eyes, nose, etc.) and the beard (for mouth features) regions. This fact leads us to use entropy as a measure for uncertainty and unpredictability. For employing entropy, we first need to provide a reasonable probability distribution function (PDF) which satisfies the following conditions: (i) for all x, $f(x) \geq 0$ and (ii) $\sum_{all x} f(x) = 1$, where $f(x)$ is a PDF.

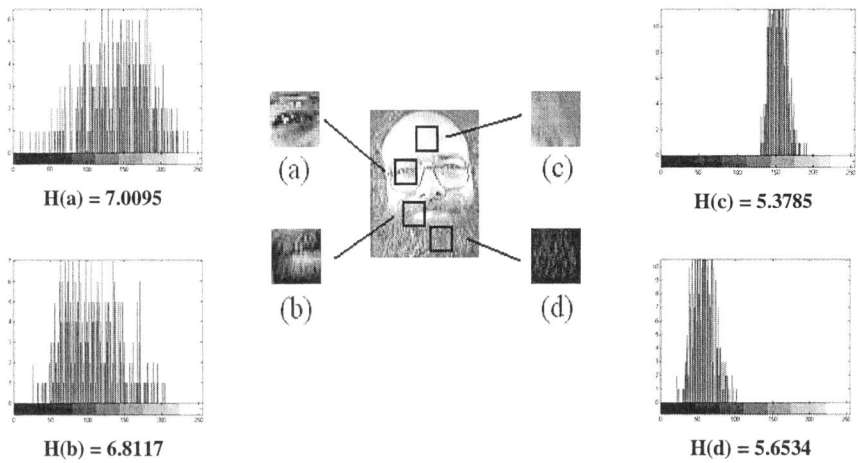

**Fig. 1.** The PDF and local entropy for four different regions of the face are shown. Facial features (a,b) indicate unpredictable local area, flatter PDF and therefore higher entropy.

In our system, to estimate the local PDF at pixel $(x, y)$, we use the histogram of pixel values within a circular window of radius $s$ and centered at $(x, y)$. Considering that the value of each bin in the histogram is greater or equal to 0, the first condition is satisfied. Then to make the second one satisfied, we divide each bin by $\pi s^2$. In our experiments we used circular windows of radius 5.

Given that $X$ is a random variable which takes on a finite set of values according to a probability distribution $p(x)$, the entropy of $X$ is defined by:

$$H(X) = -\sum_{i=1}^{n} p(x_i) \log_2(p(x_i)) \qquad (4)$$

where $X$ takes the value $x_i$ such that $0 \leq i < n$. In our case $n$ is 255, $x_i$ refers to the $i^{th}$ bin, and $p(x)$ is the value of the $i^{th}$ bin in the histogram. In Figure 1, the PDF in four different regions of a face image (eye, mouth corner, skin and beard) are shown and for each of them, the entropy measure is computed. Facial features such as the eye and the mouth corner exhibit unpredictable local intensity and therefore high entropy. However, the PDF in skin and beard regions are peaked which indicates that most of their pixels are highly predictable and hence the entropy is low.

### 2.4 Facial Feature Models

To construct a model for a particular facial feature, the system requires a set of $w \times w$ sample image regions centered at that feature point (in our experiments $w = 11$). For each of these sample images: (i) a Gabor Jet is computed at the center pixel, relative to the main orientation of the image region; (ii) The normalized histogram of the intensity (PDF) is generated; and (iii) the local entropy is calculated. The Gabor Jet and entropy value of each training sample are saved in a data structure, to be used in the detection process. Our training set consists of 20 sample images for each facial feature. In general, the training samples should be as different as possible to cover all the possible variations and reduce the redundancy. For instance, a good set of samples for constructing a model for the eye may include images of open, partially open, closed, male, female and eyes covered with glasses.

### 2.5 Detection Algorithm

After constructing the facial feature models, the system is able to detect facial features in a new face image. To locate a particular facial feature in an input image, the system does the followings.

1. Calculates the entropy value for all pixels of the input image.
2. Selects those pixels where their local entropy is above average (candidate points)
3. Assigns an orientation(s) to each candidate point and then computes the Gabor Jet for each of them relative to the assigned orientation(s).
4. Compares the Gabor Jet and the local entropy of each candidate point (at each main orientation), with the Gabor Jet and the local entropy of all trained models, using the following equation.

$$S([H_1 \ J_1],[H_2 \ J_2]) = S_{entropy}(H_1,H_2) \times S_{GaborJet}(J_1,J_2) \tag{5}$$

where:

$$S_{entropy}(H_1,H_2) = 2 \times \left[\frac{\min\{H_1,H_2\}}{H_1+H_2}\right] \tag{6}$$

$$S_{GaborJet}(J_1,J_2) = \frac{\sum x_i y_j}{\sqrt{\sum x_i^2 \sum y_i^2}} \tag{7}$$

5. Selects the candidate point which has the highest similarity (according to equation 5) to any of the trained models.

Equation (6) measures the similarity between two entropies, $H_1$ and $H_2$, based on Symmetrical Uncertainty [18]. Equation (7) measures the similarity between two Gabor Jets, $J_1$ and $J_2$, based on the similarity function used in [1]. In equation (5) multiplication is chosen experimentally, to combine these two similarities.

Our facial feature detection algorithm can be applied only on face images and provided that the facial feature is presented in the input images. However, by performing a face detection algorithm on the input images, before applying the facial feature detection, the system can accept inputs without any limitation and then be applied on the detected face regions. The face detection algorithm we have used was proposed by Viola and Jones and is discussed in [5].

## 3 Experimental Results

The above proposed method was tested on the ORL face dataset. The ORL dataset consists of 400 frontal face images from 40 individuals. Although the images were taken under controlled conditions, the dataset does contain faces with complex facial features. We trained the system for detecting the left eye and left mouth corner. We selected 20 sample images, with high variety and low redundancy, for constructing the models of each of the two facial features. After training the system, the method was tested in two phases: (i) testing the system on original ORL faces, and (ii) testing the system on randomly rotated ORL faces. For each phase 100 images were selected randomly from those images which had not taken part in the training process. Each image in each phase was tested by two methods: (i) using only a Gabor Jet for describing each facial feature, and (ii) using Gabor Jet and entropy together, for describing each facial feature. The results of the preliminary experiments are summarized in Table 1 and some of the result images with located eye and mouth corner are shown in Figure 2.

Our experimental results appear to show that local entropy can reliably guide Gabor Jet based feature detector to locate facial features in the face images. However, by studying the failure results of our method (Gabor Jet + Entropy) in phase 1, we found out that usually failure occurs when the appearance of the facial feature in the input image, is considerably different from its corresponding trained models. Besides, approximately 50% of the failure cases in phase 2 occurred due to the incorrect orientation assignment.

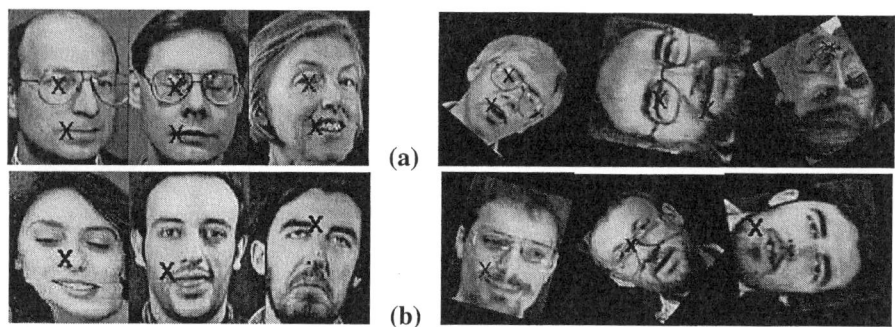

**Fig. 2.** (a) Examples of test images where their facial features are accurately localized using the Gabor Jet + local entropy method. (b) Examples of test images where one of their facial features is not located properly (only the wrong localized feature is shown).

**Table 1.** Experimental results. A feature point was counted as accurately detected if it was localized within 5 pixels of the actual position. In each phase, the test sets consisted of 100 face images.

| Methods | Phase1 (original Images) Localization % | | Phase2 (rotated images) Localization % | |
|---|---|---|---|---|
| | eye | mouth | Eye | mouth |
| Gabor Jet | 79% | 86% | 76% | 82% |
| Gabor Jet + Entropy | 97% | 98% | 92% | 95% |

## 4 Conclusions

In this paper we have presented a rotation-invariant facial feature detection system based on combining the Gabor wavelet and the entropy measure. One of the advantages of our method is that it can be trained for any individual facial feature using a small set of sample images, and once trained, without the necessity to know the approximate position of the facial feature in the face image, or relative distances to other facial features, it can find the actual position of the feature (with relatively high accuracy rate).

## Acknowledgements

The authors would like to acknowledge the Communications and Information Technology Ontario (CITO) for partially supporting this work.

## References

1. L. Wiskott, J. Fellous, N. Kruger, C. Malsburg: Face Recognition by Elastic Bunch Graph Matching. Intelligent Biometric Techniques in Fingerprint and Face Recognition (1999) 355-396
2. Liao, R., Li, S.Z.: Face Recognition Based on Multiple Features. Automatic Face and Gesture Recognition, fourth IEEE International Conference on (2000) 34-39
3. K. Toyama R. S. Feris, J. Gemmell, V. Krüger: Hierarchical Wavelet Networks for Facial Feature Localization. 5th International Conference on Automatic Face and Gesture Recognition (2002)
4. D. Cristinacce, T. Cootes: Facial Feature Detection Using AdaBoost with Shape Constraints. British Machine Vision Conference (BMVC) (2003)
5. P. Viola, M. Jones: Rapid Object Detection Using a Boosted Cascade of Simple Features. Computer Vision and Pattern Recognition Conference, Vol. 1 (2001) 511-518
6. I. Dryden, K. V. Mardia: The Statistical Analysis of Shape. Wiley, London, (1998)
7. T. D'Orazio, M. Leo, G. Cicirelli, A. Distante: An Algorithm for Real Time Eye Detection in Face Images. 17th International Conference on Pattern Recognition, Vol. 3 (2004) 278-281
8. G. Donato, M. Stewart, J. Hager, P. Ekman, T. Sejnowski: Classifying Facial Actions. IEEE Transaction on Pattern Analysis and Machine Intelligence, Vol. 21 (1999)
9. A. Z. Timor Kadir, M. Bardy: An Affine Invariant Salient Region Detector. European conference on Computer Vision (2004) 228-241
10. G. Chow, X. Li: Towards a System for Automatic Facial Feature Detection. Pattern Recognition, Vol. 26 (1993) 1739-1755
11. G. Yang, T. Huang: Human Face Detection in a Complex Background. Pattern Recognition, Vol. 27 (1994) 53-63
12. T. Chang, T. Huang, C. Novak: Facial Feature Extraction from Color Images. International Conference on Pattern Recognition (1994) 39-43
13. C. Huang, T. Cheng, C. Chen: Color Image Segmentation Using Scale Space Filter and Markov Random Field. Pattern Recognition, Vol. 25 (1992) 1217-12229
14. The ORL Face Dataset: http://www.cam-orl.co.uk/facedatabase.html
15. L. Florack, B. Romeny, M. Viergever, and J. Koenderink: The Gaussian Scale-space Paradigm and the Multi-scale Local Jet. International Journal of Computer Vision, Vol. 18 (1996) 61-75
16. J. J. Yokono, T. Poggio: Rotation Invariant Object Recognition from One Training Example. Massachusetts Institute of Technology, CBCL Memo 238 (2004)
17. D. Lowe: Distinctive Image Features from Scale-Invariant Key-points. International Journal of Computer Vision (2004)
18. D. MacKay: Information Theory, Inference, and Learning Algorithms, Cambridge University Press, ISBN 0-521-64298-1 (2003)
19. E. Hjelmas, B. Lowe: Face Detection: A Survey. Computer Vision and Image Understanding (2001) 235-274

# Face Recognition Using Optimized 3D Information from Stereo Images[*]

Changhan Park[1,2], Seanae Park[2], Jeongho Shin[1], Joonki Paik[1], and Jaechan Namkung[2]

[1] Image Processing and Intelligent Systems Laboratory, Department of Image Engineering,
Graduate School of Advanced Imaging Science, Multimedia, and Film, Chung-Ang University.
221 Huksuk-Dong, Tongjak-Ku, Seoul 156-756, Korea
http://ipis.cau.ac.kr
[2] Intelligent Image Communication Laboratory, Department of Computer Engineering,
Graduate School, Kwangwoon University, #516 Bimakwan, 447-1 Wolge-Dong, Nowon-gu,
Seoul 139-701, Korea
parkch@kw.ac.kr
http://vision.kw.ac.kr

**Abstract.** In this paper we propose a new range-based face recognition for significant improvement in the recognition rate using an optimized stereo acquisition system. The optimized 3D acquisition system consists of an eyes detection algorithm, facial pose direction distinction, and principal component analysis (PCA). The proposed method is carried out in the YCbCr color space in order to detect the face candidate area. To detect the correct face, it acquires the correct distance of the face candidate area and depth information of eyes and mouth. After scaling, the system transfers the pose change according to the distance. The face is finally recognized by the optimized PCA for each area with the facial pose elements detected. Simulation results with face recognition rate of 95.83% (100cm) in the front and 98.3% with the pose change were obtained successfully. Therefore, proposed method can be used to obtain high recognition rate with an appropriate scaling and pose change according to the distance.

## 1 Introduction

Human biometric characteristics are unique, so it can not be easily duplicated [1]. Such information includes; face, hands, torso, fingerprints, etc. Potential applications, economical efficiency, and user convenience make the face detection and recognition technique an important commodity compared to other biometric features [2], [3]. It can also use a low-cost personal computer (PC) camera instead of expensive equipments, and require minimal user interface. Recently, extensive research using 3D face data has been carried out in order to overcome the limits of 2D face detection and feature extraction [2], which includes PCA [3], neural networks (NN) [4], support vector machines (SVM) [5], hidden markov models (HMM) [6], and linear discrimi-

---

[*] This research was supported by Korean Ministry of Science and Technology under the National Research Laboratory Project, Korean Ministry of Information and Communication under HNRC-ITRC program at Chung-Ang university supervised by IITA, and the Research Grant of Kwangwoon University in 2005.

nant analysis (LDA) [7]. Among them, PCA and LDA methods with self-learning method are most widely used [3]. The frontal face image database provides fairly high recognition rate. However, if the view data of facial rotation, illumination and pose change is not acquired, the correct recognition rate remarkably drops because of the entire face modeling. Such performance degradation problem can be solved by using a new recognition method based on the optimized 3D information in the stereo face images.

This paper proposes a new face detection and recognition method using optimized 3D information from stereo images. The proposed method can significantly improve the recognition rate and is robust against object's size, distance, motion, and depth using the PCA algorithm. By using the optimized 3D information, we estimate the position of the eyes in the stereo face images. As a result, we can accurately detect the facial size, depth, and rotation in the stereo face images. For efficient detection of face area, we adopt YCbCr color format. The biggest object can be chosen as a face candidate among the candidate areas which are extracted by the morphological opening for the Cb and Cr components [8]. In order to detect the face characteristics such as eyes, nose, and mouth, a pre-processing is performed, which utilizes brightness information in the estimated face area. For fast processing, we train the partial face region segmented by estimating the position of eyes, instead of the entire face region. Fig.1. shows the block diagram of proposed algorithm.

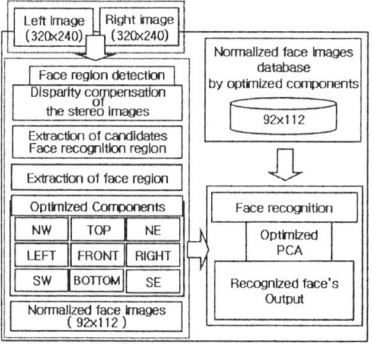

**Fig. 1.** Block diagram of the proposed algorithm

## 2 Proposed Stereo Vision System

In order to acquire the distance and depth information, we use a parallel stereo camera as shown in Fig. 2. From the stereo camera, we obtain the disparity between left and right images and estimate the distance by a stereo triangulation.

### 2.1 Disparity Compensation of Stereo Images

A block matching algorithm is used to extract the disparity in the stereo images, after applying $3 \times 3$ Gaussian noise smoothing mask.

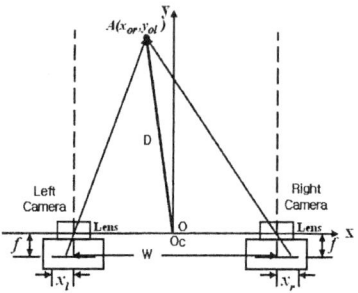

**Fig. 2.** Structure of a parallel stereo camera

In general, the block matching algorithm uses the mean absolute difference (MAD) or the mean square difference (MSD) as a criterion. However, the proposed method uses the sum of absolute difference (SAD) to reduce computational complexity as

$$SAD = \sum_i^{Nx} \sum_j^{Ny} \left| I_L(i,j) - I_R(i+k,j) \right|, \qquad (1)$$

where $I_L$ represents the $N_x \times N_y$ block of left image, $I_R$ represents the $N_x \times N_y$ corresponding block of right image, and $k$ represents the disparity between left and right images. In the stereo image matching, the disparity compensation between left and right images should be performed. When a point in the 3D space is projected on left and right images, the virtual line connecting two points is called an epipolar-line [9]. The corresponding blocks of the stereo images are matched on the epipolar-line with the same x-coordinate. The modified block matching algorithm based on 4×4 block is used for fast processing as shown in Fig. 3.

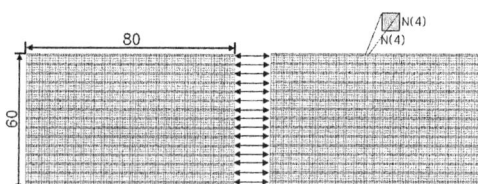

**Fig. 3.** Disparity compensation of stereo images

The proposed block matching algorithm can remove unnecessary operations and the performance of the proposed block matching algorithm is as good as the one of the global searching algorithm. The process of the proposed algorithm is as following. First, SAD is calculated at each row and then the minimum value of SAD at the corresponding row is obtained as

$$SAD_{MIN}^R = MIN \left( \sum_k \left[ \sum_i^N x \sum_j^N y \left| I_L(i,j) - I_R(i+k,j) \right| \right] \right). \qquad (2)$$

Finally, the minimum SAD of entire image can be obtained as

$$SAD_{MIN} = MIN \left( \sum SAD_{MIN}^R \right). \qquad (3)$$

Also, the disparity value between left and right images can be calculated as [2]

$$right^* = right_{t-k}, \quad left^* = left_{t+k}. \tag{4}$$

## 2.2 Scaling of the Face Images According to the Distance

320×240 RGB color images including face region are used as an input image. For fast processing and reducing the effect for illumination changes, the RGB input image is converted to YCbCr image. By defining the color range for Orientals' face skin as $R_{Cb}$ = [77 127] and $R_{Cr}$ = [133 173], a color-based image segmentation [10] is performed as

$$S(x,y) = \begin{cases} 1, & if [Cb(x,y) \in R_{Cb}] \cap [Cr(x,y) \in R_{Cr}]. \\ 0, & otherwise \end{cases} \tag{5}$$

By using the camera characteristics as given in Table 1, the distance can be measured as

$$D = \frac{bf}{x_l - x_r} \times 86.80 \times 10^3 \, [m], \tag{6}$$

where $b$ represents the width between cameras, $f$ represents the focal length, and $x_l$ and $x_r$ respectively represent the distances of left and right images. Also, the constant of $86.80 \times 10^3$ represents the effective distance per pixel.

**Table 1.** Camera's component elements

| Item | | Characteristic |
|---|---|---|
| Camera setting method | | binocular |
| Camera setting width | | 65(mm) |
| Camera focus length(f) | | 3.6(mm) |
| Size | 1 pixel | 7.2×5.6(μm) |
| Resolution | width | 512(dots) |

For the 320x240 input image, the maximum distance of the disparity, $x_l - x_r$ is equal to 1, and the minimum distance is equal to 320. The scaling according to the change of distance [11] is performed as

$$\begin{bmatrix} x' \\ y' \\ 1 \end{bmatrix} = \begin{bmatrix} s_x & 0 & 0 \\ 0 & s_y & 0 \\ 0 & 0 & 1 \end{bmatrix} \begin{bmatrix} x \\ y \\ 1 \end{bmatrix}, \tag{7}$$

where $x'$, $y'$ represent the position after scaling processing, $s_x$, $s_y$ represent the scaling factor, and $x$, $y$ represent the current position. From the obtained distance in (6), the scaling factor of face image can be calculated as

$$V_x = (B_{dist} \times V_{dist}) / A_{dist}, \tag{8}$$

where $B_{dist}$, $V_{dist}$, and $A_{dist}$, and represent the basic distance, the established value by distance, and the obtained distance, respectively.

## 2.3 Range-Based Pose Estimation Using Optimized 3D Information

In order to solve the problem of the low recognition rate due to the uncertainty of size, distance, motion, rotation, and depth, optimized 3D information from stereo images is used. By estimating the position of eyes, the proposed method can estimate the facial size, depth, and pose change, accurately. The result of estimation of facial pose change is shown in Fig. 5.

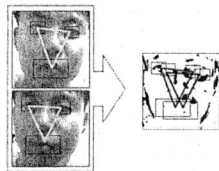

**Fig. 5.** Estimation of face rotation

In Fig. 5, the upper and lower images respectively represent the right image and the left image of frontal face. In Table 2, the range of 9 directions for face images is defined to estimate the accurate facial direction and position of stereo images.

**Table 2.** Range of face position according to direction

| NW (-15°~ -30°) | TOP (+15°~ +30°) | NE (+15°~ +30°) |
|---|---|---|
| LEFT (-15°~ -30°) | FRONT (-5°~ +5°) | RIGHT (+15°~ +30°) |
| SW (-15°~ -30°) | BOTTOM (-15°~ -30°) | SE (+15°~ +30°) |

## 3 Pose Estimation and Face Recognition

Face recognition rate is sensitive to illumination change, pose and expression change, and resolution of image. In order to increase the recognition rate under such conditions, we should consider the pose change as well as the frontal face image. The recognition rate can be increased by the 3D pose information as presented in Table 2. In order to detect face region and estimate face elements, the multi-layered relative intensity map based on the face characteristics is used, which can provide better result than the method using only color images. The proposed directional blob template can be determined according to the face size. In detail, to fit for the ratio of the horizontal and vertical length of eyes, the template should be defined so that the length of horizontal axis is longer than that of vertical one as shown in Fig. 6 (a). The central pixel of a template in a $W \times H$ image is defined as $P_c=(x_c, y_c)$. By using $W_{ff} \times H_{ff}$ directional template for face components, the average intensity $\overline{I_{Dir}}$ of 8-neighborhood pixels is calculated in the central pixel, $P_c$. As a result, the brightness value at $P_c$, $\overline{I_c}$ and the brightness difference value can be obtained. The principal direction, $\overline{d_{pr}}$, and its magnitude, $|d_{pr}|$, are determined as the direction including the biggest brightness difference as shown in Fig. 6 (b).

Fig. 7 shows the result of the face region divided by the multi-layered relative intensity map. We can build the database including 92×112 face images at each direction. The directional range of face image can be classified into 9 groups as shown in Fig. 7.

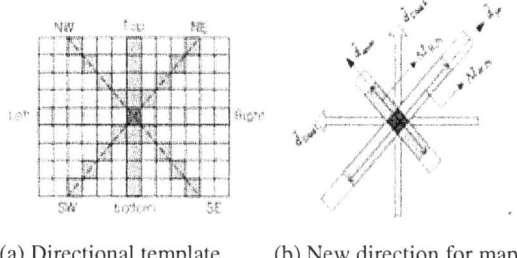

(a) Directional template    (b) New direction for map

**Fig. 6.** Directional template for estimation of position for eyes and mouth

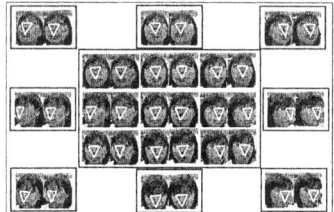

**Fig. 7.** Face area division of multi-layered relative intensity map

The classified images are trained by PCA algorithm using optimized 3D information component. The block diagram of the proposed optimized PCA algorithm is shown in Fig. 8.

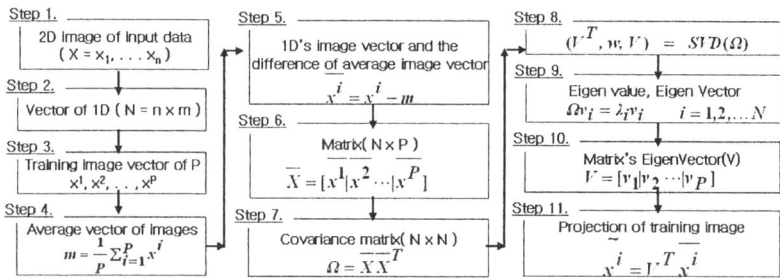

**Fig. 8.** The block diagram of PCA algorithm

## 4  Experimental Results

For the experiments, we extracted 50~400 face images from 320×240 stereo images. Fig. 9 shows the matched result of the left and right images captured at the distance of 47cm.

**Fig. 9.** The matched result of stereo image pair

Figs. 10 show the 92×112 scaled versions of the images captured at different distances. The scaling ratio of the captured face images was determined with respect to the reference image captured at the distance of 100cm. The scaling up ratios are respectively 1.2, 1.5, and 2.0 at the distances of 120cm, 150cm, and 200cm, while the scaling up ratios are 0.4 and 0.5 at the distances of 30cm and 50cm. The scaling factors were determined by experiment. Figs.11 show the samples of stereo image pairs used as input images. Figs. 12 show the some result images recognized by the proposed algorithm. The proposed algorithm can recognize the face as well as the pose of the face under pose changes.

(a) Left images　　　　　　　　　(b) Right images

**Fig. 10.** The scaled version of the face images captured at the distance of 30, 50, 100, 120, 150, and 200cm

**Fig. 11.** The samples of the input stereo image pairs

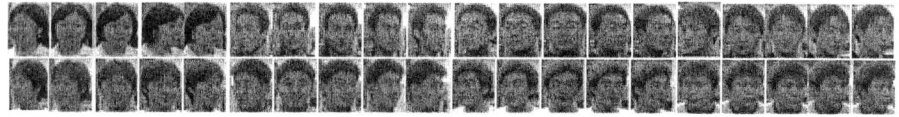

**Fig. 12.** Various pose of the result images recognized by the proposed algorithm

In Table 3, the recognition rate is compared according to the distance. As shown in the Table 3, the highest recognition rate can be obtained at the reference distance of 100cm. After training 200 stereo images, the recognition rates of the proposed methods were compared to those of the existing methods with respect to 120 test images. The recognition rate of the proposed method based on optimized 3D information is provided in Table 4. Experiment 1 and 2 respectively used frontal face images and images with various pose change. Table 4 shows that the recognition rate using the conventional PCA or HMM drops in inverse proportion to the distance. From the experiments, the proposed method can increase the recognition rate.

**Table 3.** The recognition rate according to the distance

| No. of training images (L/R) | No. of test images | Recognition rate according to distance (%) | | | | | |
|---|---|---|---|---|---|---|---|
| | | 30 (cm) | 50 (cm) | 100 (cm) | 120 (cm) | 150 (cm) | 200 (cm) |
| 200/200 | 120 | 90.00 | 93.33 | 95.83 | 91.67 | 90.00 | 87.50 |

**Table 4.** Recognition rate comparison between the proposed method and others

| | Recognition rate (%) | | | |
|---|---|---|---|---|
| Distance | Experiment-1 | Experiment -2 | PCA | HMM |
| 30cm | 90.0 | 93.3 | 90.0 | 91.7 |
| 50cm | 93.3 | 95.8 | 85.0 | 87.5 |
| 100cm | 95.8 | 98.3 | 81.7 | 87.5 |
| 120cm | 91.6 | 96.7 | 79.2 | 83.3 |
| 150cm | 90.0 | 93.3 | 68.3 | 75.8 |
| 200cm | 87.5 | 91.7 | 59.2 | 70.0 |

## 5 Conclusions

This paper proposed a new range-based face detection and recognition method using optimized 3D information from stereo images. The proposed method can significantly improve the recognition rate and is robust against object's size, distance, motion, and depth using the PCA algorithm. The proposed method uses the YCbCr color format for fast, accurate detection of the face region. The proposed method can acquire more robust information against scale and rotation through scaling the detected face image according to the distance change. Experiments were performed in the range of 30~200cm and we could get the recognition rate up to 95.8% according to the scale change. Also, we could get the high recognition rate of 98.3% according to the pose change. Experimental results showed that the proposed method can increase the low recognition rate of the conventional 2D-based algorithm.

## References

1. M. H. Yang, D. J. Kriegman, and N. Ahuja, "Detecting faces in images: a survey," IEEE Trans. Pattern Analysis, Machine Intelligence, vol. 24, no. 1, pp. 34-58, January 2002.
2. H. C. Lee, C. H. Park, Y. Namkung, and J. C. Namkung, "An object tracking method using the stereo images," J. IEEK, vol. 39 SP-5, pp. 46-58, September 2002.
3. Z. Sun, G. Bebis, X. Yuan, and S. J. Louis, "Genetic feature subset selection for gender classification: A Comparison Study," Applications of Computer Vision, 2002. (WACV 2002). Proceedings. Sixth IEEE Workshop on, 2002. pp. 165-170. December 2002.
4. H. Rowley, S. Baluja, and T. Kanade, "Neural Network-based face detection," IEEE Trans. Pattern Analysis, Machine Intelligence, vol. 20, no. 1, pp. 203-208, January 1998.

5. E. Osuna, R. Freund, and F. Girosi, "Training support vector machines: an application to face detection," Proc. of the IEEE, Computer Vision, Pattern Recognition, pp. 130-136, June 1997.
6. F. Samaria and S. Young, "HMM based architecture for face identification," Image and Vision Computing, vol. 12, no. 8, pp. 537-543, October 1994.
7. P. Belhumeur, J. Hespanha, and D. Kriegman, "Eigenfaces vs Fisherfaces: Recognition using class specification linear projection," IEEE Trans. Pattern Analysis, Machine Intelligence, vol. 19, no. 7, pp. 711-720, July 1997.
8. B. A, McLindin, "Baselining illumination variables for improved facial recognition system performance," Video/Image Processing and Multimedia Communications 2003, 4th EURASIP Conference, vol. 1, pp. 417-422, July 2003.
9. L. H. Chen and W. C. Lin, "Visual surface segmentation from stereo," Image and Vision Computing, vol. 15, no. 2, pp. 95-106, February 1997.
10. D. Chai and K. N. Ngan, "Face Segmentation Using Skin-Color map in Videophone Applications," IEEE Trans. Circuits, Systems for Video Technology, vol. 9, no. 4, pp. 551-564, June 1999,
11. O. D. Faugeras, Three-Dimensional Computer Vision, 4th edition, MIT Press, 2001.
12. W. A. IJsselsteijn, H. de Ridder, and J. Vliegen, "Subjective evaluation of stereoscopic images: effects of camera parameters and display duration," IEEE Trans. Circuits, Systems for Video Technology, vol. 10, no. 2, pp. 225-233, March 2000.

# Face Recognition – Combine Generic and Specific Solutions

Jie Wang, Juwei Lu, K.N. Plataniotis, and A.N. Venetsanopoulos

Department of Electrical and Computer Engineering, University of Toronto,
10 King's College Road, Toronto, Canada M5S 3G4
{jwang, juwei, kostas, anv}@dsp.utoronto.ca

**Abstract.** In many realistic face recognition applications, such as surveillance photo identification, the subjects of interest usually have only a limited number of image samples a-priori. This makes the recognition a difficult task, especially when only one image sample is available for each subject. In such a case, the performance of many well known face recognition algorithms will deteriorate rapidly and some of the algorithms even fail to apply. In this paper, we introduced a novel scheme to solve the one training sample problem by combining a specific solution learned from the samples of interested subjects and a generic solution learned from the samples of many other subjects. A multi-learner framework is firstly applied to generate and combine a set of generic base learners followed by a second combination with the specific learner. Extensive experiments based on the FERET database suggests that in the scenario considered here, the proposed solution significantly boosts the recognition performance.[1]

## 1 Introduction

Face recognition (FR) which has many realistic applications such as forensic identification, access control and human computer interface receives more and more attentions in both the academic and industrial areas. However it is still a difficult problem far from well solved since face objects usually exhibit various appearance due to aging, illumination and pose variations. Furthermore, image samples available for training are usually limited. Particularly, if only one image sample per subject is available, the problem becomes even more challenging.

In literature, many state-of-the-art FR algorithms have been proposed and the recent surveys could be found in[1] [2]. Among various face recognition techniques, appearance based approach which treats the face image as a holistic pattern is one of the most attractive methodologies [3]. A 2D face image is treated as a vector in the high dimensional image space and the subject identification

---

[1] This work is partially supported by a Bell University Lab research grant and CITO Student Internship Program. The authors would like to thank the FERET Technical Agent, the U.S. National Institute of Standards and Technology for providing the FERET database.

is performed by applying statistical classification methodologies, among which principle component analysis (PCA)[4], an unsupervised technique, and linear discriminant analysis (LDA)[5][6][7], a supervised technique, are most commonly used. It is generally believed that the supervised techniques are superior to those unsupervised ones for classification purposes. However, such techniques are more susceptible to the so-called "small sample size" problem, where the number of the training samples is much smaller than the dimensionality of the samples. The problem will be particularly severe when only one training sample is available for each subject. In such a case, the intra-subject information cannot be estimated which makes the supervised learning technique such as LDA based algorithms fail to apply. Thus training an unsupervised learner seems to be the only choice. However, unsupervised learning techniques are not optimal for classification tasks [5], furthermore, due to the fact that only limited number of samples are available, the estimation of the statistical model is not reliable, resulting in a poor performance.

In this paper, we proposed a scheme to solve the one sample problem by combining a generic and a specific solution. A generic FR system is built on a generic database. It is assumed that the subjects contained in the generic database do not overlap those to be identified in a specific FR task. Therefore, a generic FR system which is built to classify the generic subjects could be generalized to identify the unseen subjects in a specific FR task. This is based on a reasonable assumption, that human faces share similar intra-subject variations[8]. Thus discriminant information of the specific subjects (those to be identified) can be learned from other. It is also a realistic solution since a reasonably sized generic database is always existed. Therefore, without the one sample limitation, supervised learning techniques can be applied on the generic database. It is well known that supervised techniques are class specific and the learner which is optimal for the trained subjects may not work well with those specific subjects which are not included in the training session. In order to improve the generic behavior of the supervised algorithms and enhance the generalization power, a multi-learner framework is introduced. Generic FR system is formed by combining a set of base generic FR subsystems which are trained on different generic subsets. Since the generic learner does not target at the specific subjects, it provides a bias solution for a specific FR task. In order to further improve the recognition performance, a specific FR system is built on those specific subject images (1 image per subject) by using an unsupervised leaning algorithm. The final identification is performed by aggregating the output from both the generic and specific FR systems. Extensive experimentations on the FERET database [9] indicate that the proposed algorithm significantly improves the performance under the considered scenario which is often encountered in practice.

The rest of the paper is organized as follows: Section 2 introduces the system framework. The generic and the specific learners are described in section 3 and section 4 respectively while their combination is discussed in section 5. Experimental results obtained by using the FERET database are given in section 6 followed by the conclusion drawn in section 7.

## 2 System Framework

In order to facilitate the presentation, some terminologies are defined. Let $GalD$ be the gallery set containing the subjects of interest with the identity labels, one frontal image sample per subject. Let $PrbD$ be the probe set which includes the face images to be identified. It is assumed that there is no overlap between gallery samples and probe samples. Thus the task of a FR system is to determine which gallery subject the probe image belongs to. A generic database, denoted as $GenD$ is collected elsewhere. The subjects included in the $GenD$ do not overlap with those in the gallery set and the probe set.

In the training session, a number of generic subsets are generated from the generic database. Each training subset contains the image samples of $T$ subjects which are selected randomly from the total subjects in generic database without replacement. With each training subset, a corresponding base generic learner, denoted as $H_G^k, k = 1, ..., M$, is built which includes a feature extractor and a classifier. Similarly, the specific learner is generated from the gallery images, denoted as $H_S$. While in the operation session, both the probe **p** and the gallery samples are inputed to the base generic learners and the specific learner. A generic recognition result is obtained by aggregating the results from each base learners which is denoted as the level 1 combination. The final determination is performed by combining of the generic result and the specific result, which is denoted as level 2 combination. The system framework is depicted in Fig.1

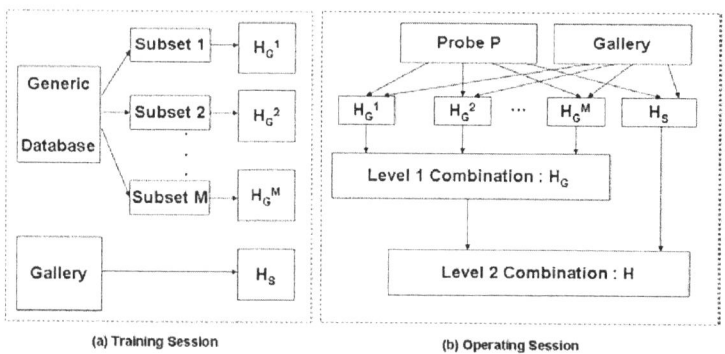

**Fig. 1.** System Framework

## 3 Generic Learner

### 3.1 Multiple Base Generic Learners

Let $GenD$ be the generic set of size $C \times L$ containing $C$ subjects $L$ images each. $\mathbf{t}_{i,j}$ is the $jth$ image of subject $i$, $i = 1, ..., C, j = 1, ..., L$. $M$ generic training subsets are generated from $GenD$, each of which contains $T$ subjects randomly selected from all $C$ subjects in the $GenD$ without replacement. Let $SGenD_k$ be the $kth$ training subset containing $T$ subjects, $L$ images each, where $k = 1, ..., M$. Therefore, a base generic learner, denoted as $H_G^k$, is trained on the subset $SGenD_k$.

In appearance approach, a learner is generally formed by a feature extractor and a classifier. Since the generic database is collected elsewhere, it is reasonable to assume that at lease two image samples are available for each generic subject. Therefore, supervised techniques can be applied. In this paper, direct linear discriminant analysis (DLDA)[10] is selected as generic feature extractor due to its good performance. Linear discriminant analysis (LDA) and its variants[5][6][10] provide class specific solutions by maximizing the so called Fisher's criterion, i.e., the ratio of the between- and within-class scatters are maximized, $A = \arg\max_A \frac{|A^T S_b A|}{|A^T S_w A|}$, where $S_b$ and $S_w$ are the between- and within-class scatter matrices of the training samples respectively and $A$ is the optimal transformation matrix from the original image space to the feature space. Direct LDA procedure solves the above optimization problem by firstly diagonalizing the between-class scatter followed by diagonalizing the within-class scatter. However, in the SSS scenario, the variance of the estimation of the small eigenvalues of $S_w$ increases significantly resulting in exaggerating the importance of the corresponding eigenvectors. Therefore, a modified but equivalent criterion is utilized, i.e., $A = \arg\max_A \frac{|A^T S_b A|}{|A^T S_w A + A^T S_b A|}$ [7]. Following the feature extractor, nearest center classifier is selected to determine the probe identity by calculating the distance between the probe and each gallery subject in the extracted feature subspace. The identity of the probe is therefore determined as the one with the smallest distance.

Let $A_G^k$ be the transformation matrix obtained from the generic training subset $SGenD_k$. Let $GalD$ be the gallery set, containing of $H$ image samples $\mathbf{s}_i, i = 1, ..., H$, one per subject, thus the generic base learner $H_G^k$ outputs the the probe identity as follows:

$$H_G^k(\mathbf{p}) = \arg\min_i D_G^k(\mathbf{p}, \mathbf{s}_i) \qquad D_G^k(\mathbf{p}, \mathbf{s}_i) = ||(A_G^k)^T \mathbf{p}, (A_G^k)^T \mathbf{s}_i|| \qquad (1)$$

where $D_G^k$ denotes the distance of the probe and the gallery subject in the feature subspace specified by $A_G^k$, and $||.||$ is the distance metric. In this paper, Euclidean distance is selected for DLDA extracted feature space.

In addition to the probe label, each base learner also makes a soft decision by providing a membership score $R_G^k(\mathbf{p}, \mathbf{s}_i)$ which indicates how the probe $\mathbf{p}$ belongs to the gallery subject $\mathbf{s}_i$. The larger the score, the higher possibility the probe belongs to the subject $\mathbf{s}_i$. Therefore, we define the membership score as follows, i.e.,

$$R_G^k(\mathbf{p}, \mathbf{s}_i) = (D_{Gmax}^k - D_G^k(\mathbf{p}, \mathbf{s}_i))/(D_{Gmax}^k - D_{Gmin}^k) \qquad (2)$$

$$D_{Gmax}^k = max(\{D_G^k(\mathbf{p}, \mathbf{s}_i)\}_{i=1}^H) \qquad D_{Gmin}^k = min(\{D_G^k(\mathbf{p}, \mathbf{s}_i)\}_{i=1}^H)$$

With such definition, small distance results in high membership score and vice versus. Therefore, the identity of the probe is equivalent to that with the highest membership score, i.e., $H_G^k(\mathbf{p}) = \arg\max_i R_G^k(\mathbf{p}, \mathbf{s}_i)$.

## 3.2 Combine Base Learners – Level 1 Combination

In order to combine multiple learners, many combination policies are developed in literature[11]. In this paper, sum rule is selected to combine the generic base learners for its simplicity and robust performance.

The final score, denoted as $R_G$, is therefore the summation of the scores obtained by all base learners and the identity is the one with the highest value, i.e., $R_G(\mathbf{p}, \mathbf{s}_i) = \sum_{k=1}^{M} R_G^k(\mathbf{p}, \mathbf{s}_i)$     $H_G(\mathbf{p}) = \arg\max_i R_G(\mathbf{p}, \mathbf{s}_i)$.

## 4 Specific Learner

The specific learner, denoted as $H_S$, is trained on the gallery set, where each subject only has one image sample. Therefore unsupervised learning techniques are selected. In this paper, PCA is adopted as the specific feature extractor resulting in a specific feature space specified by $A_S$, while the classifier is again the nearest center classifier. The membership score provided by the specific learner, $R_S(\mathbf{p}, \mathbf{s}_i)$, is defined in a similar way, i.e., $R_S(\mathbf{p}, \mathbf{s}_i) = (D_{Smax} - D_S(\mathbf{p}, \mathbf{s}_i))/(D_{Smax} - D_{Smin})$, $D_{Smax} = max(\{D_S(\mathbf{p}, \mathbf{s}_i)\}_{i=1}^{H})$ and $D_{Smin} = min(\{D_S(\mathbf{p}, \mathbf{s}_i)\}_{i=1}^{H})$, where $D_S(\mathbf{p}, \mathbf{s}_i)$ is the distance between probe $\mathbf{p}$ and gallery subject $\mathbf{s}_i$ in the specific feature space $A_S$. Here, Mahalanobis distance is selected for the PCA based feature subspace due to its good performance. Correspondingly, the probe identity is determined as: $H_S(\mathbf{p}) = \arg\max_i R_S(\mathbf{p}, \mathbf{s}_i)$.

## 5 Combine Generic and Specific Learners – Level 2 Combination

The generic leaner, trained on the samples of generic subjects, is usually bias the optimal one for a specific recognition task, since it does not target at the subjects of interest. On the other hand, the specific learner is exactly trained on the subjects of interest, however, due to the limited sample size, the estimation relies heavily on the gallery samples, giving rise to high variance. Therefore it is reasonable to combine these two learners by using a regularization factor $\eta$ to balance the bias and variance. Here, we propose to combine the generic and specific learners with the following form:

$$R(\mathbf{p}, \mathbf{s}_i) = \eta R_G(\mathbf{p}, \mathbf{s}_i) + (1 - \eta) R_S(\mathbf{p}, \mathbf{s}_i) \qquad H(\mathbf{p}) = arg\max_i R(\mathbf{p}, \mathbf{s}_i) \qquad (3)$$

where $\eta$ is the regularization factor, $0 \leq \eta \leq 1$, $R_G(.)$ and $R_S(.)$ are the membership scores provided by the generic and the specific learner and $R_G(.)$ has been normalized to 0-1. It is observed that if $\eta = 0$, the final learner results in the specific leaner which exhibits large variance. When $\eta = 1$, only generic learner affects the performance resulting in a biased solution.

# 6 Experiments

## 6.1 Experiment Setup

A set of experiments are performed on the FERET database. In the current FERET database, 3817 face images of 1200 subjects are provided with the eye coordinates information which is required to align and normalize the images. In all experiments reported here, images are preprocessed following the FERET protocol guidelines: (1) images are rotated and scaled so that the centers of the eyes are placed on specific pixels and the image size is normalized to 150 × 130; (2) a standard mask is applied to remove non-face portions; (3) histogram equalization is performed and image intensity values are normalized to zero mean and unit standard deviation; (4) each image is finally represented, after the application of mask, as a vector of dimensionality 17154.

Among these 1200 subjects, there exist 226 subjects with 3 images per subject. These 678 images are used to form the generic training database. In addition, there are 1097 images of 207 subjects each of which has 4-9 images. Of these images, we randomly select 207 frontal images, one per subject, to form the gallery set while the remaining 890 images are treated as probes.

For specific learner, PCA is applied for feature extraction denoted as $H_{S-PCA}$. As for DLDA based generic learner, $H_{G-DLDA}$, it is formed by the combination of 50 base learners generated from 50 different generic training subsets, each of which has $H$ subjects, where $H$ is varied from 30 to 110 with the interval of 10. For comparison purposes, two single generic learners trained on the whole generic training set are also generated by using PCA and DLDA respectively, denoted as $H_{G-PCA-Single}$ and $H_{G-DLDA-Single}$.

## 6.2 Results and Analysis

The comparison of the correct recognition rate (CRR) obtained by the single generic learners ($H_{G-PCA/DLDA-Single}$) and the combination of multiple base generic learners (output of level 1 combination, $H_{G-DLDA}$) is depicted in Fig.2(a). As for the single generic learners, the best CRRs are utilized for comparison. It is well-known that CRR is a function of feature number and the best found CRR is the one with the peak value corresponding to the optimal feature number ($M^*$) which is obtained by exhaustively searching all possible feature numbers. In addition, the comparison of the CRRs obtained by the specific learner ($H_{S-PCA}$), generic learner ($H_{G-DLDA}$) and their combination ($H_{S-PCA} + H_{G-DLDA}$) is depicted in Fig.2(b). It can be observed from Fig.2(a) that the introduced multi-learner framework improves the recognition performance with respect to the single generic learner. Fig.2(b) indicates that the combination of the generic and specific solution further boosts the recognition performance, outperforming either of them.

Fig.3(a) depicts the effect that the regularization factor $\eta$ has on the recognition performance. It can be observed that the best performance is between $\eta = 0$ and $\eta = 1$. The result is consistent with our claim that balancing the

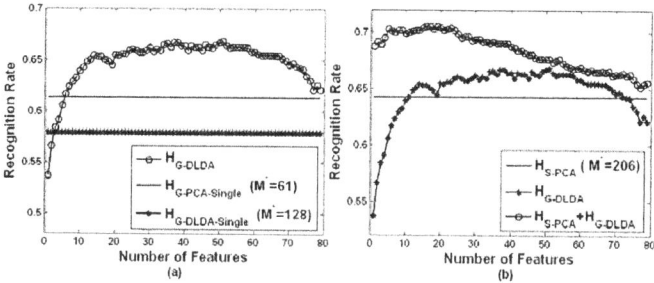

**Fig. 2.** (a) CRRs obtained by the single generic learners and the combination of multiple base learners v.s. feature number for each base learner; (b) CRRs obtained by the generic, specific learners and their combination v.s. feature number for each base learner, $\eta = 0.6$; Each base learner is trained with 80 subjects

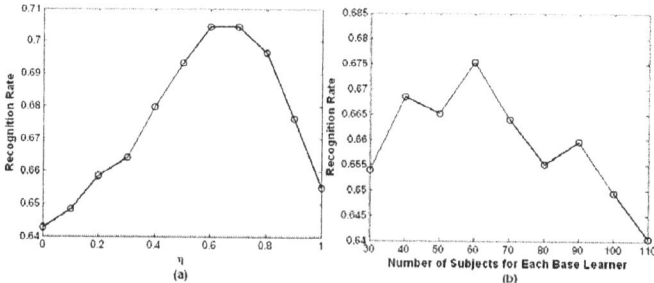

**Fig. 3.** (a) CRR obtained by the combination of generic and specific learners $H_{G-DLDA} + H_{S-PCA}$ v.s. $\eta$; Each base learner is trained with 80 subjects and retain 20 features. (b) CRR obtained by the generic learner $H_{G-DLDA}$ with 20 features v.s. number of subjects including in each training subset.

biased generic solution and the specific solution with high estimation variance can provide better performance.

The last experiment deals with the influence of the subject number in each training subset. Fig.3(b) demonstrates the relationship of the CRR obtained by $H_{G-DLDA}$ and the number of subjects used to train each base generic learner. The results indicate that the performance initially improves as the number of the training subjects increases. However, if too many subjects are included, the performance will degrade. It is well known that a necessary and sufficient condition for combining a set of learners to be more accurate than any of its individual members is if these base learners are accurate and diverse[12]. When the number of subjects are small, including more subjects and more samples could increase the learning capacity of the base learner which makes the base learner more accurate. However, since the number of the total generic subjects is fixed, continuing increasing the subjects in each training subset leads to heavier overlapping between different subsets, thereafter, the base learners trained on which become more similar. The decreasing of the base learner diversity leads to the combination effect degraded.

## 7 Conclusion

In this paper, we proposed a novel framework to combine the generic solution and the specific solution for face recognition applications when only one image sample for each subject of interest is available. A set of base generic learners trained on the generic subject samples are firstly combined to provide a generic solution followed by a combination with the specific solution obtained from the subject samples of the interest. Experimentations on the FERET database indicate that the proposed scheme significantly improves the recognition performance.

## References

1. Chellappa,R., Wilson,C.L. and Sirohey,S.,: Human and machine recognition of faces: A survey. Proceedings of the IEEE Vol.83,(1995) 705-740.
2. Zhao,W.Y., Chellappa,R., Rosenfeld,A. and Phillips,P.J.,: Face recognition: A literature survey. ACM Computing Surveys Vol.35(4),(2003) 399-458.
3. Brunelli,R., and Poggio,T.,: Face recognition: feature versus templates. IEEE Transactions on Pattern Analysis and Machine Intelligence Vol.15(10),(1993) 1042-1052.
4. Turk,M.A and Pentland,A.P.,: Eigenfaces for recognition. Journal of Cognitive Neuroscience Vol.3(1),(1991) 71-86.
5. Belhumeur,P.N., Hespanha, J.P. and Kriegman, D.J.,: Eigenfaces vs. Fisherfaces: recognition using class specific linear projection. IEEE Transactions on Pattern Analysis and Machine Intelligence Vol.19(7),(1997) 711-720.
6. Lu,J., Plataniotis,K.N. and Venetsanopoulos, A.N.,: Regularization Studies of Linear Discriminant Analysis in Small Sample Size Scenarios with Application to Face Recognition. Pattern Recognition Letter Vol.26(2),(2005) 181-191.
7. Lu,J., Plataniotis,K.N. and Venetsanopoulos,A.N.,: Face recognition using LDA-based algorithms. IEEE Transactions on Neural Networks 14(1)(2003) 195-200.
8. Wang,X. and Tang,X.,: Unified subspace analysis for face recognition. Proceedings of the Nineth IEEE International Conference on Computer Vision (2003) 679-686.
9. Phillips,P.J., Moon,H., Rizvi,S.A and Rauss,P.,: The FERET evaluation method for face recognition algorithms. IEEE Transactions on Pattern Analysis and Machine Intelligence Vol.22(10),(2000) 1090-1104.
10. Yu,H. and Yang,J.,: A direct LDA algorithm for high dimensional data - with application to face recognition. Pattern Recognitio Vol.34, (2001) 2067–2070
11. Kittler,J., Hatef,M., Duin, R. and Matas,J.,: On combining classifiers. IEEE Transactions on Pattern Analysis and Machine Intelligence Vol.20, (1998) 226–239
12. Hansen,L. and Salamon,P.,: Neural network ensembles. IEEE Transactions on Pattern Analysis and Machine Intelligence Vol.12, (1990) 993–1001

# Facial Asymmetry: A New Robust Biometric in the Frequency Domain

Sinjini Mitra[1], Marios Savvides[2], and B.V.K. Vijaya Kumar[2,*]

[1] Department of Statistics, Carnegie Mellon University, Pittsburgh, PA 15213
smitra@stat.cmu.edu
[2] Electrical and Computer Engineering Department, Carnegie Mellon University,
Pittsburgh, PA 15213
msavvid@cs.cmu.edu, kumar@ece.cmu.edu

**Abstract.** The present paper introduces a novel set of facial biometrics defined in the frequency domain representing "facial asymmetry". A comparison with previously introduced spatial asymmetry measures suggests that the frequency domain representation provides an efficient approach for performing human identification in the presence of severe expressions and also for expression classification. Feature analysis indicates that asymmetry of the different regions of the face (e.g., eyes, mouth, nose) help in these two apparently conflicting classification problems. Another advantage of our frequency domain measures is that they are tolerant to some form of illumination variations. Error rates of less than 5% are observed for human identification in all cases. We then propose another asymmetry biometric based only on the Fourier domain phase and show a potential connection of asymmetry with phase.

## 1 Introduction

Human faces have two kinds of asymmetry - intrinsic and extrinsic. The former is caused by growth, injury and age-related changes, while the latter is affected by viewing orientation and lighting direction. Intrinsic asymmetry is the interesting one since it is directly related to the individual face structure while extrinsic asymmetry can be controlled to a large extent. Psychologists say that the more asymmetric a face, the less attractive it is and more recognizable ([1], [2]), which show the potential significance of asymmetry in recognition tasks.

A commonly accepted notion in computer vision is that human faces are bilaterally symmetric ([3]) and [4] reported no differences whatsoever in recognition rates while using only the right and left halves of the face. However, a well-known fact is that manifesting expressions cause a considerable amount of facial asymmetry, they being more intense on the left side of the face ([5]). Indeed [6] found differences in recognition rates for the two halves of the face under a given facial expression.

Despite extensive studies on facial asymmetry, its use in automatic recognition started in the computer vision community only in 2001 with the seminal

---
* The authors wish to thank CyLab and Technical Support Working Group (TSWG).

work by Liu ([7]), who for the first time showed that facial asymmetry measures are efficient human identification tools under expression variations. This was followed by more in-depth studies ([8], [9]) on human as well as expression classification. But no work has yet been done on developing asymmetry measures in the frequency domain for face identification which, given the correspondence between the two domains, seems worthwhile to explore.

The paper is organized as follows. Section 2 describes the dataset used and Section 3 introduces the new asymmetry measures in the frequency domain. Section 4 presents some exploratory feature analysis and Section 5 contains the classification results. A discussion appears in Section 6.

## 2  Data

We use a part of the "Cohn-Kanade AU-coded Facial Expression Database" ([10]), consisting of images of 55 individuals expressing three different emotions - joy, anger and disgust. The data consist of video clips of people showing an emotion, each clip being broken down into several frames. The raw images are normalized using the same affine transformation as used in [8], the normalized images being of dimension $128 \times 128$. Figure 1 shows some of these. This is the only available database, as per our knowledge, for studying facial asymmetry under extreme expressions, and we use this small subset as out initial testbed.

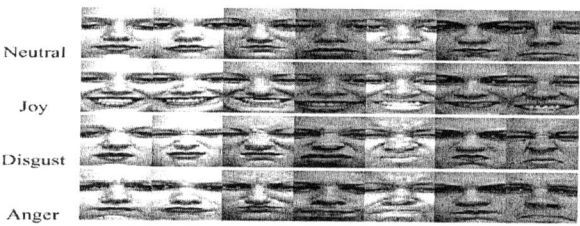

**Fig. 1.** Sample images from our database

## 3  Asymmetry in Frequency Domain

Many computer engineering applications involve the frequency-domain representation of signals. The frequency spectrum consists of two components, *magnitude* and *phase*. In 2D images, the phase captures more of the image intelligibility than magnitude and hence is very significant for performing image reconstruction ([11]). [12] showed that correlation filters built in the frequency domain can be used for efficient face-based recognition, and in fact, they perform as well as those based only on the phase ([13]). Later [14] demonstrated that performing PCA using the phase spectrum alone not only outperformed spatial domain PCA, but also are tolerant to illumination and occlusions. These point out that classification features in the frequency domain, and particularly phase, are capable of producing potentially improved results.

Symmetry properties of the Fourier transform are often very useful ([15]). Any sequence $x(n)$ can be expressed as a sum of a *symmetric* or even component $x_e(n)$ and an *asymmetric* or odd component $x_o(n)$. Specifically, $x(n) = x_e(n) + x_o(n)$, where $x_e(n) = \frac{1}{2}(x(n) + x(-n))$ and $x_o(n) = \frac{1}{2}(x(n) - x(-n))$. When a Fourier transform is performed on a real sequence $x(n)$, the even part $(x_e(n))$ transforms to the real part of the Fourier transform $R$ and the odd part $(x_o(n))$ transforms to its imaginary part $I$ (Fourier transform of any sequence is generally complex-valued). The Fourier transform of a real and even sequence is thus real; that of a real and odd sequence is purely imaginary. Now, since phase is defined as $\theta = \tan^{-1}(\frac{I}{R})$, it will be zero in case $I = 0$. In other words, a symmetric 1D sequence gives rise to zero-phase frequency spectrum. These observations imply that the imaginary components of 1D Fourier transform slices of the face can be considered as a measure of facial asymmetry in the frequency domain, and provides a scope for establishing a connection with phase as well as developing more refined classification tools.

### 3.1 The Asymmetry Biometrics

Following the notion presented in the earlier section, we define our asymmetry biometrics as:

- **I-face**: frequency-wise imaginary components of rowwise Fourier transforms - 128 × 128 matrix of features
- **Ave I-face**: frequency-wise imaginary components of Fourier transforms on averages of two-row slices of the face - 64 × 128 matrix of features
- **E-face**: sum of the *energy* of the imaginary components of the Fourier transform of averages of two-row slices of the face - a feature vector of length 64

For all three sets of features, the higher their values the greater the amount of asymmetry, and vice versa. The averaging was done in order to study if smoothing out noise in the image can reduce artificial asymmetry artifacts that gives misleading results. To the best of our knowledge, these frequency-based features as a means of representing facial asymmetry are novel in any computer vision and pattern recognition problems.

## 4 Feature Analysis

Exploratory feature analysis provides an useful insight into the nature of the different features and their utility in classification. Figure 2 shows the pattern of asymmetry variation among the different expressions of two people using the E-faces. The E-face features range from the forehead to the chin of each face. They give a preliminary but convincing idea that these measures may be helpful in recognizing people in the presence of expression variations, as well as in identifying expressions. This hence constitutes a work parallel to that of [8] and [9], in a frequency domain framework instead.

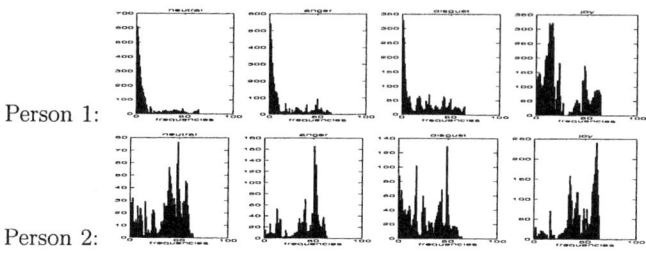

**Fig. 2.** Asymmetry of facial features for 4 expressions. X-axis shows frequencies.

### 4.1 Discriminative Feature Sets

We studied the discriminative power of these asymmetry features to determine the specific facial regions that help in identifying humans and expressions. We use a quantity known as *Augmented Variance Ratio* (AVR; also used by ([8]), which compares within class and between class variances, while penalizing features with near-equal class means. For a feature $F$ with values $S_F$, AVR is calculated as

$$AVR(S_F) = \frac{Var(S_F)}{\frac{1}{C}\sum_{k=1}^{C} \frac{Var_k(S_F)}{min_{j \neq k}(|mean_k(S_F) - mean_j(S_F)|)}},$$

where $mean_i(S_F)$ is the mean of the subset of values from feature $F$ belonging to class $i$. The higher the AVR value of a feature, the more discriminative it is for classification. For human identification, the 55 subjects form the classes and for expression classification, the classes are the 3 emotions.

Figure 3 shows the E-face AVR values for both human and expression classifications. For the former, features around the nose bridge seem to be most discriminative whereas the mouth region appeared to differ mostly across expression. Figures 3(b) and (d) respectively show the facial regions that correspond to the highest AVR values for the two classification problems. These results sug-

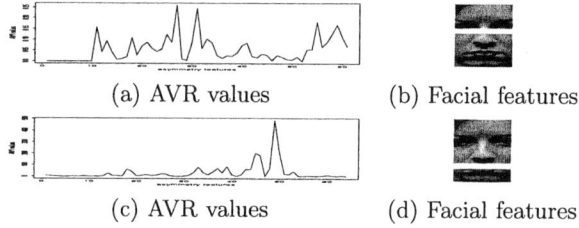

**Fig. 3.** AVR values for E-faces.(a)-(b) correspond to human identification and (c)-(d) to expression classification. The x-axis in (a) and (c) shows the different frequencies.

gest that the asymmetry of different face parts drives these two classification problems and hence may be effective for both, and is consistent with [9].

## 5 Results

Of the various classifiers tried (including SVM, LDA, FF), the best results were obtained with Individual PCA (IPCA) which we report here. The IPCA method ([13]) is different from the global PCA approach ([16]) where a subspace $W$ is computed from all the images regardless of identity. In individual PCA, on the other hand, subspaces $W_p$ are computed for each person $p$ and each test image is projected onto each individual subspace using $y_p = W_p^T(x - m_p)$. The reader is referred to [13] for more details about the procedure and its advantages over the global PCA approach.

### 5.1 Human Identification

We trained on the neutral frames from all the 55 individuals and tested on their peak frames of the 3 emotions. Hence this represents an expression-invariant human identification problem, similar to the one reported in [8] which uses a simplistic measure of facial asymmetry in the spatial domain called D-face. Statistical tests based on the results in Table 1 show that all of our proposed frequency domain measures are significantly better than original D-face (p-values <0.0001). When compared with the D-face PCs, there is no statistically significant differences (p-values>0.05). Further, the I-faces proved to be significantly better than the E-faces, which may be due to the loss of discriminative information by way of feature reduction. We will henceforth work with only I-faces.

**Table 1.** Error rates for human identification using frequency-domain measures

| I-face | Ave I-face | E-face | Spatial D-face | D-face PCs |
|--------|------------|--------|----------------|------------|
| 4.85%  | 3.64%      | 6.36%  | 17.58%         | 3.03%      |

### 5.2 Expression Classification

Our database has images with 3 different emotions: joy, anger and disgust. We used only the peak frames from the 3 emotions for this, training on a randomly selected subset of 30 people from our dataset and testing on the remaining 25. This random division of the subjects into training and test sets was repeated 20 times (in order to remove bias due to subjective selection) and the final error rates were obtained by averaging over these 20 repetitions. This experimental setup was also followed in [9], and this facilitates easy comparison of results. The results in Table 2 show that the frequency domain features outperformed both the D-face measures with significant improvements of over 10% (p-values<0.001), unlike the human identification case.

### 5.3 Illumination Variations

No experiments were performed on the illumination tolerance of the spatial measures, and hence we use a simple scheme as the first step towards studying this

**Table 2.** Misclassification rates for expression classification. The figures in the parentheses denote the standard deviations over the 20 repetitions.

| I-face | Ave I-face | D-face | D-face PCs |
|---|---|---|---|
| 26.93% (4.18%) | 27.07% (3.77%) | 39.60% (2.74%) | 36.73% (3.88%) |

for asymmetry features as such. We consider a "top-down" illumination pattern which means that the illumination gradient moves only from bottom to the top of an image (dark to light) and it is uniform over each row. We introduce this kind of illumination artificially to the images in our database, as shown in Figure 4. We considered this setup since the Cohn-Kanade database is the only

(a) Origial image  (b) Illumination matrix  (c) Illuminated Image

**Fig. 4.** Creating the "illuminated" images. $(c) = (a) \otimes (b)$.

available database with extreme expressions, and no other illumination database has the same type of controlled expression changes to facilitate studying facial asymmetry. The two experimental scenarios for human identification that we studied are as follows. **Exp. 1:** Train on all non-illuminated images, test on all illuminated ones; **Exp. 2:** Train on non-illuminated neutral frames from 3 emotions, test on illuminated peak frames from 3 emotions. Clearly, the second setup is more difficult and involves identification in the presence of both expression and illumination changes. As for expression classification, we use the same setup as before, only the test images had illumination variations and the training images did not. The results in Table 3 demonstrate that the I-faces are capable of perfect identification of the same image under illumination.

**Table 3.** Error rates for human and expression classification under illumination changes (std. deviations in parentheses)

| Features | Human (Exp.1) | Human (Exp. 2) | Expr. |
|---|---|---|---|
| I-face | 0% | 4.85% | 30.93% (4.14%) |
| Ave I-face | 0% | 4.54% | 32% (4.93%) |

The I-face human identification results are exactly the same with and without illumination variations, which can be explained as follows. By construction, the illuminated images are scaled the same way for all elements within a row (and differently for different rows). By the linearity property for Fourier transform ([15]), and considering its polar form, this implies that the I-face features for every row are now scaled versions of the original ones, and this same scaling applies to the same row in each image and hence this does not alter the classification results. This is not true for the Ave I-faces because the averaging scales the different elements of each row differently prior to applying FFT. Theoretically, expression classification results should also be same for I-face, but the random selection of training and test sets precludes the scope of exactly similar results.

### 5.4 Phase-Only Images

In order to study the connection between asymmetry and phase mentioned in Section 3 more rigorously, we constructed same features using "phase-only" images (obtained by dividing the Fourier transform by its magnitude). We call them I-face$_\theta$ and Ave I-face$_\theta$. Human and expression identification results with and without illumination changes using the same setup as before appear in Table 4. Both sets of human recognition results are comparable with those using the

**Table 4.** Misclassification rates for human and expression classifications using phase-only images. Standard deviations for the latter appear in parentheses.

| Images | Features | Human | Expr. |  |
|---|---|---|---|---|
| No | I-face$_\theta$ | 4.85% | 37.8% | (4.98%) |
| Illum. | Ave I-face$_\theta$ | 5.45% | 38.8% | (4.76%) |
| Illum | I-face$_\theta$ | 4.85% | 36.74% | (4.63%) |
|  | Ave I-face$_\theta$ | 5.76% | 40.40% | (4.76%) |

original images, but expression results are considerably worse. This shows that removing the magnitude loses relevant information for identifying expressions but not for identifying people.

As with I-face, I-face$_\theta$ gives the same human classification results with and without illumination variations. This happens since the scale factor $a$ gets absorbed completely in the magnitude (exploiting the linearity property again), keeping the phase and hence I-face$_\theta$ unchanged.

## 6 Discussion

We have shown in this paper that facial asymmetry measures in the frequency domain offer a promising potential as an useful biometric in practice, especially, in the presence of expression and illumination variations. This is an advantage over spatial measures which are particularly sensitive to illumination variations. An error rate of less than 5% for human recognition is very impressive and desirable given that the test images are very different from the training ones. This in turn is very important for recognition routines in practice, for example, surveillance photos captured at airports are expected to be quite diverse with respect to facial expressions and illumination conditions. Our features also outperformed the spatial measures in expression classification.

The phase-based measures also proved efficient for distortion-tolerant human identification, which also established a nice connection with phase. The asymmetry features based on the actual images and the phase-only images produced exactly same human classification results. This indicates (although empirically) that phase contains all the asymmetry of a face, at least to the extent that is necessary for classification purposes, and no crucial information is lost by removing the magnitude. The Ave I-face$_\theta$ results are different from the Ave I-face results and this may have arisen from the averaging.

Future research directions include studying the illumination tolerance more rigorously by considering real images with illumination changes since artificial manipulation often produces biased results. We will also consider frequency domain analogs of S-face features proposed by [9] which are based on edges.

## References

1. Thornhill, R., Gangstad, S. W.: Facial attractiveness. Transactions in Cognitive Sciences **3** (1999) 452–460
2. Troje, N. F., Buelthoff, H. H.: How is bilateral symmetry of human faces used for recognition of novel views? Vision Research **38** (1998) 79–89
3. Seitz, S.M., Dyer, C.R.: View morphing. SIGGRAPH (1996) 21–30
4. Gutta, S., Philomin, V., Trajkovic, M.: An investigation into the use of partial-faces for face recognition. In: AFGR. (2002) 33–38
5. Borod, J.D., Koff, E., Yecker, S., Santschi, C., Schmidt, J.M.: Facial asymmetry during emotional expression: gender, valence and measurement technique. Psychophysiology **36** (1998) 1209–1215
6. Martinez, A.M.: Recognizing imprecisely localized, partially occluded and expression variant faces from a single sample per class. PAMI **24** (2002) 748–763
7. Liu, Y., Schmidt, K., Cohn, J., Weaver, R.L.: Human facial asymmetry for expression-invariant facial identification. In: AFGR. (2002)
8. Liu, Y., Schmidt, K., Cohn, J., Mitra, S.: Facial asymmetry quantification for expression-invariant human identification. In CVIU **91** (2003) 138–159
9. Mitra, S., Liu, Y.: Local facial asymmetry for expression classification. CVPR (2004)
10. Kanade, T., Cohn, J.F., Tian, Y.L.: Comprehensive database for facial expression analysis. In: AFGR. (2000) 46–53
11. Hayes, M.H.: The reconstruction of a multidimensional sequence from the phase or magnitude of its fourier transform. ASSP **30** (1982) 140–154
12. Savvides, M., Vijaya Kumar, B.V.K., Khosla, P.: Face verification using correlation filters. In: 3rd IEEE Automatic Identification Advanced Technologies. (2002) 56–61
13. Savvides, M., Kumar, B.V.K.: Eigenphases vs.eigenfaces. In: ICPR. (2004)
14. Savvides, M., Kumar, B.V.K., Khosla, P.K.: Corefaces - robust shift invariant pca based correlation filter for illumination tolerant face recognition. CVPR (2004)
15. Oppenheim, A.V., Schafer, R.W.: Discrete-time Signal Processing. Prentice Hall, Englewood Cliffs, NJ (1989)
16. Turk, M.A., Pentland, A.P.: Face recognition using eigenfaces. CVPR (1991)

# Occluded Face Recognition by Means of the IFS

Andrea F. Abate, Michele Nappi, Daniel Riccio, and Maurizio Tucci

Universitá Degli Studi di Salerno,
via Ponte Don Melillo, 84084, Fisciano, Salerno, Italy
{abate, mnappi, driccio, mtucci}@unisa.it

**Abstract.** Due to growing demands in such application areas as law enforcement, video surveillance, banking, and security system access authentication, automatic face recognition has attracted great attention in recent years. The advantages of facial identification over alternative methods, such as fingerprint identification, are based primarily on the fact that face is fairly easy to use and well accepted by people. However it is not robust enough to be used in most practical security applications because too sensitive to variations in pose and illumination. During the last few years, many algorithms have been proposed to overcome these problems using 2-D images, but very few has been made in order to address the problem of partial occlusions. In this paper, a fractal based technique is presented; the face image is partitioned in different regions of interest, each one is indexed by means of an IFS system. A new distance function is then introduced, in order to discard unuseful information. The proposed method turns out to be faster and more robust than other approaches in the state of the art.

## 1 Introduction

In last years security problems are capturing increasing attention from researchers. Particularly the people authentication problem. A lot of biometrics, such as fingerprint, hand-shape and iris have been studied until today, finding that two main characteristics enact the success of a biometric: reliability and people acceptance. Indeed, iris recognition represents the most reliable approach, but it is too much intrusive. On the contrary, fingerprint are easily applicable, but it cannot be used with non consentient people. As very nice compromise between acceptance and reliability, face recognition is emerging. Recognition rate of face biometric is not comparable to that of iris and fingerprint, however the ease in taking snapshots and video capturing make this method effective also when the subject is unaware of the presence of a face recognizer. Furthermore the wide range of commercial and law enforcement applications supported by the availability of feasible technologies favor the success of the face biometric. In general, even if face recognition systems are so far from the recognition capability of humans, it is true that human brain has noticeable limitations on the number of the persons, that it can accurately remember. Therefore, research has been made attempting to make face recognition systems fully automatic, also looking for successful face classifiers. Existing approaches for Face Recognition can be classified in three principal cathegories, as suggested by [6]: **Holistic methods** - Eigenfaces, Fisherfaces, Support Vector Machine, Independent Component Analysis, **Feature-based methods** - Dynamic Link Architecture, Hidden Markov Model, Convolution Neural Networks and **Hybrid methods** - Modular eigenfaces, Component-based. All these method deal with a large set of typical drawbacks in face recognition, such as variations in expression, lighting, pose and acquisition time. Nevertheless, there exist few works about the problem of the occlusions, such as [2]. In this approach, each face image is divided into k different local parts, each of them is modeled by using a Gaussian distribution (or, equivalently, with a mixture of Gaussians), which accounts for the localization error problem. Given that, the mean feature vector and the covariance matrix for every local subspace are drawn out, while the probability of a given match can be directly associated with the sum of all $k$ Mahalanobis distances. However, to compute all the mixture of Gaussian can be computationally expensive, in some cases. Therefore, in this paper a fractal based technique is suggested, which turns out to be fast and very robust with respect to synthetic as well as natural occlusions. The new proposed strategy is based on IFS (Iterated Function Systems), largely used in image compression and indexing [1]. In this case, the affine transformation are used in order to characterize auto-similarities into a face image, extracting a compact feature vector with high discriminant power. Before introducing the new method we recall the principal concepts of the IFS theory. Given an input image $I$, it is partitioned in a set $R$ of disjoint square regions of size $r \times r$ named ranges. From the same image $I$, another set of overlapped regions (domains) of size $d \times d$ (where usually $d = 2r$) is extracted. As a domain is double sized with respect to a range, it has to be shrunk to the $r \times r$ dimension, with a $2 \times 2$ average operation on its pixels. That is made only the first time, downsampling the original image and obtaining a new face image that is a quarter of the original. However, to find the best match for each range $r$ requires an exhaustive search over all the set $D$, that is an impractical operation. Generally, ranges and domains are classified by means of feature vectors in order to throw down the cost of the linear search on the domain pool. For a range $r$, only the domains $d$, with a feature vector close to that of the range $r$ are codified. In order to compute the fractal code of an input image $I$, the DRDC method [5] has been chosen, but many other methods are available in literature. In the DRDC approach image blocks are classified defering range/domain comparisons respect to a preset block $\tilde{d}$, using the approximation error as a feature vector. The rest of this paper is organized as follows. Section 2 shows in more detail the feature extraction process, while in Section 3 a new distance function is provided in order to make robust and fast the matching operation between features vectors. Furthermore, Section 4 provides a concise description of the measures, databases and experimetal results compared to [2]. At last the conclusions are drawn in Section 5.

## 2 Features and Feature Vector Structure

In order to make method presented in this paper robust with respect to likely occlusions, the feature extraction process is made local to the region, of interest, defined as the union of four main areas, which are left eye, right eye, nose and mouth. For each of these areas, a set of fiducial point is extracted and the average approximation error is computed, so that point locations and approximation errors represent the signature for the face. The first problem to be solved is locating the face in the picture. The detection of a face is semi-automatical. The center of the eyes and baseline of the nose are manually selected, extracting a face region of size proportional to the distance among these three points. The face region extracted from the input image is normalized to 256 × 256 pixels. Nothing has been done for the original warping of the input images, which also can affect the recognition rate. Once the segmentation of the face is done, the face objects are independently indexed by means of the IFS systems as separate region of interest. For each region of interest (eyes, nose or mouth) a set of fixed points $P = \{P_1, P_2, \ldots, P_n\}$, called *entry points* is considered.

For each $P_i = (x_i, y_i) \in P$, the algorithm extracts the corresponding range $R_{x_i, y_i}$, whose upper-left corner falls in the position $P_i$. It searches for the first $n$ best fitting domains with respect to an affine transformation, as detailed in [5]. In order to render the method more robust with respect to small shifts around the entry position $(x_i, y_i)$ 18 nearest neighbors of the current entry points are considered. Starting from the current entry point, all centroids are computed by means of the above algorithm, then with a spiral visit centered in the current entry point, 8 neighbors are considered. The neighbors are looked for on an Archimede's spiral $\rho = a \cdot \theta$, where $\rho$ is the distance from the center to the tracing point, $\theta$ is the angular distance covered and $a$ is a fixed constant. With the spiral visit, the higher the distance from the entry point, the less useful is its information. This can be explained considering that the further the neighbor is from the current entry point, the less their similarity to the current range.

In order to use the information about the distribution of similarities brought out during the indexing phase, range/domain relations have to be organized so that comparisons are possible. In this case, the domains are organized in a set of clusters $C = \{C_1, C_2, \ldots, C_m\}$, each represented by its centroid $c_i$, and the centroids are stored in memory as a list. Each centroid object in the list includes its spatial coordinates, computed as the mean of the coordinates of domains to the cluster, as well as the average approximation error between the domain and the prefixed block. A detailed description of the clusterization algorithm follows:

**Domain Insertion(List of Centroids CL, Domain D)**
```
1)    Search for the centroid c_k in CL nearest to D
2)    If c_k doesn't exists
3)        create a new cluster with D as centroid c_k
4)        add c_k to CL
5)    Else
6)        c'_k(x) = (c_k(x)+D(x))/2   and   c'_k(y) = (c_k(y)+D(y))/2
```

7) $c'_k(err) = \frac{c_k(err)+D(err)}{2}$
8) If $\exists D \in$ cluster represented by $c_k \ni$ distance$\left(D, c'_k\right) > d$
9)     Annul Updating
10)    create a new cluster with D as centroid $c_k$
11)   add $c_k$ to CL
12) End

At first the list of centroids is empty; then, starting from the first entry point, the corresponding range is extracted and the $n$ best fitting domain are searched. The domains are inserted in the clusters one at a time. Initially the list of centroids is empty, then a new cluster is created and its centroid has the same coordinates of the inserted domain. The second domain fitting the current range is extracted by means of the IFS transformation and has to be inserted in the correct cluster. The algorithm scans the list of centroids searching for the centroid with minimum distance. If no suitable cluster is found, a new cluster is created and added to the list, while the corresponding centroid has the same coordinates and approximation error of the inserted domain. On the contrary, if there is a cluster whose centroid is not further than a fixed threshold $\epsilon$ from the domain to be inserted, the algorithm tries to update the cluster with the new domain. The new coordinates are computed for the centroid according to (line (6)), but taking into account also the new domain being inserted. After updating the coordinates, a check is made where there is a domain in the cluster whose distance from the centroid is greater than the fixed threshold $\epsilon$. In this case, the updating operation is canceled, and a new cluster is created with the same coordinates and approximation error of the inserted domain.

Once the list of centroids has been computed, it has to be rearranged so that a distance function can be defined for the comparisons to be performed later. The ideal way to compare two face images would be to match the respective approximation errors of corresponding centroids in the two images. Since each centroid in the list consists of two coordinates $C(x, y)$, the nearness of two centroids can be estimated in a simpler way using Euclidean norm.

Let $L_1$ be a list of centroids of length $n = |L_1|$ to be compared with another list $L_2$, of length $m = |L_2|$. An effective manner to compare the centroids in $L_1$ and $L_2$ is representing the centroids' spatial location with Peano keys. From the literature, it is known that Peano keys are useful in indexing tasks because they map a 2D space into a 1D space, while preserving most of the spatial information in the original data. Given a centroid $C(x, y)$, the correspondent Peano key $a_C$ is computed interleaving bits of $x$ and $y$, from the less significant digit to the most significant. The Peano keys so computed are then sorted. This can be done in linear time $O(n)$ with Radix Sort.

When comparing $L_1$ and $L_2$, a time $O(m)$ is spent searching for the centroid $C_{L_2}^j$ in $L_2$ nearest to the first centroid $C_{L_1}^1$ in $L_1$, keeping memory of $j$. It can be observed that the location of the next centroid in $L_2$ nearest to $C_{L_1}^k$ falls not so far from the position $j$—indeed, it is about $j + c$, where it has been found experimentally that $0 \leq c \leq 10$, and $j$ is the position in $L_2$ of the centroid nearest to $C_{L_1}^{k-1}$ in $L_1$, with $k > 1$. It can be deduced that for each centroid in $L_1$, only $c$ centroids in $L_2$ have to be tested. The overall complexity of the comparisons is then $O(n + c \cdot m) = O(n + m)$—linear, since $c$ is a constant. Low-complexity comparisons are crucial, considering that in a huge database of face images, millions of images might have to be tested.

## 3   An 'Ad Hoc' Distance Function $\Delta(A, B)$

This section defines the distance function used when comparing two feature vectors. The domain of this function consists of 2D vectors $S \in \Re^2$, where $(a, b) \in S$. The symbol $a$ represents a Peano key obtained, while the real value $b$ represents the average of the approximation error for the centroid centered in $a = P(x, y)$. Given 2 vectors $S, T \in \Re^2$, the operator $\Psi(S, T)$ is defined as follows.

$$\Psi_i(S, T) = \left| b_T^{\mu(S,T)} - b_S^i \right| \quad (1)$$

with

$$\mu(S, T) = \min_j \left\| a_T^j - a_S^i \right\|_2,$$

that is, $\mu(S, T)$ represents the index in $T$ of the point $a_T^j = P_1(x_1, y_1)$ nearest to the point $a_S^i = P_2(x_2, y_2)$ in $S$.

For each item $a_S = P(x, y) \in S$, a search is performed for the nearest item $a_T = P(x, y) \in T$ according to Euclidean norm $|P_S - P_T|_2$, and the quantity $|b_S - b_T|$ is computed. This quantity represents the absolute difference between the approximation errors corresponding to the nearest points $P_S \in S$ and $P_T \in T$.

Lastly, the values of $\Psi_i(S, T)$ are summed for all $i$. In order to make the distance function more robust to partial occlusions, it can be noted that if $\Psi_i(S, T)$ is too large, it does not supply much useful information, and this can be interpreted as a sign of possible occlusion.

More precisely, if $\bar{m} = \frac{1}{|S|} \cdot \sum_{i=1}^{|S|} \Psi_i(S, T)$ is the average value of $\Psi$ over $S$, it turns out that only the values of $\Psi_i(S, T)$ ranging from 0 to $2\bar{m}$ provide useful information. Therefore, a threshold is applied to cut all values above $2\bar{m}$, leaving smaller values untouched. This is done by means of the following function:

$$\Delta(S, T) = \frac{1}{|\tilde{S}|} \sum_i^{|S|} \gamma_S^i \cdot \Psi_i(S, T) + \frac{1}{|\tilde{T}|} \sum_i^{|T|} \gamma_T^i \cdot \Psi_i(T, S), \quad (2)$$

where

$$\gamma_S^i = \frac{(S(i) - 2 \cdot E[S]) - |(S(i) - 2 \cdot E[S])|}{2 \cdot (S(i) - 2 \cdot E[S])}$$

and

$$\tilde{S} = \left\{ (a_i, b_i) \in S \mid \gamma_S^i \neq 0 \right\}.$$

# 4 Experimental Results

There are several standard database used by the scientific community in order to assess the performances of the proposed face recognition algorithms. The AR face database was created by Aleix M. Martinez and Robert Benavente at the Computer Vision Center (CVC) [3]. It contains over 4,000 color images corresponding to 126 people's faces (70 men and 56 women). Images feature frontal view faces with different facial expressions, illumination conditions, and occlusions (sun glasses and/or scarf). The pictures were taken at the CVC under strictly controlled conditions. In general in the face authentication application the user doesn't claim his identity and the system has to compare the input face image with all the database, then it is a 1:N problem, which we refer to as identification. Another case frequently occurs in low enforcement application, in which there are huge databases containing images of criminals and when a new person is reported to the police a lot of snapshots have to be manually analyzed. In this case, it is very useful that a face authentication method guarantee that the person we are searching for is retrieved at least in the first $n$ entry, with $n$ as small as possible. Then, it makes sense to use CMS (Cumulative Match Score) [4] as a measure of the performances, while in the former case the recognition rate is applied. Experiments have been conducted on a subset of 50 subjects from the AR Faces database. Three images have been used with different facial expression: neutral, angry and smile. One of the most interesting aspects is how good are the recognition performances when the dimensions of the occluded area increase. Then in the first experiment, for each face the neutral expression is used as gallery, while neutral, angry and smile images with synthetic occlusion represent the probe. Synthetic square occlusions of $p \times p$ dimension have been added, where $p$ varies from a low of 5 to a maximum of 50. For each value of

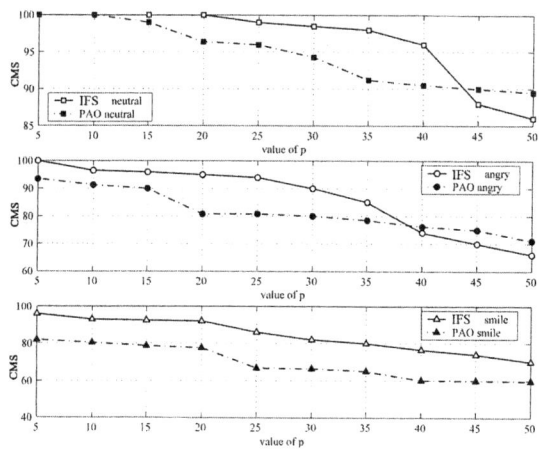

**Fig. 1.** Performances of IFS when synthetic rectangular occlusions occurr, comparison with PAO algorithm

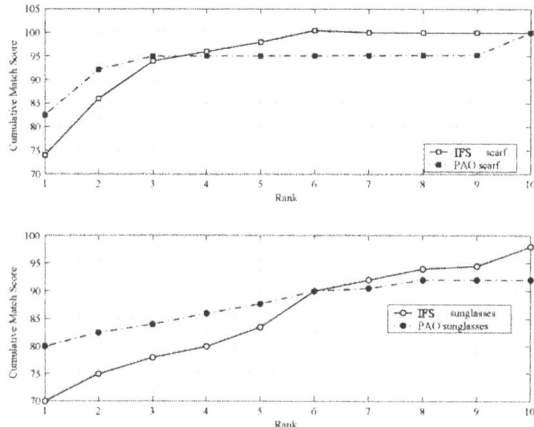

**Fig. 2.** IFS and Martinez' algorithm in the case of natural occlusions

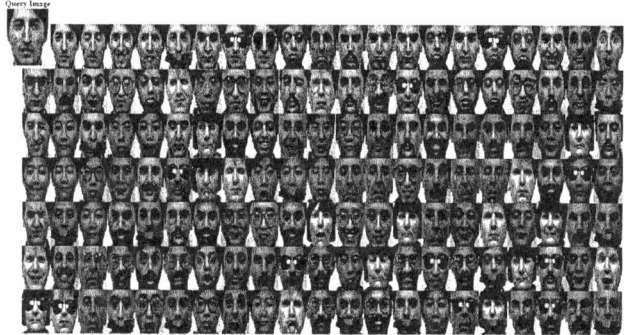

**Fig. 3.** An example of the system response. The first image is the query image.

$p$ the square is randomly localized in the image 100 times and mean results are reported in Fig. 1. For this experiment the IFS performances are compared to the probabilistic approach proposed by Martinez [2], referred as PAO, in this paper. For PAO, results are drawn out from the tables in [2]. Fig. 1 shows also drops of 10% in the CMS of the two methods confirming the robustness of the IFS with respect to the synthetic occlusions. The second experiment has the aim of testing the IFS based approach in case of natural occlusions, such as scarfs or sunglasses. In the AR Faces database, two images with accessories are provided for each person, in both sessions. A subset of 50 persons has been taken also for this experiment. The neutral image has been used as gallery, while two images with natural occlusion (scarf and sunglasses) have been used as probe. From Fig. 2 is clear that PAO start better than IFS, but for ranks greater than 6, the reverse is true. In particular for sunglasses occlusions the final gap between the methods is about 5%. Furthermore, has been observed that in the most part of the performed tests, IFS has significantly outperformed PAO. These results are particularly interesting considering applications such as low enforcement, where it is admissible that the correct answer falls at least in the first $n$ answers with $n$ as small as possible. At last, the Yale Database has been considered. It consists of 165 images, 11 for each of the 15 different subjects. They mainly differ in expressions and illumination conditions. Moreover, occluded images have been added to the database, superimposing scarf and sunglasses images to the no-glasses image in the database, for all subjects. Then, Fig. 3 shows the system responce when the neutral image of the subject $s$ is used as query image.

## 5 Conclusions

The interest of researchers for face recognition is firmly increasing in last years, so that several solution have been proposed until today. However the most part of the recent methods deal only with change in expressions and in illumination conditions, not considering the case of synthetic and natural occlusions. In particular the literature about fractals applications in Face Recognition is very poor. For these reasons in this paper a new fractal based approach, is proposed. It is shown how IFS transformations can be readapted in order to provide a good signature for face images, useful for the face recognition task. The indexing process has been made local and a new distance function is provided in order to deal with partial occlusions. Experimental results show the robustness of the proposed method with respect to synthetic occlusions (black squares randomly localized on the image) and natural occlusions such as scarfs and sunglasses. In particular, they underline that, in most cases, IFS overcomes tother methods in the state of the art.

## References

1. R. Distasi, M. Nappi, M. Tucci "FIRE: Fractal Indexing with Robust Extensions for Image Databases" , in *IEEE Transactions on Image Processing*, vol. 12, Issue: 3, pp. 373–384, March 2003.
2. A. M. Martnez "Recognizing Imprecisely Localized, Partially Occluded and Expression Variant Faces from a Single Sample per Class" , in *IEEE Transactions on Pattern Analysis and Machine Intelligence*, vol. 24, no. 6, pp. 748–763, June 2002.
3. A. M. Martnez "The AR face database" , CVC Tech. Report no. 24, 1998
4. P. J. Phillips, H. Moon, S. Rizvi and P. Rauss "The FERET evaluation methodology for facerecognition algorithms" , in *IEEE Transaction on Pattern Analysis and Machine Intelligence*, vol. 22, no. 10, pp. 1090–1104, October 2000.
5. Riccio D., Nappi M. "A Range/Domain Approximation Error Based Approach for Fractal Image Compression" , to be appear in *Transaction on Image Processing*,
6. W. Zhao, R. Chellapa, P. J. Phillips and A. RosenFeld "Face Recognition: A Literature Survey" , in *ACM Computing Surveys*, vol. 35, no. 4, pp. 399–458, December 2003.

# Verification of Biometric Palmprint Patterns Using Optimal Trade-Off Filter Classifiers

Pablo Hennings, Marios Savvides, and B.V.K. Vijaya Kumar

Carnegie Mellon University,
Department of Electrical and Computer Engineering,
5000 Forbes Avenue, Pittsburgh PA 15213, USA
msavvid@cs.cmu.edu, {phh, kumar}@ece.cmu.edu
http://www.cmu.ece.edu/~phh

**Abstract.** We present results on classification of palmprint patterns from a large number of classes for biometric verification. We train optimal trade-off correlation filter classifiers with patterns of subregions of the palm as the actual biometric for the person's identity. Our results show that with less than 5 cm$^2$ (less than 1 in$^2$) of the actual palm captured at a low resolution, correlation filter algorithms can verify the authenticity of the palmprint pattern with error rates below 0.5% from as many as 400 different patterns. There is no previous work on biometric palmprint recognition that studies pattern verification of such small palmprint regions with such large number of classes.

## 1 Previous Work on Palmprint Recognition

Palmprint recognition performs matching of patterns in a palm surface with previously learned templates. Although, these patterns, called simply *palmprints*, have fingerprint like characteristics, it is not until recently that serious research has been conducted to determine how reliable a palmprint may be for biometric recognition [1][2][3].

Palmprints contain different types of patterns, such as principal lines and smaller creases or wrinkles, textures and fingerprint-like ridges (see Figure 1). Previous approaches to palmprint recognition include techniques to effectively extract features from these different patterns [2][4][5][6], and use a specific feature or a combination of them for palmprint classification [7][8][9]. There is a major emphasis in palmprint recognition research on defining and extracting the most appropriate features for known classification techniques.

In this paper, we show that advanced correlation filter classifiers perform with very high levels of accuracy on palmprint verification. These optimal filters have many advantages [10], of which probably the most outstanding is that they are trained on the image pixels directly, reducing the feature extraction stage to image segmentation. This training advantage simplifies the problem of palmprint recognition.

Originally, the application of correlation filter classifiers for palmprint recognition was presented in [11]. Here we present a follow-up study that includes

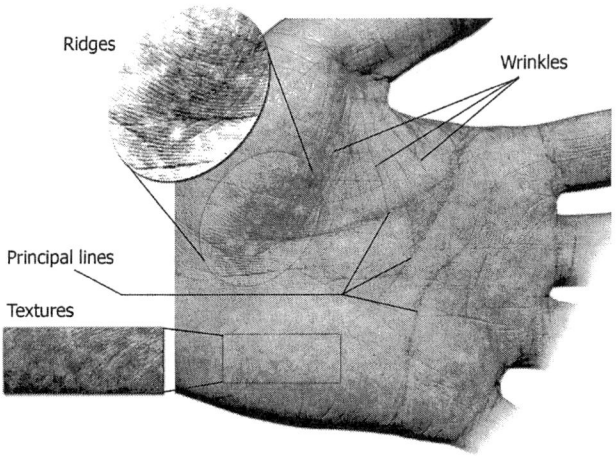

**Fig. 1.** Palmprint features of a palm captured at a high resolution

the use of a considerably larger number of palmprint classes and low-resolution image patterns from a limited palmprint area. Specifically, we show that correlation filters can achieve error rates as low as 0.1% for palmprint patterns of actual area of less than 5 cm$^2$ (less than 1 in$^2$) at a low capture resolution of 72 pixels-per-inch. A survey on the application of advanced correlation filters for classification of other biometrics can be found in [12]; recent work in face and fingerprints is presented in [13] and [14], respectively.

This paper is organized as follows. Section 2 reviews the theory of correlation filter classifiers used in this study. The specifications of the palmprint database and the image segmentation procedures are presented in Section 3. Results of the different experiments performed are shown and discussed in Section 4, and finally, conclusions are stated in Section 5.

## 2 Optimal Trade-Off Correlation Filter Classifiers

A correlation filter is designed to produce correlation outputs with high amplitude at the origin while keeping the rest of the output plane as small as possible when correlating an authentic image. Thus, the objective is to obtain strong correlation peaks when applying the (space-reversed) filter to an image of the filter's pattern class (see Figure 2). With this in mind, we use as a match metric the peak-to-correlation energy (PCE) ratio, given by

$$PCE = \frac{max_g - \mu_g}{\sigma_g} \quad (1)$$

where $g$ is the output correlation plane, $\mu_g$ is its mean, and $\sigma_g$, its standard deviation.

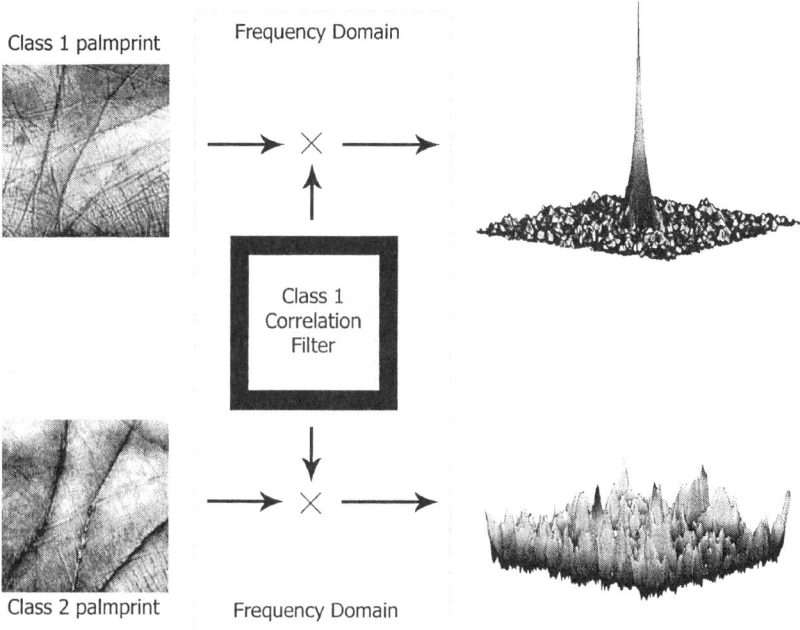

**Fig. 2.** Applying an advanced correlation filter. The palmprint on top is an authentic exemplar, and, when filtered with the correlation filter of the same class, yields a sharp peak. In contrast, the palmprint below belongs to an imposter, and it yields a plane with lower energy and no clearly-visible peak.

Different designs of correlation filters are available [10]. We briefly describe the filter design process for the minimum average correlation energy (MACE) filter, and then elaborate to describe other correlation filters known to be successful in biometrics.

Given a set of $N$ training images taking values in a $d$-dimensional image space, the MACE filter design minimizes the average energy of the output correlation planes, $g_i$, corresponding to the images $x_i$, subject to the constraints that the amplitude value at the origin of each plane, $g_i(0,0)$, is fixed to a specific value.

This result is achieved in the following manner. Let $\mathbf{D}$ be a $d \times d$ diagonal matrix carrying the average power spectrum of the training images, i.e.,

$$\mathbf{D}(k,k) = \frac{1}{N} \sum_{i=1}^{N} |\mathbf{x}_i(k)|^2, \qquad (2)$$

where $\mathbf{x}_i$ is the two-dimensional Fourier transform of $x_i$ in vector form. Then the optimal filter $\mathbf{h}$ should minimize the average correlation energy (ACE) measure, defined as $ACE = \mathbf{h}^+ \mathbf{D} \mathbf{h}$ (where $^+$ is the transpose conjugate), and meet the constraints $\mathbf{X}^+\mathbf{h} = \mathbf{u}$, where $\mathbf{X} = [\mathbf{x}_1, ..., \mathbf{x}_N]$ and $\mathbf{u} = [u_1, ..., u_n]^T$ carries the constraint values. The solution to this problem [15] is

$$\mathbf{h} = \mathbf{D}^{-1}\mathbf{X}(\mathbf{X}^+\mathbf{D}^{-1}\mathbf{X})^{-1}\mathbf{u}, \qquad (3)$$

where the filter $\mathbf{h}$ is expressed in vector form.

Robustness to noise can be achieved by minimizing the output variance of the correlation peak. If the noise in the training set is additive zero-mean and stationary, with power spectral density values arranged in a $d \times d$ diagonal matrix $\mathbf{P}$, then a measure that can also be minimized through the same process is the output noise variance, $ONV = \mathbf{h}^+\mathbf{P}\mathbf{h}$. This design is the minimum variance synthetic discriminant function (MVSDF) filter proposed by Kumar in [16].

For the palmprint classifier we propose, we use the optimal trade-off synthetic discriminant function (OTSDF) filter [17], which finds a compromise between the minimization of the ACE and ONV measures by minimizing the energy function

$$E(\mathbf{h}) = \alpha(ONV) + \beta(ACE), \qquad (4)$$

where $\beta = \sqrt{1 - \alpha^2}$. Then, the OTSDF filter is given by

$$\mathbf{h} = (\alpha\mathbf{I} + \beta\mathbf{D})^{-1}\mathbf{X}(\mathbf{X}^+(\alpha\mathbf{I} + \beta\mathbf{D})^{-1}\mathbf{X})^{-1}\mathbf{u}, \qquad (5)$$

where $\mathbf{I}$ is the identity matrix (we have further assumed the noise in the training is white). The advantage of this filter is that it allows for the minimization of the energy in the correlation plane, which produces sharp output peaks, while adjusting for noise tolerance.

## 3 Palmprint Data Set

We used the PolyU Palmprint Database [1][18]. It consists of 600 grayscale images, with 72 ppi, 6 palmprints per palm; 50 palms are right-hand palms and 50 are left-hand palms. When collecting the database, 3 palmprints are captured in a first session from each enrollee, and the other 3 in a second session about two months later. We use the set of palmprints from the first session for training and those from the second session for testing. Our method for extracting the palmprint patterns (i.e., segmentation) for the experiments is the same as and is explained in [11]. A brief description is provided in Figure 3.

## 4 Palmprint Verification Experiments and Results

The palmprint classification approach we propose is an OTSDF correlation filter classifier, and we use these filters in all the experiments presented here. In designing the filter for a given class, no information from the other classes is used, meaning that no impostor images where included in the filter design. We discuss results on two different sets of experiments.

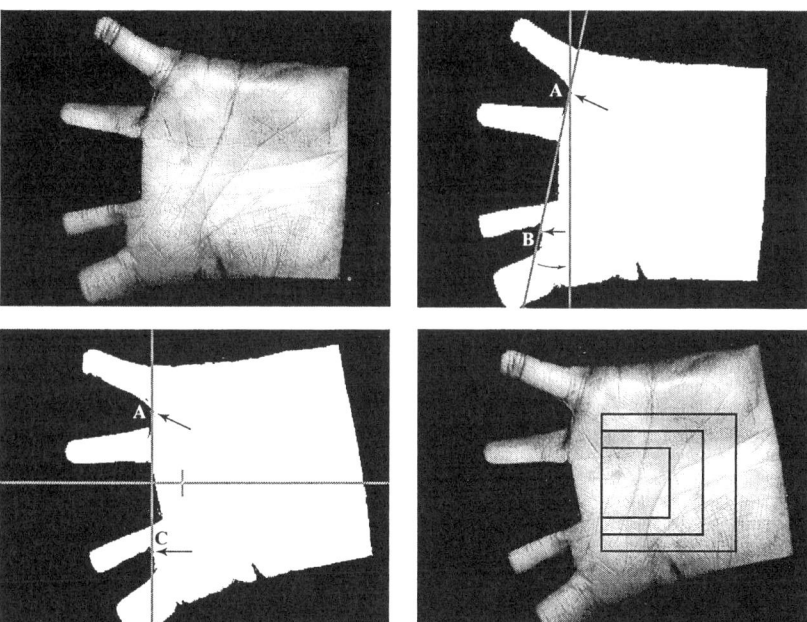

**Fig. 3.** Palmprint alignment procedure. An original image from the database *PolyU* (*top left*). Thresholded image (*top right*). Through a contour search the fiducial points at locations $A$ and $B$ are found. After computing the angle between the line through these two points and the vertical axis, the image is rotated about point $A$. The pixel at $B$ translates to location $C$ (bottom left), and the imaginary line through the two original fiducial points is now aligned to the vertical axis. Then the center between $A$ and $C$ is computed and a horizontal margin is defined to offset the box delimiting the region of interest. Finally, the palmprint regions are extracted (bottom right). Each square shown represents the regions of interest with size $64 \times 64, 96 \times 96, 128 \times 128$.

### 4.1  Experiment Set 1: Verification of 100 Classes

Our first set of experiments attempts verification of palmprint patterns from 100 users. We assume they all used their palm from the same hand, so that the principal lines of all patterns are in the same direction. Because the database consists of palmprints from 50 left hands and 50 right hands, we flipped the left-hand palmprint images to appear as captured from right-hand palms, and still consider them as a different class for a total of 100 classes. For classifiers designed to use the geometrical structure of the image patterns (such as correlation filter classifiers), this is a more difficult task as a result of the patterns increased similarity.

In this manner, we perform five experiments for classifiers using five different square regions with sides of length 64, 80, 96, 112, and 128 pixels. Results are shown in Table 1.

**Table 1.** Results of OTSDF filter classifier on 100 classes

| $n \times n$ | $64 \times 64$ | $80 \times 80$ | $96 \times 96$ | $112 \times 112$ | $128 \times 128$ |
|---|---|---|---|---|---|
| Avg FRRz ($M_1$) | 2.6% (8) | 1.0% (3) | 0.3% (1) | 1.0% (3) | 0.3% (1) |
| Avg FARz ($M_2$) | 0.07% (23) | 0.02% (6) | 0.01% (3) | 0.01% (3) | 0.03% (10) |

*Avg FRRz*: Average FRR at zero FAR. $M_1$ misses out of 300.
*Avg FARz*: Average FAR at zero FRR. $M_2$ misses out of 29,700.

A correlation filter can be considered as a two-class classifier, therefore the error rates are computed for each filter and the average of all the classes is reported. In this way, we compute the average of the FRR at zero FAR (*Avg FRRz*) and the average of the FAR at zero FRR (*Avg FARz*), which give a better interpretation of the classifier performance when either no impostor or no authentic palmprint exemplar is misclassified, respectively.

In this experiment, each correlation filter is tested to verify 3 authentic palmprints, but to reject 297 (3 images times 99 classes). The average FARz is thus computed using 29,700 match scores. Therefore, considering this average, the proposed classifier performs best with regions of size $96 \times 96$ and $112 \times 112$.

### 4.2 Experiment Set 2: Verification of 400 Classes

In this set of experiments we consider right-hand and left-hand palms from the *PolyU* database as they are and use them without flipping the left hands or performing any modification. Using a similar image segmentation method as above, we extract square palmprint patterns from different non-overlapping sections of the same palm, and consider each square section a different class. For each experiment, these square palmprint patterns have sides of length 72, 64, 56, 48, 40, and 32 pixels. We are able to extract 400 different patterns from this

**Table 2.** Results of OTSDF filter classifier on 400 classes

| $n$ | $in^2$ | $cm^2$ | Avg EER | Avg FARz |
|---|---|---|---|---|
| 72 | 1 | 6.4516 | 0.35% | 0.58% |
| 64 | 0.7901 | 5.0976 | 0.19% | 0.30% |
| 56 | 0.6049 | 3.9028 | 0.10% | 0.19% |
| 48 | 0.4444 | 2.8674 | 0.36% | 0.48% |
| 40 | 0.3086 | 1.9912 | 0.56% | 0.80% |
| 32 | 0.1975 | 1.2744 | 1.87% | 2.53% |

database, and thus we train a classifier consisting of 400 filters, one per class as before. Results are shown in Table 2, including the equivalent actual area of the patterns used. The average false acceptance rate at zero rejection rate ($Avg\ FARz$) for each experiment is computed using 478,800 match scores.

It is interesting to note that the filters do not necessarily perform increasingly worse as the area of the pattern is reduced. This shows that correlation filters make efficient use of local biometric content found in the palmprints. Although when the size of the pattern is extremely small, as expected, performance degrades.

These results are promising, considering the parameters of the experiment and the fact that the images in the database have a resolution of 72 ppi which is not high enough to capture palmprint features so accurately. We believe that increasing image resolution, and implementing more robust correlation filter designs (for example, by simply including more images in the training set) will provide classifiers with higher accuracy that will perform efficiently when the number of classes is large.

## 5 Conclusions

We have shown that the performance of correlation filter classifiers is promising regarding the implementation of palmprint verification for large data sets.

Our results show that implementation of correlation filters even with low resolution images (72 ppi), provides palmprint pattern verification that is highly accurate even for sizes of less than 1 in$^2$. This result is outstanding, considering that a whole palmprint is of approximately 5 in$^2$.

Finally, because correlation filters use image segmentation instead of feature extraction, the computational overhead and design of such preprocessing stage can be avoided. By performing verification of a new user with a single linear filtering operation of images of small size, correlation filters are a computationally efficient and reliable verification algorithm for security systems that require very high levels of accuracy.

## References

1. Zhang, D., Kong, A.W.K., You, J., Wong, M.: Online palmprint identification. IEEE Trans. Pattern Anal. Mach. Intell. **25** (2003) 1041–1050
2. Shu, W., Rong, G., Bian, Z., Zhang, D.: Automatic palmprint verification. Int. J. Image Graphics **1** (2001) 135–151
3. Duta, N., Jain, A.K., Mardia, K.V.: Matching of palmprints. Pattern Recognition Letters **23** (2002) 477–485
4. Zhang, D., Shu, W.: Two novel characteristics in palmprint verification: datum point invariance and line feature matching. Pattern Recognition **32** (1999) 691–702
5. Kong, A.W.K., Zhang, D., Li, W.: Palmprint feature extraction using 2-D gabor filters. Pattern Recognition **36** (2003) 2339–2347

6. Wu, X., Zhang, D., Wang, K.: Fisherpalms based palmprint recognition. Pattern Recognition Letters **24** (2003) 2829–2838
7. You, J., Kong, A.W.K., Zhang, D., Cheung, K.H.: On hierarchical palmprint coding with multiple features for personal identification in large databases. IEEE Trans. Circuits Syst. Video Techn. **14** (2004) 234–243
8. Kong, A.W.K., Zhang, D.: Feature-level fusion for effective palmprint authentication. In Zhang, D., Jain, A.K., eds.: ICBA. Volume 3072 of Lecture Notes in Computer Science., Springer (2004) 761–767
9. Zhang, L., Zhang, D.: Characterization of palmprints by wavelet signatures via directinal context modeling. IEEE Trans. Syst. Man, and Cyber. B **34** (2004) 1335–1347
10. Vijaya Kumar, B.: Tutorial survey of composite filter designs for optical correlators. Applied Optics **31** (1992) 4773–4801
11. Hennings, P., Vijaya Kumar, B.: Palmprint recognition using correlation filter classifiers. In: Proc. of 38th Annual Asilomar Conference on Signals, Systems, and Computers. Volume 1. (2004) 567–571
12. Vijaya Kumar, B., Savvides, M., Venkataramani, K., Xie, C., Thornton, J., Mahalanobis, A.: Biometric verification using advanced correlation filters. Applied Optics **43** (1992) 391–402
13. Savvides, M.: Reduced Complexity Face Recognition using Advanced Correlation Filters and Fourier Subspace Methods for Biometric Applications. PhD thesis, Department of Electrical and Computer Engineering, Carnegie Mellon University, Pittsburgh, Pennsylvania, USA (2004)
14. Venkataramani, K.: Reduced complexity correlation filters for fingerprint verification. Master's thesis, Carnegie Mellon University (2002)
15. Mahalanobis, A., Vijaya Kumar, B., Casasent, D.: Minimum average correlation energy filters. Applied Optics **26** (1987) 3633–3640
16. Vijaya Kumar, B.: Minimum-variance synthetic discriminant functions. J. of Opt. Soc. Am. A **3** (1986) 1579–1584
17. Refregier, P.: Filter design for optical pattern recognition: multicriteria optimization approach. Optics Letters **15** (1990) 854–856
18. The PolyU Palmprint Database, http://www.comp.polyu.edu.hk/~biometrics.

# Advanced Correlation Filters for Face Recognition Using Low-Resolution Visual and Thermal Imagery

Jingu Heo, Marios Savvides, and B.V.K. Vijaya Kumar

Department of Electrical and Computer Engineering,
Carnegie Mellon University, U.S.A.
jheo@cmu.edu, msavvid@ri.cmu.edu, kumar@ece.cmu.edu

**Abstract.** This paper presents the evaluation of face recognition performance using visual and thermal infrared (IR) face images with advanced correlation filter methods. Correlation filters are an attractive tool for face recognition due to features such as shift invariance, distortion tolerance, and graceful degradation. In this paper, we show that correlation filters perform very well when the face images are of significantly low resolution. Performing robust face recognition using low resolution images has many applications including human identification at a distance (HID). Minimum average correlation energy (MACE) filters and optimal trade-off synthetic discriminant function (OTSDF) filters are used in our experiments showing better performance over commercial face recognition algorithms such as FaceIt® based on Local Feature Analysis (LFA) using low resolution images. We also address the problems faced when using thermal images that contain eyeglasses which block the information around the eyes. Therefore we describe in detail a fully automated way of eyeglass detection and removal in thermal images resulting in a significant increase in thermal face recognition performance.

## 1 Introduction

Despite a significant level of maturity with a few practical successes, face recognition is still a highly challenging task in pattern recognition and computer vision [1]. The performance of face recognition systems varies significantly according to the environments where face images are captured and according to the way user-defined parameters are adjusted in different applications [2]. Since a face is essentially a 3D object, lighting sources from different directions may dramatically change visual appearances due to self-shadowing and specular reflections, thus face recognition accuracy degrades quickly when the lighting is dim or does not uniformly illuminate the face [3].

Illumination tolerant face recognition is an essential part of any face recognition system [4]. Currently there are many algorithms that have been developed with the aim of handling visual based face recognition in the presence of illumination variations [5]. Most algorithms developed for face recognition try to reduce the dimensionality of the face spaces in order to represent faces in a lower dimensional space. Such subspace analysis includes PCA (eigenfaces) [6], LDA (fisherfaces) [5], 3D linear Subspace [7], Local Feature Analysis (LFA) [8], and Independent

Component Analysis (ICA) [9] are still active research fields due to the unsatisfactory performance when faces in real-life practical applications.

Unlike using the visible spectrum, recognition of faces using different multi-spectral imaging modalities, in particular infrared (IR) imaging sensors [10][11] has become an area of growing interest. Thermal IR and particularly Long Wave Infra-Red (LWIR) imagery is independent of illumination since thermal IR sensors operating at particular wavelength bands measure heat energy emitted and not the light reflected from the objects. Hence thermal imaging has great advantages in face recognition under low illumination conditions and even in total darkness, where visual face recognition techniques fail. However, thermal images of a subject wearing eyeglasses may lose information around the eyes since glass blocks a large portion of thermal energy emitted by the face. Therefore, automatic eyeglass detection is important for further processing for thermal face recognition without redesigning overall face recognition system.

The use of correlation filters as a biometric verification is expanding due to their efficiency and robustness to illumination variations and other distortions. However, relatively less effort has been made to demonstrate their performance using Infra-Red facial imagery. In this paper, in an attempt to show the effectiveness of face recognition with correlation filters, we evaluate the performance of visual and thermal imagery over several different face recognition algorithms including Principal Component Analysis (PCA), normalized correlation, and Local Feature Algorithm (LFA). Co-registered visual and long-wave infrared (8-12$\mu m$) images acquired from the Equinox databases are used for the performance evaluation.

## 2 Advanced Correlation Filters

As one of the most popular correlation filters; the MACE filter [12][13] is designed to minimize the average correlation plane energy resulting from the training images, while constraining the value at the origin to certain pre-specified values. The minimization of energy is done while satisfying the linear constraints that the correlation values at the origin resulting from the training images take on pre-specified values (stored in row vector **u**), i.e.,

$$\mathbf{X}^+\mathbf{h} = \mathbf{u} \qquad (1)$$

where **X** is a $d^2 \times N$ complex matrix, where the $i$th column contains the 2-D Fourier transform of the $i$th training image lexicographically re-ordered into a column vector. Minimizing the average correlation energy while satisfying Eq. (1) leads to the following closed form solution for the MACE filter **h**.

$$\mathbf{h} = \mathbf{D}^{-1}\mathbf{X}(\mathbf{X}^+\mathbf{D}^{-1}\mathbf{X})^{-1}\mathbf{u} \qquad (2)$$

where **D** is a $d^2 \times d^2$ diagonal matrix containing the average power spectrum of training images along its diagonal. A way to optimally trade off [14] between noise tolerance (achieved through low frequency emphasis) and peak sharpness (through high frequency emphasis) producing the following optimal trade-off filter:

$$\mathbf{h} = \mathbf{T}^{-1}\mathbf{X}(\mathbf{X}^+\mathbf{T}^{-1}\mathbf{X})^{-1}\mathbf{u} \qquad (3)$$

where $\mathbf{T} = \left(\alpha \mathbf{D} + \sqrt{1-\alpha^2}\mathbf{C}\right)$, $0 \leq \alpha \leq 1$ and **C** is a $d^2 \times d^2$ diagonal matrix whose diagonal elements $\mathbf{C}(k,k)$ represent the noise power spectral density at frequency $k$. The peak-to-sidelobe ratio (PSR) and Peak-to-Correlation Energy (PCE) are one of the commonly used methods to measure the correlation output.

## 3  Eyeglass Detection and Removal in Thermal Imagery

Since thermal faces are integrated with several features comprised of different blobs, the use of an ellipse can be a powerful representation of certain features around the faces in the thermal images. Since eyeglass regions are usually cooler than any of the facial components [11], binary images can be achieved via thresholding. These binary images then are connected using the chain coding scheme; thus providing data points for fitting ellipses as shown in Figure 1.

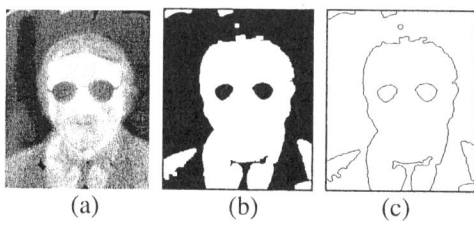

(a)    (b)    (c)

**Fig. 1.** Results of the connected components; (a) an original thermal image, (b) the thresholded thermal image, and (c) connected components

From the results provided by inter-connected components using the thresholded thermal images, each connected component is fitted with ellipses. An equation for an ellipse can be denoted as the product of a coefficient vector **a** and an independent variable (containing data points) **x** :

$$F(\mathbf{a},\mathbf{x}) = \mathbf{a}\mathbf{x} = ax^2 + bxy + cy^2 + dx + ey + f = 0 \quad (4)$$

where $\mathbf{a} = [a\ b\ c\ d\ e\ f]$ and $\mathbf{x} = [x^2\ xy\ y^2\ x\ y\ 1]^T$. Ellipse fitting is to minimize the sum squared algebraic distance $E = |F(\mathbf{a},\mathbf{x})|^2$ over the set of **N** data points in terms of least squares. This can be denoted as

$$\hat{\mathbf{a}} = \arg\min_{\mathbf{a}} \{ \sum_{i=1}^{N}(F(\mathbf{a},\mathbf{x}_i))^2 \} \quad (5)$$

Fitzgibbon et al [15] proposed direct least conic fitting algorithms while applying constraints $\mathbf{a}^T D \mathbf{a} = 1$, where D is 6*6 matrix with D(1,3) = -2, D(2,2) = 1, D(3,1) = -2, and otherwise containing zeros. This can be interpreted as applying constraints using $b^2 - 4ac = 1$ with the unique solution $\hat{\mathbf{a}}$ which minimizes the algebraic distance E. After finding solutions for fitting ellipses, it is convenient to convert into the standard form of an ellipse to use its parameters effectively. Figure 2 shows an ellipse with the parameters that are used for the eyeglass detection in thermal face images. The center of an *i*th ellipse is denoted by $C_i$, $2\alpha_i$ denotes the length of major axis, $2\beta_i$ is the length of minor axis, and $\theta_i$ indicates the orientation angle of the ellipse in the range of $-\pi/2 < \theta_i < \pi/2$.

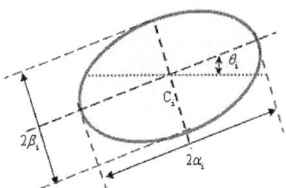

**Fig. 2.** Parameters of an ellipse used for the similarity measure

A pair of ellipses of similar shape is considered as eyeglasses in thermal images. In this paper, the similarity of $i$th and $j$th ellipsoids is defined as

$$S_{ij} = \frac{\alpha_i \beta_i}{\alpha_j \beta_j} \left( \frac{k_1}{k_1 + |\theta_{ij}|} \right) \left( \frac{k_2}{k_2 + |\theta_i + \theta_j|} \right) \quad (6)$$

where $\theta_{ij}$ represents the angle between the centers of the two ellipses $C_i$ and $C_j$ and $k_1$ and $k_2$ are weighting factors for the similarity measure. Since those features used for the similarity measure are heterogeneous, weights are applied for better similarity measure. We assume that $\alpha_j \beta_j > \alpha_i \beta_i$ so the similarity measure $S_{ij}$ is less than 1. The distance between a pair of ellipses are also considered and we discard if the major axis is five times larger than the minor axis ($0.2 < \beta/\alpha < 1$).

After detecting eyeglasses, the eyeglass regions are replaced with an average eye template in the thermal images. Manually selected landmarks points (20 points) for both left and right eye templates are used to retrieve the ellipse parameters in order to find the geometrical transformation between eyeglass candidates as shown in Figure 3.

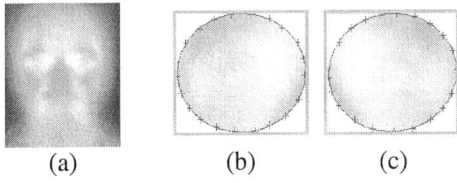

(a)    (b)    (c)

**Fig. 3.** Estimation of elliptical parameters for both left (b) and right (c) eye template acquired from the average thermal image without eyeglasses (a)

We apply an affine transformation for the replacement of the eyeglasses. Thus new points $\mathbf{x}'(x', y', 1)$ in the eyeglass can be replaced by the points $\mathbf{X}(x, y, 1)$ in the eye template. This can be denoted as $\mathbf{x}' = \mathbf{T}\mathbf{x}$ where

$$\mathbf{T} = \begin{bmatrix} s_1 * \cos(\theta) & s_2 * \sin(\theta) & t_x \\ -s_1 * \sin(\theta) & s_2 * \cos(\theta) & t_y \\ 0 & 0 & 1 \end{bmatrix} \quad (7)$$

where $s_1$ and $s_2$ are the major and minor axis size ratio between eye template and eyeglass respectively, $\theta$ is the angle of the eyeglass, and translation vector $t_x$ and $t_y$ are assumed to be zero since the transformation is processed based on the center of the two ellipses. Figure 4 illustrates an example of detecting eyeglasses in thermal images using the ellipse fitting method and the result of eyeglass replacement with a template eyeglass pattern. Only two ellipses in Figure 4(c) remained after applying the similarity measure scheme showing the true location of the eyeglasses. From the result of the similarity measure, we claim that eyeglasses are present if the score ($S_{ij}$) is larger than 0.7.

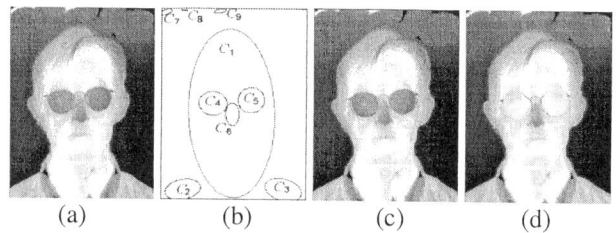

(a)  (b)  (c)  (d)

**Fig. 4.** Eyeglass detection and replacement; (a) an original image, (b) ellipse fitting results from connected components, (c) eyeglass regions detected, and (d) a face image replaced with eyeglass templates

Table 1 summarizes the performance of eyeglass detection algorithm with the ellipse fitting method. For the performance of the eyeglass detection, a subset of LWIR Equinox database (a total of 1643 images, and 536 face images with eyeglasses) is used. We calculated the False Rejection Rate (FRR) and False Acceptance Rate (FAR). We also increased the number of thresholds in the range of [0.5 0.65] and measure the performance of the eyeglass detection using multiple thresholds showing that better performance can be achieved over a single threshold scheme with an Equal Error Rate (ERR) of approximately 7.0 %. A fully automatic eyeglass replacement is achieved when the similarity score is higher than 0.9.

**Table 1.** Performance of the eyeglass detection scheme

| Number of Thresholds | True Positive | False Negative | False Positive | True Negative |
|---|---|---|---|---|
| 1 | 384 | 152 | 12 | 1095 |
| 2 | 444 | 92 | 29 | 1078 |
| 3 | 481 | 55 | 30 | 1077 |
| 4 | 485 | 51 | 32 | 1075 |
| 5 | 494 | 42 | 43 | 1064 |
| 6 | 494 | 42 | 47 | 1060 |
| 7 | 499 | 37 | 51 | 1056 |
| Total = 1643 | Eyeglass= 536 | | No eyeglass= 1107 | |

## 4 Performance Comparison

A subset of Equinox database [16] is used for the evaluation of visual and thermal face recognition performances. The database consists of visual and thermal IR images of 3,244 (1,622 per modality) face images from 90 individuals. Images taken with frontal lighting conditions are used as the gallery images. The performance is measured via the first success rates (rank-1 recognition). Manually selected eye positions from the visual images are used for the normalization of faces not only for visual images and but also for the thermal images as they were acquired using a co-registered thermal camera). This is one of the challenges of using only thermal images as it is very hard to determine where the eyes are and thus the use of a co-registered camera which can acquire both visual and thermal images is necessary to perform proper face normalization for scale, rotation using the eye locations. Figure 5 shows an example of the normalized faces acquired from both modalities.

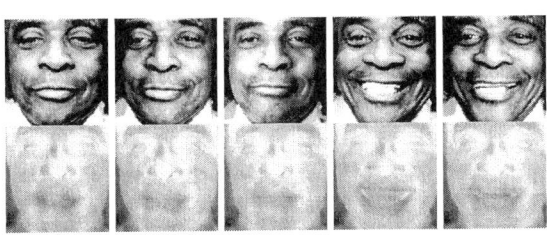

**Fig. 5.** The normalized faces: visual (top row) and thermal (bottom row) images of the same individuals taken from different conditions

The performance is evaluated while varying the face size to very low resolutions. Low resolutions also allow for using low-memory computing platforms and face recognition speed is faster with smaller image resolutions due to a lower computational demand. Also from a practical application, there are many real-world applications where the face images acquired from surveillance footage is of poor low-quality low-resolution video feed. Figure 6 shows the performance of correlation filters (MACE and OTSDF). The best performance is achieved from the thermal imagery using the OTSDF filters producing a 96.5% recognition rate when 3 images are used during training; while the visual face recognition performance performs at best 85.0%. The results show that under variations such as illumination and expression, thermal face recognition can perform better than visual face recognition which is significantly affected by variations.

In an effort to show the effectiveness of correlation filters, we compared commonly used face recognition algorithms, such as Normalized Correlation, PCA and a well-known commercial face recognition software FaceIt®, which has been highly ranked by the face recognition vendor test (FRVT) based on Local Feature Analysis (LFA) are also included in this experiment. Table 2 shows the comparison results using a low-resolution face size (32*32 pixels) and a higher resolution face size of 128*128 pixels. FaceIt® gave robust performance results with visual and thermal images when face size is large enough, however for low resolution images (such as 32x32), OTSDF filter outperforms FaceIt® recognition algorithm. Throughout the performance comparison, thermal face recognition gives better performance over visual face recognition regardless of the different algorithms.

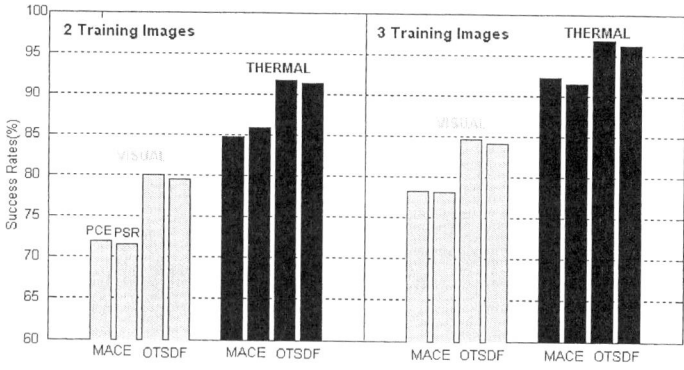

**Fig. 6.** Performance comparison with correlation filters using visual and thermal face recognition (No eyeglasses)

**Table 2.** Performance comparison using different face recognition algorithms; Recognition Rates (%), No eyeglasses

|  | Small face size (32*32) – 3 gallery | | Large face size (128*128) – 3 gallery | |
| --- | --- | --- | --- | --- |
|  | **Visual** | **Thermal** | Visual | Thermal |
| OTSDF | **84.10** | **96.84** | 79.98 | 88.83 |
| PCA | **60.85** | **90.38** | 55.53 | 91.38 |
| Normalized Correlation | **46.16** | **56.28** | 51.54 | 60.91 |
| LFA (FaceIt®) | **82.33** | **85.66** | 94.54 | 96.22 |

Table 3 shows the performance comparison results where individuals are wearing eyeglasses. We reported the best performance of different algorithms regardless of the size of the face. We also observed that visual face recognition is only slightly affected by the presence of the eyeglasses. FaceIt® shows almost similar performance

**Table 3.** Performance comparison using different face recognition algorithms; Recognition Rates (%), Eyeglass

|  | Visual | Thermal | |
| --- | --- | --- | --- |
|  | N/A | Before Removal | **After Removal** |
| OTSDF | 78.10 | 45.76 | **85.77** |
| Normalized Correlation | 50.11 | 44.72 | **50.68** |
| LFA (FaceIt®) | 90.11 | 40.56 | **80.34** |

regardless of the presence of the eyeglasses in visual images also. Without the eyeglass removal, thermal face recognition shows a very low performance rates. After our proposed eyeglass removal method, overall performance is significantly improved in thermal face recognition regardless of the different algorithms. However our proposed OTSDF filter approach performs the best among the algorithms.

## 5 Summary

This paper presents the performance evaluation of visual and thermal infrared (IR) images using correlation filters and also includes comparison with other face recognition algorithms. From the experimental results, our advanced correlation filters show that the best performance can be achieved at very low resolutions (as low as 32x32 pixels) for both visual and thermal images which are ideal for practical surveillance scenarios. Working with low resolution face images can also be an important factor for some face recognition applications where low-memory and fast speed are a critical issue. We also show that for subjects wearing eyeglasses, our proposed eyeglass replacement algorithm significantly improves the recognition accuracy in thermal images.

## References

[1] I. Craw, N. Costen, T. Kato, and S. Akamatsu, "How should we represent faces for automatic recognition?," *IEEE Trans. PAMI*, Vol. 21, No. 8, pp.725-736, 1999.
[2] P. J. Phillips, P. Grother, R. J. Micheals, D. M. Blackburn, E. Tabassi, and M. Bone, "Face Recognition Vendor Test 2002," *Evaluation Report, National Institute of Standards and Technology*, pp.1-56, 2003.
[3] Y. Adini, Y. Moses, and S. Ullman, "Face Recognition: The Problem of Compensating for Changes in Illumination Direction," *IEEE Trans. PAMI*, Vol.19, No.7, pp.721-732, 1997.
[4] R. Chellappa, C.L. Wilson, S. Sirohey, "Human and machine recognition of faces: a survey," *Proceedings of the IEEE*, Vol.83 (5), pp705-741, 1995.
[5] P.Belhumeur, J. Hespanha, and D. Kriegman, "Eigenfaces vs Fisherfaces: Recognition Using Class Specific Linear Projection," *IEEE Trans. PAMI*, Vol.19. No.7, pp.711- 720, 1997.
[6] M. Turk and A. Pentland, "Eigenfaces for Recognition," Journal of *Cognitive Neuroscience*, Vol. 3, pp.72-86, 1991.
[7] P.Belhumeur and D.Kriegman, "What is the Set of Images of an Object under All Possible Illumination Conditions," *Int. J. Computer Vision*, Vol.28, No.3, pp.245-260, 1998.
[8] P. S. Penev, "Local Feature Analysis: A Statistical Theory for Information Representation and Transmission," *Ph.D. Thesis, The Rockefeller University*, 1998.
[9] M.S.Bartlett, J.R.. Movellan, T.J. Sejnowski, "Face recognition by independent component analysis, *IEEE Trans. on Neural Networks*. Vol. 13, No. 6, pp. 1450-1464, 2002.
[10] L. B. Wolff, D. A. Socolinsky, and C. K. Eveland, "Quantitative measurement of illumination invariance for face recognition using thermal infrared imagery," *Proc. CVPR Workshop on Computer Vision Beyond the Visible Spectrum*, 2001.

[11] J. Heo, S. Kong, B. Abidi, and M. Abidi, "Fusion of Visual and Thermal Signatures with Eyeglass Removal for Robust Face Recognition," *IEEE Workshop on Object Tracking and Classification Beyond the Visible Spectrum in conjunction with CVPR 2004*, pp. 94-99, Washington, D.C., 2004.

[12] A. Mahalanobis, B.V.K. Vijaya Kumar, and D. Casasent, "Minimum average correlation energy filters," *Appl. Opt.* 26, pp. 3633-3630, 1987.

[13] M. Savvides, B.V.K. Vijaya Kumar and P. Khosla, "Face verification using correlation filters," *Proc. Of Third IEEE Automatic Identification Advanced Technologies*, Tarrytown, NY, pp.56-61, 2002.

[14] P. Refregier, "Filter Design for optical pattern recognition: Multi-criteria optimization approach," *Optics Letters,* Vol, 5, pp. 854-856, 1990.

[15] A. W. Fitzgibbon, M. Pilu, and R. B. Fisher, "Direct Least Square Fitting of Ellipses," *IEEE Trans. PAMI*, Vol. 21, No. 5, pp.476-480, 1999.

[16] http://www.equinoxsensors.com/products/HID.html

# Robust Iris Recognition Using Advanced Correlation Techniques

Jason Thornton, Marios Savvides, and B.V.K. Vijaya Kumar

Electrical & Computer Eng, Carnegie Mellon University,
Pittsburgh, PA 15213, U.S.A.
jthornto@andrew.cmu.edu, msavvid@ri.cmu.edu, kumar@ece.cmu.edu

**Abstract.** The iris is considered one of the most reliable and stable biometrics as it is believed to not change significantly during a person's lifetime. Standard techniques for iris recognition, popularized by Daugman, apply Gabor wavelet analysis for feature extraction. In this paper, we consider an alternative method for iris recognition, the use of advanced distortion-tolerant correlation filters for robust pattern matching. These filters offer two primary advantages: shift invariance, and the ability to tolerate within-class image variations. The iris images we use in our experiments are from the CASIA database and also from an iris database we collected at CMU. In this paper, we perform automatic segmentation of the iris (which surrounds the pupil) from the rest of the eye, normalizing for scale and pupil dilation. We then use these segmented iris images to compare the recognition performance of various methods, including Gabor wavelet feature extraction, to correlation filters.

## 1 Introduction

A biometric is any physical characteristic of a person which may distinguish that individual from others. Biometric recognition has obvious applications in security, as well as any task that requires authorized access via an automatic identification system. One such biometric characteristic is the iris pattern, which is contained in the colored portion of the eye. Figure 1 shows a sample image of the iris and its visible pattern, which is largely determined by a meshwork of muscle ligaments. The iris pattern is thought to be unique to each eye, with a high degree of discrimination ability [1] (note that the left and right irises from the same person are also distinct). The primary challenge is to build an iris recognition system that allows for intra-class variation resulting from pupil dilations, eyelid obstruction, camera focus, and other factors that can affect the iris pattern. We employ correlation filters to handle this type of distortion.

Most existing research in this area focuses on extracting consistent features from a segmented iris pattern. Wildes [2] decomposed the iris signal into different frequency bands, using normalized correlation with templates to perform recognition. Other feature extraction techniques have involved projecting the iris pattern onto an Independent Components Analysis (ICA) basis [3], or a Fractional Fourier basis [4]. Most recently, iris patterns have been characterized by their location in global Principal Component Analysis (PCA) subspaces [5].

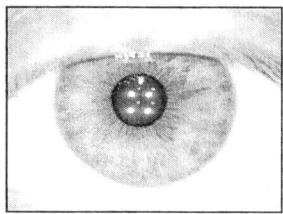

**Fig. 1.** Iris pattern, contained in an eye image

The most popular technique for feature extraction uses Gabor wavelet analysis [6] to represent the texture of the iris. Daugman [7] pioneered this type of feature extraction for irises, using the phase response of Gabor filters. His early success has popularized this recognition algorithm as a standard in the field, including attempts at practical implementation [8].

In Section 2, we discuss effective segmentation of the iris pattern from the rest of the eye image. In Section 3, we describe two variations of the Gabor encoding algorithm, and some specifics of their implementation for the purpose of testing. Section 4 explains correlation filter discriminants and their advantages when applied to iris images. Sections 5 and 6 give results and conclusions.

## 2 Iris Segmentation

Segmentation and normalization of the iris pattern are natural pre-processing steps before feature extraction. Once the iris region boundaries have been detected, we can map the iris image into polar coordinates $I(\rho, \theta)$ using the center of the pupil as the origin. In this mapping, the radial width of the iris (along the $\rho$ axis) is normalized to one. As a result, every iris pattern is mapped into the same rectangular area in the new coordinate system. Figure 2 shows an example of a segmented iris mapping. An attractive attribute of this type of segmentation is that it normalizes for translation and scale of the iris pattern, as well as pupil dilation. However, in-plane rotations of the iris image result in cyclic shifts of the polar mapping.

In order to compute the segmented mapping in Figure 2, we must find the inner and outer boundary of the iris. Daugman discovered that modeling the iris boundaries as non-concentric circles was effective and reduced the problem to the selection of 6 parameters (center positions and radii of the inner circle and the outer circle). Conceptually, each iris boundary may be detected as the location where the image intensity along an expanding contour becomes suddenly brighter.

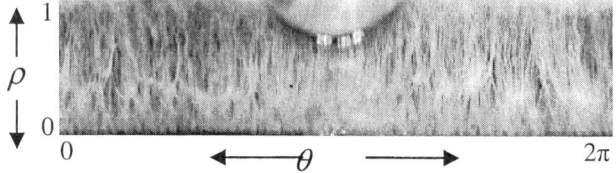

**Fig. 2.** Iris pattern mapped to a normalized rectangle in polar coordinate system

If we represent the original eye image as the intensity function $E(x, y)$, we can define a partial circular integration at the circle specified by $x_c$, $y_c$ and $r$ as

$$p(x_c, y_c, r) = \int_{I_\theta} E(x_c + r\cos\theta, y_c + r\sin\theta) \, d\theta \qquad (1)$$

where $I_\theta$ is a sub-interval of $[0, 2\pi]$ including the angles most likely to be unaffected by eyelid occlusion; this includes the left and right sides of the eye. We find our boundaries by searching for two local maxima satisfying

$$\max_{x_c, y_c, r} \left[ \frac{\partial p(x_c, y_c, r)}{\partial r} \right] \qquad (2)$$

We may think of $p(x_c, y_c, r)$ as a modified version of a circular Hough transform of the eye image (modified because we are only using a partial circle). We compute a fast approximation to $p(x_c, y_c, r)$, using a bank of contour filters as described in our earlier work [9]. After computing this space, we select the largest gradients in the radial direction, obtaining an estimate for both the inner and outer iris boundaries.

We performed boundary detection and normalized segmentation on every eye image in the two datasets we used for testing. Figure 3 shows an example of our automatic segmentation process. Our segmentation succeeded in approximately 98-99% of eye images, and tends to fail mostly in cases of heavy eyelid occlusion. Another algorithm for segmentation was developed by Masek and Kovesi [14], who publicly distribute their implementation. We found that our segmentation algorithm works approximately 60 times faster in comparison (both use un-optimized Matlab code).

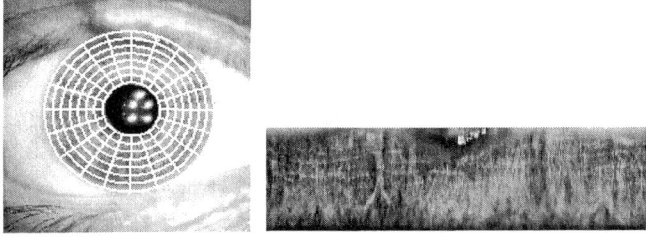

**Fig. 3.** Iris boundary detection, and mapping into normalized polar coordinates

## 3 Gabor Wavelet Iris Encoding

In this section we discuss iris encoding using Gabor wavelet analysis; specifically, we describe two types of Gabor analysis that we use as a benchmark for recognition performance. A 2D Gabor wavelet has the functional form of a complex exponential with a Gaussian envelope. Expressed in the segmented coordinate system, it is given by

$$\psi(\rho, \theta) = \exp\left[ -\frac{\rho^2}{2\sigma_\rho^2} - \frac{\theta^2}{2\sigma_\theta^2} - j\omega\theta \right] \qquad (3)$$

The Gaussian envelope, with size determined by parameters $\sigma_\rho$ and $\sigma_\theta$, localizes the wavelet in space. The complex exponential localizes the wavelet in frequency (in this definition, the center frequency is $\omega$ in the direction of the $\theta$ axis). We change the 2D frequency component by rotating the Gabor wavelet, and by scaling it by powers of 2. Figure 4 shows the real part of a Gabor wavelet, at a sample orientation. We can also change the spatial component of the Gabor wavelet by simple translation.

Choosing different parameter values for scaling, rotation, and translation generates a family of Gabor wavelets. Daugman first suggested using such a family of wavelets as a basis for representing the iris pattern (note that this basis is non-orthogonal). The iris is projected onto the Gabor wavelet basis to yield a set of complex coefficients. Each coefficient is encoded by two bits, depending on which quadrant the complex coefficient lies in. To compute a match score between two iris patterns, the percentage of matching bits of their characteristic codes is calculated.

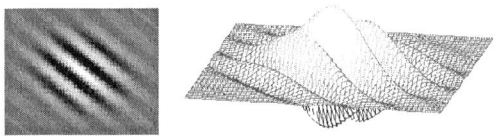

**Fig. 4.** 2D and 3D view of Gabor wavelet (real part) oriented at $\phi = \pi/4$

We implemented a Gabor wavelet encoding algorithm, selecting a basis of 2D Gabor wavelets spanning 5 scales and 12 orientations and distributed spatially across the iris pattern. This basis consists of more scales and orientations than are typically used for iris encoding [7], but we found that this basis performed better than the other wavelet family compositions we tried. The basis generates a characteristic code for each iris on the order of $10^4$ bits. An alternate implementation, also made publicly available by Masek and Kovesi [14], uses a basis of 1D log-Gabor wavelets. This basis has only one orientation (horizontal) but many translations.

Once an iris has been encoded, comparing it to template codes is very computationally efficient, requiring only bitwise operations and sums. As a result, many templates may be checked for match at a cheap computational cost. The encoding process, which involves a projection onto a large basis, does require some significant computation up front.

Gabor wavelet encoding algorithms rely on the consistency of Gabor texture features among iris patterns from the same eye. However, the amount of intra-class variation of iris patterns (and by extension, their Gabor texture features) becomes problematically high for certain subjects and camera systems. In addition, the only way that rotation of the eye image can be accounted for is to repeat the matching process for multiple rotated images during evaluation.

Correlation filter classification offers an alternative way to address these problems. We compared a Gabor wavelet algorithm to the correlation filter algorithm in [9]. Preliminary results on a dataset of artificially distorted iris patterns suggested that correlation filter recognition may improve accuracy under distortion, in part because it can handle rotation of the iris without the extra processing required by the Gabor wavelet method.

## 4 Advanced Correlation Filter Design

A correlation filter is designed specifically for the recognition of one pattern class (in this case an individual's iris), represented by a set of training images. Given a test image, we apply the correlation filter by performing cross-correlation between the test image and the filter. The resulting correlation plane $C$ should contain a sharp peak if there exists a match between the filter and image. We measure the degree of match using peak-to-correlation energy (PCE), defined here as PCE = (peak - $\mu$)/$\sigma$ where $\mu$ and $\sigma$ denote mean and standard deviation, respectively. Correlation filters are shift-invariant (which means they can handle rotation of the iris), and they are designed to recognize distorted or noisy versions of their pattern class.

There are a variety of advanced correlation filter design choices [10]. One common design technique sets constraints on the heights of the correlation peaks resulting from centered training images. For example, all authentic training images, which contain a sample of the pattern class, must result in a correlation peak at the origin of $C(0, 0) = 1$, while all imposter training images must have $C(0, 0) = 0$. Subject to this constraint, the filter design optimizes some performance criteria.

For the Optimal Trade-off Synthetic Discriminant Function (OTSDF) filter [11], we optimize a trade-off between two different criteria, namely average correlation energy (ACE) and output noise variance (ONV). ACE (given below) measures the average energy of the filter outputs resulting from our training images, which we wish to reduce to lower sidelobes. Let **h** be a vector representing the correlation filter and **D** represent a diagonal matrix carrying the average power spectrum of the training images; then the ACE can be written as

$$ACE = \mathbf{h}^+\mathbf{Dh} \qquad (4)$$

where + denotes conjugate transpose. The ONV characterizes the variance of the noise at the correlation output. If the input noise is white, ONV is given by

$$ONV = \mathbf{h}^+\mathbf{h} \qquad (5)$$

Minimizing a weighted sum (determined by a parameter $\alpha$) of ACE and ONV subject to the constraints that the correlation peak is 1 for the authentics leads to

$$\mathbf{h} = \mathbf{A}^{-1}\mathbf{X}(\mathbf{X}^+\mathbf{A}^{-1}\mathbf{X})^{-1}\mathbf{u} \qquad (6)$$

with $\mathbf{A} = \alpha\mathbf{I} + \sqrt{1-\alpha^2}\mathbf{D}$. Vector **u** holds the peak constraints mentioned above (1 for authentics, 0 for imposters), and the $i$th column of matrix **X** contains the vectorized 2D-Fourier transform of the $i$th training images denoted as $\mathbf{X}_i$.

The OTSDF filter accomplishes two goals: it produces sharp peaks for training images, by reducing ACE in Eq. (4), and it achieves tolerance to additive white noise, by reducing ONV in Eq. (5). The resulting filter gives good discrimination between authentic and imposter images, even when authentic test images are noisy.

The primary computational cost when applying a correlation filter is the Fast Fourier Transform (FFT) that generates the correlation plane $C$. This is an order $O(MN \log MN)$ operation for $M$ by $N$ images. Comparing an image to multiple filters requires one inverse FFT per filter, which is more expensive than comparing bit codes, but requires less computation up-front because there is no code to generate.

## 5 Testing and Results

We ran recognition experiments on two different iris databases: the CASIA database from the Chinese Academy of Sciences [12], and a database collected by the authors at Carnegie Mellon University (CMU). Both databases contain the sort of within-class iris image variations we would expect to encounter in a real recognition system. Adjustments in head and eye position, as well as camera position, introduce translations, rotations, and scale changes. In addition, subjects frequently dilate and contract the pupil (an involuntary reflex) as well as occlude the iris with upper and lower eyelids.

The CASIA database contains iris images collected under infrared illumination. It has 108 iris classes, each with 7 images of the same iris (the 7 images are collected in two separate imaging sessions). The resolution of each image is 280 by 320 pixels. The CMU iris database was collected under normal illumination and contains 101 iris classes. Each class consists of approximately 20 - 25 images from the same eye, collected in two different sessions up to six months apart. The original images have much higher resolution than needed (approximately 11 megapixels); consequently, they are downsampled before processing. Figure 5 shows sample images.

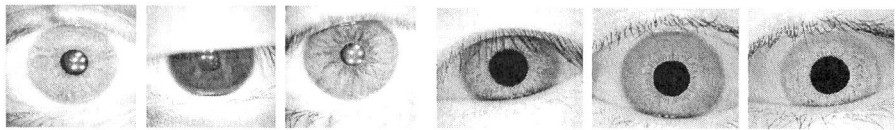

**Fig. 5.** Sample iris images from CMU (*left*) and CASIA (*right*) databases

We compared the performance of advanced correlation filter designs to other methods: primarily the Gabor wavelet encoding methods described in Section 3, but also PCA [5] and normalized correlation. We extracted sections of the iris not likely to experience eyelid occlusion and applied our classifiers to these sections.

For testing on the CASIA database, we used the first image of each class for training data, and used the other 6 images from each class as test data. In total, this allowed for 648 authentic comparisons (between irises from the same class) and 69,336 imposter comparisons (between irises from different classes). We tried 4 recognition algorithms on CASIA; results are given in the ROC curves of Figure 6, which show False Accept Rate against False Reject Rate as the match threshold is varied.

For the larger CMU database, we used 5 arbitrary images from each iris class as training data. The remaining 20 images per class were used for the testing. In total, this gave approximately 2,000 authentic comparisons and 200,000 imposter comparisons. On the CMU database, we applied OTSDF correlation filter classification and both implementations of Gabor wavelet encoding classification. The results are plotted in the ROC curves in Figure 7.

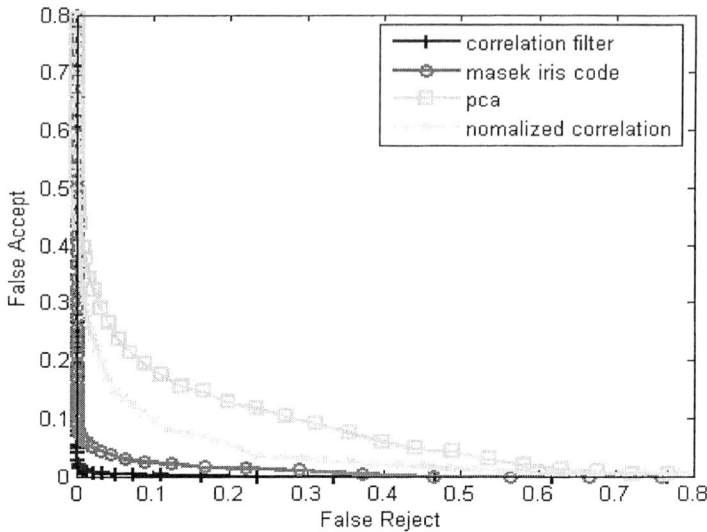

**Fig. 6.** ROC curves comparing the performance of different algorithms on CASIA database

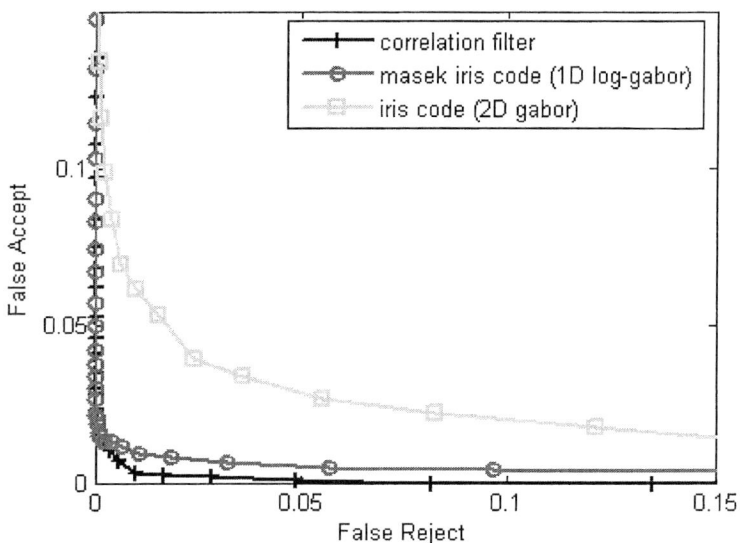

**Fig. 7.** ROC curves comparing the performance of different algorithms on CMU database

Correlation filters outperform the other methods on both datasets, giving an Equal Error Rate (EER) of 0.61% for CMU images, and 0.94% for CASIA images. If we allow match thresholds to vary from class to class (i.e., each correlation filter has its own match threshold), the average class-by-class EER drops to 0.15% for the CMU database and 0.24% for the CASIA database.

## 6 Conclusions

Iris patterns are intrinsically good biometric identifiers. However, distortions due to instrument noise, camera focus, head movement, eyelid occlusion, and pupil contraction may increase significantly the amount of within-class variation of recorded iris patterns. As a result, commonly used iris features are not always consistent enough to guarantee good recognition. Rotations of the head or eye become shifts in the segmented polar-mapped iris images. When these images are projected onto some basis for feature extraction (whether Gabor wavelets or Principal Components), even small shifts tend to perturb the projection coefficients enough to degrade recognition. Correlation filter discriminants have the natural advantage of shift invariance.

In our experiments, we show improvement in recognition accuracy on both CASIA and the CMU database by using a correlation filter method. Specifically, we use OTSDF filters that have built-in noise tolerance. Combined with fast iris segmentation pre-processing, they also offer built-in rotation invariance. These two attributes account for the advantage we see in recognition performance.

**Acknowledgement.** This research is funded in part by Carnegie Mellon's CyberSecurity Lab (CyLab).

## References

1. F.H. Adler: Physiology of the Eye. Mosby, St. Louis (1965)
2. R.P. Wildes: Iris Recognition: An Emerging Biometric Technology. Proceedings of the IEEE, vol. 85. (September 1997) 1348-1363
3. Y.P. Huang, S.W. Luo, E.Y. Chen: An Efficient Iris Recognition System. Proc. of Intl. Conf. on Machine Learning and Cybernetics, vol. 1. (2002) 450-454
4. L. Yu, K.Q. Wang, C.F. Wang, D. Zhang: Iris Verification Based on Fractional Fourier Transform. Proc. of Intl. Conf. on Machine Learning and Cybernetics. (2002)
5. V. Dorairaj, N. Schmid, G. Fahmy: Performance Evaluation of Iris Based Recognition System Implementing PCA and ICA Encoding Techniques. Proc. of SPIE Def. and Sec. Symposium (2005)
6. Y. Zhu, T. Tan, Y. Wang: Biometric Personal Identification Based on Iris Patterns. Proc. of Intl. Conf. on Pattern Recognition (ICPR), vol. 2. (2000) 801-804
7. J. G. Daugman: High Confidence Visual Recognition of Persons by a Test of Statistical Independence. IEEE Transactions on Pattern Analysis and Machine Intelligence, vol. 15, no. 11. (1993) 1148-61
8. G.O. Williams: Iris Recognition Technology. IEEE AES Systems Magazine. (1997)
9. B.V.K. Vijaya Kumar, J. Thornton: Distortion-Tolerant Iris Recognition Using Advanced Correlation Filters. Proc. of Multi-Modal User Authentication (MMUA). (Dec. 2003)
10. B.V.K. Vijaya Kumar: Tutorial Survey of Composite Filter Designs for Optical Correlators. Applied Opt., vol. 31. (1992) 4773-4801
11. B.V.K. Vijaya Kumar, D.W. Carlson, and A. Mahalanobis: Optimal Trade-off Synthetic Discriminant Function Filters for Arbitrary Devices. Optics Letters, Vol. 19. (1994)
12. CASIA Iris Image Database, http://www.sinobiometrics.com
13. Libor Masek, Peter Kovesi: MATLAB Source Code for a Biometric Identification System Based on Iris Patterns. School of Computer Science and Software Engineering. University of Western Australia. (2003)

# Secure and Efficient Transmissions of Fingerprint Images for Embedded Processors

Daesung Moon[1], Yongwha Chung[2], Kiyoung Moon[1], and SungBum Pan[3]

[1] Biometrics Technology Research Team, ETRI, Daejeon, Korea
{daesung, kymoon}@etri.re.kr
[2] Department of Computer and Information Science, Korea University, Korea
ychungy@korea.ac.kr
[3] Division of Information and Control Measurement Engineering, Chosun University, Korea
sbpan@chosun.ac.kr

**Abstract.** In this paper, we propose a secure and efficient protocol to transmit fingerprint images from a fingerprint sensor to a client by exploiting characteristics of fingerprint images. To guarantee the integrity/confidentiality of the fingerprint images transmitted, a standard encryption algorithm is employed. Because the fingerprint sensor is computationally limited, however, such encryption algorithm may not be applied to the full fingerprint images in real-time. To reduce the computational workload on the resource-constrained sensor, we apply the encryption algorithm to a nonce for integrity and to a specific bitplane of each pixel of the fingerprint image for confidentiality. Experimental results show that the integrity/confidentiality of the fingerprint images can be guaranteed without any leakage of the ridge information. Also, the image-based selective bitplane encryption can be completed in real-time on embedded processors.

**Keywords:** Biometrics, Fingerprint Verification, Embedded Processors.

## 1 Introduction

Traditionally, verified users have gained access to secure information systems, buildings, or equipment via multiple PINs, passwords, smart cards, and so on. However, these security methods have important weakness that can be lost, stolen, or forgotten. In recent years, there is an increasing trend of using **biometrics**, which refers the personal biological or behavioral characteristics used for verification[1-4].

The **fingerprint** is chosen as the biometrics for verification in this paper. It is more mature in terms of the algorithm availability and feasibility[2]. Current examples of fingerprint verification include a social services database, wherein individuals must be prevented from using multiple aliases, watch list check in an immigration office, and identity card issuance. Furthermore, we consider a **sensor-client-server model**[5] for remote user authentication. In this model, the sensor captures a fingerprint image, the client extracts some features from the image, and finally the server compares the extracted features with the stored features.

In this model, however, **security issues** ensure that the opponents will neither be able to access the individual information/measurements nor be able to pose as other individuals by electronically interjecting stale and fraudulently obtained biometrics measurements into the system[2, 5-6]. When the system and/or its communication channels are vulnerable to open physical access, cryptographic methods should be employed to protect the fingerprint information. Although either the system or the communication channel can be attacked in this model, we focus on the **attacks on the communication channels** only.

The straightforward approach to guarantee the integrity/confidentiality of the fingerprint images transmitted is to employ the standard cryptographic techniques[7]. This approach can work for the communication between the client and the server. However, a typical fingerprint sensor either does not have a processor or has a low-end, embedded processor. In this paper, we assume the sensor has a low-end processor. Thus, it may not be possible for such low-end processors to apply the standard cryptographic techniques to the full fingerprint images in real-time.

To reduce the computational workload on the resource-constrained sensor and to guarantee the integrity of the fingerprint image during the communication between a sensor and a client, we apply a standard encryption algorithm to a **nonce**, instead of the image itself. Also, to guarantee the confidentiality of the fingerprint image and to reduce the encryption time, we develop an image-based **selective bitplane encryption** algorithm for the resource-constrained sensor. We select the LSB of each pixel in the fingerprint image(called *"LSB bitplane"*) as a random noise and take the Exclusive-OR of the LSB bitplane and all the pixels of the fingerprint image. Because an opponent cannot recover the original fingerprint image without knowledge of the LSB bitplane, we need to encrypt further the LSB bitplane by using a shared session key. As the client possesses the same session key, the client can recover the original fingerprint image by decrypting the encrypted LSB bitplane and then applying the same Exclusive-OR operation.

With this image-based selective bitplane encryption, our protocol can reduce the computational workload significantly, and can guarantee the confidentiality of the fingerprint image from an opponent without any leakage of the ridge information. Based on the experimental results, we confirm that the proposed protocol can guarantee the integrity/confidentiality of the fingerprint images and provide real-time performance on embedded processors.

The rest of the paper is structured as follows. Section 2 explains the overview of a typical fingerprint verification and the attack points in remote applications, and Section 3 describes the proposed protocol based on challenge-response and image-based selective encryption. The implementation details and performance evaluation are described in Section 4. Finally, conclusions are given in Section 5.

## 2 Background

### 2.1 Fingerprint Verification

A fingerprint verification system shown in Fig. 1 has two phases: *enrollment* and *verification*. In the off-line enrollment phase, an enrolled fingerprint image for each user is preprocessed, and the minutiae are extracted and stored in a server. In the on-line verification phase, the input minutiae are compared to the stored template, and the result of the comparison is returned.

In general, there are three steps involved in the verification phase[2]: Image Pre-Processing, Minutiae Extraction, and Minutiae Matching. **Image Pre-Processing** refers to the refinement of the fingerprint image against the image distortion obtained from a fingerprint sensor. **Minutiae Extraction** refers to the extraction of features in the fingerprint image. After this step, some of the minutiae are detected and stored into a pattern file, which includes the position, orientation, and type(ridge ending or bifurcation) of the minutiae. Based on the minutiae, the input fingerprint is compared with the enrolled database in **Minutiae Matching** step.

Note that Image Pre-Processing and Minutiae Extraction steps require a lot of integer computations, and the computational workload of both steps occupies 96% of the total workload of the fingerprint verification[8]. Thus, it is reasonable to assign the time-consuming steps to a client, rather than to a resource-constrained sensor. This kind of task assignment can be found in a combination of a smart card and a card reader[9-10]. That is, the time-consuming steps are assigned to a more powerful card reader, rather than a resource-constrained smart card.

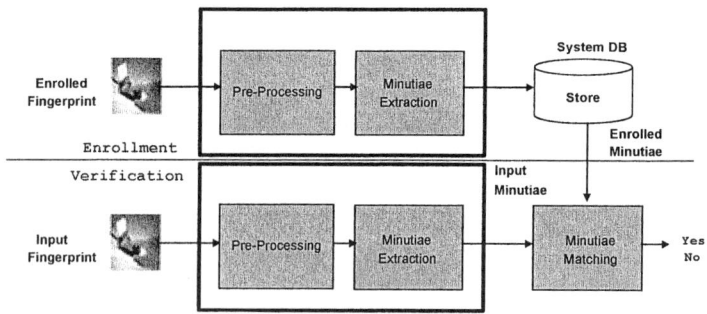

**Fig. 1.** Illustration of the Fingerprint Verification

## 2.2 Attack Points

As shown in Fig. 2, many of the possible attacks in fingerprint verification systems were identified[6]: ① *attack at the sensor*, ② *attack on the channel between the sensor and the feature extractor*, ③ *attack on the feature extractor*, ④ *attack on the channel between the feature extractor and the matcher*, ⑤ *attack on the matcher*, ⑥ *attack on the system database*, ⑦ *attack on the channel between the system database and the matcher*, ⑧ *attack on the channel between the matcher and the application requesting verification*. Details of these attacks are explained in [6].

Note that attacks ②, ④, ⑦ are launched against communication channels; they are similar in nature and can be collectively called **"replay" attacks**[2]. In this paper, we focus on this replay attack, especially attack ② where the resource-constrained sensor is involved. In general, the large-scale adoption of a security model based on an open network requires the resolution of several practical problems relative to security and information reserve issues. In order to have a high acceptability, the mechanism basic tasks should be easy, fast, and inexpensive[11].

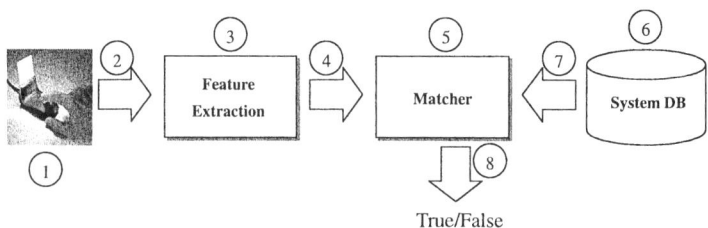

**Fig. 2.** Illustration of the Attack Points[6]

### 2.3 Previous Approaches

A typical approach to protect fingerprint information is to employ the standard cryptographic techniques such as encryption, hash, and digital signature. For instance, standard cryptographic techniques have been employed to protect biometrics information in open networks[11-12] and communication channels between smart cards and card readers[13].

Although many standard cryptographic techniques could be applied independent of the biometrics, some fingerprint-specific techniques have been reported recently. For instance, invisible watermarking of fingerprint images may assure the database administrators that all the images in the database are authentic and are not tampered with by an opponent[14]. Such mechanisms of protection reduce the risk of unauthorized insertion of spurious records into the database. The invisible watermarking can also be used to protect biometrics information over insecure communication channels by inserting it at a sender and verifying it at a receiver[15].

Treating fingerprint as a key has been reported recently. For instance, by combining an error correcting code with the IrisCode, a canonical iris feature could be generated and standard hash functions can be used[16]. Furthermore, because only a hash of the iris feature and the error correcting digits are stored in the database record, the original iris cannot be reconstructed.

In this paper, we focus on protecting fingerprint information over insecure networks by using standard cryptographic techniques, especially attack ② shown in Fig. 2.

## 3 Secure and Efficient Transmission of Fingerprint Images

The goal of this research is to transmit fingerprint images securely with the reduced amount of computational workload. Thus, a resource-constrained sensor can transmit fingerprint images securely in real time by employing the proposed protocol. In this paper, we assume that the sensor is connected physically to a specific client, and both the sensor and the client share the same master key for symmetric encryption.

## 3.1 Challenge-Response Protocol

With current technologies, a resource-constrained sensor cannot apply all the security components such as encryption module, digital signature module, hash function module, and random number generator to the full fingerprint image in real-time. Furthermore, asymmetry key encryptions such as RSA are infeasible on the resource-constrained sensor as it is slow. Symmetry key encryptions such as AES, on the other hand, can be much faster and simpler to implement. To guarantee the integrity/confidentiality of the fingerprint image and execute the required security components in real-time on the resource-constrained sensor, we propose a simple and effective protocol in terms of the computational workload and the security level. We will explain how we can achieve the goal with a standard symmetric encryption algorithm. For the purpose of explanation, we define first the following notations:

$N$ : a nonce generated randomly in the client and used as a "challenge"
$Bio$ : biometric data such as fingerprint
$K_m$ : a master key shared by both the sensor and the client
$f_1(K_m, N)$ : a simple function to generate a session key with $K_m$ and $N$
$K_s$ : a shared session key generated for each transmission
$f_2(N)$ : a simple function to generate a "response"

Fig. 3 illustrates an example of a simple **challenge-response protocol** to transmit the biometric data from a sensor to a client using a standard symmetric key algorithm only. As we mentioned, we assume that both the sensor and the client possess a master key $K_m$. For instance, the master key can be distributed when the sensor is installed on the client. As shown in Fig. 3, the client sends first a nonce $N$ encrypted with $K_m$. After receiving this message, the sensor generates a session key $K_s$ by using a simple function $f_1(K_m, N)$. Then, the sensor encrypts the input fingerprint image with the session key. The sensor also computes a response and encrypts it with the session key, and sends $E_{K_s}(Bio)$ and $E_{K_s}(f_2(N))$ back to the client. Because the client can also generate the session key, the client can confirm the source of the message.

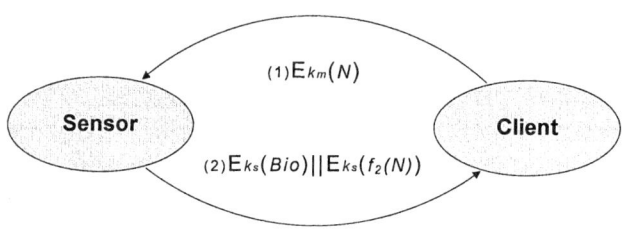

**Fig. 3.** Illustration of the Challenge-Response Protocol

This simple protocol requires only two steps of communications and guarantees both the integrity and the confidentiality of the fingerprint image transmitted. However, the sensor may not execute this protocol in real-time if it encrypts the full fingerprint image. To complete the protocol in real-time on the resource-constrained sensor, we need to reduce further the computational workload of encrypting fingerprint images.

### 3.2 Image-Based Selective Encryption

To reduce the computational workload of encrypting fingerprint images further, we proposed the image-based selective encryption that encrypts the part of fingerprint image, instead of full fingerprint image. Note that we consider not frequency but spatial domains of fingerprint images because the transform to a frequency domain is a time consuming operation for the resource-constrained processors.

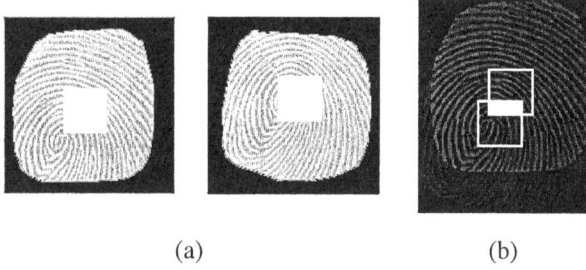

(a) (b)

**Fig. 4.** Results of the Selective Spatial Encryption. (a) Results of the Selective Spatial Encryption; (b) The Composed Image by using the Mosaic Technique.

Two approaches are possible for the image-based selective encryption. A straightforward approach, called "**Selective Spatial Encryption**", is to partition the image and encrypt the central region of the partition, instead of the full fingerprint image. Because the central region of a fingerprint image may include a lot of significant information of the fingerprint such as cores and deltas, this approach may be considered as an efficient way to conceal the fingerprint information from an opponent. However, an opponent can intercept multiple of these selectively encrypted messages and generate a composed image by using the mosaic technique[2]. Because the composed image looks similar to the original fingerprint image, this Selective Spatial Encryption cannot provide the confidentiality of the fingerprint image. Fig. 4 shows the results of the Selective Spatial Encryption and the composed image. Note that, to show the effect of the composition, the central region encrypted is shown as a white box.

The other approach is "**Selective Bitplane Encryption**"[17]. In general, a fingerprint image is given in an 8-bit/pixel(bpp) precision. We consider the 8bpp data in the form of 8 bitplanes, where each bitplane is associated with a position in the binary representation of the pixels. The selective bitplane encryption approach is to encrypt a subset of the bitplanes only, starting with the bitplane containing the Most Significant Bit(MSB) of the pixels.

Fig. 5 illustrates the Selective Bitplane Encryption approach. Fig. 5 (a) represents an original fingerprint image, Fig. 5 (b) represents a distorted image after encrypting one bitplane, and Fig. 5 (c) represents a distorted image after encrypting two bitplanes. As shown in Fig. 5, this approach can avoid the mosaic attack by distorting the whole pixel values of a fingerprint image. Also, compared to the full bitplane encryption, the computational workload of this encryption is reduced significantly.

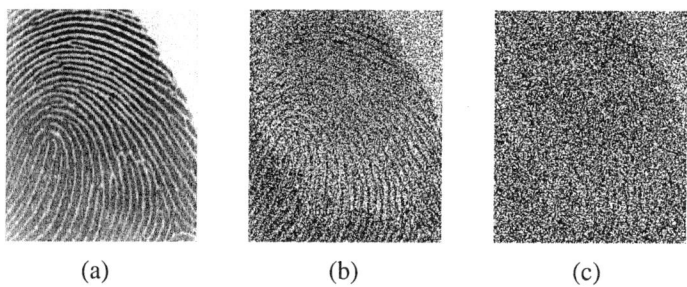

(a)  (b)  (c)

**Fig. 5.** Results of the Selective Bitplane Encryption[17]. (a) Original Fingerprint Image; (b) Result of Encrypting the MSBs only; (c) Result of Encrypting the MSBs and the Next Significant Bits.

Note that, some structural information is still visible after encrypting the MSB only, whereas encrypting two bitplanes leaves no useful information. However, the two-bitplanes encryption is not safe for fingerprint images, either. For instance, the *Replacement Attack*[17] replaces the encrypted bitplanes by constant 0's and compensates the decreased luminance by adding 96 to each pixel. As shown in Fig. 6, the Replacement Attack can reveal the structural ridge information even from the two-bitplanes encryption. Details of the Replacement Attack can be found in [17].

**Fig. 6.** Result of Replacing the MSBs and the Next Significant Bits of Fig. 5(c) with Constant 0's

To solve this problem, we use the Least Significant Bit(LSB) as the selective bitplane. Though the LSB contains the least significant information of the image, the LSB looks similar to a random number field[18] and is more suitable for our algorithm than the MSB. Also, the LSBs obtained from the fingerprint images of the same person are always different. Thus, it is natural to select the LSB as our random noise, and the LSB itself needs to be protected from an opponent. In the following, we will describe the proposed selective bitplane encryption algorithm consisting of two steps: *Image Distortion* and *LSB Encryption*.

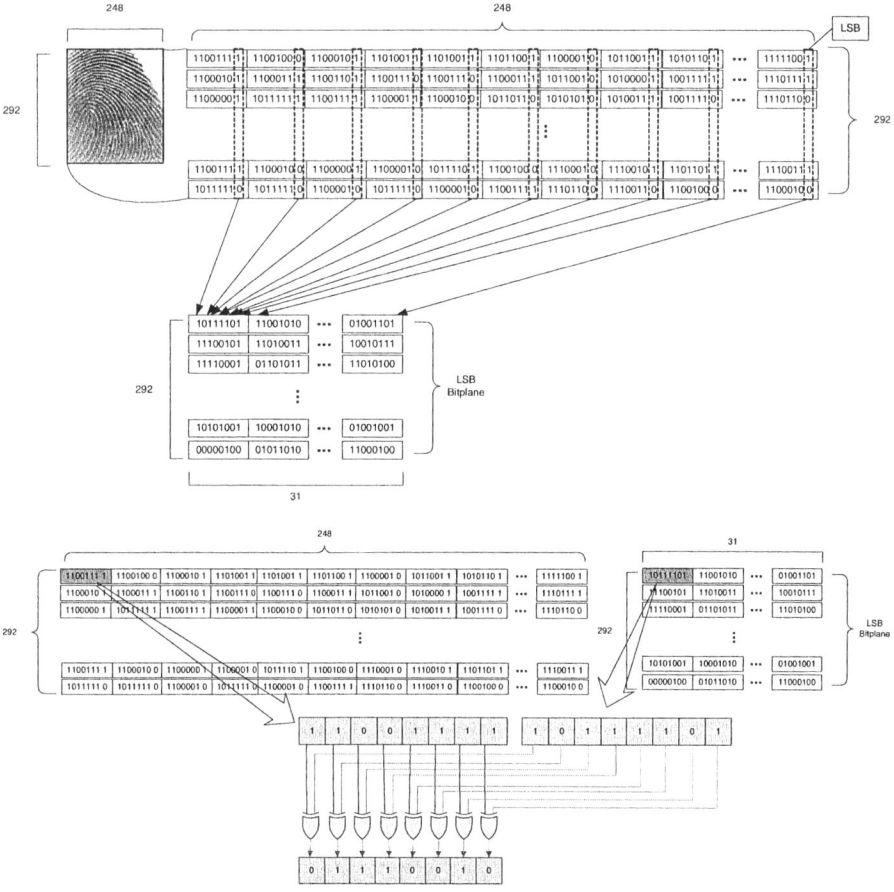

**Fig. 7.** Illustration of the Image Distortion using LSB

In **Image Distortion**, we distort the full fingerprint image by using very simple operations. For each pixel, we select the LSB of it as a random noise and generate the LSB bitplane. Then, we take a simple Exclusive-OR of the LSB bitplane and all the pixels of fingerprint image(see Fig. 7). In this design, the LSB bitplane works as a one-time pad. Because the LSB bitplane is smaller than the full fingerprint image, the LSB bitplane is reused seven times for the given fingerprint image. However, the length of the LSB bitplane is too long to predict. Without knowledge of the LSB bitplane, an opponent cannot recover the ridge structure of the fingerprint image from the result of Image Distortion. Therefore, in **LSB Encryption**, we only need to encrypt further the LSB bitplane by using a shared session key. As the client possesses the same session key, the client can recover the original fingerprint image by decrypting the encrypted LSB bitplane and then applying the same Exclusive-OR operation shown in Fig. 7.

Fig. 8 shows the proposed protocol to transmit fingerprint images by using the image-based encryption, and we call this protocol as "**Image-based Selective Bitplane Encryption Protocol**". The only difference between Fig. 8 and Fig. 3 is the second step. Instead of encrypting the full fingerprint image, the sensor generates a distorted fingerprint image $Bio \oplus LSB$ in Image Distortion. Then, the sensor encrypts the $LSB$ with the session key, and sends $Bio \oplus LSB \| E_{Ks}(LSB) \| E_{Ks}(f_2(N))$ to the client.

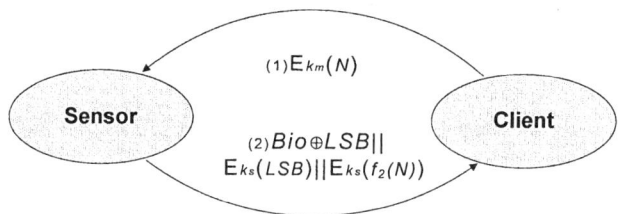

**Fig. 8.** Illustration of the Proposed Protocol

## 4 Implementation Details and Performance Evaluation

For the purpose of evaluation, a small data set of 40 fingerprint images composed of four fingerprint images per one finger was collected from 10 individuals by using the optical fingerprint sensor[19]. The resolution of the sensor was 500dpi, and the size of captured fingerprint images was 248×292. The standard symmetric encryption algorithm(*AES*) was used to guarantee both the integrity and the confidentiality.

Fig. 9 shows an input image, the LSB bitplane, and the result of the proposed encryption. As shown in Fig. 9(b), the LSB bitplane is smaller than a full fingerprint image by a factor of eight. The LSB bitplane looks like random noises and can vary at every fingerprint acquisition. Thus, unlike the Selective Spatial Encryption, it is difficult for an opponent to reveal the ridge structure of the fingerprint image even if he obtains multiple images distorted by the LSB bitplane.

The proposed algorithm is safe under the Replacement Attack because every bitplanes are modified by the Exclusive-OR operation before encrypting the LSB bitplane. Fig. 10 shows the results of the Replacement Attack on the distorted image shown in Fig. 9(c). Compared to Fig. 6, the Replacement Attack cannot reveal any ridge information of the fingerprint image.

Finally, we summarize the estimated execution times of the proposed encryption and the full encryption in Table 1. The encryption times were estimated by using the result reported in [20]. (Currently, we are porting the proposed algorithm to an ARM7 emulator board. The results of the porting will be reported in the final version of this manuscript.) As shown Table 1, the proposed encryption can reduce the time for the full encryption by a factor of eight. Furthermore, the results of Table 1 were estimated under the smart card chip environments. The encryption times can be reduced further if the proposed algorithm is executed under the embedded system(i.e., fingerprint sensor) environments having off-chip memories.

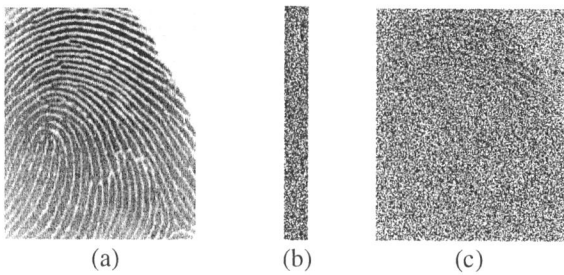

**Fig. 9.** Results of the Proposed Encryption. (a) Input Image; (b) LSB Bitplane; (c) Result of the Distortion.

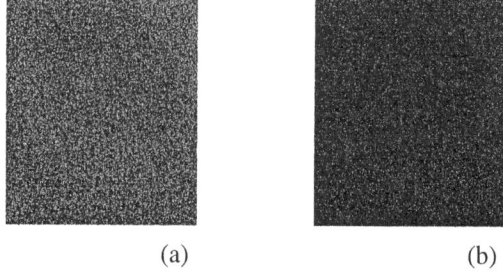

**Fig. 10.** Results of Replacement Attack. (a) Result of Replacing the MSBs of Fig. 9(c) with Constant 0's; (b) Result of Replacing the MSBs and the Next Significant Bits of Fig. 9(c) with Constant 0's.

**Table 1.** Comparison of the Estimated Times to Encrypt Fingerprint Images of Size 248×292

|  | 8051(8-bit) Processor 3.57MHz | ARM7(32-bit) Processor 28.56MHz |
|---|---|---|
| Proposed Selective Encryption | 3.01 sec | 0.03 sec |
| Full Encryption | 24.12 sec | 0.24 sec |

## 5 Conclusions

Biometrics is expected to be increasing widely used in conjunction with other techniques such as the cryptography on the network. In this paper, a secure and efficient protocol has been proposed to transmit fingerprint images from a fingerprint sensor to a client. To guarantee the integrity and the confidentiality of the fingerprint images transmitted, only a standard encryption algorithm has been employed. To reduce the computational workload on the resource-constrained sensor, however, we applied the encryption algorithm to a nonce and to the LSB bitplane of the fingerprint image.

The prototype system shows promising results. Because the full fingerprint image is distorted by applying simple Exclusive-OR operations with the LSB bitplane and then the LSB bitplane itself is encrypted, our protocol can reduce the computational workload by a factor of eight and guarantee the confidentiality of the fingerprint image. Note that our protocol can also be applied to other biometrics such as face, iris, and vein, although this paper considered fingerprint only. Also, a case where each person carries his/her sensor with a USB token[21] can be investigated as future research.

## Acknowledgement

This research was supported by the MIC(Ministry of Information and Communication), Korea, under the Chung-Ang University HNRC-ITRC(Home Network Research Center) support program supervised by the IITA(Institute of Information Technology Assessment

## References

[1] A. Jain, R. Bole, and S. Panakanti, Biometrics: Personal Identification in Networked Society, Kluwer Academic Publishers, 1999.
[2] D. Maltoni, et al., Handbook of Fingerprint Recognition, Springer, 2003.
[3] S. IM, et al., "A Direction-Based Vascular Pattern Extraction Algorithm for Hand Vascular Pattern Verification", ETRI Journal, Vol. 25, No. 2, pp. 101-108, 2003.
[4] K. LEE, et al., "A New Similarity Measure Based on Intraclass Statistics for Biometric Systems", ETRI Journal, Vol. 25, No. 5, pp. 401-406, 2003.
[5] R. Bolle, J. Connell, and N. Ratha, "Biometric Perils and Patches", Pattern Recognition, Vol. 35, pp. 2727-2738, 2002.
[6] N. Ratha, J. Connell, and R. Bolle, "An Analysis of Minutiae Matching Strength", Proc. of AVBPA 2001(LNCS 2091), pp. 223-228, 2001.
[7] W. Stallings, Cryptography and Network Security, Pearson Ed. Inc., 2003.
[8] D. Moon, et al., "Performance Analysis of the Match-on-Card System for the Fingerprint Authentication", Proc. of International Workshop on Information Security Applications, pp. 449-459, 2001.
[9] Y. Moon, et al., "Collaborative Fingerprint Authentication by Smart Card and a Trusted Host", Electrical and Computer Engineering, Vol. 1, pp. 108-112, 2000.
[10] S. Pan, et al., "A Memory-Efficient Fingerprint Verification Algorithm using A Multi-Resolution Accumulator Array for Match-on-Card", ETRI Journal, Vol. 25, No. 3, pp. 179-186, 2003.

[11] D. Maio and D. Maltoni, "A Secure Protocol for Electronic Commerce based on Fingerprints and Encryption", Proc. of Conf. on Systems, Cybernetics, and Informatics, pp. 519-525, 1999.
[12] A. Jain, S. Prabhakar, and A. Ross, "Biometrics-based Web Access", Technical Report, Michigan State U., 1998.
[13] L. Rila and C. Mitchell, "Security Analysis of Smartcard to Card Reader Communications for Biometric Cardholder Authentication", Proc. of CARDIS, pp. 19-28, 2002.
[14] M. Yeung and S. Pankanti, "Verification Watermarks on Fingerprint Recognition and Retrieval", Journal of Electronic Imaging, Vol. 9, No. 4, pp. 468-476, 2002.
[15] A. Jain and U. Uludag, "Hiding Fingerprint Minutiae in Images", Proc. of AutoID, pp. 97-102, 2002.
[16] G. Davida, et al., "On Enabling Secure Applications through Off-Line Biometric Identification", Proc. of Symp. on Privacy and Security, pp. 148-157, 1998.
[17] M. Podesser, H. Schmidt, and A. Uhl, "Selective Bitplane Encryption for Secure Transmission of Image Data in Mobile Environments," Proc. of the 5th IEEE Nordic Signal Processing Symposium, 2002.
[18] R. Gonzalez, Digital Image Processing, Addison Wesley, 1992.
[19] NiGen, http://www.nitgen.com.
[20] G. Hachez, F. Koeune, and J. Quisquater, "cAESar Results: Implementation of Four AES Candidates on Two Smart Cards," Proc. of the Second AES Conference, 1999.
[21] D. Moon, et al., "The Implementation of the USB Token System for Fingerprint Verification", Proc. of Scandinavian Conf. on Image Analysis(LNCS 2749), pp. 998-1005, 2003.

# On the Individuality of the Iris Biometric

Sungsoo Yoon[1,2], Seung-Seok Choi[1], Sung-Hyuk Cha[1], Yillbyung Lee[2], and Charles C. Tappert[1]

[1] Computer Science Department, Pace University,
861 Bedford rd, Pleasantville, NY, 10570, USA
{schoi, scha, ctappert}@pace.edu
[2] School of Engineering, Information and Industrial Engineering, Yonsei University,
134 Shinchondong, Sudaimunku Seoul, 120-749, Korea
{ssyoon, yblee}@csai.yonsei.ac.kr

**Abstract.** Biometric authentication has been considered a model for quantitatively establishing the discriminative power of biometric data. The dichotomy model classifies two biometric samples as coming either from the same person or from two different people. This paper reviews features, distance measures, and classifiers used in iris authentication. For feature extraction we compare simple binary and multi-level 2D wavelet features. For distance measures we examine scalar distances such as Hamming and Euclidean, feature vector and histogram distances. Finally, for the classifiers we compare Bayes decision rule, nearest neighbor, artificial neural network, and support vector machines. Of the eleven different combinations tested, the best one uses multi-level 2D wavelet features, the histogram distance, and a support vector machine classifier.

**Keywords:** Biometric individuality, Dichotomy model, Histogram, Iris authentication.

## 1 Introduction

This paper examines various implementations of a dichotomy model to authenticate a person based on the iris biometric, i.e., establishing a measure of discriminative power of iris that is statistically inferable. It is a method for measuring the reliability of authenticating all of the population based on information obtained from a small sample of individuals drawn from the population. This problem of establishing the individuality of a biometric has been investigated for iris [1], for handwriting [2, 3] and for fingerprints [4, 5]. Here, we consider the individuality of the iris biometric.

Establishing a measure of a certain biometric uniqueness is a challenging problem. A very small error rate of a certain performance evaluation of a biometric model can be a candidate for a measure of individuality. There are two important models in biometrics: identification (polychotomy, one-of-many decision) and verification (dichotomy, binary decision) [6, 7]. It has been argued that the verification model is clearly more suitable for establishing the individuality of a biometric rather than the identification model [7]. Consider the *many-class problem* where the number of classes is too large to be observed, such as the population of a country. Most biometric identification problems fall under the aegis of the many-class problem. Although classification techniques that assume a fixed number of classes are not useful for establishing individuality in many-class problems, most existing studies use the *identification* model and present a confusion matrix [5, 8].

In the dichotomy model [2, 7], we transform the many-class problem into a dichotomy by using a distance between two samples of the same class and between two different classe samples. Two patterns are categorized into one of only two classes – the patterns are either from the same class or from the two different classes. Given two iris samples, the feature distance between the two samples is classified as intra-person, or inter-person. We use the terms intra-person distance and inter-person distance. Two types of errors, *False Accept Rate (FAR)* and *False Reject Rate (FRR)*, are inferable to testing sets and even to the entire population.

The purpose of this paper is to investigate various combinations of features, distance measures, and classifiers used in iris authentication to find the best combination for the iris individuality. For feature extractions, we compare simple binary and multi-level 2D wavelet features. For distance measures, we examine scalar distances such as Hamming, Euclidean, feature vector, and histogram distances. Finally, for the classifiers, we compare Bayes decision rule, nearest neighbor, artificial neural network and support vector machines. Among the eleven different combinations tested, the best dichotomizer uses the multi-level 2D wavelet feature, histogram distance, and a support vector machine classifier.

The rest of the paper is organized as follows. Section 2 illustrates the *dichotomy* model which is a statistically inferable approach to establishing the individuality of a biometric. Section 3 presents the various features and distance measures explored for iris authentication. Section 4 compares the experimental results of various classifiers using different combinations of features and distance measures. Finally, section 5 draws some conclusions.

## 2 Dichotomy Model and Dichotomy Transformation

The biometric individuality problem can be described as establishing a quantitative measure of the discriminative power of biometric data. Quantitative measures can be obtained from performance evaluation of either the identification model or the verification model.

Consider the multi-class problem where the number of classes is small and one can observe many instances of each class. To establish the individuality of the classes, one can cluster the instances into classes. It is a valid method to establish the individuality as long as a substantial number of instances for each class are observable. However, consider the *many-class problem* where the number of classes is too large to be observed. Most biometric identification problems fall under the aegis of the many-class problem. Although classification techniques that assume a fixed number of classes are invalid for establishing individuality in many-class problems, most existing studies use the *identification* model [5, 8]. However, as the number of classes becomes huge – for example, in the millions – this problem is seemingly insurmountable and the error rates cannot be inferable to the entire population.

We formally state the *dichotomy* problem as follows [2,7]: given two randomly selected biometric samples, the problem is to determine whether the two samples belong to the same person or two to different people. Figure 1 depicts the two biometric verification models: (a) a traditional parametric verification model [1] and (b) the dichotomy model used in [2, 7]. Daugman proposed degrees of freedom of iris mismatch score distribution as a measure of the individuality or uniqueness of an iris pattern [1].

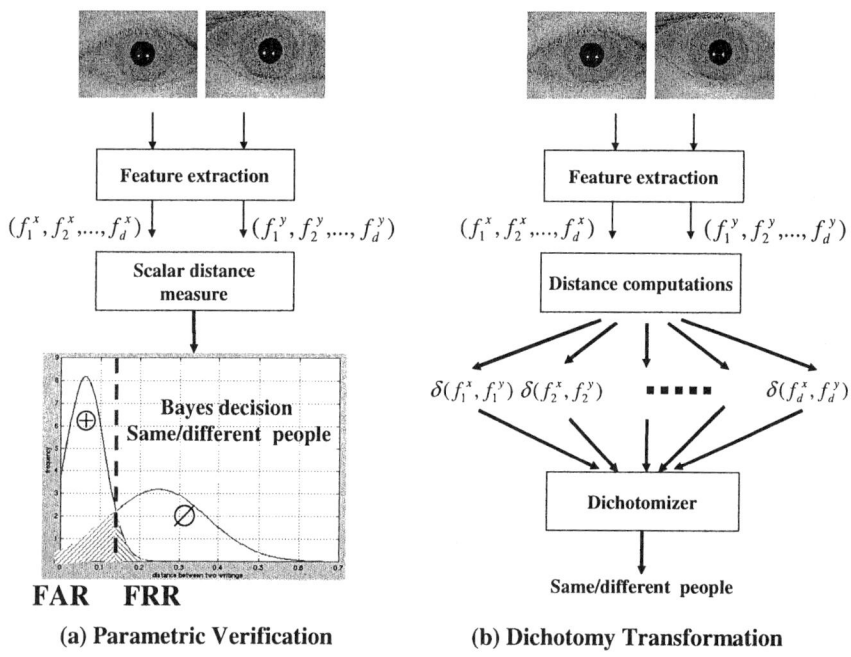

**Fig. 1.** Iris verification processes and dichotomy transformation

Let $f_i^j$ be the $i^{th}$ feature of the $j^{th}$ biometric data. First, features are extracted from both biometric data $x$ and $y$: $\{f_1^x, f_2^x, \cdots, f_d^x\}$ and $\{f_1^y, f_2^y, \cdots, f_d^y\}$. In the parametric verification model of Figure 1 (a), a scalar distance measure is applied and two distributions are generated. By assuming the two distributions are normal one can easily find the decision threshold to minimize the FAR and FRR. On the other hand, in the dichotomy model of Figure 1 (b), each feature distance is computed – that is, the feature domain is transform into a feature distance domain: $\{\delta(f_1^x, f_1^y), \delta(f_2^x, f_2^y) \cdots, \delta(f_d^x, f_d^y)\}$ where $\delta$ is a distance measure between a pair of features. Note that, in contrast to model (a) where the feature types must be homogeneous (binary or numeric), in this model (b) the features need not be homogeneous in type [7]. The *dichotomizer* takes this feature distance vector as input and outputs the decision, "same person" or "different people." These models are considered sound and valid *inferential statistical* approaches [2, 7] even though their performances may vary. Section 4 will evaluate these models.

## 3 Feature Extraction and Distance Computation

We review the features and distance measures used for iris authentication. First, we consider the *iriscode* [1], which is a binary feature vector extracted by applying a 2D Gabor wavelet filter. In [1], the *Hamming* distance in eqn (1) was used for the model in Figure 1 (a).

$$\partial(f^x, f^y) = f^x \bullet \overline{f^y} + \overline{f^x} \bullet f^y \tag{1}$$

Second, multi-level 2D wavelet features have been widely used [11-14]. The hierarchical wavelet transform decomposes an iris image into a set of frequency windows having narrower bandwidths in the lower frequency region [11]. G. Kee et al. presented a tree-structured wavelet transform in order to obtain means and standard deviations [12]. Mallat suggested that statistics obtained from wavelet decomposition are sufficient for presenting texture difference [13].

We use the 2D Daubechies wavelet transform technique to extract features from an iris image as folows. Each iris image is decomposed into 3 levels and each sub-image is divided into 2x2 windows, which results in 12 different sub-images. For each-sub image, mean and variance values are calculated. As a result, 24 numeric feature values are extracted. One can use the Euclidean distance between two vectors in eqn (2) for the Figure 1 (a) model. One can also use the absolute vector difference measure in eqn (3) for the Figure 1 (b) model. The result of the eqn (2) is a scalar value whereas that of the eqn (3) is a d-dimensional feature distance vector.

$$\partial(f^x, f^y) = \sqrt{\sum_{i=1}^{d}(f_i^x - f_i^y)^2} \tag{2}$$

$$\partial(f^x, f^y) = |f^x - f^y| = (|f_1^x - f_1^y|, |f_2^x - f_2^y|, \cdots, |f_d^x - f_d^y|) \tag{3}$$

Third, we utilize 12 linear type histograms as feature sets as previously proposed [14]. For each sub-image, the linear type of histogram is obtained as a feature from each decomposed sub image. $f_i^x$ and $f_i^y$ are ordinal histograms not simple numeric scalar values. There are numerous histogram distance measures [15] and we consider the two popular ones: eqn (4) shows the Euclidean distance and eqn (5) the histogram edit distance [15, 16]. Histogram distance measure is applied to each of the 12 histograms per iris image, resulting in a 12 dimensional feature distance vector.

$$\partial_i(f_i^x, f_i^y) = \sqrt{\sum_{j=1}^{b}(f_{i,j}^x - f_{i,j}^y)^2} \tag{4}$$

$$\partial_i(f_i^x, f_i^y) = \sum_{j=1}^{b}\left|\sum_{k=1}^{j}(f_{i,k}^x - f_{i,k}^y)\right| \tag{5}$$

## 4 Comparative Experimental Results

We compare the experimental results obtained by using several classifiers with a variety of different features and distance measures. From the iris biometric image database [12], we selected 10 left bare eye samples of 52 subjects. The intra-class distance sample is acquired by randomly selecting two iris data from the same subject while the inter-class distance sample is obtained by randomly selecting two iris data from two different subjects. We prepared three sets of inter and intra distance data for training and three independent ones for testing, each of size 1000 (500 intra-class and 500 inter-class pairs). As shown in Table 1, we examined eleven different models. Models 1 and 2 use the parametric verification model of Figure 1 (a), and the remaining models use the dichotomy transformation model of Figure 1 (b).

**Table 1.** Eleven different models

| Model | Features | Distance Measures | Classifier |
|---|---|---|---|
| 1 | Iriscode (Binary) | Hamming eqn (1) | Bayes decision |
| 2 | Wavelet means & variances | Euclidean eqn (2) | Bayes decision |
| 3 | Wavelet means & variances | Vector difference eqn (3) | Nearest Neighbor |
| 4 | Wavelet means & variances | Vector difference eqn (3) | ANN |
| 5 | Wavelet means & variances | Vector difference eqn (3) | SVM |
| 6 | Wavelet histograms | Euclidean eqn (4) | Nearest Neighbor |
| 7 | Wavelet histograms | Euclidean eqn (4) | ANN |
| 8 | Wavelet histograms | Euclidean eqn (4) | SVM |
| 9 | Wavelet histograms | Edit distance eqn (5) | Nearest Neighbor |
| 10 | Wavelet histograms | Edit distance eqn (5) | ANN |
| 11 | Wavelet histograms | Edit distance eqn (5) | SVM |

The parametric method models 1 and 2 were trained on 500 scalar distance values obtained from the intra- and inter-class sets. These scalar distance values form distributions and the mean and variance can be computed for each distribution. Assuming normal distributions, one can easily find the Bayes decision threshold. For testing, each scalar distance value is classified into the intra- or inter-distance class by comparing to the threshold value.

**Table 2.** Parametric model evaluation results on 1000 independent sample pairs per test

| Model | Sets | FRR | FAR | Performance |
|---|---|---|---|---|
| 1 iriscode + Hamming eqn (1) | Training | 19.0% | 21.5% | 79.8% |
| | Test 1 | 10.2% | 4.6% | 92.6% |
| | Test 2 | 12.0% | 3.2% | 92.4% |
| | Test 3 | 10.4% | 3.2% | 93.2% |
| 2 Wavelet means & variances + Euclidean eqn (2) | Training | 13.5% | 23.2% | 81.7% |
| | Test 1 | 4.2% | 25.6% | 85.1% |
| | Test 2 | 5.6% | 23% | 85.7% |
| | Test 3 | 4.6% | 24.2% | 85.6% |

Table 2 shows the error rates and overall performance values for models 1 and 2. Two observations can be drawn from these results. First, the results of the traditional parametric model using the scalar distance measure in Figure 1 (a) are disappointing compared to those of the other model in Figure 1 (b). The reason is that multivariate distance analysis is clearly better than a single scalar distance analysis. The other observation is that the FRR in the testing sets are much smaller than those in the training set, suggesting that the two distributions are not normal.

Models 3-11 used the dichotomy transformation to obtain 500 samples of d-dimensional feature distance vectors for intra- and inter-class sets. Regardless of the types of features, the feature distance vectors are all numeric values when proper distance measures are applied. Thus, the feature distance vectors become inputs to the dichotomizer as shown in Figure 1 (b). We tested three well-known classifiers [17] as the dichotomizer: nearest neighbor, artificial neural network (ANN), and support vector machine (SVM).

We selected the artificial neural network for a dichotomizer because it is equivalent to multivariate statistical analysis. There is a wealth of literature regarding a close relationship between neural networks and the techniques of statistical analysis, especially multivariate statistical analysis, which involves many variables [17, 18]. We selected the support vector machine because it has gained considerable popularity recently and has become state-of-the-art [19].

**Table 3.** Dichotomy model % performance results on 1000 independent sample pairs per test

|  |  | Wavelet means & variances (Models 3-5) | Histograms + eqn (4) (Models 6-8) | Histograms + eqn (5) (Models 9-11) |
|---|---|---|---|---|
| Nearest Neighbor | Test 1 | 90.5% | 81.0% | 89.9% |
|  | Test 2 | 90.8% | 80.6% | 92.6% |
|  | Test 3 | 91.0% | 81.3% | 92.0% |
| Artificial Neural Network | Training | 95.8% | 90.9% | 99.2% |
|  | Test 1 | 94.8% | 82.4% | 96.1% |
|  | Test 2 | 96.7% | 83.8% | 96.9% |
|  | Test 3 | 95.6% | 82.5% | 96.7% |
| Support Vector Machine | Training | 97.6% | 88.9% | **98.8%** |
|  | Test 1 | 96.2% | 85.7% | **97.9%** |
|  | Test 2 | 97.5% | 86.3% | **98.5%** |
|  | Test 3 | 96.7% | 86.8% | **97.9%** |

Table 3 shows performances of models 3-11. In general, SVMs outperform ANNs which, in turn, outperform nearest neighbor classifiers. The best performing SVM model was the one using the 2D three-level wavelet with the histogram distance in eqn (5).

# References

1. J.G. Daugman, "High confidence visual recognition of persons by a test of statistical independence," IEEE Transactions on Pattern Analysis and Machine Intelligence, 15(11),:1148-1161 November, 1993.
2. S.-H. Cha, "Use of Distance Measures in Handwriting Analysis," PhD dissertation, SUNY at buffalo, CSE, March, 2001.
3. S. N. Srihari, S.-H. Cha, H. Arora, and S. Lee, "Individuality of Handwriting," *Journal of Forensic Sciences*, vol. 47, no. 4, pp 856-872, 2002.
4. S. Pankanti, S. Prabhakar, and A. K. Jain, "On the Individuality of Fingerprints," *IEEE Transactions on Pattern Analysis and Machine Intelligence*, vol. 24, no. 8, pp. 1010-1025, 2002.
5. D. Stoney and J. Thornton, "A Critical Analysis of Quantitative Fingerprint Individuality Models," *Journal of Forensic Sciences*, vol. 31, no. 4, pp. 1187-1216, 1986.
6. R. M. Bolle, J. H. Connell, S. Pankanti, N. K. Ratha, and A. W. Senior, "Guide to Biometrics," Springer Professional Computing, ISBN 0-387-40089-3, 2003
7. S. Cha and S. N. Srihari, "Writer Identification: Statistical Analysis and Dichotomizer," in Proceedings of SPR and SSPR 2000 Alicante, Spain 2000, LNCS - Advances in Pattern Recognition, vol. 1876, p 123-132
8. M. Kam, B. Fielding, and R. Conn, "Writer Identification by Professional Document Examiners," *Jouranl of Forensic Sciences*, vol 42, pp. 778-786, January 1997..
9. S. Cha and S. N. Srihari, "Multiple Feature Integration for Writer Verification," in Proceedings of 7th IWFHR2000 , Amsterdam, Netherlands, September, 2000, p 333-342, ISBN 90-76942-01-3
10. John G. Daugman, High Confidence Visual Recognition of Persons by a Test of Statistical Independence, IEEE Trans. on Pattern Analysis and Machine Intelligence, 15(11), pp. 1148-1161, 1993
11. L. Ma, T. Tan, Y. Wang, and D. Zhang, Personal     Identification Based on Iris Texture Analysis, IEEE Transactions on Pattern Analysis and Machine Intelligence, Vol. 25, No, 12, 2003
12. G. Kee, Y. Byun, K, Lee and Y. Lee, Improved Techniques for an Iris Recognition System with High Performance, Lecture Notes Artificial Intelligence, 2001
13. Mallat, S.G., A theory for Multiresolution Signal Decomposition: The Wavelet Representation, IEEE Tans. Pattern Recognition and Machine Intelligence, 11(4), pp. 674-693, 1989
14. S. Choi, S. Yoon, S._H. Cha, and C. C. Tappert, "Use of Histogram Distances in Iris Authentication," in Proceedings of International Conference on Machine Learning; Models, Technologies and Applications, Jun 21-24, 2004, Las Vegas
15. S. Cha and S. N. Srihari, On Measuring the Distance between Histograms, in Pattern Recognition, Vol 35/6, pp 1355-1370, June 2002
16. S. Cha, Fast Image Template and Dictionary Matching Algorithms, in Proceedings of ACCV '98, Hongkong, LNCS -Computer Vision, vol. 1351, Springer yr. 1997, p370-377
17. R. O. Duda, P.E. Hart, and D. G. Stork, *Pattern Classification*, John Wiley & Sons, Inc.m $2^{nd}$ ed., 2000.
18. V. Cherkassky, J. H. Friedman, and H. Wechsler, *From Statistics to Neural Networks: Theory and Pattern Recognition Applications*, Springer, NATO ASI ed., 1994.
19. Edgar E Osuna, Robert Freund and Federico Girosi. *Support Vector Machines: Training and Applications*. MIT Artificial Intelligence Laboratory and Center for Biological and Computational Learning Department of Brain and Cognitive Sciences. A.I. Memo No 1602, C.B.C.L. Paper No 144, 1997.

# Facial Component Detection for Efficient Facial Characteristic Point Extraction

Jeong-Su Oh[1], Dong-Wook Kim[2], Jin-Tae Kim[3], Yong-In Yoon[4], and Jong-Soo Choi[4]

[1] Division of Image & Information Engineering, Pukyung National University, Korea
ojs@pknu.ac.kr
[2] School of Engineering, Jeonju University, Korea
dwkim@jj.ac.kr
[3] Department of Computer & Information Science, Hanseo University, Korea
jtkim@hanseo.ac.kr
[4] Graduate School of Advanced Imaging, Multimedia, and Film, Chung-Ang Univ., Korea
{yoonyi, jschoi}@imagelab.cau.ac.kr

**Abstract.** This paper proposes an algorithm detecting facial component to efficiently extract the FCP (Facial Characteristic Point). The FCP plays an important role in facial expression representation or recognition. For efficient FCP extraction using image processing, we analyze and improve the conventional algorithms detecting facial components that are the basis of the FCP extraction. The proposed algorithm includes face region detection without the effect of skin-color hair, eye region detection with weighted template, eyebrow region detection using a modified histogram, and mouth region detection using skin characteristics.

## 1 Introduction

Facial expression, together with speech, hand or body gestures, plays an important role in intentional communication. It is applied to the research that recognizes and expresses the intended meaning of the communication [1, 2, 3]. The research requires FCP extraction in preprocessing. Since a face is complex in structure and its shape and color vary according to viewpoint and lighting, it is difficult to extract the FCP from the face alone. The conventional techniques for FCP extraction require extensive processing time and use a specific hardware [2]. The hardware system is expensive devices, poses an inconvenience or psychological load to experimenters due to the markers, which are attached to the face, and it cannot detect variations of the FCP in local, but important regions. However, FCP extraction, through the use of image processing, can solve the problems in the hardware systems, since it extracts the FCP from a marker less facial picture.

This paper proposes facial component detection that is the kernel of efficient FCP extraction using image processing. The proposed algorithm analyzes and improves the conventional algorithm. It removes the effects of skin-color hair in face region detection, it detects a more accurate eye region using weighted template, and it more easily detects the eyebrow and mouth regions using a modified histogram and skin characteristics, respectively. To evaluate performance of the proposed algorithm, the facial components are detected in various images and the FCP is extracted from them. The simulation result shows that the proposed algorithm properly detects the facial components and extracts valid FCP.

## 2 Facial Component Detection

In this paper, the facial components to be greatly affected by facial expression are defined as the eye, eyebrow, and mouth. Fig. 1 shows the block diagram for the facial component detection.

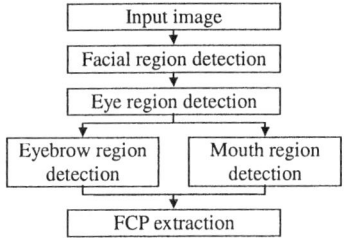

**Fig. 1.** Block diagram for facial component detection

### 2.1 Facial Region Detection

Facial region detection is important in preprocessing for the FCP extraction in face or facial expression recognition and is largely classified into two groups using facial template and color information. In the former, due to the various sizes and shapes of a face, which are dependant on viewpoint and distance, it is difficult to make an appropriate facial template [3, 4, 5]. In the latter, the face region can be easily extracted by the comparison of color information, although it is affected both by skin-color differences between races and variations in lighting [6, 7, 8]. We adopt the latter for the facial region detection, since the facial skin-color is distributed in the restricted color range and the color in an input image is easily acquired and compared with the standard facial skin-color. Additionally, we use the YCbCr color space to compute the skin-color, since it is separated by the chrominance components (Cb and Cr) and the luminance component (Y) and that can reduce the lighting effect.

To detect the facial skin-color, we use [77, 127] and [133, 173] for the ranges of Cb and Cr, respectively. Fig. 2 shows the facial region detected by the comparison of the skin-color. The facial region is well detected. However, since such an image includes skin-color outside of a face, such as golden and dyed hair, this algorithm presents a serious problem to detecting them as a facial region and that has a fatal effect on subsequent processing, such as eye or eyebrow region detection.

We solve the problem of the facial region detection using the color information by using additive hair characteristics that a hair region has a larger luminance variation than a facial region. Equation (1) represents the luminance variation at coordinates $(x, y)$. If it is larger than a specified threshold, its coordinate belongs to the hair region.

**Fig. 2.** Input image for facial region detection and a detected facial region (*left and right*)

$$V(x,y) = \frac{1}{9}\sum_{i=-1}^{1}\sum_{j=-1}^{1}|Y(x,y)-Y(x+i,y+j)| \ . \tag{1}$$

The facial region without the skin-color hair effect is derived from the logical equation between the facial region image generated by the color information and the non hair region image generated by Equation (1) as shown in Equation (2).

$$f_{RF}(x,y) = f_F(x,y) \cap \overline{f_H(x,y)} \ . \tag{2}$$

Fig. 3 shows the process of removing the skin-color hair effect by the proposed algorithm. The algorithm using only color information includes the golden hair in the facial region. However the proposed algorithm removes the skin-color hair effect by using the luminance variation additively. The final facial region is detected by the postprocessing, the largest cluster is extracted as the facial region and then the holes in the facial region are changed into the facial region.

**Fig. 3.** Images of the process of removing the skin-color hair effect, an input image with the golden hair, facial region detected by just color information, hair region detected by luminance variation, and a facial region image without the skin-color hair effect (*left to right*)

## 2.2 Eye Region Detection

Template is used to detect the eyes in the detected facial region and many eye candidate regions appear in its result. The real eye regions can be extracted by the following facts. The eyes are located symmetrically in the upper facial region and under the eyebrow if the eyes and the eyebrows are detected simultaneously [9]. Fig. 4 shows the general process of detecting eye regions. First, many eye candidate regions are extracted from the facial region by the template matching and then the eye region picked out from the candidates by means of the above-mentioned facts. However, the detected eye regions give us less accurate information regarding the facial expression, since they are detected under placing more weight on their position than their shape.

**Fig. 4.** Eye candidate regions extracted template matching and the eye region picked out from the candidates using location information on the eyes (*left and right*)

To get a more accurate eye shape, we complement the detected eye region with weighted templates. First, we assign a new eye search region: one half of width and height of the detected eye region is added to its right and left sides and its up and down sides, respectively. To provide against a much smaller search region, we also specify one fifth of the facial region width and two-thirds of height for its minimum width and height, respectively. Then we detect the edges in the eye search region with the canny edge operator and apply the weighted templates to the edge image. The weighted templates consist of four masks as shown in Fig. 5 and make it possible to detect more accurate eye shapes. In Fig. 5, a black block, a dark gray block, a light gray block, and a white block mean −1, 1, 2, and 0, respectively.

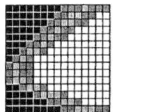  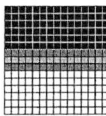 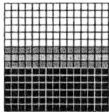

**Fig. 5.** Weighted templates for left, right, up, and down sides used to get a more accurate eye shape (*left to right*)

Fig. 6 shows the eye regions detected before and after using the weighted templates, respectively. The important corner edges are omitted in the detected eye region without the weighted templates, while the more accurate eye regions are detected by using the weighted templates.

**Fig. 6.** Detected eye regions before and after using the weighted template (*left to right*)

## 2.3 Eyebrow Region Detection

Since their shapes change according to feeling and emotion, the eyebrows play an important role in the analysis of facial expression. We specify the eyebrow search region on the basis of the detected eye region. It is located just above the eye region and its width and height are twice and one half of the width of the detected eye region, respectively. In the eyebrow search region, the eyebrow region is detected by the threshold technique using a luminance histogram. In general, the histogram has many peaks and valleys formed with one bin and they make it difficult to select the threshold fixing the eyebrow region.

We adopt a modified histogram to solve the problem of the general histogram technique. In the modified histogram, the peaks and valleys formed with one bin are changed into the larger bin and the smaller bin between both side bins, respectively. We also decide the threshold value in the limited range, that is, from 20% to 50% of the accumulated histogram, since it is experimentally investigated that the eyebrow region occupies from 20% to 50% of the eyebrow search region. The minimum bin is selected in the limited range as the threshold value. Fig. 7 shows a process of generating the modified histogram and determining the threshold value. Fig. 8 shows the detected eyebrow region. A wrong detection can occur in the eyebrow search region that includes the hair or the shade region but it is revised by using the shape information of the eyebrow.

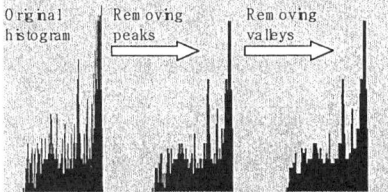 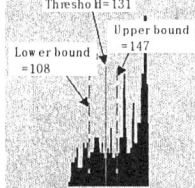

**Fig. 7.** The processes of modifying a histogram and determining a threshold value (*left and right*)

 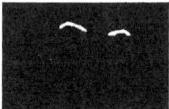

**Fig. 8.** Input image for eyebrow region detection and a detected eyebrow region (*left and right*)

### 2.4 Mouth Region Detection

A mouth search region is specified by the positions of the detected eyes and the statistical data regarding the geometric information of a face [8]. That is, the eyes and mouth are located statistically as shown in Fig. 9. The mouth search region is represented with two coordinates ($M_{left}$, $M_{top}$) and ($M_{right}$, $M_{bottom}$) by Equation (3)

$$\begin{bmatrix} M_{left} \\ M_{right} \\ M_{top} \\ M_{bottom} \end{bmatrix} = \begin{bmatrix} 0.965 x_{left} + 0.035 x_{right} \\ 0.035 x_{left} + 0.965 x_{right} \\ y_{eye} + 0.84(x_{right} - x_{left}) \\ y_{eye} + 1.24(x_{right} - x_{left}) \end{bmatrix}, \quad (3)$$

where, $Y_{eye}$ is $(Y_{left} + Y_{right})/2$.

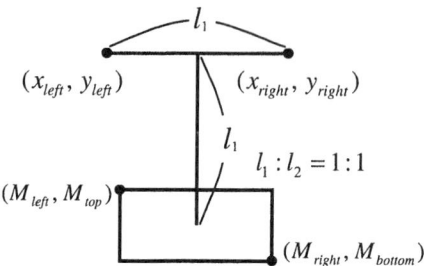

**Fig. 9.** Geometric structure of eyes and mouth

As with the hair, the mouth region also has a large luminance variance, which is in this case due to the wrinkles on lips. We can therefore detect the mouth region using the luminance variance computed by Equation (1) in the mouth search region. Fig. 10 shows the detected mouth region.

**Fig. 10.** Input image for mouth region detection and a detected mouth region (*left and right*)

## 3  FCP Extraction

We appoint 34 points for FCPs in the facial region, as shown in Fig. 11. 16, 10, and 8 FCPs are appointed in two eyes, two eyebrows, and the mouth, respectively. The x values of FCP are the right and left sides, one-fourth point, one half point, and three-fourth points from the left side of each facial component region. The y values of the right and left sides in each region and the eyebrows are the middle points of the region thickness and the others are the outline of each region.

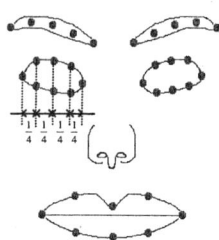

**Fig. 11.** Appointed FCPs

## 4 Results of FCP Extraction Experiment

We performed a FCP extraction experiment using the detected facial components and analyzed the results. The input image for the experiment must be a bust shot, including a front view of the face without glasses, and the background has to be simple. Fig. 12 shows the FCPs extracted by the proposed algorithm. They are located in the proper place considered in Fig. 11. Our experiment is carried out with 150 images. It extracts valid FCPs in 122 images, but invalid FCPs in the remaining 28 images.

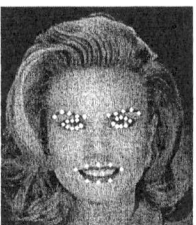

**Fig. 12.** Extracted FCPs in images

The images with the wrong FCPs are classified into four cases as depicted in Table 1. The first case was due to background effects. When the background with skin-color is detected as the facial region, the algorithm cannot detect the facial components as well as the FCP. The second case was because of long hair. Long hair covering the eyes and eyebrows causes the wrong eye region detection and makes it impossible to detect the remaining facial components. The third case was affected by viewpoint. The input image is limited but the limited images are already included in the image database for the experiment. Basically, they disagree with the geometric information of a face and as a result, the facial components cannot be normally detected in them. The fourth case regards a problem with skin-color range. The skin-color of several non-Caucasian people was out of the assumed Caucasian skin-color range and the facial region could not be detected in them. The front three cases were solved by cautious images acquisitions, and the last case solved by adjusting a skin-color range to a race. The image for facial expression representation can be generated in a less limited condition and the perfect FCP can be detected in it.

**Table 1.** Analysis of images not to extract FCP

| The causes of failure | The number of images |
|---|---|
| Skin-color background | 13 |
| Long hair | 5 |
| Viewpoint | 3 |
| Skin-color range | 7 |

## 5 Conclusion

This paper proposes the improved facial component detection algorithm for the FCP, important information for facial expression and recognition. The proposed algorithm analyzes and solves the problem of the conventional algorithm. It adopts the luminance variance, the geometric information of the facial components, the weighted template, and the modified histogram. They make it possible to detect the facial components more easily and more accurately, and that is shown in the facial component detection experiment. The FCP extraction experiment also shows valid FCP detection in most of experiment images and the possibility of a perfect FCP detection in the images acquired in less limited conditions.

## References

1. R. Chellappa, C. H. Wilson, and S. Sirohey: Human and Machine Recognition of Faces: A Survey. Proc. of the IEEE, vol. 83, no. 5 (1995) 705-740
2. Y. H. Han and S. H. Hong: Recognizing Human Facial Expressions and Gesture from Image Sequence. Journal of Biomedical Engineering Research, vol. 20, no. 4 (1999) 419-425
3. R. Brunelli and T. Poggio: Face Recognition: Feature versus Templates. IEEE Trans. PAMI, vol. 15, no. 10 (1993)
4. G. Chow and X. Li: Towards a System for Automatic Facial Feature Detection. Pattern Recognition, vol. 26, no. 12 (1993) 1739-1775
5. V. Govindaraju, S. N. Srihari, and D. B. Sher: A Computational Model for Face Location. Proc. 3rd Int. Conf. Computer Vision (1990) 718-721
6. R. C. Gonzalez and R. E. Woods: Digital Image Processing. Addison Wesley New York (1992)
7. J. C. Russ: The Image Processing Handbook, 3rd Ed.. IEEE Press (1999)
8. D. Chai and K. N. Ngan: Face Segmentation Using Skin-color Map in Videophone Application. IEEE Trans. Circuits and Systems for Video Technology (1999) 551-564
9. H-S. Yoon, M. Wang, and B-W. Min: Skew Correction of Face Image Using Eye Components Extraction. The Journal of the Korea Institute of Telematics and Electronics, vol. 33-B, no. 12 (1996) 71-83

# The Effect of Facial Expression Recognition Based on the Dimensions of Emotion Using PCA Representation and Neural Networks

Young-Suk Shin

Department of Information Communication Engineering, Chosun University,
#375 Seosuk-dong, Dong-gu, Gwangju, 501-759, Korea
ysshin@mail.chosun.ac.kr

**Abstract.** A new approach for recognizing facial expressions in various internal states that is illumination-invariant and without detectable cues such as a neutral expression is proposed. First, we propose a zero-phase whitening step of the images for illumination-invariant. Second, we developed a representation of face images based on principal component analysis(PCA) representation excluded the first 1 principle component as the features for facial expression recognition, regardless of neutral expression. The PCA basis vectors for this data set had reflected well the changes in facial expression. Finally, a neural network model for classification of facial expressions based on dimension model was created. The dimensional model recognizes not only six facial expressions related to six basic emotions (happiness, sadness, surprise, angry, fear, disgust), but also expressions of various internal states. PCA representations excluded the first 1 principle component and neural network model on the two-dimensional structure of emotion have improved the limitation of expression recognition based on a small number of discrete categories of emotional expressions, and have overcome the problems of lighting sensitivity and dependence on cues such as a neutral expression.

## 1 Introduction

The work in facial expressions for human-computer intelligent interaction did not start until the 1990s. Models for recognizing facial expressions have traditionally operated on a short digital video sequence of the facial expression being made, such as neutral, then happy, then neutral[1,2,5,6,7,8]. All require the person's head to be easily found in the video. Therefore, continuous expression recognition such as a sequence of "happy, surprise, frown" was not handled well. And the expressions must either be manually separated, or interleaved with some reliably detectable cues such as a neutral expression, which has essentially zero motion energy.

Facial expression recognition from video involves relating these patterns to a category of emotion. There are a small number of discrete categories of emotional expressions [1,2,3,4,5,6,7,8] and data in the experiments is "pure" in the sense that a user willingly or naturally tried to express exactly one emotion. There is no guarantee that the facial expression recognized as sad corresponds to any genuine affective state of sadness. Discrete categories of emotions can be treated as regions in a continuous emotion space. For example, a feeling of sadness can occur in both "lonely" and "grief". Therefore, categories may be fuzzy in the sense that an element can belong in more than one category at once.

In this paper, we present a new approach for recognizing facial expressions based on the dimensions in various internal states that is illumination-invariant and without detectable cues such as a neutral expression. The first stage employed a zero-phase whitening step of the images for illumination-invariant. Second, we developed a representation of face images based on principal component analysis representation excluded the first 1 principle component as the features for facial expression recognition, regardless of neutral expression. The PCA basis vectors for this data set had reflected well changes in facial expressions. Finally, a neural network model was created for classification of facial expressions based on the dimension model.

## 2 Database Based on the Dimensions of Emotion

The face images used for this research were a subset of the Korean facial expression database[9]. The data set contained 500 images, 3 females and 3 males, each image using 640 by 480 pixels. Examples of the original images are shown in figure 1.

Expressions were divided into two dimensions(Pleasure-Displeasure and Arousal-Sleep dimension) according to the study of internal states through the semantic analysis of words related with emotion by Younga et al. [10] using 83 expressive words. Each expressor of females and males posed 83 internal emotional state expressions when 83 words of emotion are presented. 51 experimental subjects rated pictures on the degrees of expression in each of the two dimensions on a nine-point scale. The images were labeled with a rating averaged over all subjects. Table 1 is a part list of an expressor rated for degrees of expression in each of the two dimensions on a nine-point scale.

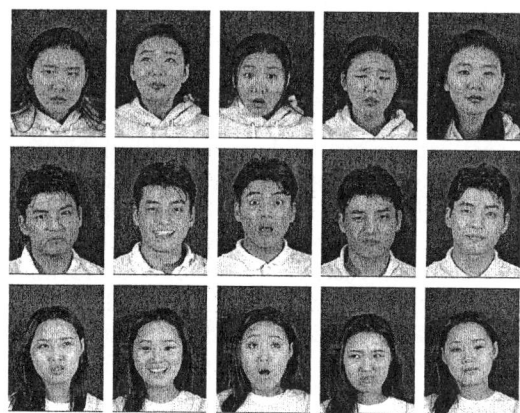

**Fig. 1.** Examples from the facial expression database containing 83 posed internal emotional state expressions

**Table 1.** A part list of an expressor rated for degrees of expression in each of the two dimensions on a nine-point scale

| Picture No. | Named emotional word of Pictures | Dimension(human rating) | | | |
|---|---|---|---|---|---|
| | | Pleasure-Displeasure | | Arousal-Sleep | |
| | | M | SD | M | SD |
| 2 | disgust | 7.5 | 1.31 | 7.07 | 1.6 |
| 4 | emptiness | 5.87 | 1.2 | 4.17 | 1.98 |
| 6 | annoyance | 7.23 | 0.82 | 5.63 | 1.54 |
| 7 | longing | 6.07 | 1.08 | 5.1 | 1.56 |
| 8 | worry | 7.4 | 0.89 | 6.03 | 1.79 |
| 11 | happiness | 2.27 | 0.83 | 4.57 | 2.28 |
| 15 | surprise | 5.27 | 1.39 | 7.97 | 1.94 |
| 18 | Fear | 7.5 | 0.82 | 7.33 | 1.06 |
| 20 | satisfaction | 2.9 | 1.03 | 4.33 | 1.86 |
| 38 | sadness | 6.07 | 0.98 | 5.37 | 1.33 |
| 49 | isolation | 6.07 | 0.78 | 4.83 | 1.23 |
| 58 | sleepiness | 5.0 | 1.26 | 1.8 | 1.37 |
| 64 | distress | 7.8 | 0.92 | 6.3 | 1.64 |
| 67 | comfort | 3.77 | 0.97 | 4.57 | 1.96 |
| 69 | tiredness | 6.17 | 0.99 | 4.3 | 2.05 |

Abbreviation: M, mean; SD, standard deviation.

## 3 PCA Representations of Facial Expressions

The face images used for this research were centered the face images with coordinates for eye and mouth locations, and then cropped and scaled to 20x20 pixels. The luminance was normalized in two steps. First, a "sphering" step prior to principal component analysis is performed. The rows of the images were concatenated to produce 1 × 400 dimensional vectors. The row means are subtracted from the dataset, $X$. Then $X$ is passed through the zero-phase whitening filter, $V$, which is the inverse square root of the covariance matrix:

$$V = E\{XX^T\}^{-\frac{1}{2}} \quad (1)$$
$$W = XV$$

This indicates that the mean is set to zero and the variances are equalized as unit variances. Secondly, we subtract the local mean gray-scale value from the sphered each patch. From this process, $W$ removes much of the variability due to lightening. Figure 2(a) shows the cropped images before normalizing. Figure 2(b) shows the cropped images after normalizing.

Some of the most successful algorithms for face recognition applied PCA representation are "eigen faces[11]" and "holons[12]". These methods are based on learning mechanisms that are sensitive to the correlations in the face images. PCA provides a dimensionality-reduced code that separates the correlations in the input.

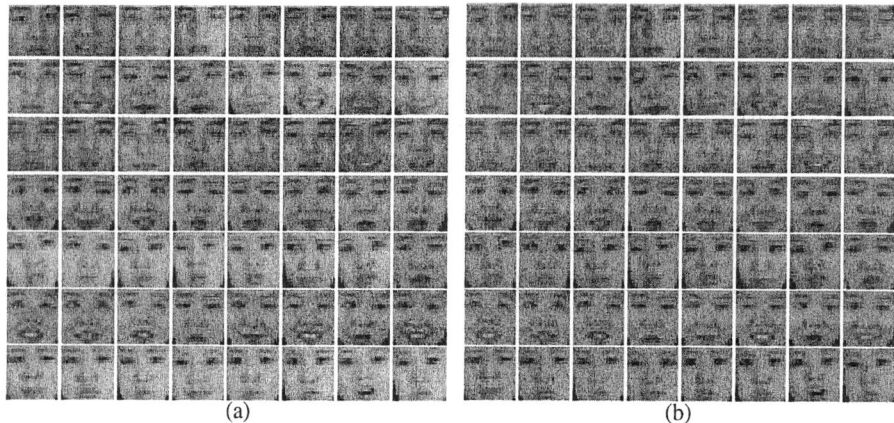

**Fig. 2.** (a) The cropped images before normalizing. (b) The cropped images after normalizing.

Atick and Redlich[13] have argued for such compact, decorrelated representations as a general coding strategy for the visual system. Redundancy reduction has been discussed in relation to the visual system at several levels. A first-order redundancy is mean luminance. The variance, a second order statistic, is the luminance contrast. PCA is a way of encoding second order dependencies in the input by rotating the axes to corresponding to directions of maximum covariance.

In a task such as facial expression recognition, the first 1 or 2 principal components of PCA do not address the high-order dependencies of the facial expression images, that is to say, it just displays the neutral face. Figure 3(a) shows PCA representation that included the first 1 principle component. But selecting intermediate ranges of components that excluded the first 1 or 2 principle components of PCA did address well the changes in facial expression (Figure 3(b)).

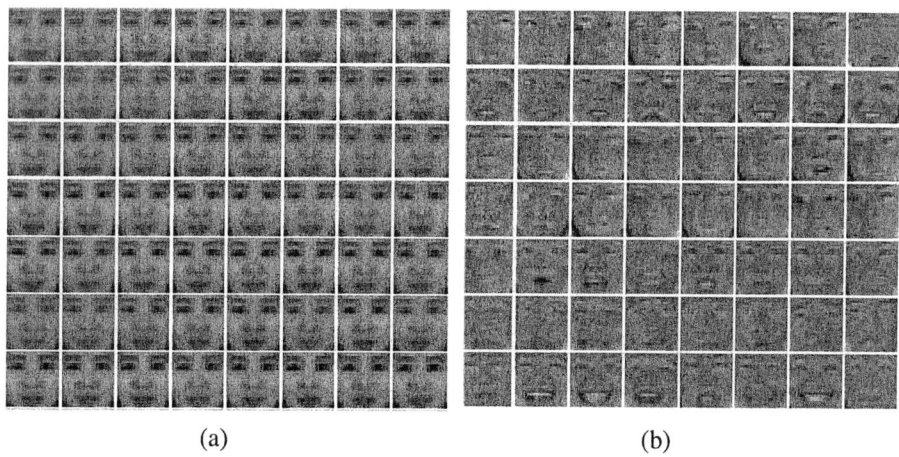

**Fig. 3.** (a) PCA representation only included the first 1 principle component (b) PCA representation excluded the first 1 principle component.

Therefore, to extract information of facial expression regardless of neutral expression, we employed the 200 PCA coefficients, $P_n$, excluded the first 1 principle component of PCA of the face images. The principal component representation of the set of images in $W$ in Equation(1) based on $P_n$ is defined as $Y_n = W * P_n$. The approximation of $W$ is obtained as:

$$\overline{W} = Y_n * P_n^T. \tag{2}$$

The columns of $\overline{W}$ contains the representational codes for the training images (Figure 3(b)). The representational code for the test images was found by $\overline{W}_{test} = Y_{test} * P_n^T$. Best performance for facial expression recognition was obtained using 200 principal components excluded the first 1 principle component.

## 4 Recognition Performance

The system for facial expression recognition uses a three-layer neural network. The first layer contained the representational codes derived in Equation (2). The second layer was 30 hidden units and the third layer was two output nodes to recognize the two dimensions: Pleasure-Displeasure and Arousal-Sleep.

Training applies an error back propagation algorithm. The activation function of hidden units uses the sigmoid function. 500 images for training and 66 images excluded from the training set for testing are used. The 66 images for test include 11 expression images of each six people. The first test verifies with the 500 images trained already. Recognition result produced by 500 images trained previously showed 100% recognition rates. The rating result of facial expressions derived from 9 point scale on two dimension for degrees of expression by subjects was compared with experimental results of a neural network(NN). The dimension values of human and NN in each of the two dimensions are given as vectors of $\overrightarrow{H}$ and $\overrightarrow{N}$. The similarity of recognition result between human and NN was obtained as:

$$S(\overrightarrow{H},\overrightarrow{N}) = \frac{\overrightarrow{H} \cdot \overrightarrow{N}}{\|\overrightarrow{H}\|\|\overrightarrow{N}\|} \min(\frac{\|\overrightarrow{H}\|}{\|\overrightarrow{N}\|},\frac{\|\overrightarrow{N}\|}{\|\overrightarrow{H}\|}) \tag{3}$$

Table 2 describes a degree of similarity of expression recognition between human and NN on the two-dimensions of emotion and indicates a part of all. The result of expression recognition of NN appears very similar to the result of expression recognition of human. In Table 2, the result of expression recognition of NN was matched to the nearest emotion word within 83 emotion words related to internal emotion states. Figure 4 and 5 show the correlation of the expression recognition between human and NN in each of the two dimensions. The statistical significance of the similarity for expression recognition between human and NN on each of the two dimensions was tested by Person correlation analysis. The correlation in the Pleasure-Displeasure dimension between human and NN showed 0.77 at the 0.01 level and 0.51 at the 0.01 level in the Arousal-Sleep dimension.

**Table 2.** The result data of expression recognition between human and NN derived from three people

| Named emotional word of Pictures(person) | Human | | Neural Network | | Recognition on Neural Network | Similarity |
| --- | --- | --- | --- | --- | --- | --- |
| | P – D | A – S | P – D | A – S | | |
| depression(a) | 6.23 | 4.43 | 5.22 | 4.41 | boredom | 0.89 |
| crying(a) | 6.47 | 4.10 | 6.16 | 5.19 | sorry | 0.94 |
| gloomy(a) | 7.37 | 5.53 | 7.53 | 6.84 | strain | 0.90 |
| strange(a) | 6.17 | 5.17 | 5.72 | 4.44 | envy | 0.89 |
| proud(a) | 3.07 | 4.47 | 1.69 | 4.54 | satisfaction | 0.86 |
| confident(a) | 3.47 | 4.57 | 2.90 | 5.35 | grateful | 0.93 |
| despair(a) | 6.23 | 5.97 | 5.35 | 5.08 | strangeness | 0.85 |
| sleepiness(a) | 5.00 | 1.80 | 3.13 | 2.96 | resting | 0.74 |
| likable(a) | 1.97 | 4.23 | 1.42 | 3.96 | warmness | 0.89 |
| delight(a) | 1.17 | 4.20 | 3.41 | 5.87 | pleasantness | 0.62 |
| boredom(a) | 6.77 | 5.50 | 5.05 | 5.65 | strangeness | 0.85 |
| pleasantness (b) | 1.40 | 5.47 | 3.12 | 4.35 | contentment | 0.88 |
| depression (b) | 6.00 | 4.23 | 7.10 | 4.28 | stuffiness | 0.88 |
| crying(b) | 7.13 | 6.17 | 7.46 | 7.07 | displeasure | 0.91 |
| gloomy(b) | 5.90 | 3.67 | 6.93 | 5.73 | sadness | 0.76 |
| strangeness(b) | 6.13 | 6.47 | 5.70 | 3.18 | boredom | 0.69 |
| proud(b) | 2.97 | 5.17 | 4.56 | 2.31 | sleepiness | 0.71 |
| confident(b) | 2.90 | 4.07 | 2.63 | 3.60 | satisfaction | 0.89 |
| despair(b) | 7.80 | 5.67 | 7.19 | 5.61 | sadness | 0.94 |
| sleepiness(b) | 6.00 | 1.93 | 6.34 | 3.07 | emptiness | 0.88 |
| likable(b) | 2.07 | 4.27 | 3.52 | 5.12 | longing | 0.75 |
| delight(b) | 1.70 | 5.70 | 1.79 | 4.92 | contentment | 0.87 |
| gloomy( c ) | 6.60 | 3.83 | 4.14 | 5.19 | longing | 0.81 |
| strangeness( c ) | 6.03 | 5.67 | 6.77 | 3.13 | intricacy | 0.85 |
| proud( c ) | 2.00 | 4.53 | 2.48 | 3.01 | satisfaction | 0.76 |
| confident( c ) | 2.47 | 5.27 | 2.30 | 3.57 | satisfaction | 0.72 |
| despair (c ) | 6.47 | 5.03 | 4.52 | 4.44 | longing | 0.77 |
| sleepiness( c ) | 6.50 | 3.80 | 5.52 | 3.82 | boredom | 0.89 |
| likable(c) | 1.83 | 4.97 | 1.54 | 5.36 | gratification | 0.95 |
| delight(c) | 2.10 | 5.63 | 2.98 | 5.30 | longing | 0.97 |
| boredom( c ) | 6.47 | 5.73 | 7.55 | 5.50 | confusion | 0.92 |
| tedious( c) | 6.73 | 4.77 | 6.98 | 6.27 | confusion | 0.87 |
| jealousy( c ) | 6.87 | 6.80 | 3.14 | 6.11 | pleasantness | 0.68 |

Abbreviation: P-D,pleasure-displeasure; A-S,arousal-sleep; Dep.,depression; Str., strangeness; Des.,despair; Del.,delight; Pro.,proud; Sle.,sleepiness; Bor.,boredom; Con.,confusion; Lik.,likable; Ted.,tedious; Int.,intricacy; Reg.,regret; Lon.,loneliness; Cry.,crying;War.,warmness; Hap.,happiness.

## 5 Discussion

Our results allowed us to extend the range of emotion recognition and to recognize on the two dimensions of emotion with illumination-invariant without detectable cues such as a neutral expression. The result of expression recognition between human and NN on the two-dimensional structure of emotion showed three significant conclusions.

The Effect of Facial Expression Recognition Based on the Dimensions of Emotion    1139

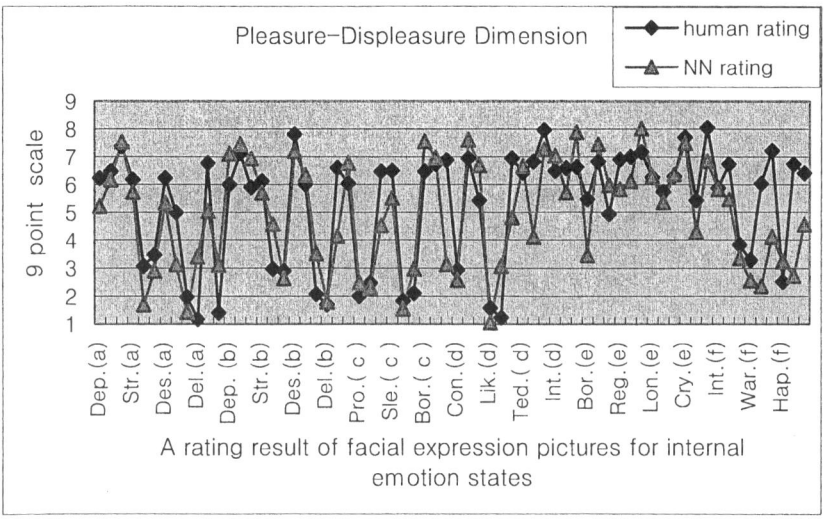

**Fig. 4.** A rating result of facial expression recognition in Pleasure-Displeasure dimension

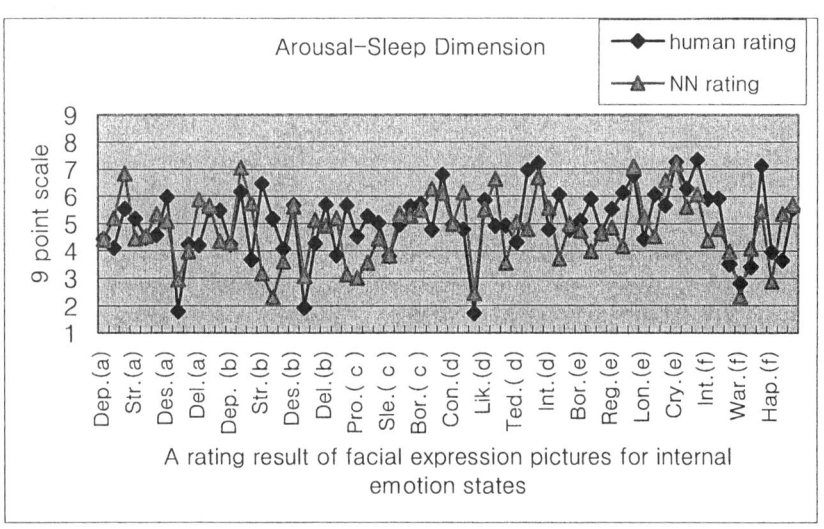

**Fig. 5.** A rating result of facial expression recognition in Arousal-Sleep dimension

First, the two-dimensional structure of emotion in the facial expression recognition appears as a stabled structure for the facial expression recognition. The correlation results of each dimension through Person correlation analysis were significant over 0.5 at the 0.01 level. Secondly, Pleasure-Displeasure dimension is analyzed as a more stable dimension than Arousal-Sleep dimension. Pleasure-Displeasure dimension was significant 0.77 at the 0.01 level, while Arousal-Sleep dimension was significant 0.51 at the 0.01 level. This result corresponds to a research for validating the stability of two-dimensional structure of emotion about emotion word[14]. Third, when the whole face was presented, facial expressions were successfully recognized. This fact was reflected by PCA representation excluded the first 1 principle component. This finding suggests that holistic analysis is important for facial expression recognition.

We propose that the inference of emotional states within a subject from facial expressions may depends more on the Pleasure-Displeasure dimension than Arousal-Sleep dimension. It may be analyzed that the perception of Pleasure-Displeasure dimension may be needed for the survival of the species and the immediate and appropriate response to emotionally salient, while the Arousal-Sleep dimension may be needed for relatively detailed cognitive ability for the personal internal states.

## References

1. Mase, K.: Recognition of facial expression from optical flow. IEICE Transactions, E 74, **10** (1991) 3473-3483
2. Yacoob, Y., Davis, L.S.: Recognizing human facial expression from long image sequences using optical flow. IEEE Trans. Pattern Anal. Machine Intell. **18**(6) (1996) 636-642
3. Bartlett, M., Viola, P., Sejnowski, T., Larsen, J., Hager, J., Ekman, P.: Classfying Facial Action. In: Advances in Neural Information Processing Systems 8. D. Touretzky et al. editors, MIT Press, Cambridge, MA (1996)
4. Essa, I., Pentland, A.:Coding, analysis, interpretation, and recognition of facial expressions. IEEE Transactions on Pattern Analysis and Machine Intelligence, **19** (1997) 757-763
5. Lien, J.: Automatic recognition of facial expressions using hidden Markov models and estimation of expression intensity. Ph.D. Thesis, Carnegie Mellon University, (1998)
6. Oliver, N. Pentland, A., Berard, F.: LAFTER:a real-time face and lips tracker with facial expression recognition. Pattern Recognition **33** (2000) 1369-1382
7. Cohen, I., Sebe, N., Garg, A., Chen, L. S., Huang, T. S.: Facial expression recognition from video sequence. Proc. Int'l Conf. Multimedia and Exp(ICME) (2002) 121-124
8. Cohen, I. :Semisupervised learning of classifiers with application to human-computer interaction. PhD thesis, Univ. of Illinois at Urbana-Champaign (2003)
9. Saebum, B., Jaehyun, H., Chansub, C.: Facial expression database for mapping facial expression onto internal state. '97 Emotion Conference of Korea, (1997) 215-219
10. Younga, K., Jinkwan, K., Sukyung, P., Kyungja, O., Chansub, C.: The study of dimension of internal states through word analysis about emotion. Korean Journal of the Science of Emotion and Sensibility, **1** (1998) 145-152
11. Turk, M, Pentland, A. : Eigenfaces for recognition. Journal of Cognitive Neuroscience **3**(1) (1991) 71-86
12. Cottrell, G., Metcalfe, J.: Face, gender and emotion recognition using holons. In Touretzky, D., editor, Advances in Neural information processing systems (3) San Maleo, CA. Morgan aufmann (1991) 564-571
13. Atic, J., Redlich, A.: What does the retina know about natural scenes?, Neural Computation (4) (1992) 196-210
14. Jinkwan, K., Hyesshin, M., Kyungja, O.: Validating the stability of two-dimensional structure of emotion. Korean Journal of the Science of Emotion and Sensibility, **2**(1) (1999) 43-52

# Enhanced Facial Feature Extraction Using Region-Based Super-Resolution Aided Video Sequences

T. Celik[1], C. Direkoglu[2], H. Ozkaramanli[2], H. Demirel[2], and M. Uyguroglu[2]

[1] Advanced Technologies Research and Development Institute (ATRDI),
[2] Deparment of Electrical and Electronic Engineering,
Eastern Mediterranean University,
Gazimagusa TRNC Mersin 10 Turkey
{turgay.celik, cem.direkoglu, huseyin.ozkaramanli,
hasan.demirel, mustafa.uyguroglu}@emu.edu.tr

**Abstract.** Facial feature extraction is a fundamental problem in image processing. Correct extraction of features is essential for the success of many applications. Typical feature extraction algorithms fail for low resolution images which do not contain sufficient facial details. In this paper, a region-based super-resolution aided facial feature extraction method for low resolution video sequences is described. The region based approach makes use of segmented faces as the region of interest whereby a significant reduction in computational complexity of the super-resolution algorithm is achieved. The results indicate that the region-based super-resolution aided facial feature extraction algorithm provides significant performance improvement in terms of correctly detecting the location of the facial feature points. There are 6.4 fold reductions in the computational cost.

## 1 Introduction

Facial feature extraction has been a topic of extensive research for several decades [7], [5]. This preprocessing is essential for the success of many applications such as recognition, teleconferencing, facial expression analysis, man machine interfacing and lip reading for the deaf etc. In facial expression analysis even the smallest errors can be interpreted differently leading to wrong facial expression recognition. In 3D model based low bit rate video coding, the correct extraction of features is imperative for the model adaptation, texture mapping and the subsequent animation.

Most facial feature extraction and tracking methods are sensitive to various non-idealities such as variations in illumination, noise, orientation and color space used. The problem becomes more challenging in adverse conditions where the resolution of the camera limits the quality of the images that one has to work with. In such adverse conditions, inserting the crucially needed details alleviates the difficulties aiding the correct extraction of features. As a technique which can produce a high resolution image from a sequence of low resolution images, super-resolution [1] fills this gap very nicely. In this paper we propose a region-based super-resolution aided facial feature extraction technique for video sequences that may not contain enough facial details. The region of interest, the human face in this paper is segmented from the incoming video. The region of interest is then super-resolved using a frequency domain registration method and the subsequent cubic interpolation [6]. The application of the super-resolution algorithm to a much smaller face region significantly reduces the computational cost of the algorithm. The facial feature extraction part is based on an efficient combination of methods such as morphology, median filtering, adaptive intensity clustering, edge detection, circle and ellipse fitting.

The proposed method was tested on two low resolution video sequences. For comparison purposes correct location of facial features are manually extracted for both low resolution and super-resolution images. Our results indicate that the region-based super-resolution aided method provides significant improvement in correctly detecting locations of the facial features in video sequences taken in adverse conditions. The computational cost of the overall algorithm is reduced from around 4040 MFLOPS ($10^6$ floating point operations per second) to around 625 MFLOPS per frame.

## 2 Region-Based Super-Resolution

The idea of super-resolution was first introduced in 1984 by Tsai and Huang [2] for multi-frame image restoration of band-limited signals. A good overview of existing algorithms is given by Borman and Stevenson [1]. Recently super-resolution image reconstruction has been a topic of active research. It promises to be a good tool which can improve the performance of many image processing applications. Super-resolution is comprised of two main steps. First, the registration of the low resolution images onto a high resolution grid and second the super-resolution image formation. Correct registration is critical for the success of super-resolution image reconstruction. If the images are inaccurately registered, the high resolution image is reconstructed from incorrect data and it is not a good representation of the original image. Popular methods for the registration are the spatial domain method of Karen [4] and the frequency domain approach as described in [6]. The subsequent reconstruction of the high resolution image can be accomplished by interpolation or iteratively as described by Peleg et. al., [3]. In this work, the incoming video is segmented to isolate the face region from every frame. Following the segmentation a frequency domain registration method and the subsequent interpolation using four consecutive frames as described in [6] is employed. It should be pointed out that the segmentation of the face from the incoming video also helps the registration process since the horizontal and vertical displacements can be directly calculated. Fig. 1(a) shows the original low-resolution frames, the segmented frames which are input to the super-resolution algorithm are depicted in Fig. 1(b) and the super-resolved face images are shown in Fig. 1(c)

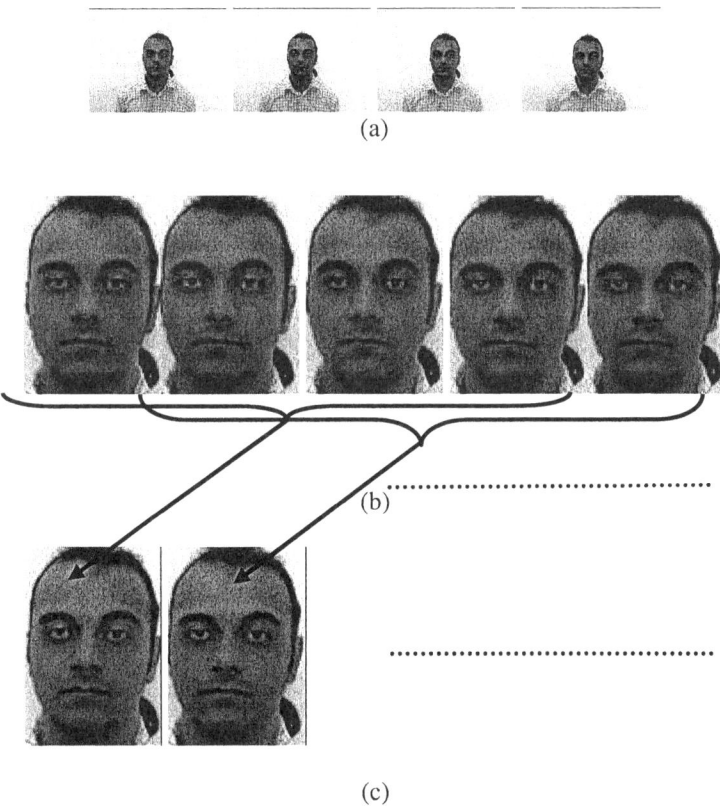

**Fig. 1.** (a) The original low-resolution frames - 240 x 320 Pixels (b) Segmented face images - 100 x 73 Pixels, (c) Super-resolved face images - 200 x 146 Pixels

## 3 Facial Feature Extraction

The facial feature extraction method uses the segmented and super-resolved faces for the processing. Fig. 2 shows the flowchart of the overall facial feature extraction algorithm. The first step is the face detection part where the feature invariant approach with multiple attributes such as skin color and shape is employed for this purpose [7]. The output of YCbCr skin color modeling is a binary image with a set of connected components. Face candidate regions from these components are processed using median filtering and morphological operations to remove the non face regions. Several heuristic criteria such as holes inside the face candidate region together with orientation and a best ellipse fitting approach constitute the two independent face candidate elimination procedures. Once the face image is obtained, the facial feature sub-images for the left and right eyes, the nose and the mouth are detected from which the feature points are extracted.

The detection of pupils involves an intensity based adaptive clustering on the gray level eye sub-images. As a result of this adaptive clustering, pupils and eyebrows remain as the two largest dark regions. Nostrils are also found by applying intensity based adaptive clustering to nose sub-image. The biggest two regions in the clustered binary image are the nostrils. More challenging problem is to find the lip corners. Lip cut formed by applying Sobel vertical derivative operator to the mouth sub image is the most important cue [5]. It limits the vertical position of lip corners. Again, intensity based adaptive clustering is applied to limit the horizontal position of right and left lip corners. A combination of lip cut information and clustered binary sub-image is used for extracting the lip corners.

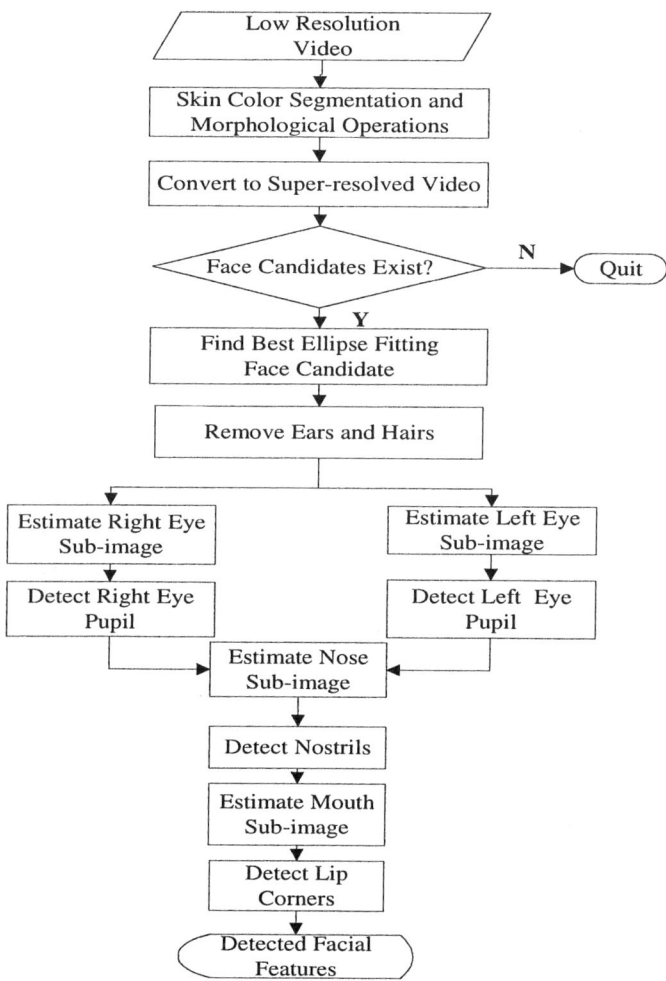

**Fig. 2.** Flowchart of the facial features detection algorithm

The pictorial results of the above method for three consecutive frames of the low resolution video sequence are depicted in Fig. 3(a). The white dots indicate the location of the detected features. In Fig. 3(b), the detected facial feature points for the same frames of the super-resolved face region are depicted.

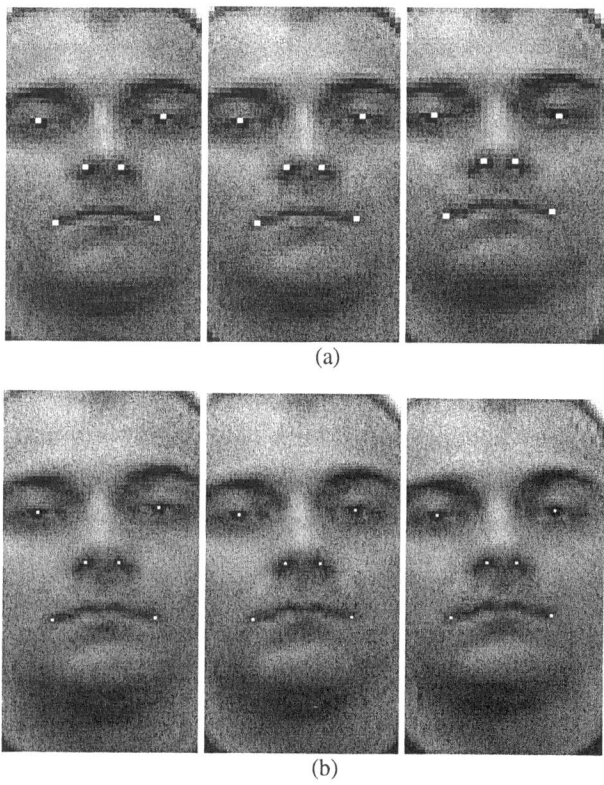

**Fig. 3.** Detection of feature points, (a) Frames 5, 6 and 7 of the low resolution sequence, (b) Frames 5, 6 and 7 of the super-resolved sequence

## 4 Results and Discussions

The detection algorithm presented above is applied to the low resolution and the super-resolved video sequences. The original low resolution video sequences used in this comparison are nine second records of a single slowly moving approximately frontal face images in constant background. Each video sequence contains 90 frames. The frames are of size 240x320. The face region constitutes a very small portion of the whole frame with approximately 100x73 pixels. Two video sequences were tested. Subject A, Fig. 4.(a), was chosen as a difficult subject in that the facial features are obstructed by illumination. He has a light beard and moustache which obstructs the nostrils and the lip corners. There is almost no skin color region between the eyebrows and the eye. On the other hand, Subject B, Fig. 4(b), is an easy subject with a distinct rounded face where the facial features are not obstructed. He has no beard and no moustache. The skin color region between the eye and eyebrows can be distinctly observed in Fig. 4b. Furthermore unlike subject A, subject B has no wrinkles on his face.

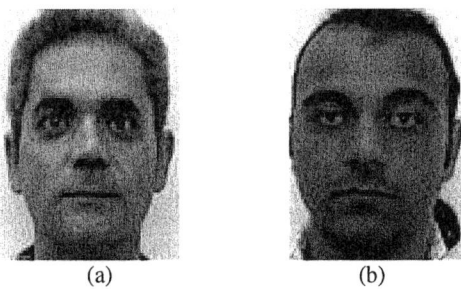

(a)　　　　　　　　(b)

**Fig. 4.** Subjects used in tests (a) Subject A, (b) Subject B

In order to assess the effectiveness of the super-resolution aided feature extraction the feature points are manually extracted from both the low and high resolution images. Facial feature points from the two low resolution sequences are first extracted. Then the segmentation aided super-resolved face sequences are obtained and the facial feature points are extracted. If a facial feature is detected to be within three pixels of the actual location (determined manually) it is declared to be a correct detection. Table 1 shows the results of this comparison. In both video sequences tested the correct detection rate increases significantly with the super-resolution aided approach. Furthermore as can be observed from Fig. 3 the feature points detected by the aid of the super-resolution approach converges to the exact feature points. This may prove to be very valuable in applications like face recognition and facial expression analysis where the accurate locations of facial feature points are of utmost importance.

The results shown in Table 1 for the low resolution sequences are quite different for the two subjects. The feature extraction algorithm performs very well for Subject B. However it does very poorly for Subject A. For the super-resolution aided approach, improvement is achieved for both subjects. Up to 18.89% improvement in correct detection is achieved for subject A. The improvement for subject B is more moderate and up to 3.34%. The large improvement in the correct detection of facial features for subject A is a good indication of the usefulness of super-resolution aided approach.

In order to evaluate the complexity of the proposed segmentation algorithm the method without segmentation is compared to the one with segmentation. Fig. 5 shows the computational cost of the super-resolution algorithm obtained using MATLAB Version 5.0. When no region segmentation is applied the computational cost is on the average 4040 MFLOPS per frame. Considering the fact that the one needs to process at least ten frames for a meaningful real time application it is obvious that with the current state of the art technology such a task is completely out of reach. When the region of interest segmentation is employed the super-resolution reconstruction takes only around 625 MFLOPS per frame. This corresponds to a computational cost reduction of approximately 85%. However this is still not within reach of the current state of the art technology. With such an approach and the current state of the art equipment one can only process approximately 3-4 frames per second. Further reduction in computational cost of the super-resolution algorithm especially the registration part is required for real time implementation.

**Table 1.** Performance of the super-resolution aided feature extraction method; (a) Subject A, (b) Subject B

| Correct Detection Rate (%) (3 Pixel Range) | Low Resolution | Super Resolution | Correct Detection Rate (%) (3 Pixel Range) | Low Resolution | Super Resolution |
|---|---|---|---|---|---|
| Left Eye | 53.33 | 57.78 | Left Eye | 98.89 | 98.89 |
| Right Eye | 64.44 | 73.33 | Right Eye | 93.33 | 95.56 |
| Left Nostril | 90.00 | 98.89 | Left Nostril | 97.78 | 98.89 |
| Right Nostril | 76.67 | 95.56 | Right Nostril | 95.56 | 97.78 |
| Left Lip Corner | 78.89 | 95.56 | Left Lip Corner | 94.44 | 97.78 |
| Right Lip Corner | 82.22 | 94.44 | Right Lip Corner | 95.56 | 98.89 |

(a)                    (b)

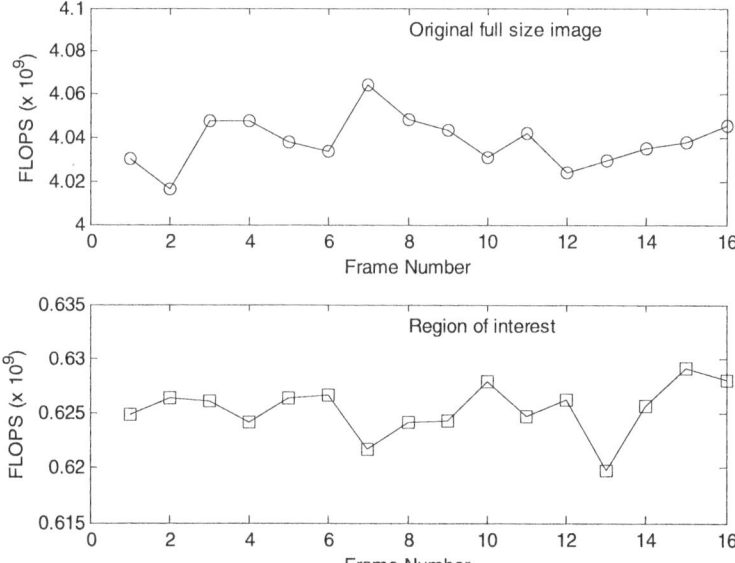

**Fig. 5.** Computational cost of super-resolution, (a) Original full-size image, (b) Region of interest

## 5 Conclusions

A region-based super-resolution aided automatic facial feature extraction method is presented. First the segmentation is carried out and head is extracted from the incoming frames. Then the consecutive frames are used to reconstruct the higher resolution image frames via a frequency domain registration algorithm and the subsequent cubic interpolation on a higher resolution grid. The facial feature extraction method involves a position, scale, shape and skin color invariant face detection part and the subsequent extraction of facial features based on an efficient combination of geometry based methods. The results indicate significant improvement in the performance of the region-based super-resolution aided extraction algorithm with approximately 6.4 fold reduction in computational cost.

## References

1. Borman S., and Stevenson R., Spatial resolution enhancement of low-resolution image sequences - a comprehensive review with directions for future research, Tech. Rep., University of Notre Dame (1998)
2. Huang, T.S., Advances in Computer Vision and Image Processing, JAI Press, vol. 1, ch. 7, pp. 317-339 (1984)
3. Irani M., and Peleg S., Improving resolution by image registration, CVGIP:Graphical Models and Image Processing, vol. 53, no. 3, pp. 231-239, May (1991)
4. Keren D.,Peleg S., and Brada R., Image sequence enhancement using sub-pixel displacement, Proceedings IEEE Conference on Computer Vision and Pattern Recognition, pp. 742-746, June (1988)
5. Lanzarotti R., Campadelli P., and Borghese N.A., Automatic features detection for overlapping face images on their 3D range models, Proceedings of the IEEE 11th International Conference on Image Analysis and Proceeding (ICIAP2001), Palermo, Italy, 26-28, pp.316-321 September (2001)
6. Vandewalle P., Süsstrunk S., and Vetterli M., Double resolution from a set of aliased images, SPIE/IS&T Electronic Imaging Conference, vol. 5301, January (2004)
7. Yang M.H., Kreigman D.J., and Ahuja N., Detecting faces in images: A Survey, IEEE Transactions on Pattern Analysis and Machine Intelligence, vol. 24, no. 1, pp. 34-58 (2002)

# Efficient Face and Facial Feature Tracking Using Search Region Estimation

C. Direkoğlu, H. Demirel, H. Özkaramanlı, and M. Uyguroğlu

Department of Electrical and Electronic Engineering,
Eastern Mediterranean University, Gazimagusa, North Cyprus
cem.direkoglu@emu.edu.tr

**Abstract.** In this paper an intelligent and efficient combination of several methods are employed for face and facial feature tracking with the motivation for real time applications. Face tracking algorithm is based on color and connected component analysis. It is scale, pose and orientation invariant, and can be implemented in real time in controlled environments. The more challenging problem of facial feature tracking uses intensity based adaptive clustering on facial feature sub-images. New search region estimation for each sub-image is proposed. The technique employs facial expression aware eye sub-image prediction. The simulation results indicate that facial feature tracking is efficient with an average tracking rate of 99% with a three pixel range under different head movements such as translation, rotation, tilt, and scale changes. Furthermore it is robust under varying facial expressions and non-uniform illumination.

## 1 Introduction

The Face tracking has become an increasingly important research topic. Many possible applications have been studied, including face or gesture recognition, teleconferencing, robotics as well as human computer interaction. Template matching using stored templates representing whole face of different people in diverse posses or expressions is a type of approach for face tracking. These templates can also be used for training a classifier, such as neural network, that can help in the face-detection process. Paul Viola and Michael Jones [1] proposed a machine learning approach for visual object detection, which is capable of processing images rapidly and achieving high detection rates. However, their framework has the disadvantage of not using temporal coherence. Any face detected in a frame provides information such as position and color, to be used in the next frames to speed up the process. The simplest approach for face tracking is skin-color. Prem Kuchi et al. [2] proposed a face tracking algorithm by using YCbCr color space. They present CbCr Gaussian skin-color model for skin and non-skin classification. The search region is estimated based on detected position and the min-max boxes for the consecutive frames. In this approach, RGB to YCbCr conversion is required and it is more complex and slow in comparison with RGB to normalized rgb conversion. Moreover, major axis is not reliable reference to estimate search region, because of its variability due to the clothes of persons in skin color applications.

In this paper, we propose a face tracking algorithm by using skin-color feature of face. Skin-color is computationally cheaper and at the same time orientation, shape, scale and translation invariant. These properties make it a good candidate for real time applications. We choose normalized r-g colorspace for skin color modeling because of its fast and simple conversion from the RGB colorspace. The other important property of normalized r-g, is that it is more tolerant in non-uniform lighting environments and one does not need to dynamically adapt its distribution. The face region, in the first frame, is located by using the algorithm explained in [3]. Once the center, minor axis and major axis are known of elliptic face, the search region is determined in the next frame by using last center position and minor axis of face. Then stochastic skin color modeling is applied to the search region and we get a set of connected components in binary format. Morphological operations are applied for smoothing and than holes inside of face candidate regions are filled. Finally the region, which includes the previous face center position, is chosen as a face. The success rate of the proposed face tracking method is on the average 93%.

Facial feature tracking is more challenging task than face tracking. Karin Sobottka and Ioannis Pitas [4] perform facial feature tracking by block (template) matching. Once, the facial features are detected, they initialize feature blocks. Then, tracking is done over time by searching for corresponding blocks in consecutive frames. Template matching or other types of appearance based techniques are computationally expensive. Jong-Gook Ko et al. [5] proposed a computationally cheap method for tracking eyes, nostrils and lip corners. In their paper, they convert grey scale frame into binary image by using intensity computation, then apply graph matching to get most similar regions in the image. The most similar regions are assigned as eyes. From the eye positions, they estimate mouth region and locate lip corners by searching most left and right columns. Finally, they determine nostrils by using eye and lip corner positions. However, in this approach, they convert whole image to binary image for graph matching and it is very critical to estimate similarity of eyes when the background is complex. Furthermore, if the lighting is not uniform around the face, there are important feature losses by this approach.

In this paper, facial feature tracking is proposed by using intensity based adaptive clustering and binary image processing. Intensity based techniques are computationally cheaper and therefore more attractive in real-time applications. Each facial feature is investigated in separate search windows. This compensates non-uniform lighting conditions on face. For each facial feature, the optimum search window is adapted dynamically in consecutive frames. After intensity based adaptive clustering for each search window, a set of connected components are obtained to determine the feature positions at that frame. Success rate of the feature tracking approach ranges from 82% to 99% for one pixel range and from 99% to 100% for 3 pixel ranges.

## 2 Face Tracking

Face tracking proposed in this paper is comprised of three main steps: search region estimation, stochastic skin color modeling and locating face region.

## 2.1 Search Region Estimation

Once the face region in the first frame is determined, one can determine the face boundary box by estimating its corner coordinates. This can be done from the knowledge of the major axis (*majax*), minor axis (*minax*) and the center ($Xc, Yc$) of the elliptic face model which can easily be calculated from the detected face region. The corner coordinates of the face region are then given by (see Fig. 1(a)).

$$(X1,Y1) = (Xc - \frac{majax}{2}, Yc - \frac{minax}{2}) \quad (X2,Y2) = (Xc - \frac{majax}{2}, Yc + \frac{minax}{2}) \quad (1)$$

$$(X3,Y3) = (Xc + \frac{majax}{2}, Yc - \frac{minax}{2}) \quad (X4,Y4) = (Xc + \frac{majax}{2}, Yc + \frac{minax}{2}) \quad (2)$$

Search region, for the next frame, is estimated by using the positions of the last frame and *minax*, depicted in Fig. 1(b). The corner coordinates of the new search region are defined by

$$(X5,Y5) = (X1 - \frac{minax}{2}, Y1 - \frac{minax}{2}); \quad (X6,Y6) = (X2 - \frac{minax}{2}, Y2 + \frac{minax}{2}); \quad (3)$$

$$(X7,Y7) = (X3 + \frac{minax}{2}, Y3 - \frac{minax}{2}); \quad (X8,Y8) = (X4 + \frac{minax}{2}, Y4 + \frac{minax}{2}); \quad (4)$$

The reason why the minor axis is used in (3) and (4) is, it is reliable. Note that major axis can vary in open throat or close throat cases of clothes, since we apply skin color modeling.

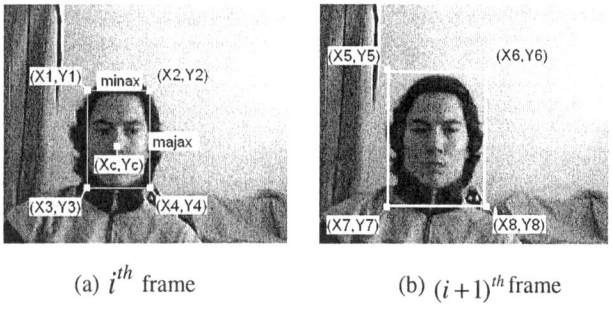

(a) $i^{th}$ frame  (b) $(i+1)^{th}$ frame

**Fig. 1.** Search region estimation for two consecutive frames

## 2.2 Stochastic Skin Color Modeling

The skin-color model is generated by supervised training of skin-color regions and the skin-color illumination brightness is reduced through normalization in Eq. (5).

$$r = R/(R - G - B)$$
$$g = G/(R + G + B) \quad (5)$$

The colors $(r,g)$ are known as chromatic colors. According to [6] the skin-color distribution in chromatic color space can be approximated by the Gaussian $N(m,\Sigma^2)$, where $m=\overline{(r,g)}$ is mean vector and $\Sigma$ is covariance matrix as shown below.

$$\bar{r} = \frac{1}{N}\sum_{i=1}^{N} r_i \qquad \bar{g} = \frac{1}{N}\sum_{i=1}^{N} g_i \qquad \Sigma = \begin{bmatrix} \sigma_{rr} & \sigma_{rg} \\ \sigma_{gr} & \sigma_{gg} \end{bmatrix} \tag{6}$$

With this Gaussian model, one can obtain the likelihood of skin color for any pixel $x = (r,g)$ of an image with Eq. (7):

$$P(r,g) = \exp(-0.5(x-m)^T \Sigma^{-1}(x-m)) \tag{7}$$

With an appropriate threshold, the image can then be further transformed to a binary image showing skin regions and non-skin regions as shown in Fig. 2.

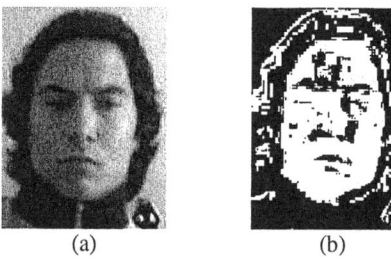

(a)  (b)

**Fig. 2.** Stochastic skin color modeling to search region

## 2.3 Locating Face Region

After the skin color modeling of the search region, we get a set of connected components in binary form. We apply median filtering and erosion morphological operation for smoothing and then fill the holes inside of face candidate regions. This is practically depicted in Fig. 3(a). Finally, the region which includes the previous center position $(Xc, Yc)$ of the face is chosen to be the new face region. This is shown in Fig. 3(b) by placing a boundary box around the region declared as the new face.

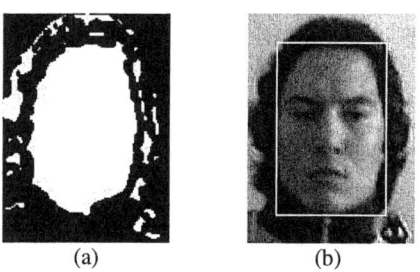

(a)  (b)

**Fig. 3.** Locating the face region

Some of the face tracking frames is shown in Fig. 4, with different scales and orientation.

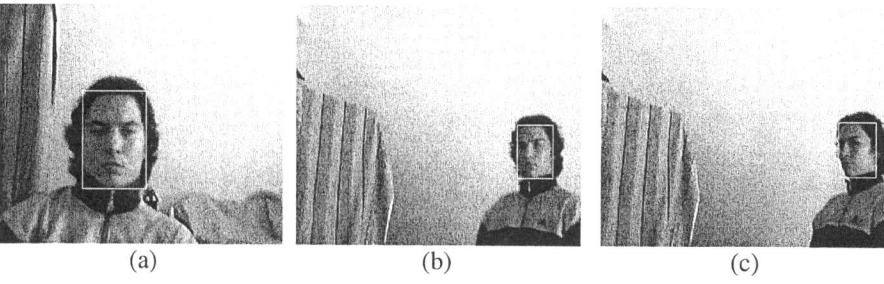

(a)  (b)  (c)

**Fig. 4.** Face tracking

The success rate of the proposed face tracking method is on the average 93%. The algorithm only fails for rapidly changing illumination or when skin colored object at the background coincides with face.

## 3 Facial Feature Tracking

Left eye pupil, right eye pupil, nostrils, left lip corner and right lip corner are the facial features that are tracked. This is achieved by using a separate search region for each of them. This compensates non-uniform lighting conditions. Once we know the facial feature positions, the Euclidean Distance (*ED*) between left eye pupil and right eye pupil is taken as a reference to determine search regions for pupils and lip corners in the next frame as shown in Fig. 5.

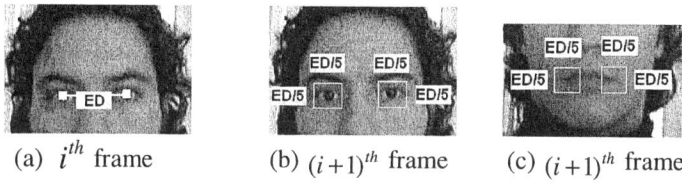

(a) $i^{th}$ frame    (b) $(i+1)^{th}$ frame    (c) $(i+1)^{th}$ frame

**Fig. 5.** Eye pupils, lip corners and nostrils search windows estimation

The Euclidean Distance between left and right eye pupil in the $i^{th}$ frame is defined by

$$ED_i = \sqrt{(xre_i - xle_i)^2 + (yre_i - yle_i)^2} \tag{8}$$

Where $(xle_i, yle_i)$ is left eye position and $(xre_i, yre_i)$ is right eye position in the $i^{th}$ frame. After determining the location of eye pupils and lip corners in the $(i+1)^{th}$ frame, this information together with $ED_i$ is used to determine the search region for nostril extraction as shown in Fig. 6.

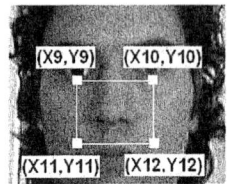

**Fig. 6.** Search window estimation for nostrils

The respective equations determining the coordinates of this region are given by

$$(X9, Y9) = (\frac{(xle_{i+1} - xre_{i+1})}{2} + \frac{ED_i}{4}, yle_{i+1}) \quad (X10, Y10) = (\frac{(xle_{i+1} - xre_{i+1})}{2} + \frac{ED_i}{4}, yre_{i+1}) \quad (9)$$

$$(X11, Y11) = (\frac{(xll_{i+1} - xrl_{i+1})}{2} - \frac{ED_i}{5}, yle_{i+1}) \quad (X12, Y12) = (\frac{(xll_{i+1} - xrl_{i+1})}{2} - \frac{ED_i}{5}, yre_{i+1}) \quad (10)$$

where, $(xle_{i+1}, yle_{i+1})$ is location of left eye pupil, $(xre_{i+1}, yre_{i+1})$ is location of right eye pupil, $(xll_{i+1}, yll_{i+1})$ is location of left lip corner, and $(xrl_{i+1}, yrl_{i+1})$ is location of right lip corner in the $(i+1)^{th}$ frame.

These processes continue dynamically. After the search region estimation, intensity based adaptive clustering on each grey scaled region and then binary image processing is applied to determine the positions of features. Intensity based adaptive clustering method is a thresholding process. The mean intensity value of the region forms the first threshold. The mean of lower values of first threshold is the second threshold. After three or more iteration we get the darkest region in the grey scaled image. The clustered image is a binary image which includes darkest regions as white connected components. Because of this adaptive process, lighting is not a problem.

### 3.1 Eye Tracking

The search window of left and right eye does not include any dark region other then pupil. After the intensity based adaptive clustering, pupil candidate regions appear. Then the possible holes inside the candidate regions are filled (see Fig. 7(b)). Finally the biggest candidate region is assigned as pupil and the center of that region is marked (see Fig. 7(c)).

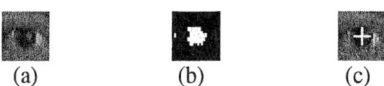

(a)　　　　　(b)　　　　　(c)

**Fig. 7.** Eye pupil detection

There are also other situations where the eyebrow falls inside the eye search region when a person smiles or annoyed. To compensate this effect, the algorithm ignores regions touching the upper border of the search window.

## 3.2 Lip Corners Tracking

To find left lip corner, intensity based adaptive clustering is performed since left lip corner is the darkest region in its search window, including smiling situations. After we get binary form, the leftmost pixel of the biggest connected component is chosen. The procedure is shown in Fig. 8. Similar procedure is applied for locating the right lip corner.

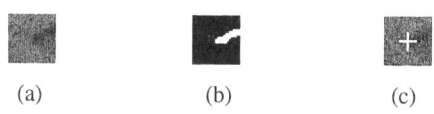

(a)            (b)            (c)

**Fig. 8.** Left lip corner detection

## 3.3 Nostril Tracking

In order to find the nostrils, intensity based adaptive clustering offers us a set of connected components, where the biggest two regions are assigned to be nostrils as depicted in Fig. 9.

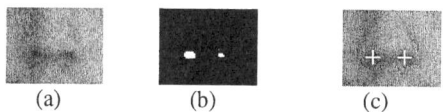

(a)            (b)            (c)

**Fig. 9.** Nostril detection

Some of the facial features tracking frames are shown in Fig. 10.

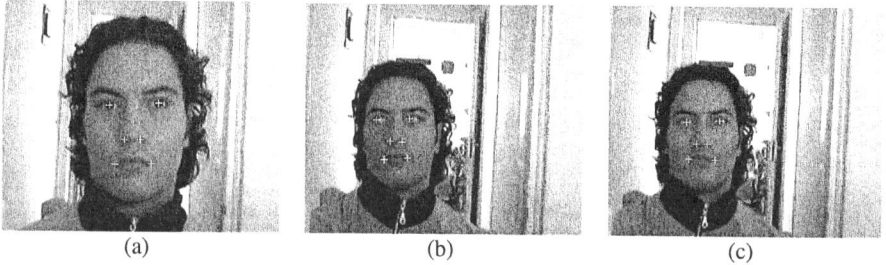

(a)                  (b)                  (c)

**Fig. 10.** Facial feature tracking

## 4 Results and Discussions

The proposed techniques for face and facial feature tracking were tested on a typical head and shoulder video sequence taken with a webcam in a non-uniformly illuminated environment. Each frame is of size 288x352 pixels. The subject in this test sequence makes translational and rotational movements; approaches and recedes from the camera; tilts his head up and down and is allowed to express facial emotion. The performance of face tracking method is 93%. The algorithm only fails for rapidly changing illumination or when skin colored object at the background coincides with face. Table 1 shows facial feature tracking simulation results which are average of two different subjects at different environments. The results in Table 1 are based on 1, 2 and 3 pixel range accuracy. The performance is obtained by comparing the simulated results to the manually extracted feature locations for all frames. Of course from this perspective the 1 pixel range is not reliable due to the human error involved in the extraction process. It should be noted that the performance tends to be almost perfect at an average tracking rate of 99% for the 3 pixel range. The various differences in the performance for 1 pixel range can be attributed mainly to the non-uniform illumination and partly to the dynamic nature of facial expressions.

**Table 1.** Facial Feature Tracking Rate Performance (%)

| Facial Features | 1 pixel range | 2 pixel range | 3 pixel range |
| --- | --- | --- | --- |
| Left eye | 92.68 | 100 | 100 |
| Right eye | 98.78 | 100 | 100 |
| Left nostril | 98.78 | 98.78 | 98.78 |
| Right nostril | 92.68 | 98.78 | 98.78 |
| Left lip corner | 81.71 | 100 | 100 |
| Right lip corner | 85.37 | 96.34 | 98.78 |

## 5 Conclusions

The present paper described intelligent combination of efficient techniques for face and facial feature tracking with the motivation for real time applications. The methods employed were computationally efficient. The proposed region estimation technique backed by facial expression aware approaches resulted in an almost perfect facial feature tracking performance where in the 3 pixel range accuracy, an average of 99% tracking rate was obtained. The performance of the face tracking technique was 93%.

## References

1. Paul Viola, Michael Jones: Rapid Object Detection Using a Boosted Cascade of Simple Features, IEEE Computer Society Conference on Computer Vision and Pattern Recognition (CVPR), ISSN: 1063-6919, vol. 1, pp. 511-518, December 2001.
2. Prem Kuchi, Prasad Gabbur, P. Subbana Bhat and Sumam David: Human Face Detection and Tracking Using Skin Color Modeling and Connected Component Operators, IETE Journal of Research, Special issue on Visual Media Processing, May 2002.
3. C. Direkoglu, H. Demirel, H. Ozkaramanli, M. Uyguroglu and A. M. Kondoz: Scale and Translation Invariant Face Detection and Efficient Facial Feature Extraction, in Proc. IASTED Int. Conf. On Signal and Image Processing (SIP'2004) ), Honollulu, Hawaii, USA August 23-25, 2004, pp. 122-128.

4. Karin Sobottka and Ioannis Pitas,: A Fully Automatic Approach to Facial Feature Detection and Tracking, International Conference on Audio- and Video-based Biometric Person Authentication (AVBPA-1997), Crans-Montana, Switzerland, 12-14 March 1997.
5. Jong-Gook Ko, Kyung-Nam Kim and R.S. Ramakrishna: Facial Feature Tracking for Eye-Head Controlled Human Computer Interface, IEEE, TENCON'99, Cheju, Korea, Sept. 1999.
6. J. Yang, W. Lu, and A. Waibel: Skin-color modeling and adaptation, Proceedings of ACCV'98, vol. II, pp. 687-694, Hong Kong, January 1998.

# A Step Towards Practical Steganography Systems

Abdelkader H. Ouda and Mahmoud R. El-Sakka, Senior Member, IEEE

Computer Science Department, University of Western Ontario, London, Ontario, Canada
{kader, elsakka}@csd.uwo.ca

**Abstract.** There has been many hidden communication techniques proposed in the last few years. The focus was given to steganography to build such techniques. Utilizing stego-key(s) to hide secret messages into images strengthen the security of these techniques. However, adopting one of the available key-agreement protocols, to distribute stego-key(s) between the communicating parties, will destroy the infrastructure of the entire communication. The reason is that, these protocols perform their transactions on sight, while the desirable communications need to be completely hidden. In this paper, a *key-generation unit* is proposed to be added to the steganography general model. This unit utilizes a new key-agreement protocol, *stego-KA*, to help support the entire class of hidden communication techniques to exchange the sego-key(s) covertly. The proposed stego-KA protocol is based on *Diffie-Hellman* key establishment protocol and has significant advantages that support hidden communications.

## 1 Introduction

It has been said throughout time that, "a picture is worth a thousand words." However, in this digital era, it could be said that, "a picture is worth a thousand *secrets*." It should come as no surprise that a picture (digital image) might be distributed while it contains a *secret message* that is hidden to the human eye. This message can be extracted only by a sophisticated image utility, using a *secret key*. These types of applications are known as *hidden communication* techniques, which utilizing a technology known by *steganography*.

One of the most realistic schemes for steganography applications goes back to Simmons in 1984 [1]. Simmons introduced his hidden communication model using the prisoner's problem, which became the most widely used scenario characterizing these models.

The *prisoner's problem* states that, there are two criminals confined in separated cells. The warden gives them the opportunity to communicate with each other through a message-exchanging channel, which is monitored by the warden. The only restriction on this channel is that it is open to the warden, and if any message is encrypted, the warden should have access to the decryption key. The main reason for this communication is that the warden will mislead the prisoners by sending them false messages in order to trick the criminals into thinking they were sent by the other party. The prisoners, on the other hand, plan to use this channel in order to arrange an escape. To do this, the prisoners will have to deceive the warden by finding a way of communicating secretly between them in full view of the warden. This means that even if a message contains secret information it would look innocuous to the warden. Since the prisoners anticipate that the warden will try to deceive them by introducing fraudulent messages, they should prepare an authentication model along with their hidden communication.

While Simmons utilized cryptography in his scheme, the vast majority of the information hiding schemes in literature [2-11] utilize steganography to solve the prisoners' problem. The main purpose of these schemes is that a secret message can be transmitted invisibly within another innocent medium, such as images. This transmission should occur so that only the sender and the receiver have the ability to insert, detect and extract the hidden message.

The rest of this paper is organized as follows. Section 2 demonstrates the general framework of the steganography model. The analysis of the related steganographic techniques is given in Section 3. Section 4 states the main problem. The proposed solution is described in detail in Section 5. The conclusion is offered in Section 6.

## 2 Framework of Steganography Model

In general, the basic framework of the image steganography model is illustrated in Fig. 1. This model consists of two main processes, namely the *embedding process* and the *extracting process*. The main function of the embedding process is to hide the secret message, called *embedded message*, in a given image, called *cover-image*. In hidden communication techniques, the cover-image is no more than an innocent (unrelated to the embedded message) piece of information that is used to hide the secret information. A secret key, called *stego-key*, is used in the embedding process such that it makes the embedded message computationally infeasible to extract without possessing this key. The output of the embedding process is called *stego-image*, which is the original image holding the hidden secret message. This output becomes, at the other end, the input of the extracting process, in which the embedded message is

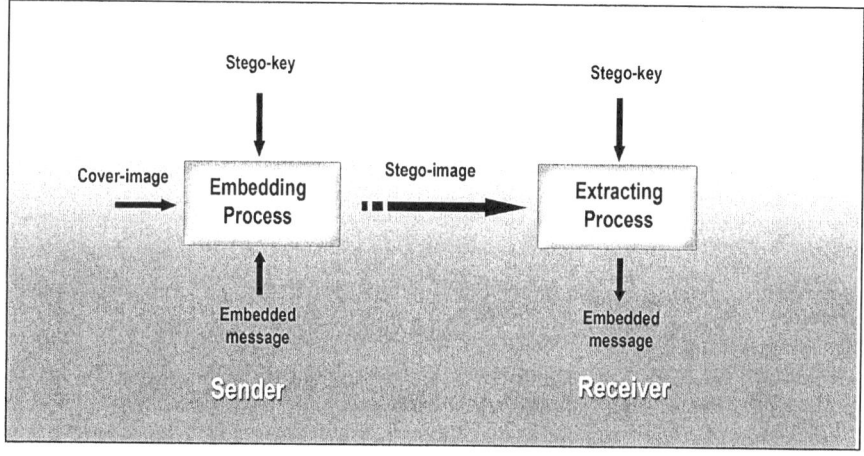

**Fig. 1.** The framework of the watermark generation and embedding process

extracted from the stego-image to complete the hidden communication process. Since the stego-key is used in the embedding process, it needs to be used in the extracting process. Note that, the notation and naming conventions that are used in **Fig. 1** are adopted after the first Information Hiding Workshop [15].

## 3 Analysis and Related Works

In this section we will study steganography techniques based on the usage of the stego-key. The reason for this is to show at what extent the stego-key is important in the entire steganography processes, including embedding, extracting, and verifications. The stego-key can be used in one or more of the following functions:

1. Determine the embedding position (the modified pixels) based on:
   - stego-key bit sequence, or
   - generated pseudo-random sequence seeded by a stego-key,
2. Scramble the embedded message (hidden information) to randomize the hidden information,
3. Scramble the cover image (pixel or block permutation) to :
   - protect the embedded message, and/or to
   - increase the embedding capacity.

### 3.1 Using the Stego-key to Determine the Embedding Positions

Kundar *et al.* [2] propose using the discrete wavelet transform (DWT) [12] to drive a multi-resolution representation of the image data. To hide one bit, the median of three coefficients will be quantized (modified) to match this bit value. These coefficients are selected based on the bit value of a stego-key. To restore the hidden message, the same stego-key is needed to the receiver.

Qi *et al.* [3] use two different stego-keys. In the embedding process, the message will be hidden in specific columns/rows of an image. The selection of these columns/rows is based on the bit sequence of one secret key. A global blur operation is then applied to the entire image in order to make the marked columns/rows unpredictable. The components of the blur kernel are also chosen based upon another secret key. Therefore, this technique has a high security level since it is based on two different secret keys. However, these keys need to be agreed in advance by the both parties.

Other kinds of applications attempt to locate an embedding position in an image using a pseudo-random sequence that is generated either by the stego-key or by any shareable seed between the sender and the receiver. Sharp [4] uses a linear feedback shift register (LFSR) [13] to generate the random sequence. This sequence is used to determine the order in which the pixels from the image are visited to embed the secret information. Therefore, the communicating parties need the same key in order to generate the same sequence.

Licks *at el.* [5] present a technique that utilizes *discrete Fourier transform* (DFT) properties [14] to embed a pseudo-random sequence as a secret message. This sequence is generated in circular form based on a stego-key. The sequence is then embedded into the magnitude part of the DFT coefficients at a specific secret radius. In the other side, this secret information is needed to verify or extract the embedded message.

### 3.2 Scrambling the Embedded Message to Randomize the Hidden Information

Some techniques attempt to protect the embedded message by scrambling the messages bits before being hidden. Liu *et al.* [6] scramble the secret message by adding to it a pseudo-random sequence generated by a shared secret key. The authors utilize the DWT coefficients to hide the message, and use a technique called error correction code and 2-D interleaving [7] to lower the detection error probability.

Marvel *et al.* [8] use a similar idea to protect the embedded message. The spread spectrum communication, error correction coding, and image processing are combined to present their technique. The embedded message is first encrypted using a secret key. Another key is used to generate a pseudo-random sequence. Then both, results are modulated using a third secret key to embed the output into the cover image. These methods are also suffering from the key-distribution problem.

### 3.3 Scrambling the Cover Image

Another way to protect the embedded message is to randomize, or permute, the cover image using the stego-key before the embedding process. Pan *et al.*, [9] propose to divide the image into subblocks. These blocks are ranked based on a specific pattern matching method so that the higher ranked block is the most suitable for data embedding. The chosen block is then permuted using a secret key before the embedding process.

Tseng *et al.* [10] propose a scheme that is able to conceal critical messages into binary images. The image is divided into small blocks; each block is scrambled by a bitwise exclusive-OR with a binary matrix of the same size. This matrix is played as a secret key. The output is then weighted by another secret integer matrix to determine which pixels need to be swapped to embed the secret message. At the end, the image pixels are modified so that the receiver can extract the message by applying reverse operation using the same secret keys.

Some other applications attempt to increase the number of the transform coefficients that may be used to hide the embedded message bits. This can be done by decorrelating the cover image samples that can result in uncorrelated and identical distributed samples over the entire image. Alturki *et al.*, in [11], use this approach to embed more data into the DCT domain of an image. The stego-key is used to decorrelate the given image. The key is used to shuffle the image pixels so that the resulting image looks like white noise to the viewer.

All these methods require that the sender and the receiver to agree upon the shared stego-key in advance.

## 4 The Major Problem

We can conclude from the above analysis that, the common requirements to achieve hidden communication are simply: 1) the cover image and the hidden messages should be unrelated, 2) the hidden message should not provide any evidence of its existence, and 3) the hidden message should not be accessible to anyone but the sender and the receiver, who possess the stego-key. We have also shown that, there are many hidden communication techniques that fulfill these requirements. However, the distribution mechanism of the stego-keys has received less attention in most of these techniques. Definitely, stego-key is an essential piece in either the embedding or the extraction process in steganographic systems available today. As a result of this, any steganographic system needs an authenticated protocol that gives the two parties (the sender and the receiver) the ability to communicate and end up with a shared secret key.

At first glance, it appears that utilizing any secure key-agreement protocol might solve this problem (the key distribution problem). As the matter of fact, an authenticated key-agreement protocol is needed, however, one should indeed note that, these protocols always have some public transactions. This of course will flaw the infrastructure of the hidden communication. It is also worse noting that, a secure solution of this problem is, in fact, a solution for the entire class of the hidden communication techniques. In this paper, a new approach that covertly enables two parties to establish a session secret key (stego-key) is proposed. More details are given in the following Section.

## 5 The Proposed Key Generation Unit

In this paper, we propose to modify the general model of the steganography, see Fig. 2, by adding a new unit called *"key generation unit"*, [16]. The main purpose of this unit is to produce a shared secret key to the communicating parties (the sender and the receiver), so that the protocol transactions are performed undercover. This unit utilizes a new hidden key agreement protocol (*stego-KA*). This protocol is based on *Diffie-Hellman* key establishment protocol [17]. It operates on the group of points of an elliptic curve over a finite field [18]. Our protocol closely follows the approach of [19], and has significant advantages that support the hidden communications.

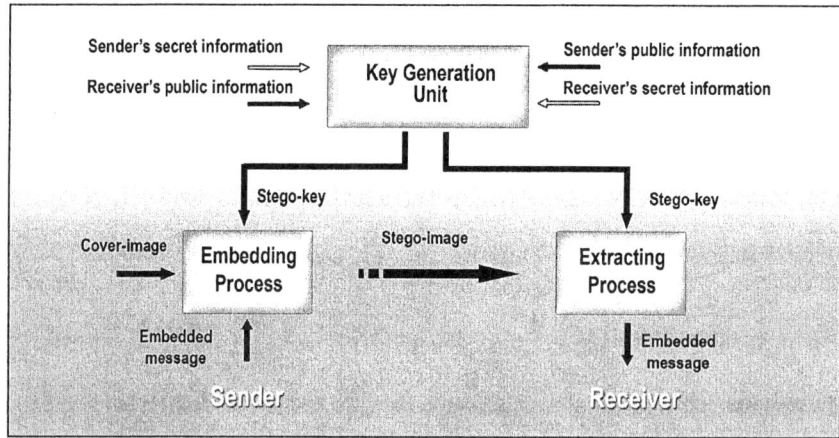

**Fig. 2.** The modified general steganography model

## 5.1 Basic Notations

Before discussing the protocol in more details, we first define some notation.

$E$ — A non-singular elliptic curve over a finite field $GF(q)$ that defines a set of points $(x, y)$, which satisfy an elliptic curve equation $y^2 = x^3 + ax + b$, where $q = p^m$ and $p$ is a large prime, $a, b \in GF(q)$

$P$ — A point $(x_p, y_p)$ of order $n$ that satisfies the elliptic curve $E$

$X(.)$ — The x-coordinate of any point on the elliptic curve $E$

$d_A, d_B$ — Long-term private keys for party A and B respectively, selected randomly from the interval $[1, n-1]$

$Q_A, Q_B$ — Long-term public keys for party $A$ and $B$ respectively, where $Q_A = d_A P$ and $Q_B = d_B P$. Note that, due to the hardness of the elliptic curve discrete logarithm problem [22], it is computationally invisible to get $d_A$ from $P$ and $Q_A$

$r_A, r_B$ — Session private keys for party $A$ and $B$ respectively, selected randomly from the interval $[1, n-1]$ at each protocol run

$R_A, R_B$ — Session public keys for party $A$ and $B$ respectively, where $R_A = r_A P$ and $R_B = r_B P$

$H(.)$ — The secure hash algorithm SHA-1 [20]. SHA-1 takes a message of an arbitrary length and produces a 160-bit output called a message digest

$I$ — Any random stego-image

$Hide_k(m, I)$ — Hiding function to conceal the data $m$ into the image $I$ using the key $k$. Note that, any of the hidden communication techniques described in Section 3 might be used.

$rh(I), lh(I)$ — The right half side and left half side of the image $I$ respectively

## 5.2 Security Attributes Requirements

Any secure key-agreement protocol should fulfill some security attributes [21]. Consequently, the hidden key agreement protocol needs to satisfy these attributes as well to be a reliable protocol. These attributes include:

***Known session keys***, the security of new session keys will not be affected if some previous session keys were disclosed.

***Forward secrecy***, the security of previous session keys will not be affected if a long-term secret key of one or more parties is compromised.

***Unknown key-share***, party $A$ cannot be forced into sharing a key with party $B$ without $A$'s knowledge, i.e., when $A$ believes the key is shared with some party $C \neq B$, and $B$ believes the key is shared with $A$. This attribute is also called man-in-the-middle.

***Key-compromise impersonation***, if $A$'s secret key is disclosed, any one who knows this key can impersonate $A$. Hence, this loss of information should not allow the adversary to impersonate other parties to $A$.

In Section 5.4 we will show how the proposed protocol satisfies these attributes.

### 5.3 The Hidden Key-Agreement Protocol, *Stego*-KA

The detail transactions of stego-KA protocol are described as follows:

1. A selects a session secret key $r_A$ and then computes a session public key $R_A$.
2. A computes the initial session key $K_0 = d_A Q_B = d_A d_B P$, $K_0$ is a point on the elliptic curve $E$.
3. A choses a random digital image $I_1$, and then hides the value $R_A$ into the $I_1$ using initial session key $K_0$. I.e., computes the function $Hide_{k_0}(R_A, I_1)$. Note that, this function might be the same as that will be used to hide the secret message in the original technique, see Section 3. Therefore the security strength of this function will be equivalent to the security of the entire technique.
4. Image $I_1$ is published somewhere in an open network such as Internet.
5. B obtains the image $I_1$ then performs the following:
   - Computes the initial session key $K_0 = d_B Q_A = d_A d_B P$
   - Uses $K_0$ to extract $R_A$ from the image $I_1$. Note that, the embedding and extracting processes are public methods, however $K_0$ is accessible only to A and B.
   - Selects a session secret key $r_B$ and then computes a session public key $R_B$
   - Generates the target session key $K = X(Q_A r_B + R_A d_B)$
   - Computes the value $Z_1 = H(lh(I_2)) \| X(R_A) \| X(R_B)$, where $\|$ be a bit-stream concatenation
   - Select a random image $I_2$, and apply the function $Hide_K (R_B \| H(Z_1), I_2)$
   - Publishes the image $I_2$ somewhere in an open network such as Internet
6. A obtains the image $I_2$ then performs the following:
   - Generates the target session key $K = X(Q_B r_A + R_B d_A)$
   - Uses $K$ to extract $R_B$ and $H(Z_1)$, which is $z$, from the image $I_2$
   - Computes the value $Z^* = H(lh(I_2)) \| X(R_A) \| X(R_B)$
   - Verifies if $H(Z^*) = z$; if the validation failed, the protocol will be ended with a failure
   - Otherwise, computes the value $Z_2 = H(rh(I_2)) \| X(R_B) \| X(R_A)$
   - Apply the function $Hide_K (H(Z_2), I_2)$
7. B extracts $H(Z_2)$, which is $z_2$, from the image $I_2$ using the session key $K$ and verify if $H(H(rh(I_2)) \| X(R_B) \| X(R_A)) = z_2$
8. If the validation failed the protocol will be ended with a failure, otherwise $K$ will be the secret session key between A and B

### 5.4 The Major Features of the Proposed Model

The key-generation unit is able to provide the communicating parties with some assurance that they know each other's true identities. Stego-KA protocol, which utilizes hidden key-confirmation transactions, has helped these parties end up sharing a common stego-key known only to them. This stego-key can then be used thereafter to establish the desirable hidden communications as it is described earlier in Section 3.

In addition to the hidden transactions property, there are other security attributes for the Stego-KA protocol.

*Known session keys*

Based on the security definition of the elliptic curve addition, losing any information about previous stego-key(s), i.e., $K = X\,(Q_A r_B + R_A d_B)$, does not affect the protocol security. I.e., it doesn't help an adversary to be able to discover a stego-key that might be generated by a fresh protocol run, especially when the session keys, i.e., $r_A$ and $r_B$ are refreshed each time the protocol is carried out.

*Forward secrecy*

Stego-KA protocol provides perfect forward secrecy. If for example the long-term secret key of the party $A$ is disclosed, i.e., $d_A$, the protocol security might be affected. However, the past produced stego-key(s) will not. The reason for this is that, the agreed stego-key $K = X\,(Q_B r_A + R_B d_A)$ is chosen also based on the values $r_A$ and $r_B$, which were chosen independently at random by parties $A$ and $B$ respectively. Therefore, the adversary will face the elliptic curve discrete logarithm problem [22] to learn any extra information about the key.

*Unknown key-share*

Stego-KA protocol will not be completed until both parties prove knowledge of the shared stego-key by using it in subsequent communications. The hidden message send from $B$ to $A$ provides key confirmation of $B$ to $A$. The hidden message embedded and send from $A$ gives an assurance to $B$ that $A$ actually possesses the key.

*Key-compromise impersonation*

Generating session keys $r_A$ and $r_B$ at each protocol run kills any hope to an adversary to impersonate any party $C$ to $A$, when $d_A$ is disclosed. Note that, if these session keys are not evolved in the stego-key, the adversary can compute the secret $X\,(Q_C + d_A)$ easily to impersonate $C$ to $A$.

## 6 Conclusion

The main goal of this paper is to make stride towards the practical use of steganography in hidden communications. The paper enhances the general steganography model by enabling the use of a hidden key-agreement protocol "stego-KA" through a new steganography unit called "key-generation unit". Stego-KA protocol is based on the idea that the communicating parties need to contribute their information, through a hidden channel, by which the stego-key will be established.

This paper also provides a new approach to classify key-based steganography techniques, which are grouped based on the usage of secret keys. This new classification facilitates the way by which these hiding techniques could be utilized in the proposed protocol.

## References

1. G. Simmons, "The Prisoners' Problem and the Subliminal Channel," CRYPTO83 - Advances in Cryptology, August 22-24. 1984. pp. 51–67.
2. D. Kundur, D. Hatzinakos, "Digital watermarking using multiresolution wavelet decomposition," In IEEE ICASSP'98, volume 5, pages 2659– 2662, Seattle, May 1998.

3. H. Qi, W. Snyder, W. Sander, "Blind Consistency Based Steganography For Information Hiding In Digital Media," IEEE International Conference on Multimedia and Expo, 2002. ICME '02. Proceedings. 2002, Volume: 1 , Page(s): 585 –588, August. 2002.
4. T. Sharp, "An Implementation of Key-Based Digital Signal Steganography," Information Hiding, LNCS 2137, pp. 13-26
5. V. Licks, R. Hordan, "On digital image watermarking robust to geometric transformations," International Conference on Image Processing, Volume: 3 , Page(s): 690–693, September. 2000.
6. H. Liu, J. Liu, J. Huang, D. Huang, Y. Shi, "A robust DWT-based blind data hiding algorithm," IEEE International Symposium on Circuits and Systems, ISCAS 2002, Volume: 2 , Page(s): II-672 -II-675, May 2002.
7. G. Elmasry, Y. Shi, "2-D Interleaving for Enhancing the Robustness of Watermark Signals Embedded in Still Images," IEEE International Conference on Multimedia and Expo (II) Page(s): 731–734, 2000.
8. M. Marvel, C. Retter, C. Boncelet, "A methodology for data hiding using images, IEEE Proceedings on Military Communications Conference, MILCOM 98, Volume: 3 , Page(s): 1044–1047, October 1998.
9. G. Pan, Z. Wu, Y. Pan, "A data hiding method for few-color images," Proceedings IEEE International Conference on Acoustics, Speech, and Signal Processing, (ICASSP '02), Volume: 4, PP 3469–3472, May 2002.
10. Y. Tseng, Y. Chen, H. Pan, "A secure data hiding scheme for binary images," IEEE Transactions on Communications, Volume: 50 Issue: 8, Page(s): 1227 -1231Aug. 2002
11. F. Alturki, R. Mersereau, "A novel approach for increasing security and data embedding capacity in images for data hiding applications," International Conference on Information Technology: Coding and Computing, Page(s): 228 –233, April 2001.
12. R. Rao, A. Bopardikar, "Wavelet Transforms", Addison Wesley Longman Inc., Reading, Massachusetts, 1998.
13. N. Zierler, "Linear Recurring Sequences", Journal of the Society for Industrial and Applied Mathematics, Vol 7, No. 1, pp. 31-48, March 1959.
14. G. Gonzalez, R. Woods, "Digital Image Processing", Addison-Wesly Publication Company. 1992.
15. B. Pfitzmann, "Information Hiding Terminology," Information Hiding: first international workshop, Proceedings LNCS 1147, Berlin: Springer, 1996.
16. A. Ouda, "Digital Watermarking Techniques for Image Security and Hidden Communications", Ph.D. Dissertation, Computer Science Department, University of Western Ontario, Canada, 2004.
17. W. Diffie, M. Hellman. New directions in cryptography. IEEE Transactions on Information Theory, IT-22: 644-654, 1976.
18. A. Menezes, P. Oorchot, and S. Vanstone, Handbook of Applied Cryptography, CRC Press, Florida, USA, 1997.
19. L. Law, A. Menezes, M. Qu and S. Vanstone. "An Efficient Protocol for Authenticated Key Agreement," Technical Report CORR 98-05, Department of C&O, University of Waterloo, 1998.
20. National Institute of Standards and Technology NIST, "Secure hash standard", Federal Information Processing Standards Publication FIPS, 180-1.
21. S. Wilson, D. Johnson and A. Menezes, "Key agreement protocols and their security analysis," proceedings of the sixth IMA international Conference on Cryptography and Coding, LNCS 1355, Springer-Verlag, pp: 30-45, 1997.
22. A. Menezes, "Evaluation of security level of cryptography: The elliptic curve discrete logarithm problem," CRYPTREC Report, December 14 2001.

# New Aspect Ratio Invariant Visual Secret Sharing Schemes Using Square Block-Wise Operation

Ching-Nung Yang and Tse-Shih Chen

Department of Computer Science and Information Engineering,
National Dong Hwa University,
#1, Sec. 2, Da Hsueh Rd., Hualien, Taiwan
Tel: +886-3-8634025, Fax: +886-3-8634010
cnyang@mail.ndhu.edu.tw

**Abstract.** An aspect ratio invariant visual secret sharing (ARIVSS) scheme is a perfectly secure method for sharing secret images, by expanding a secret pixel to $m$ sub pixels in shadow images, with $m$ being the pixel expansion; meantime the aspect ratio of the recovered secret image is fixed. The advantage of ARIVSS is that there is no loss of information when the shape of the secret image is our information; for example, a secret image of a circle is compromised to an ellipse, if $m$ does not have a square value. Two ARIVSS schemes, based on processing one and four pixel blocks, respectively, were previously proposed. In this paper, we have generalized the square block-wise approach, to further reduce pixel expansion.

## 1 Introduction

In a $(k, n)$ VSS scheme [1-7], a secret image is shared within $n$ shadows. Any $k$ ($\leq n$) shadow can be stacked to resolve the secret, but shadows of $k-1$ or less can obtain no information. When breaking a secret pixel into $m$ sub pixels in a shadow image, using VSS operation, these $m$ sub pixels should be placed in a neat rectangular block. Obviously, if the value $m$ is not a square, the block will be rectangular and the aspect ratio of the recovered image will have changed. To avoid distortion, a simple method was suggested in [1]: the authors recommended adding extra sub pixels to retain the value of $m$ as a square. This method is both trivial and easy; however for some $m$, pixel expansion can increase significantly. In previous work on this topic, an "ARIVSS scheme" using a 2×2-pixel square block was proposed to reduce pixel expansion, as well as to provide clarity in the recovered image [2].

Some other papers have also provided invariant aspect ratio features like the ARIVSS scheme [3-4]. There were no pixel expansion for these VSS schemes in [3] and [4]; the schemes in [5-7] need some simple operational logic and meantime, the size of the recovered image is completely the same as the secret image. In this paper, we have generalized the 2×2-sized square block to an $a$×$a$-sized ($a$>2) square block, to further reduce pixel expansion; our aim was to arrange the sub pixels in the shadow image, such that they have almost the same positions, relative to the pixels in the original secret image.

## 2 Preliminaries

The first VSS scheme, proposed by Naor and Shamir, can be described as a $n \times m$ Boolean matrix $S=[s_{(i,j)}]$ where $s_{(i,j)}=1$ (resp. $s_{(i,j)}=0$) denotes that the $j$th sub-pixel in the $i$th shadow is a black (resp. white) pixel [1]. When stacking arbitrary $i_1, i_2, \ldots, i_r$ shadows ($r \leq n$), by "OR"-ed Boolean operation, the "OR"-ed $m$-vector $V$ gives different contrasts where the contrast is proportional to Hamming weight $H(V)$. With the white and black whiteness $h$ and $l$, where $m > h > l \geq 0$, any $m$-vector $V$ with $H(V) \geq m-l$ can be recognized as a black color; whereas, $H(V) \leq m-h$ is regarded as a white color. Finally, we can "see" the black and white secret image without the assistance of hardware. For sharing the black (resp. white) pixels in the secret image, the dealer randomly chooses from black (resp. white) sets $C_1$ (resp. $C_0$) where all the matrices are obtained by permuting columns of basis matrix $B_1$ (resp. $B_0$).

### 2.1 Aspect Ratio of the Recovered Image

When expanding a secret pixel to $m$ sub pixels using VSS operation, the different arrangement of $m$ sub pixels in the shadow image will cause a different aspect ratio of the shadow image. Naturally, we should put these $m$ sub pixels into a neat rectangular block, such that the blocks can be arranged compactly with each other. Fig. 1 show the different arrangements of sub pixels for the pixel expansion $m=6$. In Fig. 1, the arrangement is in the proper order, a rectangular block. Fig. 1 (a) is the original secret image, a circle, and the recovered images in Fig. 1(b)-(e) are ellipses, using 1×6, 6×1, 2×3 and 3×2 rectangular blocks, respectively. However, Fig. 2 shows an improper placement of sub pixels. It is observed that the non-rectangular arrangement cannot be put together compactly and that the VSS scheme is ineffective.

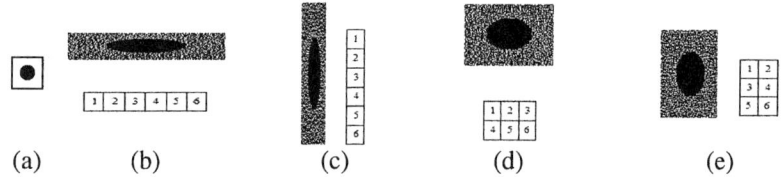

(a)  (b)  (c)  (d)  (e)

**Fig. 1.** Arrangement of six sub pixels in a rectangle block

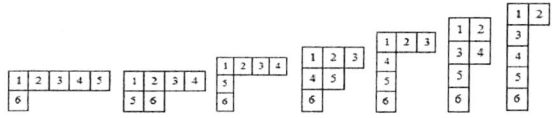

**Fig. 2.** The non-rectangle arrangement

If the value $m$ is not a square, the rectangular block cannot be arranged as a single square block; thus the distortion of the shape of the recovered image is compromised, due to the changed aspect ratio (see Fig. 1).

## 2.2 The Previous ARIVSS Schemes

Let the mapping $f(\cdot)$ be the function which shares a secret pixel $p$ into $m$ sub pixels $p_j^i$, in the $i$th shadow, $1 \leq i \leq n$ and $1 \leq j \leq m$, defined as follows.

$$f(p) = \begin{cases} p_j^i = s_{(i,j)} \text{ in } S \in C_0 \text{ for } p = 0, \\ p_j^i = s_{(i,j)} \text{ in } S \in C_1 \text{ for } p = 1. \end{cases} \quad (1)$$

Let $A_{m_1 m_2}(p_j^i; M)$ be the arranging function which arranges $m$ sub pixels into an $m_1 \times m_2$-sized rectangular block, with the position being located according the pattern $M$, where $m = m_1 \times m_2$. For example, we can use $A_{16}(\cdot)$, $A_{61}(\cdot)$, $A_{23}(\cdot)$ and $A_{32}(\cdot)$ for $m=6$; Figs. 1(b)(c) use the arrangements $A_{16}(\cdot)$ and $A_{32}(\cdot)$, respectively. The operational process of the conventional VSS scheme can be described by using functions $f(\cdot)$ and $A_{m_1 m_2}(\cdot)$, as shown in *Algorithm 1*.

*Algorithm 1: [(k, n) VSS scheme with the pixel expansion m]*
*Input: A secret pixel p in the original secret image I.*
*Output: $m_1 \times m_2$-sized rectangular blocks in n shadow images $S_i$, i=1, ..., n.*
*Step 1: $p_j^i = f(p)$, for $1 \leq j \leq m$, i=1, ..., n.*
*Step 2: Choose the proper $m_1$ and $m_2$ (the aspect ratio approximates the image I) satisfying $m = m_1 \times m_2$.*
*Step 3: Use $A_{m_1 m_2}(p_j^i; M)$, where the position in pattern M is in sequence (Note: like Fig. 1), to create n $m_1 \times m_2$-sized rectangular blocks and deliver n blocks to $S_1$, $S_2$, ..., $S_n$, respectively.*

Two previous ARIVSS schemes ([1], [2]), based on conventional (k, n) VSS schemes, with the pixel expansion $m$, are shown in *Algorithm 2* and *Algorithm 3*, respectively.

*Algorithm 2: [(k, n) ARIVSS scheme with the pixel expansion $(m_a)^2$ ]*
*Input: A secret pixel p in the original secret image I.*
*Output: $m_a \times m_a$-sized square blocks in n shadow images $S_i$, i=1, ..., n.*
*Step 1: $p_j^i = \begin{cases} f(p), \text{ for } 1 < j \leq m \\ *, \text{ for } m < j \leq (m_a)^2 \end{cases}$, i=1, ..., n, where $m_a = \lceil \sqrt{m} \rceil$ ( $\lceil \sqrt{m} \rceil$ is the smallest integer no less than $\sqrt{m}$ ) and the dummy pixel * may be "1" or "0".*
*Step 2: Use $A_{m_a m_a}(p_j^i)$ to create n $m_a \times m_a$-sized square blocks and deliver n blocks to $S_1$, $S_2$, ..., $S_n$, respectively.*

*Algorithm 3: [(k, n) ARIVSS scheme with the pixel expansion $(m_b)^2 / 4$ ]*
*Input: Four secret pixels (2×2-sized square block), $p_{(k,l)}$, where $1 \leq k, l \leq 2$, in the original secret image I.*
*Output: $m_b \times m_b$-sized square blocks in n shadow images $S_i$, i=1, ..., n.*
*Step 1: $p_{(k,l),j}^i = f(p_{(k,l)})$, for $1 < j \leq m$, i=1, ..., n.*

*Step 2:* Use $A_{m_b m_b}(\underbrace{p^i_{(1,1),j}}_{m}, \underbrace{p^i_{(1,2),j}}_{m}, \underbrace{p^i_{(2,1),j}}_{m}, \underbrace{p^i_{(2,2),j}}_{m}, \underbrace{*}_{(m_b)^2-4m}; M)$, where $m_b = \lceil \sqrt{4m} \rceil$, to create $n$ $m_b \times m_b$-sized square blocks. Pattern $M$ may be one of three patterns: a regular pattern, a partially regular pattern or a totally random pattern [2]. Then, $n$ blocks are delivered to $S_1, S_2, \ldots, S_n$, respectively. (Note: these three patterns let the sub pixels $p^i_{(k,l),j}$ in the shadow $S_i$ have almost the same geographic location, position and direction relative to $p_{(k,l)}$ in $I$.)

## 3 The Proposed ARIVSS Schemes

### 3.1 Basic Concept

From *Algorithm 2* and *Algorithm 3*, it is observed that processing an $a \times a$-sized square block of the original secret image, based on the conventional $(k, n)$ VSS scheme and using an $A_{b,b}(\cdot)$ function can construct an ARIVSS scheme, where $b$ is the smallest integer satisfying $b^2 \geq (m \times a^2)$, and the number of extra added dummy sub pixels is $b^2 - (m \times a^2)$. The pixel expansion for this scheme is $(b/a)^2$. In fact, *Algorithm 2* and *Algorithm 3* are special cases for $a=1$ and $a=2$, respectively. To achieve the minimal pixel expansion for the ARIVSS scheme, we need to find the smallest $(b/a)^2$ for $a>2$. From the above description, designing an ARIVSS scheme for $a>2$, delivers the following problems: i) How do we measure the optimization of the mapping pattern? ii) How do we find the optimal mapping pattern?

Let the mapping pattern for the arranging function $A_{b,b}(\cdot)$ for processing an $a \times a$-sized square block be $M_{a,b}=[m_{(i,j)}]$, where $m_{(i,j)}=(k, l)$ or * (dummy pixel), $1 \leq i, j \leq b$ and $1 \leq k, l \leq a$. In this paper, a measurement is defined, an average *position weighting* $\overline{W}$, to estimate the optimization of the pattern $M_{a,b}$. The higher the $\overline{W}$, the less the distortion of the recovered image. Also, two optimal patterns are given: one is the pattern $M^*_{a,b}$ with minimum normal pixel expansion, $\overline{PE}$, and the other is the pattern $M^\Delta_{a,b}$ with the maximum performance factor, $PF$; $\overline{PE}$ and $PF$ are clearly defined in Section 4.

### 3.2 Encoding Algorithm

By extending the $2 \times 2$-sized square block to an $a \times a$-sized square block in *Algorithm 3*, the encoding algorithm for our ARIVSS scheme is given below.

*Algorithm 4:* [$(k, n)$ ARIVSS scheme with the pixel expansion $(b/a)^2$ ]

  *Input:* $a^2$ pixels ($a \times a$-sized square block), $p_{(k,l)}$, where $1 \leq k, l \leq a$, in the original secret image $I$.
  *Output:* $b \times b$-sized square blocks in $n$ shadow images $S_i$, $i=1, \ldots, n$.

Step 1: $p_{(k,l),j}^i = f(p_{(k,l)})$, for $1 < j \leq m$, $i=1, ..., n$.

Step 2: Use $A_{b,b}(\underbrace{p_{(1,1),j}^i, ..., p_{(a,a),j}^i}_{m}, \underbrace{*}_{b^2 - a^2 \times m}; M_{a,b})$, where $b = \lceil a\sqrt{m} \rceil$, to create n $b \times b$-sized square blocks according the mapping pattern $M_{a,b}$. Then, deliver the n blocks to $S_1, S_2, ..., S_n$, respectively.

The remaining problem in *Algorithm 4* is how to find a good pattern, such that the distortion of the recovered image is as small as possible.

### 3.3 The Mapping Pattern $M_{a,b}$

The pattern $M_{a,b}$ of arranging ($a^2 \times m$) sub pixels and $N_d (= b^2 - a^2 \times m)$ dummy pixels in a $b \times b$-sized square block are discussed in this section. To achieve the same relative position between two square blocks, to avoid distortion, we use the re-sampling method in *image scaling* [8], [9]. The secret image is first divided into $a \times a$-sized square blocks and then $b \times b$-sized square blocks. Fig. 3 is an example for $a=4$, $b=7$, $m=3$ and $N_d = 1$ ($7^2 - 4^2 \times 3$). The dotted line and the solid line represent the sampling by $4 \times 4$-sized and $7 \times 7$-sized square blocks, respectively. The gray area is the secret pixel $p_{(1,1)}$ in the $4 \times 4$-sized square block. The four sub pixels in the $7 \times 7$-sized square block, $m_{(1,1)}, m_{(1,2)}, m_{(2,1)}$ and $m_{(2,2)}$ overlap the secret pixel $p_{(1,1)}$.

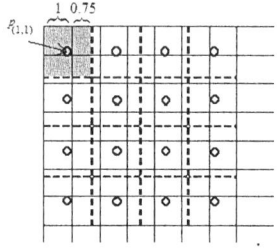

**Fig. 3.** The overlapping between the sub pixel $m_{(i,j)}$ and the pixel $p_{(k,l)}$ in the pattern $M_{4,7}$

It is obvious that choosing the three sub pixels, $m_{(1,1)}, m_{(1,2)}, m_{(2,1)}$, for $p_{(1,1)}$ will result in maximum overlapping. To give the measurement of overlapping, the weighting $W_{(k,l)}^{(i,j)}$ of a sub pixel $m_{(i,j)}$ relative to a secret pixel $p_{(k,l)}$ is defined as the percentage of overlapping between $m_{(i,j)}$ and $p_{(k,l)}$. For example, in Fig.3, the values of weighting are $W_{(1,1)}^{(1,1)} = 1$, $W_{(1,1)}^{(1,2)} = 0.75$, and $W_{(1,1)}^{(2,1)} = 0.75$. Using the weighting $W_{(k,l)}^{(i,j)}$, the weight of a secret pixel $p_{(k,l)}$ for the pattern $M_{a,b} = [m_{(i,j)}]$ is defined in (2).

$$\widehat{W}_{(k,l)} = \sum_{\text{All } i,j \text{ and } m_{(i,j)} = (k,l)} W_{m_{(i,j)}}^{(i,j)}. \quad (2)$$

Our measurement for the optimization of pattern $M_{a,b}$ is then defined as the average position weighting, as follows:

$$\overline{W} = \left(\left(\sum_{k=1}^{a}\sum_{l=1}^{a}\hat{W}_{(k,l)}\right)\bigg/\left(b^2 - N_d\right)\right). \tag{3}$$

The first problem mentioned in Section 3.1 can be solved by using the measurement defined in (3). An algorithm finding a pattern $M_{a,b}$, and the theorem shows the upper bound weighting $\overline{W}_u$ for the pattern $M_{ab}$ are shown below.

*Pattern Algorithm: [Find a pattern $M_{a,b}$ for the arranging function $A_{b,b}(\cdot)$ in the ARIVSS scheme with the average position weight $\overline{W}$ ]*
Input: The values a, b and m.
Output: $M_{a,b}=[m_{(i,j)}]$, where $m_{(i,j)}=(k, l)$ or * (dummy pixel); the average position weight $\overline{W}$.
Step 1: List the sets $R_{(k,l)}=\{m_{(i,j)},$ which overlap $p_{(k,l)}\}$.
Step 2: For k = 1 to a do
    For l = 1 to a do
    {choose at most m non-chosen $m_{(i,j)}$ with large $W_{(k,l)}^{(i,j)}$ from $R_{(k,l)}$ and let $m_{(i,j)}=(k, l)$; Let the weighting of non-chosen $m_{(i,j)}$ increase a value $\delta$, $W_{(k',l')}^{(i,j)} = W_{(k',l')}^{(i,j)} + \delta$, where $p_{(k',l')}$ are the pixels around $p_{(k,l)}$;};
/* the value $\delta$ can be used as a fixed step size or an adaptive step size */
Step 3: Let the non-chosen $m_{(i,j)}=*$;
Step 4: Output $M_{a,b}=[m_{(i,j)}]$ and $\overline{W} = \left(\left(\sum_{k=1}^{a}\sum_{l=1}^{a}\hat{W}_{(k,l)}\right)\bigg/\left(b^2 - N_d\right)\right).$

*Theorem 1*: The upper bound of the average position weighting for the pattern $M_{ab}$ with the pixel expansion m is $\overline{W}_u = \left(\lfloor b/a \rfloor^2 + (b/a - \lfloor b/a \rfloor) \times (m - \lfloor b/a \rfloor^2)\right) \times \left(a^2/(b^2 - N_d)\right)$. The proof can be found in the full version.

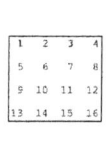 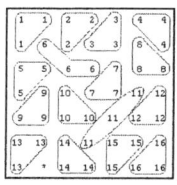 

(a)      (b) The mapping pattern $M_{4,7}$      (c) The recovered image

**Fig. 4.** The mapping pattern $M_{4,7}$ for m=3, a=4 and b=7

Consider Fig.3 (m=3, a=4 and b=7). Using *pattern Algorithm* with a fixed step size $\delta$=0.1459, the average position weighting $\overline{W}$ =0.697917. There is only one extra dummy pixel required in the mapping map $M_{4,7}$ (see Fig. 4(b)), where Fig. 4(a) is the decimal representation for (k, l) position in a 4×4-sized square block. For a (2, 3) VSS scheme with $m=3$, $B_0 = \begin{bmatrix} 110 \\ 101 \\ 011 \end{bmatrix}$ and $B_1 = \begin{bmatrix} 110 \\ 110 \\ 110 \end{bmatrix}$, our ARIVSS scheme has the small pixel expansion $(b/a)^2 = (7/4)^2 = 3.0625$ that approximates $m=3$. When using a dithered 160×160-pixeled LENA image as the secret image, the recovered image (280×280 pixels) is shown in Fig. 4(c).

## 4 Comparisons

Theorem 2 shows that our proposed ARIVSS scheme has less pixel expansion than the ARIVSS schemes in [1] and [2].

*Theorem 2*: The pixel expansions for *Algorithm 2*, *Algorithm 3* and *Algorithm 4*, are $\lceil \sqrt{m} \rceil^2$, $(\lceil 2\sqrt{m} \rceil/2)^2$ and $(\lceil a\sqrt{m} \rceil/a)^2$, respectively, where $a>2$. Then the following holds: (1) There exists at least a value $a(>2)$ such that $(\lceil a\sqrt{m} \rceil/a)^2 \leq (\lceil 2\sqrt{m} \rceil/2)^2 \leq \lceil \sqrt{m} \rceil^2$; (2) $(\lceil a\sqrt{m} \rceil/a)^2 = m$, as $a \to \infty$. The proof can be found in the full version.

**Table 1.** The normalized pixel expansion, performance factor and average position weighting for $m=2$

| a | b | $PE_a$ | $\overline{PE}$ | $\overline{PF}$ | $\overline{W}$ | $\overline{W}_u$ | a | b | $PE_a$ | $\overline{PE}$ | $\overline{PF}$ | $\overline{W}$ | $\overline{W}_u$ |
|---|---|---|---|---|---|---|---|---|---|---|---|---|---|
| 1 | 2 | 4.00 | 2.0000 | 0.500 | 1.0000 | 2.0000 | 11 | 16 | 2.12 | 1.0600 | 0.611 | 0.6472 | 0.7273 |
| 2 | 3 | 2.25 | 1.1250 | 0.667△ | 0.7500 | 0.7500 | 12 | 17 | 2.01 | 1.0050* | 0.602 | 0.6050 | 0.7083 |
| 3 | 5 | 2.78 | 1.3900 | 0.577 | 0.8025 | 0.8333 | 13 | 19 | 2.14 | 1.0700 | 0.610 | 0.6524 | 0.7308 |
| 4 | 6 | 2.25 | 1.1250 | 0.667 | 0.7500 | 0.7500 | 14 | 20 | 2.04 | 1.0200 | 0.611 | 0.6237 | 0.7143 |
| 5 | 8 | 2.56 | 1.2800 | 0.594 | 0.7608 | 0.8000 | 15 | 22 | 2.15 | 1.0750 | 0.609 | 0.6548 | 0.7333 |
| 6 | 9 | 2.25 | 1.1250 | 0.667 | 0.7500 | 0.7500 | 16 | 23 | 2.07 | 1.0350 | 0.606 | 0.6267 | 0.7188 |
| 7 | 10 | 2.04 | 1.0200 | 0.612 | 0.6243 | 0.7143 | 17 | 25 | 2.16 | 1.0800 | 0.609 | 0.6580 | 0.7353 |
| 8 | 12 | 2.25 | 1.1250 | 0.667 | 0.7500 | 0.7500 | 18 | 26 | 2.09 | 1.0450 | 0.608 | 0.6355 | 0.7222 |
| 9 | 13 | 2.09 | 1.0450 | 0.609 | 0.6360 | 0.7222 | 19 | 27 | 2.02 | 1.0100 | 0.602 | 0.6082 | 0.7105 |
| 10 | 15 | 2.25 | 1.1250 | 0.667 | 0.7500 | 0.7500 | 20 | 29 | 2.10 | 1.0500 | 0.607 | 0.6375 | 0.7250 |

Table 1 shows the pixel expansion, $PE_a = (b/a)^2$ of our ARIVSS scheme (*Algorithm 4*) for $m=2$, $1 \leq a \leq 20$; also, the values $\overline{W}$ and $\overline{W}_u$ for pattern $M_{a,b}$ are given. The trivial ARIVSS scheme in [1] (*Algorithm 2*) and the ARIVSS scheme in [2] (*Algorithm 3*) are the special cases for $a=1$ and $a=2$. In Table 1, the normalized pixel expansion is defined as $\overline{PE} = (PE_a/m)$; the performance factor $\overline{PF} = \overline{W}/\overline{PE}$ is the ratio of average position weighting to the normalized pixel expansion, used for measuring the whole performance. Two optimal schemes are defined: the superscript "*" denotes the minimum normalized pixel expansion and the superscript "△" is the scheme with the maximum performance factor. The former scheme has the small shadow size feature, while the latter has the best overall performance. It is observed that finding these two optimum schemes for $a \leq 20$ is enough, because the normalized pixel expansion was almost one and the performance factor approached a value for large $a$. The tables and the mapping patterns $M^*_{a,b}$ and $M^\Delta_{a,b}$ for other $m$ are given in the full version.

## 5 Conclusion

In this paper we introduced a generalization of the ARIVSS scheme in [2]; in such schemes the aspect ratio of a recovered image is invariant. We considered how to map the sub pixels in the shadow image to the secret pixel in the original secret image, so that their relative positions were almost the same; in this way, distortion of the recovered image was avoided.

## References

[1] M. Naor and A. Shamir, "Visual cryptography," *Advances in Cryptology - EUROCRYPT'94*, LNCS, No. 950, pp. 1-12, 1995.
[2] C.N. Yang and Tse-Shih Chen, "Aspect ratio invariant visual secret sharing schemes with minimum pixel expansion," *Pattern Recognition Letters*, Vol. 26, Issue 2, pp. 193-206, Jan., 2005.
[3] C. N. Yang, "New visual secret sharing schemes using probabilistic method," *Pattern Recognition Letters*, Vol. 25, Issue 4, pp. 481-494, Mar.,2004.
[4] R. ITO, H. Kuwakado, and H. Tanaka, "Image size invariant visual cryptography," *IEICE Trans. Fundamentals*, Vol. E82-A, No. 10, pp. 2172-2177, Oct., 1999.
[5] R. Lukac and K. N. Plataniotis, "Bit-Level based secret sharing for image encryption," *Pattern Recognition*, Vol. 38, No. 5, pp. 767-772, May, 2005.
[6] R. Lukac and K.N. Plataniotis, "Image Representation Based Secret Sharing," *Communications of the CCISA (Chinese Cryptology & Information Security Association), Special Issue on Image Secret Sharing and Quantum Cryptography*, Vol. 11, No. 2, pp. 103-114, April, 2005.
[7] R. Lukac and K.N. Plataniotis, "Colour Image Secret Sharing," *IEE Electronics Letters*, Vol. 40, No. 9, pp. 529-530, April, 2004.
[8] C. H. Kim, S. M. Seong, J. A. Lee and L.S. Kim, "Winscale: an image-scaling algorithm using an area pixel model," *IEEE Trans. on Circuits and Systems for Video Technology*, Vol. 13, No. 6, pp.549-553, June, 2003.
[9] R. C. Gonzalez and R. E. Woods, Digital Image Processing, second edition, International Edition, Prentice Hall, 2002.

# Minimizing the Statistical Impact of LSB Steganography

Zoran Duric, Dana Richards, and Younhee Kim

Department of Computer Science, George Mason University, Fairfax, VA 22030
{zduric, richards, ykim9}@cs.gmu.edu

**Abstract.** This paper explores the statistics of least-significant bit (LSB) steganography. The problem of encoding a bit sequence (message) to match the statistics of a random bit-sequence (cover) is considered. A method of hiding information in the least significant bits (LSBs) of JPEG coefficients is described; the method mimics either the chi-square statistic of JPEG coefficients or their distribution. The method uses two-bit codes to encode the message bits. It is shown to be very effective on JPEG images of natural scenes.

## 1 Introduction

The goal of digital steganography is to modify a digital object (cover) to encode and conceal a sequence of bits (message) to facilitate covert communication. The goal of steganalysis is to detect (and possibly prevent) such communication. Often, the cover media correspond to graphics files. Graphics files are the typical choice because of their ubiquitous presence in digital society, but any medium that contains a substantial amount of perceptually insignificant data can be used.

Most steganographic methods operate in two steps. First, a cover object is analyzed and the perceptually insignificant bits are identified. It is assumed that changing these bits will not make observable changes to the cover. Second, the identified bits are replaced by the message bits to create an altered cover object. In this paper, cover object is an image in either bitmap or compressed JPEG [14] formats. The perceptually insignificant bits usually correspond to the LSBs in the image representation: in bitmap images these bits correspond to a subset of the LSBs of the image pixels or the LSBs of the color palette entries, in JPEG images they correspond to a subset of LSBs of the JPEG coefficients. Our work applies to both image representations, but our empirical studies have only used the JPEG coefficients.

In Section 2 we will review related work on steganography and steganalysis. In Section 3 we will summarize a $\chi^2$ statistic-based method of detecting steganographic content. We will also show that this detection method can be easily foiled by not using all the available bits. We demonstrate, however, that the $\chi^2$ statistic can change significantly when even a small fraction of available bits is used. Although we are not aware of any published work that uses this observation, it certainly suggests a means of detecting hidden data. However, matching the statistics of the cover is easily achieved and in Section 4 we will present a method for information hiding that mimics the $\chi^2$ statistics of the cover, while placing a message that is as long as 50% of the available bits.

## 2 Literature Survey

Digital steganography is a relatively new research field [1,10,13]. The term steganalysis was introduced by Johnson and Jajodia [12] who discussed various ways that anomalies introduced by some steganographic techniques could be exploited to detect the presence of steganographic data in images. Detailed survey of early algorithms and software for steganography and steganalysis can be found in [13,11,20].

The first quantitative technique for steganalysis was designed by Westfeld and Pfitzmann [18]. They exploited the fact that many steganographic techniques change the frequencies of pairs of values (pairs of colors, gray levels, or JPEG coefficients) during a message embedding process. Their method was shown to be effective in detecting messages hidden by several steganographic techniques. This research prompted interest in both improving statistical detection techniques [4,5,6,7,21] as well as building new steganographic methods that would be difficult to detect by statistical methods [15,19,16,8].

Various attempts have been made to make steganographic content difficult to detect including reducing their capacity or payload and spreading the message across the whole carrier. Anderson and Petitcolas [1] suggested using the parity of bit groups to encode zeroes and ones; large groups of pixels could be used to encode a single bit, the bits that need to be changed could be chosen in a way that would make detection hard. Provos [15] designed a steganographic method *OutGuess* that spreads a message over a JPEG file; the unused coefficients are adjusted to make the coefficient histogram of the modified file as similar as possible to the histogram of the original image.

Westfeld [19] designed a steganographic algorithm $F5$ that uses matrix coding to minimize the modifications of the LSBs. His method first discovers the number of available bits and then spreads the message bits over the whole file. Fridrich [7,5] recently developed method for successful breaking of this algorithm. The method exploits the fact that modification of the JPEG coefficients by $F5$ produces change of *blockiness* that is strongly correlated with the embedding rate.

Sallee [16] developed a hiding method that preserves distributions of individual JPEG coefficients. On the sender's side the method estimates the distributions of the AC coefficients in JPEG images from the distribution of the most significant bits (MSBs) of the coefficients. The estimated distribution is used by an *entropy decoder* to encode compressed and encrypted messages into the LSBs of the coefficients. On the receiver's side the same distribution is estimated from the MSBs of the coefficients and the message is extracted from the LSBs of the coefficients by an *entropy encoder*. As Böhme and Westfeld [2] observed the fact that the distribution of the JPEG coefficients closely matches the distribution of the MSBs can be used to detect messages hidden by this method.

Fridrich et al. [8] have proposed an information hiding method that implements the concept of $\epsilon$-security proposed by Cachin [3]. The method makes use of the JPEG quantization error by computing all rounding error for the JPEG coefficients. Note that for some coefficients the rounding error is $0.5 \pm \epsilon$. These coefficients can be rounded either down or up without a noticeable difference and they are considered changeable. The algorithm uses a random key to generate a random binary matrix $D$ that is known to both the sender and the receiver. To embed a $q$-bit messages the sender solves a system of $q$ linear equations in GF(2).

## 3 Detecting Steganographic Content

Westfeld and Pfitzmann [18] developed a simple but effective method for detecting LSB steganographic content. The method uses a statistic that is derived from relative frequencies of conjugate pairs. It is described here for LSB steganographic insertion in JPEG image files. It was originally developed to detect messages inserted using the JPEG/JSTEG method [17].

The method begins with a histogram of JPEG coefficients that is created as they are output by the decoder. Let the JPEG coefficients be drawn from the set $A$. Even though $0 \in A$ and $1 \in A$, JPEG/JSTEG embeds messages by modifying LSBs of all coefficients, except for 0 and 1. A *conjugate pair* is the pair of coefficients that have identical binary representations except for their LSBs which are 0 and 1, respectively. For a binary number (bit string) $a$ we denote the corresponding conjugate pair with $a'$ and $a''$, where $a' = 2a$ and $a'' = 2a+1$.

Let $A \setminus \{0,1\} = \{a_1', a_1'', a_2', a_2'', a_3', a_3'', \ldots a_k', a_k''\}$ be organized into $k$ conjugate pairs. (Of course 0 and 1 also form a conjugate pair.) At any step as the decoder processes the coefficients, a histogram bin for $x \in A$ contains the number of coefficients $x$ output so far. In particular, $h_i'$ is the number of occurrences of $a_i'$ and $h_i''$ is the number of occurrences of $a_i''$.

In an unaltered image it could be expected that the frequencies of conjugate pairs significantly differ. In the portion of an image altered by JPEG/JSTEG these frequencies only depend on the relative frequencies of zeroes and ones in the hidden message. Therefore, if the frequencies of zeroes and ones in the message are approximately equal it could be expected that the conjugate pairs have similar frequencies. The $\chi^2$ statistic with $k$ degrees of freedom is given by

$$\chi_k^2 = \frac{1}{2} \sum_{i=0}^{k} \frac{(h_i' - h_i'')^2}{h_i' + h_i''}, \qquad (1)$$

The probability that the image contains steganographic content is estimated by integrating from the density function

$$p = 1 - \frac{1}{2^{\frac{k}{2}} \Gamma(\frac{k}{2})} \int_0^{\chi_k^2} e^{-\frac{x}{2}} x^{\frac{k}{2}} dx \qquad (2)$$

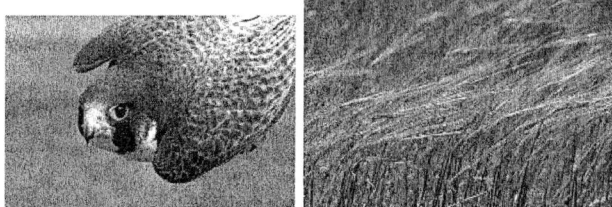

**Fig. 1.** Two natural images: a falcon (left) and a barley field (right). Image sizes are 450 × 292 (falcon) and 480 × 320 (barley).

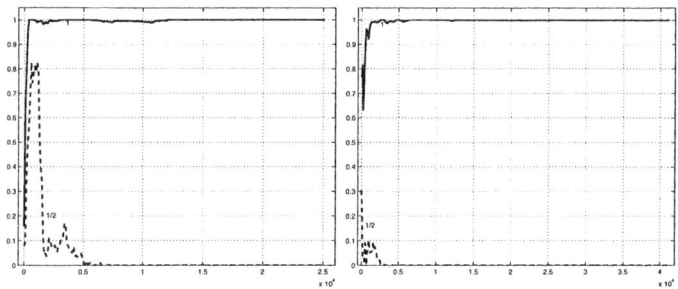

**Fig. 2.** Probabilities of detection of steganographic content for the images in Figure 1. Left: falcon, right: barley field. Graphs show the probabilities computed for full capacity insertion (1:full line) and a half capacity insertion (1/2: dashed line).

This method is illustrated on two images in Figure 1 for two cases. In the first case, a random bit sequence of the same length as the number of redundant bits (number of coefficients different than 0 and 1) was inserted in each of the images. In the second case, only 50% of the coefficients were used for insertion—i.e., every other coefficient was skipped. Probabilities computed using Equation (2) are shown in Figure 2. It can be seen that in the full capacity insertion case the probability was almost always very close to 1. However, in the half capacity case (shown by the dashed line and marked by 1/2) the probability becomes 0 after more than 4000 coefficients are used for the computation. When the density of insertion is 1/4 or less probabilities computed using Equation (2) become 0 everywhere. Based on these and other tests, it can be concluded that the method is quite effective for detecting steganographic content when all of the redundant bits are used. Similar (high detection) results can be obtained for short messages if they are inserted into available bits (coefficients) at the beginning of the image file.

When a shorter message is spread over all available bits this detection method [18] becomes much less effective. However, it is not true that $\chi^2$ statistics are not useful for detection in this situation. If $\chi^2$ statistic is computed using Equation (1) it can be seen that insertion of random bit sequences lowers $\chi^2$ considerably. Figure 3 shows $\chi^2$ curves of the original (unaltered) images in Figure 1, as well as $\chi^2$ curves of the altered images with insertion frequencies 1, 1/2, 1/4, and

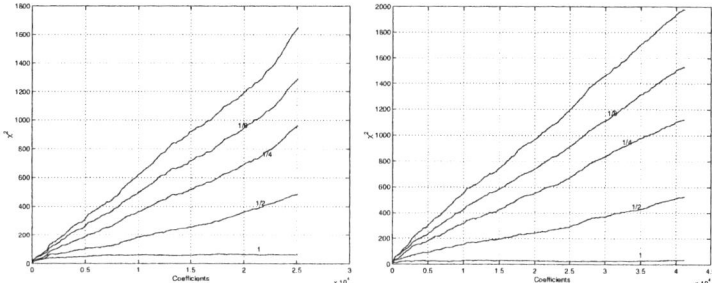

**Fig. 3.** $\chi^2$ statistic computed for the images in Figure 1. Number of skipped bits is varied. The topmost curves correspond to the original (unaltered) images, the curves marked by 1, 1/2, 1/4, and 1/8 correspond to the relative insertion frequencies, e.g. 1/4 corresponds to changing 1 out of every 4 bits. The "falcon" image (left) has 25179 coefficients available for embedding and the numbers of altered coefficients in the four cases are: 12606, 6279, 3118, and 1569. The "barley" image (right) has 41224 coefficients available for embedding and the numbers of altered coefficients in the four cases are: 20544, 10256, 5099, and 2545.

1/8. Note that bit insertion does not change the number of degrees of freedom for $\chi^2$ statistic. Since any bit insertion generally lowers $\chi^2$ statistic, a new method for detecting steganographic content based on a direct use of the statistic could possibly be designed.

In the previous discussion we tacitly assumed that it is not known which bits of the larger cover are being used. If it was known, say,that we used every other redundant bit that could be exploited. However a pseudo-random number generator can be used to determine which bits to use, so that any attempt at "guessing" which bits contain steganographic content could be expected to fail.

## 4 Embeddings That Mimic Image Statistics

Can a better method be given for hiding a message in the redundant bits? In Section 3 it was argued that while hiding a message within a cover nearly the same size was difficult, the published methods were weak when the message was shorter than the cover. However it was also shown that if only a fraction of the cover bits were used then histogram-based statistical tests are still effective.

In this section we explore embedding a message in a longer cover, but using all the cover bits in a way to avoid detection by histogram-based methods. This method begin by encoding/expanding the message $\mathcal{M}$ into a longer sequence of bits that can still be embedded in the available cover bits. The message $\mathcal{M}$ is encoded by a symbol sequence $\mathcal{S} = \langle s_1(m_1), \ldots, s_N(m_N) \rangle$ where $s_i$ encodes $m_i$. For example, since $m_i = 0$ or $m_i = 1$ this coding scheme can be used

$$s_i(0) \in \{00, 11\}, \quad s_i(1) \in \{01, 10\}, \quad i = 1, \ldots, N. \tag{3}$$

**Input:** $\mathcal{M} = \langle m_1, \ldots, m_N \rangle$ (message),
$\mathcal{B} = \langle b_1, b_2, \ldots, b_{2N}, b_{2N+1} \rangle$ (JPEG coefficients)
**Output:** $\mathcal{B}^* = \langle b_1^*, b_2^*, \ldots, b_{2N}^*, b_{2N+1}^* \rangle$ (modified JPEG coefficients)

**for** $i = 1, \ldots, N$
    $\mathcal{B}_i \leftarrow \langle b_1, b_2, \ldots, b_{2i}, b_{2i+1} \rangle$
    **if** $m_i = 0$ **then**
        $b^{11} \leftarrow b_{2i} \odot 0, \quad b^{12} \leftarrow b_{2i+1} \odot 0, \quad b^{21} \leftarrow b_{2i} \odot 1, \quad b^{22} \leftarrow b_{2i+1} \odot 1$
    **else**
        $b^{11} \leftarrow b_{2i} \odot 0, \quad b^{12} \leftarrow b_{2i+1} \odot 1, \quad b^{21} \leftarrow b_{2i} \odot 1, \quad b^{22} \leftarrow b_{2i+1} \odot 0$
    $\mathcal{B}^1 \leftarrow \langle b_1^*, b_2^*, \ldots, b_{2i-2}^*, b_{2i-1}^*, b^{11}, b^{12} \rangle$
    $\mathcal{B}^2 \leftarrow \langle b_1^*, b_2^*, \ldots, b_{2i-2}^*, b_{2i-1}^*, b^{21}, b^{22} \rangle$
    **if** $|\chi^2(\mathcal{B}_i) - \chi^2(\mathcal{B}^1)| < |\chi^2(\mathcal{B}_i) - \chi^2(\mathcal{B}^2)|$ **then**
        $b_{2i}^* \leftarrow b^{11}, \quad b_{2i+1}^* \leftarrow b^{12}$
    **else**
        $b_{2i}^* \leftarrow b^{21}, \quad b_{2i+1}^* \leftarrow b^{22}$
**endfor**

**Fig. 4.** Embedding algorithm. $x \odot i$ replaces the LSB of $x$ by $i$.

The embedding algorithm takes a message $\mathcal{M} = \langle m_1, \ldots, m_N \rangle$ and a sequence of JPEG coefficients $\mathcal{B} = \langle b_1, b_2, \ldots, b_{2N}, b_{2N+1} \rangle$ and it produces sequence $\mathcal{B}^* = \langle b_1^*, b_2^*, \ldots, b_{2N}^*, b_{2N+1}^* \rangle$. The extraction (decoding) algorithm will take the sequence of JPEG coefficients $\mathcal{B}^*$ and extract the message $\mathcal{M}$. (The encoding and decoding algorithms use bits of the message to encode $N$ and other required information.)

An *embedding algorithm* must decide for each message bit which of the allowed symbol sequences should be substituted for it. The greedy algorithm given here hopes to produce an embedding such that the $\chi^2$ statistic of the altered coefficients will be virtually the same as the original coefficients. (The algorithm can be extended to similar statistical tests.)

The greedy embedding algorithm is shown in Figure 4. It encodes each successive bit of the message in the best possible way relative the encodings of the previous message bits; that is, the new bit is encoded in a way that matches the old $\chi^2$ statistic as best as possible. Note that $\chi^2$ updates can be implemented efficiently since each embedding only affects a pair of coefficients and Equation (1) can be rewritten to first subtract the previous contribution of each affected coefficient and then add the new contribution.

The algorithm was implemented and tested using a publicly available JPEG implementation [9]. Examples of embedding messages using this algorithm into images in Figure 1 are illustrated in Figure 5. Since messages would typically be encrypted before being hidden, the experiments used random bit sequences for the messages. It can be seen that the method described here follows the original $\chi^2$ statistic very closely. The method inserts messages whose length is up to half of the available (redundant) bits. It modifies about 1/3 of all redundant bits. In the examples from Figure 5, the number of modified bits was 8361 out of 25179 for the "falcon" image and 13699 out of 41224 for the "barley" image.

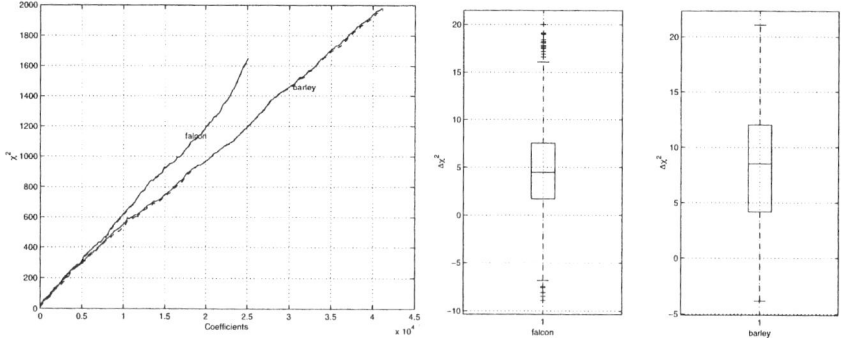

**Fig. 5.** Left: $\chi^2$ statistic for images in Figure 1 before (solid blue lines) and after embedding (dashed red lines) random bit sequences by the algorithm in Figure 4. Middle and right: boxplots of the differences between the $\chi^2$ statistics of the original and altered images for 'falcon' and 'barley'.

This can be compared to a full capacity embedding that changes roughly 1/2 of all redundant bits, and 1/2 capacity embedding that changes roughly 1/4 of all redundant bits. Both of those approaches result in $\chi^2$ statistic that is significantly different from the statistic of unaltered images.

**Fig. 6.** Examples of natural images used in our experiments

Additional experiments were performed for images in Figure 6. As can be seen in most cases the performance was similar to the results shown in Figure 5. In a few cases ("palace", "Edinburgh", "Parthenon") there is a number of points marked as outliers where the $\chi^2$ of altered images differs significantly from the $\chi^2$ of the original images; this is mostly due to the fact that a portion of each image corresponds to a uniform bright sky region. The performance was not as good on the image of the eye shown in the lower right corner of Figure 6. Our method reduced the $\chi^2$ statistic by about 20%. Since this was an anomaly we examined the histogram of the JPEG coefficients and discovered that for many conjugate pairs only one of the histogram frequencies was non-zero. Therefore, many of the insertions into those coefficients decreased the $\chi^2$ statistic for the image.

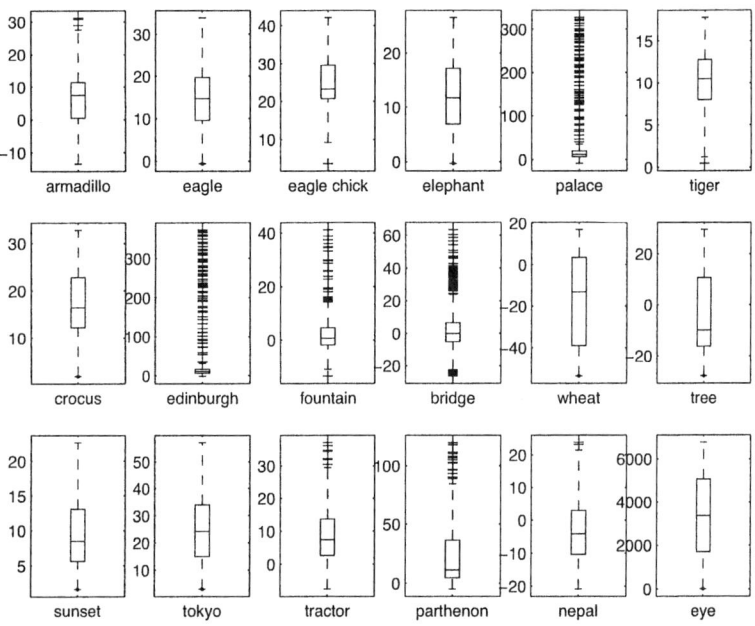

**Fig. 7.** Boxplots of the differences between the $\chi^2$ statistics of the original and altered images shown in Figure 6

## 5  Conclusions

In this paper we explored the statistics of least-significant bit steganography. We considered the problem of encoding a message to match the statistics of a cover. A method of hiding information in the LSBs of JPEG coefficients was described; the method mimics the chi-square statistic of JPEG coefficients. This is accomplished by using multiple codes for each of the output symbols. In addition, we showed how multiple codes can be used to guarantee that images with messages embedded in them have the same coefficient histograms as the original (unmodified) images. We demonstrated the effectiveness of the method on JPEG images of natural scenes. Future work will include finding more effective statistics for detecting hidden steganographic content in JPEG and other image formats as well as designing hiding techniques that mimic higher order statistics of images. In forthcoming work we will report on how these techniques can be used in conjunction with methods in the literature.

# References

1. R.J. Anderson and F. Petitcolas. "On the limits of steganography." *IEEE Journal on Selected Areas in Communications*, 16:474–481, 1998.
2. R. Böhme and A. Westfeld. "Exploiting preserved statistics for steganalysis." LNCS 3200, Springer-Verlag, Berlin Heidelberg, pp. 82–96, 2004.
3. C. Cachin. "An information-theoretic model for steganography." LNCS 1525, Springer-Verlag, Berlin Heidelberg, pp. 306–318, 1998.
4. S. Lyu and H. Farid. "Detecting hidden messages using higher-order statistics and support vector machines", LNCS 2578, Springer-Verlag, Berlin Heidelberg, pp. 34–354, 2002.
5. J. Fridrich. "Feature-based steganalysis for JPEG images and its implications for future design of steganographic schemes." *Proc. 6th Information Hiding Workshop*, Toronto, Canada, 2004.
6. J. Fridrich, M. Goljan, and R. Du. "Detecting LSB Steganography in color and gray-scale images", *IEEE Multimedia Magazine*, pp. 22–28, October 2001.
7. J. Fridrich, M. Goljan, and D. Hogea. "Steganalysis of JPEG images: Breaking the F5 algorithm", LNCS 2578, Springer-Verlag, Berlin Heidelberg, pp. 310–323, 2002.
8. J. Fridrich, M. Goljan, and D. Soukal. "Perturbed quantization steganography with wet paper codes." *Proc. ACM Multimedia Workshop*, Magdeburg, Germany, 2004.
9. Independent JPEG Group. http://www.ijg.org.
10. N. Johnson and S. Jajodia. "Exploring steganography: Seeing the unseen." *IEEE Computer*, 31:26–34, 1998.
11. N. Johnson, Z. Duric, and S. Jajodia. *Information Hiding: Steganography and Watermarking — Attacks and Countermeasures.*, Kluwer Academic Publishers, Boston, 2000.
12. N. Johnson and S. Jajodia. "Steganalysis of images created using current steganography software." *Proc. Int. Workshop on Information Hiding*, LNCS 1525, Springer-Verlag, Berlin, pp. 273–289, 1998.
13. S. Katzenbeisser and F.A.P. Petitcolas (eds.). *Information Hiding: Techniques for Steganography and Digital Watermarking*, Artech House, Norwood, MA, 2000.
14. Joint Photographic Experts Group. http://www.jpeg.org/public/jpeghomepage.htm.
15. N. Provos. "Defending against statistical steganalysis." *Proc. 10th USENIX Security Symposium*, pp. 323–325, 2001.
16. P. Sallee. "Model-based steganography." *Proc. Information Hiding Workshop*, LNCS 2939, Springer-Verlag, Berlin, pp. 154–167, 2003.
17. D. Upham. Jsteg V4. available at: http://www.funet.fi/pub/crypt/steganography.
18. A. Westfeld and A. Pfitzmann. "Attacks on steganographic systems." *Proc. Information Hiding Workshop*, LNCS 1768, Springer-Verlag, New York, pp. 61-75, 1999.
19. A. Westfeld. "F5—a steganographic algorithm: High capacity despite better steganalysis." *Proc. Information Hiding Workshop*, LNCS 2137, Springer-Verlag, Berlin, pp. 289-302, 2001.
20. P. Wayner. *Disappearing Cryptography*. 2nd ed., Morgan Kaufmann, San Francisco, 2002.
21. A. Westfeld. "Detecting low embedding rates". *Proc. Information Hiding Workshop*, LNCS 2578, Springer-Verlag, Berlin Heidelberg, pp. 324-339, 2002.

# Extended Visual Secret Sharing Schemes with High-Quality Shadow Images Using Gray Sub Pixels

Ching-Nung Yang and Tse-Shih Chen

Department of Computer Science and Information Engineering,
National Dong Hwa University,
#1, Da Hsueh Rd, Sec. 2, Hualien, 974-01, Taiwan
Tel: +886-3-8634025, Fax: +886-3-8634010
cnyang@mail.ndhu.edu.tw

**Abstract.** An extended visual secret sharing (EVSS) scheme with innocent looking (unsuspicious) cover images was firstly proposed by Naor and Shamir. Most recent papers about EVSS schemes are dedicated to get a higher contrast of the concealed secret or a less size of shadow image. The conventional EVSS scheme uses the whiteness of black and white sub pixels to represent the gray level of the covered image while we use the gray sub pixels instead to achieve the high-quality shadow image. The term "high-quality" means that the shadow has high-quality image such as a photo picture.

## 1 Introduction

A new type of secret sharing scheme called visual secret sharing (VSS) scheme [1] can conceal the secret that is an image (printed text, handwritten note, picture, etc.) and provide an unconditionally secure way to encode the secret image into $n$ shadow images given to a set $\mathcal{P}=\{1, 2, ..., n\}$ of $n$ participants. We can easily recover the secret by using the human sight without the assistance of hardware. A VSS scheme for any access structure is defined by the qualified and forbidden sets of non-empty subsets, $\Gamma_{Qual}$ and $\Gamma_{Forb}$, of $\{1, 2, ..., n\}$ to describe which combinations shall reveal a secret. We herein use Ateniese et al's general access scheme [2] to represent the VSS scheme. ($\Gamma_{Qual}$; $\Gamma_{Forb}$) for a general access structure of a VSS scheme is defined as $\Gamma_{Qual} \subseteq 2^{\mathcal{P}}$, $\Gamma_{Forb} \subseteq 2^{\mathcal{P}}$ and $\Gamma_{Qual} \cap \Gamma_{Forb}=\emptyset$. Any set $X=\{i_1, i_2, ..., i_r\} \in \Gamma_{Qual}$, where $X \subseteq \mathcal{P}$, can get the shared secret by stacking their shadow images, but any set $X=\{i_1, i_2, ..., i_r\} \in \Gamma_{Forb}$ has no information on the secret image.

Shadow images for the conventional VSS schemes are random and meaningless. The random shadow images are unusual but suspected to censors. Thus, it would be suited to design a VSS scheme with the extended ability, *"the meaningful shadow images"*. An EVSS scheme is a VSS scheme with meaningful shadow images [1, 3]. The EVSS scheme will address the problem that shadow images will be censored since they are suspected. Although the shadow images in [1, 3] are meaningful (not random), they do not have the qualities like real photographs. Desmedt proposed three visual cryptography schemes to hide the secret in the real *high-quality* shadow images

[4-6]. All of these three schemes are designed only for $n=2$ and cannot be extended to the VSS schemes for more participants. Other image secret sharing schemes with perfect quality secret image are shown in [7-9]; however they need computations for decoding.

In this paper, we use gray sub pixels instead of black and white sub pixels in the shadow image and successfully transform the VSS scheme to our new EVSS scheme with *high-quality* shadow images. In Section 2, we describe the previous VSS and EVSS schemes. In Section 3, we propose our new EVSS schemes with *high-quality* shadows based on gray sub pixels. Section 4 gives the contrasts for the proposed schemes. Section 5 concludes the paper.

## 2 The Basic VSS Scheme and EVSS Scheme

### 2.1 The VSS Scheme with Random Shadow Images

For a black and white VSS scheme, each pixel in the secret image is divided into $m$ (the pixel expansion) black and white sub pixels in $n$ shadows and shadow images are random and meaningless. The VSS Scheme is defined by $n \times m$ Boolean matrix $S = [s_{ij}]$, where $s_{ij} = 1$ if and only if the $j$th sub pixel in the $i$th shadow is black, otherwise $s_{ij} = 0$. When shadows $i_1, i_2, ..., i_r$ in a set $X \in \Gamma_{Qual}$ are stacked, we "see" a recovered secret whose black sub pixels are represented by the Boolean "OR" of rows $i_1, i_2, ... i_r$ in $S$. The gray level of this recovered image is proportional to the Hamming weight of the "OR"ed $m$-vector $V$. For the fixed threshold $1 \leq d \leq m$ and relative difference $\alpha > 0$, if $H(V) \geq d$, this gray level is interpreted by the human sight as black, and if $H(V) \leq d - \alpha m$, the result is interpreted as white.

DEFINITION 1 (VSS scheme). *A VSS scheme with a general access structure ($\Gamma_{Qual}$, $\Gamma_{Forb}$) can be shown as two base $n \times m$ Boolean matrices $B_0$ and $B_1$. When sharing a white (resp. black) pixel, the dealer randomly chooses one row of the matrix in the set $C_0$ (resp. $C_1$) including all matrices obtained by permuting the columns in $B_0$ (resp. $B_1$) to a relative shadow. The chosen matrix defines the gray level of the m sub pixels in the recovered image. A VSS Scheme is considered valid if the following conditions are met [2]:*

 1. *(contrast condition)*
 *For any $S$ in $C_0$ (resp. $C_1$), the "OR"ed $V$ of rows $i_1, i_2,..., i_r$ in a set $X=\{i_1, i_2,..., i_r\} \in \Gamma_{Qual}$ satisfies $H(V) \leq d - \alpha m$ (resp. $H(V) \geq d$).*
 2. *(security condition)*
 *For any subset $X=\{i_1, i_2,..., i_r\} \in \Gamma_{Forb}$, the two collections of $r \times m$ matrices obtained by restricting each $n \times m$ matrices in $C_i$, $i \in \{0, 1\}$, to rows $i_1, i_2, ..., i_r$ are not visual in the sense that they contain the same matrices with the same frequencies.*
 3. *(the image pattern on shadows)*
 *After the dealer's operation, the shadows are random image when $\{1\}, \{2\}, ...,$ and $\{n\}$ belong to $\Gamma_{Forb}$.*

## 2.2 The EVSS Scheme with Black and White Shadow Images

EVSS schemes can provide the shadows with arbitrary images, i.e. they are meaningful and the user will recognize the image pattern on his/her shadow. The definition of the gray level and the contrast $\alpha$ of the recovered secret are the same as the VSS scheme. Additionally, a contrast $\alpha_s$ for the shadow image that provides the meaningful image pattern is also given. An EVSS scheme with a general access structure ($\Gamma_{Qual}$; $\Gamma_{Forb}$) and $\mathcal{P}=\{1, 2, ..., n\}$ is formally defined as follows:

DEFINITION 2 (EVSS scheme). *An EVSS scheme with a general access structure ($\Gamma_{Qual}$; $\Gamma_{Forb}$) can be shown as $2^{(n+1)}$ base n×m Boolean matrices {( $B_0^{s_1...s_n}, B_1^{s_1...s_n}$ )}, and the corresponding sets are {( $C_0^{s_1...s_n}, C_1^{s_1...s_n}$ )} including all matrices obtained by permuting the columns in $B_i^{s_1...s_n}$, where $s_1,...,s_n \in \{0,1\}$. When sharing a white (resp. black) pixel and the pixel in shadow t ($1 \le t \le n$) is white ($s_t=0$) and black ($s_t=1$), the dealer randomly choose one row of the matrix in the set $C_0^{s_1...s_n}$ (resp. $C_1^{s_1...s_n}$). An VSS Scheme is considered valid if the following conditions are met* [3] :

1. (contrast condition)
   For any S in $C_0^{s_1...s_n}$ (resp. $C_1^{s_1...s_n}$ ) and $(s_1,...,s_n) \in \{0,1\}^n$, the "OR"ed V of rows $i_1, i_2,..., i_r$ in a set $X=\{i_1, i_2,..., i_r\} \in \Gamma_{Qual}$ satisfies $H(V) \le d - \alpha m$ (resp. $H(V) \ge d$).

2. (security condition)
   For any subset $X=\{i_1, i_2,..., i_r\} \in \Gamma_{Forb}$, the two collections of r×m matrices obtained by restricting each n×m matrices in $C_i^{s_1...s_n}$, $i \in \{0, 1\}$, to rows $i_1, i_2, ..., i_r$ are not visual in the sense that they contain the same matrices with the same frequencies.

3. (the extended capability: the image pattern on shadows)
   After the dealer's operation, the shadows are meaningful. This is due to $H_1(V_t) - H_0(V_t) \ge \alpha_s m$, where $H_1(V_t)$ and $H_0(V_t)$ are the Hamming weight of row t (i.e., shadow t) in $C_i^{s_1...s_{t-1} 1 s_{t+1}...s_n}$ and $C_i^{s_1...s_{t-1} 0 s_{t+1}...s_n}$.

# 3 The Proposed EVSS Scheme with High-Quality Shadow Images

## 3.1 Basic Concept

For the EVSS scheme, the image patterns on shadows are just black and white; though meaningful, they do not possess the *high-quality* image such as a photo. Here, we propose new methods to construct the EVSS schemes with *high-quality* shadow images (High-quality EVSS). The High-quality EVSS (H-EVSS) scheme uses a different structure of the sub pixel. The new gray sub pixel is shown in Fig. 1, where a sub pixel is the gray level according to the cover image of the shadow, and the operation between sub pixels is the "ADDITION". It means that a gray sub pixel "ADD" a gray sub pixel will cause a grayer sub pixel.

$\boxed{W}$ ADD $\boxed{W}$ = $\boxed{W}$    $\boxed{W}$ ADD $\boxed{G_i}$ = $\boxed{G_i}$    $\boxed{G_i}$ ADD $\boxed{G_j}$ = $\boxed{G_k}$

**Fig. 1.** "ADD" operation for gray sub pixels in the H-EVSS scheme

The major differences between our H-EVSS schemes and the conventional EVSS schemes are described as follows:

1) The H-EVSS scheme uses "ADD" operation for gray sub pixels defined in Fig. 1 and the conventional EVSS scheme uses "OR"ed operation for black and white sub pixels.

2) The H-EVSS scheme discards the criterion *"with no trace of the cover images"* when stacking the shadows associated to participants in $X \in \Gamma_{Qual}$ to recover the secret message. Note that when one discloses the shadow and stacks it with other shadows associated to participants in $X$ to recover the secret, the cover image of the shadow need not keep secret. Therefore, we can get the secret, no matter we see the remnant images of the cover image or not.

3) The H-EVSS scheme has *high-quality* shadows. (In fact, we achieve the *high-quality* shadows at the cost of recovering the secret message with trace of the cover images.)

4) The H-EVSS scheme has the less pixel expansion, because our scheme use the gray levels of sub pixel to represent the color of the shadow image while the conventional EVSS scheme uses the whiteness of the black and white sub pixels.

### 3.2 An H-EVSS Scheme with a General Access Structure

DEFINITION 3 (H-EVSS scheme). *An H-EVSS scheme with a general access structure ($\Gamma_{Qual}$; $\Gamma_{Forb}$) can be shown as two base $n \times m$ matrices $B'_0$ and $B'_1$ with element $G_i$ and white. The corresponding sets are $C'_0$ and $C'_1$ including all matrices by permuting the columns in $B'_i$. When sharing a white (resp. black) pixel, the dealer randomly chooses one row of the matrix in $C'_0$ (resp. $C'_1$) to a relative shadow. The chosen matrix defines the gray level of the m sub pixels in the recovered image. An H-EVSS Scheme is considered valid if the following conditions are met:*

*1. (contrast condition)*
*For any S in $C'_0$ (resp. $C'_1$), the "ADD" V of rows $i_1, i_2, ..., i_r$ in a set $X=\{i_1, i_2, ..., i_r\} \in \Gamma_{Qual}$ satisfies $\tilde{H}(V) \geq m-d+\alpha m$ (resp. $\tilde{H}(V) \leq m-d$), where $\tilde{H}(V)$ is the whiteness of V (i.e. the number of the white sub pixels). Note that we use the number of the dominant color of sub pixels to distinguish the "black" and "white". Here, the dominant color is "white" since it has the biggest contrast relative to other gray colors.*

*2. (security condition)*
*For any subset $X=\{i_1, i_2, ..., i_r\} \in \Gamma_{Forb}$, the two collections of $r \times m$ matrices obtained by restricting each $n \times m$ matrices in $C'_i$, $i \in \{0, 1\}$, to rows $i_1, i_2, ..., i_r$ are not visual in the sense that the whiteness of $\tilde{H}(V)$ are the same with the same*

frequencies. Although the gray sub pixels in V will disclose remnant images of the shadows; however, this does not affect the secrecy of secret sharing scheme.

3. *(the extended capability: the image pattern on shadows)*

After the dealer's operation, the shadows are with high quality image. This is due to that the $G_i$ level in the shadow $i$ is chosen according to the corresponding pixel in the cover image of the shadow $i$.

A transfer operation $\mathcal{T}(\cdot)$ is defined as follows. Let $B=[b_{ij}]$ be an $n \times m$ Boolean matrix, where $1 \le i \le n$ and $1 \le j \le m$. Then $B' = \mathcal{T}(B) = [b'_{ij}]$ is

$$b'_{ij} = \begin{cases} 255 \text{ (white subbpixel), if } b_{ij} = 0, \\ G_i, \text{ if } b_{ij} = 1, \end{cases}$$

where $G_i$ is the level of the corresponding pixel in the cover image of shadow $i$.

The idea is that we use the gray sub pixel $G_i$ to show the gray level of the pixel in the cover image and meantime the whiteness of the stacked result is used to recover the secret image.

*Construction:* Let $B_0$ and $B_1$ be the base matrices for the VSS scheme with a general access structure $(\Gamma_{\text{Qual}}; \Gamma_{\text{Forb}})$. Then, the base matrices for an H-EVSS scheme can be obtained by $B'_0 = \mathcal{T}(B_0)$ and $B'_1 = \mathcal{T}(B_1)$. (Note: the proof that the scheme from the construction is an H-EVSS scheme is shown in the full version).

*Example 1.* Construct a simple 2-out-of-2 H-EVSS scheme with $n=2$, $\mathcal{P}=\{1, 2\}$, $\Gamma_{\text{Qual}}=\{\{1,2\}\}$ and $\Gamma_{\text{Forb}}=\{\{1\},\{2\}\}$.

Use $B_0 = \begin{bmatrix} 1100 \\ 1100 \end{bmatrix}$ and $B_1 = \begin{bmatrix} 1100 \\ 0011 \end{bmatrix}$ in the VSS scheme, we have the base matrices $B'_0 = \mathcal{T}(B_0) = \begin{bmatrix} GG00 \\ GG00 \end{bmatrix}$ and $B'_1 = \mathcal{T}(B_1) = \begin{bmatrix} GG00 \\ 00GG \end{bmatrix}$. □

Fig. 2 shows the cover image, one shadow and the stacked result where the cover image is a photo picture of the members in our laboratory, and the secret image is a text image "VSS".

(a) the cover image    (b) one shadow    (c) Shadow 1 + Shadow 2

**Fig. 2.** A 2-out-of-2 H-EVSS scheme

Although the recovered image has the trace of the original cover image, there is no compromise for the secrecy. Finally, we really have the *high-quality* shadows and get the secret "VSS".

Next, we discuss how to improve the contrast of the recovered secret (Section 3.3) and the contrast of the shadow image (Section 3.4) for the proposed H-EVSS scheme.

### 3.3 Improve the Contrast of the Recovered Secret

Different transformation methods, *histogram slide to darkness*, *clipping at end* and *histogram shrink*, are used to reduce the gray levels of an image [10]. We can *darken* the cover image to reduce the gray levels such that the affection of other gray sub pixels is diminished for human sight when recovering the secret. Then, the contrast of the recovered secret is enhanced.

Fig. 3 shows the preprocessed cover images, their corresponding histogram diagrams and recovered images using different transformations. Fig. 3(a) is *histogram slide to darkness* with $DL$=100; Fig. 3(b) is *clipping at end* with $UC$=150 and $LC$=255; Fig. 3(c) is *histogram shrink* with $US$=0 and $LS$=100.

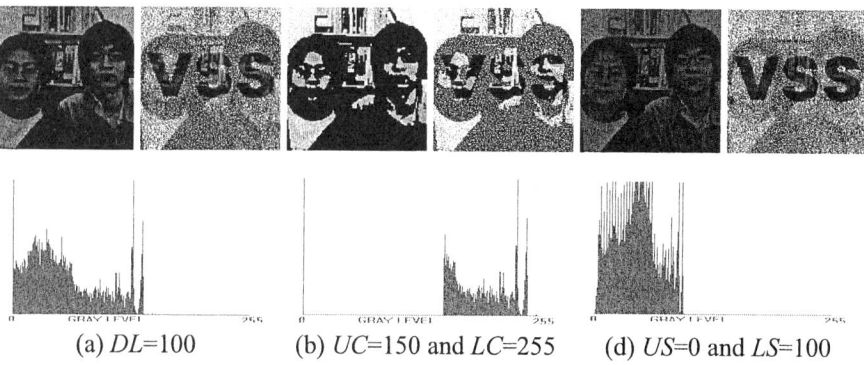

(a) $DL$=100  (b) $UC$=150 and $LC$=255  (d) $US$=0 and $LS$=100

**Fig. 3.** Preprocessed cover images and their corresponding recovered images

### 3.4 Improve the Contrast of the Shadow Image

We use the mean value of the cover image to substitute the white sub pixel to enhance the clearness of the shadow image. A new *Transfer* operation $T_m(\cdot)$ is defined. Let $B=[b_{ij}]$ be an $n \times m$ Boolean matrix, where $1 \le i \le n$ and $1 \le j \le m$, and then $B' = T_m(B) = [b'_{ij}]$ is defined as follows:

$$b'_{ij} = \begin{cases} G_m, & \text{if } b_{ij} = 0, \\ G_i, & \text{if } b_{ij} = 1, \end{cases}$$

where $G_i$ is the level of the corresponding pixel in the cover image of shadow $i$ and $G_m$ is the mean value of the gray level for the cover images of all shadows.

Consider *Example 1*. Using the mean value instead of the white pixel, the base matrices $B'_0$ and $B'_1$ can be designed as $B'_0 = T_m(\begin{bmatrix} 1100 \\ 1100 \end{bmatrix}) = \begin{bmatrix} G\ G\ G_m\ G_m \\ G\ G\ G_m\ G_m \end{bmatrix}$ and

$B'_1 = T_m(\begin{bmatrix} 1100 \\ 0011 \end{bmatrix}) = \begin{bmatrix} G\,G\,G\,G \\ G\,G\,G\,G \end{bmatrix}$. From $B'_0$ and $B'_1$ matrices, the stacked white and black pixels are 2"$G+G$" 2"$G_m+G_m$" and 4"$G+G_m$", respectively. Fig. 4(a)~(c) show Shadow 1, Shadow2 and the stacked result. Using the mean value ($G_m$=214 for the cover image Fig. 2(a)) to substitute the white sub pixel really gets a clear shadow image, and meantime the secret is still decoded by human sight.

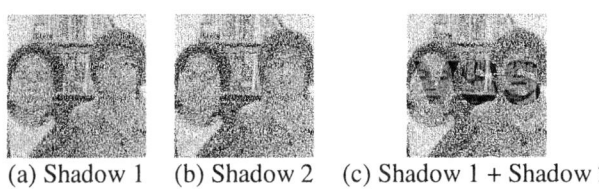

(a) Shadow 1    (b) Shadow 2    (c) Shadow 1 + Shadow 2

**Fig. 4.** Improve the contrast of the shadow image by using $G_m$

## 4   The Contrasts of Recovered Image and Shadow Image for H-EVSS Schemes

It is observed that, from the matrices $B'_0$ and $B'_1$, each shadow will have $xGyW$ sub pixels, where $x+y=m$, $G$ is the gray level of the pixel of the corresponding cover image and $W$ is the white sub pixel. The black and white pixels of the recovered image is represented as "$m$-$l$"$G$"$l$"$W$ and "$m$-$h$"$G$"$h$"$W$ sub pixels, respectively. Note that the $G$ in stacked result denotes that "ADD" all sub pixels in the same position of different shadows. Accordingly, we may define the contrasts $\alpha$ and $\alpha_s$ for our H-EVSS scheme as follows to meet the real situation.

*The Contrast of Shadow Image $\alpha_s$:*
Because the contrast of $\alpha_s$ will be different from that of using different preprocessing methods, we typically give a definition of $\alpha_s$ for using *histogram to darkness method* with the darkness value $DL$, $\alpha_s = (255 - DL)/255$.

*The Contrast of Recovered Image $\alpha$:*
The contrast of the recovered image should be proportional to the contrast $((h-l)/(m+l))$ that is defined in [11], but will be compromised by other gray sub pixels. So, we define the new contrast $\alpha$ as $((h-l)/(m+l)) \times (1/(\alpha_s+1))$.

The definitions are consistent with the real situation, e.g., $DL$=255 (the cover image is an all black image), the value $\alpha_s$=0 (all black image) and the value $\alpha = ((h-l)/(m+l))$ (the same as the definition of conventional VSS scheme). For $DL$=0 the contrast $\alpha_s$ is 1 and the value $\alpha = ((h-l)/(m+l)) \times (1/2)$ is reduced.

## 5 Conclusion

In this paper, we propose the new H-EVSS schemes. The decryption method of our new scheme is only to stack shadows. We show how to improve the contrasts of the recovered image and the shadow images. Also, the contrasts for the new H-EVSS scheme are defined. Experimental results show that our scheme is really possessed of the extended ability, the meaningful and *high-quality* shadow images. Moreover, our new H-EVSS scheme has the same pixel expansion like the VSS scheme; however the EVSS scheme will have more pixel expansion than the VSS scheme.

## References

[1] M. Naor and A. Shamir, "Visual cryptography," *Advances in Cryptology-EUROCRYPT'94*, LNCS, No.950, pp.1-12, Springer-Verlag, 1995.
[2] G. Ateniese, C. Blundo, A. De Santis, and D.R. Stinson, "Visual cryptography for general access structures," *ECCC, Electronic Colloquium on Computational Complexity* (TR96-012), 1996.
[3] G. Ateniese, C. Blundo, A. De Santis and D. R. Stinson, "Extended capabilities for visual cryptography," *Theoretical Computer Science*, 250(1-2), pp.143-161, 2001.
[4] Y. Desmedt, S. Hou, and J. Quisquater, "Audio and optical cryptography", *Advances in Cryptology-Asiacrypt'98*, Springer-Verlag, pp.392-404, 1998.
[5] Y. Desmedt, S. Hou, and J. Quisquater, "Cerebral cryptography", *Second International Workshop on Information Hiding,* LNCS, No.1525, pp.1-12, Springer-Verlag, pp.62-72, 1998.
[6] Y. Desmedt and T. Van Le., "Moire cryptography," *Seventh ACM Conference on Computer and Communications Security (CCS-7)*, pp.116-124 , 2000.
[7] R. Lukac and K. N. Plataniotis, "Bit-Level based secret sharing for image encryption," *Pattern Recognition*, Vol. 38, No. 5, pp. 767-772, May, 2005.
[8] R. Lukac and K.N. Plataniotis, "Image Representation Based Secret Sharing," *Communications of the CCISA (Chinese Cryptology & Information Security Association), Special Issue on Image Secret Sharing and Quantum Cryptography*, Vol. 11, No. 2, pp. 103-114, April 2005.
[9] R. Lukac and K.N. Plataniotis, "Colour Image Secret Sharing," *IEE Electronics Letters*, Vol. 40, No. 9, pp. 529-530, April 2004.
[10] R. C. Gonzalez and R. E. Woods, Digital Image Processing, second edition, International Edition, Prentice Hall, 2002.
[11] P.A. Eisen and D.R. Stinson, "Threshold visual cryptography schemes with specified whiteness", *Designs, Codes and Cryptography*, Vol.25, No.1, pp.15-61, Jan., 2002.

# A Steganographic Method for Digital Images Robust to RS Steganalysis

André R.S. Marçal and Patricia R. Pereira

Faculdade de Ciências, Universidade do Porto,
DMA, Rua do Campo Alegre, 687, 4169-007 Porto, Portugal

**Abstract.** Digital images are increasingly being used as steganographic covers for secret communication. The Least Significant Bit (LSB) encoding is one of the most widely used methods for embedding a message in a digital image. However, the direct application of LSB encoding is vulnerable to steganalysis. For example, RS steganalysis is very efficient in detecting the presence of a message in a digital image and to estimate its approximate size. This paper presents a method robust to RS steganalysis, that makes the presence of a message unnoticeable. The method is based on the application of reversible histogram transformation functions to the image, before and after embedding the secret message. The method was tested on 4 greyscale images, with messages of 10%, 30% and 90% of the maximum embedding size. The proposed method proved to be effective in eluding RS steganalysis for all cases tested.

## 1 Introduction

There has always been interest in safely exchanging secret messages. Throughout times, cryptographic tools have been developed and used in order to make the message exchanged incomprehensible to anyone intersecting the communication. A less known approach is steganography, although also used for thousands of years. Steganography's aim is to make the secret communication undetectable, that is, to hide the presence of the secret message. The recent development of Internet has brought new attention to both cryptography and steganography. The interest in steganography has been enhanced recently by the emergence of commercial espionage and the growing concerns about homeland security due to terrorism. The purpose of steganography is therefore to hide (or embed) a secret message into an artefact, called cover. After embedding the secret information into the cover, it becomes a stego-artefact. Almost anything can be used as cover, as long as it looks common and unsuspicious after the embedding process. With the arrival of the digital era and the generalized usage of the Internet and email for the exchange of files, digital covers such as audio, image and video files have become the most obvious choices. This is party due to their widespread use, but also because this type of media usually includes a random noise component in which the secret message may be easily hidden.

The exchange of ever-growing volumes of data through the Internet, and the widespread access to steganography software prompted the development of steganalysis tools. The goal of steganalysis is to identify the presence of secret messages embedded in an artefact. An alternative to this passive approach is to perform active or malicious attacks, with the aim of modifying or destroying a secret message that might have been embedded. From the perspective of someone wishing to send a secret message, the best protection is achieved when steganography and cryptography[1] are used together. In this case, even if steganography fails and the presence of the secret message is unveiled, there will still be an additional layer of protection, as the message embedded is ciphered. An overview of the most important topics in criptography, from a steganographer's point of view, is available in [1].

## 2 Steganography and Steganalysis on Digital Images

Digital images are considered a good choice for a steganography cover because of their insensitivity for the human visual system [2]. The most common approach is to use a substitution system, where the parts of the image considered to be redundant or noisy are replaced by the bits of the secret message [3]. This is done, most of the times, without any change in perceptual content in the cover image [4]. There is no restriction concerning the nature of the message hidden, as long as it can be represented by a stream of bits. In order to recover the message, one only has to know the method and sequence by which the stream of bits was embedded in the image. However, the stego-images produced by these methods may be vulnerable to steganalysis as the embedding process modifies the statistical properties of the cover image. Another problem is that the secret content of the stego-image might be in jeopardy when the image is subjected to manipulations such as lossy compression, denoising or image enhancement, as these operations may modify the content of the image bits, thus making the hidden message recovery impossible.

### 2.1 LSB Encoding

One of the common data hiding methods is based on manipulating the Least Significant Bit (LSB) planes, by direct replacing the LSBs of the cover image with the message bits [5]. LSB substitution can be performed on all types of images, including raw uncompressed, compressed formats and indexed images. An extended description and discussion of substitution methods, including LSB methods can be found in [3]. The maximum cover size (in bits) is the total number of bytes of the cover image. For 8-bit images, it is the total number of pixels. For example, a text of over 5000 words can be embedded on a 512x512 pixels 8-bit image by the LSB substitution method (maximum message size of 262144 bits = 32768 bytes).

The changes introduced in a 8-bit cover image by the LSB substitution process are very little. The possible swapping of a pixel's LSB results in a change of

---

[1] Criptography is here used to refer to all the widely used techniques to make information ininteligible to any person who does not hold the key to decipher it.

its Digital Number (DN) by +1 or -1. This will only occur, on average, for every other bit of the embedded message bit stream. Although the use of additional bit planes increases the embedding capacity of an image, the modification in the cover image might become more easily perceptible visually.

An important issue regarding LSB substitution steganography is the selection of the location where the secret message is to be placed in the image. The most common choices are sequential and pseudo-random methods. The sequential method starts on a specific pixel (usually the first one), using all subsequent pixels until the message is fully embedded. The pseudo-random method generate a pseudo-random sequence of values (the indices of bytes of the cover image) that determines the order by which the secret message bits are embedded.

## 2.2 Visual Steganalysis

One of the most basic forms of steganalysis for digital images is by visual inspection. This can be done directly on the image, or by the observation of a single bit plane, most commonly the LSB. The observation of periodic or other type of suspicions patterns in the image bit plane is used to reveal the presence of a secret message. An example of LSB visual inspection is presented in [6]. Visual steganalysis can be useful in the presence of a small number of suspicious images. However, as the visual inspection of images requires direct human intervention, visual steganalysis is not an effective method for scrutinizing large volumes of image data.

The direct visual steganalysis is based on the faith that the observer's attention will be called out by small discrepancies in uniform regions of the image. When LSB substitution steganography is used, the DN pixel values of the cover image will only have been changed by +1 or -1. For indexed colour images, even this small modification might be easily noticeable, if the variations in colour are not gradual in the colour palette. Colour indexed images are therefore considerably vulnerable to direct visual steganalysis, and should be avoided as cover images for LSB substitution steganography without further processing. On grey scale images, or other type of colour images, a DN change of +1 or -1 will hardly be perceptible, thus the presence of a secret message can only be noticed in very uniform or highly saturated areas.

## 2.3 Quantitative Steganalysis

Fridrich et al. [7] [8] introduced a powerful, yet complex, steganalytic method that is able to accurately estimate the length of the embedded message on a digital image, for several LSB steganographic methods. The method is based on the fact that the content of each bit plane of an image is correlated with the remaining bit planes. In particular, for an 8-bit image, there is some degree of correlation between the LSB plane and the other seven bit planes. When a message is inserted in the LSB plane, its content is considered to become randomised, and thus the correlation between the LSB plane with the remaining bit planes is reduced or lost.

The RS steganalysis method uses a discrimination function and a flipping operation to identify three types of pixel groups - Regular (R), Singular (S) and Unchanged (U) - depending on how the flipping changes the value of the discrimination function [8]. The size of the group of pixels and the corresponding flipping mask M is initially established. For example M=[010] will correspond to a test performed on groups of 3 pixels at a time, where only the middle one is flipped. In typical images, applying the LSB flipping mask to the pixels in the group will more frequently lead in an increase in the discrimination function, rather than a decrease, and thus the total number of regular groups in an image will be larger than singular groups. The randomisation of the LSB plane forces these differences to zero, as the length of the embedded message increases [8].

When a message with a relative length p is embedded in the cover image ($p = 1$ for full length embedding), the fraction of image pixels with the LSB flipped is, on average, $\frac{p}{2}$. Flipping the LSB of all image pixels will result in an image with a fraction of flipped pixels $1 - \frac{1}{2}$. In the process of steganalysing an image, the actual value of p is unknown. The relative number of R and S groups is counted for the original image, and for the flipped version of that image (with the LSB off all pixels flipped). These will result in four points for the so-called RS diagram, which are used to estimate the value of p. A detailed description of the RS steganalysis can be found in [8]. For greyscale images, the RS steganalysis method can separate cover images from stego images with a 10% embedded message [8].

## 3 Proposed Method

The standard process consists of embedding a message $t$ into a cover image $x$. The result is a new image $y_1$, the stego-image, which should ideally be very similar to the cover image. The process can be represented by equation, where $E$ is the encoding function.

$$y_1 = E(x, t) \quad (1)$$

This process may, however, be vulnerable to steganalytic methods, namely those of statistical steganalysis. The proposed method uses histogram transformation functions in order to defeat steganalysis. The idea is to break the signature that is established between neighbouring pixels in the encoding process, by means of histogram transformation pre and post encoding. Initially, a histogram transformation function $f^*$ is applied to the cover image, $x$. This function $f^*$ compresses the range of levels used in the original image, to a narrower range. The secret message is embedded in the resulting image $f^*(x)$, producing an image $E(f^*(x), t)$. The final image $y_2$ is obtained through the application of a histogram transformation function $f$ that expands the range of values back to the initial range, as expressed in Equation (2).

$$y_2 = f(E(f^*(x), t)) \quad (2)$$

A schematic representation of the encoding method is presented in Figure 1. As in the standard method, the final image should be as close as possible to the

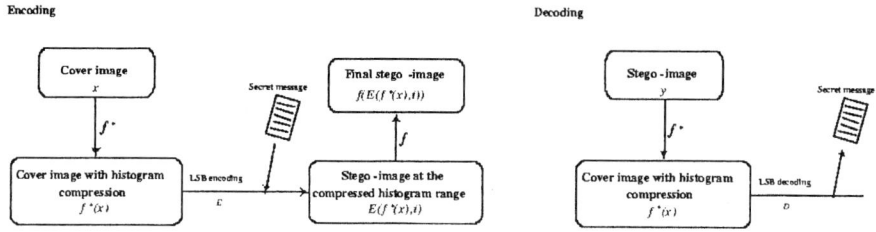

**Fig. 1.** Scheme of the proposed method

original cover image. In order to extract the message from the image, one has to apply the histogram transformation function f to compress the histogram back to the range of values present at the encoding stage. It is therefore required that the transformation function $f^*$ is the inverse of function $f$, a property stated in Equation (3).

$$f^*(f(z)) = z \qquad (3)$$

Due to the discrete nature of digital images, this property does not stand when the order of function $f$ and $f^*$ is swapped. That is, $f(f^*(z))$ is usually not equal to $z$. This is not a problem, as long as the changes introduced by the compression and decompression of the histogram are not noticeable. There are other properties that the histogram transformation functions $f$ and $f^*$ should obey to prevent strange artifacts to appear in the image. One requirement is that both functions are monotonous, either increasing (4) or decreasing (5).

$$\forall x_1, x_2; \ x_1 > x_2 \Rightarrow f(x_1) \geq f(x_2) \wedge f^*(x_1) \geq f^*(x_2) \qquad (4)$$

$$\forall x_1, x_2; \ x_1 > x_2 \Rightarrow f(x_1) \leq f(x_2) \wedge f^*(x_1) \leq f^*(x_2) \qquad (5)$$

In this work, linear histogram transformation functions of the form presented in Equations (6) and (7) were used, where $\lfloor x \rfloor$ is the largest integer below $x$, and $a$ is a constant. The number of occupied levels of $f(x)$ is the same as in $x$, but due to the discrete nature of digital images, $f(f^*(x))$ does not occupy the same number of levels as $x$. Let us consider an example with a cover image of 8-bit unsigned format and $a = 10$. The range of values in the original image $x$ is 0-255, which is reduced to 0-232 by the application of the histogram compression function $f^*$. The subsequent application of function $f$ (Equation 6) will result in an image $y$ with a range of values 0-255, but with some pairs of levels merged. For example, $f^*$ will compress both levels 219 and 220 to the same value (200), which is then expanded to the level 220.

$$f(x) = x + \left\lfloor \frac{x}{a} \right\rfloor \qquad (6)$$

$$f^*(x) = x - \left\lfloor \frac{x}{a+1} \right\rfloor \qquad (7)$$

## 4 Results

Four test images were selected to evaluate the performance of the proposed method. The test images are 512x512 pixels sections of photographs acquired by a digital camera (Peacock, Dinosaurs, Chickens) and a film camera (Falkland). In this later case the film was digitalized in a Kodak Photo Lab. The images were converted to an 8-bit grey scale from their original 24-bit colour format. Figure 2 shows the greyscale version of the test images. Text messages with 10%, 30% and 90% of the maximum embedding size were produced - messages A (3277 characters), B (9830 characters) and C (29491 characters).

**Fig. 2.** Test images (from left to right): Falkland, Peacock, Dinosaurs, and Chickens

### 4.1 Message Embedding

The messages were embedded in the cover images using LSB substitution steganography with both sequential and pseudo-random methods. The messages were embedded directly and using the histogram transformation functions (f and f*) with $a = 10$ and $a = 8$ (6,7). A total of 72 stego-images were obtained - 4 cover images, 3 messages, 3 types of functions and 2 location methods. For each test image, 2 additional images were also produced by applying functions f* and f (compression and expansion of the histogram), without embedding any message. A total of 84 images were thus available for testing.

### 4.2 Visual Tests

The direct visual inspection of the stego-images did not reveal any clues about the presence of the embedded messages, for test images. It is worth pointing out that no direct comparisons were made between the stego-images and the cover images, as in a normal scenario the cover image is not available. In fact, it is good steganography practice to avoid the use of well-known cover images.

A visual inspection of the LSB plane of the stego-images was also performed. This method proved very effective in detecting messages that were directly embedded sequentially. The use of the proposed method reduced the footprint of the sequential embedded message, but a careful observer could still detect the presence of a message. However, the visual inspection of the LSB plane was totally inefficient with pseudo-random LSB substitution steganography.

## 4.3 RS Steganalysis

The RS steganalysis method was applied to the 72 stego-images, the 4 cover images, and the cover images modified by compression and expansion of the histogram (8 images). Two flipping masks were used: M=[010] and M=[0110]. As no significant differences were obtained with the two flipping masks, the results presented throughout are for M=[010]. The differences in the message size estimation by the RS method between sequential and pseudo-random stego-images were also found to be negligible. Since the stego-images embedded sequentially are vulnerable to visual steganalysis, the results presented are all for pseudo-random LSB encoding.

The message size estimated by RS steganalysis with direct LSB encoding is presented in Table 1. As expected, the RS method proved to be very effective in estimating the message size. The difference between the estimated and the actual length of the embedded message were below 5% for all cases except one - for the test image Falkland and message C (90%) the estimated size was 83%. The results from RS steganalysis with the stego-images produced with the proposed method are considerably different, as it can be seen in Table 2. Two results are presented for each test image and message: using histogram transformation functions ($f$ and $f^*$) with $a = 10$ and with $a = 8$. When the estimated message length by RS steganalysis is below 5% (the typical range of accuracy of the method), the steganalysis fails to detect the presence of the secret message. This is achieved for all test images and message sizes, although not with every set of histogram transformation functions. For the test image Falkland, the stego-image with message C and functions $f$ / $f^*$ with $a = 10$, the estimated message length is 9.4%. For the test image Peacock, functions $f$ / $f^*$ with $a = 8$ produce high negative values for the estimated message length, even without any

**Table 1.** Estimated message length for standard (direct) encoding

| MESSAGE | FALKLAND | PEACOCK | DINOSAURS | CHICKENS |
|---|---|---|---|---|
| None | 0.1% | 3.0% | 1.3% | -1.4% |
| A (10%) | 9.7% | 12.9% | 12.1% | 9.5% |
| B (30%) | 29.1% | 31.8% | 31.8% | 29.6% |
| C (90%) | 83.0% | 87.4% | 85.4% | 89.3% |

**Table 2.** Estimated message length for the proposed method of encoding

| MESSAGE | FALKLAND | | PEACOCK | | DINOSAURS | | CHICKENS | |
| | $a = 10$ | $a = 8$ | $a = 10$ | $a = 8$ | $a = 10$ | $a = 8$ | $a = 10$ | $a = 8$ |
|---|---|---|---|---|---|---|---|---|
| None | 4.8% | -1.2% | 1.0% | -16.7% | -1.6% | 3.3% | -0.3% | -1.3% |
| A (10%) | 5.0% | 0.7% | 0.9% | -18.8% | -0.7% | 4.3% | -1.6% | -1.1% |
| B (30%) | 4.3% | -0.5% | 0.9% | -21.7% | -0.7% | 3.7% | -0.7% | -0.3% |
| C (90%) | 9.4% | 4.9% | 0.5% | -29.5% | -3.6% | 2.0% | 2.7% | 2.3% |

message. The results for the other two test images are all below the 5% mark for both sets of functions.

## 5 Conclusions

The proposed method, based on the application of reversible histogram transformation functions to the cover image, proved effective in defeating RS steganalysis. The RS steganalysis method was successful in estimating the message length embedded in standard stego-images, but failed to detect the presence of the embedded messages, when using the proposed method. The two types of functions used were effective on two test images, with messages of 10%, 30% and 90% of the maximum embedding length. On the other two test images, only one of the functions performed well for all 3 messages. The choice of the adequate set of histogram transformation functions is dependent of the cover image. The implementation of the proposed method as a robust steganography software would, therefore, require the automatic testing of various sets of histogram transformation functions, for a given cover image, selecting the set that provides the best results for that image. An indication of the histogram transformation functions used would then have to be inserted in a pre-defined location in the cover image. For example, the linear histogram transformation functions used here would be characterised by a single byte (the value of the parameter a).

## References

1. Eric Cole, Hiding in Plain Sight: Steganography and the Art of Covert Communication. Wiley Publishing, Inc., (2003)
2. Lou, D.C., Liu, J.L.: Steganographic method for secure communications. Computers and Security, **21** (2002) 449–460
3. Katzenbeisser, S., Petitcolas, F.A.P.: Information Hiding Techniques for Steganography and Digital Watermarking. Artech House (2000)
4. Chandramouli, R., Memon, N.: Analysis of LSB based image steganography techniques. Proceedings of the IEEE International Conference on Image Processing. **3** (2001) 1019–1022
5. Chan, C.K., Cheng, L.M.: Hiding data in images by simple LSB substitution. Pattern Recognition, **37** (2004) 469–474
6. Westfeld, A., Pfitzmann, A.: Attacks on steganographic systems. Lecture Notes in Computer Science, Springer-Verlag **1768** (2000) 61–75
7. Fridrich, J., Goljan, M., Rui Du: Detecting LSB steganography in color, and grayscale images. IEEE Multimedia **8** (2001) 22–28
8. Fridrich, J., Goljan, M., Hogea, D., Soukal, D.: Quantitative steganalysis of digital images: estimating the secret message length. Multimedia Systems **9** (2003) 288–302

# Estimation of Target Density Functions by a New Algorithm

Askin Demirkol[1], Zafer Demir[2], and Erol Emre[3]

[1] Department of Electrical and Computer Engineering,
University of Missouri, Rolla, MO 65409-0040 USA
[2] Dept. of Electrical Eng., Sakarya University, Sakarya, 54100 Turkey
[3] Dept. of Comp. Eng., Sakarya University, Sakarya, 54100 Turkey

**Abstract.** In this paper, a new Target Density Function(TDF) is theorized to image the radar targets by a new estimation algorithm. TDF is represented in a specified manner. This method is developed by inspiring of ambiguity functions. TDF is obtained in the range and scanning angle plane different from Fowle-Naparst's methods. Target density function is produced via a linear phased array radar system. This is another gain of the method. In addition to scanning, targeting and imaging properties, by this way, the problem associated with beamforming is bypassed.

**Keywords:** Sensor imaging, radar imaging, SAR-ISAR, phased array radar, dense-target environment, target density function.

## 1 Introduction

Radar imaging is a mapping process of 3-D object to 2-D image by extracting the echo signals off the targets. It is provided with 2-D Inverse Fourier Transform(IFT) by Inverse Synthetic Aperture Radars(ISAR) principles [20,19,5,18]. Radar image formation consists of three consecutive phases such as signal acquisition, signal processing and image processing [20,19]. This study is interested in first and second phases.

Target density function(TDF) is an important characteristic of radar imaging. TDF is known with different names such as ambiguity function, density function, target density function, object(target), object reflectivity function, doubly-spread reflectivity function, reflection coefficient [12,11]. They all seem directly relevant to the representation of the exact object.

If TDF is considered as a reflection coefficient, according to Schlumberger/ oilfield glossary and American meteorological society/glossary of meteorology, reflection coefficient is defined as the ratio of the received signal to the transmitted signal. By this definition, when the reflected signals from different directions are considered, TDF has an important role in producing of the radar images.

There are two approaches on TDF. First one considers point scatterers reflected off the target scatterer centers. Integration of all point scatterers is able to give the whole object. This approach is based on inverse Fourier transform(IFT) referred to ISAR principles [19,13,20,5,18].

Second method on TDF is dense-target environment approach credited to Fowle and Naparst [7,8]. This takes into consideration the existence of densities of the targets and it is based on the ambiguity functions with two variables as range and velocity[3].

In this study, a new TDF is theoretically developed by a new approach on range-scanning angle plane different from Fowle-Naparst and IFT-ISAR techniques. While this is obtained via by a phased array radar system, the problem associated with beamforming is bypassed. This is another advantage of this study. All details of the new method is given in section 4.

## 2 Radar Systems

A typical radar (RAdio Detection And Ranging) measures the strength and round-trip time of the microwave signals that are emitted by a radar antenna and reflected off a distant surface or target. Radar is an active sensors that provides its energy and capable of detection, tracking and targeting [1,2,13,4,6,19,20].

Let consider a point target at range $R$, with radial velocity $v$ relative to a collocated transmitter/receiver, as shown in Figure 1a.

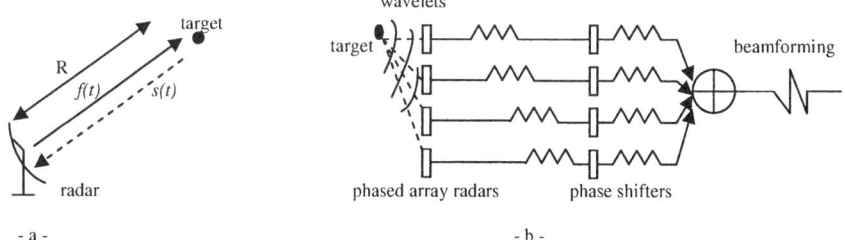

**Fig. 1.** Radar-target Detection

Suppose an arbitrary signal $f(t)$ is transmitted. The received signal after reflection from a point target is given by

$$r(t) = af(s(t-\tau)) \qquad (1)$$

where

$$\tau = \frac{2R}{c}$$
$$s = \frac{c-v}{c+v} \qquad (2)$$

Where, $a$ is an amplitude that depends on the range of the object, its reflectivity properties, and the frequency of operation among other factors; $c$ is the speed of propagation as speed of light.

The returned signal, $r(t)$ is a delayed and time-scaled version of the transmitted signal, $f(t)$.

If a SAR(synthetic aperture radar) imaging is considered, instead of a target point, if our target is composed of continuum of point targets, in receiving mode, SAR processes the returned image signal to reach the target at $x, y, z$ coordinates[19,20,10].

$$s(t) = \int_{-\infty}^{\infty} \int_{-\infty}^{\infty} \int_{-\infty}^{\infty} \rho(x,y,z) f(t - \frac{2R}{c}) dx dy dz \qquad (3)$$

Where $f$ is the transmitted signal function, $\rho$ is reflectivity function, $R$ is the range and $c$ is the speed of light. SAR is a technique which is based on multi-aperture sensing[9].

As for phased array radar systems, they perform radar functions much more rapidly and with increased accuracy. Arrays may be considered as active element or passive arrays. In the active array, a transmitter or receiver or both connected directly to each element. In the passive array, only transmitter and one receiver is used for the entire array system [1,2].

A general view of a phased array radar system is as the following Figure 1b. As can be seen, the waves reflected off the targets are received by the radar system by phase differences. The differences are matched using a phase shifter, then the process is finalized by the beam-forming.

## 3 Preliminaries of Density Functions

In radar research and applications, Target Density Function(TDF) is called with different names such as ambiguity function, density function, target density function, object(target), object reflectivity function, doubly-spread reflectivity function, reflection coefficient etc..[12,11].

According to Schlumberger/oilfield glossary and American meteorological society/glossary of meteorology, reflection coefficient is defined as the ratio of the received signal to the transmitted signal. This indicates that when TDF is considered as a reflection coefficient, it is indirectly relevant to the object or image.

As TDF definition, reflection coefficient is used in IFT and ISAR image formation. This technique defines the reflection coefficient by superposition method which is integration of all point scatterers. Summation of the point scatterers represent the whole object [19,13,20,5,18]. This is shown in the equation (3). $\rho(x,y,z)$ determines the integration of the point scatterers at the object or target.

First *Density* term related to the target density function term is called as dense and density by Fowle et all [7]. In this paper, it is used to emphasize to define complex targets and separate the single and multiple targets. In multiple case, while a high density of similar targets is defined, in single case, a single target in a dissimilar clutter background is claimed. Then *dense target environment* term is used by Naparst in his paper [8].

Fowle's approach is inspired of ambiguity functions and considers the single target. Ambiguity functions are important in radar signal design. They are capable of quantifying the behavior of a radar waveform. A typical ambiguity function describes the response of a particular range-velocity resolution of a radar to a point target [3,14,17,16,15]. This type of ambiguity function with range-velocity variables also correspond to Naparst's approach based doppler effect as well. If the ambiguity function $A(x,y)$ corresponding to a function $u(t)$ is defined by

$$A(x,y) = \int_{-\infty}^{\infty} u(t - \frac{x}{2})\hat{u}(t + \frac{x}{2})e^{-j2\pi yt}dt \qquad (4)$$

where $\hat{u}$ is the complex conjugate of $u$. This approach provided important contribution to radar applications to describe target density functions. The variables $x, y$ in ambiguity function (4), corresponds to the velocity and distance of Fowle and Naparst's models [7,8].

In addition to *dense target environment* concept, Naparst also described it as a *target density function* in the same work. This approach was on multiple and high density target environment differently from Fowle's. He defined dense-target environment that it includes a lot of targets that ranges and velocities of those targets are very close to each other. This definition has also taken advantage of Fowle's single target density properties. Definition by Naparst, density of targets at distance $x$ and velocity $y$ is $D(x,y)$. In this case, the echo or the reflected signal from targets will be

$$e(t) = \int_{0}^{\infty} \int_{-\infty}^{\infty} D(x,y)\sqrt{y}s(y(t-x))dxdy \qquad (5)$$

In this approach, it is assumed that all targets are illuminated equally. By this way, the target density function seems based on the range-velocity variables similar to ambiguity functions.

As stated, Fowle and Naparst' approaches are firstly interested in high and low dense-target environments.

## 4 Estimation of Target Density Function

Here, a new target density function(TDF) is estimated by a new algorithm. TDF is an effective tool for imaging of the radar targets in dense-target environment. A new target density estimation algorithm is theorized by making use of IFT-ISAR(point scatterers) and Fowle - Naparst' approaches. In this study, new TDF is worked for radar imaging based on a linear phased array radar system. The object at out of range is imaged by a new estimation algorithm using the target density function.

The variables of the target density function are based on the coordinates as range, $R$ and angle $\beta$. If $g(R,\beta)$ is a target density function at range $R$ with scanning angle $\beta$. In this work, by making use of the definitions of target density function above, we describe a target density function as the following;

**Definition.** Target Density Function is as the limit of the ratio of the amplitude of the signal reflected from an infinitesimally neighborhood about the point $(R,\beta)$ to the amplitude of the incoming signal.

By this definition

$$g(R, \beta) = \lim_{d(\Omega) \to 0} \frac{A_r}{A_t} \quad (6)$$

where $d(\Omega)$ is the diameter of the ball about the point $(R, \beta) \in \Omega$, $A_r$ and $A_t$ are the amplitudes of the reflected and the transmitted signals, respectively.

This definition is relevant to how much energy is reflected and it looks different from the other target density function definitions. Instead of ambiguity functions based on range-velocity variables, imaging is taken by a new target density function based on range and scanning angle. Although the new TDF is obtained in different manner, it is similar to Naparst's approach in terms of high dense target environment.

Let consider the following Figure 2, as target plane. Where $\beta$ is $cos\theta$ and $R$ is the range from the target to the radar.

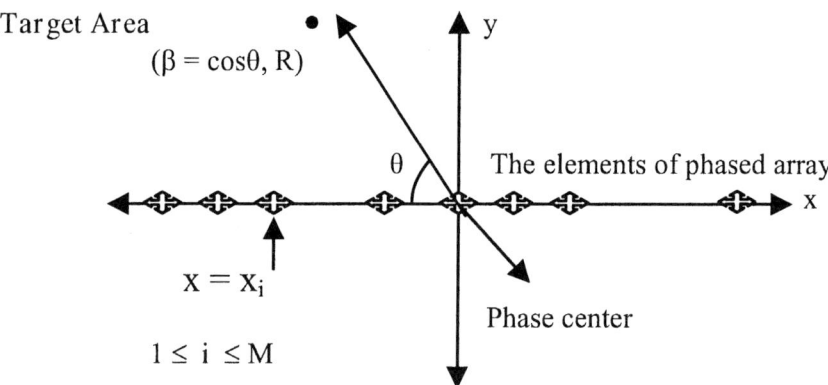

**Fig. 2.** Phased array imaging

As can be seen in Figure 2, the target density function is a function of the spatial coordinates $(R, \beta)$ in the upper semi-plane.

Now let obtain the target density function. Let $P(t)$ be any periodic function of time, such as a train of pulses, where

$$p(t) = \sum_{k=-\infty}^{\infty} \alpha_k \, e^{jk\omega_0 t} \quad (7)$$

$$\omega_0 = 2\pi \times \text{PRF}, \quad (8)$$

where PRF is the pulse repetition frequency.

$$s_c(t) = e^{j\omega_c t} \quad (9)$$

Where $s_c(t)$ is the carrier signal.

$$s_m(t) = p(t)s_c(t) \tag{10}$$

Where $s_m(t)$ is the modulated signal.
The reflectivity of one point at $g(R,\beta)$

$$y(x,t) = s_m(t - 2R/c - \beta x/c)g(R,\beta) \tag{11}$$

Let generalize (11) to the whole radar-target semi upper plane by superposition principle;

If $g(R,\beta)$ is the reflectivity of the point $(R,\beta)$, and $R_1$ is the maximum range of interest target area; then

$$\begin{aligned}y(x,t) &= \int_{-1}^{1}\int_{0}^{R_1} s_m(t - 2R/c - \beta x/c)g(R,\beta)dRd\beta \\ &= \int_{-1}^{1}\int_{0}^{R_1} p(t - 2R/c - \beta x/c)e^{-j\omega_c(2R/c-\beta x/c)}e^{j\omega_c t}g(R,\beta)dRd\beta\end{aligned} \tag{12}$$

where $y(x,t)$ is the output of the sensor located at center (the feature space), and $c$ is the speed of light.

The algorithm is as follows,

$$y(x,t) = \sum_{k=-\infty}^{\infty} \alpha_k e^{j(\omega_c+k\omega_0)t} \int_{-1}^{1}\int_{0}^{R_1} e^{-j(\omega_c+k\omega_0)2R/c} e^{-j(\omega_c+k\omega_0)\beta x/c} g(R,\beta)dRd\beta \tag{13}$$

Then, demodulation of the equation (13) via

$$s_d(t) = e^{-j(\omega_c+k\omega_0)t} \tag{14}$$

yields

$$Y(k,x) = \int_{-1}^{1}\int_{0}^{R_1} e^{-j(\omega_c+k\omega_0)2R/c} e^{-j(\omega_c+k\omega_0)\beta x/c} g(R,\beta)dRd\beta \tag{15}$$

for each $k$ and $\beta$, let be $G(k,\beta)$

$$G(k,\beta) = \int_{0}^{R_1} g(R,\beta) e^{-j(\omega_c+k\omega_0)2R/c} dR \tag{16}$$

Hence for each fixed $k$ and $\beta$ we obtain

$$Y(k,x) = \int_{-1}^{1} G(k,\beta) e^{-j(\omega_c+k\omega_0)\beta x/c} d\beta \tag{17}$$

If this equation is considered as the following,

$$Y_k(x) = \int_{-1}^{1} G_k(\beta) e^{-j(\omega_c+k\omega_0)\beta x/c} d\beta \tag{18}$$

If there are N sensors, each located at $x = x_i$, this gives us the inner product of $G_k(\beta)$ with

$$a_i(\beta) = e^{-j(\omega_c+k\omega_0)\frac{x_i}{c}\beta} \tag{19}$$

This enables us estimate $G_k(\beta)$ as

$$G_k(\beta) \cong \sum_{k=-\infty}^{M} b_i a_i(\beta) \tag{20}$$

for some constants $b_i$.

Then, if let the equation (16), consider as a

$$G_k(\beta) = G(k,\beta) = \int_0^{R_1} g(R,\beta) e^{-j(\omega_c+k\omega_0)2R/c} dR \tag{21}$$

Let consider it as a Fourier series as the following.

$$g(R,\beta) = \sum_{k=-\infty}^{\infty} G_k(\beta) e^{j(\omega_c+k\omega_0)2R/c} \tag{22}$$

If we change $k$, $-N \ll k \ll N$, ($N$ and $\omega_c$ are chosen such that $\omega_c \cong N\omega_0$), for each fixed $\beta$ we obtain the trigonometric Fourier series of $g(R,\beta)$ with respect to the variable $R$. Hence we estimate $g(R,\beta)$ (we obtain $2N+1$ terms) as,

$$g(R,\beta) \cong \sum_{k=-N}^{N} G_k(\beta) e^{j(\omega_c+k\omega_0)2R/c} \tag{23}$$

As realized that although a phased array radar system is used during the estimation of TDF, the problem associated with beamforming is bypassed. This is another gain of our technique.

## 5 Summary and Conclusion

In this paper, a new target density function(TDF) is theorized by a new estimation algorithm by utilizing the point scatterer and ambiguity functions. New target density function is based on range and angle information different from conventional approaches.

The new TDF is interpreted in a specified manner and partly inspired of IFT-ISAR and Fowle-Naparst approaches. However, it is developed based on range and scanning angle plane in high dense-target environment.

In addition to the new algorithm, second gain of this study is provided by the phased array radar system. Although TDF is produced via by the phased array radar, the problem associated with beamforming is bypassed. This is another advantage of our technique.

## References

1. Skolnik,M.I.: Introduction to radar systems, 1980.
2. Skolnik,M.I.: Radar handbook, 1970.
3. Woodward,P.M.: Probability and information theory with applications to radar,1957.
4. Cook,C.E., Bernfeld,M.: Radar signals;An introduction to theory and application,1967.
5. Chen,V.C., Ling,H.: Time-Frequency transforms for radar imaging and signal analysis,2002.
6. Hovanessian,S.A.: Introduction to synthetic array and imaging radars, Artech House, c1980.
7. Fowle,E.N., Kelly,E.J., Sheehan,J.A.: Radar system performance in a dense-target environment. IRE Int.Convention record, no.4, pp.136-145, 1961.
8. Naparst,H.: Dense target signal processing. IEEE Transactions on information theory, v.37, no.2, March, 1991.
9. Chen,V.C., R.Lipps,R., Bottons,M.: Radar imaging of ground moving targets, Radar Conference, 2001. Proceedings of the 2001 IEEE , 1-3 May 2001 pp.426 - 431, 2002.
10. Birk,R., Camus,W., Valenti,E.: Synthetic aperture radar imaging systems", Aerospace and Electronic Systems Magazine, IEEE, v.10, Issue.11, pp.15-23, Nov. 1995.
11. Chen,V.C., Qian,S.: Time frequency transform vs. fourier transform for radar imaging. Time-Frequency and Time-Scale Analysis, 1996., Proceedings of the IEEE-SP International Symposium on, pp.389-392, 18-21 June 1996.
12. Sowelam,S.M., Tewfik,A.H.: Waveform selection in radar target classification. IEEE Transactions on information theory, v.46, no.3, pp.1014-1029, May 2000.
13. Siebert,W.McC.: A radar detection philosophy. IEEE Transactions on Information Theory, v.2, Issue.3, pp.204-221, Sep 1956.
14. Blahut,R.E., Wilcox,C.H., Miller,W.: The synthesis problem for radar ambiguity functions. Springer-Verlag, Mathematics subject classifications: 78A45,22E70,43A80,pp.229-260,1991.
15. Lerner,R.M..: communication and radar, Section-B:radar waveform selection", IEEE Transactions on Information Theory, Oct 1963.
16. Auslander,L., Tolimeri,R.: Characterizing the radar ambiguity functions. IEEE Transactions on Information Theory, v.30,no.6, pp.832-836, Nov. 1984.
17. Lush,D.C., Hudson,D.A.: Ambiguity function analysis of wideband radars. Radar Conference, 1991., Proceedings of the 1991 IEEE National, pp.16-20, 12-13 March 1991.
18. Odendaal,J.W.: 2-D Radar Imaging,, Communications and Signal Processing, 1994. COMSIG-94. Proceedings of the 1994 IEEE South African Symposium on, pp.146-151, 4 Oct. 1994.
19. Prickett,M.J.: Principles of inverse synthetic aperture radar(ISAR) imaging. IEEE EASCON, pp.340-344,1980.
20. Ausherman,D.A., Kozma,A., Walker,J., Jones,H.M., Poggio,E.C.: Developments in radar imaging. IEEE Transactions on Aerospace and Electronic Systems, v.20, no.4, pp.363-400, 1984.

# A Neural Network for Nonuniformity and Ghosting Correction of Infrared Image Sequences*

Sergio N. Torres, Cesar San Martin, Daniel G. Sbarbaro, and Jorge E. Pezoa

Department of Electrical Engineering, University of Concepción,
Casilla 160-C, Concepción, Chile
sertorre@udec.cl
http://nuc.die.udec.cl

**Abstract.** In this paper, an adaptive scene-based nonuniformity and ghosting artifacts correction algorithm for infrared image sequences is presented. The method simultaneously estimates detector parameters and carry out the non-uniformity and ghosting artifacts correction based on the retina-like neural network approach. The method incorporates the use of a new adaptive learning rate rule into the estimation of the gain and the offset of each detector. This learning rule, together with the consideration of the dependence of the detector's parameters on the retinomorphic assumption used for parameter estimation, may sustain an efficient method that could not only increase the original method's ability for estimating the non-uniformity noise, but also increase the capability of mitigating ghosting artifacts. The ability of the method to compensate for nonuniformity and reducing ghosting artifacts is demonstrated by employing several infrared video sequences obtained using two infrared cameras.

**Keywords:** Image Sequence Processing, Infrared Focal Plane Arrays, Neural Network.

**Topic:** Vision and Image Processing, Signal Processing.

## 1 Introduction

Infrared (IR) imaging systems employ an IR sensor to digitize the information, and due to its high performance, the most used integrated technology in IR sensors is the Focal Plane Array (FPA). An IR-FPA is a die composed of a group of photodetectors placed in a focal plane forming a matrix of $X \times Y$ pixels, which gives the sensor the ability to collect the IR information.

---

* This work was partially supported by Grant Milenio ICM P02-049. The authors wish to thank Ernest E. Armstrong (OptiMetrics Inc., USA) and Pierre Potet (CEDIP Infrared Systems, France) for collecting the data, and the United States Air Force Research Laboratory, Ohio, USA.

It is well known that nonuniformity noise in IR imaging sensors, which is due to pixel-to-pixel variation in the detectors' responses, can considerably degrade the quality of IR images since it results in a fixed-pattern-noise (FPN) that is superimposed on the true image. Even more, what makes matter worse is that the nonuniformity slowly varies over time, and depending on the technology used, this drift can take from minutes to hours. In order to solve this problem, several scene-based nonuniformity correction (NUC) techniques have been developed [1,2]. Scene-based techniques perform the NUC using only the video sequences that are being imaged, not requiring any kind of laboratory calibration technique.

Recently our group has been given special attention to the NUC method based in a retina-like neural network approach developed by Scribner et al [3,4]. We developed an enhanced version of his NUC, which relies on the use of an adaptive learning rate schedule in the parameters estimation update process [5,6]. This adaptive learning rate is chosen to be dependent on the spatial content of the readout data, constraining thus the speed of the learning process for each detector on the IR-FPA independently. Nonetheless, in despite of the new degree of adaptiveness added to the Scribner's method, it still generates ghosting artifacts in cases such as when the infrared camera is recording objets that are not moving with respect to the camera and then they suddenly leave the field of view.

Therefore, seeking for more effectiveness in the reduction of ghosting artifacts, and also exploiting even further the exceptional potential of the original Scribner's method, in this paper, an extension of our previously developed scene-based NUC method based in Scribner's work is presented. Specifically, we include the use of a new adaptive learning rate rule into the estimation of the gain and the offset of each detector. This new learning rate is chosen to be dependent on the spatial variation of the read-out data of one frame, and on the temporal motion between consecutive frames. In this way, faster adaptation is mainly allowed for such detectors not only where the input data fits the hypothesis assumed by the retinomorphic model, but also following temporal variations in the operation point of each detector. Moreover, the estimation of each neuron's parameter is improved with the consideration in the error function of the dependence of the retinomorphic assumption on the updated detector's parameters. The foregoing could not only increase the method's scene-based ability for estimating the non-uniformity parameters, but also increase the capability of mitigating ghosting artifacts.

This paper is organized as follows. In Section 2 the new NUC method based on Scribner's work is presented. In Section 3 the NUC technique is tested with video sequences of real raw IR data. In Section 4 the conclusions of the paper are summarized.

## 2 The NUC Algorithm for Infrared Video Sequences

The aim of this paper is the development of a novel adaptive scene-based NUC method for reducing the FPN and the ghosting artifacts in a fast and reliable frame by frame basis. Formerly, we review the fundamental concepts of an avenue introduced by Scribner et al. [3,4], briefly showing his retina-like neural net for NUC, and then, we present our proposed innovations.

### 2.1 Scribner's Neural Network for NUC

First, we assume that each infrared detector is characterized by a linear model. Then, for the $(ij)^{\text{th}}$ detector in IR-FPA, the measured readout signal $Y_{ij}$ at a given time $n$ can be expressed as:

$$Y_{ij}(n) = g_{ij}(n) \cdot X_{ij}(n) + o_{ij}(n) \qquad (1)$$

where $g_{ij}(n)$ and $o_{ij}(n)$ are the gain and the offset of the $ij^{\text{th}}$ detector, and $X_{ij}(n)$ is the real incident infrared photon flux collected by the respective detector. As proposed by Scribner, equation (1) is reordered as follows:

$$X_{ij}(n) = w_{ij}(n) \cdot Y_{ij}(n) + b_{ij}(n) \qquad (2)$$

where the new parameters $w_{ij}(n)$ and $b_{ij}(n)$ are related to the real gain and offset parameters of each detector as follows:

$$w_{ij}(n) = \frac{1}{g_{ij}(n)} \qquad b_{ij}(n) = -\frac{o_{ij}(n)}{g_{ij}(n)} \qquad (3)$$

The expression presented in equation (2) is the responsible of performing the non-uniformity correction on the readout data. Then, for each $ij^{\text{th}}$ detector, the NUC model (2) can be considered as the simplest neural network structure, which consists of a single linear neuron node, with an estimate weight ($\hat{w}_{ij}(n)$) and an estimate bias ($\hat{b}_{ij}(n)$). Thus, the readout data $Y_{ij}(n)$ is the input to the $ij^{\text{th}}$ neuron, and its output $\hat{X}_{ij}(n)$ is the estimation obtained for the real infrared data. The entire array of single-input/single-output linear neurons constitutes the base for Scribner's adaptive NUC method. For a complete version of Scribner's NUC method and our previously published enhancements of such method see [3,4] and [5,6] respectively.

### 2.2 NUC Method with Ghosting Reduction Capabilities

This neural network approach allows the use of linear regression techniques to perform the estimation of each neuron parameters. The needed error function $E_{ij}(n)$ to accomplish this estimation task is defined as the difference between a desired target value $T_{ij}(n)$ and the estimated infrared data $\hat{X}_{ij}(n)$. Using an analogy with biological retina-like processes, the target value proposed by Scribner for estimating the unknown parameters can be assumed as the local spatial average (mean filter) of the output data $\hat{X}_{ij}(n)$. This assumption is based on the retinomorphic hypothesis, which states that there is a high probability for one detector, and its closest neighbors, of being illuminated by the same infrared irradiance. Therefore, the error function is finally given by:

$$E_{ij}(n) = T_{ij}(n) - \hat{X}_{ij}(n), \qquad (4)$$

where the desired target value $T_{ij}(n)$ is calculated as:

$$T_{ij}(n) = \frac{1}{(2v+1)^2} \sum_{k=i-v}^{i+v} \sum_{l=j-v}^{j+v} \hat{X}_{kl}(n), \qquad (5)$$

where $2v+1$ is the kernel neighborhood, or averaging window size.

In this paper, this is the starting point for the development of our proposed enhancements to Scribner and to our previous work. First of all, we consider that the target $T_{ij}(n)$ in the functional $J_{ij}$ depends of each detector parameter involved in the retinomorphic model, but these parameters are spatially independent. Then, its partial derivatives (gradients) relatives to the desired parameters to be estimated are expressed as follows:

$$J_{ij} = \sum_n E_{ij}(n)^2 = \sum_n (T_{ij}(n) - \hat{X}_{ij}(n))^2 \qquad (6)$$

$$\frac{\partial J_{ij}}{\partial \hat{w}_{ij}} = -\frac{8v(v+1)}{(2v+1)^2} \cdot E_{ij} \cdot Y_{ij} \qquad (7)$$
$$\frac{\partial J_{ij}}{\partial \hat{b}_{ij}} = -\frac{8v(v+1)}{(2v+1)^2} \cdot E_{ij}$$

the functional $J$ is minimized only when its both gradients in (7) are equal to zero. Even that this new functional is more accurate than the Scribner's one, we do not expect major improvements since the difference between both functionals is in the factor $\frac{8v(v+1)}{(2v+1)^2}$, which is approximate equal to the constant factor of 2 derived by Scribner in his pioneering work.

We now update the steepest descent algorithm to solve this Least Mean Square (LMS) optimization problem. In this gradient-based search algorithm, the parameters to be estimated are recursively and smoothly updated with a portion of each respective error gradient as follows:

$$\hat{w}_{ij}(n+1) = \hat{w}_{ij}(n) - \eta_{ij}(n) \cdot \frac{8v(v+1)}{(2v+1)^2} \cdot E_{ij}(n) \cdot Y_{ij}(n) \qquad (8)$$
$$\hat{b}_{ij}(n+1) = \hat{b}_{ij}(n) - \eta_{ij}(n) \cdot \frac{8v(v+1)}{(2v+1)^2} \cdot E_{ij}(n)$$

where $\eta_{ij}(n)$ is an adaptive learning rate rule. In our previous work, we proposed the use of an adaptive learning rate $\eta_{ij}(n)$, which depends on the local spatial standard deviation of the input image $\sigma_{Y_{ij}}(n)$, and it was defined as follows:

$$\eta_{ij}(n) = k_{alr} \cdot \frac{1}{1 + \sigma_{Y_{ij}}(n)} \qquad (9)$$

where $k_{alr}$ is a constant that fix the maximum allowable value for $\eta_{ij}(n)$. Therefore, if a given piece of the input image (a pixel and its neighbors) is smooth enough, then the desired averaged target value at the output is more confident, and the learning rate can get larger values. On the other hand, if the local input standard deviation in the surroundings of a certain pixel is too high, like in an object border, the learning rate get smaller values. The local standard deviation $\sigma_{Y_{ij}}(n)$ can be calculated with any desired window size, hopefully according to the window size already used to calculate the local average for the desired output.

We propose to introduce in the foregoing learning rate rule the ability of reducing ghosting artifacts. We know that ghosting is generated when a target that have being imaged for some time, suddenly leaves the field of view of the camera. In other words, the operation point of the detectors imaging such target have suddenly changed. Therefore, the adaptive learning rate rule should start learning faster globally or at least for such detectors. Thus, the adaptive learning rule designed for each neuron is expressed as follow:

$$\eta_{ij}(n) = \frac{k_{alr}}{1 + \sigma_{Y_{ij}}(n)} \times \Delta Y$$

$$\Delta Y = |p| + |q|$$

$$C_{pq}(n) = real\,\{\text{IFT}\,[\text{FT}\,(Y\,(n)) \cdot H^*\,(n)]\}$$

$$H(n) = \frac{\text{FT}\,(Y\,(n-1))}{|\text{FT}\,(Y\,(n-1))|^2}$$

where $C_{pq}(n)$ is the correlation between the frame $Y(n)$ and the frame $Y(n-1)$. FT and IFT indicate Fourier transform and inverse Fourier transform respectively. $H(n)$ is a classical adaptive correlation filter [7]. $\Delta Y$ is a global factor, which is proportional to the level of motion between the frames $n$ and $n-1$, evaluated as the distant in pixels between $(p,q) = (0,0)$(Center of $C_{pq}(n)$) and $(p,q)$ of the origin and the peak of the correlation matrix $C_{pq}(n)$ respectively. Thus, with this enhancement the learning rate $\eta_{ij}$ will not update the parameters if $\Delta Y = 0$ since there is not motion between frames $n$ and $n-1$ and will update the parameters as faster as the motion between consecutive frames required (magnitude of $\Delta Y$) eliminating ghosting artifacts by adapting the parameters to the new operation points of the detectors.

The overall fast adaptive NUC scheme is presented in figure 1, where the input image is the readout data $Y_{ij}(n)$, which enters to the adaptive NUC neural net model (represented by an array of linear neurons) that calculates the corrected image version $\hat{X}_{ij}(n)$. The local spatial average function (*Neighborhood Operation 1*) is applied to the estimated corrected image $\hat{X}_{ij}(n)$, generating thus the target $T_{ij}(n)$ in order to calculate the *Error* function $E_{ij}(n)$. The error is then feed-backed in the steepest descent *Parameters Update Algorithm*, where the adaptive learning rate $\eta_{ij}(n)$ finally uses the local spatial variance (*Neighborhood Operation 2*) of the input image and the estimation of the motion between consecutive frames for ghosting reduction.

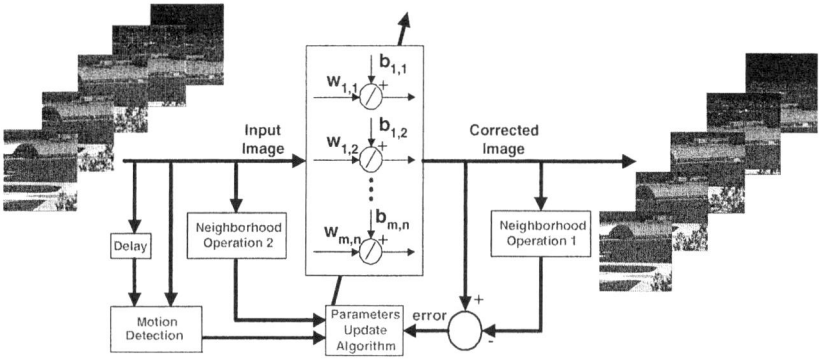

**Fig. 1.** Scheme of the proposed Scene-Based Non-Uniformity Correction Method

## 3 Performance Evaluation with Real Infrared Image Sequences

The main goal of this section is to test the ability of the proposed learning rate rule to mitigate ghosting artifacts generates by using Scribner's scene-based NUC method or our enhancement to his method. The algorithm is tested with two real infrared image sequences. The first sequence has been collected using a $128 \times 128$ InSb FPA cooled camera (Amber Model AE-4128) operating in the $3-5\mu m$ range. As an example, figure 2(a) shows from left to right a raw frame, the corresponding corrected frame by our previously published enhance version of Scribner's NUC method, and the corresponding corrected frame by the NUC method proposed in this paper. It can be seen using only the naked eye, that the ghosting artifact (the gate of the hangar) generates by the motion of the camera is only eliminated in the frame corrected by the proposed NUC method. The NUC performance is evaluated employing the index root mean square error (RMSE) computed between the reference (the real IR sequence calibrated with black bodies) and the corrected IR video sequence. Figure 3 shows the calculated RMSE for each frame corrected using our previous upgrade to Scribner's NUC method and using the proposed method. Further, the average RMSEs computed for the whole infrared sequence are equal to 79.75 and 78.61 for the sequence corrected by our previously published enhance version of Scribner's NUC method and for the sequence corrected by the proposed NUC method, respectively. Note that, we have reached an improvement of only 1.5% since a window size of $v = 3$ is used generating a factor $\frac{8v(v+1)}{(2v+1)^2} = 1.95$, which is approximate equal to the constant factor of 2 derived by Scribner in his work. Further, it can be seen in figure 2(a) using only the naked eye that the non-uniformity is notably reduced by both NUC methods.

The second sequence of infrared data has been recorded using a $320 \times 240$ HgCdTe FPA cooled camera (CEDIP Jade Model) operating in the $8-12\mu m$ range. As an example, figure 2(b)(c) shows from the left to right a raw frame, the corresponding corrected frame by our previously published enhance version

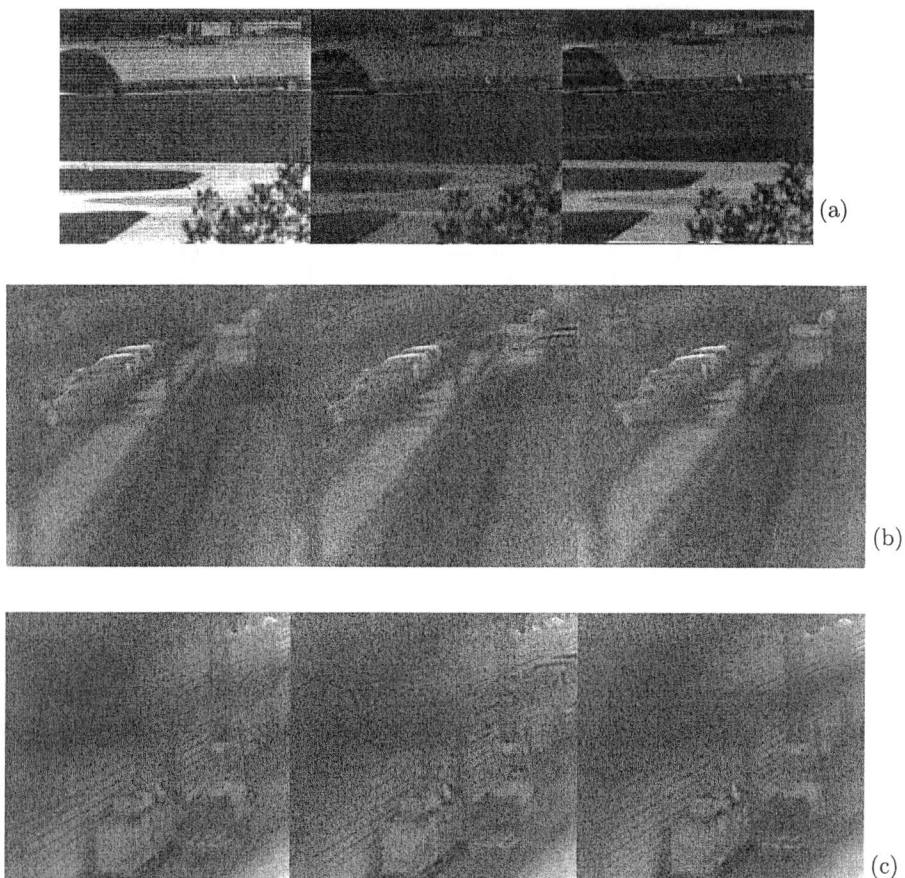

**Fig. 2.** Performance of the NUC methods under real IR data. (a)(b)(c) The $1611-th$ $(1134-th)$ $(1340-th)$ frames of the first (second)(second) set of IR data, at the left the raw frames, at the center the corresponding frames corrected by our previous enhancement to Scribner's NUC method and at the right are the frames corrected by proposed method.

of Scribner's NUC method, and the corresponding corrected frame by the NUC method proposed in this paper. Again, it can be seen by only using the naked eye, that the non-uniformity presented in the raw frame has been notably reduced by both NUC methods. Also, the ghosting artifact(see the ghost vehicle and the ghost boxes) generates by the motion of the camera is only eliminated in the frame corrected by the NUC method proposed in this paper. Thus, we have shown experimentally with real IR data that the proposed scene-based NUC method has the ability of notably reduces the ghosting artifacts and the non-uniformity noise presented in IR-FPA sensors.

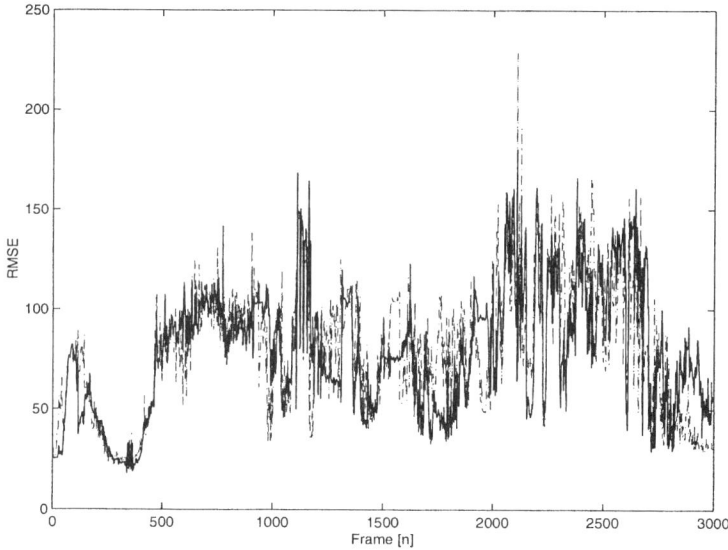

**Fig. 3.** The evolution of the RMSE between the reference (set 1 calibrated with black bodies) and the corrected frames of IR data set 1. Dashdot line represents the RMSE computed for our previous upgrade to Scribner's NUC method, and solid line represents the RMSE computed for proposed NUC method.

## 4 Conclusions

In this paper an enhanced version of our previously developed upgrade to Scribner's NUC method is proposed. The new method has the ability of not only reducing the FPN, but also eliminating ghosting artifacts efficiently. It was shown, using real IR data that the method is able to adapt the estimation of the nonuniformity parameters to abrupt changes in the scene, reducing therefore the ghosting artifacts efficiently.

## References

1. Torres, S., Hayat, M.: Kalman Filtering for Adaptive Nonuniformity Correction in Infrared Focal Plane Arrays. The JOSA-A Opt. Soc. of America. **20**. (2003) 470–480.
2. Torres, S., Pezoa, J., Hayat, M.: Scene-based Nonuniformity Correction for Focal Plane Arrays Using the Method of the Inverse Covariance Form. OSA App. Opt. Inf. Proc. **42**. (2003) 5872–5881.
3. Scribner, D., Sarkady, K., Kruer, M.: Adaptive Nonuniformity Correction for Infrared Focal Plane Arrays using Neural Networks. Proceeding of SPIE. **1541**. (1991) 100–109.
4. Scribner, D., Sarkady, K., Kruer, M.: Adaptive Retina-like Preprocessing for Imaging Detector Arrays. Proceeding of the IEEE International Conference on Neural Networks. **3**. (1993) 1955–1960.

5. Torres, S., Vera, E., Reeves, R., Sobarzo, S.: Adaptive Scene-Based Nonuniformity Correction Method for Infrared Focal Plane Arrays. Proceeding of SPIE. **5076**. (2003) 130–139.
6. Vera, E., Torres, S.: Fast Adaptive Nonuniformity Correction for Infrared Focal Plane Arrays. To be published in EURASIP Journal on Applied Signal Processing. (2005).
7. Vijaya Kumar, B. V. K.:Tutorial survey of composite filter designs for optical correlators. Appl. Opt. **31**. (1992) 4774–4801 .

# Real-Time Image Processing Using Graphics Hardware: A Performance Study

Minglun Gong[1], Aaron Langille[1], and Mingwei Gong[2]

[1] Department of Math and Computer Science, Laurentian University,
Ramsey Lake Road, Sudbury, Ontario, Canada
{gong, aaron}@cs.laurentian.ca
[2] Department of Computer Science, University of Calgary,
2500 University Dr. NW, Calgary, Alberta, Canada
gongm@cpsc.ucalgary.ca

**Abstract.** Programmable graphics hardware have proven to be a powerful resource for general computing. Previous research has shown that using a GPU for local image processing operations can be much faster than using a CPU. The actual speedup obtained is influenced by many factors. In this paper, we quantify the performance gain that can be achieved by using the GPU for different image processing operations under different conditions. We also compare the strengths and weaknesses of two of the current leaders in mainstream GPUs – ATI's Radeon and nVidia's GeForce FX. Many interesting observations are obtained through the evaluation.

## 1 Introduction

Real-time image processing has many applications in areas such as robot navigation and object tracking. In order to achieve real-time performance many custom designed SIMD systems, which tend to be costly, have been used in previous research [2].

As programmable graphics hardware increases in power and decreases in price, it is becoming a more viable option for both simple and complex image processing operations. While it is still challenging to implement some iterative algorithms for a current Graphics Processing Unit (GPU), many image processing operations are well suited for moving from the CPU to the GPU [1, 4-6, 8, 9]. Since local image processing operations can be performed on GPUs in a moderately parallel manner, considerable performance increase can be achieved over their CPU counterparts.

The total speedup obtained is influenced by many factors including the type of image processing operation and the shading language used to implement the operation. The objective of our research is to quantify the performance gain that can be achieved for different image processing operations under different conditions. The experimental results show that, for the twelve operations tested, a current GPU is on average six times faster than the reference CPU.

We also compare the strengths and weaknesses of two of the current leaders in mainstream GPUs – ATI's Radeon and nVidia's GeForce FX. While the game performance and rendering abilities of both of these product lines are well studied, very little research has been published that highlight their performance in the area of image processing. Based on a variety image processing operations, this paper provides a head-to-head comparison between the two. The results suggest that the ATI GPU gives a better overall performance.

### 1.1 Related Work

A modern GPU can be considered a streaming processor, which consists of two pipelines: the vertex pipeline and the fragment pipeline. In most 3D graphics applications, the vertex pipeline is used to calculate the transformation and lighting of each vertex and the fragment pipeline is used for calculating the shading of each rasterized pixel.

Even though they are primarily designed for 3D graphics applications, GPUs have shown to be useful for image-related applications such as fast Fourier transformation (FFT) [6], image segmentation [9], stereo matching [8], and motion estimation [5]. Using GPUs for these applications typically involves the following steps: (1) load the input images to the video memory and bind them to texture sampling units; (2) load the algorithm into the fragment processor as a pixel shader (also referred as fragment program); (3) set either the screen of a pixel buffer as the rendering target; and (4) execute the shader by rendering a image-sized rectangle.

Some recent research [1, 7] has tried to evaluate the performance of programmable graphics hardware on image processing operations. In their paper [1], Colantoni et al. compare an nVidia GeForce FX card with reference AMD and Intel CPUs on five different image processing operations. They report that the average speedup of the GPU over CPU is around ten. Our evaluation results confirm Colantoni et al.'s findings even though a different set of operations are used. However, we also found that the speedup is much lower if we compare the performance of the GPU with an optimized CPU implementation that utilizes the Multi-Media Extension (MMX) instructions.

Sugita et al. compare an ATI Radeon 9700 Pro card with Intel Pentium 4 3GHz CPU [7] on several image filtering operations, as well as a stereo matching application. Their results show that, compared to the MMX-optimized CPU implementation, the GPU implementation can achieve a speedup of three to six times on image filtering operations, and about twice on the stereo matching application.

Unlike these two papers, our research evaluates both ATI and nVidia GPUs, which makes it possible to provide a head on comparison between the two. Twelve different image processing operations have been carefully chosen. Some operations involve complex arithmetic calculations, such as image gradient magnitude calculation, while others involve comparison calculations, such as 3×3 median filtering. In addition, we also compare the two GPUs under both Direct3D and OpenGL APIs.

## 2 Performance Evaluation on Image Processing Operations

### 2.1 Image Processing Operations Selected

In order to compare the performance of the GPUs with the reference CPU on different image processing tasks, a variety of operations are selected for testing. These operations can be roughly classified into the following three categories.

**Arithmetic Operations:** For operations in this category, the output intensity $I'_{x,y}$ of pixel $(x,y)$ depends solely on the input intensity $I_{x,y}$ of the same pixel. As a result, these operations mainly test the processor's speed on arithmetic calculations. The functions involved for the different operations are listed below:

- Negative: $I'_{x,y} = 1 - I_{x,y}$
- Increase brightness: $I'_{x,y} = I_{x,y} + 0.2$
- Increase contrast: $I'_{x,y} = I_{x,y} \times 1.5$
- RGB to XYZ space: $I'_{x,y} = \begin{bmatrix} 0.412 & 0.358 & 0.180 \\ 0.213 & 0.715 & 0.072 \\ 0.019 & 0.119 & 0.950 \end{bmatrix} \cdot I_{x,y}$

**Image Convolutions:** Operations in this category calculate the linear combination of the intensities of neighboring pixels. Hence, the performance on these operations reflects how fast the processor is able to access the neighboring pixels.

- Laplacian filter: $I'_{x,y} = 4I_{x,y} - I_{x-1,y} - I_{x+1,y} - I_{x,y-1} - I_{x,y+1}$
- 3×3 mean filter: $I'_{x,y} = \frac{1}{9} \sum_{u=-1}^{1} \sum_{v=-1}^{1} I_{x+u,y+v}$
- 3×3 Gaussian filter: $I'_{x,y} = \frac{1}{16} \begin{pmatrix} 4I_{x,y} + 2(I_{x-1,y} + I_{x+1,y} + I_{x,y-1} + I_{x,y+1}) \\ + I_{x-1,y-1} + I_{x+1,y-1} + I_{x-1,y+1} + I_{x+1,y+1} \end{pmatrix}$
- Gradient magnitude: $I'_{x,y} = \sqrt{\begin{pmatrix} 2I_{x+1,y} - 2I_{x-1,y} \\ + I_{x+1,y-1} - I_{x-1,y-1} \\ + I_{x+1,y+1} - I_{x-1,y+1} \end{pmatrix}^2 + \begin{pmatrix} 2I_{x,y+1} - 2I_{x,y-1} \\ + I_{x-1,y+1} - I_{x-1,y-1} \\ + I_{x+1,y+1} - I_{x+1,y-1} \end{pmatrix}^2}$

**Comparison-Based Operations:** Different from previous operations, the operations in this category involve comparisons. Hence these operations evaluate how fast the branching calculations can be handled.

- Thresholding: $I'_{x,y} = \begin{cases} 0 & I_{x,y} < 0.5 \\ 1 & I_{x,y} \geq 0.5 \end{cases}$
- Dilation: $I'_{x,y} = \max \begin{pmatrix} I_{x,y}, I_{x-1,y}, I_{x+1,y}, I_{x,y-1}, I_{x,y+1}, \\ I_{x-1,y-1}, I_{x+1,y-1}, I_{x-1,y+1}, I_{x+1,y+1} \end{pmatrix}$
- Erosion: $I'_{x,y} = \min \begin{pmatrix} I_{x,y}, I_{x-1,y}, I_{x+1,y}, I_{x,y-1}, I_{x,y+1}, \\ I_{x-1,y-1}, I_{x+1,y-1}, I_{x-1,y+1}, I_{x+1,y+1} \end{pmatrix}$
- Median filter: $I'_{x,y} = \text{median} \begin{pmatrix} I_{x,y}, I_{x-1,y}, I_{x+1,y}, I_{x,y-1}, I_{x,y+1}, \\ I_{x-1,y-1}, I_{x+1,y-1}, I_{x-1,y+1}, I_{x+1,y+1} \end{pmatrix}$

## 2.2 The Implementations on CPU and GPU

Two different approaches are used to implement the above operations for the reference Intel CPU. The first approach uses a straightforward C++ implementation, compiled using Microsoft Visual C++ .Net. Reasonable efforts have been put in to optimize the performance of this implementation. However, attempts were not made to optimize at the assembly level.

The second approach makes use of Intel's Image Processing Library (IPL), which provides optimized image processing functions that take advantage of the MMX technology. We are able to find functions in the IPL for most of the operations listed above. For example, the Negative operation is implemented using the iplSubtractS function, which subtracts the intensity from a constant, and the Mean operation is implemented using the iplBlur function, which calculates the average intensity of nearby pixels. However, at the time of testing, we were unable to find any existing function in IPL that is optimized specifically for calculating the gradient magnitude of an image. As a result, the more general function iplConvolve2D is used to convolve the input image with two Sobel kernels and then combine the results by calculating the square root of the square sum.

As mentioned earlier, to execute an image processing operation on GPU we need to implement the operation using a pixel shader and load the shader into the fragment processor. Writing a shader in the native assembly-like shading language tends to be confusing for programmers lacking experience in other assembly languages. It also had the disadvantage that the shader needs to be rewritten if and when we want to take advantage of more complex instructions provided by newer graphics hardware. To address these problems, several high level shading languages have been developed. The shaders written in high level shading languages can be compiled into the shader assembly code according to the hardware profile specified. Which hardware profiles can be used depends on the support provided by the chosen hardware and also depends on which 3D API (OpenGL or Direct3D) is chosen for programming.

To evaluate the performance of the GPUs under different shading languages and profile settings, we implemented the previously described image processing operations using three widely used high level languages: Microsoft's High Level Shading Language (HLSL), nVidia's Cg, and OpenGL's OpenGL Shading Language (GLSL). Since HLSL and Cg are based on a common language that was co-developed by Microsoft and nVidia, our implementations for HLSL and Cg actually share the same code. The syntax for GLSL is different from that of HLSL and Cg. However, we are able to find similar functions to translate between the two. As a result, all three implementations are comparable in terms of efficiency.

Great effort was made to ensure the shaders were correct and efficient. The correctness is verified by comparing the images generated by the shaders with those generated by the corresponding functions in Intel's IPL. Wherever possible, different variations for a shader were implemented and the one that producing the fewest instructions in the compiled assembly was chosen (Table 1 shows the number of instructions used for different operations). However, two constraints were placed on our implementation: (1) use only one rendering pass even though some operations are separable and can be more efficiently implemented using two rendering passes, and (2) no bilinear texture sampling is used although it can reduce the number of instructions needed for some operations [3]. These two constraints help to minimize the overhead for setting up the rendering process and to focus on comparing the performance of the fragment processors of the GPUs with the reference CPU.

**Table 1.** The number of texture and arithmetic instructions used for different operations when the HLSL code is compiled using the pixel shader 2.0 profile

| Arithmetic Ops. | Instructions | | Convo-lutions | Instructions | | Comparison Ops. | Instructions | |
|---|---|---|---|---|---|---|---|---|
| | Tex. | Arith. | | Tex. | Arith. | | Tex. | Arith. |
| Negative | 1 | 2 | Laplacian | 5 | 9 | Thresholding | 1 | 3 |
| Brightness | 1 | 2 | Mean | 9 | 18 | Dilation | 9 | 17 |
| Contrast | 1 | 2 | Gaussian | 9 | 19 | Erosion | 9 | 17 |
| RGB2XYZ | 1 | 5 | Gradient | 8 | 30 | Median | 9 | 59 |

**Table 2.** Speed differences between the two graphics cards

| Feature | ATI Radeon 9800 XT | nVidia GeForce FX 5950 Ultra |
|---|---|---|
| GPU Clock Speed | 412 MHz | 450 MHz |
| Video Memory Speed | 730 MHz | 850 MHz |

### 2.3 Test Conditions

Two different GPUs are evaluated: The first is ATI's Radeon 9800 XT (released on September 30, 2003) and the second is nVidia's GeForce FX 5950 Ultra (released on October 23, 2003). Both graphics card have 256MB DDR RAM, were considered to be the top of their respective product line and occupied the same high-end home and small business desktop market niche at the time of their purchase. While these two video cards are considered to be in the same class, there are some key differences that should be noted (see Table 2).

In terms of hardware profiles, both cards support pixel shader 2.0 (PS2.0) under the Direct3D API and fragment program 1.0 (ARBFP1) under the OpenGL API. In addition, the GeForce 5950 also supports a vendor-specific profile named FP30 under the OpenGL API. Since both HLSL and GLSL code can only be compiled into their own APIs while Cg code can be compiled into both APIs, this gives a total of four unique language and profile combinations for the Radeon 9800 (HLSL/PS2.0, Cg/PS2.0, GLSL/ARBFP1, and Cg/ARBFP1) and five combinations for the GeForce 5950 (with an additional Cg/FP30).

The two graphics cards are installed on two identical PCs: IBM ThinkCenter M50 (model 8189-T7U). Some of the key system specifications include: Intel 3GHz Pentium 4 processor with 1 MB cache and hyper threading enabled, 512MB PC2700 DDR RAM, 800MHz Front Side Bus, and 1 AGP slot operating at AGP 8X.

For the GPU testing, in order to maximize both performance and shader language compatibility, the appropriate vendor drivers were installed[1]. Beyond the vendor drivers the software on the test system consisted of Microsoft Windows XP (Service Pack 2), Norton AntiVirus, Microsoft .Net Developer Studio, nVidia's Cg Toolkit, the OpenGL Utility Toolkit (GLUT) for Windows and the Intel IPP libraries.

---

[1] nVidia's driver (ForceWare 66.93 build 6.14.10.6693) is obtained from www.nVidia.com, and ATI's driver (Catalyst 5.1 build 6.14.10.6505) is obtained from www.ati.com

Our objective is to measure the time needed for different image processing operations on different processors. Unfortunately, directly measuring the processing time is limited by the accuracy of the system clock. Instead, the application we developed repetitively performs an image processing operation on an image and measures the frame rate. The application waits one minute for the frame rate to be stabilize, and saves the result to a text file before exiting.

## 3 Evaluation Results

### 3.1 CPU vs. GPU

Now we start to present the evaluation results. The first test compares the performance of both the nVidia GeForce 5950 and ATI Radeon 9800 with the Intel Pentium 4 on the image processing operations previously discussed. In this test, the image size is fixed at 512×512, and the shading language and profile for the GPU is set to HLSL/PS2.0.

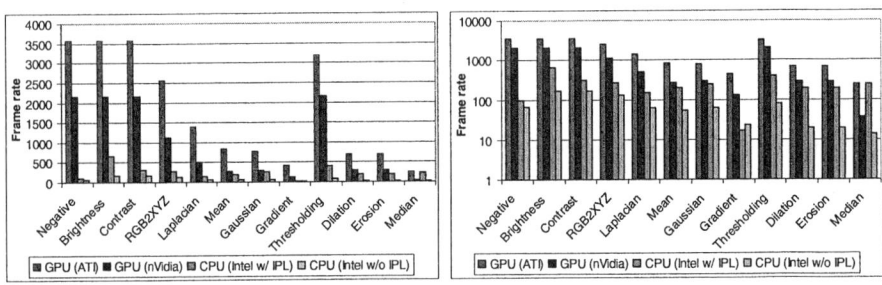

**Fig. 1.** Performance comparison among GPUs and the reference CPU, shown in both linear and log scales

The frame rates measured for different implementations are shown in Fig. 1. In order to illustrate the performance differences for both simple and complex operations, the frame rates are shown in both linear and log scales. The following observations can be made from the figure:
- Both GPUs outperform the Pentium 4 on all operations except Median. The relatively poor performance of the GPUs on the Median operation is likely caused by the lack of truth branching functionality.
- Between the two implementations for the Intel CPU, the one utilizing IPL is generally faster. However, since there is no function in IPL that is optimized for gradient magnitude calculation, the implementation for Gradient using IPL is actually slower than the straightforward C++ implementation.
- The time needed for Negative, Brightness, and Contrast operations is the same on each respective GPU, but this is not the case on Pentium 4. This suggests that the addition, subtraction, and multiplication operations require same number of clock cycles on the two GPUs, but different cycles on Pentium 4.

- As expected, the time needed for Dilation and Erosion operations is the same on all processors.
- Considering its simplicity, the Negative operation requires a surprising amount of time on Pentium 4, even though the optimized function, iplSubtractS, has been used in the implementation with IPL.

The speedup of the two types of GPUs over Pentium 4 is shown in Table 3. Two observations are worth noting here. Firstly the speedup for the Negative and the Gradient operations are somewhat inflated due to the uncharacteristically poor performance of the CPU on these operations. Secondly, for the Median operation, the Radeon 9800 is as fast as the Pentium 4, but the GeForce 5950 is actually about 6.5 times slower than the CPU.

Generally speaking, the speedup is quite effective for both GPUs, and the Radeon 9800 is the better performer between the two. Taking all twelve operations into account, the Radeon 9800 achieves an (geometric) average speedup of 6.61 while the GeForce 5950 achieves 2.70. In addition, comparison among the speedups for different types of operations indicates that using GPUs gives larger performance gains on simple arithmetic operations, but the benefit is relatively small for operations involving complex comparisons.

**Table 3.** The speed up of two types of GPUs over 3GHz Pentium 4. The comparison is based on the implementation that uses IPL since it produces better overall performance.

| Arithmetic Ops. | Speedup ATI | Speedup NV | Convolution Ops. | Speedup ATI | Speedup NV | Comparison Ops. | Speedup ATI | Speedup NV |
|---|---|---|---|---|---|---|---|---|
| Negative | 35.84 | 21.52 | Laplacian | 9.16 | 3.35 | Thresholding | 7.93 | 5.33 |
| Brightness | 5.55 | 3.33 | Mean | 4.21 | 1.39 | Dilation | 3.57 | 1.48 |
| Contrast | 11.30 | 6.79 | Gaussian | 3.15 | 1.18 | Erosion | 3.57 | 1.48 |
| RGB2XYZ | 9.38 | 4.09 | Gradient | 25.79 | 7.70 | Median | 1.03 | 0.15 |
| Geo. Mean | 12.05 | 6.68 | Geo. Mean | 7.48 | 2.55 | Geo. Mean | 3.20 | 1.15 |

### 3.2 Effects of Shading Languages and Profiles

In the previous subsection, the image processing operations are implemented using HLSL and compiled using the PS2.0 profile. This subsection evaluates the performances of the two GPUs under other shading language and profile settings on 512×512 images. Since Negative, Brightness, and Contrast operations take the exact same time to execute on both GPUs, two of the operations (Brightness and Contrast) are removed from the evaluation to avoid redundancy. Similarly the Erosion operation is also excluded since it takes the same amount of time as Dilation.

As discussed in Section 0, The Radeon 9800 supports four different language/profile combinations, while the GeForce 5950 supports five. To compare these different settings for different operations, the relative frame rate is used as the performance metric. The relative frame rate is defined as the frame rate under a given language/profile setting over the frame rate under the HLSL/PS2.0 setting. As a result, the relative frame rates for HLSL/PS2.0 setting are always 100%.

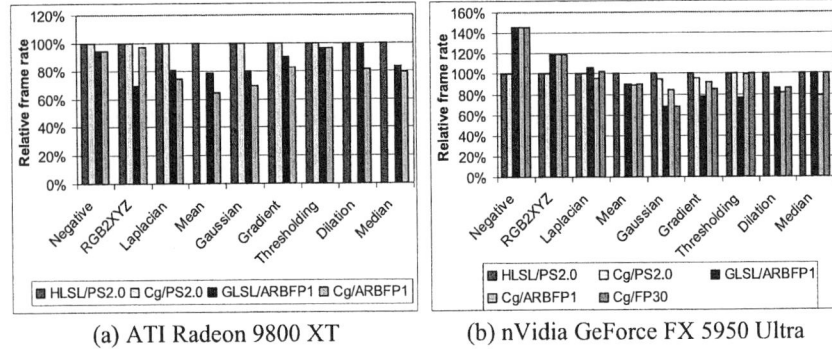

(a) ATI Radeon 9800 XT   (b) nVidia GeForce FX 5950 Ultra

**Fig. 2.** The relative frame rates under different language/profile settings for the two GPUs

The calculated relative frame rates are shown in Fig. 2. Careful readers may notice that some data is missing from the figure. This indicates that certain operations cannot be run under certain language/profile combinations. Our investigation found that these problems are caused by the following reason: When the Mean, Dilation, and Median operations are implemented using the HLSL/Cg standard and compiled into PS2.0 profile using the latest version of Cg compiler (version 1.3, released on Jan 18, 2005), the generated assembly level shader code contains dependent texture operation sequences that are longer than the forth order, which exceeds the limit of the PS2.0 profile. As a result, the code cannot be executed under the Direct3D API, regardless of which GPU is used.

If we put these aberrations aside, the following can be observed from Fig. 2:

- Under the Direct3D API, the two language/profile settings, HLSL/PS2.0 and Cg/PS2.0, have identical performance on the Radeon 9800, and their relative performances on the GeForce 5950 are also very similar.
- Under the OpenGL API, the performance differences among the three language/profile settings, Cg/ARBFP1, Cg/FP30, and GLSL/ARBFP1, are as high as 25% for some operations. However, none of the three settings give the best performance on all operations.
- For Radeon 9800, using the two settings under the Direct3D API gives better performance on all image processing operations than using those under the OpenGL API.
- No language/profile setting is a clear out-performer for the GeForce 5950. Generally speaking, the three settings under the OpenGL API give better performance on Negative and RGB2XYZ operations, while those under the Direct3D API give better performance on Mean, Gaussian, Gradient, and Dilation operations. The two groups tie on Laplacian, Thresholding, and Median operations.

## 4 Conclusions and Future Work

In this paper, we compare two popular mainstream GPUs, the ATI's Radeon 9800 XT and nVidia's GeForce FX 5950 Ultra, with Intel's 3GHz Pentium 4 on different image processing operations. The evaluation results show that, for the twelve operations tested, the Radeon 9800 is on average 6.6 times faster than the MMX-optimized implementation on Pentium 4, while GeForce 5950 is on average 2.7 times faster. We also compare the two GPUs under different shading language and profile settings and obtain many useful observations. For example, we show that the HLSL and PS2.0 is the best choice for programming on Radeon 9800 since the best performance can be achieved under this setting.

Both ATI and nVidia have released their newer generation GPUs: ATI Radeon X850 and nVidia GeForce 6800 Ultra. These GPUs are even more powerful and support the new pixel shader 3.0 profile. The performance of these GPUs on image processing operations will be studied in the future.

## References

1. P. Colantoni, N. Boukala, & J. Da Rugna. Fast and accurate color image processing using 3D graphics cards. *Proc. of International Fall Workshop Vision, Modeling, and Visualization.* 2003.
2. A. Gentile, J. Cruz-Rivera, D. S. Wills, L. Bustelo, J. J. Figueroa, J. E. Fonseca-Camacho, W. E. Lugo-Beauchamp, R. Olivieri, M. Quiñones-Cerpa, A. H. Rivera-Ríos, I. Vargas-Gonzáles, & M. Viera-Vera. Real-Time Image Processing on a Focal Plane SIMD Array. *Proc. of IPPS/SPDP Workshops.* pp. 400-405. 1999.
3. M. J. Harris, G. Coombe, T. Scheuermann, & A. Lastra. Physically-based visual simulation on graphics hardware. *Proc. of SIGGRAPH/Eurographics Workshop on Graphics Hardware.* pp. 109-118. 2002.
4. M. Hopf & T. Ertl. Accelerating morphological analysis with graphics hardware. *Proc. of Workshop on Vision, Modeling, and Visualization.* pp. 337-345. 2000.
5. F. Kelly & A. Kokaram. Graphics hardware for gradient based motion estimation. *Proc. of SPIE Embedded Processors for Multimedia and Communications, v5309.* 2004.
6. K. Moreland & E. Angel. The FFT on a GPU. *Proc. of SIGGRAPH/Eurographics Workshop on Graphics Hardware.* pp. 112-119. 2003.
7. K. Sugita, T. Naemura, & H. Harashima. Performance evaluation of programmable graphics hardware for image filtering and stereo matching. *Proc. of ACM symposium on Virtual reality software and technology.* pp. 176-183. 2003.
8. R. Yang & M. Pollefeys. Multi-resolution real-time stereo on commodity graphics hardware. *Proc. of IEEE Conference on Computer Vision and Pattern Recognition, v1.* pp. 211-220. 2003.
9. R. Yang & G. Welch. Fast image segmentation and smoothing using commodity graphics hardware. *Graphics Tools*, special issue on *Hardware-Accelerated Rendering Techniques*. 2003.

# Real-Time and Robust Background Updating for Video Surveillance and Monitoring

Xingzhi Luo and Suchendra M. Bhandarkar

Department of Computer Science, The University of Georgia,
Athens, Georgia 30602-7404, USA

**Abstract.** Background updating is an important aspect of dynamic scene analysis. Two critical problems: sudden camera perturbation and the *sleeping person* problem, which arise frequently in real-world surveillance and monitoring systems, are addressed in the proposed scheme. The paper presents a multi-color model where multiple color clusters are used to represent the background at each pixel location. In the proposed background updating scheme, the updates to the mean and variance of each color cluster at each pixel location incorporate the most recently observed color values. Each cluster is assigned a weight which measures the time duration and temporal recurrence frequency of the cluster. The *sleeping person* problem is tackled by virtue of the observation that at a given pixel location, the time durations and recurrence frequencies of the color clusters representing temporarily static objects are smaller compared to those of color clusters representing the true background colors when measured over a sufficiently long history. The camera perturbation problem is solved using a fast camera motion detection algorithm, allowing the current background image to be registered with the background model maintained in memory. The background updating scheme is shown to be robust even when the scene is very busy and also computationally efficient, making it suitable for real-time surveillance and monitoring systems. Experimental results on real traffic monitoring and surveillance videos are presented.

## 1 Introduction

Separating foreground from background (also known as figure-ground discrimination) is an important though difficult problem in computer vision. Many background models have been proposed for surveillance systems. Based on the manner in which they are generated, existing background models can be categorized as off-line (static) background models [1,2,3] or online (adaptive) background models [4,5,6,7,8,9,10]. Due to the dynamic nature of the background, online adaptive background models are usually preferred in real time video surveillance and monitoring systems. Broadly speaking, there are two categories of online methods to model the background image. The first category models the background image using a single color value at each pixel location [4,5,6,7], whereas the second category uses multiple color values at each pixel location [8,9,10]. For dynamic scenes with high levels of random noise, a single value is not sufficient to represent the background color at a given pixel location. In the context of video surveillance and monitoring in outdoor scenes, the source of random noise could be the swaying of trees and the movement of grass due to breeze.

In this paper we propose an online background updating scheme for a real-time traffic surveillance and monitoring system. The background color at a pixel location is modeled as a mixture of Gaussian distributions as in [8,9,10]. In particular, we address two critical problems that are confronted by real-world surveillance and monitoring systems. The first problem is sudden camera perturbation, which occurs occasionally but causes typical background updating schemes to fail. In the context of traffic monitoring and surveillance, cameras mounted on bridges or overpasses are typically subject to structural vibrations caused by especially heavy moving vehicles, resulting in sudden and random camera perturbations. The second problem is the *sleeping person* problem [7] where a moving object stops in the scene and becomes motionless for some duration of time. A typical adaptive background model would result in the improper merging of the temporarily stationary object with the background image. The sleeping person problem arises frequently in the context of automated traffic monitoring when moving vehicles stop temporarily at traffic lights or intersections.

## 2 Proposed Background Model

In the proposed background model, the camera perturbation is modeled as a Euclidean transformation. A background image with dimensions greater than those of the actual image frame in the video stream is generated and continuously updated. The first image frame is aligned with the center of the background image. For each successive image frame, a fast algorithm is used to estimate the camera motion (perturbation) parameters and consequently determine the alignment of the new image frame with the stored background image. The background updating procedure is performed on those locations within the background image that overlap with the new image frame.

The color values at each pixel location in the background image are modeled as a multiple Gaussian mixture (MGM). A novel weight updating scheme for the color clusters is used to address the sleeping person problem. Once every $T$ frames, the number of color values that fall into each cluster is computed and stored in a counter. The corresponding cluster weight is updated once every $T$ frames based on the counter value and the previous history of the cluster. A new cluster may be created and an old cluster deleted after comparing all the cluster weights. The cluster weight evaluation scheme takes into consideration both the cluster duration and the recurrence frequency. The key idea behind the proposed approach is to use the cluster weight to approximate the cluster duration thus enabling one to decide whether or not to adapt a new cluster into the background model. A significant advantage of the proposed approach is that since the background updating is done once every $T$ frames, it is computationally very efficient and very well suited for real-time applications.

### 2.1 Camera Motion Estimation

As is common in most surveillance systems, the camera is assumed to be stationary. However, we account for sudden camera perturbations, which occur occasionally but nevertheless cause typical background updating schemes to fail. In the context of traffic monitoring and surveillance, cameras mounted on bridges or overpasses are typically subject to structural vibrations caused by especially heavy moving vehicles, resulting in sudden and random camera perturbations. Since the range of the perturbations is typically small, we model them as a simple Euclidean transformation given by $x' = x\cos(\theta) - y\sin(\theta) + s_x$ and $y' = x\sin(\theta) + y\cos(\theta) + s_y$, where $s_x$ and $s_y$ are the translational parameters along the X axis and Y axis respectively, and $\theta$ is the angle of rotation assuming the first image frame in the video stream to be the reference image frame. We also assume that $s_x, s_y \in [-D_s, D_s]$ and $\theta \in [-D_\theta, D_\theta]$ where $D_s$ and $D_\theta$ are predefined bounds. The parameters $(s_x, s_y, \theta)$ are determined as follows:

1. For each triple $(s_x, s_y, \theta)$, compute the region of overlap between the image frames $f(0)$ and $f(t)$.
2. Compute a match metric between the two image frames within the rectangular region of overlap.
3. Output the parameters $(s_x, s_y, \theta)$ which optimize (minimize, in our case) the match metric between the two images.

Given the transformation parameters $(s_x, s_y, \theta)$, the region of overlap $R$ between $f(0)$ and $f(t)$ is computed. The match metric is given by $m = \sum_{(x,y) \in R} |f(x', y'; t) - f(x, y; 0)|/A$, where $A$ is the area of the region of overlap $R$. As an alternative to brute-force search in the parameter space $(s_x, s_y, \theta)$, a more efficient search algorithm is used. Since the camera is expected to be primarily static with a very small angle of rotation, a local search procedure is used to determine the translational parameters $(s_x, s_y)$ and $\theta$ is assumed to be 0. The algorithm is described as follows:

1. Begin with $(s_x, s_y) = (0, 0)$ and step size $\delta = \delta_0$.
2. Explore the four neighbors of $(s_x, s_y)$ in parameter space given by $(s_x + \delta, s_y + \delta)$, $(s_x + \delta, s_y - \delta)$, $(s_x - \delta, s_y + \delta)$, and $(s_x - \delta, s_y - \delta)$. If any of these neighbors results in a lower match metric, replace the current $(s_x, s_y)$ with the neighbor that results in the lowest match metric.
3. Repeat step 2 until there is no change in the match metric.
4. Update $\delta = \delta/2$, and repeat steps 2 and 3.
5. Repeat steps 2, 3 and 4 until $\delta = \delta_{min}$.

Based on empirical observations on real data, the coarse-to-fine tuning of the step size $\delta$ is seen to prevent the search from being trapped in a local minimum when the range of translational motion is small.

After the optimal translational parameters $(s_x, s_y)$ are determined, if the match metric $m$ is above a certain predefined threshold, then we search in the space of the rotational parameter $\theta$ in the range $[-D_\theta, D_\theta]$ to determine the optimal Euclidean transform parameters. If $m$ is less than the threshold, then no further search in the $\theta$ space is deemed necessary, i.e. $\theta = 0$. After the alignment of the new image frame with the background image is performed, the background updating is done at the corresponding locations in the background image.

## 2.2 Background Image Updating

A background color at a pixel location usually persists for a longer time duration than any foreground color and has a higher frequency of recurrence [1,8]. Thus, it is logical to assign to each cluster center a weight that takes into account both, the time duration of the cluster and its recurrence frequency as an alternative to the simple weight updating scheme described in [10]. Consequently, in the proposed scheme, the weight assigned to each cluster is indicative of both, the time duration of the cluster and the cluster recurrence frequency. Thus each cluster is characterized by the following parameters:

- $C_i$: Centroid or mean of the $i$th color/gray level cluster.
- $\sigma_i^2$: Variance of the $i$th color/gray level cluster.
- $N_i$: Total number of colors/gray levels that have matched the $i$th cluster. Initially, $N_i = 1$ for all clusters.
- $tl_i$: The most recent time that the $i$th cluster has been updated. Initially, $tl_i = 0$ for all clusters.
- $n_i$: The number of colors/gray levels that have matched the $i$th cluster in recent history.

Given color $X_k$ at a certain pixel location in the current frame, we compare it to the existing cluster centroids associated with this pixel location. If $X_k \in [C_i - 2.5\sigma_i, C_i + 2.5\sigma_i]$ then $X_k$ is deemed to match the $i$th cluster. The centroid and covariance of the $i$th cluster are updated as follows:

$$C_i = C_i + \frac{1}{L}(X_k - C_i) \quad (1)$$

$$\sigma_i^2 = \sigma_i^2 + \frac{1}{L}((X_k - C_i)^2 - \sigma_i^2) \quad (2)$$

where $L$ is an integer representing the inverse of the learning rate. The advantage of using an integer $L$ instead of the learning rate $\alpha$ in equations (1) and (2), is that the need for floating point computation at each update is averted. For example, in equation (1) we can accumulate the difference $(X_k - C_i)$ and decrement $C_i$ by 1 if $(X_k - C_i) < -L$ and increment $C_i$ by 1 if $(X_k - C_i) > L$. If color $X_k$ does not match an existing cluster then a new cluster is created replacing an existing cluster $j$ with minimum weight $N_j$.

In order to efficiently compute the time duration and recurrence frequency of a cluster, we quantize the time series $x(t)$ into time slices of interval $T$. For all clusters in a given time slice, if the number of colors that have been assigned to cluster $i$ in that time slice is $n_i$ then the time duration of the cluster is updated as: $N_i = N_i + T$ if $n_i > T/2$; otherwise $N_i = N_i + n_i$. Thus, if a cluster at a given pixel location is assigned more than $T/2$ colors in a given time slice, then this cluster is deemed to dominate this time slice. Consequently, we reward this cluster by adding $T$ to $N_i$ else we update its time duration by adding the actual number of matched colors $n_i$ to $N_i$.

We also check for the recurrence frequency of clusters. If a cluster has not been matched for some period of time and then matched again, it is probable that the cluster does represent the real background. If this cluster has been deemed to be sufficiently exposed during the current time slice, i.e., $n_i \geq \delta$ then we increase its weight by increasing its value of $N$. On the other hand, if $n_i < \delta$ then the cluster is deemed insufficiently exposed and its recurrence frequency ignored during the current time slice. We measure the recurrence frequency of the $i$th cluster by checking the last time $tl_i$ that the cluster was matched. If $t - tl_i > 2T$, then $N_i = N_i + T/2$, that is $N_i$ is incremented by an extra duration $T/2$ to account for the cluster recurrence and $t_l$ is set to $t$. Checking for recurrence frequency is useful when the dynamic scene is very busy. In this situation, the true background color/gray level may not persist at a given pixel location for a long time duration, however its recurrence frequency will typically be high. Increasing the value of $N$ to account for the high recurrence frequency increases the probability of this color/gray level to be considered as part of the background.

The clusters at each pixel location are ranked on the basis of their $N$ values, the higher the value of $N$, the higher the priority for the corresponding color/gray level of that cluster to be considered as part of the background. However, it is necessary to set an upper limit for the value of $N_i$ since too large a value of $N_i$ will make it difficult for an actual new background color cluster to be considered as part of the background. We set the upper limit of $N_i$ to $\Delta$. At any pixel location, if $N_{max} > 1.25\Delta$ where $N_{max} = \max_i(N_i)$, we scale down all the $N_i$ values by multiplying them by $4/5$. If $N_i = 0$ then the $i$th cluster is deleted. All the clusters which satisfy the condition $N_i > N_{max}/3$ are deemed to represent the valid background colors/gray levels. If a cluster has not been updated for a time period $\Delta$, then it is deleted. The background updating is performed once every $T$ frames.

The background updating algorithm is summarized as follows:

1. Given an observed color/gray level $X_k$ at a pixel, check all of the pixel's clusters. If $X_k$ matches cluster $i$, then update the centroid and the variance of cluster $i$ using equations (1) and (2). Set $n_i = n_i + 1$.
2. If there is no match, create a new cluster and replace an existing cluster with the smallest $N_i$ value. For the new cluster, set $C = X_k$, $N = 1$, $n = 1$, $\sigma^2 = \sigma_0^2$ and $tl = k$.
3. If $(t \mod T) \equiv 0$ and $t > 0$ then for each cluster $i$ at each pixel,
    (a) Check the value of $n_i$ and update $N_i$ as follows:
        i. If $n_i > T/2$, then $N_i = N_i + T$.
        ii. Otherwise, $N_i = N_i + n_i$.
    (b) Check for recurrence: If $n_i > \delta$ and $t - tl_i > 2T$, then $N_i = N_i + T/2$ and $tl_i = t$.
    (c) Reset all $n_i$ values to zero.
    (d) Check which clusters will be deemed as belonging to the background. All clusters $i$ such that $N_i > N_{max}/3$ where $N_{max} = \max_i(N_i)$ are considered to belong to the background.
    (e) If $N_{max} > 1.25\Delta$, then $N_i = N_i * 4/5$, for all $i$.
    (f) For any $i$, if $k - tl_i > \Delta$, then delete this cluster.

## 3 System Implementation

The background updating scheme described above was incorporated into a real-time traffic monitoring system and tested on color (RGB) and grayscale video sequences of real traffic scenes. All video sequences were sampled at a constant rate of 30 frames per second (fps). We chose values of $L = 1024$ and $k = 4$ in our implementation. Since the background is constantly refreshed, the value of $N_i$ for the cluster corresponding to the actual background eventually increases to $1.25\Delta$. In the context of traffic monitoring, we assumed that a vehicle stops temporarily for up to 2 minutes at a traffic light or intersection, which amounts to 3600 frames at a sampling rate of 30 frames per second. In order to avert the *sleeping person* problem, this delay of 3600 frames must be less than $\Delta/3$ since all clusters for which $N_i \geq \Delta/3$ are considered to be part of the background. Since we need to choose a value of $\Delta > 3 \times 3600 = 10800$, we chose a value of $\Delta = 12000$. We also chose $T = 2$ seconds (60 frames) and $\delta = 20$. Thus, if a cluster that has not been updated for the past $2T = 120$ frames, has received more than 20 updates in the current time slice, then it is treated as an instance of a recurring background color/gray level and the $N_i$ value of the cluster is incremented by $T/2$.

## 4 Experimental Results

To simulate camera perturbation, the video streams were gathered while the tripod mount of the camera was being manually shaken. Figure 1(a) shows the background image from the moving camera. The actual size of the image frame is $360 \times 240$ pixels whereas the background image size is $400 \times 280$ pixels.

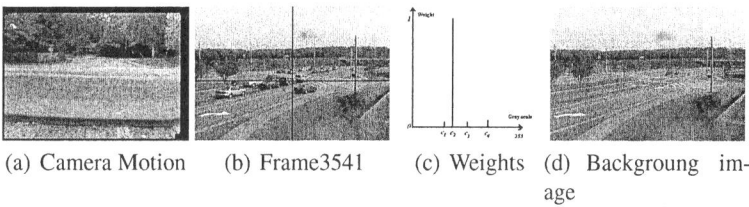

(a) Camera Motion  (b) Frame3541  (c) Weights  (d) Backgroung image

**Fig. 1.** Experimental Results

Experimental results on the captured videos captured show that the proposed scheme for camera motion compensation works well and that the background updating scheme is capable of recovering from abrupt and random camera motion, provided it is small.

A comparison between the proposed background updating scheme and that of Stauffer and Grimson [10] is performed using video streams, captured by a static camera, of a busy traffic scene containing several vehicles and with traffic lights present. Figures 1(b), 1(c) and 1(d) summarize the experimental results on a grayscale video sequence. Figure 1(b) shows a grayscale image frame at time $t = 3541$ where time is measured in terms of the frame number in the video sequence. In this frame it is evident that some cars have stopped at a traffic light. Figure 1(c) shows the weights $N_i$ of each of the $k = 4$ gray level clusters associated with pixel location $(180, 134)$ at time $t = 3541$. In Figure 1(c), the cluster centroids are denoted by $C_1$, $C_2$, $C_3$ and $C_4$ and the maximum cluster weight $N_{max}$ is marked as 1 with the other cluster weights scaled in proportion. In Figure 1(b), the pixel location $(180, 134)$ is marked by the intersection of the corresponding vertical and horizontal lines for the sake of clarity. It can be seen that although there is a stationary car at this pixel location for some length of time, the weight of the corresponding gray level cluster is small compared to that of the gray level cluster which denotes the actual background. Hence the gray level of the stationary car

(a) Our scheme  (b) Grimson's scheme

**Fig. 2.** Background image and object segmentation at time 3841 with learning rate $\alpha = 1/1024$

at this pixel location is not treated as a background gray level. Figure 1(d) shows the background image generated with the proposed background model where, at each pixel location, the gray level displayed is the one corresponding to the cluster center with the maximum weight $N_{max}$. Since none of the stationary vehicles are merged with the background image, the background updating scheme can be seen to be robust in the face of the *sleeping person* problem. It is also adaptive since the cluster parameters are periodically updated. However, since the updating is done once every $T = 60$ frames (i.e., 2 seconds at 30 fps), the proposed scheme is also computationally efficient.

In an RGB color video sequence, each color cluster is represented as $C = \{c_r, c_g, c_b, \sigma^2\}$, that is, the same $\sigma^2$ value is used to represent the variance of the cluster along each of the R, G and B axes. Given a new observation $X = (r, g, b)$ and a cluster $C = \{c_r, c_g, c_b, \sigma^2\}$, if the condition $d < 2.5\sigma$ is satisfied, where $d = \max(d_r, d_g, d_b)$ and $d_r = |r - c_r|, d_g = |g - c_g|, d_b = |b - c_b|$, then $X = (r, g, b)$ is deemed to have matched the cluster $C$. Furthermore, the parameters of cluster $C$ are updated as follows: $c_r = c_r + (r - c_r)/L$, $c_g = c_g + (g - c_g)/L$, $c_b = c_b + (b - c_b)/L$ and $\sigma^2 = \sigma^2 + (1/L)(d_r^2 + d_g^2 + d_b^2 - 3\sigma^2)$.

Figures 2(a) summarize the results of our scheme for an RGB color video sequence. The image on the left in Figure 2(a) is the background image generated at time $t = 3841$, and the image on the right is the result of foreground object segmentation at the same time instant. It is evident that the stopped cars can be detected using background subtraction.

Figure 2(b) depicts the background image and the result of foreground segmentation at time $t = 3841$ using the background updating scheme proposed by Stauffer and Grimson [10] with the same learning rate of $1/1024$. It is evident that the objects that become temporarily motionless are partially merged into the background and cannot be extracted. More results on real traffic monitoring videos are available online at *http://www.cs.uga.edu/~xingzhi/research/bkg/demo/*. From these videos it can be seen that, the proposed scheme suffers from the sleeping person problem initially when little information about the background is known. However, the proposed scheme is observed to eventually overcome this problem and converge to a stable background image. Stauffer and Grimson's scheme, in contrast, is observed to suffer from the sleeping person problem from time to time.

## 5 Conclusions

In this paper we proposed a background updating scheme for a real-time traffic monitoring system. Specifically, we addressed the camera perturbation problem and the *sleep-*

*ing person* problem. To make the background updating scheme adaptive to gradual changes in the background, we used a multi-color model where multiple color clusters were associated with each pixel location in the background image. The cluster parameters were updated periodically to adapt to gradual changes in the background. To make the proposed background updating scheme robust in the face of the *sleeping person* problem, the color clusters at each pixel location were assigned weights based on the observation that the clusters corresponding to the real background colors were likely to persist for a longer time duration and also have a higher recurrence frequency compared to the clusters that correspond to colors from temporarily motionless objects. The camera perturbation was modeled as a Euclidean transformation and the camera perturbation compensation procedure was modeled as a fast local search procedure in the perturbation parameter space to optimize an image match metric. Experimental results on grayscale and color video sequences obtained from real traffic scenes showed that the proposed background updating scheme could adapt to gradual or long-term changes in the background while ignoring short-term changes arising from the sleeping person problem. The proposed scheme was also shown to be computationally efficient since most of the computation was performed once every 60 frames (or 2 seconds at 30 fps). Moreover, the background update equations were optimized by greatly reducing the floating point computation, thus making the scheme well suited for real-time applications. Although the proposed real-time background updating scheme was specifically designed for a real-time traffic monitoring system, it is nevertheless applicable to most surveillance systems, in which the *sleeping person* problem is seen to occur but the time period for which a moving object is temporarily stationary has a definite upper bound.

## References

1. D. Farin, P.H.N. deWith and W. Effelsberg, Robust Background Estimation for Complex Video Sequences, *Proc. IEEE ICIP*, Barcelona, Spain, Sept. 2003, pp. 145-148.
2. M. Isard and J. MacCormick, BraMBLe: A Bayesian Multiple-Blob Tracker, *Proc. ICCV*, Vancouver, Canada, July 2001, Vol. 2, pp. 34-41.
3. M. Massey and W. Bender, Salient stills: Process and Practice, *IBM Sys. Jour.*, 1996, Vol. 35, Nos. 3&4, pp. 557-573.
4. D. Koller, J.W. Weber and J. Malik, Robust Multiple Car Tracking with Occlusion Reasoning, *Proc. ECCV*, Stockholm, Sweden, 1994, pp. 189-196.
5. C. Ridder, O. Munkelt and H. Kirchner, Adaptive Background Estimation and Foreground Detection Using Kalman Filtering, *Proc. of Intl. Conf. Recent Adv. Mechatronics*, Istanbul, Turkey, 1995, pp. 193-199.
6. S. Kamijo, Traffic Monitoring and Accident Detection at Intersections, *IEEE Trans. Intell. Transp. Sys.*, Vol. 1, No. 2, June 2000, pp. 108-118.
7. K. Tooyama, J. Krumm, B. Brumit, and B. Meyers, Wallflower: Principles and Practice of Background Maintenance, *Proc. ICCV*, Corfu, Greece, Sept. 1999, pp. 255-261.
8. D. Butler, S. Sridharan and V.M. Bove, Jr., Real-time Adaptive Background Segmentation, *Proc. IEEE ICME*, Baltimore, MD, July 2003.
9. P. KaewTraKulPong and R. Bowden, An Improved Adaptive Background Mixture Model for Real-time Tracking with Shadow Detection, *Proc. Wkshp. Adv. Vision-based Surveillance Sys.*, Kingston, UK, Sept. 2001.
10. C. Stauffer and W.E.L. Grimson, Adaptive Background Mixture Models for Real-time Tracking. *Proc. IEEE Conf. CVPR*, Ft. Collins, CO, June 1999, pp. 246-252.

# Evaluation and Improvements of a Real-Time Background Subtraction Method

Donatello Conte[1], Pasquale Foggia[2], Michele Petretta[1], Francesco Tufano[1], and Mario Vento[1]

[1] Dipartimento di Ingegneria dell'Informazione ed Ingegneria Elettrica,
Università di Salerno Via P.te Don Melillo 1 I-84084 Fisciano (SA), Italy
{dconte, mpetretta, ftufano, mvento}@unisa.it
[2] Dipartimento di Informatica e Sistemistica, Università di Napoli "Federico II",
Via Claudio 21 I-80125 Napoli, Italy
foggiapa@unina.it

**Abstract.** In a video surveillance system, moving object detection is the most challenging problem especially if the system is applied in complex environments with variable lighting, dynamic and articulate scenes, etc.. Furthermore, a video surveillance system is a real-time application, so discouraging the use of good, but computationally expensive, solutions. This paper presents a set of improvements of a basic background subtraction algorithm that are suitable for video surveillance applications. Besides we present a new evaluation scheme never used in the context of moving object detection algorithms.

## 1 Introduction

In the last decade the improvement of computer performance has made real time video analysis affordable on commonly available hardware. Thus there has been a growing interest in low-cost in video analysis applications. Among them, a central role is played by intelligent video surveillance systems, i.e. system able to detect a set of predefined events related to object moving in the scene, and to trigger an appropriate reaction.

Usually a video analysis system may be split into two main steps: localization of the objects of interest and object tracking, i.e. following the object trajectory trough successive images in the video sequence. The object detection step plays an important role in video surveillance systems. For the time being all the techniques of object detection supply good results under particular circumstances, where the environment is completely controlled with respect to key factors such as the lighting or the position of the camera. For video surveillance applications these conditions can not be assumed in the general case because the environment in which the system has to work is typically characterized by variable lighting, dynamic and articulate scenes and a set of problems due to meteorological events that affect the detection performance.

This paper, after a description of the overall proposed system, describes a novel object detection algorithm based on background subtraction that results more robust in real applications. In particular our approach presents an innovative procedure for updating the reference image, that is robust with respect to sudden lighting changes or to structural scene changes; we will also propose novel corrective algorithms, that will allow the correction of the object detector results in order to assure good outputs for the subsequent processing stages. The effectiveness of our approach is validated by means of a new evaluation scheme. The experimentations are performed on the standard PETS database [2] which is recognized to be a benchmark for object detection.

## 2 Related Works

Video surveillance applications need to work in the absence of detailed a priori knowledge about the objects of interest, and this reason makes it preferable the use of segmentation algorithms working without models. These algorithms, usually, try to segment the frame of the video into two regions: foreground (pixels belonging to the objects of interest) and background (all the others). In a second phase the foreground pixels are grouped to determine the blobs representing the objects.

In video surveillance systems, background subtraction is the most used approach for the object detection step. The basic idea is to obtain the foreground region comparing current image with reference image. The pixels of the background can be either represented by a single color value [8] or by a probabilistic distribution. In [5] the authors use an uniform distribution; this choice is effective only if the background model is always perfectly synchronized with scene changes. Alternatively, in order to reduce the sensitivity to the variation of the light conditions or to mitigate *waving tree* problems (they occurs when part of the background of the scene is detected as object of interest because it is performing little movements), a simply statistical model is used introducing a Gaussian description of the background pixel [13]. Although this solution mitigates errors due to a not perfectly synchronized reference image, on the other side it produces a system less sensitive in the regions where a great variance of colors has been calculated (also for the detection of the objects of interest). To avoid this loss of sensitivity, a more complicated statistical model for pixel representation, Mixture of Gaussian (MOG) has been proposed ([10]). For outdoor scenes, illumination conditions, usually, change significantly during the day because of sun position or meteorological events; some false positives (objects detected by the system that do not truly exist) derive by these circumstances: this problem is commonly referred to as *light of day problems* [11]. In fact, if the background is not accurate or consistent with current scene condition, the detection cannot result reliable. Background model, essentially, may be updated using two different ways: non recursive [11, 7] and recursive techniques [5, 13, 6]. The first ones process, for each frame, a sliding window of $N$ past frames and calculate the median value [7] or a linear prediction [11] of the background parameters. The second technique updates the background model using current frame and previous background information; it is used as input of a Wiener filter in the Pfinder system [13]. In [6], instead, the reference image is updated using an Infinite Impulse Response filter. Others algorithms, similarly to our approach, in order to manage also sudden illumination changes. [5, 4, 1] apply fast update rate only to the pixels belonging to instantaneous background region, while the regions belonging to the detected object are not updated. The drawback of these approaches is that errors in the objects detection may produce an erroneous reference image compromising the detection performance of the successive frames.

In this paper we present an algorithm, belonging to the last category, suitable for real time applications and robust enough for outdoor scenes. In real time applications more performance constraints have to be considered than in the case of post-processing applications. An adequate frame-rate has to be obtained in order to preserve the continuity of the video information to analyse. For this reason the used algorithms in addition to resulting reliable must not be excessively time consuming. An improvement of the algorithm of background maintenance has been developed and a set of heuristics have been added at the plain background based approach. Furthermore, the results of an extensive experimentation process (described in detail), are shown, in order to validate the effectiveness of the heuristics within real applications.

## 3 System Architecture

The object detection is divided into three steps (Fig. 1): the pixel segmentation processes the input frames producing a foreground pixel mask, that is obtained thresholding the absolute difference between the current image frame and the reference image; then, a morphological dilatation filter is applied to the foreground pixel mask; finally, by a connected components labelling algorithm the blob segmentation step identifies the semantically separated objects and localizes them.

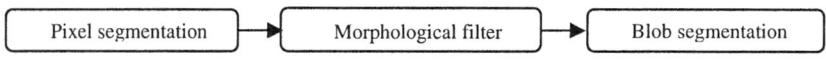

**Fig. 1.** Object detection flowchart

Each detected object is described by means of its *bounding box*. The latter is evaluated as the smallest rectangle, whose sides are parallel to the edges of the frame in which the object is inscribed. In the following the bounding boxes will simply called *boxes*. Then an object tracking block preserves the identity of objects across the frames assigning them univocal IDs. In this way we obtain the trajectories of every object and after a perspective correction a classification of the objects behavior can be done. If some behaviors are classified as interesting events, the system reacts appropriately on the basis of the application context. For the foreground detection step an adaptive background based algorithm has been implemented. In our model the background pixels are represented by their RGB values. Finally, a tracking algorithm has been implemented, in particular this system uses an overlap – based algorithm [3] because of the high frame-rate (16 f/s for 384x288 resolution on a P4 2.8Ghz).

## 4 Algorithm Improvements

First at all, let us introduce some definitions. We indicate the background image used for computing the differences with the term *reference image,* to distinguish it from instantaneous background that we will define later. Since we do not deal with occlusions (that are a tracking level problem), in the following, we will use the words "object" and "blob" with the same meaning.

Regarding the foreground detection step, we have already mentioned in section 2 that the basic background subtraction algorithm only works acceptably in very limited circumstances. In order to make the system robust also in outdoor conditions, in the following we will propose a set of improvements. The values of the parameters were chosen on the basis of a training phase. In the simplest algorithms for the object detection [8] the threshold for the pixel segmentation is chosen statically depending on the scene. As regards the definition of the threshold, we have chosen an algorithm that differs from the basic approach for the introduction of a dynamic strategy to update the threshold in order to adapt it to the reference image changes. The main idea is to increase or decrease the threshold on the basis of the brightness changes of the scene. A similar strategy is shown in Gupte et al. [4]. But whereas in [4] the authors change the threshold on the basis of the static distribution of intensity levels in the current frame, we adapt the threshold on the basis of the variation of the intensity during the image sequence. The threshold is updated according to this formula:

$$Th = Th \cdot (1 - \Delta_L) \quad if \quad \frac{|I^t| - E^{t-n}[t]}{E^{t-n}[t]} < \chi \quad \vee \quad Th \cdot (1 + \Delta_H) \quad if \quad \frac{|I^t| - E^{t-n}[t]}{E^{t-n}[t]} > \chi \quad (1)$$

Where $Th$ is the current threshold; $I^t$ is the average of the pixels intensity; $E^{t-n}[I]$ is the moving average of $I$ calculated by the last n frames; $\chi$ is a percentage (we have chosen a value of 25%); $\Delta_L$ and $\Delta_H$ are the percentage respectively of the decrement and increment of the threshold (for both 0.3). The value of threshold has an upper and a lower bound.

In the pixel analysis, often, some conditions cause little isolated background areas to be detected as foreground pixels. We have added a noise filter that operates at blob level to remove the spurious objects according to their dimensions.

The *shadows* problem is very hard to solve at pixel level. In [1] the authors try to detect the shadows considering the properties of the HSV color space. A very interesting approach [9] considers three properties for the detection of the shadows: the presence of a uniform dark region, the luminance changes with respect to the previous frame and the shadow's edges. We propose a technique for the shadow suppression that results very little time consuming but which performances are comparable whose [1, 9] for the proposed application. For each object, bounded by its box, we define its *histogram* as the function that associate for a box abscissa *x*, the number of foreground pixels over that column; this histogram is normalized by the relative box height. A foreground pixel is recognized as shadow pixel if:

$$H(x) < T_h \wedge B(x,y) - I(x,y) > T_i \quad (2)$$

Where $H(x)$ is the histogram value at x abscissa, $T_h$ is the histogram threshold (equal to 0.4), $B(x,y)$ and $I(x,y)$ are the image reference and current frame intensity, and finally $T_i$ (35) is the intensity threshold. So the recognized shadow pixels are eliminated from the foreground mask.

When a foreground mask depurated from shadows pixels has been obtained, the connected component labelling is executed again on the regions interested by shadow removal. In Fig. 2 it is clear the effectiveness of our algorithm.

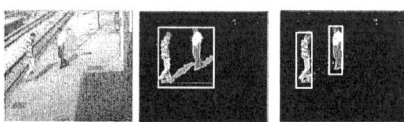

**Fig. 2.** Foreground mask before (left) and after (right) shadow filtering

As regard the image reference updating strategy we use the algorithm proposed in [4] with some improvements. After pixel segmentation, we have the binary object mask to distinguish the moving pixels from the others. We call *instantaneous background* those locations where the mask is 0 and *detected objects region* those location where the mask is 1. The basic updating formula (IIR filter) used as a starting point is:

$$B_{n+1}(x, y) = (1-\alpha) * B_n(x, y) + \alpha * I(x, y) \quad (3)$$

Where $B_n(x,y)$ is a background pixel at time $n$, $I(x,y)$ is a current frame pixel and $\alpha$ is a coefficient representing the update speed. The first difference in comparison with the author of the work [4] is that we chose to use two different updating speeds depending on the region: for the instantaneous background pixels, the new values are updated very quickly using $\alpha=0.5$; instead for the detected objects region a very slow update policy is needed, $\alpha$ value depends on the application, we choose it equal to 0.0001. The above-mentioned solution needs that in the start-up period a coherent background can be obtained: this means that the system must start in a condition in which a number of free scene frames can be obtained. Even so a problem afflicts this approach: it is represented by the condition in which during a quick illumination change, such as the transit of a cloud in front of the sun, a slowly moving or stopped object is present in the scene. In this case the scene area under this stopped object is not updated. This inconsistency causes the creation of a wrong foreground blob in the mask when the above-mentioned object leaves its position. In [4] this problem is not solved, so we have introduced a new processing step. Specifically, for each object, it is calculated, for the pixels adjacent to its bounding box, the average variation ($\Delta$) between the image reference at frame $n$ and $n+1$. On the basis of this variation we update the region under the identified object according to this formula:

$$b_{n+1}(x, y) = b_n(x, y) + \Delta \quad (4)$$

It is worth to notice that in a real context the problem of object camouflage is very frequent. In fact for a wrong detection it is not needed that the whole object camouflages itself with the scene. If only a part of it is similar to the background, it may be broken, after foreground detection, into two or more blobs. This causes a serious loss of precision for the detector and it may affect successive tracking and classification steps. The problem cannot be solved by any pixel level algorithm and only a little number of works faces this problem at higher levels. Marcenaro et al. [8] deal with this problem merging regions that are partially overlapped or near; the main drawback of this approach is that it can merge different objects in an unique blob.

We present a slight improvement that try to solve this drawback. The base hypothesis is that, if the video frame rate is higher than 6-7 fps, object dimensions cannot change suddenly. In fact the algorithm uses the following idea: if the height of an object decreases suddenly and a new object is detected where the old object should be positioned, it is classified as a broken object. In details, the system calculate the moving average of the height, over a sliding window, for each object. If the current object height results lower by a fixed percentage than the average height, the system checks whether there is a new object (an object that is appeared in the current frame) within the bounding box of the object modified according to the calculated average height. If this check succeeds, the new object is removed and the old one is extended to enclose the corresponding region.

## 5 Experimental Results

Whereas there are several approaches to evaluate the performances of the tracking algorithms (the second step of a complete tracking system), it has not been made much effort (besides some exceptions [11]) to evaluate the performances of the moving object detection step. One reason is the huge effort needed to produce the ground truth. In fact a detailed ground truth requires the evaluation of each pixel of each frame. Furthermore, an evaluation at pixel level, i.e. counting misdetected pixels (as in [11]), provides measure that is not so meaningful, and it cannot be intended to be a good ranking of the algorithms. Here we use a quantitative method, widely used in other contexts, but never in the evaluation of this kind of algorithms. The method is described in the following. The ground truth is defined, for each frame, as the box coordinates representing the real moving objects present in the frame. Traditionally, the performance of an information retrieval system is evaluated with the measures of precision and recall.

For object detection systems, the notion of correct detection does not have a precise, suitable definition; the question cannot be answered with a simple "yes" or "no", since objects may be partially detected. We used an evaluation scheme (presented in [12] in the context of text detection in video sequences) which exploits geometrical information (overlap) in the precision and recall measures. The goal of a detection evaluation scheme is to take a list of ground truth boxes $G_i = 1..|G|$ and a list of detected boxes $D_j = 1..|D|$ and to measure the quality of the match between the two lists. From the two lists G and D of detected boxes and ground truth boxes, two overlap matrices $\sigma$ and $\tau$ are created. The rows $i = 1..|G|$ of the matrices correspond to the ground truth boxes and the columns $j = 1..|D|$ correspond to the detected boxes. The values are calculated as follows:

$$\sigma_{ij} = \frac{Area(G_i \cap D_j)}{Area(G_i)} \qquad \tau_{ij} = \frac{Area(G_i \cap D_j)}{Area(D_j)} \tag{5}$$

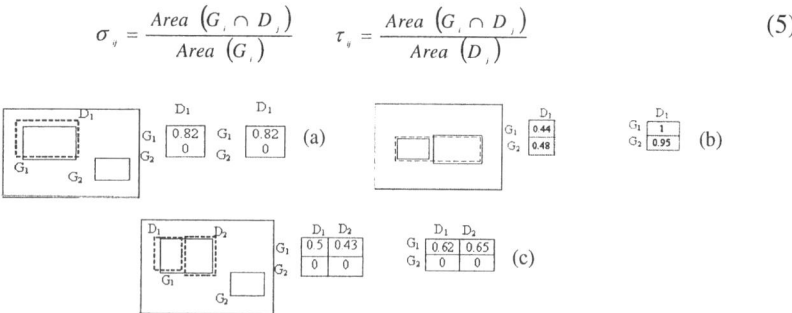

**Fig. 3.** a) One-to-one matching; b) One-to-many matches with one detected box; c) One-to-many matches with one ground truth box

The matrices can be analyzed for determining the correspondences between the two lists:

**One-to-One Matches:** $G_i$ matches against $D_j$ if row $i$ of both matrices contains only one non-zero element at column $j$ and column $j$ of both matrices contains only one non-zero element at row $i$. The overlap area needs to have a certain size compared to the rectangle in order to be considered successful ($\sigma_{ij} \geq e_1$ and $\tau_{ij} \geq e_2$).

**One-to-Many Matches with One Ground Truth Box:** $G_i$ matches against several detected boxes if row $i$ of the matrices contains only one non-zero element at column $j$. The two additional constraints of $\Sigma_j\, \sigma_{ij} \geq e_3$ and $\forall j : \tau_{ij} \geq e_4$ ensure respectively that the single ground truth rectangle is sufficiently detected and that each of detected rectangles is precisely enough.

**One-to-Many Matches with One Detected Box:** $D_j$ matches against several ground truth boxes if column $j$ of the matrices contains only one non-zero element at row $i$. Also here we add the constraints of $\Sigma_i\, \tau_{ij} \geq e_5$ and $\forall i : \sigma_{ij} \geq e_6$.

Based on this matching strategy, the recall and precision measures are given as follows:

$$recall = \frac{\sum_i Match_G(G_i)}{N},\ precision = \frac{\sum_j Match_D(D_j)}{M} \quad Match_G(G_i) = \begin{cases} 1 & \text{if } G_i \text{ matches against a single detected box} \\ 0 & \text{if } G_i \text{ does not match against any detected box} \\ 0.8 & \text{if } G_i \text{ matches against several detected boxes} \end{cases} \quad (6)$$

The function $Match_D(D_j)$ is defined accordingly. This evaluation takes into account one-to-many matches, but "punish" them slightly. These measures provide an intuitive measure of how many boxes have been detected correctly and how many false alarms have been produced.

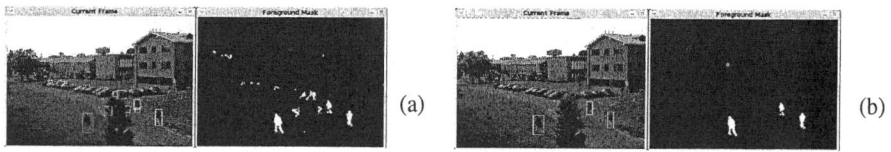

**Fig. 4.** Results on PETS dataset: a) Standard Algorithm; b) Improved Algorithm

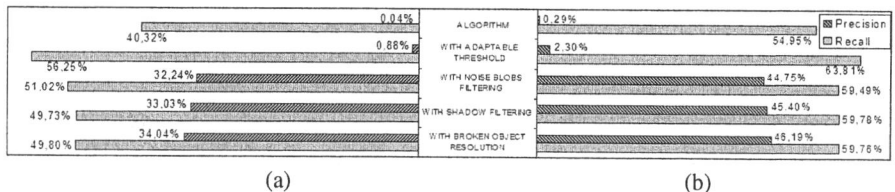

**Fig. 5.** Results on PETS 2001: a) Dataset 2 Camera 1; b) Dataset 4 Camera 1

Two sequences from PETS2001 dataset have been chosen as testing set. Some other sequences from the same database have been used to tune our algorithm parameters. The two test sequences are: the "testing" sequence – dataset 2 – camera 1 from 80 to 1487 and the "testing" sequence – dataset 4 – camera 1 from 1 to 1082. In Fig. 4 one example showing the foreground mask and the moving objects detected by the basic and the improved algorithms on PETS dataset, is provided. In the results of the basic algorithm and the algorithm with the novel heuristics, added step by step, are shown.

First of all we want to remark that the absolute values cannot be taken into account in a comparison with other algorithms because of the different evaluation schema used. You can notice that the original algorithm has performances surely improvable, especially for the precision index. Adding the improvement on the threshold the indexes increase a lot. This proves the effectiveness of the novel improvement. The noise filter raises enormously the precision index because of the reduction of numerous false positive. The drawback is a slight reduction of the recall index. Finally, with the other heuristics (shadow filtering and broken object resolution) the precision index continue to increase. Here we want to underline that in a video surveillance system we are interested to recognize the events occurring in the scene avoiding false alarms (i.e. inexistent events). Therefore the effort to try new solution for the last two problems has been justified by the most favourable precision index obtained.

## 6 Conclusions

In this paper we discussed some improvements of a classical background subtraction algorithm. Furthermore we have shown the application of an evaluation scheme never used in moving object detection algorithms. The results, within the video surveillance framework, are promising. In the future we want to assess the performances of our approach carrying out a comparison with other algorithms using the presented evaluation scheme.

## References

1. R. Cucchiara, C. Grana, M. Piccardi, A. Prati, Detecting Moving Objects, Ghosts, and Shadows in Video Streams. IEEE Trans. PAMI. Vol. 25-10, pp. 1337-1342. 2003.
2. ftp://pets.rdg.ac.uk/PETS2001/
3. L. M. Fuentes, S. A. Velastin, People Tracking in Indoor Surveillance Applications. Workshop on Performance Evaluation of Tracking Systems (PETS2001). 2001.
4. S. Gupte, O. Masoud, R. F. K. Martin, N. P. Papanikolopoulos, Detection and Classification of Vehicles. IEEE Transac. on ITS. Vol. 3-1, pp. 37-47. 2002.
5. I.Haritaoglu, D. Harwood, L.S. Davis. "W4: real-time surveillance of people and their activities". IEEE Transac. on PAMI. Vol. 22 - 8 , pp. 809 – 830. 2000.
6. J. Heikkilä, O. Silvén, A Real-Time System for Monitoring of Cyclists and Pedestrians. IEEE Workshop on Visual Surveillance, (VS'99), pp. 74 - 81. 1999.
7. B. Lo, S. Velastin, Automatic congestion detection system for underground platforms. 2001 International symposium on intelligent multimedia, video, and speech processing, pp. 158 - 161. 2001.
8. L. Marcenaro, M. Ferrari, L. Marchesotti, C.S. Regazzoni. "Multiple object tracking under heavy occlusions by using Kalman filters based on shape matching". IEEE International Conference on Image Processing. Vol. 3, pp. 341 – 344. 2002.
9. J. Stauder, R. Mech, J. Ostermann, Detection of moving cast shadows for object segmentation. IEEE Transac. on Multimedia. Vol. 1 - 1, pp. 65 - 76. 1999.
10. C. Stauffer, W.E.L. Grimson. "Learning patterns of activity using real-time tracking". IEEE Trans. on PAMI. Vol. 22 – 8, pp. 747 – 757. 2000.
11. K. Toyama, J. Krumm, B. Brumitt, B. Meyers, Wallflower: Principles and Practice of Background Maintenance. Seventh IEEE International Conference on Computer Vision. Vol. 1, pp. 255 - 261. 1999.
12. C. Wolf, "Text Detection in Images taken from Videos Sequences for Semantic Indexing", Ph.D. Thesis at INSA de Lyon, 20, rue Albert Einstein, 69621 Villeurbanne Cedex, France. 2003.
13. C. R. Wren, A. Azarbayejani, T. Darrel, A. P. Pentland, Pfinder: Real-Time Tracking of the Human Body. IEEE Trans. PAMI. Vol. 19-7, pp. 780-785. 1997.

# Fixed Pixel Threshold PDC Algorithm and Its Implementation for Full Search Block Matching Motion Estimation

Lynn Yang and Majid Ahmadi

Department of Electrical and Computer Engineering, University of Windsor
401 Sunset Ave, Windsor, ON, Canada N9B 3P4
(lyang, ahmadi)@uwindsor.ca

**Abstract.** A hardware-oriented block matching algorithm and its area-efficient VLSI implementation are presented. The proposed technique benefits from the simplicity of the Pixel Difference Classification algorithm (PDC), further exploits the inherence of the characteristics of the data being processed, and the goal of an area-efficient implementation is reached. A quality investigation based on processing video sequences confirms the stability and performance of the proposed algorithm when compared with the conventional full-search as well as low-complexity techniques. Realized in TSMC 0.18-micron CMOS technology the chip has a core area of 1.01 $mm^2$. For a comparable video quality, the proposed implementation has shown a significant silicon area deduction compared with the recently published conventional implementations.

## 1 Introduction

Motion estimation (ME) is the most time consuming task in encoding video of today's hybrid video coding standards such as MPEG. As portable HDTV systems, such as MPEG cameras, become more popular, high-efficiency, small-area and good picture quality ME processor is essential, since ME technique requires more than 80% performance of the codec. However, the existing motion estimation algorithms and hardware design methods are not well fitted into high-level design smoothly. Existing designs are mostly based on the matching criterion called mean absolute error (MAE) [1] as defined below

$$MAE(k,l) = \sum_{i=0}^{N-1}\sum_{j=0}^{N-1} |a(i,j) - b(i+k, j+l)|,$$
$$-p: k,l: p-1, \qquad (1)$$

$$v = \arg \min_{-p \leq k, l \leq p-1} MAE(k,l) \qquad (2)$$

where $a(i,j)$ represents pixels of the reference block, $b(i,j)$ are pixels of the candidate block, the position $(k,l)$ of a candidate block that results in the minimum distortion denotes the motion vector $v$.

By exhaustively searching all candidates within the search window, full search (FS) method provides the most optimal solution among all block-matching search strategies. But its high computational complexity made it difficult to be implemented compact enough to fit in a single-chip MPEG2 encoder [4,5].

In order to reduce the computational complexity of FS, many fast search methods have been developed [2]. Among them, the 3-step search (3SS) is the most adopted for modification and implementation. Recently published ME processors designed within single-chip encoders for MPEG@HL are based on modified 3SS [4,5]. By using a large search pattern in the first step, the 3SS is very efficient to find the global minimum especially for those sequences with large motion. On the other hand, it becomes inefficient in estimating of small motions since it will be trapped into a local minimum. Although computations are cut down, all fast search methods including 3SS suffer video quality degradation.

Previous work focus on the MAE criterion, in which the 16-bit accumulators take large silicon area, and become bottleneck of the entire architecture [8]. In this paper, we propose a new approach: by modifying the pixel difference classification algorithm (PDC)[7], a new hardware-oriented matching criterion has been developed. It replaces the 16-bit accumulators with 8-bit counters and has comparable and stable video quality as the MAE. Combined with the FS, an area efficient motion estimator has been implemented, the test chip core implementation has shown a significant silicon area deduction compared with the recently published conventional implementations. For a resolution of $1920 \times 1080$ HDTV format, search window size of $-8/7$, clock rate of 100MHz, it is capable to process 50 frames per second, make single-chip realization of MPEG@HL codec an easy job.

In the following parts, the proposed algorithm — simplified PDC (SPDC) is presented in section 2; section 3 compares video processing quality of SPDC with conventional algorithms; Hardware implementation results are discussed in section 4, and section 5 concludes the paper.

## 2 Proposed Algorithm

In order to understand the proposed algorithm, it is necessary to give a brief description of the PDC algorithm first. In the PDC algorithm described in Eq. (3)-(5), instead of accumulating, the absolute errors are at first compared with a threshold $t_p$, then the results $p(i,j,k,l)$, which is a binary representation for "no or yes", are counted together to form average cost functions $PDC(k,l)$. The largest $PDC(k,l)$ represents the best match.

$$\begin{aligned} p(i,j,k,l) &= 1 \quad if\ |a(i,j)-b(i+k,j+l)| \le t_p \\ &= 0 \quad if\ |a(i,j)-b(i+k,j+l)| > t_p \end{aligned} \tag{3}$$

$$PDC(k,l) = \sum_{i=0}^{N-1}\sum_{j=0}^{N-1} p(i,j,k,l)\ ,\quad -p\colon k,l\colon p-1 \tag{4}$$

$$v = \arg \max_{-p \le k, l \le p-1} PDC(k,l) \qquad (5)$$

From the above description we know that the pixel threshold $t_p$ is a constant 8-bit value lies between $(00 \sim FF)_{16}$, and this value is not fixed by the original algorithm. For design of architectures, a fixed value of the pixel threshold will save an 8-bit input port and simplify the circuits. In order to reach this goal, several video sequences with different grades of dynamism have been used to evaluate the performance of the PDC algorithm under different pixel thresholds.

First, 15 points distributed among the 256 $t_p$ values are selected; and then, motion vectors are calculated by the algorithm under these values. The PSNR (peak signal-noise-ratio) of the reconstructed frames based on the motion vectors are reported as an objective measure of the processing quality. Some of the results are shown in Figure 1 and 2. The following phenomena have been observed:

1) For all video sequences tested, when the pixel threshold $t_p$ takes the values within the range of 15 ~ 31, the performances have shown quite stable.
2) For scenes contain large motions and many moving objects such as Football, the bigger the value of $t_p$ is, the better the performance.
3) For video sequences with small motions and only one moving object, such as Miss America and Claire, the opposite result has been observed, e.g. the smaller the $t_p$ is, the better the estimation.
4) For most video sequences contain moderate background and several objects' motions such as Table Tennis, Flower Garden and Salesman, performance within the above mentioned range are quite stable and close to each other.

Based on the investigation and hardware design consideration, we have chosen the value of $15 = (0F)_{16}$ as the fixed value for the pixel threshold. Once the value of the pixel threshold is fixed, Equation (3) can be replaced by Equation (6). Observing this equation, we found a coincidence can be used to cut down hardware further without degrading the video quality of the algorithm. Here the value 0F acts as a low-pass filter, it blocks bigger errors of the pixels. In another word, we need only checking the 4 MSB of the absolute difference of pixels, only when these 4 bits are all 0, this pair of pixels is counted as matching pixels.

$$\begin{aligned} p(i,j,k,l) &= 1 \quad if\,|a(i,j)-b(i+k,j+l)| \le 0F \\ &= 0 \quad if\,|a(i,j)-b(i+k,j+l)| > 0F \end{aligned} \qquad (6)$$

Therefore calculations described in Eq. (3) can be further simplified by truncating the 4 LSB bits of the pixel difference, omitting the comparator, checking only the 4 MSB bits of the pixel difference. In this way, the 8-bit comparator is replaced by a 4-input OR gate, circuits is therefore further simplified. Consider parallel implementation, hundreds of processing elements are needed, so the hardware cut down is quite significant. This part of the hardware benefit we got was not at the expense of the video quality.

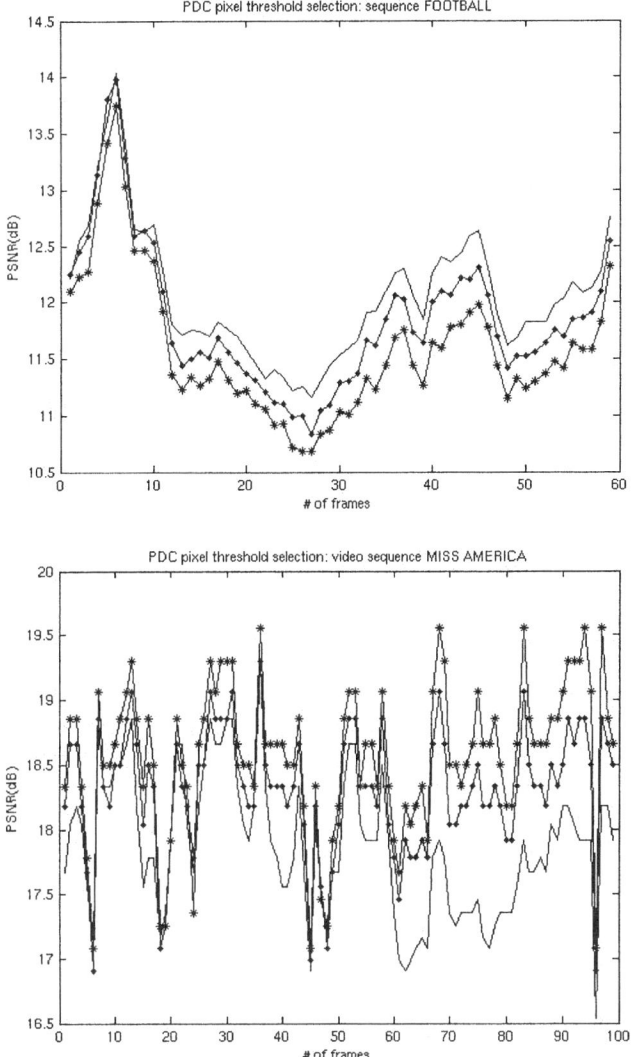

**Fig. 1.** Performance of PDC at selected 3 values of pixel threshold corresponding to video frames

where ——— $t_p = (1F)_{16}$, •-•-•- $t_p = (0F)_{16}$, *-*-*- $t_p = (07)_{16}$

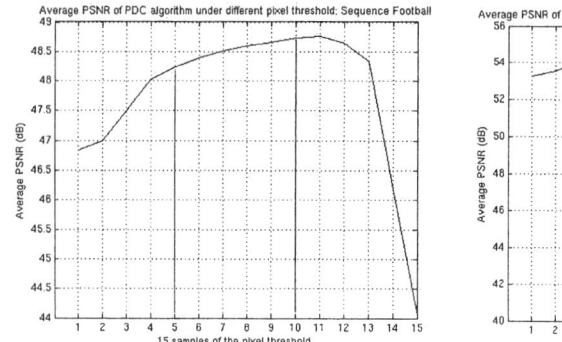 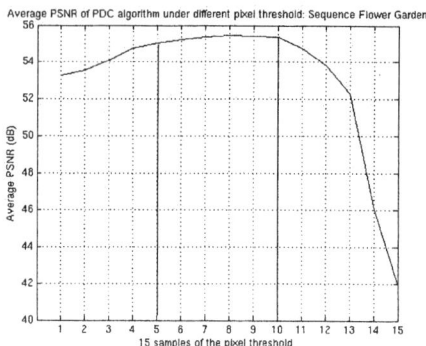

**Fig. 2.** Performance of PDC at different values of pixel threshold for the sequences of Football, Flower Garden, Claire and Table Tennis

## 3 Performance Comparison

Performance of the proposed SPDC algorithm is compared with the MAE, both by full search method. Because the 3SS combined with the MAE is the most adopted for fast and cost effective hardware implementations, so it has been included in our comparison too.

Several video sequences are used including Football, Table Tennis, Flower Garden, Miss America and Salesman. Motion vectors of each frame are estimated against its previous frame. A comparison between the PSNR of the reconstructed frames is reported as an objective measure of the visual quality achieved, some of the results are shown in Figure 3.

Figure 3 compares the PSNR of the reconstructed frames processed by different algorithms. For the Football sequence, which contains fast motions, the proposed algorithm shows a less than 0.5dB average degradation compared with the MAE algorithm. For the sequence Flower Garden, which contains camera panning, performance of the proposed algorithm is even closer to the MAE algorithm. However the 3SS low-complexity algorithm shows a very poor quality, its PSNR shows unstable and unreliable performances of this kind of fast search methods. Due to the page limitation, the reconstructed frames and their error images for different video sequences compared with the proposed SPDC and other algorithms cannot be shown here.

## 4 Implementation Result

Based on the proposed algorithm, we have designed and implemented a systolic array architecture. For this architecture, the number of processing elements (PE) needed by the systolic array is the parameter of the search area. For a search area of $2p-1$, the required PEs are $(2p)^2$; this number has also to be selected for the reference block size to avoid data management problems resulting in idle cycles and decreasing of the hardware efficiency. For the test chip, block size is chosen at 16×16, search area $-8/7$, therefore 256 PEs are needed.

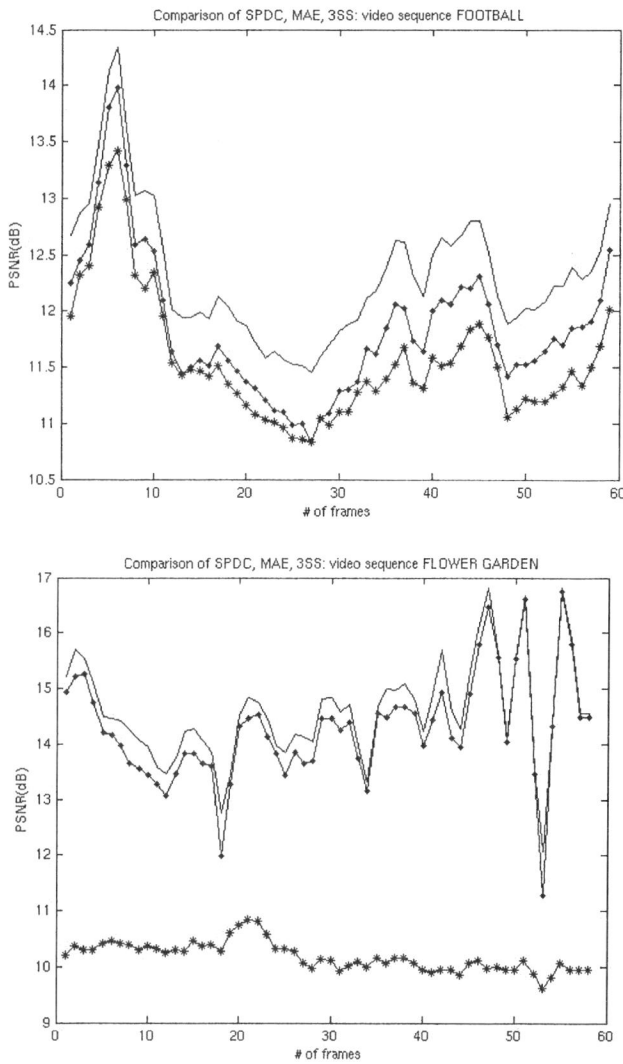

**Fig. 3.** Comparison of performance

where •-•-•- proposed SPDC + FS, _____ MAE+ FS, *-*-*- MAE+ 3SS

A comparison of one PE hardware cost for the proposed SPDC and the conventional MAE is given in Table 1. Architectures of the proposed PE and the conventional one for the MAE are shown in Figure 4. The PE structure for the MAE is obtained from [3, 6]. The proposed PE uses an 8-bit counter replaced the 16-bit accumulator in the PE for MAE. The fixed pixel threshold technique proposed in this work cut down further more hardware cost. Generally for every PE, a 30~40% of area and about 60% of power is saved by the proposed design.

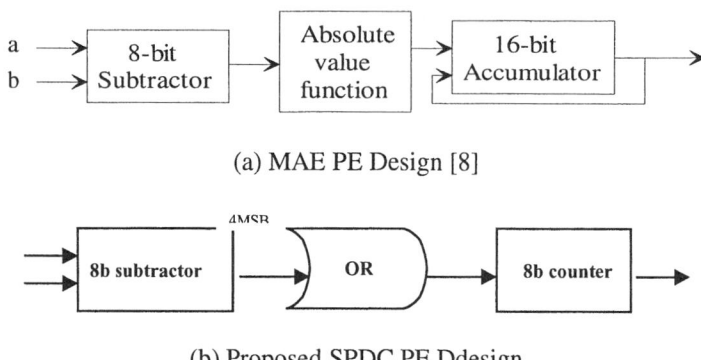

(a) MAE PE Design [8]

(b) Proposed SPDC PE Ddesign

**Fig. 4.** Comparison of processing element structure

The chip layout is obtained by TSMC 0.18-micron CMOS technology. It has a core size of 1.01 $mm^2$, 32 signal pins, which shows a motion estimator with full-search quality, suitable for HDTV applications at about 1/4 of the silicon area of the conventional MAE realization [3].

## 5 Conclusions

In this paper, we present a hardware-oriented block-matching algorithm and its implementation with full search quality for HDTV applications. The architecture is highly regular and modular, saves tremendous designing time. For a video format of 1920×1080 pixels resolution, the proposed implementation can process as many as 50 frames / sec (fps), fast enough for 30fps HDTV applications.

**Table 1.** Comparison of Processing Element Design Technology: 0.18 $\mu m$ CMOS, 6 metal layers

| Clock Cycle | Algorithm | Cell Area ($\mu m^2$) | Dynamic Power(mW) |
|---|---|---|---|
| 5ns | MAD | 10127.40 | 13.08 |
|  | TPC | 6809.88 | 4.94 |
| Savings |  | 32.8% | 62.2% |
| 10ns | MAD | 8216.58 | 6.30 |
|  | TPC | 4890.92 | 2.07 |
| Savings |  | 40.5% | 67.1% |

Compared with conventional algorithms and their implementations in terms of video quality and cost, contributions of the proposed work are significant. It brings a fresh new approach to the research field of algorithms and their implementations for motion estimation.

# References

[1] H. G. Musmann, P. Pirsch, H. - J. Grallert, "Advances in Picture Coding," in *Proceedings of the IEEE,* vol. 73, no. 4, April 1985, pp. 523-548.
[2] Peter Kuhn, Algorithms, Complexity Analysis and VLSI Architectures for MPEG-4 Motion Estimation, Kluwer Academic Publishers, Boston, 1999.
[3] N. Roma, L. Sousa, "Efficient and Configurable Full-Search Block-Matching Processors," in IEEE Trans. on Circuits And Systems For Video Technology, vol. 12, no. 12, Dec. 2002, pp. 1160-1167.
[4] M. Mizuno, et al, "A 1.5-W Single-Chip MPEG-2 MP@ML Video Encoder with Low Power Motion Estimation and Clocking," in IEEE Journal of Solid-State Circuits, vol. 32, no. 11, November 1997, pp.1807~1814.
[5] H. Sato, H. Ohira, et al, "MPEG-2 4:2:2@HL Encoder Chip Set," Proceedings of ISCAS'00, pp. IV-41~44.
[6] L.P.Chau and X. Jing, "Efficient Three-Step Search Algorithm for Block Motion Estimation in Video Coding," in ICASSP'03, pp.III-421~424.
[7] H. Gharavi, M. Mills, "Block-matching Motion Estima-tion Algorithms--New Results," in IEEE Trans. on Circuits And Systems, vol. 37, no. 5, May 1990, pp. 649-651.
[8] KM. Yang, MT. Sun, L. Wu "A Family of VLSI Designs for the Motion Compensation Block-Matching Algorithm," in *IEEE Trans. on CAS,* vol 36, no. 10, Oct. 1989, pp. 1317-1325.

# Robust Global Mosaic Topology Estimation for Real-Time Applications

Nuno Pinho da Silva and João Paulo Costeira

ISR - Instituto Superior Técnico,
Torre Norte, Piso 7
Av.Rovisco Pais, 1 1049-001 Lisboa, Portugal
{nmps, jpc}@isr.ist.utl.pt
http://www.isr.ist.utl.pt

**Abstract.** This paper proposes an iterative methodology for real-time robust mosaic topology inference. It tackles the problem of optimal feature selection (*optimal sampling*) for global estimation of image transformations. This is called IGLOS: iterative global optimal sampling. IGLOS is a unified framework for robust global image registration (optimum feature selection and model computation are considered within the same methodology). The major novelty is that it does not rely on random sampling procedures. Furthermore, by considering an optimal subset of the total number of correspondences, it naturally avoids trivial solution. IGLOS can cope with any motion parameterization and estimation technique. Applications to underwater linear global mosaics and topology estimation are presented.

## 1 Introduction

In underwater activities, globally coherent seabed maps are useful tools to a human operator on a survey mission. Also, they have been used as spatial representations to support underwater autonomous navigation [?,5,10]. In building image mosaics there are two main tasks: image registration and image rendering. If only pair-wise registration is performed, small levels of noise in the estimation process may lead to large accumulated error, particulary if there are loops in the trajectories where non time consecutive frames overlap [1,8]. Furthermore, underwater applications are particulary prone to outliers due to independent moving objects (e.g., fishes or algae), poor lighting condition and mismatches. Therefore, robust global registration is required. Traditionally, this is accomplished with random sampling based algorithms between overlapping pairs followed by mosaic global topology estimation, in particular, with linear models [3,6].

This paper addresses the problem of robust global mosaic topology inference in real-time operations. Instead of removing outliers by random sampling, our methodology tackles the problem of optimal feature selection by sorting. An iterative approach is propose: from a set of correspondences and a model, we choose a subset of points that minimize the regression error. This methodology is called IGLOS: iterative global optimal sampling. Feature selection process is the same as the one used in least trimmed squares [7]. IGLOS depends upon one single parameter that needs no estimation: *pt*, the required number of features to compute the model (*pt* parameter). Usually, trivial solution is avoided by introducing penalizing terms on the cost function [6,8] or using restrict motion models [2]. In our method, by imposing the choice of *pt* optimal features, spread over the image, we not only increase robustness to outliers but also avoid degeneracy. The major contributions are robustness, optimality and low complexity, which makes it suitable for real-time topology estimation.

## 2 Iterative Global Optimal Sampling (IGLOS)

### 2.1 Problem Formulation

Consider the image registration example of Figure 1. For the sake of clarity, assume that camera motion between $I_k$ (image $k$) and the reference image $I_0$ is adequately described by an affine transformation $\mathbf{H}_{0k}$[1], and that $p$ correspondences were found between pairs of images $(I_i, I_j)$. Let $h_k = row(\mathbf{H}_{0k})$ be a column vector formed by stacking the first two rows of $\mathbf{H}_{0k}$ (see [4] for details on *row* operator). In matrix form:

$$\mathbf{H}_{0k} = \begin{bmatrix} \alpha_1^k & \alpha_2^k & \alpha_3^k \\ \alpha_4^k & \alpha_5^k & \alpha_6^k \\ 0 & 0 & 1 \end{bmatrix}$$

$$h_k = [\alpha_1^k, \alpha_2^k, \alpha_3^k, \alpha_4^k, \alpha_5^k, \alpha_6^k]^t$$

$$h_0 = [1, 0, 0, 0, 1, 0]^t$$

Using the notation $x = [u \; v \; 1]^t$ and $\mathbf{C}(x) = \begin{bmatrix} u & v & 1 & 0 & 0 & 0 \\ 0 & 0 & 0 & u & v & 1 \end{bmatrix}$ the registration error between a pair of corresponding points, measured in the reference image $I_0$ is given by $\varepsilon_{ij}^n = \|\mathbf{C}(x_{ij}^n) \cdot h_i - \mathbf{C}(x_{ji}^n) \cdot h_j\|_2^2$, where $x_{ij}^n \leftrightarrow x_{ji}^n$ is the $n$th $(n \leq p)$ pair of corresponding points between images $I_i$ and $I_j$, in homogenous coordinates. The global residue is written as:

$$\varepsilon = \left\| \begin{bmatrix} \mathbf{C}(x_{01}^1) & -\mathbf{C}(x_{10}^1) & 0 \\ \vdots & \vdots & \vdots \\ \mathbf{C}(x_{01}^p) & -\mathbf{C}(x_{10}^p) & 0 \\ \mathbf{C}(x_{02}^1) & 0 & -\mathbf{C}(x_{20}^1) \\ \vdots & \vdots & \vdots \\ \mathbf{C}(x_{02}^p) & 0 & -\mathbf{C}(x_{20}^p) \\ 0 & \mathbf{C}(x_{12}^1) & -\mathbf{C}(x_{21}^1) \\ \vdots & \vdots & \vdots \\ 0 & \mathbf{C}(x_{12}^p) & -\mathbf{C}(x_{21}^p) \end{bmatrix} \cdot \begin{bmatrix} h_0 \\ h_1 \\ h_2 \end{bmatrix} \right\|_2^2 = \|\mathbf{A} \cdot \bar{h}\|_2^2 = \|\bar{\varepsilon}\|_2^2 \quad (1)$$

---

[1] This is the most general collineation allowing for the residual vector to be expressed as a linear combination of the motion parameters, for more than 2 images.

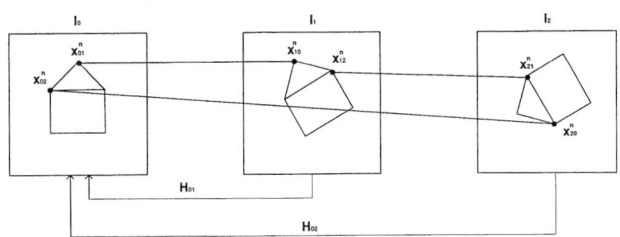

**Fig. 1.** Image registration example with three images

Note that each row of matrix $\mathbf{A}$ is related to the coordinates of a single matched pair. Given a model estimate $\bar{h}$, finding the optimum set of inliers is tantamount to choosing the entries of $\bar{\varepsilon}$ such that the global error $\varepsilon$ is minimum in the least squares sense. This can be done by left multiplying $\mathbf{A}$ by a diagonal matrix $\mathbf{P}$ with $1, 0$ entries respectively. Thus, the problem of global robust registration can be stated through the following optimization problem:

Problem 1. $\quad (\mathbf{P}^*, \bar{h}^*) = \underset{\mathbf{P} \in \mathcal{D}_{01}^{pt}, \ \|\bar{h}\| = 1}{\arg\min} \{\|\mathbf{P} \cdot \mathbf{A} \cdot \bar{h}\|_2^2\}$

where $\mathcal{D}_{01}^{pt}$ is the set of diagonal matrices with $\{0, 1\}$ entries and rank $pt$ (to avoid null solution). The $pt$ parameter is the total number of required inliers (the number of 1's in $\mathbf{P}$). If $p_{min}$ is the minimum number of features to instantiate some model (e.g., $p_{min} = 3$ for affine or $p_{min} = 4$ for the general homography) and $p_k$ correspondences were found between each image pair $M_k$, in a total of $M$ matched pairs, then $pt$ is the sum of all $pt_k : p_{min} \leq pt_k \leq p_k$ correspondences between all matched frames. In the example of Figure 1, $pt_k = p_{min} = 3$, $\forall k$ then $pt = \sum_{m=1}^{3} pt_k = 9$.

Since $(\mathbf{P}^*$ and $\bar{h}^*)$ are unknowns, this problem is a nonlinear optimization problem. Furthermore, it is an integer problem in the $\mathbf{P}$ variable. Its combinatorial nature requires exhaustive search to finding a solution. To avoid this exhaustive search issue, some algorithms randomly sample the search space which is equivalent to randomly assign 1's and 0's in matrix $\mathbf{P}$. Though complex, Problem 1 is separable, in the sense that knowing one variable we can easily compute the other. Decoupling Problem 1, makes possible to avoid combinatorial explosion.

### 2.2 Iterative Approach for Solving Problem 1

Assume that, at iteration $q$, one knows an estimate $\mathbf{P}^q$ of $\mathbf{P}$, that is, a subset of correspondences. Knowing $h_0$ (e.g., for affine transformation $h_0 = [100010]$), the registration error is $\varepsilon = \|(\mathbf{P}^q \cdot \mathbf{A}) \cdot \bar{h} - (\mathbf{P}^q \cdot \mathbf{A}_0) \cdot h_0\|_2^2$, where $\mathbf{A}_0$ collects the columns correspondent to the reference image, $\mathbf{A}$ the remaining columns and $\bar{h}$ is the frame-to-mosaic global model for the remaining frames. Writing $b_0 = (\mathbf{P}^q \cdot \mathbf{A}_0) \cdot h_0$, Problem 1 reduces to

Problem 2. $\bar{h}^* = \arg\min_{\bar{h}} \{\|(\mathbf{P}^k \cdot \mathbf{A}) \cdot \bar{h} - b_0\|_2^2\}$

which solution gives an optimal $\bar{h}$ for the considered set of features. Note that $\mathbf{P}^q$ is idempotent $((\mathbf{P}^q)^t \cdot \mathbf{P}^q = \mathbf{P}^q)$. As long as $\mathbf{A}$ is full rank ($p_k \geq p_{min}$) and assuming affine motion, the solution to Problem 2 is

$$\bar{h}^* = (\mathbf{A}^t \cdot \mathbf{P}^q \cdot \mathbf{A})^{-1} \cdot (\mathbf{P}^q \cdot \mathbf{A})^t \cdot b_0 \qquad (2)$$

Given $\bar{h}^*$, an optimal set of correspondences can be found by solving

Problem 3. $\mathbf{P}^* = \arg\min_{\mathbf{P} \in \mathcal{D}_{01}^{pt}} \{\|\mathbf{P} \cdot \bar{\varepsilon}\|_2^2\}$

If an efficient solution for the above problem exists, one may iterate between choosing the optimum set of features with known motion and computing the best global transformation from a set of $pt$ correspondences. Initialization and other implementation issues are discussed in Section 3.

### 2.3 Optimal Sampling: Inlier Selection

Optimal sampling refers to the selection of the inliers that minimizes $\varepsilon$, that is, efficient solution of Problem 3. Reshape $\bar{h}$ by reintroducing $h_0$ into the proper entries (considering a sequence of $N$ frames, $\bar{h} = [h_0\ h_1\ ,\ldots,\ h_N]^t$ for $I_0 = I_1$). Given the transformation, all pair-wise residues measured in the mosaic frame $\varepsilon_{ij}^n$ are stacked into the residual vector $\bar{\varepsilon}$ in ascending image order. Recalling that $\mathbf{P}$ is idempotent, the global registration error can be expressed as

$$\varepsilon = \|\mathbf{P} \cdot \bar{\varepsilon}\|_2^2 = \sum_j^{T_p} (\bar{\varepsilon}_j)^2 \cdot \mathbf{P}_{jj} \qquad (3)$$

Thus, optimal sampling is accomplished by *sorting the residual vector and choosing the first $pt_k$ entries between each matched pair $M_k$*. Sorting $\bar{\varepsilon}$ is performed in $\sum_{k=1}^{M} \mathcal{O}(p_k \log p_k)$ complexity, where $p_k$ are the correspondences found in each matched pair $M_k$, $k = 1, \ldots, M$. $pt_k$ is the number of required inliers, that is, $p_{min} \leq pt_k \leq p_k$. It turns out that this process leads to the criterium of the least trimmed squares [7]. Figure 2 outlines the methodology.

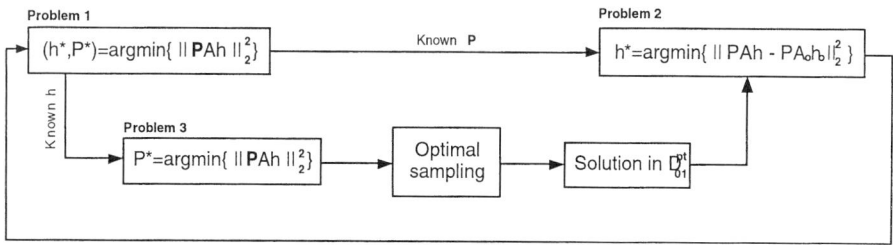

**Fig. 2.** Outline of the methodology

## 3 Implementation

Section 2.3 describes how to efficiently solve Problem 3. Given some initial feature subset (or motion estimation), one may iterate between find the optimal subset of features and compute the model with the selected subset until the following is verified

$$| \; \|\mathbf{P}^q \cdot \mathbf{A} \cdot \bar{h}^{q-1}\|_2^2 - \|\mathbf{P}^q \cdot \mathbf{A} \cdot \bar{h}^q\|_2^2 \; | \leq \theta \qquad (4)$$

or a $q = K_{max}$ iterations ($N$ is the total of frames in the sequence).

By defining regions on the image, features may be selected by constraining them to these regions in order to avoid degeneracy. Also, in Problem 2, $b_0$ is null everywhere except for the entries correspondent to coordinates in the reference frame. Therefore, reducing the number of selected features introduces less zeros in $b_0$, thus avoiding a solution close to the trivial solution ($\bar{h} = 0$).

Note that by decoupling Problem 1, inlier selection and motion computation are made independent. Extending IGLOS for accurate global registration is done by replacing Equation 2 with a nonlinear method.

To decrease computational burden, one may consider only the frames that overlap with the last one acquired. This considerably reduces the dimension of $\mathbf{P}$, consequently, the computational cost. Furthermore, instead of using batch least squares, model can be obtained using recursive least squares [3], making IGLOS suitable for real-time applications.

### 3.1 Initialization

We propose an *iterative initialization*[2]. In case of image mosaicing, we used the assumptions that image motion is smooth. In fact, one reasonable assumption is that the transformation between consecutive image is (picewise) constant. In other words, initial motion estimates between consecutive images are given by $\mathbf{H}_{(l-1)l} = \mathbf{H}_{(l-2)(l-1)}$, where $I_l$ is the last acquired frame. If the transformation between the first 2 frames is known (a global translation which can be easily estimated or computed by other methods), frame-to-mosaic initialization proceeds as follow:

$$\begin{aligned}\mathbf{H}_{0l} &= \mathbf{H}_{0(l-2)} \cdot \mathbf{H}_{(l-2)(l-1)} \cdot \mathbf{H}_{(l-1)l} \\ \mathbf{H}_{(l-2)(l-1)} &= (\mathbf{H}_{0(l-2)})^{-1} \cdot \mathbf{H}_{0(l-1)} \\ \mathbf{H}_{(l-1)l} &= \mathbf{H}_{(l-2)(l-1)} \\ \mathbf{H}_{(l-1)l} &= (\mathbf{H}_{0(l-2)})^{-1} \cdot \mathbf{H}_{0(l-1)}\end{aligned} \Rightarrow \mathbf{H}_{0l} = \mathbf{H}_{0(l-1)} \cdot (\mathbf{H}_{0(l-2)})^{-1} \cdot \mathbf{H}_{0(l-1)} \qquad (5)$$

for $l \geq 3$.

## 4 Experimental Results

Consider that a planar seabed is filmed by a moving camera pointing downwards. In each selected frame, a set of features were matched with a correlation based

---

[2] The authors acknowledge Prof. José Santos-Victor for this contribution.

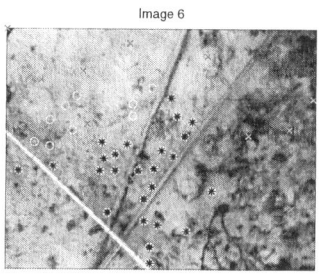
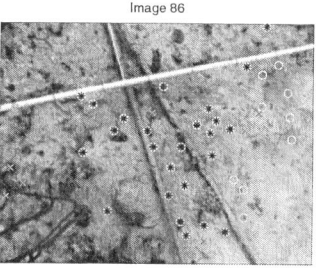

**Fig. 3.** Two images from the rock sequence, taken at non consecutive time. Superimposed inliers are depicted as circles 'o', outliers as crosses 'x' and IGLOS optimum set as asterisks '*'. No outlier was returned in the optimum.

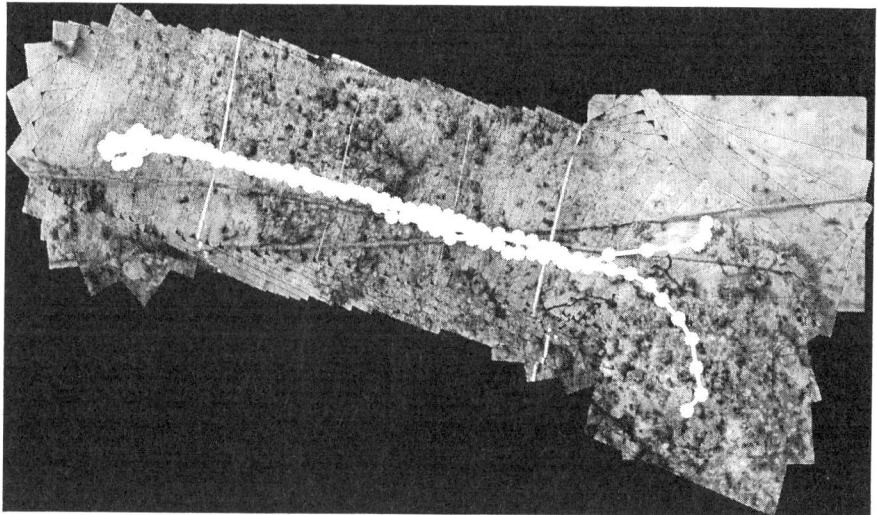

**Fig. 4.** Global IGLOS mosaic image. Topology is superimposed.

matcher as in [2]. The mosaic in Figure 4, constructed from a N=96 frames sequence[3], contains 610 overlapping pairs (Figure 3). Besides the real outliers, the set was contaminated with 30% of outliers, randomly taken from a uniform distribution over the image plane, to give a benchmark for performance. We require $pt_k = 25$ inliers for every $M_k$ matched pair and affine model was assumed. Setting the first image as the reference frame $I_0$, we assume $h_2$ and $h_3$ (the transform from frames $I_2$ and $I_3$ to $I_0$, respectively) to be a global translation, after which initializations proceed as described in Section 3.1. Images were rendered with the use-last operator.

Figure 4 presents the correctly estimated topology superimposed. The maximum number of iterations per frame was set to $K_{max} = 50$ but the average

---

[3] The authors acknowledge Nuno Gracias for the image set and rendering procedures.

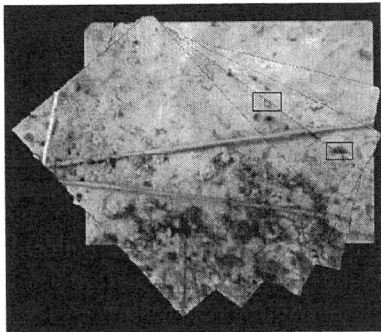 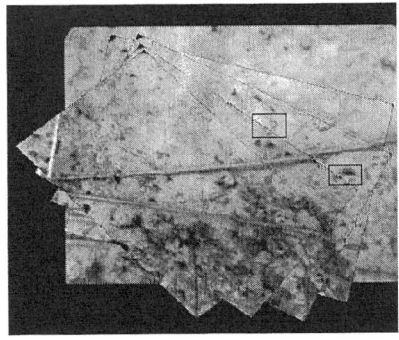

**Fig. 5.** Details from resulting mosaics. **Left:** from IGLOS mosaic. **Right:** from linear least squares mosaic.

number of iterations per frame was $K = 42.7345$. In the same conditions, a random sampling algorithm would have done $K_p = 24$ iterations per overlapping pair, meaning that $K = \frac{24 \cdot 610}{96} = 152.5$ iterations per frame would be necessary to assure, with 95% of probability (not optimal), that all points sampled i one sample would contain no outliers. The returned optimal set contains no outliers (Figure 3). Besides efficiency, selecting an optimum set of features promotes accuracy on linear mosaic construction, which is important in survey missions. Figure 5 illustrates details of the resulting mosaics with IGLOS and linear least squares. Superimposed boxes highlight the differences. Despite outliers, in the left image it is possible to observe that only one rock and sea weed exist. IGLOS provides a methodology for real-time robust mosaic topology estimation and improves accuracy in the resulting mosaic.

## 5 Summary and Conclusions

We have formulated the problem of global robust registration as a nonlinear mixed-integer optimization problem. To avoid NP hard problem, an iterative methodology was proposed, IGLOS: *iterative global optimal sampling*. Outliers rejection is performed through pair-wise sorting and model is globally estimated. The applicability of IGLOS to robust global consistent mosaics was discussed.

The methodology presented does not rely on random sampling procedures or on any estimate of the inlier standard deviation to assure robustness. Other motion parameterizations (e.g., similarity or full collineation) and non-linear estimation are straightforwardly introduced in the methodology. Major contributions are robustness with low complexity and optimality in the least squares sense. The tradeoff is dependence of initialization. IGLOS provide a unified framework for robust global registration (optimum feature selection and model computation are performed within the same methodology). In autonomous navigation, IGLOS allows for real-time robust mosaic topology inference.

# References

1. Duffin, K., Barret W.: Globally optimal image mosaics. Graphics Interface, pp.217-222, 1998.
2. Gracias, N.: Mosaic-based Visual Navigation for Autonomous Underwater Vehicles. Phd Thesis, Instituto Superior Técnico. Universidade Técnica de Lisboa, 2002.
3. Gracias, N., Costeira, J., Santos-Victor, J.: Linear Global Mosaics for Underwater Surveying. 4th IFAC/EURON Symposium on Autonomous Vehicles, IAV04, Lisbon, Portugal, 2004.
4. Llkepohl, H.: Handbook of Matrices. Springer, 1996.
5. Negadahripour, S., Horn, B.: Direct passive navigation. PAMI, 9(1), January, 1987.
6. Pizarro, O. and Singh, H.: Toward large-area mosaicing for underwater scientific applications. IEEE journal of oceanic engineering, vol. 28(4), October, 2003.
7. Rosseeuw, P.J., Leroy, A.M.: Robust Regression and Outlier Detection. John Wiley and Sons, 1987.
8. Sawhney, H., Hsu, S., Kumar, R.: Robust video mosaicing through topology inference and local to global aligment. Proc. European conference on computer vision, Springer-Verlag, June, 1998.
9. Torr, P.H.S., Murray, D.W.: The Development and Comparison of Robust Methods for Estimating the Fundamental Matrix. IJCV, 24(3),271-300, 1997.
10. Unnikrishnan, R., Kelly, A.: Mosaicing large cyclic environments for visual navigation in autonomous vehicles. Proc. International conference o robotics and automation (ICRA2002), pp. 4299-4306, Washington DC, USA, May, 2002.

# Real-Time Digital Image Warping for Display Distortion Correction

Dongil Han

Vision and Image Processing Lab.,
Sejong University,
Seoul, Korea
dihan@sejong.ac.kr

**Abstract.** This paper describes a digital image warping method which reduces the geometric and optical distortions in several display devices such as wide screen CRTs, Projection TVs and Projectors. The 2-pass scan line warping algorithm is introduced and it effectively reduces the typical type of display distortions such as keystone, pincushion, or barrel types. The proposed warping algorithm also considers the image scaling function and renders arbitrary image scaling up or down with display distortion correction. The proposed architecture is successfully implemented in hardware and operates at the clock speed around 40 ~ 160MHz. Finally, it is successfully adopted in display distortion correction purposes.

## 1 Introduction

Recently, digital TV enables high quality display resolutions according to the development of innovative display devices such as flat panel PDP, LCD, ELD(Electro Luminescent Display) and several kinds of projection TV sets based on the PRT, LCD, DLP and LCoS. The advantage of projection system is that the large screen can be obtained easily compared to the flat panels or direct view display devices. But the projection display system tends to be bulky compared to the plat panel display systems. Therefore, extensive development efforts are being conducted into large screen display systems with light weight and small volume and depth.

The low cost display system uses direct-view CRT screens and the maximum 34" or 36" CRT size is used for wide screen display. As the screen size gets larger, the CRT also has larger display distortions. The traditional CRT uses the DY(Deflection Yoke), CPM (Convergence and Purity Magnet Rings) and magnetic tapes to reduce and correct the several kinds of geometric distortions[1]. But, the adjustment of DY and CPM gets more complex as the size of CRT gets bigger. Thus, to solve these problems systematically, the imaginary position coordinate is introduced in [2]. By using a DSP technology, this system realizes a microcomputer controlled multi-scan monitor system with geometry correction and deflection control. But this kind of control methods cannot be applied to the other kind of display distortion correction [3].

The digital image warping technique can be a good solution for solving the above mentioned display image distortion problems [4][5]. The image warping is a key feature for implementing image morphing which has proven to be a powerful tool for visual effects in film and television, enabling the fluid transformation of one digital image into another. Image morphing is realized by coupling image warping with color interpolation. Image warping applies 2-D geometric transformations to the images to retain geometric alignment between their features.

A number of methods for correcting the lens distortion in real-time or embedded applications have been reported. Especially, a lens geometric and photometric distortion correction method to obtain a high quality image with low cost digital cameras is introduced in [6]. Lens geometric distortion coefficient of a digital camera is estimated using a simplified camera calibration technique. Based on the estimate of the lens geometric distortion coefficients, image warping adapted for DSP architecture is applied in this method.

Wu [7] presents an efficient inverse warping algorithm for generating novel views from multiple reference images taken from different viewpoints. His method proceeds in three steps: preprocess for edge-pixel extraction, inverse warping from the primary image, and hole filling from remaining reference images. Using the algorithm, two virtual offices have been tested and they can navigate virtual environments at an interactive rate.

In this paper, we adopted the digital image warping techniques in low cost display equipment and described the hardware architecture of the proposed method. Due to the characteristics of display equipment, digital image warping should be implemented in real-time. Therefore, we introduced the two-pass scan line warping algorithm which can be implemented in real-time hardware for correcting the typical types of display distortions such as keystone, pincushion, or barrel.

## 2 Digital Image Warping for Display Distortion Correction

The typical geometrical and optical distortion examples in display devices are shown in Figure 1. The real-world restrictions of manufacturing tolerances result in display devices that deviate from the ideal case. Depending on the type of display device, one or more geometrical distortions can be occurred. The CRT type displays tend to show the tilt and pincushion type distortions. The projector typically shows the keystone type distortions. The projection type displays tend to show the tilt, keystone, barrel and pincushion. These distortions usually require external correction logic to perform the device to operate within tolerances demanded by the end-user.

Figure 2 shows the block diagram of proposed digital image scaling and warping system. The resolution of input image can be different compared to the resolution of display devices. Thus the image-scaling block is also an essential part of the proposed digital warping system.

By using the 2-pass scan line algorithm, the warping function is operated in the horizontal and vertical directions, separately. This operation should consider with the image scaling function to minimize the required hardware cost. In the warping mode, as shown in figure 2, the input image is scaled into the display size in horizontal direction and stored to the video memory. After that, the image is scaled into the display size in vertical direction in the vertical scaling block. And then, the image is warped in the vertical direction and stored to the video memory. Finally, the image is warped in the horizontal direction and the proposed block generates the video which is the image scaled to the display resolution and intentionally added distortions which reduces the display distortions in final display stage.

The detailed description of the vertical and horizontal warping block is shown in figure 3 and figure 4.

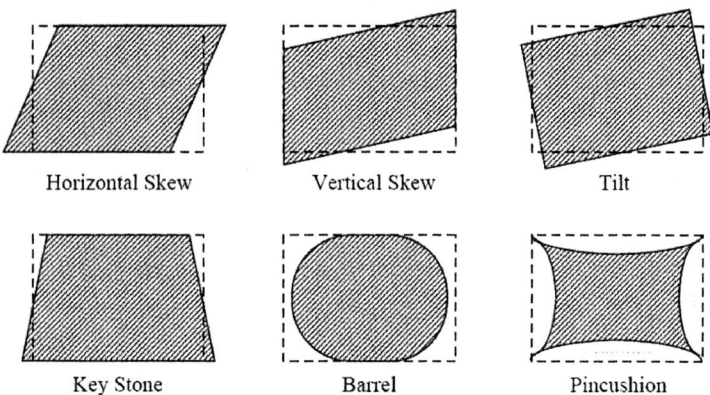

**Fig. 1.** The typical display distortion examples

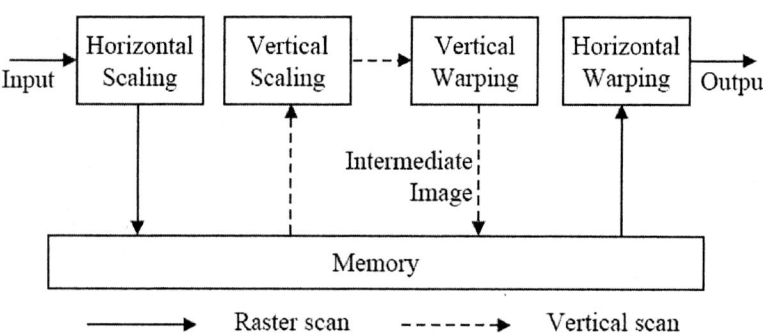

**Fig. 2.** The overall warping system

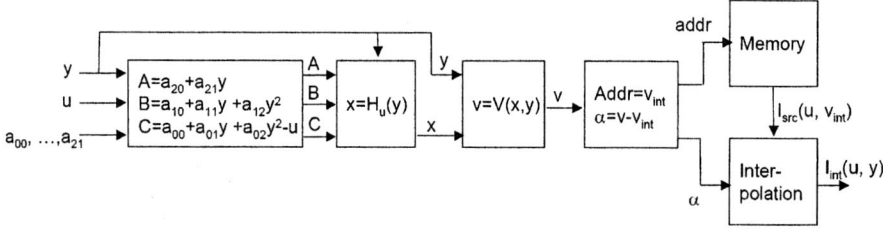

**Fig. 3.** The vertical warping block diagram

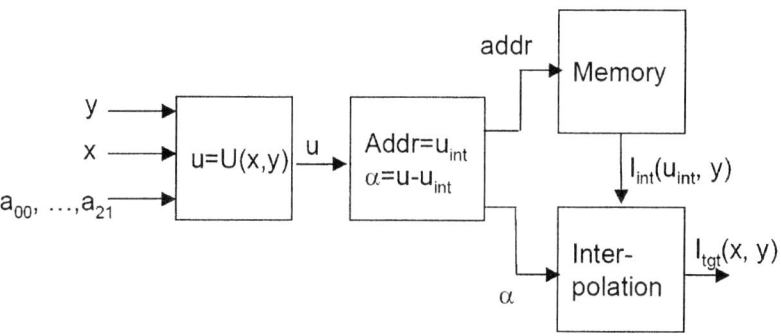

**Fig. 4.** The horizontal warping block diagram

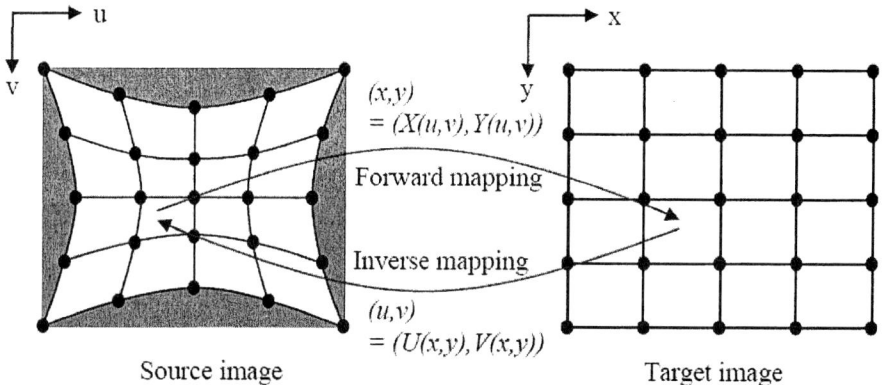

**Fig. 5.** Source and destination image coordinates

As shown in figure 5, suppose that a source image $I_{src}$ with pixel coordinates (u, v) undergoes geometric transformation to produce a target image $I_{tgt}$ with coordinates (x, y). This inverse mapping function can be expressed as the following polynomial equations.

$$u = U(x, y) = \sum_{i=0}^{N} \sum_{j=0}^{N-i} a_{ij} x^i y^j \tag{1}$$

$$v = V(x, y) = \sum_{i=0}^{N} \sum_{j=0}^{N-i} b_{ij} x^i y^j \tag{2}$$

The transform can represent more complex shape of distortion when selecting the large number of N. But the hardware complexity for implementing the transform also increases. The typical shapes of distortions in conventional display devices were introduced in figure 1 and the relations between the orders of polynomial N and the possible shape of correctable distortions are summarized in Table 1.

**Table 1.** The correctable distortion shapes with the different selection of N

| The order of polynomial, N | The type of correctable distortions |
|---|---|
| 1 | Horizontal Skew, Vertical Skew, Tilt |
| 2 | Keystone |
| 3 | Pincushion, Barrel |

For correcting the pincushion and barrel distortion, N = 3 is selected in our implementation.

The reverse mapping scan line algorithm has the following three steps.

Step 1. From the equation 1, derive the auxiliary function $x = H_u(y)$ which can be obtained by solving the x position of target image with respect to target y positions by holding u constant.

When the order of polynomial N equals 3, the equation (1) and (2) can be rewritten as following equations.

$$u = U(x,y) \\ = a_{00} + a_{01}y + a_{02}y^2 + a_{03}y^3 + a_{10}x + a_{11}xy + a_{12}xy^2 + a_{20}x^2 + a_{21}x^2y + a_{30}x^3 \quad (3)$$

$$v = V(x,y) \\ = b_{00} + b_{01}y + b_{02}y^2 + b_{03}y^3 + b_{10}x + b_{11}xy + b_{12}xy^2 + b_{20}x^2 + b_{21}x^2y + b_{30}x^3 \quad (4)$$

In above equations, the $y^3$ and $x^3$ terms are not required for correcting the pincushion and barrel type distortions. Thus, we can get more compact and simple forms.

$$u = U(x,y) = a_{00} + a_{01}y + a_{02}y^2 + a_{10}x + a_{11}xy + a_{12}xy^2 + a_{20}x^2 + a_{21}x^2y \quad (5)$$

$$v = V(x,y) = b_{00} + b_{01}y + b_{02}y^2 + b_{10}x + b_{11}xy + b_{12}xy^2 + b_{20}x^2 + b_{21}x^2y \quad (6)$$

In order to calculate the auxiliary function $H_u(y)$, let's hold u constant in equation (5). Then the equation (5) can be rewritten as a simple quadratic equation.

$$Ax^2 + Bx + C = 0 \quad (7)$$

Here,

$$A = a_{20} + a_{21}y \quad (8)$$

$$B = a_{10} + a_{11}y + a_{12}y^2 \quad (9)$$

$$C = a_{00} + a_{01}y + a_{02}y^2 - u. \quad (10)$$

By solving the quadratic equation, we can get auxiliary function $H_u(y)$ as follows.

$$x = H_u(y) = \frac{-B \pm \sqrt{B^2 - 4AC}}{2A} \quad (11)$$

Step 2. Once $x = H_u(y)$ is determined, the second step plugs it into the equation (2). And then we can get $v = V(H_u(y), y)$ which can evaluate the source $v$ coordinate of all pixels with respect to target $y$ position. From this mapping function, we can get vertically warped intermediate image $I_{int}$ as follows.

$$I_{int}(u, y) = I_{src}(u, V(H_u(y), y)) = I_{src}(u, v) \quad (12)$$

Step 3. The mapping function $u = U(x, y)$ is applied to the vertically warped image $I_{int}$ and finally we can get vertically and horizontally warped image $I_{tgt}$.

$$I_{tgt}(x, y) = I_{int}(U(x, y), y) = I_{int}(u, y) \quad (13)$$

## 3 Experimental Results

The proposed hardware architecture is firstly simulated in C. The simulation includes the image scaling and display distortion correction and these functions are conducted in x and y direction, independently. The display distortion correction functions

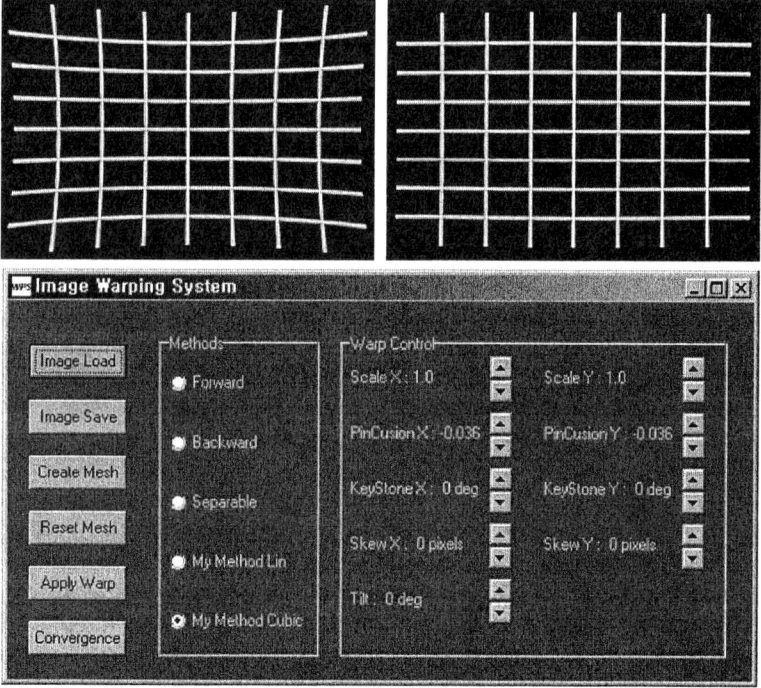

**Fig. 6.** C simulation window with source and destination images

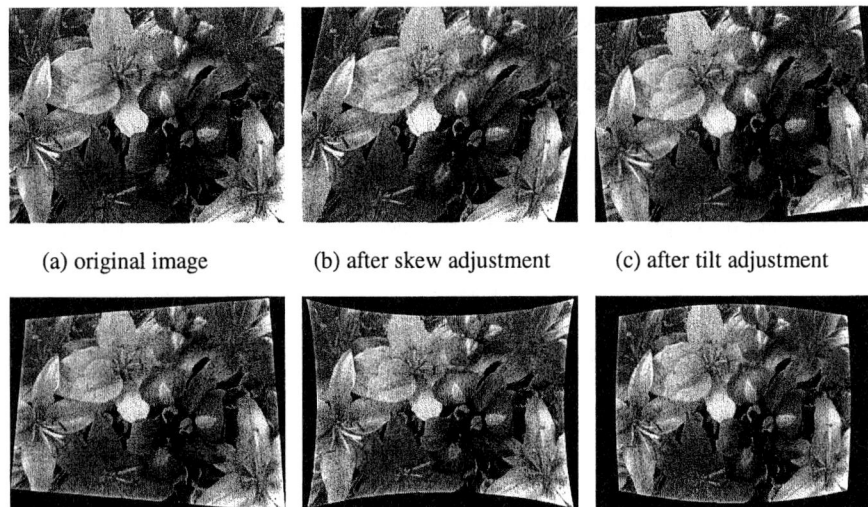

(a) original image   (b) after skew adjustment   (c) after tilt adjustment
(d) after keystone adjustment   (e) after pincushion adjustment   (f) after barrel adjustment

**Fig. 7.** VHDL simulation results

include pincushion, keystone, skew, tilt and convergence correction. Figure 6 shows a snap shot of simulation window with the source image is located in top left position. After the adjusting the warp variables in simulation window and clicking the "Apply Warp" button, the target image is generated in the right side of the source image. Horizontal and vertical pincushion control function is used in this figure.

The proposed hardware architecture is implemented in VHDL and the VHDL simulation shows the same result compared to the C simulation. Using the hardware emulation, many still and moving images are tested. Figure 7 shows VHDL simulation result of several types of display distortion correction. The first image shows original flower image. The next images show the results of skew, tilt, keystone, pincushion and barrel warp control.

Finally, the proposed hardware architecture is implemented in FPGA. The operation frequency of the proposed 2-pass scan line digital image warping system is faster than 162MHz and can be applied for UXGA resolution display system.

## 4 Conclusion

We have described the 2-pass scan line digital image warping method and real-time hardware architecture. For integrating the image scaling and digital image warping, the warping system is separated into two parts and generates intermediate image. This intermediate image enables raster-scan input and raster-scan output and also enables the overall system working in real-time. Most of the distortion types of display devices such as skew, tilt, keystone, pincushion and barrel are considered and the proposed image warping method can adjust and correct all of these display distortions in real-time.

The camera lens system also has a similar kind of geometric and photometric distortions. The rectification of stereo matching system also has a similar problem. Therefore, the future work will investigate these application areas and find solutions for correcting these problems by using the developed real-time digital image warping method.

## Acknowledgments

This work is supported by grant No R01-2003-000-10785-0 from the Basic Research Program of the Korea Science & Engineering Foundation, System IC 2010 program and by the IC Design Education Center.

## References

1. Zeungnam Bien, Dongil Han, Jongcheol Park, Jong-Woon Lee, Changsuk Oh: Real time color purity and convergence measurement algorithms for automatic ITC adjustment system. in IEEE Workshop on Applications of Computer Vision, Proceedings, pp. 274 – 281, 30 Nov.-2, Dec.1992.
2. N. Yamazaki, K. - I. Shibuya, T. Nagamine, H. Sakurai and H. Takegoshi: Digital geometry correction and deflection control system for multi-scan monitors. in IEEE Trans. on Consumer Electronics, vol. 41, no. 3 Aug. 1995, pp. 540-549.
3. Jerry C. Whitaker: Video Display Engineering. in McGraw-Hill, 2001.
4. George Wolberg: Digital Image Warping. in IEEE Computer Society Press, Los Alamitos, California, 1990
5. George Wolberg and Terrance E. Boult: Separable image warping methods and systems using spatial lookup tables. in U. S. patent 5,204,944
6. Wonpil Yu: An embedded camera lens distortion correction method for mobile computing applications. in IEEE Trans. on Consumer Electronics, vol. 41, no. 3 Aug. 1995, pp. 540-549.
7. Enhua Wu and Xin Zheng: Composition of novel views through an efficient image warping. in The Visual Computer, vol. 19, no 15 Aug. 2003, pp.319-328

# Complexity-Controllable Motion Estimation for Real-Time Video Encoder

Zhi Yang, Haixiang Zhang, Jiajun Bu, and Chun Chen*

College of Computer Science, Zhejiang University,
310027 Hang zhou, P.R. China
{yangzh, bjj, chenc}@zju.edu.cn
zhhx@vip.sina.com

**Abstract.** Motion estimation (ME) is the main bottleneck and by far the most time-consuming module in real-time video coding application. Based on sufficient statistical analysis, a novel complexity-controllable ME algorithm is presented in this paper. The proposed algorithm consists of three effective stages: 1) initial stage with zero-motion detection, 2) predictive stage with early termination scheme, and 3) local refined stage by small diamond search. Furthermore, with given complexity constraints, a complexity-controllable scheme is introduced into the search process, which can achieve the preferable tradeoff between motion accuracy and ME complexity. Experimental results demonstrate that our proposed algorithm achieves similar performance with significantly reduced number of search points in comparison with some well-known ME algorithms, such as diamond search, hexagon-based search and enhanced hexagon-based search, etc. Moreover, due to its complexity-controllable feature, our algorithm can be adapted to various devices with a wide range of computational capability for real-time video encoder.

## 1 Introduction

With the rapid development of networks, more and more real-time video coding applications come into being. Because of complexity constraint, many highly efficient but complex algorithms cannot be directly used in real-time video encoder. Although specific fast algorithms can be adopted to satisfy a specific scenario, it is not a cost effective way since there are so many different scenarios. Therefore, it is desirable to design complexity-controllable algorithms which can adapt to the available computational resources dynamically.

Motion estimation (ME) plays an important role in video coding system to eliminate temporal redundancy between video pictures. Because of simplicity and effectiveness, block-matching ME has been widely adopted by video coding standards, such as MPEG-x and H.26x[1]. Meanwhile, ME is computationally intensive, e.g. the full search algorithm consumes up to 80% of computing time.

---

* The work was supported by National Natural Science Foundation of China (60203013), 863 Program (2004AA1Z2390) and Key Technologies R&D Program of Zhejiang Province(2005C23047 & 2004C11052).

For this reason, many fast ME algorithms have been developed to alleviate the heavy computation load, such as new three-step search (TSS)[2], four-step search (FSS)[3], diamond search (DS)[4] and hexagon-based search (HEXBS)[5]. Furthermore, some predictive ME algorithms[6][7] use spatio-temporal correlation to ulteriorly reduce the search points. However, despite the significant speedup, ME still consumes the largest amount of computational resources, especially in real-time video coding.

In order to further reduce the complexity, complexity-scalable ME has been studied, which can provide a proper tradeoff between motion accuracy and computational-complexity. In reference [8], a partial-distance metric is used to limit the number of candidates through a threshold-process that enables complexity scalability. In reference [9], complexity scalability is obtained by scaling the number of the processed motion vector (MV) fields and the number of vector evaluations.

Different from previous works, in this paper, we present a novel complexity-controllable ME (CCME) algorithm. In the proposed algorithm, the ME process consists of three stages, called initial stage, predictive stage and refined stage. The search process of each block can be terminated at any aforementioned stage due to zero-motion detection and early termination schemes. Withal, different texture and motion within block lead to different search complexity. Therefore, a complexity-controllable scheme is used to adaptively allocate resources to each block and controls the entire complexity of all ME in one picture is up-bounded, which is crucial for real-time video coding application to avoid delay and jitter.

The rest of the paper is organized as follows. Sufficient statistical analysis and the three-stage ME algorithm are presented in *Section 2*. In *Section 3*, the complexity-controllable scheme is proposed. Experimental results and comparative analysis are shown in *Section 4* and conclusions are drawn in *Section 5*.

## 2 Proposed Motion Estimation Algorithm

### 2.1 Initial Stage with Zero Motion Detection

The block motion in real world video sequences is usually gentle, smooth, and varies slowly. Most of blocks can be regarded as stationary or quasi-stationary. *Fig. 1* shows the MV distribution based on full search algorithm for three test sequences. For "News"and "Silence"with movement restricted to the center area, nearly 80% blocks can be regarded as stationary. And for "Foreman"which consists of disordered motion in all directions, the MV distribution is still center-biased. Commonly, macroblock (MB) with the size of $16 \times 16$ is used to perform ME, and the sum of absolute difference ($SAD$) is used to measure the matching error. After analysis of other ten sequences, we also observed that the average $SAD$ of the stationary MB is within the range of 500–1300. Therefore, we choose a threshold $T_1$ used to detect the stationary MB. If $SAD$ in MV(0,0) is less than $T_1$ ($SAD_{(0,0)} < T_1$), we can figure out that the MB is stationary (zero-motion). Higher threshold will result in larger detection error, so we set $T_1 = 550$, which achieves good speedup with negligible ME accuracy degradation.

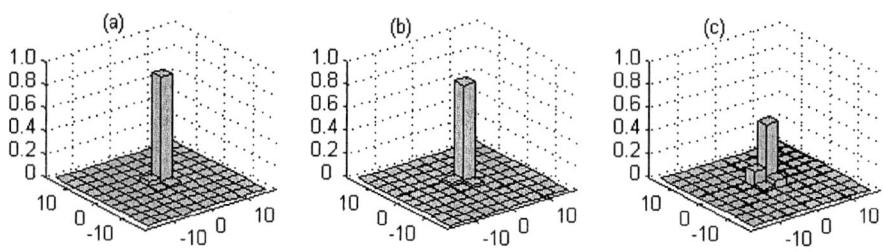

**Fig. 1.** MV distribution through full search for (a)News (b)Silence (c)Foreman

So the initial stage can be summarized as follows. Check the $SAD$ of $MV(0,0)$. If $SAD_{(0,0)} < T_1$, the MB can be regarded as zero-motion, otherwise go to the next stage.

### 2.2 Predictive Stage with Early Termination Strategy

For those video sequences, such as "Foreman", "Mobile&Calendar (M&C)" and "Coastguard", which contain large or global motion contents, they cannot benefit much from the initial stage by zero-motion detection because the percentages of stationary MB are only 25.8%, 22.4% and 11.3% respectively.

From previous research[6][7], the spatio-temporal correlation can be used to predict the MV of current MB because the MV always varies slowly both spatially and temporally. To minimize the computational cost and storage requirement for the prediction, in our predictive stage we only consider the spatial correlation and MVs of three adjacent blocks (left, top, and top-left) are chosen as the predictors (*Fig. 2*).

| P3 | P2 |
|----|----|
| P1 | C  |

**Fig. 2.** Candidate predictors P1, P2 and P3 for current macroblock C

We also analyze the prediction accuracy for these sequences and *Table 1* shows the results. It can be seen that the prediction becomes more accurate when more predictors are evaluated. Moreover, we also find that if the three predictors have the same MV, the MV of the current MB is the same with a very high probability, e.g. 90.5%, 93.3% and 93.7% for "Foreman", "M&C" and "Coastguard" respectively. Furthermore, we analyze the $SAD$ correlation between adjacent blocks through full search algorithm. After prediction, if minimal predictive

$SAD$ of current block is less than minimal $SAD$ of adjacent blocks, continued search can achieve little benefit. In order to ensure the search accuracy, we set up the early termination strategy with two necessary conditions: if the three predictors have the same MV and the predictive $SAD$ is less than threshold $T_2$ (*formula (1)*), the search can be early terminated. $\rho$ is a scale parameter, through exhausted experiments and statistical analysis, we set $\rho = 1.2$ which can achieve good speedup without much ME accuracy degradation.

**Table 1.** Percentage of prediction accuracy with each predictor and their combinations

| Sequence | P1 | P2 | P3 | P1&P2 | P1&P2&P3 |
|---|---|---|---|---|---|
| Foreman | 57.0% | 58.9% | 53.7% | 71.7% | 79.3% |
| M&C | 77.6% | 78.4% | 71.4% | 89.1% | 90.2% |
| Coastguard | 81.8% | 71.7% | 75.2% | 90.8% | 92.3% |

Through the aforementioned analysis, the predictive stage can be summarized as follows. Three adjacent predictors are selected to predict the MV of current MB. If the three predictors have the same MV and the predictive $SAD$ value of current MB is less than threshold $T_2$, set the MV of current MB as the same and early terminate the search. Otherwise, calculate the $SAD$ value of the predictive MVs and select the one which obtain the minimal $SAD$ as the starting point for next refined stage.

$$T_2 = \max\{T_1, \rho \times \min\{SAD_{left}, SAD_{top}, SAD_{topleft}\}\} \quad (1)$$

### 2.3 Refined Stage by Small Diamond Search

After prediction, there is still some displacement between the best predictive MV (starting point) and the final MV. An additional local refinement search can be used to eliminate the displacement. Due to spatial correlation, after prediction the displacement should be small. The displacement can be defined by *formula (2)*.

$$D = \min_{1 \leq i \leq 3}\{\max\{|MV_{C_x} - MV_{P_{i_x}}|, |MV_{C_y} - MV_{P_{i_y}}|\}\} \quad (2)$$

Where $D$ denotes the displacement, $MV_{C_x}, MV_{C_y}$ denote the $x$ and $y$ components of final MV of the current macroblock $C$ and $MV_{P_{i_x}}, MV_{P_{i_y}}$ denote the $x$ and $y$ components of predictive MV, $1 \leq i \leq 3$. Table 2 shows the probability within different displacement. The statistical results also demonstrate that $D = 4$ is a nearly best choice to confine the search area for the local refinement search. In refined stage, we use small diamond search (*Fig. 3*) to complete the refinement.

So the local refined stage can be summarized as follows. Check the four points around the center (starting point) as *Fig. 3 (a)*. If the center is still the best point, the search is finished. Otherwise, perform the recursive search as *Fig. 3 (b)* until the best point lies in center or until the recursive search time exceeds four.

**Table 2.** Probability within different displacement

| Sequence | $D=0$ | $D \leq 1$ | $D \leq 2$ | $D \leq 3$ | $D \leq 4$ |
|---|---|---|---|---|---|
| Foreman | 75.1% | 86.8% | 90.1% | 93.7% | 95.3% |
| M&C | 92.6% | 97.4% | 98.4% | 98.8% | 99.2% |
| Coastguard | 93.2% | 98.6% | 99.6% | 99.8% | 99.9% |

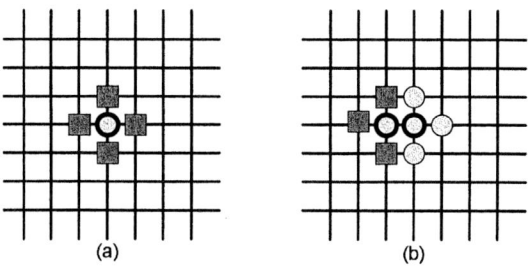

**Fig. 3.** Small diamond search pattern (a) first step (b) recursive step

## 3  Complexity-Controllable Scheme

In order to define effective complexity for ME algorithm, we set the search points ($SP$) as the uniform complexity measurement. For every search point, $SAD$ value must be calculated and evaluated, which is the most time-consuming and high-frequency operation in ME process.

Our proposed ME algorithm consists of three stages and each stage has its own complexity. The initial stage has fixed complexity ($1_{SP}$). In predictive stage, the best case is that the three predictors have the same MV, the complexity is $1_{SP}$; the worst case is that the three predictors have different MVs, every predictor should be evaluated to decide the starting point for refined stage and the complexity is $3_{SP}$. In refined stage, the complexity range from $4_{SP}$ to $16_{SP}$ in terms of small diamond search pattern and four recursive search time limit. Therefore, the complexity of ME for one MB can be defined by *formula (3)*.

$$C_{MB} = 1 + \alpha(p + \beta(4 + 3r)) = 1 + \alpha p + \alpha\beta(4 + 3r) \qquad (3)$$

Where $C_{MB}$ denotes the complexity, $\alpha$ and $\beta$ are binary coefficients ($\alpha = 0$ means zero-motion and $\alpha = 1$ means non-zero-motion; $\beta = 0$ means early-termination and $\beta = 1$ means non-early-termination), $p$ denotes the number of evaluated predictors and $1 \leq p \leq 3$, $r$ denotes the recursive search time in small diamond search and $0 \leq r \leq 4$. Therefore, the $C_{MB}$ can range from $1_{SP}$ to $20_{SP}$. In order to realize complexity-controllable feature, we can adjust parameters $p$ and $r$ to control the complexity and ensure complexity-bounded. For example, if we limit $p = 2$ and $r = 2$, the $C_{MB}$ is limited to $13_{SP}$.

Through the complexity-controllable scheme, we set the parameters $p$ and $r$ so as to limit the ME complexity and ensure real-time for video coding. Since different MB contains different texture and motion, uniformly allocating computational resources may bring about some resource wasting. Because of zero-motion detection and early termination scheme adopted in our proposed algorithm, we can easily realize resource adaptive allocation by a simple controller. Before ME, every MB is uniformly allocated the computational resources ($SP$) according to computational capability. A controller contains the available $SP$ which can be used to perform ME of current MB. The controller must guarantee that the ME complexity of the current MB cannot exceed its own available $SP$ through aforementioned complexity-controllable scheme. Due to zero-motion detection and early termination strategy, the residual $SP$ of current MB can be added to the available $SP$ of next MB. As a result, the simple controller not only ensures the total complexity upper-bounded, but also realizes resource adaptive allocation.

After adding resource allocation scheme to the ME process, the CCME algorithms can be described as *Fig. 4*.

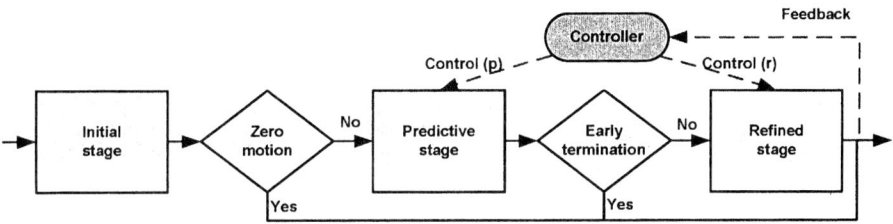

**Fig. 4.** Process of the proposed CCME algorithm

## 4 Experimental Results

To evaluate the performance of the proposed CCME algorithm, we first compare it with DS[4], HEXBS[5] and predictive enhanced HEXBS[7] algorithms without complexity constraint. And second, we add complexity constraint into the algorithm to evaluate the complexity-controllable feature. The experimental setup is as follows: the distortion measurement of mean square error ($MSE$) used, block size of 16 × 16, and search window size of ±15. Three groups of sequences (CIF format) have been chosen, because they present different kinds of motion which can achieve the comprehensive evaluation.

The average $MSE$ values and average number of $SP$ are summarized in *Table 3* for different algorithms without considering the complexity constraint. It is very clear that the CCME achieves considerable speedup in terms of $SP$ with almost the same or better $MSE$ distortions compared to the DS, HEXBS and enhanced HEXBS algorithms. For "News" and "Silence", with motion limited within a small region, the CCME achieves averagely 4 times faster with about 2% $MSE$ distortion increasing. For "Foreman", with disordered large motions, the CCME achieves averagely 2 times faster and lower $MSE$ distortion. For

"M&C" and "Coastguard", with large or global motion, the CCME also achieves significantly speedup with negligible $MSE$ change.

**Table 3.** Average $MSE$ per pixel and average $SP$ per MB for different algorithms

| | Average MSE per pixel | | | | |
|---|---|---|---|---|---|
| | News | Silence | Foreman | M&C | Coastguard |
| DS | 24.24 | 22.40 | 74.14 | 239.77 | 65.82 |
| HEXBS | 24.66 | 22.67 | 78.26 | 249.40 | 67.89 |
| Enhanced HEXBS | 24.95 | 23.01 | 61.87 | 241.01 | 67.73 |
| Proposed algorithm | 25.08 | 23.18 | 59.66 | 240.87 | 67.72 |
| | Average SP per MB | | | | |
| DS | 12.80 | 13.34 | 17.52 | 13.63 | 15.01 |
| HEXBS | 10.69 | 11.02 | 13.75 | 10.79 | 12.96 |
| Enhanced HEXBS | 8.35 | 9.01 | 11.37 | 8.89 | 9.15 |
| Proposed algorithm | 2.39 | 3.19 | 6.82 | 6.52 | 6.27 |

The complexity-controllable feature is described in *Fig. 5*. Given different complexity constraints, our proposed algorithm can adapt to a wide range of computational capability and achieve a preferable tradeoff between ME accuracy and complexity due to resource adaptive allocation scheme. Two sequences, "Foreman" and "Coastguard" are selected to accomplish the test. It can be seen that with multilevel predefined complexity constraint ($SP$ per MB), our proposed algorithm with resource adaptive allocation (RAA) scheme is obvious better than the one without RAA scheme.

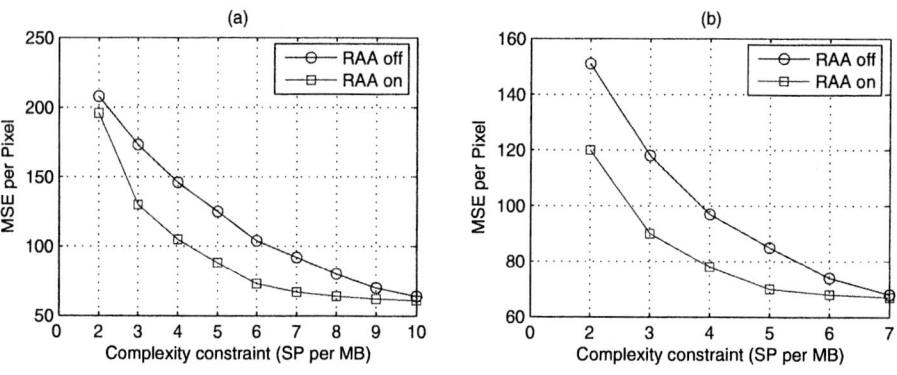

**Fig. 5.** Complexity-controllable feature of the proposed algorithm with and without the resource adaptive allocation (RAA) for (a) Foreman (b) Coastguard

## 5 Conclusions

In this paper, we proposed a novel complexity-controllable motion estimation algorithm. The proposed CCME algorithm makes use of three effective stages to achieve superior search performance. Moreover the complexity-controllable scheme can achieve a preferable tradeoff between ME accuracy and complexity. As for the performance, the CCME algorithm speeds up the search about 2–5 times faster than the well-known DS, HEXBS and enhanced HEXBS algorithms without any motion accuracy degradation. Furthermore, given different complexity constraints, the complexity-controllable scheme represents good performance and decreases 15%–30% $MSE$ distortions comparing to the one without this scheme. And also, we believe that the performance of the CCME algorithm could still be improved by using a more intelligent resource allocation scheme.

## References

1. Rao, K.R., Bojkovic, Z.S., Milovanovic, D.A.: Multimedia Communication Systems: Techniques, Standards, and Networks, Prentice Hall PTR, (2002)
2. Li, R., Zeng, B., Liou, M.L.: A New Three-Step Search Algorithm for Block Motion Estimation, IEEE Transactions on Circuits and Systems for Video Technology, Vol. 4, (1994), 438–422
3. Po, L.M., Ma, W.C.: A Novel Four-Step Search Algorithm for Fast Block Motion Estimation, IEEE Transactions on Circuits and Systems for Video Technology, Vol. 6, (1996), 313–317
4. Zhu, S., Ma, K.K.: A New Diamond Search Algorithm for Fast Block-Matching Motion Estimation, IEEE Transactions on Image Processing, Vol. 9, (2000), 287–290
5. Zhu, C., Lin, X., Chau, L.P.: Hexagon-based Search Pattern for Fast Block Motion Estimation, IEEE Transactions on Circuits and Systems for Video Technology, Vol. 12, (2002), 349–355
6. Namuduri, K.R.: Motion Estimation Using Spatio-Temporal Contextual Information, IEEE Transactions on Circuits and Systems for Video Technology, Vol. 14, August (2004), 1111–1115
7. Zhu, C., Lin, X., Chau, L., Po, L.M.: Enhanced Hexagonal Search for Fast Block Motion Estimation, IEEE Transactions on Circuits and Systems for Video Technology, Vol. 14, (2004), 1210–1214
8. Lengwehasatit, K., Ortega, A.: Computationally Scalable Partial Distance Based Fast Search Motion Estimation, Proceedings of International Conference on Image Processing, Vol. 1, (2000), 824–827
9. Mietens, S., de With, P.H.N., Hentschel, C.: Computational-Complexity Scalable Motion Estimation for Mobile MPEG Encoding, IEEE Transactions on Consumer Electronics, Vol. 50, (2004), 281–291

# Author Index

Abate, Andrea F. 1073
Abdel-Dayem, Amr R. 869
Aguiar, Rui 974
Ahmadi, Majid 1242
Ahmed, M. 415
Alajlan, N. 399, 415
Ali, Mortuza 302
Almaoui, Mazen 191
Anderson, Ryan 490
Andra, Srinivas 754
Antunes, Mark 174
Apalkov, Ilia V. 223
Aribisala, Benjamin S. 914
Arica, Nafiz 431

Badura, Stanisław 516
Bao, Hujun 107
Bauckhage, Christian 456
Benoit, Stephen 770
Bhandarkar, Suchendra M. 836, 1226
Bhattacharya, Prabir 601
Borges, Janete S. 447
Bouchafa, Samia 391
Boudihir, M. Elarbi 575
Bougleux, Sébastien 651
Bourbakis, Nikolaos 1
Bres, Stéphane 737
Brittain, Nathanael J. 328
Bu, Jiajun 383, 1266
Bui, Tien D. 91, 133, 746
Bulacu, Marius 625
Bunyak, Filiz 820
Buxton, Bernard F. 407

Cai, Canhui 351
Campilho, Aurélio 949, 958, 974
Cao, Guitao 762
Cao, Guo 423
Celik, T. 1141
Cha, Sung-Hyuk 1118
Chang, Yuchou 24
Chen, Bin 659
Chen, Chun 383, 1266
Chen, Guangyi 91

Chen, Jing 351
Chen, Li 40
Chen, Shoushui 423
Chen, Tse-Shih 1167, 1184
Cheriet, Farida 938
Cho, Dongwook 91
Choi, Jae-Young 1023
Choi, Jong-Soo 1125
Choi, Seung-Seok 1118
Choi, Woong Il 207
Chung, Yongwha 1106
Claridge, Ela 914
Cong, Lin 32
Conte, Donatello 1234
Costeira, João Paulo 1250
Cruz-Enriquez, Héctor 247
Cuesta Frau, David 55

Dadgostar, Farhad 804
De Witte, Valérie 667
Demirel, Hasan 335, 1141, 1149
Demirkol, Askin 1200
Demir, Zafer 1200
Desai, Bipin C. 601
Dias, Jorge 617
Dios, Juan José de 1032
Direkoğlu, C. 1141, 1149
Du, Zhenlong 107
Duric, Zoran 1175

Eglin, Véronique 737
El Badawy, O. 399, 559
El Rube, I. 415
Elmoataz, Abderrahim 651
El-Saadany, E.F. 903
El-Sakka, Mahmoud R. 328, 869, 1158
Emre, Erol 1200
Ensafi, P. 159

Fauqueur, Julien 490
Fazl Ersi, Ehsan 1040
Ferreira, João Filipe 617
Ferrie, Frank P. 770
Fexa, Ales 1014
Fieguth, Paul 73, 861, 1006

Figueiredo, M.A.T.  9
Foggia, Pasquale  1234
Fraser, Ian  694
Freeman, G.H.  149, 399, 415

Gao, Qigang  567
Gao, S.  133
Gao, Xin-bo  231
García, Narciso  1032
Ghazel, M.  149
Gomes e Silva, André R.  278
Gong, Minglun  1217
Gong, Mingwei  1217
Gouton, Pierre  635
Greenspan, Michael  694
Gregori, Valentín  81
Grimard, Guy  938
Grzegorzek, Marcin  481
Gu, Qian  729
Guan, Ling  593
Guo, Feng  844

Ha, Sang-An  540
Hafiane, Adel  17
Han, Bing  231
Han, Dongil  473, 643, 1258
Han, Yutao  585
He, Lei  659
Hennings, Pablo  1081
Heo, Jingu  1089
Hernández-Cisneros, Rolando  998
Hernández-Fenollosa, María Ángeles  55
Hocanin, Aykut  335
Hong, Jinkeun  343
Hosic, Sabina  335
Hu, Bing  762
Huseh, Min-Yu  255
Hwang, Dae-Hwan  643
Hwang, Sunghyun  125

Jang, Soo-Wook  375, 712
Jayas, Rajat  499
Jeon, Byeungwoo  207
Jervis, Eric  861
Ji, Hong-bing  231
Jiao, Licheng  32, 48, 239, 263
Jin, Fu  73
Jin, Hai-yan  239

Jodoin, Pierre-Marc  778
Jung, Gwang-Seok  294
Jung, Tae-Yeon  812

Kachouie, Nezamoddin N.  861, 1006
Kamel, Mohamed S.  182, 399, 415, 559
Kang, Kyung-Won  294
Kaye, Cam  499
Kaye, John E.  499
Kerre, Etienne E.  667
Khelifi, Samia F.  575
Khryashchev, Vladimir V.  223
Kim, Dong-Wook  1125
Kim, Duk-Gyoo  812
Kim, Eun-Su  375, 712
Kim, Jin-Tae  1125
Kim, Jong-Nam  294
Kim, Ju-Young  812
Kim, J.Y.  286
Kim, Kihong  343
Kim, Kwang-Baek  540
Kim, Minhwan  532
Kim, Nak-Bin  1023
Kim, Sungshin  540
Kim, Yong Se  473
Kim, Younhee  1175
Kingsbury, Nick  490
Ko, Hanseok  852
Kolesnik, Marina  1014
Konishi, Ryosuke  507
Koo, Kyongmo  532
Kwon, Ohyun  141
Kwon, Sang Gu  207
Kyan, Matthew J.  593

Langille, Aaron  1217
Lathuiliere, Alexandra  635
Latorre, Pedro  9, 81
Lee, Gwang-Soon  375
Lee, Heungkyu  852
Lee, Seong-Whan  182
Lee, Seong-Won  125
Lee, Sung-Hak  375, 712
Lee, Yillbyung  1118
Leszczynski, Mariusz  516
Li, Haiyan  367
Li, Hui  99
Li, J.S. Jimmy  703
Li, Li  367
Li, Yupeng  593

Li, Zhi-gang  359
Linares-Pellicer, Jordi  55
Ling, Jianguo  215
Lin, Hai  107
Lins, Rafael Dueire  278, 310
Liu, Chaoqiang  99
Liu, Fang  239
Liu, Ping  659
Liu, Xin-Gang  320
Liu, Yazhou  255
Lorenzo-Ginori, Juan V.  247
Lu, Juwei  729, 1057
Lu, Ye  828
Lukac, Rastislav  879
Luo, Limin  524
Luo, Xingzhi  836, 1226

Makrogiannis, Sokratis  1
Mansouri, Alamin  635
Marçal, André R.S.  447, 1192
Markham, Richard  894
Martin, Cesar San  1208
Marzani, Franck S.  635
Matsuda, Tetsuya  549
Melkemi, Mahmoud  651
Mendonça, Ana Maria  974
Mignotte, Max  778
Mitra, Sinjini  1065
Mizuta, Shinobu  549
Mohamed, S.S.  903
Mo, Linjian  383
Moon, Daesung  1106
Moon, Kiyoung  1106
Moon, Kwang-Seok  294
Morillas, Samuel  81
Murshed, Manzur  302

Nachtegael, Mike  667
Namkung, Jaechan  1048
Nappi, Michele  1073
Niemann, Heinrich  481
Nikitenko, Dennis  966
Nourine, Rachid  575

Oh, Jeong-Su  1125
Ohn, Syng-Yup  676
Oliveira, Daniel Marques  310
Oporto-Díaz, Samuel  998
Orchard, Jeff  116, 439
Osareh, Alireza  894

Ouda, Abdelkader H.  1158
Özkaramanlı, H.  1141, 1149

Paik, Joonki  125, 141, 1048
Palenichka, Roman M.  464
Pan, SungBum  1106
Pan, Wumo  746
Park, Changhan  1048
Park, Changmin  532
Park, Seanae  1048
Pavan, S.  270
Peng, Ningsong  215
Pereira, Patricia R.  1192
Peris-Fajarnés, Guillermo  9, 81
Petretta, Michele  1234
Pezoa, Jorge E.  1208
Pinho da Silva, Nuno  1250
Plataniotis, Konstantinos N.  191, 686, 729, 879, 990, 1057

Qian, Gang  844
Qin, Li  886
qin, Xueying  107
Qi, Xiaojun  585

Rahman, Md. Mahmudur  601
Rahnamayan, S.  930
Ramunas, John  861
Randhawa, Sharmil  703
Reznikova, Irina V.  223
Riccio, Daniel  1073
Richards, Dana  1175
Rivero-Moreno, Carlos Joel  737
Rocha, Rui  949
Rueda, Luis  886, 982

Sá Miranda, C.  974
Saitoh, Takeshi  507
Salama, M.M.A.  903, 930
Salgado, A.  609
Sánchez, J.  609
Sanfeliu, Alberto  720
Sarrafzadeh, Abdolhossein  804
Savvides, Marios  1065, 1081, 1089, 1098
Sbarbaro, Daniel G.  1208
Schomaker, Lambert  625
Schulte, Stefan  667
Seo, Kwang-Deok  320
Seo, Kyung-Sik  922
Sha, Yuheng  32

## Author Index

Shadgar, Bita 894
Shah, Mubarak 167
Shan, Tan 48, 263
Shi, Pengfei 762
Shin, Jeongho 125, 141, 1048
Shin, Young-Suk 1133
Shoa, Tina 174
Shu, Huazhong 524
Silva, Jorge 949
Skarbek, Władysław 516
Smolka, Bogdan 686, 990
Sohng, Kyu-Ik 375, 712
Sousa, António V. 974
Sridhar, G. 270
Sridhar, V. 270
Subramanya, S.R. 820
Suen, C.Y. 746
Suh, Il Hong 473
Sun, Qiang 32
Suvonvorn, Nikom 391

Tappert, Charles C. 1118
Terashima-Marín, Hugo 998
Thomas, Gabriel 174, 499
Thornton, Jason 1098
Tizhoosh, H.R. 159, 930
Tormos, Pau Micó 55
Torres, Sergio N. 1208
Toumoulin, Christine 524
Trachtenberg, Michael 174
Tsotsos, John K. 456
Tucci, Maurizio 1073
Tufano, Francesco 1234

Uyguroğlu, M. 1141, 1149

Van der Weken, Dietrich 667
Venetsanopoulos, A.N. 1057
Vento, Mario 1234
Vergés–Llahí, Jaume 720
Vidyadharan, Vidya 982
Vijaya Kumar, B.V.K. 1065, 1081, 1089, 1098
Vinhais, Carlos 958
Viswanathan, Murlikrishna 1023
Voisin, Yvon 635
Vrscay, E.R. 63, 149

Wang, Jie 729, 1057
Wang, Shuang 48

Wang, Yonggang 24, 40
Ward, R.K. 149
Wen, Mei 367
Whangbo, Taeg-Keun 1023
Wilkie, K.P. 63
Windisch, Luke 938
Winger, Lowell 73
Wirth, Michael 966
Wu, Biao 359
Wu, Mei 567
Wu, Nan 367
Wu, Q.M. Jonathan 828
Wu, Yin 199
Wu, Yongjun 754

Xia, Tao 99
Xi, Dihua 182
Xun, Changqing 367
Xu, Shu-Chang 199

Yang, Ching-Nung 1167, 1184
Yang, Jie 215
Yang, Lei 215
Yang, Lynn 1242
Yang, Xiao-hui 239
Yang, Xin 423
Yang, Young-Gyu 1023
Yang, Zhi 1266
Yao, Guilin 255
Yao, Hongxun 255
Yarman Vural, Fatos T. 431
Ye, Xiuzi 199
Yoo, Kook-Yeol 320
Yoon, Sungsoo 1118
Yoon, Yong-In 1125
You, Bum-Jae 473
Youssef, A.M. 903

Zaremba, Marek B. 464
Zavidovique, Bertrand 17, 391
Zelek, John S. 1040
Zhai, Yun 167
Zhang, Chunyuan 367
Zhang, Haixiang 383, 1266
Zhang, Hong 789
Zhang, Jason Z. 828
Zhang, Q.H. 133
Zhang, Sanyuan 199
Zhang, Xiangrong 48
Zhang, Ying 359

Zhang, Yunjun  796
Zhang, Zhao-yang  359
Zhou, Dongxiang  789
Zhou, Jian  524

Zhou, Yue  24, 40
Zhu, Hongqing  524
Zografos, Vasileios  407
Zvonarev, Pavel S.  223

# Lecture Notes in Computer Science

For information about Vols. 1–3618

please contact your bookseller or Springer

Vol. 3728: V. Paliouras, J. Vounckx, D. Verkest (Eds.), Integrated Circuit and System Design. XV, 753 pages. 2005.

Vol. 3718: V.G. Ganzha, E.W. Mayr, E.V. Vorozhtsov (Eds.), Computer Algebra in Scientific Computing. XII, 502 pages. 2005.

Vol. 3715: E. Dawson, S. Vaudenay (Eds.), Progress in Cryptology – Mycrypt 2005. XI, 329 pages. 2005.

Vol. 3714: H. Obbink, K. Pohl (Eds.), Software Product Lines. XIII, 235 pages. 2005.

Vol. 3713: L. Briand, C. Williams (Eds.), Model Driven Engineering Languages and Systems. XV, 722 pages. 2005.

Vol. 3712: R. Reussner, J. Mayer, J.A. Stafford, S. Overhage, S. Becker, P.J. Schroeder (Eds.), Quality of Software Architectures and Software Quality. XIII, 289 pages. 2005.

Vol. 3711: F. Kishino, Y. Kitamura, H. Kato, N. Nagata (Eds.), Entertainment Computing - ICEC 2005. XXIV, 540 pages. 2005.

Vol. 3710: M. Barni, I. Cox, T. Kalker, H.J. Kim (Eds.), Digital Watermarking. XII, 485 pages. 2005.

Vol. 3708: J. Blanc-Talon, W. Philips, D. Popescu, P. Scheunders (Eds.), Advanced Concepts for Intelligent Vision Systems. XXII, 725 pages. 2005.

Vol. 3706: H. Fuks, S. Lukosch, A.C. Salgado (Eds.), Groupware: Design, Implementation, and Use. XII, 378 pages. 2005.

Vol. 3703: F. Fages, S. Soliman (Eds.), Principles and Practice of Semantic Web Reasoning. VIII, 163 pages. 2005.

Vol. 3702: B. Beckert (Ed.), Automated Reasoning with Analytic Tableaux and Related Methods. XIII, 343 pages. 2005. (Subseries LNAI).

Vol. 3699: C.S. Calude, M.J. Dinneen, G. Paun, M.J. Pérez-Jiménez, G. Rozenberg (Eds.), Unconventional Computation. XI, 267 pages. 2005.

Vol. 3698: U. Furbach (Ed.), KI 2005: Advances in Artificial Intelligence. XIII, 409 pages. 2005. (Subseries LNAI).

Vol. 3697: W. Duch, J. Kacprzyk, E. Oja, S. Zadrożny (Eds.), Artificial Neural Networks: Formal Models and Their Applications – ICANN 2005, Part II. XXXII, 1045 pages. 2005.

Vol. 3696: W. Duch, J. Kacprzyk, E. Oja, S. Zadrożny (Eds.), Artificial Neural Networks: Biological Inspirations – ICANN 2005, Part I. XXXI, 703 pages. 2005.

Vol. 3695: M.R. Berthold, R. Glen, K. Diederichs, O. Kohlbacher, I. Fischer (Eds.), Computational Life Sciences. XI, 277 pages. 2005. (Subseries LNBI).

Vol. 3694: M. Malek, E. Nett, N. Suri (Eds.), Service Availability. VIII, 213 pages. 2005.

Vol. 3693: A.G. Cohn, D.M. Mark (Eds.), Spatial Information Theory. XII, 493 pages. 2005.

Vol. 3691: A. Gagalowicz, W. Philips (Eds.), Computer Analysis of Images and Patterns. XIX, 865 pages. 2005.

Vol. 3690: M. Pěchouček, P. Petta, L.Z. Varga (Eds.), Multi-Agent Systems and Applications IV. XVII, 667 pages. 2005. (Subseries LNAI).

Vol. 3687: S. Singh, M. Singh, C. Apte, P. Perner (Eds.), Pattern Recognition and Image Analysis, Part II. XXV, 809 pages. 2005.

Vol. 3686: S. Singh, M. Singh, C. Apte, P. Perner (Eds.), Pattern Recognition and Data Mining, Part I. XXVI, 689 pages. 2005.

Vol. 3685: V. Gorodetsky, I. Kotenko, V. Skormin (Eds.), Computer Network Security. XIV, 480 pages. 2005.

Vol. 3684: R. Khosla, R.J. Howlett, L.C. Jain (Eds.), Knowledge-Based Intelligent Information and Engineering Systems, Part IV. LXXIX, 933 pages. 2005. (Subseries LNAI).

Vol. 3683: R. Khosla, R.J. Howlett, L.C. Jain (Eds.), Knowledge-Based Intelligent Information and Engineering Systems, Part III. LXXX, 1397 pages. 2005. (Subseries LNAI).

Vol. 3682: R. Khosla, R.J. Howlett, L.C. Jain (Eds.), Knowledge-Based Intelligent Information and Engineering Systems, Part II. LXXIX, 1371 pages. 2005. (Subseries LNAI).

Vol. 3681: R. Khosla, R.J. Howlett, L.C. Jain (Eds.), Knowledge-Based Intelligent Information and Engineering Systems, Part I. LXXX, 1319 pages. 2005. (Subseries LNAI).

Vol. 3679: S.d.C. di Vimercati, P. Syverson, D. Gollmann (Eds.), Computer Security – ESORICS 2005. XI, 509 pages. 2005.

Vol. 3678: A. McLysaght, D.H. Huson (Eds.), Comparative Genomics. VIII, 167 pages. 2005. (Subseries LNBI).

Vol. 3677: J. Dittmann, S. Katzenbeisser, A. Uhl (Eds.), Communications and Multimedia Security. XIII, 360 pages. 2005.

Vol. 3675: Y. Luo (Ed.), Cooperative Design, Visualization, and Engineering. XI, 264 pages. 2005.

Vol. 3674: W. Jonker, M. Petković (Eds.), Secure Data Management. X, 241 pages. 2005.

Vol. 3672: C. Hankin, I. Siveroni (Eds.), Static Analysis. X, 369 pages. 2005.

Vol. 3671: S. Bressan, S. Ceri, E. Hunt, Z.G. Ives, Z. Bellahsène, M. Rys, R. Unland (Eds.), Database and XML Technologies. X, 239 pages. 2005.

Vol. 3670: M. Bravetti, L. Kloul, G. Zavattaro (Eds.), Formal Techniques for Computer Systems and Business Processes. XIII, 349 pages. 2005.

Vol. 3666: B.D. Martino, D. Kranzlmüller, J. Dongarra (Eds.), Recent Advances in Parallel Virtual Machine and Message Passing Interface. XVII, 546 pages. 2005.

Vol. 3665: K. S. Candan, A. Celentano (Eds.), Advances in Multimedia Information Systems. X, 221 pages. 2005.

Vol. 3664: C. Türker, M. Agosti, H.-J. Schek (Eds.), Peer-to-Peer, Grid, and Service-Orientation in Digital Library Architectures. X, 261 pages. 2005.

Vol. 3663: W.G. Kropatsch, R. Sablatnig, A. Hanbury (Eds.), Pattern Recognition. XIV, 512 pages. 2005.

Vol. 3662: C. Baral, G. Greco, N. Leone, G. Terracina (Eds.), Logic Programming and Nonmonotonic Reasoning. XIII, 454 pages. 2005. (Subseries LNAI).

Vol. 3661: T. Panayiotopoulos, J. Gratch, R. Aylett, D. Ballin, P. Olivier, T. Rist (Eds.), Intelligent Virtual Agents. XIII, 506 pages. 2005. (Subseries LNAI).

Vol. 3660: M. Beigl, S. Intille, J. Rekimoto, H. Tokuda (Eds.), UbiComp 2005: Ubiquitous Computing. XVII, 394 pages. 2005.

Vol. 3659: J.R. Rao, B. Sunar (Eds.), Cryptographic Hardware and Embedded Systems – CHES 2005. XIV, 458 pages. 2005.

Vol. 3658: V. Matoušek, P. Mautner, T. Pavelka (Eds.), Text, Speech and Dialogue. XV, 460 pages. 2005. (Subseries LNAI).

Vol. 3656: M. Kamel, A. Campilho (Eds.), Image Analysis and Recognition. XXIV, 1279 pages. 2005.

Vol. 3655: A. Aldini, R. Gorrieri, F. Martinelli (Eds.), Foundations of Security Analysis and Design III. VII, 273 pages. 2005.

Vol. 3654: S. Jajodia, D. Wijesekera (Eds.), Data and Applications Security XIX. X, 353 pages. 2005.

Vol. 3653: M. Abadi, L. de Alfaro (Eds.), CONCUR 2005 – Concurrency Theory. XIV, 578 pages. 2005.

Vol. 3652: A. Rauber, S. Christodoulakis, A. M. Tjoa (Eds.), Research and Advanced Technology for Digital Libraries. XVIII, 545 pages. 2005.

Vol. 3650: J. Zhou, J. Lopez, R.H. Deng, F. Bao (Eds.), Information Security. XII, 516 pages. 2005.

Vol. 3649: W.M. P. van der Aalst, B. Benatallah, F. Casati, F. Curbera (Eds.), Business Process Management. XII, 472 pages. 2005.

Vol. 3648: J.C. Cunha, P.D. Medeiros (Eds.), Euro-Par 2005 Parallel Processing. XXXVI, 1299 pages. 2005.

Vol. 3646: A. F. Famili, J.N. Kok, J.M. Peña, A. Siebes, A. Feelders (Eds.), Advances in Intelligent Data Analysis VI. XIV, 522 pages. 2005.

Vol. 3645: D.-S. Huang, X.-P. Zhang, G.-B. Huang (Eds.), Advances in Intelligent Computing, Part II. XIII, 1010 pages. 2005.

Vol. 3644: D.-S. Huang, X.-P. Zhang, G.-B. Huang (Eds.), Advances in Intelligent Computing, Part I. XXVII, 1101 pages. 2005.

Vol. 3642: D. Ślezak, J. Yao, J.F. Peters, W. Ziarko, X. Hu (Eds.), Rough Sets, Fuzzy Sets, Data Mining, and Granular Computing, Part II. XXIII, 738 pages. 2005. (Subseries LNAI).

Vol. 3641: D. Ślezak, G. Wang, M. Szczuka, I. Düntsch, Y. Yao (Eds.), Rough Sets, Fuzzy Sets, Data Mining, and Granular Computing, Part I. XXIV, 742 pages. 2005. (Subseries LNAI).

Vol. 3639: P. Godefroid (Ed.), Model Checking Software. XI, 289 pages. 2005.

Vol. 3638: A. Butz, B. Fisher, A. Krüger, P. Olivier (Eds.), Smart Graphics. XI, 269 pages. 2005.

Vol. 3637: J. M. Moreno, J. Madrenas, J. Cosp (Eds.), Evolvable Systems: From Biology to Hardware. XI, 227 pages. 2005.

Vol. 3636: M.J. Blesa, C. Blum, A. Roli, M. Sampels (Eds.), Hybrid Metaheuristics. XII, 155 pages. 2005.

Vol. 3634: L. Ong (Ed.), Computer Science Logic. XI, 567 pages. 2005.

Vol. 3633: C. Bauzer Medeiros, M. Egenhofer, E. Bertino (Eds.), Advances in Spatial and Temporal Databases. XIII, 433 pages. 2005.

Vol. 3632: R. Nieuwenhuis (Ed.), Automated Deduction – CADE-20. XIII, 459 pages. 2005. (Subseries LNAI).

Vol. 3631: J. Eder, H.-M. Haav, A. Kalja, J. Penjam (Eds.), Advances in Databases and Information Systems. XIII, 393 pages. 2005.

Vol. 3630: M.S. Capcarrere, A.A. Freitas, P.J. Bentley, C.G. Johnson, J. Timmis (Eds.), Advances in Artificial Life. XIX, 949 pages. 2005. (Subseries LNAI).

Vol. 3629: J.L. Fiadeiro, N. Harman, M. Roggenbach, J. Rutten (Eds.), Algebra and Coalgebra in Computer Science. XI, 457 pages. 2005.

Vol. 3628: T. Gschwind, U. Aßmann, O. Nierstrasz (Eds.), Software Composition. X, 199 pages. 2005.

Vol. 3627: C. Jacob, M.L. Pilat, P.J. Bentley, J. Timmis (Eds.), Artificial Immune Systems. XII, 500 pages. 2005.

Vol. 3626: B. Ganter, G. Stumme, R. Wille (Eds.), Formal Concept Analysis. X, 349 pages. 2005. (Subseries LNAI).

Vol. 3625: S. Kramer, B. Pfahringer (Eds.), Inductive Logic Programming. XIII, 427 pages. 2005. (Subseries LNAI).

Vol. 3624: C. Chekuri, K. Jansen, J.D. P. Rolim, L. Trevisan (Eds.), Approximation, Randomization and Combinatorial Optimization. XI, 495 pages. 2005.

Vol. 3623: M. Liśkiewicz, R. Reischuk (Eds.), Fundamentals of Computation Theory. XV, 576 pages. 2005.

Vol. 3622: V. Vene, T. Uustalu (Eds.), Advanced Functional Programming. IX, 359 pages. 2005.

Vol. 3621: V. Shoup (Ed.), Advances in Cryptology – CRYPTO 2005. XI, 568 pages. 2005.

Vol. 3620: H. Muñoz-Avila, F. Ricci (Eds.), Case-Based Reasoning Research and Development. XV, 654 pages. 2005. (Subseries LNAI).

Vol. 3619: X. Lu, W. Zhao (Eds.), Networking and Mobile Computing. XXIV, 1299 pages. 2005.